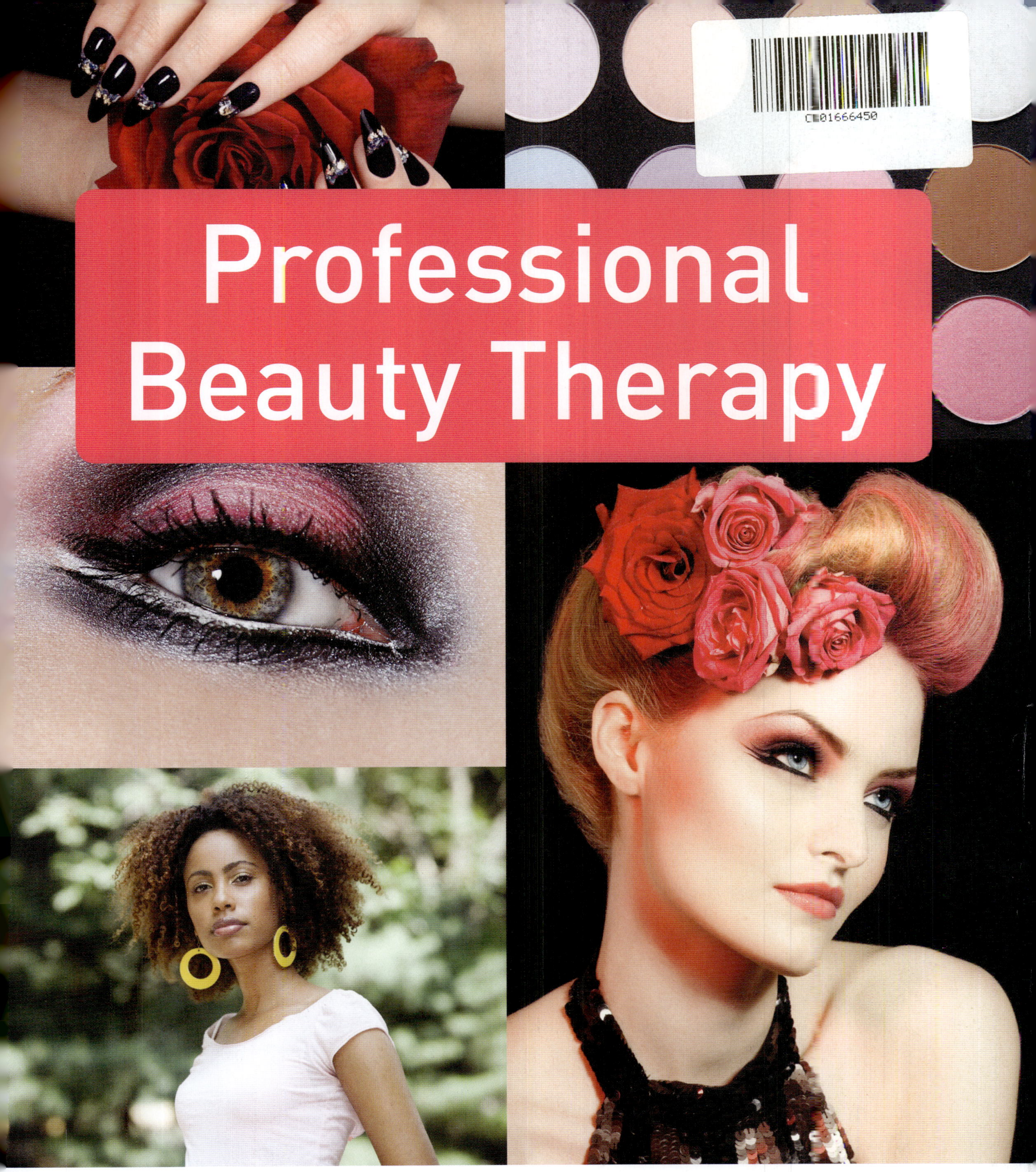

Professional Beauty Therapy

HABIA SERIES LIST

Hairdressing

Student textbooks

Begin Hairdressing: The Official Guide to Level 1 3e *Martin Green*

Hairdressing – The Foundations: The Official Guide to Level 2 6e *Leo Palladino and Martin Green*

Professional Hairdressing: The Official Guide to Level 3 7e *Martin Green and Leo Palladino*

The Official Guide to the City & Guilds Certificate in Salon Service 1e *John Armstrong with Anita Crosland, Martin Green and Lorraine Nordmann*

The Colour Book: The Official Guide to Colour for NVQ Levels 2 and 3 1e *Tracey Lloyd with Christine McMillan-Bodell*

eXtensions: The Official Guide to Hair Extensions 1e *Theresa Bullock*

Salon Management *Martin Green*

Men's Hairdressing: Traditional and Modern Barbering 3e *Maurice Lister*

African–Caribbean Hairdressing 3e *Sandra Gittens*

The World of Hair Colour 1e *John Gray*

The Cutting Book: The Official Guide to Cutting at S/NVQ Levels 2 and 3 *Jane Goldsbro and Elaine White*

Professional Hairdressing titles

Trevor Sorbie: The Bridal Hair Book 1e *Trevor Sorbie and Jacki Wadeson*

The Art of Dressing Long Hair 1e *Guy Kremer and Jacki Wadeson*

Patrick Cameron: Dressing Long Hair 1e *Patrick Cameron and Jacki Wadeson*

Patrick Cameron: Dressing Long Hair 2 1e *Patrick Cameron and Jacki Wadeson*

Bridal Hair 1e *Pat Dixon and Jacki Wadeson*

Professional Men's Hairdressing: The Art of Cutting and Styling 1e *Guy Kremer and Jacki Wadeson*

Essensuals, The Next Generation Toni and Guy: Step by Step 1e *Sacha Mascolo, Christian Mascolo and Stuart Wesson*

Mahogany Hairdressing: Steps to Cutting, Colouring and Finishing Hair 1e *Martin Gannon and Richard Thompson*

Mahogany Hairdressing: Advanced Looks 1e *Martin Gannon and Richard Thompson*

The Total Look: The Style Guide for Hair and Make-up Professionals 1e *Ian Mistlin*

Trevor Sorbie: Visions in Hair 1e *Trevor Sorbie, Kris Sorbie and Jacki Wadeson*

The Art of Hair Colouring 1e *David Adams and Jacki Wadeson*

Beauty therapy

Beauty Basics: The Official Guide to Level 1 3e *Lorraine Nordmann*

Beauty Therapy – The Foundations: The Official Guide to Level 2 5e *Lorraine Nordmann*

Professional Beauty Therapy – The Official Guide to Level 3 4e *Lorraine Nordmann*

The Official Guide to the City & Guilds Certificate in Salon Services 1e *John Armstrong with Anita Crosland, Martin Green and Lorraine Nordmann*

The Complete Guide to Make-up 1e *Suzanne Le Quesne*

The Encyclopedia of Nails 1e *Jacqui Jefford and Anne Swain*

The Art of Nails: A Comprehensive Style Guide to Nail Treatments and Nail Art 1e *Jacqui Jefford*

Nail Artistry 1e *Jacqui Jefford*

The Complete Nail Technician 2e *Marian Newman*

Manicure, Pedicure and Advanced Nail Techniques 1e *Elaine Almond*

The Official Guide to Body Massage 2e *Adele O'Keefe*

An Holistic Guide to Massage 1e *Tina Parsons*

Indian Head Massage 2e *Muriel Burnham-Airey and Adele O'Keefe*

Aromatherapy for the Beauty Therapist 1e Valerie Worwood

An Holistic Guide to Reflexology 1e *Tina Parsons*

An Holistic Guide to Anatomy and Physiology 1e *Tina Parsons*

The Essential Guide to Holistic and Complementary Therapy 1e *Helen Beckmann and Suzanne Le Quesne*

The Spa Book 1e *Jane Crebbin-Bailey, Dr John Harcup, and John Harrington*

SPA: The Official Guide to Spa Therapy at Levels 2 and 3, *Joan Scott and Andrea Harrison*

Nutrition: A Practical Approach 1e *Suzanne Le Quesne*

Hands on Sports Therapy 1e *Keith Ward*

Encyclopedia of Hair Removal: A Complete Reference to Methods, Techniques and Career Opportunities, *Gill Morris and Janice Brown*

The Anatomy and Physiology Workbook: For Beauty and Holistic Therapies Levels 1–3. *Tina Parsons*

The Anatomy and Physiology CD-Rom

Beautiful Selling: The Complete Guide to Sales Success in the Salon *Ruth Langley*

The Official Guide to the Diploma in Hair and Beauty Studies at Foundation Level 1e *Jane Goldsbro and Elaine White*

The Official Guide to the Diploma in Hair and Beauty Studies at Higher Level 1e *Jane Goldsbro and Elaine White*

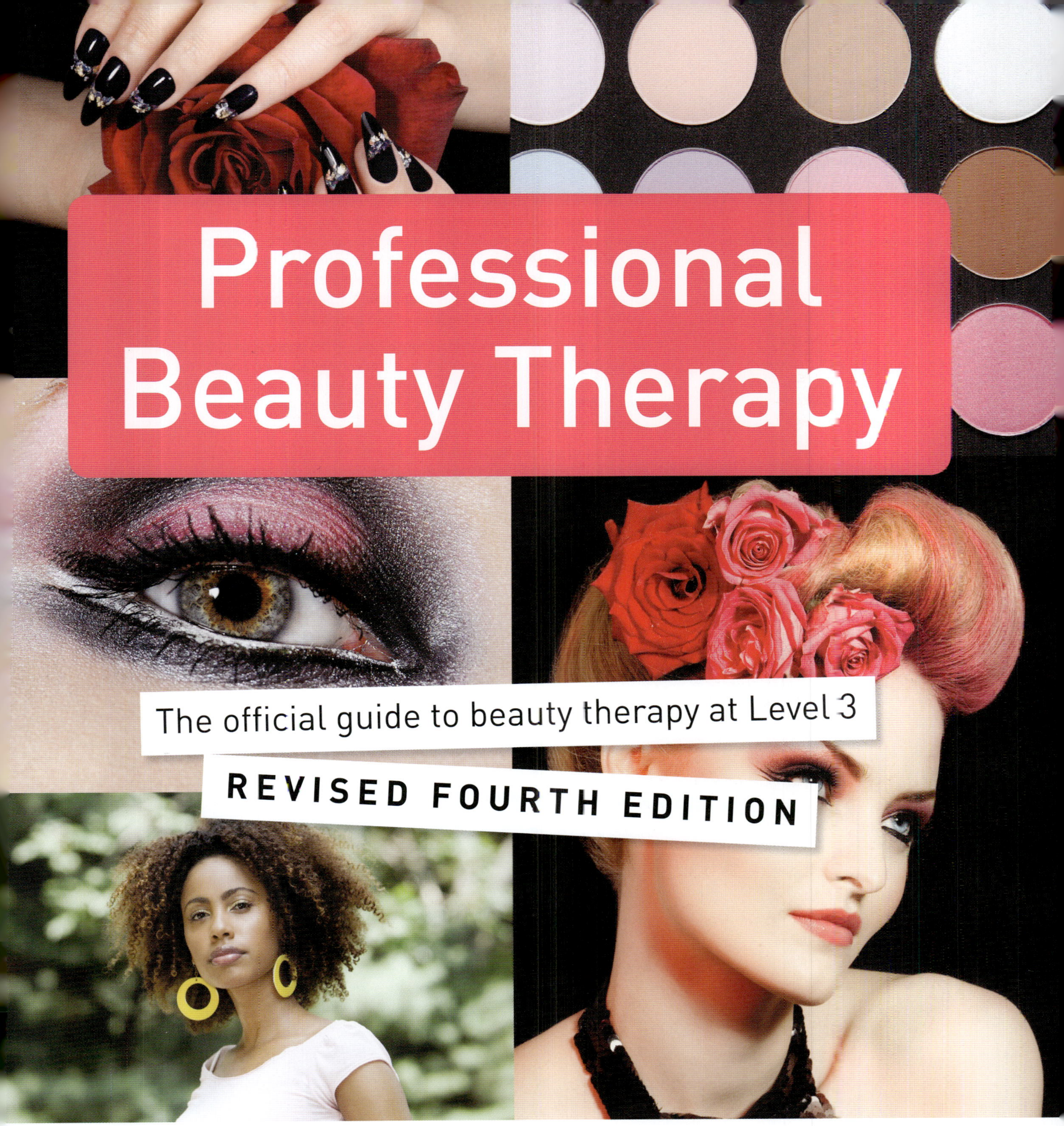

Professional Beauty Therapy

The official guide to beauty therapy at Level 3

REVISED FOURTH EDITION

LORRAINE NORDMANN

CENGAGE Learning

Australia • Brazil • Japan • Korea • Mexico • Singapore • Spain • United Kingdom • United States

CENGAGE Learning

Professional Beauty Therapy
Revised Fourth Edition
Lorraine Nordmann

Publisher: Melody Dawes
Development Editor: Lauren Darby
Publishing Assistant: Claire Whittaker
Content Project Editor: Sue Povey
Production Controller: Eyvett Davis
Typesetter: MPS Limited
Cover design: HCT Creative

British Library Cataloguing-in-Publication Data
A catalogue record for this book is available from the British Library.

ISBN: 978-1-4737-1063-4

Cengage Learning EMEA
Cheriton House, North Way, Andover, Hampshire, SP10 5BE
United Kingdom

Cengage Learning products are represented in Canada by Nelson Education Ltd.

For your lifelong learning solutions, visit **www.cengage.co.uk**

Purchase your next print book, e-book or e-chapter at
www.cengagebrain.co.uk

Printed in China by RR Donnelley
Print Year: 2015 Print Number: 02

Contents

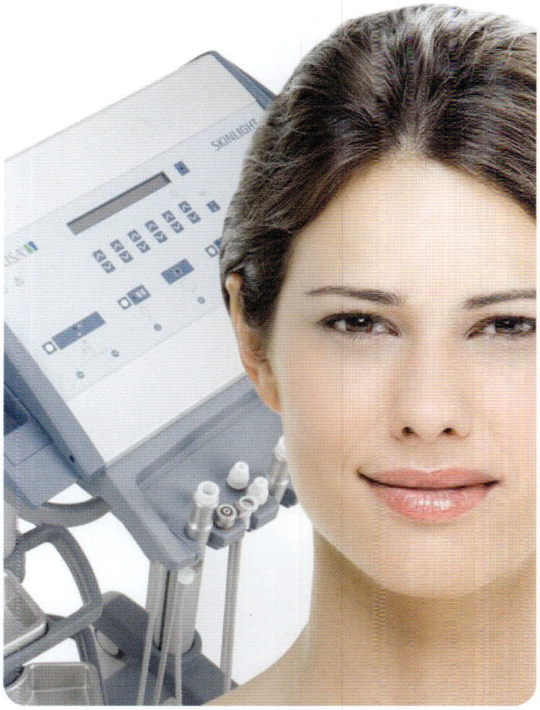

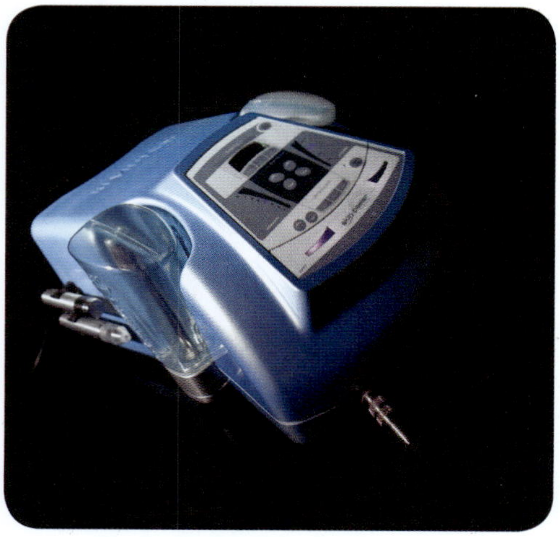

9 Electrical epilation 294

10 Body massage 332

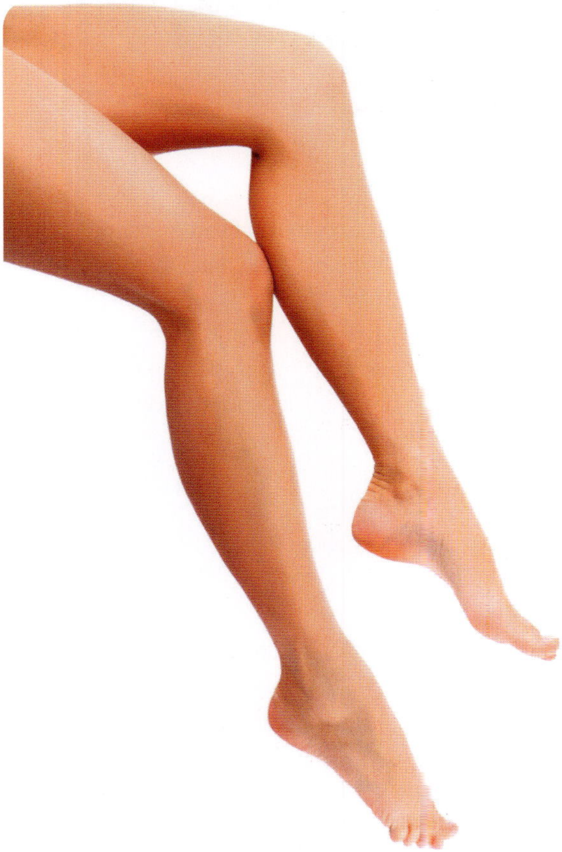

TISSERAND
LAMP VAPORISING RING
LAVENDER

COURSEMATE

CourseMate: Online chapters

Foreword from our partners

Nothing stands still; time has the effect of showing your age, not necessarily in a positive way. One beneficial aspect of the beauty industry is that advances in products and techniques with well trained beauty therapists mean that, as an industry, we can offer clients a service that not only provides them with positive results but has a cascading effect on their family, friends and ultimately the general public.

So it's no surprise that the number one beauty author, Lorraine Nordmann, takes all of this in her stride and produces a superb book that reflects industry expectations, best practice and a strong focus on client care and professional attitudes.

Lorraine is never one for holding back, and her sense of understanding the complexity of the industry shows by the way she has the ability to write in an engaging style; keeping the content simple yet making you feel that her considerable knowledge and experience are at your fingertips and you're fired up ready to go. Lorraine has excelled herself again, making sure that this edition will be well read and will leave a lasting impression on what the industry requirements are.

As Director of Standards and Qualifications for Habia, I'm delighted that Lorraine reflects the standards and ethos of Habia.

Jane Goldsbro
Director of Standards & Qualifications
Habia

About VTCT

VTCT is a government approved specialist awarding organisation responsible for qualifications in the beauty therapy, complementary therapy, hairdressing, sports, fitness, hospitality and catering sectors.

VTCT has been in existence for over 50 years, and in fact it was VTCT who originally coined the phrase *Beauty Therapy*. VTCT has remained at the forefront of developing the vocational system of qualifications in the UK and internationally.

VTCT invests in many charitable projects which support education and training in the beauty therapy industry. VTCT is the main sponsor and organiser of Worldskills UK (Beauty Therapy competitions) and VTCT also fund the development of the European and British Standard for Beauty Salon Services. In addition, VTCT donates charitable funds to disfigurement charities, prison education and other worthwhile causes linked to the beauty therapy sector.

VTCT has the widest and most diverse range of qualifications in the beauty industry and are leading on many new initiatives in education, including online assessment and registration, e-portfolio and e-resources.

VTCT develops innovative, fit for purpose qualifications via beauty therapy technical expert panels made up of employers, industry experts and educationalists from all over the UK.

About this book

Industry role models feature throughout the book and are your insight into the exciting beauty industry. Their profile is included at the start of the chapter and they provide subject-specific tips that are both practical and inspiring.

ROLE MODEL

Janice Brown

Director, HOF Beauty (House of Famuir Ltd)

" My career journey has taken me from working in (and later managing) a group of salons, through sales, teaching, training, research and development. I am currently Director of HOF Beauty Ltd. Along the way I have specialized in electrolysis and hair removal. I am the co-author of the *Encyclopaedia of Hair Removal*, along with Gill Morris. I am proud to say that I have been able to make a real difference to people's lives by helping to correct skin, body and hair growth issues. I hope I have also been able to inspire and encourage fellow therapists through the training I have provided. In the course of my career I have been fortunate enough to travel the world and work with wonderful people. Beauty therapy for me is not only a career but a true passion.

ACTIVITY

Where would you find guidance and if applicable legislation on the following health and safety hazards in the workplace?

- manual handling;
- noise levels;
- hazardous substances;
- use of computers;
- first aid;
- accidents.

Activity boxes feature within all chapters and provide additional tasks for you to further your understanding.

FUNCTIONAL SKILLS

Functional skills icons show where your information communication technologies (ICT), maths, and English skills can be developed by using the suggestions or activities suggested.

" Alcohols such as surgical spirit should not be used to clean equipment and furniture in the salon, particularly those with laminated or painted surfaces as they have a stripping effect over time. Alcohol is also flammable and so should never be used to clean wax heaters that are switched on or not cool.

Janice Brown

Role model quotes are included throughout a number of core chapters. Each quote provides valuable insight into the world of work, providing helpful and practical advice about working in such a varied and innovative industry.

A & P icon

A & P icons highlight essential anatomy and physiology knowledge needed for the unit

Anatomy and physiology essential knowledge for unit

The beauty therapy units covered in this book with an essential anatomy and physiology knowledge requirement are:

- Body electrical services
- Facial electrical services
- Single eyelash extensions
- Body massage

BEST PRACTICE

It is good practice to have a health and safety information file storing all current information including any updates to legislation.

Best practice boxes suggest good working practice and help you develop your skills and awareness during your training.

ALWAYS REMEMBER

Cleaning with surgical spirit

Before sterilization, surgical spirit applied with clean cotton wool may be used to clean small objects.

Always remember boxes draw your attention to key information or helpful hints that will help you prepare for assessment.

TOP TIP

Health and safety resource packs are available from Habia providing guidance in implementing health and safety policy and legislation in the beauty therapy workplace.

Top tips share the author's experience and provide positive suggestions to improve knowledge and skills for each unit.

EQUIPMENT AND MATERIAL LIST

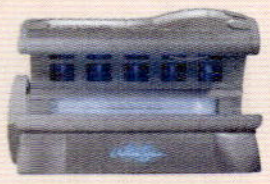

Sunbed equipment Sited in a fully screened area to avoid irradiation of other clients or therapists

Sunbed cleaning agent To clean the UV tanning system

Towels To dry the skin and protect the hair

YOU WILL ALSO NEED:

Disposable tissue roll Such as bedroll

Towels (2) Freshly laundered for each client

Flat mask brushes (3) Disinfected

Trolley To display all facial treatment products to be used in the facial service

Client's record card To record all the details relevant to the client's service

Facial toning lotions (a selection) To suit various types of skin

Equipment lists help you prepare for each practical treatment and show you the tools, materials and products required.

HEALTH & SAFETY

UV lamp record of usage

UV light is dangerous, especially to the eyes. The UV lamp must be switched off before opening the cabinet. A record must be kept of usage, as the effectiveness of the lamp decreases with use.

Health & Safety boxes draw your attention to related health and safety information essential for each technical skill.

Sample client record card

Date	Beauty therapist name	
Client name		Date of birth (Identifying client age group.)
Home address		Postcode
Landline phone number	Mobile phone number	Email address
Name of doctor	Doctor's address and phone number	
Related medical history (Conditions that may restrict or prohibit service application.)		
Are you taking any medication? (This may affect the condition of the skin or skin sensitivity.)		

Client record cards illustrate what you need to assess and gain from the client at consultation and also provide guidance on information following a treatment.

ASSESSMENT OF KNOWLEDGE AND UNDERSTANDING

Having covered the learning objectives for **monitoring safe work operations** – test what you need to know and understand by answering the following short questions below.

Check that health and safety instructions are followed:

1. It is important to have current knowledge of health and safety regulations, where can you source reliable information from?
2. What are the main responsibilities of the employers and employees in the workplace under the Health and Safety at Work Act 1974)?
3. Name four pieces of health and safety legislation and identify how they should be complied with.
4. How can information relating to health and safety workplace instructions be passed on?
5. How and when can issues of health and safety be fed back from staff to prevent a hazard becoming a risk?

Step-by-step: Massage routine for the back

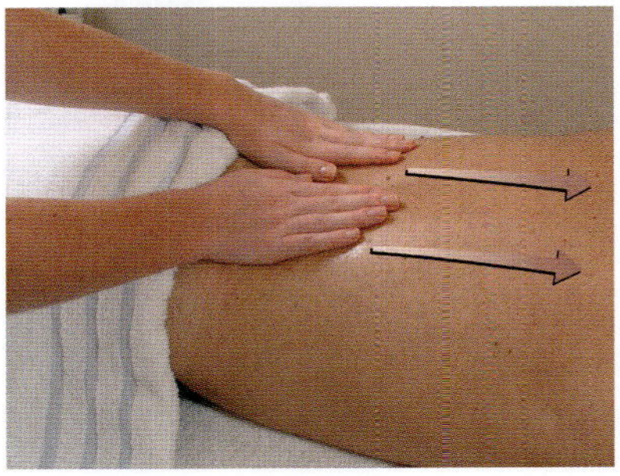

1. **Effleurage** From the base of the back, effleurage up the erector spinae area, across the shoulders and back down to the base of the spine. Repeat this step a further two times.

Step-by-step sequences demonstrate the featured practical skills using colour photographs to enhance your understanding.

Assessment of knowledge and understanding questions are provided at the end of all core chapters. You can use the questions to prepare for oral and written assessments and help test your own knowledge throughout. Seek guidance from your supervisor/assessor if there are areas you are unsure of.

COURSEMATE

CourseMate video boxes highlight certain techniques which are available to view online.

About the website

CourseMate

- Online Chapter 1 Freelance work
- Online Chapter 2 Fashion and photographic make-up
- Online Chapter 3 Airbrush make-up
- Online Chapter 4 TV, film and special effects make-up
- Online Chapter 5 Specialist skin camouflage

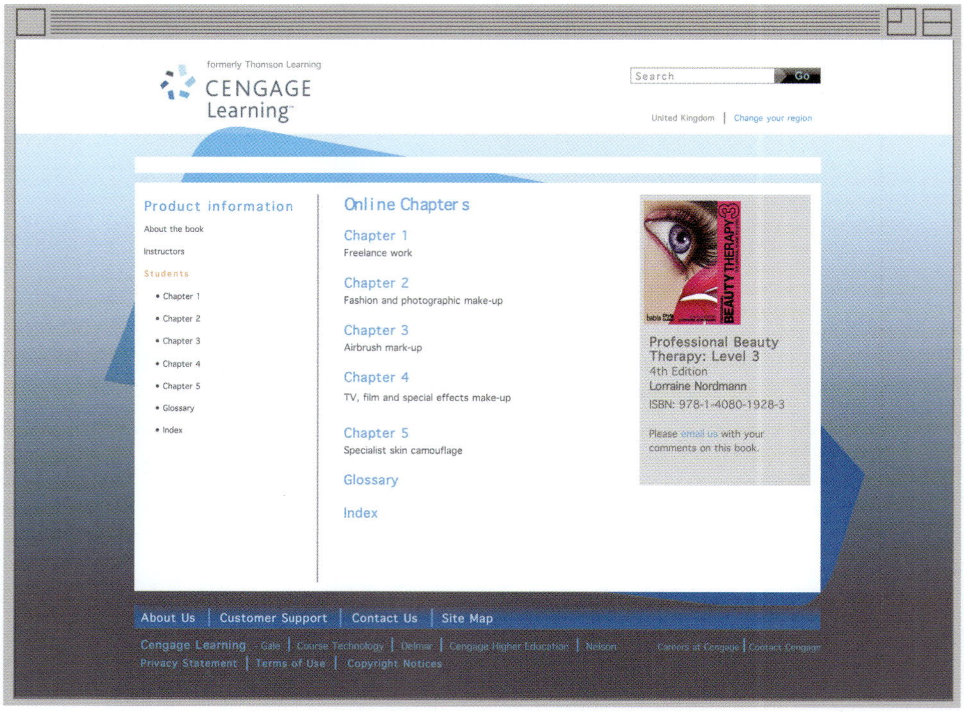

Use the *Professional Beauty Level 3* CourseMate alongside the *Professional Beauty Therapy: The Official Guide to Level 3, Revised Fourth Edition* textbook for a complete blended learning solution!

This highly interactive resource brings course concepts to life and is designed to support lecturers and students through the range of online resources which can be perfectly integrated into the classroom to cover the guided learning hours for each unit.

For Students:

- Searchable eBook
- Step-by-step videos
- Interactive multiple choice quizzes
- Interactive activities and games

For Lecturers:

- Lessons plans
- PowerPoint slides
- Activity handouts
- 'Engagement Tracker' tools so students' progression and comprehension can be fully monitored

For further information about CourseMate, please contact **emea.fesales@cengage.com**

About the author

Lorraine Nordmann has worked in the beauty therapy industry for the past 30 years and has witnessed significant technological advances of benefit to both the client and industry. Her commitment to the industry and passion for learning is evident in every page of her publications. As well as this Level 3 book, Lorraine is also the author of *Beauty Basics* and *Beauty Therapy: The Foundations*, covering the latest industry standards at Levels 1 and 2.

A note from the author

The industry has become diverse allowing specialism in micro-industries traditionally termed beauty therapy, i.e. make-up services, massage therapies and nail services. With this in mind the revisions to *Professional Beauty Therapy* and online materials have been written to support the training routes beauty therapy general, beauty therapy massage and beauty therapy make-up in line with the current national occupational standards. This allows you to excel in the area of the industry that you feel passionate about. Industry role models feature in each chapter to share their experiences, offering practical advice throughout.

The revisions to this book *Professional Beauty Therapy, fourth edition,* will support you attaining your qualification and develop the skills and attributes needed to meet current industry requirements whichever your training route (NVQ/SVQ or VRQ).

Enjoy your training and I wish you success in the industry.

Lorraine Nordmann

About the contributors

Jo Crowder is an international freelance make-up artist and hairstylist who has been actively involved in the make-up industry for the last 20 years. Her work has appeared extensively on TV, films and theatre, and graced the pages of magazines, national newspapers and books. She developed and ran the make-up artistry department at Liverpool Community College for 6 years, before taking on new challenges in Bulgaria. She now spends her time between the two countries, where she continues to work in the industry.

Pamela Linforth is the Human Resources and Training Director at Ellisons. A fully qualified beauty therapist, electrologist, lecturer and member of the Chartered Institute of Personnel and Development, she has made her career in the beauty therapy industry. Pamela was instrumental in Ellisons achieving and maintaining the Investor in People standard and is a champion of training and development for customers and staff.

Joan Scott has over 20 years of experience in the health and beauty sector. Her many and varied roles include beauty therapist, massage therapist, physiotherapy assistant, salon owner, lecturer, external examiner/verifier and curriculum manager. She is currently Assistant Principal at Trafford College and is the Chair of Habia's UK Beauty Forum.

Joan is co-author of *Spa*: *The Official Guide to Spa Therapy*, and of the Lecturer's Resource Packs for *Beauty Therapy* Levels 2 and 3. She has a passion for the spa and wellness sector, and combines a wealth of knowledge, with both an industry and education perspective.

Acknowledgements

The author and publishers would like to thank the following

Elizabeth Rose Whiteside for her ongoing love, support and passion for the industry.

Norman Whiteside for being the perfect father and critique.

Helen Green for her professionalism and commitment to the achievement of every goal.

Lauren Darby for her ultimate support and dedication.

Lucy Mills for her professional vision.

Lorraine Onorato for her industry expertise and contributing towards the Threading chapter.

For providing the cover image

Getty Images

For providing pictures for the book

Adele O'Keefe
The Airbrush Company Ltd, www.airbrushes.com
Dr Andrew Wright
Aqua Sana, Center Parcs, www.aquasana.co.uk
American Academy of Dermatology
Australian Bodycare
Babor
BABTAC, the British Association of Beauty Therapy and Cosmology
Beauty Express Ltd
Bella Vou, www.bellavou.co.uk
Clare Kirkman
CACI International
Carlton Beauty + Spa Ltd
Chubb Fire Ltd
Clean+Easy
Collin UK © Collin Paris
Cosmopro Inc
Corbis Covermark, Farmeco, www.farmeco.com
Daylight Company Ltd
Delmar Cengage Learning
Depilex
Ellisons
Everlash
Finders/Spa Find
GiGi
Gill Morris and Janice Brown for images from their book *Encyclopedia of Hair Removal*
Gail Proudman, SPMU Technical and Medical
Helen Eastwood
Habia
Health and Safety Executive (HSE)
Helionova Ltd
HMSO (Her Majesty's Stationery Office)
House of Famuir, www.hofbeauty.co.uk
Hugh Rushton
istockphoto
Janine Rigby and Andrea Dowdall
Dr John Gray, *The World of Skin Care*
jPb-imagery.com
Jacqui Wilson
Mavala Mediscan Milady, www.milady.cengage.com
Dr M. H. Beck
MiniKini
Moom waxing, www.moom-uk.com
Shane Noden – Personal Trainer and Club Manager, Haydock Spirit Health Club

Oxford Designers and Illustrators
The Sanctuary at Covent Garden Ltd, www.thesanctuary.co.uk
Simon Jersey Ltd, www.simonjersey.com
Saks Covent Garden
Salon System (Original Additions) Ltd
Silhouette-Dermalift
Simon Jersey, www.simonjersey.com
Smart Buy
Smith and Nephew, Hull
Sterex Electrolysis
St Tropez, The Skin Finishing Experts
Sukar (Nagwa Trading Co. Ltd)
SunChic Tanning, www.sunchic.com
Sunquest Tanning Ltd
Sarah Clough and Vicky Unsworth, beauty therapists, Evolve, New Woman/New Man Beauty Clinic
Thalgo UK Ltd, www.thalgo.com
Thermal Stones, www.ThermalStones.co.uk
Thinkstock Tisser and Aromatherapy
Mike Turner- Photographer
United Beauty/SolGlo, www.miketurner-photography.co.uk
UV-Power UK
Vital Touch
Wellcome Trust
Valerie Ann Worwood
Vicky Kennedy, Evolve, New Woman/New Man Beauty Clinic
Elizabeth and Norman Whiteside

For their contribution as industry role models

Tammy Baker
Janice Brown
Claire Burrell
Annette Close
Zoe Crowley
Sam Davies
Kerry Davis
Lisa Fulton
Alice Guise
Katie Harris
Gill Morris
Mary Overton
Andy Rouillard
Shavata Singh
Alex Widdows
Katie Whitehouse

For providing the student case study

Coral Sharp

For their help with the review process

Debbie Le Grave, Newham College, London
Joanne Mackinnon, London College of Beauty Therapy

Every effort has been made to trace the copyright holders, but if any have been inadvertently overlooked the publisher will be pleased to make the necessary arrangements at the first opportunity. Please contact the publisher directly.

1 Introduction

SHUTTERSTOCK/MONKEY BUSINESS IMAGES

There is a choice of five employment routes to achieve an NVQ/SVQ Diploma at Level 3, a work-related, competency-based qualification:

- beauty therapy general
- nail services
- beauty therapy make-up
- spa therapy
- beauty therapy massage

This book covers the current practical skills that you must be able to perform and the essential knowledge you need to know to become qualified for employment in either the **Beauty Therapy General** or **Beauty Therapy Massage** industry. It also may be used as a reference text for non-NVQ/SVQ qualifications such as VRQs (vocationally related qualifications, which are becoming increasingly popular, focussing their content on the development of the underlying skills and abilities required for progression into the workplace. It may also support study for internationally recognized qualifications such as CIBTAC and CIDESCO. An NVQ/SVQ qualification in General Beauty Therapy or Beauty Therapy Massage may be gained through different government-approved awarding bodies. These are listed below with their website addresses and include:

- VTCT – www.vtct.org.uk
- CGLI – www.cityandguilds.com
- Edexcel – www.edexcel.com
- ITEC – www.itecworld.co.uk

VTCT logo

Each awarding body is required to cover the same standards, describing what an individual needs to do, know and understand – referred to as National Occupational Standards (NOS) – in the design of their qualification. The Standards are provided by the government-approved standards setting body for hairdressing, beauty therapy, nails and spa therapy, Habia (Hairdressing and Beauty Therapy Industry Authority). This ensures an employer can be confident of the skills an employee will be able to perform competently in accordance with what NVQ/SVQ level they have achieved, whichever awarding body has accredited it.

Habia provides an updated list of the the National Occupational Standards on their website www.habia.org.

NVQs/SVQs are required to be studied, combining both 'on-the-job' and 'off-the-job' training, with the emphasis being that you are working towards a work based qualification, therefore spending the majority of your time in the workplace

Habia logo

ALWAYS REMEMBER

Habia Sector Skills Body

Habia is the Sector Skills Body for the hair, beauty, nails, spa, industries. The role of the Sector Skills Body Habia is to represent the industry on matters such as training, skills and business development.

TOP TIP

Apprenticeships

Apprenticeship is the training route for an NVQ. You will study *on-the-job* in the work-place as an apprentice to achieve your work-based qualification at Level 3. You will have the benefit of contributing to the business, using and developing your skills while training. You will also study *off-the-job* to attain your technical and functional skills qualifications, communication, and application of number and ICT. At the end you will be job ready, having all the necessary skills required by an employer.

To find out more about apprenticeships visit the Habia website at www.habia.org.

COURTESY OF WORLD OF BEAUTY BY KATY, LONDON

Certificates from different awarding bodies

NVQs and SVQs

National Vocational Qualifications (NVQs) and Scottish Vocational Qualifications (SVQs) in Scotland are nationally recognized qualifications which have a similar format. The award of an NVQ/SVQ demonstrates that the person has the competence (having sufficient skill and knowledge) to perform job roles/tasks effectively in their occupational area. An NVQ/SVQ at Level 3 involves the application of knowledge in a wide range of varied work activities, most of which are complex and non-routine and require the employee to use their initiative and make independent decisions. Supervision and guidance for others may be required.

Each NVQ/SVQ is made up of a number of units and outcomes. The unit structure differs between an NVQ and SVQ.

The **unit** relates to a specific task or skill area of work. It is the smallest part of an award that can be accredited separately. The **learning outcomes** describe in detail the skill and knowledge components of the unit, and what is required to be completed (but not how).

An example of a unit and its outcome from NVQ/SVQ Level 3 Beauty Therapy General route is shown below:

The title of the unit is **Provide self-tanning services**.

The outcomes for the unit detail the practical skills and knowledge requirements essential to provide self-tanning services.

The outcomes that detail the unit components include:

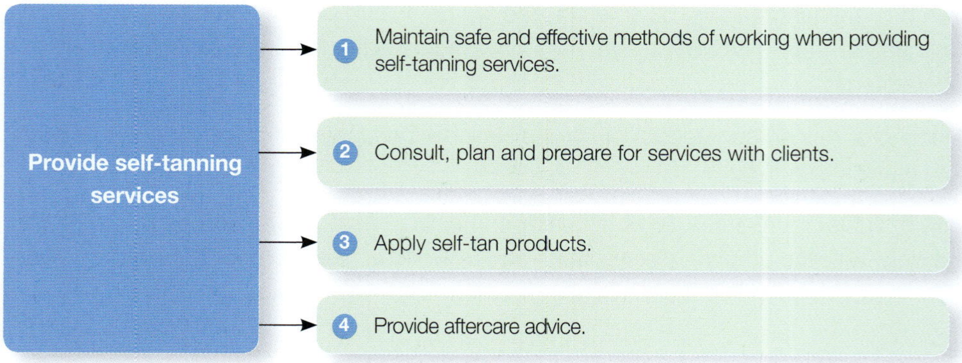

Units and outcomes

For each unit, when all competence evidence requirements have been achieved, a unit of certification may be awarded, such as **Provide self-tanning services**. This is a mini-qualification in itself.

Each NVQ/SVQ is made up from a specific number of units required for the occupational area. Some of the units are termed **mandatory** (compulsory), some are **optional** (not compulsory).

Mandatory units must be competently achieved to gain the NVQ/SVQ award.

Optional units are selected for study by the candidate in addition to the mandatory units to attain the qualification.

The NVQ/SVQ will state which are the mandatory, compulsory units to achieve the qualification, plus the number of optional units which must be successfully completed in order to achieve the full NVQ/SVQ qualification. Remember, this choice will differ dependant upon if you are studying towards an NVQ or SVQ.

The Level 3 NVQ qualification structure is shown in the following table to achieve the Beauty Therapy General employment route. Each qualification structure shows the compulsory mandatory units and optional units to be achieved whichever route is chosen. The optional units chosen should complement and ideally be relevant to the employment route being studied towards.

National Occupational Standards: Level 3 Beauty Therapy Proposed NVQ Qualification Structure Candidates must complete all **6 mandatory units** totalling 55 credits and in addition a further 10 credits from the optional units to achieve an overall total of 65 credits.

Mandatory units (all must be completed):
Monitor procedures to safely control work operations (4 credits) (ENTO HSS3)
Contribute to the planning and implementation of promotional Activities (5 credits)
Provide body electrical treatments (12 credits)
Provide facial electrical treatments (12 credits)
Provide body massage treatments (10 credits)
Provide electrical epilation treatments (12 credits)

ENTO – Employment National Training Organization

ALWAYS REMEMBER

What can I study?

For information on all the Level 3 Beauty Therapy units, including NVQ, SVQ, general massage and nail routes, go to the Habia website, www.habia.org.

PLUS a minimum of 10 optional credits from the list below:
Contribute to the financial effectiveness of the business (4 credits)
Plan and provide airbrush make-up (8 credits)
Provide single eyelash extension treatments (5 credits)
Provide UV tanning services (2 credits)
Provide Indian head massage (7 credits)
Carry out massage using pre-blended aromatherapy oils (8 credits)
Provide self-tanning services (3 credits)
Provide female intimate waxing services (5 credits)
Provide male intimate waxing services (5 credits)
Provide stone therapy treatments (10 credits)

ENTO – Employment National Training Organization

Performance criteria

The performance criteria lists the necessary actions that you must achieve to complete the task competently (demonstrating the required practical skills and experience to the assessor).

It is necessary that you are able to meet the expected standard for each performance criteria outcome that makes up the unit to which you are to be assessed against.

The **performance criteria** requirements for Provide self-tanning services, Outcome 4: Provide aftercare advice are as follows:

- **a** giving advice and recommendations accurately and constructively
- **b** giving your clients suitable advice specific to their individual needs.

Range

Range statements are often identified for each outcome. The assessment range relates to the different conditions or applications in which a skill must be demonstrated competently for the outcome and on what occasions.

For example, the range assessment requirements for Outcome 1, **Equipment**, are shown below:

> Range: Your performance must cover the following situations
>
> 1 Equipment covers:
>
> a spray gun
> b compressor
> c buffing mitt

It is not sufficient only to be able to practically perform the task: you must understand why you are doing it and be able to apply this competence to a variety of situations. This is referred to as your knowledge and understanding.

Further assessment of your **knowledge and understanding** of the skill, the knowledge specification, may be assessed through written tests, assignments and oral questioning.

The **knowledge and understanding** requirements that you are required to know for Provide self-tanning services, aftercare for clients are listed below:

- Products for home use that will benefit the client, and those to avoid and why.
- The contra-actions that could occur after self-tanning and what advice to give clients.
- The post-service restrictions applicable to self-tanning.
- Suitable types of follow-on services, their benefits and costs.

What often occurs is that the same knowledge and understanding may be necessary for similar units. This can be seen, for example, in the knowledge and understanding for **Organizational and legal requirements**. This duplication is necessary because some units may be studied and accredited as an individual skill/unit.

Where evidence has been achieved this speeds up the learning process.

To achieve unit competence, all performance criteria, range and knowledge and understanding requirements must have been met and evidence presented as necessary. Evidence is usually provided in your assessment log book and portfolio: either paper based or electronic.

Where there is evidence of previous experience and achievement this may be presented to the assessor for consideration for accreditation. This is called recognition of prior learning (RPL).

Professional Beauty Therapy follows the Beauty Therapy NVQ/SVQ Level 3 syllabus for the Beauty Therapy General and Beauty Therapy Massage route and covers both the practical and theoretical requirements for both the mandatory and optional units.

In addition to the NVQ/SVQ termed job-ready qualifications, there is the option to study towards a nationally recognized Vocational Related Qualification (VRQ). VRQs relate to a specific occupational area NOS and are taken by learners wanting to develop the skills and gain the knowledge to enter a particular industry or by learners working already within that industry to accredit or update their skills.

Professional Beauty Therapy provides essential information whichever your qualification.

Job-ready (competence based) means that you are ready for work when qualified. All awarding bodies will use the same assessment criteria for the job-ready qualifications they offer.

VRQ qualifications provide knowledge, understanding and capability for your occupation but without the ability to be immediately ready for work.

BEST PRACTICE

Service standards

As a senior beauty therapist you will be expected to ensure that services are delivered to a consistently high standard, following all relevant legislation, with codes of practice and work-related policies and procedures applied.

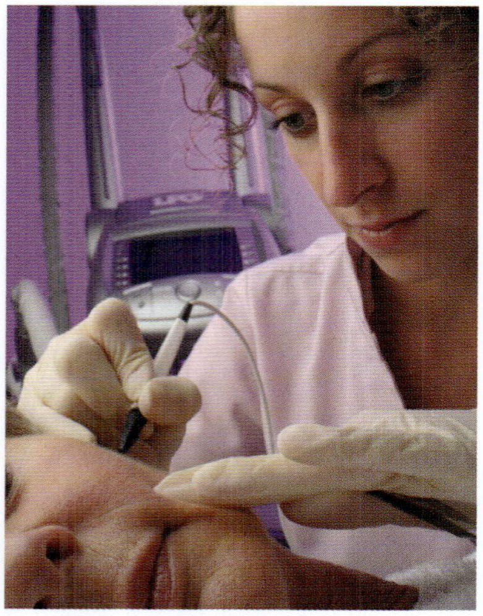

BELLA VOU WWW.BELLAVOU.CO.UK

Professional Level 3 beauty therapist at work

ACTIVITY

Professionalism

Give three examples of professional 'best practice' which you consider you have provided in your work role delivering Level 3 beauty therapy or beauty therapy massage services.

ACTIVITY FUNCTIONAL SKILLS

Employability skills

Write a list of the personal strengths you feel you have that would make you successful and an asset as a beauty therapist/massage therapist employee.

Do you have any weaknesses, for example, poor listening skills, which need to improve to develop your employability skills? What can you do to improve the identified weakness?

A successful career in beauty therapy and massage

A beauty/massage therapist qualified to Level 3 will carry out advanced techniques and, as a senior beauty therapist, will be capable and usually expected to perform additional management responsibilities in the workplace.

To gain employment and become a business asset, you must have excellent employability skills. An employer regards these as being just as important as your qualification. Employability skills include attitudes and actions often referred to as 'soft skills':

- appearance – being always professionally presented
- being reliable (including an excellent attendance and punctuality record)
- having a positive attitude
- being self-motivated
- using your initiative – solving problems, suggesting solutions!
- being involved in decision-making (relevant to your experience and within your responsibility)
- having good interpersonal skills with all of whom you come into contact with
- being a good communicator, considering at all times the diversity of your clientele
- working well in a team – building a team 'ethos' which strives to fulfil the business objectives

On successful completion of your NVQ/SVQ in Beauty Therapy or Beauty Therapy Massage at Level 3 you can gain employment or progress your training, obtaining a further or higher qualification.

Employment opportunities include:

Beauty therapy

- business owner
- freelance (working for yourself)
- senior beauty therapist in a salon
- specializing in a particular area of beauty therapy, such as electrical epilation
- employment in a department store, spa, leisure centre or club providing beauty therapy services
- college lecturer
- a technician for a manufacturer providing training on products, equipment and services
- sales and marketing manager
- cruise ship or airline beauty therapist

- working in the media: magazines, advertisements and television
- trainer

Massage therapy

- business owner
- freelance (working for yourself)
- senior massage/beauty therapist post
- employment in a complementary therapy clinic, hotel, spa, gym leisure centre or club
- providing onsite services in the workplace, for example **Indian head massage** for **stress**
- sales and marketing manager
- cruise ship or airline delivering beauty therapy massage
- working in the media: magazines, advertising and television
- trainer

Progression opportunities When you achieve your Level 3 qualification in General Beauty Therapy or Beauty Therapy Massage you can continue to update and advance your skills as relevant to your future career path/goals.

This will include:

- Study of other associated industry qualifications in hairdressing, nails, make-up or spa services.
- Further training to gain advanced practical techniques to maintain **continuing professional development** (CPD). CPD is important to keep yourself up-to-date and be responsive to the emerging trends of the industry.
- Attainment of a higher level beauty therapy and complimentary therapy qualification to broaden your career progression into areas such as the National Health Service.
- Assessor training when you have attained substantial occupational experience.
- Level 4 management qualifications to develop skills in: business planning; financial management; sales and marketing; and leadership. This will provide the skills necessary to manage people and run a business.
- Higher education: you could study towards a degree or attain a teaching qualification.

ALWAYS REMEMBER

Senior beauty therapist's role

Senior beauty therapists are likely to take on a leadership role to monitor and bring about changes in delivery of products, services, resources or systems. While operating within their role and responsibility they will report progress regularly to their supervisors. This may include areas such as quality of service delivery, performance against targets, for example sales, marketing strategies, colleague performance and health and safety.

It is possible to attain a supervisory or management work role within approximately 2 years of qualifying if you gain evidence of your experience. NVQ units you will study towards will develop such skills, for example mandatory units **Monitor procedures to safely control work operations** and **Contribute to the planning and implementation of promotional activities** help you gain evidence and experience.

TOP TIP

Practical experience

While training, take every opportunity to practice your skills; this is vital to improve your confidence and practical skills when working 'on the job'.

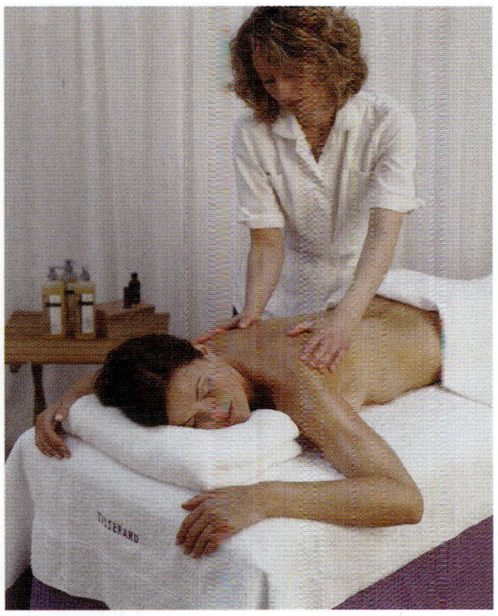

TISSERAND

Extending your beauty therapy proficiencies to include massage therapy opens many doors

TOP TIP

Keep up-to-date

Visiting trade shows, lectures and seminars provides an excellent opportunity to keep up-to-date in new products, equipment and services, as well as subscribing to professional trade magazines.

STUDENT CASE STUDY

A student who has recently completed Level 3 in massage explains her personal development, work experiences and the next steps.

Name: Coral Sharp

Title of Qualification:
NVQ Level 3 Beauty Therapy

Name of College: Bolton Community College

What did you enjoy most about studying, and what did you find most challenging?

The unit that I enjoyed the most was the body massage unit. As a beauty therapist I found this a relaxing treatment to both give and the client to receive and I felt that I always met my client's needs. I also enjoyed the non-surgical micro-current facial treatments, as every client has a different need and a different condition. The unit which was the most challenging for me was the epilation, as this involved more practice and I felt this was the most advanced skill on the course.

What are your next steps in your career development, and where would you like to see yourself in the future?

The next step for me in my career development is to complete Level 4 in Salon Management and to gain further hands-on experience. In the future, I would like to have my own business in a salon where I will specialize in the more advanced treatments such as micro-pigmentation and red vein removal. Sometime in the future I would like to have experienced working on a cruise ship to gain additional experience of the beauty industry.

Describe your work experience so far.

I have previously worked in a hairdressing salon offering nail services, in which I was self-employed. There, my duties were to provide manicures, pedicures and acrylic nails on a daily basis. My main responsibilities were to provide nail services and to ensure that the salon was kept extremely clean and tidy at all times to implement high standards of hygiene. I was also responsible for client welfare whilst ensuring that they were comfortable and relaxed during their treatments. It was also important that I gave the clients aftercare advice to ensure they gained the maximum benefit from the service and it was important to remain professional at all times.

What is your job role and where do you work?

I am currently working for a large retail company whilst a full-time student completing my Level 4 in Salon Management at Bolton Community College. In my role as a sales assistant and cashier I endeavour to provide excellent customer service and to take leads on showroom sales. I am also responsible for cash control, banking and placing orders over the phone for delivery.

What do you find rewarding about your current job, and what do you find challenging about your job?

I find that, in retail, being able to help a customer and to provide them with the best possible service by answering any questions and resolving any problems that they have is essential. It is rewarding knowing that the customer is satisfied. I find that customer complaints can sometimes be challenging but if handled professionally the problem can be rectified.

What do you think makes a good beauty therapist?

I think that excellent customer care is essential as a beauty therapist and professionalism is critical. As a good therapist you should be able to guarantee commitment and a high standard of work to ensure that the client's needs are met. Not only the treatment but the manner in which you present yourself is just as important.

ACTIVITY

FUNCTIONAL SKILLS

Planning your dream job

While training towards your Level 3 qualification consider your 'dream job'. Using professional journals/magazines or online job advertisements, search for a vacancy and obtain a job description so you can see the qualifications, experience and personal attributes that you will be requried to have. You can then draw up a plan of what you will need to achieve, when and how to gain the necessary evidence of your qualifications and experience. This is your career path, the journey required to achieve your career aspirations.

BABOR

Demonstration skills and services at a trade exhibition

Industry role models

In the beauty therapy and massage industry there are many role models who have extensive experience, which has helped raise the industry profile, and they have a passion for their work, which is inspirational to our beauty therapists and massage therapists of the future.

Industry role models have contributed 'tips of the trade' in this book, sharing their expertise and valued knowledge, explaining how they achieved the industry status that they have today. These include:

Chapter 3 – Janice Brown, HOF Beauty (House of Famuir Ltd)

Chapter 4 – Kerry Davis, The Sanctuary Spa

Chapter 5 – Lisa Fulton, FakeBake (UK) Ltd

Chapter 6 – Alice Guise, Salon Synergy

Chapter 8 – Mary Overton, CACI International and Claire Burrell, CACI International

Chapter 9 – Gill Morris, GMT TEC

Chapter 10 – Katie Harris, Equilibrium Complementary Health Centre

Chapter 11 – Zoe Crowley, Elveden Forest Center Parcs

Chapter 12 – Katie Whitehouse, Vital Touch Ltd

Chapter 13 – Sam Davies, Ki Day Spa

Chapter 14 – Alex Widdows, 'Sun Chic', Luxury Tanning Salon

Chapter 15 – Tammy Baker, St Tropez

Chapter 16 – Andy Rouillard, Axiom Bodyworks and Annette Close, Australian Bodycare UK Ltd

Chapter 17 – Shavata Singh, Shavata UK

The following role model examples show case studies of the career journey of two of our industry experts, detailing how they achieved their status in the industry.

ROLE MODEL

MARY OVERTON, CACI

Mary Overton

Export Manager for CACI International

" I started my career in the beauty industry 26 years ago upon the recommendation of a relative who at that time was working as the Beauty Editor for a leading women's magazine. I felt that a career in beauty would offer me many varied and exciting opportunities. This has certainly proved to be the case!

In 1981, after graduating from the Shaw College of Beauty Therapy and Micheline Arcier Aromatherapy School, I worked as a beauty therapist/aromatherapist for several years. After gaining additional qualifications in media studies and a City & Guilds qualification in teaching I then worked for several multinational companies including the skincare company Guinot as a company trainer/training manager.

For the past 9 years I have been responsible for developing the export business for CACI International and raising the profile of the CACI brand overseas, including new product launches in Asia, Australasia, the Americas, Middle East, Scandinavia, and Central and Eastern Europe. During my career I have enjoyed representing my company on television both at home and abroad, contributing to beauty articles in the trade press, and was a judge for the Professional Beauty Awards for 2 years running.

Mary shares her expertise in Chapter 8, **Facial and body electrical services**.

ROLE MODEL

KATIE WHITEHOUSE, VITAL TOUCH

Katie Whitehouse

Director of Vital Touch Ltd and Complementary Therapist: Sports and Holistic Massage, Aromatherapy, Pregnancy Massage and Reflexology

" I am a founder Director of Vital Touch Ltd. We are based in Devon where we make gorgeous organic skincare and aromatherapy products which are sold to beauty therapists, spas and retail outlets nationwide and abroad. Our passion is positive touch and our mission is to promote the benefits of this through the use of our natural products and massage guides.

I have been a practising massage therapist, aromatherapist and reflexologist for 20 years. I have taught massage, sports massage, anatomy and physiology in many colleges in the UK and currently run courses specializing in training therapists to be confident in massaging pregnant clients.

I am also involved in training for midwives, doulas and antenatal teachers – enabling fathers-to-be to connect with their partner and unborn baby through simple touch and massage.

Currently Vice Chair of the APNT (Association of Physical and Natural Therapists) I am also an assessor for the Association. I have also been involved with the Aromatherapy Consortium where I was Secretary for the Research and Scientific Subcommittee.

Katie shares her expertise in Chapter 12, **Aromatherapy massage using pre-blended oils**.

TOP TIP

Top jobs!

Survey shows beauty therapists are happy in their work

Beauty therapy is one of the UK's 20 happiest sectors to work in, according to the City & Guild's annual happiness survey 2012.

***Source:* Career Happiness Index 2012, City & Guilds.**

As you can see from these role models, upon successful completion of your Level 3 qualification you will be able to work in a rewarding job which is full of variety and has endless career possibilities.

2 Anatomy and physiology

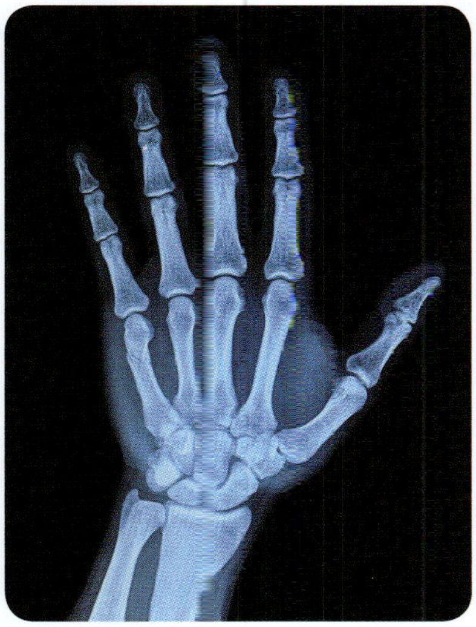

SHUTTERSTOCK/HUANG YUETAO

This chapter covers the essential anatomy and physiology requirements for students studying for an NVQ/SVQ or equivalent accredited course in Beauty Therapy at Level 3. It covers the following topics:

- the cells and **tissues**
- the skin
- **adipose tissue**
- the hair
- the nails
- the **skeletal system**
- the nervous system
- the urinary system
- the **digestive system**
- the **respiratory system**
- the endocrine system
- the **reproductive system**
- the muscular system
- the heart and circulatory system
- the lymphatic system
- the brain
- the **olfactory system**
- the limbic system

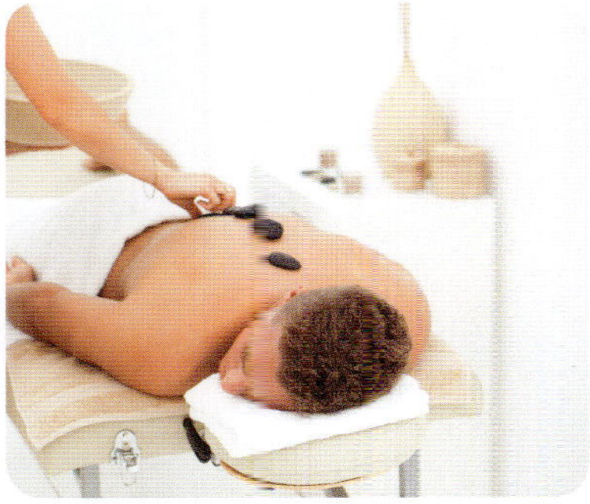

SHUTTERSTOCK/MIKLAV SHUTTERSTOCK/HUANG YUETAO

Your services will have a physiological effect on the area being treated

Anatomy and physiology (A&P) knowledge and understanding are located in this chapter, and a brief discussion can also be found within each of the chapters where essential anatomy and physiology are identified using the symbol shown.

As a beauty therapist it is important that you have a good understanding of anatomy and physiology, as many of your services aim to improve the particular functioning of systems of the body. For example, a body massage will improve blood and lymph circulation locally, as you massage the skin's surface, and increase cellular renewal as you improve nutrition to the living cells and remove dead skin cells. The result is healthier-looking skin.

Anatomy and physiology knowledge and understanding requirements

It is necessary for you to know and understand anatomy and physiology as relevant to each unit. This may be assessed through oral questioning, a written test or assignment. To guide you in your studies, the **essential** anatomy and physiology you need to know and understand for each unit has been identified with a ✓ symbol in the table below. Look for the A&P symbol to remind you to check back here for your essential anatomy and physiology knowledge!

Anatomy and physiology essential knowledge for unit
The beauty therapy units covered in this book with an essential anatomy and physiology knowledge requirement are:
Provide body electrical services
Provide facial electrical services
Provide single eyelash extension services
Provide body massage services
Provide UV tanning services
Provide Indian head massage
Carry out massage using pre-blended aromatherapy oils
Provide self-tanning services
Provide female intimate waxing services
Provide male intimate waxing services
Provide stone therapy service
Provide electrical epilation services

Anatomy and physiology essential knowledge for each topic:

Topic:	*Body electrical*	*Facial electrical*	*Single lash extension*	*Body massage*	*UV tanning*	*Provide Indian head massage*	*Massage using pre-blended aromatherapy oils*	*Self-tanning*	*Female intimate waxing*	*Male intimate waxing*	*Stone therapy*	*Electrical epilation*
Structure and function of cells and tissues	✓	✓		✓	✓	✓	✓	✓	✓	✓	✓	✓
Skin structure and function	✓	✓		✓	✓	✓	✓	✓	✓	✓	✓	✓
Factors affecting skin condition	✓	✓		✓	✓	✓	✓	✓	✓	✓	✓	✓
Structure and type of hair			✓						✓	✓		✓
Hair growth cycle			✓						✓	✓		✓

Topic:	Body electrical	Facial electrical	Single lash extension	Body massage	UV tanning	Provide Indian head massage	Massage using pre-blended aromatherapy oils	Self-tanning	Female intimate waxing	Male intimate waxing	Stone therapy	Electrical epilation
Muscle groups in parts of the body, position, structure and function	✓	✓		✓		✓	✓				✓	
Muscle tone	✓	✓		✓		✓	✓				✓	
Bones in parts of the body, position, structure and function	✓	✓		✓		✓	✓				✓	
Structure and function of the heart	✓	✓		✓			✓					
Principles of the blood circulatory system	✓	✓		✓		✓	✓				✓	✓
Principles of the lymph system	✓	✓		✓		✓	✓				✓	✓
Composition and function of blood and lymph	✓	✓		✓		✓	✓				✓	✓
Blood flow and pulse rate	✓	✓		✓		✓	✓				✓	✓
Central nervous system and autonomic system	✓	✓		✓		✓	✓				✓	
Endocrine system	✓	✓		✓		✓	✓				✓	✓
Respiratory system				✓		✓	✓				✓	
Olfactory system							✓					
Digestive system	✓			✓			✓				✓	
Excretory system				✓			✓				✓	
Reproductive system				✓			✓					
Structure and function of female and male genitalia									✓	✓		
Basic structure and function of the eye			✓		✓							

Cells and tissues

The human body consists of many trillions of microscopic cells. Each cell contains a chemical substance called **protoplasm**, which contains various specialized structures the activities of which are essential to our health. If cells are unable to function properly, a disorder results.

Surrounding the cell is the **cell membrane**: this forms a boundary between the cell contents and their environment. The membrane has a porous surface which permits food to enter and waste materials to leave.

In the centre of the cell is the **nucleus**, which contains thread-like structures called **chromosomes**. On these are the **genes** we have inherited from our parents making us who we are. The **genes** are ultimately responsible for cell reproduction and cell functioning.

The liquid within the cell membrane and surrounding the nucleus is a gel-like substance called **cytoplasm**. Scattered throughout this are other small bodies, the **organelles** or 'little organs'; each has a specific function within the cell.

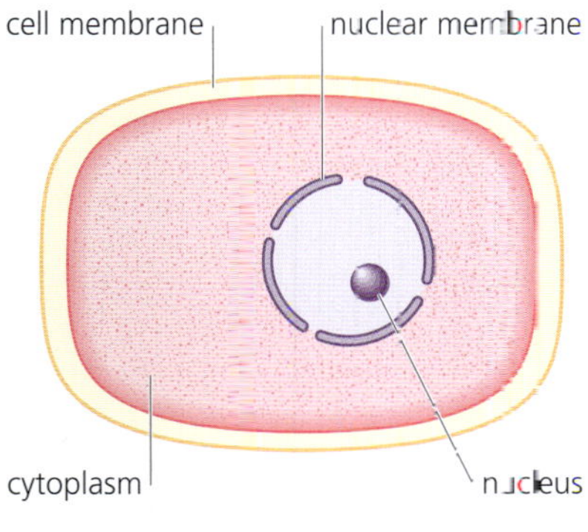

A basic cell

ALWAYS REMEMBER

Did you know?

The skin accounts for one-eighth of the body's total weight. It measures approximately 1.5 m^2 in total, depending on body size. It is thinnest on the eyelids (0.05 mm), and thickest on the soles of the feet (approximately 5 mm).

Cells in the body tend to specialize in carrying out particular functions. Groups of cells that share function, shape, size or structure are called **tissues**. Tissues, in turn, may be grouped to form the larger functional and structural units we know as **organs**, such as the heart.

If the tissues are damaged, for example if the skin is accidentally broken, the cells divide to repair the damage – called regeneration.

The body is composed of four basic tissues. These are described below.

Types of tissue and general function

Name of tissue	*Examples*	*General functions*
Epithelial tissue 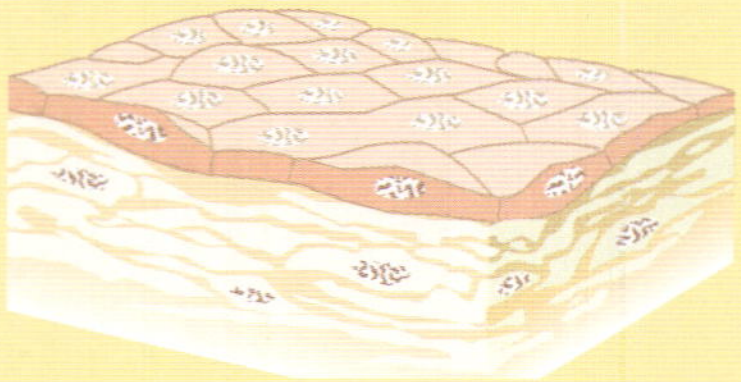	Epidermis.	Forms surfaces and linings for protection.
Connective tissue 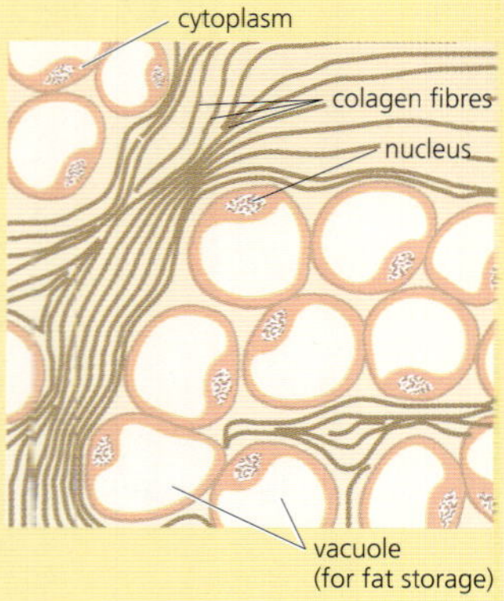	Dermis layer of skin Collagen fibres Bone Ligaments Tendons	A structural tissue that supports, surrounds and connects different parts of the body.
Muscular tissue 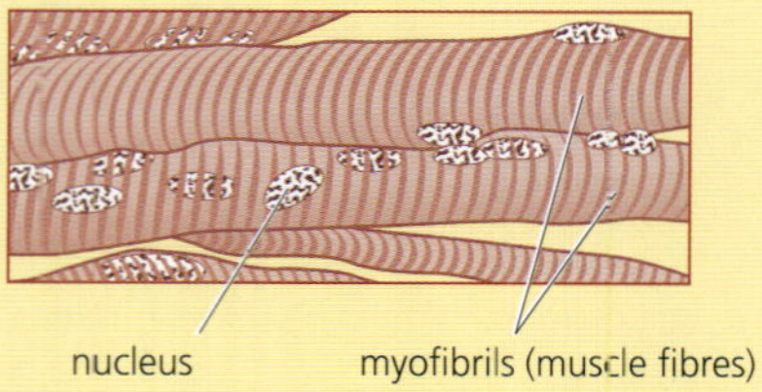	Voluntary or skeletal, muscle tissue Involuntary or smooth muscle tissue	Contracts and shortens producing movement. Skeletal muscle tissue moves the body and maintains posture. Smooth muscle tissue moves substances through the body.
Nervous tissue 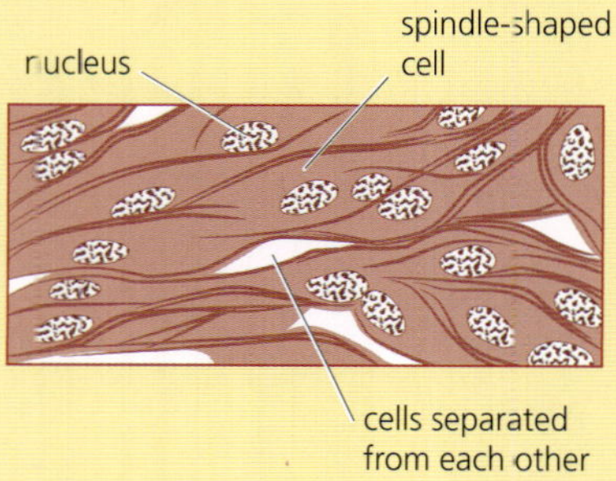	Neurones (nerve cells).	Forms a communication system between different parts of the body, controlling and co-ordinating most body processes.

Functions of the skin

The human skin is an organ – the largest of the body. It provides a tough, flexible covering, with many different important functions. Its main functions are:

- protection
- heat regulation
- excretion
- sensitivity
- nutrition
- moisture control

The skin varies in appearance according to our ethnicity, gender and age. It also alters from season to season and from year to year, and reflects our general health, lifestyle and diet.

Protection

The skin protects the body from potentially harmful substances and conditions.

- The outer surface is **bactericidal**, helping to prevent the growth of harmful microorganisms. It also prevents the absorption of many substances (unless the surface is broken) because of the structure of the cells on its outer surface, which form a chemical and physical barrier.
- The skin cushions the underlying structures from physical injury.
- The skin provides a **waterproof coating**. Its natural oil, **sebum**, prevents the skin from losing essential water, and therefore preventing skin dehydration.
- The skin contains a pigment called **melanin**. This absorbs harmful rays of UV light.
- The skin uses a warning system to defend against outside invasion. Redness and inflammation of the skin indicate that the skin is intolerant or allergic to something, this may be either external or internal.

Heat regulation

Humans have a normal body temperature maintained at 36.8–37°C. Body **temperature** is controlled in part by heat loss through the skin and by sweating. If the temperature of the body is increased by 0.25–0.5°C, the sweat glands secrete sweat to the skin's surface. The body is cooled by the loss of heat used to evaporate the sweat from the skin's surface.

If the body becomes too warm, there is an increase in blood flow into the blood capillaries in the skin. The blood capillaries widen (dilate) and heat is lost from the skin. If the external temperature becomes low and the body needs to conserve heat there is a reduction in blood flow into the blood capillaries in the skin. The blood capillaries become narrower (constrict) so less blood is brought to the skin's surface. Hair also limits heat loss from the scalp.

Excretion

Small amounts of certain **waste products**, such as urea, water and salt, are removed from the body in sweat by a process called excretion from sweat glands through the surface of the skin from the skin's pores.

ALWAYS REMEMBER

Did you know?

Although the skin has a waterproof property, it allows water to be lost from the tissues through evaporation every day, approximately 500 ml.

You need to keep your skin hydrated.

TOP TIP

Functions of the skin

By remembering the word *SHAPES* this will help you remember the functions of the skin:

- **S Sensation**
- **H Heat regulation**
- **A Absorption**
- **P Protection**
- **E Excretion**
- **S Secretion**

HEALTH & SAFETY

Skin protection

Although the skin is structured to avoid penetration of harmful substances by absorption, certain chemicals can be absorbed through the skin. Always protect the skin when using potentially harmful substances, e.g. wear gloves when using harsh chemical cleaning agents.

This complies with the legislative regulations Personal Protective Equipment at Work Regulations 2002 (as amended).

HEALTH & SAFETY

Temperature control

If the external temperature becomes low, blood flow nearer the skin's surface is decreased and the blood capillaries narrow (constrict), preventing heat loss and conserving heat.

ALWAYS REMEMBER

The skin's correct functioning is essential to life. It becomes darker to protect against excessive UV exposure but can also produce **vitamin D**. A fatty substance in the skin is converted to vitamin D with UV light from the sun. This circulates in the blood and with the mineral salts calcium and phosphorus helps the formation and maintenance of the health of the body's bones. Lack of vitamin D can lead to bone softening disease.

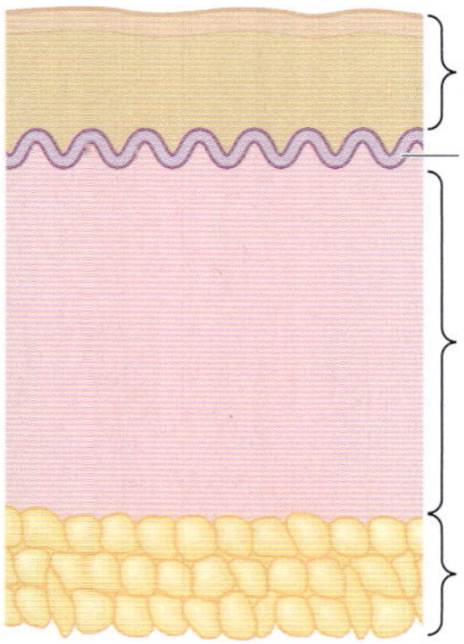

Skin structure

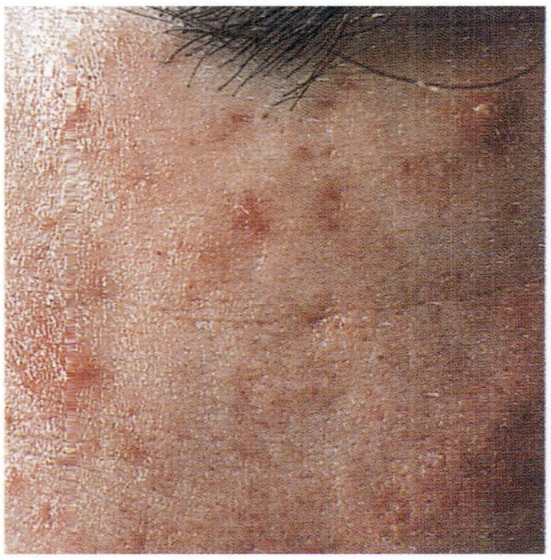

DR M H BECK

Skin's surface (showing acne scarring)

Sensitivity

The skin is a sensory organ, and the sensations of **touch**, **pressure**, **pain**, **heat** and **cold** are identified by **sensory nerves** and receptors in the skin. This information is then sent to the brain for decoding and initiating the appropriate bodily response. It also allows us to recognize objects by their feel and shape and helps prevent injury by alerting us to dangers including sharp objects and hot surfaces.

Nutrition

The skin provides storage for **fat**, which provides an energy reserve. It is also responsible for producing a significant proportion of our **vitamin D**, which is essential for healthy bones which is created by a chemical action when sunlight is in contact with the skin.

Absorption

Although the skin is structured to protect itself from penetration by harmful substances, absorption may take place through the sweat glands, hair follicles and epidermal cells for a beneficial effect. Water and fat soluble substances such as essential oils are examples of products used that can be absorbed by the skin.

The structure of the skin

If we looked within the skin using a microscope, we would be able to see two distinct layers: the **epidermis** and the dermis. Between these layers is a specialized layer which acts like a 'glue', sticking the two layers together: this is the **basement membrane**. If the epidermis and dermis become separated, body fluids fill the space, creating a **blister**, a small pocket of fluid in the top layers of the skin.

Situated below the epidermis and dermis is a further layer, the **subcutaneous tissue** or **fat layer**. The fat layer consists of cells containing fatty deposits, called adipocyte cells. It is supplied with a network of arteries that run parallel to the skin's surface. The thickness of the subcutaneous layer varies according to the body area, and is, for example, very thin around the eyes.

The fatty layer has a protective function and:

- acts as an insulator to conserve body heat
- cushions muscles and **bones** below from injury
- acts as an energy source, as excess fat is stored in this layer

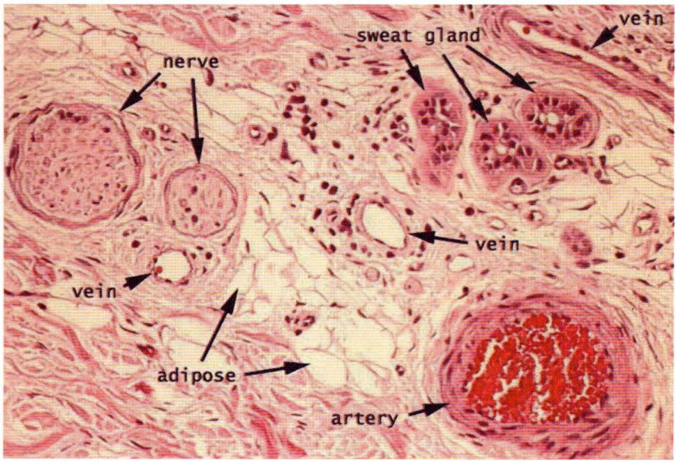

Adipose tissue – the empty-looking structures are fat cells

ALWAYS REMEMBER

Liposuction

Liposuction is a cosmetic surgery treatment that involves the removal of fat cells by suction from any area of the body. Tiny incisions are made where the fat removal is required. Fat is then removed through a hollow surgical tube. The tube is moved around in the skin, breaking up the fat, which is then sucked out.

A new treatment uses ultrasound waves applied to the skin's surface to liquefy fat. The fat is then naturally excreted.

The epidermis

The epidermis is located directly above the dermis. It is composed of five layers, with the surface layer forming the outer skin – what we can see and touch. The main function of the epidermis is to protect the deeper-living structures from invasion and harm from the external environment.

There is no blood supply in the epidermis. Nourishment of the epidermis, essential for growth, is received from a liquid called the **interstitial fluid** formed from blood plasma. This acts as a link between the blood and cells.

Each layer of the epidermis can be recognized by its shape and by the function of its cells. The main type of cell found in the epidermis is the **keratinocyte**, which produces the protein **keratin**. It is keratin that makes the skin tough and that reduces the passage of substances into or out of the body.

Over a period of about 4 weeks, cells move from the bottom layer of the epidermis to the top layer, the skin's surface, changing in shape and structure as they progress. The process of cellular change takes place in stages.

- *The cell is formed at the bottom layer* – by division of an earlier cell, called mitosis.
- *The cell matures* – it changes structure and moves upwards and outwards.
- *The cell dies* – it moves upwards and becomes an empty shell, which is eventually shed from the top layer.

ALWAYS REMEMBER

The epidermis

The epidermis is the most significant layer of the skin with regard to the external application of skincare cosmetics and services such as micro-dermabrasion due to the immediate effect on its appearance.

The layers and zones of the epidermis

There are five layers or *strata* (the Latin word for layer) that make up the epidermis. The thickness of these layers varies over the body's surface.

Each layer is found either in the germinative zone or keratinization zone. This is illustrated and described below.

ALWAYS REMEMBER

Did you know?

Every 5 days we shed a complete surface layer. About 80 per cent of household dust is composed of dead skin cells

ALWAYS REMEMBER

Psoriasis

With the skin disorder psoriasis, cell division occurs much more quickly, resulting in clusters of dead skin cells appearing on the skin's surface.

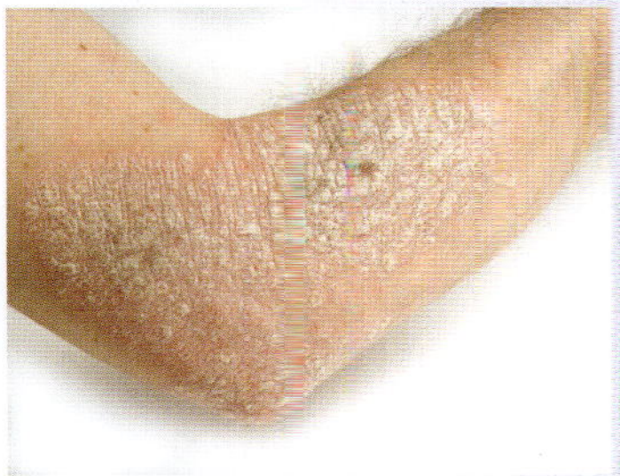

SHUTTERSTOCK/KENXRO

Surface plaques of psoriasis skin condition

HEALTH & SAFETY

Allergic reactions

Most people will be unaware that a foreign body has invaded the skin. Sometimes, however, the skin's surface intolerance to a substance is apparent. It shows as an allergic reaction, in which the skin becomes red, itchy and swollen.

Product ingredients are being sourced all the time that aim to reduce the possibility of skin sensitivity. It is important to keep up to date.

Skin testing is essential where recommended by a manufacturer to avoid an allergic reaction.

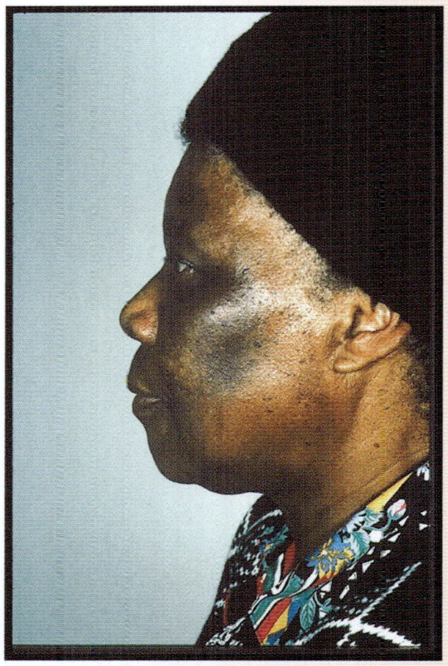

DR JOHN GRAY, THE WORLD OF SKIN CARE

Allergic reaction to an ingredient in hair dye

ALWAYS REMEMBER

Artificial skin tanning

Self-tanning products contain an ingredient called dihydroxyacetone (DHA), this provides an artificial tanned appearance to the skin. DHA reacts with the skin's amino acids, chemical protein chains in the stratum corneum. Through desquamation the colour is lost as the skin's surface cells are removed.

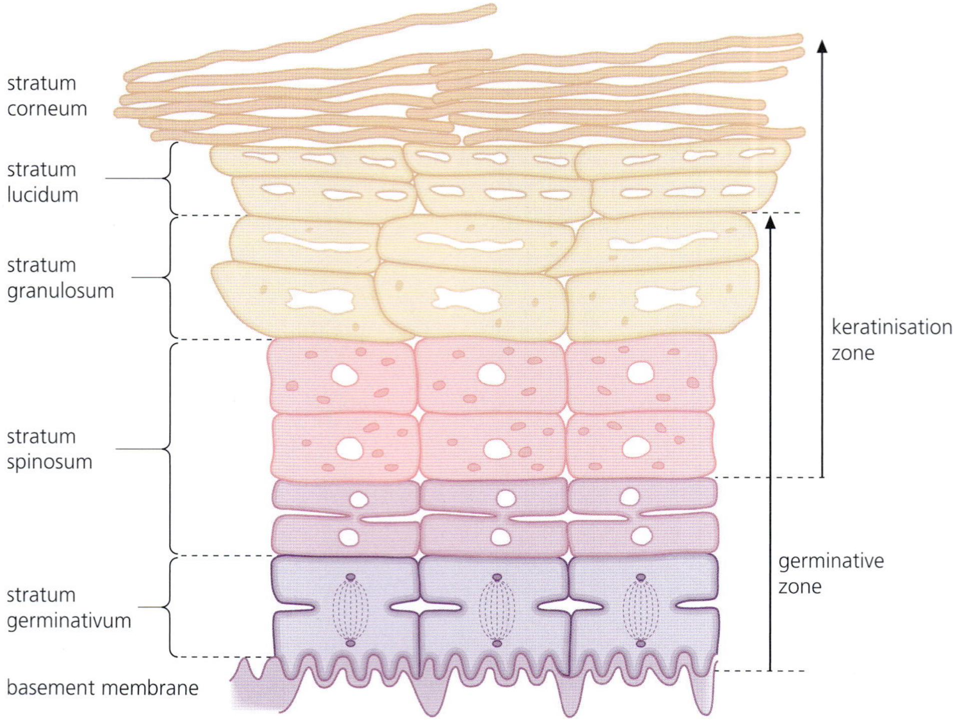

The layers of the epidermis

The germinative zone In the **germinative zone** the cells of the epidermis layers are living cells. The germative zone layers of the epidermis are the *stratum germinativum*, *stratum spinosum* and *stratum granulosum*.

Stratum germinativum The **stratum germinativum**, or **basal layer**, is the lowermost layer of the epidermis. It is formed from a single layer of column-shaped cells joined to the basement membrane. These cells divide continuously and produce new epidermal cells (keratinocytes). This process of cell division is known as **mitosis**.

Stratum spinosum The **stratum spinosum**, or **prickle-cell layer**, is formed from two to six rows of cells which appear long in relation to their width termed elongated. These have a surface of spiky spines which connect to surrounding cells. Each cell has a large nucleus and is filled with fluid.

Two other important cells are found in the germinative zone of the epidermis: langerham cells and melanocyte cells.

Langerhan cells Specialized defence cells which absorb and remove foreign bodies that enter the skin. They then move from the epidermis to the dermis below, and finally enter the lymph system (the body's waste-transport system) where the foreign bodies are made safe by neutralizing them.

Melanocyte cells produce the skin pigment melanin, which contributes to our skin colour. About one in every ten germinative cells is a melanocyte. Melanocytes are stimulated to produce melanin by UV rays, and their main function is to protect the other epidermal cells in this way from the harmful effects of UV.

The quantity and distribution of melanocytes differs according to race. In a white person the melanin tends to be destroyed when it reaches the stratum granulosum layer. With stimulation from artificial or natural UV light, however, melanin will also be present in the upper epidermis.

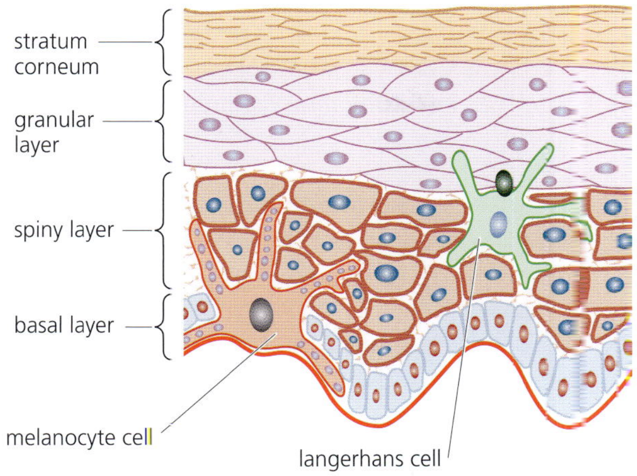

Melanocyte and langerhan cells

In contrast, black skin has melanin present in larger quantities throughout *all* the epidermal layers, a level of protection that has evolved to deal with bright UV light. This increased protection allows less UV to penetrate the dermis below, reducing the possibility of premature ageing from exposure to UV light. The more even quality and distribution of melanin also means that people with darker skins are less at risk of developing some skin cancers.

Another pigment, **carotene**, which is yellowish, also occurs in epidermal cells. Its contribution to skin colour lessens in importance as the amount of melanin in the skin increases.

Skin colour also increases when the skin becomes warm. This is because the **blood** capillaries at the surface dilate, bringing blood nearer to the surface so that heat can be lost. This is called **vasodilation**. If the temperature is cold the blood capillaries become narrower so less blood is brought to the skin's surface to conserve heat, called **vasoconstriction**. The skin will then lose colour.

HEALTH & SAFETY

Potential dangers and risks of over-exposure to UV radiation

- **Vitiligo**: lack of skin pigment is called vitiligo or leucoderma. It can occur with any skin colour, but is more obvious on a dark skin. Avoid exposing such skin to UV light as it does not have the melanin protection.
- **Sunburn**: if the skin becomes red on exposure to sunlight, this indicates that the skin has been over-exposed to UV. It will often blister and shed itself.
- **Keratitis**: inflammation of the cornea (the transparent front to the eye).
- **Conjunctivitis**: inflammation of the conjunctiva (the thin skin covering the cornea and eyelids).
- **Cataracts**: changes to the lens of the eye, making it opaque.
- **Skin cancer**: this is more common in fair-skinned people and those who have suffered episodes of sunburn during childhood. It can take many years to develop.
- **Skin ageing**: changes to connective tissues in the dermis make skin less elastic, showing more wrinkles and folds. The epidermis becomes thicker and more leathery.
- **Allergic reactions**: exposure to sunlight may induce allergic reactions including **prickly heat** – a prickly, burning sensation accompanied by a rash, and **polymorphic light eruption** which can produce itchy, red blisters.

ALWAYS REMEMBER

When the epidermis cell dies and is eventually shed from the skin's surface this is termed *desquamation* by the beauty therapist.

BEST PRACTICE

Cosmetic sunscreens

Many hair and skincare products and cosmetics including lipsticks and mascaras, now contain sunscreens. This is because research has shown that UV exposure is the principal cause of skin ageing called photoageing, resulting in loose skin and wrinkling and can also cause the skin and hair to become dry.

Following a service such as microdermabrasion the skin's defence is reduced and cosmetic sunscreens should be applied.

BEST PRACTICE

Calluses

Constant friction causes the skin to thicken as a form of protection, developing calluses. A client with a manual occupation may therefore develop hard skin (calluses) on their hands. The skin condition can be treated with an emollient preparation, which will moisturise and soften the dry skin.

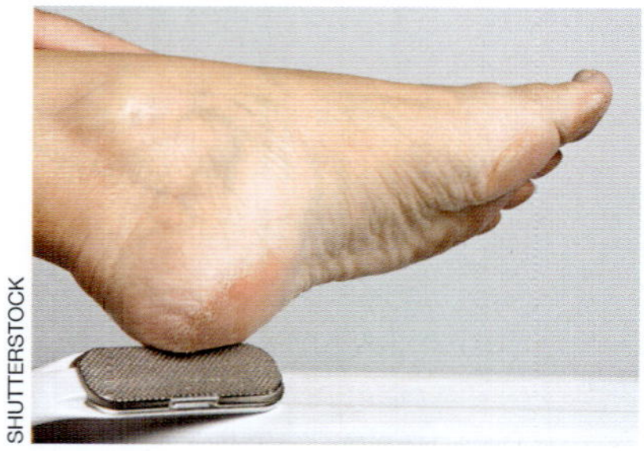

Hard skin on feet

Stratum granulosum

The **stratum granulosum**, or **granular layer**, is composed of one, two or three layers of **cells** which have become much flatter. The nucleus of the cell has begun to break up, creating what appear to be granules within the cell cytoplasm. These are known as **keratohyaline granules** and later form keratin. At this stage the cells form a new, combined layer.

The keratinization zone

The **keratinization zone**, or **cornified zone**, is where the cells begin to die and where finally they will be shed from the skin. The cells at this stage become progressively flatter, and the cell cytoplasm is replaced with the hard protein **keratin**.

Stratum lucidum

The **stratum lucidum**, **clear layer** or **lucid layer**, is only seen in non-hairy areas of the skin such as the palms of the hands and the soles of the feet. The cells here lack a nucleus and are filled with a clear substance called **eledin** produced at a further stage of keratinization.

Stratum corneum

The **stratum corneum**, **cornified** or **horny layer**, is formed from several layers of flattened, scale-like overlapping cells, composed mainly of keratin. These help to reflect UV light from the skin's surface; black skin, which evolved to withstand strong UV, has a thicker stratum corneum than does white skin.

The stratum corneum is up to 20 per cent thicker in men than women. Male skin also contains more collagen, the skin protein providing strength. Collagen production in females slows at the menopause which can result in sudden skin ageing. As such, skin ageing appears faster in females than males. Males produce more of the skin natural oil sebum making it appear oilier and have less sweat glands.

It takes about 3 weeks for the epidermal cells to reach the stratum corneum from the stratum germinativum. The cells are then shed, a process called **desquamation**.

The dermis

The **dermis** is responsible for the elasticity of the skin. It also contains the skin appendages – nerves, **blood vessels**, glands and hair follicles.

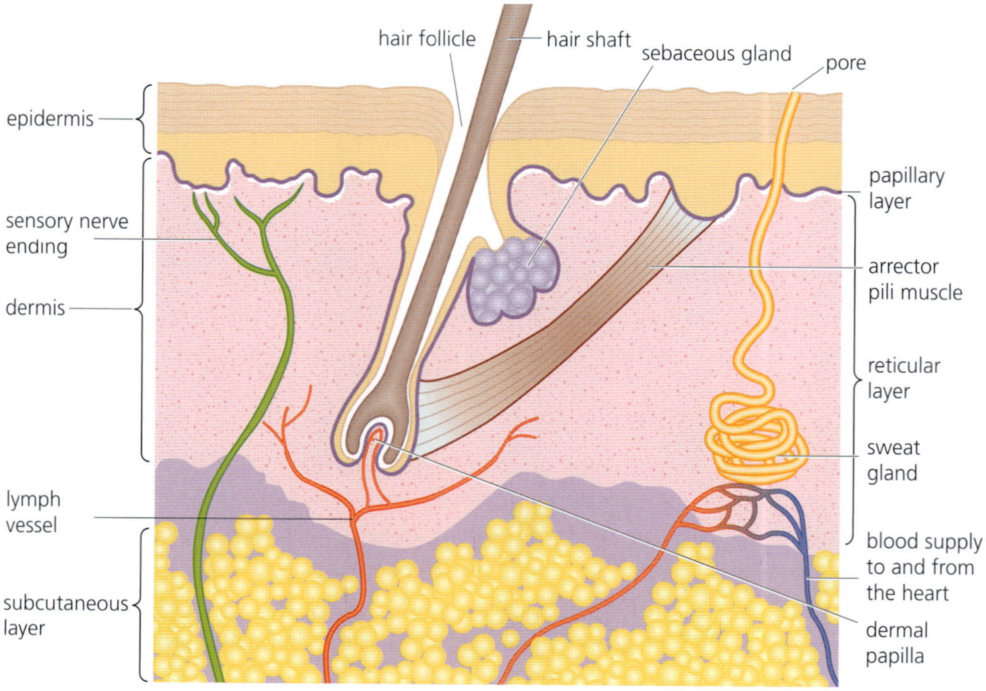

The skin

The dermis is the inner portion of the skin, situated underneath the epidermis and composed of dense connective tissue containing other structures such as the lymphatic system, blood vessels and nerves. It is much thicker than the epidermis and has two distinct layers: the papillary layer and the reticular layer.

The papillary layer Near the surface of the dermis are tiny projections called **papillae**; these contain both nerve endings and blood and lymph capillaries. This part of the dermis also supplies the epidermis above with its nutrition and removes waste away through the associated lymphatic circulation.

The reticular layer Underneath the papillary layer, the reticular layer contains a dense network of protein fibres. These fibres allow the skin to expand, to contract and to perform intricate, supple movements. The reticular layer contains sweat glands, blood vessels, hair follicles, lymph vessels, the arrector pili muscles and sebaceous glands.

This network is composed of two sorts of protein fibre: yellow **elastin** fibres and white **collagen** fibres. Elastin fibres give the skin its elasticity, and collagen fibres give it its strength. The fibres are produced by specialized cells called **fibroblasts**, and are held in a gel called the **ground substance**. While this network is strong, the skin appears youthful and firm. As the fibres harden and fragment, however, the network begins to collapse, losing its elasticity. The skin then begins to show signs of ageing. Male skin contains more collagen and appears to age slower.

A major cause of damage to this network is unprotected exposure of the skin to UV light and to weather. Sometimes, too, the skin loses its elasticity because of a sudden increase in body weight, for example at puberty or pregnancy. This results in the appearance of **stretch marks (striations)**, streaks of thin skin which are a different colour from the surrounding skin: on white skin they appear as thin reddish streaks; on black skin they appear slightly lighter than the surrounding skin. The lost elasticity cannot be restored. Micro-dermabrasion service may be applied to improve their appearance supported by cosmetic skincare preparations.

Nerve endings The dermis contains different types of sensory **nerve endings**, which register the sensations of touch, pressure, pain and temperature. These send messages to the **central nervous system** and the **brain**, informing us about the outside world and what is happening on the skin's surface. The appearance of each of these nerve endings is quite varied. The sensory nerve endings in the skin cause us to have an involuntary reflex reaction to unpleasant stimuli, thereby protecting the skin from injury.

Growth and repair The body's blood system of arteries and veins brings blood to capillary networks in the skin and takes it away again. The blood carries the nutrients and oxygen essential for the skin's health, maintenance and growth, and takes away waste products.

Defence Within the dermis are the structures responsible for protecting the skin from harmful foreign bodies and irritants.

HEALTH & SAFETY

Repair

Repair occurs if the skin becomes damaged. Blood transports repair cells which covers the site of the injury. Behind this, blood cells form a clot which dries and prevents infection from germs entering the skin. Collagen fibres are secreted by fibroblast cells in the dermis which bind the surface of the wound together. Epithelial cells of the dermis cover the wound underneath the clot. The clot or scab is lost. The cells of the dermis grow upwards until the skin's thickness is restored.

ALWAYS REMEMBER

The formation of the papillae ridges in the dermis are unique to each individual, and this provides our fingerprint.

HEALTH & SAFETY

Scars

When the surface has been broken, the skin at the site of the injury is replaced but may leave a scar. This initially appears red, due to the increased blood supply to the area, required while the skin heals. When healed, the redness will fade. If the skin's healing process continues for longer than necessary, too much scar tissue will be formed resulting in a raised scar called a 'keloid scar'. Keloid scarring is more typical in people of Eastern Asian or African–Caribbean descent, rather than Caucasian descent; due to uncontrolled fibrous growth in the skin tissue during healing.

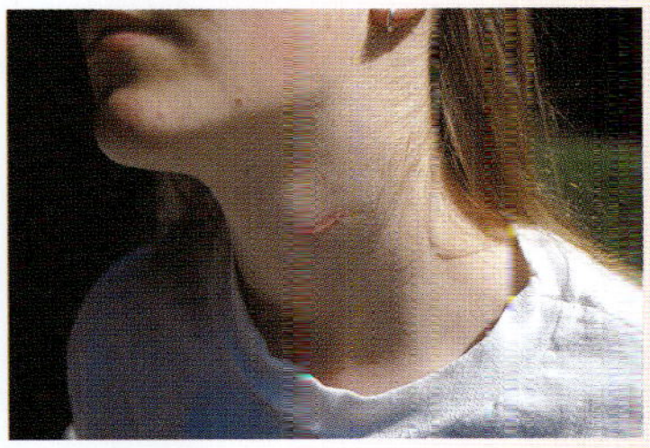

DR JOHN GRAY, *WORLD OF SKIN CARE*

Keloid scar

HEALTH & SAFETY

Sunbathing

If sunbathing, always protect the skin with an appropriate protective sunscreen product according to skin type and natural hair/skin colouring. After UV exposure always use an emollient aftersun preparation to minimize the cumulative effects of premature ageing, by rehydrating and soothing the skin.

ALWAYS REMEMBER

Sensory nerve endings

Sensory nerve endings are most numerous in sensitive parts of the skin, such as the fingertips and the lips.

TOP TIP

Massage

Appropriate external massage movements can be used to increase the blood supply within the dermis, bringing extra nutrients and oxygen to the skin and to the underlying muscle. At the same time, the lymphatic circulation is increased, improving the removal of waste products that may have accumulated.

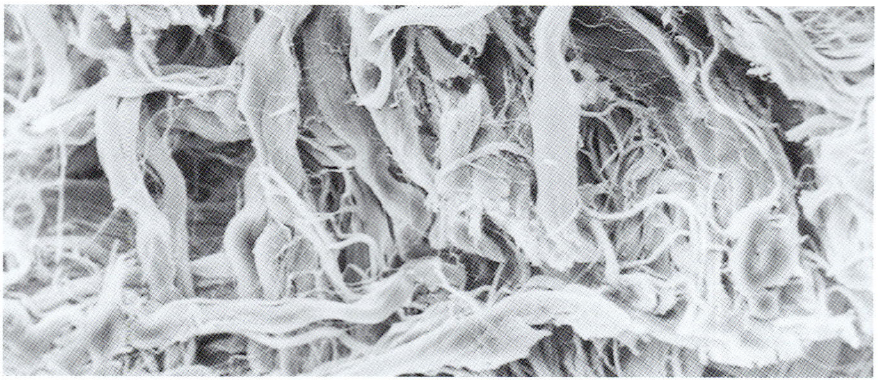

Collagen and elastin fibres in the dermis

One set of cells, the **mast cells**, burst when stimulated during inflammation or allergic reactions, and release a chemical substance called **histamine**. This causes the blood vessels nearby to enlarge, thereby bringing more blood to the site of the irritation to limit skin damage and begin repair.

In the blood, and also in the lymph and the connective tissue, is another group of cells: the **macrophages**. These destroy microorganisms and engulf dead cells and other unwanted particles. They form a role in the immune system that protects the body from disease-causing microorganisms.

Collecting waste Lymph vessels in the skin carry a fluid called lymph, a straw-coloured fluid similar in composition to blood plasma. Plasma is the liquid part of the blood that disperses from the blood capillaries into the tissue spaces. Lymph is composed of water, lymphocytes (a type of white blood cell that plays a key role in the immune system), oxygen, nutrients, hormones, salts and waste products such as used blood cells. The waste products are eliminated, and usable protein is recycled for further use by the body. It acts as a link between the blood and the cells.

Control of skin functioning **Hormones** are chemical messengers transported in the blood. They control the activity of many organs in the body, including the cells and glands in the skin. These include **melanosomes**, which produce skin pigment, and the **sweat glands** and **sebaceous glands**.

Hormone imbalance at different times of our life may disturb the normal functioning of these cells and structures, causing various **skin disorders**, for example acne vulgaris during puberty.

Skin appendages Within the dermis are structures called **skin appendages**. These include:

- sweat glands
- sebaceous glands
- hair follicles, which produce hair
- nails

Sweat glands **Sweat glands** or **sudoriferous glands** are composed of **epithelial tissue**, a specialized lining tissue which extends from the epidermis into the dermis.

These glands are found all over the body, but are particularly plentiful on the palms of the hands and the soles of the feet. Their function is to regulate body temperature through the evaporation of sweat from the surface of the skin. Fluid loss and control of body temperature are important to prevent the body overheating, especially in hot, humid climates. For this reason, perhaps, sweat glands are larger and more abundant in black skin than white skin as a result of evolution.

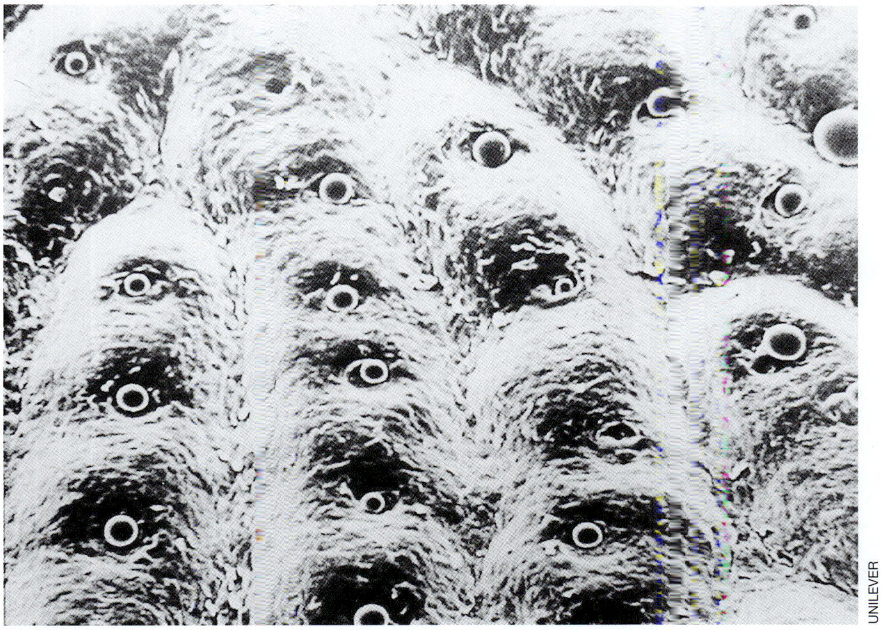

Sweat pores on the skin's surface

TOP TIP

Pores

Pores allow the absorption of some facial cosmetics into the skin. Many facial treatments are therefore aimed at cleansing the pores, some with a particularly deep cleansing action, as with galvanic desincrustation and micro-dermabrasion.

The pores may become enlarged, because of congestion caused by dirt, dead skin cells, cosmetics and ageing. The application of an *astringent* skincare preparation creates a tightening effect upon the skin's surface, slightly reducing the size of the pores.

There are two types of sweat glands: *eccrine glands* and *apocrine glands*. **Eccrine glands** are simple sweat-producing glands, found over most of the body, appearing as tiny tubes (**ducts**). The eccrine glands are responsive to heat. These are straight in the epidermis, and coiled in the dermis. The duct opens directly onto the surface of the skin through an opening called a **pore**.

Eccrine glands continuously secrete small amounts of sweat, even when we appear not to be perspiring. In this way they maintain the body temperature at a constant 36.8°C.

Apocrine glands are found in the armpit, the nipples and the groin area. This kind of gland is larger than the eccrine gland, and is attached to a hair follicle. Apocrine glands are controlled by hormones, becoming active at puberty. They also increase in activity

HEALTH & SAFETY

Moisture balance

Excessive sweating, which can occur through exposure to high temperatures or illness, can lead to *skin dehydration* – insufficient water content. Fluid intake must be increased to rebalance the body fluids. Skin care products, services and routines should be changed to ensure the skin is rehydrated. Client recent health history should be checked at every consultation.

ACTIVITY

The emotions

Emotions can affect blood supply to the skin: blood vessels in the dermis may enlarge or constrict. Think of different emotions, and how these might affect the appearance of the skin.

ALWAYS REMEMBER

Did you know?

We each have approximately 2–5 million sweat glands.

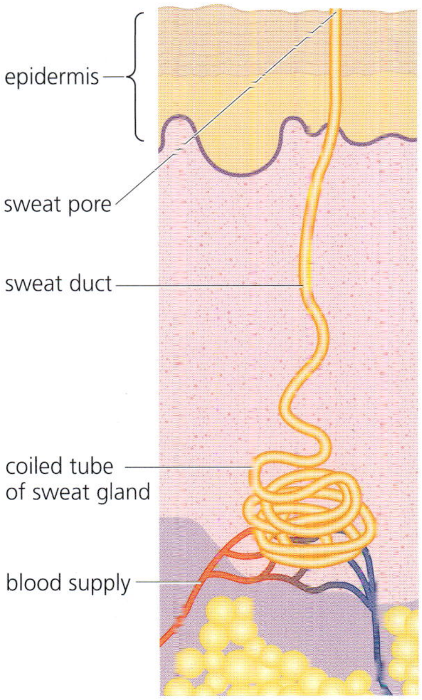

An eccrine sweat gland

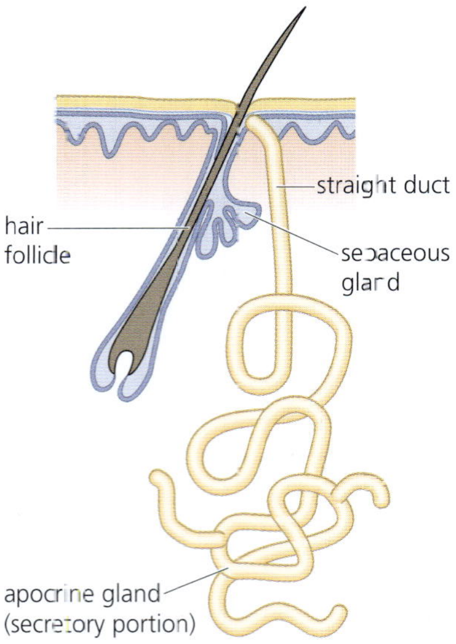

An apocrine gland

when we are excited, nervous or stressed. The fluid they secrete is thicker than that from the eccrine glands, and may contain urea, fats, sugars and small amounts of protein. Also present are traces of aromatic molecules called **pheromones**, which are thought to cause sexual attraction.

An unpleasant smell – **body odour** – develops when apocrine sweat is broken down by skin bacteria. Good habits of personal hygiene will prevent this.

Cosmetic perspiration control To extend hygiene protection during the day, apply either a deodorant or an antiperspirant. **Antiperspirants** reduce the amount of sweat that reaches the skin's surface: they have an astringent action which closes the pores. **Deodorants** contain an active antiseptic ingredient which reduces the skin's bacterial activity, thereby reducing the risk of odour from stale sweat.

HEALTH & SAFETY

Antiperspirants

The active ingredient in most antiperspirant products is aluminium chlorohydrate. This is known to cause contact dermatitis in some people, especially if the skin has been damaged by recent removal of unwanted hair. Bear this in mind if you are performing an underarm depilatory wax service or an electrical epilation service in this area.

BEST PRACTICE

Skin problems at puberty

Skin problems are common at puberty when changes in hormone levels cause sebaceous glands to produce excess sebum and the skin's surface becomes oily. Growth of skin bacteria can increase in the sebum causing inflammation of the surrounding tissues. This can lead to the skin disorder acne vulgaris, see page 22. The skin should always be kept clean and handled with clean hands.

Sebaceous glands The **sebaceous gland** appears as a minute sac-like organ. Usually it is associated with the hair follicle with which it forms the **pilosebaceous unit**, but the two can appear independently.

Sebaceous glands are found all over the body, except on the palms of the hands and the soles of the feet. They are particularly numerous on the scalp, the forehead, and in the back and chest region. The cells of the glands decompose, producing the skin's natural oil, sebum. This empties directly into the hair follicle.

The activity of the sebaceous gland increases at puberty, when stimulated by the male hormone **androgen**. In adults, activity of the sebaceous gland gradually decreases again. Men secrete slightly more sebum than women; and on black skin the sebaceous glands are larger and more numerous than on white skin.

Sebum is composed of fatty acids and waxes. These have **bactericidal** and **fungicidal** properties, and so discourage the multiplication of microorganisms on the surface of the skin. Sebum also reduces the evaporation of moisture from the skin, and so prevents the skin from drying out.

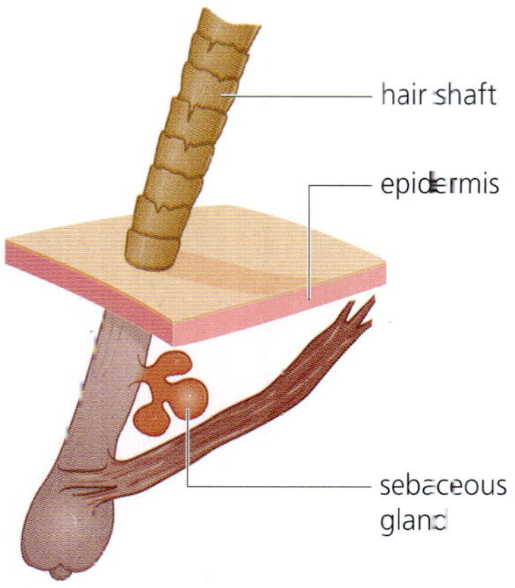

Sebaceous gland

Acid mantle Sweat and sebum combine on the skin's surface, creating an acid film. This is known as the **acid mantle**, and discourages the growth of bacteria and fungi.

Acidity and alkalinity are measured by a number called the pH. An *acidic solution* has a pH of 0–7; a *neutral solution* has a pH of 7; and an *alkaline solution* has a pH of 7–14. The acid mantle of the skin has a pH of 5.5–5.6.

Mature skin

The change in appearance of women's skin during ageing is closely related to the altered production of the hormones oestrogen, progesterone and androgen at the menopause.

Mature skin has the following characteristics:

- The skin becomes dry as the sebaceous and sudoriferous glands become less active.
- The skin loses its elasticity as the elastin fibres harden, and wrinkles appear due to the cross-linking and hardening of collagen fibres.
- The epidermis grows more slowly and the skin appears thinner, becoming almost transparent in some areas such as around the eyes, where small veins and capillaries show through the skin.
- Broken capillaries appear, especially on the cheek area and around the nose.
- The facial contours become slack as muscle tone is reduced.
- The underlying bone structure becomes more obvious, as the fatty layer and the supportive tissue beneath the skin grow thinner.
- Blood circulation becomes poor, which interferes with skin nutrition, and the skin may appear sallow.
- Due to the decrease in metabolic rate, waste products are not removed so quickly, and this leads to puffiness of the skin.
- Patches of irregular pigmentation appear on the surface of the skin, such as lentigines and chloasmata.

The skin may also exhibit the following skin conditions, although these are not truly *characteristic* of ageing skin:

- Dermal naevi may be enlarged.
- Seborrhoeic warts may appear on the epidermal layer of the skin.
- Verruca filliformis warts may increase in number.
- Hair growth on the upper lip or chin, or both, may become darker or coarser, due to hormonal imbalance in the body.
- Dark circles and puffiness may occur under the eyes.

TOP TIP

AHAs

Mild acids, such as the natural fruit acids used in face creams and known as AHAs, allow the removal of surface cells by dissolving the compounds holding them together. A stronger AHA called glycolic acid is used in some anti-ageing preparations. These are designed to remove the dull outer layer of cells and reveal fresher skin beneath but continuous use can make the skin sore.

Stronger acids have a shrinking or drying effect on the skin. The very strong AHA, salicylic acid, is included in some preparations and is used to destroy warts.

BEST PRACTICE

The lips

Sebaceous glands are not present on the surface of the lips. For this reason the lips should be protected with a lip emollient preparation to prevent them from becoming dry and chapped.

TOP TIP

Cosmetic moisturisers

Cosmetic moisturizers copy the action of sebum in providing an oily covering for the skin's surface, reducing moisture loss and keeping the skin soft and supple.

HEALTH & SAFETY

Using alkaline products

Because the skin has an acid pH, if alkaline products are used on it the acid mantle will be disturbed. It will take several hours for this protective film to be restored; during this time, the skin may be irritated and sensitive.

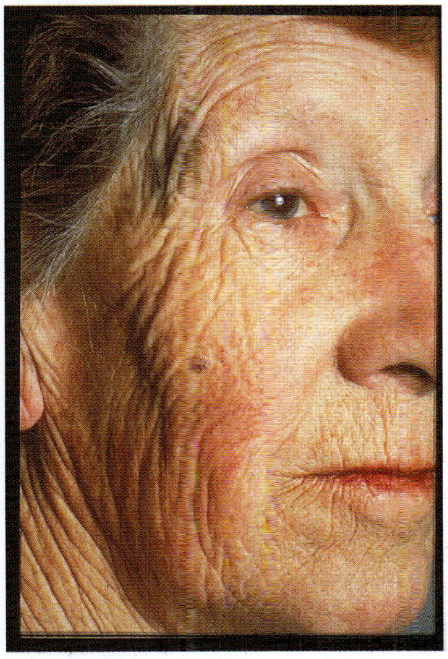

DR JOHN GRAY, THE WORLD OF SKIN CARE

Mature skin

HEALTH & SAFETY

Ultraviolet light and ageing
The ageing process is accelerated when the skin is regularly exposed to UV light.

ACTIVITY
FUNCTIONAL SKILLS

The ageing process
Find images showing men and women from different cultures and at various ages.
1 Can you identify the visible characteristics of ageing?
2 Does ageing occur at the same rate in men and women and in different cultures?
3 Which services could be offered in a treatment plan, the main objectives of which are to treat signs of ageing?
4 Discuss your findings with your assessor.

The hair

The structure and function of hair and the surrounding tissues

A hair is a long, slender structure which grows out of, and is part of, the skin. Each hair is made up of dead skin cells, which contain the protein called keratin.

Hairs cover the whole body, except for the palms of the hands, the soles of the feet, the lips and parts of the sex organs.

Hair has many functions:

- *scalp hair* insulates the head against cold, protects it from the sun and cushions it against bumps
- *eyebrows* cushion the brow bone from bumps and prevent sweat from running into the eyes
- *eyelashes* help to prevent foreign particles entering the eyes
- *nostril hair* traps dust particles inhaled with the air
- *ear hair* helps to protect the ear canal. Hair cells in the inner ear send signals to the brain when the head moves; this information is used to help the body maintain balance
- *body hair* helps to provide an insulating cover (though this function is almost obsolete in humans), has a valuable sensory function and is linked with the secretion of sebum onto the surface of the skin. Terminal hair in the pubic and underarm areas has a purpose to protect the underlying glands and organs

Hair also plays a role in social communication.

ALWAYS REMEMBER

Did you know?
There are approximately 100 000 hairs on the scalp.

TOP TIP

Did you know?
A strand of hair is stronger than an equivalent strand of nylon or copper. However, repeated chemical treatments weaken the hair. Consider this when booking appointments for services such as single lash extensions. Allow the recommended intervals between each treatment.

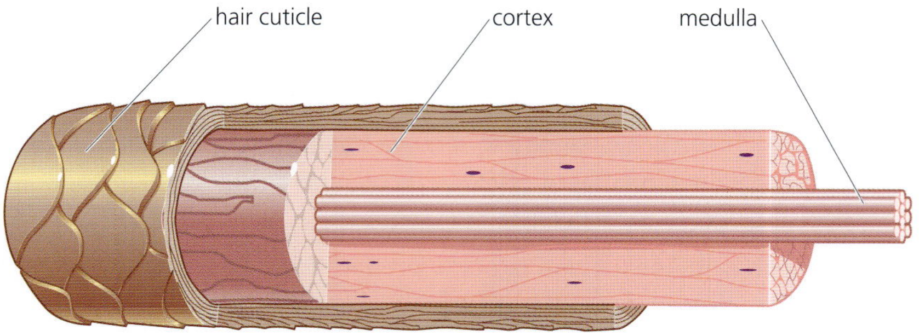

Cross-section of the hair

The structure of hair Most hairs are made up of three layers of different types of epithelial cells: the *medulla*, the *cortex* and the *cuticle*.

The **medulla** is the central core of the hair. The cells of the medulla contain soft keratin, and sometimes some pigment granules. Air spaces between the cells allow light to pass through, giving a shiny appearance to the hair. The medulla only exists in medium-to-coarse hair – there is usually no medulla in thinner hair.

The **cortex** is the thickest layer of the hair, and is made up of several layers of closely packed elongated cells. These contain pigment granules and hard keratin, giving the hair its strength.

It is the **pigment** in the cortex that gives hair its colour. When this pigment is no longer made, the hair appears white. As the proportion of white hairs rises, the hair seems to go 'grey'; in fact, however, each individual hair is either coloured as before, or white.

The **cuticle** is the protective outer layer of the hair, and is composed of a layer of thin, unpigmented, flat, scale-like cells. These contain hard keratin, and overlap each other from the base to the tip of the hair.

The parts of the hair and related skin Each hair is recognized by three parts: the *root*, the *bulb* and the *shaft*:

- the **root** is the part of the hair that is in the follicle
- the **bulb** is the enlarged base of the hair root
- the **shaft** is the part of the hair that can be seen above the skin's surface

Each hair grows out of a tube-like indentation in the epidermis, the **hair follicle**. The walls of the follicle are a continuation of the epidermal layer of the skin.

The **arrector pili muscle** is attached at an angle to the base of the follicle. Cold, aggression or fright stimulates this muscle to contract, pulling the follicle and the hair upright creating a bumpy appearance on the skin's surface referred to as goose bumps.

The sebaceous gland is attached to the upper part of the follicle; from it, a duct enters directly into the hair follicle. The gland produces an oily substance, sebum, which is secreted into the follicle. Sebum waterproofs, lubricates and softens the hair and the surface of the skin; it also protects the skin against bacterial and fungal infections. The contraction of the arrector pili muscle aids the secretion of sebum.

There are two types of **sudoriferous** (sweat) **glands**: the *eccrine* and the *apocrine* glands. The **eccrine glands** are simple sweat-producing glands, distributed over most of the body's surface and responsive to heat. The **apocrine glands** are larger and deeper.

Associated with the hairs in the groin and underarm, their ducts open directly into the hair follicles near to the surface of the skin. These glands, which are under hormonal control, become active at puberty. They also become more active in response to stress. Apocrine glands produce sweat, which decays with a characteristic smell.

The **dermal papilla**, is connective tissue surrounded by the hair bulb. It provides an excellent blood supply, necessary to provide nutrition and hormones for the growth of the hair. It is not itself part of the follicle, but a separate tiny organ of blood capillaries which transports blood to the follicle.

The **bulb** is the enlarged base of the hair root. A gap at the base leads to a cavity inside, which houses the dermal papilla. The bulb contains in its lower part the dividing cells that create the hair. The hair continues to develop as it passes through the regions of the upper bulb and the root.

ACTIVITY

The function of hair

Humans are not very hairy but their hairs sometimes stand on end! How do you know when this occurs? How does the appearance of skin change? What is the purpose of hair standing on end?

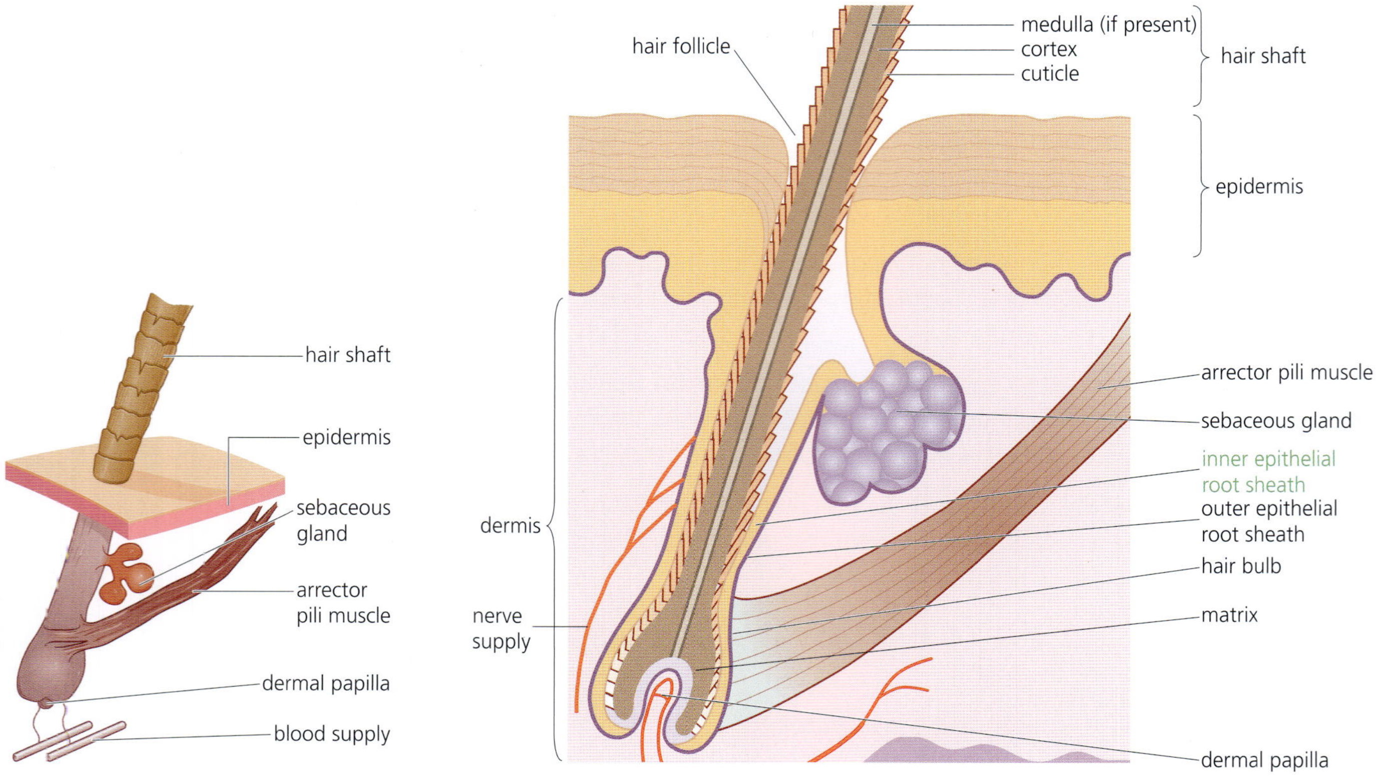

Cross-section of the skin, hair and hair follicle and its associated structures

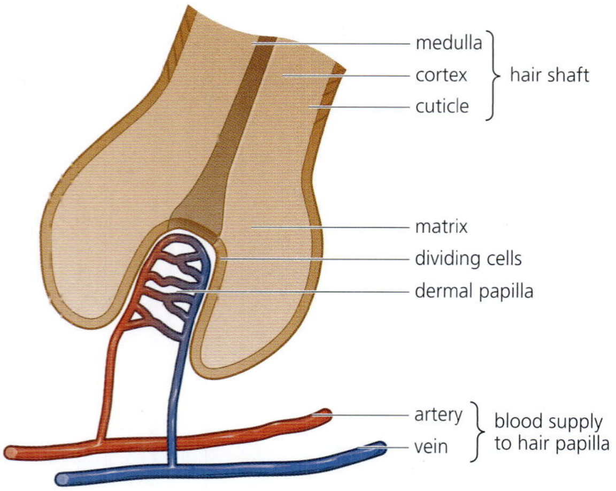

The hair bulb

ALWAYS REMEMBER

Broken hairs

When hairs break off due to incorrect waxing technique, they will break at the level at which they are locked into the follicle by the cells of the inner root sheath.

ALWAYS REMEMBER

Associated beauty therapy services

Epilation using diathermy or galvanism involves destroying matrix cells of the hair root. Heat can be used to destroy the cells. The two methods can be combined, called 'blend'.

Diathermic epilation causes the contents of the cells to coagulate due to heat produced caused by friction at the point of the epilation needle. This is similar to egg white coagulating as you cook it.

Galvanic epilation induces an alkali, sodium hydroxide, to form around the needle situated at the hair root which, given a little time, affects the proteins of cells and destroys them. The same alkali is also responsible for the removal of sebum in desincrustation and loosening of cells in galvanic services, promoting skin peeling.

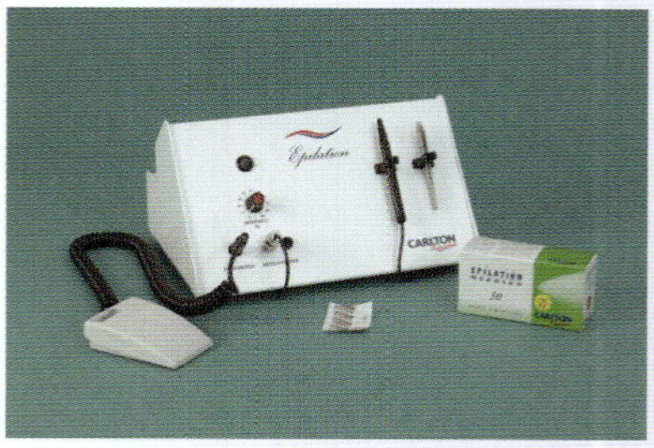

SILHOUETTE-DERMALIFT

Electrical epilation unit

The **matrix** is the name given to the lower part of the bulb, which comprises actively dividing hair germ cells from which the hair is formed. The hair germ cells grow downwards in a column called the **dermal cord**. The dermal cord surrounds the dermal papilla and when this occurs cellular changes cause a new hair to grow

The hair follicle

The **hair follicle** extends into the dermis, and is made up of three sheaths: the *inner epithelial root sheath*, the *outer epithelial root sheath* and the surrounding *connective-tissue sheath*.

The **inner epithelial root sheath** grows from the bottom of the follicle at the papilla; both the hair and the inner root sheath grow upwards together. The inner root sheath encloses the hair root in three separate layers:

- The cuticle layer, which is covered with cuticle cells in the same way as the outer surface of the hair. These cells lock together, anchoring the hair firmly in place.
- The **Huxley's** layer, which is the thickest of the three inner root sheath layers.
- The **Henle's** layer, which is the inner final layer of the inner root sheath composed of a single layer of cells.

The inner root sheath ceases to grow when level with the sebaceous gland.

The **outer epithelial root sheath** forms the follicle wall. This does not grow up with the hair, but is stationary. It is a continuation of the growing layer of the epidermis of the skin.

The **connective-tissue sheath** surrounds both the follicle and the sebaceous gland, providing both a sensory supply and a blood supply. The connective-tissue sheath includes, and is a continuation of, the papilla.

The *shape* of the hairs is determined by the shape of the hair follicle – an angled or bent follicle will produce an oval or flat hair, whereas a straight follicle will produce a round hair. Flat hairs are curly, oval hairs are wavy, and round hairs are straight. As a general rule, curly hairs break off more easily during waxing than straight hairs.

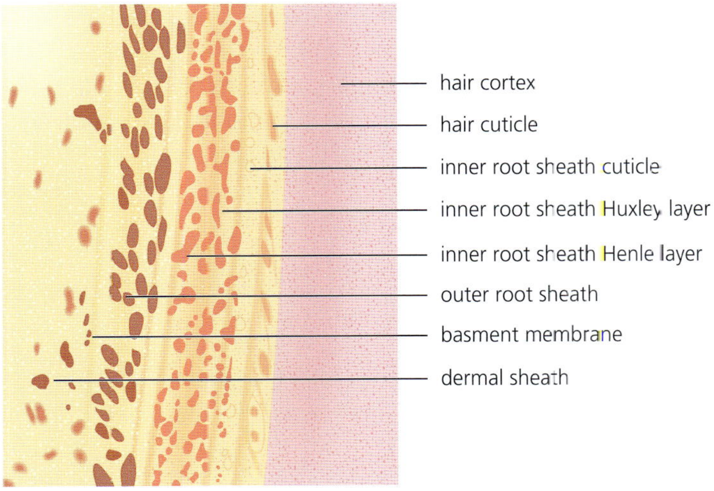

The hair in skin

The nerve supply

The number, size and type of nerve endings associated with hair follicles is related to the size and type of follicle. The follicles of vellus hairs have the fewest nerve endings; those of terminal hairs have the most.

TOP TIP

The inner root sheath can be seen on hairs removed by both temporary and permanent hair removal techniques.

BEST PRACTICE

The shape of the hair will determine what electrical epilation service would be more suitable to use for effective hair removal: shortwave diathermy, blend or galvanic.

It will also influence your choice of waxing product and application technique for intimate waxing.

TOP TIP

Angled or distorted follicle

An angled follicle may cause the hair to be broken off at the angle during waxing, instead of being completely pulled out with its root. If this happens, broken hairs will appear at the skin's surface within a few days. This will affect service application technique for electrical needle epilation.

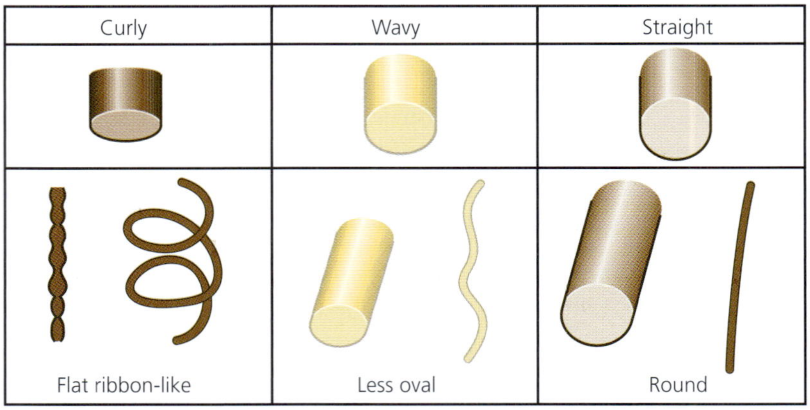

Hair shapes

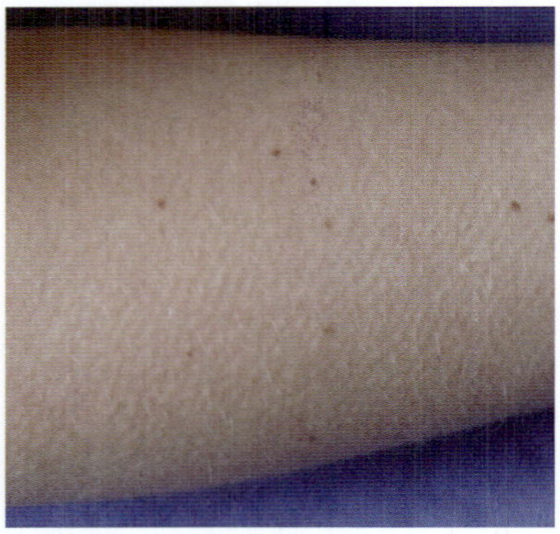

Vellus hair

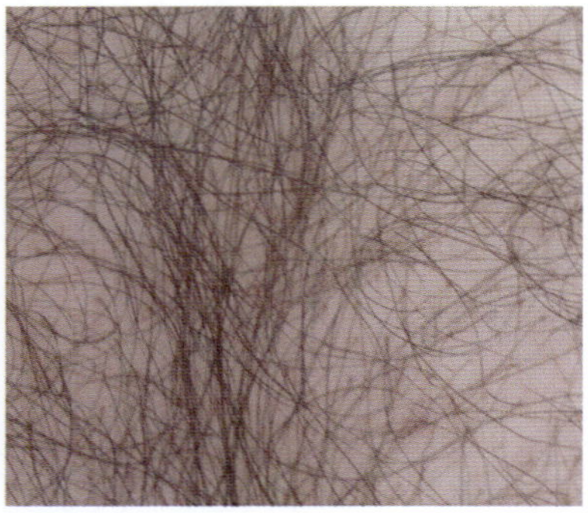

Terminal hair

ALWAYS REMEMBER

Terminal hairs

Some areas of the body – for example, the pubic area and underarm areas – often have terminal hairs with very deep follicles. When these hairs are removed, the resulting tissue damage may cause minor bleeding from the entrance of the follicle. Removal of these deep-seated hairs is obviously more uncomfortable than the removal of shallower hairs.

The nerve endings surrounding hair follicles respond mainly to rapid movements when the hair is moved. Nerve endings that respond to touch can also be found around the surface openings of some hair follicles, as well as just below the epidermis.

The three types of hair

There are three main types of hair: *lanugo, vellus* and *terminal*.

Lanugo hairs are found on the body prior to birth. They are fine and soft, do not have a medulla, and are often unpigmented. They grow from around the third to the fifth month of pregnancy, and are shed to be replaced by the secondary vellus hairs around the seventh to the eighth month of pregnancy. Lanugo hairs on the scalp, eyebrows and eyelashes are replaced by terminal hairs.

Vellus hairs are fine, downy and soft, and are found on the face and body. They are often unpigmented, rarely longer than 20 mm, and do not have a medulla or a well-formed bulb. The base of these hairs is very close to the skin's surface. If stimulated, the shallow follicle of a vellus hair can grow downwards and become a follicle that produces terminal hairs.

Terminal hairs are longer and coarser than vellus hairs, and most are pigmented. They vary greatly in shape, in diameter and length, and in colour and texture. The follicles from which they grow are set deeply in the dermis and have well-defined bulbs. Terminal hair is the coarse hair of the scalp, eyebrows, eyelashes, pubic and underarm regions. It is also present on the face, chest and sometimes the backs of males.

Hair growth

All hair has a cyclical pattern of growth, which can be divided into three phases: *anagen, catagen* and ***telogen***.

Anagen is the actively growing stage of the hair – the follicle has reformed; the hair bulb is developing, surrounding the life-giving dermal papilla; and a new hair forms, growing from the matrix in the bulb.

Catagen is the changing stage when the hair separates from the papilla. Over a few days it is carried by the movement of the inner root sheath, up the follicle to the base of the sebaceous gland. Here it stays until it either falls out or is pushed out by a new hair growing up behind it.

This stage can be very rapid, with a new hair growing straight away; or slower, with the papilla and the follicle below the sebaceous gland degenerating and entering a resting stage, telogen.

Telogen is a resting stage. Many hair follicles do not undergo this stage, but start to produce a new hair immediately. During resting phases, hairs may still be loosely inserted in the shallow follicles.

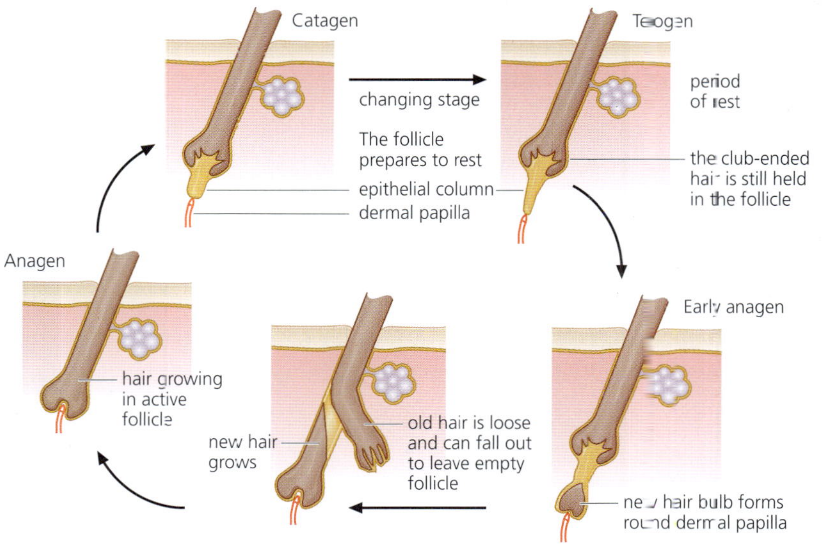

The hair growth cycle

Speed of growth The anagen, catagen and telogen stages last for different lengths of time in different hair types and in different parts of the body:

- *scalp* hair grows for 2–7 years, and has a resting stage of 3–4 months
- *eyebrow* hair grows for 1–2 months, and has a resting stage of 3–4 months
- *eyelashes* grow for 3–6 weeks, and have a resting stage of 3–4 months

After a waxing service, body hair will take approximately 6–8 weeks to return.

Because hair growth cycles are not all in synchronization, we always have hair present at any given time. On the scalp, at any one time for example, 85 per cent of hairs may be in the anagen phase. This is why hair growth after waxing starts within a few days: what is seen is the appearance of hairs that were already developing in the follicle at the time of waxing.

Types of hair growth **Hirsutism** is a term used to describe a pattern of hair growth that is abnormal for that person's sex, such as when a woman's hair growth follows a man's hair-growth pattern. The hair growth is usually terminal when it should be of a vellus type.

Hypertrichosis is an abnormal growth of excess hair for a person's sex, age and race. It is usually due to abnormal conditions brought about by disease or injury.

Superfluous hair (excess hair) is unwanted hair growth perfectly normal for the age, sex or gender of the person. For example, at certain periods in a woman's life, such as during puberty or pregnancy. Terminal hair can form at these times usually disappearing once the normal hormonal balance has returned. Hair newly formed during the menopause is often permanent unless treated with a permanent method of hair removal, such as electrical epilation or laser service.

Factors affecting the growth rate and quantity of hair Hair does not always grow uniformly:

- *Time of day.* Hair grows faster at night than during the day.
- *Weather.* Hairs grow faster in warm weather than in cold.

TOP TIP

Stages of hair growth

Because of the cyclical nature of hair growth, the follicles are always at different stages of their growth cycle. When the hair is removed, therefore, the hair will not all grow back at the same time. For this reason, waxing can appear to reduce the quantity of hair growth. This is not so; given time, all the hair would regrow. Waxing is classed as a temporary means of hair removal.

The average time for hair regrowth following temporary methods of hair removal are:

Terminal hair	5–6 weeks
Vellus hair	8–10 weeks

ALWAYS REMEMBER

Male facial hair

Male facial hair growth grows at a rate of approximately 10 mm a month.

ALWAYS REMEMBER

Anagen

A hair pulled out at the anagen stage will be surrounded by the inner and outer root sheaths and have a properly formed bulb.

Catagen or telogen

A hair pulled out at the *catagen* or *telogen* stage can be recognized by the brush-like appearance of the root.

ALWAYS REMEMBER

Vellus hairs

Vellus hairs grow slowly and take 2–3 months to return after waxing. They can remain dormant in the follicle for 6–8 months before shedding.

ALWAYS REMEMBER

Alopecia

This is often caused by a nervous disorder and is where there are round patches of smooth scalp as the hair follicles are not producing new hairs.

ALWAYS REMEMBER

Hair growth cycle

Normally about 90 per cent of scalp hair is in the anagen growth phase.

As you age, the anagen stage becomes shorter and the telogen stage longer.

HEALTH & SAFETY

African hair type

The body hair type of African clients is prone to breaking during waxing, and to ingrowing after waxing. Skin damage can result in the loss of pigmentation (hypo-pigmentation).

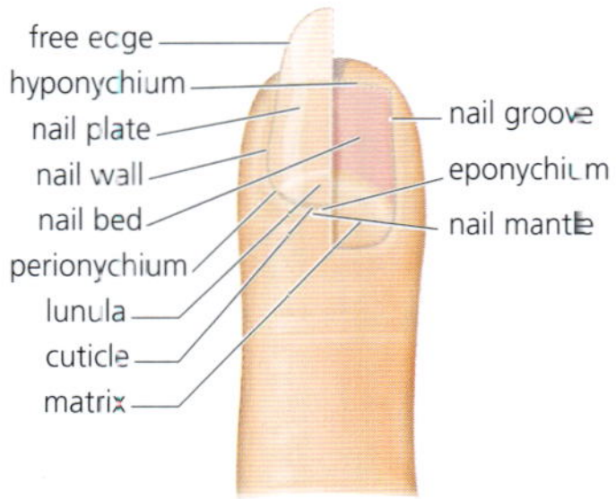

The structure of the nail

ALWAYS REMEMBER

Dark streaks caused by pigmentation are common on the nail plate of black-skinned clients. These tend to increase with age.

- ***Hormones***. In women, hairs grow faster between the ages of 16 and 24, and (frequently) during mid-pregnancy. Hormone imbalances can lead to excessive hair growth.
- *Age.* The rate of hair growth slows down with age. In women, however, facial hair growth continues to increase in old age, while trunk and limb hair increases into middle age and then decreases.
- *Colour.* Hairs of different colour grow at different speeds – for example, coarse black hair grows more quickly than fine blonde hair.
- *Part of the body.* Hair in different areas of the body grows at different rates, as do different types and thicknesses of hair. The weekly growth rate varies from approximately 1.5 mm (fine hair) to 2.8 mm (coarse hair), when actively growing.
- *Heredity.* Various members of a family may have inherited growth patterns, such as excess hair that starts to grow at puberty and increases until the age of 20–25.
- *Health and diet.* Health and a varied, balanced diet are crucial in the rate of hair growth and appearance. A person suffering from the eating disorder anorexia nervosa will suffer from a fine growth of hair all over the body.
- *Stress.* Emotional stress can cause a temporary hormonal imbalance within the body, which may lead to a temporary growth of excess hair.
- *Medical conditions.* A sudden unexplained increase of body hair growth may indicate a more serious medical problem, such as malfunction of the endocime glands, i.e. ovaries, thyroid gland and adrenal gland; or result from the taking of certain drugs, such as corticosteroids, certain birth control pills and high blood pressure medication.

The quantity as well as the type of hair present may vary with race:

- *People of Latin extraction* tend to possess heavier body, facial and scalp hair, which is relatively coarse and straight.
- *People of Eastern Asian extraction* tend to possess very little or no body and facial hair growth, and usually their scalp hair growth is relatively coarse and straight. This gives the appearance of greater hair density, but they have a lower hair density than Caucasian, Latin and African–Caribbean people.
- *People of Northern European and Caucasian extraction* tend to have light-to-medium body and facial hair growth, with their scalp hair growth being wavy, loosely curled or straight.
- *People of African–Caribbean extraction* tend to have little body and facial hair growth, but usually their scalp hair growth is relatively coarse and curled.

The nails

The structure and function of the nail

Nails grow from the ends of the fingers and toes and serve as a form of protection. They also help when picking up small objects. The different components of the nails and surrounding tissues are discussed below.

As part of your consultation you may look at the appearance of the nail as an indicator of a person's health.

Nails should be a healthy pink colour, with supple cuticles. Disease or disorder can show itself in different ways on the nail. This should be referred to the clients GP for diagnosis.

Structure and function of the nail

Nail part	*Function*
The nail plate nail plate 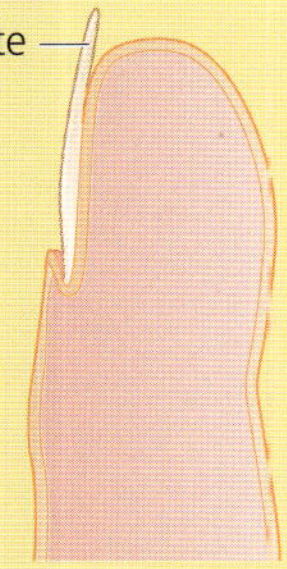	The **nail plate** is composed of compact translucent layers of keratinized epidermal cells: it is this that makes up the main body of the nail. The layers of cells are packed very closely together with fat but very little moisture. The nail gradually grows forwards over the nail bed, until finally it becomes the free edge. The underside of the nail plate is grooved by longitudinal ridges and furrows, which help to keep it in place. In normal health the plate curves in two directions: ● transversely – from side to side across the nail ● longitudinally – from the base of the nail to the free edge There are no blood vessels or nerves in the nail plate: this is why the nails, like hair, can be cut without pain or bleeding. The pink colour of the nail plate derives from the blood vessels that pass beneath it – the nail bed. *Function*: To protect the living nail bed of the fingers and toes.
The free edge free edge 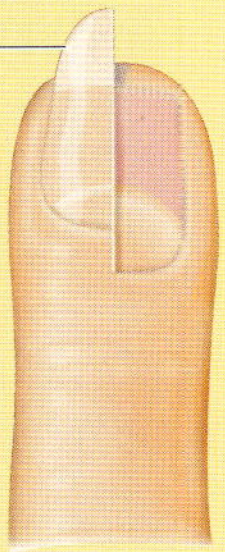	The **free edge** is the part of the nail that extends beyond the fingertip; this is the part that is filed. It appears white as there is no nail bed underneath. *Function*: To protect the tip of the fingers and toes and the hyponychium.
The matrix 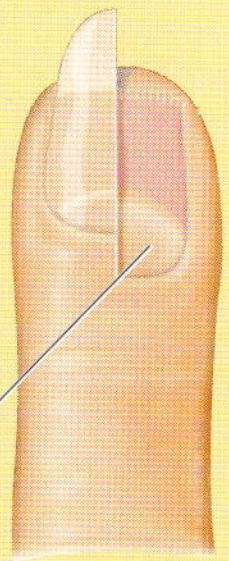 matrix	The **matrix**, sometimes called the nail root, is the growing area of the nail. It is formed by the division of cells in this area, called mitosis, and is part of the stratum germinativum layer of the epidermis. It lies under the eponychium, at the base of the nail. The process of keratinization takes place in the epidermal cells of the matrix, forming the hardened tissue of the nail plate. *Function*: To produce new nail cells.
The nail bed 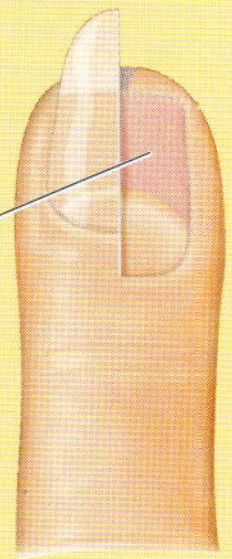 nail bed	The **nail bed** is the portion of skin upon which the nail plate rests. It has a pattern of grooves and furrows corresponding to those found on the underside of the nail plate; these interlock, keeping the nail in place, but separate at the end of the nail to form the free edge. The nail bed is liberally supplied with blood vessels, which provide the nourishment necessary for continued growth; and sensory nerves, for protection. *Function*: To supply nourishment and protection.

Nail part	*Function*
The nail mantle 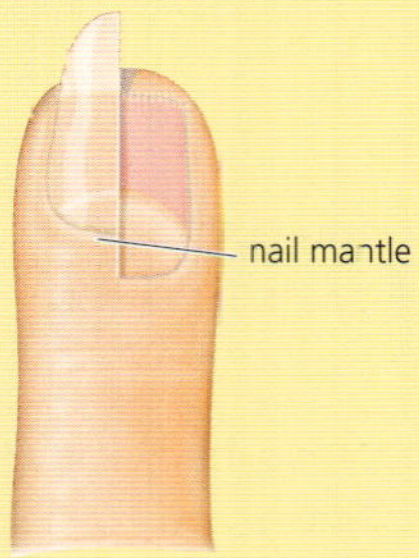	The **nail mantle** is the layer of epidermis at the base of the nail above the matrix, before the cuticle. It appears as a deep fold of skin. *Function*: To protect the matrix from physical damage.
The lunula 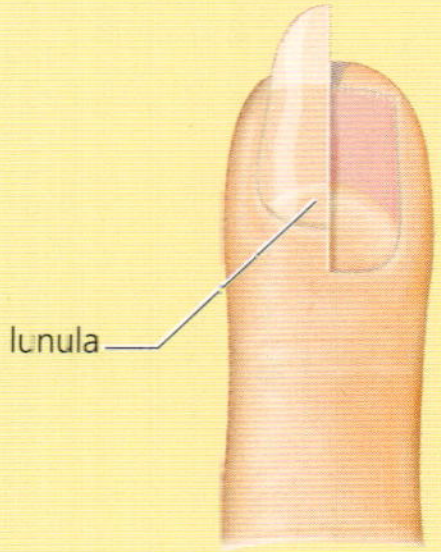	The crescent-shaped **lunula** is located at the base of the nail. These cells gradually harden through keratinization. It is white, relative to the rest of the nail, and there are two theories to account for this: • Newly formed nail plates may be more opaque (less transparent) than mature nail plates. • The lunula may indicate the extent of the underlying matrix – the matrix is thicker than the epidermis of the nail bed, and the capillaries beneath it would not show through as well. *Function*: None.
The hyponychium 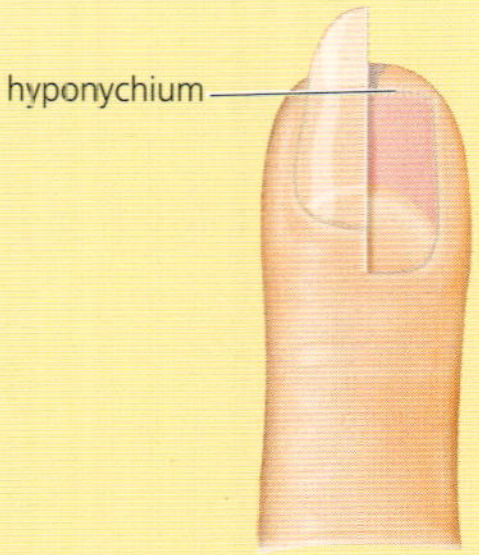	The **hyponychium** is part of the epidermis under the free edge of the nail. *Function*: To protect the nail bed from infection by preventing dirt and bacteria getting underneath the nail plate by forming a waterproof barrier.
The nail grooves 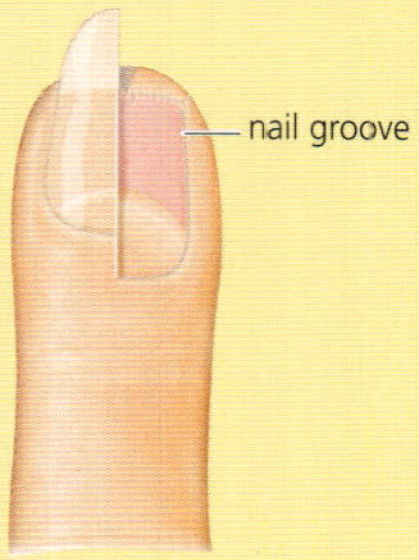	The **nail grooves** run alongside the edge of the nail plate. *Function*: To guide the body of the nail plate as it grows forwards over the nail bed.

Nail part	*Function*
The perionychium 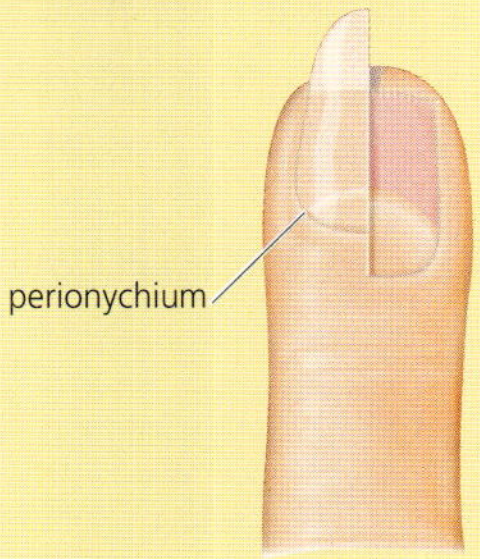	The **perionychium** is the collective name given to the nail walls and the cuticle at the sides of the nail. *Function*: To protect the nail bed from infection by preventing dirt and bacteria getting underneath the nail plate by forming a waterproof barrier.
The nail walls 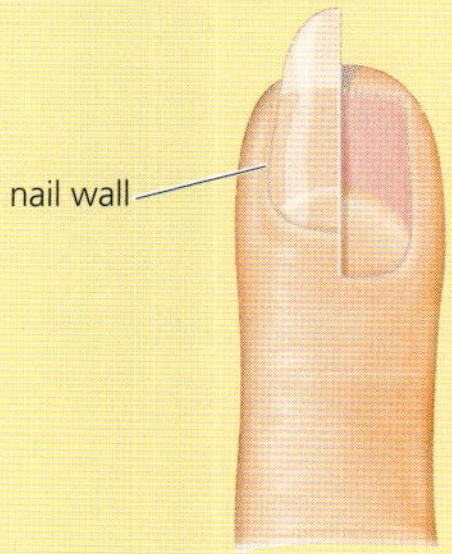	The **nail walls** are the folds of skin overlapping the sides of the nails. *Function*: To cushion and protect the nail plate and grooves from damage.
The eponychium 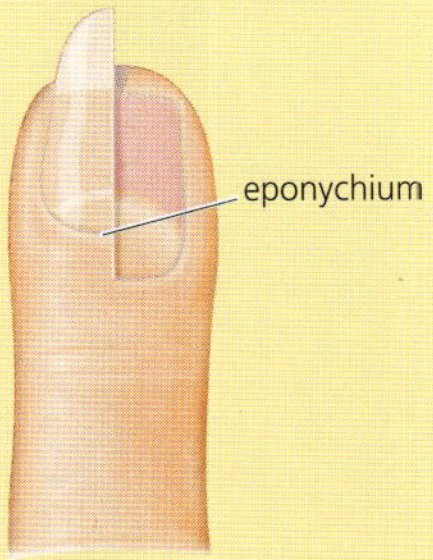	The **eponychium** is the extension of the cuticle at the base of the nail plate, under which the nail plate emerges from the matrix. *Function*: To protect the matrix from infection by preventing dirt and bacteria getting underneath the nail plate by forming a waterproof barrier.
The cuticle 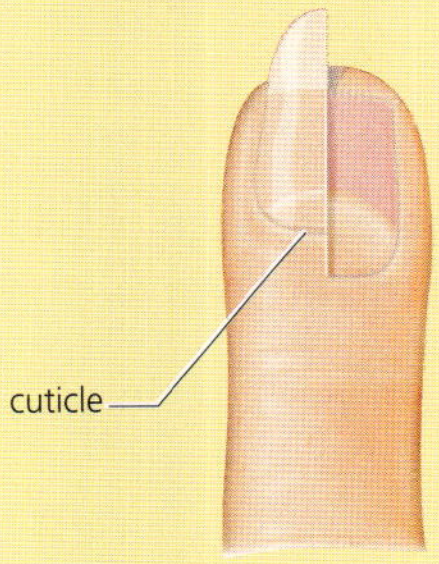	The **cuticle** is the overlapping epidermis around and extending onto the base of the nail, developing from the stratum corneum. When in good condition, it is soft and loose. *Function*: To protect the matrix and nail bed from infection by preventing dirt and bacteria getting underneath the nail plate by forming a waterproof barrier.

Nail growth

Cells divide in the matrix and the nail grows forwards over the nail bed, guided by the nail grooves, until it reaches the end of the finger or toe, where it becomes the free edge. As they first emerge from the matrix the translucent cells are plump and soft, but they get harder and flatter as they move towards the free edge. The top two layers of the epidermis form the nail plate; the remaining three form the nail bed.

The nails' cells die in a process called keratinization, where the cells become filled with a protein called **keratin**.

The nail bed has a pattern of grooves and furrows corresponding to those found on the underside of the nail plate: the two surfaces interlock, holding the nail in place.

Fingernails grow at approximately twice the speed of toenails. It takes about 6 months for a fingernail to grow from cuticle to free edge, but about 12 months for a toenail to do so.

ALWAYS REMEMBER

If the nail bed is pink this means the blood circulation to the nail bed is good. Poor health disorders such as respiratory illness and anaemia can affect the appearance of the nail colour, called 'blue nail'.

ALWAYS REMEMBER

Did you know?

Fingernails grow more quickly than toenails. Fingernails grow about 0.1 mm each day or 3 mm to 4 mm per month (4 cm per year), they grow faster in summer than in winter.

The eye

Basic structure and function of the eye

The eye is positioned in a protective socket formed from the bone of the skull called the orbital cavity. It is cushioned by a layer of fat inside the eye socket and surrounded by a tough outer layer of tissue called the **sclera**, the white part of the eye. The eye is shaped like a ball, and is referred to as the eyeball. It is responsible for providing our vision, collecting light and converting it via nerve impulses, which when received by the brain decode it and inform us what we can see.

The eyeball moves all the time, controlled by six small striated strap-shaped muscles attached to the eyeball and the walls of the orbital cavity. Eye movement is under voluntary control when looking in a particular direction but when looking at differences in distance and in different lighting conditions this is under autonomic control.

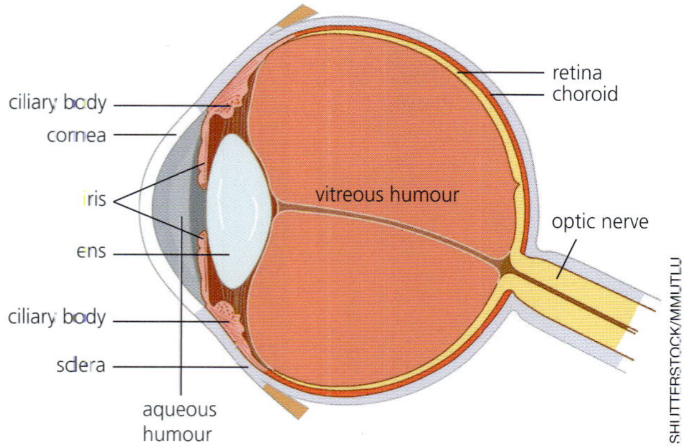

Parts of the eyeball

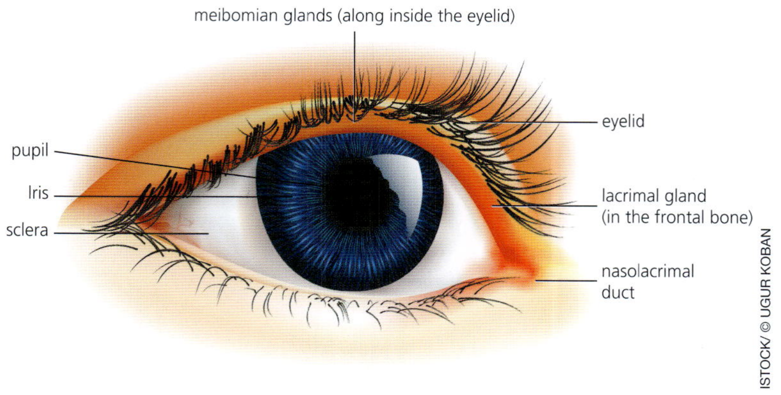

Parts of the eye

The eyeball

The eyeball is made up of a semi-solid clear gel called **vitreous humour** which gives the eye its shape and keeps structures such as the retina in place. It is made up of two cavities, front and rear, either side of a structure called the lens.

The main structures and their functions are discussed below.

Optic nerves (2nd cranial nerves) Optic nerves transport the nerve impulses from the eye to the brain.

Retina The retina is situated in the rear cavity of the eye. It is directly connected to the optic nerve. It detects light rays and these are transformed into nerve signals that the brain can understand. The retina contains two kinds of light-sensing cells called **rods** and **cones**. Cone cells detect colour when in bright light and daylight vision, rod cells detect black and white when in dim light and night vision. Impulses from rod and cone cells pass to connecting nerve cells which send signals to the optic nerve. The area of the retina that receives light is called the **fovea** and is packed with cone cells.

Cornea The cornea is a clear domed-shaped, transparent layer, covering the front coloured part of the eye, which receives light rays and directs them onto the retina.

Lens The lens is shaped like a disc and is made up of transparent fibres called **crystallins**, which allow light through. They are also, allowing the lens to change shape to direct incoming light into the eye, to the retina, to enable us to identify objects at different distances, both near and far. The lens focuses the image.

Iris The iris is the coloured part of the eye, in the middle of the iris is the pupil. This can adjust the amount of light allowed into the eye by changing the size of the pupil. When the light is bright the pupil contracts (goes smaller), letting less light into the eye. If the light is dim the pupils dilate (go larger) to allow more light into the eyes.

Pupil The pupil is a hole that allows light to enter the eye in the middle of the iris.

Optic nerve The optic nerve transports nerve signals from the retina of the eye to the brain.

Aqueous humour The aqueous humour is a clear watery fluid found between the cornea and lens that keeps the cornea curved outwards, helping to give the eye its shape. The aqueous humour is found at the front cavity of the eye.

Parts of the eye area

Ciliary muscles Ciliary muscles form a ring around the eye and focus light by changing the shape of the lens. When looking at far away objects, the ciliary muscles relax and ligaments pull on the lens changing its shape which becomes slimmer and flatter, receiving less light rays. When looking at objects which are near, the ciliary muscles contract and the eye returns to its rounded shape which receives more light rays.

Choroid The choroid is a dark membrane containing blood vessels that lies between the retina and the sclera. It cuts down reflection inside the eye and provides nutrients and oxygen for the surrounding parts of the eye, including the retina.

Blood vessels Blood vessels are found in all parts of the eye except the lens, which is transparent.

The eyelid The eyelid is composed of skin and connective tissue; these movable lids are situated above and below the eye. They protect the eyes from bright light, dust and debris. When we blink, the surface of the eye is cleaned. A membrane lining called the **conjunctiva** lines the eyelids protecting the cornea and front of the eye. The edges of the eyelids contain numerous sebaceous glands some open into the hair follicles of the eyelash hair and some directly onto the edge of the eyelids between the hairs.

Meibomian glands Meibomian glands are modified sebaceous glands which open directly onto the inside of the edge of the eyelid and secrete an oily substance when blinking that provides a protective film over the conjunctiva. This oily substance also prevents the eyes becoming dry by reducing the evaporation of tears.

The eyelids open and close, either by the voluntary action of opening and closing the eyes or the involuntary action of blinking, by the contraction of the orbicularis occuli muscle which closes the eyelid and the contraction of the levator palpebrae superioris muscle which opens and lifts the eyelid.

Lacrimal gland The lacrimal gland is situated above the outer corner of each eye in the frontal bone and it secretes tears composed of water, salt and a bactericidal enzyme called lysozyme.

Nasolacrimal duct The nasolacrimal duct drains tears into the nasal cavity.

Eyebrows Eyebrows are short, coarse terminal hairs situated above the bony orbits of the eyes, the eyebrow hair protects the front of the eye from sweat, dust and debris.

Eyelashes Eyelashes are short, coarse terminal hairs situated on the outer portion of the eyelid in rows of three to five. The eyelash hairs protect the eyes from bright light, dust and debris. There are up to 150 lashes on the upper lid and 80 on the lower eyelid. They are between 7 mm and 9 mm in length.

Organ systems of the body

The human body is made up of organ systems that work together to ensure healthy functioning of the body overall. The major organ systems of the body are described below.

Organ systems

Organ system	*Functions*	*Diagram*
Skeletal	Forms a strong framework which supports the softer tissues and maintains the shape of the body. Internal organs are suspended from the skeleton which keeps them anchored in position. Muscles are attached to the bones which contract and relax allowing movement. Together with the muscles and joints, the skeleton allows movement. Many organs are surrounded by a protective cage of bone. Many of the blood cells are made in bone marrow (found inside the bones).	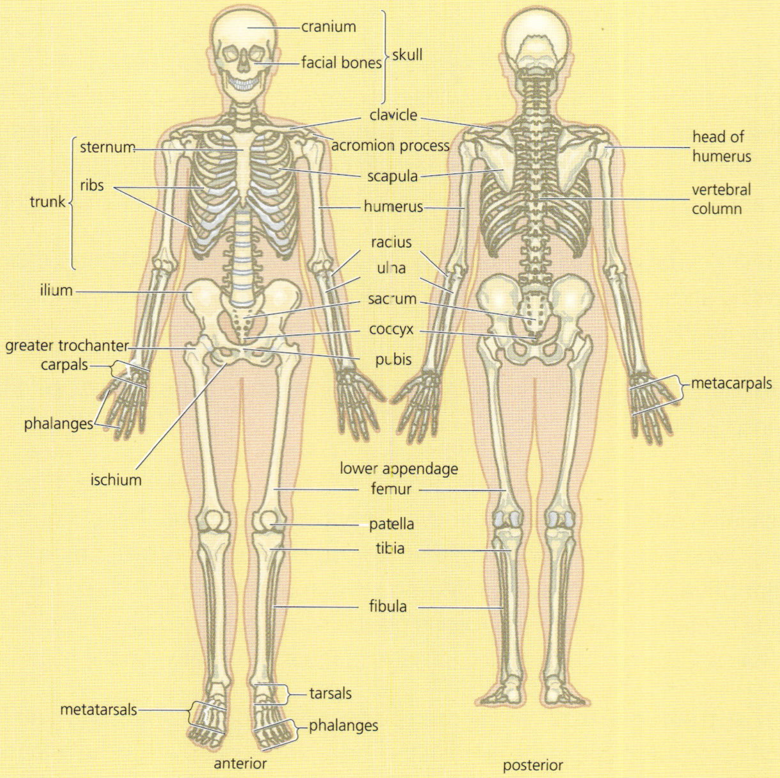

Organ system	*Functions*	*Diagram*
Muscular	Muscles attach to bones and help to maintain the body's posture. Muscles cause movement as they contract and relax. This may be *voluntarily* – where we can control the movement – or *involuntarily* – where we have no conscious control. Muscles also cause heat in the body created by energy in the muscular tissue. This is transported to other body parts by the blood.	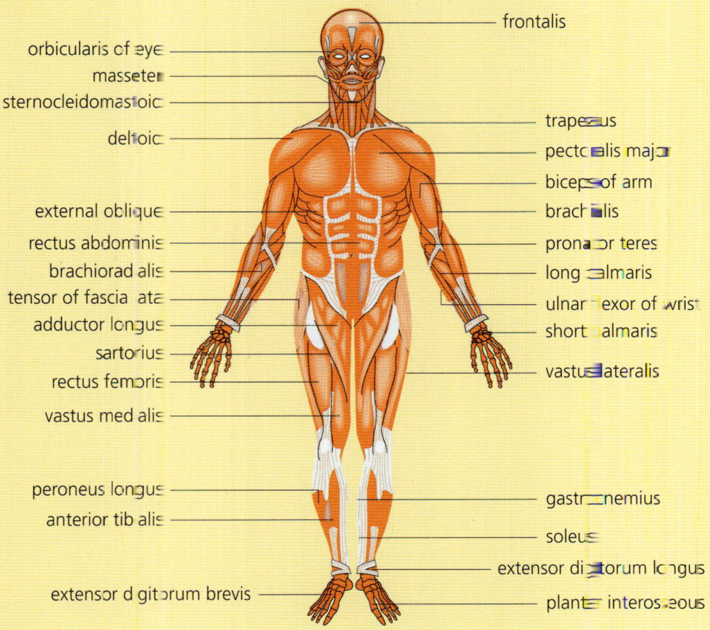
	There are three types of muscular tissue: ● cardiac ● involuntary, visceral (smooth) muscle ● voluntary, skeletal (striated) muscle	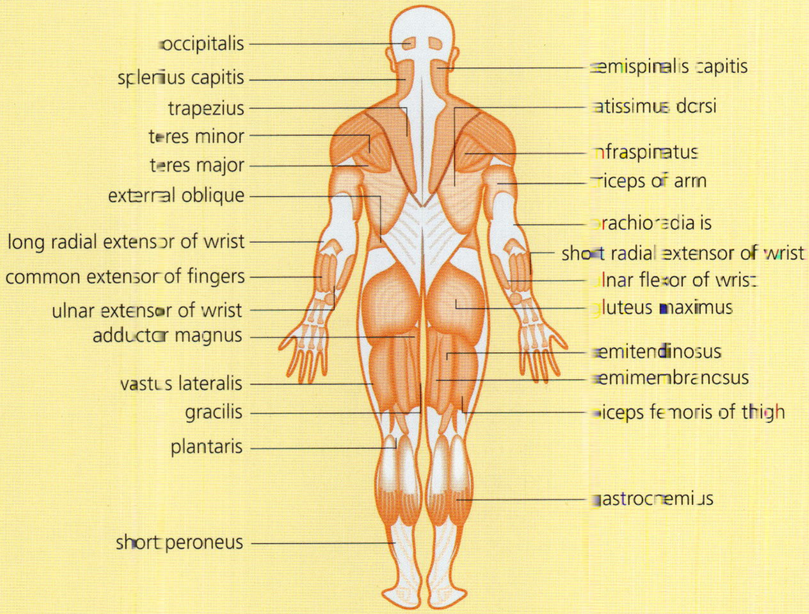

Organ system	*Functions*	*Diagram*
Nervous	Coordinates the activities of the body by responding to stimuli received by the five sense organs: eyes, ears, nose, tongue and skin.	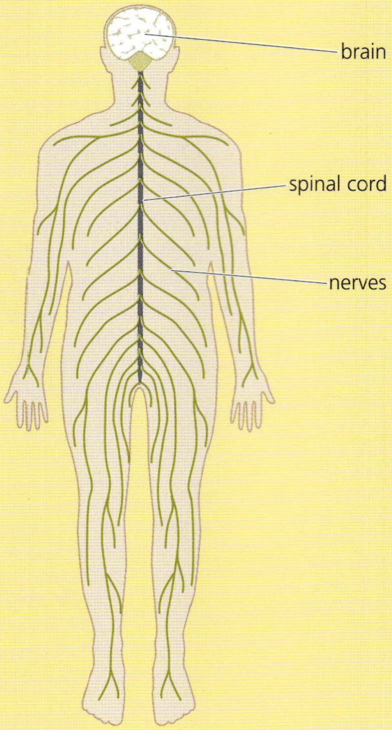
Urinary (excretory system)	Filters toxins and waste products from the blood through the kidneys (two bean-shaped organs), thus maintaining its normal composition. Waste material is filtered out of the blood by the kidneys and made into urine. It is then carried through two tubes, the ureters, to the bladder. Urine is stored in the bladder and leaves the body via the urethra. The waste is the end product of cellular metabolism.	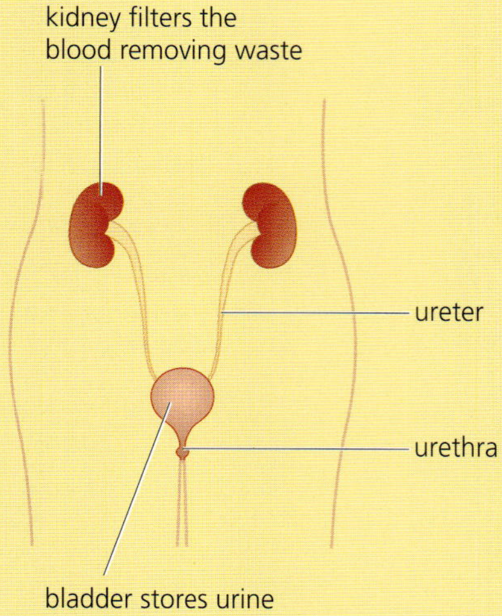

Organ system	*Functions*	*Diagram*
Digestive	Breaks down food into simpler substances so that nutrients can be absorbed into the bloodstream by the body. Food is digested in the alimentary canal, which is divided into several regions. ● The buccal cavity: the space where food is chewed in the mouth and which connects to the pharynx. ● The pharynx (throat) links with the oesophagus, a muscular tube which passes food to the stomach. Food spends a few hours in the stomach before it passes to the intestines, small and large, before finally leaving the alimentary canal via the anus.	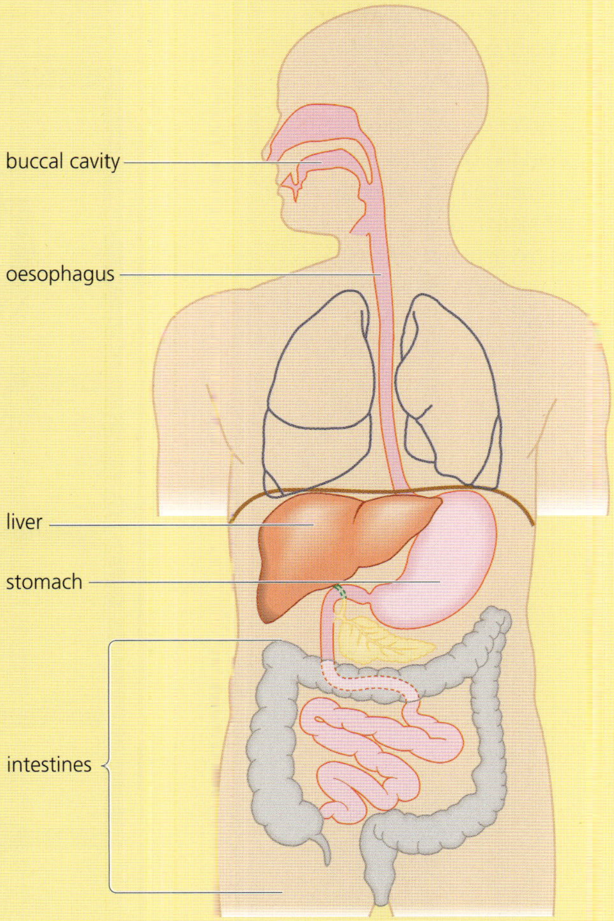
Respiratory	Ensures oxygen collected from the lungs by the blood reaches all cells of the body, where it can be used to provide energy by cell respiration. The waste product from cell respiration, carbon dioxide, is breathed out through the lungs. Air enters the lungs by the movement of the intercostal muscles expanding the ribcage and the contraction of the diaphragm.	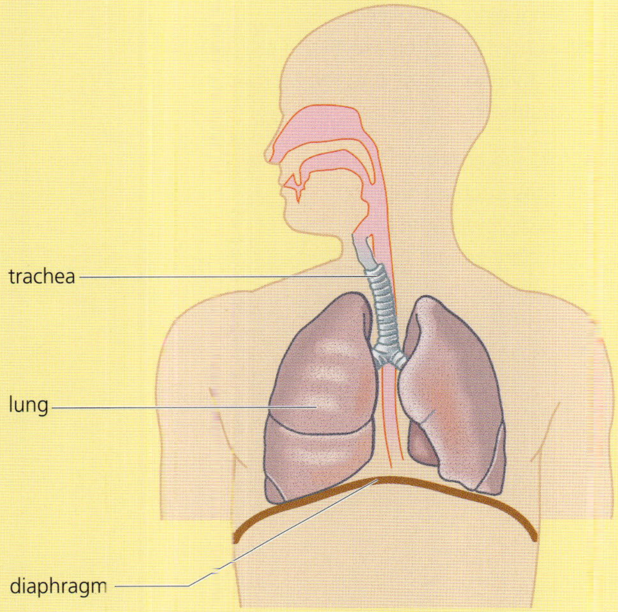

Organ system	*Functions*	*Diagram*
Circulatory	Transports materials around the body so that it can function properly. The heart pumps blood around the body, transporting materials so that the body can function properly. It supplies oxygen and nutrients, then carries away waste products.	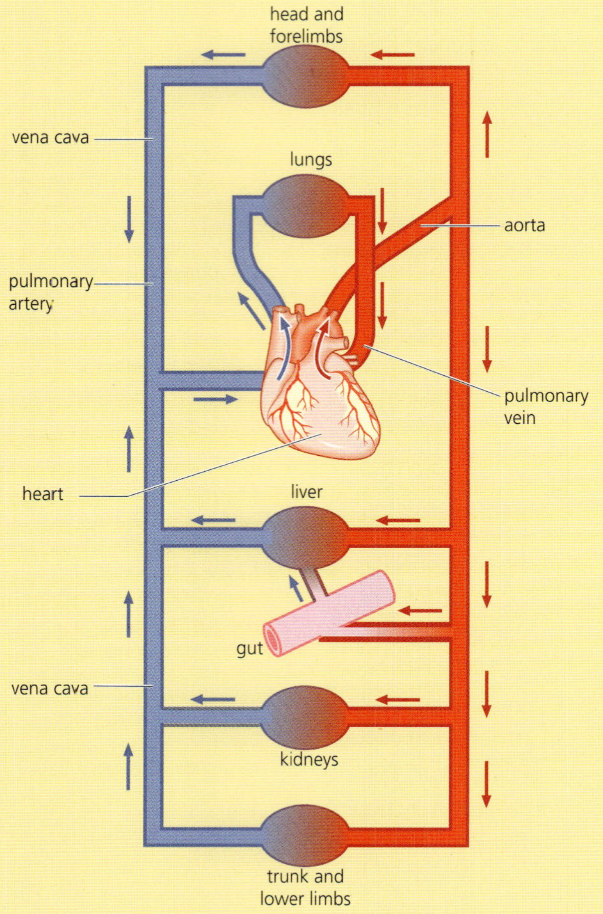
Endocrine	Coordinates and regulates processes in the body by producing chemicals called hormones released by endocrine glands into the bloodstream. Hormones control activities such as growth or the development of secondary sexual characteristics.	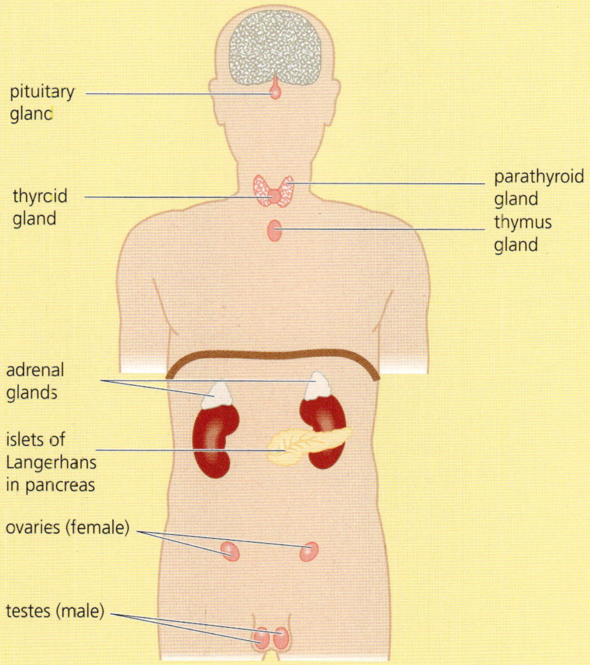

<table>
<tr><th>Organ system</th><th>Functions</th><th>Diagram</th></tr>
<tr><td>Reproductive (the sex glands)</td><td>Produces new humans.

The ovaries produce female sex hormones – oestrogen and progesterone – which stimulate the development of the female physique and are important in the menstrual cycle and pregnancy. They produce the egg required for sexual reproduction.</td><td>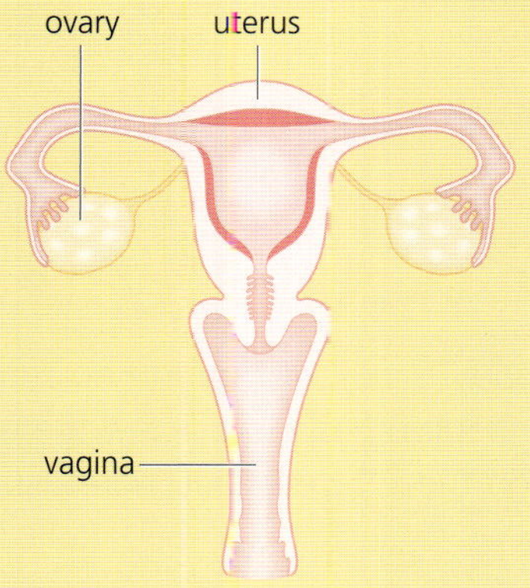
</td></tr>
<tr><td></td><td>The testes are two organs lying outside the body which produce the male sex hormones – androgens (testosterone). These hormones stimulate the development of male characteristics, hair growth, deepening of the voice and development of the male physique. They also produce sperm, which is required for sexual reproduction.</td><td>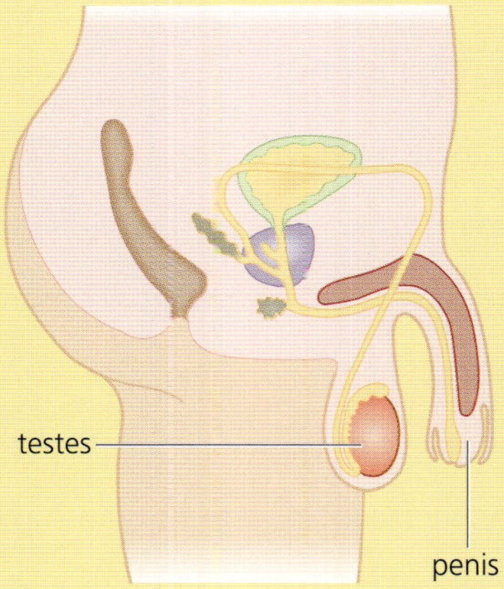
</td></tr>
</table>

Anatomical terminology

Anatomical terminology is used to describe the location, function and description of a body part. It is useful to know these terms, as it will assist your anatomy understanding. As you read through this chapter you will notice those terms.

Anterior	Front (usually refers to front of the body)	**Superficial**	Near the surface
Posterior	Back (usually refers to the back of the body)	**Superior**	Above
Proximal	Nearest to	**Inferior**	Below

Medial	Middle	**Plantar**	Front surface
Distal	Furthest away	**Dorsal**	Back surface
Lateral	Side		

The skeletal system

The body is covered by the epidermis. Beneath the epidermis is the dermis (a layer of connective tissue). In a few areas of the body, such as the scalp, bone can be felt through these layers, but more usually a padding of fat (adipose tissue) covers bony areas.

Bone is a specialized form of connective tissue, the hardest structural tissue in the body that supports, surrounds and connects different parts of the body.

ALWAYS REMEMBER

The human skeleton is made up of two parts, the **axial** and **appendicular** skeleton.

The axial skeleton is made up of the:

- skull – cranium and facial bones
- spine – the neck and back
- ribs and sternum

The appendicular skeleton is made up of the:

- shoulder girdle (the clavicle and scapulae bones) and the arms and hands
- pelvic girdle (ilium, ischium and pubis-fused bones and the sacrum bone) and the legs and feet

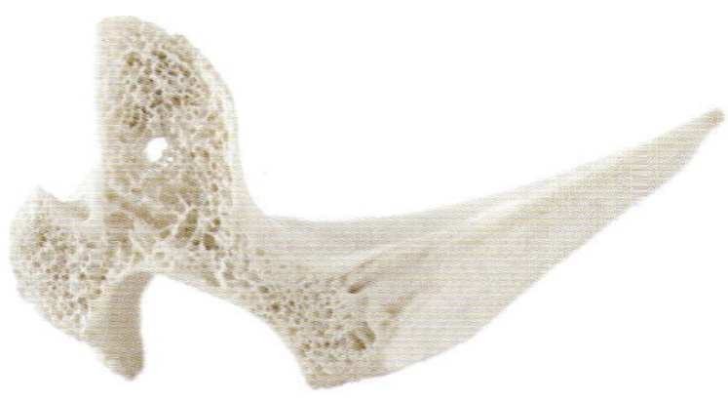
SHUTTERSTOCK
Bone tissue

It is made up of water, non-living (inorganic) material including calcium and phosphorus, and living (organic) material such as the cells which form bones called **osteoblasts**.

There are two main classifications of bone tissue, **compact** and **cancellous** (spongy). Bones are made up of both types of tissue which varies according to size and function.

Compact appears to have no visible spaces and is solid in structure making it strong and hardwearing. However, under a microscope it can be seen that it is supplied with blood and lymph vessels and nerves.

Cancellous (spongy) has many spaces which contain red and yellow bone marrow. Red bone marrow produces new red blood cells and yellow bone marrow stores fat cells.

Bones are covered with a connective tissue called the **periosteum** which has an outer layer that provides a protective function and an inner layer that receives a rich blood supply essential for the nutrition of the bone.

Bones can be classified as: flat; short; irregular; long; and sesamoid.

ALWAYS REMEMBER

Mineral stores

Bone acts as a reservoir for important minerals such as calcium and phosphorus and also makes new cells for the blood in certain bones in tissue called bone marrow.

Examples are shown below:

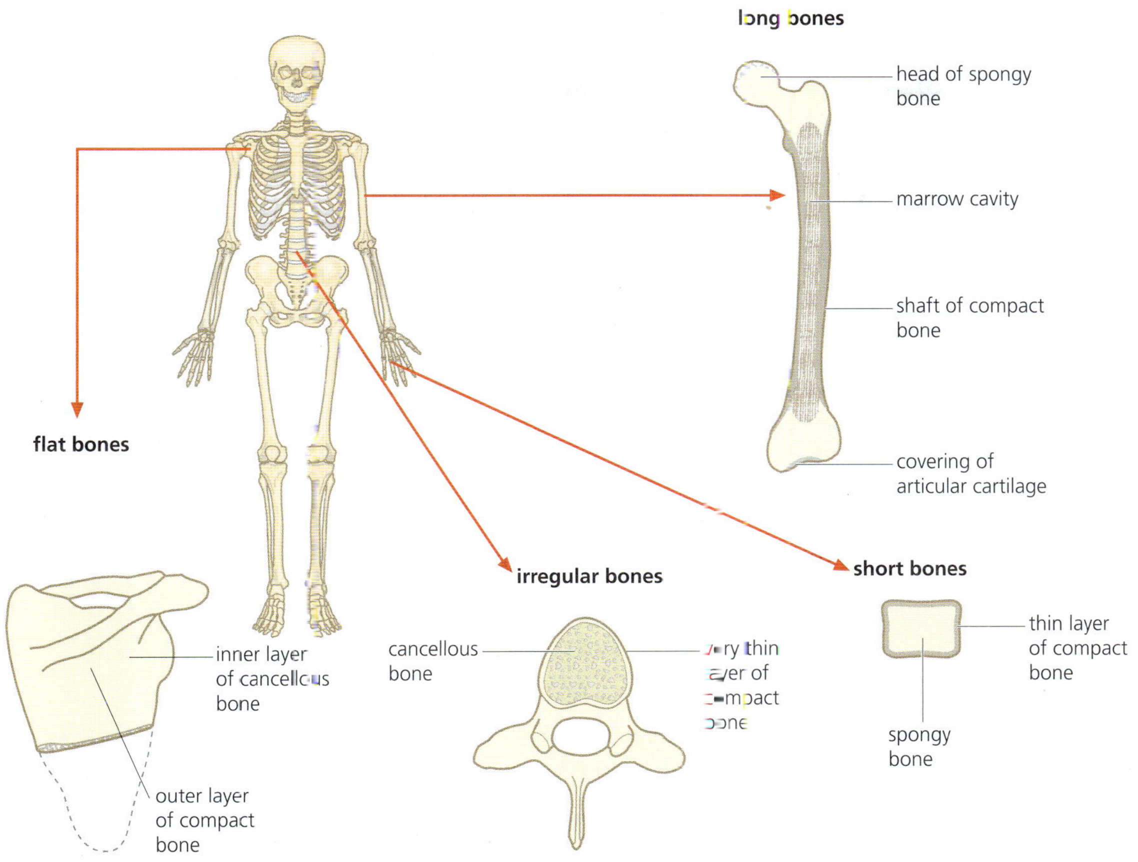

Types of bones

Bones and joints

The skeleton is made up of many bones to facilitate movement. Each bone is connected to its neighbour by connective tissue. Fibrous connective tissue is used for immovable joints such as those in the cranium. Fibro-cartilage is used for semi-moveable joints such as those between the bodies of the vertebrae. The most common joints are freely moveable. They are called **synovial joints** and are loosely held together by a form of connective tissue called **ligaments**.

Bones get stronger when they are moved regularly by muscles. Load-bearing activity is useful in helping to prevent osteoporosis (thinning and weakening of the bone tissue) in older people.

Synovial joints In a typical synovial joint a sleeve-like ligament joins one bone loosely to the next. This forms a fibrous **capsule** which is flexible enough to permit free movement, but strong enough to resist dislocation.

Lining this capsule is the **synovial membrane** which secretes synovial fluid into the joint. Synovial fluid looks and feels like egg white. It lubricates the joint, becoming less viscous as movement at the joint increases. It also contains phagocytic cells (white blood cells that protect the body by ingestion) to remove debris caused by wear and tear at the joint and it nourishes the **articular cartilage** that covers the ends of each bone. Articular cartilage provides a smooth coating at the ends of the bones, protecting them from wear by reducing friction.

Extra ligaments may run around the outside of the articular capsule or inside the joint, providing extra strength. Some joints may also contain discs of cartilage to help maintain their stability.

ALWAYS REMEMBER

Shivering

When the body temperature falls an involuntary action of the muscles causes rapid contraction – the shivering action, to make heat

ALWAYS REMEMBER

The body has 206 bones with the important functions of: support; protection; movement; blood cell production; and mineral storage.

The main support for joints is provided by the muscles that surround them. Very mobile joints such as the shoulder rely heavily on muscles as well as ligaments to hold the joint together.

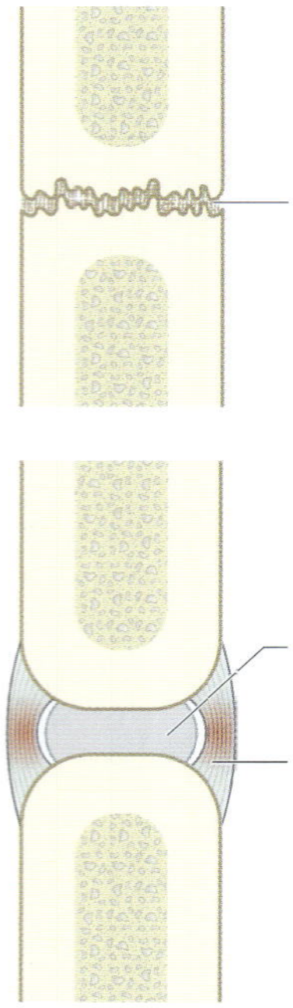

Bone connections

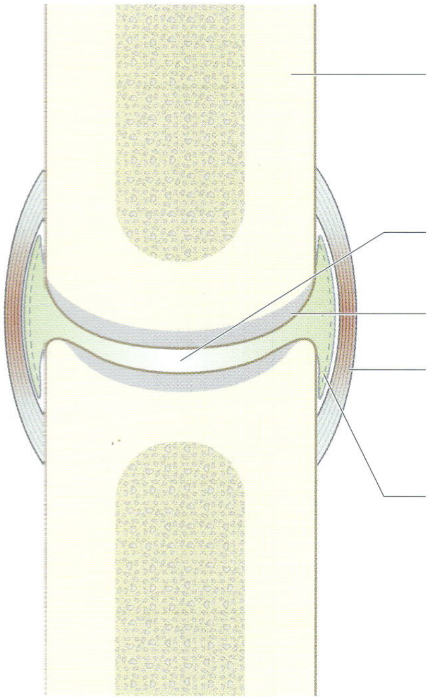

A synovial joint

Specific synovial joints in the body

Position	*Type*	*Movement*
Hip 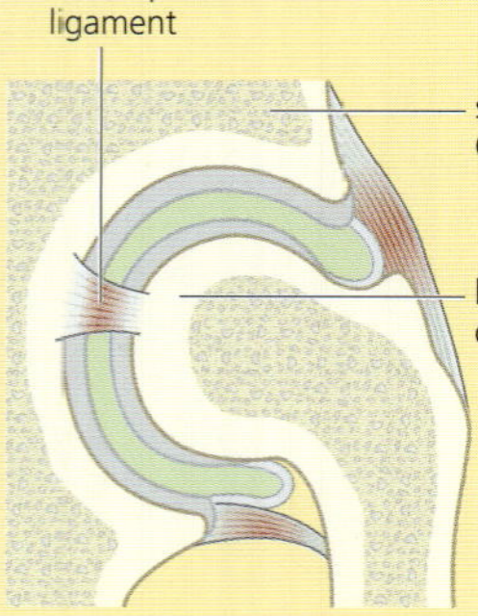	Ball and socket: the head of the femur forms the ball which fits into a socket on the pelvis.	Abduction, adduction, extension, flexion, rotation.
Shoulder 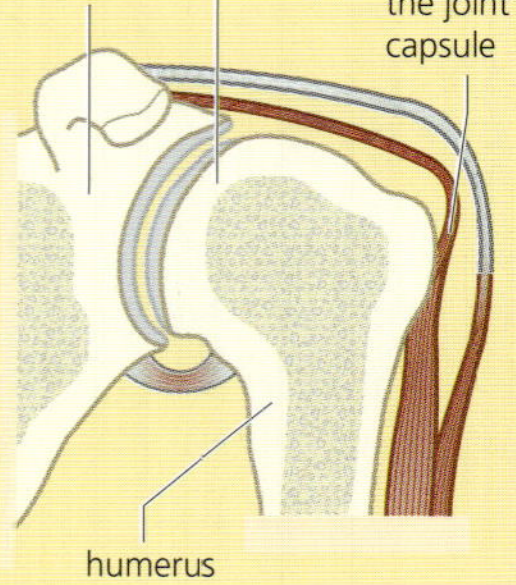	Ball and socket: the head of the humerus forms the ball that fits into a shallow socket on the scapula.	As hip Arm circling involves movement of this joint together with that of the shoulder (pectoral girdle).

Position	*Type*	*Movement*
Knee 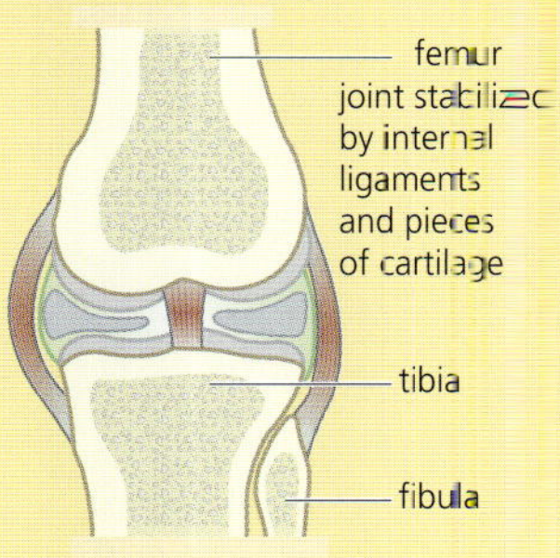	Hinge: formed between the femur and the tibia.	Flexion, extension.
Elbow 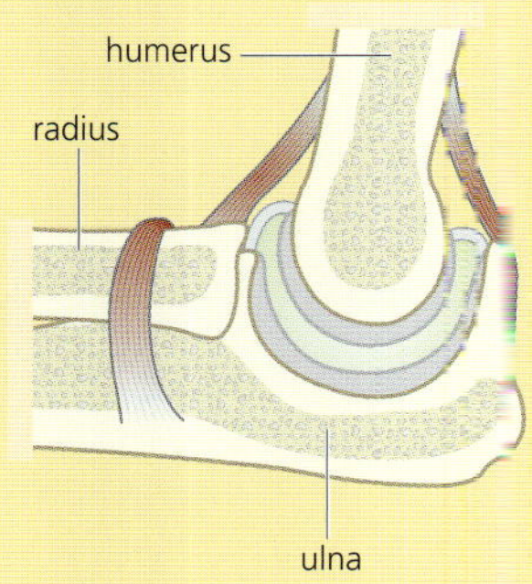	Hinge: formed between the humerus and the ulna.	As knee.
Forearm	Pivot: formed between the ulna and head of the radius.	Supination (turning the hand palm up), pronation (turning the hand palm down).
Ankle	Hinge: formed between the bones of the lower leg (tibia and fibula and the talus of the foot).	Dorsiflexion (foot pulled up toward knee), plantar-flexion (pointing the foot).
Wrist	Condyloid: formed between the bones of the lower arm (radius and ulna) and the bones of the wrist (carpals)	Flexion, extension, abduction, adduction.
Foot	Gliding.	Inversion, eversion.
Hand	Gliding.	Flexion or clenching, extension or stretching.
Toe	Hinge.	Flexion, extension, the joint at the base of the toes allows abduction and adduction.
Finger	Hinge.	As toe.

Bones of the head

The bones which form the head are collectively known as the **skull**. The skull can be divided into two parts, the face and the cranium, which together are made up of 22 bones:

- the 14 facial bones form the face
- the eight cranial bones form the rest of the head

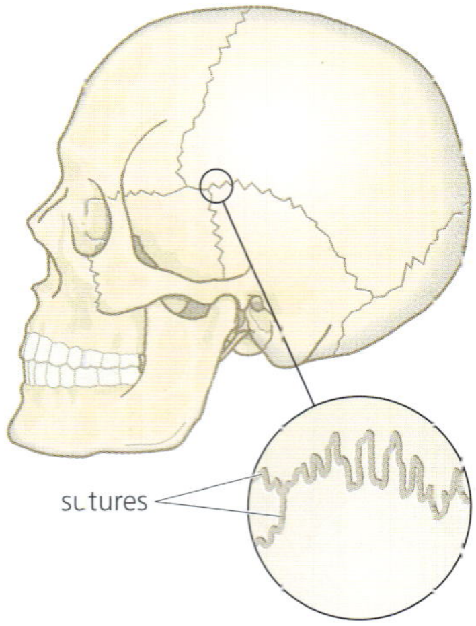

Sutures

As well as forming our facial features, the facial bones support other structures such as the eyes and the teeth. Some of these bones, such as the nasal bone, are made from **cartilage**, a connective tissue that is softer than bone.

The cranium surrounds and protects the brain. The bones are thin and slightly curved, and are held together by connective tissue. After childhood, the joints become immovable, and are called **sutures**, appearing as wavy lines.

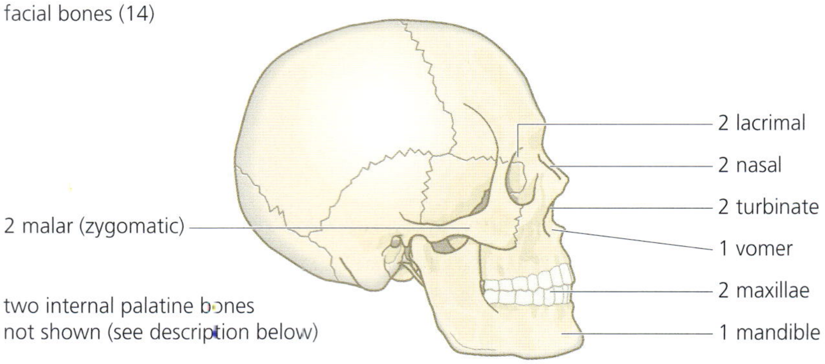

Bones of the face

Facial bones

Bone	*Number*	*Location*	*Function*
Nasal	2	The nose.	Form the bridge of the nose.
Vomer	1	The nose and palate.	Forms the dividing bony wall of the nose.
Palatine	2	The nose.	Internal bones. Form the floor and wall of the nose, the roof of the mouth and bottom of the eye orbits.
Turbinate	2	The nose.	Form the outer walls of the nose.
Lacrimal	2	The eye sockets.	Form the inner walls of the eye sockets; contain a small groove for the tear duct.
Malar (zygomatic)	2	The cheek.	Form the cheekbones.
Maxillae	2	The upper jaw.	Fused together, to form the upper jaw, which holds the upper teeth.
Mandible	1	The lower jaw.	The largest and strongest of the facial bones; holds the lower teeth.

Cranial bones

Bone	*Number*	*Location*	*Function*
Occipital	1	The lower back of the cranium.	Contains a large hole called the *foramen magnum*: through this pass the spinal cord, the nerves and blood vessels.
Parietal	2	The sides of the cranium.	Fused together to form the sides and top of the head (the 'crown').

Bone	*Number*	*Location*	*Function*
Frontal	1	The forehead.	Forms the forehead and the upper walls of the eye sockets.
Temporal	2	The sides of the head.	Provide two muscle attachment points: the mastoid process and the zygomatic process.
Ethmoid	1	Between the eye sockets.	Forms part of the nasal cavities.
Sphenoid	1	The base of the cranium the back of the eye sockets.	A bat-shaped bone which joins together all the bones of the cranium

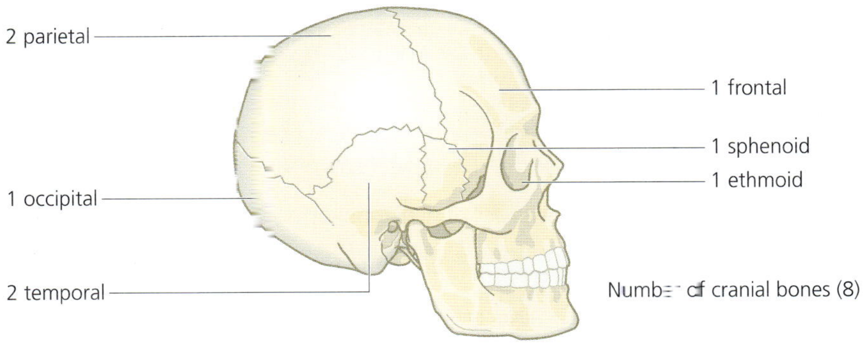

Bones of the cranium

Bones of the neck, chest and shoulder

Bone	*Number*	*Location*	*Function*
Cervical vertebra	7	The neck.	These vertebrae form the top of the spinal column: the *atlas* is the first vertebra, which supports the skull; the *axis* is the second vertebra, which allows rotation of the head.
Hyoid	1	A U-shaped bone at the front of the neck.	Supports the tongue.
Clavicle	2	Slender long bones at the base of the neck.	Commonly called the *collar bones*: these form a joint with the sternum and the scapula bones, allowing movement at the shoulder.
Scapula	2	Triangular bones in the upper back.	Commonly called the *shoulder blades*: the scapulae provide attachment for muscles that move the arms. The *shoulder girdle*, which allows movement at the shoulder, is composed of the clavicles and the scapulae.
Humerus	2	The upper bones of the arms.	Form ball-and-socket joints with the scapulae: these joints allow movement in any direction.
Sternum	1	The breastbone.	Protects the inner organs; provides a surface for muscle attachment; and supports muscle movement.

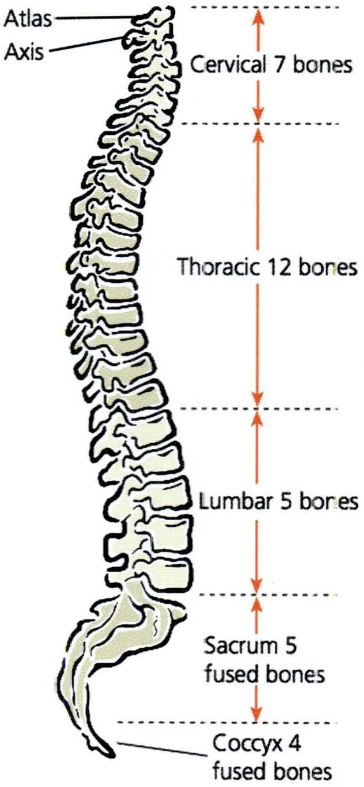

Vertebral column

Bones of the spine The spine is also referred to as the vertebral column. It is made up of 24 separate, irregular, moveable bones which support the skull, protect the spinal cord and give attachment to other bones. It is bound together by powerful ligaments. The curves in each area give the spine an 'S' shape which helps balance the body's weight.

Bone	*Number*	*Location*	*Function*
Cervical	7	Neck and upper back.	The first bone (1st cervical vertebra) is called the *atlas* and supports and connects with the skull which allows a nodding movement. The second bone (2nd cervical vertebra) is the *axis* which moves with the atlas to rotate the head side to side.
Thoracic	12	Upper and middle back.	The rib cage joins to the thoracic vertebra and protects the body's vital organs, i.e. heart and lungs.
Lumbar	5	Lower back.	Bears the body's weight and allows attachment of powerful back muscles allowing bending movements.
Sacrum	5	Base of spine.	These bones are fused and keep the pelvic girdle in place.
Coccyx	4	The tail of the spine.	These bones are fused – it has no known function.

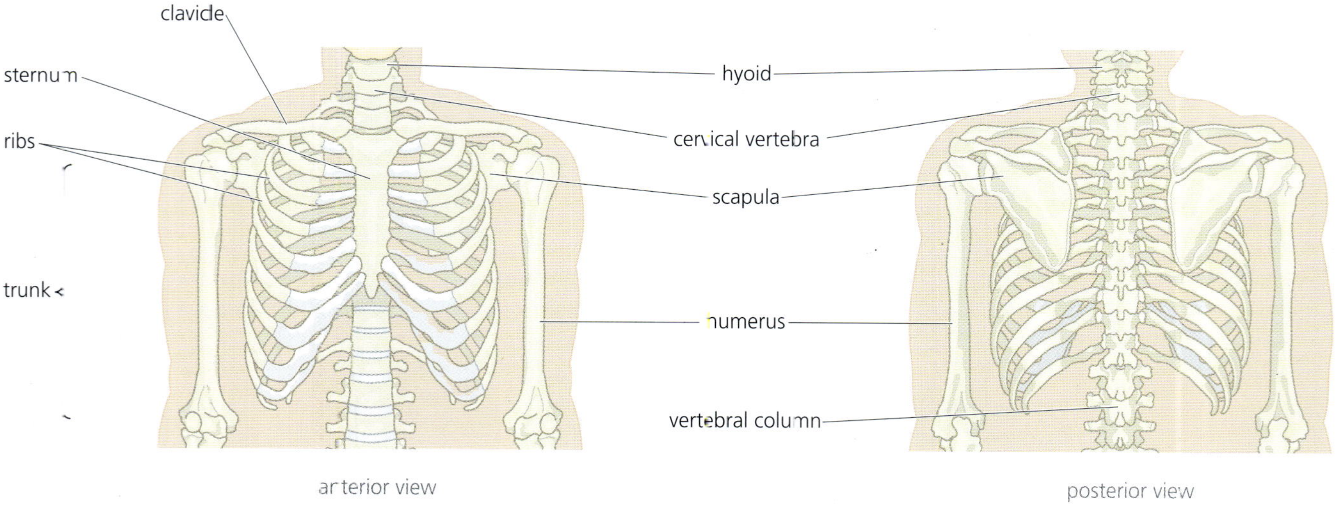

Bones of the neck, chest and shoulder

Bones of the hand and forearm

The wrist consists of eight small **carpal** bones, which glide over one another to allow movement. This is called a **condyloid** or **gliding joint**.

There are then five **metacarpal** bones that make up the palm of the hand.

The fingers are made up of 14 individual bones called **phalanges** – two in each of the thumbs and three in each of the fingers.

The arm is made up of three long bones: the **humerus** is the bone of the upper arm, from the shoulder to the elbow; the **radius** and **ulna** lie side by side in the lower arm, from the elbow to the wrist.

Having two bones in the lower arm makes it easier for your wrist to rotate. The movement that causes the palm to face downwards is called **pronation;** the movement that causes it to face upwards is called **supination.**

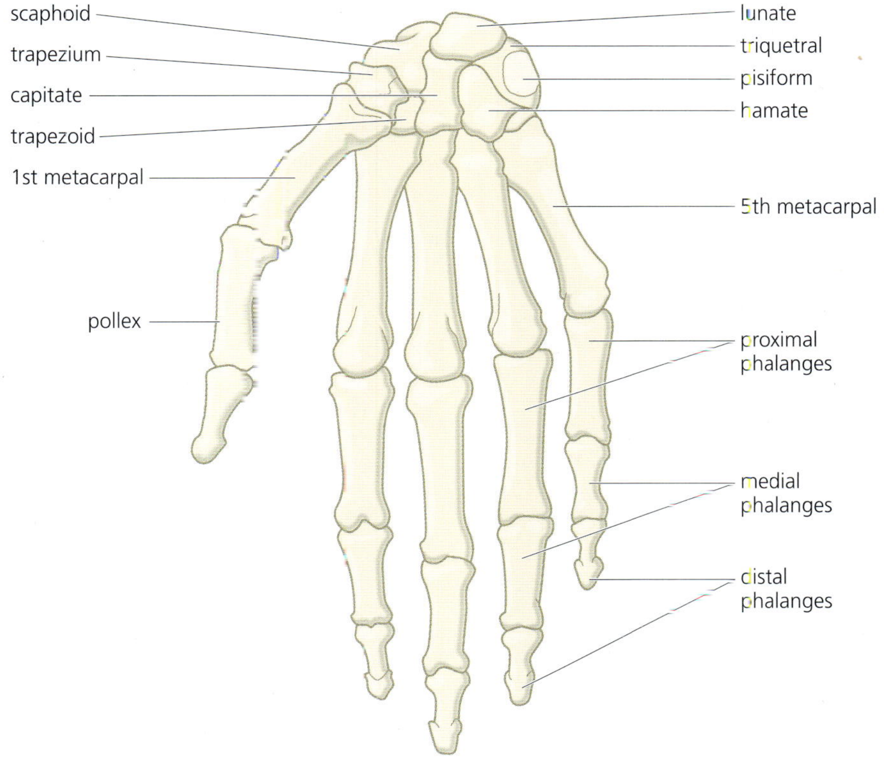

Bones of the hand and wrist

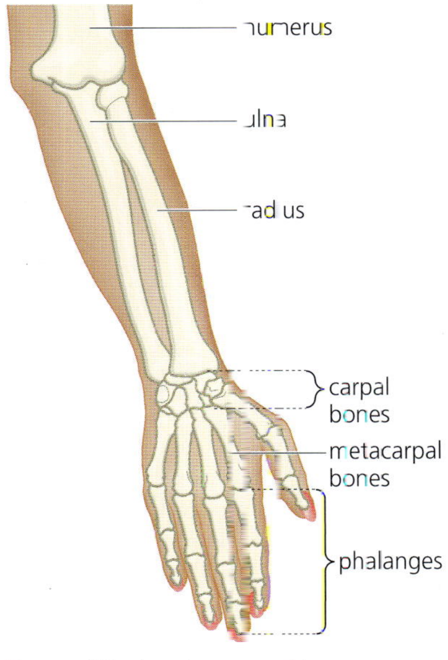

Bones of the hand, wrist and lower arm

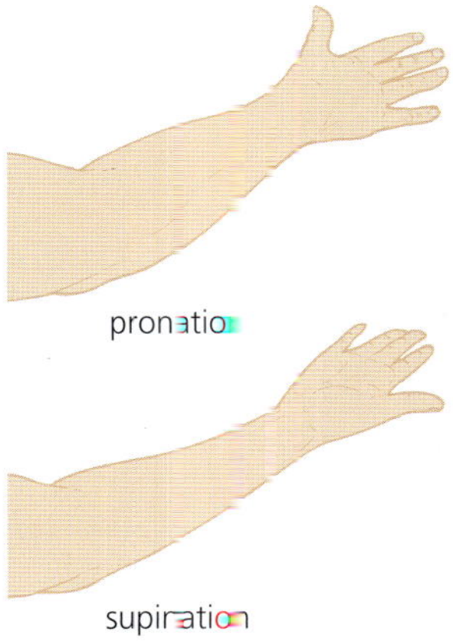

Pronation and supination

ACTIVITY

Identifying bones in the hand

Look very closely at your hand. Can you identify where the bones are? Try feeling the bones with your other hand. How many can you feel?

Bones of the foot and lower leg

The foot is made up of seven **tarsal** (ankle) bones, five **metatarsal** (ball of the foot) bones and 14 **phalanges (toe bones)**. These bones fit together to form arches which help to support the foot and to absorb the impact when we walk, run and jump.

ALWAYS REMEMBER

Anatomical definitions

Medial: towards the midline (middle) of the body.

Lateral: away from the median (middle) line of the body. The outer side of the body.

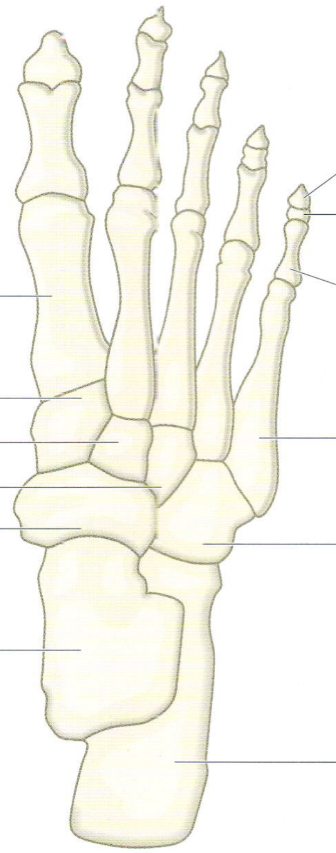

Bones of the foot

The arches of the foot The **arches** of the foot are created by the formation of the bones and joints, and supported by ligaments. These arches support the weight of the body and help to preserve balance when we walk on even surfaces. The longitudinal arch runs longitudinally from the calcaneus to the metatarsals. The arch on the inside aspect of the foot is the medial longitudinal arch, on the outside aspect it is the lateral longitudinal arch. The transverse arch lies perpendicular or at right angles to this in the metatarsal area, as shown below.

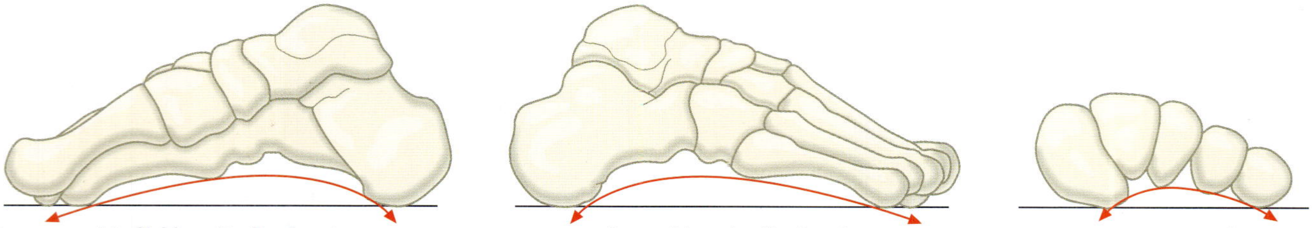

Arches of the foot

ALWAYS REMEMBER

Arches

Footprints made by bare feet show that only part of the foot touches the ground. Weight transfers from the heel to the big toe when walking. Feet with reduced arches are referred to as 'flat feet', caused by weak ligaments and tendons.

The bones of the lower leg The lower leg is made up of two long bones, the **tibia** and the **fibula**. These bones have joints with the upper leg (at the knee) and with the foot (at the ankle). Having two bones in the lower leg – as with the forearm – allows a greater range of movement to be achieved at the ankle.

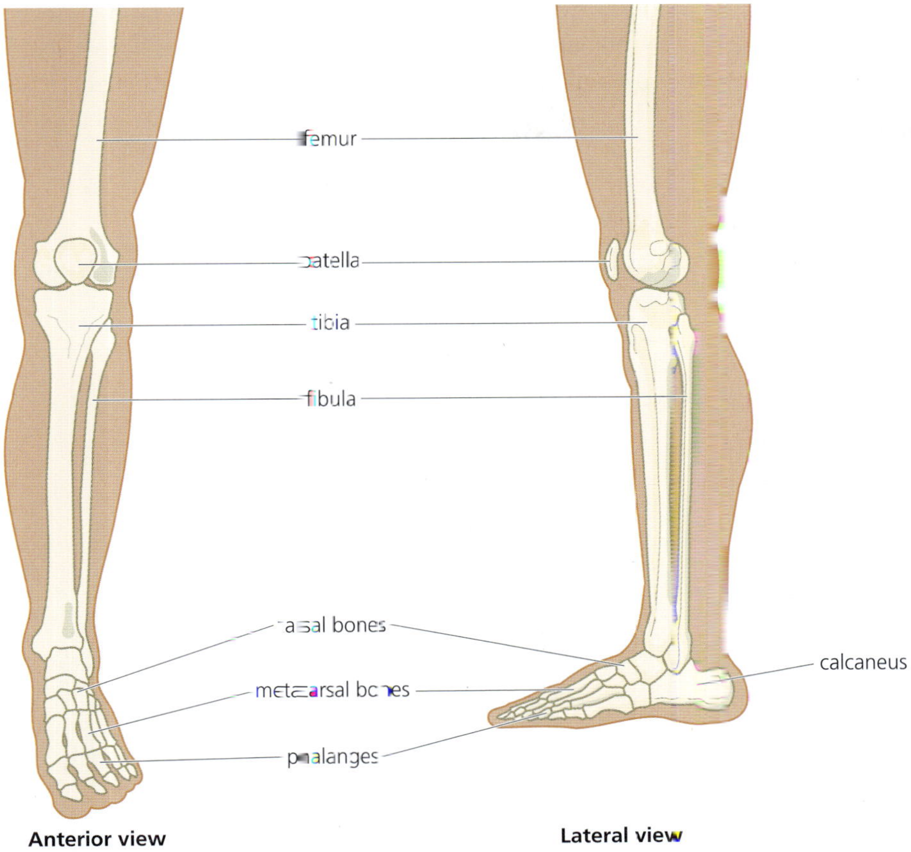

Bones of the lower leg

The muscular system

Muscles are responsible for the movement of body parts. Each muscle is made up of a bundle of elastic fibres bound together in a sheath, the **fascia**. Muscular tissue contracts (shortens) and produces movement. Muscles never completely relax – there are always a few contracted fibres in every muscle. These make the muscles slightly tense and this tension is called **muscle tone**.

Muscle tissue has the following properties:

- it has the ability to contract
- it is extensible (when the extensor muscle in a joint contracts the corresponding flexor muscle will be stretched or lengthened)
- it is elastic – following contraction or extension it returns to its original length
- it is responsive – it contracts in response to nerve stimulation

A muscle is usually anchored by a strong tendon to one bone: the point of attachment is known as the muscle's **origin**, normally the stationary end of the muscle. The muscle is likewise joined to a second bone: the attachment in this case is called the muscle's **insertion**, the end of the bone that moves. It is the second bone that is moved: the muscle contracts, pulling the two bones towards each other. (A different muscle, on the other side of the bone, has the contrary effect.) Not all muscles attach to bones, however: some insert into an adjacent muscle, or into the skin itself. The muscles with which we are concerned here are those of the face, the neck and the shoulders.

ALWAYS REMEMBER

Shivering

When the body temperature falls, an involuntary action of the muscles causes rapid contraction – the shivering action, to make heat

Muscles can also be felt under the skin – those near the surface are called **superficial muscles**. While these are the muscles you can feel when massaging, deeper muscles lying beneath these may be equally important at producing movement. Connective tissue is used to wrap bundles of muscle fibres and to surround the entire muscle. This connective tissue is drawn together at the ends of the muscle to form **tendons** which attach the muscles to the bones. These are very strong attachments. Tuberosities (thickened and strengthened areas of bone) develop where the muscles are attached.

Muscular work also increases muscle size. With lack of use, muscles lose their strength and waste away.

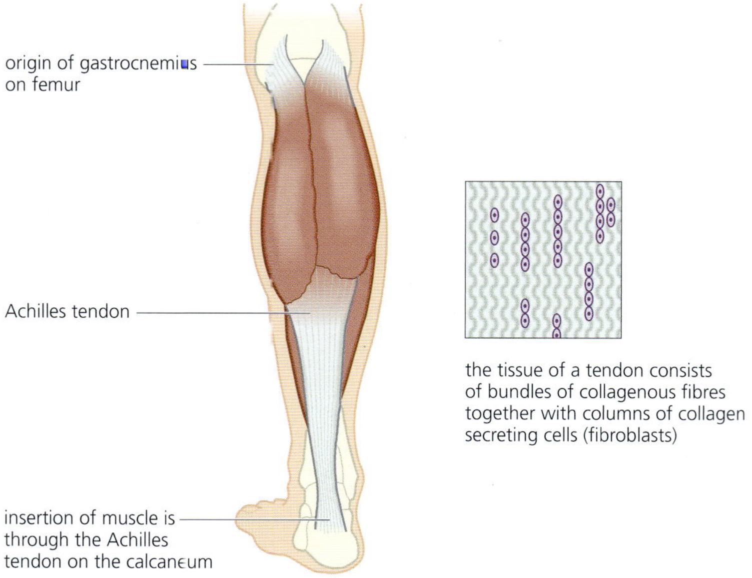

Achilles tendon attaches muscle to the calcaneum bone

The following diagrams show the main muscle actions and the terminology used to describe them.

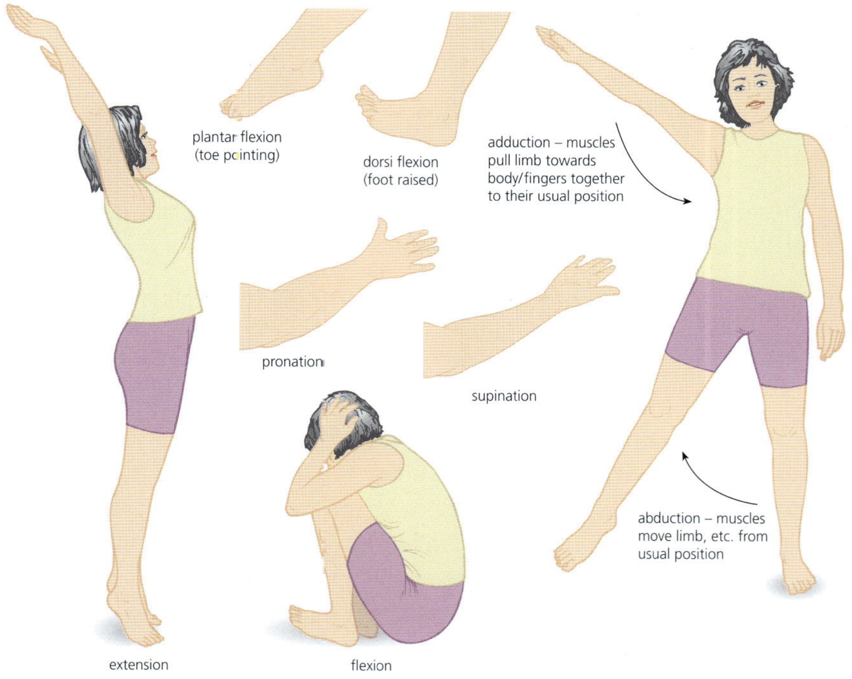

Diagrams showing the main muscle actions

ACTIVITY

Tendons

Straighten your fingers and stretch them apart. Can you see and feel the tendons that pass over the back of your hand?

Muscle tissue

There are three different types of muscle tissue:

- **Cardiac muscle tissue:** found only in the heart and responsible for keeping the heart beating rhythmically.
- **Involuntary muscle tissue:** also known as smooth muscle because of its appearance. The cells are spindle shaped and formed into bundles. They carry out automatic functions in the body such as maintaining blood pressure, movement of substances by peristalsis (moving food through the digestive system) and controlling the size of the pupil of the eye.
- **Voluntary muscle tissue:** also known as striated muscle because of its stripy appearance. This tissue is usually attached to the skeleton causing movement of parts of the skeleton, so it is referred to as skeletal muscle. This type of muscle tissue is made up of many strands lying parallel to one another. The small muscle fibres may be up to 30 cm long and around 10- to 100-thousandths of a millimetre in diameter. Each fibre is composed of even smaller strands called **myofibrils** and when these are examined closely the mechanism of how muscles contract can be deduced.

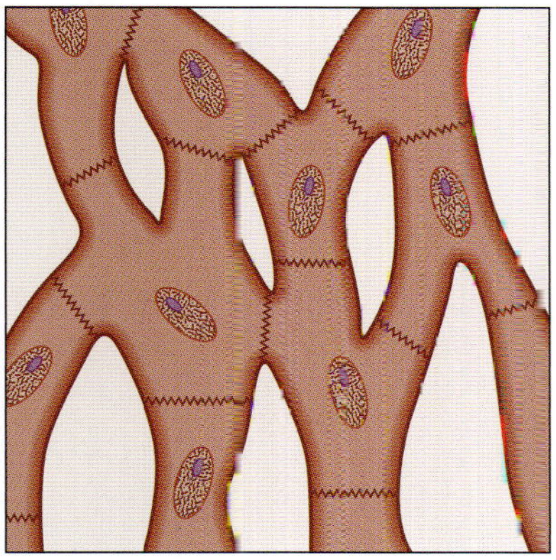

Cardiac muscle

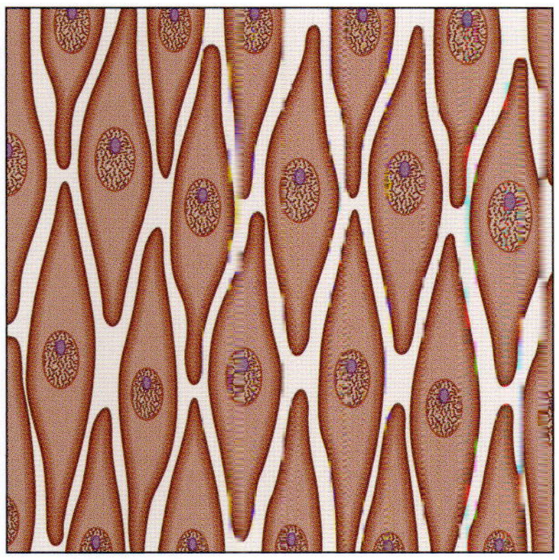

Involuntary muscle tissue

Voluntary muscle tissue

How do voluntary muscles contract?

Voluntary muscles contract by a system of sliding filaments. Each myofibril is made up of two types of filament – thin ones composed mainly of a protein called **actin** and thick ones composed mainly of a protein called **myosin**. These filaments partially overlap. When the muscle is stimulated to contract, the filaments pull over each other and overlap more. This shortens the muscle and increases its tension. The more the fibres pull together and overlap (until the actin fibres touch) the more tension is produced. Force increases as the muscle gets shorter and shorter.

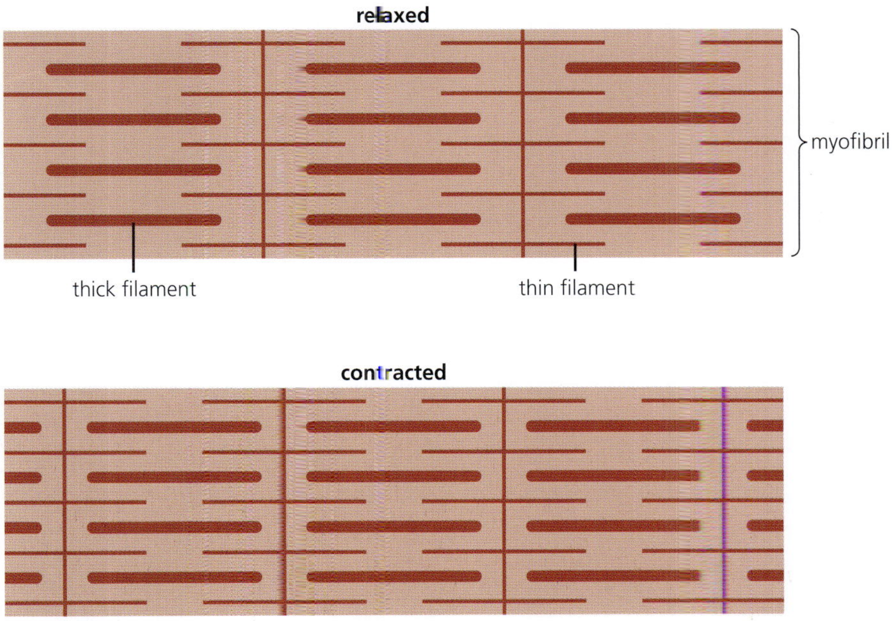

The sliding filament theory of muscle contraction

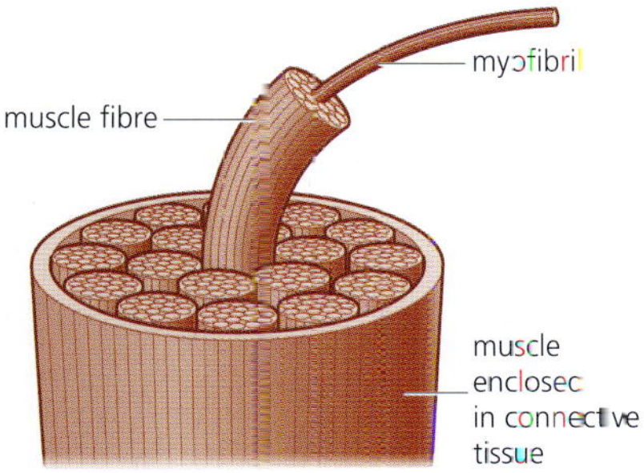

Muscle enclosed in connective tissue

TOP TIP

FUNCTIONAL SKILLS

Measuring microscopic structures

If you look at your ruler you will see that it is marked off in centimetres. Each centimetre is divided into ten parts. Each one of these is a millimetre. You will not see any divisions smaller than a millimetre on a ruler. Cells and small structures of the body are measured in micrometers (μm). There are 1000 μm in 1 mm. If you laid the muscle fibres across your ruler there would be between 10 and 100 in each 1 mm gap.

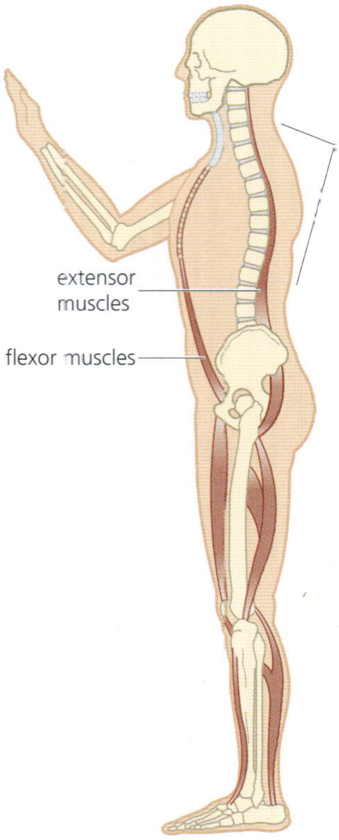

Main extensors and flexors used in posture

Muscle tone

Muscles never completely relax – there are always a few contracted fibres in every muscle. These make the muscle slightly tense and this muscular tension is called **muscle tone**.

Muscle tone helps the body to stand upright and keeps the muscles prepared for immediate action. A flaccid muscle is one with less than normal tone. Sometimes this is due to damage to the motor nerve supply. A muscle that is not used will become flaccid and then atrophy or waste away. **Flexors** are muscles that bend a limb; **extensors** are muscles that straighten a limb. We can only keep upright if the flexor and extensor muscles of joints are both partially contracted to keep the joints steady.

- **Good posture:** the body is held upright with little muscular effort as the head is balanced on top of the spine, all the vertebrae are balanced on each other, the spine is balanced on top of the hip bone and the feet are square on the ground.
- **Poor posture:** if the body is not balanced then the muscles must work harder to keep the unbalanced posture and can start to tire and ache. The back and neck muscles are the ones most likely to be affected by stooping or sitting over a desk. Poor posture also compresses the internal organs and affects their function. This can cause breathing difficulties and digestive problems. Poor posture can be corrected by conscious effort and by regular exercise.

HEALTH & SAFETY

Poor posture will also affect the curvature of the spine. If a person works over a computer for long periods, they may suffer from an exaggerated curve in the thoracic area and tension in the cervical vertebrae.

Always check posture when performing body treatment services.

The properties of muscle tissue

Muscular tissue has the following properties:

- it has the ability to contract (shorten)
- it is extensible (when the extensor muscle in a joint contracts, the corresponding flexor muscle will be stretched or extended)
- it is elastic (it can return to its original length following contraction or extension)
- it is responsive (it contracts in response to nerve stimulation)

Voluntary muscles contract only when stimulated by their nerve supply Muscle contraction requires energy and this is supplied by tissue respiration taking place inside muscle cells. In this reaction, glucose and oxygen are used to supply the energy, and carbon dioxide and water are released as waste products. Muscles need a good blood supply when a person is exercising, in order to bring the oxygen and glucose and to carry away the waste products.

The muscles can respire anaerobically (without oxygen), for short periods if the blood cannot supply enough oxygen. Glucose is then broken down to lactic acid. As it builds up in muscle tissue, lactic acid causes fatigue. When muscles become fatigued they stop contracting and become painful.

It is essential that the muscle receives a good blood supply after anaerobic exercise, as oxygen is required to complete the breakdown of lactic acid to carbon dioxide and water, and to remove all traces of lactic acid which can cause stiffness in muscles if allowed to remain.

ALWAYS REMEMBER

Muscle attachment

Muscles are attached at both ends to ligaments, tendons, bones, skin and even each other. The **origin** is the part of the muscle that is attached to a bone; the **insertion** is the other end, which is attached to a moveable part. During muscle contraction this part of the muscle moves.

TOP TIP

Exercise

Cooling-down exercises and massage are also useful in maintaining a good blood supply to the muscle following strenuous exercise. This ensures that the accumulated waste products continue to be removed quickly so as not to cause cramps or lactic acid building up, leading to sore stiff muscles.

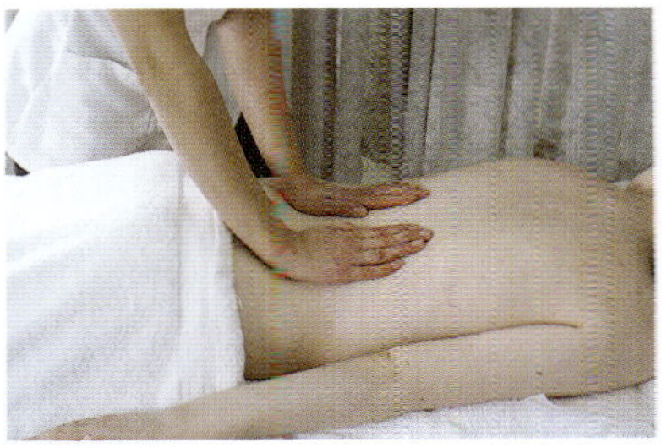

Massage

Massage helps to warm and relax muscles and improve their blood flow. When a muscle is warmer it responds more quickly and more strongly, giving a stronger contraction. Warming-up exercises are always advised before more vigorous activity in order to improve the blood flow through the muscles and prepare the muscles for more vigorous action.

ACTIVITY

Muscle fatigue

Hold one hand above your head and the other by your side. Make a fist with each hand and then release. Keep doing this until you have to stop – until your muscles become fatigued. Do the muscles in the arm above your head, with a slower blood supply (because you are holding it up), become fatigued first?

Disorders of the muscular system

- *Fatigue.* Lack of response by a muscle to continuous stimulation (i.e. it stops working) due to a lack of oxygen or the build up of lactic acid and carbon dioxide.
- *Cramps.* An involuntary complete tetanic contraction in a muscle.
- *Shivering.* Tone increases as the muscles become colder. Shivering is due to these 'prepared' muscles contracting spasmodically. This produces heat and therefore helps to raise the body temperature.

Facial muscles

Many of the muscles located in the face are very small and are attached into another small muscle or the facial skin. When the muscles contract, they pull the facial skin in a particular way: it is this that creates the facial expression.

With age, the facial expressions that we make every day produce lines on the skin – frown lines. The amount of tension, or **tone**, also decreases with age. When performing facial rejuvenating services, the aim is often to improve the general tone of the facial muscles.

ALWAYS REMEMBER

Hypothermia

As muscle tissue is cooled the chemical reactions slow and contractions take longer to occur. In hypothermia, the body temperature is so low that the muscles may become rigid, preventing the person moving.

Muscles of facial expression

Muscle	*Expression*	*Location*	*Action*
Frontalis 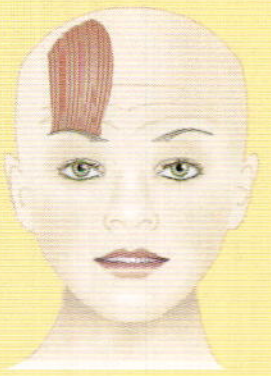	Surprise 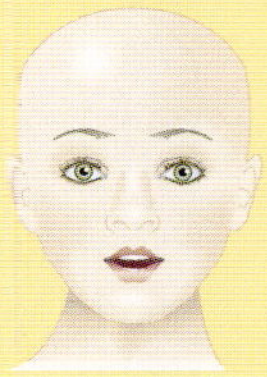 	The forehead.	Raises the eyebrows causes wrinkling across forehead.
Corrugator 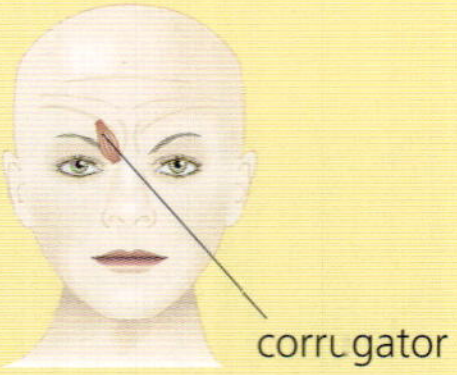 	Frown 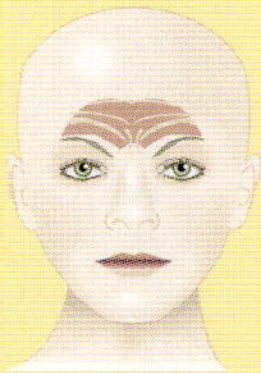	Between the eyebrows.	Draws the eyebrows down and together.
Orbicularis oculi 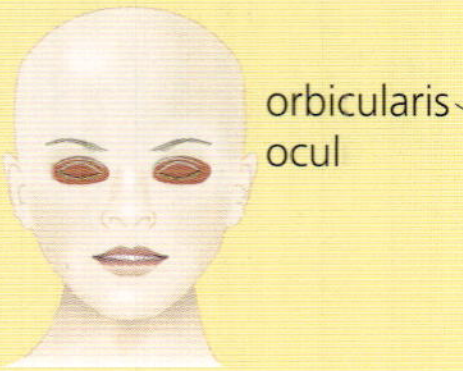 	Winking 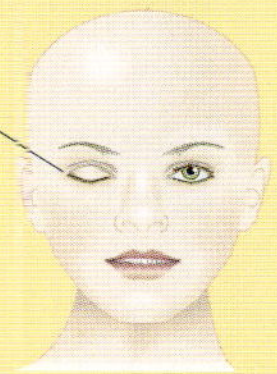	Surrounds the eyes.	Closes the eyelid.
Risorius 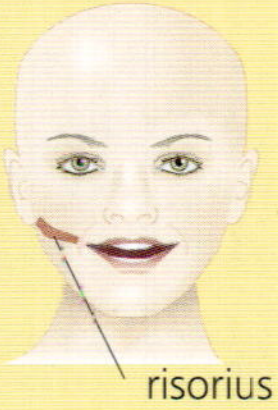 	Grinning 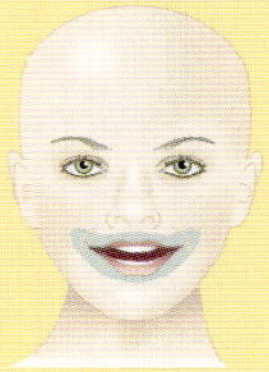	Extends diagonally, from the masseter muscle to the corners of the mouth.	Draws mouth corners outwards and backwards.
Buccinator 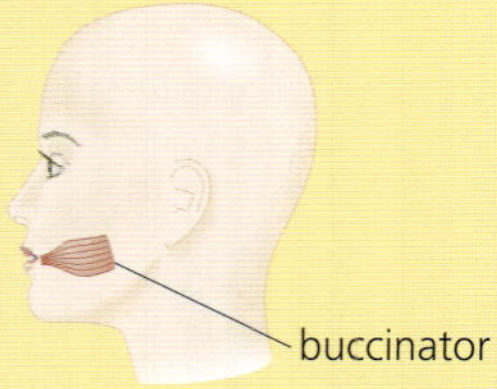 	Blowing 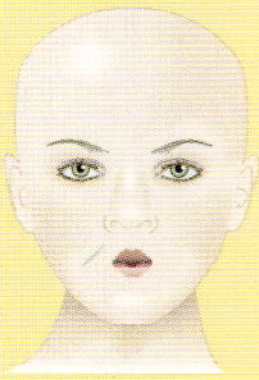	Inside the cheeks between the upper and lower jaw.	Compresses the cheeks.
Zygomaticus, made up of major and minor muscles 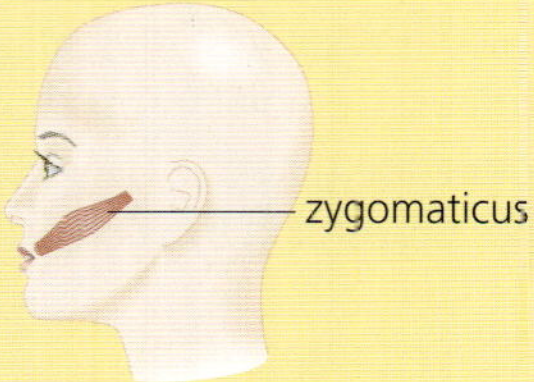 	Smiling, laughing 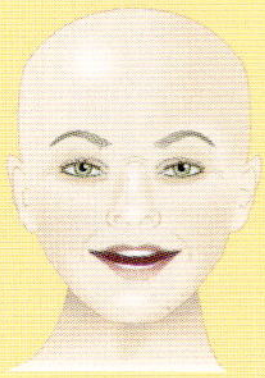	Extend diagonally from the zygomatic (cheekbone) to the corners of the mouth.	Lifts the corners of the mouth backwards and upwards.

Muscle	*Expression*	*Location*	*Action*
Procerus 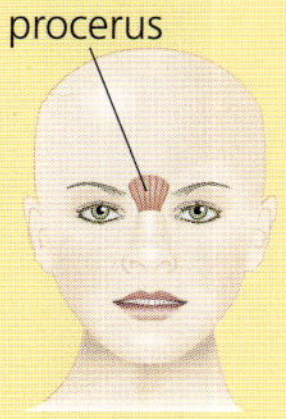	Distaste 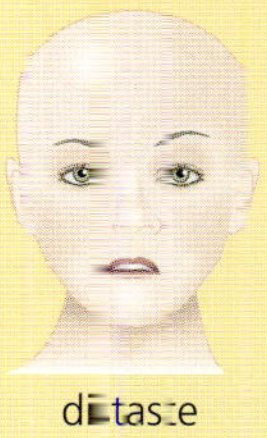	Covers the bridge of the nose.	Draws down eyebrows and wrinkles the skin over the bridge of the nose.
Nasalis 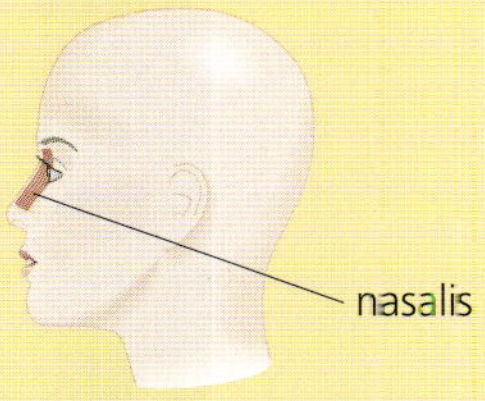	Anger 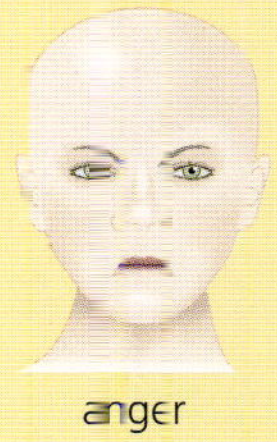	Covers the front of the nose and surrounds the nostrils.	Opens and closes the nasal openings.
Levators labii 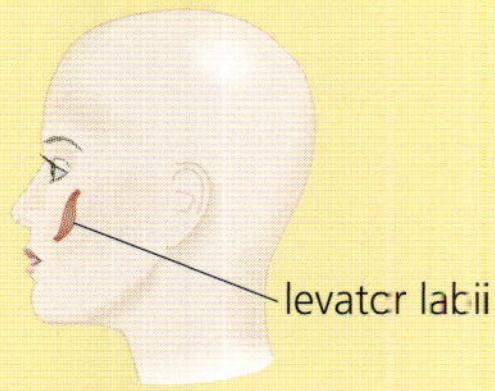	Distaste 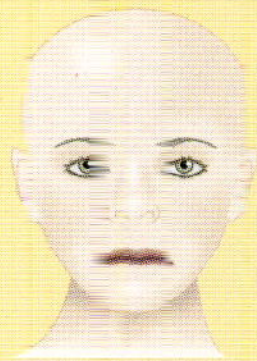	Surrounds the upper lip.	Raises and draws back the upper lips and nostrils.
Depressor labii 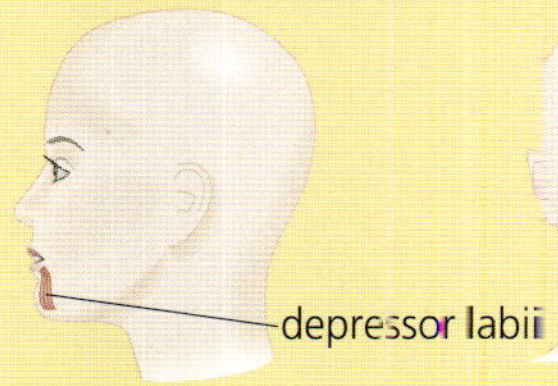	Sulking 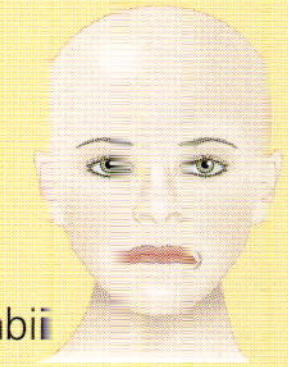	Surrounds the lower lip.	Pulls down the lower lip and draws it slightly to one side.
Orbicularis oris 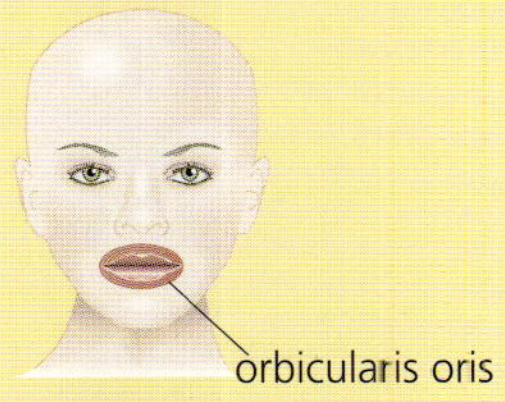	Pout, kiss, doubt 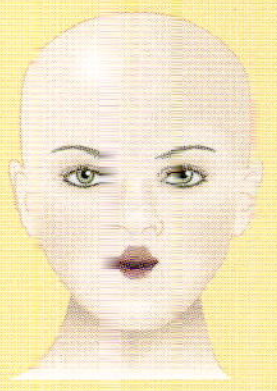	Surrounds the mouth.	Purses the lip (as in blowing), closes the mouth.
Triangularis 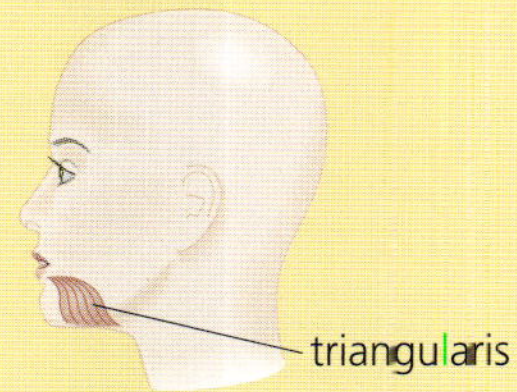	Sadness 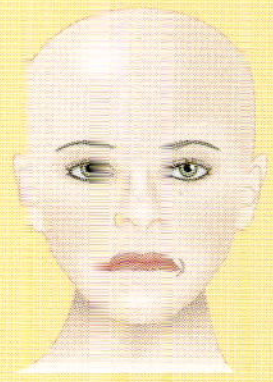	The corner of the lower lip extends over the chin.	Draws down the mouth's corners.

Muscle	*Expression*	*Location*	*Action*
Mentalis 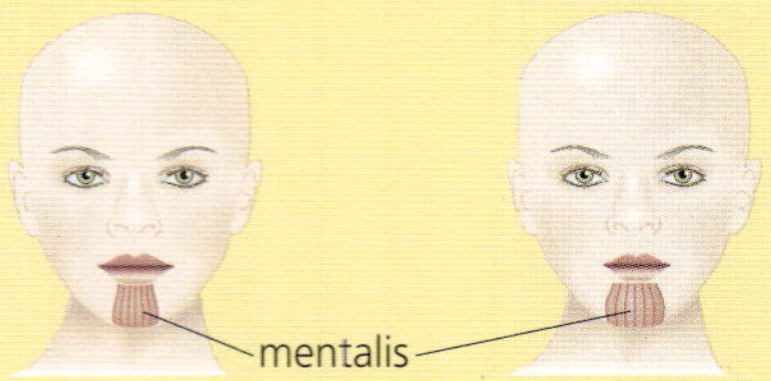	Doubt	Covers the front of the chin.	Raises the lower lip, causing the chin to wrinkle.
Platysma 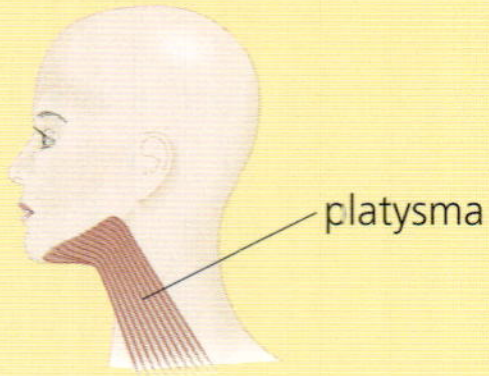	Fear, horror 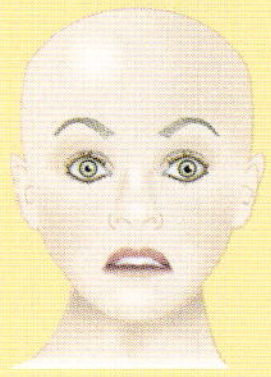	The sides of the neck and chin.	Draws the mouth's corners downwards and backwards.

ALWAYS REMEMBER

Nerves of the face

Almost all facial muscles are controlled by the 7th cranial or facial nerve.

To balance and move the head and facial features, the muscles of the head, face and neck work together.

ACTIVITY FUNCTIONAL SKILLS

Facial expressions

It is important to provide the client with facial exercises they can practise at home to exercise the muscles! Practise these exercises yourself so you will be able to accurately demonstrate them to the client.

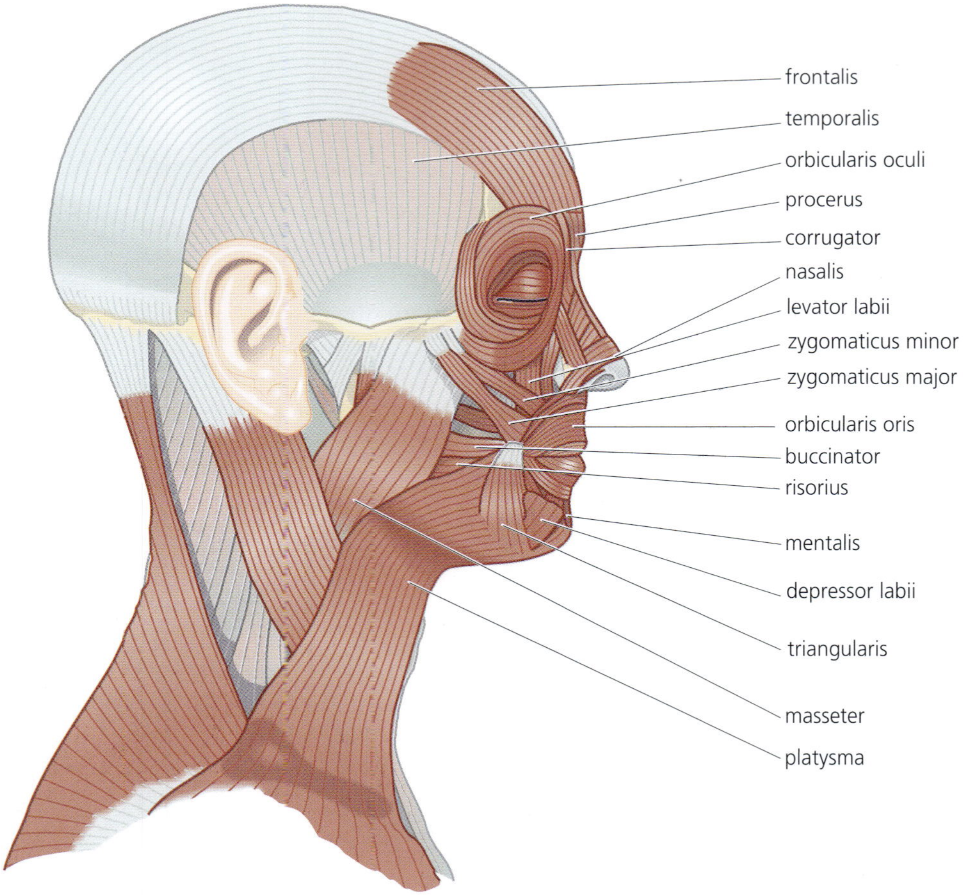

Muscles of the face and neck

Muscles of mastication The muscles responsible for the movement of the lower jawbone (the **mandible**) when chewing are called the **muscles of mastication**.

Muscle	*Location*	*Action*
Masseter	The cheek area: extends from the zygomatic bone to the mandible.	Clenches the teeth; closes and raises the lower jaw.
Temporalis	Extends from the temple region at the side of the head to the mandible.	Raises the jaw and draws it backwards, as in chewing.

Muscles that move the head

Muscle	*Location*	*Action*
Sterno-cleido-mastoid	Runs from the sternum to the clavicle bone and the temporal bone.	Flexes the neck; rotates and bows the head.
Trapezius	A large triangular muscle, covering the back of the neck and the upper back.	Draws the head backwards and allows movement at the shoulder.
Occipitalis	Covers the back of the head.	Draws scalp backwards.

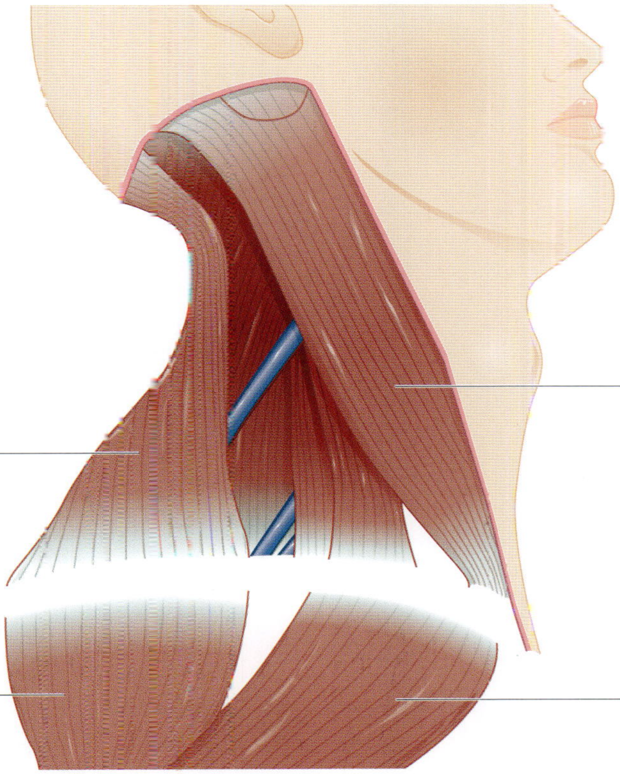

Muscles that move the head and of the upper body

TOP TIP

An adult head weighs about 5 kg, strong muscles of the neck and back are required to allow movement of the head. Remember that these areas will often suffer from tension in the muscles when performing head and neck massage.

ALWAYS REMEMBER

Muscles that move the head assist those of facial expression when communicating, for example nodding the head.

Abdominal muscles

Muscle	*Location*	*Action*
Rectus abdominis	Front of abdomen from the pelvis cartilages of the lower ribs.	Flexes the spine, compresses the abdomen, tilts the pelvis upwards.
Obliques	The internal obliques lie to either side of the rectus abdominis, running downwards and outwards; the external obliques lie on top of the internal obliques, running downwards and forwards.	Both compress the abdomen and twist the trunk, the left internal oblique working with the right external oblique.

ALWAYS REMEMBER

Terms

- Rectus: muscle fibres run straight up and down.
- Oblique: muscle fibres run diagonally.
- Aponeurosis: muscles which are flat and thin usually have a very thin tendon in the shape of a broad sheet called aponeurosis.

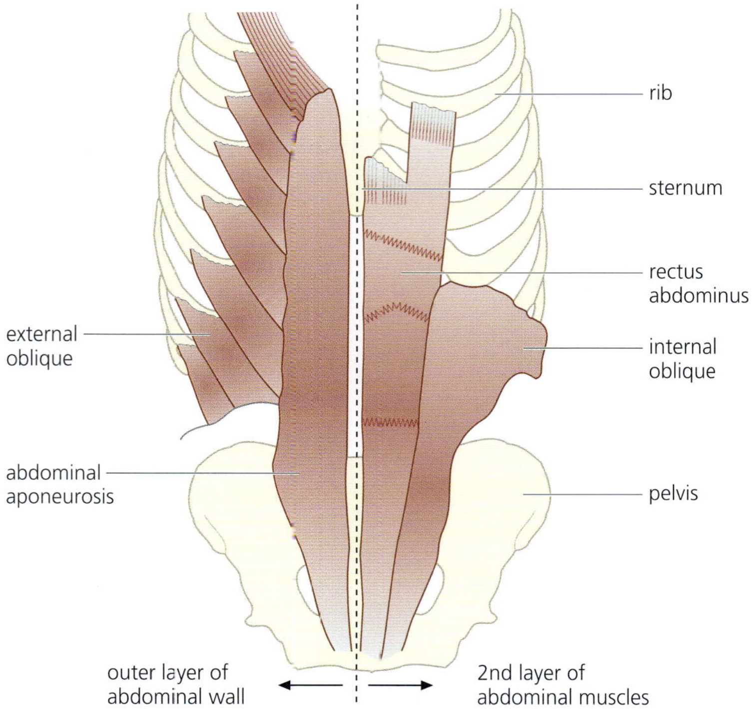

Abdominal muscles

Muscles of chest and upper arm

Muscle	*Location*	*Action*
Pectoralis major	Across the upper chest (underneath the breasts) from the clavicle, sternum and ribs to the top of the humerus, forming the front wall of the axilla.	Used in throwing and climbing to adduct the arm, drawing it forwards and rotating it medially.
Pectoralis minor	Underneath the pectoralis major. Its origin is the third, fourth and fifth ribs and it inserts into the outer corner of the scapula.	Draws the shoulder downwards and forwards.

Muscle	*Location*	*Action*
Deltoid	Over the top of the shoulder from the clavicle and scapula to the upper part of the humerus.	Abducts the arm to a horizontal position; aids in further abduction and in drawing the arm backwards and forwards.
Bicep	Lies over the front of the upper arm. Its two origins are on the scapula and its insertion is on the radius.	Flexes the elbow; supinates the forearm and hand.
Tricep	The only muscle at the back of the upper arm. It has three origins – one on the scapula and two on the humerus. It inserts into the ulna.	Extends the elbow.
Brachialis	Under the biceps at the front of the humerus from halfway down its shaft to the ulna near the elbow joint.	Flexes the elbow.
Brachio radialis	On the thumb side of the forearm, its origin is at the shaft of the humerus, its insertion is at the end of the radius bone.	Flexes the arm at the elbow.
Flexors	Middle of the forearm.	Flexes and adducts the wrist, drawing it towards the forearm.
Extensors	Little finger side of the forearm.	Muscles which extend and abduct the wrist and hand.
Thenar muscles	In the palm of the hand, below the thumb.	Flexes the thumb and moves it outwards and inwards.
Hypothenar muscles	In the palm of the hand, below the little finger.	Flexes the little finger and moves it outwards and inwards.

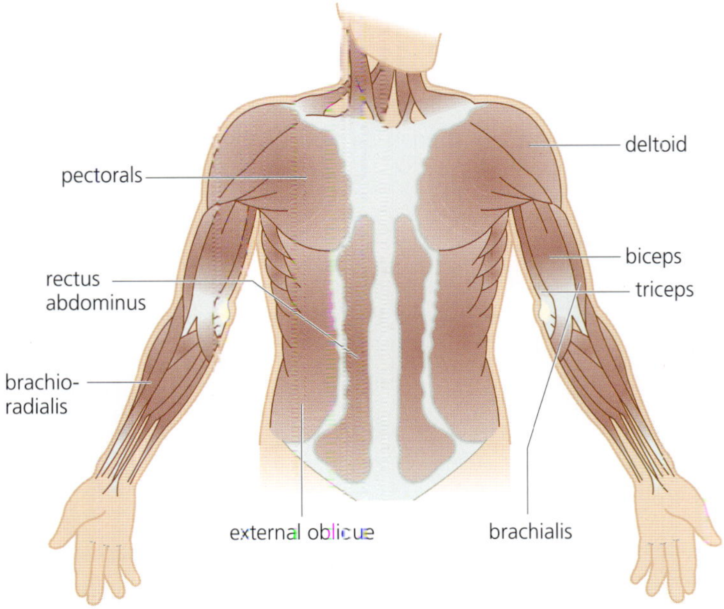

Anterior view muscles of the arm and trunk

ACTIVITY

Observing the tendons

Hold your palm face upwards, with your sleeve pulled back so that you can see your forearm. Move the fingers individually towards the palm. Can you see the tendons moving?

The muscles of the hand and forearm

The hand and fingers are moved primarily by muscles and tendons in the forearm. These muscles contract, pulling the tendons, and thereby move the fingers much as a puppet is moved by strings.

The muscles that bend the wrist drawing it towards the forearm, are **flexors;** other muscles, **extensors,** straighten the wrist and the hand.

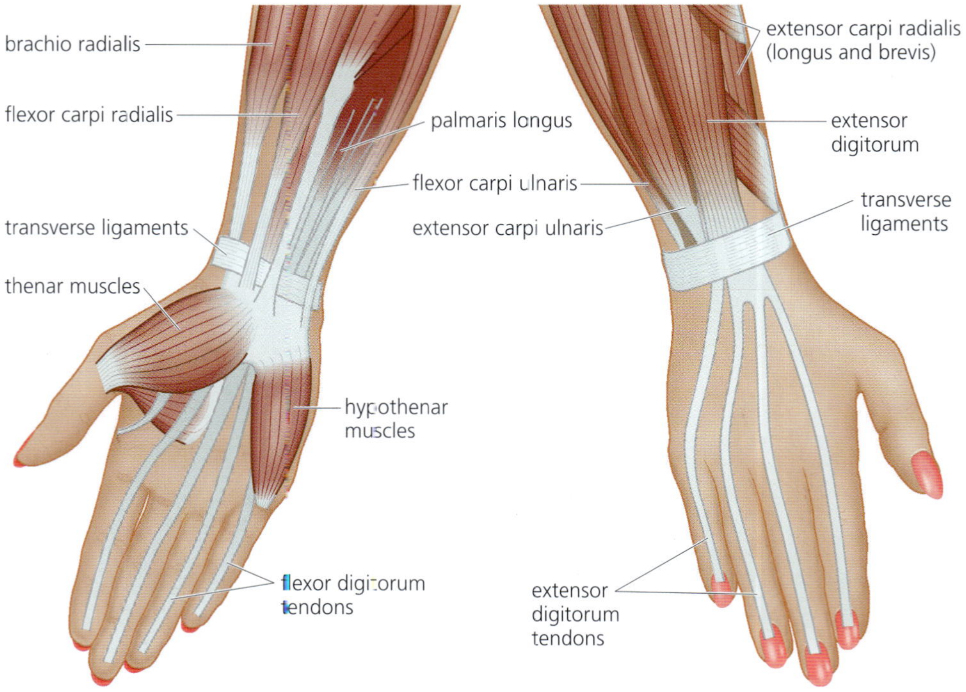

Muscles of the arm and hand

Muscles of the back (shoulder and trunk)

Muscle	*Location*	*Action*
Trapezius	The back of the neck and chest with its origin running from the base of the skull (the occipital bone) down the spines of the thoracic vertebrae. It inserts into the scapula and clavicle.	Moves the scapula up, down and back; raises the clavicle; can also be used to extend the neck.
Latissimus dorsi	Crosses the back from the lumbar region up into the top of the humerus. It forms the back wall of the axilla (armpit).	Used in rowing and climbing; it adducts the shoulder downwards and pulls it backwards.
Erector spinae	Three groups of overlapping muscles which lie either side of the spine from the neck to the pelvis.	Extends spine; keeps the body in an upright position.
Rhomboids	Between the shoulders originating from the thoracic vertebrae and inserting to the scapula bone.	Braces the shoulder and rotates the scapula, moving the shoulder.

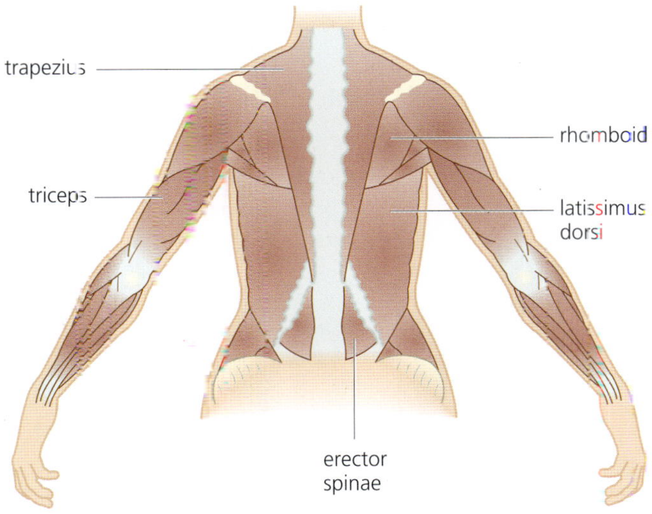

Posterior view muscles of the arms and trunk

Muscles used in breathing

Muscle	*Location*	*Action*
External intercostals	Connect the lower border of one rib to the one below with the muscle fibres running downwards and forwards.	Used in breathing movements to draw the ribs upwards and outwards when breathing in.
Internal intercostals	Between the ribs with the fibres running upwards and forwards to the rib above when breathing out (both sets of intercostals maintain the shape of the wall of the thorax).	Draw the ribs downwards and inwards when breathing out.
Diaphragm	Divides the thorax from the abdomen.	Contraction of this muscle increases the volume of the thorax.

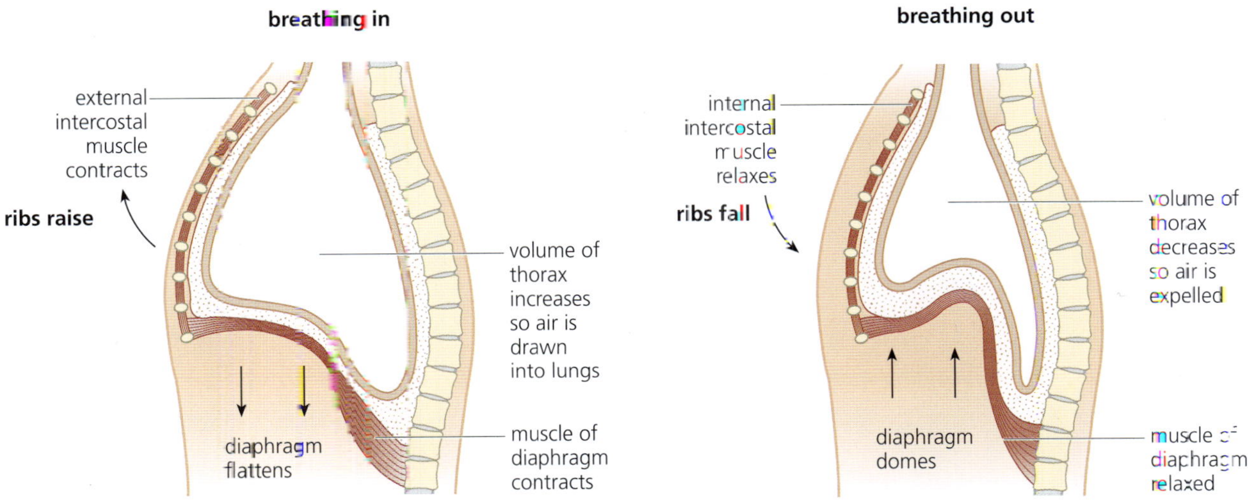

Diagrams to illustrate inspiration and expiration

es of the buttocks and legs

scle	Location	Action
Gluteals	In the buttock connecting the pelvis and femur. There are three layers of gluteal muscles.	Abduct and rotate the femur; used in walking and running and to raise the body to an upright position.
Hamstrings	Back of the thigh from the pelvis and the top of the femur to the bones of the lower leg below the knee.	Flex the knee; extend the thigh; used in walking and jumping.
Gastrocnemius	Calf of the leg.	Flexes the knee; plantar-flexes foot.
Soleus	Calf of the leg, below the gastrocnemius (both calf muscles insert through the Achilles tendon into the heel).	Plantar-flexes foot (flexes and points toe down) both calf muscles are used to push off, assisting forwards motion when walking and running.
Quadriceps extensor	Front of the thigh. A group of four muscles running from the pelvis and top of femur to the tibia through the patella and patellar ligament.	Extend the knee; used in kicking. The rectus fibres from the pelvis help to flex the hip.
Sartorius	Crosses the front of the thigh from the outer front rim of the pelvis to the tibia at the inner knee.	Flexes the knee and hip; abducts and rotates the femur; used to sit cross-legged.
Adductors	Inner thigh.	Adducts the hip; flex and rotate the femur.
Tibialis anterior	Front of the lower leg.	Inverts the foot (turns sole inwards); dorsiflexes the foot (flexes and points the toes up); rotates foot outwards. Supports the medial longitudinal arch of the foot when walking or running.

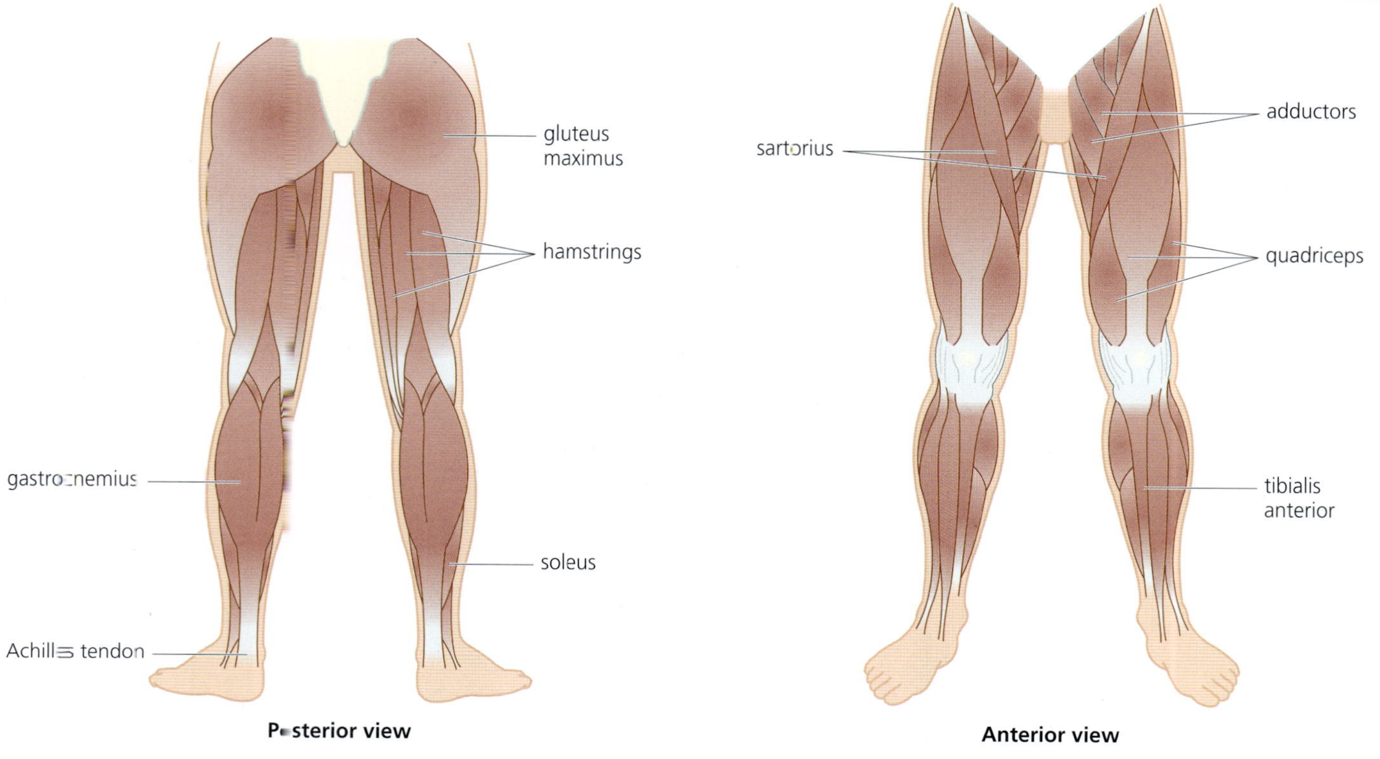

Muscles of the thigh and lower leg

The muscles of the foot

The muscles of the foot work together to help move the body when walking and running. In a similar way to the movement of the hand, the foot is moved primarily by muscles in the lower leg; these pull on tendons, which in turn move the feet and toes.

Muscles and tendons of the lower leg and foot

Muscle	*Location*	*Action*
Extensor digitorum longus	Lateral side of the front of the lower leg.	Dorsi flexes the foot up at the ankle and extends the toes.
Flexor digitorum longus	Front of lower leg to the toes.	Plantar flexes foot downwards and inverts the foot. Helps the toes to grip. Supports the lateral longitudinal arch of the foot.
Achilles tendon	Attached to the soleus and gastrocnemius down to the heel.	Raises the foot when related muscle contracts.
Extensor digitorum tendons	Tops of toes.	Straightens the toes when related muscle contracts.
Flexor digitorum tendons	Underneath the toes.	Bends the toes when related muscle contracts.

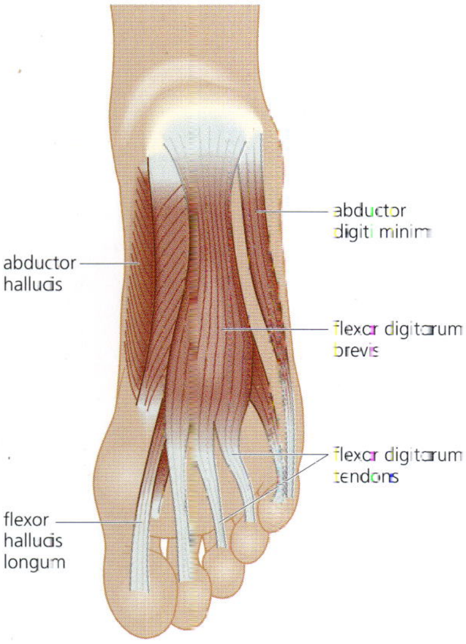

Muscles of the foot plantar view

The nervous system

The nervous system transmits messages from the brain to other parts of the body and is vast and complex. It controls everything the body does with another body system, the **endocrine system**, which secretes hormones that are chemical messengers. The nervous system is made up of a network of nerve cells, called **neurones**, which transmit messages to and from the **central nervous system** (CNS) in the form of electrical impulses.

Divisions of the nervous system The nervous system is made up of two main divisions:

- the CNS
- the autonomic nervous system

All muscles are made to work by electrical stimulation via the nerves. A nerve is a collection of nerve fibres. All nerves emerge from the CNS. Sensory (receptor) nerves are linked to sensory receptors, while motor (effector) nerves end in a muscle or gland.

The central nervous system

The CNS is composed of the brain and spinal cord. The CNS coordinates the activities of the entire body. The brain transmits impulses to all parts of the body in order to stimulate other organs to act and is protected is the bones of the cranium. The spinal cord runs along inside the vertebral column and is protected by the bones (vertebrae) of the spinal column. The brain is composed of several parts, each of which performs several functions.

Neurones Nervous tissue is made up of nerve cells or neurones. These cells connect all parts of the body to the CNS and conduct impulses throughout these organs.

Nerve cells are long, narrow and delicate. They are made up of a cell body containing a large central nucleus and nerve fibres that transmit messages to other neurones.

Sensory receptors or afferent nerves are found in many areas of the body including the dermis of the skin, muscles, tendons and joints, nose, mouth, eyes and eara, where they receive information and relay it to the brain and spinal cord. When stimulated, impulses pass from the receptor along the fibre of a **sensory (receptor) neurone** to the CNS, giving us sensations such as touch, taste, smell and hearing. Being fed such information about our environment enables us to make suitable responses.

When neurotransmitters land at their receptor sites they can stimulate or inhibit the receiving cell. Both responses are important to relay the correct message through the nervous system.

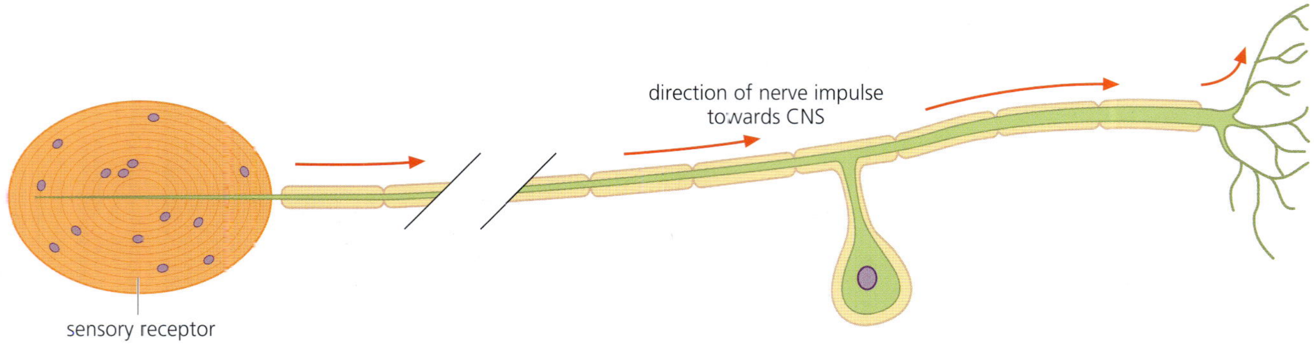

A sensory neurone

Motor (effector) neurones conduct impulses from the CNS to muscles or glands of the body. Motor neurones that initiate voluntary muscle contractions form motor end plates on the muscle fibres. They act on information sent from the brain or spinal cord to a muscle or gland to carry out a particular response, typically muscle movement. Each neurone stimulates between 10 and 2000 muscle fibres depending on whether the muscle makes very precise, fine movements or gross ones.

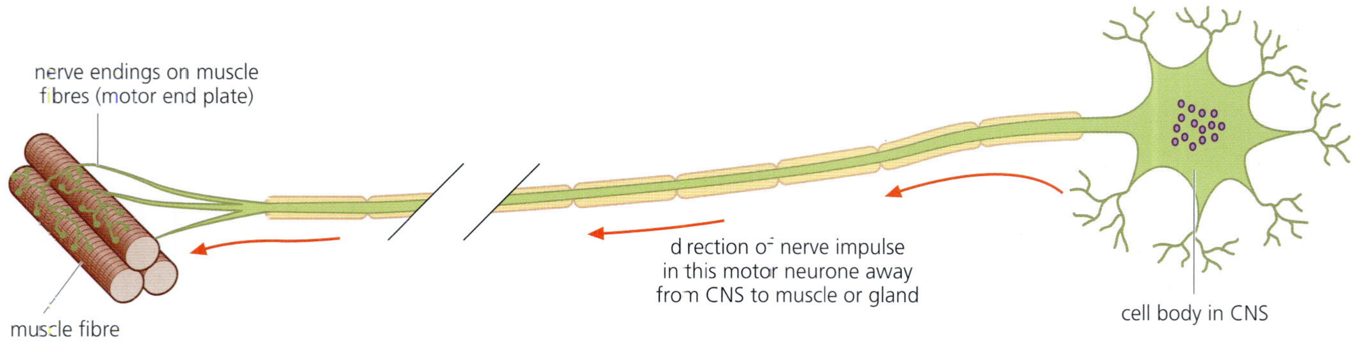

A motor neurone

HEALTH & SAFETY

Nerve damage

Nerve cells do not reproduce; when damaged, only a limited repair occurs.

A **nerve** is a collection of single neurones surrounded by a protective sheath. Sensory nerves contain only sensory neurones, **motor nerves** contain only motor neurones and mixed nerves contain both sensory and motor neurones.

Kinds of nerves There are two types of nerves: *sensory nerves* and *motor nerves*. Both are composed of white fibres enclosed in a sheath.

- *Sensory nerves.* These receive information and relay it to the brain. They are found near to the skin's surface and respond to touch, pressure, temperature and pain.
- *Motor nerves.* These are situated in muscle tissue and act on information received from the brain, causing a particular response, typically muscle movement.

TOP TIP

Massage

Appropriate massage manipulations, when applied to the skin, produce a stimulating or relaxing effect on the nerves.

Nerves of the face and neck These nerves link the brain with the muscles of the head, face and neck.

Cranial nerves control muscles in the head and neck region, or carry nerve impulses from the sense organs to the brain. Those of concern to the beauty therapist when performing a facial service are as follows:

- the 5th cranial nerve, or **trigeminal**, controls the muscles involved in mastication (chewing) and passes on sensory information from the face, such as the eyes
- the 7th cranial nerve, or **facial**, controls the muscles involved in facial expression
- the 11th cranial nerve, or **accessory**, controls the muscles involved in moving the head, the sternocleido mastoid and trapezius muscle.

5th cranial nerve This nerve carries messages to the brain from the sensory nerves of the skin, the teeth, the nose and the mouth. It also stimulates the motor nerve to create the chewing action when eating. The 5th cranial nerve has three branches:

- the **ophthalmic nerve** serves the tear glands of the eye, the skin of the forehead and the upper cheeks
- the **maxillary nerve** serves the upper jaw and the mouth
- the **mandibular nerve** serves the lower jaw muscle, the teeth and the muscle involved with chewing

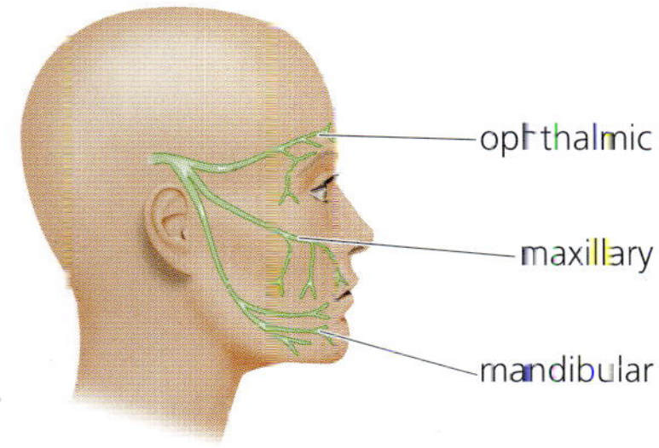

5th cranial nerve

7th cranial nerve This nerve passes through the temporal bone and behind the ear, and then divides. It serves the ear muscle and the muscles of facial expression, the tongue and the palate.

The 7th cranial nerve has five branches:

- the **temporal nerve** serves the orbicularis oculi and the frontalis muscles
- the **zygomatic nerve** serves the eye muscles
- the **buccal nerve** serves the upper lip and the sides of the nose
- the **mandibular nerve** serves the lower lip and the mentalis muscle of the chin
- the **cervical nerve** serves the platysma muscle of the neck

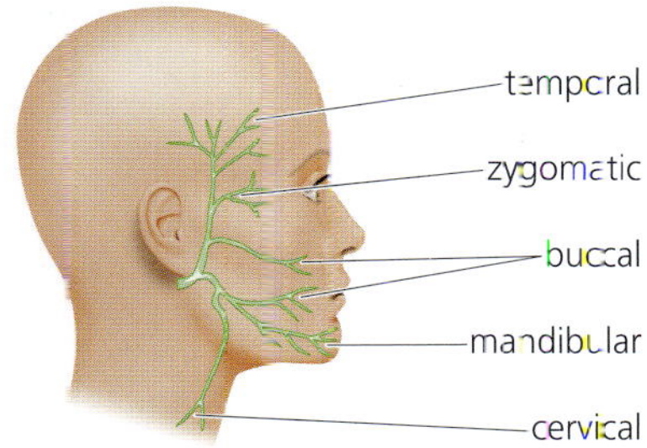

7th cranial nerve

11th cranial nerve This nerve serves the sternomastoid and trapezius muscles of the neck and its function is to move the head and shoulders.

The brain The brain is composed of several parts, each of which performs specific functions as described in the table on page 70.

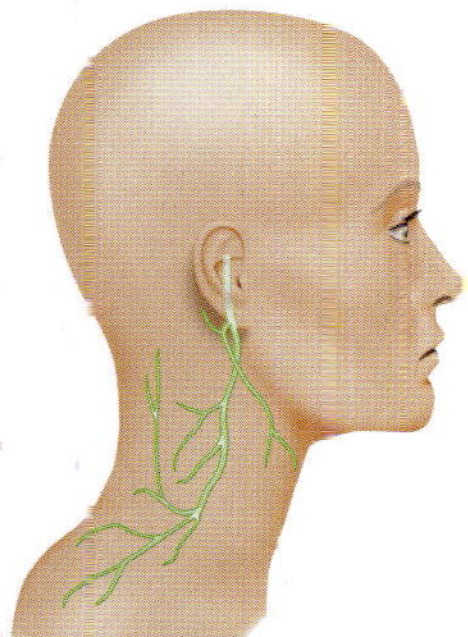

11th cranial nerve

Brain function

Part of the brain	*Position*	*Function*
Cerebrum	Consists of two hemispheres; the major part of the forebrain.	Initiates and controls all voluntary muscular movement; receives sensory information (enabling us to feel, see, smell, hear and taste); the centre of thought, memory and intelligence.
Cerebellum	Situated at the back of the brain butterfly-shaped with two lateral wings.	The motor coordinating centre, maintaining posture and controlling motor skills.
Medulla oblongata	A continuation of the spinal cord.	Controls the autonomic nervous system (e.g. heart rate and movement of food through the body); also controls involuntary reflex actions such as coughing, sneezing and swallowing.
Hypothalamus	Situated above the pituitary gland to which it is linked.	Contains centres controlling body temperature, thirst and hunger.
Ventricle	A cavity in the brain containing cerebrospinal fluid.	The fluid acts as a shock absorber, delivers nutrients and removes waste.

ALWAYS REMEMBER

Nerves of the face

Almost all facial muscles are controlled by the 7th cranial or facial nerve.

Twelve pairs of cranial nerves emerge from the brain. Some cranial nerves are sensory nerves. The second cranial nerve (the optic nerve) contains only sensory nerve fibres. It supplies the eye and is the nerve of sight. The twelfth cranial nerve is primarily a motor nerve. It contains mainly motor fibres and supplies the tongue muscles. (The sensory fibres in this nerve transmit information about the position of the tongue.) Other cranial nerves such as the fifth (trigemina) nerve are called mixed nerves as they contain both motor fibres (to supply muscles) and sensory fibres (to relay sensations).

Thirty-one pairs of spinal nerves emerge from between the vertebrae of the spinal column. All the spinal nerves are mixed nerves.

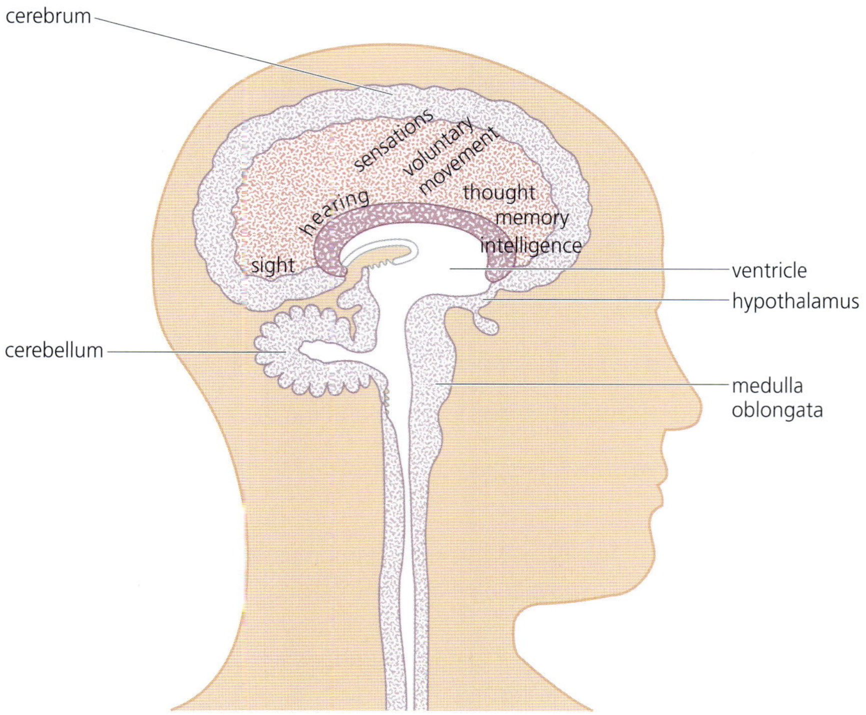

A vertical section through the brain

Transmission of nerve impulses Nerve fibres are individual neurones. Messages pass along nerve fibres as electrical impulses. These electrical impulses are the result of changes to the charges present on the inside and outside of the membrane of the nerve fibre. The membrane of a resting nerve fibre is said to be polarized when there are more positive ions present on the outer surface and more negative ions present inside the membrane. Sodium and potassium ions present in all body fluids are positively charged, while chloride ions are negatively charged. When the neurone is stimulated, a wave of depolarization passes along the fibre as the charges become temporarily reversed.

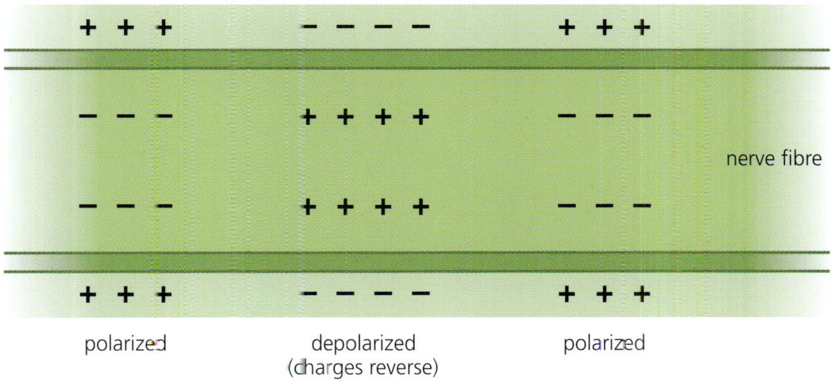

Conduction of nerve impulses

Local anaesthetics block the passage of electrical impulses by preventing depolarization. Some medical terms which relate to the nervous system are:

- anaesthesia: the loss of sensation
- analgesia: the loss of sensation to pain
- hyperesthesia: over-sensitization to touch

Passage of impulses from one neurone to another Information passes along neurones to and from the CNS. Inside the CNS, impulses pass from one neurone to another even though individual neurones never touch. When an impulse reaches the end of the nerve fibre a chemical is released. This chemical is called a **neurotransmitter** substance. An example is acetylcholine. The chemical passes across a tiny gap and is taken up by an adjacent neurone, generating an electrical impulse in that neurone. The gap between adjacent neurones is called a **synapse**.

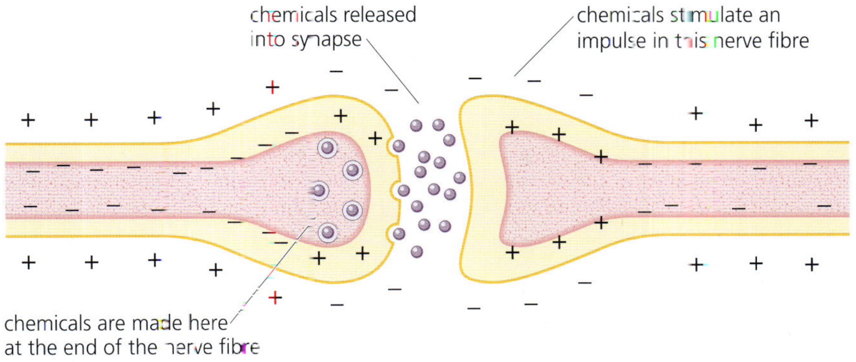

Passage of an impulse across a synapse

ALWAYS REMEMBER

Epilepsy

Epilepsy is a common disorder which occurs as a result of abnormal discharges of electricity across the brain. The symptoms vary from short lapses of attention to violent seizures (fits) resulting in unconsciousness. It does not affect intelligence, and seizures can successfully be prevented by drug therapy.

Passage from a neurone to a muscle fibre This is similar to passage across a synapse and takes place with the use of chemical transmitter substances. These are released from the end of the motor neurone into the muscle. All muscle fibres stimulated by that neurone will then contract.

The **motor point** is where a motor nerve enters a muscle. A muscle only contracts if stimulated by a motor nerve. Each individual neurone branches, making contact with individual muscle cells. One neurone together with the muscle fibres it stimulates is called a **motor unit**. The area of contact between the neurone and the muscle fibre is called the **motor end plate** or **neuromuscular junction**.

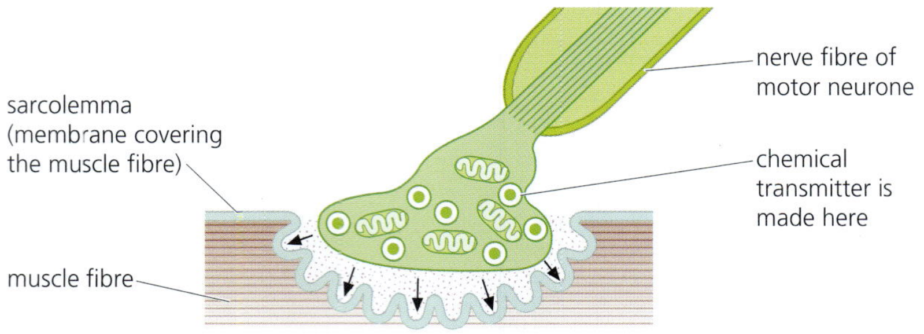

Diagram of the synapse and neuromuscular junction (motor end plate)

Voluntary and reflex actions Voluntary actions are always initiated by the brain and we can control these actions. Examples are speaking and walking. A reflex action is a quick involuntary response to a stimulus. For example, on picking up an unexpectedly hot plate you may quickly drop it. This happens because pain receptors in your hand have been stimulated. Impulses pass via sensory nerve fibres to the spinal cord and are transmitted via relay neurones to motor neurones. Impulses pass to the arm muscles which are stimulated to contract and the plate is dropped. A reflex involving the spinal cord is called a **spinal reflex**. Impulses will also pass up the spinal cord to the brain so you become aware of what you have done. This may stimulate a secondary response such as yelling OW!

Coughing, sneezing, blinking and swallowing are also reflexes but these are cranial (involving the brain) rather than spinal reflexes.

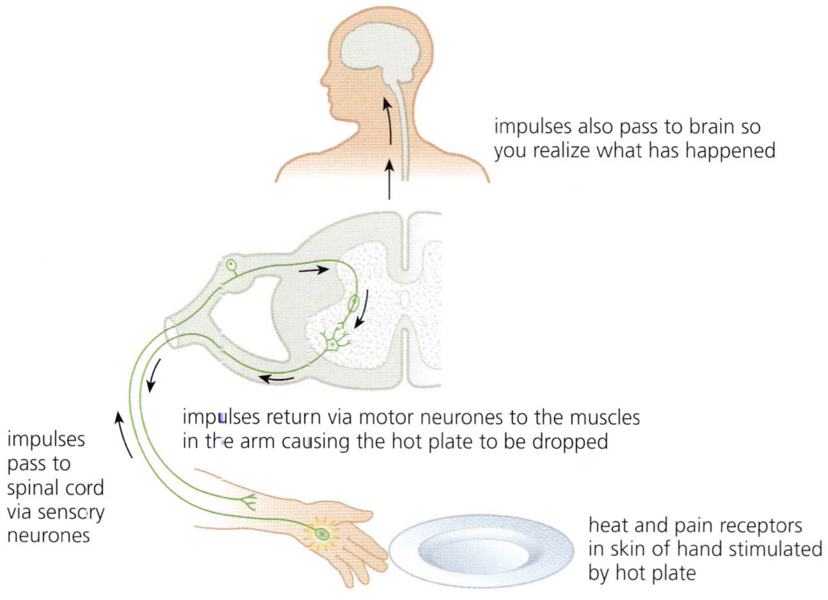

Diagram of a simple reflex arc

The olfactory system The first cranial nerve is called the olfactory nerve. It is a sensory nerve, giving us our sense of smell. Olfactory receptors are present in the upper nasal passages which are coated with watery mucus. Some chemicals dissolve in this watery mucus and stimulate the receptors of the sensory cells. Nerve fibres from the receptors join to form the olfactory nerves, which pass through the ethmoid bone into the olfactory bulbs. These lie below the frontal lobes of the cerebrum.

From the olfactory lobes, nerve fibres run to the olfactory centre of the cerebral cortex along the olfactory tract. Here in the olfactory centre, the impulses are interpreted as sensations of smell.

Smells may influence the behaviour of a person. Pheromones are scents given off by animals (including humans) to encourage sexual attention. They may be responsible for male–female attraction and male–male acts of aggression. Food must have a pleasant aroma for us to enjoy it.

The **limbic system** is involved in emotions such as pain, pleasure anger, fear, sorrow, sexual feelings and affection. It consists of a group of structures that encircle the brain stem. It also plays a part in memory and behaviour. Aromatherapy takes advantage of this limbic response, using the effects of the aroma of essential oils to produce a range of responses. These may involve feelings of relaxation and well-being.

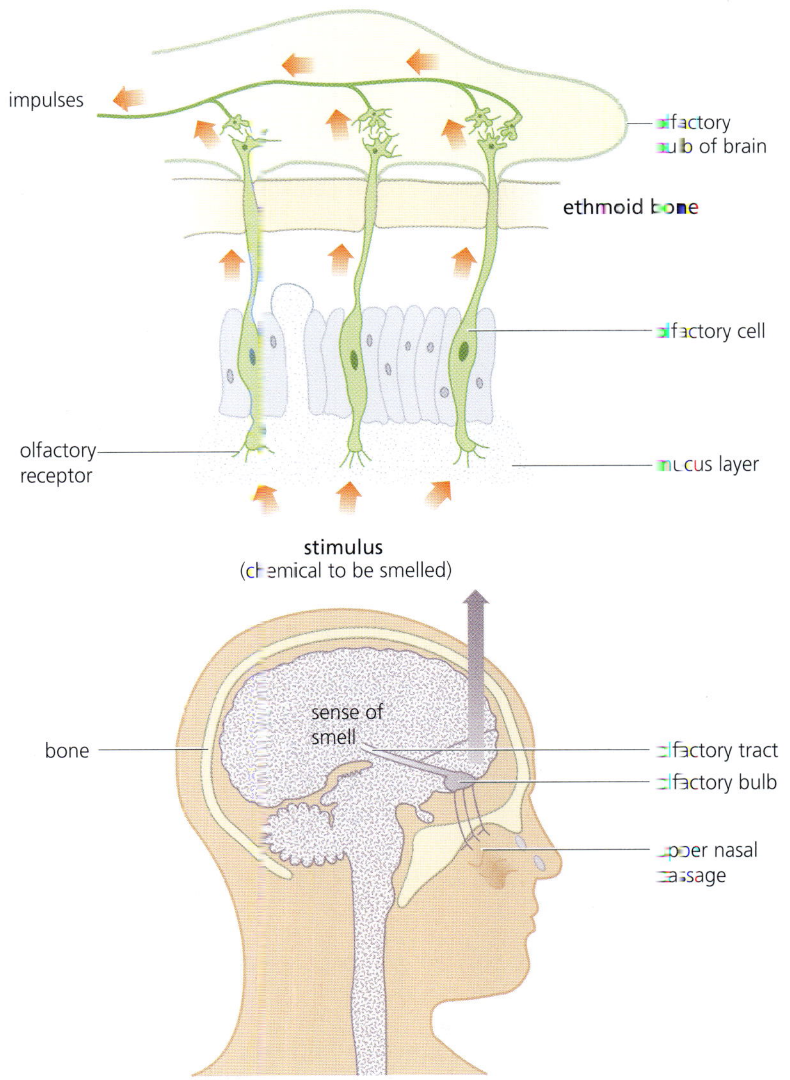

Position of olfactory centre and diagram of olfactory nerve and receptors

The autonomic nervous system

The autonomic nervous system controls the involuntary activities of smooth muscle, cardiac muscle and glands. It therefore regulates the size of the pupil, vasodilation and vasoconstriction (see page 78), the heart rate, movements of the gut and the secretion of most glands. There are two divisions, called the **sympathetic** and **parasympathetic.** Many organs receive a supply from each division. **Fibres** from one division stimulate the organ while fibres from the other division inhibit it.

The sympathetic division is stimulated in periods of stress or danger and prepares the body for physical activity in case fighting or escape becomes necessary. Fibres of the sympathetic division will therefore increase the rate and force of the heartbeat, dilate the bronchioles of the lungs, dilate the pupils of the eyes and increase sweating. Blood supply through the muscles is increased and blood sugar levels rise. Activities that are not essential in this stressful situation are inhibited, so digestion and gut movements are slowed and urine production is decreased.

The parasympathetic division is stimulated in times of relaxation. Fibres of this division stimulate digestion and absorption of food.

Although this system is called autonomic, suggesting that we exert no conscious control over its activities, research has shown that transcendental meditation (yoga) seems to inactivate the sympathetic division and has a calming effect on the body.

ALWAYS REMEMBER

If cold, vasoconstriction occurs, where the capillaries narrow to conserve blood flow and prevent heat loss form the skin's surface.

TOP TIP

Memory aide

The sympathetic division is associated with stress.

The parasympathetic division is associated with peace.

The effect of heat on the body Our body attempts to keep its temperature at a constant 36.8°C, whatever the environmental temperature. When the skin experiences high temperatures, skin receptors are stimulated and impulses pass to the hypothalamus of the brain to bring about cooling mechanisms. These are involuntary actions beyond our control and are part of the autonomic nervous system.

The skin reddens as **vasodilation** occurs. Vasodilation involves opening up of the skin capillaries near the surface so that hot blood can flow through them and radiate excess heat to the outside. (Radiation of heat from the skin will only take place if the environmental temperature is less than body temperature.)

We also sweat more. When sweat evaporates it cools the skin surface. If the surrounding air is very dry causing evaporation to take place quickly, the body can tolerate temperatures of up to 130°C for as long as 20 minutes. If the air is moist, reducing the rate of evaporation, then a person can only tolerate a temperature of 46°C for a few minutes.

Yoga/meditation

HEALTH & SAFETY

Heat

Heat services to even a small area of the body will eventually cause heating of the whole body, as blood passing through the treated area will be warmed and will distribute heat elsewhere.

The circulatory system

Fluids of the body

All cells need a constant supply of energy and raw materials, and a means of removing waste products.

- Epidermal cells need energy to continue dividing, and supplies of raw materials to manufacture new cells.
- Muscle cells need energy to contract and become fatigued if their waste products are not removed efficiently.
- Neurones need energy in order to transmit impulses.

The fluids of the body are responsible for delivering whatever the cells require and for removing any waste products. The three principle body fluids are:

- blood
- tissue fluid
- lymph

Blood

Functions of blood Inside the tissues, some fluid leaks from the capillaries as blood passes through them. When this fluid leaves the capillaries to enter the tissues it becomes tissue fluid.

Blood circulates through the blood vessels (arteries, capillaries and veins), collecting oxygen from the lungs and delivering it to the cells of the body.

Blood transports various substances around the body:

- Glucose is carried in the blood to be used by the cells together with the oxygen to supply energy.
- Blood supplies other raw materials to build or maintain cells or to manufacture products such as secretions.
- Blood carries oxygen from our lungs and nutrients from our digested food to supply energy – these allow the cells to develop and divide, and the muscles to function.
- Blood carries waste products and carbon dioxide from the cells and tissues away for elimination from the body.
- Blood carries various cells and substances which allow the body to prevent or fight disease and heal injuries.
- Blood transports hormones, the body's chemical messengers, to their target tissue to cause a particular response.

The main constituents of blood Blood consists of the following:

- **Plasma:** constitutes 55 per cent of blood and is a straw-coloured liquid: mainly water with foods and carbon dioxide.
- **Red blood cells (erythrocytes):** constitute 40–50 per cent of blood. These cells appear red because they contain haemoglobin, a protein responsible for their colour, that carries oxygen from the lungs to the body cells.
- **White blood cells (leucocytes):** there are several types of white blood cells; their main role is to protect the body by destroying foreign bodies and dead cells, and carry away the debris (a process known as **phagocytosis**).
- **Platelets (thrombocytes):** when blood is exposed to air, as happens when the skin is injured, these cells bind together to form a clot. White blood cells and platelets constitute 1–2 per cent of blood.
- **Other chemicals:** hormones also are transported in the blood – chemical messages to target tissues.

ALWAYS REMEMBER

Blood

Blood helps to maintain the body temperature at 36.8°C: varying blood flow near to the skin surface increases or diminishes heat loss.

ALWAYS REMEMBER

The blood

Blood is made up of a collection of specialized cells suspended in liquid called plasma supplying the needs of the body's cells keeping the body healthy. It is transported around the body by a network of vessels (arteries, capillaries and veins) with a length of 90 000 miles.

Tissue fluid

This fluid carries essential oxygen and nutrients to the cells. These useful substances are taken up by the cells and exchanged for waste products such as carbon dioxide. Some of the fluid containing waste products will then re-enter the capillaries and be carried by the blood back to the **heart**.

Lymph

It is not as easy for the fluid to get back into the blood capillaries as it is to leave them, so excess fluid, together with waste products, collects in **lymph capillaries** and is carried though lymph vessels. Lymph passes through lymph nodes for processing before it is emptied back into the blood circulation close to the heart.

Tissue fluid as an electrolyte

Tissue fluid is a solution of many salts carried in the form of ions. It conducts electricity. When a direct current, such as that used in galvanism, is applied to the body, the ions present in tissue fluid move. Positive ions like sodium, potassium and calcium move towards the negative electrode, making this region alkaline. Negative ions like chloride and hydroxide move towards the positive electrode, making this region acidic.

The diagram illustrates the exchange of blood, tissue fluid and lymph as blood flows through the capillaries.

Exchange of blood, tissue fluid and lymph

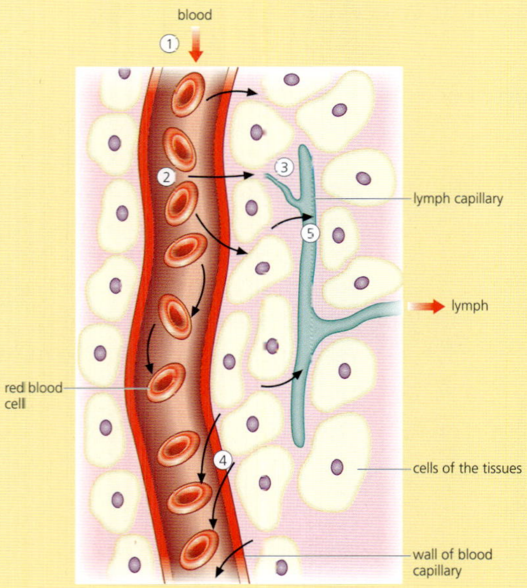

1 The blood flowing into the capillary network is under high pressure. The liquid part of the blood is forced through the walls of the capillary.

2 Larger proteins and blood cells remain in the capillaries.

3 The fluid has now become tissue fluid. It supplies the cells and removes the waste.

4 Some fluid will be drawn back into the capillaries.

5 Other fluid, together with large molecules like proteins from the cells, is drawn into the very porous lymph capillaries.

The heart

The circulation of blood is under the control of the heart. The heart is a muscular pump the size of a clenched fist which keeps the blood circulating. During diastole, the heart fills with blood from the veins. At systole, forceful contractions of first the atria and then the ventricles force blood out of the heart through the arteries. The pulmonary artery carries blood from the right ventricle to the lungs to absorb oxygen, while the aorta carries oxygenated blood from the left ventricle around the rest of the body.

Blood vessels

There are three main kinds of blood vessel: **arteries**, **veins** and **capillaries**. Arteries are thick, elastic-walled vessels that carry blood away from the heart. Every time the heart contracts to pump blood around the body, the elastic walls become stretched and then recoil. This absorbs and smoothes the surges from the heart and helps to push the blood forwards. This stretching and recoiling is felt as a pulse.

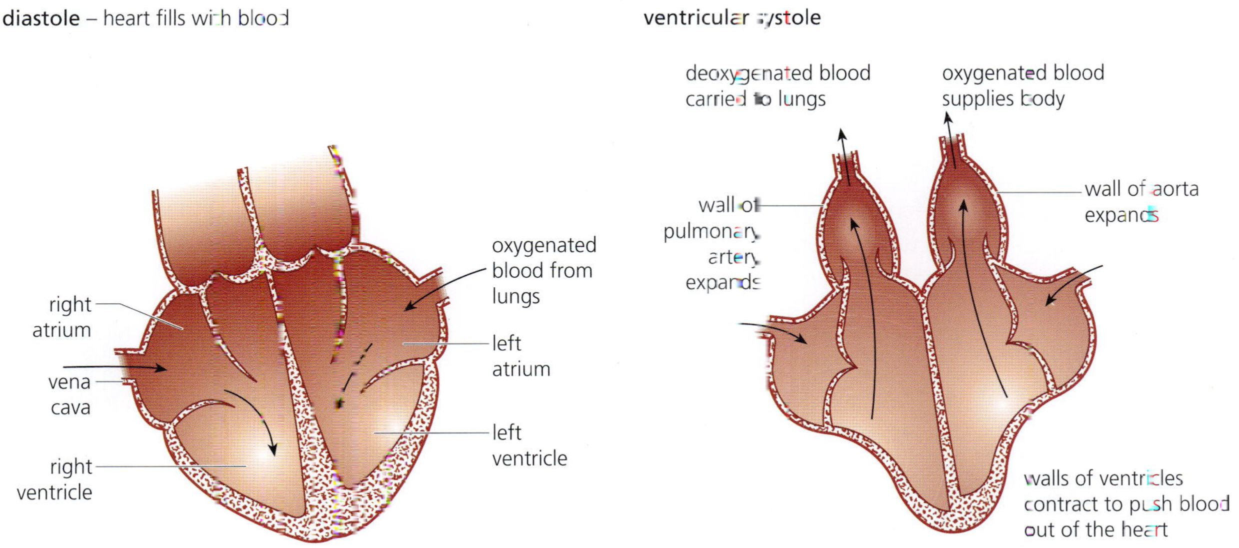

Stages of the heartbeat

Arteries lead into the main organs where they divide into smaller and smaller vessels. The smallest blood vessels are called capillaries. Capillaries are about the size of a hair. They are close to all the cells of the body, bringing supplies of oxygen and nutrients and carrying away products from the cells.

The capillary network then reforms into larger vessels called veins to deliver blood back to the heart. The blood flows much more slowly and evenly in veins. They do not pulsate like arteries. The veins often pass through the muscles. Each time muscles contract, veins are squeezed and blood is pushed along. To make sure the blood is squeezed along in the right direction, many veins have valves to stop blood flowing backwards. The veins have much thinner walls than arteries. This means that they are more easily compressed by the muscles they pass through.

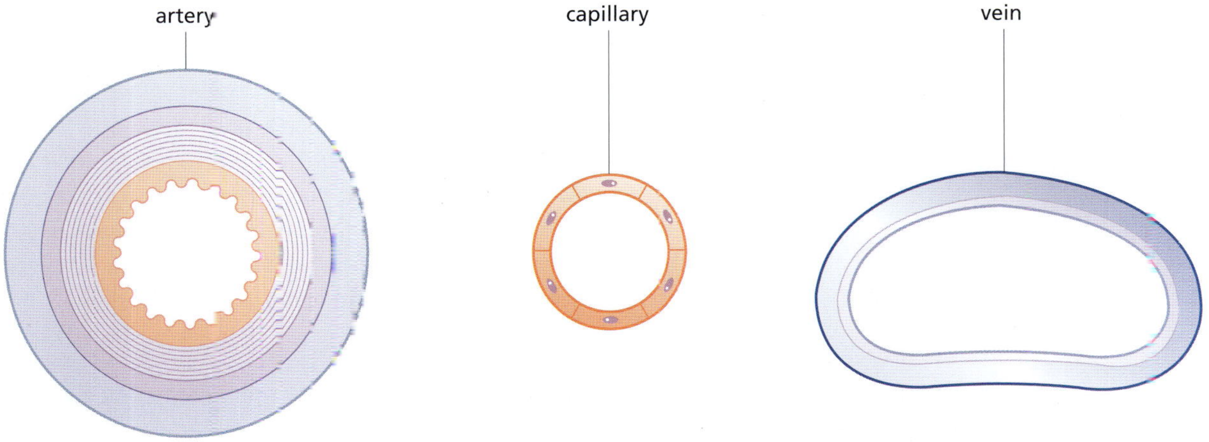

Blood vessels

ACTIVITY

Pulse rate

Take your pulse and find your resting heart rate. The normal rate is around 75 beats per minute

TOP TIP

Varicose veins

If your occupation requires you to sit or stand for long periods, you may get swollen feet and ankles or even varicose veins. Keep the blood circulating by exercising those leg muscles.

Flow of blood in arteries

The flow of blood in the arteries is maintained by blood pressure caused by the forceful contractions of the ventricles of the heart pushing blood into them. Blood pressure is maintained by the elastic walls of the large arteries, which stretch to accept the blood from the ventricles and then recoil to push the blood on its way.

Blood pressure is measured in the arteries. Normal blood pressure has a value of about 115 mm mercury over 70 mm mercury. The first value refers to the pressure reached when the heart is contracting and pushing blood around the body, and the second to the pressure when the heart is relaxed and filling up with blood. The blood pressure is always higher when someone is standing rather than lying down, and it increases with exercise or anxiety. A value of 100 over 60 would be low; a value of 160 over 100 would be high. A person with high blood pressure is said to be suffering from **hypertension**.

Hypertension needs to be treated as it can damage the heart, brain and kidneys. It is often without symptoms and can only be detected by routine blood-pressure checks. Low blood pressure may cause a person to faint easily.

Heat services may cause dizziness and fainting as blood is diverted to the skin (to reduce the rising body temperature) causing a fall in blood pressure and reduced flow to the head and brain. This fall in blood pressure can also occur when a client stands up following a service in the prone position.

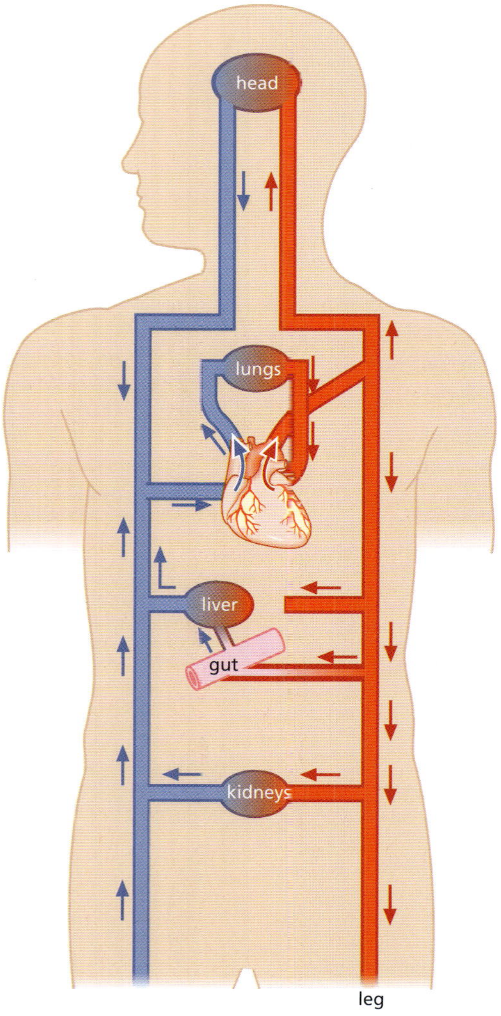

Diagram of the circulatory system

Blood flow through the organs

Arterioles are the smaller arteries which feed the capillary networks. Capillary networks are found through each major organ of the body including the skin. Arterioles are very important because they control blood flow through the organs. They have smooth muscle fibres in their walls which can contract to constrict the size of the lumen and reduce blood flow, or relax to cause dilation of the lumen and increase blood flow. The lumen is the cavity through which the blood flows.

Blood flow through the muscles is controlled by this process. It is increased during exercise when muscles are contracting, in order to bring supplies of oxygen and glucose and to carry away the waste products – mainly carbon dioxide and heat and perhaps lactic acid.

Blood flow through the skin

Normal body temperature is 36.8°C. Blood circulating through the internal organs or through working muscles therefore becomes warm. If the body temperature starts to rise, then allowing blood to pass near the skin surface releases some of this heat to the environment. This will check the rise in temperature. The skin will appear red and may feel warm to the touch.

The blood vessels in the skin are organized so that blood can either flow near the skin surface or can pass through shunt vessels which lie deeper in the dermis. The skin capillaries are used to help regulate body temperature. If the body temperature begins to drop, then blood flows deeper through the dermis, releasing less heat to the environment. This process of **vasodilation** and **vasoconstriction** is controlled by the autonomic nervous system – nerves control the arterioles that feed the capillary networks through the skin.

Erythema is reddening of the skin caused by dilation of the blood vessels controlling local capillary networks in areas of the skin affected by injury or infection.

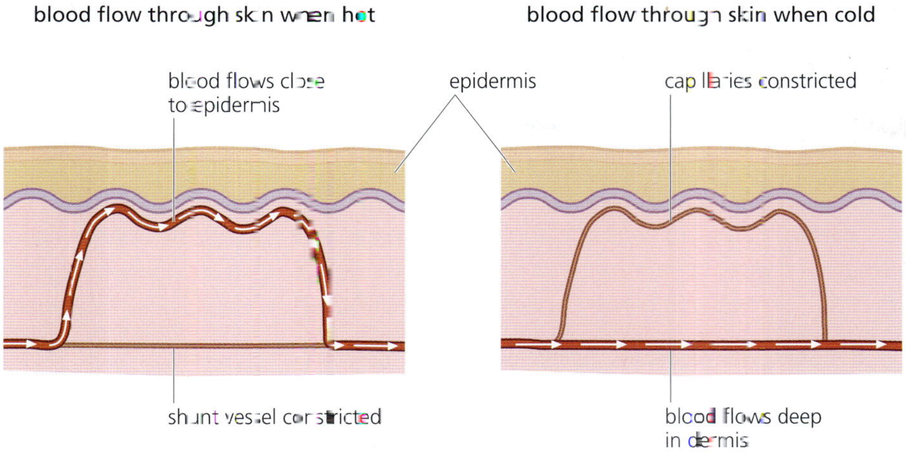

Vasoconstriction and vasodilation

Flow of blood in veins

The flow of blood in veins is slower and under less pressure than the flow in arteries. Veins tend to pass through muscles of the body where they can be squeezed so that the blood is helped along. This is especially important in the legs, where blood is being returned against gravity.

Varicose veins are a result of incompetent valves which allow blood to flow backwards, stretching and weakening the walls of the vein. The veins on the surface of the leg (and therefore not surrounded by muscle tissue) are the ones most commonly affected as gravity forces the blood back down the leg.

TOP TIP

Blood pressure

Pulse rate relates to the speed of the heartbeat. The strength of the pulse relates to the pressure of blood flow leaving the heart. The heart on average beats 70 times per minute.

Blood pressure increases during activity and decreases during rest.

Relaxing services such as Indian head massage lowers the blood pressure.

ALWAYS REMEMBER

Thrombosis

Thrombosis is the formation of a thrombus (a clot) in the blood vessels. A thrombus in a deep vein of the leg may cause pain in the calf. Pieces of the thrombus can break off and get carried through the blood stream until they wedge in tiny capillaries. If this happens in the lungs, oxygen absorption decreases and breathing is affected. A coronary thrombosis (blockage of coronary arteries supplying blood to the heart) can cause a heart attack.

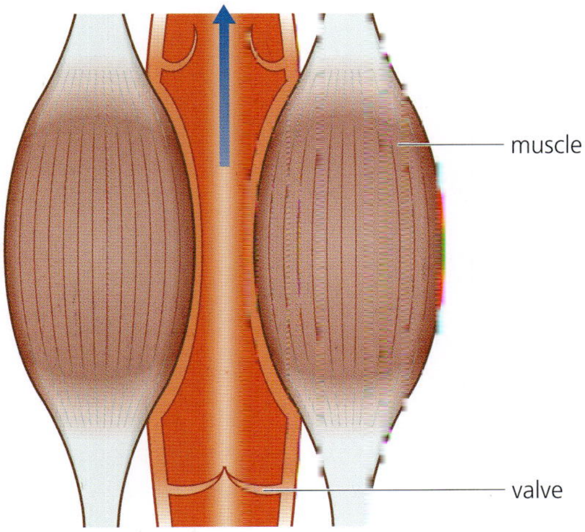

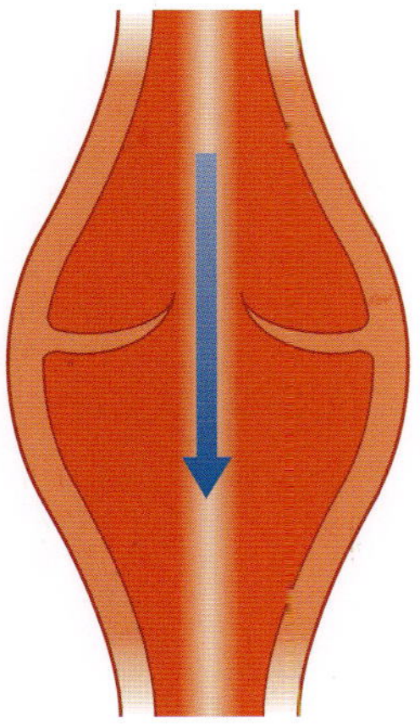

Control of blood flow by valves

Blood supply to and from the head

As previously stated, blood leaving the heart is carried in large, elastic tubes called **arteries**. The blood to the head arrives via the **carotid arteries**, which are connected via other main arteries to the heart. There are two main carotid arteries, one on each side of the neck.

These arteries divide into smaller branches, the *internal carotid* and the *external carotid*. The **internal carotid artery** passes the temporal bone and enters the head, taking blood to the brain. The **external carotid artery** stays outside the skull and divides into branches:

- the **occipital branch** supplies the back of the head and the scalp
- the **temporal branch** supplies the sides of the face, the head, the scalp and the skin
- the **facial branch** supplies the muscles and tissues of the face
- the **posterior auricular** branch supplies the scalp, back and above the ear.

ALWAYS REMEMBER

Temporal branches

Some of its important temporal branches are:

- Frontal: supplies the forehead.
- Parietal: supplies the top and sides of the head.
- Transverse: supplies the masseter muscle.
- Middle temporal: supplies the temples and the eyelids.
- Anterior auricular: supplies the front part of the ear.

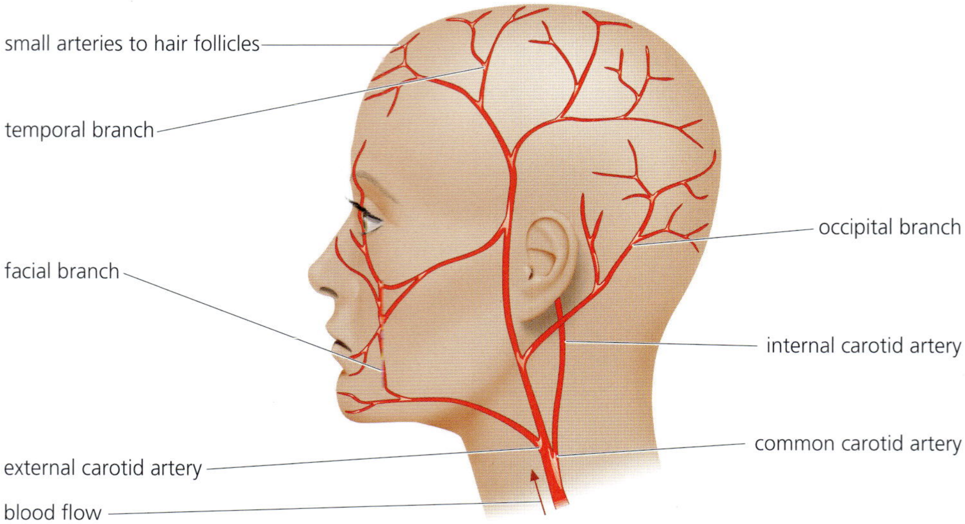

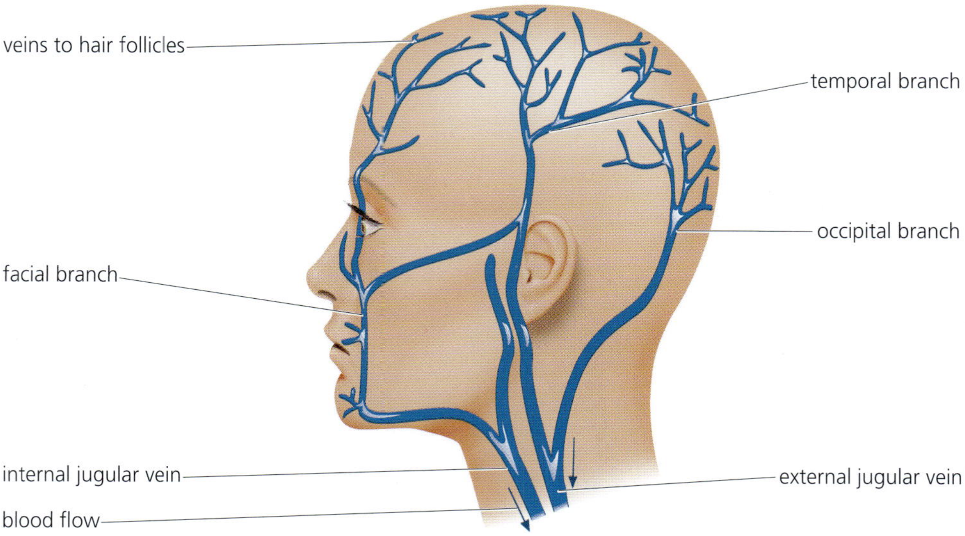

The blood supply to and from the head

These arteries also divide repeatedly, successive vessels becoming smaller and smaller until they form tiny blood **capillaries**. These vessels are just one cell thick, allowing substances carried in the blood to pass through them into the **tissue fluid** which bathes and nourishes the cells of the various body tissues.

The blood capillaries begin to join up again, forming first small vessels called **venules**, then larger vessels called **veins**. These return the blood to the heart.

Veins are less elastic than arteries and are closer to the skin's surface. Along their course are **valves** which prevent the backflow of blood.

The main veins are the external and internal jugular veins. The **internal jugular vein** and its main branch, the **facial vein**, carry blood from the face and head. The **external jugular** vein carries blood from the scalp and has two branches: the **occipital branch** and the **temporal branch**. The jugular veins join to enter the **subclavian vein**, which lies above the clavicle.

Blood returns to the heart, which pumps it to the lungs, where the red blood cells take on fresh oxygen and where carbon dioxide is expelled from the blood. The blood returns to the heart and begins its next journey round the body.

HEALTH & SAFETY

Capillaries

The strength and elasticity of the capillary walls can be damaged, for example by a blow to the tissues. Broken capillaries are capillaries whose elasticity is damaged and they remain constantly dilated with blood.

Blood supply to and from the arm and hand The arm and hand are nourished by a system of arteries which carry oxygen-rich blood to the tissues. You can see the colour of the blood from the capillaries beneath the nail: these give the nail bed its pink colour.

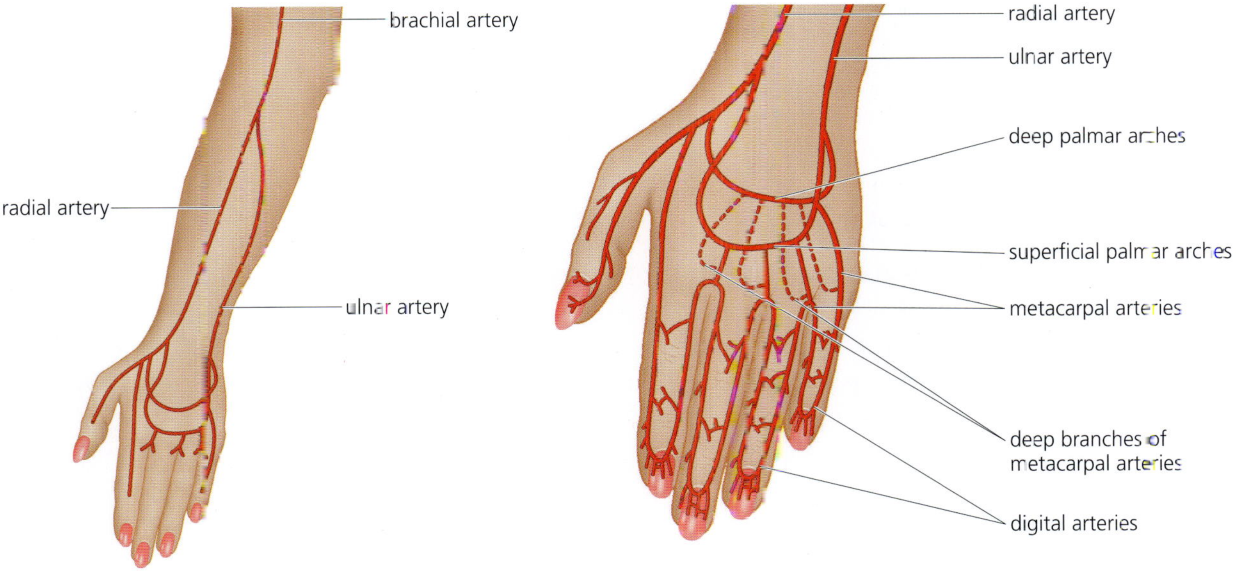

Arteries of the arm and hand

The brachial artery supplies blood to the upper arm. This branches into the ulnar and radial artery, which supplies the forearm and fingers. The radial and ulnar arteries are connected across the palm by the superficial and deep palmar arches. These arteries divide to form the metacarpal and digital arteries, which supply the palm and fingers.

Veins of the arms and hands Veins deliver deoxygenated blood back to the heart. Blood with its oxygen removed appears blue. Veins often pass through muscles. Each time muscles contract, veins are squeezed and the blood is pushed along. Massage is particularly beneficial in this process.

Blood in the digital veins drains blood from the fingers. The palmar venous arches drains blood from the hands. The cephalic and basilic veins drain blood from the forearm.

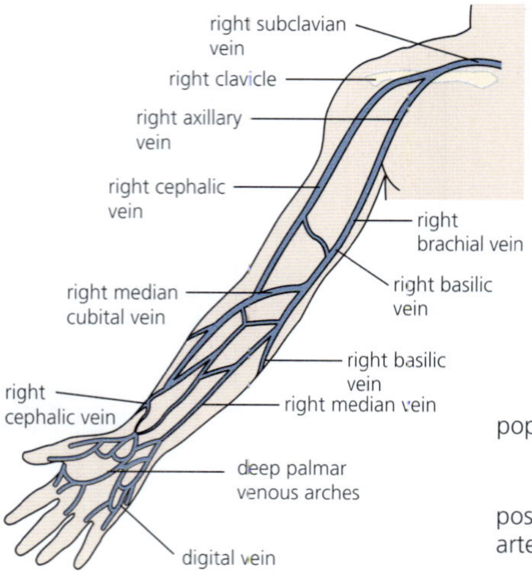

Veins of the arms and hands

Blood supply to and from the foot and lower leg The lower leg and the feet are nourished by a system of arteries that carry oxygen-rich blood to the tissue.

When it is cold, and when the circulation is poor, insufficient blood reaches the feet and they feel cold. Severe circulation problems in the feet may lead to **chilblains**.

The anterior and tibial artery supplies blood to the lower leg and foot. The peroneal artery branches off the posterior tibial artery. At the ankle the anterior tibial artery becomes the dorsalis pedis artery. The posterior tibial artery divides at the ankle to form the medial and lateral plantar arteries. The plantar and dorsalis pedis arteries supply the digital arteries of the toes.

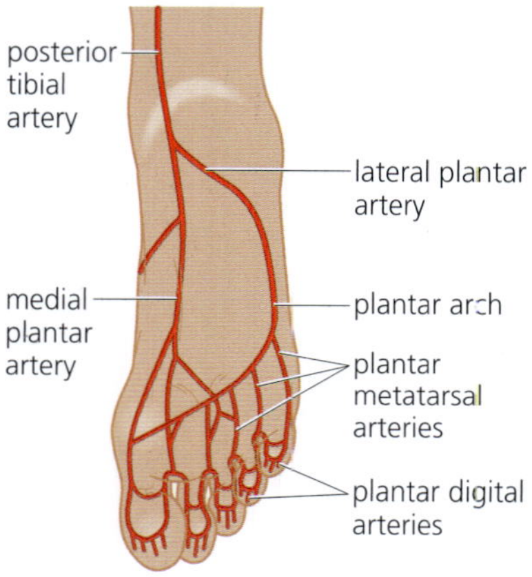

Arteries of the foot

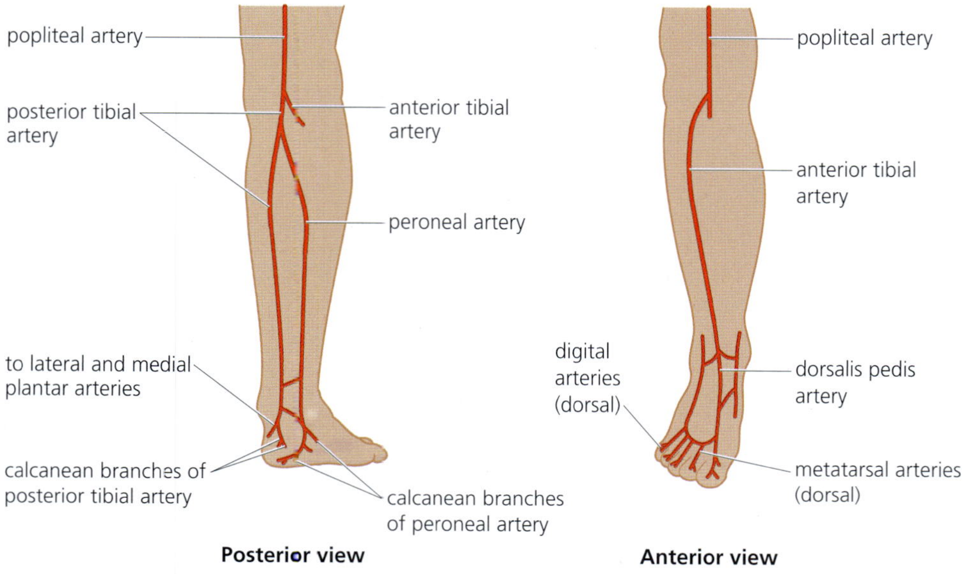

Arteries of the lower leg

The veins of the foot and lower leg The digital veins from the toes drain into the plantar and dorsal venous arch. The dorsalis pedis veins drain to the saphenous vein. The following deep veins drain the lower leg: the posterior tibial vein at the back of the leg, the peroneal vein; and the anterior tibial vein at the front of the leg. The deep tibial veins join to form the popliteal vein.

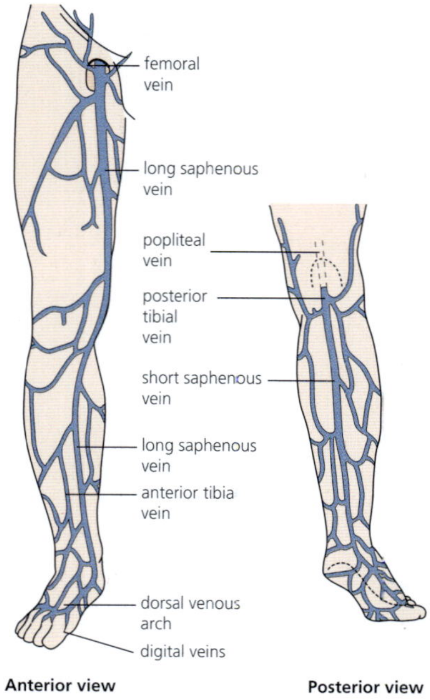

Veins of the foot and lower leg

The lymphatic system

The **lymphatic system** is closely connected to the blood system, and can be considered as supplementing it. Its primary function is defensive: to remove bacteria and foreign materials, thereby preventing infection. It also drains away excess fluids for elimination from the body.

The lymphatic system consists of the fluid **lymph**, the **lymph vessels** and the lymph nodes (or glands). You may have experienced swelling of the lymph nodes in the neck when you have been ill.

Unlike the blood circulation, the lymphatic system has no muscular pump equivalent to the heart. Instead, the lymph moves through the vessels and around the body because of movements such as contractions of large muscles. Massage can play an important part in assisting this flow of lymph fluid, thereby encouraging the improved removal of the waste products transported in the lymph.

Lymph

Lymph is a straw-coloured fluid, derived from blood plasma, which has filtered through the walls of the capillaries. Contractions of the body muscles push the lymph through a series of one-way valves. The composition of lymph is similar to that of blood, although less oxygen and fewer nutrients are available. In the spaces between the cells where there are no blood capillaries, lymph provides nourishment. It also carries **lymphocytes** (a type of white blood cell), which plays an important role in the immune system. It can destroy dangerous cells and disease causing bacteria and viruses directly before it returns to the bloodstream.

Lymph travels only in one direction from body tissue back towards the heart.

Lymph vessels

Lymph vessels are similar in structure to veins, having valves at intervals along their length. They collect lymph from the lymph capillaries. Lymph is squeezed along the vessels by pressure from the muscles they run through. It is important when massaging to make sure movements are compatible with aiding the flow of blood and lymph back

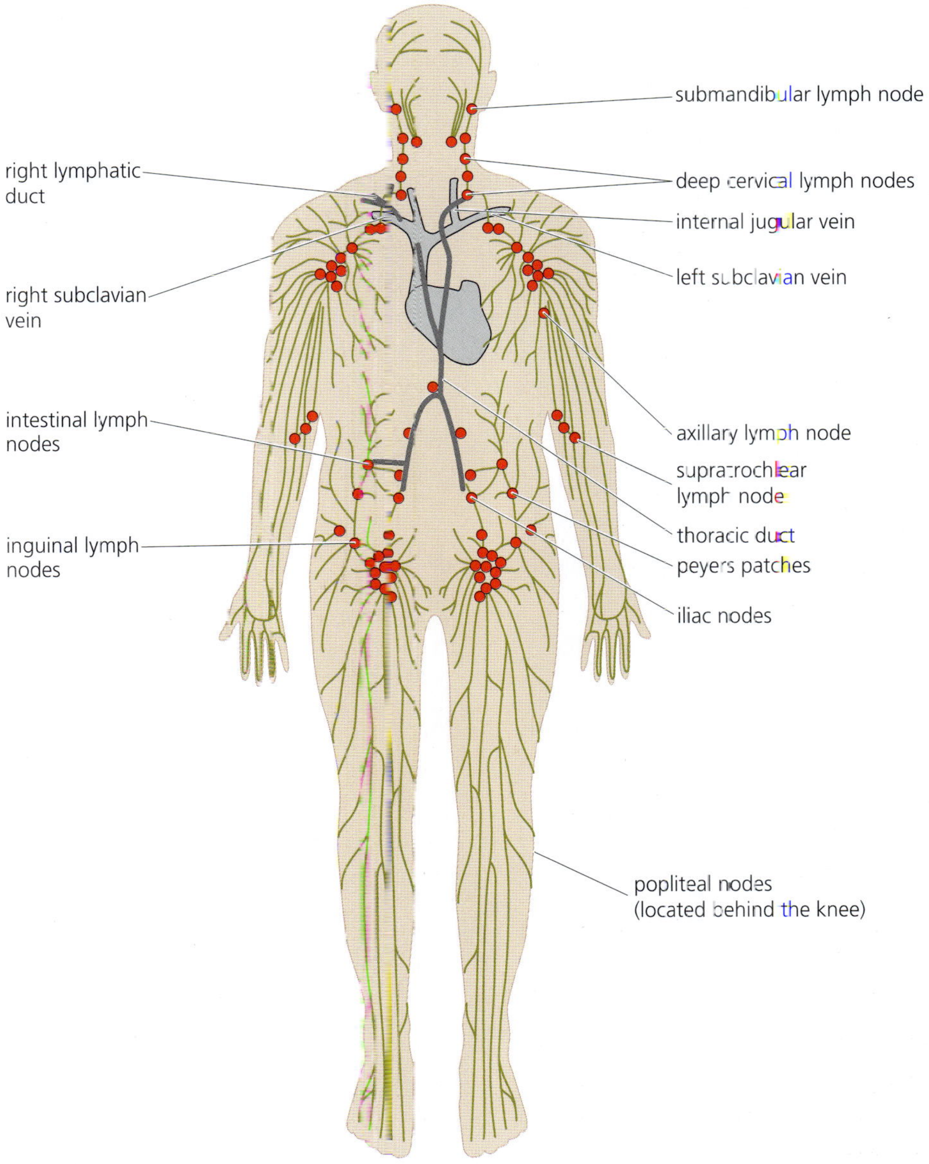

Lymph vessels and nodes (glands) in the body

A lymph vessel

towards the heart. **Oedema** is swelling of the tissues which occurs when fluids accumulate rather than returning to the bloodstream. This can be due to a failure of the circulation or to an imbalance in the composition of the blood. If an operation for breast cancer has included removal of lymph tissue, oedema sometimes affects the arm on that side.

Lymph vessels often run very close to veins, forming an extensive network throughout the body. The lymph moves quite slowly and the valves along the lymph vessels prevent backflow of the lymph.

The lymph vessels join to form larger lymph vessels, which eventually flow into one or other of two large lymphatic vessels: the **thoracic duct** (or **left lymphatic duct**) and the **right lymphatic duct**. The thoracic duct receives lymph from the left side of the head, neck, chest, abdomen and lower body; the right lymphatic duct receives lymph from the right side of the head and upper body.

These principal lymphatic vessels then empty their contents into a vein at the base of the neck, which in turn empties into the **vena cava**. The lymph is mixed into the venous blood as it is returned to the heart.

Lymph nodes

Lymph vessels take lymph through a series of lymph nodes on its way back to the blood circulation. Lymph nodes are small, oval structures between 1 mm and 25 mm in length. Lymph enters a node through an **afferent** vessel and leaves through an **efferent** vessel.

There are two types of white blood cell present inside the lymph node: **macrophages** line the walls and **lymphocytes** may detach from the lymph nodes and be taken out of the node with the lymph. Macrophages engulf and destroy any foreign particles or debris carried in the lymph. This may include bacteria. Lymphocytes manufacture antibodies to fight bacteria. They pass into the bloodstream along with the circulating lymph. When we suffer an infection, the lymph nodes closest to the site of infection may swell up and become tender as the white cells attempt to destroy the germs.

Lymph filters through at least one lymph node before returning to the bloodstream. Various groups of lymph nodes drain the different parts of the body.

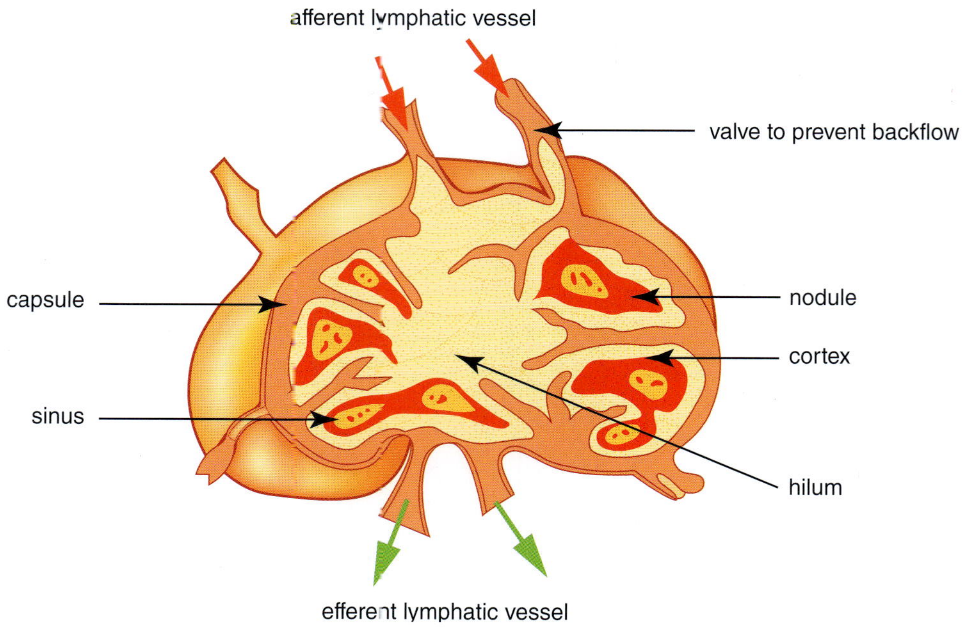

Lymph node structure

Lymph nodes of the head

- The **buccal group** drains the eyelids, the nose and the skin of the face.
- The **mandibular group** drains the chin, the lips, the nose and the cheeks.
- The **mastoid group** drains the skin of the ear and the temple area.
- The **occipital group** drains the back of the scalp and the upper neck.
- The **submental group** drains the chin and the lower lip.
- The **parotid group** drains the nose, eyelids and ears.

Lymph nodes of the neck

- The **superficial cervical group** drains the back of the head and the neck.
- The **lower deep cervical group** drains the back area of the scalp and the neck.

Lymph nodes of the chest and arms

- The nodes of the armpit area drain various regions of the arms and chest.

TOP TIP

Frontal – Temporal – Parietal – Occipital – Mandible (mandibular) – Cervical

Learn and remember these names of the main regions of the head and neck. Not only will this assist you in recalling the names and locations of the bones, it will also help you greatly with the names and locations of muscles, arteries, veins, nerves and lymph nodes.

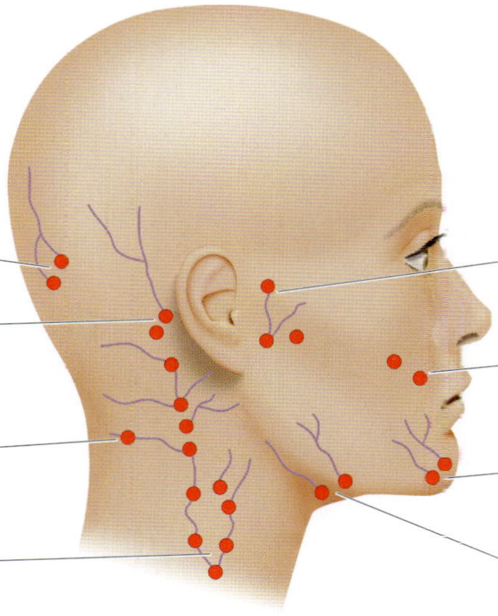

Lymph nodes of the head and neck

TOP TIP

When performing massage, the hands should be used to apply pressure to direct the lymph towards the nearest lymph node: this encourages the speedy removal of waste products.

Digestive system

The digestive system is known as the **alimentary canal**. Most foodstuffs such as carbohydrates, fats and proteins need digesting. Minerals and some vitamins do not need digesting.

Digestion starts in the mouth where food is broken down mechanically by the teeth and then chemically by the body's digestive juices so that it can be absorbed and used by the body's cells and ends at the large intestine.

The alimentary canal consists of the:

- mouth
- pharynx (throat)
- oesophagus (gullet)
- stomach

- small intestine
- large intestine

The mouth Food enters the mouth or buccal cavity, here the teeth, palate (roof of the mouth) and tongue are used to hold, taste and chew the food, called **mastication**.

The pharynx and oesophagus Glands in the mouth called salivary glands secrete a fluid called saliva which contains an enzyme called salivary amylase responsible for starch digestion.

The food then enters the pharynx and then the oesophagus where through muscular contractions in the oesophagus it enters into the stomach through a ring of muscle called the cardiac sphincter, controlling the opening. The muscular contractions are called **peristalsis**.

Stomach The stomach is a pouch J-shaped organ under the liver and diaphragm. Food stays in the stomach for several hours where it is mixed by muscular contractions of the stomach walls which liquefies the food. An acid called gastric juice containing pepsin, lipase and hydrochloric acid is added to the food from gastric glands which helps digest protein and help kill bacteria.

The food is then moved at the end of the stomach another ring of muscles called the pyloric sphincter, controlling the opening into the small intestine. This is made up of three parts the duodenum, jejunum and ileum. Here further digestion occurs through the secretion of mucus and digestive enzymes making carbohydrates into glucose, and protein into amino acids.

ALWAYS REMEMBER

Muscles of mastication
The muscles of mastication are the masseter, buccinator and temporal muscles. Feel them move when you chew.

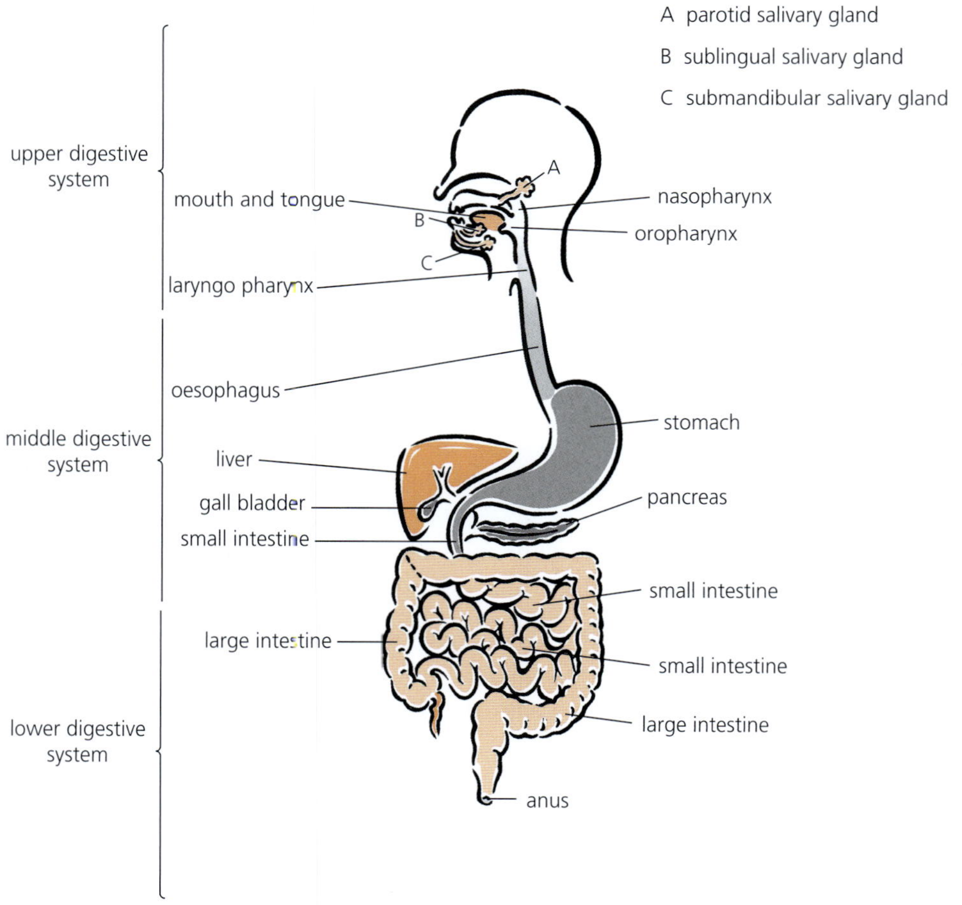

Digestive system

Pancreatic juice and insulin is released from the pancreas. Bile is required from the liver, it is stored in the gall bladder and released to emulsify (break down) fat. Villi – finger-like projections in the small intestine – help to increase the surface area to absorb digested food which is then passed into lacteal lymph capillaries to absorb fat, and blood capillaries which absorb nutrients. Lymph nodes are present in this area known as peyers patches which help destroy any harmful bacteria.

The small intestine joins the large intestine through a ring of muscle called the ileocaecal sphincter, controlling the opening.

The large intestine is also known as the colon. Here indigested food leaves the rectum and faeces are removed finally from the colon through the anus.

Excretory system The excretory system removes the waste products of metabolism from the cells. The system includes the:

- skin – sweat
- lungs – carbon dioxide
- large intestine – faeces
- kidneys – urine

The skin, lungs and large intestine have already been discussed.

The urinary system

The urinary system controls the fluid balance of the body keeping homeostasis – stability in the body.

It consists of the:

- kidneys
- ureters
- bladder
- urethra

Kidneys The kidneys are two bean-shaped, dark-red organs either side of the spinal column at the back of the abdomen. They filter out unwanted waste products as blood passes through them.

For protection they are covered in a membrane called the renal capsule and a layer of adipose fat and are protected by the lower ribs and muscles of the abdominal wall. Each kidney has two hollow concave central parts, the inner medulla and outer cortex. Each kidney contains a million small thin-walled coiled tubes called **nephrons**, situated in the cortex. They receive blood from capillaries within the kidneys delivered by the renal artery and removed by the renal vein. Each nephron filters the fluid, substances needed by the body are reabsorbed. The waste fluid opens into a common collecting duct in the medulla, then is moved to the outer part of the kidney, the pelvis. This is then transported into collection tubes called ureters becoming further concentrated. The ureters are attached to the kidneys at a point called the hilum.

Ureters There are two ureters, a muscular tube carrying urine, one is attached to each kidney which leads into the bladder.

The bladder The bladder stores urine until it is passed out of the body. When the bladder is full, nerves in the bladder inform the brain. This relaxes an internal sphincter muscle which is controlled by the autonomic nervous system.

Urethra Urine is removed from the body when an external sphincter muscle is relaxed, controlled by the conscious part of the brain, through the single urethra. Fluid excreted is called urine which is made up of 95 per cent water, urea, uric acid and ammonia. Only one type of fluid can pass through the urethra so in males the vas deferens joins the urethra which allows the passage of semen or urine from the penis. In females the urethra is close to the vaginal opening.

ALWAYS REMEMBER

Anti-diuretic hormone

The concentration and volume of urine is under the control of the anti-diuretic hormone (ADH). The brain monitors the amount of water levels in the blood, if more water is required, i.e. after a heat service such as sauna where sweat has been lost, the hypothalamus will initiate the pituitary gland to release more ADH to collect more water to return to the blood.

ALWAYS REMEMBER

Cystitis

1500 ml of urine is passed each day.

Cystitis is common and can cause discomfort in females with increased, painful urination caused by inflammation of the bladder wall.

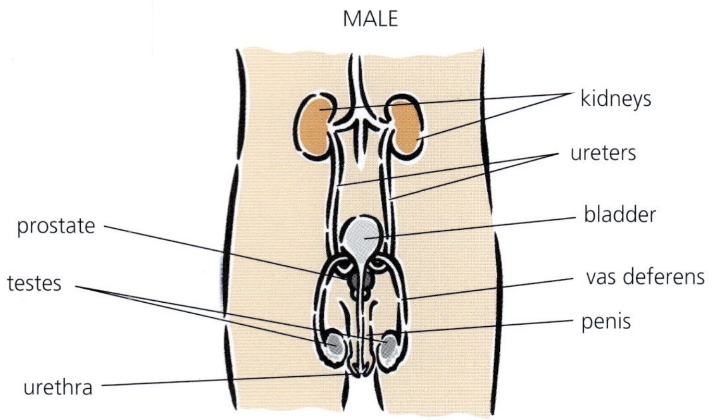

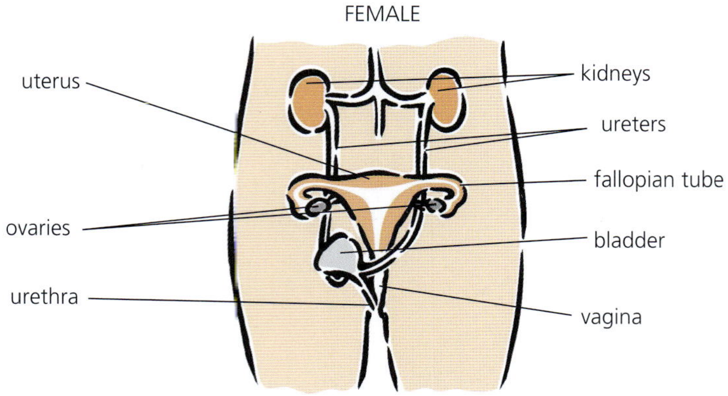

Urethra

Respiratory system

The cells of the body tissues require oxygen for metabolism in addition to food and water. Oxygen is needed to digest food to provide energy which produces by-products of water and carbon dioxide. The respiratory system takes in oxygen and transports it by red blood cells, erythrocytes from the lungs to the cells and returns carbon dioxide and moisture back to the lungs from the cells to be removed. The respiratory system works with the **circulatory system** and muscular system enabling the exchange of gases between air, blood and cells.

It consists of the:

- nose
- pharynx (throat)

- larynx (voice box)
- trachea (windpipe)
- bronchi
- bronchioles
- alveoli
- lungs
- muscles of respiration – intercostals muscle and the diaphragm

Nose Air is inhaled into the nose. Here, the air is warmed and moistened by ciliated mucous membranes which contains mucus-secreting cells inside the nose. Air is filtered by cilia, hair inside the nose and mucus which removes particles such as dust, pollution, pollen and bacteria as it enters. The mucous membrane also lines the sinuses, air-filled bony cavities called the nasal cavity located in the face and skull adjacent to the nose. The cilia move the mucus towards the throat.

The pharynx Air then passes in the same course as food for a short way to the pharynx which is connected to the nose and mouth. This is also lined with ciliated mucous membrane. It is then routed to the larynx (voice box).

Larynx The larynx continues filtering the air. The epiglottis made from cartilage is located at the entrance to the larynx which helps prevent food entering the airways.

Trachea Air leaves the larynx and passes into the trachea. The trachea is kept open by rings of flexible hyaline cartilage. This then divides into two branches, called bronchi which enter the lungs.

Bronchi The tubes entering each lung transporting air which divide further to form smaller tubes called bronchioles made of involuntary, smooth muscle. At the end of the smallest tubes, small air sacs are formed called alveoli.

Alveoli These minute air sacs are surrounded by blood-filled capillaries which allow oxygen to pass through them into the bloodstream. Carbon dioxide leaves the blood and enters the lungs where it is breathed out, exhaled through the trachea and nose or mouth.

Lungs The lungs are spongy organs located within the chest cavity, the thorax. Their base rests on the diaphragm, a muscular partition above the abdomen; their upper part is behind the clavicle bones. They are covered in a double-layered membrane called the pleura lubricated by fluid in-between to prevent friction with the chest walls.

Muscles of respiration The muscles of respiration are the diaphragm and the intercostals, see page 41.

When breathing in, inhaling called **inspiration**, the diaphragm contracts, moves down and flattens and the intercostal muscles contract to raise the ribs, increase the volume of the thorax allowing air to enter the lungs.

TOP TIP

Aromatherapy

The sensation of smell is detected in the nose. Nerves are stimulated by chemicals released from smells. Nerve impulses are conveyed by the olfactory nerves to the brain where the information is received. This is important to consider when selecting pre-blended aromatic oils for massage to create different psychological states, i.e. relaxation or stimulation.

ALWAYS REMEMBER

The larynx, often referred to as the 'Adams apple', is larger in males than females, hence the deeper voice.

ALWAYS REMEMBER

When eating, breathing temporarily stops to allow the epiglottis to fold downwards allowing food to pass the opening to the larynx and enter the oesophagus. If food enters the larynx, choking could occur.

HEALTH & SAFETY

Client comfort during massage
Pressure must not be applied over the trachea when performing massage.

HEALTH & SAFETY

Respiratory infections

Infections include the common cold, influenza and tonsillitis. If a client is unwell they should not be treated to prevent cross-infection.

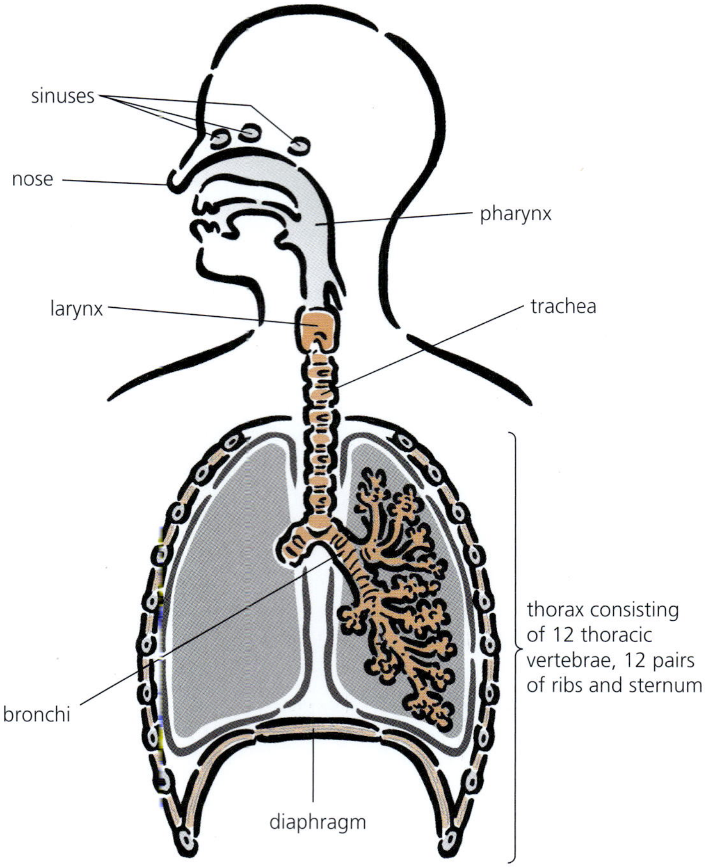

Muscles of respiration

When breathing out, exhaling called **expiration**, the diaphragm relaxes turning upwards becoming dome-shaped, intercostal muscles relax and the ribs fall, the volume of the thorax is decreased and air is expelled.

The organ affected by a particular hormone is called a **target organ**. The endocrine system works with the nervous system to bring about coordination. Hormones tend to be associated with long-term changes, such as growth, rather than the quick response expected from nerve stimulation.

The endocrine system

While the nervous system uses electrical signals to initiate a response the endocrine system uses hormones.

Endocrine glands secrete chemical messengers called **hormones** directly into the bloodstream where they circulate around the body and affect certain organs. The glands are commonly referred to as ductless glands because the hormones are secreted directly into the bloodstream.

The hypothalamus is the hormone-producing part of the brain and works with the nervous system and endocrine system to regulate the chemical processes in the body to keep them stable. This is referred to as homeostasis. The hypothalamus links with the pituitary gland which controls other glands. A low level of hormones detected by the hypothalamus will trigger the pituitary to increase hormone levels released from a 'target' gland.

Endocrine glands and their functions

Name of gland	*Hormones secreted*	*Function*
Pituitary gland	Trophic hormones.	Act on and regulate the activities of the other endocrine glands.
	FSH (follicle-stimulating hormone) and LH (luteinizing hormone).	Control reproduction.
	ADH (anti-diuretic hormone).	Affects water balance.
Thyroid gland	Thyroxine.	Controls the rate of metabolism.
Parathyroid	Parathormone.	Controls blood calcium levels.
Thymus gland (both an endocrine and lymphatic gland)	Various hormones.	Stimulates lymphoid cells responsible for antibody production against disease.
Pancreas (islets of Langerhans)	Insulin.	Controls blood sugar levels.
Adrenal (medulla)	Adrenalin.	Prepares the body for sudden stressful events.
Adrenal (cortex)	Glucocorticoids.	Reduce stress responses such as inflammation.
	Aldosterone.	Controls level of sodium and potassium in the blood.
	Oestrogens and androgens.	As other sex hormones.
Ovary	Oestrogens and progesterones.	Control female reproductive events including puberty, menstruation, pregnancy and the menopause.
Testes	Testosterone (an androgen).	Controls male fertility.

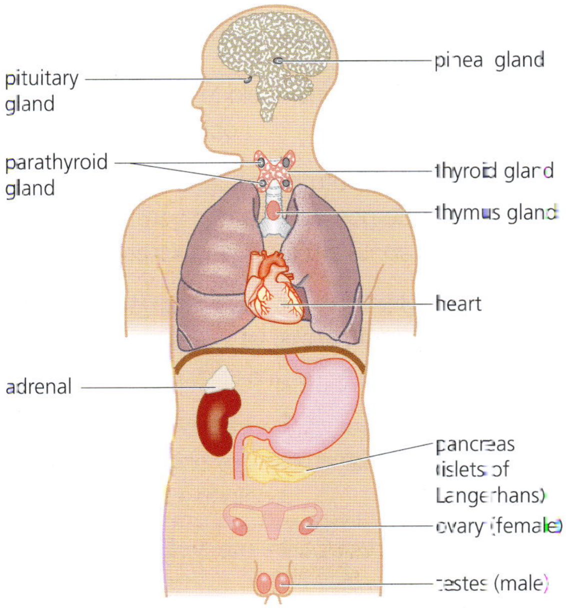

Glands of the endocrine system

The effect of hormones on hair, skin and body shape

Gland	*Name of hormone*	*Effect*
Pituitary	GH (growth hormone).	Excess (in adults) causes coarsening of skin, increased hair growth and more muscular appearance.
Thyroid	Thyroxine.	Excess causes a warm, moist, flushed skin with thin hair and loss of body weight; deficiency causes swelling and puffiness of the face, weight gain and muscular weakness.
Parathyroid	Parathormone.	Lack of hormone not only affects the bones but causes abnormal production of keratin, affecting hair, skin and nails.
Adrenal	Glucocorticoids.	Excess causes Cushing's syndrome, characterized by a redistribution of fat producing a 'moon face', 'buffalo hump', large abdomen and thin limbs; purple stretch marks and bruises may appear on the skin; deficiency causes Addison's disease with weight loss and darkening of the skin.
	Aldosterone	Excess can cause oedema.
	Corticosteroids (sex hormones).	Excess of androgens causes virilism in women (deepening of the voice, growth of facial and body hair, muscle development and sometimes male pattern baldness); excess of oestrogens causes feminization in men – breasts will enlarge.
Ovary	Oestrogen and progesterone.	Keep skin and hair in good condition; control distribution of body hair at puberty and influence the typical 'female' shape by causing fat to be stored in breasts, hips and thighs.
Testes	Testosterone.	Causes growth of facial and body hair at puberty; causes muscular development influencing 'male' body shape; encourages fat to be deposited around the waist and abdomen.

The ovaries and testes secrete hormones which influence the reproductive system and body shape. This is shown below.

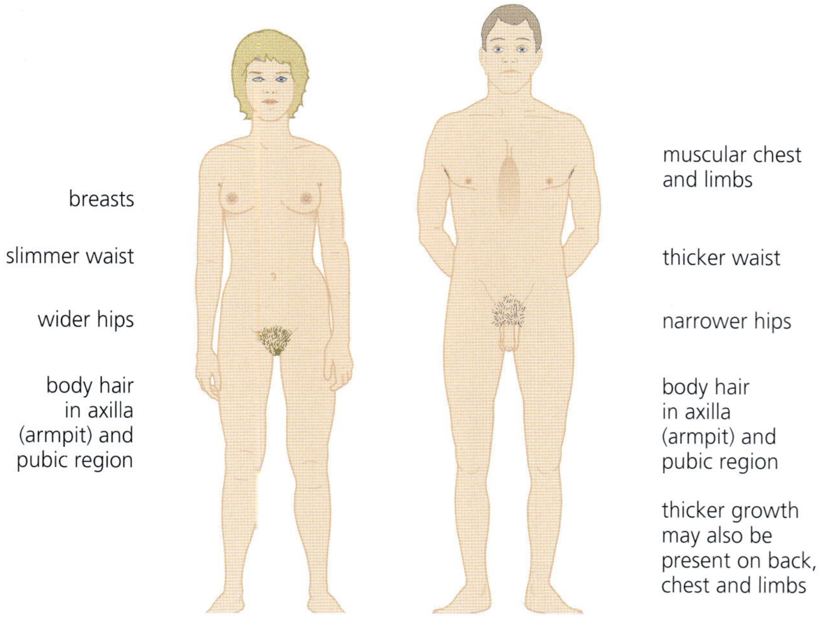

Typical male and female body shapes

Disorders of the endocrine system are caused by hypersecretion or hyposecretion of one or more hormones. These are discussed further in Chapter 9 in relation to electrical epilation services.

The reproductive system

Structure and function of the female and male external genitalia

Female external genitalia	*Description*
Labia major	Two large folds of skin composed of skin, fibrous tissue and fat. They have a high number of sebaceous glands. The lateral side is covered by pubic hair.
Labia minor	Two thin, smaller folds of skin found between the labia major.
Clitoris	Erectile tissue located above the opening of the vagina.
Vestibule	Area between the labia minor where the vaginal and urethra orifice and greater vestibule glands can be found.
Greater vestibule glands	These lie in the labia major, one on each side near the vaginal opening. They have ducts which secrete mucus to keep the vaginal area moist.
Vaginal orifice	The vagina opening found in the vestibule.
External urethral orifice	Part of the urinary system where urine is passed from.
Vulva	The collective name for the labia major, minor, clitoris and vaginal orifice
Mons pubis (pubic mound)	A fatty layer lying over pubic bone. At puberty, hair grows over this area
Anus	Opening at the end of the alimentary canal where faeces are discharged.

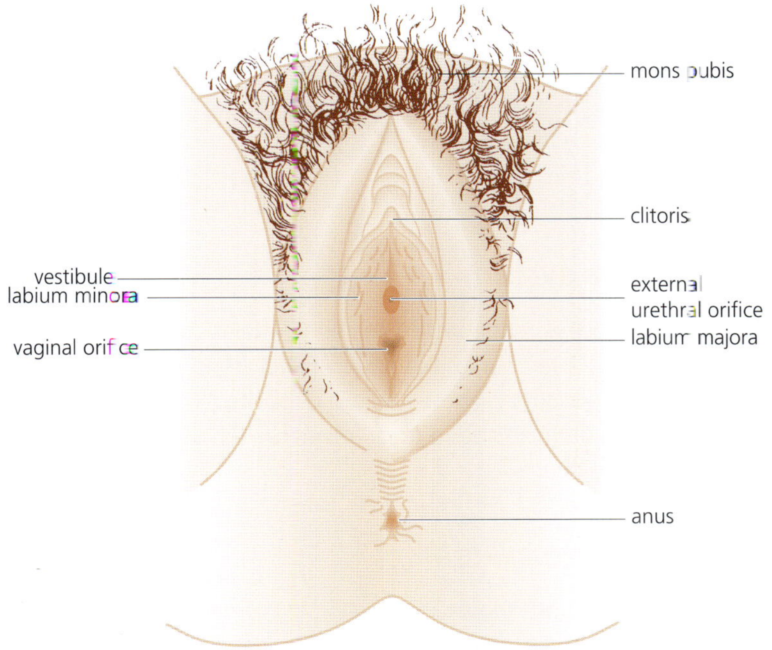

Female genitalia

Male external genitalia	*Description*
Penis	Formed of erectile tissue and involuntary muscle. The erectile tissue is supported by fibrous tissue and covered with skin.
Glans penis	Head of the penis which is triangular-shaped. A loose fold of skin called the foreskin covers and protects the head of the penis (this is absent in men that have been circumsized).
Scrotum	Skin that forms a sac-shaped pouch divided into two, each pouch containing one testis.
Testes or testicles	Two glands suspended in the scrotum surrounded by three layers of tissue. They contain interstitial cells that secrete the hormone testosterone and sperm responsible for reproduction.
Anus	Opening at the end of the alimentary canal where faeces are discharged.

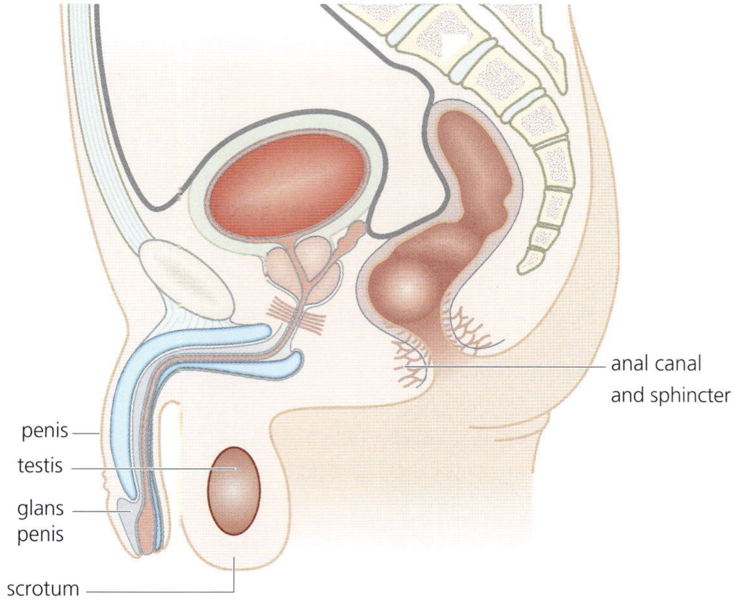

Male genitalia

Male reproductive system

Sperm are continually being made in the testes of males from puberty onwards. At ejaculation, during sexual intercourse, the sperm travel along the sperm duct, mix with secretions from the reproductive glands, and are deposited in the vagina of the female. To fertilize an ovum, one of these sperm must travel through the cervix and uterus to the oviduct and penetrate an ovum.

Female reproductive system

Ova or eggs are released from the ovary. Usually, in women of child-bearing age, one ovum is released approximately every 4 weeks. The ovum travels down the oviduct. This is where it may be fertilized if sexual intercourse has taken place and sperm are

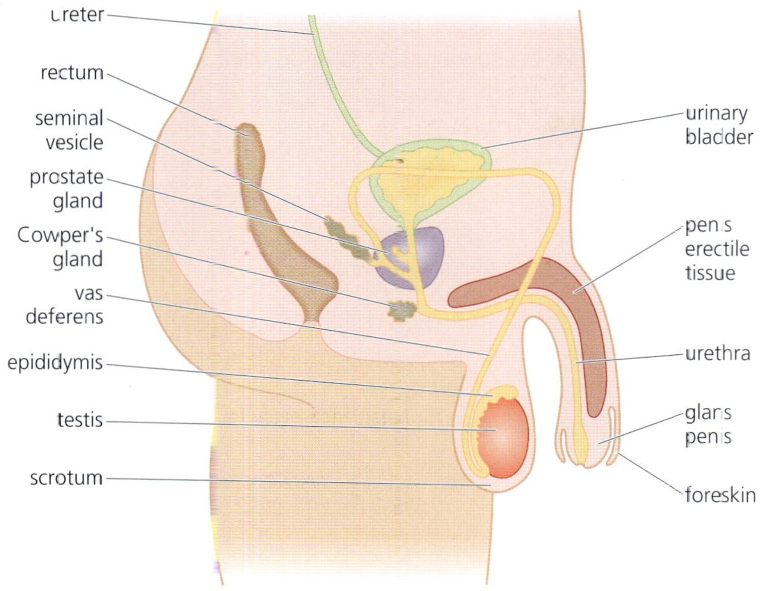

Male reproductive organs

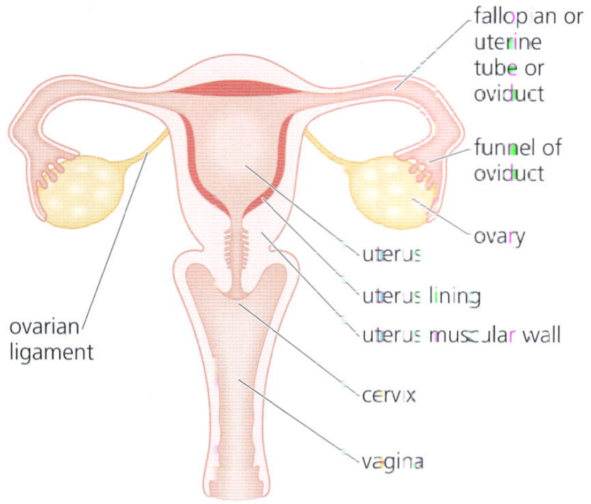

Female reproductive organs

present. A fertilized ovum embeds in the wall of the uterus where it will develop until birth in approximately 38 weeks. An unfertilized ovum will travel through the uterus and be shed with the next menstrual flow.

Menstruation This occurs from the onset of puberty until the menopause. Each menstrual cycle lasts on average for 28 days and involves changes in the ovaries and uterus controlled by hormones released from the ovary (oestrogen and progesterone) and from the pituitary gland (FSH and LH).

The menopause After the menopause the menstrual cycle ceases, ovaries become inactive and atrophy (shrink), and ovarian production of the hormones oestrogen and progesterone ceases. The other reproductive organs (uterus, vagina, oviducts, breasts) also begin to atrophy. Bones become more brittle. Blood cholesterol levels and the risk of suffering a heart attack increase. Hormone replacement therapy (HRT) delays these changes.

Female reproductive disorders

- **Amenorrhoea** the absence of menstruation. Extreme weight changes or excessive exercise can inhibit menstruation. People suffering from anorexia or taking part in strenuous athletic training often find that their periods stop.
- **Dysmenorrhoea:** painful menstruation. This may be due to reproductive disorders but also affects young adults while the hormone changes affecting menstruation and the response by reproductive organs are becoming fully established.
- **Ovarian cysts** a cyst is a fluid-filled swelling. Ovarian cysts are common and often without symptoms. They can, however, become infected, twist and cause pain, bleed, or grow to an uncomfortable size causing swelling of the abdomen.
- **Pre-menstrual tension:** a collection of symptoms which appear a few days before the onset of menstruation each month when progesterone levels are high. Symptoms may include headaches, irritability, fluid retention and sore breasts.

The breasts The main function of the breasts or mammary glands is to produce milk for the offspring. The glandular tissue of the breast is similar to that found in sweat glands. The milk-secreting cells (acini) are embedded in connective tissue and arranged as lobules separated by adipose (fat) tissue. The amount of adipose tissue present determines the size of the breast. Milk is produced under the influence of the hormone prolactin and passes through ducts to the nipple. It is ejected during breast-feeding in response to the hormone **oxytocin**, produced as the baby starts to suckle. Oxytocin also causes uterine contractions, so breast-feeding can help the uterus return to its normal size more quickly following birth.

The breasts lie over the pectoral and serratus anterior muscles. They are attached to them by a layer of connective tissue. Strands of connective tissue called suspensory ligaments run through the breast tissue, anchoring the skin to the connective tissue layer covering the muscles. This support is relatively fragile.

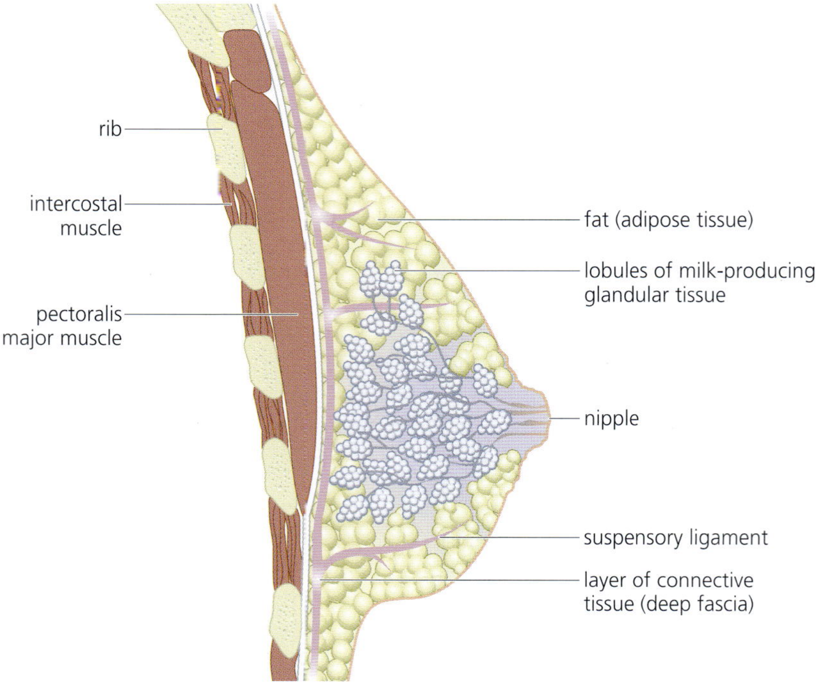

Vertical section showing breast tissues

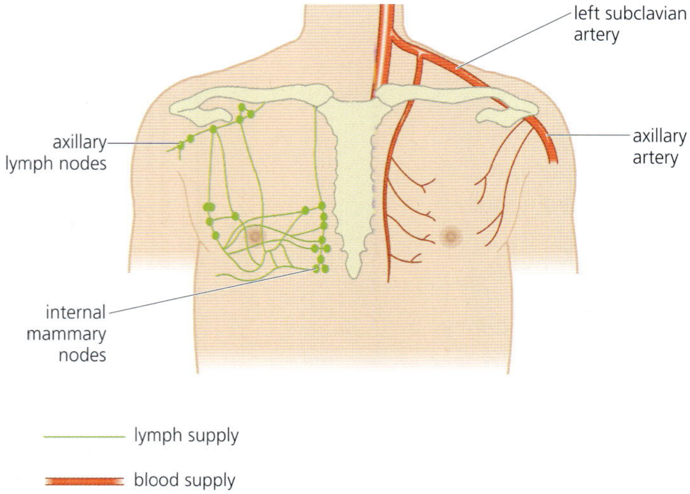

Lymph and blood supply to breast area

Breast tumours Breast tumours are felt as lumps in the breast tissue. Benign tumours are very common. They remain only in the breast and can be removed easily by minor surgery. Cysts are hollow tumours containing fluid. Fibroadenomas feel firm and rubbery.

Malignant tumours occur in breast cancer. A malignant tumour can spread quickly and easily to other tissues of the body when small parts of it break off and travel via the lymph system (metastasis). Early detection and treatment is vital. It is rarely painful so any breast changes including thickening, swelling, lumps, dimpling of the skin, nipple changes, discharge, scaliness or skin irritation should be reported to a doctor.

Ageing

Ageing is associated with a loss of body cells. Cells reproduce more slowly, die more quickly and malfunction more often. This means that all body tissues and organ systems deteriorate and the body responds less well in all situations. The maximum force generated by a muscle decreases by 30–40 per cent between the ages of 30 and 80 years, and muscles adapt less easily to increased activity. (In a young person, muscle performance improves rapidly in response to training.)

Reproductive function decreases with age. This is a gradual process in men as testosterone secretion slowly declines from about the age of 40; in women the changes are more dramatic. The menopause occurs around the age of 50. Menstruation stops and there is a significant decline in the amount of oestrogen circulating in the body. Reproductive organs, including breast tissue, start to atrophy (shrink). There is also a loss of bone mass. Connective tissues become less elastic, affecting skin, blood vessels, ligaments and even the lens of the eye.

ASSESSMENT OF KNOWLEDGE AND UNDERSTANDING

FUNCTIONAL SKILLS

You have now learnt about the related anatomy and physiology for the beauty therapy units with an essential knowledge requirement.

To test your level of knowledge, answer the following short questions. These will prepare you for your summative (final) assessment.

1 Make a large, labelled diagram to show the structure of the skin. Include on your diagram the five layers of the epidermis, a hair follicle, sweat and sebaceous glands, nerve endings and capillaries.

2 Describe the connective tissue of the dermis.

3 Which structures are found beneath the dermis?

4 What is the endocrine system?

5 Name the three main types of blood vessels.

6 Which type of blood vessel carries blood away from the heart?

7 Why do veins have valves?

8 Why do all cells in the body need a blood supply?

9 Where does lymph come from and where does it go?

10 Name the lymph nodes on this diagram.

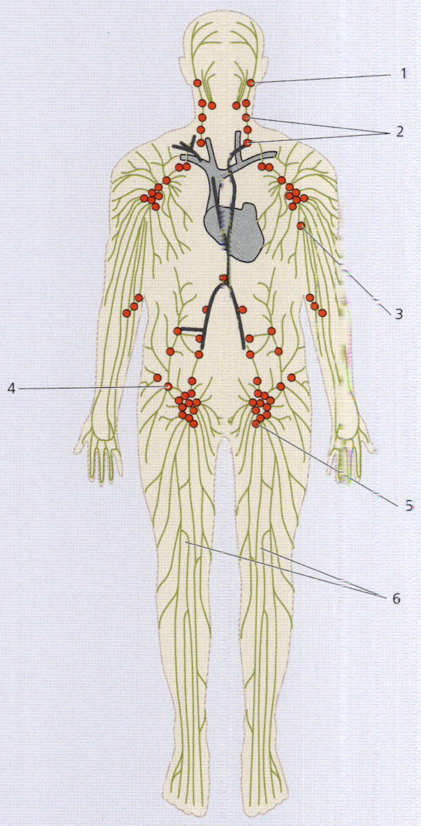

11 a Describe erythema.
b What are its possible causes?

12 Label the organs on this diagram of the digestive system.

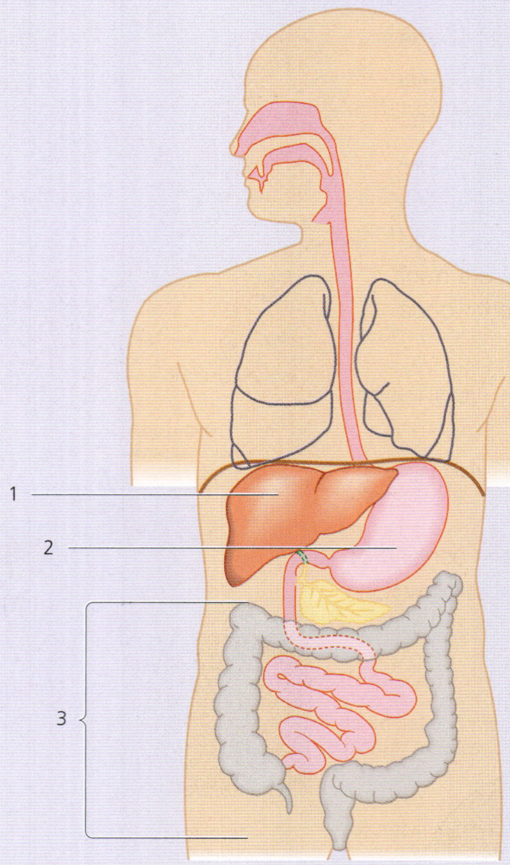

13 **a** Label the kidneys and bladder on this diagram of the urinary system.

b What is the function of each?

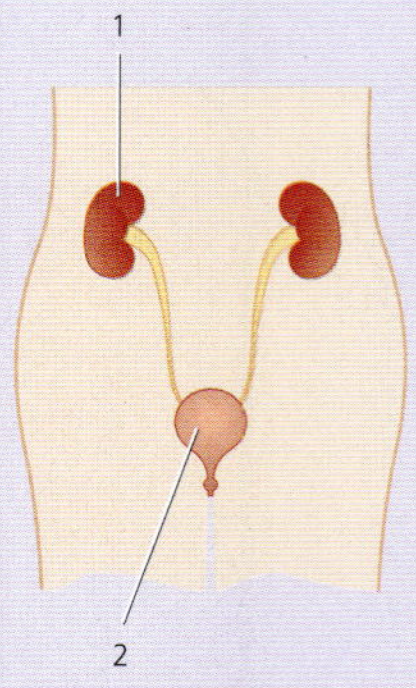

14 In which areas of the body would you find each of the following bones? tibia, carpal, vertebra, sternum, scapula, humerus, clavicle, femur, phalange, cranium.

15 **a** In which areas of the body would you find each of the following muscles? deltoid, gastrocnemius, pectorals, hamstrings, tibialis anterior, gluteals, quadriceps, rectus abdominus, latissimus dorsi.

b State an action for each.

16 How is a tendon different from a ligament?

17 Describe the structure of voluntary muscle tissue.

18 What is meant by muscle tone and how can tone be lost or improved?

19 Name the type of joint found (a) in the cranium, (b) at the hip, (c) at the elbow.

20 At a synovial joint, what are the functions of the synovial fluid, ligaments and articular cartilage?

21 How do nerve impulses pass along nerve fibres?

22 How do nerves stimulate muscles to contract?

23 What is meant by the autonomic nervous system?

24 Name the main organs on the diagram of the respiratory system.

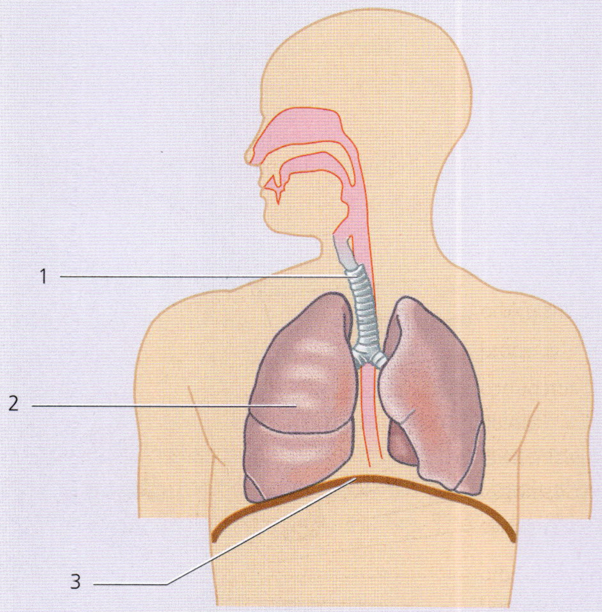

25 Where are the olfactory bulbs situated and what is their function?

26 Which area of the brain interprets the sensation of smell?

27 What is the importance of the limbic system to a beauty therapist using pre-blended massage oils?

28 **a** Name the organs of the endocrine system on the diagram.

b Name the hormones produced by each.

c What effect does each hormone have in the body?

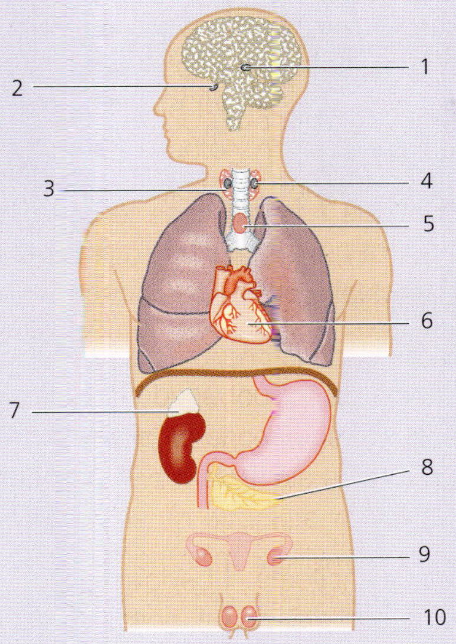

29 Name the female external genitalia where pubic hair may be removed from when performing intimate waxing using medical terminology.

30 Name the male external genitalia where pubic hair may be removed from when performing intimate waxing using medical terminology.

31 Name the **three** stages of the hair growth cycle.

32 State the difference between vellus hair and terminal.

33 Referring to the cross-section of the hair follicle below, briefly describe the name and function of each of the numbered areas.

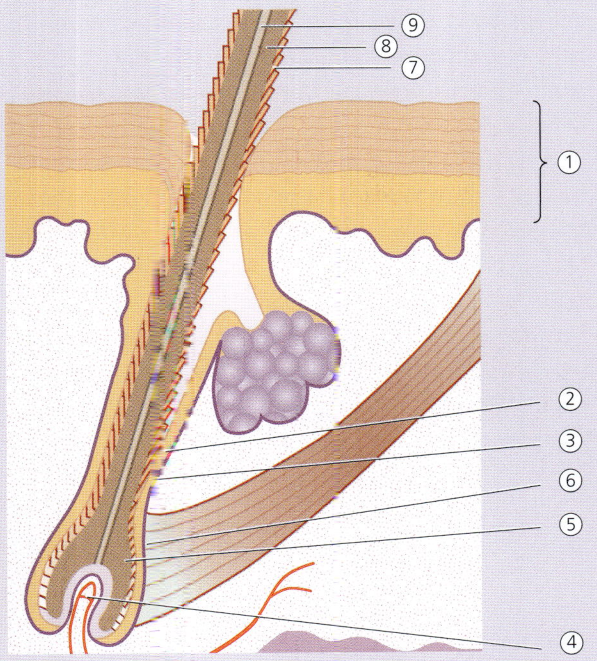

34 Why is knowledge of the hair growth cycle important when applying single eyelash extensions?

35 Name the parts of the eye labelled and briefly explain their function.

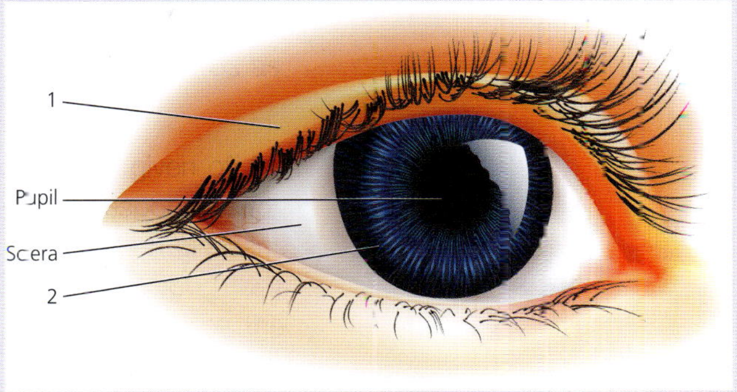

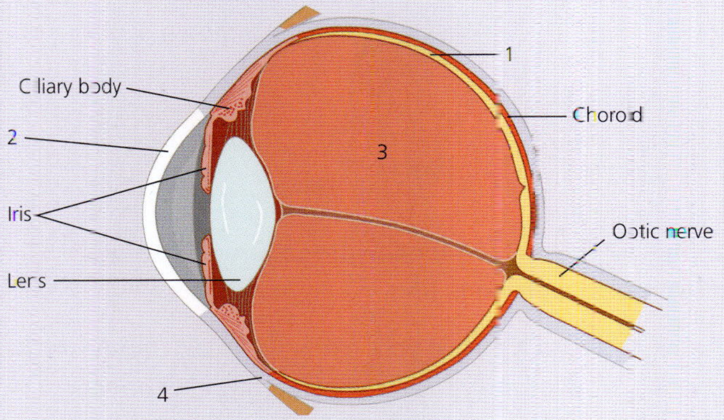

36 What physical affect can single eyelash extension application have on the eye itself?

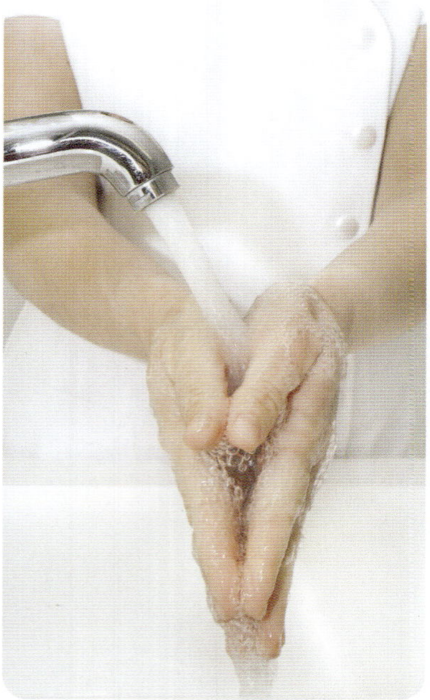

ISTOCK/RICH LEGG

3 Monitoring safe work operations

Learning Objectives

This chapter covers the **Monitor procedures to safely control work operations unit**.

This unit is all about how in your role as a senior beauty therapist you have a duty to ensure safe working practice is complied with by yourself and colleagues at all times. This is to guarantee the safety of all staff and also any visitors to the workplace premises.

The chapter covers health and safety legislative law, duties and responsibilities that you must implement and check for compliance, taking appropriate action when necessary.

There are **two** learning outcomes for this unit which you must achieve competently:

1. **Check that health and safety instructions are followed.**
2. **Make sure that risks are controlled safely and effectively.**

Health and safety practice should be considered at all times within all areas of competence.

ROLE MODEL

Janice Brown

Director, HOF Beauty (House of Famuir Ltd)

"My career journey has taken me from working in (and later managing) a group of salons, through sales, teaching, training, research and development. I am currently Director of HOF Beauty Ltd. Along the way I have specialized in electrolysis and hair removal. I am the co-author of the *Encyclopaedia of Hair Removal*, along with Gill Morris. I am proud to say that I have been able to make a real difference to people's lives by helping to correct skin, body and hair growth issues. I hope I have also been able to inspire and encourage fellow beauty therapists through the training I have provided. In the course of my career I have been fortunate enough to travel the world and work with wonderful people. Beauty therapy for me is not only a career but a true passion.

Taking care of all in the workplace

When working in a service industry, you are legally obliged to provide a **safe and hygienic environment**. This applies wherever you are working in a hotel, a spa, a leisure centre or a private beauty salon, or operating a freelance beauty therapy service. You must pay careful attention to health and safety to minimize risk. Exactly the same is true when working in clients' homes: it is essential to follow the required health and safety guidelines, just as you would when working in the beauty workplace.

Your role in health and safety practice at Level 3 is that you are responsible in a supervisory capacity to check that all statutory and workplace practices are in place, being complied with and carried out correctly on a daily basis. Workplace practices are all activities, procedures and use of resources that are carried out by staff in the workplace.

You have the responsibility for having

- current knowledge of all relevant health and safety legislation and any updates
- an understanding of identifying and eliminating risks in the workplace
- an awareness of the current health and safety training provided and future requirements
- that all health and safety legislative documentation is recorded as required and is available for audit

To ensure staff are kept informed and follow health and safety procedures you can:

- have health and safety as an agenda item at your staff meetings
- obtain and display current health and safety posters to keep health and safety in high profile
- provide on-going training and ensure staff have access to health and safety update training when necessary
- challenge any non-compliance issue if observed – health and safety practice is not optional!

ISTOCK/© MARTIN PURMENSKY

At Level 3 you may be responsible for training your staff in health and safety law and ensuring their compliance

HSE

Bad Hand Day: Campaign to raise awareness of work-related dermatitis. Pioneered by Habia

Outcome 1: Check that health and safety instructions are being followed within the work areas

Learn how to check that health and safety instructions are being followed:

1. Keep up-to-date with health and safety regulations and workplace instructions, making sure that information is from reliable sources.
2. Conduct your monitoring of workplaces at agreed intervals and in accordance with workplace instructions.
3. Confirm that worker health and safety competence is up-to-date.
4. Confirm that the health and safety training needs of other people have been identified and met.
5. Effectively communicate workplace instructions to other people and obtain feedback from them.

(Continued) Learn how to check that health and safety instructions are being followed:

6. Respond promptly to any breaches of health and safety instructions in a way which meets workplace and legal requirements.
7. Make recommendations for changes to workplace instructions to the responsible people.
8. Maintain records relating to health and safety matters that:
   - comply with legal and workplace requirements
   - are accessible to those who are authorized to use them

Outcome 2: Make sure that risks are controlled safely and accurately

Learn how to control risks to health and safety through ensuring safe working practice by:

1. Keep accurate and legible records of workplace risks identified or reported to you.
2. Report the existence of hazards in accordance with workplace health and safety instructions.
3. Confirm that appropriate precautions to control these risks have been agreed with the people responsible for health and safety.
4. Confirm that the precautions are in accordance with legal and workplace health and safety instructions.
5. Check that other people are aware of the risks and know the actions to be taken to minimize them.
6. Review the operational controls to make sure that workplace hazards are eliminated or controlled.
7. Report promptly and accurately any conflicts which still exist between workplace and legal requirements to the people responsible for health and safety.

ALWAYS REMEMBER

Safely controlling risks

Employees must work together to provide a safe and healthy workplace. As soon as a **hazard** is observed (anything that has potential to cause harm), this must be dealt with dependant upon the level of responsibility or reported to the designated authority so that the problem can be put right preventing a risk. A risk is the likelihood of potential harm from that hazard happening.

Legal responsibilities

If you cause harm to your client, or put them at risk, you will be held responsible and you will be liable to **prosecution**, with the possibility of being fined.

As a senior member of staff you will be required to implement and monitor health and safety for everyone.

FUNCTIONAL SKILLS

There is a good deal of **legislation** relating to health and safety. You will need to know about the laws relating to beauty therapy. Details are widely available, and you must be aware of your responsibilities and your rights. It is important that you obtain and read all relevant publications from your local Health and Safety Executive (HSE) office. The HSE provides guidance and information on all aspects of health and safety legislation.

This chapter looks at the current legislation relating to your workplaces working practices.

In addition, as the standards setting body for beauty therapy, the hair and beauty industry authority, Habia, provides health and safety working guidelines and legislative requirements. **Codes of practice** are also available from Habia, sharing best and mandatory working practice approved by both industry experts and health and safety advisors. Approved codes of practice are recognized by the HSE.

Ensure that health and safety information and any updates are obtained from a reliable source such as the HSE, your local authority and Habia.

ACTIVITY

CTIONAL SKILLS

Know your responsibilities – keep up-to-date

Health and safety information is continually updated. Write to your local Health and Safety Executive office, the body appointed to support and enforce health and safety law, to ask for a pack of relevant health and safety information, or visit their websites, **www.hse.gov.uk** and **www.hsedirect.gov.uk**. Legislation relevant to business operation can also be found in the Health and Safety pack for salons.

Visit Habia.org to research current beauty therapy health and safety legislation and minimum compliance standards.

The Health and Safety at Work Act (1974)

The **Health and Safety at Work Act (1974) (HASAWA 1974)** is continually reviewed with the introduction of new legislation as necessary. It is the main piece of legislation for this area. It lays down the minimum standards of health, safety and welfare required in each area of the workplace – Approved Codes of Practice (ACOP) are provided that detail the expected standards for compliance. It is the employer's legal responsibility to implement the Act and to ensure that, so far as is reasonably practicable, they manage the health and safety at work of the people for whom they are responsible and of those who may be affected by the work they do. Your role is to implement these requirements within your job responsibilities.

Officers from the Health and Safety Executive (HSE) or your Local Authority (LA) enforce health and safety law by visiting the workplace to check compliance with all relevant health and safety legislation. If non-compliance or any area of dangerous work practice is identified, an improvement notice issued and it is the responsibility of the employer to remove this danger within a designated period of time. Failure to comply with the notice will lead to prosecution. A business can be forced to stop providing a particular product or service or closed completely until all danger to employees/clients has been removed. Such workplace closure involves the issuing of a prohibition notice.

Each employee will have a job description. This specifies the main purposes and functions expected within a job. This will include expected standards, including health and safety operations. A good health and safety education will help you meet the required responsibilities to make staff aware of health and safety legislation to be adhered to and workplace practices to be adopted. The Health and Safety at Work Act covers many other smaller health and safety regulations which are also discussed.

Check the following health and safety induction activities have been covered for each staff member, examples include:

- read and understand the workplace health and safety policy
- know who to inform if there is any health and safety hazard issue they cannot resolve within their level of authority

TOP TIP

Guidance

Health and safety resource packs are available from Habia, providing guidance in implementing health and safety policy and legislation in the beauty therapy workplace.

ACTIVITY

Workplace health and safety rules

Identify the rules, practices and procedures that apply to you in your workplace's health and safety policy. The health and safety policy identifies how health and safety is managed, who does what, when and why.

HEALTH & SAFETY

The Health and Safety Information for Employees Regulations (1989) (HSIER 1989): Health and safety notice

Every employer is obliged by law to display the health and safety law poster in the workplace. This explains the responsibilities of employees, what actions to take if a health and safety problem arises and employment rights. A leaflet is available called *Your health and safety – a guide for workers*. Both poster and leaflet are available from the HSE. The poster and leaflet were updated in 2009 to reflect the main changes in health and safety legislation.

“Clients have a vast choice of salons, so by creating the right atmosphere, giving excellent service and paying attention to detail you will encourage the client to return to YOU.

Janice Brown

- have received a copy of the Health and Safety Law leaflet or have been referred to the location of the Health and Safety Law poster
- are aware of where health and safety guidance publications are stored
- emergency procedure training, i.e. action to take in the event of a fire
- first aid and accident procedures including who to inform
- manual handling best practice techniques and correct use of display screen equipment
- COSHH guidance
- personal protective equipment requirements

Health and Safety (Information for Employees) Regulations (1989)

The regulations require the employer to provide employees with health and safety information in the form of posters, notices and leaflets. The Health and Safety Executive provides relevant publications.

Each employer of more than five employees must formulate a written **health and safety policy** for their business. Habia have resources providing guidance on creating a written policy. The policy must be issued and discussed with each employee at induction and outlines the health and safety responsibilities they should undertake. It should also include items such as:

- details of the storage of chemical substances
- details of the stock cupboard or dispensary
- details and records of the checks made by a qualified electrician on specialist electrical equipment
- names and addresses of the keyholders
- escape routes and emergency evacuation procedures
- whom to report emergencies and significant risks to
- health and safety training should also be recorded once carried out

The health and safety policy should be reviewed regularly to ensure it meets all relevant legislation guidelines, including updates.

Regular health and safety checks should be made and procedures reviewed to ensure that safety is being satisfactorily maintained.

Health and safety rules and regulations and examples of compliance to be displayed include:

- the fire evacuation procedures
- Public Liability Insurance certificate
- Health and Safety (Information for Employees) Regulations (1989) poster updated April 2009
- health and safety policy (dependent upon employee numbers)
- risk assessment records and guidance
- COSHH assessment records and guidance
- first aid records and guidance

BEST PRACTICE

It is good practice to have a health and safety information file storing all current information including any updates to legislation.

HEALTH & SAFETY

Lone workers

If you are self-employed and work alone, consider your safety. Guidance is provided in *Working alone in safety – controlling the risks of solitary work*, INDG73(rev).

HEALTH & SAFETY

An example of the need to be responsive to safe working conditions and practices is the no-smoking legislation in the workplace introduced on 1 July 2007.

SHUTTERSTOCK/ SUSAN MONTGOMERY

No smoking sign

BEST PRACTICE

Provide regular training

Ensure staff know how to deal with low-risk hazards within their responsibility, following workplace policy and legal requirements.

Hazard examples include:

- obstructions to corridors, stairways and fire exits
- spillages and breakages

Obstructions An obstruction is anything that blocks the traffic route in the salon work environment. In an emergency, such as a fire, an obstruction could delay people leaving the building, cause injury or prevent the emergency services entering the premises. All staff should be trained in the importance of keeping walkways and doorways clear at all times.

Spillages and breakages Any breakage or spillage should be dealt with immediately and in the correct way. For example, breakage of glass can cause cuts, while spillages may cause somebody to slip and fall.

You must determine whether the spillage is a potential hazard to health and what action is necessary.

Staff should know who to report it to, what equipment must be used to remove the spillage and how the materials should be disposed of.

COSHH data should always be checked to confirm how the product should be handled and disposed of.

Reporting of Injuries, Diseases and Dangerous Occurrences Regulations (RIDDOR) (1995) RIDDOR requires the reporting and recording of work-related deaths and serious major injuries, cases of diagnosed industrial disease and certain 'dangerous occurrences' (near miss accidents) to the HSE. Employers, the self-employed and those in a position of control for the workplace, in cases where employees or trainees suffer personal injury at work, notification their HSE. Cases where employees suffer personal injury resulting in seven consecutive days' absence from work (including non-working days) requires notification within 15 days of the initial incident. When this occurrence results in death, major injury or more than 24 hours in hospital, it must be reported by telephone immediately, followed by a written report on the appropriate HSE documentation, within 10 days of it happening. In all cases where personal injury occurs, an entry must be made in the workplace accident book. It is a legal requirement to keep an accident book. Where visitors to the work premises, such as clients, are injured and taken to hospital, this must be reported also. This information assists the HSE in investigation of serious accidents.

HEALTH & SAFETY

Breakages and spillages

When dealing with hazardous breakages and spillages, the hands should always be protected with gloves. To avoid injury to others, broken glass should be put in a secure container prior to disposing of it in a waste bin in compliance with the Controlled Waste Regulations (1992).

First aider competence

This requires all staff in charge of and administering first aid to hold valid first aid qualifications.

If there is not a qualified first aider, there ideally should be an appointed person who will take responsibility if an accident occurs.

Injury prevention

The recording of accidents enables the HSE to identify risks and advise on how these can be prevented in the future.

ACTIVITY

Hazard rating

What would be a medium or high risk hazard? Give two examples of each. Remember the risk is the likelihood of potential harm from the hazard happening.

ISTOCK/© NICK SCHLAX

Any breakages or spillages must be cleaned up immediately

HSE

RIDDOR guide

TOP TIP

Riddor

If you are unsure if you need to report an incident, seek advice from the HSE who will make appropriate recommendations.

The HSE website provides guidance of what constitutes a reportable major injury, occupational disease and dangerous occurrence.

Also contact your insurance company if you think they need to be aware of a workplace injury incident.

HEALTH & SAFETY

HSE Five steps to risk assessment

Gain more information on how to access health and safety risks in the workplace. Look at the publication from the HSE – you can access a free version of the leaflet (INDG163) from the HSE website.

Certain work-related industrial diseases such as asthma and contact dermatitis are also reportable, but statements must be supported by the employee's GP. Dangerous workplace occurrences where there is no personal injury should also be reported, e.g. significant workplace structural damage.

A record of any reportable injury, disease or dangerous occurrence must be kept for 3 years after it happened in any appropriate form, i.e. accident book or computer. Include:

- the date, time and place
- how it was reported
- personal details of persons involved; and
- a brief description of the injury, disease or dangerous occurrence

The Management of Health and Safety at Work Regulations (1999) These require employers to make formal arrangements for maintaining and improving safe working conditions and practices under the Health and Safety at Work Act. This includes training for employees to ensure competency and the monitoring of risk in the workplace (including product use) that could cause harm on an ongoing basis, known as **risk assessment**, and performed by a competent staff member. This requires:

- identification of potential hazards
- an assessment of the potential risks associated with the hazard
- identifying who is at risk from the hazard
- identifying how risk is to be minimized or eliminated
- training staff to identify and control risks
- set up emergency procedures
- reviewing the risk assessment process regularly

When an employee becomes pregnant, the potential risks should be reviewed and appropriate action taken.

Where there are five or more people employed the Act this also includes a requirement to:

- introduce a health monitoring system, making the change if the risk assessment monitoring system identifies a need
- record the risk assessment details

Compliance with this Act will help to ensure that risks are controlled safely and effectively.

ACTIVITY

During the working week identify any hazards. For each one, identify the risk that could occur and what action needs to be taken to control this risk. If this is within your job role responsibility you could action this immediately, or if not you may need to pass it onto your employer.

Follow up this task by discussing your findings with your employer.

This is a compliance measure for the **Management of Health and Safety at Work Regulations (1999)**.

Date	*Hazard*	*Risk*	*Control action required/taken*

Young workers at risk When employing a young person under the age of 18, whether for work or work experience, employers have the same responsibilities for their health, safety and welfare as they do for other employees. There is a requirement to carry out a risk assessment for young people in the workplace if they are under school leaving age due to their immaturity and the associated risks that could occur. This must be formally recorded and kept.

Personal Protective Equipment (PPE) Regulations (2002) The **Personal Protective Equipment (PPE) Regulations (2002)** require employers to identify through a risk assessment those activities or processes which require special protective clothing or equipment to be worn. This clothing and equipment must then be made available, be suitable and in adequate supply. Employees must understand the reason and importance for using it, wear the protective clothing and use the protective equipment provided, and make employers aware of any shortage so that supplies can be maintained. Instructions should be provided on how the PPE should be used/worn to be effective.

PPE should be 'CE' marked, this indicates that it complies with the Personal Protective Equipment Regulations (2002), and satisfies basic safety requirements.

Workplace (Health, Safety and Welfare) Regulations (1992) The **Workplace (Health, Safety and Welfare) Regulations (1992)** cover a broad range of basic health, safety and welfare issues and require all at work to maintain a safe, healthy and secure working environment. These regulations aim to ensure the workplace meets the health, safety and welfare needs of all employees including those with disabilities, and accessibility should be made where practicable.

The Equality Act 2010 requires the access and facilities provided at the workplace premises must be equal for all, regardless of age, disability, gender reassignment, marriage and civil partnerships', pregnancy and maternity, race, religion or belief, sex or sexual orientation. The regulations include legal requirements in relation to the following aspects of the working environment:

- maintenance of the workplace and equipment in efficient working order
- adequate ventilation to ensure the air is changed regularly and hazardous vapours and materials are removed. Fresh air should be drawn from outside the workplace
- working temperature should be regulated by how physically demanding the work being carried out is. For work that is not severely physical, the temperature should be a minimum of 16°C for employees to be comfortable without requiring additional clothing. If the temperature becomes too high or too cold, temperature stress can be suffered
- lighting should be adequate to enable people to move safely and perform tasks competently
- cleanliness of furniture, equipment, furnishing and fittings and correct handling and disposal of waste materials
- floors and traffic routes should be of an even, safe surface to prevent trips and falls and strong enough for any weight they are required to support. Traffic routes should enable people to move easily. Dimension of doors and stairways are an important consideration, especially for disabled access
- safe workplace premises layout, and dimensions adequate for people to move about and for services being carried out
- windows, doors, gates and walls should be safe and fit for purpose

ACTIVITY

PPE risk assessment

Carry out your own risk assessment on risks of cross-infection by contamination. List the potentially hazardous substances that you may be required to handle. What protective clothing should be available?

ALWAYS REMEMBER

Training should be provided on the correct use and application of PPE and its use should be monitored. If not used the reason should be investigated as this then becomes a risk. Compliance should be monitored.

HEALTH & SAFETY

Gloves

If you are to come into contact with body tissue fluids or with chemicals, wear protective disposable surgical gloves. It has been proved that latex gloves can cause allergies, and in some cases asthma. An alternative choice of glove, i.e. nitrile or PVC formulation, should be selected that will provide adequate protection from contamination.

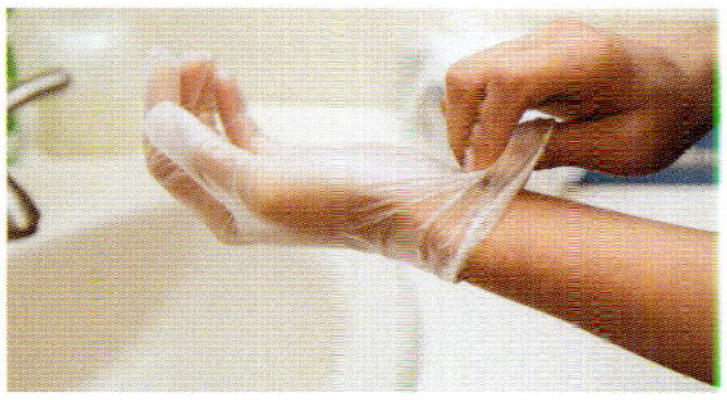

SHUTTERSTOCK/SANDHA VAN DER STEEN

Gloves – PPE resource used when carrying out wax depilation service

ALWAYS REMEMBER

Potentially hazardous substances include:

- aerosols – causing respiratory breathing difficulties
- disinfectants – causing chemical irritation to the skin
- water treatment chemicals used in the **spa pools** – causing eye or skin irritation
- false lashes adhesives – causing skin irritation and allergy
- body tissue fluids – causing skin infection and disease

HEALTH & SAFETY

Suitable rest facilities should be produced for pregnant women. They should be near sanitary facilities.

ACTIVITY

Moving objects in the workplace

Equipment or objects are often required to be moved on a daily basis. Identify three examples from your workplace and how best each item should be transported and handled safely.

TOP TIP

Safety when lifting and handling

When lifting, reduce the risk where possible; break up larger items into more manageable loads; lift from the knees, not the back. When carrying, balance weights evenly in both hands and carry the heaviest part nearest to your body.

HEALTH & SAFETY

Workplace regulations

FUNCTIONAL SKILLS

Obtain a copy of the *Workplace (Health & Safety & Welfare) Regulations 1992 HSE Approved Code of Practice.* Look through the code of practice guidelines, and ensure your workplace practice complies with the code.

- workstations should be suitable for people using them and the work being carried out. Adequate postural support should be provided
- Escalators and moving walkways should operate safely and have appropriate safely mechanism
- washing facilities with hot and cold running water should be available with hand detergent and a hygienic means of drying hands provided
- drinking water with adequate high quality supply and hygienically dispensed should be available.
- Facilities for changing and storage of clothing should be adequate and secure
- sanitary conveniences for all staff and clients should be suitable and sufficient. Males and females should have a separate room unless it can be used by only one person at a time and can be locked.
- fire exits should be clearly located and accessible and firefighting equipment available and maintained.

Manual Handling Operations Regulations (1992) The **Manual Handling Operations Regulations (1992)** apply in all occupations where manual lifting occurs, the aim being to prevent skeletal and muscular disorders and repetitive strain disorders due to poor working practice. The employer is required to carry out a risk assessment of all activities undertaken which involve manual lifting.

The risk assessment should provide evidence that the following have been considered:

- risk of injury
- the manual movement involved in performing the activity
- the physical constraint the load incurs
- the environmental constraints imposed by the workplace
- workers' individual capabilities
- action taken in order to minimize potential risks

Keep records of the risk assessment available for audit.

Manual lifting and handling Always take care of yourself when moving goods around the salon, assess the risk. Do not struggle or be impatient: get someone else to help.

ALWAYS REMEMBER

Temperature and lighting

The salon temperature should be a minimum of 16°C within 1 hour of employees arriving for work. The salon should be well ventilated, or carbon dioxide levels will increase, which can cause nausea. Many substances used in the salon can become hazardous without adequate ventilation. Where necessary, mechanical ventilation systems should be provided where windows offer inadequate ventilation. If the working environment is too warm, this can cause heat stress, a condition recognized by the HSE.

Lighting should be adequate to ensure that services can be carried out safely and competently, with the minimum risk of accident or injury.

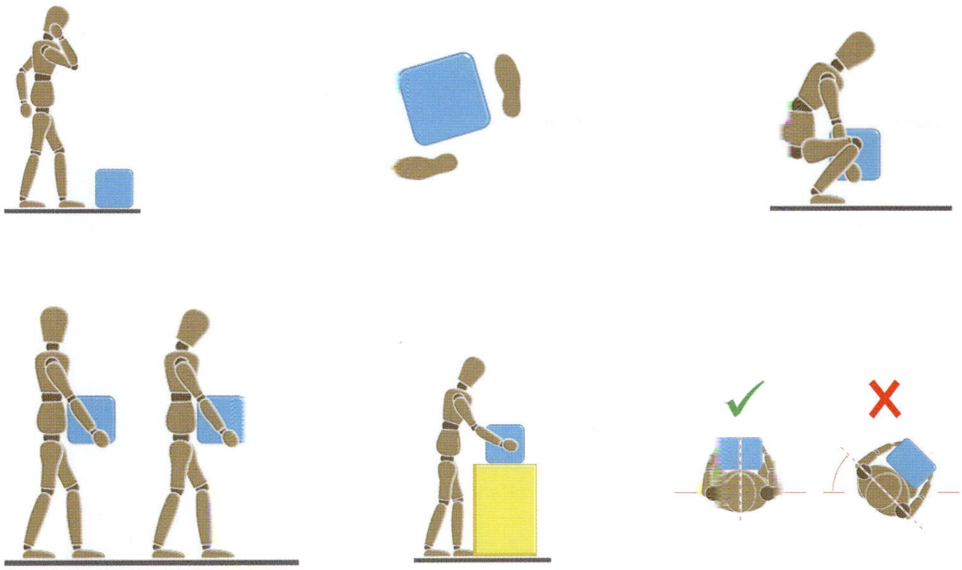

HMSO

Lifting and carrying

BEST PRACTICE

Unpacking deliveries

When you unpack a delivery, make sure the product packaging is undamaged, to avoid possible personal injury from broken goods. Wear PPE if the substance could be hazardous.

GETTY IMAGES/ PHILIP AND KAREN SMITH

Receptionists in the workplace often use a computer throughout the working day

Provision and Use of Work Equipment Regulations (PUWER) (1998) The **Provision and Use of Work Equipment Regulations (PUWER) (1998)** lay down the important health and safety controls on the provision and use of work equipment to prevent risk. They state the duties for employers and for users, including the self-employed. They affect both old and new equipment. They identify the requirements in selecting suitable equipment and in maintaining it. They also discuss the information provided by equipment manufacturers, and that adequate instruction and training in the safe use of equipment is provided. Specific regulations address the dangers and potential risks of injury that could occur during operation of the equipment.

Suitable safety measures should be in place, such as protective devices and warning signage as appropriate.

Health and Safety (Display Screen Equipment) Regulations (1992) The **Health and Safety (Display Screen Equipment) Regulations (1992)** cover the use of visual display units and computer screens. They specify acceptable levels of radiation emissions from the screen, and identify correct posture, seating position, permitted working heights and rest periods. Employers have a responsibility to comply with this regulation to ensure the welfare of their employees, avoiding the potential risks of eyestrain, mental stress and muscle fatigue.

> Always have a tidy work area and consider storage of clients' bags and clothes.
>
> **Janice Brown**

Control of Substances Hazardous to Health (COSHH) Regulations (2002) (as amended) The **Control of Substances Hazardous to Health (COSHH) Regulations (2002)** are designed to make employers consider the substances used in their workplace and assess their possible risks to health. Many substances that seem quite harmless can prove to be hazardous if used or stored incorrectly. Hazardous substances remember is anything that can harm your health.

Employers are responsible for assessing the risks from hazardous substances and controlling exposure to them to prevent ill health. Any hazardous substances identified must be formally recorded in writing and given a hazard risk rating. Safety precaution procedures should then be implemented and training given to employees to ensure that the procedures are understood and will be followed correctly.

ACTIVITY

COSHH risk assessment

Using the headings of the COSHH risk assessment, think of further hazards in the workplace, their risk, identify who could be at risk, the level of the risk and action to be taken to reduce the risk.

Step 1	Assess the risks.	Assess the risks to health from hazardous substances used in or created by your workplace activities.
Step 2	Decide what precautions are needed.	You must not carry out work which could expose your employees to hazardous substances without first considering the risks and the necessary precautions, and what else you need to do to comply with COSHH.
Step 3	Prevent or adequately control exposure.	You must prevent your employees being exposed to hazardous substances. Where preventing exposure is not reasonably practicable, then you must adequately control it (e.g. shampooing – wear non-latex gloves).
Step 4	Ensure that control measures are used and maintained.	Ensure that control measures are maintained properly and that safety procedures are followed.
Step 5	Monitor the exposure.	Monitor the exposure of employees to hazardous substances, if necessary.
Step 6	Carry out appropriate health surveillance.	Carry out appropriate health surveillance where your assessment has shown this is necessary or where COSHH sets specific requirements.
Step 7	Prepare plans and procedures to deal with accidents, incidents and emergencies.	Prepare plans and procedures to deal with accidents, incidents and emergencies involving hazardous substances, where necessary.
Step 8	Ensure employees are properly informed, trained and supervised.	You should provide your employees with suitable and sufficient information, instruction and training.

Process for undertaking COSHH risk assessment

HEALTH AND SAFETY FOR HAIRDRESSERS

COSHH RISK ASSESSMENT

habia
hair and beauty industry authority

Staff Member Responsible: Date: Review Dates:

Hazard	What is the risk?	Who is at risk?	Degree of risk High/Med/Low	Action to be taken to reduce/control risk
Aerosols (list aerosols used in your salon)	These can contain flammable gases and irritant chemicals. There is a risk of fire, explosion and intoxication.	Everyone in the salon, but in particular the user of the aerosol and the client.	Low	Look for aerosols with non-flammable gases if possible. Do not expose to temperatures above 50 C. Do not pierce or burn containers. Do not inhale.
Nail polish remover (list products used in your salon)	Irritant to the skin and eyes. Moderately toxic if swallowed or inhaled.	Beauty therapists, juniors, trainees and clients.	Medium	Store in a cool place. Reseal after use. Do not use on damaged or sensitive skin. Avoid breathing in. Never place in an unlabelled container.

EXAMPLE

 HSIP 2a HABIA

A COSHH risk assessment

Hazardous substances are usually identified through the use of known symbols, examples of which are shown on page 112. Any substance in the workplace that is hazardous to health must be identified on the packaging and stored and handled correctly.

Hazardous substances may enter the body via:

- the eyes
- the skin
- the nose **inhalation** – breathing in
- the mouth **ingestion** – swallowing
- piercing the skin

Each beauty product supplier is legally required to make available guidelines called material safety data sheets (MSDSs) on how materials should be used and stored; these will be supplied on request. When a product is 'dangerous for supply', i.e. with a hazard symbol, by law a safety data sheet must be provided.

REACH 2007 is a European Union Regulation concerning the:

Registration,

Evaluation,

Authorization; and restriction of,

CHemicals.

It operates alongside COSHH and is designed to improve the information provided by chemical manufacturers through the provision of adequate safety data sheets.

Cosmetic Products Enforcement Regulations (2013) This piece of legislation consolidates earlier regulations and incorporates current European Market Directives. Part of consumer protection legislation, it requires that cosmetics and toiletries are safe in their formulation and are safe for use for their intended purpose as a cosmetic before being placed on the market, and comply with labelling requirements, instructions for use and disposal.

It is an offence to supply cosmetic products that are likely to cause damage to human health.

Certain substances are prohibited, e.g. certain fragrances, preservatives and colourings. Specific labelling is required.

TOP TIP

Cosmetic Products (Safety) Regulations labelling information requirement includes

- The name and address of the supplier is required.
- The package must list the ingredients in descending order of weight.
- A best before date must be provided if there is an expiry date.
- Ingredients.
- The preservatives and UV filters used should be identified.
- The batch code must be shown.

ALWAYS REMEMBER

You need COSHH control measures that prevent risk and do so everyday – review your control measures regularly. Everybody must be familiar with the COSHH assessment risk reports in order that any risk is actively reduced.

C.O.S.H.H.
CONTROL OF SUBSTANCES HAZARDOUS TO HEALTH

Health and Safety Information for the Beauty Salon and Beauty Therapist.

Compiled by The Sterex Academy

Contents:

50 x Product assessment record forms
1 x 'How to' fill in/use your product assessment record forms
1 x Daily/monthly/quarterly/annual Check List
1 x Ellisons Booklet COSHH and the Beauty Salon

COSH

Sterex – COSHH leaflet available from beauty suppliers

TOP TIP

REACH

Further guidance can be found on the HSE website: www.hse.gov.uk/reach/.

ACTIVITY

Identifying hazards

Make a list of potential electrical hazards in the workplace, e.g. damaged plugs. Who would this be reported to?

HEALTH & SAFETY

COSHH assessment

All hazardous substances must be identified when completing the risk assessment. This includes cleaning agents such as a wax equipment cleaner. Where possible, high-risk products should be replaced with lower-risk products. The COSHH assessment should be reviewed on a regular basis, and updated to include any new products.

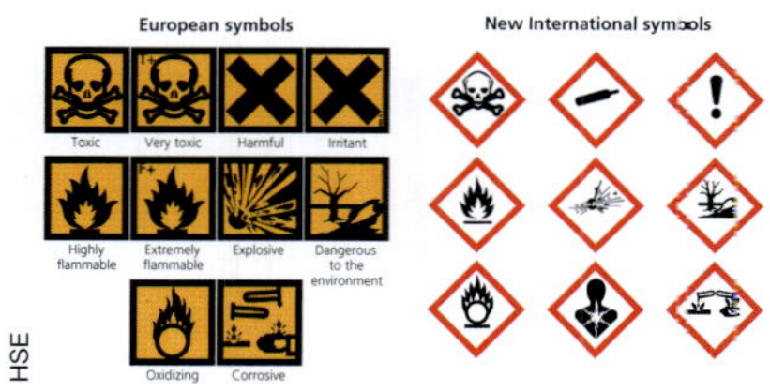

International hazard symbols

ACTIVITY

Hazard checklist

- Does any product that you use have a hazard symbol?
- Does any procedure you provide produce a hazardous substance, i.e. dust or fumes?
- Can the substance enter the body in any way?
- Currently is there a risk of injury or harm in how you use the product?
- What action do you need to take to change your current practice in the use of a product to prevent injury or harm?

HEALTH & SAFETY

COSHH

A COSHH essentials information document is available at www.coshh-essentials.org.uk. It covers a broad range of activities and provides advice for products that have data sheets.

HSE publication ISBN 9780717627851 gives details on COSHH assessment.

General COSHH Code of practice: Control of Substances Hazardous to Health regulations 2002 L5 (Sixth Edition) HSE Books, ISBN 9780717665822.

Electricity at Work Regulations (1989) The Electricity at Work Regulations (1989) cover the installation, maintenance and use of electrical equipment and systems in the workplace.

These regulations state that every piece of electrical equipment in the workplace should be tested every 12 months by a qualified electrician. This is called portable appliance testing or PAT. A written record of testing must be retained and made available for inspection.

In addition to annual testing, a trained member of staff should regularly check all electrical equipment for safety. This is recommended every 3 months. Records must be kept of the check, including:

- electrician's name/contact details
- itemized list of electrical equipment complete with each piece's unique serial number for identification purposes
- date of purchase/disposal
- date of inspection

Report on, remove from use and make safe as immediately as practicable any of these potential hazards:

- exposed wires in flexes
- cracked plugs or broken sockets
- worn cables
- overloaded sockets

Although it is the responsibility of the employer to ensure all equipment is safe to use, it is also the responsibility of the employee to always check that equipment is safe before use, and to never use it if it is faulty. This complies with the requirements of public liability insurance. Failure to do so could lead to an accident which could be considered careless or negligent.

Any pieces of equipment that appear faulty must be immediately checked and repaired before use. They should also be labelled to ensure that they are not used by accident.

Ensure all staff are trained in the procedure.

First aid Employers must have appropriate and adequate first aid arrangements in the event of an accident or illness occurring.

What is adequate first aid will depend upon each workplace and requires an assessment of first aid needs.

Detailed information can be found in the *Approval Code of Practice and Guidance: First Aid at Work*. The Health and Safety (First Aid) Regulations (1981).

It is recommended that at least one person holds an HSE approved basic first aid qualification.

All employees should be informed of the first aid procedures including:

- where to locate the first aid box
- who is responsible for the maintenance of the first aid box
- which staff member to inform in the event of an accident or illness occurring
- the staff member to inform in the event of an accident or emergency

The **Health and Safety (First Aid) Regulations (1981)** state that workplaces must have first aid provision. An adequately stocked first aid box should be available that complies with health and safety first aid regulations. This should contain a minimum level of first aid equipment.

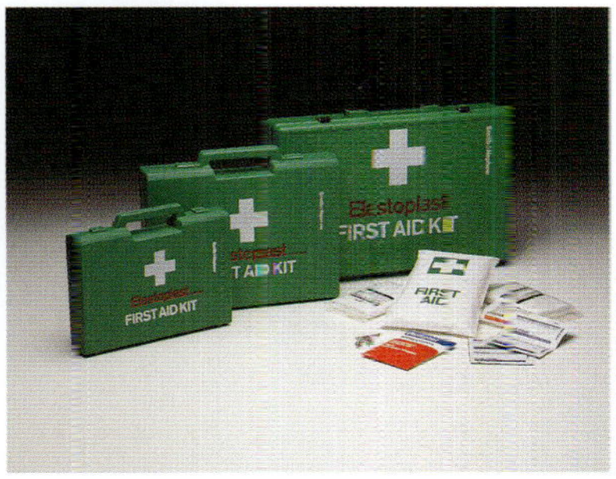
SMITH & NEPHEW, HULL

First aid kits

Contents of the first aid box

No. of employees	*1–5*	*6–10*	*11–50*
First aid guidance notes	1	1	1
Individual sterile adhesive dressings	20	20	40
Sterile eye pads	1	2	4
Sterile triangular bandages	1	2	4
Safety pins	6	6	12
Medium size sterile unmedicated dressings	3	6	8
Large size sterile unmedicated dressings	1	2	4
Extra-large size sterile unmedicated dressings	1	2	4

HEALTH & SAFETY

First aid

- This should only be given by a qualified first aider.
- A first aid certificate is only valid for 3 years and must be renewed after this period. This may mean additional first aid training.
- Know what action you can take *within your responsibility* in the event of an accident occurring.
- An accident book should be available to record details of any accident that has occurred.

TOP TIP

First Aid Booklet

HSE Guidance publication

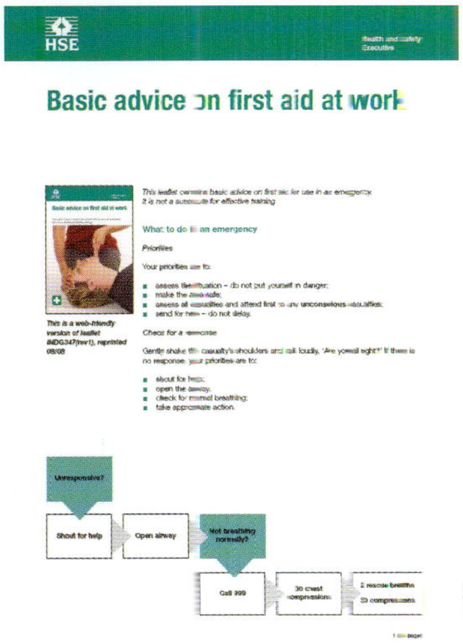

HSE

ISBN: 9780717665600

This can be stored in the first aid box.

Further examples of first aid procedure

Problem	*Action to be taken*
Casualty is not breathing	1 Immediately contact emergency services. Place the casualty on their back. Open and clear their mouth. Shout for help. 2 Tilt head backwards to open airway (maintain this position throughout). Support the jaw. 3 Kneel beside casualty, while keeping head backwards. Open mouth and pinch nose. 4 Open your mouth and take a deep breath. Seal mouth with yours and breathe firmly into it. Casualty's chest should rise. Remove your mouth and let their chest fall. If chest does not rise, check head is tilted sufficiently. Repeat at a rate of ten times a minute until the casualty is breathing alone. 5 Place them in the recovery position.
Unconscious	Immediately contact emergency services. Place into recovery position.
Severe bleeding	Immediately contact emergency services. Put on disposable non-latex gloves, then control by direct pressure using fingers and thumb on the bleeding point. Apply a dressing. Raising the bleeding limb (unless it is broken) will reduce the flow of blood.
Suspected broken bones	Immediately contact emergency services Do not move the casualty unless they are in a position which exposes them to immediate danger.
Burns and scalds (due to heat)	Do not remove clothing sticking to the burns or scalds. Do not burst any blisters. If burns and scalds are small, flush them with plenty of clean, cool water for ten minutes before applying a sterilized dressing. If burns and scalds are large or deep, wash your hands and apply a dry sterilized dressing. The casualty must be medically professionally attended to.
Burns (chemicals)	Avoid contaminating yourself with the chemical. Remove any contaminated clothing that is not stuck to skin. Flush area with plenty of cool water. Apply a sterilized dressing and the casualty must be medically professionally attended to.
Foreign body in eye	Wash out eye with clean, cool water or sterile fluid in a sealed container. A person with an eye injury should be sent to hospital with the eye covered with an eye pad. Never attempt to remove the foreign body.
Chemicals in eye	Wash out the open eye continuously with clean, cool water for 10–15 minutes gently holding the eyelid open. A person with an eye injury should be sent to hospital with the eye covered with an eye pad.
Electric shock	Don't touch the casualty until the current is switched off. If the current cannot be switched off, stand on some dry insulating material and use a wooden or plastic implement to free the casualty from the electrical source. If breathing has stopped start mouth-to-mouth breathing and continue until the casualty starts to breathe by themself or until professional help arrives.
Gassing	Use suitable protective equipment. Move casualty to fresh air. If breathing has stopped start mouth-to-mouth breathing and continue until the casualty is breathing themself or until professional help arrives. Send to hospital with a note of the gas involved.
Minor injuries	Casualties with minor injuries of a nature they would normally attend to themselves may wash their hands, wear single-use disposable non-latex (synthetic) powder-free gloves if necessary and apply a small sterilized dressing to the area from the first aid box. Keep wounds clean and dry.

Accidents Accidents in the workplace usually occur through negligence by employees or unsafe working conditions.

Any accidents occurring in the workplace must be recorded on a **report form**, and entered into an **accident book**. Incidents in the accident book should be reviewed regularly to see where improvements to working practice can be made. The report form requires more details than the accident book – you must note down:

- the date and time of accident
- the date of entry into the accident book
- the name of the person or people involved
- the accident details
- the injuries sustained
- the action taken
- what happened to the person immediately afterwards (e.g. went home or to hospital)
- name and address of the person providing service should be entered into the accident book
- the signature of the person making the entry

In the instance of an accident, first aid should only be administered by employees qualified to do so.

Disposal of waste All **waste** and litter should be disposed of in an enclosed waste bin fitted with a polythene bin liner, durable enough to resist tearing. The bin should be regularly disinfected in a well-ventilated area: wear protective gloves while doing this. Hazardous waste must be disposed of following the COSHH procedures and training by the employer.

Clinical waste Clinical (contaminated) waste is waste derived from human tissues; this includes blood and tissue fluids. This should be disposed of as recommended by the environment agency in accordance with the Controlled Waste (Amendment) Regulations (1993). Items which have been used in the skin, such as needles, should be safely discarded in a disposable **sharps container**. Again, contact your environmental health department to check on disposal arrangements.

Environmentally friendly working practices Being environmentally friendly, also known as 'eco friendly' or 'green', means that you consider how you can help to minimize harm to the environment and put this into practice in your everyday working practice. Consider the following changes:

- use biodegradable packaging for disposal of non-contaminated waste
- for hospitality drinks, rather than disposable plastic cups revert back to cups and glasses that can be washed
- dispose of chemicals safely, not down the sinks
- use wooden spatulas from sustainable wood sources
- use recycled consumable materials where possible, i.e. bed-roll, tissues and cleaning products
- use light bulbs that minimize energy use
- switch off lights in rooms not being used and also equipment when not in use – if safe to do so
- turn down the heating thermostat rather than opening windows, this will save money too

HSE

HSE accident book

ACTIVITY

Accidents

Discuss potential causes of accidents in the workplace. How could these accidents be prevented?

When would you report an accident or injury in the workplace?

ALWAYS REMEMBER

Control measures to prevent risk must be complied with consistently:

- good cleanliness
- appropriate consent procedures according to local guidance
- sterilization and disinfection procedures followed

Training must be adequate and constantly monitored for compliance.

ALWAYS REMEMBER

Each local authority is able to introduce its own bye-laws under the Miscellaneous Provisions Act.

Always check the bye-laws of your local authority.

ACTIVITY

Obtain a copy of your local authority bye-laws for skin piercing. Note the recommendations and check your compliance.

ACTIVITY

Noise levels

Assess the noise level at your workplace. Are there any interfering noise levels to normal communication, e.g. do voices need to be raised?

Is any equipment noisy? How long is this used for?

Can the risk, if identified, be controlled?

HSE

Noise at work guidance booklet

ACTIVITY

Fire drill

Each workplace should have a fire drill regularly. This enables staff to practise so that they know what to do in the event of a real fire. What is the fire drill procedure for *your* workplace?

- buy in bulk, reducing trips to the wholesaler and buy locally
- recycle your waste and packaging where possible, use colour-coded waste bags that are of course made from recycled materials
- recycle used printer cartridges
- some beauty companies will provide a free product on the return of a used product packaging

Small steps can make a big difference.

ALWAYS REMEMBER

Waste Electronic and Electrical Equipment Regulations (2007)

These regulations place duties on manufacturers, importers, retailers and salons to ensure the safe disposal of electrical products. Unwanted items must be disposed of at registered sites which are able to accept electrical waste. Reputable retailers may belong to the national 'take back scheme' and dispose of your items for you when you are replacing them with new.

Control of Noise at Work Regulations (2005)

- Loud noise can damage hearing. Noise is measured in decibels (db). A-weighting is sometimes written as 'dB(A)' which is average noise level. C-weighting is 'dB(C)' noise which is at its highest point, i.e. explosive.
- As an employer, a safe working environment should be provided, therefore noise levels should be kept within safe levels, this does not include low-level noise.
- At all workplace practices there is a duty to assess any risks in the workplace, in this case noise levels. If a risk is identified, action should be taken to correct it. This could be PPE hearing protection to be worn if you work in a noisy environment at any time in your work role.
- Information, instruction and training must be provided, which is monitored.

ACTIVITY

Health and safety staff awareness training

Where are the following found in your workplace and how are staff informed of this?

1. fire extinguisher(s)
2. information sheets stating how products should be stored/used (MSDS – Material Safety Data Sheets)
3. health and safety workplace information
4. first aid kit
5. sterilization/disinfection equipment
6. PPE
7. fire exit(s)
8. accident book
9. sharps box and waste bags for contaminated waste

Fire

The **Regulatory Reform (Fire Safety) Order (2005)** replaces all previous legislation relating to fire, including fire certificates which no longer have any validity. This law is applicable to England and Wales only. Northern Ireland and Scotland have their own similar legislation.

The Regulatory Reform (Fire Safety) Order (2005) places responsibility for fire safety onto the 'responsible person' which is usually the employer. The 'responsible person' will have a duty to ensure the safety of everyone who uses their premises and those in the immediate vicinity who may be at risk if there is a fire. The 'responsible person' must carry out a fire safety risk assessment.

Fire risk assessments will include:

- Identifying and removing any obstacles that may hinder fire evacuation
- Ensuring that suitable fire detection equipment is in place, such as a **smoke alarm**
- Making sure that all escape routes are clearly marked and free from obstacles
- Testing fire alarm systems regularly to ensure they are in full operational condition

All staff must be trained in fire and emergency evacuation procedures for their workplace. The **emergency exit route** will be the easiest route by which staff and clients can leave the building safely. Fire action plans should be prominently displayed to show the emergency exit route. Fire fighting equipment should be available and maintained, to be used only by those trained to use it.

Firefighting equipment Firefighting equipment must be available, located in a specified area. The equipment includes fire extinguishers, blankets, sand buckets and water hoses. Firefighting equipment should be used only when the cause of the fire has been identified – using the wrong extinguisher could make the fire worse. There are four classifications of fires, class A, B, C and D. Symbols are used to identify these classifications and choice of fire extinguisher as shown below. Never use firefighting equipment unless you are trained in its use.

Fire extinguishers Fire extinguishers are available to tackle different types of fire. These should be located in a set place known to all employees. It is important that these are checked and maintained as required.

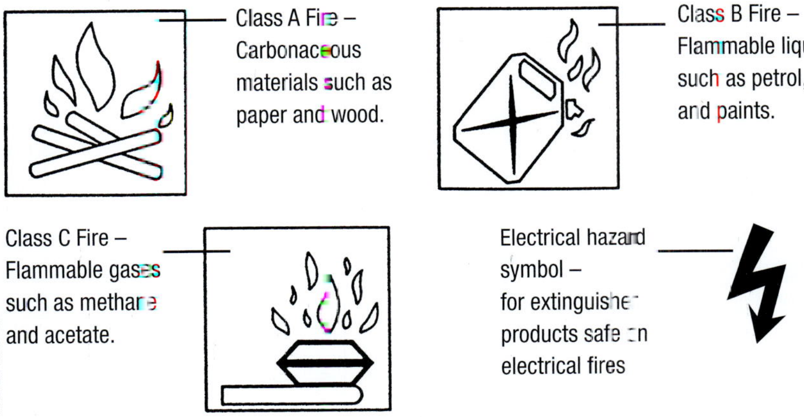

CHUBB FIRE LTD

Fire extinguisher symbols

HEALTH & SAFETY

Fire

If there is a fire, never use a lift. A fire quickly becomes out of control. You do not have very long to act!

Fire/break glass

Fire exit sign

CHUBB FIRE LTD

Fire blankets

HEALTH & SAFETY

Fire exits

Fire exit doors must be clearly marked and remain unlocked during working hours, and be free from obstruction.

ALWAYS REMEMBER

Fire extinguishers

Label colours and symbols indicate the use of particular fire extinguishers. Make sure you know the meaning of each of the colours and symbols.

Which Extinguisher to use	A Freely burning materials	B Flammable liquids	C Flammable gases	D Flammable metals	Electrical Hazards
Water	Red				
Water with Additive	Red				
Spray Foam	Cream	Cream			
ABC Dry Powder	Blue	Blue	Blue		Blue
Dry Powder Special Metal				Blue	
Dry Powder Special Monnex		Blue	Blue		Blue
CO_2 Gas		Black			Black
Hose Reels	Red				
Wet Chemical	Yellow				

For Alcohol fires use Alcohol Resistant Foam, CO_2 or Dry Powder

CHUBB FIRE LTD

Causes of fire and choice of fire extinguishers

CHUBB FIRE LTD

Firefighting equipment

Fire blankets are used to smother a small, localized fire or if a person's clothing is on fire. **Sand** is used to soak up liquids if these are the source of the fire, and to smother the fire. **Water hoses** are used to extinguish large fires caused by paper materials and the like – buckets of water may be used to extinguish a small fire. *Turn off the electricity first!*

Never put yourself at risk – fires can spread quickly. Leave the building at once if in danger, and raise the alarm by telephoning the emergency services on the emergency telephone numbers, **999** or **112**.

ACTIVITY

Causes of fires

Can you think of several potential causes of fire in the salon? How could each of these be prevented?

Complete this with the staff you have responsibility to train to raise their awareness.

Other emergencies

Other possible emergencies that could occur relate to fumes and flooding. Learn where the water and gas stopcocks are located. In the event of a gas leak or a flood, the stopcocks should be switched off and the appropriate emergency service contacted.

In the event of a bomb alert, staff must be trained in the appropriate emergency procedures. This will involve recognition of a suspect package, how to deal with a bomb threat, evacuation of staff and clients and contacting the emergency services. Your local Crime Prevention Officer will advise on bomb security.

Inspection and registration of premises Inspectors from the HSE of your local authority enforce the Health and Safety law. They visit the workplace to ensure compliance with government legislation.

If the inspector identifies any area of danger, it is the responsibility of the employer to remove this danger within a designated period of time. The inspector issues an **improvement notice**. Failure to comply with the notice will lead to prosecution. The inspector also has the authority to close a business until they are satisfied that all danger to employees and public has been removed. Such closure involves the issuing of a **prohibition notice**.

Certain services carried out in beauty therapy, such as ear piercing, semi-permanent make-up and electrical hair epilation techniques, pose additional risk as they may produce blood and body tissue fluid. Inspection of the premises is necessary before such services can be offered to the public. The inspector will visit and observe that the local bye-laws guidelines and those in the **Local Government (Miscellaneous Provisions) Act (1982)** relating to this area are being complied with as well as other relevant health and safety laws. When the inspector is satisfied, a **certificate of registration** will be awarded. This usually lasts for as long as the individual registered remains in the district.

ACTIVITY

Where would you find guidance and, if applicable, legislation on the following health and safety hazards in the workplace?

- manual handling
- noise levels
- hazardous substances
- use of computers
- first aid
- accidents
- electricity
- fire
- stress
- waste
- environmental
- working conditions, i.e. heating, lighting and ventilation

FUNCTIONAL SKILLS

Insurance

Public liability insurance protects employers and employees against the consequences of death or injury to a third party while on the premises. It is a requirement of the law that employers have liability insurance.

Professional indemnity insurance extends the public liability insurance to cover named employees against claims. This is an important consideration when performing high-risk services such as electrical epilation.

Product and **treatment liability insurance** is usually included with your public liability insurance, but you should check this with the insurance company.

Every employer must have **employer's liability insurance**. This provides financial compensation to employees should they be injured as a result of an accident in the workplace. It is required by law. This certificate must be displayed indicating that a policy of insurance has been obtained.

Personal health, hygiene and presentation

As discussed, it is essential that workplace instructions relevant to each job role are followed by all staff. The following section reviews personal health and hygiene.

Provide training and inform staff of any recommendations for change if they arise. This will help to control further risks that could occur because of negative health practice and poor hygiene standards.

Personal appearance enables the client to make an initial judgement about both staff and the salon, so make sure that the staff create the correct impression! Employees in the workplace should always reflect the desired image of the profession that they work in.

Because of the type of activities a beauty therapist will undertake, their workwear is also PPE and should be worn at all times.

Personal presentation

Beauty therapist Due to the nature of many of the services offered, the beauty therapist must wear protective, hygienic workwear. The cotton overall is ideal; air can

COURTESY OF SIMON JERSEY. WWW.SIMONJERSEY.COM

Female workwear

COURTESY OF SIMON JERSEY. WWW.SIMONJERSEY.COM

Male workwear

ACTIVITY

Fit and healthy for work

Ask your tutor for guidelines before beginning this activity.

1. Write down all the foods and drinks that you consume typically before work and during the working day. Do you think they are healthy and will provide you with the energy and hydration you require? If you are unsure, discuss the food diary with your tutor.
2. How much exercise do you take weekly?
3. How much sleep do you regularly have each night?
4. Do you think you could improve your health and fitness levels?

There may be some lifestyle changes that will help you feel fitter, healthier and with more energy.

HEALTH & SAFETY

Personal Protective Equipment (PPE) at Work Regulations (2002)

For certain services, such as electrical epilation, it is necessary to wear a protective apron over the overall. Assistant beauty therapists may wear an apron while preparing and cleaning the working area, to protect the overall and keep it clean.

circulate, allowing perspiration to evaporate and discouraging body odour. The use of a colour such as white immediately shows the client that you are clean. A cotton overall may comprise a dress, a jumpsuit or a tunic top, with coordinating trousers, length suited to work role.

Overalls should be laundered regularly and a fresh, clean overall worn each day.

Receptionist

If a receptionist is employed solely to carry out reception duties, they may wear a different salon dress/uniform, complementary to those worn by the practising beauty therapists. As they will not be as active, it may be appropriate for them to wear a smart jacket or cardigan. If on the other hand they are also carrying out services at some times, the standard salon overall must be worn.

General rules for employees

Facial make-up An appropriate make-up should be worn according to your work role, and always use the correct skincare cosmetics to suit your skin type. A healthy facial appearance will be a positive advertisement for your work. First impressions count!

Jewellery Keep jewellery to a minimum, such as a wedding ring, a watch and small earrings.

Nails Beauty therapist work requires nails to be short, neatly manicured and free of nail polish. Nail polish contains ingredients which can cause an allergic reaction in some people. Nail length can interfere with the application of the service, such as massage.

Artificial nails if worn must be short to avoid potential harm and ineffective treatment application when applying services to delicate areas such as the eyes during facial service and when performing electrical ep lation.

Shoes Ideally you should wear flat, well-fitting, comfortable shoes that enclose the feet fully but allow the toes to spread. This will help prevent future foot and postural disorders caused by ill-fitting shoes!

Ethics

Beauty therapy has a code of ethics. This is a code of behaviour and expected standards for the professional beauty therapist to follow, which will uphold the reputation of the industry and ensure best working practice for the safety of the industry and members of the public. Professional bodies produce codes of practice for their members. Each workplace may have its own code of practice which, although not a legal requirement, is a code which may be used in criminal proceedings as evidence of unacceptable work practice.

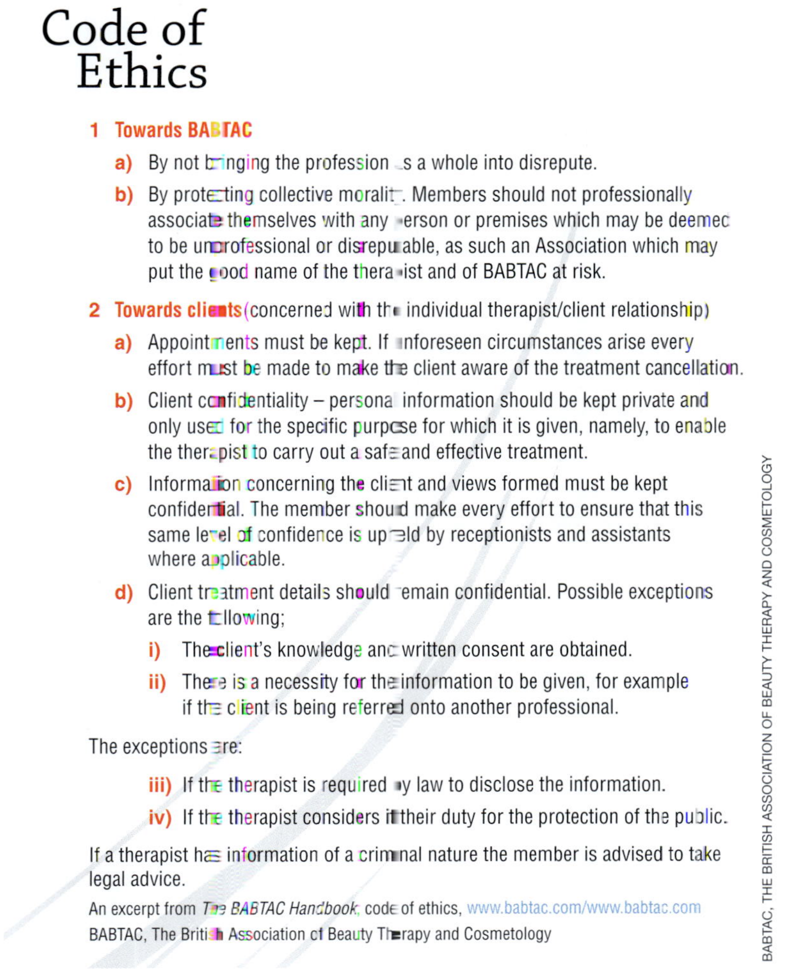

Code of Ethics

1 Towards BABTAC

a) By not bringing the profession as a whole into disrepute.

b) By protecting collective morality. Members should not professionally associate themselves with any person or premises which may be deemed to be unprofessional or disreputable, as such an Association which may put the good name of the therapist and of BABTAC at risk.

2 Towards clients (concerned with the individual therapist/client relationship)

a) Appointments must be kept. If unforeseen circumstances arise every effort must be made to make the client aware of the treatment cancellation.

b) Client confidentiality – personal information should be kept private and only used for the specific purpose for which it is given, namely, to enable the therapist to carry out a safe and effective treatment.

c) Information concerning the client and views formed must be kept confidential. The member should make every effort to ensure that this same level of confidence is upheld by receptionists and assistants where applicable.

d) Client treatment details should remain confidential. Possible exceptions are the following;

i) The client's knowledge and written consent are obtained.

ii) There is a necessity for the information to be given, for example if the client is being referred onto another professional.

The exceptions are:

iii) If the therapist is required by law to disclose the information.

iv) If the therapist considers it their duty for the protection of the public.

If a therapist has information of a criminal nature the member is advised to take legal advice.

An excerpt from *The BABTAC Handbook*, code of ethics, www.babtac.com/www.babtac.com BABTAC, The British Association of Beauty Therapy and Cosmetology

BABTAC Code of Ethics

ACTIVITY

Code of ethics

As a professional beauty therapist it is important that you adhere to a code of ethical practice. You may wish to join a professional organization, which will issue you with a copy of its agreed minimum standards.

ALWAYS REMEMBER

Correct posture benefits

Correct posture enables you to work longer without becoming tired; it prevents muscle fatigue, repetitive strain injury (RSI) and stiff joints and it also improves your appearance.

Diet, exercise and sleep

A beauty therapist requires lots of energy. To achieve this you need to eat a healthy, well-balanced diet, take regular exercise and have regular sufficient sleep – 7–8 hours per night is recommended.

Posture

Posture is the way you hold yourself when standing, sitting and walking.

Good standing posture If you are standing with good posture, this will describe you:

- head up, centrally balanced
- shoulders slightly back and relaxed
- chest up and out
- abdomen flat
- hips level
- fingertips level
- bottom in
- knees level
- feet slightly apart, and weight evenly distributed

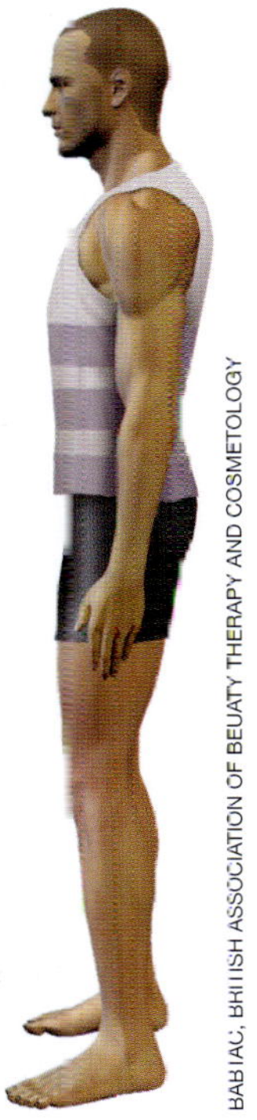

Good posture – standing

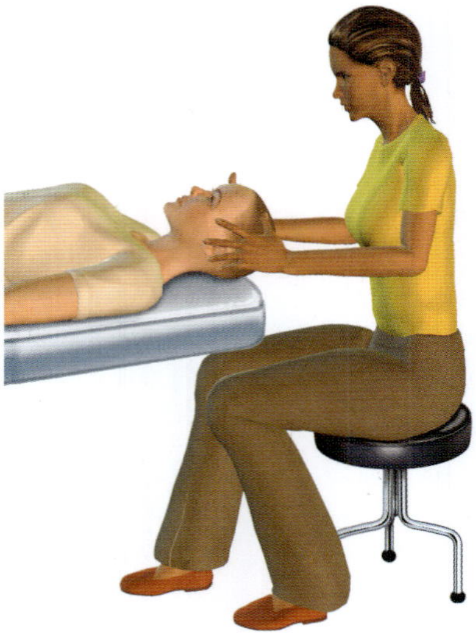

Good posture – sitting

Good sitting posture Sit on a suitable chair or stool with a good back support:

- sit with the lower back pressed against the chair back
- keep the chest up and the shoulders back
- distribute the body weight evenly along the thighs
- keep the feet together and flat on the floor
- do not slouch or sit on the edge of your seat

ACTIVITY

The importance of posture and position when working

1 Which services will be performed sitting and which standing?

2 In what way will your services be affected if you are *not* sitting or standing correctly?

3 How can incorrect sitting and standing affect you physically?

4 What training will you provide in respect of posture and position? How will this benefit the beauty therapist when working?

HEALTH & SAFETY

Repetitive strain injury (RSI)

If you do not follow correct postural positional requirements when performing services, muscles and ligaments may become overstretched and overused resulting in repetitive strain injury (RSI). This may result in you being unable to work in the short term – and potentially in the long term – in the occupation!

Personal hygiene

It is vital that staff have a high standard of personal **hygiene**. They are going to be working in close proximity with people. Guidance should be provided when necessary to reinforce the need.

Bodily cleanliness is achieved through daily showering or bathing. This removes stale sweat, dirt and bacteria, which cause body odour. An antiperspirant or deodorant may be applied to the underarm area to reduce perspiration and thus the smell of sweat. Clean underwear should be worn each day.

Cross-contamination can be avoided with a high compliance with personal hygiene practice.

Hands The hands and everything touched are covered with germs. Although most are harmless, some can cause ill health or disease. Hands should be washed regularly, especially after using the toilet and before eating food. Hands must always be washed before and after treating each client, and during service if necessary. Washing the hands before treating a client minimizes the risk of cross-infection, and presents to the client a hygienic, professional, caring image. Disinfecting hand gel may also be available to use before services are delivered, applied to clean hands.

TOP TIP

Personal hygiene

If a beauty employee has a personal hygiene problem this should be discussed immediately to avoid embarrassment and offence. Tactfully state the problem and resolve how it can be corrected.

HEALTH & SAFETY

Hand cleanliness

Wash your hands with liquid soap from a sealed dispenser. This should take 10–20 seconds. Don't refill disposable soap dispensers when empty: if you do they will become a breeding ground for bacteria.

Disposable paper towels or warm-air hand dryers should be used to thoroughly dry the hands.

Feet Feet can be kept fresh and healthy by washing them daily and then drying them thoroughly, especially between the toes to avoid foot disorders such as athlete's foot. Deodorizing foot powder may then be applied.

Oral hygiene Avoid bad breath by brushing teeth at least twice daily and flossing the teeth frequently. Use breath fresheners and mouthwashes as required to freshen the breath. Visit the dentist regularly, to maintain healthy teeth and gums. Avoid eating strong flavoured foods which could cause offence in close proximity.

Hair Hair should be clean and tidy. Hair should be cut regularly to maintain its appearance, and shampooed and conditioned as often as needed.

Hair, if long, should be worn off the face, and taken to the crown of the head. Medium-length hair should be clipped back, away from the face, to prevent it falling forwards.

Hygiene in the workplace

Infections Effective hygiene is necessary in the salon to prevent *cross-infection* and *secondary infection*. These can occur through poor practice, such as the use of implements that are not sterile. Infection can be recognized by red and inflamed skin, or the presence of pus.

Cross-infection occurs because some microorganisms are contagious – they may be transferred through personal contact or by contact with an infected instrument that has not been sterilized. **Secondary infection** can occur as a result of injury to the client during the service, or if the client already has an open cut, if bacteria penetrate the skin and cause infection. **Sterilization** and **disinfection** procedures (below) are used to minimize or destroy the harmful microorganisms which could cause infection – bacteria, viruses and fungi.

Infectious diseases that are contagious **contra-indicate** beauty services: they require medical attention. People with certain other skin disorders, even though these are not contagious, should likewise not be treated by the beauty therapist, as services might lead to secondary infection.

Sometimes people may have a contra-indication they are not aware of, such as a blood virus. If hygiene practice is not followed there is a risk of contamination from blood-borne virus transmission including hepatitis B and C and HIV/Aids. Hepatitis B can be transmitted in small volumes of blood too small to be visible, so effective sterilization methods and hygiene practice is essential.

Sterilization and disinfection Sterilization is the total destruction of all living microorganisms. **Disinfection** is the destruction of some, but not all, microorganisms. Sterilization and disinfection techniques practised in the beauty work environment involve the use of *physical* agents, such as radiation and heat; and *chemical* agents, such as antiseptics and disinfectants.

Radiation A quartz mercury-vapour lamp can be used as the source for **UV light**, which destroys harmful microorganisms. The object to be disinfected must be turned regularly so that the UV light reaches all surfaces. (UV light has limited effectiveness, and cannot be relied upon for sterilization.)

The UV lamp must be contained within a closed cabinet. This cabinet is an ideal place for storing sterilized objects.

HEALTH & SAFETY

Protecting the client

If you have any cuts or abrasions on your hands, cover them with a clean dressing to minimize the risk of secondary infection. Disposable gloves may be worn for additional protection.

Certain skin disorders are contagious. If the beauty therapist is suffering from any such disorder they must not work, but must seek medical advice immediately.

Face masks may be worn when working in close proximity to the client.

TOP TIP

Fresh breath

When working, avoid eating strong-smelling, highly spiced food. The remaining odours may be offensive to the client when working in close proximity.

HEALTH & SAFETY

Long hair

If long hair is not taken away from the face, the tendency will be to move the hair away from the face repeatedly with the hands, and this in turn will require that the hands be washed repeatedly.

ACTIVITY

Avoiding cross-infection

1. List the different ways in which infection can be transferred in the salon.
2. Can you explain simply how cross-infection can be avoided in the workplace?

HEALTH & SAFETY

UV lamp record of usage

UV light is dangerous, especially to the eyes. The UV lamp must be switched off before opening the cabinet. A record must be kept of usage, as the effectiveness of the lamp decreases with use.

> When using a UV cabinet, it is important to remember to turn the objects regularly, in order to ensure that the entire surface area of the items is disinfected.
>
> **Janice Brown**

TOP TIP

HSE advice on cleaning

Advice on cleaning work surfaces and equipment can be found at COSHH essentials – www.coshh-essentials.org.uk.

HEALTH & SAFETY

Hepatitis B immunization

It is recommended that if you are performing services such as electrical epilations, where you may come into contact with blood, you receive immunization against hepatitis B to protect both beauty therapist and client.

Contamination could occur from needle stick injuries from electrical epilation if risks are inadequately controlled.

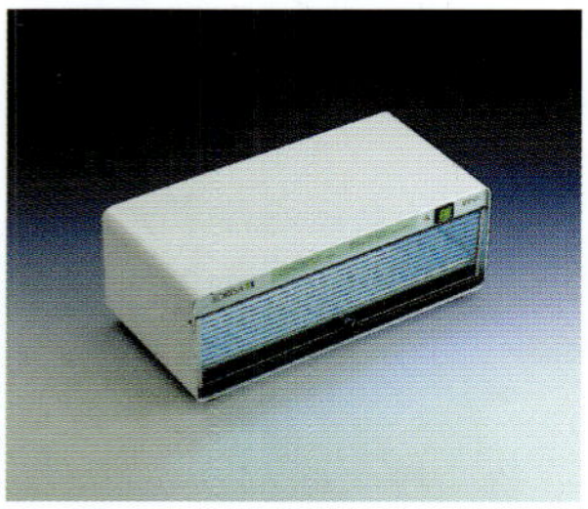
BEAUTY EXPRESS LTD

UV light cabinet

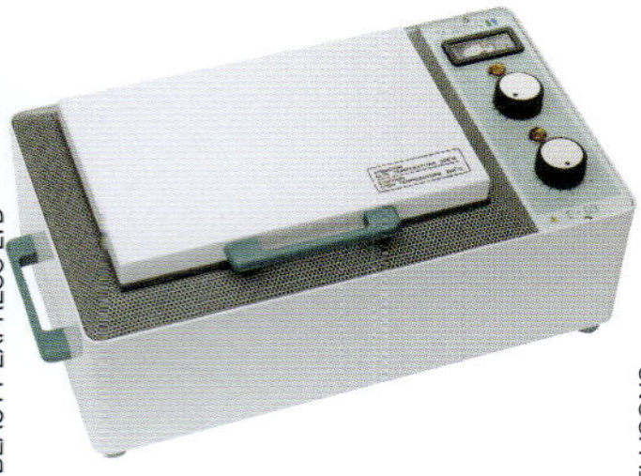
BEAUTY EXPRESS LTD

Dry-heat sterilizing cabinet

ELLISONS

Glass-bead sterilizer

Heat Dry and moist heat may both be used in sterilization. One method is to use a dry **hot-air oven**. This is similar to a small oven, and heats to 150–180°C. It is seldom used in the salon.

More practical is a **glass-bead sterilizer**. This is a small electrically heated unit which contains glass beads heated to between 190–300°C: these transfer heat to objects placed in contact with them. This method of sterilization is suitable for small tools such as tweezers and scissors. All objects should be cleaned before placing in the glass-bead sterilizer to remove surface dirt and debris.

Water is boiled in an **autoclave** (similar to a pressure cooker): because of the increased pressure, the water reaches a temperature of 121–134°C. Autoclaving is the most effective method for sterilizing objects in the salon.

HEALTH & SAFETY

Using an autoclave

- The autoclave should only be used by those trained to do so.
- Not all objects can safely be placed in the autoclave. Before using this method, check whether the items you wish to sterilize can withstand this heating process.
- All objects should be cleaned, using an effective cleaning agent, e.g. surgical spirit, to remove surface dirt and debris before placing in the autoclave
- To avoid damaging the autoclave, always use distilled deionized water.
- To avoid rusting, metal objects placed in the sterilizing unit must be of good-quality stainless steel.
- Never overload the autoclave; follow manufacturer's instructions in its use.

> Alcohols such as surgical spirit should not be used to clean equipment and furniture in the salon, particularly those with laminated or painted surfaces as they have a stripping effect over time. Alcohol is also flammable and so should never be used to clean wax heaters that are switched on or not cool.
>
> **Janice Brown**

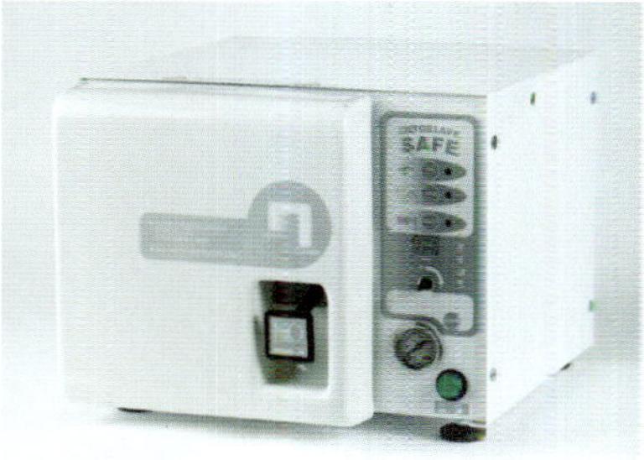

BEAUTY EXPRESS LTD

Automatic medical autoclave

Disinfectants and antiseptics If an object *cannot* be sterilized, it should be placed in a chemical disinfectant solution. A disinfectant destroys most microorganisms, but not all. **Hypochlorite** is a disinfectant; bleach is an example of a hypochlorite. It is particularly corrosive and therefore unsuitable for use with metals. Use on hard surfaces, such as work surfaces, and non-corrosive materials such as plastic tools. Always use as directed by the manufacturer.

> Remember:
> Smoking, eating and drinking during the course of a service allows close contact with the mouth, transferring microorganisms to the hand, which can then spread from or to the client.
>
> **Janice Brown**

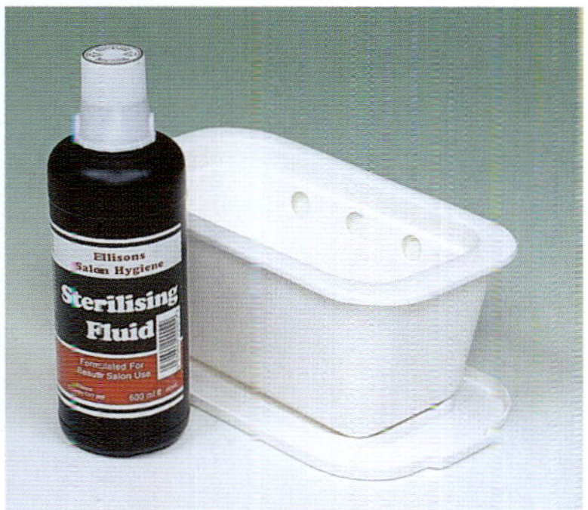

DEPILEX

Disinfection tray with liquid

HEALTH & SAFETY

Using disinfectant

Disinfectant solutions should be changed as recommended by the manufacturer to ensure their effectiveness.

After removing the object from the disinfectant, rinse it in clean water to remove traces of the solution. These might otherwise cause an allergic reaction on the client's skin.

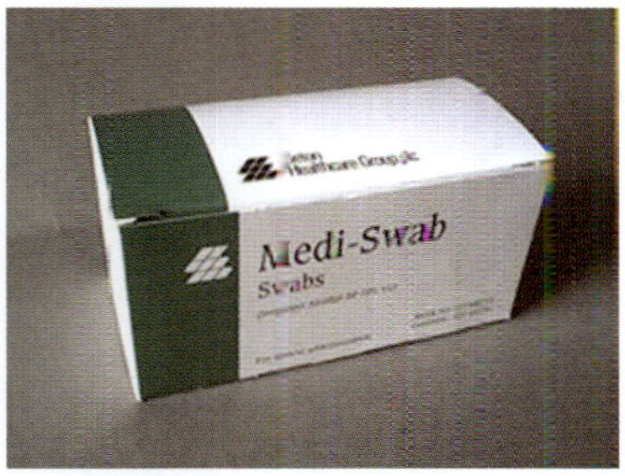

ELLISONS

Medi-Swabs (sterile isopropyl tissues)

Alcohol-impregnated wipes are popular to clean the skin using a disinfectant such as isopropyl alcohol.

An **antiseptic** prevents the multiplication of microorganisms. It has a limited action, and does not kill all microorganisms.

All sterilization and disinfection techniques must be carried out safely and effectively:

1. Select the appropriate method of sterilization or disinfection for the object. *Always* follow the manufacturer's guidelines on the use of the sterilizing unit or agent.
2. Clean the object in clean water and detergent to remove dirt and grease. Dirt left on the object may prevent effective sterilization.
3. Dry it thoroughly with a clean disposable paper towel.

> Hand washing is the single most important procedure for preventing cross-infection! You have close contact with your clients, so it is vital that your standards of personal presentation and hygiene are always of the highest standards.
>
> **Janice Brown**

4 Sterilize the object, allowing sufficient time for the process to be completed.

5 Following disinfection/sterilization, handle the object with clean tongs or protective gloves. Place objects that have been sterilized or disinfected in a clean, covered container, ideally labelled. After 24 hours the object will be clean but not disinfected.

Keep several sets of the tools used regularly, This will allow you to carry out effective sterilization following each use.

Workplace policies Each workplace should have its own workplace policy identifying hygiene rules.

- *Health and safety.* Follow the health and safety policies for the workplace.
- *Personal hygiene.* Maintain a high standard of personal hygiene. Wash your hands with a detergent containing **chlorhexidine gluconate**, which protects against a wide range of bacteria. The addition of isopropyl alcohol provides a stronger hand disinfectant removing surface bacteria and fungi and is widely used for skin **sanitization**.
- *Cuts on the hands.* Always cover any cuts on your hands with a protective waterproof dressing.
- *Cross-infection.* Take great care to avoid cross-infection in the salon. Never treat a client who has a contagious skin disease or disorder, or any other contra-indication. Refer the client tactfully to their GP.
- *Use hygienic tools.* Never use an implement unless it has been effectively sterilized or disinfected, as appropriate.
- *Disposable applicators.* Wherever possible, use disposable products.
- *Working surfaces.* Clean all working surfaces (such as trolleys and couches) with a chlorine preparation, diluted to the manufacturer's instructions. Cover all working surfaces with clean, disposable paper tissue.
- *Gowns and towels.* Clean gowns and towels must be provided for each client. Towels should be laundered at a temperature of 60°C.
- *Laundry.* Dirty laundry should be placed in a covered container.
- *Waste, including clinical waste and non-contaminated waste.* Must be disposed of following the COSHH procedures and guidelines provided by the environmental health department and training by the employer. For contaminated waste comply with the Controlled Waste Regulations (1992). Put waste in a suitable container lined with a disposable waste bag. A yellow **'sharps' container** and heavy duty yellow bag should be available for clinical waste contaminated with blood or tissue fluid, such as needles used in electrical hair epilation techniques. Protective gloves should be worn to avoid risk of contamination.
- *Eating and drinking.* Never eat or drink in the service area of the salon. It is unprofessional and harmful chemicals may be ingested.
- *Drugs and alcohol.* Never carry out services in the workplace under the influence of drugs or alcohol. Your competence will be affected, putting both yourself, clients and possibly colleagues at risk. Any accident as a result would be termed negligence and you would be liable. Ensure that your behaviour at work is in accordance with workplace policies and does not endanger yourself and others.

ALWAYS REMEMBER

Cleaning before sterilization

Before sterilization, wash and clean the object requiring sterilization. Surgical spirit applied with clean cotton wool or isopropyl impregnated tissues may be used to clean the object's surface, removing dirt and debris which would create a barrier to effective sterilization.

HEALTH & SAFETY

Damaged equipment

Any equipment in poor repair must be repaired or disposed of. Such equipment may be dangerous and may harbour germs.

HEALTH & SAFETY

Cuts on the hands

Open, uncovered cuts provide an easy entry for harmful bacteria, and may lead to infection. Always cover cuts.

HEALTH & SAFETY

Misuse of Drugs Act (1971)

This Act categorizes drugs into classes and details the penalties for those caught possessing them. It controls not just medicinal drugs (which will also be in the Medicines Act) but also drugs with no current medical uses. Therefore, you may be acting illegally if using them.

Skin diseases and disorders

The beauty therapist must be able to distinguish a healthy skin from one suffering from any skin disease or disorder. Certain skin disorders and diseases contra-indicate a beauty service: the service would expose the beauty therapist and other clients to the risk of cross-infection. It is therefore vital that you are familiar with the skin, hair and nail diseases and disorders and parasitic infections with which you may come into contact within the workplace: those that are a risk, those that are not and the correct action to take.

Relevant skin diseases and disorders are also discussed in each service chapter.

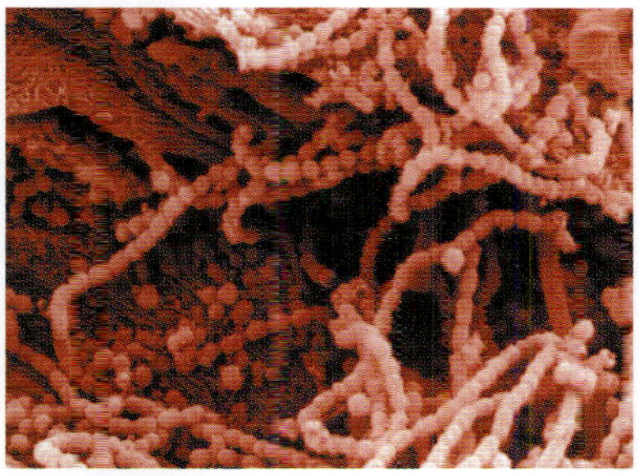

WELLCOME PHOTO LIBRARY

Microscopic bacteria

Bacterial infections

Bacteria are minute single-celled organisms of varied shapes. Large numbers of bacteria inhabit the surface of the skin and are harmless (**non-pathogenic**); indeed some play an important positive role in the health of the skin. Others, however, are harmful (**pathogenic**) and can cause skin diseases.

Impetigo An inflammatory disease of the surface of the skin, usually appearing on exposed areas.

Infectious? Yes.

Appearance: Initially the skin appears red and is itchy. Small thin-walled blisters appear; these burst and form into crusts. Untreated, small pus-filled ulcers can occur with a dark thick crust which can lead to scarring.

Site: The commonly affected areas are the nose, the mouth and the ears, but impetigo can occur on the scalp or the limbs.

Treatment: Medical – usually an antibiotic or an antibacterial ointment is prescribed containing corticosteroids such as hydrocortisone.

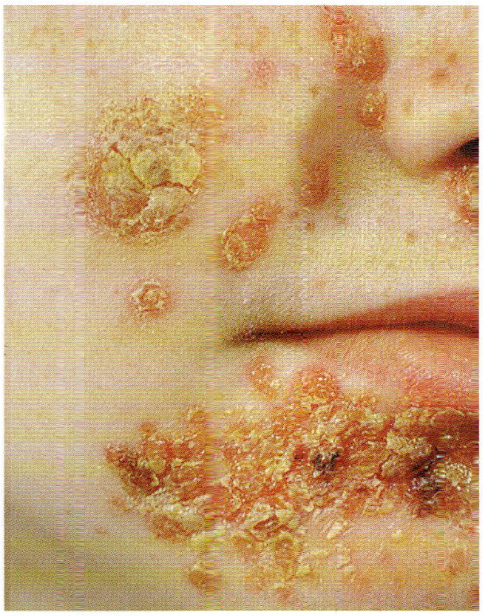

DR M H BECK

Impetigo

Conjunctivitis or pink eye Inflammation of the mucous membrane that covers the eye and lines the eyelids.

Infectious? Yes.

Appearance: The skin of the inner conjunctiva of the eye becomes inflamed, the eye becomes very red and sore, water and pus may exude from the area leaving a sticky coating on the lashes.

Site: The eyes, either one or both, may be infected.

Treatment: Medical – usually an antibiotic lotion is prescribed. However, in some cases medical treatment will not be necessary and the infection will heal independently.

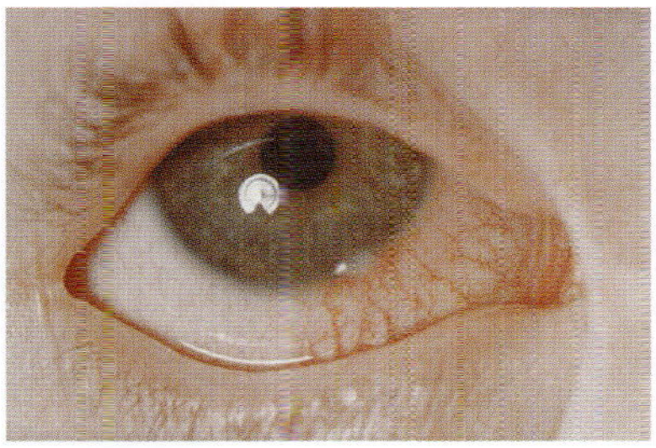

WELLCOME PHOTO LIBRARY

Conjunctivitis or pink eye

HEALTH & SAFETY

Skin problems – refer

If you are unable to identify a skin condition with confidence, so that you are uncertain whether or not you should treat the client, don't! Tactfully refer her to her GP before proceeding with the planned service.

HEALTH & SAFETY

Using chemical agents

Always protect your hands with gloves before immersing them in chemical cleaning agents, to minimize the risk of an allergic reaction. Wet work can lead to contact dermatitis, so gloves are to be worn to protect the skin of the hands.

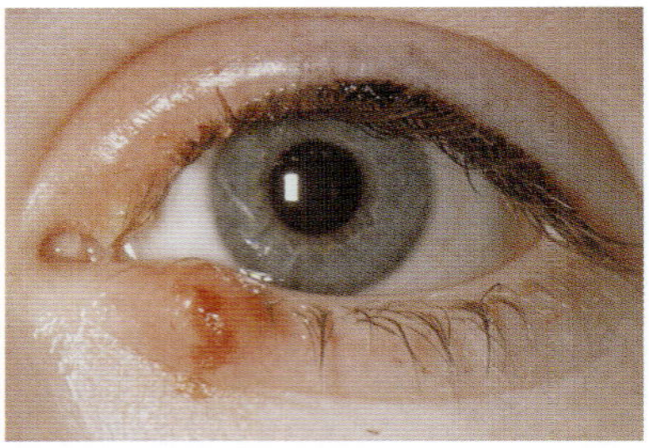

DR A L WRIGHT

Hordeola or styes

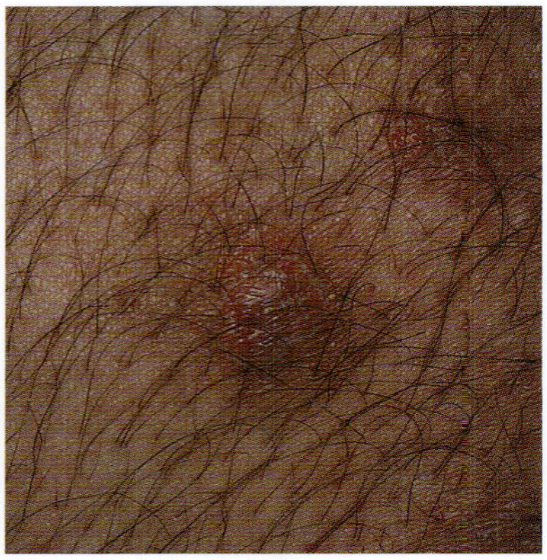

DR A L WRIGHT

Boil

HEALTH & SAFETY

Boils

Boils occurring on the upper lip or in the nose should be referred immediately to a GP. Boils can be dangerous when near to the eyes or brain.

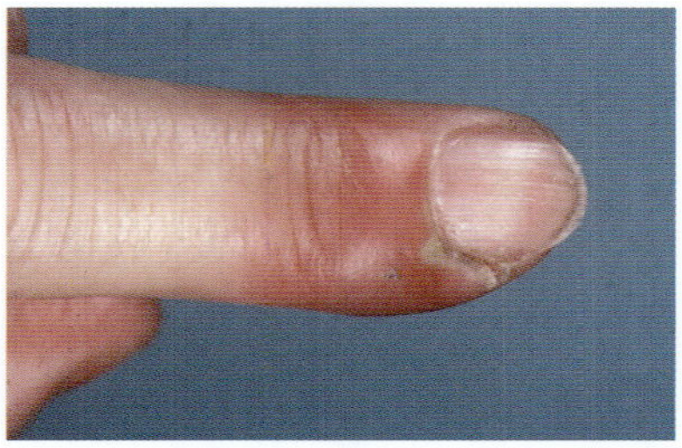

WELLCOME PHOTO LIBRARY

Paronychia

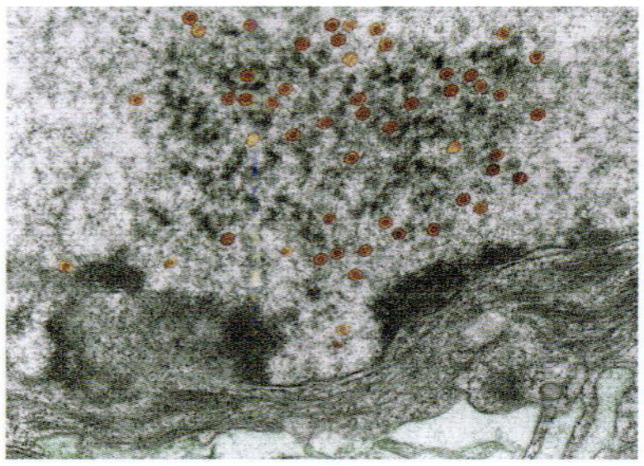

ROB YOUNG/WELLCOME PHOTO LIBRARY

Example of a microscopic virus – herpes simplex virus particles (orange) in the nucleus of an epithelial cell

Hordeolum or styes

Infection of the sebaceous glands of eyelash hair follicles. It can be an effect of blepharitis (inflammation of the eyelids).

Infectious? Yes.

Appearance: Small red, inflamed lumps containing pus, a sign of infection.

Site: The inner rim of the eyelid.

Treatment: Medical – usually an antibiotic is prescribed.

Furuncles or boils Infection affecting the hair follicle.

Infectious? Yes.

Appearance: A localized red lump appears around the hair follicle; this then develops a core of pus, yellowish-white fluid formed in infected tissue. Scarring of the skin often remains after the boil has healed.

Site: The back of the neck, the armpits and the buttocks and thighs are common areas, but furuncles can occur anywhere

Treatment: Medical. Antibiotics may be prescribed to help to control infection.

Carbuncles Infection of numerous hair follicles.

Infectious? Yes.

Appearance: A hard, round abscess, larger than a boil, which oozes pus from several points upon its surface. Scarring often occurs after the carbuncle has healed.

Site: In particular where there is friction, such as the back of the neck or on the thighs. However, they can occur anywhere.

Treatment: Medical – usually involving incision, drainage of the pus, and a course of antibiotics.

Paronychia Infection of the tissue surrounding the nail (the nail fold). If left untreated the nail bed may become infected

Infectious? Yes.

Appearance: Swelling, redness and pus in the nail fold and in the area of the nail wall.

Site: The skin surrounding the nail plate.

Treatment: Medical – usually a course of antibiotics. Incision and drainage of pus is necessary if it collects the skin next to the nail plate.

Viral infections

Viruses are minute entities, too small to see even under an ordinary microscope. They are considered to be **parasites**, as they require living tissue in order to survive. Viruses invade healthy body cells and multiply within the cell: in due course the cell walls break down, liberating new viral particles to attack further cells, and thus the infection spreads.

Herpes simplex This is commonly referred to as a cold sore and is a recurring skin condition, appearing at times when the skin's resistance is lowered through ill health or stress. It may also be caused by exposure of the skin to extremes of temperature or to UV light.

Infectious? Yes.

Appearance: Inflammation of the skin occurs in localized areas. As well as being red, the skin becomes itchy and small vesicles appear. These are Herpes simplex followed by a crust, which may crack and weep tissue fluid.

Site: The mucous membranes of the nose or lips; herpes can also occur on the skin generally.

Treatment: There is no specific treatment. They usually clear in 7–10 days. A proprietary brand of anti-inflammatory antiseptic drying cream is usually prescribed. These must be applied in the early stages of the condition when a tingling, itching sensation is experienced.

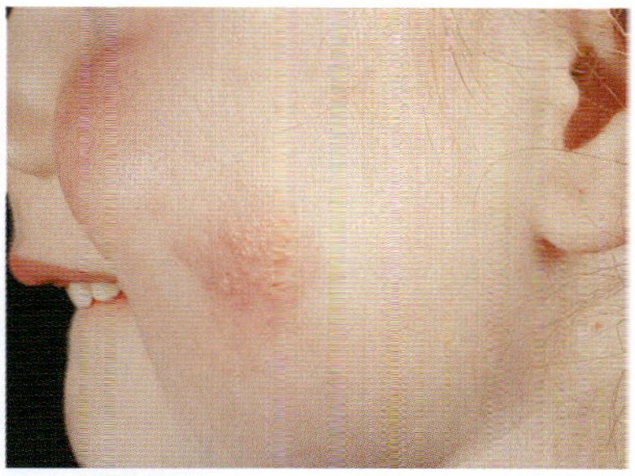

DR M H BECK

Herpes simplex

Herpes zoster or shingles In this painful disease, from the virus that causes chickenpox, the virus attacks the sensory nerve endings and is thought to lie dormant in the body and be triggered when the body's defences are lowered.

Infectious? Yes.

Appearance: Redness of the skin occurs along the line of the affected nerves. Blisters develop and form crusts, leaving purplish-pink pigmentation.

Site: Commonly the chest and the abdomen.

Treatment: Medical – usually including anti-viral medicines. Calamine lotion can soothe the irritation. If there are complications with bacterial infection, antibiotics will be prescribed.

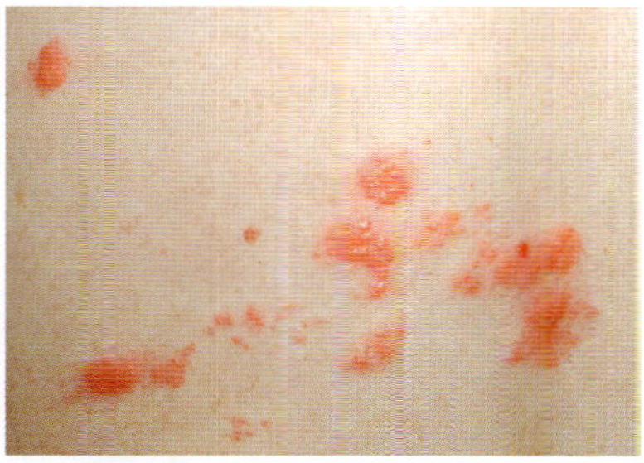

MEDISCAN

Herpes zoster or shingles

Verruca or warts Small epidermal skin growths. Warts may be raised or flat, depending upon their position. There are several types of wart: plane, common and plantar.

Infectious? Yes.

Appearance: Warts vary in size, shape, texture and colour. Usually they have a rough surface and are raised. If the wart occurs on the sole of the foot it grows inwards, due to the pressure of body weight.

Site:

- plane wart (flat wart): the fingers, either surface of the hand, face or legs
- common wart (verruca vulgaris): the face, hands, elbows and knees
- plantar wart (verruca): the sole of the foot and toes
- mosaic (palmar warts): hands and feet

Treatment: Medical – using acids, i.e. salicylic acid, solid carbon dioxide, cryotherapy or electrocautery.

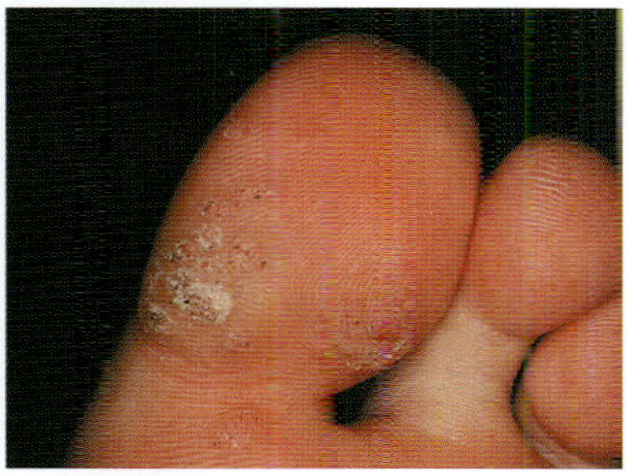

DR A L WRIGHT

Verruca

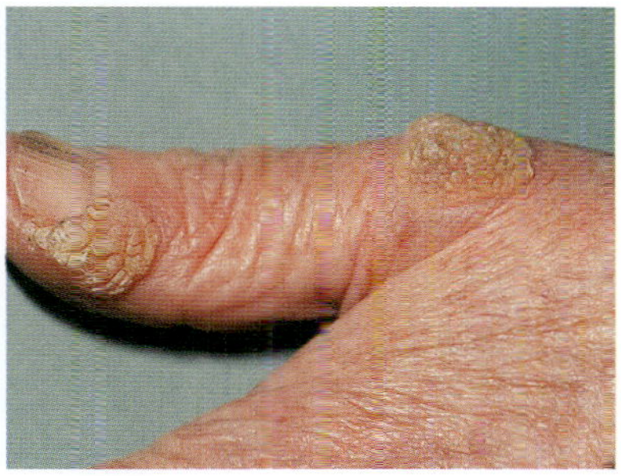

DR M H BECK

A wart

Infestations

An infestation is where animal parasites live off and invade the host's tissue to gain all their nutrients.

Scabies or itch mites (sarcoptes scabiei) A condition in which tiny mites burrow beneath the skin and invade the hair follicles. The mites feed on tissue and fluid as they burrow into the skin.

Infectious? Yes.

Appearance: At the onset, minute papules and wavy greyish lines appear, where dirt has entered the burrows. Secondary bacterial infection may occur as a result of scratching.

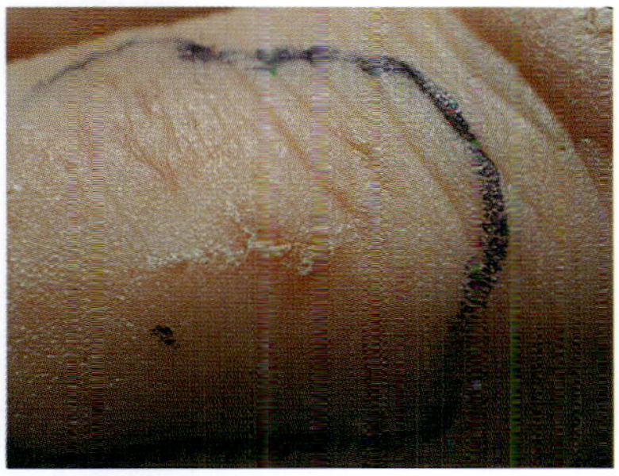

DR M H BECK

Scabies burrow

Site: Usually seen in warm areas of loose skin, such as the webs of the fingers, under the fingernails and the creases of the elbows.

Treatment: Medical – an anti-scabetic lotion containing an insecticide.

WELLCOME PHOTO LIBRARY

Pediculosis capitis or head lice

Pediculosis capitis or head lice A condition in which small lice parasites infest scalp hair.

Infectious? Yes.

Appearance: The lice cling to the hair of the scalp. Eggs are laid, attached to the hair close to the skin. The lice bite the skin to draw nourishment from the blood; this creates irritation and itching of the skin, which may lead to secondary bacterial infection.

Site: The hair of the scalp.

Treatment: Medical – an appropriate medicated insecticidal lotion or rinse.

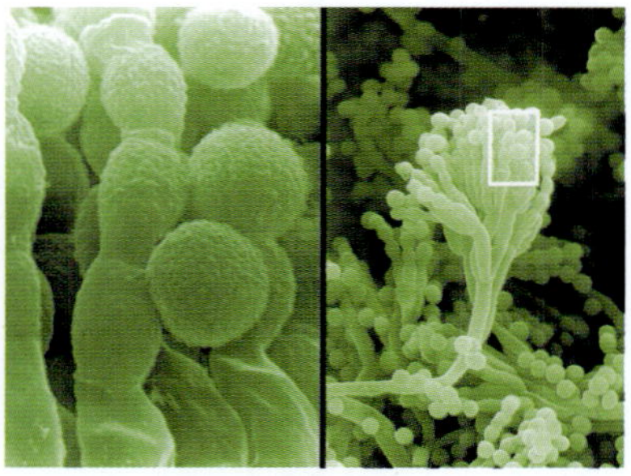

WELLCOME PHOTO LIBRARY

Example of a microscopic fungi – Penicillium mould producing spores, plus very close-up view of spore formation

Pediculosis pubis or pubic lice A condition in which small lice parasites infest body hair.

Infectious? Yes.

Appearance: The lice cling to the hair of the body. Eggs are laid, attached to the hair close to the skin. The lice bite the skin to draw nourishment from the blood; this creates irritation and itching of the skin, which may lead to secondary bacterial infection.

Site: Pubic hair, eyebrows and eyelashes.

Treatment: Medical – an appropriate insecticidal lotion.

Pediculosis corporis A condition in which small parasites live and feed on body skin.

Infectious? Yes.

Appearance: The lice cling to the hair of the body. Eggs are laid, attached to the hair close to the skin. The lice bite the skin to draw nourishment from the blood; this creates irritation and itching of the skin, which may lead to secondary bacterial infection. Where body lice bite the skin, small red marks can be seen.

Site: Body hair.

Treatment: Medical – an appropriate insecticidal lotion.

ACTIVITY

Avoiding cross-infection

1. List the different ways in which infection can be transferred in the salon.
2. How can you avoid cross-infection in the workplace?

Fungal diseases

Fungi are microscopic plants. They are parasites, dependent upon a host for their existence. Fungal diseases of the skin feed off the waste products of the skin. Some fungi are found on the skin's surface; others attack the deeper tissues. Reproduction of fungi is by means of simple cell division or by the production of spores.

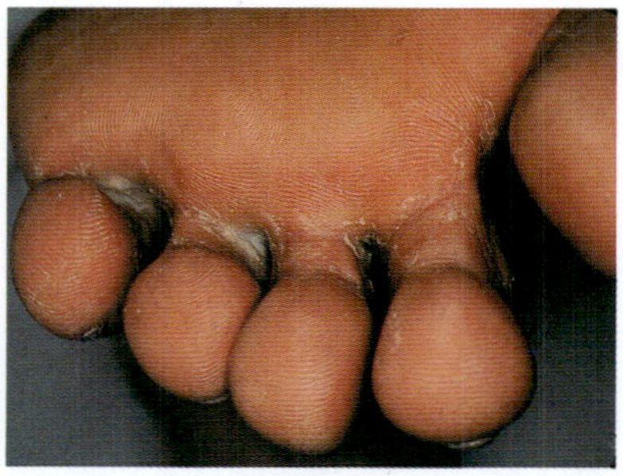

DR A L WRIGHT

Tinea pedis or athlete's foot

Tinea pedis or athlete's foot A common fungal foot infection.

Infectious? Yes.

Appearance: Small blisters form, which later burst. The skin in the area can then become dry, giving a scaly appearance.

Site: Commonly affects the webs of skin between the toes.

Treatment: Thorough cleansing of the area. Medical application of fungicides. Untreated infections such as bacterial infections may occur. It can also lead to infection of the toe and fingernails.

Tinea corporis or body ringworm A fungal infection of the skin.

Infectious? Yes.

Appearance: Small scaly red patches, which spread outwards and then heal from the centre, leaving a ring.

Site: The trunk of the body, the limbs and the face.

Treatment: Medical – using a fungicidal cream. Oral anti-fungal medication is necessary if there are several infection sites.

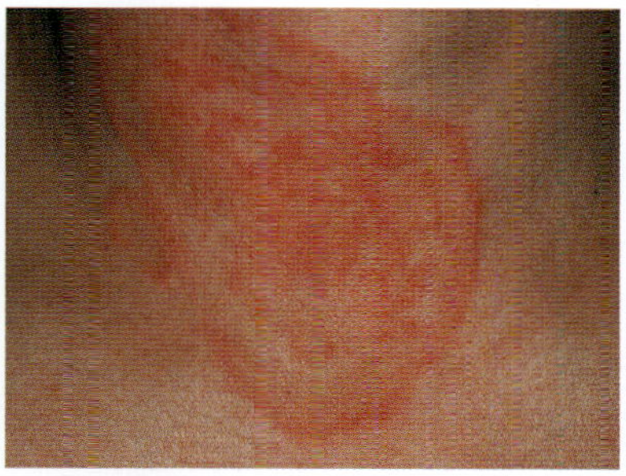

DR A L WRIGHT

Tinea corporis or body ringworm

Tinea unguium or onychomycosis Fungal infection of the fingernails.

Infectious? Yes.

Appearance: The nail plate is white and opaque. Eventually the nail plate becomes brittle and separates from the nail bed.

Site: The nail plates.

Treatment: Medical application of fungicides.

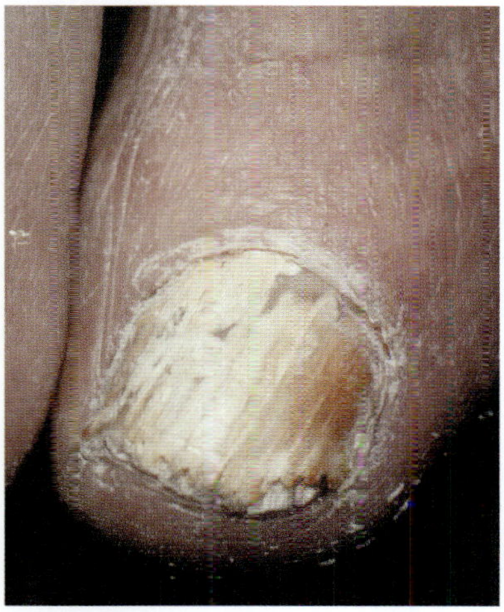

WELLCOME PHOTO LIBRARY

Tinea unguium or ringworm of the nail plate

Sebaceous gland disorders

The sebaceous glands produce sebum, the skin's natural oil which has bactericidal and anti-fungal properties. This helps to keep the skin healthy and also to prevent the skin from drying out. They are also the cause of the following disorders

Milia Keratinization of the skin over the hair follicle occurs, causing sebum to accumulate in the hair follicle. This condition usually accompanies dry skin.

Infectious? No.

Appearance: Small, hard, pearly-white cysts.

Site: The upper face or close to the eyes.

Treatment: The milium may be removed by the beauty therapist (if qualified to do so) or by a GP, depending on the location. A sterile lancet is used to pierce the skin of the overlying cuticle and thereby free the milium.

Micro-dermabrasions may be used to avoid their development. Also, retinoid creams may be applied which remove the outer epidermal layers.

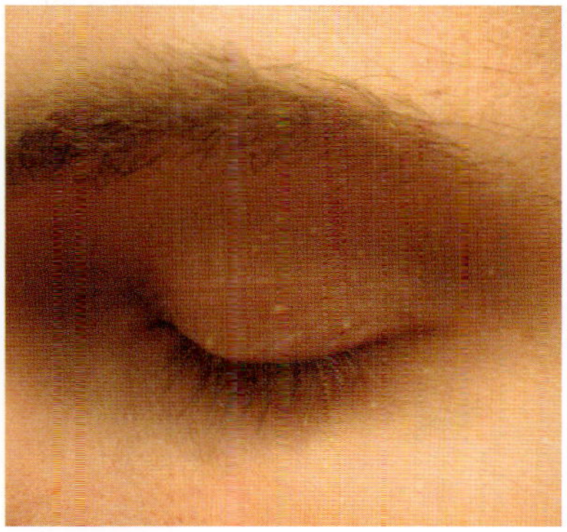

WIKIMEDIA COMMONS

Milia

Comedones or blackheads Excess sebum and keratinized cells block the mouth of the hair follicle.

Infectious? No.

Site: The face (the chin, nose and forehead), the upper back and chest.

Treatment: The area should be cleansed, and an electrical vapour service or other pre-heating service should be given to relax the mouth of the hair follicle; a sterile comedone extractor should then be used to remove the blockage. A regular cleansing service should be recommended by the beauty therapist to control the production of comedones.

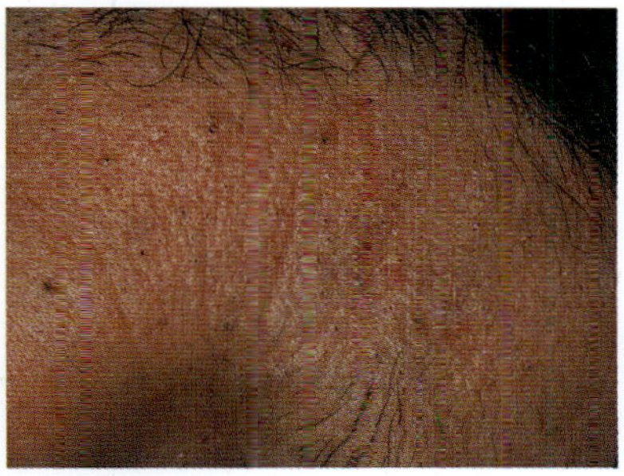

DR A L WRIGHT

Comedones or blackheads

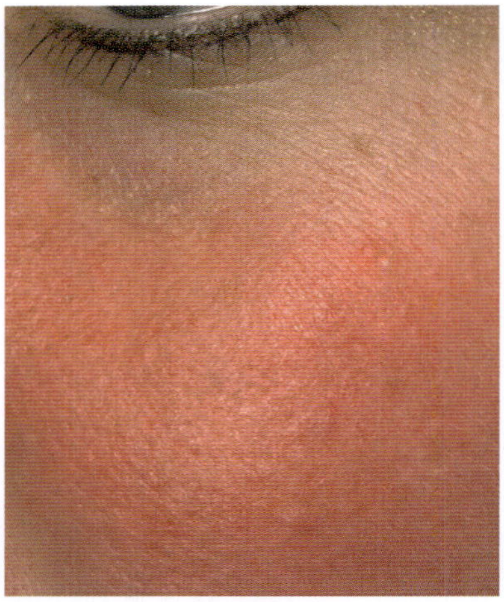
MEDISCAN

Seborrhoeic skin

Seborrhoea Excessive secretion of sebum from the sebaceous gland. This usually occurs during puberty, as a result of hormonal changes in the body.

Infectious? No.

Appearance: The follicle openings enlarge and excessive sebum is secreted. The skin appears coarse and greasy; comedones, pustules and papules are present.

Site: The face and scalp. Seborrhoea may also affect the back and the chest.

Treatment: The area should be cleansed to remove excess grease. Medical treatment may be required – this would use locally applied steroid creams.

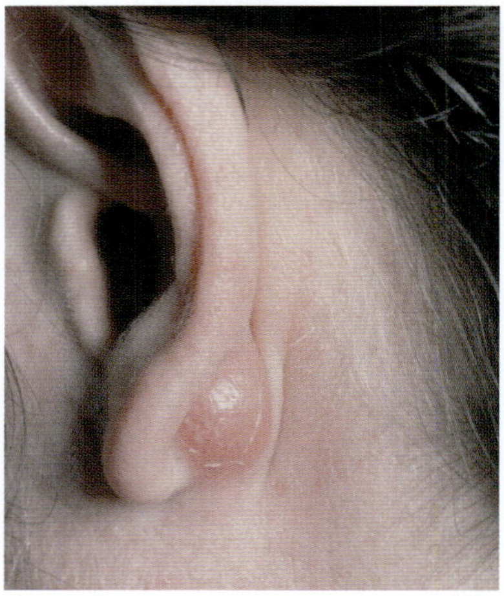
WELLCOME PHOTO LIBRARY

Sebaceous cyst

Steatomas, sebaceous cysts or wens Localized pockets or sacs of sebum, which form in hair follicles or under the sebaceous glands in the skin. The sebum becomes blocked, the sebaceous gland becomes enlarged and a lump forms.

Infectious? No.

Appearance: Semi-globular in shape, either raised or flat, and hard or soft. The cysts are the same colour as the skin, or red if secondary bacterial infection occurs. A comedone can often be seen at the original mouth of the hair follicle.

Site: If the cyst appears on the upper eyelid, it is known as a **chalazion** or **meibomian cyst**.

Treatment: Medical – often a GP will remove the cyst under local anaesthetic. Small inflamed cysts can be medically treated with steroid medications or antibiotics.

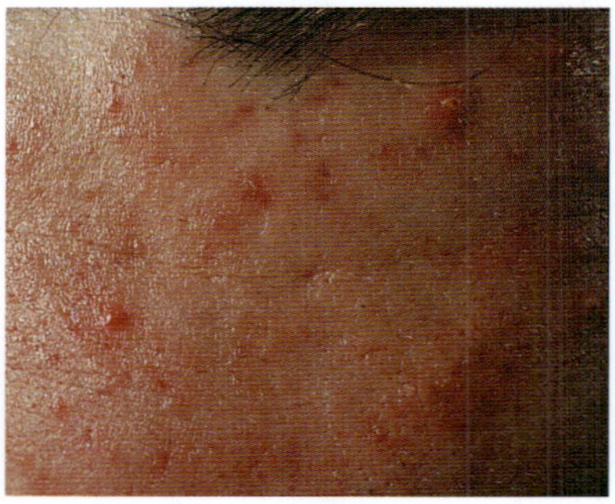
DR MH BECK

Acne vulgaris

Acne vulgaris Hormone imbalance in the body at puberty influences the activity of the sebaceous gland, causing an increased production of sebum. The sebum may be retained within the sebaceous ducts, causing congestion and bacterial infection of the surrounding tissues.

Infectious? No.

Appearance: Inflammation of the skin, accompanied by comedones, pustules, papules and possibly cysts. Scarring of the skin can be associated with this skin disorder following skin healing after bacterial infection.

Site: Commonly on the face, on the nose, the chin and the forehead. Acne may also occur on the chest and back.

Treatment: Medical – oral antibiotics may be prescribed, as well as antibiotic skin preparations. Other preparations which may be prescribed aim to unblock the skin and destroy bacteria. With medical approval, regular salon services may be given to cleanse the skin deeply, and also to stimulate the blood circulation.

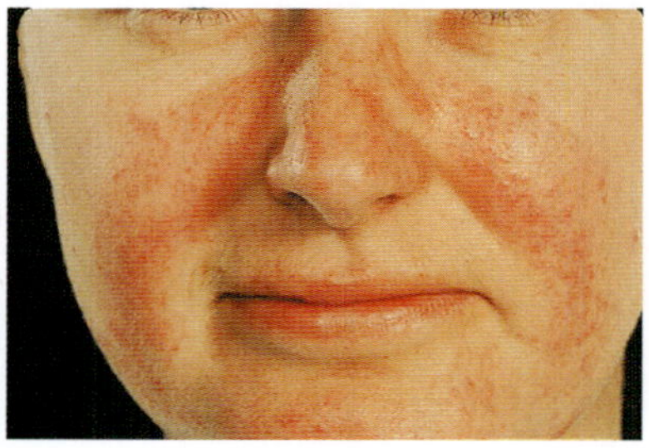
DR MH BECK

Rosacea

Rosacea Excessive sebum secretion combined with a chronic inflammatory condition, caused by dilation of the blood capillaries. Their appearance is referred to as telangiectasis.

Infectious? No.

Appearance: The skin becomes coarse, the pores enlarge and the cheek and nose area becomes inflamed, sometimes swelling and producing a butterfly pattern. Blood circulation slows in the dilated capillaries, creating a purplish appearance. Pustules and papules may also be present in severe cases.

Treatment: Medical – usually including antibiotics.

Pigmentation disorders

Pigmentation of the skin varies, according to the person's genetic characteristics. In general the darker the skin, the more pigment is present, but some abnormal changes in skin pigmentation can occur.

- **hyper-pigmentation** – increased pigment production
- **hypo-pigmentation** – loss of pigmentation in the skin

ISTOCK/© FANELIE ROSIER

Freckles

Ephelides or freckles Multiple small hyper-pigmented areas of the skin. Exposure to UV light (as in sunlight) stimulates the production of melanin, intensifying their appearance.

Infectious? No.

Appearance: Small, flat, pigmented areas, darker than the surrounding skin.

Site: Commonly the nose and cheeks of white-skinned people. Freckles may also occur on the shoulders, arms, hands and back.

Treatment: Freckles may be concealed with cosmetics. A sun block or high sun protection factor (SPF) sunscreen can be recommended, to prevent them intensifying further.

TOP TIP

Hypo-pigmentation may result from certain skin injuries, disorders or diseases.

Lentigo (lentigines) Hyper-pigmented areas of skin, slightly larger than freckles. Lentigo simplex occur in childhood. Actinic (solar) lentigines occur in middle age as a result of sun exposure.

Infectious? No.

Appearance: Brown, slightly raised, pigmented patches of skin, ranging in size.

Site: The face, hands and shoulders.

Treatment: Application of cosmetic concealing products.

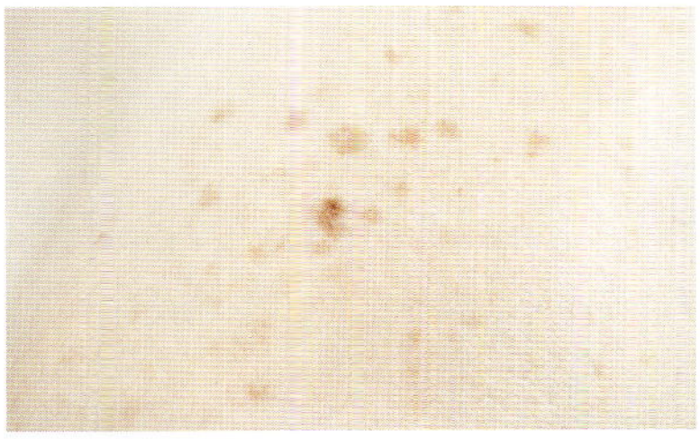

ISTOCK/© ZIGA LISJAK

Lentigo

Chloasmata or liver spots Hyper-pigmentation in specific areas, stimulated by a skin irritant such as UV usually affecting women and darkly pigmented skins. The condition often occurs during pregnancy, and usually disappears soon after the birth of the baby. It may also occur as a result of taking oral contraceptive pills. The female hormone oestrogen is thought to stimulate melanin production.

Infectious? No.

Appearance: Flat, smooth, irregularly shaped and sizes, pigmented areas of skin, varying in colour from light tan to dark brown. Chloasmata are larger than ephelides.

Site: The back of the hands, forearms, upper chest, temples and forehead.

Treatment: A barrier cream or a total sun block will reduce the risk of the chloasmata increasing in size or number.

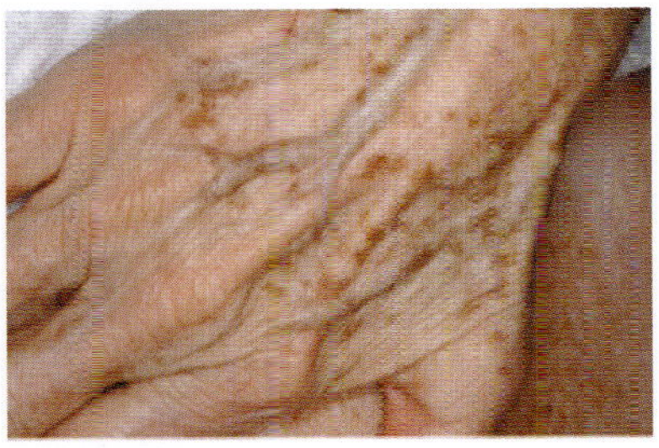

DELMAR CENGAGE LEARNING

Chloasmata or liver spots

Dermatosis papulosa nigra Often called flesh moles, characterized by multiple benign, small brown to black hyper-pigmented papules, common among black-skinned people.

Infectious? No.

Appearance: Raised pigmented markings resembling moles.

Site: Usually seen on the cheeks and forehead, although they may appear on the neck, upper chest and back.

Treatment: Apply camouflage products to even skin colour; or skin-staining preparations to de-pigmented areas. If the skin is exposed to UV light, it will not have the same protection in the areas lacking pigment and will require protection.

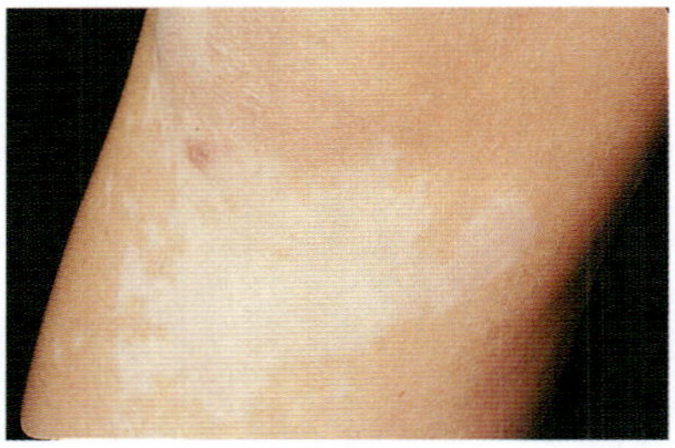
DR M H BECK

Vitiligo or leucoderma

Vitiligo or leucoderma The skin is unable to produce the melanin pigment and the hair and eyes are also affected, lacking colour. The eyes are often very pale blue or red in appearance due to lack of pigment

Infectious? No.

Appearance: Well-defined patches of white skin, lacking pigment.

Site: The face, the neck, the hands, the lower abdomen and the thighs. If vitiligo occurs over the eyebrows, the hairs in the area will also lose their pigment.

Treatment: Apply camouflage products to even skin colour; or apply skin-staining preparations in the de-pigmented areas. If the skin is exposed to UV light, it will not have the same protection in the areas lacking pigment and will require protection.

DR JOHN GRAY, THE WORLD OF SKIN CARE

Albinism in someone of African descent

Albinism The skin is unable to produce the melanin pigment, and the skin, hair and eyes lack colour.

Infectious? No.

Appearance: The skin is usually very pale and the hair is white. The eyes also are pink, and extremely sensitive to light.

Site: The entire skin.

Treatment: There is no effective treatment. Maximum skin protection is necessary when the client is exposed to UV light, and sunglasses should be worn to protect the eyes.

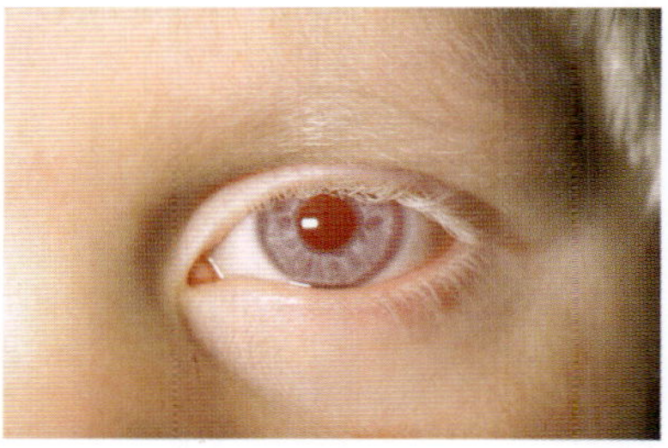
MEDISCAN

Albinism showing pink eye

Vascular (circulatory disorders) There are two types of naevus of concern to beauty therapists: vascular and cellular. **Vascular naevi** are skin conditions in which small or large areas of skin pigmentation are caused by the permanent dilation of blood capillaries.

Erythema Increase in blood to the area causing the blood capillaries to dilate. The cause can be due either to injury or inflammation as the body's immune system responds to infection or irritation.

Infectious? No.

Appearance: The skin appears red.

Site: Erythema may affect one area (locally) or all of the skin (generally).

Treatment: Identify the cause. In the case of a **skin allergy**, the client must not be brought into contact with the irritant again. If unknown, refer the client to their GP.

TOP TIP

Vascular circulatory skin disorder

If there is a vascular skin disorder, avoid overstimulating the skin or the problem will become more noticeable and the service may even cause further damage.

Dilated capillaries or telangiectasis Capillaries near the surface of the skin that are permanently dilated.

Infectious? No.

Appearance: Small red visible blood capillaries.

Site: Areas where the skin is neglected, dry or fine, such as the cheek area.

Treatment: Conceal using pigmented camouflage product, or removal by a qualified electrologist using advanced electrologist techniques or laser.

Spider naevi or stellate haemangiomas Dilated blood vessels, with smaller dilated capillaries radiating from them.

Infectious? No.

Appearance: Small red capillaries, radiating like a spider's legs from a central point.

Site: Commonly the cheek area, but may occur on the upper body, the arms and the neck. Spider naevi are usually caused by an injury to the skin.

Treatment: Spider naevi can be concealed using a camouflage cosmetic, or treated by a qualified beauty therapist using advanced electrologist techniques with diathermy or laser.

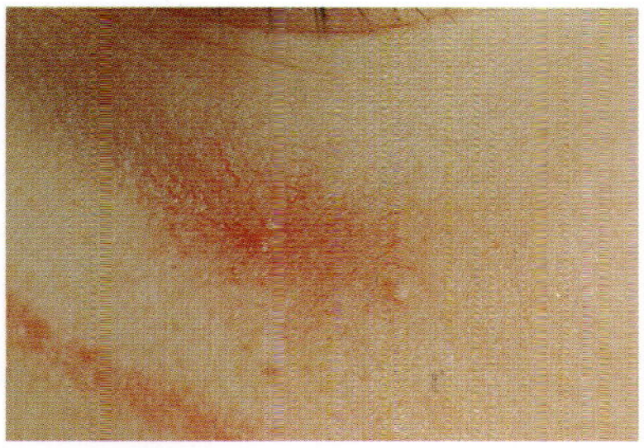

DR M H BECK

Spider naevi or stellate haemangiomas

Naevi vasculosis or strawberry marks Red or purplish raised marks which appear on the skin at birth.

Infectious? No.

Appearance: Red or purplish lobed mark, of any size.

Site: Any area of the skin.

Treatment: About 60 per cent disappear by the age of six years. Treatment is not usually necessary; concealing camouflage cosmetics can be applied if desired. A sunblock is also recommended.

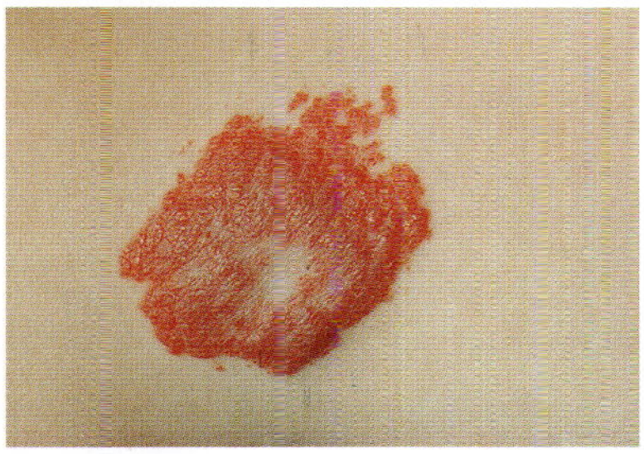

DR M H BECK

Naevi vasculosis or strawberry marks

Capillary naevi or port-wine stains Large areas of dilated capillaries, which contrast noticeably with the surrounding areas.

Infectious? No.

Appearance: The naevus has a smooth, flat surface.

Site: Some 75 per cent occur on the head; they are probably formed at the foetal stage. Naevi may also be found on the neck and face.

Treatment: Camouflage cosmetic products can be applied to disguise the area.

Cellular naevi or moles **Cellular naevi** are skin conditions in which changes in the cells of the skin result in skin malformations.

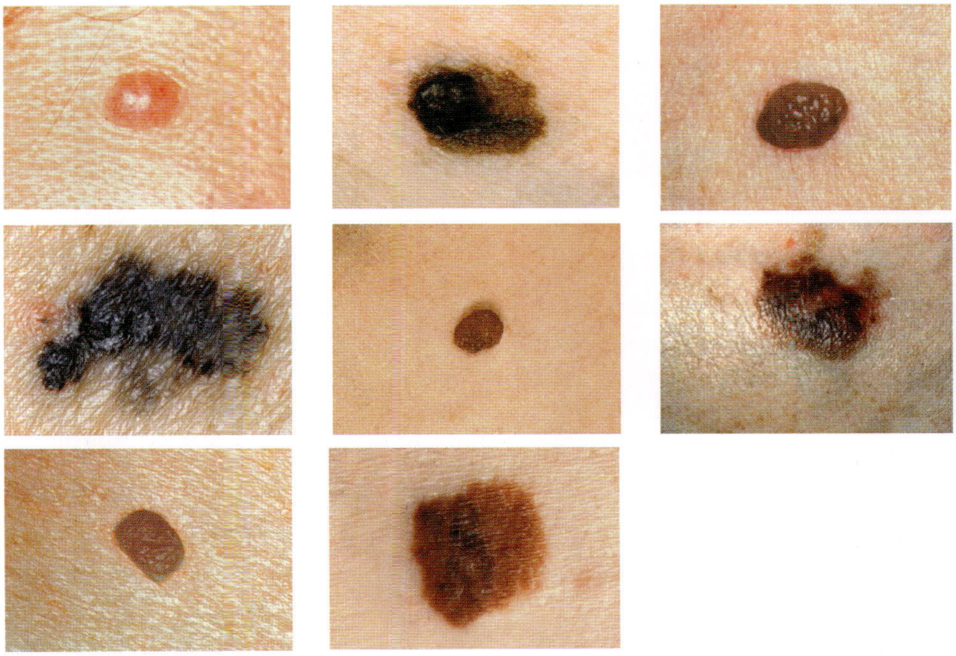

Moles

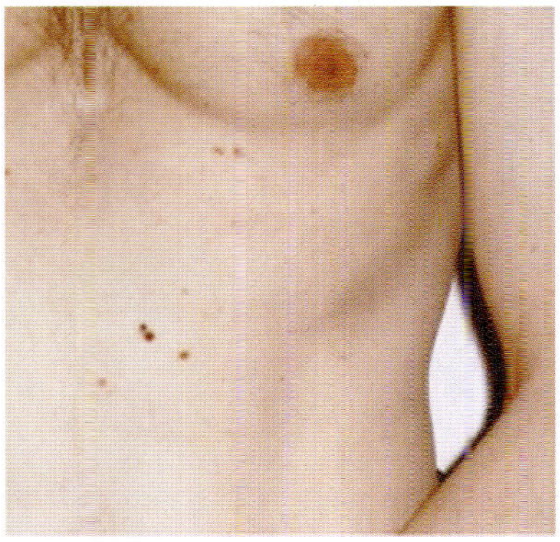

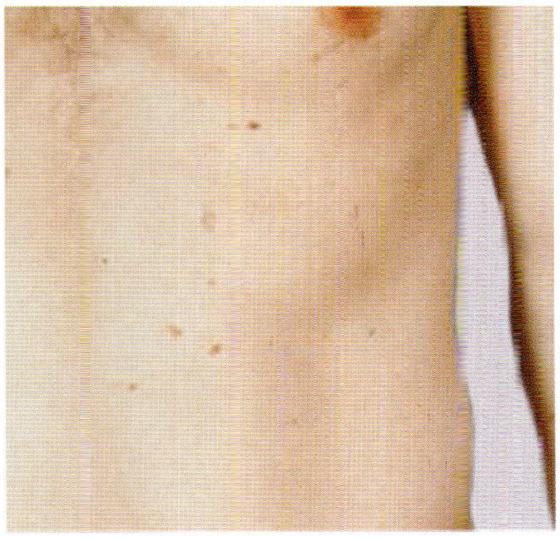

DELMAR CENGAGE LEARNING

HEALTH & SAFETY

Malignant melanoma mole

The risk of melanoma increases as the number of naevi increases. Therefore, clients with lots of naevi or moles are at higher risk.

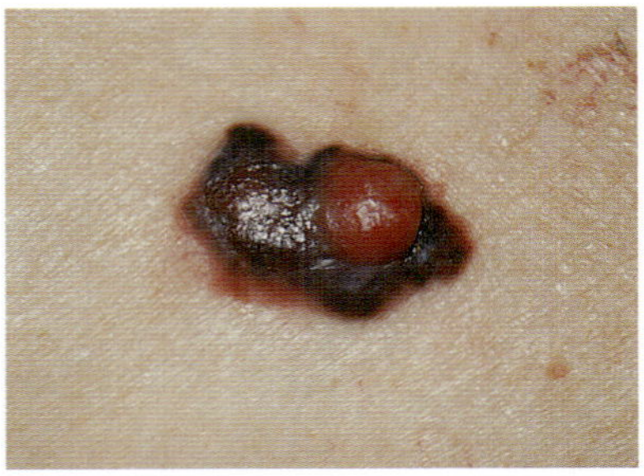
DR M H BECK

Malignant melanoma

HEALTH & SAFETY

Moles

If moles change in shape or size, if they bleed or form crusts, seek medical attention.

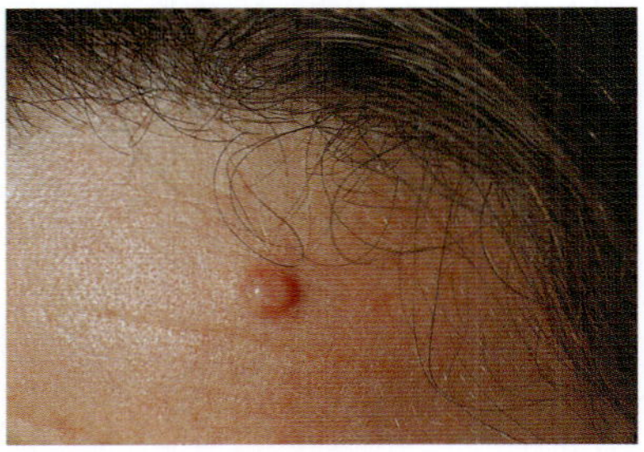
DR M H BECK

Benign naevus

TOP TIP

Naevi numbers and skin colour

A white skin normally has up to four times as many naevi as black skin.

Malignant melanomas or malignant moles Rapidly growing skin cancers, usually occurring in adults.

Infectious? No.

Appearance: Each melanoma commences as a bluish-black mole, which enlarges rapidly, darkening in colour and developing a halo of pigmentation around it. It later becomes raised, bleeds and ulcerates. Secondary growths will develop in internal organs if the melanoma is not treated.

Site: Usually the lower abdomen, legs or feet.

Treatment: Medical – always recommend that a client has any mole checked if it is changing in size, structure or colour, or if it becomes itchy or bleeds.

Junction naevi Localized collections of naevoid cells that arise from the mass production locally of pigment-forming cells (melanocytes).

Infectious? No.

Appearance: In childhood, junction naevi appear as smooth or slightly raised pigmented marks. They vary in colour from brown to black.

Site: Any area.

Treatment: Camouflage cosmetics can be used to conceal the area and the application of sunblock can prevent further pigmentation or skin darkening.

Dermal naevi Localized collections of naevoid cells.

Infectious? No.

Appearance: About 1 cm wide, dermal naevi appear smooth and dome-shaped. Their colour ranges from skin tone to dark brown. Frequently, one or more hairs may grow from the naevus.

Site: Usually the face.

Treatment: None.

Hairy naevi Moles exhibiting coarse hairs from their surface.

Infectious? No.

Appearance: Slightly raised moles, varying in size from 3 cm to much larger areas. Colour ranges from fawn to dark brown.

Site: Anywhere on the skin.

Treatment: Hairy naevi may be surgically removed where possible, and this is often done for cosmetic reasons. Hair growing from a mole should be cut, not plucked: if plucked, the hairs will become coarser and the growth of further hairs may be stimulated.

Skin disorders involving abnormal growth

Psoriasis Patches of itchy, red, flaky skin, the cause of which is unknown.

Infectious? No. Secondary infection with bacteria can occur if the skin becomes broken and dirt enters the skin.

Appearance: Red patches of skin appear, covered in waxy, silvery scales. Bleeding will occur if the area is scratched and scales are removed.

Site: The elbows, the knees, the lower back and the scalp.

Treatment: There is no known treatment. Medication including steroid creams can bring relief to the symptoms. Medically administered UV treatment is also found to be beneficial.

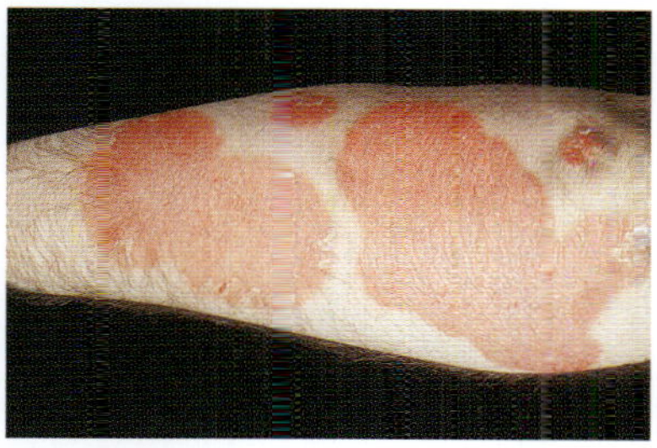

DR M H BECK

Psoriasis

Seborrhoeic or senile warts Raised, pigmented, benign tumours occurring in middle age.

Infectious? No.

Appearance: Slightly raised, brown or black, rough patches of skin. Such warts can be confused with pigmented moles.

Site: The trunk, the scalp and the temples.

Treatment: The warts can be cauterized where the tissue is destroyed by a GP using heat or cold

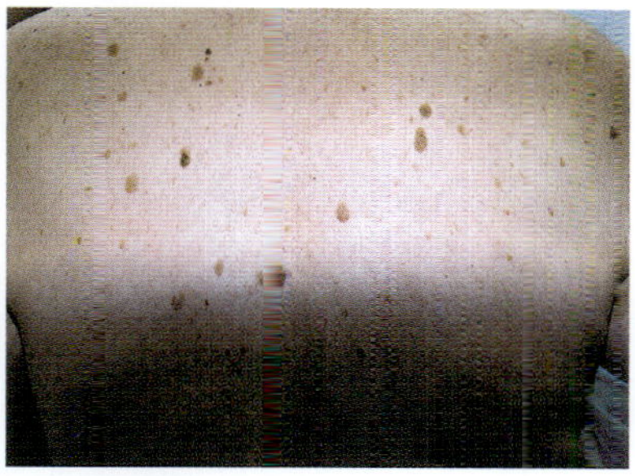

DR JOHN GRAY, THE WORLD OF SKIN CARE

Seborrhoeic or senile warts

Verrucae filliformis or skin tags These verrucas appear as threads projecting from the skin.

Infectious? No.

Appearance: Skin-coloured threads of skin 3–6 mm long.

Site: Mainly seen on the neck and the eyelids, but may occur in other areas such as under the arms.

Treatment: Medical – removal using cauterization where the tissue is destroyed using heat or cold, diathermy, either by a GP or by a qualified electrologist.

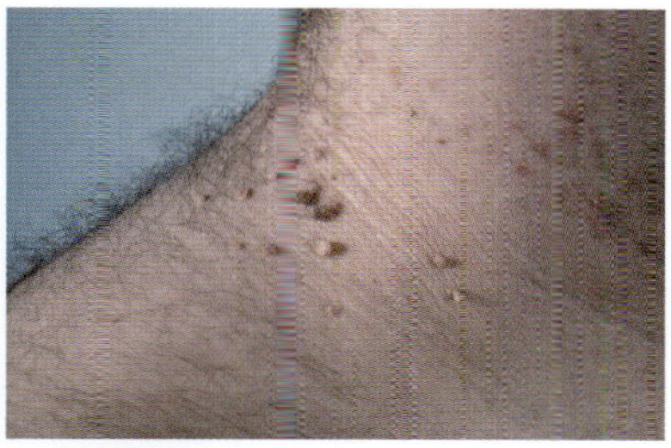

WELLCOME PHOTO LIBRARY

Verrucae filliformis or skin tags

Xanthomas Small yellow growths appearing upon the surface of the skin made up of cholesterol deposits.

Infectious? No.

Appearance: A yellow, flat or raised area of skin.

Site: Commonly the eyelids, but can occur anywhere on the body.

Treatment: Medical – the growth is thought to be connected with certain medical diseases, such as diabetes or high or low blood pressure; sometimes a low-fat diet can correct the condition.

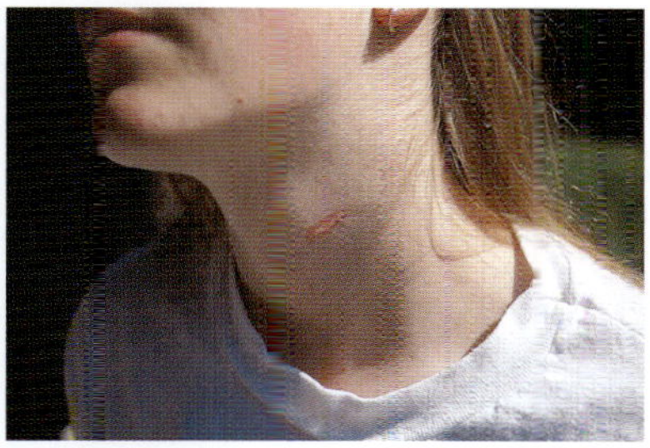

DR JOHN GRAY, THE WORLD OF SKIN CARE

Keloid scar

Keloids Keloids occur following skin injury and are overgrown abnormal scar tissue which spreads, characterized by excess deposits of **collagen**. To avoid skin discoloration the keloid must be protected from UV exposure.

Infectious? No.

Appearance: The skin tends to be red, raised, shiny and ridged.

Site: Located over the site of a wound or other lesion.

Treatment: Medical–by drug therapy, such as cortisone injections, or surgery.

HEALTH & SAFETY

Skin tags

Skin tags often occur under the arms and in the groin area. If present, take care when carrying out a wax depilation service in this area: do not apply wax over tags. If the hair is long, trim the hair instead of waxing over skin tags.

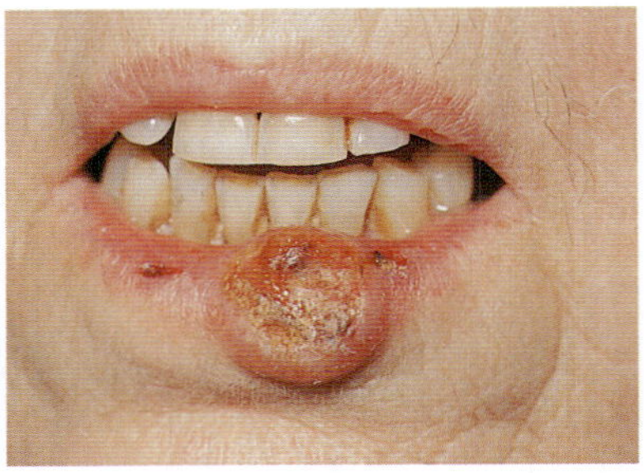

DR A L WRIGHT

Squamous cell carcinomas

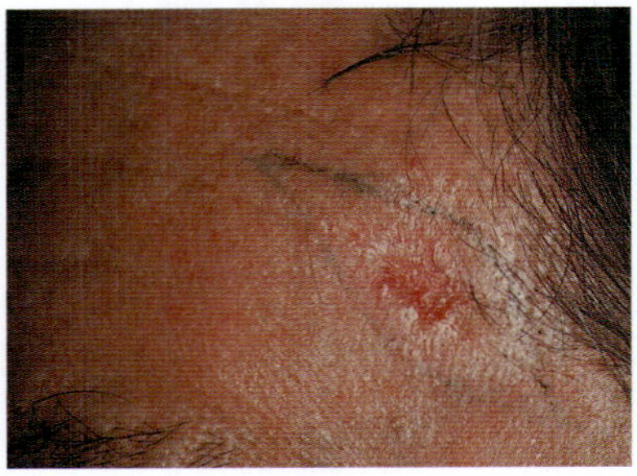

DR M H BECK

Basal cell carcinomas

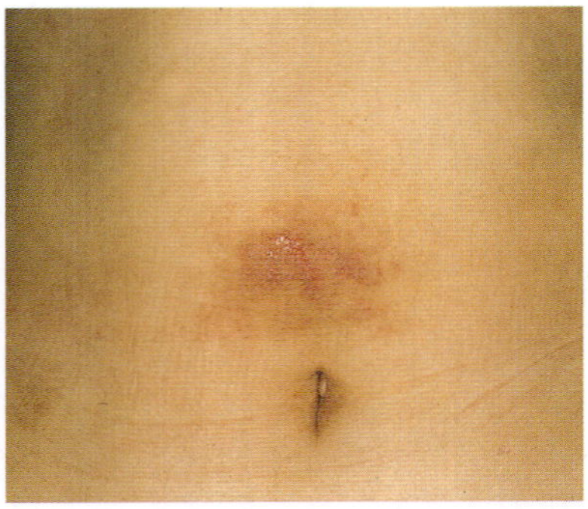

DR JOHN GRAY, THE WORLD OF SKIN CARE

Allergic reaction to a nickel button

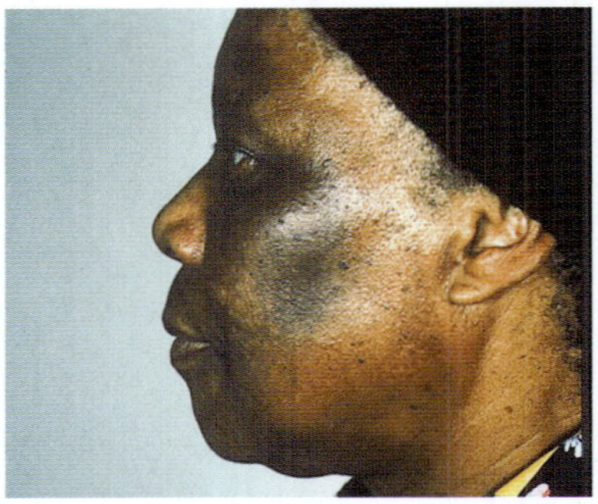

DR JOHN GRAY, THE WORLD OF SKIN CARE

Allergic reaction to an ingredient in hair dye

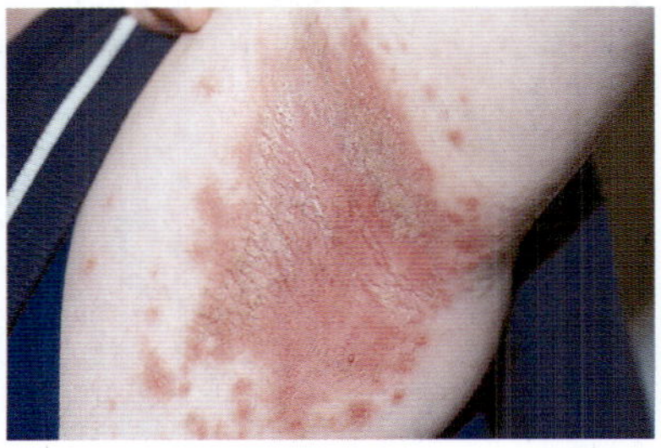

DR JOHN GRAY, THE WORLD OF SKIN CARE

Allergic reaction to an antiperspirant

Malignant tumours

Squamous cell carcinomas or prickle-cell cancers Malignant growths originating in the epidermis.

Infectious: No.

Appearance: When fully formed, the carcinoma appears as a raised area of skin.

Site: Anywhere on the skin.

Treatment: Includes surgical removal, also radiotherapy (treatment with X-ray) or treatment with drugs as necessary.

Basal cell carcinomas or rodent ulcers Slow-growing malignant tumours, occurring in middle age.

Infectious? No.

Appearance: A small, shiny, waxy nodule with a depressed centre. The disease extends, with more nodules appearing on the border of the original ulcer.

Site: Usually the face.

Treatment: Includes surgical removal, also radiotherapy (treatment with X-ray) or treatment with drugs as necessary.

Skin allergies

The skin can protect itself to some degree from damage or invasion. **Mast cells** detect damage to the skin; if damage occurs, the mast cells burst, releasing the chemical histamine into the tissues. Histamine causes the blood capillaries to dilate, giving the reddening we call 'erythema'. The increased blood flow transports materials in the blood which tend to limit the damage and begin repair.

If the skin is sensitive to and becomes inflamed on contact with a particular substance, this substance is called an **allergen**. Allergens may be animal, chemical or vegetable substances, and they may be inhaled, eaten or absorbed following contact with the skin. An **allergic skin reaction** appears as irritation, itching and discomfort, with reddening and swelling (as with nettle rash). If the allergen is removed, the allergic reaction subsides.

Each individual has different tolerances to the various substances we encounter in daily life. What causes an allergic reaction in one individual may be perfectly harmless to another.

Here are just a few examples of allergens known to cause allergic skin reactions in some people:

- metal objects containing nickel
- sticking plaster
- rubber
- lipstick containing eosin dye
- nail polish containing formaldehyde resin
- hair and eyelash dyes
- lanolin, the skin moisturizing agent
- detergents that dry the skin

- foods – well-known examples are peanuts, cow's milk, lobster, shellfish and strawberries
- plants such as tulips and chrysanthemums

HEALTH & SAFETY

Allergies

You may suddenly become allergic to a substance that has previously been perfectly harmless. Equally, you may over time *cease* to be allergic to something.

Infection following allergy

Following an allergic skin reaction in which the skin's surface has become itchy and broken, scratching may cause the skin to become infected with bacteria.

HEALTH & SAFETY

Record any known allergies

When completing the client record card, always ask whether your client has any known allergies.

HEALTH & SAFETY

Hypoallergenic products

The use of hypoallergenic products minimizes the risk of skin contact with likely irritants. Select these products for clients with skin allergies and hypersensitive skin.

Dermatitis An inflammatory skin disorder in which the skin becomes red, itchy and swollen. There are two types of dermatitis. In *primary dermatitis* the skin is irritated by the action of a substance upon the skin and this leads to skin inflammation. In *allergic contact dermatitis* the problem is caused by intolerance of the skin to a particular substance or group of substances. On exposure to the substance the skin quickly becomes irritated and an allergic reaction occurs.

Infectious? No.

Appearance: Reddening and swelling of the skin, with the possible appearance of blisters.

Site: If the skin reacts to a skin irritant outside the body, the reaction is localized. Repeated contact with the allergen will lead to a general hypersensitivity. If the irritant gains entry to the body, it will be transported in the bloodstream and may cause a general allergic skin reaction.

Treatment: Barrier cream can be used to help avoid contact with the irritants. PPE should be worn in the case of occupational hazard, i.e. gloves should be worn by a hairdresser to avoid developing contact dermatitis in the nature of the work – contact with water for long periods. When an allergic dermatitis reaction occurs, however, the only 'cure' is the absolute avoidance of the substance. Steroid creams such as hydrocortisone are usually prescribed, to sooth the damaged skin and reduce the irritation

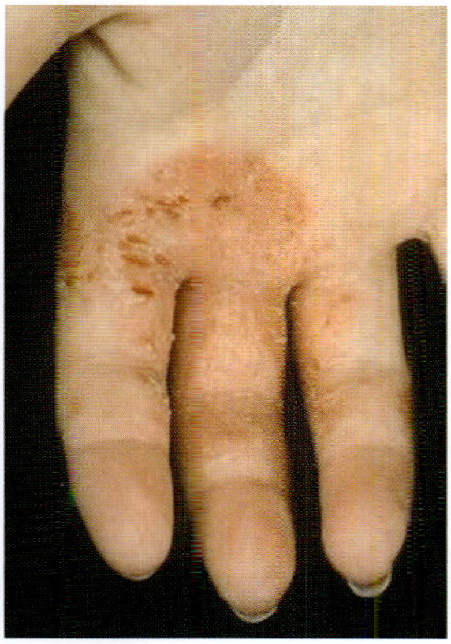

DR JOHN GRAY, THE WORLD OF SKIN CARE

Contact dermatitis on the hands

Eczema Inflammation of the skin caused by contact, internally or externally, with an irritant.

Infectious? No.

Appearance: Reddening of the skin, with swelling and blisters. The blisters leak tissue fluid which later hardens, forming scabs.

Site: The face, the neck and the skin, particularly at the inner creases of the elbows and behind the knees.

Treatment: Refer the client to their GP. Eczema may disappear if the source of irritation is identified and removed. Steroid cream may be prescribed by the GP and special diets may help. If the area is small and the skin unbroken, the service may go ahead; just avoid contact with the area

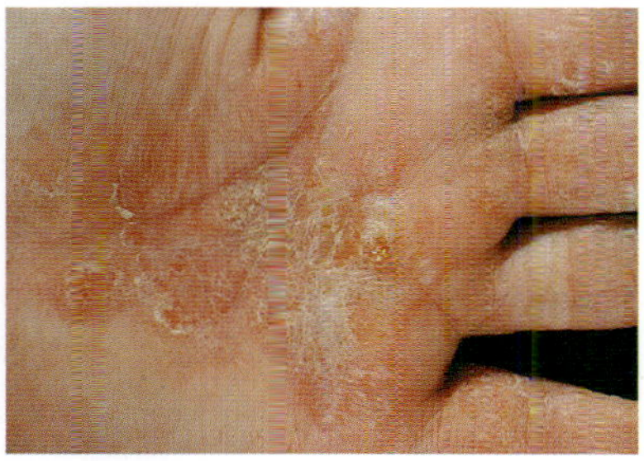

DR M H BECK

Eczema

Urticaria (nettle rash) or hives A minor skin disorder caused by contact with an allergen, either internally (food or drugs) or externally (for example, insect bites).

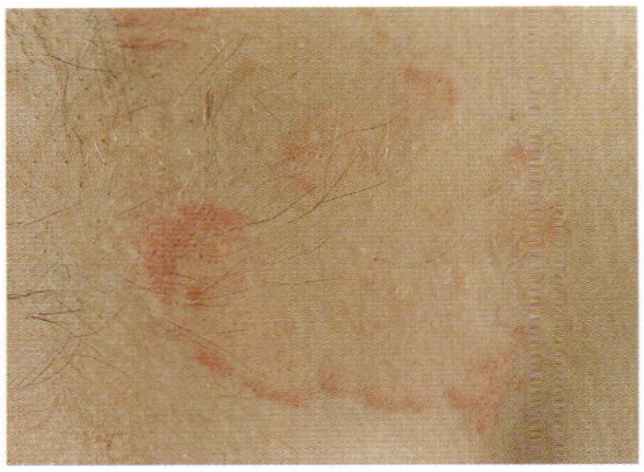
DR M H BECK
Urticaria (nettle rash) or hives

Infectious? No.

Appearance: Erythema with raised, round whitish skin weals. In some cases the lesions can cause intense burning or itching, a condition known as **pruritis**. Pruritis is a *symptom* of a disease (such as diabetes), not a disease itself.

Site: At the point of contact.

Treatment: Antihistamines may be prescribed to reduce the itching. The visible skin reaction usually disappears quickly, leaving no trace. Complete avoidance of the allergen 'cures' the problem.

ALWAYS REMEMBER

To avoid potential hazards and risks in the workplace staff should:

1. Be aware of the workplace health and safety policy and their legal responsibility in its implementation.
2. Ensure their personal presentation at work meets health and safety and legislative requirements in accordance with workplace policies.
3. Follow the most recent workplace policies for their job role and manufacturers' instructions for the safe use of resources.
4. Follow the latest health and safety legislation related to their work.
5. Know who is responsible for health and safety in the workplace.
6. Pass on any suggestions for reducing health and safety risks within their job role.
7. Report or deal with immediately any risk which could be a hazard complying with workplace policies and legal requirements.
8. Be aware of first aid arrangements in the event of an accident or illness.
9. Know the workplace fire evacuation practice and procedure.
10. Ensure their working practice minimizes the possible spread of infection or disease.

Staff training must ensure hazards are identified and their risk controlled effectively in the workplace.

ASSESSMENT OF KNOWLEDGE AND UNDERSTANDING

FUNCTIONAL SKILLS

Having covered the learning objectives for **monitor procedures to safely control work operations** – test what you need to know and understand answering the following short questions below.

Check that health and safety instructions are followed:

1. It is important to have current knowledge of health and safety regulations: where can you source reliable information from?
2. What are the main responsibilities of the employers and employees in the workplace under the Health and Safety at Work Act (1974)?
3. Name four pieces of health and safety legislation and identify how they should be complied with.
4. How can information relating to health and safety workplace instructions be passed on?
5. How and when can issues of health and safety be fed back from staff to prevent a hazard becoming a risk?

6 You may be required to complete and maintain records relating to health and safety. Give **three** examples of legislation where records should be completed and accessible for audit.

7 How and when can you identify workplace health and safety competence with staff? If a skills gap is identified, what actions must you take and why?

8 What is the purpose of the workplace health and safety policy? When must an employer have one and what information should it include?

9 Why must regular health and safety checks be carried out in the workplace?

10 Why is staff personal conduct important to maintaining the health and safety of themselves, clients and colleagues?

Make sure that risks are controlled safely and effectively

1 The air conditioning system in the salon has broken. In what way is this a hazard and how should this be reported in accordance with workplace health and safety instructions?

2 Why is it necessary to keep accurate and legible records of any risks reported and the action taken?

3 Why must staff always be aware of potential hazards?

4 What is the purpose of a risk assessment and when should this be completed?

5 Why is it important to follow manufacturers' instructions for the safe use of equipment and products?

6 In the event of a fire, after having safely evacuated the building, how would you contact the appropriate emergency service?

7 What is the procedure for dealing with an accident in the workplace? When would it need to be reported to the HSE incident contact centre?

8 When precaution procedures need to be put in place when a hazard is identified, who should these be agreed with initially?

9 Why is it important for staff to know the extent of their health and safety responsibilities and competency requirements and why should their capabilities and training received be monitored?

10 What health and safety guidance should be available for reference for the correct use and storage of hazardous substances?

BABOR

4 Promotional activities

Learning Objectives

This chapter covers the **Contribute to the planning and implementation of promotional activities** unit. This unit is all about how to plan and carry out successful promotional activities for the workplace. This will require the setting of clear objectives to be achieved, realistic timescales to work to, attention to detail when planning, and effective communication with all those involved with the implementation of activities. Finally, engaging successfully with your audience to ensure that the promotion is a success and achieves its objectives.

There are **three** learning outcomes for this unit which you must achieve competently:

1 **Contribute to the planning and preparation of promotional activities**

2 **Implement promotional activities**

3 **Participate in the evaluation of promotional activities**

For each unit your Assessor will observe you, on **at least one occasion**, of your performance when planning and implementing promotional activities. In addition, you will need to collect further documentary evidence to show you have met all the standard requirements.

From the **range** statement, you must show that you have implemented the following promotional activities:

- **demonstrations**
- **displays**
- **advertising campaigns**

(continued on the next page)

ROLE MODEL

Kerry Davis

Spa Operations Manager, The Sanctuary

"Over 30 years ago, The Sanctuary was established in the heart of London's Covent Garden to provide powerful relaxing and rejuvenating treatments. On the back of the initial success of the business, in 1998 we perfected a series of products which can be used at home without the need of a beauty therapist or special equipment. Available in Boots, and a few select locations around the world, these products allow all women to treat themselves to a touch of spa luxury, whether it's a sensual bath float or a rejuvenating pro-collagen face mask, wherever their location!

(continued)

Also that you have met the following promotional objectives:

- to enhance business image
- to increase business

When providing promotional activities it is important to use the skills you have learnt in the following unit:

Monitor procedures to safely control work operations.

Outcome 1: Contribute to the planning and implementation of promotional activities

Learn how to contribute to the planning and preparation of promotional activities by:

1. Making recommendations to the relevant person for suitable **promotional activities** and identifying the potential benefits for the business.
2. Identifying and agreeing specific measurable, achievable, realistic and time-bound **objectives** and target groups for the activity with the relevant person(s).
3. Agreeing requirements for the activity with all relevant persons in sufficient detail to allow the work to be planned.
4. Producing an agreed plan showing the:
   - type of promotional activity
   - **objectives** of the activity
   - roles and responsibilities of others involved
   - resource requirements
   - preparation and implementation activities
   - timescales
   - the budget
   - methods of evaluation
5. Agreeing a plan that takes into account any legal requirements, when necessary.
6. Ensuring resources are available to meet the planned timescale.

Promotion refers to marketing activities carried out that helps raise awareness of your business and/or product/service.

These activities let existing and potential new clients know what you can provide. They can take place on-site at the business premises or off site at an external venue.

Promotions are essential to the success of the business, they achieve the following benefits:

- Raise the profile of the business both locally and further, dependent upon the type of promotional activity carried out and advertising media used.
- Showcase your skills and provide professional advice and guidance to the client.
- Increase financial revenue to meet (or exceed) business financial targets.
- Maintain client enthusiasm and motivation in the use of a product or service, i.e. the launch of a new skincare range to enhance that already available or an upgrade in a piece of electrical equipment already offered.
- Maximize the potential for a particular event. e.g. single lash extensions for the Christmas party season.
- Reward employees if there is a target incentive to the promotion and they meet it.
- Promote clients to use the services at quieter trading periods.
- Provide feedback from the client on their future needs.
- They can target groups who do not currently use your services.
- Ultimately, promotions can increase your client base.

ACTIVITY

Target groups

From your current experience of working in industry, what target groups could be encouraged to engage with your salon services/ products that are possibly not already doing so?

How could you promote their engagement?

Types of promotional activities

There are different types of promotional activities that you may become involved with or initiate, these include:

Demonstrations

A **demonstration** enables you to show clients the product/services and the benefits of using them. You may be able to engage the clients with the product by allowing them to sample the product/service. Its success will be how you present this to the client, your enthusiasm and confidence with the product/service, overall professionalism and the promotion of its features and benefits.

ALWAYS REMEMBER

A **feature** is the uniqueness or individuality of a product or service, e.g. design technology of a new piece of equipment.

A **benefit** is the gain to be made from using the product or service.

TOP TIP

Always pay careful attention to your client and their responses when engaging in conversation with clients about products or services.

Remember to question, listen and answer:

- ***Question* your clients to find out their needs.**
- ***Listen* to the answer.**
- ***Answer* with the relevant information and advice.**

CACI

CACI trade show in Bologna

TISSERAND

Display provided by Tisserand, a natural beauty product company

Displays

Displays are good to raise client interest and awareness of products or services you want to showcase. A display is there to be looked at and as such should look professional. Testers are great if a product is being displayed, as the client can touch and smell the product. This should be placed where there is a high volume of traffic – where clients walk past it. Some displays allow products to be picked up for purchase. Displays holding retail stock should always be well stocked, with smart undamaged packaging. Eyelevel displays are best. Displays should be changed regularly according to the promotion.

Also use eye-catching promotional material (usually provided by the product supplier).

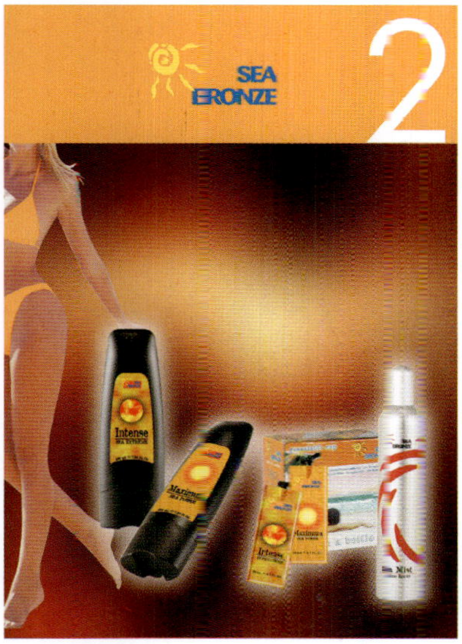

SMART BUY

Professional company promotional material

SMART BUY

Promotional tester display for self-tanning products

> Ensure that everyone knows the company business mission statement or company vision so that everyone knows what we are all trying to achieve.
>
> **Kerry Davis**

Advertising campaigns

Advertising campaigns raise client awareness of a particular product or service and intend to increase interest. A budget should be allocated to advertising and your choice of advertising will depend upon how much money you have to spend and which is most cost-effective.

TOP TIP

Advertising campaigns should be changed regularly to maintain client interest.

Methods of advertising include using signage in the business, fliers, direct mailings, email, text phone messaging, website advertisement and media such as advertisements in newspapers, commercial journals, radio and television. Your advertising campaign needs a specific goal. This could be a short-term goal, e.g. the launch of a new product, discounted services, etc. or a long-term goal such as establishing the business name and familiarity with its product and services: 'the brand'. This would be achieved through repeat advertising.

The best advert is your clients who, if happy, advertise through positive word-of-mouth, which may include a social media comment!

The above are all examples of public relation activities that help clients to understand what your business has to offer and how they might benefit from engaging with it and using its services.

The choice of advertising will depend on the marketing budget that you have available and the type of promotion activity.

The annual business plan should identify what promotions are intended to be implemented – an event list. This will be based upon a promotion strategy to reach target markets in order to achieve a specific objective(s).

When finalized this will allow you to plan effectively, briefing others of the intended schedule and their involvement. This may include a contribution from sponsors such as skincare companies who will play a part in supporting the success of the event.

Ideas from staff are important and appraisals provide a good opportunity for staff to offer their ideas such as how a new client target group can be reached or how the profile of the services that are on offer can be raised.

If you have ideas you would like to share, these should be discussed with the relevant person. Choose the correct time and way to communicate your ideas such as face-to-face at a team meeting, or appraisal review, or indirectly via email.

In presenting your ideas to the person responsible for decision-making:

- State clearly the objectives of the promotion.
- Identify when it will take place and where.
- State what can be achieved by running the promotion, the specific benefits to the business it will bring.
- Identify what and who will need to be involved.
- Identify your target clientele.
- How the promotion will need to be marketed.
- Explain how the success of the event will be measured.
- Project the anticipated budget – this must be realistic and cost-effective.
- The practicalities of how you will prepare for the promotion – when this will need to commence.

It may be that feedback following your presentation is that your ideas require more work. Agree a date which allows you to respond to and resolve the actions required.

ALWAYS REMEMBER

Planning promotion tips

You must have a plan of how and if you will be able to deal with increased business from a promotion.

- Will you need more resources? For example, following the promotion for products or services.
- Will you be able to respond to enquiries timely and efficiently? This includes telephone and website communication.

FUNCTIONAL SKILLS

SHUTTERSTOCK/ANDRESR

Presenting your ideas

FUNCTIONAL SKILLS

TOP TIP

Presenting information

Present your information to best effect to enable understanding and engagement. This can be pictorially, using pictures, graphically using graphs, etc. and verbally.

ALWAYS REMEMBER

Demonstration styles vary

Are you working on one client to demonstrate a particular product/service, or demonstrating to a group? Is it a range of products to be demonstrated or just one item?

Planning and preparing for a promotion

TOP TIP

Presenting your promotion ideas

FUNCTIONAL SKILLS

- Agree a time to present your ideas if required to the relevant person or group of people.
- Prepare and ensure that you have all resources and facts at hand to refer to.
- Provide a professional, short, concise presentation of your ideas. This should be what you feel is appropriate and should be what you are most comfortable with, e.g. flipchart or PowerPoint presentation.
- Present your ideas confidently.
- Offer the opportunity for questions to clarify any queries.
- Welcome feedback both positive and negative.

It is essential that the promotion is well organized. An initial planning meeting date will need to be arranged, attended by all people involved. Here the promotion objectives will be agreed and a schedule of activities will be drawn that need to be completed, by identified people and by a specific time. There should be an overall promotion organizer, who will coordinate the plan and activities required. Tasks should only be allocated to those competent to complete the activity.

The timescale of each activity will need to be prioritized in order of immediacy. You will also need to decide on the content and timings for the event, a programme of activities.

TOP TIP

Making a positive contribution

You may wish to charge for invitations to an event with a nominal amount supporting a charity of your choice. You would need to share this with the customers. This also provides a further PR opportunity as you can advertise how much was raised at the event for the charity.

This would need to be agreed with your line manager in the promotion proposal.

> Have standard operating procedures for everything so that everyone has clear guidelines for every task that they undertake.
>
> **Kerry Davis**

COURTESY COLLIN UK © COLLIN PARIS

Joyfully wrapped up!

An example is provided below.

Example of an internal promotional event Aim to promote new service single lash extensions; raise awareness of the immediate effect and convenience of a spray-tanning service and provide a retail sales opportunity for Christmas gift sets.

It will be necessary to have a maximum number of invites for reasons of health and safety, visibility for demonstrations and catering. You will need to decide how your guest list will be created for an invitation, ticket purchase, etc.

ALWAYS REMEMBER

Ask for advice from experienced staff

If there are staff who have had experience of running promotions, ask their advice when planning your promotion presentation. Ask them to have a look at your proposals when prepared for any further suggestions.

TOP TIP

Think outside the box

Set out to make your promotion different and interesting to capture the interest of your clients.

Christmas beautifully wrapped up

7.00pm– Arrival, guests will receive a glass of champagne and festive refreshments

7.30pm– Demonstrations by our expert team of beauty professionals, find out more about:

- single lash extensions
- spray-tanning
- party make-up tips
- party nails

8.30pm– Discounted Christmas skincare product gift sets with complimentary gift wrapping service

9.00pm– Prize drawer for a £100 service or product/s of your choice

* A goody bag of self-tanning preparations and other skincare products will be provided to all our guests.

* 10% discount on all services booked on the evening.

ACTIVITY

FUNCTIONAL SKILLS

For the example, *Christmas beautifully wrapped up*, consider **when** you would have to start planning for this event, when would you hold your initial meeting and what planning activities would be required?

Complete a planning activity schedule, listing the activities and using the following headings

Planning activity	*Responsible person*	*Date action required*	*Comment on progress*	*Activity confirmed and completed*

ACTIVITY

Anticipating problems and changes to circumstances

For the *Christmas beautifully wrapped up* promotion. What things would you need to plan for the unexpected to ensure it all ran smoothly?

You will also need to have a time schedule for the day of the event, consider:

- When do you need to start preparing?
- Who will be needed when?
- What responsibilities will staff have?

Have a contingency plan also – expect the unexpected. What if your demonstration model was ill? What if staff have not got transport to the venue? Think of the possible scenarios.

Ordering resources

You will note that for the promotion above that it is necessary to have stock available to purchase as there is an associated retail opportunity linked to the promotion. Ensure in advance that you will have adequate stock to avoid missed sales and disappointing the customers.

ELLISONS

ELLISONS

Christmas gift sets

Planning activity schedule An example, *planning activity schedule,* is shown below where a promotional event is being held at an external venue:

Planning activity	*Responsible person*	*Date action required*	*Comment on progress*	*Activity confirmed and completed*
Initial planning meeting				
Set further planning progress meeting dates				
Promotion objectives identified, these must be SMART				
Planning team established				
Promotion event programme				
Allocate responsibilities				
Identify sponsors				
Staff training requirements				
Set date(s) for promotion				
Set budget				
Locate and book venue if required				
Facilities and services checked				
Hire of equipment				
Check legal recuirements to be completed				
Check insurance requirements				
Signage requirements				
Invite VIPs				

Planning activity	*Responsible person*	*Date action required*	*Comment on progress*	*Activity confirmed and completed*
Book artists				
Update website				
Inform media local papers, television				
Order stationery, i.e. invitations				
Send out invitations				
Organize catering				
Promotion resource requirements				
Check quantity of resources required and order as necessary				
Management of promotional activities at the venue				
Clearing away products and equipment at venue post promotion				
Evaluation				
Feedback to team				

TOP TIP

Catering arrangements

Consider catering for people who have special dietary requirements, e.g. vegetarian, wheat intolerance, etc.

TOP TIP

Booking the venue

Ensure that it has access for visitors with disabilities.

Are the facilities and services available adequate?

Check health and safety. It will be necessary to perform a health and safety risk assessment in advance to check suitability.

BEST PRACTICE

Roles and responsibilities

Provide staff with an assistant – a newer staff member, who can shadow an experienced member of staff, will gain confidence and experience of the skills the activity requires and can therefore take on extra responsibility in the future.

> Ensure that all clients complete a medical form before you undertake any services.
>
> **Kerry Davis**

All objectives set should be **smart**.

- **S** specific
- **M** measurable/manageable
- **A** achievable
- **R** realistic/relevant
- **T** time bound

ALWAYS REMEMBER

A promotion can take place in the workplace or if necessary at an external venue, this will depend on audience numbers, the profile and purpose of the promotion.

Choosing a venue

Choice of venue for an external event is important; there is a lot to consider:

- Check the venue is available when you want it.
- Cost – is it within your budget?
- Capacity – will it accommodate the anticipated number of people on site?
- Suitability – does the layout meet your requirements?
- Accessibility – is it easy to get to?
- Does it meet the standards for your risk assessment?
- Are there adequate services and facilities, e.g. toilets, car parking?
- What are the facilities for emergencies, e.g. first aid?
- What insurance requirements are required and need to be put in place?
- Will sub-contractors be required to provide resources? For example, electricians for lighting/audio systems. If so, are they qualified and do they have the necessary insurance? It is necessary that you obtain copies of such documentation.

ACTIVITY FUNCTIONAL SKILLS

Venue research

Look at the cost of hiring a venue for a specific promotion of your choice aimed at a specific client group. Decide upon a budget and decide from an initial selection of three which would be best based upon your findings.

Consider:

- the promotion event
- cost of hire
- facilities, e.g. size of room for presentation, suitability, etc.
- accessibility/parking
- catering facilities

Insurance and legal requirements

Health and safety and other legal requirements must be checked in the early stages of planning. You must know the health and safety procedures for the venue you are using this will include:

- Fire drill.
- Who is responsible for public and staff safety?
- Who is responsible for emergencies?

Also be aware of all government legislation that applies to the promotion activity.

ALWAYS REMEMBER

The promotional activity planner should show:

- type of promotional activity
- objectives
- roles and responsibilities
- resources required
- planning and implementation activities
- timescales
- budget
- evaluation

COURTESY COLLIN UK © COLLIN PARIS

Peter Schmidinger demonstrating for product company BABOR

COLLIN UK

Venue for promotion at a trade show

ACTIVITY FUNCTIONAL SKILLS

Government legislation

What legislation would you need to ensure that you complied with the *Christmas beautifully wrapped up* event?

Make a list, e.g.

Sales and Supply of Goods Act (1994).

TOP TIP

Check contracts

Read the small print when checking contracts.

HEALTH & SAFETY

HSE risk assessment guidance

This leaflet obtained from the HSE aims to help you assess health and safety risks in the workplace, necessary before running a promotion where there will be a change to normal day-to-day business operations.

HSE

Five steps to risk assessment publication

HEALTH & SAFETY

Risk assessment – look for potential hazards

- A **hazard** is anything that may cause harm, such as electricity, moving heavy objects, using chemicals.
- The **risk** is the chance, high or low, that somebody could be harmed by the hazard and how serious that harm could be.

Risk assessment

Here you must identify any potential risks in order to obtain public liability insurance.

ALWAYS REMEMBER

Public liability insurance

Public liability insurance is required if members of the public visit your business premises or at an external event you organize.

Public liability insurance will cover you if someone is accidentally injured by you or your business activity. The cover should include any legal fees and expenses which result from any claim by a third party.

Check you have adequate cover in place. Remember to check if you are adequately covered if you are using your business premises.

If the venue has provided the type of activity before they may have the necessary documentation available. You will need to obtain a copy later for your records if you decide to use the venue. Check the venue has got its own public liability insurance.

You may also require an entertainment license which is when members of the public pay an admission fee or pay to use any facilities for the purposes of entertainment. The HSE has provided guidance on 'Electrical Safety for Entertainers', stating the requirements for safety standards for electrical equipment when used in public.

Check any contractual obligations. There may be local bye-laws written by the local authority you may need to be aware of in terms of parking, noise, etc. Non-compliance could invalidate insurance!

In the case of cancellation when using a service provider there may be financial penalties – check.

The HSE provide information following five steps to explain this process:

1. identify the hazards
2. decide who might be harmed and how
3. evaluate the risks and decide on precaution
4. record your findings and implement them
5. review

When the venue is confirmed have a meeting with their event coordinator to discuss your requirements further and any necessary health and safety checks, using your planning schedule. Listen also to their ideas. Identify the names of key contacts who they will interact with at the event.

Confirm:

- the agreed time you will have access to the venue from
- the programme of activities
- catering arrangements, numbers and timings
- first aid provision
- how communication will occur if immediate assistance, including emergency is required

- set up, decoration and layout for the event
- music requirements
- electrical requirements, e.g. projection equipment, lighting, electricity supplies for beauty equipment
- provision of a hospitality area to meet guests

Advertising the event

Allow sufficient time to advertise the promotion using the most efficient method. This will allow you to ensure you have reached your target audience. It will also avoid you having to cancel the event due to insufficient interest due to inadequate planning.

Methods of evaluation

Consider how you are going to evaluate the success of the event. The method must be suited for the gathering of information you need to obtain.

You may need to prepare evaluation forms that are provided on the day of the event which you will collect and analyse.

If using your business website, you may welcome electronic feedback.

You may collect immediate word-of-mouth feedback, with staff designated to ask customers at the event of their satisfaction with the organization leading up to the promotion and the event itself.

You may invite a sample of visitors to a later 'client focus group meeting' to gather their important views and opinions.

Checking progress

Planning progress meetings are important as they allow you to check that:

- Activities are being completed as per the activity schedule.
- You are keeping within your budget. Overspending may result in failure to achieve the promotions objectives and could create future cash flow problems!
- Members of the promotion team are on target with their responsibility.
- Check the priority actions such as legal responsibilities have been carried out.
- Raise any issues that need to be rectified and agree a solution.
- Update the activity plan with new actions required.

An agenda should be drawn for this meeting based on the activities on the schedule.

Notes should be recorded with updated actions required.

Before the promotional event

- Brief the team, ensuring everyone knows who is doing what and when.
- Ensure you have all the necessary resources required.
- Finalize all arrangements.

HEALTH & SAFETY

First aid qualifications

Check that whoever is appointed to administer first aid is qualified to do so and has a current recognized first aid qualification. You could be prosecuted if this is not the case.

ACTIVITY — FUNCTIONAL SKILLS

Advertising

Provide a list of reasons why you may advertise to promote the business. For example:

- To interest clients who currently use only one service.

> Have regular meetings and keep everyone informed of important information.
>
> **Kerry Davis**

> Keep client records and medical forms.
>
> **Kerry Davis**

TOP TIP

Practice makes perfect!

Practise the key parts of the demonstration presentation beforehand to ensure you are confident and that your timings will be accurate.

ALWAYS REMEMBER

Temperature at the venue

The audience will become miserable if too cold and lethargic if too warm.

TOP TIP

First impressions count

You need to make a positive impression in the first 10 seconds!

ALWAYS REMEMBER

Additional information

You may need to pass on information such as fire drill, designated smoking areas, etc. Plan how you will cover this.

Outcome 2: Implement promotional activities

Learn how to implement promotional activities by:

1. Implementing **promotional activities** to meet the agreed plan.
2. Effectively adapting **promotional activities**, when necessary, in response to changed circumstances and/or problems.
3. Using resources effectively throughout the **promotional activities**.
4. Clearly and accurately communicating the essential features and benefits of products and services to the target group.
5. Using methods of communication that are suitable for the type of promotional activity being undertaken.
6. Presenting information in logical steps.
7. Encouraging the target group to ask questions about the services and products being promoted.
8. Responding to questions and queries in a way which promotes goodwill and enhances the business image
9. Actively encouraging the target group to take advantage of the services and products being promoted
10. Clearing away products and equipment at the end of the **promotional activity**, when necessary, to meet the requirements of the venue.

Think carefully about your promotion, activities and timings to ensure the event runs smoothly on the day.

Planning requirements for the day will vary dependent upon the numbers being catered for, the location of the venue, the resources to be prepared and the programme content.

On the promotion day start your preparations at the agreed time as planned to set up your equipment and resources, testing it to check and allow for any problems.

Check all environmental conditions are appropriate for the event including temperature, ventilation and lighting.

Check the layout and seating plan (if used) for the demonstration area is appropriate to your needs. A theatre 'U' shape is useful to maximize visibility and audience participation.

Provide all the relevant literature for your clients' reference in advance of the presentation. You may leave a 'goody bag' of information and beauty samples on the chairs, which the audience can be looking at before you start. Alternatively, if to a smaller group, you can hand out information at an appropriate point during the demonstration. Samples may be passed around the audience to try while they are being discussed. Remember with larger audiences this may be impractical. However, a screen would be useful to display products if used and to show clearly the demonstration.

Be ready to meet the audience on their arrival. Have staff designated to 'meet and greet'. All staff interfacing with visitors should be enthusiastic, friendly and helpful. Name badges are useful for staff to wear for clear identification.

Provide adequate signage.

Presenting information

The time schedule and programme that the audience has for the activities should be kept to. This will avoid audience irritation and boredom; remember you want to create the right environment for your event – fun or relaxing while being sociable.

Engage with our audience as quickly as possible, this will create a relaxed atmosphere.

CACI

Mary Overton from CACI skincare and equipment supplie

Presentation Good presentation, style should be entertaining.

Introduce yourself and the team, and provide an overview of what the audience can expect – the expectations for your target audience.

Have good posture and move around (although not too much!) so that you are looking at all areas of the audience.

Explain what you will be demonstrating and what you will achieve.

Present information to your audience at a suitable pace, avoid being too wordy – this can become boring and the audience may become distracted, avoid technical jargon. The demonstration should be clear, simple and not too long. The audience must be able to see what is being done and hear the commentary.

Explain the features and benefits of the product or service as you demonstrate it. A **feature** is the uniqueness or individuality of the product or service, the **benefit** is the gain to be made from using the product or service. Maximize the impact of the demonstration by giving the audience the opportunity to buy the product/service immediately.

Use resources throughout to ensure you can maintain the interest of your audience. Change the topic every 5 minutes and include something new – new information, interesting related facts, different media to keep your audience attentive. Audience engagement can only remain for up to 20 minutes.

Think of innovative ways to keep your audience listening: perhaps audience participation prizes including 'spot prizes' for the correct answers to questions asked. You may request volunteers from the audience to model or comment on the stages of the demonstration for you in some way.

Communication both verbal and non-verbal is important. Establish a rapport early on with your audience. Observe verbal and non-verbal communication, i.e. body language, to check audience response. Smile, this will show confidence and make you more 'personable' to the audience.

Ask questions at the appropriate time and encourage questions to be asked, answering these confidently. You are the expert, show your knowledge. Ask 'open' questions that cannot be answered with yes or no, encouraging audience communication. Open questions usually start with *why*, *how*, *when*, *what* and *which*.

Listening is a skill. Listen to your audience; this will enable you to adapt to your audience. Sometimes you may have an awkward person in the audience, deal with them with good will and keep to your 'script'!

TOP TIP

Presentation planning:

- **be organized**
- **know your audience**
- **look your best**
- **practice your presentation and time yourself**

ALWAYS REMEMBER

Retail planning

An effective demonstration will always create sales. Have the product or service ready to sell. Do **not** over-project sales; this could be costly leaving you with excess stock.

Ensure there is a definite close to your demonstration. However, let the audience know where you and perhaps your team will be to answer any questions.

Marketing the promotion

If possible, video the event, you may show it on your website or as an information medium in the business reception area to maintain interest and awareness.

Do not miss any marketing opportunities for your business when holding a promotion.

Inform the local press, if invited inform them of the best time to be there and who to contact.

You could also raise awareness in the *trade press* who will feature new developmental areas within the trade and commentary on items such as charity-based events.

If you have something new and innovative this could be reviewed by the *consumer press* who will then put it into the public domain, so the potential to raise the business profile from this opportunity is much higher.

At the end of the promotional event, the premises should be left in an acceptable way. This will have been agreed if using an external venue. This is included in your planning activity schedule with tasks allocated to staff. This is both professional and ensures security of stock and equipment which require collection at the end of an event. Any waste should be collected and disposed of in the correct legislative manner.

> Have check lists for daily, weekly, monthly tasks.
>
> **Kerry Davis**

Outcome 3: Participate in the evaluation of promotional activities

Learn how to participate in the evaluation of promotional activities by:

1. Using the methods agreed in your promotional activity plan to gain feedback from the relevant sources.
2. Collating and recording the information gained from the feedback using a clear and concise format and method of presentation.
3. Drawing accurate and clear conclusions on the effectiveness of the promotional activity in meeting the agreed **objectives**.
4. Participating in discussions by giving a clear and well structured summary of the results of the evaluation.
5. Making recommendations for improvements to any future **promotional activities** based upon the outcomes of your evaluation.

> Encourage feedback, both negative and positive, to improve the level of service offered and know what you are doing right.
>
> **Kerry Davis**

> Ensure that employees sign for training that they have undertaken and have training task lists.
>
> **Kerry Davis**

Post-promotion evaluation

In your initial promotion proposal you will have identified objectives for its need. You also identified how success would be measured.

Following implementation you will be able to gauge its success by how those objectives have been achieved or progress towards them is being made.

In addition, it provides the important opportunity to gain feedback from the clients on other aspects of the business and what they would like to see changed, developed or improved.

Gaining feedback Methods of gaining evaluative feedback include:

- **Interviews** – this would be with people involved in both the planning and the implementation stages.
- **Focus discussion groups** – this could include any group such as clients from the target group, sponsors, etc.
- **Written questionnaire** – this could be completed at the event by the client group.
- **Telephone questionnaire** – this could be completed using standard questions to a specific or randomly selected client group.
- **Sales reports and summaries** – checking the financial impact of implementation of the promotion.
- **Increase in clients/services** – a database system would be required to specifically measure the percentage increase.

The type of evaluation method(s) you select will depend on what would be most appropriate to gather the information you need.

From your evaluation you could find out further:

- How is the current business meeting the needs of its clients?
- Are there further business opportunities to be explored?
- Is there a staff training need in any areas of its delivery to improve its customer care profile or meet the service delivery needs?

Gain feedback from all those involved such as guest speakers, sponsors, venue management and clients.

Arrange a meeting as soon as possible following the event with the planning team where you can review the success of your event and evaluate any feedback gained.

Consider the effects on the business since your promotion – what impact has been seen?

TOP TIP

Evaluation

If you have videoed the event you can also view this later and assess its strengths and weaknesses.

SHUTTERSTOCK/ DASHA RUSANENKO

Organize and examine your data in a spreadsheet program, which can output useful graphs

Collating, analysing and summarizing the evaluation feedback

FUNCTIONAL SKILLS

Analyse all your records and data and present it in a suitable format. It is easier to input information on a computer using a spreadsheet and database program where it can be organized and examined.

Present your information in the most appropriate way. Most spreadsheets have functions that create graphs to facilitate comparing columns of data.

Producing an evaluation report

FUNCTIONAL SKILLS

Close after the event provide initial feedback, followed by formal feedback referring to evidence you have collected including your evaluations. Agree a date and time for this and prepare a professional summary of your conclusions.

Prepare and present your results providing a report on what has been achieved including both negative and positive findings and your recommendations. Your information should be clear and concise.

> Encourage feedback from your team. Some of the best ideas come from people that are working in the daily operation.
>
> **Kerry Davis**

The areas that should be evaluated and measured could include:

- have the objectives been met?
- benefits seen;
- success of the event;
- cost-effectiveness;
- issues and how these were dealt with.

To follow this up, an action plan could be prepared with your recommendations, with new or revised targets, with dates of what has to be achieved against the performance indicators.

Answer questions honestly. Have all you records available for reference. These will provide an excellent plan for preparing future promotions.

ASSESSMENT OF KNOWLEDGE AND UNDERSTANDING

FUNCTIONAL SKILLS

Having covered the learning objectives for **contribute to the planning and implementation of promotional activities** test what you need to know and understand by answering the following short questions below. The information covers:

- venue and legal requirements
- promotional event planning and preparation
- services and products
- selling skills
- communication techniques
- evaluation techniques

Venue and legal requirements

1. What should be considered in the choice of venue for an external promotional event?
2. Health and safety and other legal requirements must be checked in the early stages when planning a promotion. What are the health and safety procedures you **must** know for the venue you are to be using?
3. What steps can you take to minimize risks when running a promotion at an external venue?
4. Why must contractual obligations be checked when planning your choice of venue?

Promotional event planning and preparation

1. You have a great idea for promoting a new service in the workplace. What should you include when presenting your ideas to the person responsible for decision-making?
2. What are the different types of promotional activities?
3. A planning activity schedule should be made before a promotion to ensure that it is well organised. What key things should the schedule include?
4. All objectives set must be SMART; what does this mean? Write several SMART objectives for a fictitious promotional activity.

Services and products

1. Why are retail sales important to the business?
2. Why is it important that you have a good knowledge of the products and services in your workplace?
3. How can you ensue that you are up-to-date with current beauty products and services? Why is this important?
4. Why is it important to explain the features and benefits of the products or service to a client?

Selling skills

1. What are the opportunities that a promotion can provide to the business?
2. Clients have 'consumer rights'. Why is it important to give accurate information about products or services promoted?
3. Name three pieces of legislation/regulations relating to the way products or services are delivered to clients to protect their legal rights.
4. What are the benefits of set sales targets for employees to the individual and the business?

Communication techniques

1. Communication is important when promoting a product/service. How do you think speaking with authority and confidence on a product or service will influence the client?
2. What should be considered when presenting information to maintain client interest?
3. Why is it important to pay careful attention to your client and their responses to your questions when asking questions?
4. How can you plan to present with confidence and make a positive visual impact?

Evaluation techniques

1. What methods of evaluation can be used following a promotional activity to measure its success?
2. What areas of a promotional activity should be evaluated?
3. What system can be used to collate and analyze promotion evaluation feedback? What are the benefits of using this method?
4. To summarize your evaluation findings an evaluation report should be presented. What should this report include in order to benefit the planning for future promotions?

ISTOCK/© PGIAM

5 Financial effectiveness

Learning Objectives

This chapter covers the **Contribute to the financial effectiveness of the business** unit. This unit is about the monitoring and effective use of salon resources and meeting productivity and development targets to make a positive contribution to the effectiveness of the business. You are also required to ensure that individuals who may assist you to deliver services to clients work effectively.

The main outcomes of this unit are:

1 **Contribute to the effective use and monitoring of resources**

2 **Meet productivity and development targets**

Your assessor will make **one** observation of your contribution to monitoring and effective use of resources. In addition where required you will need to collect additional product evidence. You should allow yourself sufficient time to collect documentary evidence as this may take up to 3 months.

From the **range** you must show that you have:

- monitored and effectively used all the **resources** listed
- set and achieved your **productivity targets** for technical services and retail sales and personal learning

For this unit it is likely you will be provide additional product evidence in your portfolio to meet the requirements of the unit.

When providing promotional activity services it is important to use the skills you have learnt in the following units:

Monitor procedures to safely control work operations.

ROLE MODEL

Lisa Fulton

International Training Manager, FakeBake (UK) Ltd

"I am the International Training Manager for FakeBake. I started working for the brand over 7 years ago, not long after the brand was brought from the USA.

My main job role is travelling around beauty colleges in Scotland, delivering lotion and spray-tan training courses to the beauty therapy students. We also have training schools in Glasgow, Warrington and London, where we offer tanning courses to salon and mobile professionals.

I travel a lot and get to do jobs in LA, NYC – tanning celebrities all over the globe.

I also work in product development, and have recently been on the design team for our brand new 'POD', which is the ultimate in spray-tan technology.

We do beauty shows all over the world, showcasing our amazing products, creating a buzz for our brand, spreading the word on our 'SYS' campaign SAVE YOUR SKIN, through this we educate teenagers on the dangers of sun beds and sunbathing, encouraging them to use the safe alternative in creating a sun kissed glow to their skin, our motto is FAKE don't FRY, LIVE THE LIE, with FAKEBAKE.

I will always enjoy my teaching role, as I can see the excitement on students' faces when they have achieved a flawless tan, and just how good they look when they have the perfect tan on.

Effective use of resources

Resources and how effectively and efficiently they are used contribute to the financial effectiveness of the business. Procedures should be followed according to your salon's requirements.

Resources contributing to the financial effectiveness of the business include:

- human resources (HR)
- stock
- tools and equipment
- time

Outcome 1: Contribute to the effective use and monitoring of resources

Contribute to the effective use and monitoring of resources

1. Correctly follow your salon procedures for monitoring the use of **resources**.
2. Ensure information relating to stock levels is obtained from colleagues in time to coincide with your salon ordering system.
3. Using **resources** in a way which complies with legal and salon requirements.
4. Checking all deliveries are accurate and complete against order documentation and promptly report any inaccuracies and/or damages.
5. Identifying and resolving any problems with **resources** within the limits of your authority.
6. Promptly report any **resource** problems you cannot resolve to the relevant person.
7. Making constructive recommendations to improve the use of **resources** to the relevant person.
8. Making recommendations which clearly show the benefits of implementing your suggestions.
9. Ensuring records for which you are responsible are accurate, legible and up-to-date.

ALWAYS REMEMBER

Business resources requiring monitoring

Your salon procedure for monitoring the use of resources includes human resources, stock, tools, equipment and time.

Human resources

Human resources (HR) are the people employed in the business. HR is the term used to refer to their qualifications, talents and abilities. HR are the most important asset in the business, which profits from services and retail sales. Staff should work together to maximize the performance of the business. Each employee should have responsibility to complete their allocated duties and responsibilities to the best of their ability. At induction, new staff are familiarized with their job. It is important that each member of staff has a written **job description**; this should detail their specific role, duties and responsibilities.

> Why not incentivize your staff, running weekly or monthly competitions? Ensure that all your staff have an equal chance of winning, rather than it always being won by one person.
>
> **Lisa Fulton**

They will also have personal productivity and development **targets**, for which their performance will be reviewed at regular intervals.

This ensures that each member of staff knows what is expected of them and that they work within their limitations, involving others when their expertise is required. It is important that staff are aware of where their responsibilities begin and end.

There should be a **grievance** and **disciplinary** procedure provided to each employee, which will emphasize the importance of staff discipline. This is vital in the case of complaints, poor performance, staffing issues and misconduct.

ALWAYS REMEMBER

Payment

- A statutory national minimum wage was introduced on 1 April 1999. For further information, obtain the Department of Trade and Industry (DTI) national minimum wage guide.
- As part of an employee's contract of employment, bonuses and commission are identified if applicable.
- A detailed written pay statement should be provided before or when an employee is paid. This should identify any deductions and what they are for.
- Sick pay may be provided by the employer identified in the employment contract, or if this has not been agreed, an employee may be entitled to statutory sick pay (SSP). For more information on SSP see the Inland Revenue National Insurance Contributions (IRNIC) Statutory Sick Pay leaflet.

Working conditions

A **written statement of the terms of employment** or **contract of employment** (which includes all terms and conditions listed below) should be given to an employee within 2 months of them starting work.

The statement or contract includes the employer's and employee's name, when employment commenced, and when the period of continuous employment began.

Terms and conditions should be listed including:

- scale or rate of pay
- payment interval, i.e. weekly, monthly
- hours of work
- holidays, including bank holidays, and how holiday pay is calculated
- place of work
- job title and roles and responsibilities
- information should also be provided on eligibility for sickness pay, pension schemes, etc.

Planning the most efficient use of HR is essential, and a rota is required to ensure there are always sufficient, experienced staff available.

Careful rota adjustment is important to allow for holidays, sickness, maternity leave and time off during the week. Certain periods of the year are busier than others, e.g. Christmas and during special promotions. It may be necessary to recruit staff during these periods to maintain an efficient service and avoid loss of clients and revenue.

Staff training

Investment in staff training is important. Time should be spent on staff training. This time may be used to update staff on new service techniques or salon policy. Although this is a time when direct income is not incurred, it has long-term benefits.

ISTOCK/© KATERYNA GOVORUSHCHENKO

Invest in staff training

> Update your skills, keep one step ahead at all times, learn constantly! As new developments within your industry become available to learn about, go on the courses. Know everything – this comes across when talking to clients.
>
> **Lisa Fulton**

Sample job description

	Job description – Beauty therapist
Location:	Based at salon as advised.
Main purpose of job	To ensure customer care is provided at all times. To maintain a good standard of technical and client care, ensuring that up-to-date methods and techniques are used following the salon training practices and procedures.
Responsible to:	Salon manager.
Requirements:	To maintain the company's standards in respect of beauty services. To ensure that all clients receive service of the best possible quality. To advise clients on services. To advise clients on products and aftercare. To achieve designated performance targets. To participate in self-development or to assist with the development of others. To maintain company policy in respect of: • personal standards of health/hygiene • personal standards of appearance/conduct • operating safely while at work • public promotion • corporate image as laid out in the employee handbook. To carry out client consultation in accordance with company policy. To maintain company security practices and procedures. To assist your manager in the provision of salon resources. To undertake additional tasks and duties required by your manager from time to time.

Ineffective staff training will affect the quality of services, productivity and financial performance. If staff carry out services in which they are inexperienced, the results will not be as effective, resulting in client dissatisfaction and potential loss of clientele.

TOP TIP

Communication

When communicating over the telephone, your face cannot be seen, therefore it is important to consider your tone of voice and speak clearly.

BEST PRACTICE

Meetings

It is good practice to allocate time for each agenda item. This will avoid the meeting overrunning. Items other than those on the agenda are raised at the end of the meeting. Time should be allocated for this under 'any other business'.

TOP TIP

Encouraging ideas

When working as a team, ideas are often generated. Ideas should never be rejected without clearly explaining why.

Product knowledge, both technical and retail, is important – poor product knowledge will hinder effective sales and lose client confidence.

Good working relationships between colleagues are essential. Every member of staff, or the *team*, plays a different role, each ensuring the success of the business. Poor working relationships create an unpleasant environment for both staff and clients. Good communication systems are important, especially when staff responsibilities are shared.

Communication systems

Information may be written or orally communicated.

Oral information may be provided via the telephone or given to a client at consultation or during the service. If you are in a position of responsibility, oral information may be used to deal with a complaint, when liaising with external bodies or during communication with staff on occasions such as discussing a grievance, appraisal and training. Oral information is important when advice is required quickly, which will improve both performance and productivity.

When communicating orally, consider:

- the tone of your voice and body language; gestures if face to face
- the setting in which the information is given
- how clearly and concisely the information is given

It is important to keep a written record of any formal communication with staff or clients for future reference. Staff communication can be improved through regular individual and group **staff meetings**. These enable the supervisor of the salon to update the staff on new initiatives, as well as providing an opportunity to share ideas for system and individual performance improvements, and to raise and discuss any concerns.

Meetings may be **informal** (unplanned) or **formal** (planned), with a purpose, usually for decision-making and action. Successful formal meetings should have:

- an identified purpose
- an agenda, indicating all topics for discussion forwarded to those participating (this should be circulated in advance of the meeting)
- a suitable venue – it may be necessary to arrange the seating to encourage participation and; if delivering a presentation; to ensure all can see and hear clearly
- a person allocated to lead the meeting, called the **chairperson**
- a person allocated to take the minutes of the meeting, which are later circulated to those who attended and those who were unable to attend. Minutes can be distributed by traditional methods, such as paper copies, or electronically by email

Working relationships

Professional relationships with colleagues should be maintained at all times. Good working relationships will improve productivity towards individual and business targets.

General codes of conduct

Be polite and courteous with colleagues at all times:

- Never talk down to colleagues.
- Never lose your temper with a colleague in front of a client.
- Never ridicule a colleague in front of a client or other colleagues.
- If there are any personal issues between yourself and a colleague, do not show these in front of a client. Settle grievances (reasons for complaint) as soon as possible, or job satisfaction and productivity can be affected.

Grievances

It is important to understand the salon's staffing structure. If you feel you are in conflict with other staff or are being treated unfairly, you can report the incident to the appropriate supervisor. All staff should be made aware of the grievance and appeals procedure at induction. The procedures aim to address situations as soon as they arise, investigating and where possible resolving the problem.

Employment and equal opportunities legislation

The government has set into law certain legislative requirements to protect employees from harm and from discrimination. Discrimination on grounds of sex, race, disability, marital status or union membership is against the law.

Working Time Directive (1998)

The Working Time Directive (WTD) aims to ensure that employees are protected against adverse conditions with regard to their health and safety, caused by working excessively long hours with inadequate rest or disrupted work patterns.

The Working Time Directive provides for:

- Working hours must be limited to an average of no more than 48 hours per week. An employee can agree to work more but it must be in writing.
- Employees are entitled to one uninterrupted rest day in every seven.
- A working day should be no longer than 13 hours, although this will depend upon the agreed break between each shift.
- Night workers are entitled to a break of 11 consecutive hours in each 24-hour period.
- If working more than 6 hours per day, employees are entitled to a minimum 20-minute break.
- After 3 months employment employees are entitled to 4 weeks paid holiday a year. Holiday pay is pro rata for part-time employees.

SHUTTERSTOCK/ BRIAN A JACKSON

Discrimination is against the law

Sex Discrimination Acts (1975 and 1985) and the Equal Pay Act (1970)

These pieces of legislation were implemented to prevent discrimination or less favourable treatment of a man or woman on the basis of gender. The Acts cover pay and conditions as well as promotion of equal opportunities.

ALWAYS REMEMBER

Equality Act 2010

This Act protects those who have a protected characteristic to ensure they are not treated less favorably because of that characteristic. The characteristics that are protected by the Equality Act 2010 are:

- age
- disability
- gender identity and gender reassignment
- marriage or civil partnership (in employment only)
- pregnancy and maternity
- race
- religion or belief
- sexual orientation

TOP TIP

Computers

Computerized systems are quick and efficient ways of running any size of business, including stock control.

ALWAYS REMEMBER

Audit stock control

Have a policy of regular stock takes to ensure the information on your computer system is correct.

TOP TIP

Stock orders

Some companies require a large minimum set-up order. This means that your money will be tied up in stock. It is important that you are confident that it will sell and will match your client market.

Capital should not be tied up unnecessarily and unproductively.

Race Relations Act (1976)

Implemented to prevent discrimination on the basis of colour, race, ethnic or national origins. The Commission for Racial Equality has produced a code of conduct to eradicate racial discrimination practice.

Disability Discrimination Act (1995)

Implemented to prevent disabled persons being discriminated against during both recruitment and employment.

Employers have a responsibility to remove physical barriers and to adjust working conditions to prevent discrimination on the basis of having a disability.

Trade Union and Labour Relations (Consolidation) Act (1992)

To prevent trade union members being treated less favourably than non-members, or vice versa. If penalized, the employee can complain to an employment tribunal.

Information systems

FUNCTIONAL SKILLS

Information systems ensure the smooth running of the business and provide data for the supervisor and external agents as legally required; for example to Customs and Excise and the Inland Revenue at the end of the financial year.

Information systems can be manual or computerized. If using a manual system, you will need an index of filing to access information quickly. Computerized systems allow you to input and access information in relation to:

- client information, personal details, records of services, retail sales, etc.
- management information, data on staff and salon performance
- current stock levels and ordering systems
- daily till reports

Stock

Stock is the total amount of consumables for use on clients within salon services plus retail products for client purchase.

Information systems should be in place for stock maintenance, which should be accurate, up-to-date and legible. One staff member should be responsible for:

- ordering stock
- maintaining stocking records and levels
- receiving incoming stock, checking deliveries for quality and discrepancy
- unpacking stock and locating it in the correct storage/display area

Salon ordering systems

Stock can be ordered from different places and in different ways.

Wholesalers These are cash-and-carry outlets which sell wholesale products to businesses. Some companies offer internet and mail order facilities.

Representatives from companies Some companies have sales representatives who will regularly visit the business and with whom you can place purchase orders. The order is returned to the company to be processed and despatched. Representatives are useful as they can advise you of new product ranges and promotions that you may wish to take part in, to help increase financial productivity.

Ordering stock

When you make an order, the supplier will normally open a credit account for you and provide information on how to order and pay. Cash-and-carry wholesalers do not normally have minimum orders. Mail order and internet companies usually charge postage on small orders. It is important to consider which is the most cost-effective way to order. When placing an order ensure sufficient time is allowed to avoid running out of stock.

Principles of stock control Stock levels can only be maintained if accurate records are kept of how much stock the business has. The records will identify stock used, and what needs to be reordered. Maintaining accurate records means you don't have to count all stock. Importantly, you also avoid running out of stock, especially of popular items, and avoid over-ordering products.

A good **stock-keeping** checklist: FUNCTIONAL SKILLS

- *Anticipate needs.* Stock must be ordered regularly, *before* it runs out. Orders should be placed as stock becomes low so new stock will be arriving as the existing stock is being used or sold. There may be short-term influences on needs such as seasonal factors, for example there may be an increased demand for cosmetic UV-screening preparations in summer or following a promotion. Regularly review order levels for stock to anticipate and accommodate demand.
- *Check incoming stock.* What has been ordered should be checked against a delivery note when it arrives. The delivery note lists all the items that have been despatched and any that are to follow, such as items that are out of stock. Never assume that the order received will be correct. Inaccuracies must be reported to the supplier immediately, before countersigning the order and confirming the delivery. Any damaged goods must be dealt with and either returned to the sender or replaced, according to the policy of the supplier. Never return anything without the relevant paperwork or without confirmation from the supplier.

  Inform your supervisor of any discrepancies as applicable.
- *Rotate the stock.* Stock must be stored and used in rotation so that new items go to the back of the shelf and older items are used first. This is often referred to as FIFO – 'first in first out'.
- *Keep accurate and up-to-date records.* Stock levels may be recorded manually or electronically. Whichever method is used, records must be accurate and updated regularly as per the business policy, usually weekly.

Manual and computerized stock-control systems The two main types of stock control systems used to collect and collate stock information are *point-of-sale systems* and *stock-check systems*, which can be manual or computerized.

Point-of-sale systems Point-of-sale systems collect information concerning sales at the time the sale is made. The person making the sale has to complete a form, such as a sales bill, which includes stock information.

TOP TIP

Supplier reliability

It is important that your supplier is reliable. An efficient business cannot afford uncertain delivery schedules, which if late may mean certain stock items have been exhausted, affecting retail and service sales!

ELLISONS

A promotion for retail – summer

ELLISONS

Salon wholesaler's showroom

HEALTH & SAFETY

Damaged stock

Handle broken containers with care as they could cause harm. Before touching them or clearing up, check that the contents are not hazardous, and whether they have spilt. Always dispose of damaged stock safely and quickly.

HEALTH & SAFETY

Duty of care

Employees should be made aware that they can be fined for breaking safety rules.

TOP TIP

Returning goods

Goods may have to be returned to the supplier:

- if they were damaged
- if they were not what was ordered
- if they had been incorrectly ordered

Goods returned to the supplier should be logged using either a manual or electronic system.

BEAUTY WORKS

CASH SALE INVOICE

Date and Tax Point:

Invoice No: 32622

Quantity	Description	Price £	p	
1	Moisturiser (sensitive) – 20 g	12	50	
1	Toner (oily) – 200 ml	9	50	
1	Nail varnish – tropical red	7	50	

The Beauty Garden
Mytown
The Midlands
Tel: 01234 456789

Goods 29.50
VAT 5.16
Invoice Total £34.66

A typical sales bill

ISBN 0-333-68902-X
9 780333 689028
901C1

Barcodes

Computers can read price tickets coded by means of barcodes printed on the packaging. As the products are sold, the code numbers are read by the computer via a scanning barcode reader, which recognizes the product and automatically updates its records. This system is essential for large businesses with a high rate of stock turnover.

Stock-check systems ***Stock-check systems*** allow the stock-keeper to refer quickly to the quantity of stock available. If you have a record of how many stock items you started with and what is left, you will know immediately how many you have sold.

With a regular stock check you can set a reorder level: whenever the quantity of goods falls to a predetermined level, it is time to reorder this product.

A simple stock-check system is the stock record card. With a regular stock check you can set a reorder level. Whenever the quantity of goods falls to a predetermined level, it is time to reorder this product. Alternatively, stock information is fed into the computer, which analyses the sales details, recalculates stock levels and calculates when to reorder, and other details as required. This provides automated stock-control information and printouts for use when performing manual stock-taking checks.

The stock-taking record needs to show:

- a description of the product and its size
- how much is in stock
- what has been sold and used
- what has come in
- the minimum and maximum holding levels
- the point at which the product is to be reordered

HEALTH & SAFETY

Avoid hazards

All packing materials must be tidied away immediately. They are a hazard and might cause accidents.

Precious Skin Care
Ellisons
TEL: 361619

REP: Susan Green

		Min	Max	Mar	Apr	May	Jun
Coral							
Cleanser	500 ml	10	20	5 / 15	10 / 10	12 / 8	9
	200 ml	20	30	22 / 8	20 / 10	19 / 11	20
Toner	500 ml	10	20	10 / 10	11 / 9	9 / 11	10
	200 ml	20	30	20 / 10	20 / 10	21 / 9	9
Moisture	250 ml	5	10	5 / 5	6 / 4	5 / 5	7
Cream	50 ml	15	25	12 / 13	16 / 9	15 / 10	1
Night	250 ml	5	10	5 / 5	8 / 2	5 / 5	5
Cream	50 ml	15	25	14 / 11	16 / 9	14 / 11	10

Manual stock-recording system

Stock rotation When new stock arrives it must go to the back of the shelf and existing stock should be brought forward: remember the rule of FIFO.

Many products have a shelf life or best before date. This is because many products contain the minimum amount of preservatives in their formulation.

Products that have exceeded their shelf life should be disposed of.

If the company updates its packaging, request any stock you hold is replaced to maintain currency of image.

Moving and storing stock Stock should be taken to the appropriate storage area following checking. This may be into storage, into the retail area or into the service area for use within the service.

Always take care of yourself when moving goods around the salon. Do not struggle: get assistance as necessary.

The Health and Safety at Work Act (1974) relates to all work-place health and safety. Both employers and employees have a duty to work in as safe and healthy a way as possible. Employees have a responsibility not to endanger their own health and safety, but the employer must ensure that rules are laid down for safe working practices. They must:

- train staff in safe working practices
- provide safe systems for the handling, transit and storage of all materials

The legislation to ensure safe working practice when handling resources is the Manual Handling Operations Regulations (1992).

Manual handling in the workplace can be described as the transporting or supporting of loads by hands or by bodily force. The employer is required to carry out a risk assessment of all activities undertaken which involve manual lifting.

ALWAYS REMEMBER

Stock records

- All stock records can suffer from human error. Make sure that those responsible understand the business system.
- Careful records ensure enough stock is held until the next reorder and delivery. Regular supplies of stock keep the stock turning over and reduce the amount of money tied up on the shelf.

HEALTH & SAFETY

Stock deterioration

Stock that is deteriorating may change in consistency, look discoloured and the smell may change or become unpleasant. Bacterial or fungal growth may even be seen on the product surface.

Ensure that stock is stored to maintain its quality and shelf life.

HEALTH & SAFETY

Employer's liability insurance

An employer must have employer's liability insurance to provide cover for any injury or disease an employee may suffer from as a result of their work. The latest certificate must be displayed.

HEALTH & SAFETY

RIDDOR

Manual handling injuries account for 25 per cent of injuries reported to enforcing authorities each year.

In the case of employees suffering a personal injury at work which results in:

- major injury
- more than 24 hours in hospital
- an incapacity to work for more than 3 calendar days

this must be reported under the **Reporting of Injuries, Diseases and Dangerous Occurrences Regulations 1995 (RIDDOR)**.

The risk assessment should provide evidence that the following have been considered:

- risk of injury
- the manual movement involved in performing the activity
- the physical constraint that the load incurs
- the environmental constraints imposed by the workplace
- workers' individual capabilities
- action taken in order to minimize potential risks

HSE Health & Safety Executive

Health and Safety at work etc Act 1974
The Reporting of Injuries, Diseases and Dangerous Occurrences Regulations 1995

Click here for report guidance

Report of an injury or dangerous occurrence

Filling in this form
This form must be filled in by an employer or other responsible person.

Part A

About you

1 What is your full name?

2 What is your job title?

3 What is your telephone number?

About your organisation

4 What is the name of your organisation?

5 What is its address and postcode?

6 What type of work does the organisation do?

Part B

About the incident

1 On what date did the incident happen?

2 At what time did the incident happen?
(Please use the 24-hour clock eg 0600)

3 Did the incident happen at the above address?

Yes ☐ Go to question 4

No ☐ Where did the incident happen?

☐ elsewhere in your organisation - give the name, address and postcode

☐ at someone else's premises - give the name, address and postcode

☐ in a public place - give details of where it happened

If you do not know the postcode, what is the name of the local authority?

4 In which department, or where on the premises, did the incident happen?

F2508 (05.00)

Part C

About the injured person

If you are reporting a dangerous occurrence, go to Part F. If more than one person was injured in the same incident, please attach the details asked for in Part C and Part D for each injured person.

1 What is their full name?

2 What is their home address and postcode?

3 What is their home phone number?

4 How old are they?

5 Are they

☐ male?

☐ female?

6 What is their job title?

7 Was the injured person (tick only one box)

☐ one of your employees?

☐ on a training scheme? Give details:

☐ on work experience?

☐ employed by someone else? Give details of the employer:

☐ self-employed and at work?

☐ a member of the public?

Part D

About the injury

1 What was the injury? (eg fracture, laceration)

2 What part of the body was injured?

Next Page

HMSO

Injury report under RIDDOR

Safe practice advice when lifting includes: stand in front of the object with feet a shoulder width apart, assess the weight of the load and only lift if it is safe to do so.

Take a firm grasp of the object. Lift from the knees, not the back. Avoid twisting the body: this may lead to injury (see page 108).

When carrying, balance weights evenly in both hands and carry the heaviest part nearest to your body (see page 108).

Stock must be easily accessible and products need to be found easily. Place the stock labels towards the front.

Remember the oldest stock should be issued first – first in, first out: 'FIFO'. Therefore, place new stock at the back of the shelves.

Certain substances may require special storage and handling requirements. Legislation relating to the storage and handling of resources is located in the Control of Substances Hazardous to Health Regulations (COSHH) (2002). All cosmetic products come under the strict legislation of the **Cosmetics Products (Safety) Regulations (2004)**. Written by the Cosmetic, Toiletry and Perfumery Association (CTPA), with the cooperation of the Hairdressing and Beauty Suppliers' Association (HBSA), this piece of legislation consolidates earlier regulations and incorporates current European Directives. Part of consumer legislation, it requires that cosmetics and toiletries are safe for use for their intended purpose as a cosmetic and comply with labelling requirements.

Security Security concerns should be taken into consideration to prevent loss of stock through theft. Regular stock checks may identify loss of stock.

- The retail area should be designed to be in full view of staff, with a security camera placed where possible for additional security.
- Retail and product resources should be kept in a secure area, accessed only by those with authority to do so.
- Open display areas should be stocked with replica 'dummy' products and minimal sample products.
- All staff at their induction should be made aware of the consequence of theft. Theft is often referred to as gross misconduct and may lead to dismissal and prosecution.

Dealing with theft If you suspect a client of stealing and you have reasonable evidence, you have the right to make a citizen's arrest under the Police and Criminal Evidence Act (1984). Theft is a criminal offence. You must know your employer's policy on theft and apprehending a thief.

Below is additional legislation relevant to beauty therapy salons relating to technical services and retail resources.

Consumer protection legislation

You must be aware of current legal requirements relating to the sale and retail of goods. Look at the consumer protection legislation relating to the beauty therapy trade, such as the Cosmetic Products (Enforcements) Regulations (2013).

Consumer Protection Act (1987)

This Act follows European laws to protect the customer from unsafe, defective services and products that do not reach safety standards. It also covers misleading price indications about goods or services available from a business.

Tools and equipment

All physical resources should be provided in sufficient quantity and of a suitable standard to comply with all relevant health and safety requirements and legislation. Adequate staff training should be given to ensure staff use equipment in the most efficient, safe manner.

When purchasing equipment it is important to consider the following:

- Is there a client demand for it?
- Is it possible to lease the equipment? (This is useful when the equipment is very expensive.)
- Is it durable? In the event of it breaking, what back-up support is provided?

Adequate records should also be kept to show when equipment has been electrically checked and serviced, usually every 12 months in compliance with the **Electricity at Work Regulations Act (1989)** (EAW Regulations), by a qualified electrician. An electrical testing record should be kept for each piece of equipment.

If equipment appears faulty in any way staff should report it to the supervisor immediately.

All tools and equipment should be cleaned after every use, then sterilized or disinfected in an appropriate way.

Time management

Time management is important. Ensure that you manage your time effectively to ensure that all your responsibilities are fulfilled. Look at your daily workload schedule and identify all the important tasks that need to be completed. A diary is a useful *aide-mémoire* to record tasks that need to be completed, or your computer may have a 'to do list' software task feature that you can use. Tasks need to be prioritized in order of importance; the important tasks need to be completed first as their completion is more urgent. Any tasks not completed should be carried forward to the next day. Managing your time effectively makes you more productive; you achieve more from the day as you waste less time on less important non-urgent tasks.

Working in an efficient, tidy manner will save time, as your work area will need minimal preparation for each client. It will also prevent resources being mislaid if they are kept in the correct designated place.

Effective delegation of tasks ensures the smooth running of the salon. All staff should have a job description that clearly defines their work role. It is important that you only keep tasks to complete yourself if nobody else can do them. For example, colleagues may be responsible for looking at your work schedule and supporting you, ensuring that all resources are available for you at the designated time. Cumulatively, this creates more time for you to be more productive, which will benefit the business financially.

When booking clients for a service it is essential that sufficient time is allocated to the service. In a salon, therefore, the receptionist's role is important ensuring that clients are booked correctly for their service.

BEST PRACTICE

Efficiency
Being tidy, putting things back where they should be after use, will mean the next beauty therapist to use them will be able to get straight on with the service. One of the most annoying losses of time is caused by careless use of equipment.

It is also important to carry out services in the allocated time and not to overrun, to avoid keeping future clients waiting for their service.

If a client is late, the booking schedule will need to be checked to see if the service can be accommodated without compromising the quality.

The table below is a list of commercial times allocated to different Level 3 services.

	Service (excluding consultation and preparation)	*Max time (mins)*
1	Facial electrical services	no set time
2	Nail extensions	120
3	Partial body massage	30
4	Full body massage without head	60
5	Full body massage including head	75
6	Body massage using pre-blended aromatherapy oils	60
7	Face and body massage using pre-blended aromatherapy oils	75
8	Indian head massage	45
9	Single lash extension services	120

Note: Standard service times have not been specified for the following services:

10 Epilation

11 Body electrical treatments

12 Spa services

This is because service times will vary dramatically according to client needs, service requirements and service delivery.

“Link sell products to the services you are doing. When a client receives a spray-tan service, link sell a spray-on moisturiser, this will maintain the client's tan.

Lisa Fulton

“Provide advice: Once they have had their tanning service, they will have a different skin tone so they will have to adapt their make-up accordingly. They should have two shades of foundation, one for the days when the tan is at its darkest and one for when it starts to fade.

Lisa Fulton

Ensure that you regularly check scheduled appointments and plan ahead where you can see any potential problem – put a strategy in place to rectify it. This may involve asking others to help you.

BEST PRACTICE

Time management

In the case of overrunning, seek and follow the supervisor's advice on the most effective remedial action. If the client cannot wait, the solution may be to offer an alternative beauty therapist or an alternative service time. If the client is able to wait, make the wait as enjoyable as possible, for example offer refreshments or magazines. Another beauty therapist may be able to prepare the client for you.

Working under pressure

Sometimes you will be extremely busy and may be feeling tired and irritable. This is not your client's or colleague's problem! Remain cheerful, courteous and helpful. You should also use your initiative in helping others, for example preparing a colleague's work area when you are free and they are busy.

You must be able to cope with the unexpected:

- clients arriving late for appointments
- clients' services overrunning the allocated service times
- double bookings, with two clients requiring service at the same time
- the arrival of unscheduled clients
- changes to the bookings

With effective teamwork such situations can usually be overcome.

Avoiding client dissatisfaction

Some dissatisfied clients will voice their displeasure; others will remain silent and simply not return to the salon. The situation can often be prevented through good customer care and effective communication.

- Always ensure that a client has a thorough consultation before any new service. This should be carried out by a colleague with appropriate technical expertise.
- Regularly check client satisfaction. If there is any concern, notify the supervisor of this immediately.

HEALTH & SAFETY

Reception

Relevant health and safety requirements should also be considered at reception. If the client requires a skin test or consultation before the service is received, this should be discussed when the client makes the appointment. Income will be lost and the client will be disappointed if when they arrive for the service they find they are unable to have it because of poor reception management.

ISTOCK/© AMANDA ROHDE

Create your personal targets

Outcome 2: Meet productivity and development targets

Meet productivity and development targets

1. Setting, agreeing and recording your **productivity and development targets** with the relevant person to meet the needs of the business.
2. Actively seek opportunities which will help you to meet your **productivity and development targets**.
3. Ensuring those who assist you with services to clients work effectively to enable you to meet your **productivity and development targets**.
4. Regularly review and record your progress towards the achievement of your **productivity and development targets**.
5. Adjusting your activities in a way that will help you to meet your **productivity and development targets**.
6. Meeting your set **productivity** and **development targets** consistently and within the agreed timescale.

- Inform the client of any disruption to service – do not leave them wondering what the problem may be. Politely inform them of the situation.
- Inconvenience caused by disruption to service can usually be compensated in some way. It is important to resolve problems and keep clients satisfied.

Unfortunately problems in which the client cannot be appeased do sometimes arise. A **complaints procedure** is a formal standardized approach accepted by the business to handle any complaints. It is important all staff are trained in the correct implementation of the complaints procedure.

Customer care is vital: clients provide the salon's income and the staff's wages. The success of the business depends upon the client's satisfaction.

Utilities

Utilities include power and water. It is important that these are used in the most economic way to contribute to the profitability of the business.

Targets

In order to develop personally and to improve your skills professionally, it is important to have personal targets against which you can measure your achievement.

If these are confidential, salon policy regarding confidentiality should be observed.

> Determine why the client is having the tanning service, then recommend products that will help give them the desired results. Prescribe specific tanning formulas that match each individual skin tone for the most natural result. The whole point of faking it is that it is supposed to look natural!
>
> **Lisa Fulton**

Targets should follow the **SMART** principle:

- **Specific** – clearly defined
- **Measurable** – quantifiable in some way
- **Agreed** – between both parties
- **Realistic** – achievable
- **Timed** – for the duration of a fixed period

To an employer it is important that you are consistent. You must always perform your skills to the highest standard, and present and promote a positive image of the industry and the business in which you are employed and which you represent.

Productivity

Productivity targets are set for the business through strategic plans, budgets and sales targets and from these they are broken down to team and individual targets.

For instance, if there is a new service that has been decided upon for the business to offer, then a decision will be made as to how that new service will pay for itself and bring more

TOP TIP

Improve your skills

- In quieter periods observe colleagues who have more advanced qualifications and experience.
- Practise your skills! The more you practise, the more skilled and efficient you will become.

HEALTH & SAFETY

First aid at work

The Health and Safety (First Aid) Regulations (1981) require employers to provide adequate facility resources and staff to enable first aid to be given to employees if they are injured or become ill at work.

Further guidance can be found in HSE document, *First Aid at Work. The Health and Safety (First Aid) Regulations (1981) L74.*

ALWAYS REMEMBER

Productivity targets

Productivity targets are for: retail sales, technical services and personal learning.

ALWAYS REMEMBER

Employee incentives
Certain companies provide rewards for employees who develop ideas for increased productivity.

Commission is a method of rewarding individuals who achieve and exceed targets.

When making recommendations, clearly show the benefits of implementing your suggestions.

money into the business. This is a financial target. In order to achieve this, a productivity and development target will be needed for the individual beauty therapist. It is likely that there will be training needed on the service and then sales targets set for the numbers of services performed and the sales targets for the product sales that go with the service.

This shows how the productivity targets for technical (the service) and product sales go together and also how the individual training all link up.

Personal development plans are necessary to make sure that the individual beauty therapist is always learning and improving, bringing more added value to the business and also preventing the individual from becoming stale and bored.

Personal targets will include:

- *Technical sales*, i.e. individual services and courses, link selling of services such as recommending a body massage for someone who has a facial and complains of back ache and stress. Or encouraging someone who has half leg waxing to have underarm and bikini waxing when they mention going on holiday. Each beauty therapist will have their own targets which will be linked to their ability to perform the services, their expertise and experience.
- *Retail sales*, i.e. the products that go with the services for **aftercare** or to continue the maintenance programme at home. If the salon also has a retail sales section for customers who can just walk in without having services this is a good extra way of achieving revenue. Each salon employee should have a retail sales target and see it as a professional way of supporting their services and part of their job description.
- *Standards of work* are essential to be professional and to give exceptional customer service and care.
- *General tasks* that are needed to be done around the salon including stock taking, hygiene maintenance, keeping equipment in good condition.
- *Personal development targets* (personal learning) such as improving confidence, selling skills, customer care skills and communication, and training targets such as new services or learning existing services that the salon offers but you have not been trained to use need to be agreed.

“Always sell the products' **benefits** first, don't just list ingredients. For example, 'This product will help reduce lines and wrinkles if used regularly, as it contains Matrixyl–3000® which is a strong anti-ageing peptide.'

Lisa Fulton

“Refer to celebrity users when recommending a product. This gives your client someone to associate with and aspire to.

Let's face it we all want to achieve the flawless results that we see in magazines and the media.

Lisa Fulton

ALWAYS REMEMBER

Productivity targets
Productivity targets can be achieved by being aware of retail opportunities. For example, when a client receives artificial nails, you can sell them recommended products and tools to care for their nails at home. An appointment should be made for a maintenance service.

Keep clients informed of any special offers and promotions.

Keep abreast of current and seasonal trends.

Appraisals

Appraisals or progress reviews are an important method of communication, where one member of staff looks at the way another member of staff is performing in their job role. It is usual for an employee to receive an appraisal from their supervisor on a regular basis.

Appraisals provide an opportunity to review individuals' performance against targets set. Each member of the team will have their own strengths and weaknesses and it is important to utilize their strengths and action plan to improve weaknesses with appropriate personal goals.

Performance appraisal will look at:

- results achieved against agreed targets set
- additional accomplishments and contributions

This may seem daunting, but it is an important and useful process. You can also use it to your advantage:

- Identify with your supervisor the tasks you see that need to be accomplished, and how these will be met.
- Identify staff development training needs: this will provide you with a greater range of skills and expertise. This will ultimately improve your opportunities for promotion, giving you increased responsibilities.
- Identify obstructions which are affecting your progress. Look for guidance and support on how these will be overcome.
- Identify and amend any changes to your work role.
- Identify what additional responsibilities you would like.
- Identify and focus on your achievements to date against targets set.
- Update your action plan, which will help you achieve your targets.

If personal targets are not being met it is important to identify the problem. Following this, new performance targets should be put in place to resolve any difficulties.

At the next appraisal the agreed objectives and targets set for the previous period will be reviewed.

ISTOCK/© KIRBY HAMILTON

Employee evaluation form

ALWAYS REMEMBER

Responding to feedback

Take on board negative feedback and use it as constructive criticism and work hard to improve it.

Being positive about negative feedback

Your appraisal may not always be a positive experience. It is important to be positive about improvements and any recommendations to improve your performance, and to work towards achieving these.

Not meeting targets may ultimately result in disciplinary procedure which can lead to dismissal.

Your achievement of the productivity targets set leads to the financial effectiveness of the business.

Why it is necessary to manage the resources such as human, stock, tools and equipment and time effectively.

There are many reasons for having a business such as a beauty salon but if your business is not profitable then you are not able to run it. The finances underpin everything else that is done. If the resources are not managed effectively then the business will lose money. If the business loses money and more money is going out than coming in then it will have to stop and bankruptcy may even be the result.

> Why not designate and empower product or brand champions within your salon? This doesn't have to be the lead beauty therapist. Ensure the product champion receives full training by the supplier and remains in regular contact with that supplier to keep informed of promotions and new products. It's then the product champion's responsibility to educate the rest of the staff about these developments.
>
> **Lisa Fulton**

ACTIVITY

Group activity

Research what might happen as a result of not managing the resources effectively. Split the group into four so each group can look at one range statement.

Give examples for the range human, stock, tools and equipment and time. Bring the group back together again to discuss findings and come to conclusions as to why each resource needs to be managed effectively.

TOP TIP

Internal promotion

Internal promotion may require an employee to put in extra work, take on more responsibility or come up with new ideas.

ASSESSMENT OF KNOWLEDGE AND UNDERSTANDING

FUNCTIONAL SKILLS

Having covered the learning objectives for **contribute to the financial effectiveness of the business** – test what you need to know and understand answering the following short questions below. This will help you to prepare for your summative (final) assessment.

Salon procedures and legal requirements

1 Give **two** examples of your salon's requirements relating to the use of resources (human, stock, tools and equipment, time).

2 What are the critical aspects of current legal requirements relevant to beauty salons relating to the use of the following resources? Use of personal protective equipments, use of products, tools and equipment, disposal of waste and sharps.

3 Which resources relate to the following legislation? (i.e. Health and Safety at Work relates to Human Resources)
- Health and Safety at Work legislation
- COSHH Regulations
- Manual Handling Operations Regulations
- Electricity at Work Regulations
- RIDDOR, Workplace Regulations
- Data Protection Act
- Working Time Directives
- Cosmetic Product Regulations

4 Give a brief explanation of the current legal requirements relating to the sales of retail goods for each of the following:
- Sale and Supply of Goods Act
- Distance Selling Act
- Trade Descriptions Act
- Consumer Protection legislation

5 In your work place give examples of your own limits of authority in relation to the use of the following resources:
- Human resources, i.e. can you ask people to do things for you, can you agree holiday requests or working hours?
- Stock control, i.e. can you order stock?
- Tools and equipment, i.e. are you competent to use all the tools and equipment?

6 To whom would you report recommendations in your workplace?

Resource use, monitoring and recording

1. How does the effective use of resources contribute to the profitability of the business?
2. State what are the **three** key principles of stock control?
3. What are the stocking levels for your salon? i.e how many days worth of stock is normally kept? Enough to keep working for a week or longer?
4. What is the monetary value of the stock you keep in the salon?
5. How should an effective salon ordering system work and how can you ensure that reordering occurs when it is needed?
6. Why is it important to keep accurate records for the use and monitoring of resources?
7. Why must you know which resources you are responsible for?
8. Can you think of common problems associated with salon resources?

Communication

1. Why is it important to communicate effectively in the workplace with the following?
   - your clients
   - your colleagues
   - your boss
2. If you have recommendations for improvements which you feel would benefit the workplace, how would you present these to your boss and colleagues in a positive manner?
3. How and when would you best negotiate and agree productivity and development targets?
4. How should instructions be given to those assisting you? i.e. how can you check they are clear?
5. How can you encourage others to work effectively on your behalf?
6. How can you respond positively to negative feedback?

Work and time management

1. What are the general principles of time management that are applicable to the delivery of salon services?
2. Give an example of how you can plan and reschedule your own work and that of those who may assist you in order to maximize any opportunities to meet your targets? i.e. adding a new service, or allowing some extra time at the end of a service to recommend and sell products.

Productivity and development targets

1. How would you know and understand your productivity and development targets and the associated timescales for their achievement?
2. Why is it important to meet your productivity and development targets?
3. What would be the consequences of your failure to meet your productivity and development targets?
4. What types of opportunities could you use to achieve the productivity and development targets? i.e. add-on services and sales.
5. Why should you regularly review your targets?
6. Why is it important to gain feedback on your performance and development from others?

SHUTTERSTOCK/ BRENDAN HOWARD

6 Successful business ideas

Learning Objectives

This chapter covers the **Check the likely success of a business idea** unit. This unit is about the need to check a new business idea to see if it will succeed, and will form a valuable part of your self-employment.

There are **two** learning outcomes for this unit which you must achieve competently:

1. **Help you know if an idea is worth developing further**
2. **Stop you wasting time and money on an idea if it will not succeed**

You might choose to do this if you are setting up a new business, expanding your business or looking to change or adapt the products and services that you are offering.

To achieve this you should be able to:

- Look at your business idea as a whole, in an open-minded way and identify how it will work in practice.
- Develop a clear understanding of your customers' needs, your competitors' activities and the market for your business idea.
- Identify the implications of any laws you will need to meet, resources you will need to buy and skills you or others will need to develop.
- Decide whether your business idea is likely to make you enough money to cover your costs and any profits that you need to make.

ROLE MODEL

Alice Guise

Business Development Consultant, Salon Synergy

"I am currently working in the hair and beauty industry as a consultant both for manufacturers and salon owners on a range of topics from designing and writing course material, developing the skills of salon managers, assisting in focusing and targeting salon owners towards their goals, putting in place new systems, training and incentives to increase business both for services and retailing.

Prior to this I was Business Development Manager for Toni and Guy, responsible for the performance of 63 salons in the UK. I was able to take on this role as I had 17 years' salon experience behind me, having run my own hair and beauty business which grew from two staff and four dressing chairs, to 20 staff with 12 chairs, two beauty rooms, tanning, and a large retail area.

I have developed my own managerial and business skills through a range of industry courses, external material which in the main has been self-sought, and of course the invaluable knowledge and experience which real-life situations expose one to, enabling me to have immediate empathy with other salon owners who too are risking their own money and livelihood.

Introduction

TOP TIP

Explain your business idea

1. Know what type of business you want.
2. Know why it will be successful.
3. Discuss the skills that you have to operate a successful business.
4. Know how the business will be financed.
5. Know realistically how profitable the business will be when operating.
6. Know how much your clients will need to be charged to be profitable.
7. Have a contingency plan for unseen circumstances.

Types of business that could be suitable for the beauty therapist:

- setting up a new business from scratch such as an independent room within an existing business, a salon or a freelance therapist
- an existing single business that you might buy
- a franchise operation, which you could buy into

Explaining your business idea

Describing what your business will be is necessary if you are to have a clear idea of what you want to achieve. There are a number of options including a beauty therapy salon offering a full range of services through to a more specialist service offering massage services only. More specialist services will narrow down the number of potential clients you have, so it is especially important to do your market research to make sure this is viable.

ISTOCK/© IZVORINKA JANKOVIC

Plan your business with the help of a trusted adviser

Being able to explain why your business is going to be successful will take research into all areas of setting up and running your business including how you are going to finance it, where the money will come from, where it will be situated and how profitable it will be when it is running.

The skills you will need to run your business successfully will include:

- managing finances
- managing people
- managing workflow and resources
- managing information
- a good knowledge of law and regulations that affect business
- marketing skills
- qualifications in the service areas you intend to provide if working yourself
- to be able to stay motivated even when things are not easy and to be a self-starter who wants to succeed

ALWAYS REMEMBER

Leasehold

You do not own the property outright. You buy the right to use it for business (or living in) for a specified number of years, usually 99 to 125 years. Leasehold is usual for business premises. You will also pay a rent (ground rent) to the freeholder and sometimes service charges, e.g. for maintenance.

Freehold

You own the property outright. This is usual for a house you are going to live in.

TOP TIP

Work with wholesalers

If you are starting up and need everything then good wholesalers will give you help, information and quotes at good rates in order to gain your new and ongoing business.

"When recruiting your team, remain fixed on the skills and personality you need to fill any particular role. Do not become set on employing people you LIKE. Yes, you must trust and respect them, but will they be good at that job? The best teams are those that mix up different skills and thinking. You are paying them to carry out tasks, but you can also have their imagination and ideas for free!

Alice Guise

Financing the start up of your business

FUNCTIONAL SKILLS

You will need to have clear costings for how much money is needed to start your business. This will include:

- how much any equipment will cost
- how much your products will cost
- how much your consumables will cost
- the cost of the business building (leasehold or freehold) or room
- the price you will pay if you are buying an existing business
- how much you will need if you are doing building alterations or decoration
- marketing costs
- money you will need to run as you start up but are not making any profit, this includes your own and any employees' wages
- a personal survival budget so you can still afford your own living expenses
- a crisis fund or budget so you have extra money in case of an unforeseeable event

How much should you charge your clients in order to be profitable?

FUNCTIONAL SKILLS

This will vary depending upon your overheads, but it is important not to undercharge. You must cover your running costs for each service and also meet the profit targets you have set yourself in order to be successful.

Example You have worked out that your overheads, that is the cost of everything from your heating and lighting through to your products, average out at £10.00 an hour if you are open for 40 hours a week.

This means you must take more than £10.00 an hour if you are to start to make a profit. You will not be able to have every single hour booked so this must be taken into account. You may decide that you therefore need to be taking at least £20.00 an hour in order to meet your costs and make some profit. Services such as waxing, where you would charge £12.00 for a half-leg wax, which takes 20 minutes, would therefore be profitable if you could fit three into an hour. A full facial which takes an hour but which you only charge £15.00 for would not be profitable.

Market research is essential in order to make sure you can charge enough to make your business work. Check local prices to see where you can position your own prices. It is possible to be easily affordable and work at getting a lot of clients through the door or go to the other end of the market and be expensive but have fewer clients. Either way can be successful.

The contingency fund

FUNCTIONAL SKILLS

It is a good idea to have a fund of money that is for emergencies and unforeseen problems. This can be the difference between success or failure if you hit a problem. There are a number of things that may affect your business that are beyond your control.

For example:

- You may be unable to work due to ill health or an accident.
- Business rates may be increased beyond your budget.
- There may be a downturn in the economy, which results in fewer people coming into the salon.
- A service or product that brings in a lot of revenue may go out of fashion.

ACTIVITY

Knowledge of the economic climate

Research the local and national business economy and see how many things that are beyond your control could possibly have an affect on your proposed business. For example, a downturn in the economy resulting in people not having so much money to spend, or proposed plans for a new shopping centre that may take trade away from where you might situate your business.

Deciding on the kind of business that you want

This could be as simple as having a personal preference. It is necessary however to make sure that it is viable. If you dream of a make-up studio but there are already strong competitors in your local area, it may be that you would not be able to find enough clients. It is also important that you decide on a type of business that really interests you and motivates you to do well. If massage therapy is your real interest then it is unlikely that you will be happy doing a lot of leg waxing and eyelash tinting. Make sure that the services you offer are ones that your clients want but also that you enjoy.

ACTIVITY FUNCTIONAL SKILLS

SWOT Analysis

Do a SWOT analysis to help you plan for business success.

Strengths. What are the strengths of your business idea? i.e. what are the unique selling points, how is it better than other local businesses? Are your people better?

Weaknesses. What are the weaknesses? Are there areas that can be improved on such as a better service selection or different products?

Opportunities. What opportunities for improvement are there? Can you offer a new service that others don't have? Has a local competitor begun to lose business, which you could pick up?

Threats. Is there a new competitor? Has a larger chain moved into the area or a new spa/gym opened up?

> Remember – you are not only selling smooth skin, or a bottle of something; you are selling the hope and the dream of being and feeling beautiful.
>
> **Alice Guise**

How will you run your business?

There are several ways you can run your business:

- The **owner/operator.** This is the most usual, particularly in a new business. The owner also does all the services and often works on their own to build up the business to begin with.
- As a **manager/administrator** who either does not do any services or only a few of the more technical or expensive ones. This gives time to run the business side and is often the best way if a number of beauty therapists are employed.
- By **employing a manager** to run the business from day to day so you are only involved in the ownership duties such as the finances. This is normally suitable when you have a well-established business and possibly several salons.

ISTOCK/© LAURI WIBERG

Sharing location with an associated business will gain clients and reduce overheads

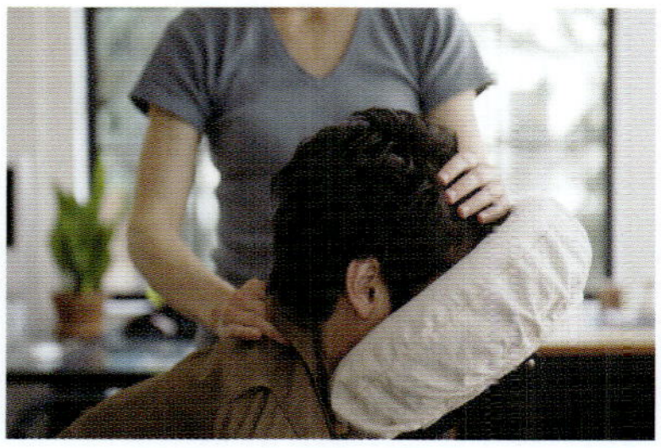

ISTOCK/© NIGHTANDDAYIMAGES
ISTOCK/© LAURI WIBERG

Many offices hire mobile therapists for their staff

BEST PRACTICE

Check out your ideas with others

You need to have an open mind about identifying if your business idea will work. Be realistic and do not assume that customers will think your idea is good just because you do. Get impartial advice from trusted sources such as your friends and family already successful in business.

Deciding where to base your business

Location is important for the success of the salon or clinic. A high street shop front location will give high visibility and walk in trade but will also be more expensive in business rates or rent (it is unlikely that you will be able to buy a high street building).

It is sometimes possible to have a first floor high street location, which is more affordable but still has the advantages.

You could be situated within an associated business such as a gym/spa, hairdressing salon, chiropractor or physiotherapist. This way both businesses can gain clients from each other and share overheads.

You could be based in your own house and have a converted room for your business.

It is also possible to have a freelance beauty therapist business, which does not have a base at all.

The location you decide upon will be as a result of what sort of business you want to run and how much you have in your start up budget.

Parking for your clients should always be considered. Most will want the convenience of being able to park close by to come in and out for their services.

ALWAYS REMEMBER

Knowledge of competitors

It is easy enough to do some market research in your area. Go and visit other salons and have services. Observe what is popular, listen to comments from other beauty therapists and clients. Very fashionable services such as single eyelash extensions will work in areas such as city centres but may not be popular in small towns or country areas. Know who lives in your area and what sort of money they have to spend and how they would like to spend it.

TOP TIP

Make sure there is a market for your business

1 Know where your business clients will be based in the market and who your potential clients will be.
2 Gather and carry out market research to confirm business viability.
3 Consider market and business trends to ensure it will have long lasting appeal.

How to make sure there is a market for your business

A market for your business is the potential clientele that may be in the area that you want to set your business up in. There are a number of ways of trying to find out if that market actually exists.

It is necessary to make the decision as to where you are going to position your business in the market. Are you going to aim for the less expensive services or the more expensive ones? If there are a number of businesses locally that are all much the same is that because it is the only sort of market or is it because no-one has thought of being different?

ELLISONS

Ellisons Academy

> You will hope that all your staff will be able to work on their own initiative, but, for them to feel comfortable with that, they need to know that it's OK to make a little mistake sometimes. You need to be forgiving and help them learn from any possible mistakes which may occur. If you display angry and displeased responses, nobody will want to act on their initiative for fear of soliciting that response from you. This takes strength of character, but is the way to develop a self-reliant team and staff which will not be calling you and asking for answers every minute of the day!
>
> **Alice Guise**

Unique selling point (USP) You need to decide what your USP will be for your new business idea. This is the reason why your new business, product or service is different from anything else being offered. If you are offering something different from other businesses and something that people actually want, then you are going to have people coming to your business as they cannot get it anywhere else. Your USP may be a service, a product or your facilities and customer service. Whatever it is you must make it the thing that you use to sell your business to your customers.

Examples of USP services could be:

- a brand which no-one else has in your area, e.g. skin and body care products and services, body wraps, nail enhancements. Some high quality brands will restrict the number of businesses in an area that offer the products.

Examples of USP facilities could be:

- a whirlpool spa, light therapy relaxation room, a café bar

Examples of USP customer service could be:

- additional free services such as hand and foot massage while a facial is being done, a walk in 'no appointment' service for a quick eyebrow shape and lash tint.
- staff trained in customer service who really enjoy looking after customers.

There are a lot of things that can be offered to make you different from the competition, one of the best things is to make sure that everything goes so well at every visit that your customers always come back.

SHUTTERSTOCK/CHUBYKIN ARKADY

A whirlpool spa offers USP facilities

Market research

You can do your own research with questionnaires and interviews, this is called primary research. You get the information first hand and it is specifically for what you want.

You can use existing information such as local government statistics on households, incomes, types of business and so on, this is secondary research.

You must look at the other businesses in the area that are competitors and carefully analyse what they are offering and how they are doing it. This could be from price lists or from going and having services done yourself. This will show you what their strengths and weaknesses are. This will help you to decide what sort of business will be needed and what variety of services will sell well.

ACTIVITY

USP

Research your local salons and see if you can tell immediately what each one's USP is.

ACTIVITY

Trends

Research past trends in services to see what is currently in fashion and what has now gone out of fashion See if you can predict what will be the next really desirable service to be offered in salons. What factors help to make a service fashionable and desirable? Consider, for example, celebrity endorsement, health conscious services.

Market and business trends also need to be taken into account. Beauty therapy and associated services are fashion led and so things can come and go in popularity. It is not always a good idea to offer only the latest trend as it may be that it will soon be out of fashion.

It is always possible that other trends which are beyond your control might affect your business proposal. This is particularly so when the national economy rises and falls. It is necessary as a businessperson to be up-to-date with business trends and so you should read good quality newspapers and watch current affairs television programmes.

Market review

This should include the following:

- Which market position is going to be best for your proposed business?
- A clear understanding of what your potential clients' likely needs are.
- What trends in fashion and the economy may affect your business?
- What possible factors beyond your control may affect your business?

ACTIVITY

Special offers

You have been asked to do special offers for the salon to celebrate an event such as Mother's Day What offers would be suitable? How would you go about promoting them? How would you make sure that you made a profit from the offers?

ACTIVITY — FUNCTIONAL SKILLS

Group activity

Research how to set up a new product range in the business. This could be skincare, body care or self-tanning, for example.

These are some of the considerations: How much would it cost? How much is the mark-up and profit margin? How much do you need to sell to start to make a profit? Is it suitable for your business? Make a business case for the product range you decide on.

> How will you get your team to work together? Answer: Get them to WORK TOGETHER! Yes – it's that simple. Any project, task, event and the like which needs working on can be taken to the team and used to (A) get the task done and (B) bring their skills and relationships together for the purpose of a common goal. Don't be afraid of letting your people grow, think and take responsibility.
>
> **Alice Guise**

TOP TIP

Identify your skills

Identify skills you and others may need to develop to make your business a success by:

1. **Making a list of what you can do, e.g. services, calculating profit, using the IT system.**
2. **Making a list of what you need to be able to do, e.g. banking, cash flow forecasts, knowing about laws and regulations that affect your business.**

Then look at where the gaps are and plan how you can train and develop to meet all the needs. You can start at your accountant and business adviser and also the local Chamber of Commerce and Small Firms Enterprise Initiative to get support.

Check what laws and regulations would affect your business idea and how you might meet them

There are a number of laws and regulations that affect the business owner whether they are alone or in partnership. Businesses that are properly set up within the law quickly build and maintain an honest and trustworthy reputation, which improves their chances of long-term success. No one starts a business with the intention of failing

The laws and regulations that are important to you cover building regulations and planning permission, licence to trade, company law, health and safety, fire safety, employment law, taxes, the selling of goods, the supply of goods and services, insurance requirements. There are general laws that affect all businesses like health and safety and taxes and there are local regulations like planning permission and licences, which may be different in various regions, cities and towns.

If you are trading as a sole trader or partnership you can use your own name or a different business name. However, the name must not be offensive or use inappropriate words or expressions. You cannot use the words Limited or plc. Always check first if someone else is using the name you want to use. It may cause you a real problem if a national company is already using it, they tend to guard their names and you may be sued. You can easily do a search on the Companies House website to check this and save yourself problems in the future.

Setting up a Limited Company means you will need to register your name and other details with Companies House. Your name must end with Limited, Ltd, plc (or Welsh equivalent) and must not, like the sole trader names, be inappropriate or offensive.

There are rules about displaying your business name as well as including where you run your business and on all stationery such as orders, invoices, business letters and so on. Don't get anything printed before you are certain you can use your proposed name.

TOP TIP

Choosing a business name

It is not a good idea to name your business after something that is very fashionable because it will quickly date. Try to make sure it has a timeless quality and reflects what you are offering.

TOP TIP

Checking a business name

Check your local phone directories to see if anyone else is already using your proposed name. Check the Patent Office website to see if your proposed name is already registered by someone else.

Running your business

Once you have got through setting up your business to suit your requirements you must then be able to run your business successfully and legally.

Areas that you need to know about are:

- providing goods and services to your clients – the Sales of Goods and Services Act – Trading Standards
- terms and conditions you will offer your clients, e.g. guarantees, payment facilities
- terms and conditions that you will have from your suppliers and will offer to them
- if you need to copyright or patent any new part of your business
- employment law if you are employing anyone, even if they are self-employed
- tax that will be payable on your income, VAT Regulations
- preparing and keeping accounts records
- insurance that you must have by law and as a sensible precaution

ACTIVITY FUNCTIONAL SKILLS

Research where you can get free advice and information from such as Gov.uk, Camber of Commerce, Companies House, Patent Office, Federation of Small Businesses, Office of Fair Trading.

It is a legal requirement for every business whether you are a mobile therapist or an owner of a chain of salons to ensure that the products or services you sell meet minimum standards. All goods that you sell must correspond to any description given, be of satisfactory quality and be fit for their purpose. All services you supply must be carried out with reasonable care and skill, within a reasonable time and for a reasonable charge. Customers have a range of rights if they are unhappy with goods or services and may be able to claim compensation or replacements.

ACTIVITY FUNCTIONAL SKILLS

Find out about your local Trading Standards from the Trading Standards website and the Sale of Goods Act and how it applies to you at the DTI website.

Payment of bills on time is not only professional and good practice but a legal requirement (Late Payment of Commercial Debts (Interest) Act (1998)). It is possible to charge

ACTIVITY FUNCTIONAL SKILLS

Taxation

Depending upon the type of business you are running you will be liable for different types of taxation. Using the HMRC website, research which types of taxation will be relevant to your proposed business.

HEALTH & SAFETY

The Health and Safety at Work Act (1974)

Under this Act you have a duty of care towards your employees, your clients, yourself and anyone else who may come into your business premises such as a contractor, maintenance person or electrician. Employees also have a duty of care to work in such a way as to look after themselves and their colleagues and clients. Health and safety is therefore the responsibility of everyone not just one individual. You have to have a health and safety policy and if you employ five or more people it has to be written down. Your local Environmental Health Officer will want to inspect your premises from time to time and you must be able to show, with the correct documentation, that you are following the guidelines.

ACTIVITY

Fire extinguishers

Research what sort of fire extinguishers should be available in a beauty therapy salon.

PHOTOGRAPH REPRODUCED BY KIND PERMISSION OF CHUBB FIRE

Fire extinguishers

interest on debts over 30 days but most businesses choose not to do this in the interest of good relations.

Always pay your bills on time and do not make the mistake of overtrading. This is when you are spending more than you have coming into the business. It is possible for your business to fail if you then cannot pay future bills and it is illegal to do this. It is best to have good, independent financial advice about cash flow. This is freely available from your high street bank or you may choose to pay a financial adviser.

Employment law is very detailed and is regularly updated and changed. As an employer you will have a number of responsibilities to your employees including if they are self-employed or temporary. These include:

- recruitment and selection
- data protection
- pay
- maternity and paternity rights
- termination of contract

There is good free advice available from ACAS (Advisory, Conciliation and Arbitration Service). It is also possible to visit its website for details on contracts of employment and statutory holiday requirements, minimum wage levels and so on. As employment law is very detailed it will be worth using an employment law legal specialist if you have any problems. For general information the Citizens Advice Bureau can also be useful.

A contract of employment should be a written contract or statement (see Chapter 5 Financial effectiveness).

Financial regulations It is essential to get advice on financial regulations including Income Tax from a professional adviser. It is very difficult to do this yourself. There is free advice available from high street banks and other similar sources and it is normal to have an accountant who will keep the business financial records and deal with income and business taxes. If you are employing people then you need to set yourself up as an employer with HMRC.

Environmental impact Everyone has an impact on the environment. It is important to save energy, recycle and to keep the use of packaging and non-essential materials to a minimum. Check with the local council to see if there are any local regulations you need to be aware of. General good housekeeping practices such as switching off lights and having appliances such as wax pots on time switches are good for the environment and your bills and expenses.

Fire The Regulatory Reform (Fire Safety) Order (2005) replaces all previous legislation and places responsibility for fire safety onto the 'responsible person', which is usually the employer.

Checklist of legislation affecting employers and employees

NB: This is regularly changed and expanded so make sure you do your up-to-date research.

1970 Equal Pay Act

1974 Health and Safety at Work Act

1975	Sex Discrimination Act
1976	**Race Relations Act**
1995	Disability Discrimination Act
1998	National Minimum Wage Act
1998	Working Time Regulations
1998	**Data Protection Act**
1998	Employment Rights Act
1998	Human Rights Act
1999	Employment Relations Act
2000	Part-time Workers Regulations
2000	**Consumer Protection (Distance Selling) Regulations**
2002	Control of Substances Hazardous to Health Regulations (COSHH)
2004	Cosmetic Products (Safety) Regulations
2010	Equality Act

Deciding if your business idea will be worth developing

Once you have your business idea and your market research you can then make a decision as to whether it has the potential for success. There are business consultants who can also give you an objective and impartial view on whether or not your idea has potential. There are small business advisers in local banks who can help you and this is usually provided free.

Your business must be profitable in order to succeed. Working out the likely profits from your business idea will also help you to make the decision.

If you discover from your research that there is a lot of competition, that prices are very low and that you cannot make a profit, then you will need to either adapt your plan or discard it as an idea that won't succeed. You must be ruthless about this to avoid unnecessary waste of time and money in pursuing it.

ACTIVITY FUNCTIONAL SKILLS

Business potential

Using this checklist see if your business idea has potential:

- Does the cash flow forecast add up to profit? Yes/No
- Do I have a USP? Yes/No
- Does anyone else in the area offer exactly the same? Yes/No
- Am I offering services and products that people actually want? Yes/No
- Is there already a lot of competition? Yes/No
- Do I have the skills to make a success? Yes/No

If you have more Yes than No answers your business idea may have potential.

TOP TIP

Decide if your business will be a success

1. **Confirm if your idea has potential. You may like to employ a business consultant to give you their impartial opinion.**
2. **Estimate carefully the expected profitability of the business.**
3. **Carry out further market research as necessary to confirm data.**
4. **Identify your own personal cash flow needs.**
5. **Consider how your business will be funded.**
6. **Decide on your business aims this is important to successful business planning.**

ISTOCK/© DMITRY ERSLER

Does your business idea have potential?

FUNCTIONAL SKILLS

Cash flow forecast

You will need to do one of these to estimate the cash and profitability of the business. This is normally done for 6 to 12 months.

This can then be used when looking for finance, to plan your future business and as a way of checking that your business is going to plan.

Cash is normally the term used for money paid in and also paid out of the business. This includes:

- receipts: money expected in from clients
- payments: money spent on various things to keep the business going, e.g. products, running costs, wages.

Always be careful in estimating how much money you could have coming in to the business. Predicting too much coming in too quickly will be unrealistic. If you are buying an existing business, the cash flow history is important to know.

ACTIVITY FUNCTIONAL SKILLS

Cash flow

Using the table work out the cash flow and decide whether or not this new business, owned and operated by one person, will be a success.

The beauty salon

Cash flow forecast/cash budget

	Jan	*Feb*	*March*	*April*	*May*	*June*
Income						
Sales	NIL	200	300	400	400	400
Services	300	500	2000	2500	3000	3000
Total income	300	700	2300	2900	3400	3400
Expenditure						
Rent	300	300	300	300	300	300
Salary	800	800	800	1000	1000	1000
Expenses	100	200	200	200	200	200
Purchases	NIL	100	200	200	300	300
Total expenditure	1200	1400	1400	1700	1800	1800
Opening balance						
Net cash flow						
Closing balance						

You must also have a budget for your own personal survival and living expenses. Work out what money you need in order to have somewhere to live, food, transport and so on. Everyone's needs will be different so it is necessary to put together your own personal cash flow plan to make sure you are meeting your needs and can pay yourself enough.

ACTIVITY FUNCTIONAL SKILLS

Budgeting

Write down how much money you have coming in each month. Then work out what you have to pay out each month to maintain your lifestyle. This will give you a basic idea of your personal budget needs.

Funding your business

It is likely that you will need to borrow money from an outside source in order to get your business going.

Money provided by you is considered to be capital and is an asset.

Money borrowed from other sources is called liabilities.

Borrowing money A business can borrow money from:

- banks
- finance houses
- building societies
- creditors
- government sponsored schemes
- the Prince's Trust

ISTOCK/© YANIK CHAUVIN

You may be drawn to offer wellness therapy in a holistic spa

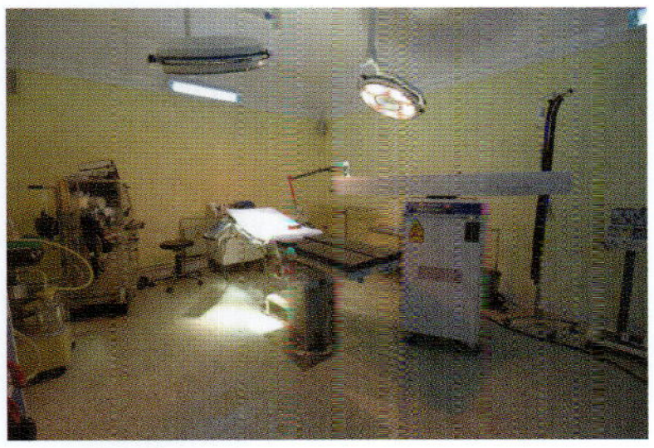
SHUTTERSTOCK/ DRAGAN TRIFUNOVIC

You could work alongside the medical profession in a laser clinic

Deciding on the business aims

Successful planning and start up of the business should include a set of business aims. Ask yourself what you want the business to achieve. This could be simple or ambitious. There are several examples:

- to support yourself, living costs and enable you to be your own boss
- to make a good profit so that you can afford to have a comfortable lifestyle
- to be the best beauty therapy salon in the city and to have a high profile with a celebrity clientele
- to be a fully committed holistic clinic where clients are treated for general day-to-problems
- to offer a specialist electrolysis and laser clinic working alongside the medical profession

Remember that whatever you decide upon as the aim of your business it must always be profitable in order to survive.

ASSESSMENT OF KNOWLEDGE AND UNDERSTANDING

FUNCTIONAL SKILLS

Having covered the learning objectives for **check the likely success of a business idea** – test what you need to know and understand by answering the following short questions below. These will prepare you for your summative (final) assessment.

Business focus

1 How would you identify a business idea's USP and why would it be successful?

2 How would you judge whether a business idea was worth developing, adapting or stop going any further with it to avoid wasting time and money on it as it will not succeed?

Market research

1 What do you need to research, how can you carry out your own research and how do you get hold of published market research?

2 How might your customer's actions and choices affect the success of your business?

Competitors

1 How could you assess if your competitors may affect your business? e.g. by having the same services at cheaper prices, by copying your advertising, by being better at customer service.

Market and business trends

1 How can political and commercial changes affect a business idea? e.g. tax changes, environmental concerns, health issues, fashion trends.

2 Could events which are local, national or even international improve your business opportunities? e.g. a local Summer Carnival might give an opportunity to promote the salon with free services for the Carnival Queen and her entourage, a national celebration such as the Olympics or Queen's Birthday could be used to give special offers, an International World Wildlife Fund fund-raising activity could get you and your customers involved by raising money and the salon profile in the local press. What other instances can you think of?

3 Could events which are local, national or even international limit your business opportunities? e.g. international terrorism may affect travel badly and so business if you are attached to a hotel spa. A national flu outbreak or bad weather may prevent clients attending the salon or locally having road works right outside your business may prevent clients from coming in or parking. What other instances can you think of?

Law and regulations

1 Which laws will need to be considered alongside your business idea and how might they affect the success of it? e.g. there can be additional costs to adhere to health and safety requirements, employment law will concern you if you employ people, and tax laws also need careful adherence.

Skills and abilities

1 How can you assess your own and other people's skills, abilities and knowledge when planning what you need to be able to do to successfully get your business started? i.e. you will not know everything about starting a business so where would you go for professional advice?

2 What should you have in place in the workplace to make sure that people can be trained and developed and constantly improve their skills and abilities?

Resources

1 How can you identify what resources and of which type you will need and their costs? e.g. people, products.

Finances

1 How do you know how much profit you should aim to make when you are planning your business idea?

2 How can you then use this to plan your budget and sales forecast?

3 How do you work out the selling price of your products and services to ensure you achieve your sales forecast?

4 What is a cash flow forecast and profit and loss accounts and what information would you need to produce them?

7 Diagnostic consultation

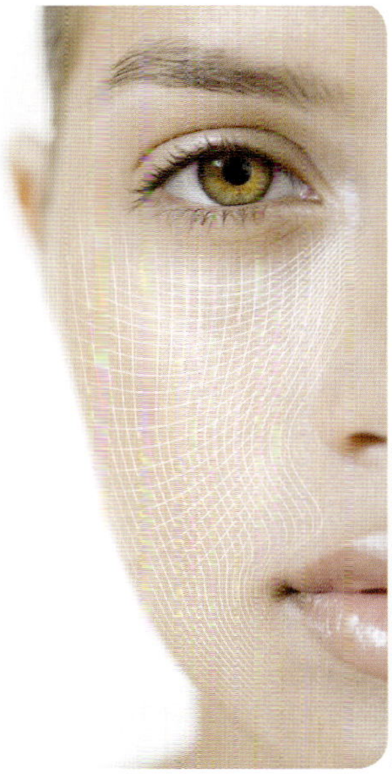
SHUTTERSTOCK/DRAGAN TRIFUNOVIC

Assessing the client and preparing service plans

Consultation and plan for services

Through the consultation process you assess the needs of the client and ascertain the service. As a Level 3 beauty therapist you will be performing many different services. The objectives of these services will be generally:

- to improve skin condition and texture
- to improve contour and muscle condition
- to aid relaxation, improve feelings of well-being and reduce symptoms of stress

Assessment techniques

Often there may be an underlying cause not immediately obvious that will only become apparent through:

- questioning
- observation and diagnostic **assessment**
- **skin analysis**
- body figure analysis

Questioning techniques It is necessary to ask the client a series of questions before the service plan can be finalized. This must be carried out in a private area to maintain client confidentiality and the details recorded on the client **record card**. The information is confidential: the client must be made aware of how the information is to be used and it should be stored in a secure area following client service. This is enforced through the Data Protection Act (1998) – legislation designed to protect the client's privacy and confidentiality.

The client should understand the reason behind the questions asked and feel comfortable when answering them. As such, they should be asked in a sensitive and supportive manner. Avoid technical terms, choosing commonly understood words to ensure client understanding. Ask 'open' questions which will encourage the client to give more than a one-word response of 'yes' or 'no', which will help you to make informed decisions based on the information provided.

If, after the consultation, you are unsure of the client's suitability for service, tactfully explain to the client why this is and ask them to seek permission from their GP before the service is given. Some clients' expectations may be unrealistic. If this is the case, tactfully explain why and aim to agree to a realistic service programme.

DERMALOGICA

Facial diagnostic consultation

ALWAYS REMEMBER

Data Protection Act (1998)
The Data Protection Act requires anyone who processes personal data to inform the Information Commissioner's Office (ICO) how you will use this information. For advice, contact the Information Commissioners' Office at www.ico.gov.uk.

HEALTH & SAFETY

Client suitability for service

If there is a contra-indication, you will require a letter of consent from your client's GP before commencing any service.

Never diagnose contra-indications when referring a client to their GP. This is not within your professional responsibility, you are not qualified to do so.

The health of the client should be checked at each service as their health or medication may change at any time.

ALWAYS REMEMBER

Service plans

Designing an effective service plan includes:

- completion of the client record card
- checking for client suitability to services
- diagnostic techniques
- design of a suitable, realistic, agreed service plan

BEST PRACTICE

Open questions

Open questioning techniques may begin with 'how', 'what', 'when' or 'where', for example 'How do you want to improve your skin's appearance?' 'What facial services have you received before?'

Records on computer should be password protected to ensure only those permitted to access them can do so.

Suitable questions for consultation and assessment

Questions for the client	*Information required*
What is your service need? (e.g. slimming, hair removal, improved facial muscle tone, improved relaxation)	Is this realistic for this client? The beauty therapist can consider appropriate services.
What area requires service?	Never presume the area to be treated! The service area may require an intensive approach through selected services in order to achieve maximum results. A longer service time and cost may be necessary, e.g. the removal of superfluous hair with epilation.
What services have you received previously? Were you satisfied with the service results? If not, why? (A client may be nervous of electrical services because of a previous bad experience.)	Discuss the benefits of the service choice you are able to offer to meet their service needs. Where necessary, reassure the client and regain their confidence in the service through your knowledge and professionalism.
Are you undergoing any current service for the area? (e.g. temporary methods of hair removal, restylane injections, current skincare routine.)	You may find that the area of service has become worse through neglect or inappropriate service methods. Advise the client accordingly.
Describe your lifestyle.	These factors will directly affect the client's health, general appearance and well-being.
Do you take regular exercise?	It may be necessary for the client to take regular exercise to improve fitness, muscle tone, circulation and increase calorie expenditure.
What is your occupation?	The client's occupation may be stressful or contribute to poor posture, muscle fatigue, etc. Discuss relevant services and supportive home-care advice.

Questions for the client	*Information required*
Are there any external factors that may limit your commitment to the service programme?	The client's domestic situation or employment hours may present restrictions to the programme required.
Describe your diet.	Is the client's diet healthy and balanced? If not, offer a healthy alternative which is relevant to their needs. Take into consideration any special dietary requirements.
Do you take part in any leisure activities?	Are these offering an effective means of relaxation? Offer suggestions where relevant, such as relaxation exercises.
Do you smoke?	Smoking has a detrimental effect on health and fitness. Tactfully discuss these issues.
Check the client's suitability for service – the client may have known contra-indications or contra-actions to services.	The client's health may contra-indicate service, e.g. medical history, current medication, recent operations, allergies, etc. Explain the reason and offer alternatives.
Inspect the service area and question the client if there are any evident conditions that cause concern.	There may be visible contra-indications to service application. The service may require modification to accommodate contra-indications present, e.g. varicose veins in the service area.
Suggest a realistic service plan and discuss service attendance, period of time and cost.	You need to know if the client can commit themself to the plan, in terms of time and cost.
Question the client to ensure they understand all aspects of the service plan, e.g. aims, outcomes.	This should provide an opportunity to answer relevant questions and will ensure client satisfaction.

Lifestyle factors After questioning, consider whether the client's current lifestyle habits have contributed to the condition:

- *Alcohol*. Alcohol is a toxin (poison) and deprives the body of its vitamin reserves, especially vitamins B and C, which are necessary for a healthy skin. It also causes skin dehydration and premature ageing.
- *Smoking*. Smoking interferes with cell respiration and slows down the circulation. This makes it more difficult for nutrients to reach the skin cells and for waste products to be eliminated. As such, the skin looks dull with a tendency towards open pores. Cigarette smoking also releases a chemical that destroys vitamin C. This interferes with the production of collagen and elastin and contributes to premature ageing of the skin. Nicotine is also a toxic substance.
- *Recreational drugs*. Drugs are chemical substances that affect the homeostasis – the regulation and maintenance of balance of the internal systems of the body. Drugs enter the blood and are transported to the cells of the body affecting the body in different ways. This can lead to skin disorders caused by side-effects of the drugs such as dry skin, premature aging, skin rashes and infections from scratching the skin.
- *Stress*. **Stress** can occur any time a person becomes pressurized. The symptoms of stress are seen in many different forms, including insomnia, poor digestion, headaches, muscular tension, and skin disorders such as psoriasis and eczema. If someone is suffering from stress, they may drink more alcohol and smoke more cigarettes, causing further stress to the skin. At the consultation, try to determine if the client is suffering from symptoms of stress. Very often the

TOP TIP

Food and exercise diary

Encourage the client to keep a food and exercise diary if the client needs to review the quality and regularity of their nutrition and exercise.

Good and poor patterns can become evident which you could review with the client for improvement.

client will offer this information and the service objective will be to induce relaxation through its therapeutic effect.

- *Sedentary lifestyle*. Lack of exercise results in poor blood and lymph circulation and poor muscle tone, resulting in slack contours, the appearance of a 'cellulite' condition and weight gain due to inactivity. A feeling of well-being is achieved when taking part in exercise. Lack of exercise also results in lethargy. Aim to improve the client's motivation by educating them in the benefits to be achieved from a balanced diet, regular exercise and specific salon services.
- *Diet*. A nutritionally balanced diet is vital to the health of the body and the appearance of the skin. A healthy diet contains all the nutrients we need for health and growth. Lack of energy, skin allergies and disorders are, in part, the result of a poorly balanced diet.
- *Health*. The diagnosis of the client's health is important before considering any service plan. Medication and ill health can contra-indicate certain services or be a contributory cause of the problem. Always confirm the client's general health while completing the record card.
- *Ageing*. With ageing, there is a decrease in bone density (osteoporosis) so that bones become brittle and are easily fractured. Exercise and a diet containing plenty of calcium-rich foods can guard against this. The change in appearance of women's skin during ageing is closely related to the altered production of the hormones oestrogen, progesterone and androgen at the menopause. The skin loses its elasticity, becomes dry, appears thinner and the facial contours become slack. Services which accelerate the skin's natural functioning by nourishing and firming are recommended.
- *Exposure*. Unprotected exposure to the environment allows evaporation from the epidermis, which results in a dry, dehydrated skin condition. UV exposure causes premature ageing of the skin as the UVA rays penetrate the dermis. Free radicals – highly reactive molecules which can cause skin cells to degenerate – are also formed. These molecules disrupt the production of the collagen and elastin that give skin its strength and elasticity. Environmental pollutants such as lead, mercury and aluminium can accumulate in the body, where they attack protein in the cells. The skin should always be protected. Advise the client on suitable skincare and cosmetics that offer maximum protection. Antioxidant nutrients in the form of vitamins C, E and beta-carotene are beneficial in that they reinforce the effects of the skincare routine and service plan.
- *Pregnancy*. Clients may feel they need pampering during pregnancy. It is a time when the body undergoes significant bodily changes, which can cause sensitive and pigmented skin, fluid retention, insomnia, nausea, constipation and back ache. Caution is needed in the choice of services, but there are many services available that may be of significant help to the client.
- *Superfluous hair*. In women, superfluous hair is considered to be in excess of that of normal downy hair. Unwanted hair may be caused by *topical stimulation*. This is where stimulation or friction to an area of skin may cause excessive hair growth. Women under considerable stress may have excessive hair growth due to high levels of adrenalin, which also stimulates androgen production.

  Certain prescribed drugs, such as anabolic steroids, can also cause superfluous hair. Diet can affect hair growth. People suffering from the eating disorder anorexia nervosa become very thin and undernourished. It is quite common to see excessive hair growth all over the face and body. This is a result of a shutdown in the ovaries, reducing the oestrogen levels and stimulating the circulating androgens.

BEST PRACTICE

Client advice

If the client's expectations from the service are unrealistic, tactfully advise them why this is so. For example, the client is seriously overweight and the slimming service will not be of beneficial effect unless there is substantial weight loss.

Remember, there are always alternative services that can be offered which will support the client in achieving their service goal.

HEALTH & SAFETY

Alcohol

Alcohol intake is measured in units – 1 unit is 1 centilitre of alcohol and is equivalent to:

- 1 single measure of spirits
- ½ pint lager, beer or cider
- 1 small glass of wine

A maximum of **3–4** units a day are recommended for men and a maximum of **2–3** units for women.

ALWAYS REMEMBER

Ageing skin service considerations

As the skin ages it will be necessary to advise the client that the results achieved will be limited; they will take longer to achieve the optimum effect and care will be necessary by the beauty therapist performing services such as micro-dermabrasion as the skin is less resistant to the skin thinning effect which can lead to excessive redness, sensitivity and poor skin healing.

ALWAYS REMEMBER

Vitamins

Vitamins can be sourced in the diet. For instance:

Vitamin C is found in a wide variety of fruit and vegetables, such as:

- peppers
- broccoli
- sweet potatoes
- oranges
- kiwi fruit

Vitamin E

- nuts
- seeds
- spinach
- vegetables
- sardines
- egg yolks

Beta-carotene

This is turned into **Vitamin A** and is sourced from yellow and green vegetables and yellow fruit, e.g. mango and melon.

HEALTH & SAFETY

Pregnancy

Miscarriage is most likely during the first 3 months of pregnancy. Regular monitoring of the client's health is important before every service, as medical conditions may occur, such as changes in blood pressure and diabetes.

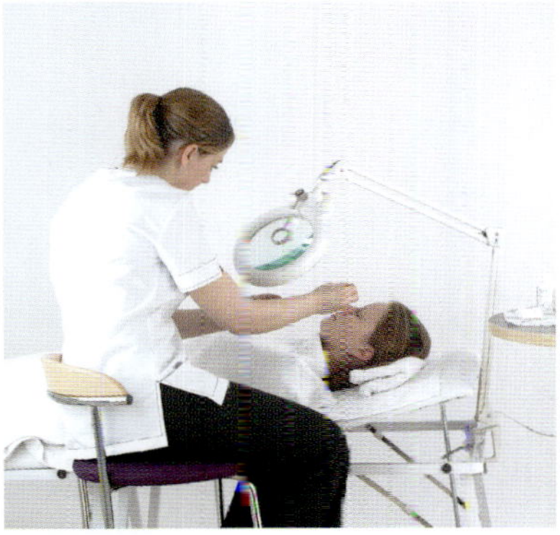

DAYLIGHT COMPANY

Skin being viewed for skin type with a magnifying lamp

TOP TIP

UV exposure

UV exposure is a primary cause of skin ageing. Recommend the client wears a suitable UV sun block at all times. This will be necessary following services such as micro-dermabrasion.

Observation and diagnostic assessment

Specific diagnostic procedures will enable you to identify any underlying condition or cause which may be creating or contributing to the condition identified. These must be carried out in a way that ensures the client's modesty and privacy is maintained at all times.

Skin analysis

Following facial cleansing, inspect the skin's surface using a magnifying lamp.

Assessing skin type The skin is the largest organ of the body. Its basic structure does not vary from person to person in health, but the physiological functioning of its different features does and this gives us different **skin types**.

Skin reflects general health and responds quickly to any changes. This must be taken into consideration. For example, hormonal changes at puberty or in pregnancy may cause the sebaceous glands to become more active, resulting in oilier skin. During this time, the service routine must, therefore, be altered to suit the skin's needs. However, when the hormonal balance is settled, the skin type may change completely.

Skin tone A healthy young skin will probably have good skin tone and will be supple and elastic. This is because the collagen and elastin fibres in the skin are strong. The skin loses its strength with age as collagen production slows and elasticity is lost. Poor skin tone is recognized by the appearance of facial lines and wrinkles. To test skin tone, gently lift the skin at the cheeks between two fingers and then let go. If the skin tone is good, the skin will spring back to its original shape. The longer it takes to return to its original position the poorer the **skin tone**.

TOP TIP

Assessing skin moisture content

Equipment is available which can assess the hydration level of the skin by analyzing how effectively current is passed through the tissues, providing a value for hydration.

This enables the correct diagnosis of the skin's needs and choice of therapeutic ingredients.

ALWAYS REMEMBER

Collagen

Collagen fibres provide skin with strength and elastin fibres with elasticity.

Collagen accounts for up to 75 per cent of the weight of the dermis, elastin accounts for 5 per cent.

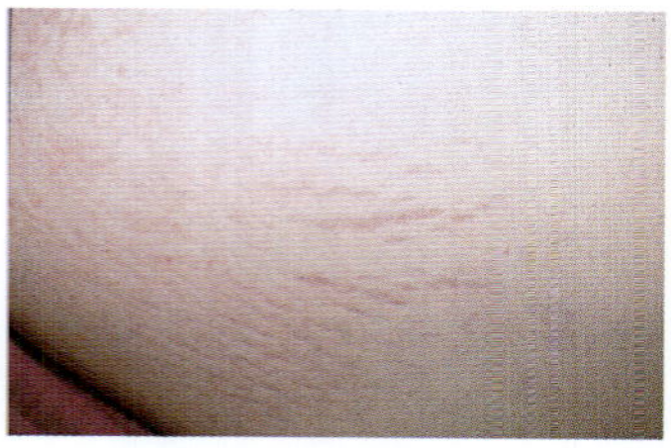

DR JOHN GRAY, THE WORLD OF SKIN CARE

Stretch marks

Stretch marks (striations) Stretch marks appear on the skin as long, faint scars. They occur as a result of the skin breaking beneath the surface, in the dermal layer. Stretch marks are permanent and are caused by fluctuations in body weight as the skin stretches with weight gain, for example, during pregnancy. They are commonly seen on the breasts, abdomen, inner upper arm and inner thigh.

Services that improve skin tone through firming will improve the appearance of stretch marks, for example micro-current body application supported by the application of skin-strengthening creams or oils. Pregnant clients and clients with fine skin or sun-damaged skin should be encouraged to keep the skin supple with regular application of skincare emollients.

TOP TIP

Stretch marks

If a client has stretch marks, services that stretch the skin further will be contra-indicated, for example vacuum suction and skin-stretching massage manipulations. A healthy, balanced diet is important – low levels of zinc, vitamins B6 and C are thought to contribute to the formation of stretch marks.

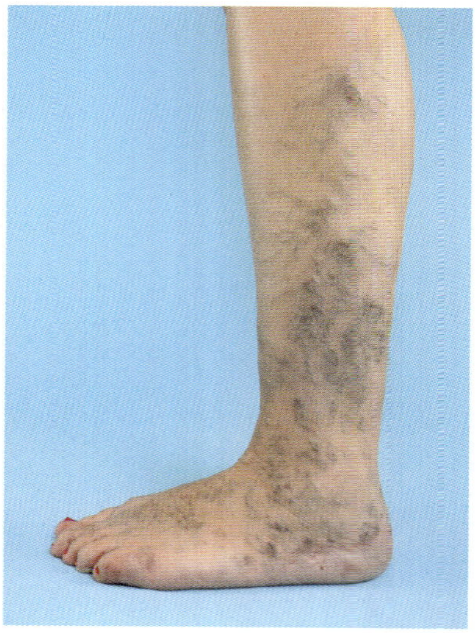

DR JOHN GRAY, THE WORLD OF SKIN CARE

Varicose veins

Varicose veins Veins have valves to prevent backflow as they carry blood under low blood pressure back towards the heart. An occupation requiring you to sit or stand for long periods may lead to varicose veins, a condition where the veins' valves have become weak and lost their elasticity. The area appears knotted, swollen and bluish/purple in colour. Where varicose veins are present, services that put further pressure on the weakened vein, such as the mechanical service vacuum suction, will be unsuitable.

Muscle tone Observe the facial contours when the client is semi-reclined on the service couch. Poor muscle tone will be recognized by slack facial contours. The service

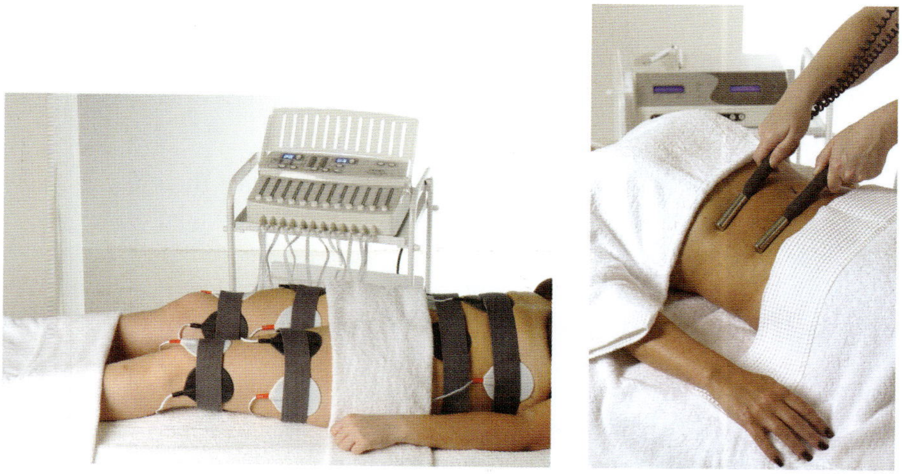

DEPILEX

Muscle tone can be improved significantly by targeting individual muscles or groups of muscles with electrotherapy services, such as electro-muscle stimulation (shown) which improves muscle tone aim will be to strengthen the muscles by shortening them, which will tighten and firm the muscles and contours. Suitable services include facial electrical muscle stimulation and micro-current, supported by facial exercises which the client can perform at home.

A healthy diet, effective skincare routine and supportive beauty service plan all help to delay the effects of ageing.

Body analysis

Body analysis follows the completion of personal details on the client record card. Further details are recorded from each stage of the analysis.

Clients will have different body shapes, referred to as *somatotypes*. Each body shape can be classified as one of three body types.

Body type There are three main body types, but most people are a combination of these.

- **ectomorph** a lean and angular body shape – long limbs, slim narrow shoulders, hips and chest
- **mesomorph** strong athletic body shape – muscular build, well-developed shoulders and slim hips; an inverted triangle shape
- **endomorph** a large body frame – short limbs, plump, rounded body, often pear-shaped hips are wider than the shoulders

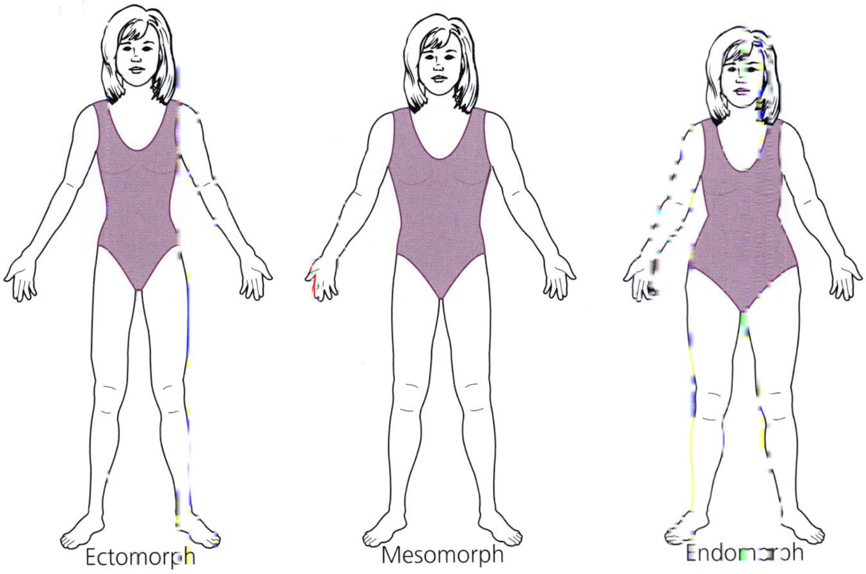

Body types

Specific target areas for service and figure correction will be common to each figure type.

Muscle tone Exercising a muscle causes it to become firm, with improved metabolism, responsiveness and blood supply. Lack of exercise results in the muscle becoming stretched and slack. It is also less responsive and has a reduced rate of metabolism. Even when relaxed, a muscle that is regularly exercised will appear toned. Many services will require the muscle to have its tone improved. This will involve the client physically exercising or passive exercise where the use of electrical equipment causes the muscles to contract and relax, thus improving their tone.

To assess muscle tone, simple exercises may be performed either on the service couch or on the floor. Sample exercises are described in the table below.

ALWAYS REMEMBER

Assessment exercises will also assess joint mobility. Clients with postural or joint mobility issues will be restricted in the movement range they will be able to perform.

Simple exercises to assess muscle tone

Area	*Exercise*
Abdominals	Ask the client to perform a sit-up (legs bent at knee) from the lying position. Feel the strength in the anterior abdominal muscles. With the client standing, ask the client to breathe in – the abdomen should become flatter, possibly concave.
Legs	While lying on their back, ask the client to perform leg raises, slowly lifting one leg at a time and holding each at its raised position. Feel the tone in the quadriceps group.
Arms	The client holds their hand to their shoulder while the beauty therapist attempts to move the arm from position. You can feel the strength in the biceps and triceps as the arm extends while performing this movement.

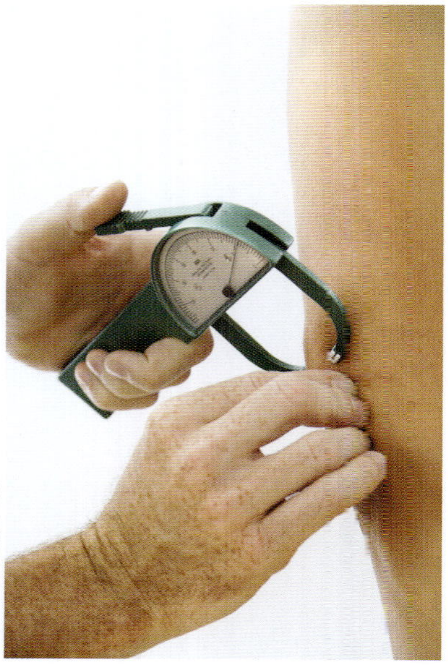

SHUTTERSTOCK/IOFOTO

Measuring percentage of body fat using skin fold calipers

Body fat The amount of body fat stored underneath the skin in the subcutaneous layer will depend upon the weight of the client. This will make a difference to the body shape. It is not always evenly distributed, leading to problem areas – usually the thighs and bottom in women. In men it is predominantly in the upper back and abdominal regions.

Body fat can be measured using:

A **skin fold calliper:** used to pinch the skin at selected points on the body. These include the triceps, beneath the scapula, abdomen, below the navel, bi-and suprailiac, at the hip and front of thigh. The skin is picked up using the index finger and thumb of one hand that is then pinched 1 cm away from the finger and thumb between the callipers. The callipers pull the fat away from the muscles and bones. A gauge on the callipers measures the thickness of that pinch. The measurements obtained are then calculated to identify the percentage body fat.

A bioelectrical impedance device uses a very low level electrical impulse. Electrodes are placed on the body which pass an electrical impulse through the body. The signal travels quickly through muscle tissue which has a high percentage of water and is a good conductor of electricity, and slowly through fat, which has less water and is a poor conductor of electricity offering resistance to the current. The bioelectrical impedance device uses the information from the current to calculate body fat percentage.

Hand-held body fat monitor measures the conduction of electricity through the tissues of the body and calculates body fat.

FUNCTIONAL SKILLS

Body mass index The measure of how healthy a person's weight is can be measured by their body mass index. The body mass index (BMI) is a height–weight measure often used to determine if a client is overweight.

A formula used to calculate this is as follows:

$$\frac{\text{Weight in kilograms}}{\text{Height in metres squared}}$$

The average adult BMI is between 20–25; in excess of 26 is considered a health risk.

$$\text{BMI} = \frac{\text{Wt}}{\text{Ht}^2}$$

Once the BMI is calculated you can refer to a BMI chart to find out if the client is underweight, normal range-healthy, overweight or obese.

Cellulite Cellulite is a term used to describe fatty tissue that causes the overlying skin to appear dimpled, like 'orange peel' in appearance. Common places for the occurrence of cellulite are the thigh, buttock, knee and triceps areas.

To assess for cellulite, gently squeeze the client's skin. If cellulite is present, small lumpy nodules will be seen. In advanced cases this will be obvious without squeezing the skin.

Cellulite is caused by:

- poor venous and lymphatic circulation, providing poor elimination of waste products
- a sedentary lifestyle, resulting in weight gain caused by low energy expenditure and sluggish circulation due to inactivity
- poor diet and metabolism problems due to hormonal imbalance

However, slim women who exercise regularly can also be affected. Therefore a specific service should be advised, with supporting retail products. The service plan will be to stimulate the lymphatic circulation, increase exercise and improve the diet, with a reduction in processed foods and toxins, and an increase in water consumption to flush out excess toxins.

Beauty therapy services that are beneficial for the treatment of cellulite are those that improve circulation, mobilize fatty tissue and generally improve skin appearance. These include manual and mechanical massage, micro-dermabrasion, vacuum suction, galvanic body therapy and micro-current.

Advise the client on the application of any retail preparations recommended. Often the cost of the service will include the supporting home-care preparations.

Fluid retention Tissue fluid can accumulate, causing swelling (oedema). The beauty therapist must assess if this has a medical or non-medical cause. This will be determined at the consultation stage while completing the client record card.

Normal swelling can occur around the ankles if a person stands for long periods. It is common before menstruation, affecting the abdomen and breasts. Fluid retention can also be caused by allergies and a diet with excessive processed foods, high salt intake and insufficient water. To test for fluid retention, press the client's skin. If it remains indented and does not immediately spring back, this is a sign of fluid retention.

Fluid retention in the face is often caused by poor hydration, leading to dehydration. It can also be caused by poor lymphatic circulation where excess fluid appears in the spaces between the adipose tissue.

Weight When weighing the client, ideally weigh them at the same time of day in the same clothing. Usually this will be with the client in their underwear, but, if not, allow 1 kg (2 lbs) for outer clothing. Record the weight on the client record card. The weight should then be measured against the desirable weight range tables for the client's height and frame size.

If the client wishes to lose weight, a realistic target should be set. This should be monitored weekly to maintain motivation.

Height Using a fixed scale attached to the wall, measure the client's height without shoes, heels together and the back as straight as possible. The shoulders should touch the wall while the client looks ahead.

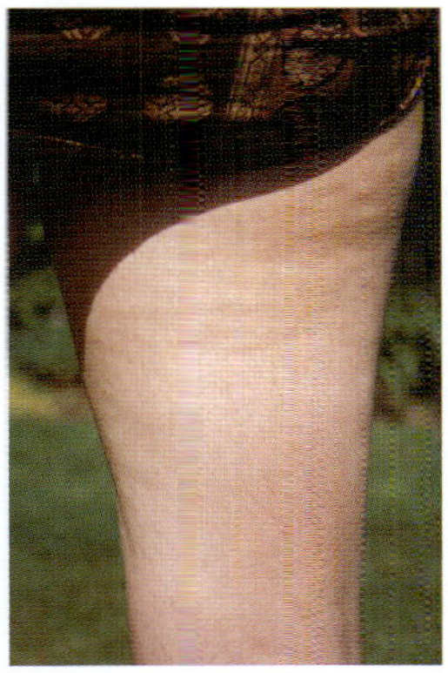

DR JOHN GRAY, THE WORLD OF SKIN CARE

Cellulite

TOP TIP

Massage

Specific types of massage, such as mechanical massage or manual lymphatic drainage (MLD), improve the efficiency of the lymphatic system. Cypress, lemon and lavender are essential oils which may be used in conjunction with manual massage on a cellulite condition.

HEALTH & SAFETY

Fluid retention

Fluid retention may be symptomatic of a serious underlying cause requiring medical attention, such as cardiac, kidney or metabolic problems.

TOP TIP

Reducing puffy facial features

Facial exercises, manual massage techniques and electro-muscle stimulation services help to reduce fluid retention leading to puffy tissue in the face.

BEST PRACTICE

A healthy diet

Advice for a client – eight guidelines for a healthy diet:

1. Enjoy your food.
2. Eat a variety of different foods.
3. Eat the right amount to maintain a healthy weight.
4. Eat plenty of starchy and high-fibre foods.
5. Avoid eating too much saturated fat.
6. Avoid eating too much sugary foods.
7. 'Look after' the vitamins and minerals in your food.
8. If you drink alcohol, keep consumption within recommended unit limits.

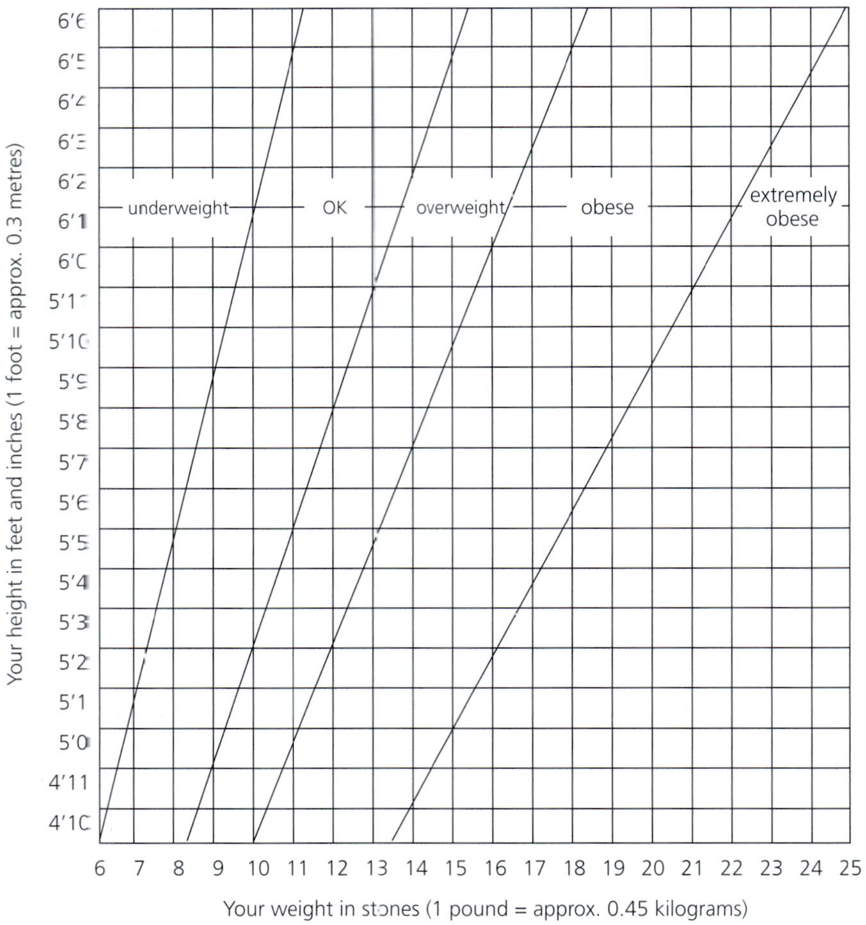

Height–weight range chart

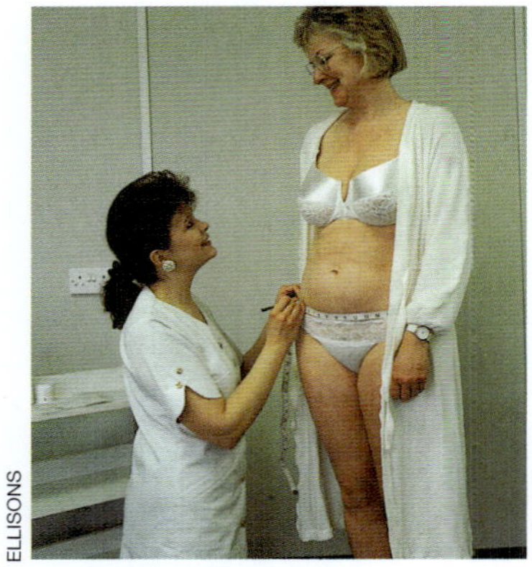

Taking measurements

TOP TIP

Measurement

For accuracy when measuring, always take measurements from the same place – ideally fixed bony points. For example, any vertebrae may be used as these points remain static. Record the results on the client record card.

Taking measurements Measurement records provide evidence of inch loss, the aim of many figure body services. They may be performed before and immediately after certain body services where the aim is to achieve immediate inch loss, e.g. a slimming body wrap. Normally, if the client is regularly attending the salon, once a week is sufficient. Frame size is identified by measuring the size of the client's bones – small, medium or large.

Assessing posture

TOP TIP

Postural alignment

Another method of checking postural alignment is to use a weighted plumb line (a string with an attached weight). This line is the line of gravity, and should appear to pass through the centre of the earlobe, the centre of the shoulder, behind the hip joint, in front of the knee joint and in front of the ankle joint.

The client is checked from the side, front and back for any exaggerated protrusion against the line of gravity created by the weighted plumb line.

Posture varies from person to person and is affected by the client's:

- occupation
- health

- psychological state
- muscular strength

Good posture is recognized when the body is in alignment:

- head held up
- arms loose at the sides of the body
- back held straight but not stiff
- abdomen pulled in
- hips held at the same level
- bottom pulled in
- feet – body weight equally distributed

Observe your client from the front, side and back. Make notes on the record card of any exaggerated curves or alignment imbalance of the body. Areas of postural imbalance will result in muscle strain, tightening and fatigue.

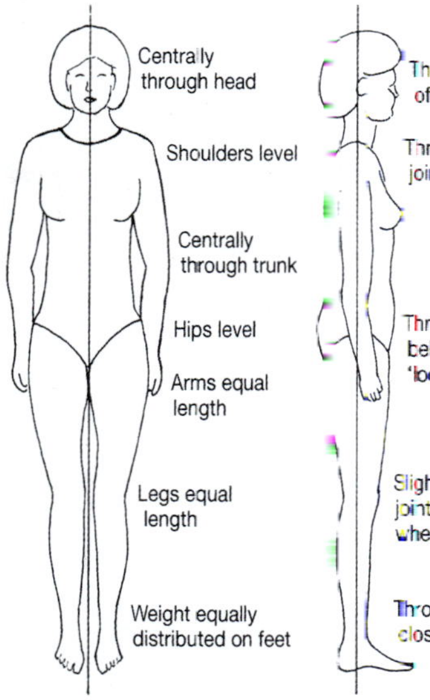

Good posture

Common figure faults

Fault	Cause	Service	
Poking chin: If the head pokes forwards it distorts the ligaments of the neck, leading to neck and shoulder pain. Headaches, tiredness and backache can result due to unnecessary strain on the ligaments and muscles.	High heels, which alter balance, throwing the body weight forwards; occupation, where the head protrudes forwards for long periods; associated postural problems – round shoulders.	Heat service to the upper back followed by manual massage; stretching and mobility exercises for the shortened muscles; education of correct posture.	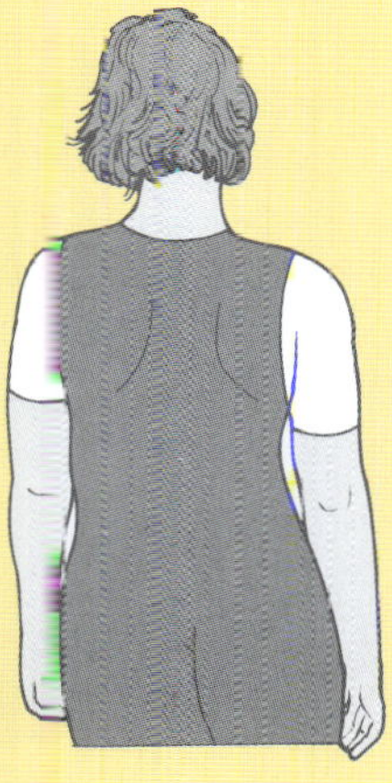
One shoulder higher than the other: This can lead to the postural condition 'scoliosis' where there is a sideways deviation of the vertebral column. This is commonly seen with one hip being higher than the other.	Uneven distribution of weight when carrying loads, e.g. carrying a bag on one shoulder; standing with the weight on one hip, affecting postural alignment.	Shortened muscles will require lengthening and lengthened muscles will require shortening to correct the lateral deviation; stretching and mobility exercises; education of correct posture.	Scoliosis
Rounded shoulders. The shoulders sag forwards, shortening the chest muscles and lengthening the muscles of the upper back. This leads to sagging breasts in women and often a dowager's hump occurs in old age. Here, fatty deposits accumulate over the thoracic and cervical area of the upper back and neck. This is commonly associated with the postural condition 'kyphosis' where there is an exaggerated outward curve in the thoracic area of the vertebral column.	Occupation, where the shoulders tend to be rounded for long periods, e.g. computer operators, hairdressers; psychological, e.g. lack of confidence or a postural attempt to disguise a large chest or minimize height.	Mechanical massage or vacuum suction may be of benefit following a preheating service applied to the area; stretching and mobilizing exercises; muscle-toning services for the stretched muscles; education of correct posture.	 Kyphosis

Forwards or backwards tilt of the pelvic girdle: This pelvic deviation affects body alignment, causing back strain and muscle fatigue. A forward pelvic tilt is commonly referred to as the postural condition 'lordosis', where the client will appear to have a hollow back in the lumbar region.	Poor posture, e.g. slouching; poor muscle tone of the anterior abdominal walls; post-pregnancy or operation in the area.	Manual massage to stretch the tightened muscles and increase mobility; active exercise or passive exercise using electrical muscle stimulation or micro-current service to strengthen the abdominal muscles.
Hips not level: This is also commonly seen as one hip and one knee being higher than the other. This can lead to or be caused by the postural condition 'scoliosis' where there is a sideways deviation of the vertebral column to the left or right.	Standing with the body weight on one hip; uneven distribution of weight when carrying loads.	Shortened muscles will require lengthening and lengthened muscles will require shortening to correct the lateral deviation; education of correct posture.

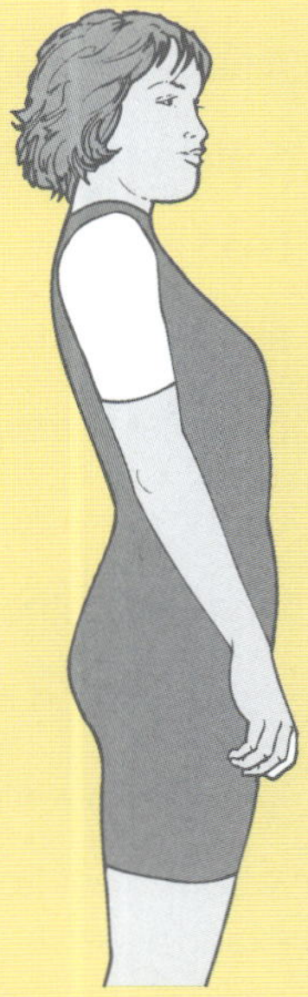

Lordosis

HEALTH & SAFETY

Spinal curvatures and postural disorders

Certain spinal curvatures and postural disorders require medical attention and cannot be treated by the beauty therapist. If unsure, always recommend GP approval before services are given.

HEALTH & SAFETY

Pregnancy

Avoid leaning back. Keep the back straight, which is less tiring. Strengthen the muscles following the birth, avoiding slouching.

HEALTH & SAFETY

Postural disorders

While some postural disorders are caused through bad habits, others are genetic postural deformities which cannot be corrected or remedied.

Sitting, standing and walking Assess and correct the client's sitting, standing and walking stance:

- *Sitting*. Ensure the knees are parallel to the floor. Ideally the knees should be higher than the hips; this avoids unnecessary back strain. The bottom should be pressed against the back of a chair. Feet should be flat on the floor.
- *Standing*. The body should be held upwards yet not stiff. Spinal curvatures must not be exaggerated. The weight should be balanced between both feet. Hips should be level, with the stomach and bottom pulled in. Shoulders should be relaxed and set back a little; arms loosely at the sides.
- *Walking*. The body should be tilted slightly forwards as each step is taken. The toes should point forwards and the heel should be lifted well off the ground as the weight is transferred to the front foot. Arms should swing freely.

Postural education requires emphasizing to the client poor postural habits which require correction. To improve posture, strengthening and stretching exercises may be recommended which tone weak muscles, increase mobility and support salon services. Having carried out a thorough consultation, reviewed lifestyle factors and established any required service objectives, you will be able to select an appropriate service plan. The service may require modification – adaptation in some way because of the client's physical condition or lifestyle factors such as occupation.

Discuss the aims of the service. All details should be recorded on the client record card. Agree the service plan with the client and ensure that the client understands what commitment the service plan requires in terms of cost, frequency and duration.

Allow time and invite the client to ask questions before the service commences.

Prepare the client for the service including removal of outdoor clothing, assisting the client onto the couch and covering the client to ensure modesty and privacy is maintained.

8 Facial and body electrical services

CACI

Learning Objectives

This chapter covers the **Provide body electrical services** and **Provide facial electrical services** units.

These units are all about how to apply electrical services by selecting and using different equipment and techniques to improve face, body and skin condition.

Consultation techniques are important to select the appropriate service to achieve the client service objectives.

There are **four** learning outcomes which you must achieve competently:

Provide body electrical services:

1. **Maintain safe and effective methods of working when providing body electrical services.**
2. **Consult, plan and prepare for services with clients.**
3. **Carry out body electrical services.**
4. **Provide aftercare advice.**

Provide facial electrical services:

1. **Maintain safe and effective methods of working when providing facial electrical services.**
2. **Consult, plan and prepare for services with clients.**
3. **Carry out facial electrical services.**
4. **Provide aftercare advice.**

For each unit your Assessor will observe you on **at least five separate occasions which must involve at least three different clients**.

(continued on the next page)

CACI

ROLE MODEL

Mary Overton

Export Manager for CACI International

“I started my career in the beauty industry 26 years ago upon the recommendation of a relative who at that time was working as the Beauty Editor for a leading women's magazine. I felt that a career in beauty would offer me many varied and exciting opportunities. This has certainly proved to be the case.

In 1981, after graduating from the Shaw College of Beauty Therapy and Micheline Arcier Aromatherapy School, I worked as a Beauty Therapist/Aromatherapist for several years. After gaining additional qualifications in media studies and a City & Guilds qualification in teaching I then worked for several multinational companies including the skincare company Guinot as a company trainer/Training Manager.

For the past 9 years I have been responsible for developing the export business for CACI International and raising the profile of the CACI brand overseas including new product launches in Asia, Australasia, the Americas, Middle East, Scandinavia, Central and Eastern Europe. During my career I have enjoyed representing my company on television both at home and abroad, contributing to beauty articles in the trade press, and was a judge for the Professional Beauty Awards for 2 years running.

(continued)

The range to be completed is listed separately for both units below:

Provide body electrical services.

From the **range** statement, you must show that you have:

- used all types of equipment such as galvanic unit, electro-muscle stimulator (EMS), micro-current unit, lymphatic drainage equipment, micro-dermabrasion unit
- used all consultation techniques
- treated all body types
- treated all body conditions
- taken the necessary action where a contra-action, contra-indication or service modification occurs
- applied services to meet required assessment service objectives
- provided all types of relevant aftercare advice

Provide facial electrical services.

From the **range** statement, you must show that you have:

- used all types of equipment such as direct high-frequency unit, galvanic unit, EMS, micro-current unit, lymphatic drainage equipment, micro-dermabrasion unit and micro-lance tool
- used all consultation techniques
- treated all skin types
- treated all skin conditions
- taken the necessary action where a contra-action, contra-indication or service modification occurs
- applied services to meet required assessment service objectives
- provided all types of relevant aftercare advice

When providing body and facial electrical services it is important to use the skills you have learnt in the following units:

Monitoring safe work operations

Promotional activities

CACI

ROLE MODEL

Claire Burrell

Trainer for CACI International

"I have been in the beauty industry for 9 years. I graduated from the London College of Fashion where I studied a HND in Beauty Therapy and Health Studies. Once I graduated I worked as a beauty therapist within a health club, moving up the ladder to head therapist and then manager. I managed the salon for a number of years and then decided to take another path within the Industry and studied for a teaching qualification. I worked at a college teaching beauty therapy for a short period of time and then started my career with CACI International as a trainer.

As one of the company trainers at CACI, I train beauty therapists on a variety of electrotherapy treatment systems. The famous micro-current non-surgical facelift being one system, as well as micro-dermabrasion, IPL [intense pulsed light] and endermologie systems. I often travel overseas to deliver training and perform demonstrations. Most recently I demonstrated our new CACI Ultimate system on Channel 4's *10 Years Younger*, which was an amazing experience.

Studying beauty therapy has opened up many avenues for me, so don't think your only option is to work in a salon – there are many career paths you can take.

Essential anatomy and physiology knowledge requirements for these units are identified on the checklist in Chapter 2, pages 12 and 13. This chapter also discusses anatomy and physiology specific to these units.

This chapter covers the equipment required to be studied for the unit on **Body Massage Service**, which includes gyratory massage and audio sonic massage service.

It is important that the preparation of the client, yourself and the service area is set up by implementing all health and safety regulations, related legislation and following manufacturers' service instructions.

Specific, safe and effective working guidance is discussed in the chapter, alongside discussion of each service.

Electrical services for the face and body

Electrical services produce intensified results in a short period of time compared with those that can be achieved manually.

Service objectives for electrical services for the face and body include:

- improved skin condition
- improve skin texture
- improved contour and muscle condition
- improved body condition

Electrical science

Matter

Everything is made up of **matter**, which in turn is composed of over 100 basic substances called **elements**. All matter, whether solid, gaseous or liquid, is made up of tiny particles called **atoms**.

Each atom is made up of three types of particles. It has a nucleus containing particles called **protons** which have a positive electric charge, and **neutrons** which have no electric charge. Around the nucleus is an outer layer containing continually orbiting particles with a negative electric charge called **electrons**. Each element has atoms which differ in their make-up of protons, neutrons and electrons.

Where atoms have the same number of protons (+) and electrons (–) they have overall no electric charge, but sometimes electrons can be lost or added to the atom. When this occurs the atoms become particles with an electrical charge and are called ions. This normally happens when substances are dissolved in water. It makes the water able to conduct electricity.

If an atom gains an electron then the particle will contain more electrons than protons and will be a negative ion called an **anion** with a negative charge. If it loses an electron then the particle will have more protons than electrons and will be a positive ion called a **cation** with a positive charge.

Ions can interact with each other. Ions of the same charge are repelled by each other, while ions of different charges attract each other.

HEALTH & SAFETY

Manufacturer's instructions

Although guidance has been provided regarding service application techniques, always read the manufacturer's instructions provided with each piece of electrical equipment you use before you attempt to use it.

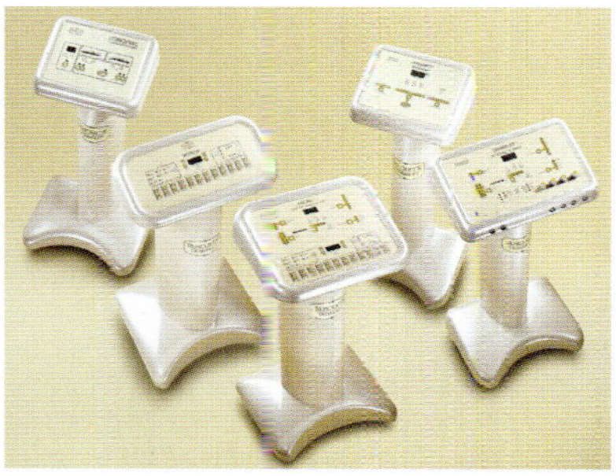

SILHOUETTE-DERMALIFT

Electrical facial and body equipment

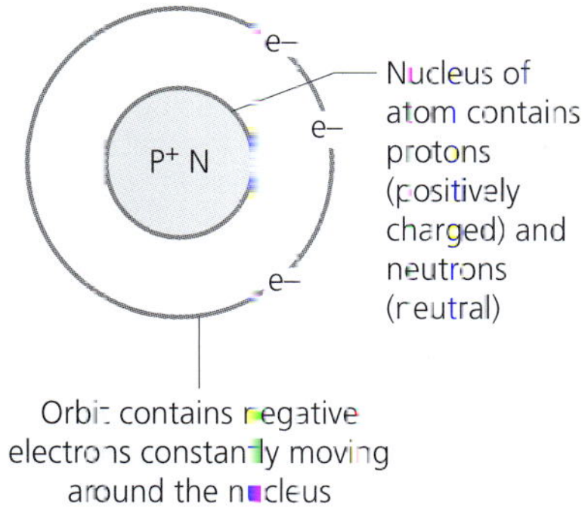

Structure of an atom

ALWAYS REMEMBER

A negatively charged ion is called an **anion** (–).

A positively charged ion is called a **cation** (+).

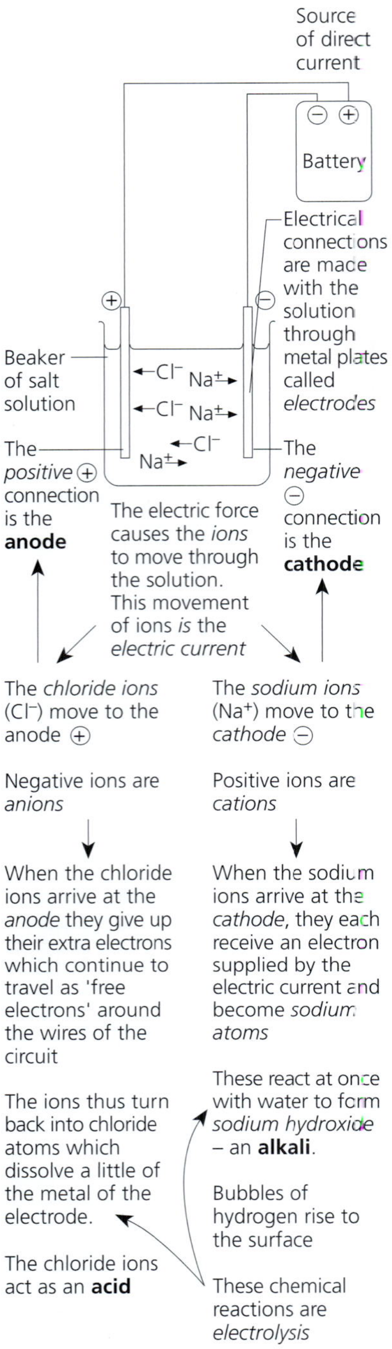

Galvanic electrolysis

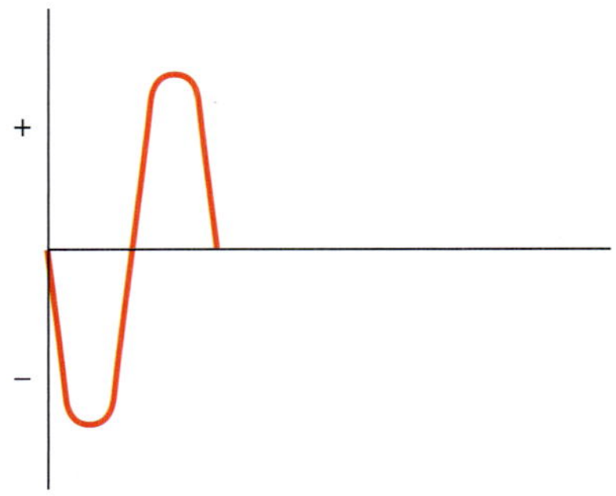

Electric current

HEALTH & SAFETY

Familiarization

Different manufacturers' equipment may vary in its application, e.g. the micro-current. Always familiarize yourself with each piece of equipment, especially the setting requirements, before using it on a client in order to apply it effectively and safely.

> It is essential to familiarize yourself with every service being offered on your salon price list as ignorance is no excuse in the eyes of your client.
>
> **Mary Overton**

When an **electric current** is passed through water containing ions, the ions are made to move. Positive ions – cations – are attracted to the negative electrode, called the **cathode**. Negative ions – anions – are attracted to the positive electrode, called the **anode**.

When the ions arrive at their respective electrodes, chemical reactions occur – acids are formed at the anode and alkalis at the cathode. This process is called **electrolysis**. Galvanic electrolysis is illustrated here, showing what happens to the movement of ions when an electrical current is passed through a solution of salt (sodium chloride) and water.

Electric current

An electric current occurs when there is a flow of charged particles in a **conductor**.

When an electric current flows through a metal wire, a conductor, the electrons pass from atom to atom through the metal. The flow of electrons along the wire of the electric circuit between the electrical supply and the appliance is called an **electric current**. The circuit is the route travelled by an electric current. There must be a positive electrode (anode) and a negative electrode (cathode) to complete the circuit.

What is happening is a connection between the different electrical charges. The electrons will flow from the negative pole or positive pole to whichever has an excess or a shortage of them. The factor essential for the production of an electric current is the difference of potential. The potential is where we use the + sign to mean higher potential and – sign to show lower potential. Electrons will move from the lower to the higher potential. To ensure the flow of electric current it is necessary to maintain this difference of potential so the electrons keep flowing. This can be achieved by the use of a chemical action such as using a battery, it provides a potential difference. Your equipment will be equipped with the facility to initiate polarity change.

Types of electrical current There are different types of currents available and these are used to create different physiological effects in electrical beauty therapy services.

They are classified according to the:

- waveform used
- polarity
- **frequency** – low, medium or high frequency

Batteries A battery is a device which produces electricity by chemical reactions and delivers a dc. The stored chemical energy in the battery is converted into electrical energy. The connections of the battery are identified by their polarity – a positive terminal (+) and a negative terminal (–). There is a transfer of electrons between the terminals which powers the flow of electrons.

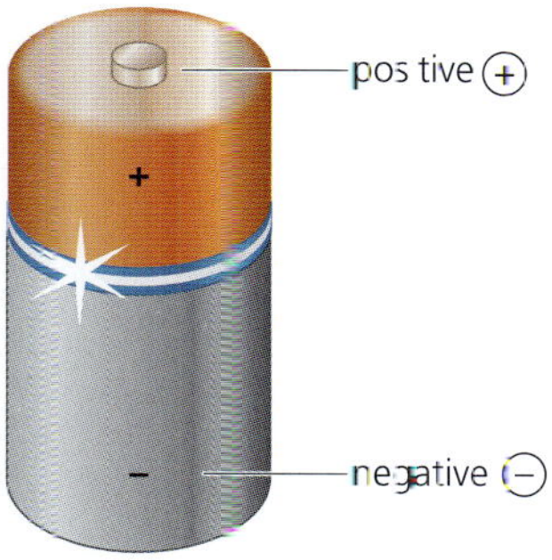

A battery

Electric power Electricity to power electrical equipment is taken from the 'mains' supply via the sockets in buildings, at 230 volts (an electric measure to register the flow of electric current). Alternatively, a battery might be used to power items of equipment.

Mains electricity is an alternating current (ac) moving back and forth. In most countries mains alternates five times of current flow each second. This is referred to as a frequency of 50 cycles per second, measured in **hertz** (Hz) (see page 212).

ALWAYS REMEMBER

Batteries

- Dry cell batteries (non-rechargeable) are used for some portable equipment. The cost of running battery-operated equipment is much higher than that of mains operated. Always consider this when purchasing new equipment.
- Batteries must be removed once exhausted or they may leak, damaging the equipment.
- Always insert the batteries correctly to avoid damage to the equipment.

TOP TIP

Internal batteries

Some items of therapy equipment have specially designed internal batteries. These are charged from the mains supply by a transformer which reduces the mains voltage and a rectifier to convert the ac to dc. Such batteries should be fully discharged before they are recharged, otherwise they will fail to operate at their full capacity.

Electrical measurement

FUNCTIONAL SKILLS

The pressure creating the flow of electrical current around the circuit is the difference of potential and is measured in volts (V). Voltage causes the current to flow. The rate of flow of electric current around a circuit when the electrical force or voltage is applied, is measured in amperes or **amps** (A), a measure of electrical strength.

The power or energy used by electrical equipment is measured in **watts** (W) and kilowatts (kW): 1000 watts = 1 kilowatt.

As watts are relatively small units, powerful appliances need several thousands of them. For this reason the larger unit of energy, kilowatt, is used.

Watts can be calculated by measuring volts and amps, and using the following equation:

$$\text{watts} = \text{volts} \times \text{amps}$$

This equation enables you to calculate the power of an appliance. However, each item of equipment is usually labelled with the voltage it is designed to work from, and either the power rating in watts or kilowatts, or the current it consumes in amps. Sometimes the value for amps is not shown and requires calculation in order to select the correct fuse, and to prevent overloading a socket.

To calculate amps knowing volts and watts, use the following equation:

$$\text{amps} = \frac{\text{watts}}{\text{volts}}$$

Resistance Electrical resistance is the resistance offered by the circuit to the flow of electrons. Resistance is measured in **ohms** (Ω) after Gustaf Ohm.

ALWAYS REMEMBER

Measures of electrical strength

Microampere: current 0.001 amperes less or 1/1 000.000 of an amp.

Milliampere (mA): current is 1.0 ampere or less or 1/1000 of an amp.

Milliamp is used to measure output on galvanic services.

HEALTH & SAFETY

Currents of 1.0 amp are unsafe to use on the human body.

Ohm's law **Ohm's law** relates to the current, voltage and resistance in an electrical circuit and states that 'the ratio between the voltage and the current flowing in a conductor is constant'. This ratio is called the resistance of the conductor.

To calculate the resistance of a piece of equipment use the following equation:

$$\text{resistance} = \frac{\text{volts}}{\text{amps}}$$

Every substance has a resistance to the flow of electrons passing through it. In order to transfer the electrical energy, electrical resistance must be reduced and a good conductor of electricity is necessary.

Electrical conductors and insulators

FUNCTIONAL SKILLS

A conductor is a substance which easily transmits an electric current.

Good conductors include metals such as copper, gold and aluminium and solutions which contain conducting properties such as acids, salts and alkalis, known as electrolytes (a compound which in solution conducts an electric current and contains ions).

Good conductors have a nucleus with free electrons which are able to travel. The material has a small resistance, offering little opposition to the moving electrons so that the electric current can pass freely through it. Although electricity passes through a conductor, it has to be forced through it by a battery or the mains supply and as such it offers some resistance.

Poor conductors include rubber, plastic and wood, and are often used to prevent the flow of electrons. They are known as **insulators**. These are materials which have a nucleus with few electrons able to travel so that electricity can only pass through them with difficulty.

Pure water has a high resistance to electricity, but when another compound is dissolved in it, it becomes a good conductor, for example a saline solution, where sodium chloride is dissolved in water.

In beauty therapy, an electrode is used to conduct electric current. The positive electrode and the negative electrode serve as points of contact when electricity is applied to the body.

TOP TIP

Gold needles

Gold is used for electrical epilation needles used in the treatment of sensitive skin, as it is a good conductor of electricity allowing for the smooth application of the current.

BEST PRACTICE

EMS electrodes

The surfaces of EMS electrodes are prepared with a conducting gel before application or the layer of air and the dry surface of the electrode will act as insulators.

Fuses Fuses protect electrical appliances from excess current. Wire in the fuse melts if excessive current occurs. This breaks the electric current. A fuse is fitted in the plug to protect the cable from overheating. It is a **cartridge** fuse, where the fuse wire is in a glass or porcelain tube.

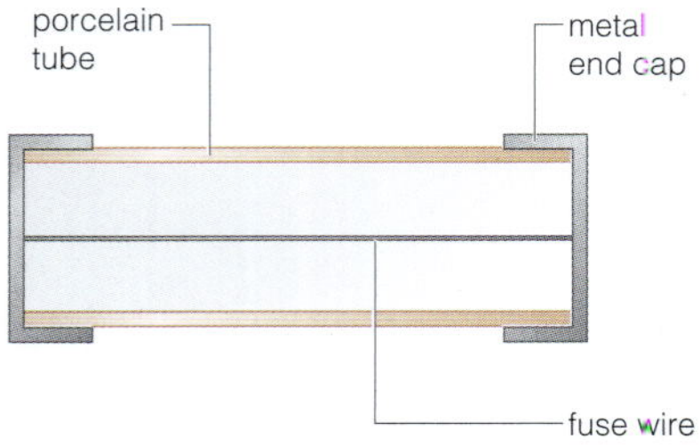

A cartridge fuse

Some items of electrical equipment also have fuses fitted inside them to give extra protection.

The plug connected to an appliance should contain the correct size of cartridge fuse is calculated using the following formula:

$$\text{watts} = \text{amps} \times \text{volts}$$

TOP TIP

Typical plug, showing fuse placement.

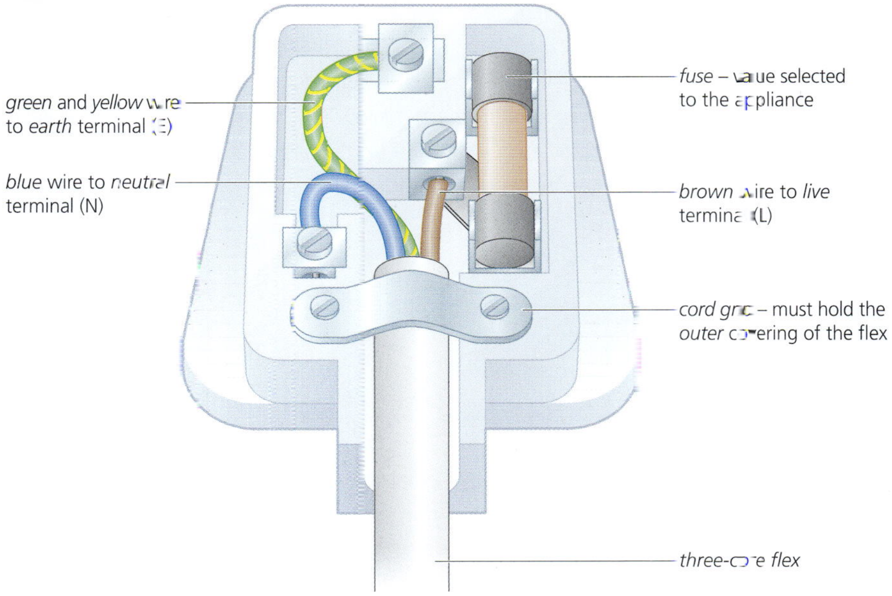

All plugs must comply with the Plugs and Sockets etc. (Safety) Regulations 1994 The law regulates safety of electrical plugs, sockets and adaptors for use in the UK.

Fuses in plugs are generally 3 amp or 13 amp and have different current ratings:

- 3 amp for appliances up to 700 watts
- 13 amp for appliances over 700 watts
- 5 amp fuses are available for older equipment and are still available to buy.

HEALTH & SAFETY

Moulded plug

All new equipment must be fitted with a 'moulded on' plug on its flex. All plugs must meet British Standard BS 1363 – this will be marked on the back of the plug. This will contain the correct value fuse. Should it blow, it must be replaced with another one of the same value. Should it be necessary to replace the plug, the old one should be cut off, its fuse removed and the plug disposed of.

Electrical machines in beauty therapy

In beauty therapy machines, the electricity is applied to achieve specific effects:

- EMS equipment and micro-current stimulate muscles to contract and shorten, improving their tone.
- Galvanic service creates a cleansing action on the skin's surface – electrically charged cosmetics are introduced into the skin's surface to produce specific therapeutic effects.

HEALTH & SAFETY

Fuses and earthing

All electrical appliances must be correctly fused and earthed in accordance with the British Standards Institution (BSI) recommendations. The earth wire in a plug takes away stray electricity should a fault develop in an appliance, preventing electric shock and protecting the flex and equipment.

HEALTH & SAFETY

Safety visual checks

Visually check equipment regularly for mains-powered equipment. Equipment must not be used if the plug or connector is damaged, the cable has been repaired with tape, is not secure, or internal wires are visible. Discoloured plug casing or cable may indicate overheating – have equipment professionally checked by a competent person. Comply with the law Electricity at Work Regulations (1989)

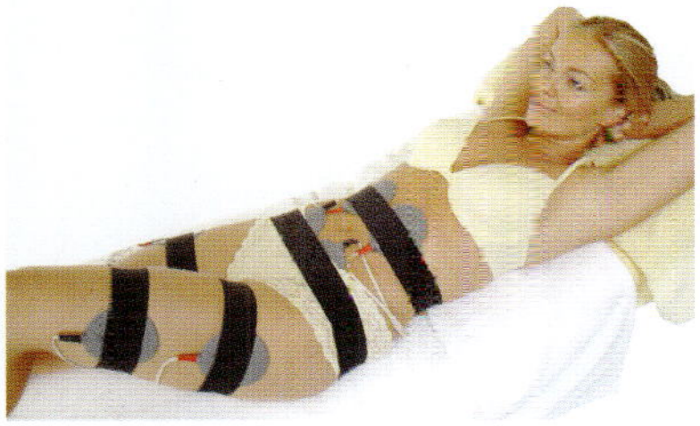

SILHOUETTE-DERMALIFT

EMS body electrical equipment

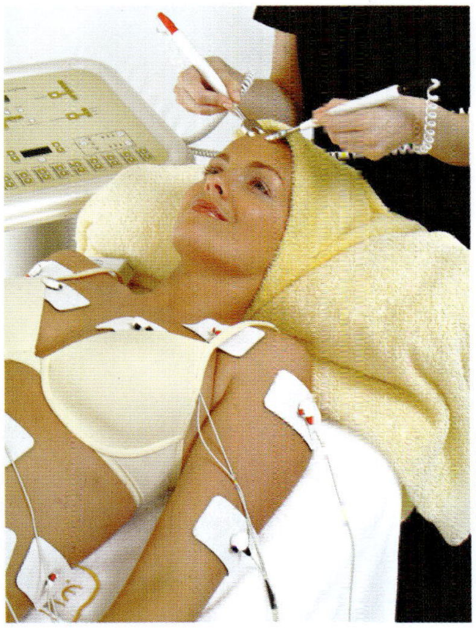

SILHOUETTE-DERMALIFT

Micro-current facial electrical equipment

ALWAYS REMEMBER

Gels

Water-soluble ingredients are often used in gel form to improve the conduction of electricity for services such as muscle stimulation. The gel prevents the evaporation of water and therefore removes the need to keep moistening the surface of the skin or electrode during service application.

The electrical resistance of the skin can be greatly reduced by dampening its surface, as water is a conductor of electricity. There are two forms of electricity, alternating current (ac) and **direct current (dc)**.

> Staff training is fundamental to the success of a business, and it is important that it is ongoing. By ensuring that beauty therapists have additional skills as a salon manager/owner you are both satisfying your ongoing business needs, motivating your staff and ensuring loyalty by investing in their continuous professional and personal development.
>
> **Mary Overton**

FUNCTIONAL SKILLS

Alternating current

Alternating current (ac) is an interrupted electrical current which reverses its direction of flow of electrons, flowing first in one direction around the circuit and then the opposite way at a fixed frequency. The **frequency** tells us how many complete cycles occur each second. The unit for frequency is the hertz (Hz).

The width, depth and frequency of electrical impulses can be varied to achieve different effects. The **frequency** of the ac may be high or low, dependent upon the number of alternate cycles or oscillations per second.

- ac alternating *a few times each second* is *low* frequency
- ac alternating at *a few thousand hertz* is *medium* frequency
- ac alternating at *100 000 hertz or more* is *high* frequency

Examples of usage:

- EMS causes nerve and muscle stimulation and is used to improve skin and muscle tone. (EMS actually originates as an interrupted dc but becomes ac after passing through a special transformer.) The current is surged in stimulation periods with alternate pulses, and intervals with no pulses.
- **High-frequency service**, both direct and indirect technique, creates the warming effect of friction for skin stimulation, cellular regeneration and healing.
- Short-wave diathermy electrical epilation uses the heating effect created by a high-frequency ac for superfluous hair removal.

ALWAYS REMEMBER

Competence

Many suppliers will only provide training to beauty therapists who have achieved competence in their occupation. Insurance also will only be provided for those who can provide evidence of their competence.

TOP TIP

EMS therapy

Most machines have a biphasic option in which each alternate pulse is in the reverse direction. This reduces the effect of skin resistance so that a lower intensity produces a greater effect.

ALWAYS REMEMBER

Electrical epilation techniques

Short-wave diathermy – high-frequency ac

The wave size is constant. The voltage is low but the frequency higher – 27 million alternations per second.

Blend

Blend superimposes high-frequency ac on top of a galvanic dc to combine the chemical effect of galvanic with the heating effect of diathermy.

Direct current

Direct current (dc) is an electrical current using the effects of polarity. The electrons flow constantly, uninterrupted in one direction from positive to negative. Two electrodes which conduct electricity are necessary: the anode electrode, positive (+ve) – attached to the positive lead, and the cathode electrode, negative (–ve) – attached to the negative lead. Its source is usually a battery. Electrodes are the applicators which direct the electricity through the client.

One electrode acts as the active electrode achieving the effects on the body; the other acts as the inactive electrode, its purpose being to complete the electrical circuit.

While the current flows, chemical changes occur at the electrodes:

- Acids are produced at the anode, these chemicals have an astringent, toning effect on the skin.
- Alkalis are produced at the cathode, these chemicals have a cleansing, softening action on the skin.

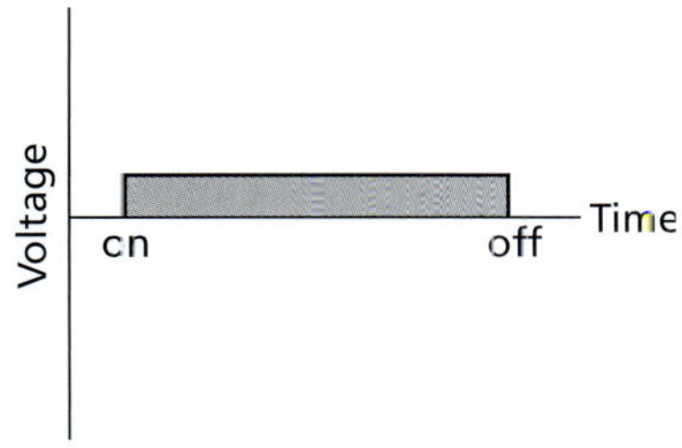

Direct current

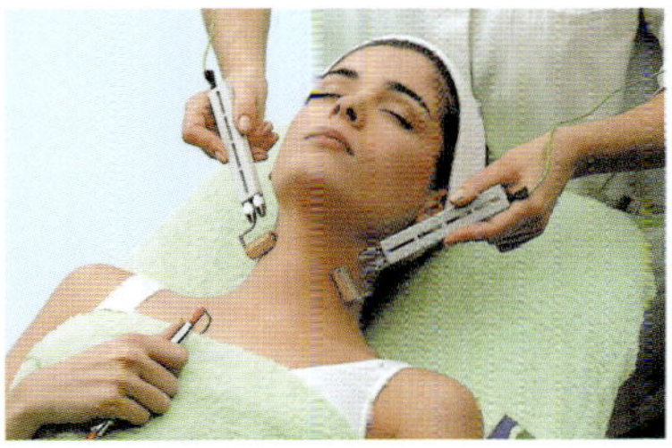

Galvanic-iontophoresis application

Examples of usage: galvanic services and electrolysis

- Galvanic services – to introduce water-soluble ingredients into the skin, iontophoresis; to cleanse the skin of excess sebum, dirt and dead skin cells (disincrustation)
- Galvanic electrolysis – alkalis are created to chemically destroy superfluous hair

The dc may be modified to create pulses of current. These then may be used for the purpose of muscle stimulation and contraction:

- electrical muscle stimulation for the face and body
- micro-current – to improve general muscle tone and improve circulation

Other equipment powered by electricity includes vacuum suction and gyratory massager equipment. Electricity is used to drive a motor which produces the effects created by the attachment heads on the tissues. Vacuum suction creates reduced pressure in cups that are applied to the skin, lifting the tissues, improving lymphatic drainage. Gyratory massage attachment heads cause vibration in the tissues in the service area.

ALWAYS REMEMBER

Micro-current

This is basically a dc, interrupted at low frequencies of 1 to a few hundred times per second. It combines the muscle stimulation of a pulsed current with the galvanic effects of a dc.

Current levels are low – 300–500 microamps (µA) (hence the name micro-current!).

Changing the electrical current

The electricity for each **electrotherapy** service can be changed to achieve different effects. A cathode ray oscilloscope can be used to show the differences in ac and dc by graphical display.

Different components are used in electrical appliances to change the electrical current and the equipment's function:

- *Transformer*. This alters the voltage in ac circuits from one value to another without changing the frequency. The voltage may be increased with a step-up transformer or decreased with a step-down transformer.
- *Rectifier*. This changes the ac to a dc. Electrons are only able to flow in one direction.
- *Capacitor*. This stores electrical energy and discharges it when required. It is used to provide a smooth impulse pattern after rectification.
- *Rheostat*. This controls the amount or strength of current flowing through a circuit. It varies the resistance to the current to increase or decrease the strength of the current.

HEALTH & SAFETY

Chemical tissue damage

Both acids and alkalis cause tissue destruction when current intensity is in excess of the service requirements.

ALWAYS REMEMBER

Blend epilation

Blend epilation uses both ac and dc, combining heat and chemical effects for hair removal.

HEALTH & SAFETY

Suppliers should always ensure that there are user instructions of all appliances.

The CE mark

- *Potentiometer*. This varies the voltage in the circuit. It is used to control the intensity of service application such as in electrical muscle stimulation.

Choosing your equipment

Electrotherapy equipment is costly, and careful consideration should be made before purchase. Always:

- purchase from a reputable company, whose equipment has proved suitable for its purpose
- check that the machine is safe; look for the CE mark, which is awarded only if electrical safety standards have been reached, meeting the provisions of the relevant European Directives legislation. By affixing the CE mark the manufacturer or supplier who places the product on the market takes on responsibility for the conformity of the product.

The Health and Safety Executive is responsible for enforcing safety standards through the various legislation standards. As well as the Consumer Protection Act (1987). If people are injured by defective equipment they have the right to sue.

For further information about your legal responsibilities when using electrical equipment refer to chapter 3 monitoring safe work operations, pages 103–119.

Also, when choosing your equipment always:

- check that it carries a guarantee
- ensure you have written guidance instructions
- consider whether it is financially viable
- question whether the equipment supplier will support you with advertising and training
- ask if a temporary replacement will be provided should the equipment become faulty
- ensure you are provided with sufficient materials. Often materials may need to be washed or sterilized between clients, therefore have several sets available. This will also reduce wear and tear.

Obviously, care and consideration are necessary when using any piece of equipment to ensure that clients receive safe and effective service.

> Competition is healthy and helps you to raise your game. Keep knowledgeable and current about new equipment in the market place.
>
> **Mary Overton**

> Don't be afraid of your machine. Electrical equipment does seem daunting in the beginning but confidence in its use comes with experience.
>
> **Claire Burrell**

HEALTH & SAFETY

Refer to the HSE website for guidance on how to comply with legislation to **maintain portable electrical equipment in low risk environment**. A portable or movable electrical appliance is any item that can be moved.

General electrical safety precautions

The following safety guidelines should always be followed:

- Ensure the equipment is at the correct height to use to avoid postural damage or repetitive strain injury (RSI) to the beauty therapist.
- Always keep water away from electrical equipment to avoid electrical shock.
- Avoid trailing wires, to prevent damage to the machine and personal injury caused through tripping over them.
- Check wires are not damaged.
- Always check that the current controls are at zero before service commences, to avoid accidental current transfer.
- Check leads are fitted correctly before use.
- Store and place all equipment on a sturdy surface.
- Always perform a skin sensitivity test to ensure the client can indicate their physiological tolerance to the service.
- Position equipment so that the current intensity reading is clearly visible.
- Check the performance of the machine on yourself if possible before use on a client, to make sure it is in good working order.
- Sufficient plug sockets should be provided to avoid overloading and possible fire.
- Wires should not become twisted or this can lead to poor electric circuitry and breakage of the wires. Consider storage to keep all accessories in optimum condition.
- Clean the equipment with products suitable to the finish of the product or damage could occur to the finish, e.g. visibility to read gauges and settings features.

> Always gain your client's trust and advise them on the appropriate retail products that will benefit their service results – NEVER pressure clients into buying!
>
> **Claire Burrell**

TOP TIP

Exhibitions

Exhibitions are ideal places to visit to view equipment, talk directly to the suppliers and compare benefits and costs with other suppliers in order to reach the best deal.

HEALTH & SAFETY

Put safety first at all times

Do not:

- use equipment from a socket where the mains lead is likely to be overstretched
- use a twisted, torn flex or cable
- handle plugs or sockets with wet hands
- overload a socket

HEALTH & SAFETY

Electrical fires

A fire extinguisher must be available to deal with electrical fires. This will usually be CO_2 colour coded black or a dry powder type, colour coded blue.

Safety features

In the case of non-computerised equipment, most pieces of electrical equipment now have a safety feature whereby the current will not flow if any amplitude dials are not set at zero.

HEALTH & SAFETY

Equipment testing intervals

- A maintenance plan must be in place for all portable electrical equipment.
- Training and information should be provided to all employees in order to carry out regular visual safety checks.
- The person assigned to carry out inspection and test for equipment that is considered broken, has been repaired or requires a routine safety check should be identified. This must be a competent person, means having suitable training, skill and knowledge for the task to prevent injury to themselves or others.

> Always take advantage of any training courses offered by your company this will keep you motivated and up-to-date with the latest technology.
>
> **Claire Burrell**

Legal requirements

The **Electricity at Work Regulations (1989)** imposes duties on employers and self-employed persons to comply with specific health and safety regulations within their control and responsibility. Electrical equipment must be safe; equipment must therefore be regularly inspected by a qualified electrician. Accurate records listing the date of inspection, the test results and next test date must be available for inspection by the Environmental Health Officer (EHO).

The **Health and Safety at Work Act (1974)** states that:

- all equipment should meet safety standards, be regularly checked and be in good working order
- consideration of handling and application of equipment is the responsibility of the employer to avoid possible employee injury, and adequate training should be given
- trailing leads should not pose a threat to the welfare of employees or clients

Disposal of equipment

If you have to dispose of a piece of electrical equipment this should be done safely. This may be at your local waste recycling department or alternatively, if purchasing a new piece of equipment, the supplier may take your old equipment off you for recycling. If the equipment contains a battery, this is termed hazardous waste and should be disposed of appropriately in compliance with the Hazardous Waste Regulations.

Outcome 1: Maintain safe and effective methods of working when providing facial and body electrical services

Learn how to maintain safe and effective methods of working when providing facial and body electrical services by:

1. Setting up and monitoring the service area to meet organization procedures and manufacturers' instructions.
2. Wearing suitable personal protective equipment, when necessary.
3. Making sure that environmental conditions are suitable for the client and the service.
4. Ensuring your personal hygiene, protection and appearance meet accepted industry and organizational requirements.
5. Effectively disinfecting your hands prior to service.
6. Ensuring your own posture and position minimizes fatigue and risk of injury while working.
7. Ensuring all **tools and equipment** are cleaned using the correct methods.
8. Positioning **tools and equipment** and products for ease and safety of use.

***(Continued)* Learn how to maintain safe and effective methods of working when providing facial and body electrical services by**

9. Ensuring the client is in a comfortable and relaxed position suitable for the service.
10. Maintaining accepted industry hygiene and safety practices throughout the service.
11. Adopting a positive, polite and reassuring manner towards the client throughout the service.
12. Maintaining the client's modesty, privacy and comfort at all times.
13. Checking the client's well-being at regular intervals according to organizational policy.
14. Disposing of waste materials safely and correctly.
15. Ensuring the service is cost-effective and carried out within a commercially viable time.
16. Ensuring client record cards are up-to-date, accurate, complete, legible and signed by the client and practitioner.
17. Leaving the service area and **tools and equipment** in a condition suitable for future services.

The service area should be clean and warm; a comfortable working temperature for both client and beauty therapist is between 18 and 21°C.

Adequate ventilation should be provided to create a hygienic environment, preventing cross-infection through viral airborne spores, drowsiness through carbon dioxide-saturated air and the removal of stale smells and odours.

The service area should induce relaxation and comfort. Lighting should be soft, the decor subtle and non-gender biased. Sound levels should be low and chosen for relaxation.

Before the client is shown through to the cubicle, it should be checked to ensure that it is clean and tidy and that all the required equipment, accessories and consumables are available.

All equipment should be placed in a position for ease and safety when in use. Poor positioning can lead to short-term and long-term **repetitive strain injury (RSI)** leading to poor postural, muscular strain, pain and health problems which may not be able to be corrected. Examples include bursitis and tenosynovitis which lead to stiffness and mobility problems and epicondylitis also known as 'tennis elbow', resulting in pain and stiffness in the elbow, forearm and ring finger.

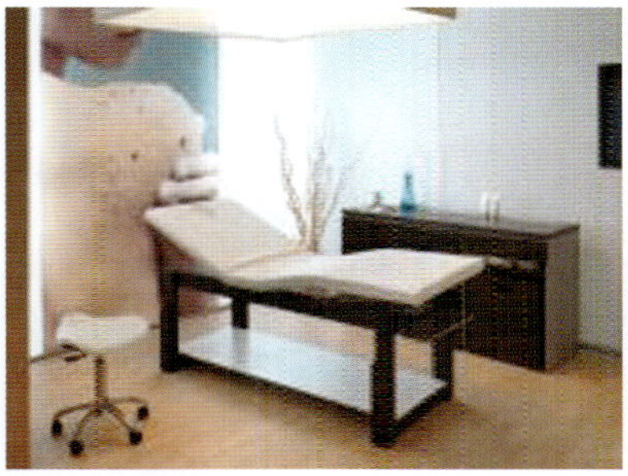

BEAUTY EXPRESS LTD

Service couch

HEALTH & SAFETY

Avoiding contact with metal

No metal should come into contact with the client during electrical services to the face or body. Ensure the metal frame of the couch is covered with an insulating material.

Preparation

All materials and equipment must meet hygiene, legal and salon policy requirements.

BEST PRACTICE

keep up-to-date with your legal responsibilities

Keep up-to-date with all the health and safety beauty therapy occupational guidance by regularly checking the Habia website, www.habia.org. Habia offers a range of guidance and support to ensure best practice and compliance with mandatory legislation.

EQUIPMENT AND MATERIALS LIST

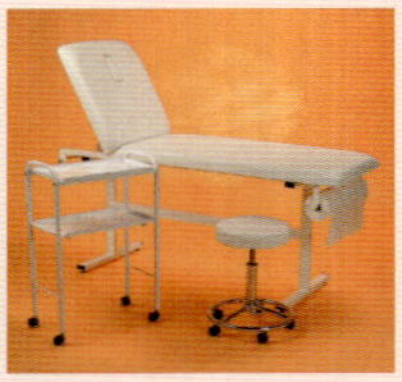
BEAUTY EXPRESS LTD

Couch or beauty chair
With sit-up and lie-down positions and an easy-to-clean surface. For the beauty therapist's comfort it should be adjustable in height to avoid future postural problems and muscle strain

Beauty stool (with or without backrest)
This may or may not have a back-rest; in some designs the backrest is removable. For the comfort of the beauty therapist it should be adjustable in height; to allow mobility it should be mounted on castors

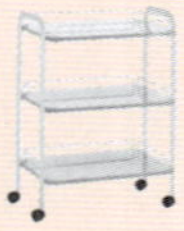
ELLISONS

Trolleys (two trolleys are necessary)
One to display service products and consumables; the other to place small pieces of electrical equipment on

ELLISONS

Magnifying lamp
This is used to magnify the skin's surface during facial services

BEAUTY EXPRESS LTD

Towels
These should be clean for each client. Small and large towels must be available to drape across the client as necessary and an easily accessible hand towel for the beauty therapist

ELLISONS

Gown for client
To maintain client modesty

ELLISONS

Headband or cap
A clean headband or disposable cap is used to protect the client's hair from cosmetic creams

ELLISONS

Cotton wool
A plentiful supply of both damp and dry, sufficient for the service to be carried out. Dry cotton wool should be stored in a covered container; damp cotton wool is usually placed in a clean bowl

BEAUTY EXPRESS LTD

Tissues
Large and of a high quality; stored in a covered container

ELLISONS

Spatulas
Several clean spatulas (preferably disposable) should be provided for each client. These are used mainly to remove products from their containers

ELLISONS

Waste bin
Placed unobtrusively within easy reach and lined with a disposable bin liner

ELLISONS

Record card
For facial and body services

BEAUTY EXPRESS LTD

Sharps box
For disposal of micro-lances used within services

YOU WILL ALSO NEED:

Facial/body sponges or mitts To remove products from the skin during service

Petroleum jelly Available to protect the client's skin where necessary, forming a barrier to electric current

Adhesive plaster To cover any metal jewellery in the area that cannot be removed. Ensure client is not allergic to plaster adhesive

Tools/equipment To perform a thermal and tactile test to check client's skin response to heat and pressure stimuli

Mirror Clean hand mirror or access to a mirror should be available for use in consulting with the client before, during and after their service

Disposable slippers These protect and prevent the spread of infection from contact with foot disorders when walking on the floor barefoot

Container for jewellery For the safe storage of removed jewellery

Reception

When booking a client for an electrical **facial** or body service you must select equipment that will achieve the results that you require. The application of each service may need to be adapted for differing skin or body types, while also selecting appropriate cosmetic therapeutic ingredients.

There are certain conditions which may be present that will prevent you from selecting a piece of electrical equipment. These contra-indications must be checked for before booking the client for an appointment and an alternative service offered in such cases.

If a client is a minor, under the age of 16 years of age, it is necessary to obtain signed written consent before the service is carried out. It is also necessary that the parent or guardian is present when the service is given.

Several different electrical services may be selected when planning a service programme for your client in order to achieve optimum results and to add variety to the programme.

The common performance criteria for **Outcome 2** are listed below for both body and facial electrical services, where they differ they are identified (body) or (facial).

Outcome 2: Consult, plan and prepare and plan for service with clients

Learn how to use consultation techniques to effectively plan and prepare for facial and body services by:

1. Using **consultation techniques** in a polite and friendly manner to determine the client's service needs.
2. Ensuring that informed and signed parent or guardian consent is obtained for minors prior to any service.
3. Ensuring that a parent or guardian is present throughout the facial electrical service for minors under the age of 16.
4. Obtaining signed, written informed consent from the client prior to carrying out the service.
5. Clearly explaining to the client what the service entails in a way they can understand.
6. Encouraging clients to ask questions to clarify any points.
7. Asking your client appropriate questions to identify their medical history, **skin type**, **skin condition** and lifestyle pattern (facial) or asking your client appropriate questions to identify their medical history, **body type**, **body condition** and lifestyle pattern (body).
8. Asking your client appropriate questions to identify if they have any contra-indications to facial electrical service (facial).

BEST PRACTICE

Disposable headbands

To reduce laundering costs always ensure a new headband is available for each client. Disposable headbands are ideal.

HEALTH & SAFETY

Heavy duty yellow plastic sacks

Heavy duty yellow plastic sacks should be available for clinical contaminated waste.

Make arrangements for collection and disposal with the local environmental health office.

TOP TIP

Multi-service units

You may prefer to purchase a multi-unit which will offer a wider service choice for the client and will also save space. However, if the machine becomes faulty, the disadvantage is that you cannot offer any of the other services until it is repaired!

BEST PRACTICE

Jewellery

Jewellery in contact with electrical current can cause the current to concentrate as metal is a good conductor of electricity. Also, burning could occur to the client's skin if receiving a pre-heating service such as in infrared service application. Always ensure jewellery is removed in the service area. Follow your salon policy on what responsibility is given to the client for security of jewellery removed.

(*Continued*) Learn how to use consultation techniques to effectively plan and prepare for facial and body services by:

- 9 Asking your client appropriate questions to identify if they have any contra-indications to body electrical service (body).
- 10 Accurately recording your client's responses to questioning.
- 11 Taking the **necessary action** in response to any identified contra-indications.
- 12 Accurately carrying out a test patch to accurately determine the client's skin response to heat and pressure stimuli (facial).
- 13 Accurately carrying out thermal and tactile tests to accurately determine the client's skin response to heat and pressure stimuli (body).
- 14 Recommending alternative services which are suitable for the client's condition and needs if contra-indicated for facial electrical service (facial).
- 14 Recommending alternative services which are suitable for the client's condition and needs if contra-indicated for body electrical service (body).
- 15 Ensuring client advice is given without reference to a specific medical condition and without causing undue alarm and concern.
- 16 Clearly explaining and agreeing the projected cost, likely duration, frequency and types of service needed.
- 17 Agreeing in writing to the client's needs, expectations and **service objectives**, ensuring they are realistic and achievable.
- 18 Ensuring that the client's skin is clean and prepared to suit the type of equipment to be used.
- 19 Selecting suitable **tools and equipment** and related products for the facial service and client's skin type and condition (facial).
- 19 Selecting suitable **equipment** and related products to suit the **service objectives** (body).

Consultation and planning for facial and body electrical services

By the time the client is shown through to the service cubicle, their record card may have been partly filled in at reception by the receptionist. General personal details will be recorded for the client and comments recorded relating to their current lifestyle habits. The card should be collected by the beauty therapist, who will add to it during and after the service.

In the privacy of the service cubicle, carry out a service consultation and assess the client's needs, following accepted codes of practice. This should take place when the client first meets the beauty therapist and again whenever a new service is to be carried out. All details must be recorded on the client's record card.

Consultation techniques to assess the client's needs and suitability for service include questioning the client and examining the client both visually and manually as necessary. See Diagnostic consultation, Chapter 7.

It is important to wash your hands before any client contact, demonstrating that you work hygienically.

The client is prepared for the electrotherapy service, which may include:

Face service:

- *Cleansing*. To remove dead skin cells, sebum debris and make-up if worn.
- **Exfoliation**. This may include an exfoliating facial cosmetic, or facial brush to remove debris and dead skin cells which would act as a barrier offering initial resistance.
- *Pre-heating service*. Such as steam and warm towels. The increase in skin temperature makes the skin more receptive.

Body service:

- *Exfoliation*. May include an exfoliating body cosmetic or body brush.
- *Pre-heat service*. May include, **infrared**, steam, **sauna**, spa service.
- It may be necessary to shower before service to cleanse the skin, remove other body products, apply an **exfoliant** or remove a body preparation.

Sample record cards are shown for body and face electrical services.

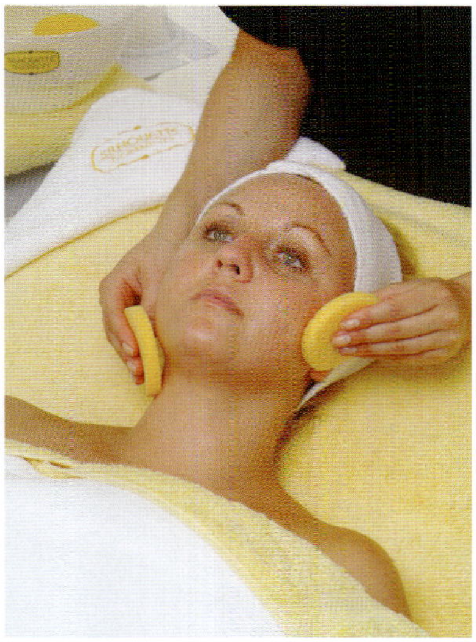
SILHOUETTE-DERMALIFT

Preparing the client for facial electrical service

Contra-indications

The consultation will draw your attention to any specific contra-indications to electrical services or aspects which require special care and attention and may require service modification. The following contra-indications are relevant to all electrical services:

- Cuts and abrasions: if the skin is broken, the electrical current will concentrate in that area as body fluid is a conductor of electricity.
- Severe bruising would make a service uncomfortable and harmful to the client.
- Skin disease/disorder: may be contagious or could be aggravated by a service.
- Recent scar tissue: scar tissue will have less strength than healthy skin; avoid services that will involve stretching the skin.
- Malignant melanoma, cancer of the skin making cells abnormal in the area.
- Inflammation or swelling of the skin: the condition could be made worse.
- Operation in the service area: if recent, wait for 6 months.
- High or low blood pressure: this could be made worse.
- Circulatory disorder.
- Hepatitis, inflammation of the liver caused by a virus, can make the client feel very ill.

- Defective sensation: the client must be able to tell you of the sensation experienced.
- Metal plates or pins within the service area.
- Heart disease/disorder.
- Electronic implants: can be affected by the electric current.
- Spastic condition: dysfunction of the **nervous system**.
- Epilepsy.
- Botox® (botulinum toxin A) is a neurotoxin that affects the nervous system paralysing muscles temporarily, reducing the appearance of lines and wrinkles in the area of application. Immediate side-effects include redness and swelling at the site of Botox® injection. As the service paralyzes the muscle, services to exercise muscle would be ineffective.
- Dermal fillers, i.e. Restylane® is a rejuvenating cosmetic treatment where an injectable gel containing hyaluronic acid is placed in the tissues. This substance occurs naturally in the body in connective tissue and synovial fluid. Its effects are to hydrate, keeping cell plump and assists joint lubrication. This effect degenerates with age. Injectable fillers aim to lift the skin, increase the volume of the tissues and are used to plump the lips. Electrical facial treatment is initially restricted and should not be applied immediately after an injection as skin sensitivity and lymphatic drainage treatments could cause displacement of the filler.
- Botox® and Restylane® are popular cosmetic enhancers, check if these have been received.
- Intense pulsed light (IPL) or laser would initially restrict treatment due to the thermal damage to the skin which can lead to erythema and small blisters on certain skins. Follow your manufacturer's guidelines.
- Epilation due to the damage caused by destruction of the hair follicle tissue. Secondary infection could occur if applied immediately following service. Service may follow following skin healing.
- Retinol® or Retin® A products before micro-dermabrasion service: allow one month before the end of the course because of its skin-thinning effect which could lead to skin damage.
- HIV (human immunodeficiency virus) damages the body's defence system so that it cannot fight certain infections. Certain side-effects of the disease would contra-indicate service. Cross-infection can occur if there is contact with infected blood or serum.
- History of thrombosis or embolism, as the formation of a thrombus (blood clot) can occur. Pieces of the thrombus can break off and are transported in the bloodstream becoming wedged in capillaries, affecting the lungs or heart. Blockage of the coronary arteries can lead to a heart attack!
- Metal pins or plates may cause electrical current concentration.
- Piercings in the area may cause electrical current concentration.
- Highly anxious client: the service may be ineffective or too uncomfortable for the client.
- Certain medication may cause an unwanted skin reaction or be the cause of the skin/body condition.

BEST PRACTICE

Contra-indications

In the event of a client having a contra-indication:

- Encourage the client to seek medical advice: never make a personal judgement.
- Explain professionally why the service cannot be carried out: because you would not wish to harm the client or make the condition worse. If contagious there is also a risk of cross-infection!
- Service may be possible if the service is adapted, e.g. avoiding areas such as a mild bruise If GP consent is obtained after medical advice has been sought, service may be given.

" Being punctual and reliable, as well as professional, presentable and confident are important employability skills.

Claire Burrell

Record card for providing body electrical services

Date | Beauty therapist name

Client name | Date of birth (identifying client age group.)

Home address | Postcode

Email address | Landline | Mobile phone number

Name of doctor | Doctor's address and phone number

Related medical history (Conditions that may restrict or prohibit service application.)

Are you taking any medication? (This may affect the appearance of the skin or skin sensitivity.)

CONTRA-INDICATIONS REQUIRING MEDICAL REFERRAL
(Preventing **body electrical** service application.)

☐ bacterial infection (e.g. impetigo)
☐ viral infection (e.g. herpes simplex)
☐ fungal infection (e.g. tinea corporis)
☐ parasitic infection (i.e. pediculosis and scabies)
☐ skin disorders
☐ skin disease (e.g. malignant melanoma)
☐ high or low blood pressure
☐ heart disease/disorder
☐ medical conditions under supervision
☐ pacemaker
☐ recent scar tissue
☐ dysfunction of the nervous system
☐ epilepsy
☐ HIV

SERVICE AREAS

☐ trunk ☐ limbs ☐ full body

SKIN SENSITIVITY TEST

☐ thermal ☐ tactile
☐ patch test

EQUIPMENT

☐ electro-muscle stimulator (EMS) ☐ galvanic unit
☐ micro-dermabrasion ☐ micro-current unit
☐ lymphatic drainage equipment

CLIENT PREPARATION

☐ exfoliation ☐ pre-heat services
☐ skin cleansing ☐ showering

CONTRA-INDICATIONS THAT RESTRICT SERVICE
(Service may require adaptation.)

☐ cuts and abrasions
☐ bruising and swelling
☐ recent scar tissue (avoid area)
☐ undiagnosed lumps, bumps, swellings
☐ recent injuries to the service area
☐ mild eczema/psoriasis
☐ high or low blood pressure
☐ history of thrombosis/embolism
☐ menstruation, over the abdomen
☐ varicose veins
☐ medication ☐ diabetes
☐ metal pins or plates ☐ pregnancy
☐ body piercings ☐ highly anxious client
☐ Botox® service
☐ injectable fillers, i.e. Restylane®
☐ electrical epilation

LIFESTYLE

☐ occupation ☐ family situation
☐ dietary and fluid intake ☐ sleep patterns
☐ exercise habits ☐ smoking habits
☐ hobbies, interests, means of relaxation

BODY TYPES AND CONDITION

☐ endomorph ☐ mesomorph
☐ ectomorph ☐ cellulite
☐ poor muscle tone ☐ sluggish circulation
☐ uneven skin texture

OBJECTIVES OF SERVICE

☐ improved skin and body condition
☐ improved contour and muscle condition

Beauty therapist signature (for reference)

Client signature (confirmation of details)

Record card for providing body electrical services (continued)

SERVICE ADVICE

Body electrical services – *varies according to the service.*

The service time will vary according to the client's needs, service requirements and type of service received.

SERVICE PLAN

Record relevant details of your service and advice provided for future reference.

Ensure the client's records are up-to-date, accurate and fully completed following service. Non-compliance may invalidate insurance.

DURING

- photograph the service area in accordance with organizational requirements
- explain the sensation of the equipment being used
- explain the service procedure at each stage of the service
- explain how the skincare products should be applied and removed at home
- adjust current intensity and duration according to the service needs
- note any adverse reaction, if any occur, and action taken

AFTER

- photograph the service area post-service in accordance with organizational requirements
- record the areas treated
- provide advice where lifestyle changes could be made to maximize the results, e.g. posture, diet, exercise and skincare
- record any modification to service application that has occurred
- record what products have been used in the service as appropriate
- provide advice to follow immediately following service, to include increased fluid intake following lymphatic drainage services
- recommended time intervals between services
- discuss the benefits of continuous services
- record the effectiveness of service
- record any samples provided (review their success at the next appointment)

RETAIL OPPORTUNITIES

- provide guidance on progression of the service plan for future appointments
- advise on products that would be suitable for home use and how to gain maximum benefit from their use to care for their skin and continue the service benefits
- advise on further products or services that you have recommended that the client may or may not have received before
- note any purchase made by the client

EVALUATION

- record comments on the client's satisfaction with the service
- record if the service objectives were achieved, and if not explore why and make appropriate recommendations
- record how you will progress the service to maintain and advance the service results in the future

HEALTH AND SAFETY

- advise on avoidance of any activity or product application that may cause a contra-action
- advise on appropriate necessary action to be taken in the event of an unwanted reaction (e.g. a skin reaction)

SERVICE MODIFICATION

Examples of service modification include:

- altering pressure or current intensity where the skin appears sensitive
- adapting the padding technique to accommodate the size of the client and muscular toning requirements

Record card for providing facial electrical services

Date | Beauty therapist name

Client name | Date of birth (Identifying client age group.)

Home address | Postcode

Email address | Landline | Mobile phone number

Name of doctor | Doctor's address and phone number

Related medical history (Conditions that may restrict or prohibit service application.)

Are you taking any medication? (This may affect the condition of the skin or skin sensitivity.)

CONTRA-INDICATIONS REQUIRING MEDICAL REFERRAL
(Preventing **facial electrical** service application.)

☐ bacterial infection (e.g. impetigo)
☐ viral infection (e.g. herpes simplex)
☐ fungal infection (e.g. tinea corporis)
☐ parasitic infection (e.g. pediculosis and scabies)
☐ skin disorders
☐ skin disease (e.g. malignant melanoma)
☐ high or low blood pressure
☐ heart disease/disorder
☐ medical conditions under supervision
☐ pacemaker
☐ recent scar tissue
☐ dysfunction of the nervous system
☐ epilepsy
☐ HIV

CONTRA-INDICATIONS THAT RESTRICT SERVICE
(Service may require adaptation.)

☐ cuts and abrasions
☐ bruising and swelling
☐ recent scar tissue (avoid area)
☐ undiagnosed lumps, bumps, swellings
☐ recent injuries to the service area
☐ high or low blood pressure
☐ history of thrombosis/embolism
☐ menstruation, over the abdomen
☐ mild eczema/psoriasis
☐ medication
☐ metal pins or plates
☐ facial piercings
☐ Botox® service
☐ injectable fillers, i.e. Restylane®
☐ electrical epilation
☐ varicose veins
☐ diabetes
☐ pregnancy
☐ highly anxious client

SKIN SENSITIVITY TEST

☐ thermal
☐ patch test
☐ tactile

LIFESTYLE

☐ occupation
☐ dietary and fluid intake
☐ current skincare routine
☐ hobbies, interests, means of relaxation
☐ family situation
☐ sleep patterns
☐ smoking habits

EQUIPMENT

☐ direct high frequency
☐ electro-muscle stimulator (EMS)
☐ lymphatic drainage equipment
☐ micro-lance
☐ galvanic unit
☐ micro-current unit
☐ micro-dermabrasion

SKIN TYPES AND CONDITIONS

☐ oily
☐ combination
☐ mature
☐ congested skin
☐ dry
☐ sensitive
☐ dehydrated

CLIENT PREPARATION

☐ exfoliation
☐ skin cleansing
☐ pre-heat services

OBJECTIVES OF SERVICE

☐ improved skin and body condition
☐ improved contour and muscle condition
☐ impaired skin texture

Beauty therapist signature (for reference)

Client signature (confirmation of details)

Record card for providing facial electrical services (continued)

SERVICE ADVICE

Facial electrical service – *varies according to the service.*

The service time will vary according to the client's needs, service requirements and type of service provided.

SERVICE PLAN

Record relevant details of your service and advice provided for future reference.

Ensure the client's records are up-to-date, accurate and fully completed following service. Non-compliance may invalidate insurance.

DURING

- photograph the service area in accordance with organizational requirements
- explain the sensation of the equipment being used
- explain the service procedure at each stage of the service
- explain how the skincare products should be applied and removed at home
- adjust current intensity and duration according to the service needs
- note any adverse reaction, if any occur, and action taken

AFTER

- photograph the service area post-service in accordance with organizational requirements
- record the areas treated
- provide advice where lifestyle changes could be made to maximize the results, e.g. posture, diet, exercise and skincare
- record any modification to service application that has occurred
- record what products have been used in the service as appropriate
- provide advice to follow immediately following service, to include increased fluid intake following lymphatic drainage services
- recommended time intervals between services
- discuss the benefits of continuous services
- record the effectiveness of service
- record any samples provided (review their success at the next appointment)

RETAIL OPPORTUNITIES

- provide guidance on progression of the service plan for future appointments
- advise on products that would be suitable for home use and how to gain maximum benefit from their use to care for their skin and continue the service benefits
- advise on further products or services that you have recommended that the client may or may not have received before
- note any purchase made by the client

EVALUATION

- record comments on the client's satisfaction with the service
- record if the service objectives were achieved, and if not explore why and make appropriate recommendations
- record how you will progress the service to maintain and advance the service results in the future

HEALTH AND SAFETY

- advise on avoidance of any activity or product application that may cause a contra-action
- advise on appropriate necessary action to be taken in the event of an unwanted reaction (e.g. a skin reaction)

SERVICE MODIFICATION

Examples of service modification include:

- altering pressure or current intensity where the skin appears sensitive
- choice of service cosmetic products for galvanic service to suit the facial skin characteristics
- adapting the padding technique to accommodate the size of the client and muscular toning requirements

A skin sensitivity test is necessary to test if the client's sensory nerve endings are responsive to stimuli such as heat and touch and will respond to electrical pulse stimuli to cause muscle contraction for the service to be both safe and effective.

> "By understanding the needs of the customer and her needs and desires, you will be able to determine the best means of generating interest so as to make an appointment.
>
> **Mary Overton**

Skin sensitivity tests

When performing a **skin sensitivity test**, use a sharp and smooth object, lightly stroke this over the skin (usually the area of the service). This is called a **tactile skin sensitivity test**. Hold a test tube containing warm water followed by cold water next to the skin. This is called a **thermal skin sensitivity test**. Ask the client to differentiate between the different sensations.

Patch test

If a client has indicated intolerance to any product, a patch test may be performed to check skin reaction 24–28 hours before the service. A small amount of the product is applied to an area where the skin is thinner and will show a reaction more quickly, i.e. behind the ear or the inner crease of the elbow.

Once the consultation is complete, the beauty therapist should ensure that all details are recorded accurately and that the client has signed their record card. This enables continuity of service and up-to-date tracking of the services received.

Equipment

The pieces of facial and body electrical equipment that the NVQ Level 3 beauty therapist may become competent in using are as follows:

- *Mechanical equipment*. Which use electricity (to power electric motor pumps) to produce the effects, gyratory massage, audio sonic, **vacuum suction** and micro-dermabrasion.
- *Electronic equipment*. These pass various types of electric current through the client for a variety of effects: high frequency, galvanic, faradic, micro-current, epilation.
- *Ray therapy equipment*. These use electricity to produce electromagnetic rays to treat the client: infrared, UV lamps, sun beds/booths.

The beauty therapy units that assess electrotherapy are:

Provide body electrical services

Provide facial electrical services

The following discussion of both these units explain the differences in their application to both body and face as relevant, and the aftercare advice to provide your clients to complete the service.

The common performance criteria for **Outcome 3** are listed below for both body and facial electrical treatments, where they differ they are identified (body) or (facial).

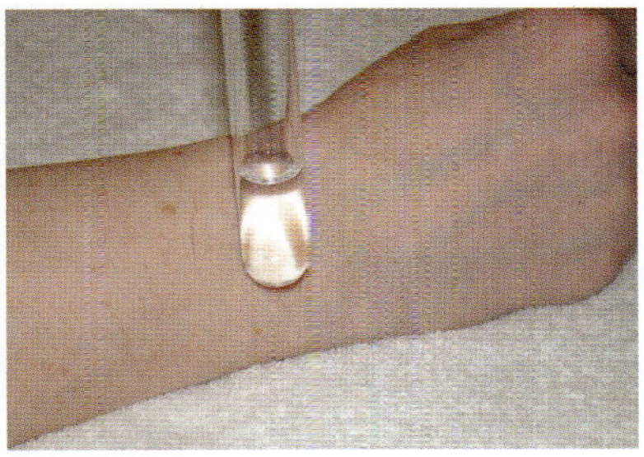

LORRAINE NORDMANN

Thermal skin sensitivity test

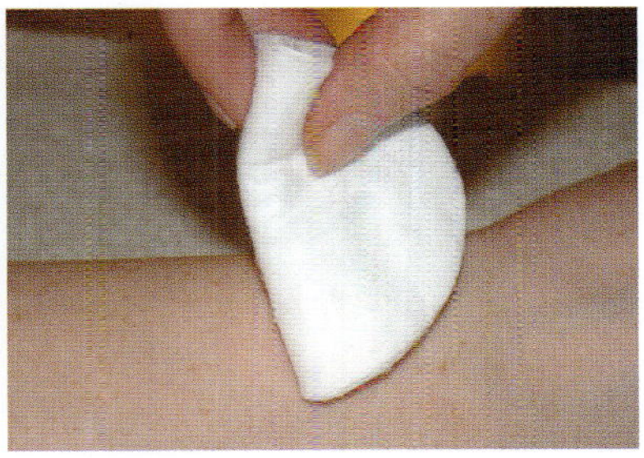

Tactile skin sensitivity test

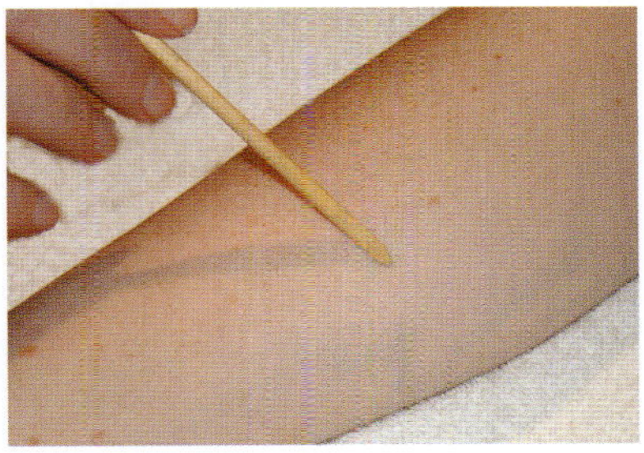

Tactile skin sensitivity test

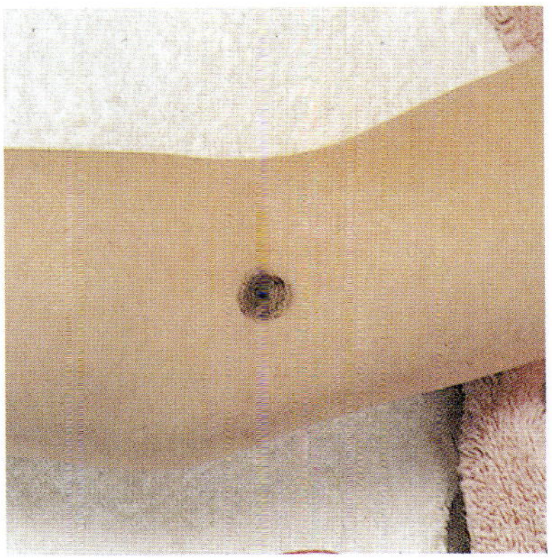

LORRAINE NORDMANN

A skin sensitivity patch test shown to assess skin tolerance for eyelash/brow tinting service

TOP TIP

Equipment

You are able to purchase electrical equipment individually or as a equipment system that has multi-service selection.

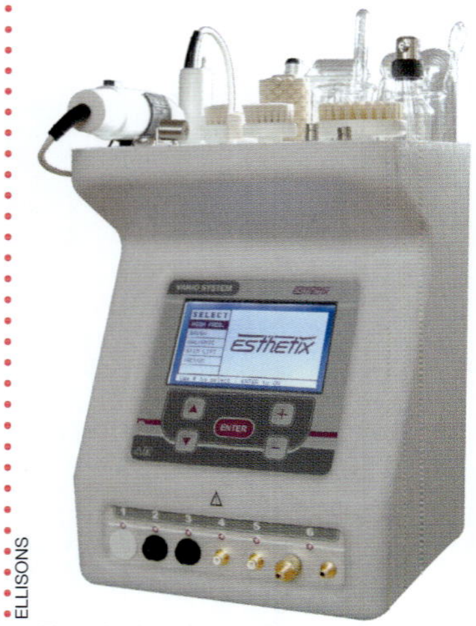

Electrical multi-service equipment

Outcome 3. Carry out body and facial electrical treatments

Learn how to carryout body and facial electrical services by:

1. Clearly explaining the sensation created by the equipment being used.
2. Explaining the service procedure to the client in a clear and simple way at each stage in the process.
3. Safely using the correct service settings, applicator and accessories on the body throughout the service in accordance with manufacturer's instructions.
4. Adjusting the intensity and duration of the service to suit the client's **body type** and **condition** and the areas of the body being treated (body).
4. Adjusting the intensity and duration of the service to suit the client's facial **skin type** and **condition** (facial).
5. Carrying out necessary comedone and milia extraction, when required, minimizing discomfort to the client and minimal damage to the skin (facial).
6. Taking prompt remedial action if the client experiences discomfort or contra-actions.
7. Applying a suitable post-service product to the treated area, if required.
8. Ensuring the finished result is to the client's satisfaction and meets the agreed **service objectives**.

Outcome 4. Provide aftercare advice for body and facial electrical service

Learn how to provide aftercare for body and facial electrical service by:

1. Giving advice and recommendations accurately and constructively.
2. Giving your clients suitable **advice** specific to their individual needs.

Equipment to be studied includes:

- high frequency
- galvanic
- faradic
- **micro-current**
- micro-dermabrasion

- EMS
- vacuum suction
- micro-lance (non-electrical)

Note: Gyratory massage and audio sonic service is discussed and is referenced in **Chapter 10 Body massage**. They can be recommended as a pre-heating service for electrical services but are not assessed as part of body and facial electrical services.

Electro-muscle simulator service

Electro-muscle stimulation, is an electrical service, applied to both the face and body. An electrical current is used to simulate the effect of isometric exercise, that is exercise requiring repetitions. Specific muscles are repeatedly exercised by stimulation by the electrical current, which creates a tightening, toning effect.

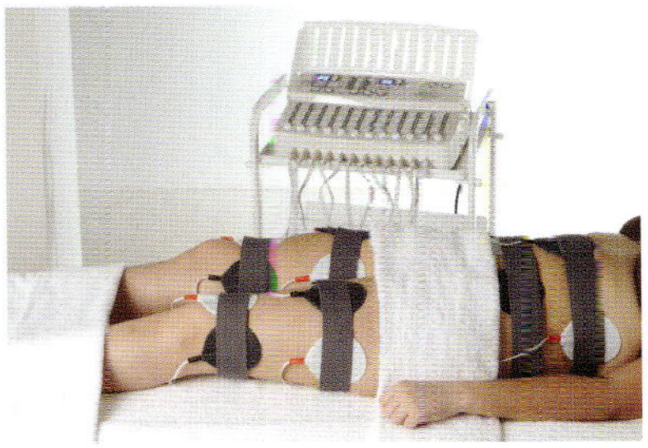

Client receiving body EMS

General effects:

- improved tone of specific muscles, producing a reshaping effect for figure correction and face lifting
- increased metabolism of the stimulated muscles
- waste products are more readily eliminated from muscles by the pumping action on the lymph vessels and veins as the muscles contract and relax

Body use:

- increased fluid and waste elimination through an improved lymphatic circulation, beneficial to improve the appearance of a cellulite condition
- posture improvement achieved through increasing muscle tone in overstretched muscles
- improved appearance of the body contour as the muscles tighten, having a slimming effect
- beneficial for clients contra-indicated to active exercise

Facial use:

- improved firmness of slack facial muscles
- improved skin colour through improved blood circulation

COURSEMATE

For a video on the EMS service please visit this book's accompanying CourseMate.

Anatomy and physiology

Muscles are composed of bundles of muscle fibres. Each fibre is supplied with many nerves which, when stimulated by the electrical current, cause the muscle fibres to shorten and the muscle to contract. The nerves creating movement are called motor nerves, and repeated stimulation by the electrical current causes the muscle fibres to improve in tone. The result is increased firmness of the tissues and a reshaping of body contours.

The positioning of the electrode which passes the electrical current is important. It should be as close as possible to the muscle's **motor point**. This is the point where the motor nerve enters the muscle. This ensures that stimulation occurs with minimum current intensity.

Initially, the skin will resist the current as the surface epidermal cells contain little moisture and the underlying adipose layer is also a poor conductor of electric current. Once the current has overcome the skin's resistance the electrical pulses bring about muscle contraction.

ALWAYS REMEMBER

The EMS is known by different terms. This includes faradic after the original type of current used for improving muscle tone or by the manufacturers' trade names.

ALWAYS REMEMBER

With advances in technology, many units are now computerized and contain a microprocessor which produces quite complex routines. These are programmed to suit different parts of the body.

A light emitting diode (LED) will show intensity levels.

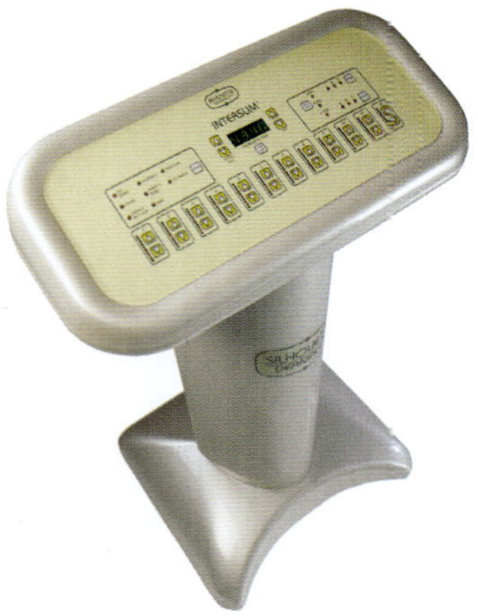
SILHOUETTE-DERMALIFT

Silhouette muscle toning machine

TOP TIP

Stimulation and interval periods

Set the stimulation period long enough for the muscle fibres to be stimulated and shorten. Set the interval period of a sufficient duration to allow all the muscle fibres to relax and lengthen, or muscle fatigue will occur A client with poor muscle tone or excessive adipose tissue will require longer stimulation and relaxation periods.

Electro-muscle stimulator equipment

Equipment uses an alternating low frequency, surged and interrupted dc. The current is applied through paired carbon pad electrodes.

A typical machine has the following features:

- *Mains switch.* For turning the machine on and off.
- *Pulse control.* This varies the length of time for which the stimulation and relaxation periods occur. This is variable between 0.5–2.5 seconds. In the stimulation period, the current flows and the muscle fibres contract. In the interval period, the current ceases to flow and the muscle is allowed to rest.
- *Frequency control.* Controls the number of electrical pulses per second. This is commonly adjustable between 65–135 Hz pulses per second. The frequency setting alters the depth of stimulation and the stimulation of different groups of fibres within the muscle. Therefore the lower frequency is selected for the service of deeper muscles and for clients with excessive adipose tissue. The higher frequency is selected for superficial fascia and muscle.
- *Amplitude.* Regulates the intensity of power to each electrode(s). This is usually adjustable from 0–10.
- *Pulse width.* This changes the width of each pulse, which affects the period of stimulation within the muscle. The higher the setting of the pulse, the greater the stimulation. A lower pulse is selected for facial application and a higher setting for body application.
- *Mode control.* This is used to select the polarity. There are usually two options. In unidirectional or monophasic mode, pulses are of the same polarity. One electrode has a negative charge and the other a positive charge; the current flows in one direction between the two. In bidirectional or biphasic mode, impulses are of reversed polarity. This minimizes the skin's resistance, making it possible to stimulate the muscles with a lower current intensity. Each electrode can have the same polarity, the current flows in one direction and then the other. A pull sensation is experienced after each contraction. Monophasic is always used on facial EMS, as this sequence is always required.
- *Gain control.* This dial increases all the intensity dials without the need for turning them up individually.
- *Variable control.* A feature used on the body which randomly changes the pattern of the stimulation and interval period. This ensures that the client can relax as they will not be able to anticipate the contraction period.
- *Electrodes.* Composed of rubber, these enable the current to flow to selected muscles usually containing carbon to improve conductivity. For body there are two leads: the red lead is placed near the origin of the muscle and the black lead near the insertion. The facial block electrode contains both the positive and negative electrode.

Reception

- Complete personal details on the client's record card.
- Question the client to check for possible contra-indications.

TOP TIP

Memory card system

Electronic cards are a development in technology available with some computerized units. They are able to store details of the client's service programme, improving efficiency of data retrieval and for the service to be performed quickly.

BEST PRACTICE

EMS frequency settings

Frequency setting for the face usually select 120 Hz. For the body usually select 60–100 Hz. Always follow your manufacturer's instructions.

Facial service Allow 15 minutes for the service application itself. As the service is usually applied following other preparatory facial services, a 45-minute appointment is normally booked. The client should attend twice a week for a course of 10 and then continue with a maintenance facial once every month.

Body service An initial service assesses the client's tolerance to the service and should be given for 15–20 minutes. Future service time increases to 30–40 minutes. The client should attend the salon two to three times per week for a course of 10 services. They should then continue with a maintenance service once every 1–2 weeks.

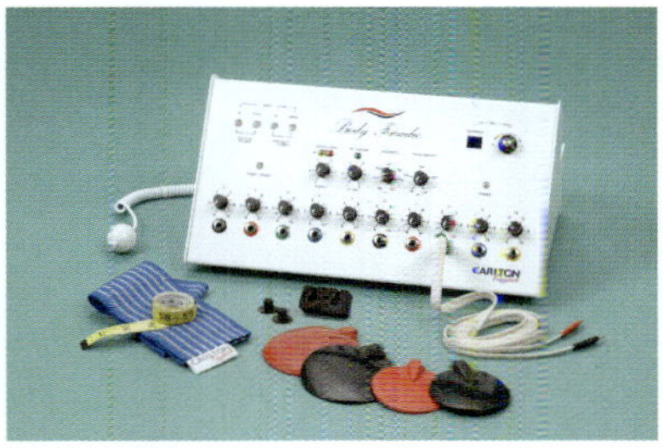

CARLTON PROFESSIONAL

Combined body and face EMS unit

EQUIPMENT AND MATERIALS LIST

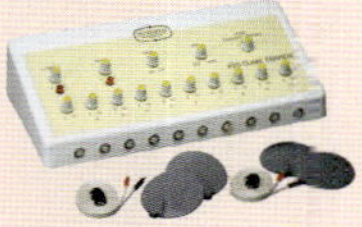

EMS machine facial/body or combined unit

Record card
Confidential record of details of each client registered at the salon

YOU WILL ALSO NEED:

Electrodes Commonly composed of electrically conductive carbon-impregnated rubber. The electrodes are used in pairs for body application. Small, single block containing twin electrodes is used to stimulate the muscles for facial service or a facial mask electrode may be used to treat several facial muscles at once

Elasticated straps To hold the electrodes in place (body application)

Electrical leads Paired to transport the electric current to the electrodes

Skincare preparations To cleanse the skin prior to service

Ionized solution Such as conducting gel applied directly to the skin or surface of the electrode to ensure effective conduction of the current

Unperfumed talc To soothe the skin after body application if necessary

Contra-indications

During the client assessment, if you find any of the following in the service area, EMS service must not be carried out or the service modified:

- broken skin
- defective skin sensation, one that cannot detect different sensations

- metal plates or pins in the service area
- excessive dental fillings, (facial application)
- nerve or muscular disorders
- migraine sufferers (facial application)
- thrombosis or phlebitis
- heart disorders
- high blood pressure
- pacemaker
- IUD coil
- varicose veins
- pregnancy
- recent injectable cosmetic services (usually facial services)
- facial/body piercings

Sterilization and disinfection

After use, clean the surface of the electrodes in warm, soapy water. Dry naturally and disinfect in an UV sterilizing cabinet. Additional electrodes are necessary to allow for effective disinfection between the service of clients.

Wash the elasticated straps in warm water, anti-bacterial detergent and dry.

If a sponge is placed underneath the electrode surface this must be washed after every use.

HEALTH & SAFETY

Hygiene

Any materials such as sponge envelopes and elastic straps should be washed in an anti-bacterial detergent to prevent spread of infection, referred to as cross-infection.

ALWAYS REMEMBER

Facial block electrode

The facial electrode has a twin electrode, as two connections are necessary to complete a circuit.

BEST PRACTICE

Dealing with obesity and allergies

If the client is obese it may be necessary to place a sponge dampened with warm water underneath each body electrode to ensure even contact with the skin and to guard against a concentration of current. This technique may also be used if the client is allergic to the surface of the electrodes. This would be recognized by red circles of erythema.

HEALTH & SAFETY

After surgery

Wait approximately 6 months before treating a client following any surgery such as a caesarean section. If in doubt, always consult the client's GP.

Preparation of the service area

- Cover the service couch with a clean towel.
- Ensure that the metal frame of the couch will not come into contact with the client.
- Check all general electrical safety precautions.
- **Test the electrode(s)** to ensure they are in good working order.

Dampen the surface of the electrode(s) and hold against the palm of one hand. With the other hand, turn up the current intensity until you can feel a mild tingling sensation indicating that the current is flowing.

Facial application

- Prepare the facial electrode for service.
- Secure the electrode firmly to the electrical leads.
- Insert the lead into the relevant outlet connection.
- Select the frequency required for facial application

Body application

- Place the elasticated straps on the couch, ready for positioning for the service.
- Prepare the electrode(s) for service.
- Secure the electrodes firmly to the electrical leads.
- Insert the leads into the relevant outlet(s) of the unit.
- Select the frequency required for the client according to the client requirements.

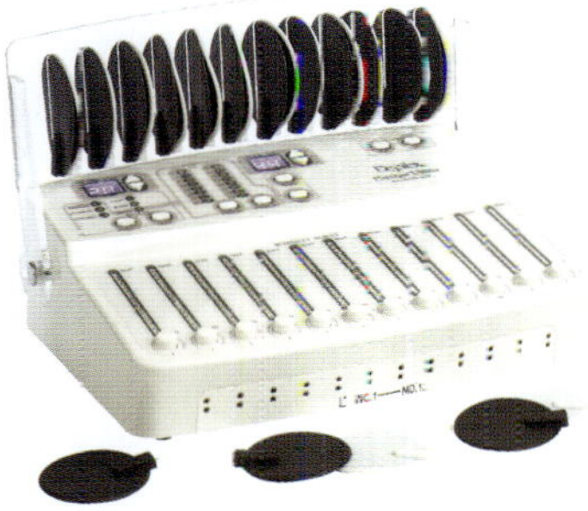

DEPILEX

Physique Ultima

Preparation of the beauty therapist

- Collect the client's record card.
- Disinfect your hands before handling the client.
- Assess the client, discuss the client's lifestyle and objectives for the service if this is the initial service. Agree on an appropriate service plan.
- If a service has a slimming requirement it will be necessary to measure the client at the beginning of the service course and once every week (see page 202).
- If this is a repeat service, check the client's progress against targets set and provide support and advice as necessary.

HEALTH & SAFETY

Lead attachment
Ensure that the leads are firmly attached to the electrodes to be certain of effective current transfer.

BEST PRACTICE

Testing electrodes
Testing the electrodes before application ensures that service is not delayed before facial application or after padding if an electrode is not working for body application.

Preparation of the client

Facial application

1. Perform skin sensitivity tests in the area to be treated.
2. Remove all jewellery from the service area.
3. Cleanse and tone the skin of the face and neck. Blot the skin dry with a soft facial tissue.
4. Analyze the client's skin using a magnifying lamp, and question the client further where necessary to check information in relation to the client's skin condition.
5. Explain the service sensation to the client. The client will initially feel a prickling sensation as the sensory nerve endings in the skin are stimulated, followed by a gentle tightening of the skin as the muscle contracts. Explain to the client that the skin may appear reddened in the area following service. This is a reflex action causing the capillaries in the area temporarily to dilate called a reflex vasodilation.

TOP TIP

Straps
The elasticated straps must not be too tight. Have a range of strap sizes available.

TOP TIP

Pre-heating service

It is beneficial to perform a pre-heating service before the EMS service as this will optimize response to the current. For the face this may be a steam service, for the body it may be a sauna, infrared or massage (without use of an oil base massage medium which would inhibit the current application).

Body application

1. Perform a sensitivity test in the area to be treated.
2. Remove all jewellery from the area.
3. Instruct the client to remove all clothing except underwear.
4. Measure the client (if required).
5. Position the client on the service couch. This will be in a supine or prone position depending on the padding layout selected. The couch may be slightly elevated at the head.
6. Cleanse the skin using a non-oily detergent cleanser to remove body creams, etc. These would create a barrier to effective current conducting if present. Cover any minor cuts or abrasions with petroleum jelly or a small surgical plaster to form a barrier to the electric current.
7. Secure the elasticated straps around the parts to be treated. These must not be too tight or too loose.

HEALTH & SAFETY

Level of movement

A gentle pulling of the skin in the area of stimulation is sufficient. Exaggerated facial movements should be avoided, especially around the eye area.

Service application

Facial application

1. Position the client in a semi-reclined position with gravity acting on the facial contours. It is easier to exercise and observe the muscles in this position.
2. Ensure all intensity dials are at zero.
3. Switch the machine on at the mains.
4. Select the frequency setting according to the service requirements.
5. Set the stimulation and interval period. The stimulation period is set longer than the interval period.
6. Apply a conducting ionized solution to the electrode surface.
7. Switch on the machine. Place the electrode on the skin at first motor point to be stimulated. Working from the neck upwards, increase the current intensity slowly, during the stimulation period. When the intensity gauge registers (if available), wait approximately 30 seconds to allow the current to overcome the skin's resistance. Alternatively, ask the client when she can feel the current.
8. Increase the current intensity until the client experiences the prickling sensation. Continue increasing the current until a visible contraction can be seen in the area of stimulation.

TOP TIP

Electrode pairs

It is important that the pairs of electrodes do not touch each other in body application as the current will not enter the muscle efficiently if this happens.

BEST PRACTICE

Facial EMS application

As the muscle becomes warm due to increased blood flow and relaxed as a result of the service, discomfort may be experienced as a surge of current is felt. Reduce the current intensity in this case during the interval period and then increase to a level to obtain the desired contraction.

ALWAYS REMEMBER

Facial muscles

- As facial muscles insert into the facial skin or other adjacent muscles it is often difficult to treat individual muscles. Therefore, appropriate facial nerves are stimulated to ensure an effective service of groups of muscles.
- Because the facial muscles are difficult to isolate, the pair of facial electrodes are small and close together.
- By stimulating the facial nerve, 7th cranial nerve, by placing the electrode at the side of the face below the ear, all the superficial muscles of facial expression may be stimulated at the same time.

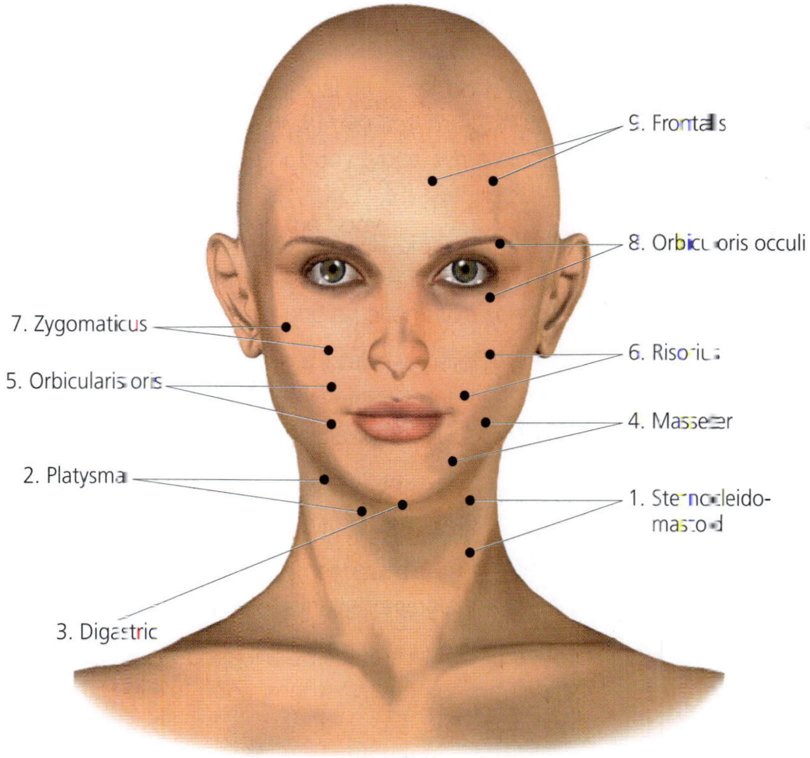

EMS facial muscle application technique

HEALTH & SAFETY

Motor points

It is important to know the position of different muscles' motor points or the service will be less effective and possibly uncomfortable for the client.

HEALTH & SAFETY

Underwear

Ensure the client does not have any metal contained in underwear, when performing body EMS in contact with the electrodes.

9 Reposition electrode and exercise each muscle motor point 6–10 times.

10 Repeat the whole facial sequence three times.

11 Turn the intensity control to zero and switch the unit off.

12 Complete details of the service on the client's record card.

Body application This service is usually aimed at general muscle toning improvement. The beauty therapist is able to concentrate on improving problem areas of particular concern to the client. This is commonly known as **spot reduction**. Other services may also be offered which achieve a different complimentary effect.

1 Place the electrodes in pairs, secured with the elasticated straps, selecting the padding technique to achieve the required results:

- *Longitudinal.* An electrode is placed near the origin and insertion of a particular muscle. This method specifically shortens muscles but is less economical on electrodes.
- *Split motor point.* An electrode is placed on the motor point of the same muscle but on each side of the body. This method is suitable for treating smaller muscles where the actual motor point is difficult to locate. It is efficient on electrodes so more areas of the body can be treated at once.
- *Duplicate.* An electrode is placed on the motor point of two different muscles that are adjacent to each other. This allows for differing muscle strengths on either side of the body.

2 Apply the ionized solution to the surface of each electrode. Select the appropriate padding technique for the body part to be treated. Place in position and secure with the straps.

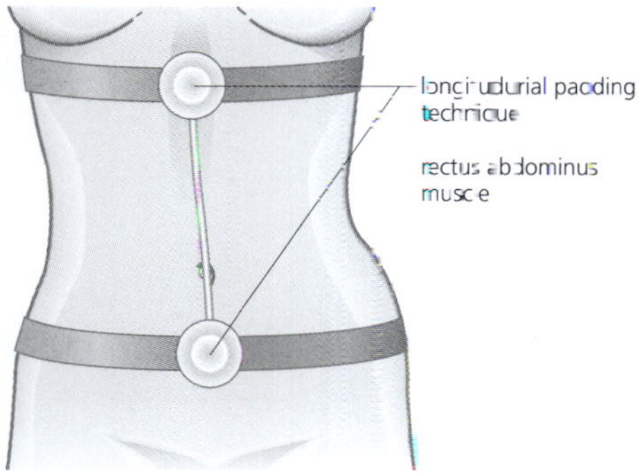

Longitudinal padding technique – rectus abdominus

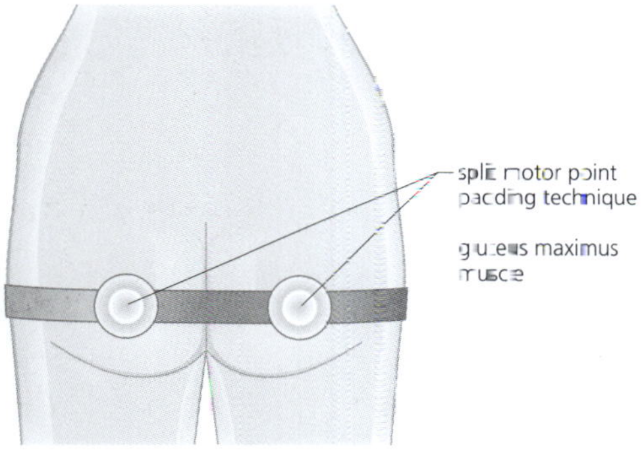

Split motor point padding technique – gluteus maximus

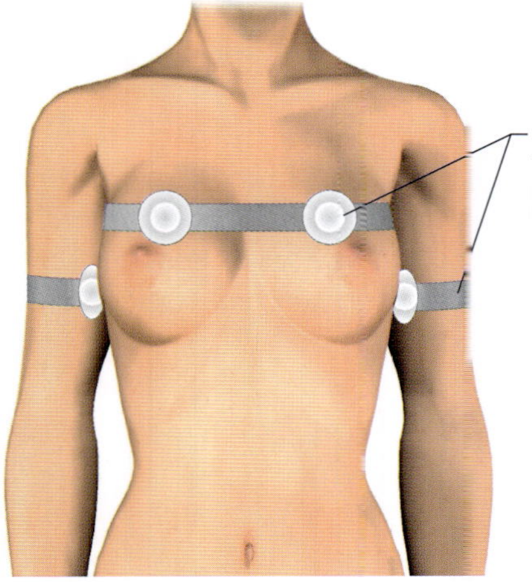

Duplicate padding technique – pectoralis major and biceps

3 Ensure all dials are at zero and then turn on the current at the mains and switch the machine on.

4 Set the stimulation, interval, frequency, pulse sequence and mode according to the needs of the client.

5 Explain the service sensation to the client again, you will have referred to this at consultation. The client initially will feel a prickling sensation as the sensory nerve endings in the skin are stimulated, followed by a tightening of the muscle as it contracts.

A visible contraction of the muscle will be seen as it is stimulated.

The client may be covered to maintain modesty and to keep them warm – essential for effective muscle contraction.

6 Increase the intensity of each electrode outlet during each stimulation period until the client feels the tingling sensation. The current continues to be increased until visible, even contractions are achieved.

During service it may be necessary to increase or decrease intensity further as the muscles become receptive to the service. Only increase the current intensity during the contraction (stimulation) period to avoid excessive intensity application.

EMS Faradic machine

7 Apply the service according to the service plan. At the end of the service, reduce the level of current intensity simultaneously until all outlets are at zero. Some machines will be automatically timed and will switch off at the end of the timed period.

8 Switch off the machine at the mains.

9 If the client's skin appears reddened in the service area, explain that this is a reflex action causing the capillaries in the area to temporarily dilate.

10 Complete details of the service on the client's record card.

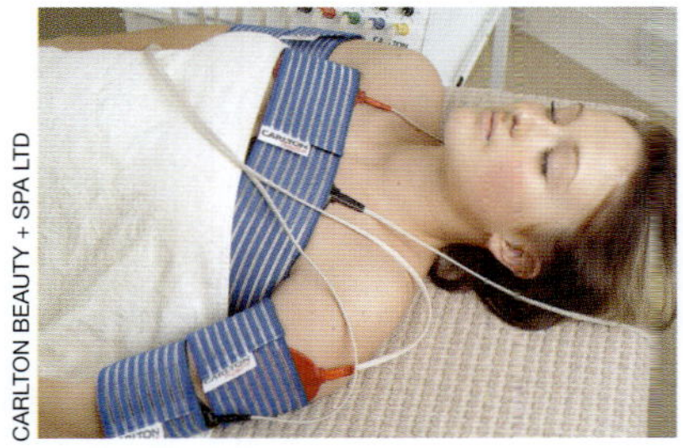

EMS service to the upper body pectoralis major and tricep muscles

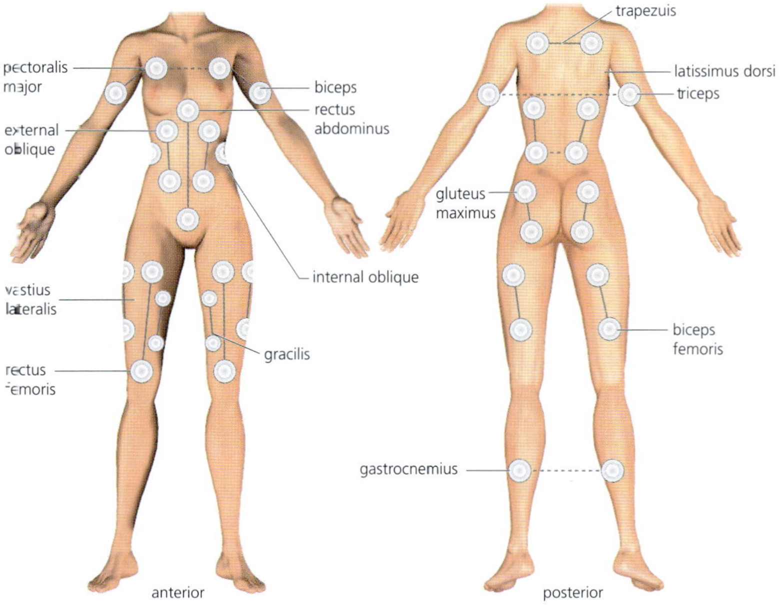

Sample EMS padding techniques to anterior and posterior body

Aftercare

If this was a single treatment, recommend the benefits of a course to optimize results. Advise the client on purchase and correct application of commercial face and body cosmetic skincare preparations. Nutritional advice should be given if the client is on a weight-reducing diet. Supportive exercises for the face or body may also be given. Offer the client water for hydration.

The service should be seen as a support to active exercise rather than a replacement. Reinforce the importance of regular service as part of a course to gain maximum benefit. Measure the client if the client is on a weight reduction programme.

TOP TIP

Improving tone

Settings to improve muscle tone for EMS body application should have intense contractions with longer resting periods. This improves muscle bulk.

BEST PRACTICE

Non-response of muscles

If a muscle is not responding check the following possibilities:

- the surface of the electrode has become dry and requires moistening
- the electrode is not in good contact with the skin
- the unit setting or application technique is incorrect for the clients needs
- faulty connections on the unit or leads
- grease on the surface of the electrode or client's skin

Always reduce the current intensity to zero before checking for the fault. Never move electrodes while the electrical current is flowing.

ACTIVITY

FUNCTIONAL SKILLS

Facial exercises

Design a supporting exercise sheet that the client can use at home to support the salon service. Research and illustrate the exercises suitable to improve tone of the neck and face.

Contra-actions

- **Muscle fatigue** caused by over-stimulation of weak disused muscles: this can be recognized by erratic contractions of the muscles or poor response to the stimulation. The muscles will feel sore and stiffened following service. This can be avoided by ensuring an effective consultation and communication with the client during service.
- **Excessive reddening of the skin** caused occasionally by an allergic reaction to the graphite contained in the rubber electrode. *Action*: place a dampened sponge beneath the electrode to enable the service to continue.
- **Erythema** caused by reflex vasodilation If the reaction does not disappear following 24 hours, the clients should be advise to seek the advice of their GP. *Action*: apply unperfumed talc or cooling compress to soothe the skin.

TOP TIP

Mineral make-up

Increasingly, mineral make-up is applied following facial services as it has the benefit that skin respiration is not hindered. The make-up enhances the overall appearance of well-being where a skin cleansing effect is required.

Galvanic service

Galvanism is an electrical service which can be applied to both the face and body. Therapeutic substances are introduced into the skin using a direct current to create specific effects upon the surface and underlying tissues. General effects are:

- increased blood and lymphatic circulation
- reduction of non-medical swelling and puffiness by improving the dispersal of accumulated tissue fluids and waste products from the area
- improved function and appearance of the skin by the introduction of water-soluble substances

HEALTH & SAFETY

Client supervision

Never leave a client unsupervised during an electrical body service; check comfort periodically as the muscles may become fatigued.

COURSEMATE

For a video on the galvanic body service please visit this book's accompanying CourseMate.

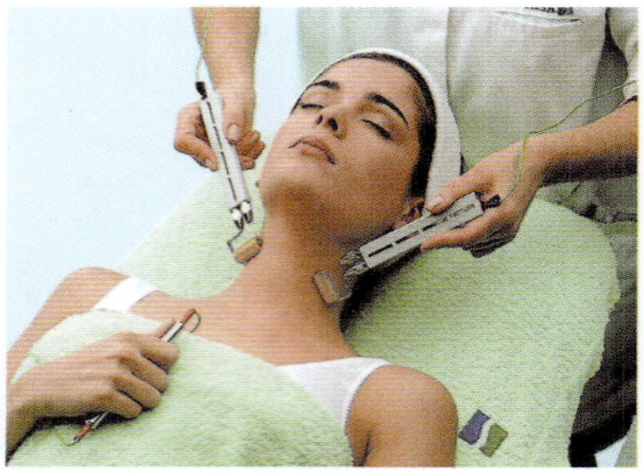
BEAUTY EXPRESS LTD

Galvanic facial service

Body use:

- used in slimming services as fat is more readily transported for use in the increased lymphatic flow
- improves the appearance of cellulite

Facial use:

- improved skin texture through removal of the surface dead skin cells (desquamation)
- introduction into the skin of regulating therapeutic ingredients enables different skin types and conditions to be treated

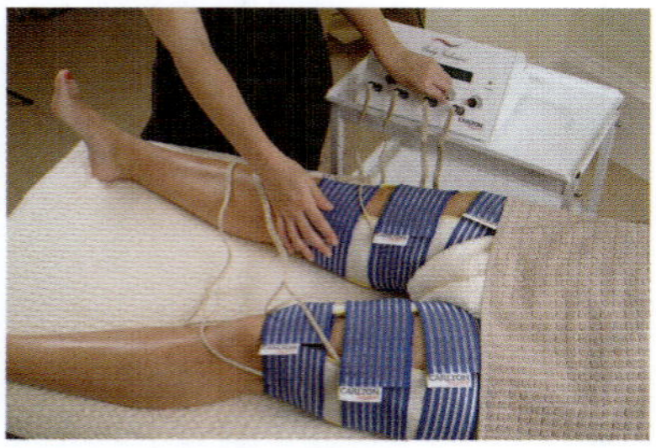
CARLTON BEAUTY + SPA LTD

Galvanic body service

Anatomy and physiology

The chemical effects of the substances produced beneath the electrodes are used to improve the general functioning of the skin. Acids are produced under the positive pole (the anode), and alkalis are formed under the negative pole (the cathode).

The irritant effect of the alkaline chemical formation stimulates the blood flow and causes the superficial blood capillaries to dilate, thus causing the deeper blood vessels to dilate as a reflex action. The astringent effect of the acid chemical formation reduces redness of the skin and firms the tissues.

The movement of ionized ingredients into the skin is called **iontophoresis**. The cells are nourished by the improved circulation and the skin benefits from the therapeutic effects of the substances which have been introduced.

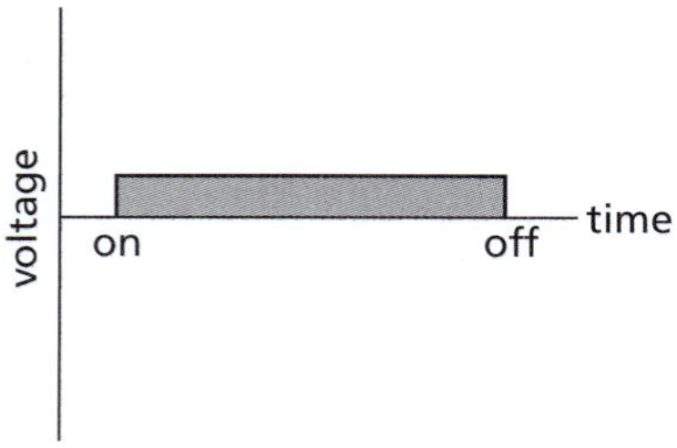

Direct current

Electrical and chemical effects

The galvanic unit produces a smooth-flowing, uninterrupted dc. It converts the mains ac at 230 volts to a smooth dc at up to 100 volts. This is achieved in three stages:

- a **transformer** reduces the voltage of the ac mains supply
- a **rectifier** changes ac to dc
- a **capacitor** smoothes any irregularities in that dc

A **rheostat** is used to set the required intensity. A **milliammeter** shows the flow of current through the client and an **electronic circuit** keeps the current at the required level, even though the skin's resistance will change during the course of the service.

A low-intensity dc is used, measured in milliamps (mA – one-thousandth of an amp) to introduce into the skin electrically charged, water-based solutions containing therapeutic ingredients from plants, herbs, flowers and fruit. These solutions are known as **electrolytes**. They contain acids and salts which increase electrical conductivity, helping to break down the skin's resistance and create chemical changes when the **galvanic current** is passed through them.

When dissolved in water, an electrolyte partly splits and forms ions which carry either a positive charge (cation) or negative charge (anion). When electrodes carrying a continuous dc are introduced into the electrolytic solution, the ions in the solution begin to move and are attracted to either the positive pole (anode) or negative pole (cathode).

The service effectiveness works upon the electrical principle:

- like charges repel
- opposite charges attract

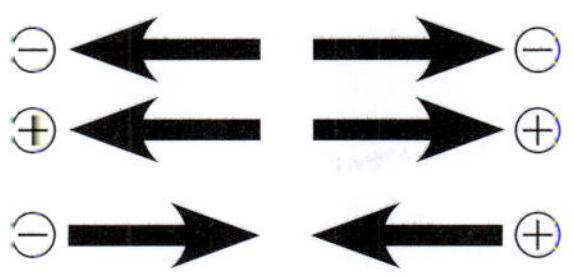

The tissue fluids of the human body have electrolytic properties. They contain ions and therefore allow the current to pass through the human body. Both positive and negative connections are required when performing the service. You select the appropriate pole according to the effect you want to create upon your client's tissues. The electrode then creates the chemical effects of this pole and is known as the **active** electrode. The other electrode is known as the **indirect** or **indifferent** pole and is used to complete the electrical circuit.

The polarity of the active ingredients in galvanic solutions is usually indicated with a ⊕ or ⊖ symbol. The solutions are repelled into the skin by the active electrode which must be the same polarity as the solution.

Chemical effects created at the poles

Effects at the anode (positive pole)	*Effects at the cathode (negative pole)*
Acid reaction (hydrochloric acid	Alkaline reaction (sodium hydroxide)
Vasoconstrictive, decreases blood supply which reduces redness of the skin	Vasodilative, increases blood supply which increases the redness of the skin
	Improves lymphatic circulation which reduces non-medical swelling in tissues
Astringent effect – pores tighten	Pores relax
Soothing effect on nerve endings	Stimulating effect on nerve endings
Firms tissues	Softens tissues

ALWAYS REMEMBER

Sebum

Because the superficial layers of the epidermis have a low water content and are coated with sebum, they offer resistance to the current. The current applied must be sufficient to pass through them. As the service progresses, sebum will be cleansed from the skin and the resistance will fall.

Reception

- Complete personal details on the client's record card.
- Question the client to check for possible contra-indications.

Facial service Explain that it is inadvisable to wear make-up for at least 8 hours after service due to its cleansing action. Other facial services may be received between services according to the client's requirements. It is recommended that the client receives this service every 4–6 weeks. Allow 1 hour when booking the service.

Body service Explain that it is inadvisable to receive UV or a heat service directly after this service due to the heating effect created in the tissues. It is recommended that the client undergoes service two to three times per week for a course of 10 sessions. Allow 30 minutes when booking the service.

HEALTH & SAFETY

Deterioration of electrodes

Electrodes can suffer in time from corrosion and should be replaced when this becomes obvious. Cracked electrodes should not be used as they would not maintain good contact with the skin or ensure even current application.

EQUIPMENT AND MATERIALS LIST

ELLISONS

Client record card
Confidential record of details of all clients registered at the salon

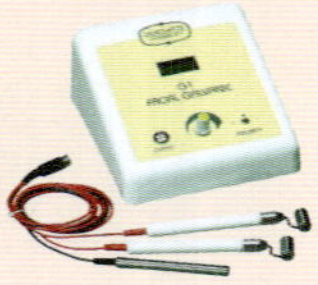

SILHOUETTE DERMALIFT

Facial galvanic unit

SILHOUETTE DERMALIFT

Body galvanic unit

YOU WILL ALSO NEED:

Electrodes A number of different electrodes are used in **galvanic therapy** which act as active or indifferent electrodes; the electrodes may be composed either of rubber impregnated with carbon or stainless steel

Dampened sponge envelopes or cotton wool Selected to cover the electrodes according to the type of electrode and the area of service

Elasticated straps As necessary to hold electrodes in place

Leads Attach to the electrodes and connect to the machine. These are often colour coded as follows:

red = positive (anode)

black = negative (cathode)

Warm water To dampen the sponge envelopes and to remove facial products

As advised by the manufacturer's instructions:

Skincare preparations To cleanse the skin

Soothing and moisturising skincare preparations To apply to the skin following service

Ionized solution For desincrustation (facial) and iontophoresis (both facial and body). These will indicate the polarity they have (=) or (–).

Petroleum jelly or small surgical dressing to cover minor cuts and abrasions

HEALTH & SAFETY

Smooth materials
Ensure all conductive materials are smooth so that the current is conducted evenly. Galvanic chemical burns could also occur due to a concentration of current.

ALWAYS REMEMBER

Saline
Saline is an electrolyte, i.e. a conductor of electricity which can be ionized. This is a mixture in which salt (sodium chloride) has been dissolved in water. It may be used for desincrustation or the treatment of poor lymph circulation in body iontophoresis.

TOP TIP

Diuretic effects
Body iontophoresis preparations tend to have diuretic properties (elements which help the body naturally to release retained fluids). These include citrus oils, and herbal and marine elements. Warn the client they may need to pass water following service.

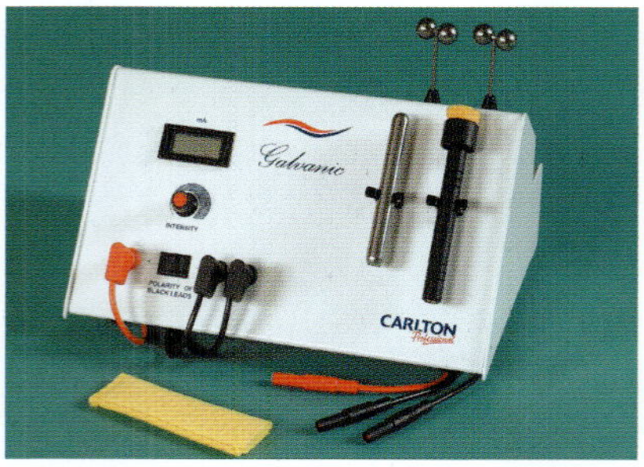

CARLTON PROFESSIONAL

Facial galvanic unit

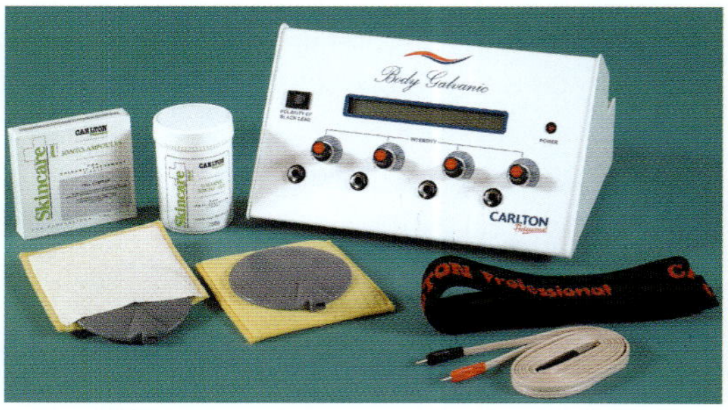

CARLTON PROFESSIONAL

Body galvanic unit

Electrodes for galvanic therapy

Electrode	*Illustration*	*Use and effect*
Indifferent metal bar electrode	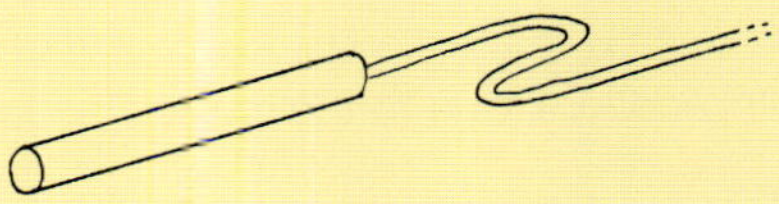	A metal bar contained within a damp sponge envelope is held by the client; this completes the electrical circuit. Used in facial service.
Facial indifferent electrode	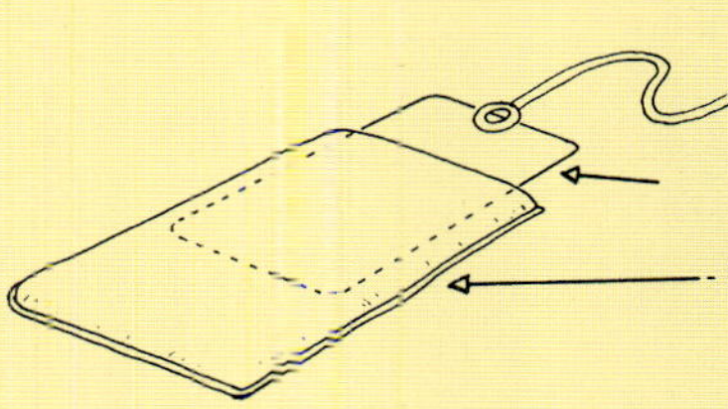	An alternative to the indifferent metal bar electrode. A small electrode contained in a damp sponge envelope completes the electrical circuit. This is placed firmly in contact with the client's skin, usually behind the shoulder. Used in facial service.
Ball electrode	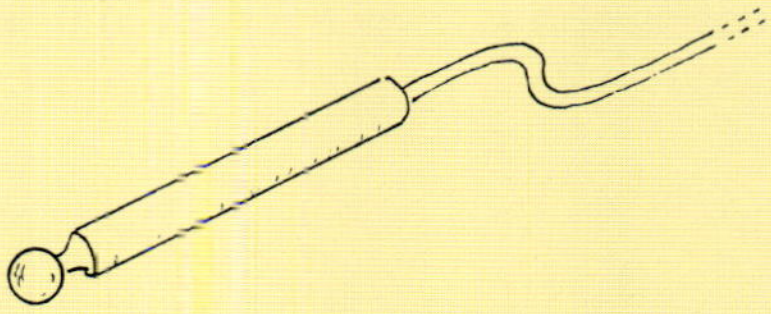	Double or single, used to treat smaller areas in facial service such as the sides of the nose, around the eyes and chin area. Single flat electrode and single dome electrode are also available for targeted facial application.
Roller electrode	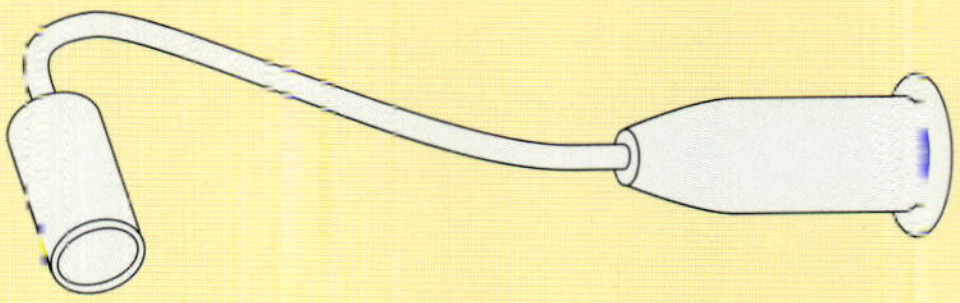	The most frequently used electrodes for the face and upper body; held one in each hand, they move over the skin surface with a slow even rhythm. Single rollers are also available.
Tweezer (pincer) electrode	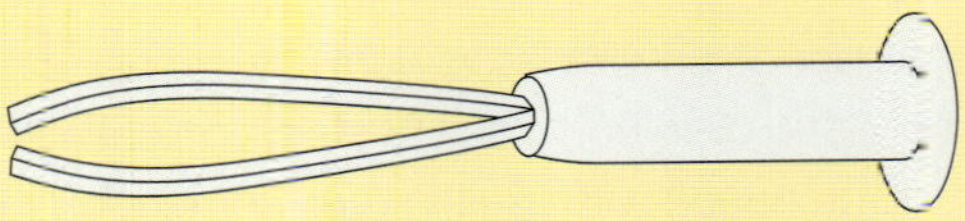	Used for desincrustation; its points are protected with cotton wool or lint soaked in desincrustation solution. Applied to problem areas, e.g. around the chin area.
Carbon-impregnated electrodes	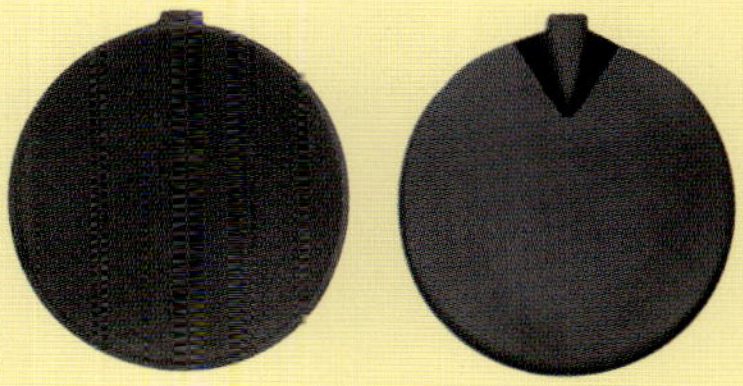 BEAUTY EXPRESS LTD	Used in pairs for service of the body.
Body electrodes	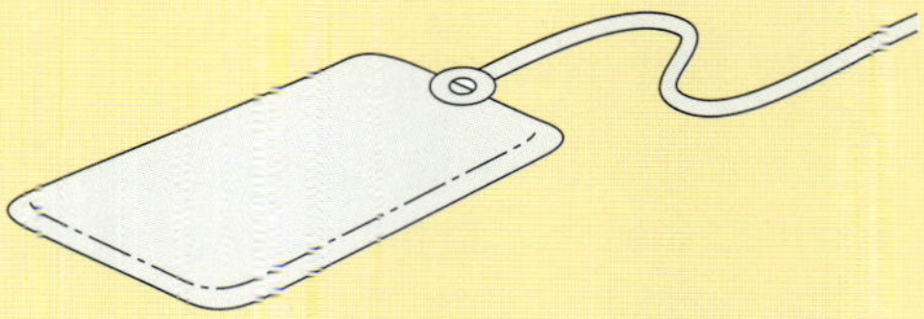	Larger electrodes used in pairs covered with damp sponge envelopes for service of the body.

Contra-indications

During the client assessment, if you find any of the following in the service area, galvanic service must not be carried out:

- excessive dental fillings
- broken skin

HEALTH & SAFETY

Internal metal
Internal metal may cause a localized concentration of current, possibly resulting in internal burning.

HEALTH & SAFETY

Cleaning electrodes
Poor cleaning of electrodes can lead to a build-up of debris, which in turn will lead to poor conductivity.

BEST PRACTICE

Elasticated straps
Several sets of elasticated straps will be required to allow for effective cleaning following client service.

ELLISONS

Galvanic products selected for their therapeutic properties i.e. toning, nourishing, treatment of sensitivity, etc.

- heart conditions
- low/high blood pressure
- defective sensation
- diabetes
- kidney disorder (body application), due to the diuretic action
- metal plates or pins within the area
- pacemaker
- IUD coil
- varicose veins
- pregnancy
- facial body piercings

Body galvanic service should not be applied over the kidney, sciatic nerve or breast area.

HEALTH & SAFETY

Skin disorders
Any skin disorder where the skin is broken, such as eczema, should not be treated as the skin's resistance to the current would be reduced, resulting in a concentration of current in the area.

Sterilization and disinfection

After each service, wash the sponge envelopes in warm, water using an anti-bacterial and detergent agent. Dry naturally, and disinfect in an UV sterilizing cabinet. Store in polythene bags to keep clean. Poor maintenance will result in replacement due to deterioration.

Clean the electrodes thoroughly, removing any cosmetic preparations and chemical formations with warm, soapy water. Dry, and place in an UV sterilizing cabinet. Wash the elasticated straps in warm water using an anti-bacterial agent and dry thoroughly.

Preparation of the service area

- Cover the service couch with a clean towel.
- Check all general electrical safety precautions.
- Use test facility feature if available to ensure the machine is in good working order. For galvanic test button machines: switch the machine on, turn the amplitude dials up slightly and press the test buttons. The mA gauge should rise, showing the machine is working. Return the amplitude to zero.
- Dampen the sponge coverings evenly in warm water.

Facial application

- Prepare the electrodes for the service area. All metal electrodes except the active roller electrodes should be covered with dampened sponge sleeves. (However, if using a tweezer electrode this will require covering to avoid galvanic burns caused by a concentration of current.)

- Secure the electrodes firmly to the electrical leads.
- Insert the leads into the relevant connections.

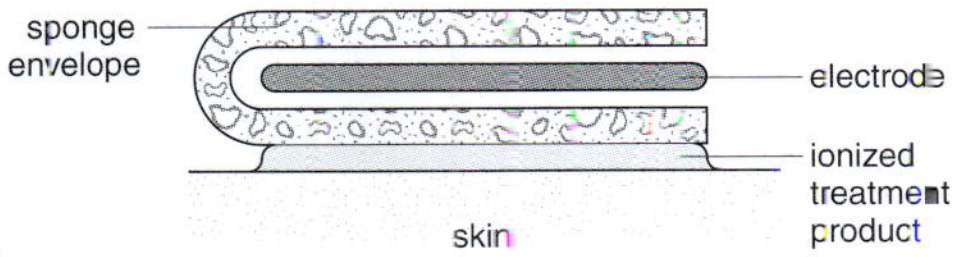

Preparation of body electrodes

Body application

- Place the elasticated straps on the couch in position for the service.
- Prepare the electrodes for the service. All electrodes should be covered with dampened sponge sleeves.
- Secure the electrodes firmly to the electrical leads.
- Insert the leads into the relevant connections.

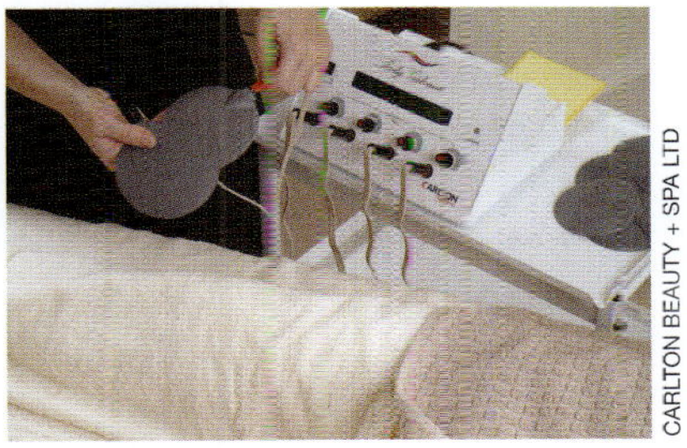

Securing the electrical leads to the electrodes

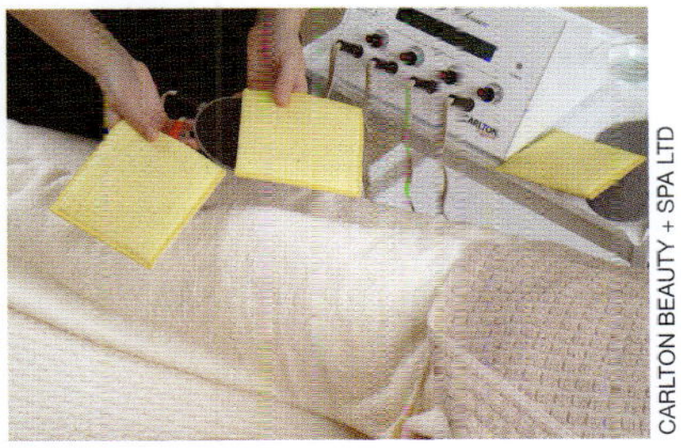

Preparation of the electrodes

Preparation of the beauty therapist

- Collect the client's record card.
- Wash your hands before handling the client.
- Assess the client. Discuss the client's lifestyle and objectives of the service if this is the initial service. Agree on an appropriate service plan.
- If a service has a slimming requirement it will be necessary to measure the client at the beginning of the service course and once every week.
- If this is a repeat service, check the client's progress against targets set and provide support and advice as necessary.

Preparation of the client

Facial application

1. Remove the client's upper clothing to underwear. Position the client comfortably on the couch in a supine position and cover with a clean towel.
2. Remove all jewellery from the service area.
3. Perform skin sensitivity and thermal tests if it is the client's first service. Record the results on the client's record card.
4. Cleanse and tone the skin of the face and neck. Blot the skin dry with a soft facial tissue.
5. Analyze the client's skin using a magnifying lamp. Question the client further where necessary to check information in relation to the client's skin condition.
6. Cover any minor cuts or abrasions with petroleum jelly or a small surgical plaster to form a barrier to the electric current.
7. Explain the service sensation to the client. A slight prickling sensation in the skin will be experienced as the skin resistance drops and the lotion penetrates the skin. This will be followed by a feeling of warmth as the skin becomes stimulated and the circulation increases.

HEALTH & SAFETY

Galvanic burns

A galvanic burn, caused by a concentration of chemicals (acids or alkalis), may be caused due to poor preparation of the electrodes such as:

- tucks or folds in the covering
- unevenly moistened viscose covers
- inadequate electrode insulation
- exposure of skin to metal points of facial tweezer electrodes

HEALTH & SAFETY

Metal couch frame

The client must not come into contact with the metal frame of the couch. As a safety precaution you may choose to drape an insulating fabric over the couch underneath the towel.

HEALTH & SAFETY

Broken skin
Broken skin exposes the living tissues of the epidermis. Unless protected, the higher water content of these tissues will encourage a concentration of the current in the area and may cause a burn.

HEALTH & SAFETY

Hot spots
The client should not feel any 'hot spots'. These may be chemical burns. Question the client during service to check.

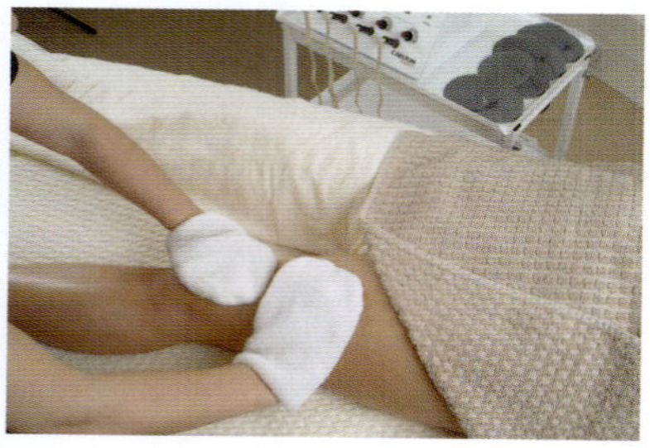
CARLTON BEAUTY + SPA LTD

Cleaning the skin

BEST PRACTICE

Professional questioning and recommendations
Question the client further where necessary to check information in relation to the client's service objectives during service application. You will then be able to offer supportive advice and recommend the sale of professional retail products for home use.

TOP TIP

Exfoliation
The skin will have increased resistance if it is dehydrated, very dry or very oily, as lack of moisture, dead skin cells and sebum act as an initial barrier to current flow. A mild exfoliating skin preparation may be applied before service commences to remove dead skin cells, sebum and cosmetic ingredients' residue. This will reduce the skin's resistance initially to the electric current and facilitate absorption of the galvanic solution.

For body service the skin may benefit from gentle body brushing.

Body application

1. Perform a skin sensitivity and thermal test if it is the client's first service. Record the results on the client's record card.
2. Remove all jewellery from the service area.
3. Instruct the client to remove all clothing except underwear.
4. Measure the client (if required).
5. Position the client on the service couch. This will be in a supine or prone position depending on the padding layout selected.
6. Cleanse the skin using a non-oily detergent cleanser and blot dry with paper tissue.
7. Cover any minor cuts or abrasions with petroleum jelly or a small surgical plaster to form a barrier to the electric current.
8. Explain the service sensation to the client. A slight prickling sensation in the skin will be followed by a feeling of warmth.

Galvanic service application: facial

After analyzing the client's skin you may select to choose either the positive or negative pole. The **positive pole** is used to:

- close the pores
- reduce skin redness
- introduce acid preparations into the skin

The **negative pole** is used to:

- improve circulation – the current passing through the skin acts as an irritant, causing the superficial blood vessels to dilate
- remove the surface dead skin cells and sebum
- open the pores
- introduce alkaline preparations into the skin

The service techniques are described as **desincrustation** and **iontophoresis**.

- *Desincrustation.* The negative pole is selected. As the solution is ionized, alkalis form which soften the dead skin cells and fatty acids of sebum. This has a cleansing action upon the skin's surface which is suitable for most skin types except those which are highly sensitive.

- *Iontophoresis*. Manufactured water-soluble preparations are introduced into the skin. These may be either creams or gels which assist rehydration and increase cellular metabolism in the area.

Service technique is given according to the skin type and the results to be achieved.

ALWAYS REMEMBER

A metallic taste in the mouth

A metallic taste may be experienced by the client. Through the initial consultation reassure the client that this is simply a reaction between the saliva in the mouth and the electric current.

TOP TIP

Booking considerations

This is not a suitable service to have immediately before a special occasion as it is inadvisable to wear make-up for 8 hours afterwards and sometimes a few pustules may also occur.

Desincrustation service

1. The client firmly holds a clean, damp, sponge envelope containing the indifferent electrode, or alternatively the indifferent facial electrode is secured in contact with the client's body, usually behind the clients shoulder. (It may also be secured with a strap to the clients upper arm.)
2. Dependent upon the electrodes used, the desincrustation solution is applied directly to the skin of the face and neck with a mask brush, or by cotton wool, gauze soaked in a desincrustation solution which then covers the active electrode. General desincrustation may be applied with the roller electrodes followed by application to areas of congestion using the ball/tweezer electrode.

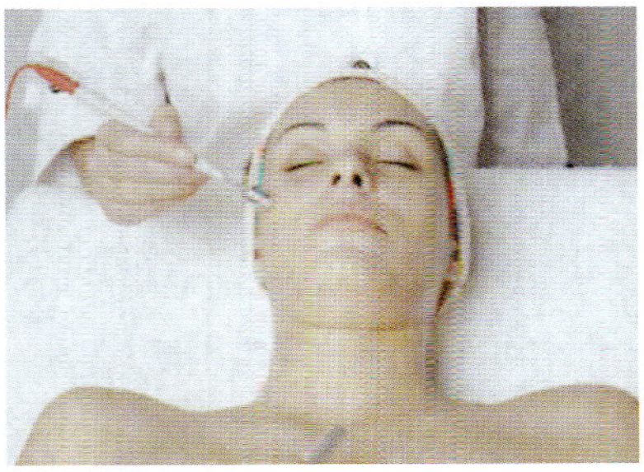

SMART BUY

Desincrustation application

BEST PRACTICE

Even current

Apply sufficient solution to provide even current flow. A solution provided in an ampoule is usually liquid. This is best poured over gauze in a bowl, then the gauze is placed directly over the face. This is not necessary with gels, providing a thick enough layer is applied. If the skin or environment is warm this will require renewal as the water content of the gel will evaporate.

BEST PRACTICE

Sebaceous gland activity

Avoid excessive application of desincrustation service or the skin's sebaceous glands will become over-stimulated, producing more sebum as a result!

3. Switch on the machine at the mains. Select the negative pole and switch the machine on.
4. Place the electrode(s) on the skin's surface and keep it moving while the current intensity is gradually increased until the amperage meter registers. Then increase the intensity further until the client experiences a mild tingling sensation. The skin's resistance varies for this service but the current should not exceed 1.5 mA. The electrode(s) should not break contact with the skin while the current flows or discomfort may be experienced by the client.
5. Apply the current to the skin for 3–5 minutes. The service should not be uncomfortable and the client's comfort should be checked during application. Suggested desincrustation application technique using the tweezer or ball electrode is illustrated (or alternatives as discussed previously your machine may be equipped with). The smaller surface area requires you to reduce current intensity. It is ideal to work within areas of congestion as shown.
6. Reduce the current intensity slowly with one hand. Remove the active electrode(s) from the skin. Switch off the machine.

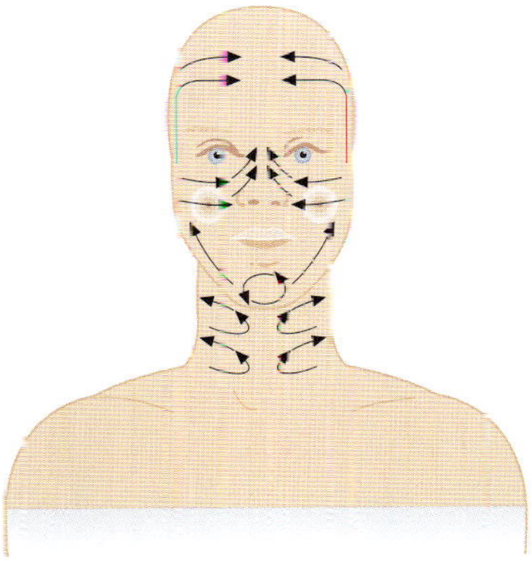

→ = roller electrode application

Desincrustation application using roller electrodes

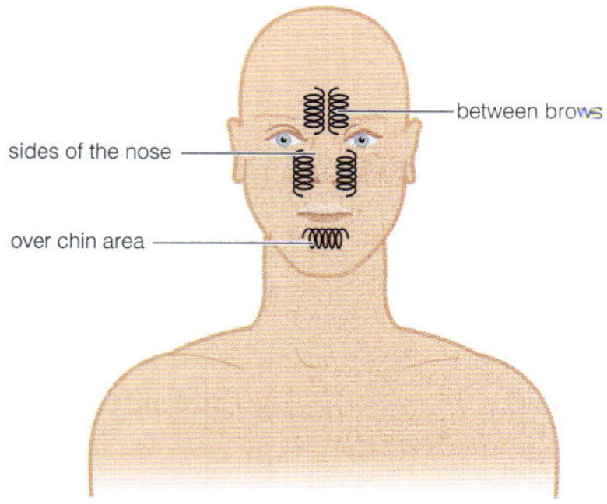

Desincrustation application using tweezer or ball/probe electrode – commonly treated areas

TOP TIP

Combined unit

If using a combined electrical unit, high frequency may be applied following desincrustation or iontophoresis if appropriate to the client's service needs.

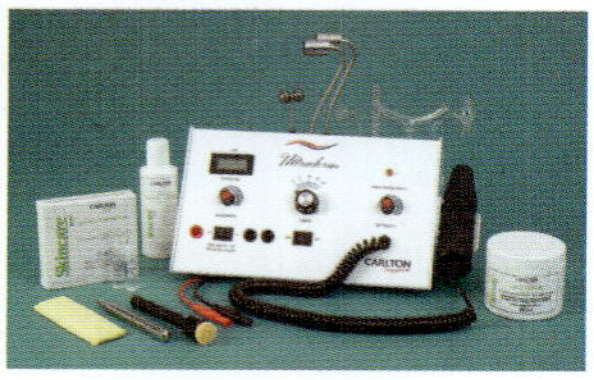

CARLTON BEAUTY + SPA LTD

Ultraderm unit

TOP TIP

Acne vulgaris

You may recommend the benefits of the cleansing and healing action of galvanic therapy for the service of a congested, pustular or mild acne vulgaris condition.

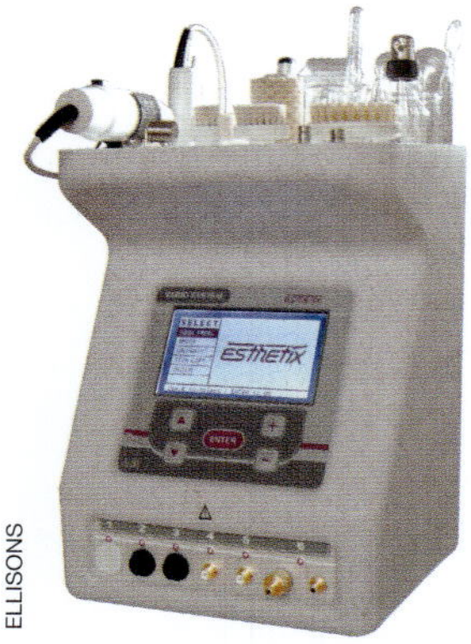

ELLISONS

Combined computerised unit offering galvanic facial service

7 Remove the indifferent electrode from the client.

8 Switch off the machine at the mains.

9 Remove the remaining solution from the client's skin using damp sponges or damp cotton wool.

10 As the skin's pores are relaxed, gentle comedone removal may be performed.

If milia require removal, this is completed at the end of the service to avoid secondary infection using a micro-lance (see page 247).

11 Iontophoresis may follow, selecting suitable service products for the client's skin type.

12 A facial **mask** may be applied, followed by the application of toning lotion and a service **moisturiser**.

13 Record the service details on the client's record card.

BEST PRACTICE

Manual adjustment

Although most machines can adapt the current to within 5 per cent of the initial setting, it may be necessary to manually reduce the current over bony areas which offer less resistance to the electrical current.

Intensity and timing

The intensity of the current and the timing of the service are important. Too low a current intensity and too short an application renders the service ineffective. Too high a current may be uncomfortable for the client.

BEST PRACTICE

Electrode application

The application of the electrodes should follow movements which will induce client relaxation. Be firm in application but without applying unnecessary pressure.

Iontophoresis service

1 The client firmly holds a clean, damp, sponge envelope containing the indifferent electrode, or alternatively the indifferent electrode is secured in contact with the client's body, usually the upper arm.

2 An appropriate iontophoresis solution is applied to the skin of the face and neck in accordance with its opacity.

3 Switch the machine on at the mains. Select the relevant pole according to the iontophoresis solution chosen and switch the machine on.

4 Place the active electrode(s) on the skin's surface and reassure the client of the sensation to be experienced. Increase the current intensity gradually until the mA meter gauge registers, keeping the electrode moving all the time. Wait

30 seconds before increasing the current until the client experiences a tingling sensation. Then gradually increase the current to a level where the tingling sensation subsides. The current should not exceed 1.5 mA.

5 Continue the service, moving the electrodes slowly over the skin's surface. Suggested iontophoresis application using roller electrodes is illustrated.

6 Apply the service for between 5–7 minutes, depending on the effect required and the client's skin tolerance.

7 Reduce the current very slowly to allow the chemical effects to be completed. When using the roller electrode it is necessary to remove one hand to reduce the current intensity while keeping the other electrode in contact with the skin. You may reverse the polarity and apply the current on the reverse pole for a further 2 minutes. This will neutralize any chemical residue on the skin's surface which may cause sensitivity.

8 Switch off the machine.

9 Switch off at the mains.

10 Remove the indifferent electrode from the client.

11 Remove remaining solution from the skin's surface with clean, damp sponges or cotton wool.

12 A facial mask may be applied, followed by the application of toning lotion and a moisturiser.

13 Record the details of the service on the client's record card.

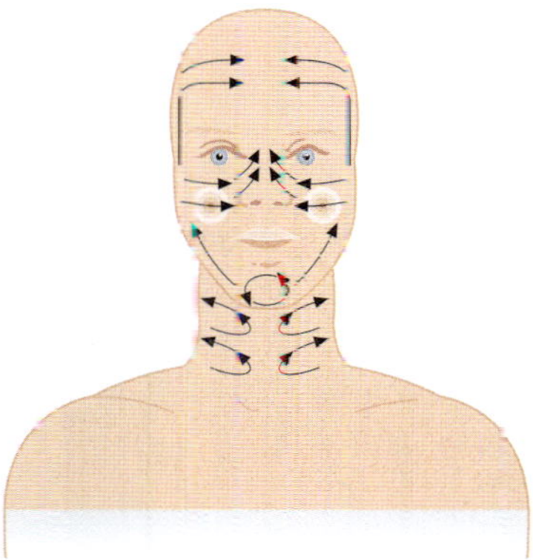

Iontophoresis application using roller electrodes

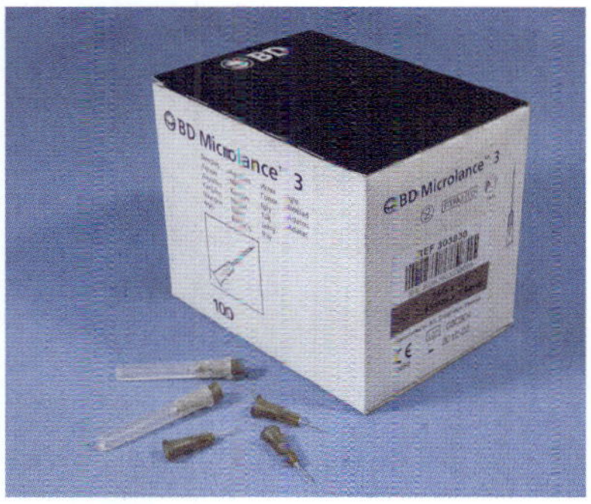

Micro-lance

Micro-lance A micro-lance is a pre-sterilized needle designed to be used to scrape the surface of the skin to release skin blockages such as in growing hairs and the sebaceous skin matter milia. The skin should be prepared before skin piercing, ideally following cleansing treatments such as steam exfoliation or galvanic desincrustation where the skin epidermis is softened.

Disposable gloves should be worn when executing this service due to the risk of contact with body tissue fluids

The skin should be first disinfected using a cleaning agent such as isopropyl alcohol individually wrapped tissues.

The skin is held taut and the surface of the skin gently scraped until broken. If removing an ingrowing hair which is still living, this is released and the skin then cleaned and an antiseptic lotion applied to promote skin healing. If the hair is dead, this is removed using sterile tweezers.

If removing a milia, the skin is gently scraped until broken and then the milia is gently removed using a rolling movement with the index and middle fingers either side of the milia until it is extracted. The fingers should be protected with facial tissue, alternatively cotton buds may be used if the skin is sensitive.

Follow with the application of a sterile cleaning agent and antiseptic soothing lotion.

All contaminated waste should be disposed off in a yellow sack for later collection and incineration. The micro-lance should be placed in a yellow sharps box container.

The client must be advised to avoid touching the area with unclean hands and if a scab occurs this must not be removed, it must be shed naturally.

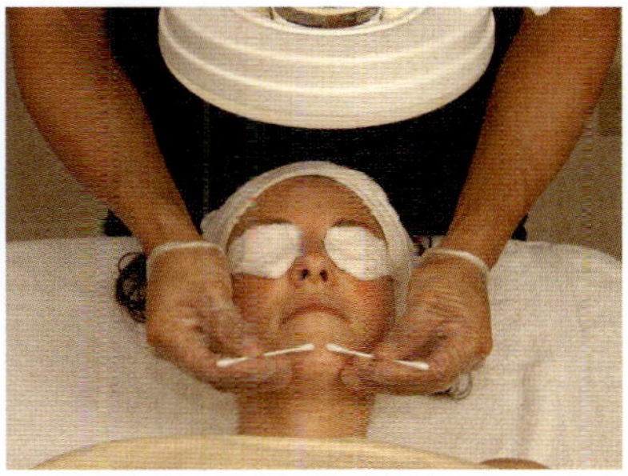

Extractions

COURSEMATE For a video on micro-lance (also showing disposal of medical waste) please visit this book's accompanying CourseMate.

TOP TIP

Combined therapy

Combining galvanic therapy followed by high-frequency currents produces a skin-toning effect when used with skin-firming ingredients. A small electrode is used to introduce the gel into the skin. This is followed by a low-intensity application of high frequency. This may be offered as a service for the eye tissue.

HEALTH & SAFETY

Increasing current

- Never increase the current until the electrode is in contact with the skin's surface.
- Turn up the current very slowly until the amperage meter begins to register. The client's skin offers an initial resistance to the current through its dead skin cells and adipose tissue.

HEALTH & SAFETY

Irritation for the client

If a client finds the service is causing intolerable irritation of the skin, reduce the current very slowly and cease service. You may wish to reverse polarity and apply the current on the reverse pole for a few moments to neutralize the chemicals that are causing the irritation.

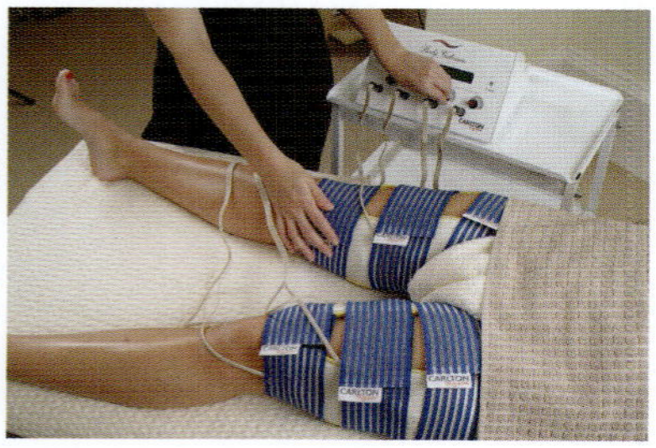

CARLTON BEAUTY + SPA LTD

Turning up intensity

Galvanic service application: body

Body galvanic service is usually applied for the service of cellulite and a sluggish lymphatic circulation. The combination of the physiological effects created and the penetration of active therapeutic ingredients gives an immediate improvement to skin appearance. The galvanic current stimulates the metabolism in the tissues and the localized movement of tissue fluids through the cell membranes. Tissue fluids are drawn towards the negative pole (known as **electro-osmosis**), which may help improve the appearance of lumpy tissue.

The deeper blood vessels dilate due to a reflex action to the stimulation of the superficial capillaries. The whole area becomes warm but the erythema is greater under the negative electrode due to the alkaline skin irritant effect.

After assessing the client's skin condition and service needs you may select either the positive or negative pole according to the physiological effects required.

The **positive** pole is used to:

- reduce skin redness
- introduce acid preparations into the skin

The **negative** pole is used to:

- open the pores to enable penetration of the active ingredients
- stimulate blood and lymph circulation to help improve a sluggish circulation
- introduce alkaline preparations into the skin which claim to break down the metabolites by ionization
- improve the appearance of cellulite – the increased tissue fluids to the active pole plump out the skin and improve circulation

How to provide galvanic body service

1. The appropriate active solution should be placed under the negative or active electrode – this is usually the area requiring attention. A suitable conducting solution must be placed at the positive or indifferent electrode. This is placed opposite the active pad.
2. Firmly strap the electrodes in place so that they make firm, even contact with the skin. The electrodes must not touch each other or the service will be ineffective as the current will pass straight from one to the other without ionization occurring. Sample padding arrangements are illustrated.
3. Switch the machine on at the mains.
4. Select the negative pole and switch the machine on.
5. Slowly increase each intensity dial until the mA meter registers and the skin's resistance is reduced, causing the client to feel a tingling sensation. Wait approximately 30 seconds before increasing the current intensity. The tingling sensation will disappear as the current intensity is increased, being replaced by a feeling of warmth. A final amperage reading of 3.00 mA is not normally exceeded.
6. Increase the service time from an initial 10 minutes to 20 minutes for future services. The polarity may be reversed for the final 2–3 minutes to neutralize the chemicals which have been formed in order to reduce skin irritation.

7 At the end of the service, slowly reduce the current intensity to zero to avoid client discomfort. A noticeable erythema will be seen on the skin when the electrodes are removed as a result of chemical formation.

8 Switch the machine off at the mains.

9 Remove the straps and electrodes from the service area.

10 Wash the skin in warm water to remove the galvanic solution and acids and alkalis which will have formed.

11 A light application of unperfumed talc may be applied to soothe the skin and reduce the erythema.

12 Record details of the service on the client's record card.

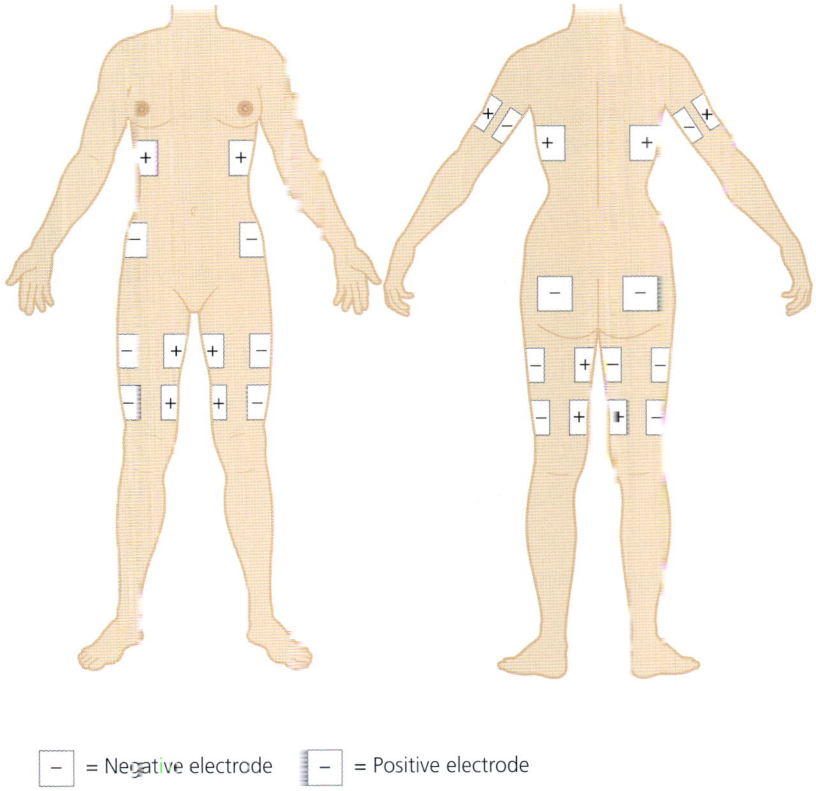

Sample galvanic body padding techniques

BEST PRACTICE

Increasing current

Turn up the current very slowly until the milliammeter begins to register. The client's skin offers an initial resistance to the current through its dead skin cells and adipose tissue.

HEALTH & SAFETY

Irritation for the client

If a client finds the service is causing intolerable irritation of the skin, reduce the current very slowly and cease the service. You may wish to reverse polarity and apply the current on the reverse pole for a few moments to neutralize the chemicals which are causing the irritation.

Aftercare

Following facial service, advise the client to avoid make-up for up to 8 to 12 hours to support the skin-cleansing effect.

It is normal for a few pustules or papules to occur following facial service. The client must not touch the area but allow the skin to heal without intervention.

Following body service, the client should be advised to drink plenty of water. The client may need to pass urine immediately after service because of increased fluid elimination. Inform them that this is a normal effect after this service. If treating a cellulite condition, daily body brushing should be advised to stimulate lymphatic circulation followed by application of a cellulite skincare product.

Offer the client water for hydration.

BEST PRACTICE

Intensity and timing

The intensity of the current and the timing of the service are important. Too low a current intensity and too short an application renders the service ineffective. Too high a current intensity and too long an application can sensitize the skin resulting in possible skin injury.

HEALTH & SAFETY

Galvanic burn

To minimize the risk of a galvanic burn always consider the following:

- reduce the current when applying electrodes over bony areas
- body sponge envelopes should be evenly moistened to ensure even distribution of the current
- body sponge envelopes should be cleaned effectively following service to remove chemicals
- poor communication with the client could result in the client not informing you of discomfort
- the current intensity should not be too high for the size of the electrodes

TOP TIP

Erythema

If the client has a noticeable erythema following service, explain that this is due to increased blood stimulation which will reduce in a few hours. Explain also that exposure to warmth directly after service will increase the colour further.

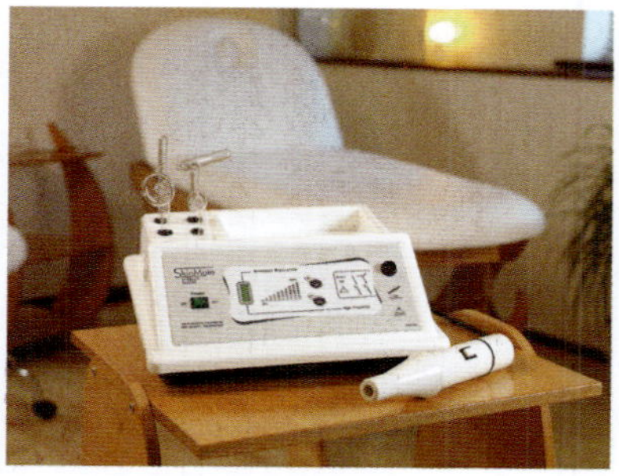

HOF BEAUTY

High-frequency unit service

Contra-actions

- **Galvanic burn**: a chemical burn caused by a concentration of alkali formation on the skin. It is recognized by a darkish split in the skin surrounded by a red, inflamed ring. *Action*: sterile, cold water should be applied to the area followed by a sterile, dry dressing. Medical advise should be sought.
- **Sensitization**: if the facial skin shows excessive erythema it is indicating a release of histamine showing that the skin is distressed. *Action*: cease the service, or reverse the current for a short time and apply a cosmetic containing a cooling, soothing ingredient. Apply a cool compress.

Note any contra-action, advice provided and related updates on the record card.

High-frequency service

High frequency may be applied directly or indirectly to the skin of the face or body to stimulate, disinfect and heal the skin. Indirect high frequency is not a competence requirement for your assessment evidence but is provided for you as additional knowledge on how this service may be applied.

Direct high-frequency application

In the direct method, the beauty therapist places a high-frequency electrode in contact with the client's skin in the service area.

- increases blood circulation, resulting in erythema and warms the skin tissues
- increases lymph circulation, resulting in absorption of waste products
- increases metabolism in the area
- stimulates superficial nerve endings
- generates ozone which has a germicidal action on the surface of the skin, which is both healing and refining

Uses:

- treatment of oily skin
- treatment of mild acne vulgaris
- treatment of dry skin – stimulates sebaceous gland activity

Indirect high-frequency application

In the indirect method the client holds an electrode while the beauty therapist massages their skin. The high-frequency current is transferred between the client's skin and the beauty therapist's fingers.

Effects:

- increases the activity of the sebaceous and sudoriferous glands
- improves blood circulation, nourishing the skin
- improves the lymphatic circulation, speeding up the elimination of waste products

Uses:

- treatment of dry and dehydrated skin
- tightening effect to improve the appearance of fine lines and wrinkles
- improves the appearance of the skin

Anatomy and physiology

The high-frequency current generates warmth in the skin and stimulates the nerve endings. This in turn causes reflex vasodilation of the blood capillaries leading to increased blood circulation.

Metabolism in the area is increased which encourages healthy cell function and promotes skin healing. With the direct method of application, sparking beneath the electrode generates ozone which has a mild antiseptic, drying effect, making the direct method beneficial for the service of a blemished skin.

A dry skin benefits from the stimulation of the sebaceous and sudoriferous glands with indirect high frequency, through its skin-warming effect.

ALWAYS REMEMBER

Electrode colour

High-frequency glass electrodes may show different colours when in use. This depends on the gas they contain:

- violet – electrode containing argon
- blue – electrode containing mercury vapour
- orange – electrode containing neon

Electrical and chemical effects

A high-frequency current is an electrical current which moves backwards and forwards at very high speed. The current is termed as an **alternating** or **oscillating** current. This rapid backwards and forwards movement creates high-frequency vibrations over the skin's surface of between 10 000 and 250 000 vibrations per second. We say it has a frequency of 100 000 to 250 000 cycles per second or **hertz**. The result is a heating, stimulating effect.

Reception

Complete personal details on the client's record card. Question the client to check for possible contra-indications.

High frequency may be offered as an individual service or may be incorporated into a programme with other services. As such 1 hour is usually allowed when booking this service. The service should be received once every 4–6 weeks.

ALWAYS REMEMBER

High-frequency current

The ac operates at high voltage – up to 200 000–300 000 volts, alternating at a high frequency – 100 000–250 000 Hz, but at low current, so its energy/power is low.

EQUIPMENT AND MATERIALS LIST

ELLISONS

Client record card
Confidential record of details for all clients registered at the salon

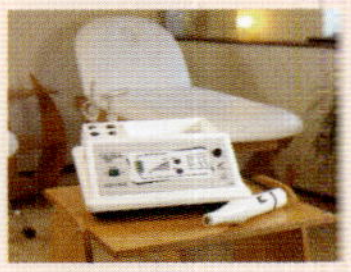

HOT BEAUTY

High-frequency unit

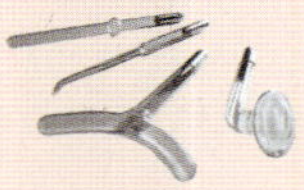

Selection of both glass and metal high-frequency electrodes
The electrodes have a metal cap which inserts into the electrode holder; this allows conductivity of the current. Inside the glass electrodes is a near vacuum. A tiny amount of a gas is contained in the electrode which allows the current to pass through and create energy in the form of light and UV rays. When the current passes through the glass electrode and the oxygen on the skin's surface, ozone is created

YOU WILL ALSO NEED:

Cosmetic preparation for direct high frequency Oxygenating cream (which encourages the production of oxygen), or talc on an excessively oily skin. The cream has a soothing, nourishing effect on the skin whereas talc is more stimulating and drying. A specialised face mask or gauze can be applied over the face providing a gap between the skin and electrode which encourages ozone production

Massage medium for indirect high frequency e.g. a cream emulsion

> If a piece of equipment is faulty, inform your manager as soon as possible. This ensures that they can quickly solve any ensuing problems thereby preventing future treatment downtime and loss of revenue for the salon.
>
> **Mary Overton**

Electrodes for galvanic therapy

Electrode	*Illustration*	*Use and effect*
Mushroom electrode	 ϕ 47 mm 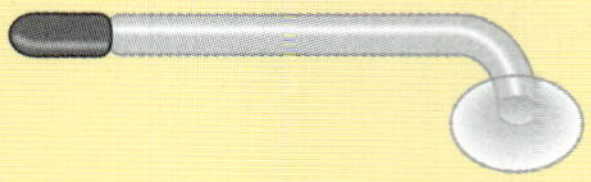 ϕ 30 mm	A glass electrode available in different sizes, selected according to the part to be treated – the smaller the electrode the more stimulating the effect.
Horseshoe electrode	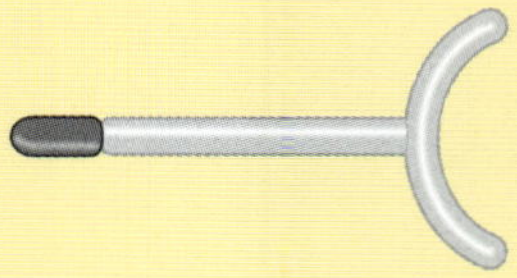	A glass electrode shaped to contour the neck area. Moved over the skin of the neck, it has a sedative effect on the nerve endings.
Saturator electrode		A metal bar which is placed into the high-frequency applicator. Held by the client and used in indirect high frequency.
Spiral intensifier electrode	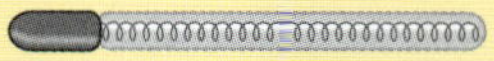	A metal coil contained in a cylindrical glass electrode which intensifies the effect. Held by the client and used in indirect high frequency.
Roller electrode		Glass roller-shaped electrodes which may be freely moved along the skin's surface. Used for general service application to the face and body.

Contra-indications

During the client assessment, if you find any of the following in the service area, high-frequency service must not be carried out:

- skin inflammation
- skin disorder or disease
- excessive dental metalwork

- hypersensitive skin
- acne rosacea
- oedema
- migraine sufferers
- lack of tactile sensation
- severe headaches
- nervous client
- heart condition
- recent injectable cosmetic service
- facial-body piercings

Sterilization and disinfection

After use:

- the electrodes should be cleaned according to their type
- glass electrodes should have any massage medium removed and be wiped with disinfectant
- the electrodes should then be placed in an UV sterilizing cabinet, turning the electrodes to ensure thorough disinfection after 20 minutes

Preparation of the service area

- Cover the service couch with a clean towel.
- Check all general electrical safety precautions.
- Test the equipment and machine to ensure they are in good working order.
- Select a suitable electrode for the service area and effect to be created.
- Switch on the machine and place the electrode directly on your skin's surface.
- Gradually increase the current intensity until a low buzzing noise occurs.
- Return the current intensity to zero.
- Disinfect the surface of the electrode after testing, before client application.

Preparation of the beauty therapist

- Collect the client's record card.
- Disinfect your hands before handling the client.
- Assess the client's skin and determine the objectives of the service.

Preparation of the client

- Instruct the client to remove upper clothing to underwear.
- Position the client comfortably on the service couch in a supine position and cover her with a clean towel.

TOP TIP

Skin disorders

Although most skin disorders contra-indicate service, mild infections such as pustules and papules benefit from direct high-frequency service due to its skin-disinfecting effect.

HEALTH & SAFETY

Electrode holders

It is essential to make sure that any moisturising creams or talcum powder are cleaned off the electrode holder. Both are very conductive to high frequency and can result in the beauty therapist feeling more of the high-frequency current than they should.

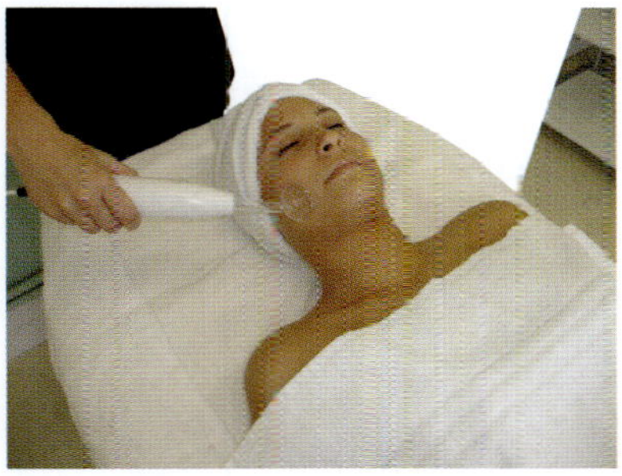

ELLISONS

Direct high-frequency service

HEALTH & SAFETY

Jewellery

Wedding bands and metal nail jewellery must be covered with an insulating material if they cannot be removed if carrying out indirect high frequency where the client is required to hold the indifferent electrode.

- Remove all jewellery from the service area.
- Cleanse and tone the area of skin to be treated, and apply a suitable therapeutic cosmetic skin preparation.
- Analyze the skin using a magnifying lamp. Question the client further where necessary to check information in relation to the client's skin condition.
- Explain the service procedure. A new client will need to be reassured of the buzzing noise, glowing colour of the electrode and the mild ozone smell.
- If performing indirect high frequency, ask the client to remove all jewellery from the hand and wrist area. A small amount of talc can be applied to the client's hand to absorb perspiration during the service.

Direct high-frequency service application

1. Switch on the power at the mains.
2. Switch on the machine.
3. Hold the selected active electrode in contact with the service area, increase the current intensity to the desired level.
4. Move the electrode over the skin's surface in a rotary fashion, creating a stimulating, warming effect. Reduce current intensity over areas which offer less skin resistance to the current such as the forehead, nose and cheekbones.
5. The service is applied according to the needs of the client's skin. Generally, the electrode is applied to the skin for 8–10 minutes for oily skin, and 5 minutes for dry skin.
6. Check the client's comfort and observe skin reaction during application.
7. Remove excess cream or talc from the client's skin.
8. Follow with a service mask, toner and suitable moisturiser.
9. Record details of the service on the record card.

HEALTH & SAFETY

Sparking

Do not spark near the client's eyes, where the skin is delicate.

COURSEMATE

For a video on direct high-frequency (using several different tools) please visit this book's accompanying CourseMate.

TOP TIP

Sparking

'Sparking' may be incorporated to dry up and sanitize any pustules that might be present. The electrode is lifted approximately 7 mm away from the skin, and then quickly replaced on the skin's surface. This is repeated in a gentle tapping motion approximately six to eight times. The oxygen in the air becomes ionized and creates ozone, which destroys bacteria, promoting skin healing.

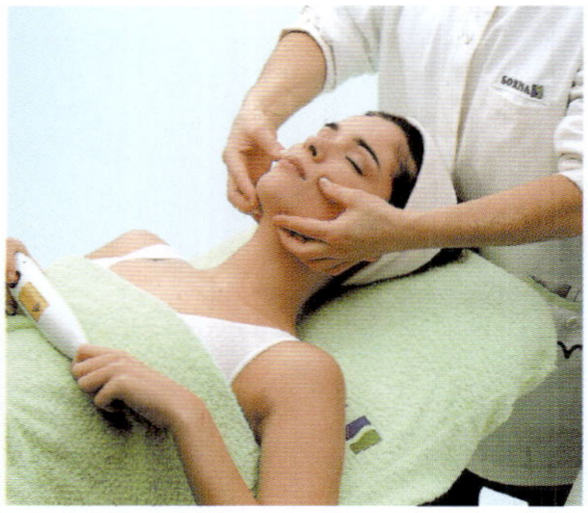

BEAUTY EXPRESS LTD

Indirect high-frequency application

Indirect high-frequency service application

1. Switch on the power at the mains.
2. Place the saturator electrode into the handle and place firmly into the client's hand.
3. Place one hand on the client's face, performing small circular massage movements. With the other hand switch on the machine.

4 Increase the current slowly until the client experiences a tingling sensation and gentle warmth as your hands act as the electrode and the current flows from the client to your fingers.

5 Place both hands on the client's face and perform a face, neck and shoulder massage using effleurage and petrissage movements but omitting tapotement movements. When massaging over bony areas and around the eye area, remove one hand from the client's face and reduce the current intensity.

6 Check the client's comfort and skin reaction during service application.

7 Service times will differ according to skin type and skin tolerance. Generally the massage is performed for 8–10 minutes with the electrical current.

8 At the conclusion of the service, remove one hand while keeping the other hand in contact with the client's skin. Remove massage medium from this hand before slowly reducing the current intensity.

9 Switch the machine off.

10 Switch the power off at the mains.

11 Remove the saturator from the client's hand and continue with a light massage without electrical current for a further 5–8 minutes.

12 Remove all massage medium from the electrodes, particularly the electrode holder, to avoid the current going astray and giving you accidental shocks.

13 Remove excess cream from the skin's surface.

14 Follow with a service mask, toner and suitable moisturiser.

15 Record details of the service on the client record card.

HEALTH & SAFETY

Tapotement

Tapotement must be avoided in your massage of the skin for indirect high frequency as it would cause the current to jump between the gap created between the beauty therapist's hands and the client's skin, causing a sparking effect and irritation.

BEST PRACTICE

Less fatty areas

Areas with little fatty tissue offer less resistance to the current, intensifying the sensation experienced by the client in these areas. Therefore, always reduce the current intensity accordingly.

Aftercare

The client should be advised against applying make-up for up to 8 hours following the service, to support the skin-cleansing effect. Advise on the correct application of skincare preparations appropriate to their needs. Recommend other facial services to complement the effects of high frequency.

Avoid other heat services for 24 hours.

Offer the client water for hydration.

Contra-actions

- *Excessive erythema*. Indicates over-stimulation of the skin.
- *Tissue destruction*. Caused by sparking for too long or electrode held too far from the skin's surface.

Gyratory vibratory service

Gyratory vibratory service is an electrical body massage service which produces friction on the skin's surface, creating a heating effect. It provides a deep massage and is often used as a slimming service where the aim is to soften fatty tissue and stimulate the lymphatic circulation. The benefits resemble those created by manual massage but with less effort required by the beauty therapist! (Gyratory massage is also required for the unit Provide body massage services – see page 365.)

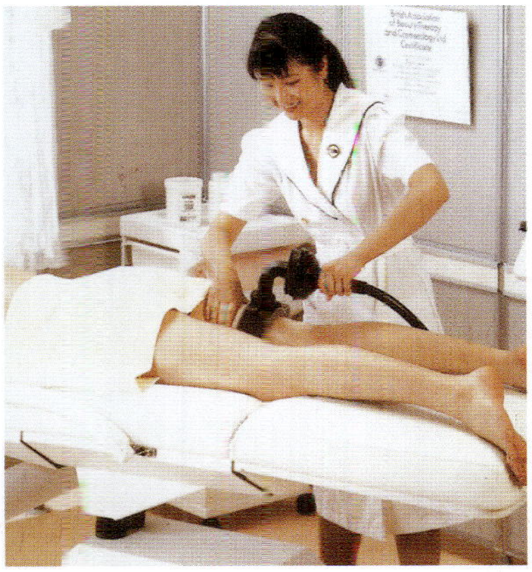

CARLTON PROFESSIONAL

Gyratory vibratory service

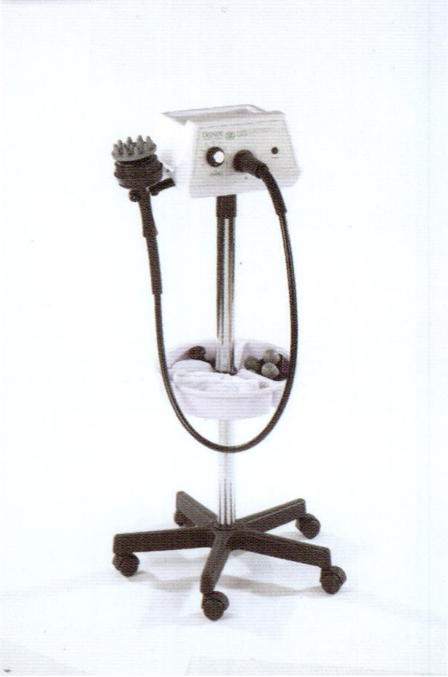

DEPILEX

Gyratory vibratory massage equipment

General effects:

- increased blood circulation which improves the skin colour and transports nutrients and oxygen to the skin cells and muscles
- increased venous blood and lymph circulation, which increases the removal of toxins and waste materials
- improved skin texture by removal of the surface dead skin cells (desquamation)
- relaxing of tense muscles due to the heating effect
- softening of areas of soft and hard adipose tissue
- stimulation of sensory nerve endings
- stimulation of skin function, increasing sebaceous gland activity

Body use:

- to reduce localized fatty deposits. This is commonly referred to as 'spot reduction'
- to improve areas of cellulite
- to stimulate a sluggish lymphatic and blood circulation, improving cellular metabolism
- to improve a dry skin condition by removing dead skin cells and improving sebaceous gland activity

TOP TIP

Hand-held massager

The hand-held gyratory vibratory massager is suitable for the mobile beauty therapist. It has less choice in applicator heads than the floor-standing type.

Anatomy and physiology

The warmth generated by the service increases metabolic activity in the service area. The combination of warmth and the stimulation of superficial nerve endings causes reflex vasodilation – the blood vessels and capillaries expand and there is an immediate increase in the blood flow producing an erythema. Muscles are relaxed by the warmth of the increased blood circulation through the area. The increase in skin temperature stimulates the sweat glands and sebaceous glands.

Gyratory vibratory equipment

The gyratory vibrator machine may be floor-standing or hand-held. The gyratory vibration of the massage head is driven by a powerful electric motor. An internal fan draws air through the motor to keep it cool. The air vents on the motor unit must not be obstructed.

Floor-standing vibratory machine The electric motor is supported on a pedestal. A flexible drive shaft connects the motor to the vibratory head creating a gyratory effect. Various applicators are attached to the head – these simulate the therapeutic effects of manual massage. The applicators may be made from sponge, rubber or polyurethane.

Hand-held vibratory machine The hand-held vibratory massage has a variable speed controller that creates either a deeper, soothing massage or a more superficial, stimulating effect.

Reception

- Complete personal details on the client's record card.
- Question the client to check for possible contra-indications.

The effects, although similar to manual massage, are created much more quickly, therefore service time is shorter. Allow 30–45 minutes for a full-body application and 20 minutes for specific areas such as the thighs and gluteals. The client should attend two to three times per week for the service.

EQUIPMENT AND MATERIALS LIST

ELLISONS

Client record card
Confidential record of the details of each client registered at the salon

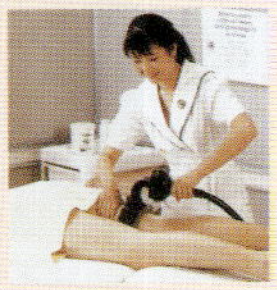
DEPILEX

Gyratory vibratory machine
Floor-standing or hand-held

ELLISONS

A selection of applicators
Appropriate for the service (see tables below)

ELLISONS

Disposable applicator covers
Recommended to avoid cross-infection; ideal to place over sponge heads

YOU WILL ALSO NEED:

Purified, unperfumed talc To allow the applicator to move easily across the skin's surface

Clean cotton wool To cleanse the skin and apply talc to the service area

Witch hazel or eau de cologne To cleanse the skin

Clean tissues To blot the skin dry

Common applicator attachments for floor-standing model

Name of attachment	*Illustration*	*Use and effect*
Round smooth rubber applicator	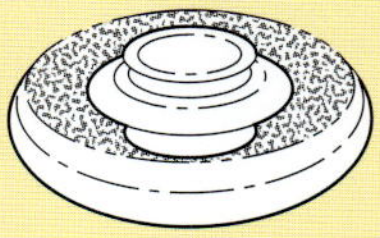	Client who has sensitive skin which may be irritated by sponge; used for effleurage and petrissage effects.
Round smooth water massage head		Warm or crushed ice water creates a stimulating/invigorating or relaxing effect; used for effleurage and petrissage effects.
Round sponge applicator	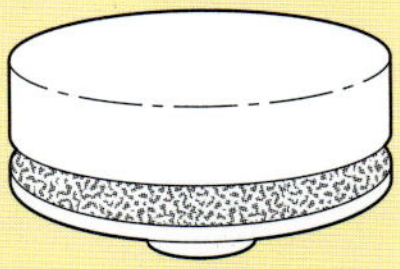	Used on the trunk to induce relaxation at the start and end of massage of the service part; used for effleurage and stroking effects. A coarse disposable sponge is also available, used with creams and gels.
Curved sponge applicator	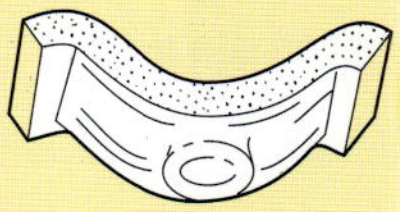	Used on the arms and legs to induce relaxation at the start and end of massage of the service part; used for effleurage and stroking effects.

Name of attachment	*Illustration*	*Use and effect*
'Eggbox' rubber applicator		Used on bulky muscular areas and fatty tissue such as the gluteals and thighs; used for petrissage effect. NB: A two-ball rubber applicator is available to provide a deep localized massage for bulky muscular areas.
'Pronged' rubber applicator		Used on bulky muscular areas and fatty tissue such as the gluteals and thighs; used for petrissage effect.
'Football' rubber applicator		Used on loose flabby areas of the skin such as the abdominal walls; also used over the colon to promote peristalsis; used for petrissage effect.
Directional stroking applicator	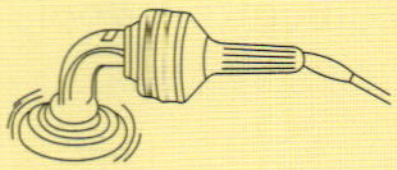	Allows the application of tapotement massage technique on the tissues. It also enables the movement of fluid tissue, this having a lymphatic drainage effect by directing the movement of tissue fluids.
'Spiky' rubber applicator	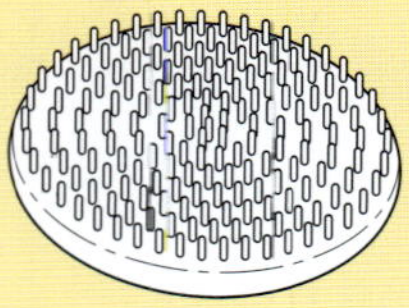	Used generally over the body to stimulate the nerve endings and create a rapid hyperemia; improves a dry skin condition by removing surface dead skin cells; used for percussion effect.
'Lighthouse' rubber applicator	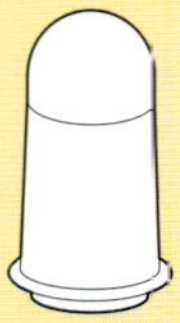	Used to treat tension nodules on the upper trapezius and may be used either side of the spine and around the knee; used for friction effect.

Common applicator attachments for hand-held model

Name of attachment	*Picture*	*Use and effect*
'Egg box' applicator	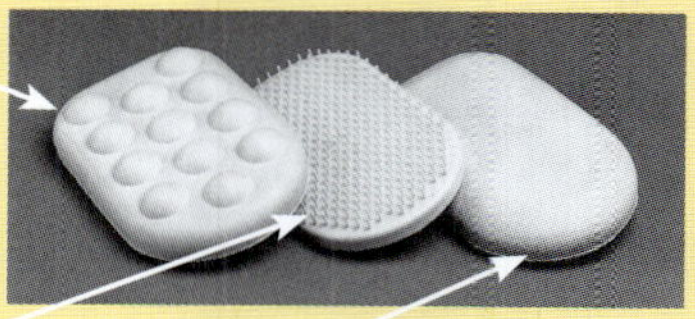	Used on bulky muscular areas and fatty tissue such as the gluteals and the thighs.
'Spiky' applicator		Used generally over the body to stimulate the nerve endings and create a rapid hyperemia.
'Smooth' applicator		Used for effleurage and petrissage effects.

Contra-indications

During the client assessment, if you find any of the following in the service area, gyratory massage service must not be carried out:

- skin inflammation
- broken skin
- highly vascular skin
- hypersensitive skin
- painful joints
- recent fractures
- excessively hairy areas
- thrombosis/phlebitis
- bony areas
- varicose veins
- medical oedema
- senile skin
- skin tags, moles

Gyratory massage service must not be carried out over the abdomen of a pregnant client or during menstruation.

Sterilization and disinfection

After use, attachments should be washed in warm soapy water to remove talc, dead skin cells and sebum. They should then be dried and disinfected in an UV cabinet. Disposable protective attachment coverings may be purchased from larger wholesalers.

Preparation of the service area

- Cover the service couch with clean towels.
- Check all general electrical safety precautions.
- Select applicator attachments for the area(s) to be treated. These should be placed on a trolley or in the equipment tray provided if using the floor-standing unit.
- Ensure there is enough floor space in the service area for your equipment when performing the service

Preparation of the beauty therapist

- Collect the client's record card
- Sanitize your hands before handling the client.
- Assess the client, discuss the client's lifestyle pattern and the objectives for the service.
- Agree on an appropriate service plan.

ALWAYS REMEMBER

Gyratory massage suitability
Gyratory massage is indicated for larger areas of the body and areas of excess adipose tissue and muscle bulk. It is not suitable for the chest area and other bony areas.

HEALTH & SAFETY

Attachments hygiene
It will be necessary to have several sets of attachments to allow for effective cleaning and disinfection and to maintain their durability and quality.

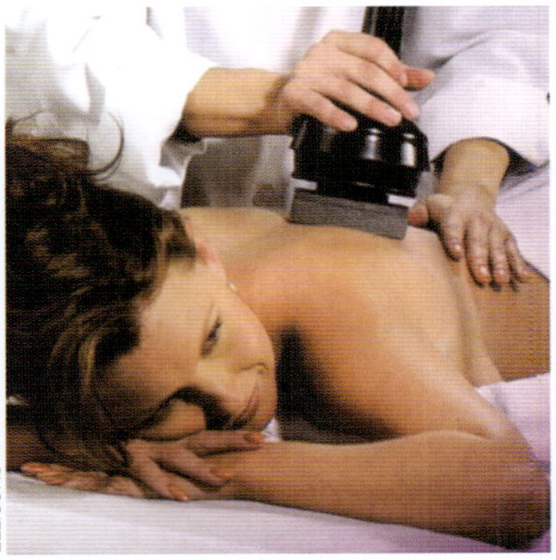
ELLISONS

Gyratory massage to the back

HEALTH & SAFETY

Electrical leads

Ensure the electrical lead cannot be tripped over. Floor-standing equipment should be on a stable surface.

TOP TIP

Pre-heating

A pre-heating service is beneficial before application as the therapeutic effects are created more rapidly when the tissues have been warmed.

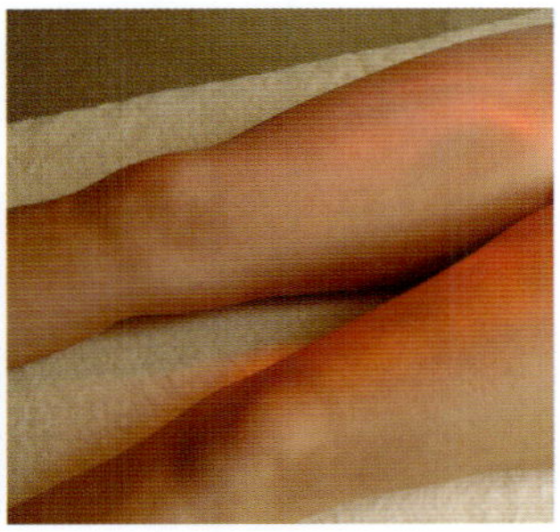
CARLTON BEAUTY + SPA LTD

Pre-heating infrared service

- If this is a repeat service, check the client's progress against targets set and provide support and advice as necessary.

Preparation of the client

- Remove all jewellery from the service area.
- Explain the service sensation to the client, explaining how the skin will become warm and reddened. Demonstrate the noise of the motor to the client.
- Expose the part of the body to be treated and cover all other areas.
- Cleanse and dry the client's skin.
- Apply a dry medium, such as an unperfumed talc, to aid service application.

Body service application

The order of service application is usually as follows: arms, abdomen, front of the legs. The client then turns over and the back of the legs, gluteals and back are treated.

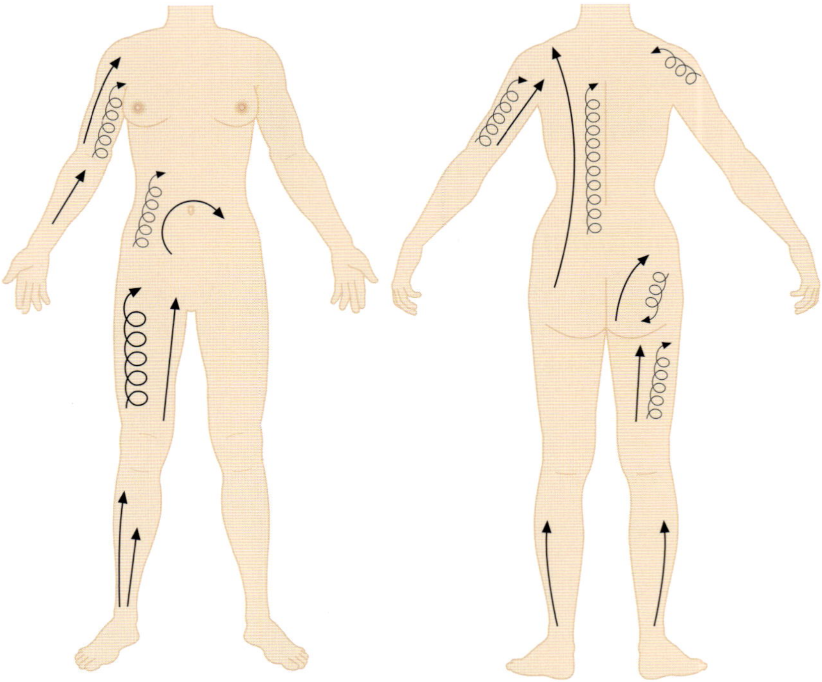

Gliding strokes towards the venous return lymphatic nodes

Round smooth sponge applicator
Round smooth massage head
Curved sponge applicator
Spiky rubber applicator
Two-ball rubber applicator

Rotary movements along muscle length or localized area

Round smooth applicator

Eggbox rubber applicator
Two-ball rubber applicator
Pronged rubber applicator
Football rubber applicator
Lighthouse rubber applicator (used on upper fibres of trapezius muscle)

Sample application to anterior and posterior body

Floor-standing model Attachments must be securely fixed to the head before switching the motor on.

1 Switch the machine on at the mains and at the mains switch on the machine.

2 Commence service with the effleurage applicators in the direction of lymphatic and venous flow. When treating the limbs, always apply effleurage strokes towards the trunk in one direction.

3 Apply four to six strokes to cover the whole service area. One hand may be used to lead or follow the applicator head to soothe the skin.

Effleurage to the abdomen is to the lateral abdominal wall and following the direction of the colon to aid peristalsis.

4 Switch off the machine to change applicator heads.

5 Cover each part as treated with a clean towel for modesty and to keep the client warm.

6 Follow with the petrissage applicators. Petrissage commences at the upper service part and descends in a rotary application.

7 Lift and guide the tissues under the applicator head with one hand.

8 Continue application until a mild erythema is created upon the skin's surface.

9 Follow with the friction applicator. Small, localized rotary movements are applied to the service area. Common areas of service include:

- the upper fibres of the trapezius – to relieve tension
- either side of the spine – to stimulate and induce relaxation
- around the knee – for the mobilization of adhesions or stiffness

10 Follow with the percussion applicator. Percussion is applied in one direction in a flowing stroke as with effleurage. Use one hand to lead or follow each application stroke. Complete each service area with the effleurage applicator head to soothe the skin.

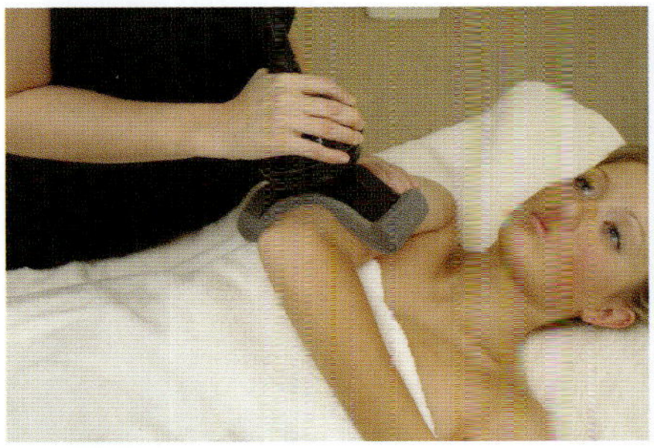

CARLTON BEAUTY + SPA LTD

Effleurage to the arms

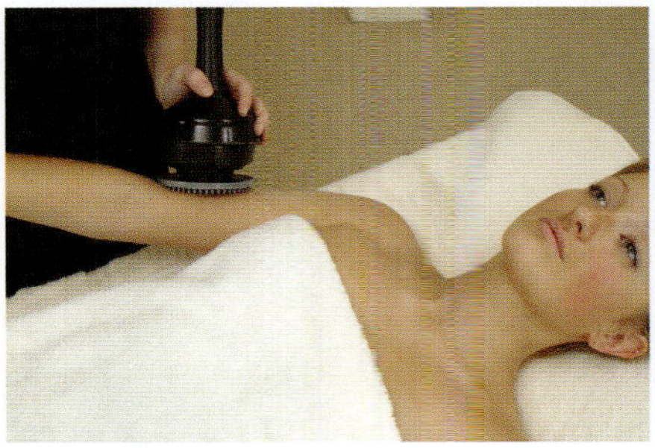

CARLTON BEAUTY + SPA LTD

Percussion 'spiky' application

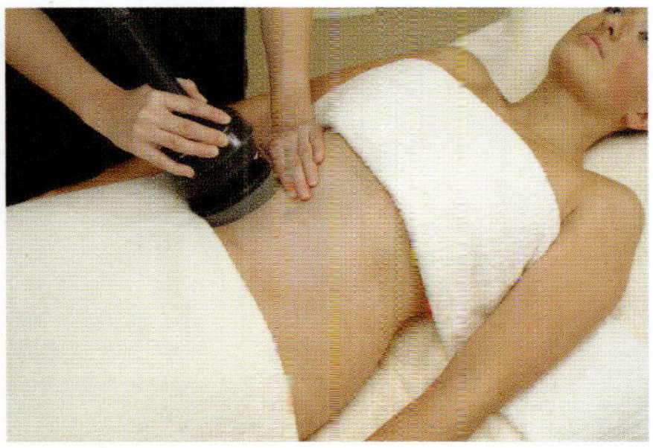

CARLTON BEAUTY + SPA LTD

Effleurage to the abdomen

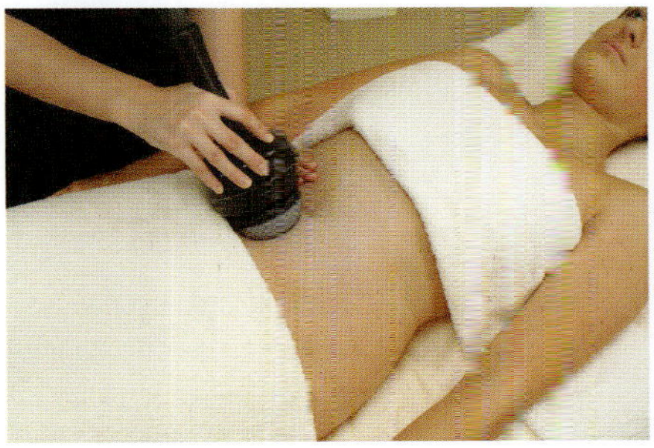

CARLTON BEAUTY + SPA LTD

Petrissage 'football' application to aid peristalsis

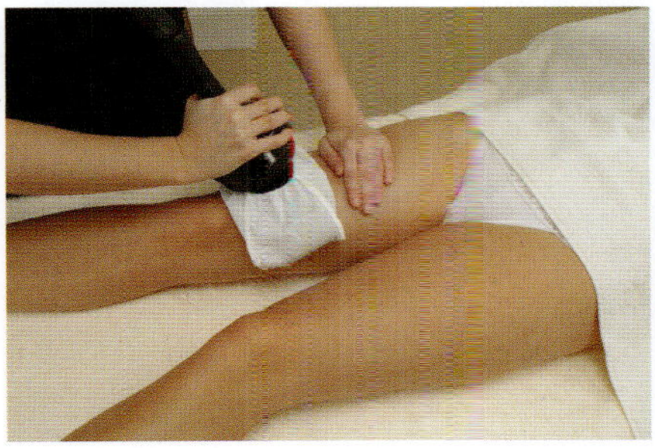

CARLTON BEAUTY + SPA LTD

Effleurage to the front (anterior) legs

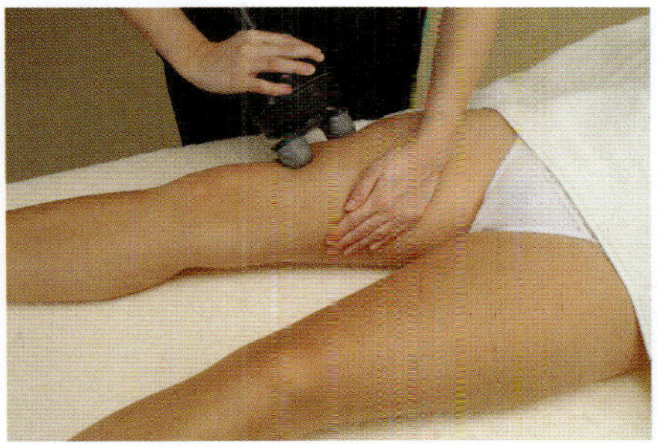

CARLTON BEAUTY + SPA LTD

Petrissage two-ball rubber application

11 Switch off the machine.

12 Remove the massage medium as necessary on completion of service.

13 Switch off and unplug the machine at the mains.

14 Complete details of the service on the client's record card.

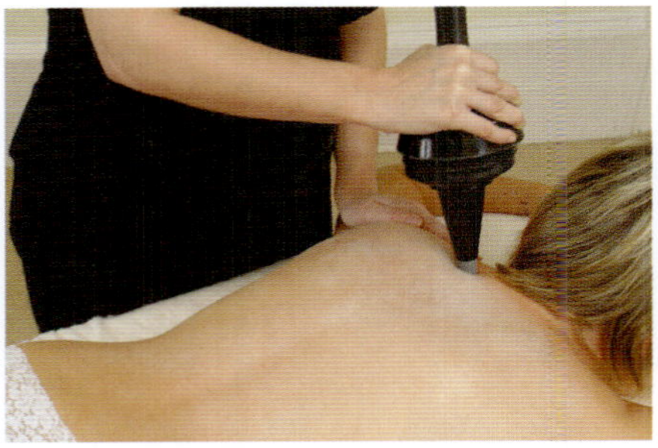
CARLTON BEAUTY + SPA LTD

Friction 'lighthouse' application to upper fibres of the trapezius

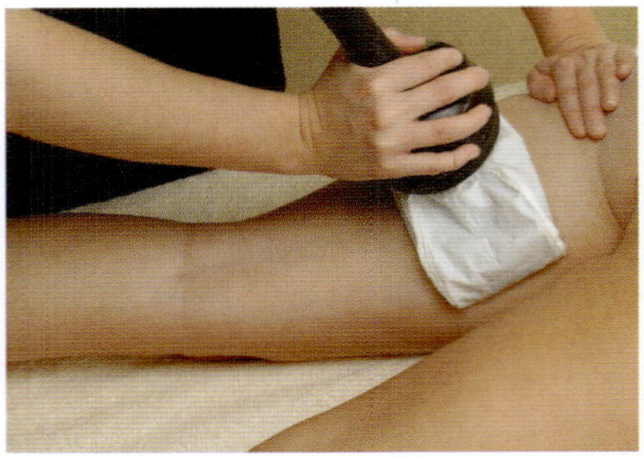
CARLTON BEAUTY + SPA LTD

Effleurage to the back (posterior) thigh (disposable covering shown)

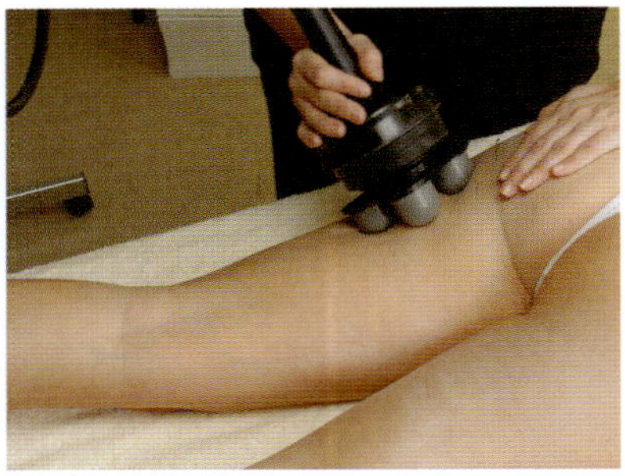
CARLTON BEAUTY + SPA LTD

Petrissage 'eggbox' application to legs, hip and gluteal area

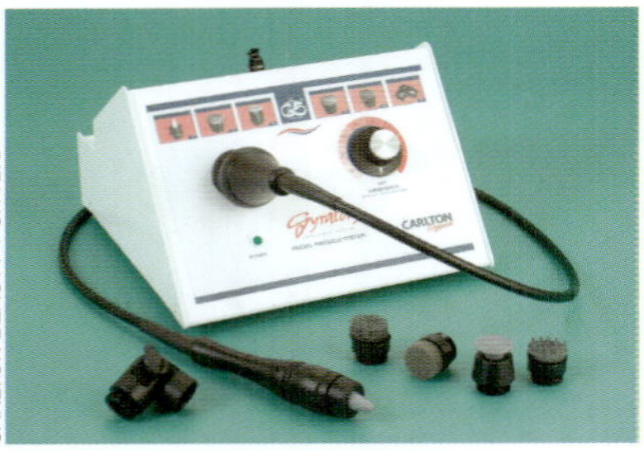
CARLTON BEAUTY + SPA LTD

Gyratory massage machine

Step-by-step: Gyratory massage facial application

Gyratory massage is available for face, neck and chest application. These areas are not a competence requirement for your assessment evidence but are provided for you as additional knowledge on how this service may be applied.

The applicator heads can be applied to achieve a deep cleansing, skin toning and lymphatic drainage effect. Maximum service time 35 minutes in total.

CARLTON BEAUTY + SPA LTD

1 Cleanse – A manual cleanse starts the treatment. Reapply cleansing milk and select sponge applicator. Moving in small circular movements, work from the neck up to the forehead for 3–5 minutes.

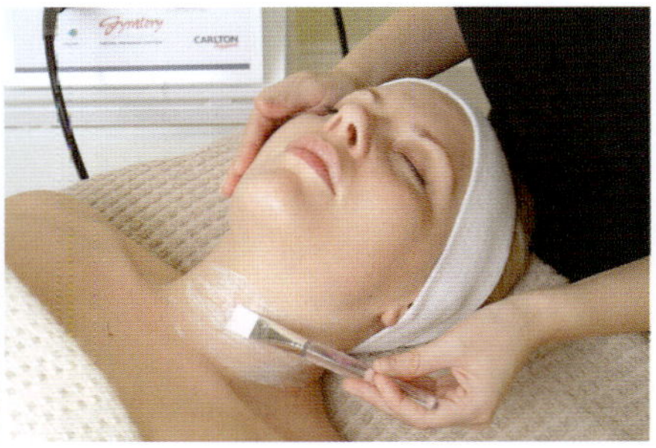
CARLTON BEAUTY + SPA LTD

2 Exfoliation – Remove cleansing milk and apply exfoliating cream to the area.

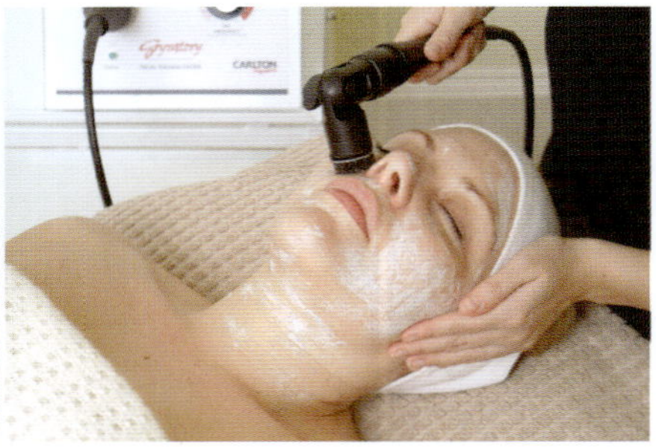
CARLTON BEAUTY + SPA LTD

3 Exfoliation – Select coarse foam sponge. Using the same movements as in the cleansing stage, work for 3–5 minutes. Remove excess cream and skin debris from the skin.

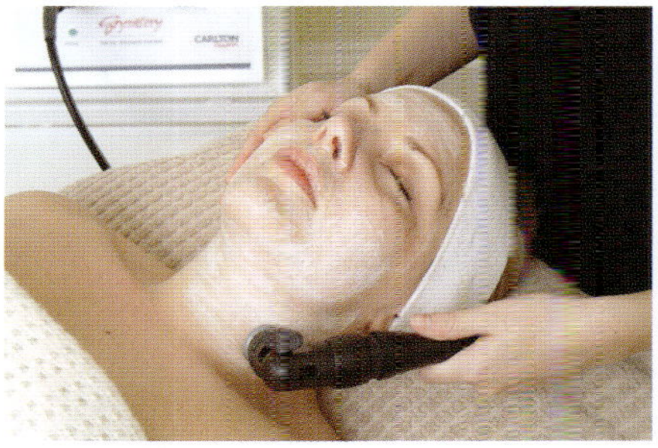

CARLTON BEAUTY + SPA LTD

4 Lymphatic drainage – Apply massage cream to face and neck. Select rubber applicator. Starting at the base of the neck work upwards towards the relevant lymph nodes, using a lymphatic drainage technique for 5 minutes.

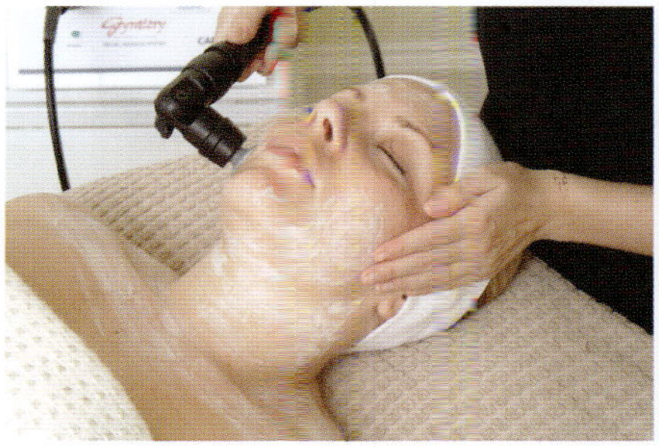

CARLTON BEAUTY + SPA LTD

5 Facial massage – Using rubber applicator perform an effleurage movement working over the face and neck for 2 minutes. Apply more massage cream if required to provide adequate slip.

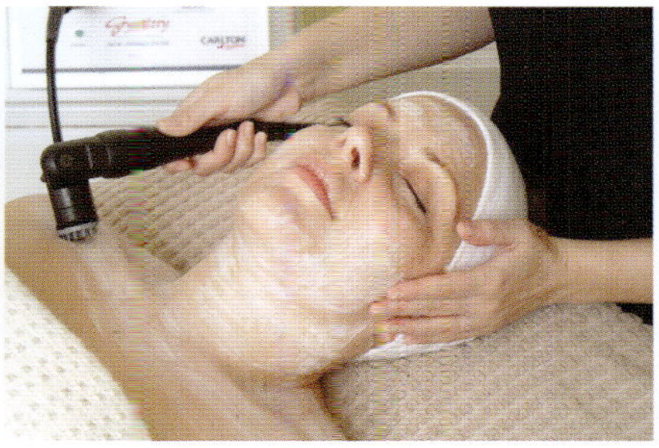

CARLTON BEAUTY + SPA LTD

6 Stimulating – Select multiple prong applicator. Using circular sweeping movements work across chin, neck, chest, shoulders and face for 3 minutes. Using the rubber applicator, work with stroking movements from the centre of the forehead outwards for 3 minutes. Then perform effleurage movement as before for 2 minutes. Remove massage cream.

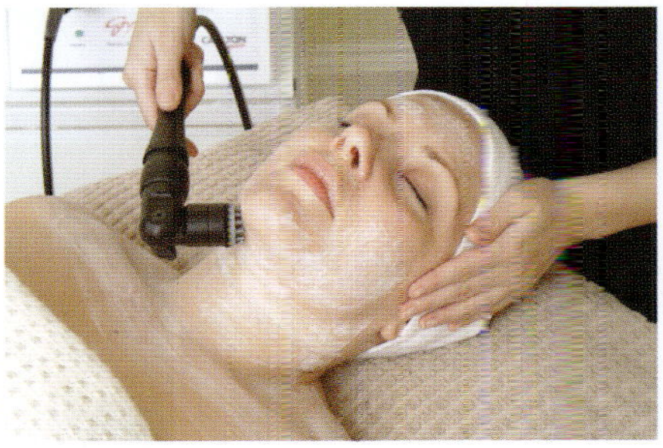

CARLTON BEAUTY + SPA LTD

7 Penetration of product – Apply appropriate moisturising skin preparation to the face and neck. Select multiple prong applicator. Working from the neck to the forehead use soothing strokes to penetrate cream into the skin for 3–5 minutes.

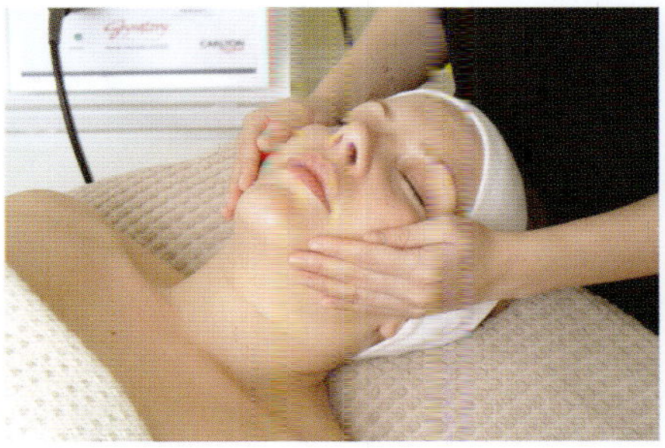

CARLTON BEAUTY + SPA LTD

8 Manual massage – Manually massage the remaining moist. using into the face, neck and chest.

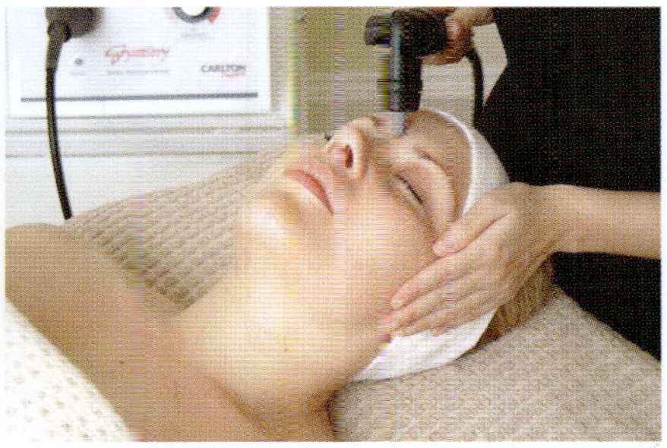

CARLTON BEAUTY + SPA LTD

9 Anti-wrinkle – Select firm rubber tip applicator. Work in straight lines along fine lines and wrinkles on neck and face for 2 minutes.

10 Anti-wrinkle – Using firm rubber tip applicator work on wrinkles and fine lines using a zig-zag movement on face and neck for 3 minutes.

Aftercare

Manual massage may be applied to soothe the skin following service application. This will also increase the lymphatic drainage effect. Other services may also be offered which achieve a different complimentary effect.

Offer client water for hydration.

The use of skincare preparations designed to increase skin firmness or tone a localized problem area should be encouraged to support the salon service. These include gels and creams which are applied in light circular movements, working in an upwards direction. Nutritional advice should be given if the client is on a weight-reducing diet. Supportive exercises for the body may also be given.

HEALTH & SAFETY

Kidneys and breast area

Avoid application over the kidneys and breast area.

TOP TIP

Technique

Ensure each part of the applicator is in contact with the part being treated to avoid uneven pressure of application, which could result in bruising. Support the tissues with one hand to maximize the effect.

BEST PRACTICE

Apply the applicator heads according to their use and effect, see pages 257–258.

Contra-actions

Bruising, caused by:

- too heavy an application
- incorrect choice of applicator head for service area
- too lengthy a service application

Skin scratching and irritation caused by:

- incorrect choice and application of applicator head (usually the sponge and spiky applicator)

Excessive erythema caused by:

- incorrect choice and application of applicator head
- too lengthy a service application
- skin allergic to sponge if used
- too heavy an application

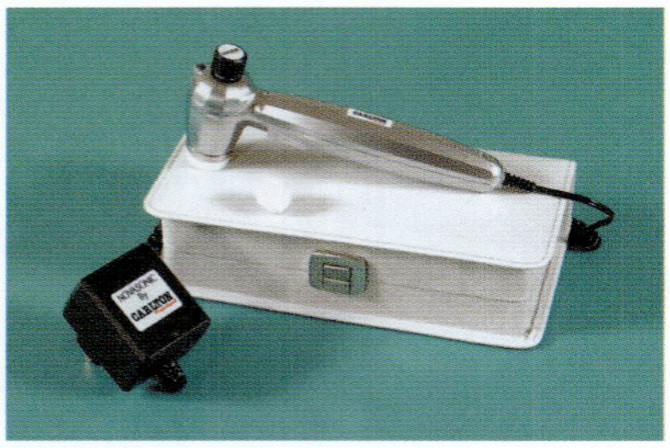

CARLTON PROFESSIONAL

Audio sonic machine

Audio sonic

Audio sonic is a hand-held electrical massage service which is applied to localized areas of the face or body. The equipment produces sound waves, of 100–10 000 Hertz heard as a humming noise, which vibrate through the skin's cells and tissues. The vibrations travel approximately 5 cm into the skin without any tissue damage. It is particularly beneficial for the service of sensitive areas or hypersensitive skin, because no surface friction is created as with other massage services.

General effects:

- increases blood circulation, which improves skin colour and transports nutrients and oxygen to the skin's cells and muscles
- increases venous and lymph circulation which enhances the removal of waste and toxins
- improves skin texture by removal of surface skin cells (desquamation)
- relaxation of tense muscles
- softening of areas of soft adipose tissue
- stimulation of skin function, increasing sebaceous gland activity

Body use:

- cellulite, particularly soft fat which offers less resistance than hard fat
- deep relaxation of contracted muscle tissue
- fibrositis nodules in the trapezius muscle

Facial use:

- hypersensitive or vascular skin conditions
- mature skin

Anatomy and physiology

Nodules are shaken and vibrated by the sound waves. These compress and decompress the soft tissues. During compression the cells press together, moving tissue fluid including waste and toxins. Decompression of the tissues allows fresh blood to circulate through the area bringing fresh oxygen and nutrients.

Audio sonic effects

An electromagnet is used in audio sonic therapy. The current flows first in one direction and then the other, which causes a coil of the electromagnet to move backwards and forwards. This movement passes to the head of the appliance which, when applied to the skin, transmits to the tissues as a vibration. The depth of sound pitch creating the vibrations can be increased or decreased affecting the depth of travel into the tissues. Intensity is controlled by an adjustment knob. Frequency is the number of vibrations per second.

Reception

- Complete personal details on the client's record card.
- Question the client to check for possible contra-indications.

The service is usually applied to localized areas and effects are achieved quickly. Allow 10 minutes for the service depending on the service area. The client may receive the service as necessary.

EQUIPMENT AND MATERIALS LIST

ELLISONS

Record card
Confidential record of details of each client registered at the salon

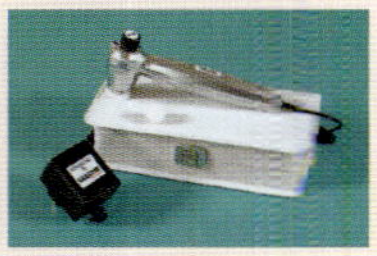

CARLTON PROFESSIONAL

Audio sonic machine with attachment heads

YOU WILL ALSO NEED:

Skincare preparation To cleanse the skin

Talc, oil or cream To allow the attachment head to move easily across the skin's surface

Clean cotton wool To cleanse the skin and apply talc to the service area

Clean tissue To blot the skin dry

Surgical spirit To clean heads after use

Attachment heads for audio sonic

Name of attachment	*Use and effect*
Flat plate or disc	Facial and body use. Used over larger areas.
Hard ball	Fibrositis nodule and deep body service. Used over smaller areas for an intensified effect.

Contra-indications

During the client assessment, if you find any of the following in the service area, audio sonic service must not be carried out:

- skin inflammation
- skin disorder such as psoriasis and eczema
- excessive broken veins
- bony area
- very slim clients
- broken skin
- painful inflamed joints
- varicose veins
- metallic implants
- recent fractures
- the eye area, because the skin is fine and sensitive so bruising may occur

Sterilization and disinfection

After use, attachment heads should be washed in warm soapy water to remove talc/cream, dead skin cells and sebum. Wipe over the heads with surgical spirit applied with clean cotton wool. They should then be disinfected in the UV cabinet.

> Always check settings on face and body electrical equipment before commencing the service.
>
> **Claire Burrell**

Preparation of the service area

- Cover the service couch with clean towels and disposable paper roll.
- If the client is to be seated, ensure the seat is at the correct height and placed in an area close to the electrical point.
- Check all electrical safety precautions.
- Select applicator heads for the area(s) to be treated. These should be placed on a clean trolley surface.

Preparation of the beauty therapist

- Collect the client's record card.
- Wash your hands before handling the client.
- Assess the client, discuss the client's lifestyle pattern and objectives for the service.
- Agree on an appropriate service plan.
- If this is a repeat service, check the client's progress and provide advice as necessary.

Preparation of the client

- Remove all jewellery and accessories from the service area.
- Explain the service sensation to the client, and how the skin will become warm and slightly reddened. Demonstrate to the client the noise the equipment will make.
- Expose the service area: all other areas should be covered.

- Cleanse and dry the client's skin.
- Apply a medium to the skin to aid the service application

Service application

Attachments must be securely fixed to the head before switching the motor on.

1. Switch the machine on at the mains and at the switch on the machine.
2. Test the machine and adjust the intensity as appropriate. Clean the attachment head with surgical spirit.
3. Select the head to be used and attach it securely to the equipment.
4. For full body application commence service with the soles of the feet, calves, thighs, hand, forearm and upper arm.
5. Apply the head to the skin and follow the muscle length where tension is present, moving in a vertical or horizontal direction in straight lines or in a circular movement upwards towards the heart.
6. Increase or decrease sound frequency as you work over different areas using the adjustment control. It is necessary to reduce the frequency over bony areas.
7. Switch off the machine to change applicator heads.
8. Cover the body part when treated, for modesty and to keep the client warm.
9. Switch off the machine.
10. Remove the massage medium as necessary on completion of the service. If applied as part of a facial service you may wish to apply a mask.
11. Switch off and unplug the equipment at the mains.
12. Complete details on the client's record card.

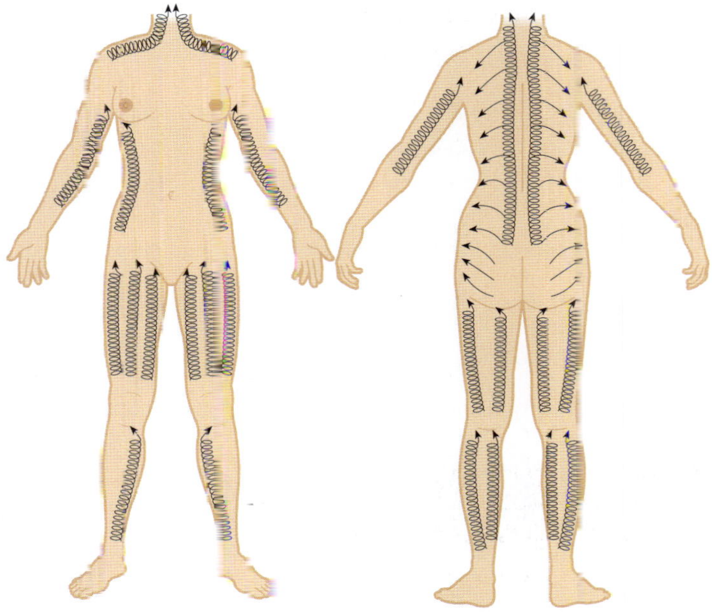

Audio sonic application to body – anterior and posterior, using vertical, horizontal and circular movements

HEALTH & SAFETY

Application pressure
Never apply pressure, this is unnecessary and may cause skin irritation.

TOP TIP

Treating bony areas
Place your free hand over the bony area and apply the applicator head over the hand. This will reduce the vibrations and avoid irritation.

This is particularly beneficial when treating the facial area.

Aftercare

The use of facial and body skincare preparations designed to treat the skin should be encouraged to support the service. Advice on correct posture and exercises may be given when this is the cause of the problem, such as tension nodules in muscles. If the service was for relaxation, you might give advice on relaxing bath products and massage techniques that could be used at home.

Contra-actions

- discomfort caused by insufficient protection and incorrect frequency when treating bony parts
- excessive erythema caused by too lengthy treatment of the skin
- skin irritation caused by excessive pressure during application
- excessive frequency intensity leading to bruising on delicate areas

Vacuum suction service – lymphatic drainage equipment

Vacuum suction is a mechanical service which can be applied to either the face or the body. External suction is applied to the surface tissues causing lift and stimulation of the underlying structures.

There are two methods of application: **static**, where the cup is held in one position; and **gliding**, where the cup is moved in the direction of the local lymphatic flow to the nearest lymph node. A deep lymphatic massage is provided.

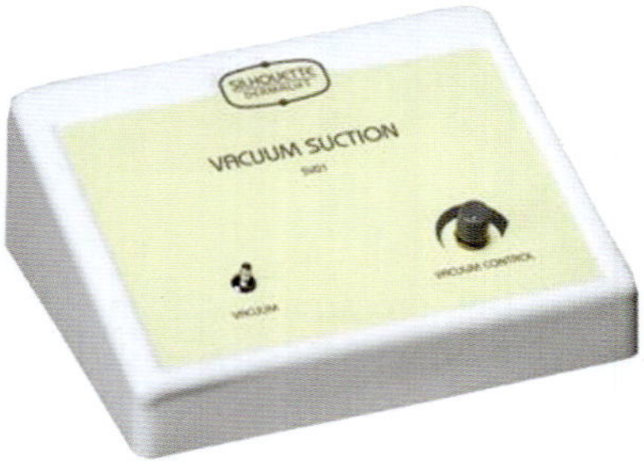

SILHOUETTE-DERMALIFT

Vacuum suction unit

General effects:

- The blood and lymphatic vessels dilate, improving blood and lymphatic circulation.
- Non-medical swelling and puffiness is reduced, by improving the dispersal of accumulated tissue fluids and waste products from the area.
- Localized fatty deposits can be softened. The fat is more readily transported for utilization in the increased lymphatic flow.
- Skin texture is improved by absorption of the specific oils/creams and removing the surface dead skin cells (desquamation).

COURSEMATE

For a video on vacuum suction service – lymphatic drainage, please visit this book's accompanying CourseMate.

Body use:

- to improve a sluggish circulation, increased blood and lymphatic flow
- to reduce fatty deposits on the thighs, abdomen and buttocks
- to improve areas of 'cellulite'
- to treat areas of non-medical swelling; this tissue fluid accumulation is described as **oedema**

Facial use:

- cleansing action, to remove surface cells and to gently draw out sebum, make-up and impurities
- to improve the appearance of skin and reduce fine lines

- to stimulate a sluggish lymphatic circulation and promote skin respiration
- to treat a dry skin condition by stimulating the activity of the sebaceous glands

Anatomy and physiology

Vacuum suction is aimed at improving the circulation of **lymph**. Lymph fluid, which is transported in the lymphatic system is composed of water, salts and waste products and fatty materials of body metabolism and digestion.

Lymph vessels have valves at intervals along their length to prevent backflow. Under normal circumstances lymph flow is caused by pressure applied on the vessels as nearby muscles contract and relax, either in normal movement or when exercising. As vacuum suction service is applied, it too alternately applies and releases pressure over the lymphatic vessels, thereby moving the lymph.

Directing the gliding movements in the direction of the lymphatic flow towards the nearest lymph node (gland) enhances the effect and result. Therefore, when applying the service to the face or body it is necessary to know where the relevant lymph nodes are situated (see Chapter 2, pages 83–85).

Vacuum suction equipment

The vacuum suction unit comprises a vacuum pump driven by an electric motor. Dome-shaped glass cups are attached to the machine by plastic tubing. As the vacuum pump reduces atmospheric pressure, air is sucked out of the cup which draws the skin and subcutaneous tissues into the cup. The degree of suction is indicated by a gauge, and the vacuum level should be set according to the part being treated. This is set by the control valve.

In some machines, the static vacuum suction is pulsed in differing levels of vacuum intensity, causing the skin and subcutaneous tissue to rise and fall underneath each cup.

Some machines blow air, which is used to apply cosmetic oils and liquids. This feature, created by a pulsation valve, can also be used to create the effect of 'air massage', where the vacuum is pulsed and the degree of suction rises and falls as it travels over the skin's surface, creating a toning effect.

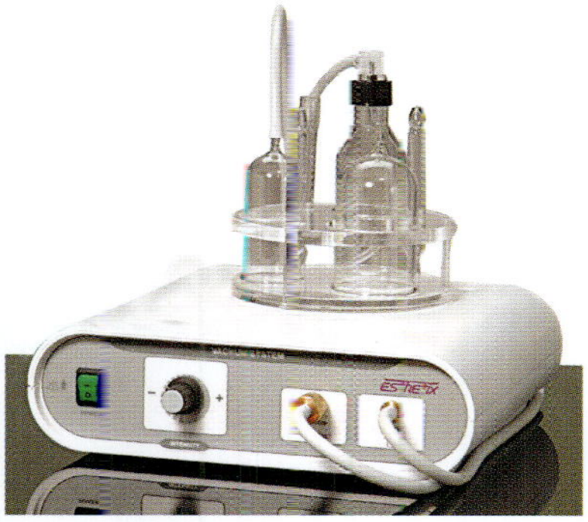
ELLISONS

Vacuum suction unit

TOP TIP

Finger holes

Some glass cups have finger holes. By covering the holes, the vacuum is created and the tissue is lifted. By removing the finger the vacuum is released and the tissue is lowered.

Reception

Vacuum service is usually given as part of a programme in conjunction with other services as planned by the beauty therapist. Generally, 20–40 minutes is allowed for body application, 5–12 minutes for facial application.

Body vacuum is usually booked as a course of ten services, applied two to three times per week. Facial vacuum suction service may be applied every 4–6 weeks.

TOP TIP

Effort required

Less effort is required by the beauty therapist when performing static pulsating vacuum suction service, although practice is required to select the correct pressure in each individual cup.

TOP TIP

Size of cup

Cups should be selected according to the size of the part being treated; the larger the part, the greater the diameter of the cup.

EQUIPMENT AND MATERIALS LIST

ELLISONS

Record card
Confidential record of the details of every client registered at the salon

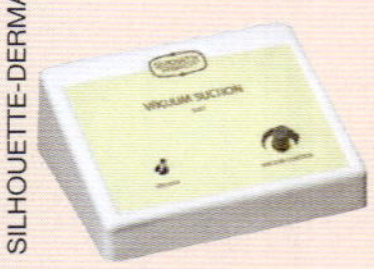

SILHOUETTE-DERMALIFT

Vacuum suction facial/body or combined unit

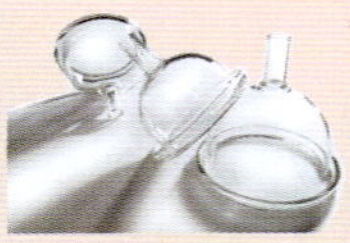

SILHOUETTE-DERMALIFT

Glass cups of various sizes
Glass apertures known as ventouses are also available for facial application. The cups must be clear to allow you to see the degree of suction at all times

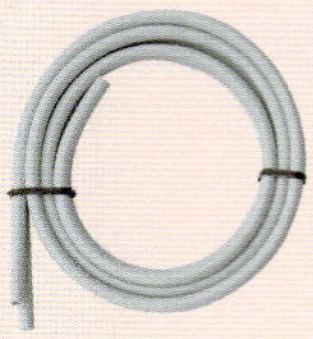

SILHOUETTE-DERMALIFT

Plastic or silicone tubing attached to vacuum outlet

YOU WILL ALSO NEED:

Oil or cream To act as a lubricant and provide movement of the cup, and to act as a seal between the skin and the cup and may contain therapeutic ingredients

Tissues For protection of the client's clothes (body service)

Damp cotton wool To cleanse skin and remove excess lubricant

Different types of vacuum cup

Glass cup	*Picture*	*Use and effect*
Body cup: various diameters available from 2–10 cm	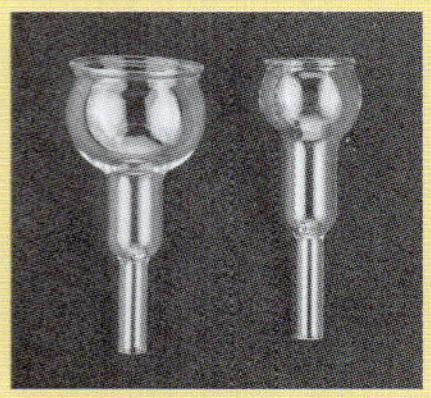 SILHOUETTE-DERMALIFT	All areas of the body including the back where muscular tension may also be relieved.
Facial cup: various diameters available from small to medium	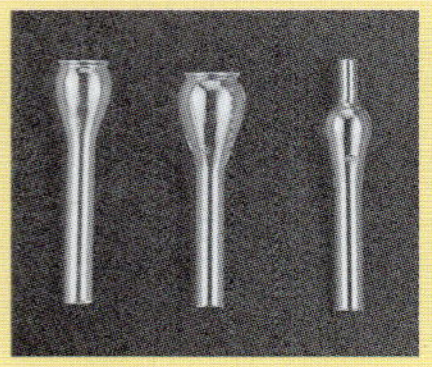 SILHOUETTE-DERMALIFT	General skin cleansing; lymphatic drainage of the face and neck; treatment of fatty deposits (double chin condition).
Comedone ventouse	 SILHOUETTE-DERMALIFT	Mechanical comedone extraction; congested areas around the chin and nose.
Flat ventouse	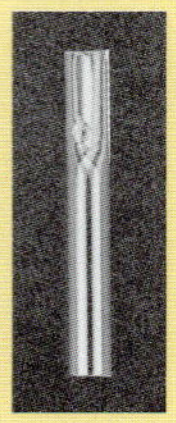 SILHOUETTE-DERMALIFT	Treatment of expression lines; can also be used for general skin cleansing and superficial lymphatic drainage.

Contra-indications

If the client has any of the following, vacuum suction service should not be carried out:

- reduced (poor) skin elasticity (including stretch marks and scar tissue) – the skin will be damaged by the stretching action on the tissues
- broken veins and capillaries – as the skin is delicate the condition may be worsened
- senile skin – as the skin ages it loses both strength and elasticity and the service may cause discomfort and damage
- hypersensitive skin and skin inflammation
- varicose veins – the service would put unnecessary pressure on the veins
- bruised skin
- thrombosis, phlebitis
- glandular swelling
- over infected pustular areas, e.g. accompanying an acne vulgaris skin condition.

Vacuum suction service should not be carried out on breast tissue.

Sterilization and disinfection

After service, remove oil from the cups and plastic tubes with warm water and detergent. The cups should then be thoroughly rinsed, dried and disinfected in an UV sterilizing cabinet.

Preparation of the service area

- Cover the service couch with a clean towel.
- Check all general safety precautions.
- Test the machine to ensure it is in good working order.
- Select cups of appropriate size and type to treat the client's needs. Ideally this should be one size smaller than the part to be treated. Attach the cups and tubing to the machine.
- Switch on the machine at the mains and check the vacuum setting of the unit on your own skin; this is usually done on the relaxed upper arm for a body cup or on the lower arm for a facial cup/ventouse. Slowly increase the intensity until the skin visibly rises into the cup.
- Return the vacuum intensity to zero and switch off the machine.
- Clean the cup/ventouse with a disinfectant agent after testing.

Preparation of the beauty therapist

- Collect the client's record card.
- Wash your hands before handling the client.
- Assess the client; discuss the client's lifestyle and the objectives for the service.
- Agree on an appropriate service plan.
- If this is a repeat service, check the client's progress against targets set and provide support and advice as necessary.

HEALTH & SAFETY

Removing the cup

Always remember to release the vacuum before removing the cup from the skin to avoid skin damage such as bruising and thread veins.

BEST PRACTICE

Cleaning

Use a small, flexible spiral brush to clean the inside of facial ventouses where dead skin cells and oil will readily accumulate. Glass cups may be sterilized in the autoclave.

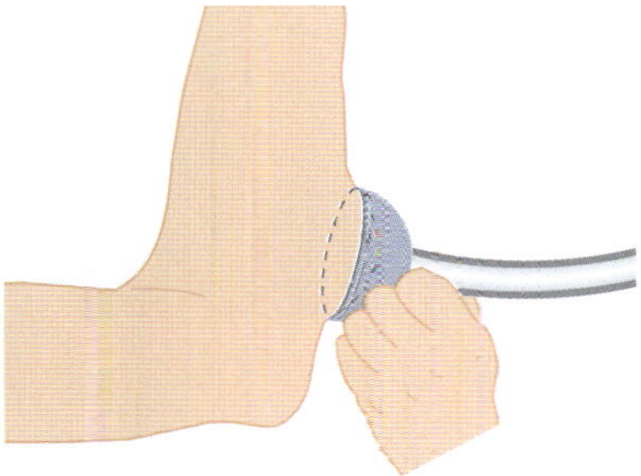

Checking the vacuum setting pressure of the unit before use

TOP TIP

Pre-heating

A pre-heating service to prepare for facial vacuum service may be steam; for body service, a sauna or steam service may be given. Remember, though, that the vacuum effects will be achieved more quickly so service time must be reduced accordingly.

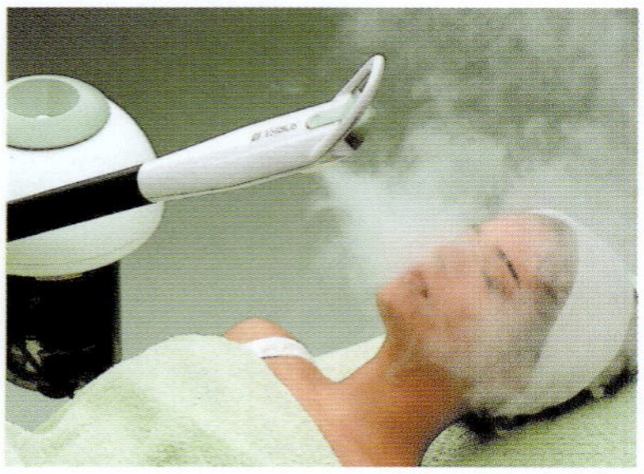

BEAUTY EXPRESS LTD

Steam pre-heating service

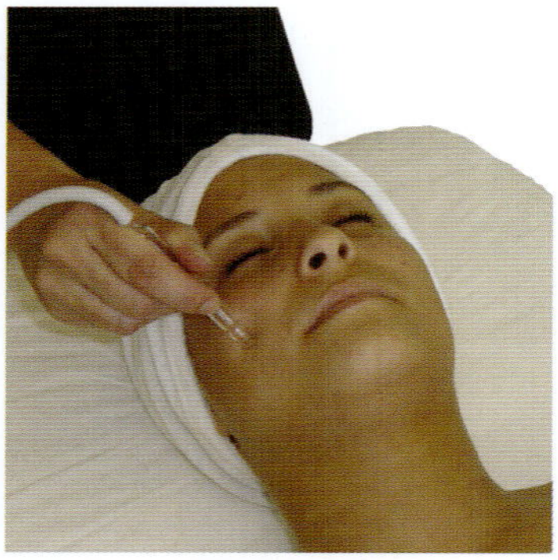

ELLISONS

Facial vacuum suction

HEALTH & SAFETY

Eyes

Avoid excessive treatment around the delicate eye tissue to prevent stretching. Only use a flat head ventouse for the treatment of lines in this area.

Preparation of the client

Facial service

- Instruct the client to remove upper clothing to underwear. Position the client comfortably on the couch in a supine semi-reclined position and cover with a clean towel.
- Remove all jewellery from the service area.
- Check the area of service for visible contra-indications.
- Cleanse and tone the skin of the face and neck. Blot the skin dry with a soft facial tissue.
- Analyze the client's skin using a magnifying lamp. Question the client further where necessary to check information in relation to the client's skin condition.
- Discuss the service effect and explain the service sensation to the client, i.e. that there will be a gentle pulling of the skin, creating a warming, stimulating effect.
- Usually a pre-heating service is carried out to prepare and stimulate the service area so that it is more receptive. If a client has had a pre-heating service, ensure that they are kept warm to maximize the effect.
- Apply sufficient lubricant to the service area to allow easy movement across the skin.

Body service

- Remove all jewellery from the service area.
- Instruct the client to remove all clothing except underwear.
- If the purpose of the service is for body contouring, measure the client and record this on the client's record card.
- Position the client on the service couch. This will be in a supine or prone position depending on the part to be treated.
- Cleanse the skin using witch hazel and blot dry with paper tissue.
- Discuss the service effect and explain the service sensation to the client, i.e. there will be a gentle pulling of the skin, creating a warming, stimulating effect.

Service application

Facial gliding technique Facial vacuum suction may be applied for the purpose of facial cleansing, skin toning, improving skin functioning and facial contouring.

1. Select a suitable cosmetic lubricant and apply this in an even layer to the face and neck.
2. Switch the machine on at the mains.
3. Select the vacuum intensity for the part to be treated. Always begin the service on the lowest degree of vacuum until a comfortable level is reached (usually the cup is 20 per cent full with flesh), moving the cup at all times. Remember, less suction is required over the neck and bony areas of the face as there is less subcutaneous tissue here.
4. Starting at the base of the neck, direct each stroke in an upwards direction towards the relevant lymphatic node. Release the vacuum at the end of the stroke before removal of the cup.

5 Repeat each stroke on average four times.

6 Depending on the cup or ventouse used, break the vacuum by inserting the fingertip of the opposite hand underneath the cup, or lift the finger over the hole to release the vacuum.

7 Move the cup by half a width each time, repeat the stroke and continue application upwards to cover the facial area.

8 Return the vacuum intensity dial to zero and switch the machine off at the mains.

9 Remove the massage medium from the skin or follow the service with another complimentary service such as facial massage. Complete the service with a face mask, toning lotion and service moisturiser.

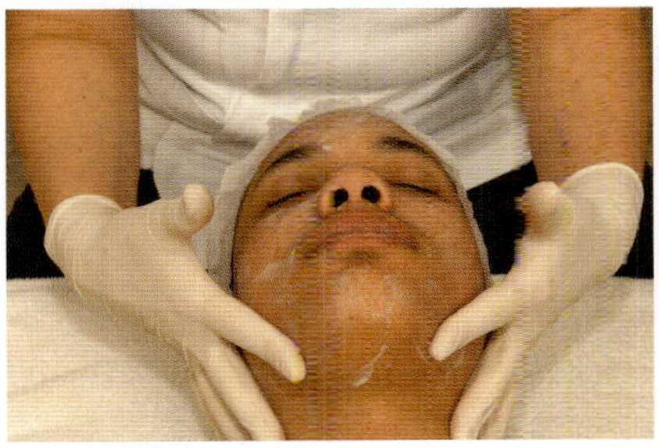

Pre-cleanse client

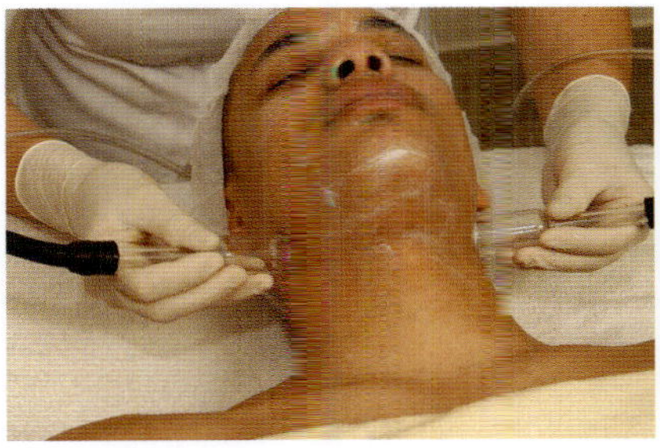

Direct each stroke upwards from the supra-clavicular lymph node towards the ub-mandibular lymph nodes shown

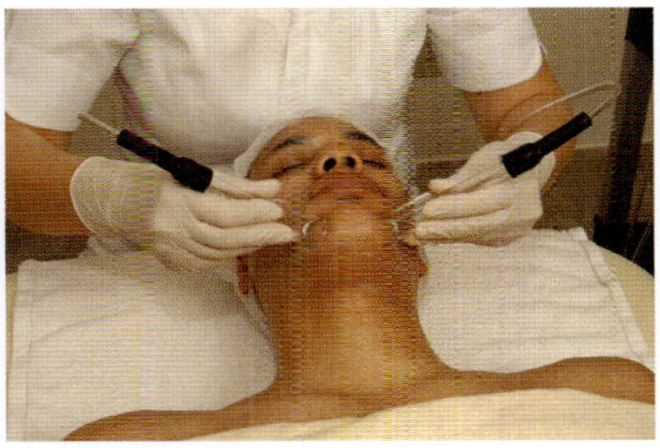

Move the cup upwards by half a width of previous stroke each time

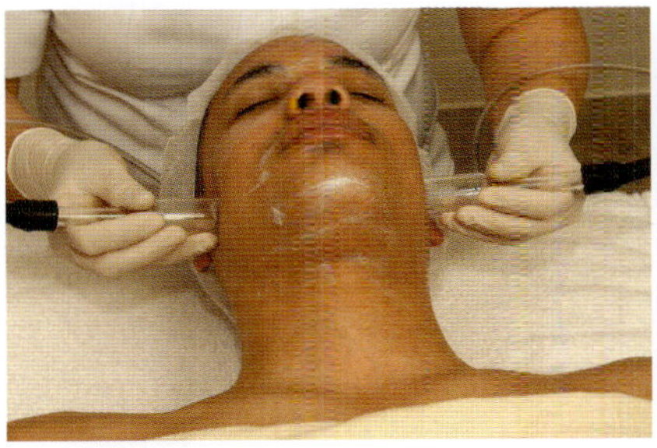

Direct strokes outwards from the centres of the face towards the parotid lymph nodes

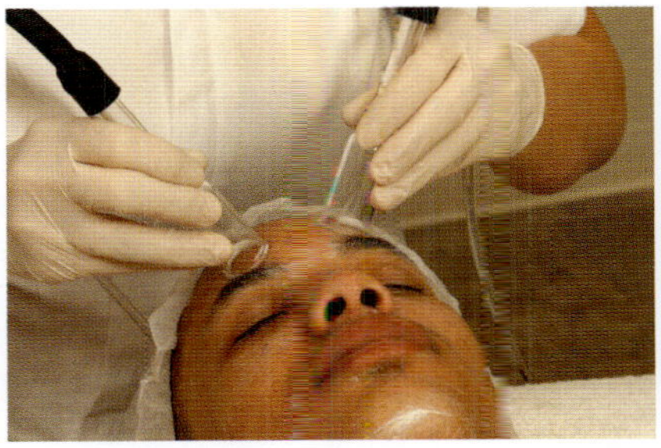

Direct strokes across forehead, downwards towards temple and return to supra-clavicular node

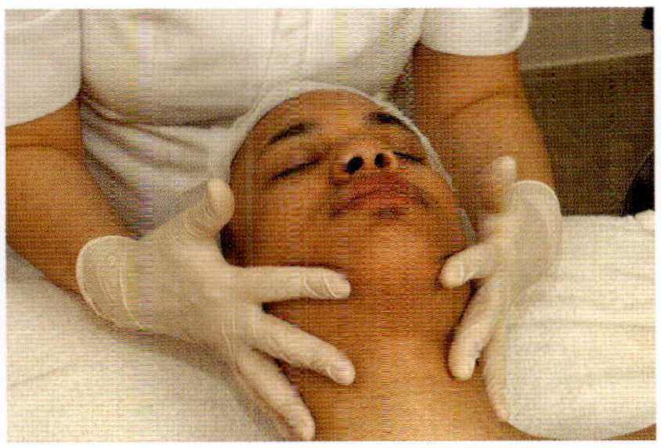

Follow with another service such as facial massage/mask if required.

ALWAYS REMEMBER

Technique

- Strokes should be rhythmical and flowing.
- Do not apply the strokes too fast as this will make the results less effective.
- Do not apply strokes directly over lymph nodes.
- Overlap each stroke by half the previous stroke.
- If contact with the skin is broken during the application of a stroke, commence the stroke again.

HEALTH & SAFETY

Facial comedone ventouse

The facial comedone ventouse must not be moved in a gliding action over the skin's surface. Hold it static while operating the vacuum and release the vacuum before removal to avoid bruising or stretching the skin.

Skin blockages To remove signs of congestion such as comedones, select a small ventouse. The small diameter of the aperture increases the suction effect on the skin and the comedone is loosened.

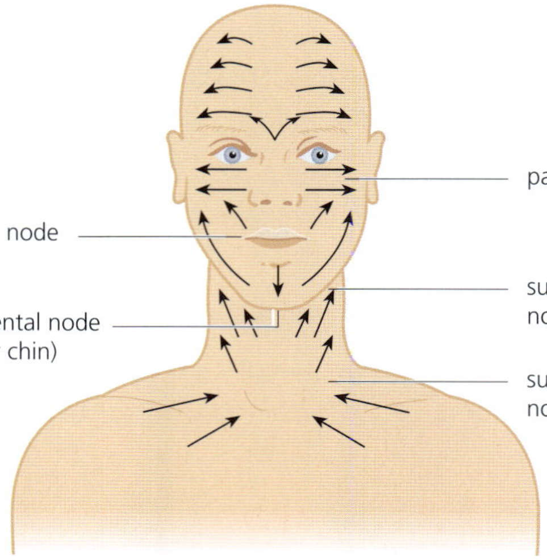

Face and neck applications

Body gliding technique A poor diet, sedentary lifestyle and stress can cause sluggish lymphatic circulation. Toxins become stored, causing puffy and tender tissue.

The body gliding technique is used to increase dispersal of accumulated fluid in the tissues and to soften areas of fatty tissue, improving the general functioning and appearance of the skin.

1. Place tissues along the edges of underwear to prevent staining with the lubricant.
2. Apply oil to the area to be treated, either manually or with the vacuum spray attachment if available.
3. Switch on the machine at the mains.
4. Place the cup on the border of the area to be treated and increase the vacuum suction intensity until the tissue fills the cup by 20 per cent.
5. Starting at the boundary of the area to be treated, gently lift the cup away from the skin without breaking the seal and glide it in a straight line towards the nearest lymphatic node.
6. At the end of the strip, depending on the cup chosen, break the seal by inserting the tip of a finger of the opposite hand underneath the edge of the cup or uncovering the hole which releases the vacuum. Return the cup to the beginning of the strip.
7. Perform the gliding action over each strip of skin four to six times, then move onto the next strip, overlapping the previous strip by half its width.
8. Adjust the vacuum intensity according to the area being treated; the suction may be increased or decreased during application.
9. Continue until all the service area has been covered.
10. Return the vacuum intensity to zero and switch the machine off at the mains. The skin should have become warm with a visible mild erythema and the area should feel smooth and invigorated.
11. At the end of the service you may perform a manual massage effleurage stroke to reinforce the lymphatic drainage effect.

TOP TIP

Avoid excessive oil

Avoid the use of excessive oil as this will make the cup difficult to control.

HEALTH & SAFETY

High suction

If the suction is too high, break the seal immediately to avoid a contra-action, e.g. bruising.

TOP TIP

Soft tissue

Loose, soft-fat areas of tissue require less suction than other areas.

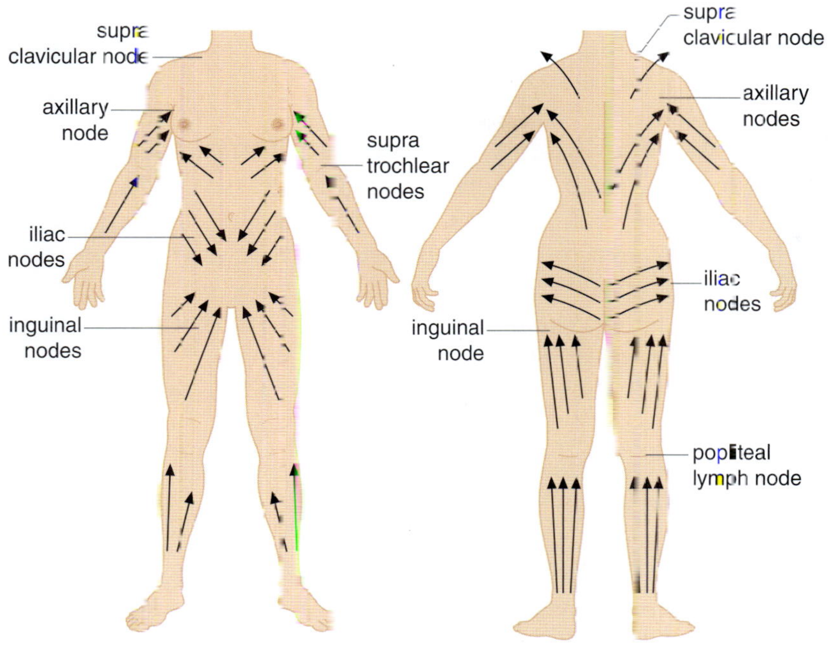

Application to body – anterior and posterior

BEST PRACTICE

Alternative services

Other services you may offer:

- Micro-current machines are aimed at the effective drainage of the lymphatic system. The current is directed at the problem areas.
- Inflatable air-pressure massage body envelopes treat localized cellulite and poor lymphatic-drained areas. External pressure on the tissues increases the flow of lymph.

Body pulsating multi-cup vacuum technique With multi-cup vacuum suction, up to eight cups are placed on the skin's surface. These operate simultaneously. This method is suitable for larger clients and for specific problem areas of stubborn fat such as the abdomen and thighs.

1. Switch on the machine at the mains.
2. Switch on the pulsation control operated by the pulsator valve. This controls the degree of suction and also the length of pulsation periods.
3. Place the cups on the skin, not too close together, a rocking action is used to ensure the seal of the cup makes good contact with the skin's surface and the vacuum created draws the tissues into the cup.
4. The lower degree of pulsation must be sufficient to ensure the cups remain in contact with the skin. During the release period the cup may be moved along the area being treated.
5. Increase the degree of lift (intensity) and duration of pulsation period according to the effect required.
6. The cups may be moved to other service areas during application. Gliding technique may be used to reinforce the removal of tissue fluid in the area.
7. Apply the service for 10–15 minutes.
8. Remove the cups during the lower degree pulse.
9. Return the vacuum intensity to zero and switch off at the mains.
10. Remove the oil thoroughly from the skin and follow with further complementary service if required.

TOP TIP

Slimmer clients

When treating the abdominal area of slimmer clients, select the gliding technique, as suction will become difficult on the low-pulsed vacuum periods.

Static vacuum massage technique On areas of hard fat or cellulite, static vacuum is beneficial. Multiple cups are applied to the area attached to plastic tubing and

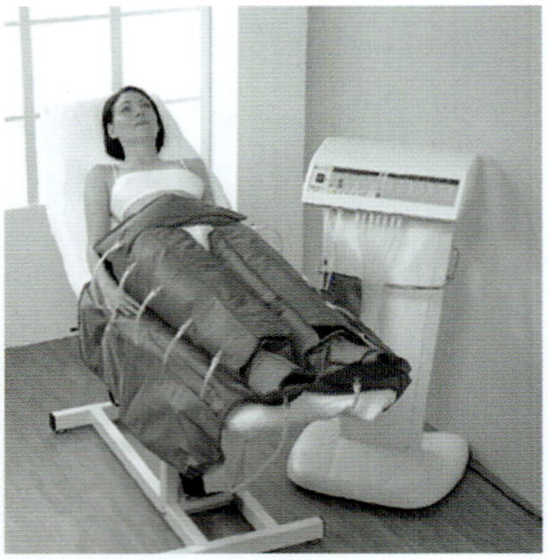
BEAUTY EXPRESS LTD

Inflatable air pressure massage envelope – pressotherapy

adaptors. Independent controls are selected for the vacuum intensity and release period that will need to be of sufficient intensity to keep the cups in place on the release period. The service time is approximately 10 minutes.

Pressotherapy – lymphatic drainage equipment Pressotherapy is a cosmetic service used to improve non-medical venous and lymphatic oedema. It acts by applying pressure and increasing absorption of interstitial fluid – the liquid between the cells of the body. The equipment has a **compressor** which blows air into boots or sleeves covering the limbs and an abdominal section can be attached which aids absorption of tissue fluid in the buttocks and lower abdominal area. The inside of the chambers inflate separately, draining the limb from the lower extremity to the upper. The client will want to pass urine immediately following the service because of the diuretic effect, so this must be explained.

Aftercare

Complete details of the service on the client's record card and include details of home-care advice and any product samples provided.

Offer client water for hydration.

Advise the client to increase fluid intake to help the lymphatic cleansing effect. Also advise the client of an effective service plan combining diet and exercise appropriate to their needs. Retail products support the effectiveness of the service. These include exfoliating and body contour products. These often contain anti-diuretic ingredients such as seaweed, ivy, ginseng and horsetail, which aim to increase the skin's metabolism and lymphatic circulation.

Contra-actions

Bruising and thread veins caused by:

- pulling the cup off without reducing the vacuum
- vacuum pressure being too high
- over-treatment of an area
- cup too small for area of the service
- increasing the vacuum while the cup is stationary (gliding technique)

Overstretching of the skin caused by:

- over-treatment of the area
- failure to reduce vacuum over looser areas of skin

Micro-current service

COURSEMATE

For a video on micro-current service please visit this book's accompanying CourseMate.

Micro-current therapy is an electrical service with an immediate skin toning and firming effect. It may be offered as a service for either the face or body and is available as a single or combined unit. It is very popular as its results are immediate. It may be offered to a wide client group, including those who wish to use the service as a preventative measure against premature ageing as well as to re-educate and strengthen muscles.

General effects:

- stimulation of cellular functioning of the epidermal and dermal layers – this naturally slows through the ageing process
- improved blood circulation, increasing the transportation of oxygen and nutrients to the skin's cells
- improved lymphatic circulation, speeding the elimination of waste and toxins which accumulate, causing puffy skin tissue (non-medical oedema)
- shortening of muscles and improvement in tone

Body use:

- for its skin rejuvenation effect
- to improve the appearance of a cellulite condition
- to improve the appearance of skin tone in specific problem areas, being especially beneficial for scar tissue
- to improve the appearance of stretch marks by the effect of skin tightening
- to improve the bust contour

Facial use:

- skin rejuvenation through an improved muscle and skin tone; lines and slack facial contours will appear less obvious
- frown lines resulting from tense muscles are softened if the current is used to relax the muscles
- skin type characteristics may be treated specifically, such as the open pores of oily skin, which may be tightened
- skin colour is improved by the improved blood circulation and improved elimination of waste products and toxins
- dark circles and puffiness around the eyes may be treated

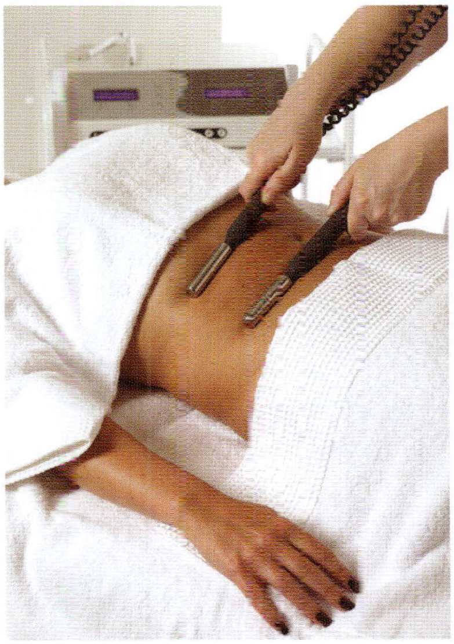

DEPILEX

Micro-current application to the body using probes

Anatomy and physiology

Cells degenerate with ageing, resulting in reduced nutrition and oxygen which affects the cellular metabolism. The electrical current stimulates cell metabolism and increases the permeability of cell membranes to improve movement of materials in and out of the cells. The application of a small electrical current directly stimulates the muscle fibres, but because the micro-current operates at a low intensity it does not cause visible contraction as seen in faradic service. Myofobrils, the very fine contractile fibres found in the muscle length (see page 55), are stimulated moving only the protein filament structures actin and myosin. In response to electrical impulses the myosin filaments pull on the actin, causing the muscle to shorten.

Electrical science

Micro-current is based on a modified dc and as such creates the same effects as a galvanic current. It is basically a dc interrupted at low frequencies of one to a few hundred times per second.

The modern micro-current delivers currents which are measured in microamps (millionths of an amp) shown as μA. Output strengths are typically 300–600 μA (0.3–0.6 milliamps),

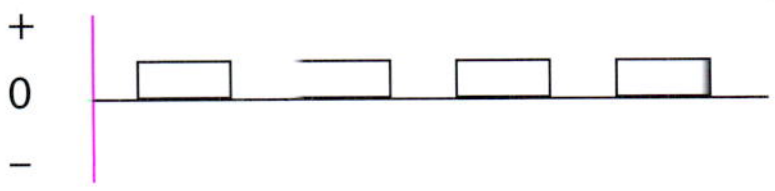

Micro-current waveform

although in alternating mode 1200 μA (1.2 mA) can be reached. The voltage adjusts itself to give the required safe current level. The μA setting should be set according to the manufacturer's procedure.

A negative polarity stimulates the nervous response and dilates the vessels of the blood and lymphatic circulatory systems. This has a beneficial warming effect on the tissues. In the treatment of a cellulite condition, sluggish circulation is increased, causing waste toxins to be eliminated more rapidly. To eliminate the effects of the galvanic current, each alternate electrical pulse can be modified to an ac. Other machines operate on ac and then electronically reverse each alternate pulse. The micro-current therefore oscillates back and forth between positive and negative charges.

TOP TIP

Battery operation

Micro-current equipment for convenience may operate from a rechargeable battery; the client may see it psychologically as safer because it is not directly connected to the mains.

The frequency of the current or speed of the electrical pulses per second is measured in hertz (Hz). The frequency selected sets the number of contractions per second, which will either relax (lengthen) or tighten (shorten) muscle tissue. This may be changed manually with some micro-current machines during the service application. At a lower setting, 1–5 Hz, the muscles are specifically shortened to improve tone. As the Hz is increased, to, say, 30Hz and above, muscles are lengthened.

A very low, computerized micro-current sends electrical impulses which stimulate the skin's nerve endings. This causes the muscles to contract and shorten, which strengthens them and increases tone. This results in a firmer facial skin appearance.

A dc galvanic current may be incorporated to stimulate the blood and lymph circulation to treat the general functioning of the skin and cellulite conditions.

Micro-current uses different combinations of current intensity, frequency and waveform to achieve its different effects of skin toning, muscle toning and improving the skin's appearance.

Reception

- Complete personal details on the client's record card.
- Question the client to check for contra-indications.
- The number of sessions required will vary for each client. Ageing clients will require more treatments to achieve the immediate visible results seen on a younger client.
- It is important that the client first receives a one-off service to observe the result. A course of treatment should then be recommended.
- Inform the client of any pre-service considerations such as avoiding a meal 1 hour before body abdomen applications.

"Look after your machine and it will look after you! Maintenance, cleanliness and storage of your machine is very important."

Claire Burrell

Facial service Allow 30–60 minutes for a facial application, depending on the service application technique chosen. The client should attend two to three times per week. Usually the service is given as a course of 12.

Body service Allow half an hour for a body application. The client should attend on average two to three times per week. The service is usually given as a course of ten.

For both facial and body services, once the contours have been improved in tone, a general maintenance plan of two to three courses a year is advised.

EQUIPMENT AND MATERIALS LIST

ELLISONS

Record card

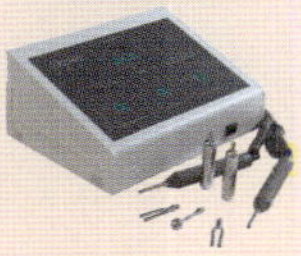

ELLISONS

Micro-current Unit with probes, double or single adhesive pad electrodes

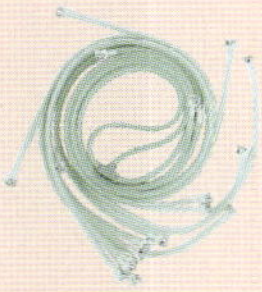

SORISA

Facial leads

SORISA

Conducting ionized gel This may contain specific therapeutic ingredients to enhance the effects achieved for each given skin type/condition

YOU WILL ALSO NEED:

Conductive gloves (if required)

Surgical spirit (to clean the probes)

Disposable cotton buds Cut to 1.5 cm (if required)

ALWAYS REMEMBER

Probes

The probe electrodes are available with or without the requirement for the inserting of cotton buds soaked in conducting ionized gel.

Electrodes are available which, when the bud is snapped in half, each bud receives a lifting formula which is absorbed by the cotton bud tip.

ALWAYS REMEMBER

Needles

Some machines use needles to pass the current directly into the skin. The needle is inserted into the epidermis and this transmits the current to the muscle for a few minutes. Probes are usually made of stainless steel as it is a good conductor of electrical current.

Contra-indications During the client assessment, if you find any of the following in the treatment area, micro-current service must not be carried out:

- epilepsy
- Botox® or collagen injections and fillers (on area of treatment)
- skin disorder or disease – these could be aggravated by the service or cross-infection could occur
- electrical implants, e.g. pacemakers – the micro-current could cause interference with other electrical sources
- metal plates and pins – these will conduct the current and cause discomfort
- severe varicose veins
- excessive dental metal work – these conduct a minute current transfer to the tooth nerve
- IUD coil when working over the abdominal area
- loss of tactile skin sensation

Clients who suffer from migraines should not be treated around the eye or forehead area.

HEALTH & SAFETY

Dental work

If the client has dental work such as fillings which may cause possible discomfort, place the electrodes above or below the gum area.

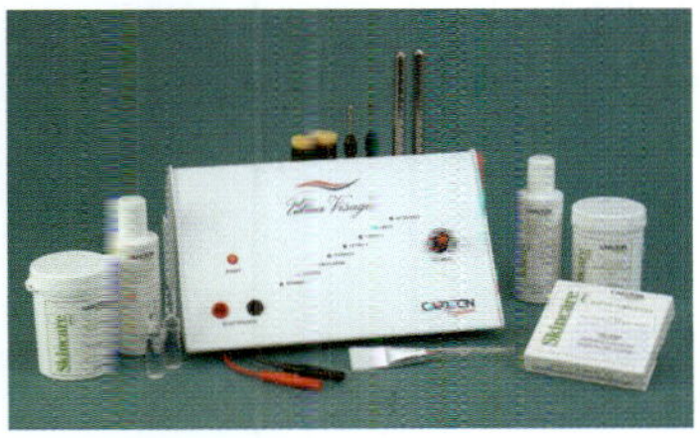

DEPILEX

Micro-current unit

Sterilization and disinfection

Disposable cotton buds must be used for each client. After each service the probes should be cleaned thoroughly, removing the conducting gel with surgical spirit. Place in an UV sterilizing cabinet and then store in a sealed container. Facial pads, if used, should be replaced after each client.

Preparation of the service area

- Cover the couch with a clean towel.
- Check all electrical safety precautions.
- Test the machine to ensure it is in good working order. If battery operated, the equipment will only work if the unit is fully powered up.

Facial application

- Prepare the cotton buds for facial service if used. These are cut and shortened for insertion into the facial electrode probes.
- Prepare the facial electrode pads for face and neck service.
- Select the probes according to the area to be treated.
- Secure the probe electrodes firmly to the electrical leads.
- Insert the leads into the relevant connections.

Body application

- Collect clean conductive gloves if used.
- Select the probes according to the area to be treated.
- Secure the probe electrodes/gloves firmly to the electrical leads.
- Insert the leads into the relevant connections.

Preparation of the beauty therapist

- Collect the client's record card.
- Wash your hands before handling the client.
- Assess the client; discuss the client's lifestyle and objectives of the service if this is the initial service. Agree an appropriate service plan.
- If a service has a slimming requirement it will be necessary to measure the client at the beginning of the service course and once every week thereafter.
- If this is a repeat service, check the client's progress against targets set and provide support and advice as necessary.
- Often with a course of facial service a 'before' and 'after' photograph may be taken.

TOP TIP

Waveforms

The waveforms produced may be an ac or a dc. The benefit of the dc is that it has both muscle stimulation and galvanic service effects.

Preparation of the client

- After an initial consultation, the correct service for the client's needs is identified. This consultation evaluates the client's lifestyle. Factors such as smoking, alcohol and stress are discussed and a relevant service programme is reached.
- Discuss the aims of the service with the client.
- For facial application, a photograph could be taken before to show the results that have been achieved after the **micro-current therapy** service.
- For body application take the client's measurements before and after each session.

- Instruct the client to remove upper clothing to underwear. Position the client comfortably on the couch in a supine position and cover with a clean towel.
- Perform a skin sensitivity test to ensure the client can detect different skin sensations.
- Record the results on the client's record card.
- Remove all jewellery from the service area.
- For facial applications, cleanse the skin area with cleanser and toner and blot the surface dry. A facial exfoliation is beneficial before the service to allow the current to flow easily.
- For body applications, cleanse the skin with witch hazel or eau de cologne applied with clean cotton wool.
- Analyze the client's skin using a magnifying lamp. Question the client where necessary to check information in relation to the client's skin condition.
- Cover any minor cuts or abrasions with petroleum jelly or a small surgical plaster to form a barrier to the electrical current.
- Explain the sensation to the client. A slight prickling sensation will be experienced in the skin. Also, if your equipment uses the sound of a beep to follow as a guide in service applications, timing, inform the client of this.
- It is advisable to recommend a pre-service of facial peeling or body exfoliation to reduce the skin's resistance to the current.

TOP TIP

Facial pads

If used in the service, facial pads will fail to stick to the skin if the skin is not dry. This will result in service interference and uneven current application.

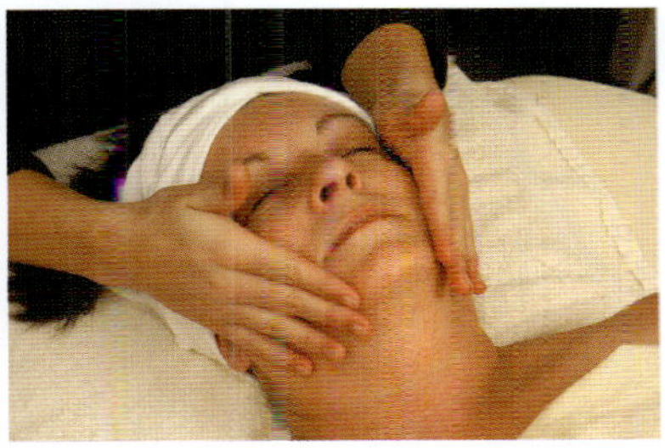

Facial exfoliation before a service

Service application

The current intensity, frequency (pulses per second), waveform and duration should be selected as appropriate to treat the client's skin condition and for client comfort. This may need to be varied for each side of the face or body. The current levels may be kept low – intensity does not have to be high to achieve the best results.

TOP TIP

If your machine provides an audio 'beep' sounding guide, move at a pace synchronised with this, over the skin. This will assist you in providing the correct pressure and pace of application.

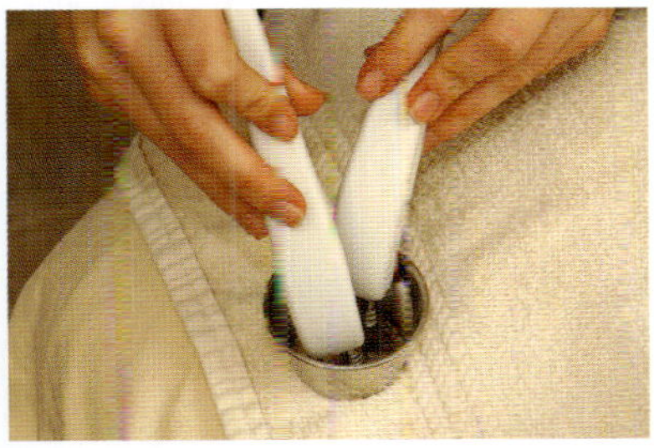

Moisten the applicator probes

BEST PRACTICE

No muscle contractions

In contrast to EMS service there will be no visible contraction of the muscle with the electrical current application. It is important to consider this when using facial electrodes. Also warn the client that flashing lights can be experienced when working around the eye area. This is not harmful!

Always check that the pressure applied is not uncomfortable for the client when performing facial toning techniques.

Facial application

1 Apply an electrolyte such as ionized gel in a thick layer specifically to the area being treated.

Moisten the conducting probes or cotton buds that are inserted into the conducting probes.

2 Select the treatment electrode. These will be either probes or facial pads.

The specific application of the single probes in various strokes, or placement of the facial pads over the skin's surface achieve increased blood and lymph

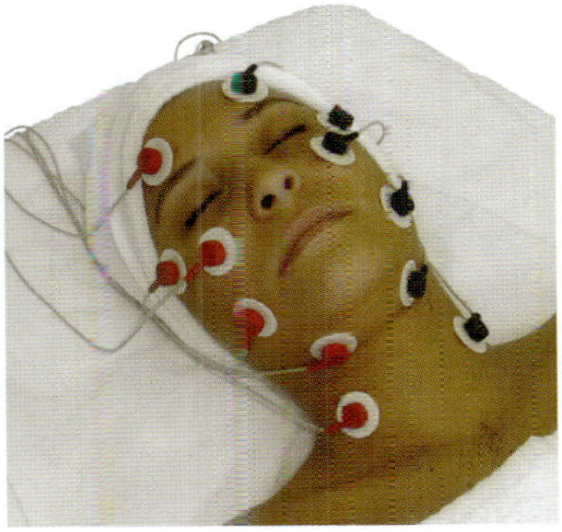

Micro-current using facial pad technique

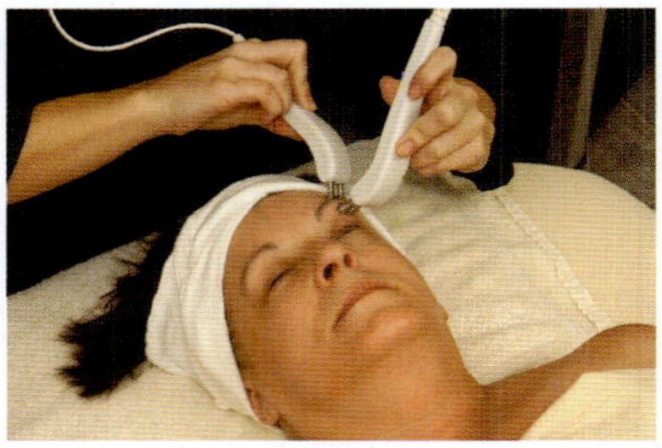

Compression using facial micro-current service

circulation. Also, specific muscles are tightened and relaxed as the electric current flows, creating an immediate lifting effect. The process helps to soften the appearance of fine lines and wrinkles. Probes are normally used on delicate areas such as around the eye area. Application must be firm to ensure effective current application.

Dual probes may be used on larger muscles of the face and are especially beneficial along the jaw area in the treatment of jowls, the result of poor muscle tone along the jaw-line.

3 Commence service application.

When working on toning muscles, techniques include relaxing, strengthening and tightening. Current intensity, frequency and wave form will be altered dependent upon which technique is used and the facial area being worked upon. Your equipment supplier will provide guidance on where the movements are to be performed, in which direction, how quickly and how much pressure should be applied.

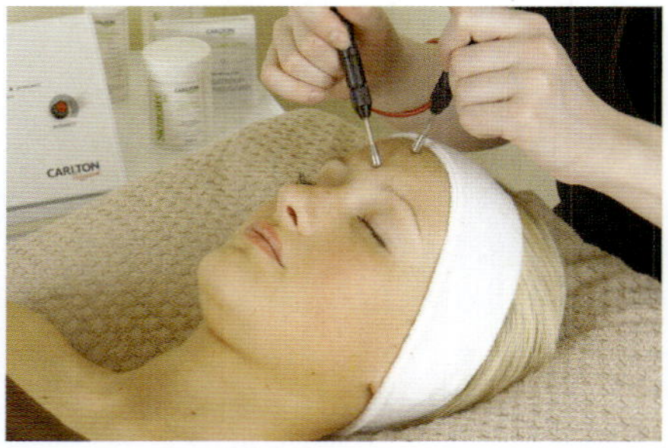

Relaxing The electrodes start at the centre of the muscle, its belly, both electrodes are moved towards the origin and insertion of the muscle, lengthening the muscle following the recommended speed and timing guidelines.

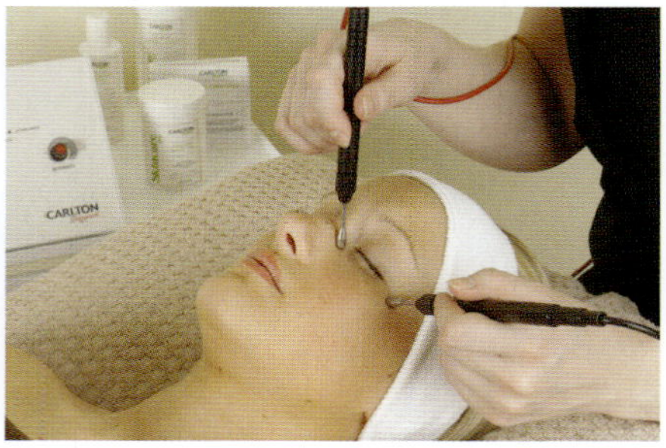

Strengthening One electrode remains stationary at the origin whilst the other moves towards it at the recommended speed and timing. Near the end of the movement approximately 1cm of tissue is compressed between the tips of the probes.(The neck is not usually included until the 7th session.)

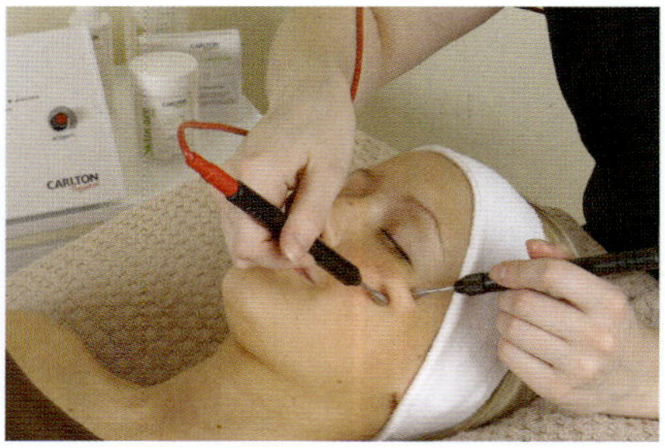

Tightening Both electrodes are moved simultaneously towards the centre of the muscle belly. Near the end of the movement 1 cm of tissue is compressed between the tips of the probes.

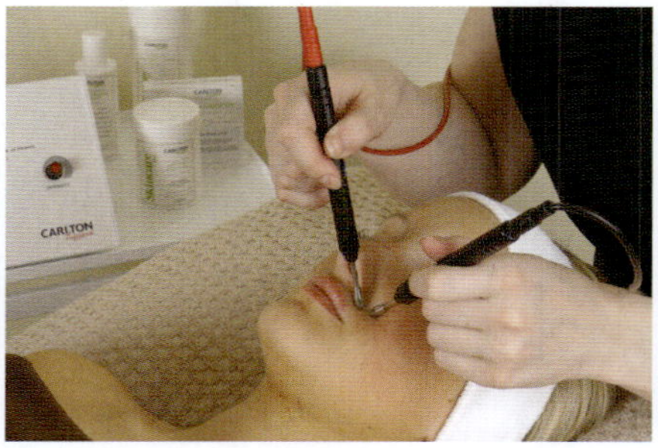

Muscle toning is often followed by skin toning using gliding and compression movements. Again, guidance on application will be provided.

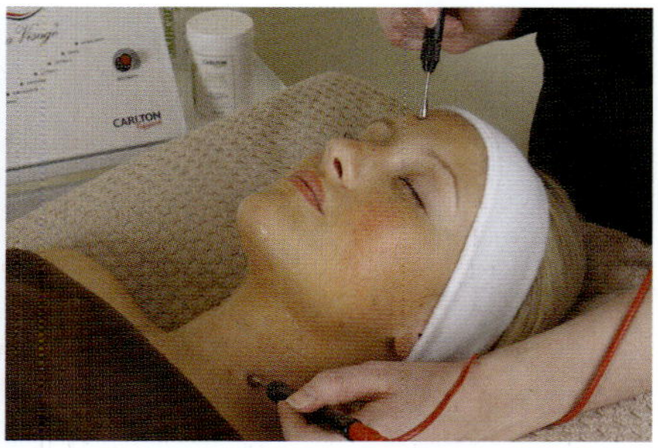

Gliding One electrode is stationary at a selected starting position and the other electrode moves towards it compressing 1 cm of tissue between the tips of the electrodes.

4 After treatment using electrode pads or facial probes, return all control settings to zero.

5 The facial may be completed with ionisation, where ionised substances are passed into the epidermis with an uninterrupted dc. Blood circulation is increased and the skin may appear slightly reddened following treatment due to the irritant effect of the galvanic current.

6 Remove excess conducting gel from the skin's surface.

7 Record the treatment details on the client's record card.

Body application

1. Select the current, frequency and wave-form appropriate to the part of the body to be treated.
2. Apply conductive gel to the skin.
3. Apply probes or conductive gloves. Hold one probe stationary with light pressure, hold the other probe firmly in an opposing position. The application of the probes or conductive gloves over the skin firms the tissues and soft fatty areas are broken down. Application must be firm to ensure effective current application. The positive bar is usually placed at the top of the treatment area, with the negatively charged bar moving firmly over the skin towards the nearest lymph node.
4. Stretch marks and scar tissue improve in appearance as the micro-current tightens the collagen fibres that give strength to the skin and stimulates cell and collagen renewal. The tissues will appear firmed.
5. Often, a manual massage is used to conclude the service to ensure the absorption of all the service gel and remove lymph waste in the area.
6. Alternatively, a specialized skin-toning service product may be applied with the aim of improving a cellulite appearance.

TOP TIP

If your machine provides an audio 'beep' sounding guide, move at a pace synchronised with this over the skin. This will assist you, providing the correct pressure and pace of application.

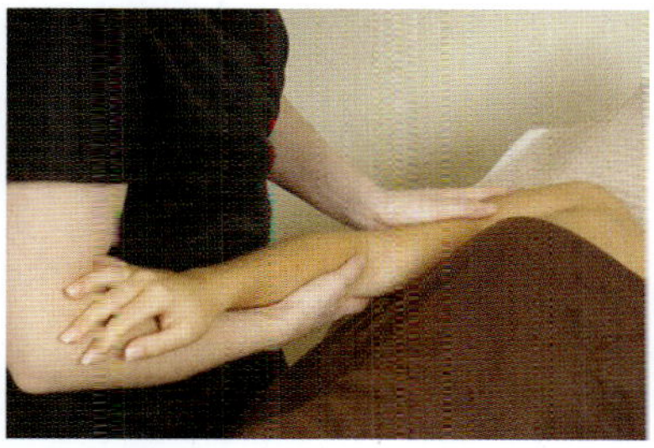
CARLTON BEAUTY + SPA LTD

Manual massage may be applied to conclude the service

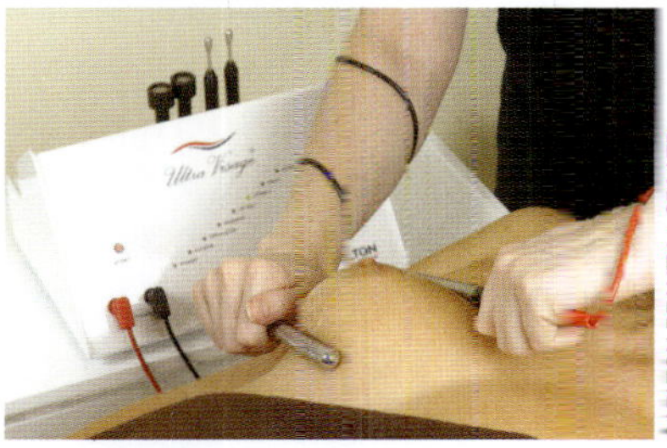
CARLTON BEAUTY + SPA LTD

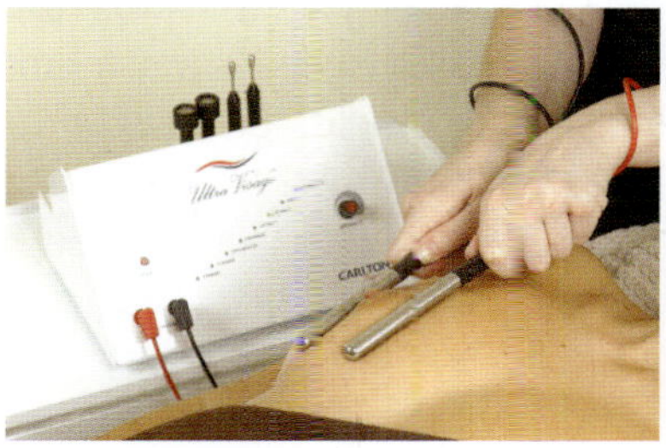
CARLTON BEAUTY + SPA LTD

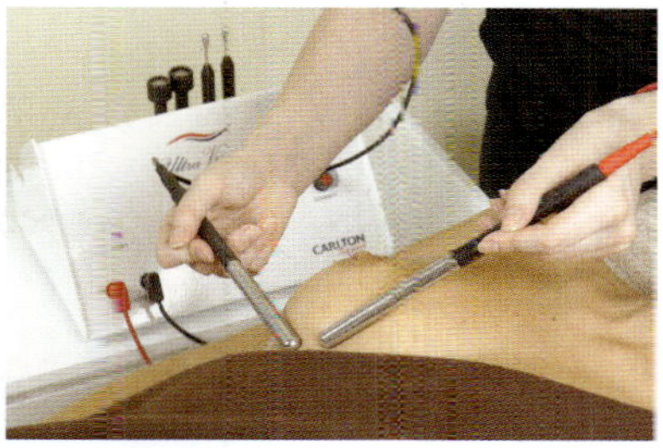
CARLTON BEAUTY + SPA LTD

Application of probes – bust tightening procedure

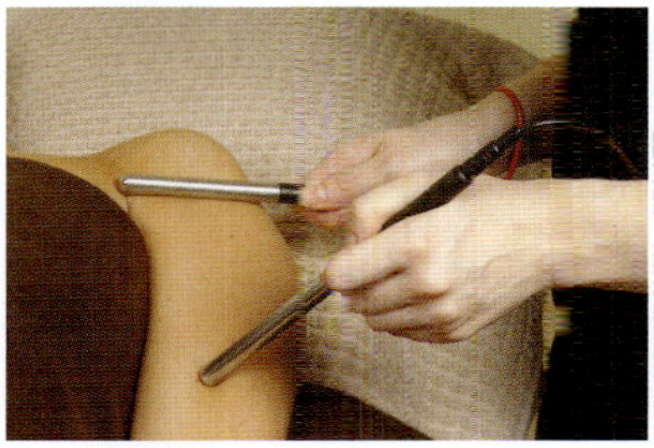
CARLTON BEAUTY + SPA LTD

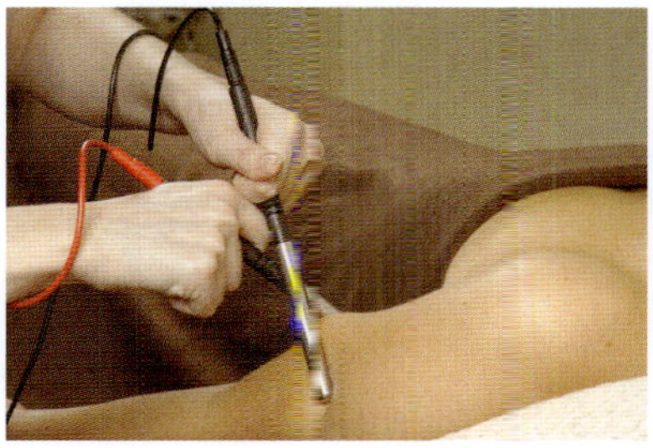
CARLTON BEAUTY + SPA LTD

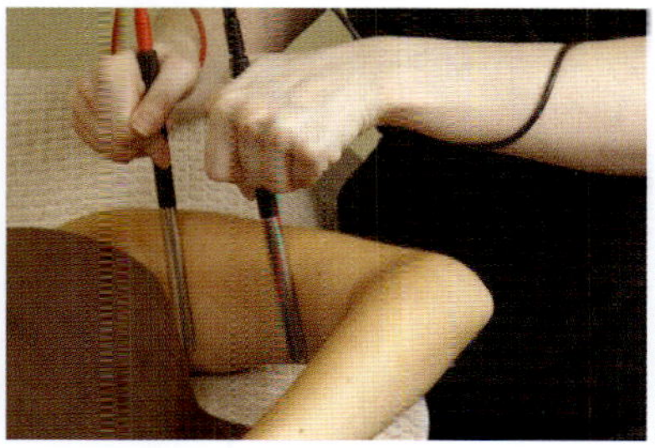
CARLTON BEAUTY + SPA LTD

Application of probes arm bicep tightening procedure

Aftercare

To continue the treatment process the beauty therapist should discuss the benefits of home care with the client. Ideally, facial cosmetic creams and make-up must not be applied directly after service. The skin needs to be able to 'breathe'. However, as some services only take 30 minutes, some clients may wish to take advantage of receiving their service during a lunch-break. The negative effects on the skin of alcohol, smoking and UV radiation should be discussed with the client. The drinking of natural, uncarbonated water should be encouraged following service to help remove toxins, and the benefits of a healthy diet should also be discussed.

TOP TIP

Skin dragging

More gel may be applied if the skin drags, as the gel absorbs and dries during application.

TOP TIP

Glove system

The glove system is useful on the face, hips and thighs where specific muscles are stimulated by electric pulses emitted through silk-like gloves. The gloves are dampened with water.

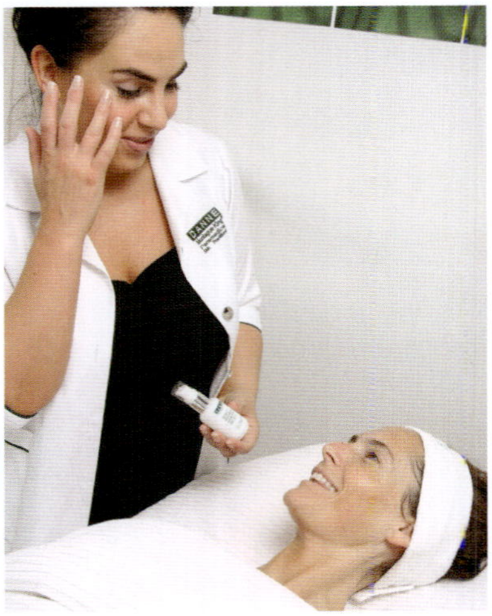

LORRAINE NORDMANN

Home care routine supports and enhances the service

"Take up a language – I wish I had known how useful this would be when I was younger!

Mary Overton

Simple, facial exercises should be recommended to the client. These will continue to firm the facial muscles and reinforce the firming effects of the micro-current service.

Clients should be offered retail cosmetic skincare preparations to support and enhance the effects achieved. Alpha hydroxy acid (AHA) services are beneficial to cosmetically remove surface dead skin cells and improve the skin's appearance, reducing the skin's resistance to the service.

Following course completion, the client should be advised of the benefit of maintenance services.

Contra-actions

- **Muscle fatigue** caused by incorrect choice of current intensity, frequency and waveform.
- Excess stimulation when introducing ionized substances into the skin which stimulates circulation in the epidermal layer using galvanic, direct current. A cool compress should be applied and a note made on the clients record card. GP referral is necessary if it does not subside in 24 hours.

Micro-dermabrasion

Micro-dermabrasion service

Micro-dermabrasion is a mechanical exfoliating or skin-peeling facial and body service where a controlled high-speed flow of microcrystals is applied under pressure over the skin's surface through an applicator probe which gently breaks down the skin cells. The crystals are usually made from the mineral aluminum oxide, the second hardest mineral – the other being diamond, which some manufacturers use! An immediate vacuum effect then occurs: while applying the crystals to the skin, the applicator probe also removes dead skin and excess microcrystals through a vacuum system. The service also has a cellular regenerative effect, improving both cellular renewal and repair and the tone and elasticity of the skin.

General effects

Face and body:

- desquamation effect, due to the exfoliation of the skin surface, specifically improving the appearance of:
  - coarse skin with open pores – regular service will help remove excess dead skin cells and cleanse the pores
  - fine lines and wrinkles around the eyes, lips and neck
  - scar tissue, e.g. acne scarring, stretch marks – their appearance will be less noticeable
  - superficial hyper-pigmentation (only if the pigmentation is located in the epidermis)
- improved blood circulation locally, increasing the transportation of oxygen and nutrients to the skin's cells
- stimulation of cellular functioning of the epidermal and dermal layers – (this naturally slows as part of the ageing process) creating a skin rejuvenating effect
- improved lymphatic circulation and drainage locally through its vacuum suction action, speeding the elimination of waste and toxins which cause puffy skin tissue when they accumulate (non-medical oedema).

Anatomy and physiology

The service is termed *mechanical*: the microcrystals mechanically remove cells from the skin's surface, removing 0.06 mm (superficial dermabrasion) to 0.45 mm (medium dermabrasion) of skin in a single service. The applicator probe stimulates cells called fibroblasts in the connective tissue of the dermis, held in a substance called the ground substance. These cells are responsible for the production of collagen and elastin protein fibres. Elastin gives the skin elasticity, while collagen fibres give it strength. Thus the service improves the strength and elasticity of the skin. The vacuum suction feature stimulates both blood and lymphatic circulation locally.

Micro-dermabrasion effects

A compressor, a device that compresses gas, draws atmospheric air through the hole in the applicator when not in contact with the skin. A vacuum occurs when the applicator is then placed in contact with the skin. This causes the microcrystals located at the other end of the system to be sucked by negative pressure until they reach the applicator probe. When the applicator head is in contact with the skin, this closes the air outlet hole. Microcrystals will only flow when the outlet hole is closed onto the treatment area.

Reception

Allow 15–20 minutes for micro-dermabrasion service application depending upon the service area. However, to allow for cleansing, and additional cosmetic service applications, 50 minutes is normally booked for this service. A course of 10–20 services is generally recommended every 7–10 days. The length of course and interval will depend upon the condition being treated, skin sensitivity and the reaction of the skin to service. Following the course, maintenance service should be recommended once per month. As the skin continuously renews and replaces, service must be repeated in order to maintain the result. When booking this service advice should be given as to aftercare requirements.

The service record card covering micro-dermabrasion can be found on pages 223–226.

TOP TIP

One single service

When promoting micro-dermabrasion, remind the client that one single service will remove excess dead skin cells and sebum making the skin appear brighter and healthier, whatever the skin type.

When demonstrating the effectiveness of the service you could treat half the face and then show the client the difference it has made to the skin's appearance.

ALWAYS REMEMBER

Storage of microcrystals

These must be kept dry. Store in a dry atmosphere to avoid them becoming damp, which would affect flow of crystals during service application.

EQUIPMENT AND MATERIALS LIST

SILHOUETTE DERMALIFT

Record card

SILHOUETTE-DERMALIFT

Micro-dermabrasion unit

SILHOUETTE DERMALIFT

Applicator probe

SILHOUETTE DERMALIFT

Disposable heads
For the probe

SILHOUETTE DERMALIFT

Microcrystals
Made of aluminium oxide (corundum)

YOU WILL ALSO NEED:

Protective eye shields Mask and gloves, e.g. goggles for client wear, mask and gloves for beauty therapist wear

Facial sponges To remove skincare preparations

Complimentary skincare Cosmetic skincare preparation, i.e. service mask, skin calming strengthening preparations

HEALTH & SAFETY

Medication

Some oral and topical medication can cause increased skin sensitivity. Examples include Retinol® or Retin A® products and roacceutane medication prescribed for the service of acne vulgaris. One to three months should be left after a course of prescribed medication as described above has been completed before micro-dermabrasion is received. However, GP approval should be sought.

SILHOUETTE-DERMALIFT

Micro-dermabrasion unit

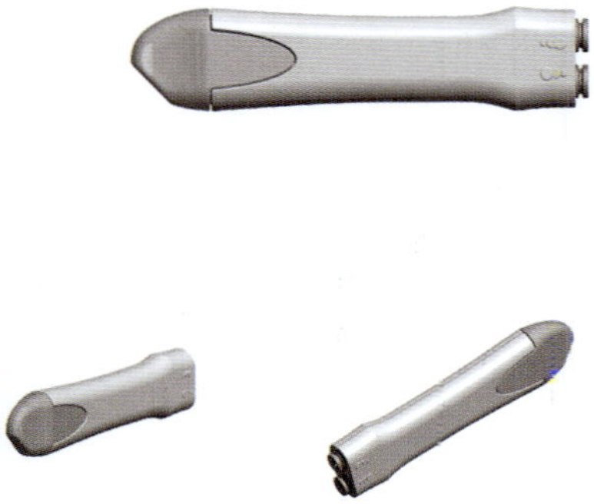

BEAUTY EXPRESS LTD

Applicator probe attachments

Contra-indications

During the client assessment, if you find any of the following, micro-dermabrasion service must not be carried out:

- skin disorder or disease – these could be aggravated by the service, or cross-infection could occur; e.g. herpes simplex
- recent laser surgery or chemical peel, e.g. glycolic peel. Check the recommended period to wait between these services and micro-dermabrasion service.
- hypersensitive skin
- highly vascular skin, e.g. acne rosacea or broken capillaries:
- erythema caused by recent UV exposure
- loss of tactile skin sensation
- anti-coagulation drugs as prescribed to treat cardiovascular conditions as these will interfere with the skin coagulation process
- diabetic condition: poor skin healing makes the client vulnerable to infection
- pigmentation disorders such as moles and birthmarks
- keloid scarring: this could make the condition worse
- blood disorders such as hepatitis B and AIDS caused by the virus HIV (human immunodeficiency virus) – there may be a risk of cross-infection as the viruses are transmitted by body fluids
- do not apply immediately to an area following wax depilation
- recent injectable cosmetic treatments, i.e. Botox® collagen or fillers. Check the recommended period to wait between these services and micro-dermabrasion service.

Sterilization and disinfection

The crystals are sterile; once applied to the skin they are returned with any waste materials from the skin to the waste crystal container. place used crystals in a strong clinical (yellow) waste disposal bag or clinical waste container before disposal. Dispose of and replace the active probe cap after each client service.

Filters should be changed and replaced as guided by the equipment manufacturer.

PPE gloves must be worn when performing this service due to the risk of contamination with tissue fluid.

Preparation of the service area

- Cover the service couch with a clean towel.
- Check all electrical safety precautions.

- Test the machine to ensure it is in good working order.
- Ensure the crystal level in the active container is filled with sterile crystals, observing the minimum and maximum levels as a guide. Remove any crystal residue from the cap of the bottle with a dry brush, insert the suction tube in the crystals and close cap securely.
- The waste crystal bottle must be emptied regularly, observing the maximum level as a guide. Empty the used crystal bottle before use and clean its filter following manufacturer's instructions.

Preparation of the beauty therapist

- Collect the client's record card.
- Wash your hands before handling the client. Collect PPE gloves to wear before commencing service application.
- Assess the client; discuss the client's lifestyle and the objectives of the service if this is the initial service. Agree an appropriate service plan.
- Features of this service may include taking a photograph to show skin appearance comparison before and after service.

Preparation of the client

- After an initial consultation, the correct service for the client's skin needs is identified and agreed with the client.
- Instruct the client to remove clothing according to the area being treated.
- Position the client comfortably on the couch and cover with a clean towel.
- All jewellery must be removed from the service area. Ensure that the ears are covered and fully protected form the crystals.
- Question the client further where necessary to check information in relation to the client's skin condition.
- Cleanse and tone the client's skin using appropriate skincare preparations and then blot the skin dry. *Dry skin is essential* to ensure effective exfoliation.
- For safety test the compressor suction power setting on your inner wrist before use on the client.
- Inform the client of the noise.
- Inform the client of the sensation and expected appearance of the skin following service.
- Provide protective eye shields to prevent irritation of the eyes from the crystals and any skin debris during facial application.
- Perform a patch test to assess skin tolerance. If suitable to receive the service, proceed.

Service application

- Start equipment.
- Select the programme according to the area being treated and the pressure required. White skin often has a lower level of abrasion setting than black skin. Reduce pressure for sensitive skin.

TOP TIP

Loss of suction

Loss of suction, check tube air outlets are clear; container lids are secure or the filter beneath the crystal waste container may require replacement.

HEALTH & SAFETY

Crystal hygiene

The jars containing sterile and unused crystals are sealed so that there is no cross-contamination during the service process.

BEST PRACTICE

Avoid overworking an area

Avoid overworking an area by moving the applicator too slowly or applying the vacuum suction pressure too high or skin bleeding may occur as excessive skin cells are removed.

On a sensitive skin increase the speed of application, resulting in superficial exfoliation. This will allow you to assess skin tolerance.

Care should be taken when working on thinner areas of skin such as the neck area to avoid excessive erythema.

HEALTH & SAFETY

Eyes
Avoid service on delicate eye tissue.

HEALTH & SAFETY

Medication
If the client is taking medication to thin the blood, service pressure must be lighter as the blood will reach the skin's surface much more quickly. If unsure, always confirm client suitability for service with their GP.

COURSEMATE

For a video on the micro-dermabrasion service please visit this book's accompanying CourseMate.

- Stretch and support the skin in the area of service.
- The attachment probe is continuously moved over the skin's surface, following lymphatic flow. The crystals are directed onto the skin's surface and a mild suction is applied. The slower the movement the greater the degree of abrasion in the area.
- For general facial service, movements are from the centre of the face outwards.
- For hyper-pigmentation marks, wrinkles and scarring, treat each individually, following general movements to the area.
- For stretch marks work over the skin at the outside of the scar first as the stretched skin has less resistance and will readily bleed.
- For areas of callused skin, incorporate micro-dermabrasion service. Typically this may be the hand or foot area.
- Compressor suction setting should be selected according to the skin condition being treated, effect to be achieved and skin sensitivity. The higher the suction, the stronger the speed of crystal abrasion. Reduce the compressor suction setting on finer areas of the skin such as around the eyes. The number of strokes applied to an area of skin is usually 2–3.
- Service time varies according to the area of the body being treated. Clean the skin's surface while dry after service application to observe the results achieved, further service may be required.
- Allow between 10–20 minutes for the face/body and 5–10 minutes for the hands.
- Excess crystals may be gently removed from the skin surface using cleansing lotion and damp sponges.
- A calming service mask is applied to the skin to calm and desensitize. As the skin is more permeable following exfoliation and vacuum service the products will work more efficiently.
- It is good practice to apply a sun protection screen of SPF30 to protect the skin following service.

Step-by-step: Micro-dermabrasion service

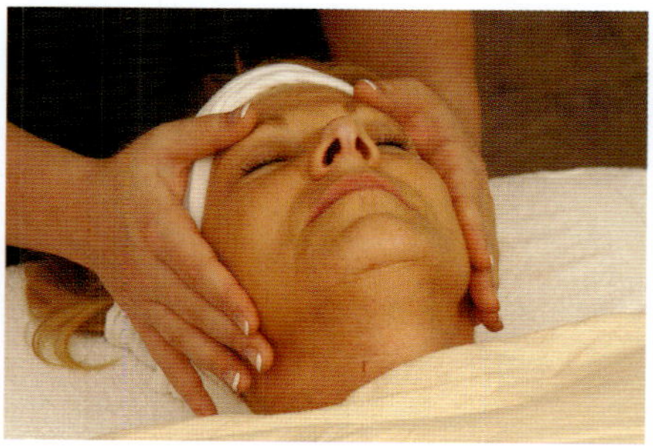

1 Position the client comfortably in a relaxing, reclining position with hair protected.

2 Make sure the client has removed all facial piercings, jewellery and contact lenses.

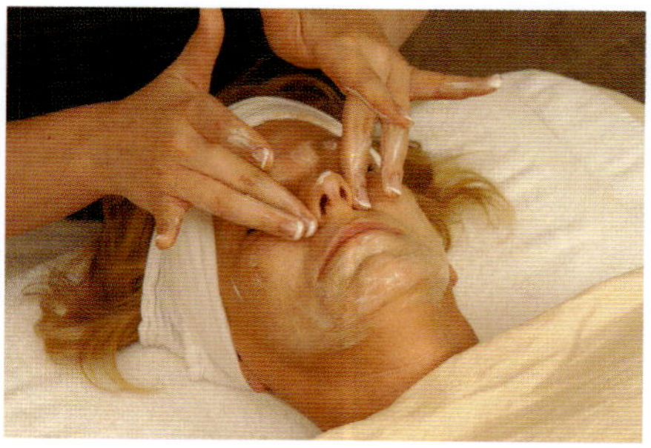

3 Remove the client's make-up with appropriate cleanser.

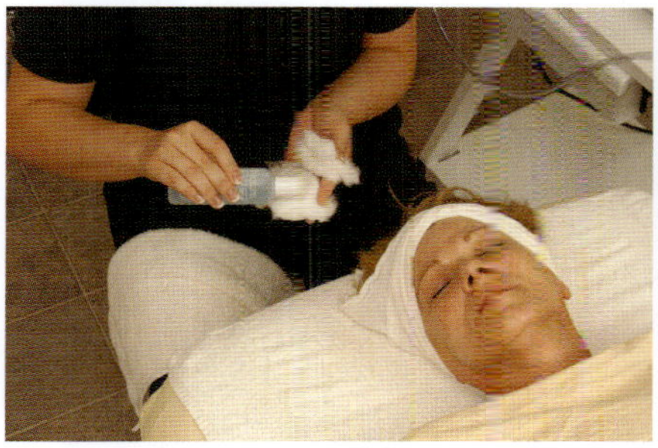

4 Cleanse the client's skin following manufacturer's recommendations. Dry the skin.

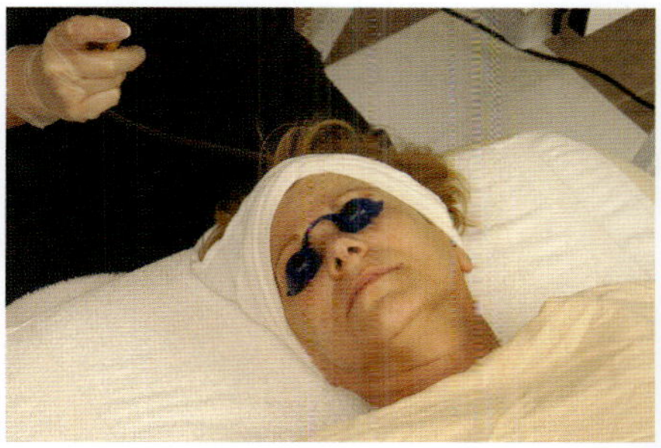

5 Cover client's eyes with occlusive protective eyewear, or eyepads. (*NOTE*: Goggles are not needed unless you are using crystals.)

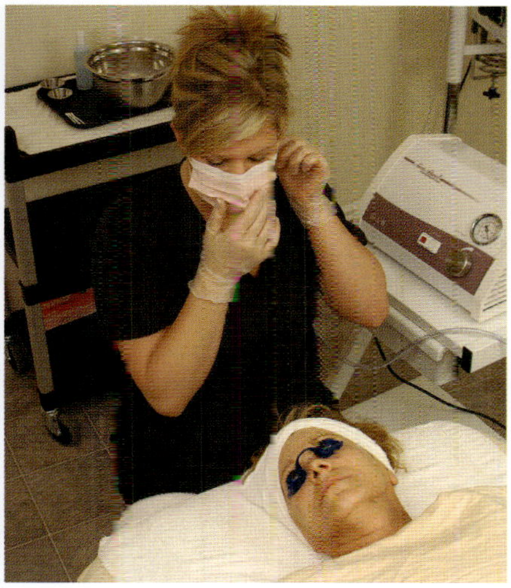

6 Put on protective mask and gloves.

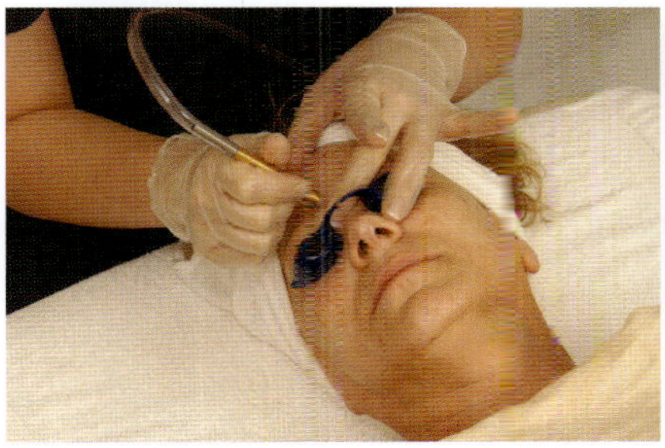

7 Conduct a patch test to assess skin suitability for the service. Skin should be slightly pink and comfortable. Start with settings low and increase as you determine how the client is tolerating the strokes.

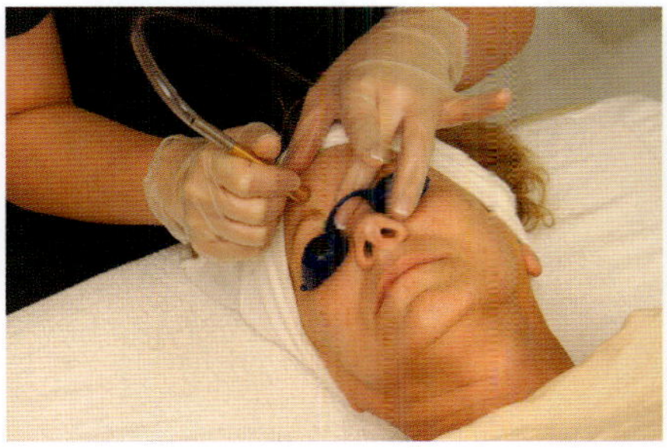

8 Start the procedure on the right half of the forehead. Using your non-dominant hand, hold the skin taut between your fingertips.

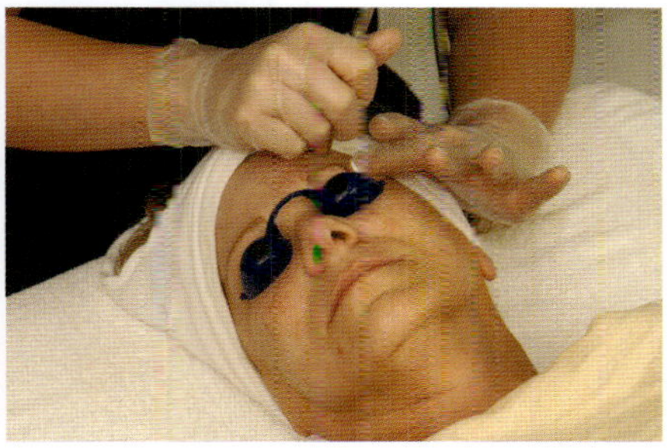

9 The next set of strokes should be a horizontal pattern. Repeat.

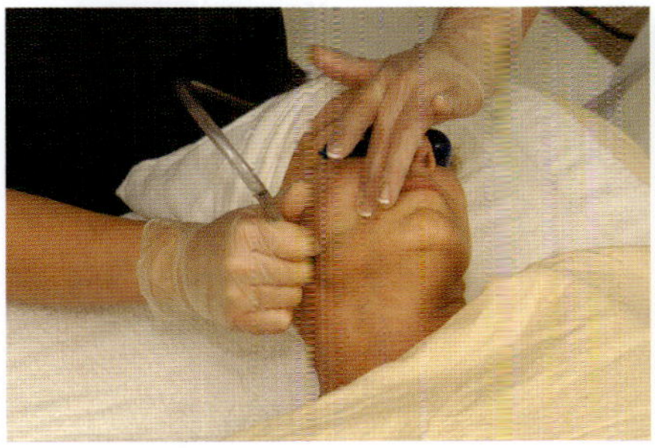

10 Repeat both sets of strokes on each cheek, working from the nose to jaw outwards and from the eye orbital bone to the chin. Repeat on chin and nose.

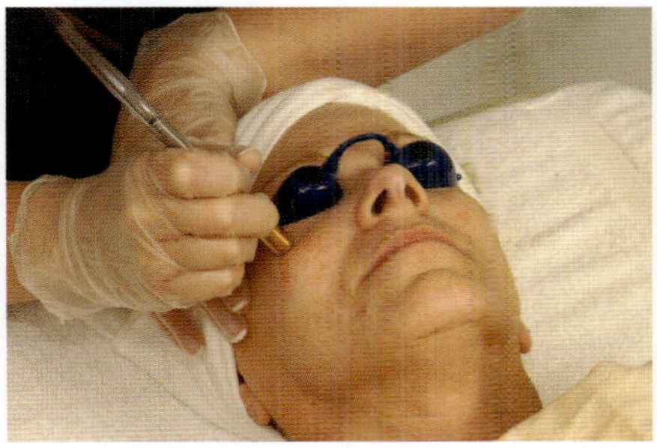

11 Reduce the vacuum pressure to the lowest level in the orbital areas. Never work on the eyelid itself. Use the orbital bone as a guideline for how close to the eye to go.

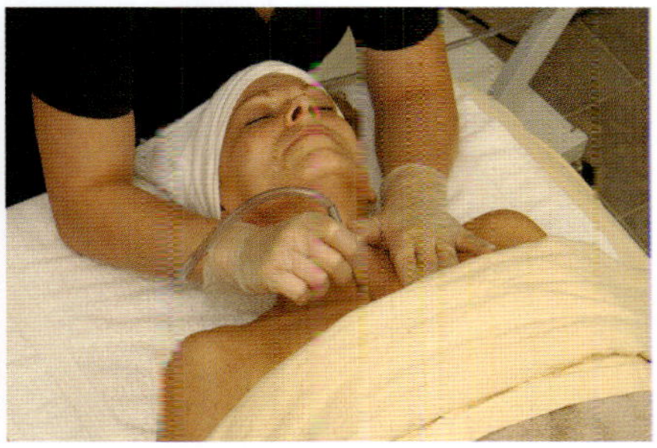

12 For the chest, start in the centre of the chest and stroke outward, holding the skin taut.

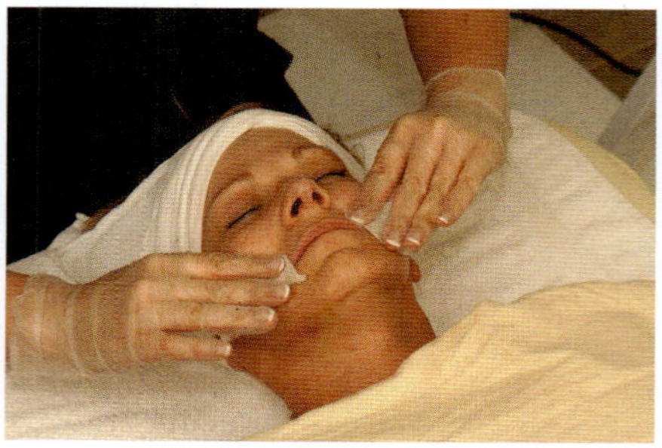

13 Wipe over the face to ensure that you have removed all crystals.

14 Follow with normal facial routine procedure, i.e. mask application according to manufacturer's instructions.

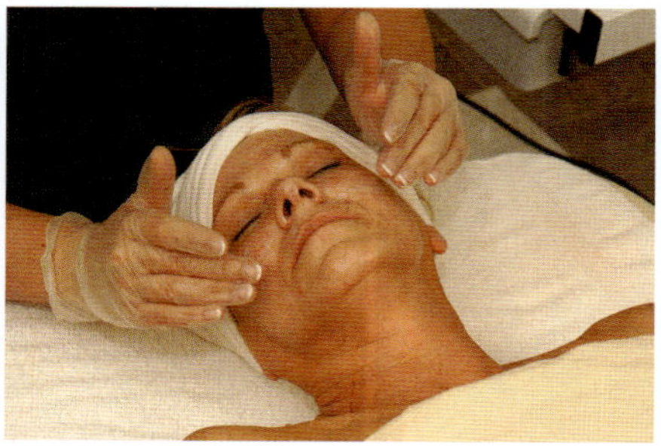

15 Conclude the treatment with soothing serum or lotion and sun protection.

Aftercare

Inform the client that following the service they may experience signs of skin irritation such as redness, dryness and itching. This will vary according to the service application technique applied or the skin type treated. Soothing, nourishing skincare preparations should be recommended and the client must not scratch the skin.

Promote other electrotherapy services such as facial/body **faradic** therapy or microcurrent or body wraps which will provide a skin/muscle firming effect. Encourage the retail sale of sun protection creams and relevant skincare.

If a contra-action occurs, advise the client to contact the salon immediately to receive appropriate professional advice.

> You should expect your customer to treat you as they would treat any other professional – such as an accountant or a lawyer. All professionals sell things, they sell their advice, their time and expertise – just like you.
>
> But the process starts with and depends on you. If you value yourself as a professional then your customers will value you too.
>
> Remember that most people will form an initial opinion about someone within 30 seconds of meeting them. First impressions last – if you do not look or act the part then you will not be taken seriously.
>
> **Mary Overton**

> Broaden your outlook by reading trade magazines, attending trade exhibitions and taking up any courses offered by your employer.
>
> Good editorial coverage in local papers is a superb medium by which to promote your business and should be pursued with enthusiasm, as the rewards are high. I would recommend you approach the editor of the Women's page and offer a free facial or body treatment and build on your relationship by approaching them regularly with fresh information, news flashes and ideas. This can be about you as a beauty therapist or your salon as a whole.
>
> **Mary Overton**

The client should:

- Avoid UV exposure for up to 7 days following service, as the skin is more susceptible to sun damage.
- Not apply self-tan preparations to the area for 48 hours.
- Wear an UV sun block on exposure to sunlight at all times.
- Use recommended retail products to care for the skin at home, to soothe and nourish the skin.
- Avoid full make-up application for 24 hours following service: eye and lip make-up may be worn.
- Avoid heat services and self-tan application for 24–48 hours following service to avoid skin sensitization.

Contra-actions

- excessive erythema, skin irritation
- excessive skin bleeding

Do not treat the skin again until skin healing has occurred. In cases of extreme skin reaction to service it will be advisable that the client does not receive the service again due to unsuitability.

BEST PRACTICE

Fair skinned and post-acne clients

Care should be taken when treating fair skin types as this skin has less tolerance and may suffer from excessive erythema.

Do not treat a client who has post-acne scars if there are any pustules present to avoid sensitization and infection.

ASSESSMENT OF KNOWLEDGE AND UNDERSTANDING

FUNCTIONAL SKILLS

You have now learnt about the effects of the different electrical facial and body services and how to select and adapt your technique of application to meet the client's service requirements. These skills will enable you to improve face, body and skin condition using electrical services.

To test your level of knowledge and understanding, answer the following short questions. These will prepare you for your summative (final) assessment.

Anatomy and physiology questions required for these units are found on pages 98–99.

Organizational and legal requirements

1. Which legislation are you responsible for implementing when performing electrotherapy services?
2. How can cross-infection be avoided when carrying out electrotherapy service?
3. What action should be taken to safeguard others in the event of faulty equipment?
4. How often should electrical equipment be checked and by whom?
5. State four general electrical safety precautions which should be taken when using electrotherapy equipment.
6. Why is it important to allow sufficient time to complete a service?
7. Why is it important to keep detailed records of the clients' service(s)?
8. How can repetitive strain injury be avoided when performing electrotherapy services?

Client consultation

1. To perform an effective consultation you need the client to feel confident about providing you with positive, honest answers to your questions. You should have good:
   - communication skills
   - questioning techniques
   - listening skills
   - answering techniques

   Give examples of what you understand by good skills and techniques for each of the above.
2. What details are required on your client's record card?
3. Why is it important to discuss the client's lifestyle?
4. How would you recognize the following skin types/conditions:
   - dry?
   - oily?
   - sensitive?
   - congested?
   - dehydrated?

5 How would you recognize:
- poor muscle tone of the abdomen?
- kyphosis?
- cellulite?
- fluid retention?
- the body type mesomorph?

Preparation for service

1 How should the service environment be prepared to ensure client comfort and maximum benefit from the service? Consider temperature, lighting and sound.

2 Why is it beneficial to perform a pre-heating service before certain electrotherapy services?

3 How should the client be positioned to gain maximum benefit from:
- micro-current service to the face?
- audio sonic service to the shoulders?

4 Why is it important to discuss the expected service sensation with the client?

Anatomy and physiology

1 Name four facial bones.

2 Name the bones that form the shoulder girdle.

3 Name the location and action of the following muscles:
- buccinator
- sternocleido mastoid
- masseter
- trapezius
- rectus abdominus
- biceps

4 How does ageing affect the skin and how may this influence your choice and suitability of electrotherapy services?

5 What is the function of:
- arteries
- veins
- capillaries

6 Name four essential parts of the lymphatic system.

7 Name the two main veins which return blood from the head and face back towards the heart.

8 Name four lymphatic glands and state where they are located.

9 Name the main cranial nerves relevant to facial electrotherapy facial service.

10 State three effects on the skin of the services:
- galvanic
- high frequency
- micro-dermabrasion

Contra-indications and contra-actions

1 Why is it important to refer clients to their GP if you identify a contra-indication?

2 When would you need to refer a client to their GP before service could be given?

3 State three contra-indications to facial electrotherapy service.

4 State three contra-indications to body electrotherapy service.

5 List the possible contra-actions that may occur during both facial and body application and how you would deal with them. Provide three examples for both facial and body application.

Equipment and products

1 How is the following equipment cleaned to prevent cross-infection:
- vacuum suction ventouses?
- gyratory massage heads?
- faradic pad electrodes?

2 Why are water-based solutions used for galvanic service?

3 Name a suitable product to use for facial vacuum suction service.

4 How can a high standard of personal hygiene be maintained when performing electrotherapy services?

Service-specific knowledge

1 Why are skin sensitivity tests, both tactile and thermal, performed before service application?

2 How should the skin be prepared for:
- audio sonic body application?
- body galvanic iontophoresis?
- facial indirect high frequency?
- facial micro-dermabrasion?

3 How would the following contra-actions be recognized:

- galvanic burn?
- EMS or micro-current muscle fatigue?
- bruising from a vacuum suction service?
- skin bleeding from a micro-dermabrasion? What actions should be taken?

4 Considering the differences between male and female skin, how would this affect the application of facial vacuum suction in terms of vacuum intensity?

5 What type of electric current is used for the following services:

- faradic?
- galvanic?
- high frequency?

6 Give four physiological benefits that the client may expect from the following services:

- gyratory massage
- EMS service
- facial iontophoresis
- micro-dermabrasion

7 In which direction and at what system of the body is facial vacuum suction service directed?

8 Over what areas of the face may galvanic current intensity have to be produced and why?

9 Why is it important to gain feedback from the client and give relevant advice to them following service?

10 Why is it important to record any contra-action either during or following service on the client's record card?

11 After the electrotherapy service the client should be given advice to follow to ensure that they gain maximum benefit from the service. Discuss the advice to be given following:

- facial galvanic desincrustation
- facial micro-current
- body gyratory massage
- body faradic service

12 What recommendations to lifestyle habit would enable a client to continue the benefits from the service for:

- body faradic, the client wishes to improve his muscle tone?
- facial vacuum suction, the client wishes to improve her sluggish, congested skin type?
- micro-dermabrasion?

13 How often would you recommend a client receive micro-current electrotherapy service for rejuvenation?

14 What intervals would you recommend between micro-dermabrasion services?

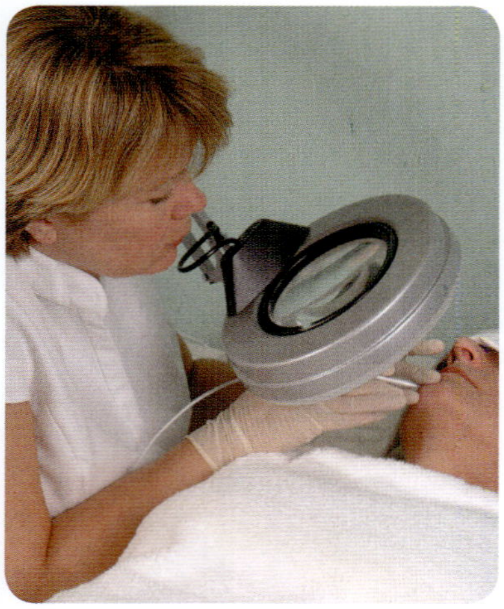

© CENGAGE LEARNING LTD

9 Electrical epilation

Learning Objectives

This chapter covers the **Provide electrical epilation treatments unit**.

This unit is about the skills involved in assessing, preparing for and carrying out electrical epilation services to permanently remove hair, using ac and blend techniques. You will also need to show you can competently advise clients on the aftercare needed following electrical epilation.

To carry out this unit you will need to maintain effective health, safety and hygiene throughout your work. You will also need to maintain a high standard of personal appearance and use good communication skills with the client.

There are **four** learning outcomes for this unit which you must achieve competently:

1 **Maintain safe and effective methods of working when providing electrical epilation services.**

2 **Consult, plan and prepare for services with clients.**

3 **Carry out electrical epilation.**

4 **Provide aftercare advice.**

For each unit your Assessor will observe you on **at least six separate occasions working on at least four different clients**. This will include **two** observations each for the upper lip, chin and bikini line.

(continued on the next page)

GILL MORRIS

ROLE MODEL

Gill Morris MCIM, FSA

Director GMT TEC

"Gill Morris is a Chartered Marketer, Fellow of the Royal Society of Arts and a Director of GMT TEC. She offers management and marketing consultancy services, plus is responsible for delivering business training specifically to the world of spa and beauty. In her past career she has been a General Beauty Therapist, owned two salons, worked for the supply side of the industry in research and development, new product development and general marketing, she has travelled extensively internationally and lectured in many countries, including America, Japan, South Africa and across Europe. Gill is an author of textbooks, distance learning workbooks and industry articles as well as being a judge of industry awards, member of college and exhibition advisory committees, is a sought after speaker, plus a Founding Director of Habia.

(continued)

From the **range** statement you must show that you have:

- used all **consultation techniques**
- dealt with **at least one of the necessary actions** where a contra-action, contra-indication or service modification occurs
- covered all the **areas** to be treated
- used all **types of needle**
- dealt with all of the **hair types**
- dealt with all the **skin types and conditions**
- carried out all of the **electrical epilation services**
- provided all types of relevant **advice**.

However, you must prove that you have the necessary knowledge, understanding and skills to be able to perform competently across the range.

When providing electrical epilation services it is important to use the skills you have learnt in the following units:

Monitoring safe work operations.

Promotional activities.

Essential anatomy and physiology knowledge requirements for this unit are identified on the checklist in Chapter 2, pages 12 and 13. This chapter also discusses anatomy and physiology specific to this unit.

Electrical needle epilation

Electrical needle **epilation** is used to permanently remove unwanted superfluous (excess) hair. A fine needle is used to deliver an electrical current into the hair follicle to destroy the hair root and this eventually destroys the hair follicle tissue, preventing the hair from regrowing.

This is a popular salon service and is usually carried out for cosmetic reasons. It is used on occasions to remove excessive hair growth resulting from certain medical conditions and has psychological benefits, as clients can often be very distressed by the hair growth. Clients experience great improvement in self-esteem and self-confidence following this service.

Being able to provide electrical epilation services can make you very employable. It shows that you can provide a technically skilled service and that your communication skills are good.

Superfluous hair is perfectly normal at certain stages of a woman's life, such as during puberty, pregnancy and menopause. Hair found during these times can disappear once the normal balance has returned. However, hair newly formed during the menopause is often permanent. Unwanted hair on the face is the area most often treated by epilation, but body hair can be removed from areas such as the breasts, underarms, bikini lines and legs. Male clients may also have hair permanently removed either for cosmetic reasons or because of irritation or that they suffer from ingrowing hairs. Clients undergoing gender reassignment from male to female may also want to change their hair growth pattern into a more female one.

Causes of hair growth

Excess hair growth can be either normal or abnormal, and may stem from a number of causes:

- *Topical.* Hair growth can be caused by irritation of the skin caused by friction, resulting in an increased blood supply. The hair follicles receive more nutrients and grow thicker, longer hairs. A plaster cast on a broken arm, for example, can result in increased hair growth when the cast is removed. This is soon shed. Moles and birthmarks or edges of scars often have longer hairs growing due to the increased blood supply in the area. People who work outdoors may grow longer hairs on areas that have been regularly sunburnt, like the top of the nose.
- *Congenital.* Congenital hair growth is an inherited predisposition (tendency) to excessive hair all over the body. A person can be born with this or it can appear later in life, which is very unusual.
- *Systemic.* This includes normal hair growth caused by hormones at puberty, pregnancy and menopause, and abnormal hair growth caused by a hormonal imbalance due to disease, tumour, surgery, medicine or emotional stress.

TOP TIP

Hereditary factors

Hereditary factors must be taken into account when assessing what is normal for a particular client.

Malfunctions of the endocrine system and the effects on hair growth

Abnormal hair growth is often the result of an abnormal change in the endocrine system causing a hormonal imbalance. This may be due to illness, tumours, dietary disorders or medication.

Virilization With **virilization**, the female body becomes more masculine and as a result, heavy facial and body hair growth can be seen in a masculine pattern. A hormone imbalance which may be due to a tumour of the adrenal cortex or a tumour of the ovaries will influence the hypersecretion of androgens and the reduction in the secretion of oestrogen. This will produce the male pattern of hair growth in females. This condition is known as **abnormal systemic hair growth**.

ALWAYS REMEMBER

Recognizing virilization

Virilization is recognized by a deepening of the voice, cessation (stopping) of menstruation causing infertility, loss of scalp hair and the development of acne vulgaris. The breast tissue reduces and the body thickens in shape.

TOP TIP

Stress

Women under considerable stress have excessive hair growth due to high levels of adrenalin which also stimulates androgen production.

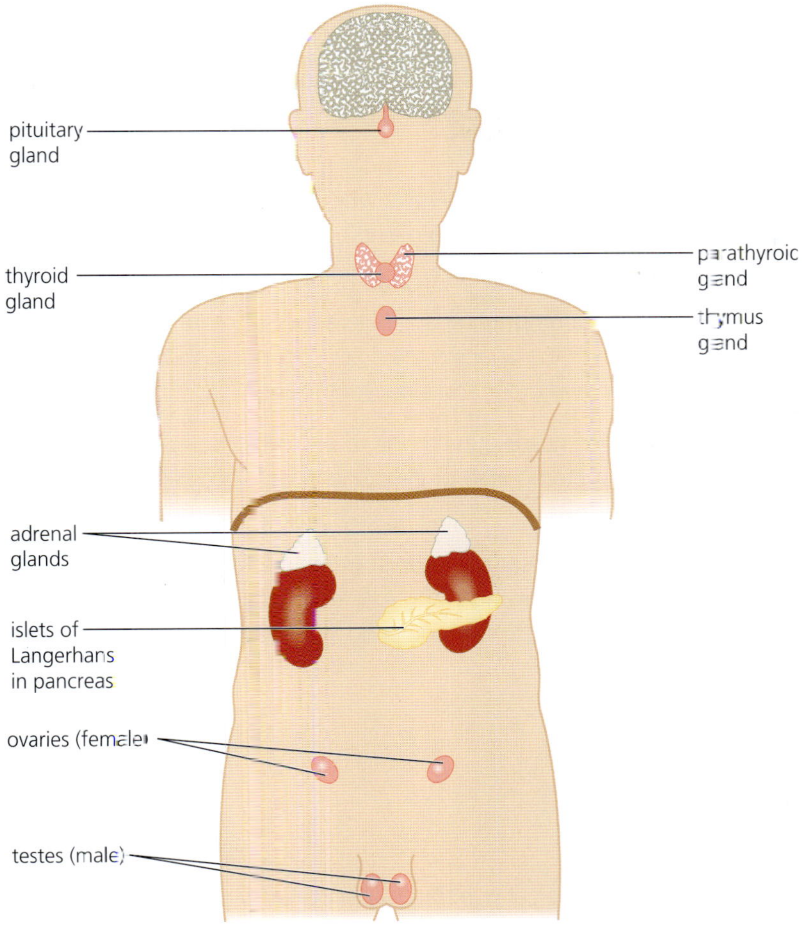

The endocrine system

Polycystic ovary syndrome (Stein–Leventhal syndrome) A variety of symptoms can result from this condition, including infertility, heavy periods, irregular periods and excessive growth of facial and body hair. The cause is cysts or growths, on the ovaries which develop due to non-completion of the ovulation process. This is not uncommon.

Cushing's syndrome This condition is often due to tumours on the adrenal cortex, where too much cortisol is produced. There is an associated over-production of androgens as a result and a heavy masculine hair growth can be seen. Other symptoms include a thickened trunk, round face, dowager's hump and thin legs and arms.

Anorexia nervosa People suffering from the eating disorder anorexia nervosa become very thin and undernourished. It is quite common to see excessive hair growth all over the face and body. This is a result of a shutdown in the ovaries, reducing the oestrogen level and stimulating the circulating androgens. Also, women and girls who have a high level of athletic training with low levels of body fat (e.g. gymnasts) may also be affected by the ovaries shutting down. Both processes will result in varying degrees of virilization.

Effects of medication Certain prescribed drugs, such as androgens and anabolic steroids, have a secondary effect of causing excessive hair growth. The beauty therapist needs to determine the effect of the drug with the client's doctor so that an effective service plan can be devised.

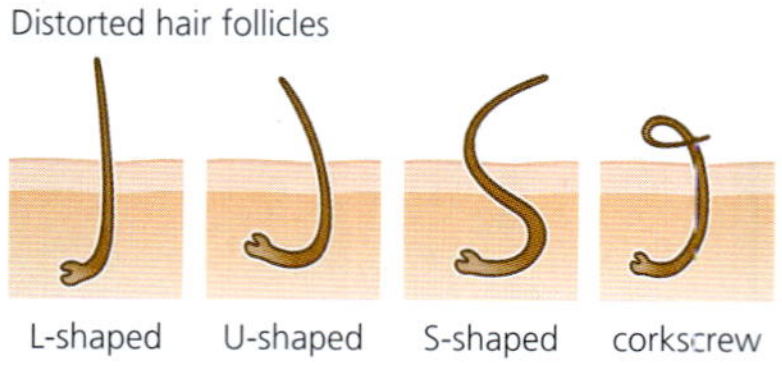

Distorted hair follicles. Direction of hair growth and angle as it leaves the hair follicle are important to consider when inserting the needle into the hair follicle. Hairs that grow from a distorted hair follicle, as shown, are more difficult as insertion depth is limited only to where the angle of the follicle changes. These types of hair follicles are best treated with galvanic or blend methods to enable treatment application to the target area

HEALTH & SAFETY

Releasing an ingrowing hair

To free an ingrowing hair the skin's surface should first be sanitized. Wearing disposable gloves, the beauty therapist should gently pierce the surface of the skin to free the hair using a sterile disposable needle. The hair should then be cut, not removed, to allow the skin to heal around it. All contaminated waste should be disposed off correctly and the needle placed in a sharps box. An antiseptic product should be applied to the area to promote skin healing. When the skin has healed the hair can be treated as normal.

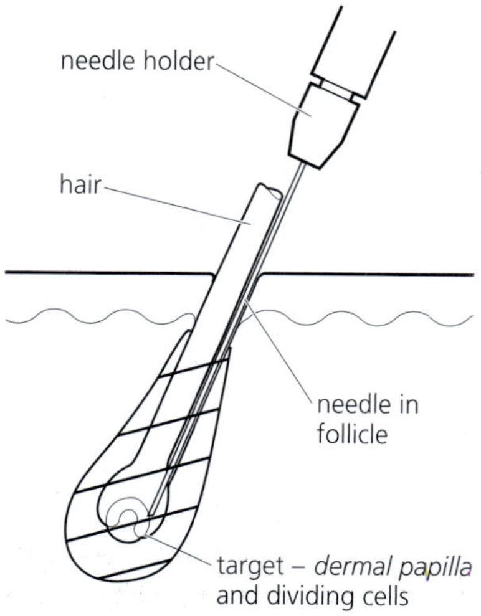

Galvanic current action occurs throughout the length and width of the follicle (indicated by a dark diagonal lines)

Unusual hair growth

- *Ingrowing hairs.* These are hairs which have not grown above the surface of the epidermis and are still in the follicle. If left the hairs can become infected so they need to be freed.
- *Embedded hairs.* These again are hairs which have become trapped below the skin. They should be treated as ingrowing hairs. When the skin is pierced, the hair usually will uncoil from underneath.
- *Pili multigemini hairs (compound hairs).* Here, two or more hairs grow out of a single follicle. Beneath the opening there are separate papillae for each hair, and the hairs have their own outer and inner root sheath.
- *Corkscrew hairs.* This hair is curved due to the follicle being distorted in shape. Over-treatment using temporary or permanent hair removal methods can cause this condition.
- *Tombstone hairs.* If the beauty therapist treats a telogen hair and there is an early anagen hair also growing in the follicle, the anagen hair will work its way to the skin's surface and will appear dull and thicker than normal. It will eventually fall out.

Electrical science

Epilation service

Epilation services rely on electrical currents to permanently alter the hair follicle, making it unable to produce new hairs. There are three types of epilation services: galvanic, diathermy and blend. These are described in the table below.

Service	*Action*
Galvanic current	dc flows in one direction
	negative pole = needle
	positive pole = indifferent electrode
	chemical action sodium hydroxide 'lye' occurs
ac	High-frequency ac (diathermy)
	Produces heat in tissues
	Electro-coagulation occurs
Blend	Combination of diathermy and galvanic
	Heating the tissues makes the lye more effective and quicker acting

Direct or galvanic current

A dc is one where electrons flow in one direction. This current uses the negative pole (cathode) and positive pole (anode) to complete a circuit.

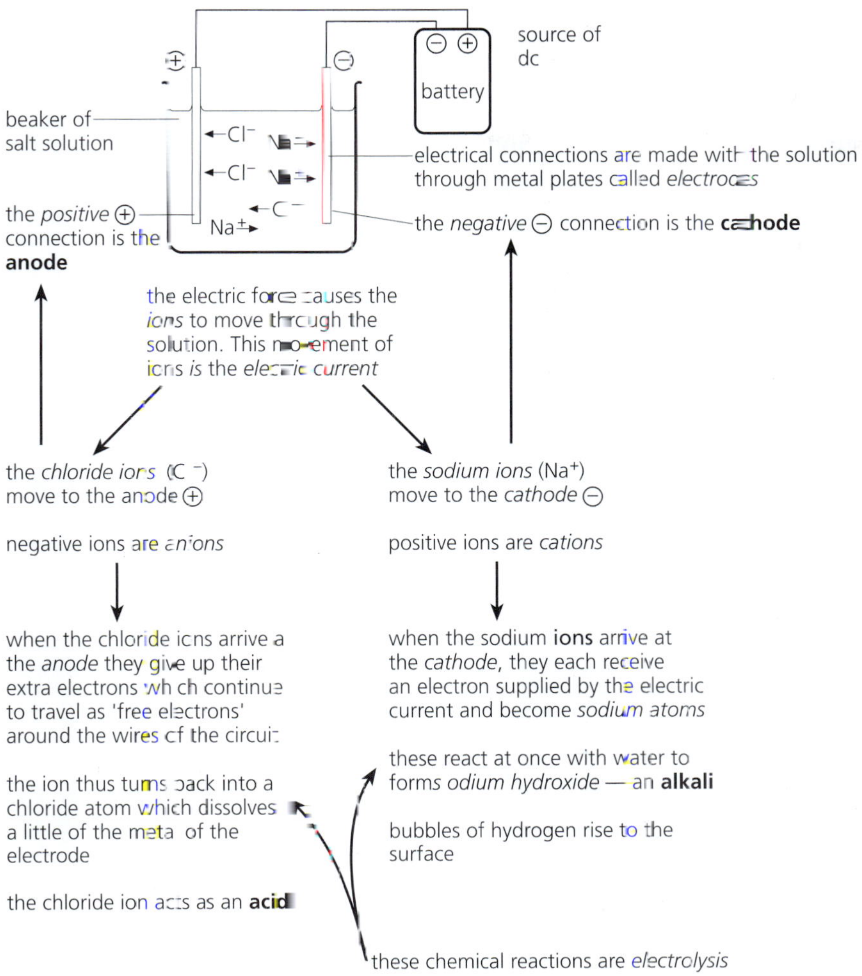

The process of electrolysis

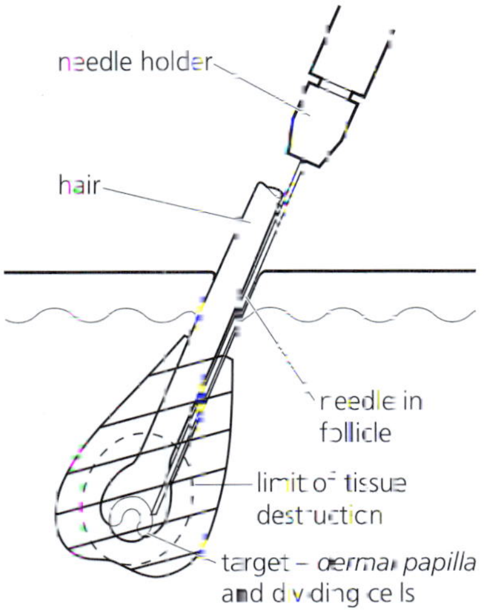

Diathermy current action is restricted to the base of the hair follicle. Blend current action combines the effects of galvanic and diathermy, producing both heat (dashed line) and lye (dark diagonal lines)

The client holds the indifferent electrode (anode) and the needle holder is attached to the negative outlet (cathode). The negative pole is the active pole and the positive pole is used to attract and complete the circuit.

When dc electrons go through a salt water solution, the salt and water molecules become chemically rearranged and form new substances. The salt and water are changed into sodium hydroxide and hydrogen gas. This reaction is called electrolysis.

The needle from the dc electrical epilation machine is inserted into the follicle; dc flows out over the length of the needle. Because of the moisture in the follicle, sodium hydroxide (lye) is formed within it. This chemically decomposes the follicle tissue and then remains in the follicle to continue to destroy the cells.

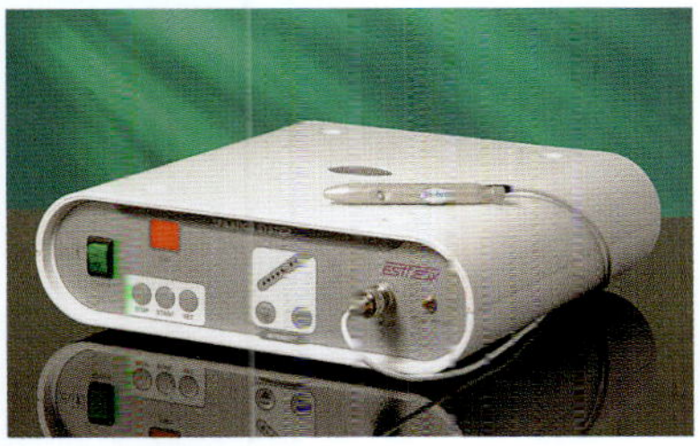

ELLISONS

Short wave diathermy machine

High-frequency ac or short-wave diathermy

Short-wave diathermy uses a high-frequency ac oscillating at millions of cycles per second. High-frequency epilating machines work on 13.56 and 40.68 MHz (the higher the frequency the more comfortable the sensation).

A high-frequency ac is introduced into the skin via a needle, heat is produced as the water molecules in the cells are agitated by the high-frequency energy.

The needle itself is not hot. Low level tissue destruction occurs as proteins in the cells coagulate on heating, called electro-coagulation, and blood vessels in the area are cauterized.

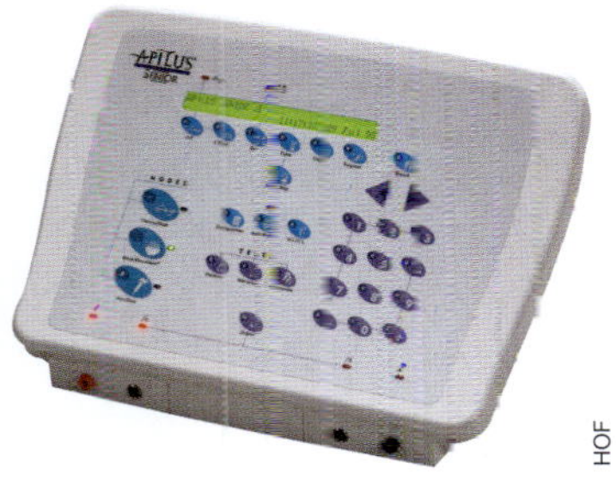

HOF

Blend epilator

Blend current In the blend method, both ac and dc flow from the needle at the same time. Both currents still retain their individual effects in the skin follicle.

The dc produces sodium hydroxide (lye) that chemically decomposes the follicle, while the high-frequency current coagulates the follicle. The interaction of the two currents produces better results than either current on its own. The heating of the tissue makes the sodium hydroxide more effective.

There are many variations of electrical epilation machine available. Each manufacturer will have different ways of using the machine for the best results.

There are three types of electrical epilation current available:

- The ac machine usually known as a diathermy machine. These are usually machines which use the lower frequency band of 13.56 MHz. They are simple to use with a button or dial to adjust to increase the current intensity. They may have an automatic timer for the current duration, e.g. 1 second, 2 seconds, and they may have a choice of finger switch or foot switch control to switch the current on or off. This is known as manual alternating or diathermy service. A low level of intensity and a longer time to treat each follicle.
- The galvanic current machine is rarely used and not easily available mainly due to its very slow hair removal rate due to the galvanic procedure technique.
- The blended current machines which use ac and galvanic current blended together are most commonly used. This is because they give the beauty therapist a choice of ac, galvanic current and blend current. This means you can treat all different types of hair with the best current combination for the most effective service. The more advanced and therefore expensive blend machines will have a large number of automatic settings. The beauty therapist can choose the current settings for the hair problem (see table on page 324). These machines usually use the higher frequency ac band of 40.68 MHz. The settings are all applied with a foot pedal and can include constant blend, blend followed by galvanic or even galvanic with pulses of ac. It is recommended that you have the training provided by the suppliers of these more complex machines to get the best out of them. The higher-frequency auto-timed units can also be used for the flash technique which is a high-intensity ac on a microsecond time. This can vaporize (change from a solid and liquid into a gas) miniscule amounts of follicle tissue without triggering the pain nerves so avoiding discomfort. This is a technique which is generally used only by experienced beauty therapists.

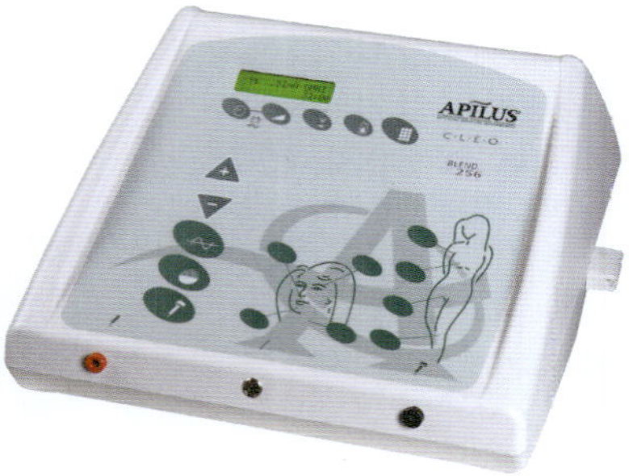

HOF

Blend epilation unit

ALWAYS REMEMBER

The equipment, no matter how simple or complicated is only as good as the person providing the service. The skill is to make the needle insertions into the follicle accurate and comfortable so the current is delivered to the right area to destroy the follicle and stop the hair from growing again.

ALWAYS REMEMBER

Consent

You will need a signed consent form from a parent or guardian for treating minors. A minor is classed as under 16 in Scotland, and under 18 in England.

Outcome 1: Maintain safe and effective methods of working

Maintain safe and effective methods of working when providing electrical epilation services

1. Setting up and monitoring the service area to meet organization procedure and manufacturers' instructions.
2. Making sure that environmental conditions are suitable for the client, the service and meet legal and safety requirements.
3. Ensuring your personal hygiene, protection and appearance meet accepted industry and organizational requirements.
4. Effectively disinfecting your hands throughout the service as required.
5. Wearing the recommended personal protective equipment to avoid cross-infection and exposure to hazardous waste.
6. Ensuring your own posture and position minimizes fatigue and risk of injury while working.
7. Ensuring all reusable tools and equipment are disinfected or sterilized using the correct methods.
8. Positioning equipment and products for ease and safety in use.
9. Ensuring the client is in a comfortable and relaxed position suitable for the service.
10. Maintaining accepted industry hygiene and safety practices throughout the service.
11. Maintaining the client's modesty, privacy and comfort at all times.
12. Checking the client's well-being at regular intervals according to organizational policy.
13. Disposing of single-use items, hazardous waste and waste materials safely and correctly.
14. Ensuring the service is cost-effective and is carried out within a commercially viable time.
15. Ensuring client records are up-to-date, accurate, complete, legible and signed by the client and practitioner.
16. Leaving the service area and equipment in a condition suitable for future services.

Before beginning the electrical epilation service check that you have the necessary equipment and materials to hand and that they meet legal, hygiene and industry requirements for electrical epilation.

EQUIPMENT AND MATERIALS LIST

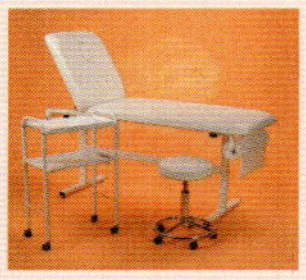
BEAUTY EXPRESS LTD

Couch, stool and trolley
Couch and stool adjustable height; trolley to hold equipment

ELLISONS

Magnifying lamp (normally 0.3 dioptre fluorescent)
This allows a slight magnification of three-quarters the normal size and a clear cold light

ELLISONS

Client record card

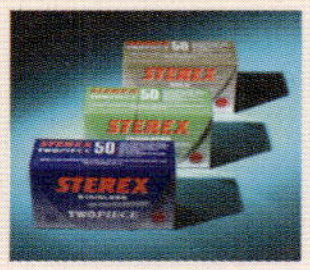

COURTESY OF STEREX ELECTROLYSIS

Pre-sterilized needles
In assorted sizes – 002–006 and types one piece, two piece, insulated and gold

BEAUTY EXPRESS LTD

Stainless steel tweezers
Six pairs are usually required to allow for sterilization between each client

BEAUTY EXPRESS LTD

Sharps box
For the disposal of used needles
Yellow sac required for contaminated (clinical) waste disposal

ELLISONS

Covered, lined foot pedal bin
For contaminated waste

ELLISONS

Autoclave
Used to sterilize tweezers, scissors and chuck caps for epilation service

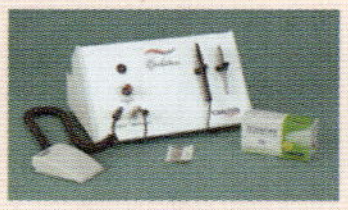
CARLTON PROFESSIONAL

ELLISONS

Your workplace may use any of the following equipment for permanent hair removal:

Galvanic/dc epilation unit

Short wave diathermy/high-frequency epilation unit

HOF

Blend epilation unit

YOU WILL ALSO NEED:

Disposable surgical gloves (nitryl or PVC formulation) To avoid cross-infection to the client or beauty therapist. A fresh pair is used for each client

Kidney bowl To store the sterile tweezers and needle holder

Pre-service antiseptic skin cleanser or swabs To cleanse and disinfect the service area

Post-service antiseptic soothing lotion or gel To soothe the skin and promote skin healing, avoiding secondary infection

Cotton wool To apply skin-service preparations (stored in a covered container)

Tissues To blot the skin dry after cleansing and to shield the eyes from the magnification lamp (stored in a covered container). Eye shields are available and the tissue may be placed under these before wearing.

Stainless steel scissors To trim hairs as necessary.

Bowls To hold client jewellery as necessary

Hand mirror To discuss and show the client the epilated area before and after service

Antiseptic wipes (unscented) To disinfect the service area

Cold sterilizing solution Such as sodium hyperchlorite and small container to hold it in, to keep tweezers and scissors sterile

Additional equipment for dc galvanic service

Hand-held indifferent electrode Necessary to complete the circuit

Needle holder With finger button or foot switch to control current application

Additional equipment for diathermy high-frequency service

Needle holder With finger button or foot switch to control current application

Additional equipment for blend service

Hand-held indifferent electrode Necessary to complete the circuit. A cover is often provided for this electrode which may require to be dampened before use.

Needle holder With finger button or foot switch to control current application

Preparation of the service area

- The service area should be clean.
- All towels should be replaced with clean ones after each client.
- Clean paper tissue bedroll should cover the surface of the service couch.
- Time should be spent cleaning the couch, magnifying lamp and trolley.
- The needle holder, lamp edges and any other surface touched during the previous service should be wiped over with disinfectant.
- Sterile equipment should be collected in a clean kidney bowl lined with a clean paper tissue. Your hands must be protected with clean gloves when handling sterile equipment.

Positioning of the equipment The service trolley should be placed on the side that the beauty therapist is working from. This prevents trailing wires or leads stretching across the client when adjusting machine settings. The magnifying lamp should be placed so that it can illuminate the area without being knocked when the beauty therapist is working, or spring back because it has been overstretched. A pedal bin should be placed under the couch within the beauty therapist's reach, lined with a disposable bin bag. If possible, the couch should be pulled away from the wall at the head so that the beauty therapist can move around the top when epilating the eyebrows or when wishing to work from the opposite side. This creates minimal disturbance to the client when working.

The trolley should be prepared with all the equipment required.

Preparation of the beauty therapist

The beauty therapist should present a professional, clean appearance at all times. Creating a good impression promotes good working practice and confidence in the client.

- A clean overall and tights or trousers should be worn daily.
- Minimal or no perfume should be worn to avoid client allergy and overpowering the client while in close contact.
- Nails should be short, clean and free of polish.
- Long hair should be tied back at the nape of the neck to prevent it falling forward. Long fringes should be secured back away from the face.
- Minimal jewellery should be worn – i.e. a wedding band and small stud earrings.

Preparation of the client

The beauty therapist should greet the client and put them at ease. The client record card should be collected and completed if this is the consultation, or referred to if this is a follow-up service.

Positioning of the client is important for effective service. Depending on the area being treated, the client should be positioned on the couch comfortably and any clothing removed from the body part to be treated as relevant. If the face is to be treated, any make-up or lotions should be cleansed from the face by wiping over with antiseptic pre-electrolysis lotion.

Disposable eyepads or disinfected protective eye shields can be used to cover the eyes to protect them from the bright light of the magnifying lamp. This also encourages the client to relax.

HEALTH & SAFETY

PPE

Wear personal protective equipment provided. Gloves must not be latex because it is a known allergen. This means your clients may be allergic to it and you may be also. Use nitryl or PVC gloves instead which are less likely to cause reactions on the skin. Get the best fitting ones you can.

> People working not just together but for each other is a key skill which employers look for.
>
> The ability to quickly become part of a team with the minimum amount of disruption to a business is very important to an employer, as disruption costs money.
>
> **Gill Morris**

> A person who comes for a consultation is not yet a client, they are a potential client only.
>
> Do not take it for granted during the consultation that they are already a client as this is where you 'sell' yourself, your knowledge and your ability.
>
> **Gill Morris**

BEST PRACTICE

Client confidence

The client must feel that they have confidence in the beauty therapist. This will be demonstrated by:

- a professional appearance
- high standards of hygiene practice
- good organizational skills
- a positive, knowledgeable consultation
- conversation to reassure the client and put them at ease

Remember what it's like not to know

Be aware that a potential client can be nervous as he/she won't know what to expect, ensure you ask if they have any questions and that you go through all their concerns.

Gill Morris

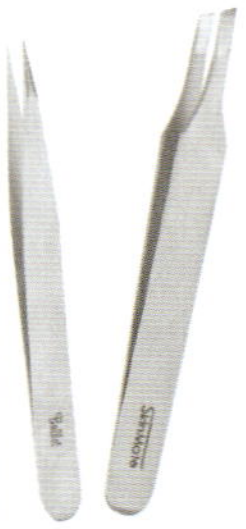

BEAUTY EXPRESS LTD

Electrolysis tweezers

BEAUTY EXPRESS LTD

Automatic medical autoclave

HEALTH & SAFETY

Sterilization

Sufficient resources should be available for effective sterilization of equipment between clients.

TOP TIP

Service area

The area which has been wiped and cleansed with antiseptic lotion should be dried before epilation is performed. If this is not done, the moisture can conduct a sudden surge of current up the follicle, which may cause surface burning.

BEST PRACTICE

Showing improvement

Before the service begins take close-up photos of the area, but make sure that the client cannot be recognized. This shows improvement during and after. Permission must be obtained from the client first.

Disposable bedroll should be placed in the area to be treated so that it protects the client's modesty and area being treated.

Sterilization and disinfection

As electrical epilation involves possible blood contact, a high standard of hygiene and sterilization should be adhered to at all times to prevent infection. Hepatitis and AIDS are common today and stringent measures must be followed to prevent cross-infection of the virus to the clients and beauty therapist. Bacterial and viral strains can be prevented from spreading by sterilizing equipment effectively and keeping all surfaces clean.

The couch, trolley, magnifying lamp and floor should be cleaned daily with disinfectant. Cleaning requirements should be checked with your local authority health department. Manufacturer's instructions should be followed for diluting substances for effective destruction of bacterial and viral spores. The couch should not have a cover, but be protected with clean disposable bedroll for each client.

Antiseptic wipes should be available to clean the couch or equipment before and during service as necessary.

Tweezers and scissors These should be made of good quality stainless steel to prevent rusting. These must be cleaned first with a disinfectant wipe to remove dirt and debris and then and placed in the autoclave to sterilize prior to service.

Probe and chuck The probe should be cleaned with disinfectant before each client. Several chuck caps should be available, sterilized in the autoclave and placed in the UV cabinet for the recommended time. Place the needle holder on clean cotton wool in the kidney bowl.

HEALTH & SAFETY

Autoclave

Tweezers and chuck caps are sterilized between clients, using an autoclave. These must be washed in a soapless cleanser, carefully rinsed in cold water and wiped with a disinfectant wipe before being placed in the autoclave. For best practice use an ultrasound cleaning bath to ensure all microscopic debris is removed before sterilizing.

Sterilized instruments

When removing the sterilized tweezers from the autoclave, use the appropriate tool for this purpose. Never handle them as not only will this contaminate them, but they will also be extremely hot.

Needles Needles can be bought from different companies but all come pre-packed and sterilized and are disposed of after each client.

The needle has three parts – the shank, shaft and tip. Most needles are made from stainless steel. If the client has very sensitive skin, a 24 carat gold-plated, stainless steel needle is available, which is considered to reduce irritation as it is a good conductor of electricity and thought to facilitate insertion.

There are two piece needles as shown in the diagram and one piece needles which are shaped more like a javelin and are more durable than two piece.

Insulated needles which are preferable for the treatment of diabetic clients but can only be used with short-wave diathermy technique. These have a coating covering the shaft, leaving only the tip exposed, which concentrates the current at the base of the hair follicle. This reduces heat/chemical sensitisation to the upper hair follicle, whilst you concentrate tissue destruction where required.

Many needles are supplied with a protective plastic covering, which prevents contamination of the needle during loading. Care should be taken when loading the needles to prevent contamination. Needles must always be in perfect condition.

All other **aseptic** methods those that try to eliminate all bacteria are followed as for all beauty therapy services.

When booking the initial appointment for epilation service, sufficient time should be allocated to perform the consultation, which normally takes 15 minutes. This is usually complimentary. This is followed by a test of the area to assess skin tolerance or sensitivity to the service and check the client's suitability for the service. It also gives the client an indication of the sensation to expect during the service process. After the first consultation, service times will vary according to the area to be treated and the amount of hair to be removed.

- Small areas such as the upper lip and chin are usually treated within 10 to 15 minutes.
- Larger areas such as the back, forearm and lower limbs may take up to an hour.

The client should be advised to wear loose-fitting clothing if body hair is to be removed, to prevent rubbing and irritation of the area following the service.

If the facial area is to be treated advise the client to avoid wearing heavy facial make-up and high-necked clothes or scarves, which may irritate the area. The skin must be kept clean to avoid secondary infection. Advise against activities such as swimming or skin services such as exfoliation on the same day, as these may cause skin sensitization.

Skin healing intervals must be allowed between services. This will prevent infection and scarring. Dependent upon the area to be treated, hair growth and skin type, this may be between 1–2 weeks.

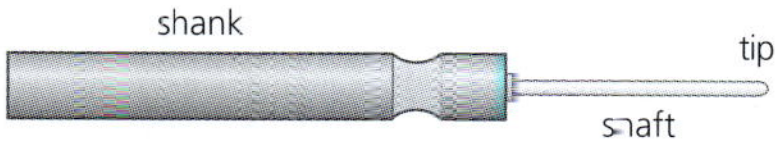

Parts of a needle

HEALTH & SAFETY

Needle sterilization methods

Gamma irradiation is sterilization using short wavelength radiation. A visible red spot on each packet identifies it has been through this process. Ethylene oxide, a highly poisonous gas, is also used to sterilize pre-packed needles.

HEALTH & SAFETY

Sharps disposal

Sharps boxes must be disposed of by a reputable hygiene disposal company. Contact your local environmental health authority for guidance.

Sharps box

Outcome 2: Consult, plan and prepare for services with clients

Consult with the client for epilation service

- Using **consultation techniques** a polite sensitive and supportive manner to determine the client's service needs.
- Obtaining signed, written informed consent from the client prior to carrying out the service.
- Ensuring that informed and signed parent or guardian consent is obtained for minors prior to any electrical epilation services.

***(continued)* Consult with the client for epilation service**

4. Ensuring that a parent or guardian is present throughout the electrical epilation service for minors.
5. Clearly explaining to the client what the service entails in a way they can understand.
6. Using suitable visual aids effectively to aid client understanding.
7. Using **consultation techniques** which accurately identify the client's medical history, hair type, causes of hair growth, skin type and condition and emotional state.
8. Establishing and recording the client's past and present hair management techniques and the implication for services.
9. Asking your client appropriate questions to identify if they have any contra-indications to electrical epilation services.
10. Accurately recording your client's responses to questioning.
11. Taking the **necessary action** in response to any identified contra-indications.
12. Actively encouraging the client to ask questions and clarify any points of which they are unsure.
13. Encouraging clients with suspected contra-indications to seek medical advice without reference to specific conditions and without causing undue alarm or concern.
14. Taking consistent, clear high quality pre-service photographs of the area(s) to be treated with the consent of the client as and when required.
15. Clearly explaining the physical sensation created by the service.
16. Correctly preparing the area to be treated and carrying out a test patch to establish suitability for service.
17. Ensuring written aftercare procedures are given to the client following the test patch.
18. Recommending alternative services or products which are suitable for the client if contra-indicated for electrical epilation service.

(continued) Consult with the client for epilation service

- **19** Clearly explaining and agreeing the projected cost, likely duration, frequency, types of service and client commitment needed.
- **20** Clearly identifying and agreeing in writing the area(s) to be treated, client expectations and service objectives, ensuring they are realistic and achievable.
- **21** Selecting and preparing equipment to meet legal and safety requirements and service objectives.

The consultation is an important part of a successful electrical epilation service. The information gained will allow you to assess whether the client is suitable for service and devise a service plan to suit each client.

Use your communication skills when conducting the consultation. These must be verbal, visual and body language, you must explain the service programme clearly and use your pamphlet which explains the procedure and related advice and skin poster to illustrate the procedure. Explain about the hair growth cycle and how the service slows down and stops the hair regrowing with the help of a skin visual aid.

You and your client should sit together, on the same level, to discuss the service. Be relaxed, smile and show you are friendly and at ease to put your client at ease. Be reassuring but not patronizing. Listen actively to your client and answer questions thoroughly. Use your client record card as an additional means of explaining the services, contra-indications and contra-actions. Be clear about the important aftercare advice and again use your pamphlet and give it to the client to reinforce what you have said. At all times be aware of your client's body language and check for signs of them being fearful, nervous or anxious.

The beauty therapist will consider the client's medical history, emotional condition, general health and well-being, any contra-indications present, current hair growth and their suitability for service. Time should be spent explaining the service procedure and what is achievable with regular services, so that the client is aware of their commitment in relation to time and costs.

Explain the sensation of the service to the client:

- High-frequency or – short-wave diathermy technique: a slight stinging 'irritating' sensation will be experienced.
- dc – galvanic technique: there will be a sensation of warmth which will gradually increase in intensity.
- Blend technique: a slight stinging 'irritating' sensation will be experienced.

TOP TIP

Body language

Always observe the client's body language while taking personal details. If the client appears uneasy, reassurance may be needed, otherwise they might be deterred from proceeding with the service.

> **All students leave with the same qualification, why are you different?**
>
> How are you going to stand out to a potential employer? Employers want to see someone who'll fit in well, contribute to the business, someone who's prepared to go the extra mile, someone who can communicate with clients, someone who is professional, dedicated and friendly. Is that you and how will they know?
>
> **Gill Morris**

BEST PRACTICE

Sensitivity

If the client has sensitive skin or finds the service sensation very uncomfortable, shorter, more regular services should be booked.

TOP TIP

Service times

Service booking times are normally assessed during the consultation.

BEST PRACTICE

Personal experience

Experience each method of electrical epilation yourself. You can then describe the different sensations to your clients.

ALWAYS REMEMBER

Hair growth cycle

Approximately 20 per cent of hairs lie dormant below the skin's surface at any given time. Only those hairs visible above the skin's surface are able to be treated. At the next service, previously dormant hairs will now be visible and may be treated – these will not be the same hairs that were removed in the previous service.

TOP TIP

Waxing

If a client has no hair at all on the area you are working on when they come for their service, not even the fine vellus hairs, then it's likely they are waxing.

During the consultation, the client should be encouraged to discuss the service and ask questions. The following questions should be asked of the client during the consultation in order to obtain relevant information:

- *When did the problem start?* This will give an indication of the cause of the unwanted hair growth, e.g. common times for unwanted hair to appear for a female are during puberty, pregnancy and the menopause. Such hair, although unwanted, is normal. If the hair appears for no apparent reason it may indicate an underlying medical cause.
- *How is your general health?* This may give you an indication as to the cause of hair growth. Details of the client's medical history and medication taken need to be recorded. This is necessary because some medication may cause unnatural hair growth and the client's medical history may indicate the cause.
- *Is your menstrual cycle normal?* An unusual menstrual cycle may indicate a medical problem resulting in unwanted hair growth.
- *How many children? What are their ages?* Occasionally pregnancy can initiate an unwanted hair growth problem due to hormonal imbalance. This usually diminishes after the birth, but the client may require temporary removal.
- *Which methods of hair removal have you used previously?* Removing hair from the root with temporary methods of hair removal, such as tweezing, threading and waxing, can increase hair growth due to stimulation of the dermal papillae and blood supply. These measures may also have distorted the follicle, therefore it may take longer to achieve success with this service. Such methods must be stopped as soon as service commences.
- *Which area do you want to have treated?* This will allow you tactfully to determine the problem area and the psychological effect on the client. Never presume the area to be treated!
- *Have you had epilation before?* The beauty therapist needs to know when, why and what method was used and how successful it has been. Be professional and discreet at all times when discussing other beauty therapists.
- *Name, address and telephone number.* This is necessary in case the client needs to be contacted in order to change their appointment.
- *Visual examination of the area to be treated.* This is necessary for the beauty therapist to note the areas, the type and amount of hair growth and the general skin condition.

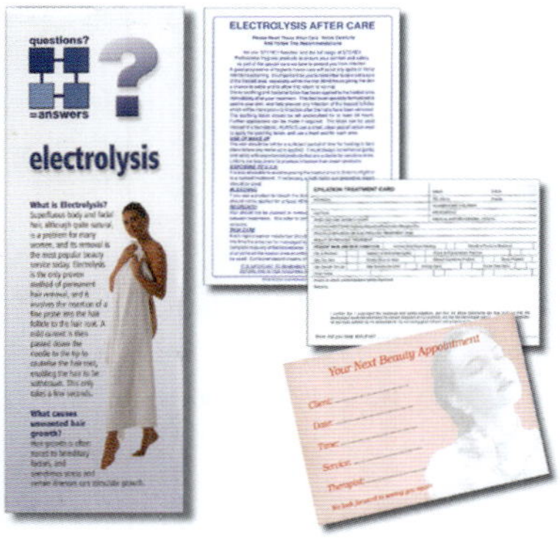

ELLISONS

Provide information so clients can make informed choices

Discuss with your client:

- how to manage the hair growth between services – plucking and waxing are not recommended as they may in some people, encourage the hair to grow. Bleaching, trimming or sometimes shaving may be suitable. Ensure the client knows that the hairs need to be long enough to see the angle and direction of growth for them to be treated
- what other services the client may be having done, e.g. facials or skin peeling. Some salon services need to be done at different times, e.g. some facials and sun beds should not be received at all
- your recommendation for which technique will be best for the hair type

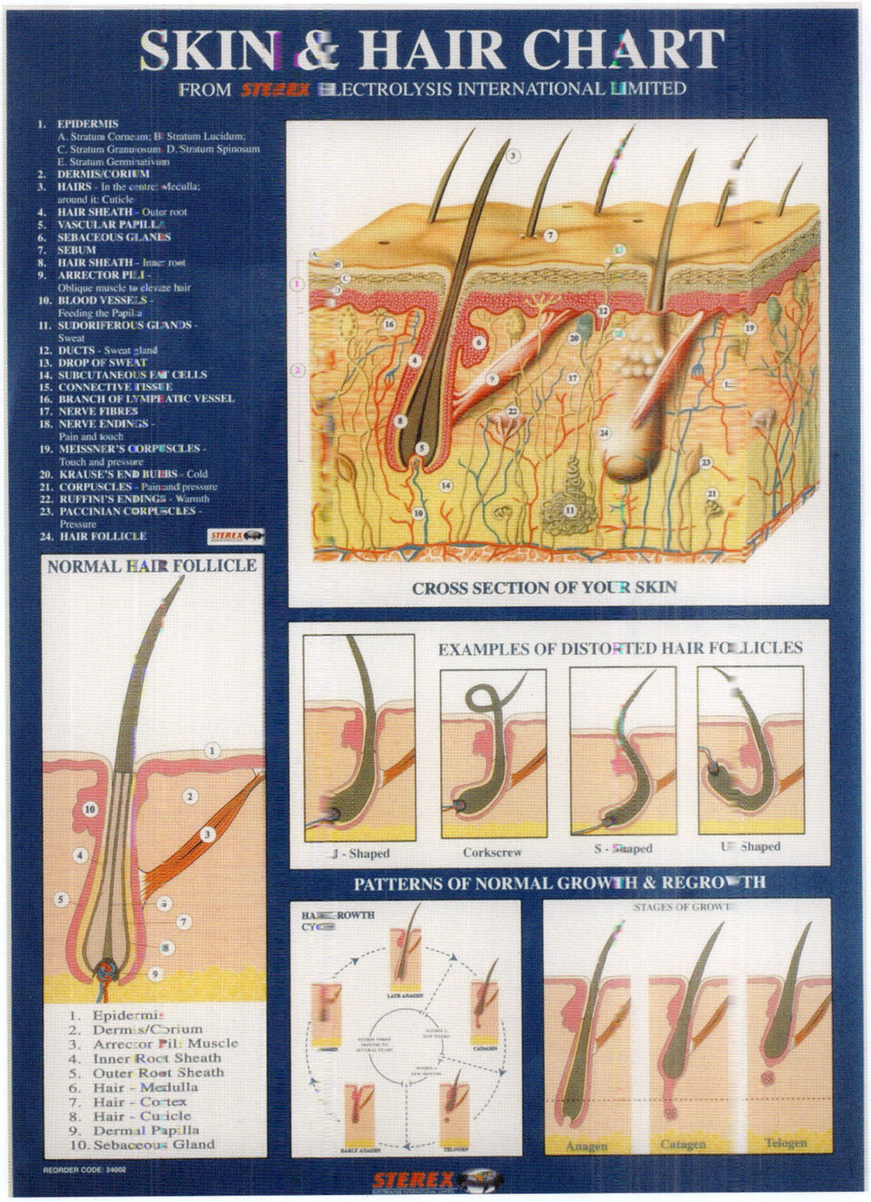

COURTESY OF STEREX ELECTROLYSIS

Skin poster the skin structure and the hair growth cycle which can be used at consultation when explaining the process

TOP TIP

Contact with clients

Before contacting a client by telephone or email you must confirm that this is acceptable. Some clients may wish to keep their services confidential.

TOP TIP

Probing technique

It is often best to learn probing techniques using a two piece needle. The flexibility of the needle shows if you are inserting well or not. It slides in easily in the right place but will bend if there is too much resistance. This helps you develop a sensitive touch and accurate insertion.

> **The two most important things you need to get right**
>
> The right amount of current discharged in the right place.
>
> **Gill Morris**

Diathermy is quick, removes a lot of hairs in one service and is particularly suitable for a fine, long growth which is fairly shallow and on dry skin. This makes it ideal for a lot of

ACTIVITY

Consultation questions

State how your consultation questions would differ when treating a female client, male client and gender dysphoria client.

facial hair growths presented, especially on the upper lip and sides of the face. More hairs are removed each service but it is considered that there is a larger percentage that regrow although they are finer each time.

Blend is very thorough, slower but with very little regrowth. It is suited to a full-terminal type of hair growth such as strong hair on the chin and body areas. It is ideal for deep, moist follicles.

Galvanic is slow but thorough and often has less pain sensation so it is good for very sensitive people who have particularly strong hair growth.

Most epilation services are carried out using the blend technique.

The physical sensation of the service will vary from client to client and area to area. The face is a sensitive area with the upper lip being most sensitive. The body is less sensitive but areas such as the upper thigh and bikini line can be very reactive to the current and the client may feel more sensitive. Toes are very sensitive; do not sit where you can be accidentally kicked by an involuntary twitch in reaction to the service sensation.

It is obvious that the higher intensity of the current, the more the client will feel it. Therefore strong, dense hair growths such as those found due to hormone imbalances or gender disphoriac clients are the most difficult to treat causing the most discomfort.

During a woman's menstrual cycle her reaction to the pain sensation can be different. Some women feel pain more when ovulating mid cycle, others just before a period is due, especially if they also have other premenstrual tension symptoms.

Transgender consultation considerations

There are several stages to the transgender (changing from male to female) client's service. It is important that you treat your clients with tact and consideration but no differently from your other clients.

During the consultation you should explain that you will need to know what stage the client is at for their transgender treatment. This will make a difference as to the amount of hair regrowth that they experience during their course of treatment.

At the beginning of their change they may have started female hormone treatment which will help to lessen the regrowth.

However, if they have had the full surgical procedure and are now completely physically female and also taking the female hormones then the hair regrowth during the treatment will be even less.

It is important to explain this and also to make sure that your client can talk to you and their doctor freely about the progression of the treatment and any concerns they may have.

Facial hair removal is usually the most asked for with transgender clients but other areas may also be treated such as neck and chest.

A patch test of the service is very useful as it is possible that transgender clients can have sensitive skin due to the female hormone treatment. It must also be explained that the service must be done carefully and with suitable gaps for healing in between to prevent skin damage.

BEST PRACTICE

Safe working practice

Some clients may ask for too much hair to be removed as they are very keen to have their problem hair removed. Do not be pushed into doing more than you know will be safe and effective.

ACTIVITY

Popular permanent hair removal systems

Research the availability of electrical epilation services in your local salons.

- Which types of services are offered?
- Which services are most asked for?
- What are the range of prices and times available?
- What sort of qualifications do the people have who are offering the service?
- Is the service popular?

Look at how much it would cost in equipment to set up the service and work out if it would be profitable and what the pay back time on the equipment would be.

ACTIVITY

Consultation role play

Working in pairs, write a case study of a client who may come in for an electrical epilation service. Role play this with another pair who then have to do the consultation with you. See if they can get all the relevant information from you which would give a full and thorough consultation.

Client record card

A client record card should always be completed prior to the service being given. This enables the beauty therapist to ensure that the client is suitable for service. Once the client has verified the details given they must sign the card. This protects the beauty therapist and client from undesirable service outcomes caused by misinformation. An **evaluation** of the information will form the basis of the service plan.

Once the consultation is completed, make sure that the client is satisfied with the information given and the service plan, and encourage the client to ask any further questions. Full and accurate record cards are necessary for insurance purposes.

TOP TIP

Needle fear

Needles are usually called probes as this sounds less alarming to most people. A lot of people are naturally very nervous of needles.

ALWAYS REMEMBER

Modification of service

Examples of epilation service modification include:

- shortening or lengthening the service time
- choosing a different service type (galvanic, diathermy or blend) to better suit the client's hair growth removal and tolerance
- changing the probe type or needle size
- treating hairs either further apart or more closely together depending upon skin tolerance and reaction
- changing the frequency of services to weekly or fortnightly

TOP TIP

Review of progress

Always check the record card at the beginning of every service. Encourage the client to tell you about how the skin and hair growth has been since the last service.

Record card for provide electrical epilation services

Date	Beauty therapist name	
Client name	Date of birth (Identifying client age group.)	
Address	Postcode	
Email address	Landline phone number	Mobile phone number
Name of doctor	Doctor's address and phone number	
Related medical history (Conditions that may restrict or prohibit service application.)		
Are you taking any medication? (This may affect the appearance of the skin or skin sensitivity.)		

CONTRA-INDICATIONS REQUIRING MEDICAL REFERRAL
(Preventing **electrical epilation** service application.)

- ☐ epilepsy
- ☐ diabetes
- ☐ hormone imbalance
- ☐ cardiovascular conditions
- ☐ nervous system dysfunction
- ☐ highly nervous client
- ☐ asthma
- ☐ pregnancy
- ☐ metal plates or pins in the service area
- ☐ skin disorders
- ☐ skin diseases
- ☐ pacemaker
- ☐ moles
- ☐ loss of skin sensation
- ☐ hemophilia

SERVICE AREAS
face:
☐ upper lip ☐ chin ☐ sides of face ☐ hair line
☐ neck/nape ☐ eyebrow

body:
☐ chest/breast ☐ back ☐ bikini line ☐ abdomen
☐ arms ☐ hands ☐ legs ☐ feet
☐ underarm

HAIR TYPE
☐ coarse ☐ fine ☐ curly

Amount of hair:
☐ dense ☐ medium ☐ sparse

SKIN TYPE
☐ oily ☐ dry ☐ sensitive
☐ dehydrated ☐ mature

CONTRA-INDICATIONS THAT RESTRICT SERVICE
(Service may require adaptation.)

- ☐ cuts and abrasions
- ☐ bruising
- ☐ localized eczema/psoriasis
- ☐ piercings
- ☐ slow healing
- ☐ highly sensitive skin
- ☐ psoriasis
- ☐ eczema
- ☐ diabetes
- ☐ acne vulgaris
- ☐ epilepsy

EQUIPMENT

- ☐ diathermy, galvanic or blend machine
- ☐ one-piece needle
- ☐ two-piece needle
- ☐ insulated, gold

Beauty Therapist signature (for reference)

Client signature (confirmation of details)

Record card for provide electrical epilation services (continued)

SERVICE ADVICE

Full facial – *allow up to 1 hour*
Upper lip – *allow 10–15 minutes*
Chin – *allow 15 minutes*
Sides of face – *allow 30 minutes each side*
Eyebrows – *allow 10 minutes each side*
Neck – *allow 30 minutes*
Large body areas (e.g. abdomen, shoulders, forearms, legs, feet, bikini line) – *allow 1 hour*

SERVICE PLAN

Record relevant details of your service and advice provided for future reference.
Ensure the client's records are up-to-date, accurate and fully completed following service. Non-compliance may invalidate insurance. The client should sign the record card after each service to show it has been agreed.

DURING

Find out:

- find out what products and skincare routine the client uses
- discuss the client's lifestyle and desire for hair removal
- explain what you are doing and how the sensation will feel
- reassure the client as you are working because it may be uncomfortable

Note:

- any extreme reddening
- if any areas are more moist and react more quickly than others
- which areas have stronger hairs, needing more current intensity
- if there are areas where the hairs are finer, needing a smaller probe size

AFTER

- record the results of the service and how many hairs you were able to remove successfully
- note if there were any adverse reactions or contra-actions, e.g. tiny bruises, blood spots
- record any modification of the service as you worked
- record the effectiveness of the service and the amount of hairs removed
- discuss and record the frequency of the services necessary for success

RETAIL OPPORTUNITIES

Advise on:

- provide the client with aftercare products suitable for their skin type
- discuss further skincare necessary to keep the skin in the best condition during the course of the service
- advise on further facial services to encourage good skin health

EVALUATION

- record the client's satisfaction with the service
- if the results are not as expected record the reasons why
- if applicable record how the service may be altered to improve the result in the future

HEALTH AND SAFETY

- give aftercare advice to avoid any infection in the area
- advise what not to apply to the area to avoid any irritation while the skin is healing
- advise on good hygiene procedures while treating the area at home
- advise what to do if there is any adverse skin reaction or irritation between services

ACTIVITY

Contra-indication to service

Explain when you would decide that the service could not be carried out. Discuss the ways in which you should explain to your client that you would like them to seek medical advice.

ALWAYS REMEMBER

Areas not recommended for the service

Areas which are not recommended for the service are inside the ear, inside the nose and genitals. These areas are all very sensitive and also may have healing and infection problems.

BEST PRACTICE

Diabetes

In persons with diabetes, the skin is slow to heal. To enable effective skin healing, the service time should be shorter and over longer periods. Service applications must be well spaced.

TOP TIP

GP referral

Acknowledge a GP referral with thanks. This will maintain a positive, professional relationship between yourself and the medical profession.

Clients need you every day, not just in the salon

Ensure they buy and use the correct products at home on a daily basis – you will get the credit for the improvement, you will earn more money through commission and your employer will be very pleased.

Gill Morris

Plan and prepare for the epilation service

Contra-indications

If, while completing the record card or on visual inspection of the skin, the client is found to have any of the following in the area of the service, then electrical epilation service must not be carried out without medical referral.

Contra-indications requiring medical referral

- epilepsy – a fit would put the client at risk of injury
- diabetes – poor skin healing makes the client vulnerable to infection
- hormone imbalance (abnormal hair growth) – the service will be ineffective unless the hormonal imbalance is treated and controlled
- cardiovascular conditions – the anti-coagulant drugs prescribed for these conditions interfere with the effectiveness of the service as coagulation is required in the follicle
- nervous system dysfunction or highly nervous clients – it is important that the client is able to detect sensations in order that the skin is not over-treated
- pregnancy – after the birth of the child, any excess hair growth often disappears naturally as the hormones stabilize
- metal plates and pins in the area being treated – if being treated with galvanic technique, current concentration may occur causing tissue burning around the metal
- skin disorders such as psoriasis, eczema, naevi, keloids, scarring, cuts, abrasions, recent wounds, bruising – there is a risk of infection or further skin damage
- skin disease, infectious conditions such as herpes simplex and scabies – there is a risk of cross-infection
- pre-malignant moles – the cells may become damaged and become malignant as a result
- blood disorders such as hepatitis B and AIDS caused by the virus HIV – there is a risk of cross-infection as the viruses are transmitted by body fluids
- loss of skin sensation or hypersensitive skin – the skin may become damaged
- asthma – the stress of the service may cause an attack
- electrical implants such as a pacemaker – their efficiency may be affected by the electrical current

Clients who have contra-indications must be referred to their GP prior to the service. This must be done without specifically naming a condition and must not cause concern or alarm. The GP will diagnose professionally and will be able to determine whether the client is able to have electrical epilation service. A note from the GP is then needed before the service commences. These contra-indications apply to all three types of electrical epilation.

The following skin services may inhibit your electrical epilation service. This means that you may have to stop the service programme or you may have to wait to start it until the other services have finished.

- Glycolic peel, will remove the superficial skin's surface resulting in very smooth but possibly sensitive skin. This may also be prone to pigmentation.
- Micro-dermabrasion, also removes the superficial skin's surface with crystals or mechanical sloughing. Will result in smooth but possibly sensitive skin.
- Laser skin resurfacing. This is a medical procedure which can take months to heal.

With all services that have the effect of removing the skin's surface whether by chemical or abrasive actions you should wait until the service has finished healing before electrical epilation is started or continued. You must refer your client to their beauty therapist or medical practitioner for advice as to when you can start electrical epilation.

HEALTH & SAFETY

The Environmental Health Officer (EHO)

EHOs are inspectors appointed to verify standards of hygiene and safety in the salon. They will advise and support the implementation of the necessary bye-laws relating to skin piercing and electrical epilation. A copy of the local bye-laws can be obtained from the Local Authority where you are licensed.

You must be licensed with your local authority to perform electrical epilation. There will be a charge for this which varies between areas and there may be some differences in the regulations so make sure you are aware of them.

> Employers need people who have the ability to manage themselves, e.g. do things without having to be asked.
>
> An interviewee who acts as though they would only do the minimum amount of work required and who has to be hand-held all the time is unlikely to get a job.
>
> **Gill Morris**

ACTIVITY FUNCTIONAL SKILLS

Needle suitability

Draw and describe the different types of needle (one-piece, two-piece, insulated, surgical steel, gold-plated) available for epilation service. Research the cost of each of the different types of needle and state for which hair and skin types they are most suitable.

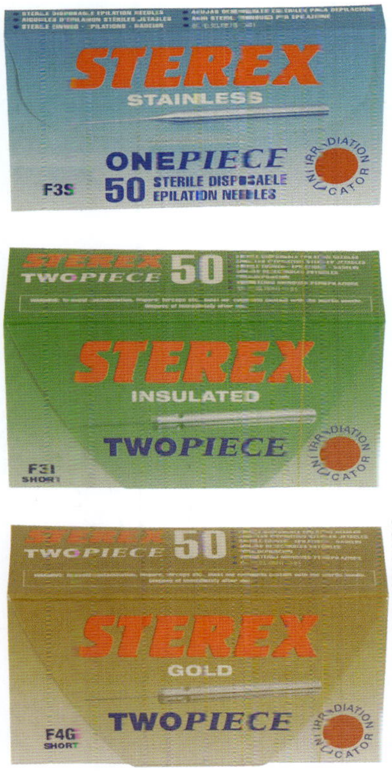

COURTESY OF STEREX ELECTROLYSIS

Electrolysis needles: one-piece, insulated, gold

Service application

Magnifying lamps

Magnifying lamps are normally used to ensure that the hairs can be clearly seen so that insertions are accurate and service effective. Most lamps have a magnification of 1.75 or dioptre of 3 which means they show things as 75 per cent larger than life. This also gives a good depth of field, the distance between the magnifying lens and the skin, so you can get your hands and the probe holder and tweezers underneath easily.

It is best to keep the lens as near to level with the area being treated as possible as this gives a clear, undistorted view.

Stronger magnification is not suitable for epilation as the depth of field is too small to allow you to get your hands under the magnifier.

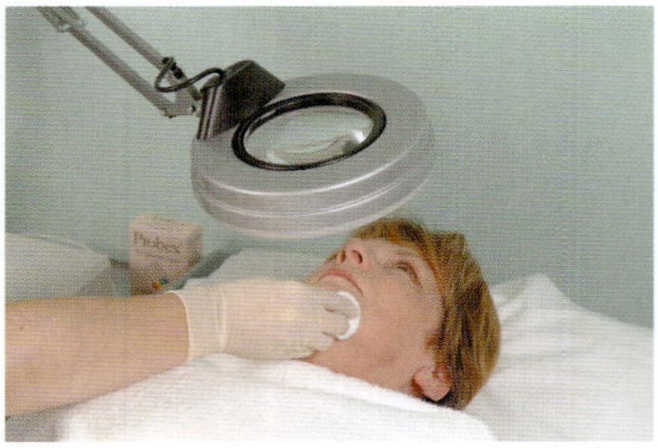

Preparing the client

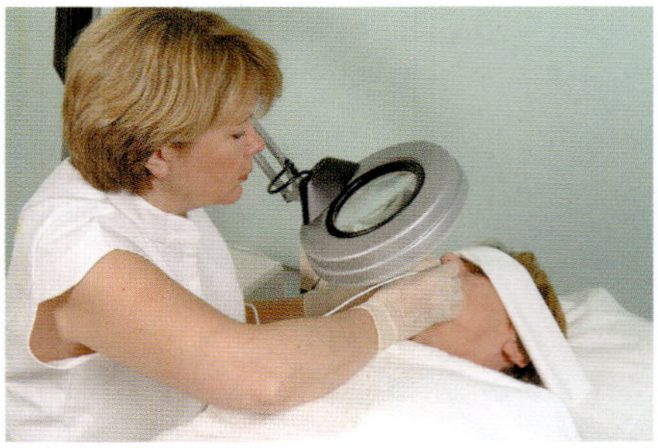

Upper lip

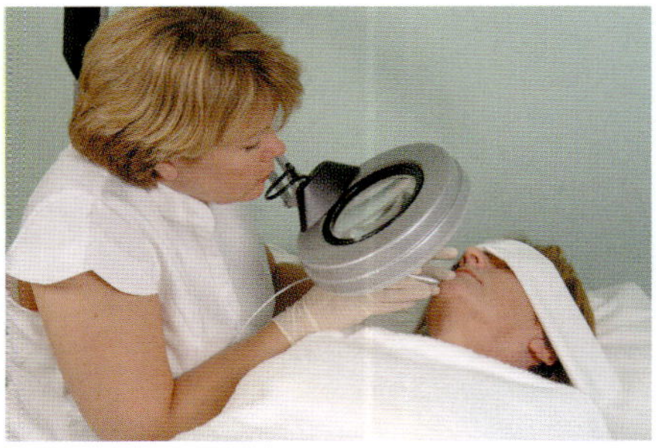

Chin

TOP TIP

Eye care - health and safety

Ask your optician for advice on glasses for epilation if you feel that it would be better for your comfort and vision. There are also lenses with lamps attached to headbands which can be used. These look very medical, so can be alarming to some clients.

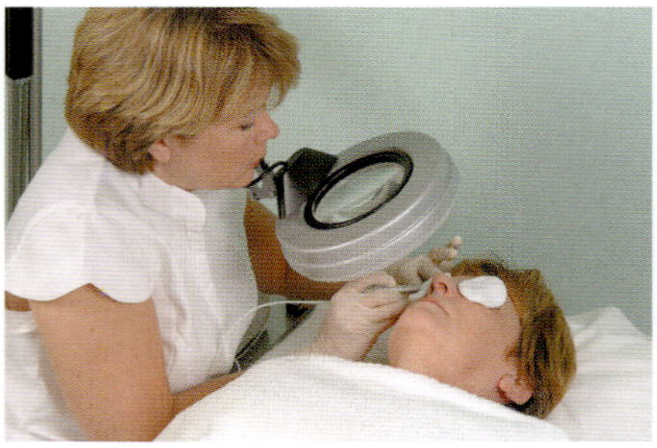

Eyebrows

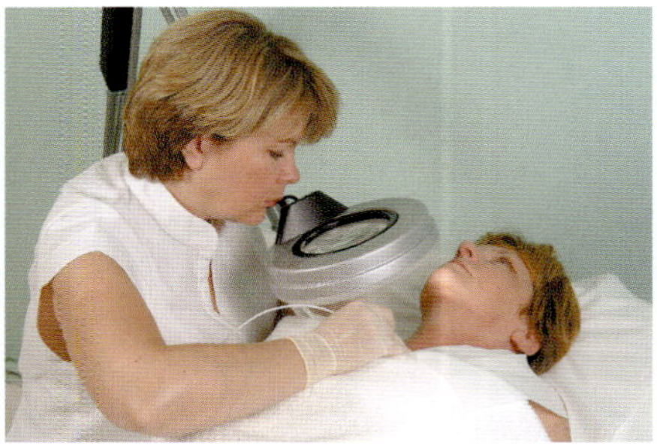

Chest

For an effective service, the following factors need to be taken into consideration:

- The client's skin type – this will affect the selection of current intensity and duration of application.
- Follicle size – this should be observed because it will determine the choice of needle size and length for effective destruction of the lower follicle and destruction of the dermal papillae. Having chosen the correct needle size, the beauty therapist will need to only stretch the skin lightly without distorting the hair follicle. This enables ease of insertion. Sufficient current needs to be applied for the correct amount of time for effective destruction of the lower follicle. The hair should then slide out of the follicle easily without any traction.
- Hair type – hairs vary in length and thickness according to race and different parts of the body. Consider this when selecting needle size and needle insertion. Hair type will be different for the body and face. Most facial hair growths are divided into finer hair on cheeks, upper lips and stronger pigmented hair on the chin, neck and sides of face. Hairline and eyebrow hairs will be fully pigmented terminal hairs. Body hair will almost always be strong, fully pigmented terminal hair. Gender disphoriac clients will have strong, fully pigmented terminal hair on the face.
- Racial hair types vary. African hair type can be strong, dark and curly, Asian and South East Asian hair type can be dark, strong or fine and straight, Northern European hair can be fair, fine or strong and straight.
- Position of the client and beauty therapist – this is important because it can hinder effective removal. The beauty therapist should be able to achieve ease of insertion without compromizing the service.

The beauty therapist's technique, rhythm and continuity should be accurate. Mis-probing can lead to the client's skin becoming damaged and scarred.

Note: Gender disphoriac clients must be treated with sensitivity and empathy. They will normally be undergoing hormone therapy for feminization, which will help the hair growth to become finer and fairer. However, initial services will need to be extensive

“Position your client so you can easily gain access to the follicle.

Use folded towels or bolsters to support the client. Position yourself so your muscles are not under stress, i.e. keeping your elbows down. Electrologists who have bad posture and positioning will find they can't insert correctly as their hands will shake, their shoulder muscles will ache and burn and they are prone to RSI.

Gill Morris

with possibly high current levels to remove the hairs. This can be uncomfortable and stressful. To minimize this it is preferable to use the blend technique and to keep the client comfortable and relaxed. Work on the upper lip and sides of face during one service and the chin and neck during the next service. Alternate weekly so the client can have as many services as possible, as you would do for any client with an extensive hair growth. It is not advisable to treat an area more than once every 2 weeks as the skin needs to recover and heal fully before the next service to avoid marking or scarring.

Skin sensitivity test

It is essential to carry out a skin sensitivity test on a small area to decide if the client is suitable for an electrical epilation service.

Possible allergies include:

- electrical epilation needles
- pre-service and post-service lotions

It is also possible to have adverse reactions to the service itself, see the contra-actions table for full details of these.

Skin sensitivity test procedure

- Clean and prepare the skin area with the lotions you would normally use. Blot the skin dry.
- Remove a few hairs using the correct size stainless steel needle.
- Remove a few hairs using a gold-plated needle.
- The use of the different needle types will help you to assess which needle type will cause least reaction while still being effective.
- Apply the post-service lotion you would normally use.
- Check for any excessive reddening or swelling. To be certain that the client is not going to have any adverse healing reaction it is best to leave the area for a full week and then check.

Current application for different skin types

Oily skin Oily skin is thick and coarse, with open follicles. Excess sebum present on the skin's surface will act as an insulator to the current, maintaining the intensity of the current in the lower follicle. The slightly wider follicles give the beauty therapist ease of insertion.

There will usually be a higher level of moisture in the skin's lower tissues, making the service more effective.

Dry skin The upper layers of the epidermis can be dry or dehydrated due to a lack of sebum or moisture. Dead skin cells can build up and block the follicle opening, making needle insertion more difficult. The current intensity must be set at a level to avoid burning in the upper follicle where there is a lack of moisture.

Sensitive skin This type of skin is thin and very fine. It has a translucent appearance and red, broken capillaries may be present. When using high-frequency epilation

TOP TIP

Needle choice

Needle choice is determined by the size of the follicle, hair type being treated, i.e. vellus or terminal, and the thickness and diameter of the hair.

ACTIVITY

Service modification

When working on different types of hair, note how the service needs to be varied in order to successfully epilate them. Describe the current intensities, service times and the types of epilation service that seem to suit each type of hair best.

ALWAYS REMEMBER

Correct needle choice for the follicle size

- If the needle chosen is too large it can stretch the follicle and cause bruising and burning.
- If the needle chosen is too small the current will not destroy the dermal papilla and the service will be ineffective.

BEST PRACTICE

Assess client suitability

Do not be persuaded by a client who is trying to insist you do a full service straight away. If there are any problems it is your responsibility to assess clients and skin tolerance to the service.

technique, the application of heat can make the skin react quickly, creating a sudden erythema. Sensitive skin can be associated with both dry and oily skin so care should be taken when choosing current intensity.

Moist skin This has a high water content through the epidermis and dermis layers. The beauty therapist should be careful when applying the current because it can have a tendency to shoot back up the follicle to the surface of the skin, causing surface burning. Accuracy needs to be maintained on application of current and duration of the service as different parts of the body have differing moisture gradients.

Client groups

Different ethnic backgrounds will result in different types of hair growth. Caucasian clients often have a lot of excess facial hair growth, which can be very obvious and distressing, particularly during and after the menopause. Black clients can have coarse, terminal hair growth which is pigmented. The follicles may be curved but respond well to a blend or galvanic service. It is generally found that the curve or curl of the hair above the skin is more exaggerated than the curve of the follicle below the skin.

Oriental clients do not generally have a lot of facial hair. The hair is generally straight, dark and simple to treat.

Asian clients often have a lot of long, dark but fine hair on the face as a norm. This type of hair responds particularly well to diathermy as it is often shallow with dry follicles.

Gender disphoriac clients may be at the beginning, middle or end of their gender change service programme. The hair growth is likely to be coarse and pigmented. Listen carefully to their concerns; treat the areas they are most worried or self-conscious about first and be a friendly, warm and welcoming person for them. Do not do too much on one area even if the client pressures you to carry on despite reddening or swelling. The higher currents and amount of services needed to remove the growth can easily result in marking or scarring of the skin.

HEALTH & SAFETY

Perspiration

If the client is warm when being treated, this could lead to perspiration (sweat) on the skin's surface. This must be removed by blotting the skin dry otherwise surface burning may result when the current is applied.

Beauty therapist's posture

The beauty therapist should maintain a good working position throughout the service to avoid fatigue, repetitive strain injury and postural problems. A height-adjustable stool should be placed at the correct height and side of the couch. This will enable the beauty therapist to maintain a steady position and facilitate accurate insertion into the hair follicle. Leaning on the client should be kept to a minimum as the client may become uncomfortable. If right-handed, the beauty therapist should work from the left side and if left-handed, from the right side.

Positioning of the client

The client should be placed on the couch in a position that enables ease of insertion in the area being treated. If the client suffers from respiratory disorders, the head of the couch must be elevated into a sitting position to enable the client to breathe properly. The client must feel comfortable and relaxed throughout the service. Depending on the area to be treated, a pillow or bolster may be required for support.

Lips The client should lie on the couch in a comfortable position and the beauty therapist should work from the side. The client is treated from the corners of the mouth

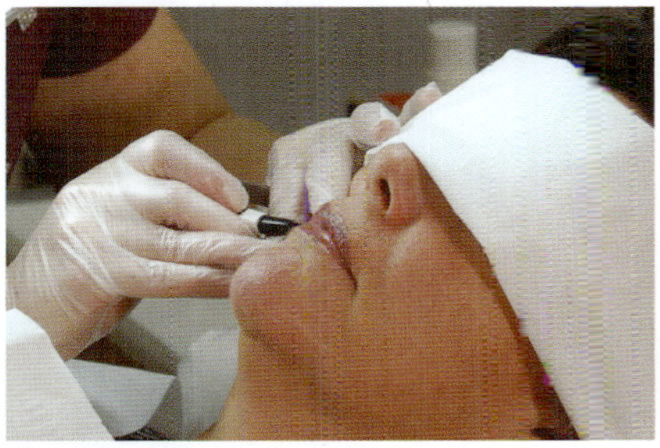

Position for insertion: right-hand side upper lip

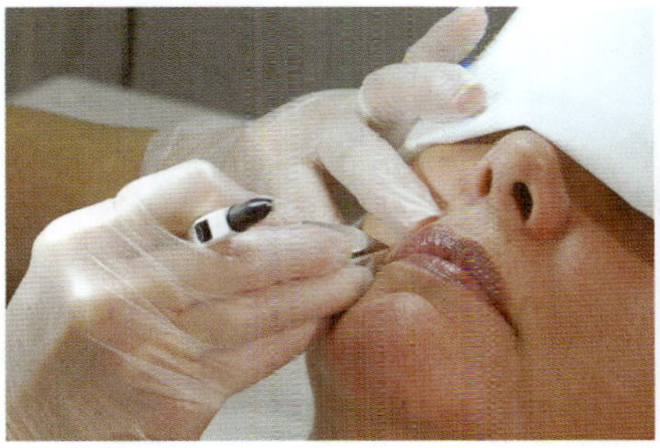

Removing treated hair

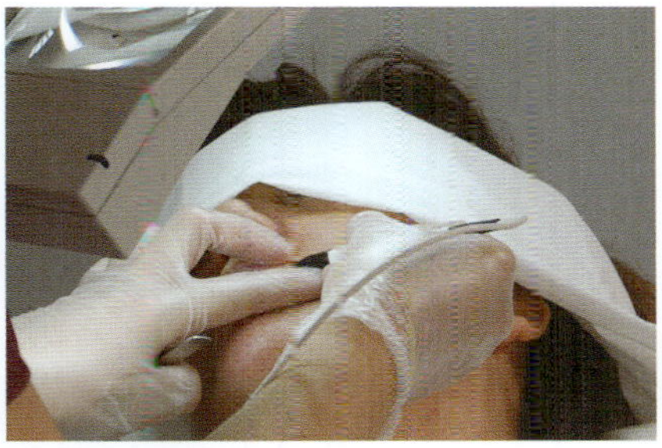

Position for insertion: left-hand side upper lip

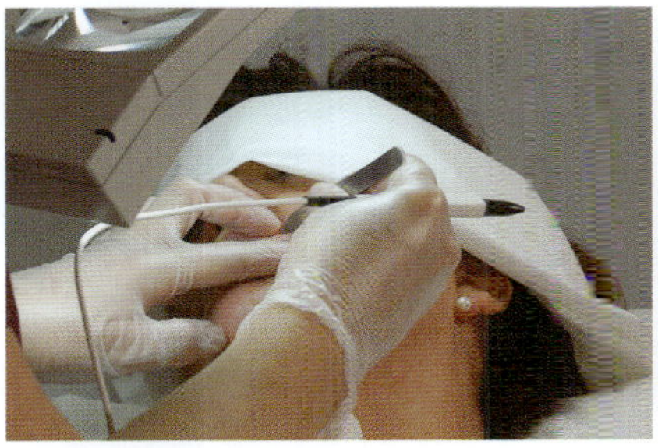

Removing treated hair

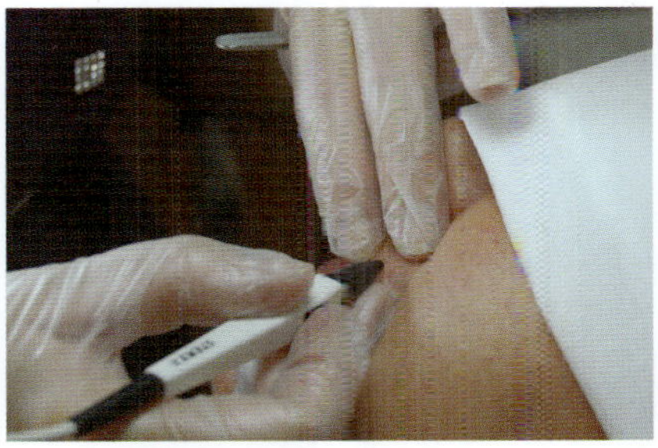

Applying current

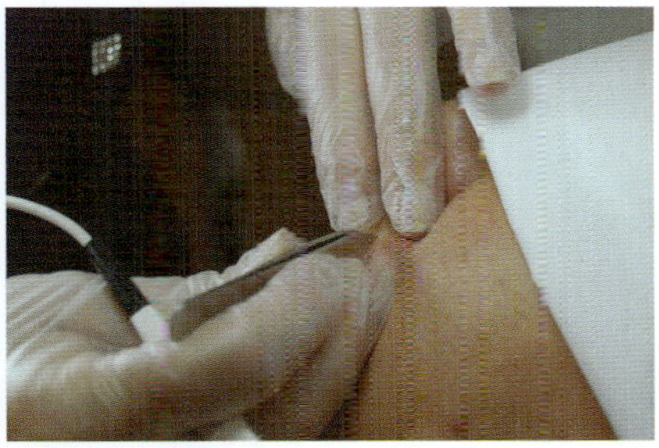

Removing hair

alternately until the middle is reached under the nose. This area is treated last because it is very sensitive, and the client will have become more accustomed to the current intensity.

Chin The client is positioned on the couch. If the client has a thick neck, a roll can be placed behind the neck to extend the chin upwards. Hairs normally grow at random, so the coarser darker hairs should be removed first to thin the area out.

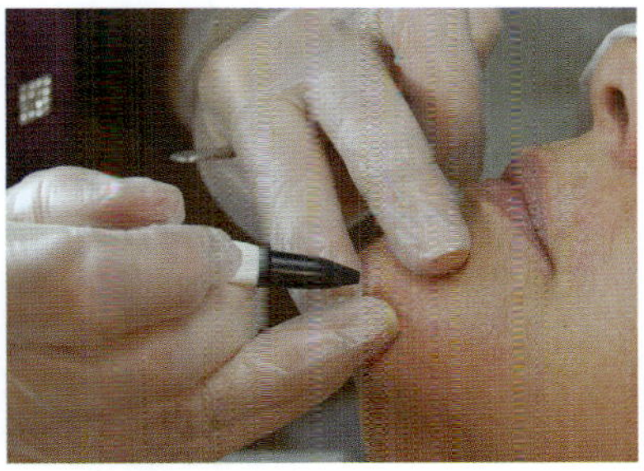

Inserting probe on chin

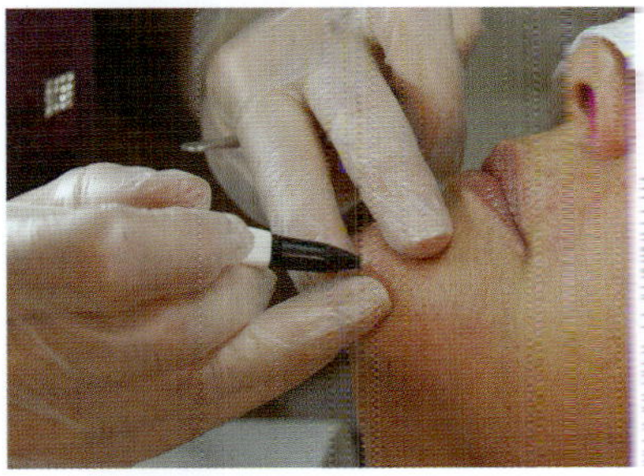

Applying current

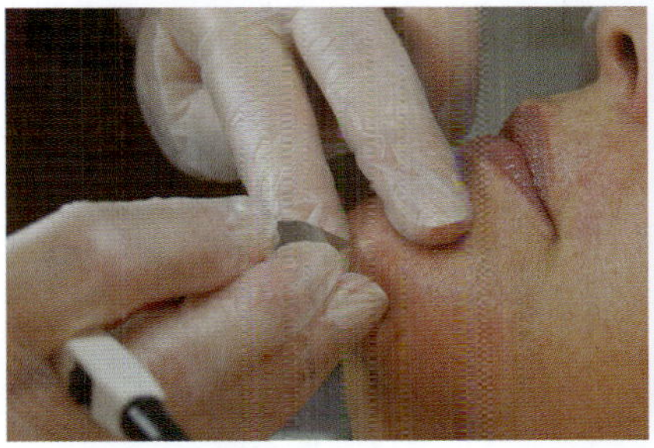

Grasping hair with tweezers

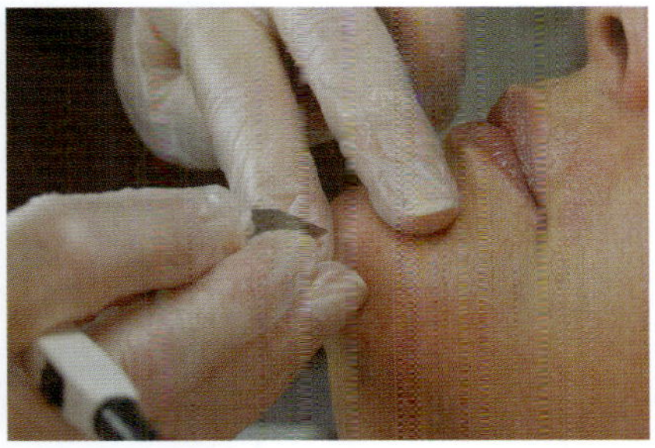

Removing treated hair

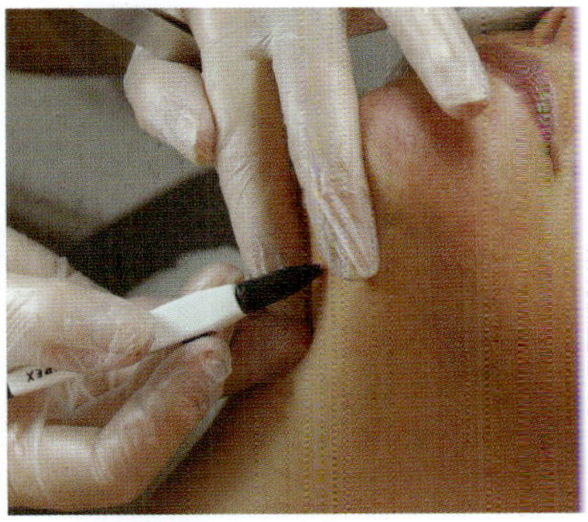

Position for insertion: neck

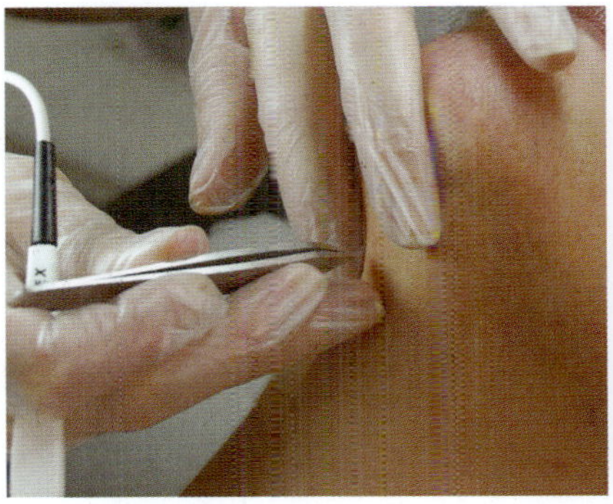

Removing treated hair

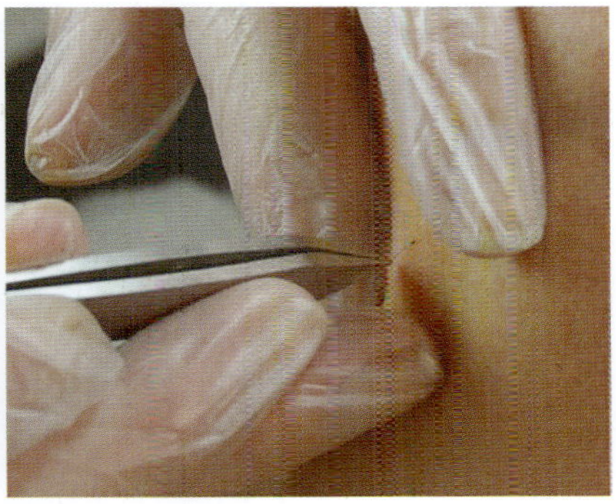

Treated hair showing the bulb

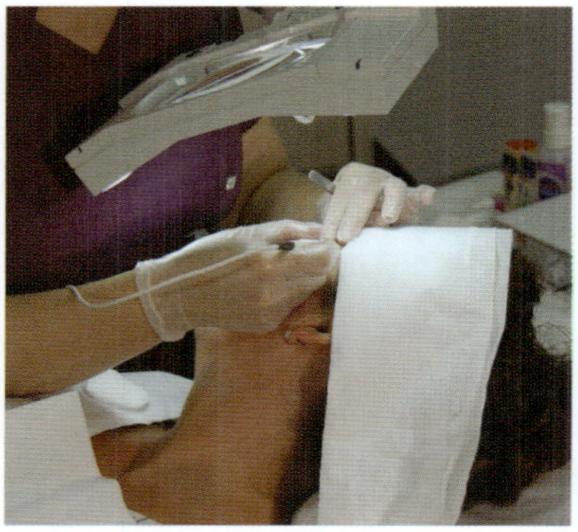

Client position for treating left eyebrow

Eyebrows These can be treated from the head of the couch or the side. The client's hair must be secured away from the face with a clean headband. The beauty therapist should work from the outside of the brows inwards towards the nose. Care should be taken when epilating between the brows because it is very vascular and moist. If incorrect technique is used, bruising or a black eye can occur.

Chest/nipples The hair on the chest grows either towards the face or towards the waist. The client should be positioned with pillow support. The beauty therapist may work from the top of the couch or at the side. Observe the client for sensitivity at all times. The breast and chest area are extremely sensitive areas but are suitable to treat.

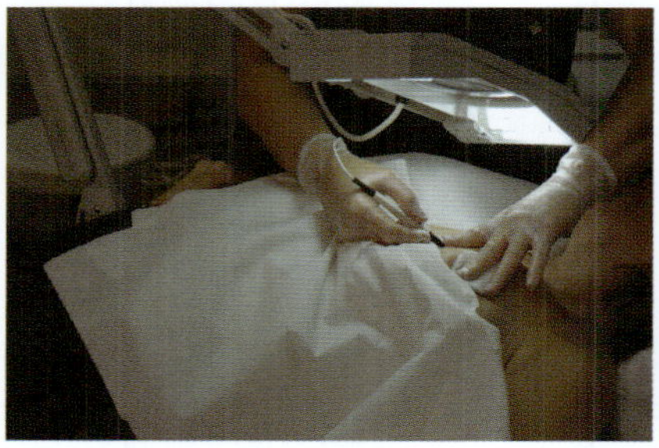

Position and covering for breast service

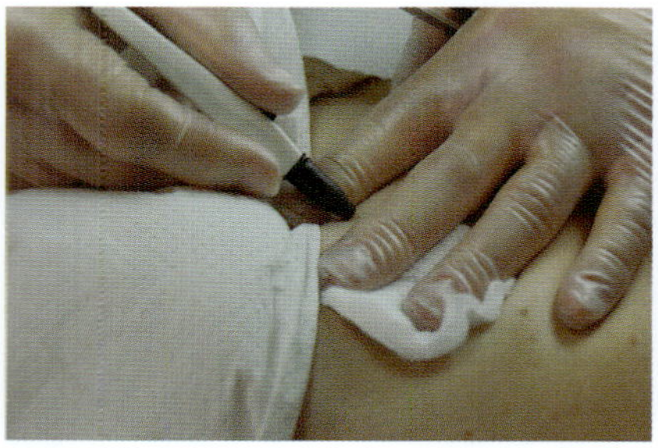

Insertion on breast

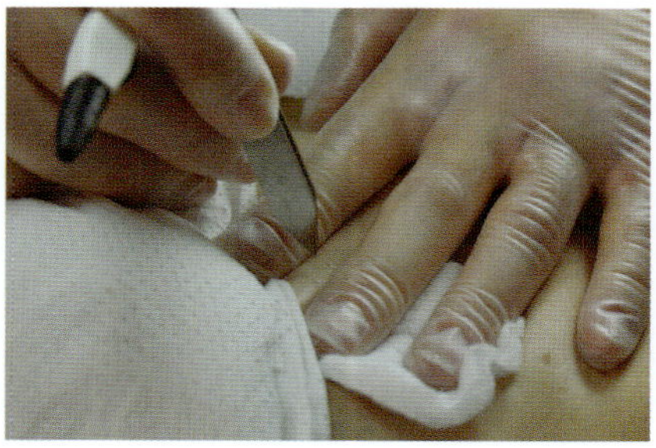

Removal of treated hair

Bikini line Support the limb being treated with a pillow. Hairs grow in varying directions dependent upon the area and are normally embedded in deep follicles.

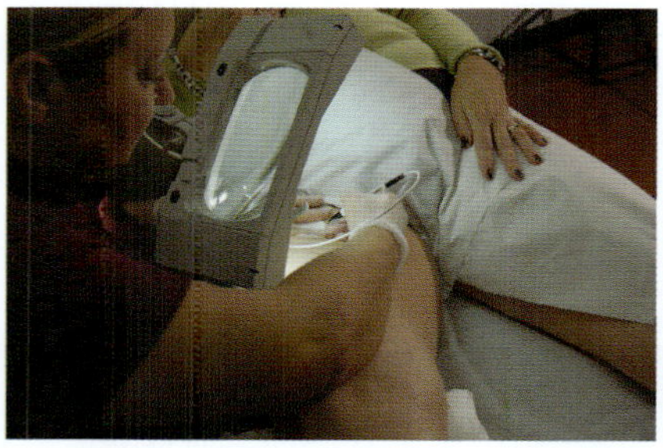

Position of client for bikini line service

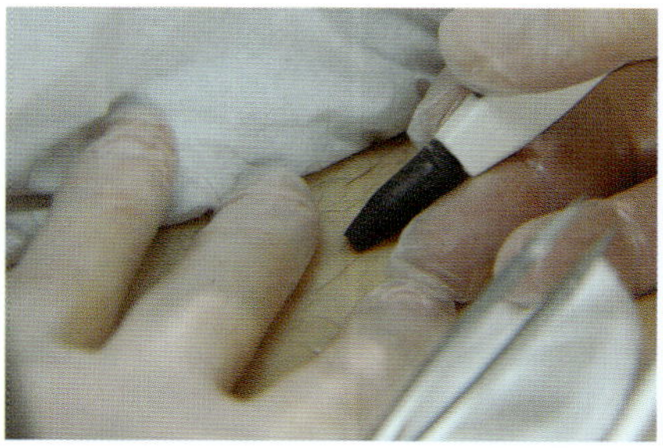

Insertion: bikini line

Underarms Support the arm with the client's hand placed behind their head on the side being treated. For comfort, support the arm being treated on a pillow. The armpit is very moist so care should be taken when selecting the current intensity. The hairs under the arm grow in different directions so the beauty therapist will have to change their positioning to gain accurate insertion.

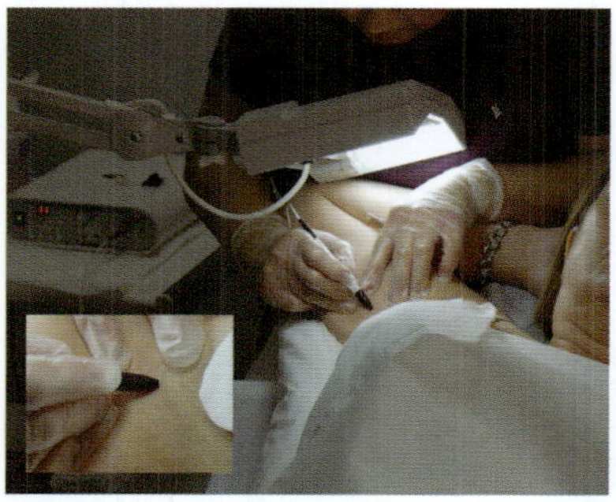

Position for underarm service

Outcome 3: Carry out electrical epilation

Carry out electrical epilation

1. Leaving the area to be treated clean, oil free and dry prior to service.
2. Using the size and **type of needle** which is appropriate for treating the client's follicle size, **hair type** and **skin type** and the type of **electrical epilation service**.

(Continued) Carry out electrical epilation

- 3 Loading and using needles avoiding damage and contamination throughout the service.
- 4 Illuminating and magnifying the service area to ensure maximum visibility during treatment.
- 5 Stretching and manipulating the skin in a way suitable for the area to be treated.
- 6 Ensuring the needleholder and needle is used at the correct angle, direction and needle depth for the hair follicle and the area to be treated.
- 7 Adjusting the intensity and duration of current flow to ensure effective hair release to suit client tolerance, sensitivity and safety.
- 8 Smoothly removing the hair from the treated follicle without traction.
- 9 Working systematically to remove hair within the **area**(s) **to be treated** and the skin's tolerance.
- 10 Discontinuing service where contra-actions occur in accordance with manufacturer's instructions.
- 11 Soothing the treated area using suitable techniques and products.
- 12 Taking service progress photographs of the area(s) treated with consent of the client as and when required.
- 13 Ensuring that the finished result is to the client's satisfaction and meets the agreed service plan.

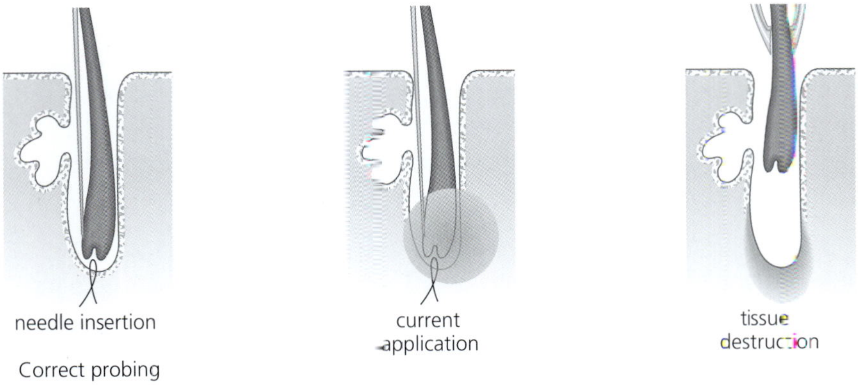

Correct probing technique

TOP TIP

Consultation

On a client's first service session, space out the epilation. Do not attempt to clear an area – this will occur over future services. Explain this to the client.

TOP TIP

Selection of hair

For the first few minutes, remove finer hairs. This will enable the client to adjust to the service sensation. Coarser hairs require a higher current intensity.

TOP TIP

Technique

Transfer the tweezers into the working hand to remove the treated hair, keeping the skin taut. Do not lose sight of the hair to be removed!

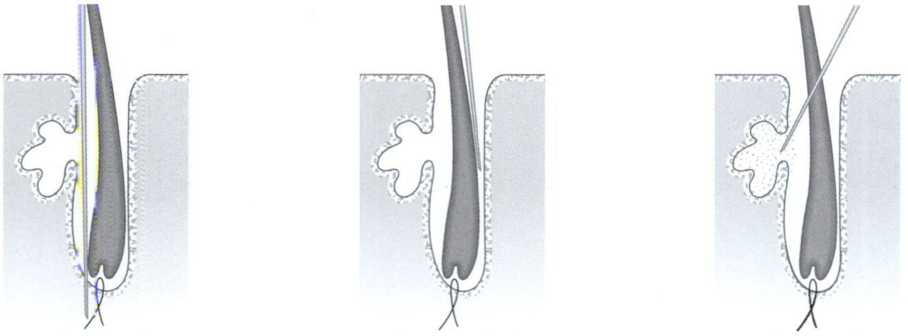

Incorrect probing technique

How to provide high-frequency ac or short-wave diathermy epilation

1. Check the client for contra-indications.
2. Ensure the record card is up-to-date and signed.
3. Wash your hands using a disinfectant wash and dry thoroughly using a warm air hand drier or disposable paper roll.
4. Protect the hands with clean disposable gloves.
5. Disinfect the area with pre-epilation skin cleaning lotion.
6. Using a magnifier, assess the skin type, hair type and follicle size. Blot the skin surface dry with a clean tissue as necessary.
7. Place the selected disposable needle into the needle holder. Ensure the needle is securely fastened into the probe.
8. Switch the machine on at the mains and unit.
9. Stretch the follicle open slightly without distorting the follicle with the index and middle finger of the left or right hand.
10. Probe the follicle, inserting the needle underneath the hair with the direction and angle of hair growth. This will prevent you piercing the follicle wall.
11. Set the current low and then gradually increase the intensity to the correct setting until the hair comes out without resistance.
12. When the needle is at the base of the hair follicle, apply the high-frequency current to enable the hair to be removed from the hair follicle without traction. The current should be set at the lowest intensity setting possible, using the shortest amount of time to effectively remove the hair. The client should not feel too uncomfortable during the service when being removed.
13. Remove the epilated hair using the tweezers and place on tissue or cotton wool kept within range of the area being treated. The hair should slide easily from the follicle when being removed.
14. Treat the area, observing skin reaction and adjust the current intensity to correspond with differing hair types and areas being treated.

> To insert the needle correctly you need the right *direction*, *angle* and *depth*. Without all three the insertion will be ineffective at best and can cause scarring at worst.
>
> **Gill Morris**

15 Check client satisfaction with the area treated. Show the client the area if facial in a mirror.

16 At the end of the epilation period, reduce the current intensity to zero and switch the unit off.

17 Remove the contaminated needle and place in the sharps box. Place the contaminated waste in the lined waste bin.

18 Apply post-epilation soothing antispetic lotion to the area treated with clean, sterile cotton wool.

19 Discuss aftercare advice with the client.

20 Complete details of the service on the record card, including: date; area treated; service duration; needle type and size; current intensity; skin reaction; your signature and client signature.

21 Help the client from the couch. Book the next appointment for the client to ensure continuity of service.

22 File the record card at reception.

How to provide dc – galvanic epilation

1 Repeat steps 1 to 8 from page 320.

2 The client must hold the indifferent electrode in their hand. Protect this with a dampened tissue or as directed by the manufacturer.

3 Attach the needle holder to the negative pole.

4 Set the current intensity to 0.10 milliamps and the duration to 10 seconds.

5 Insert the needle into the follicle, apply the current intensity by pressing the foot pedal. Most equipment will automatically switch off after the allotted time.

6 Remove the probe from the follicle, use the tweezers to remove the hair from the follicle and place it onto a clean piece of tissue or cotton wool.

7 The effect continues after the current stops because of the chemical action on the tissues in the follicle. To maximize this effect you may leave a treated hair in place while treating another to ensure effective removal.

It may be necessary to increase the intensity or lengthen the time to allow the hairs to be easily removed.

8 Continue working across the area until the service has been completed.

9 Repeat steps 14 to 21 from page 321.

How to provide blend epilation

1 Repeat steps 1 to 8 from page 320.

2 The client will hold the indifferent electrode protected with a dampened tissue or as advised by the manufacturer.

3 Set the blend machine with the high frequency on low and the galvanic current on 0.10 milliamps. Set the timer for 5 seconds.

ALWAYS REMEMBER

Number of insertions

The current should be adjusted throughout the service for effective removal of different types of hair growth. If the hair cannot be removed after the second attempt, assess the area for any reaction. If it is not sensitized, a third insertion may be performed although this is not desirable. If the hair still cannot be removed, tweeze the hair to avoid infection caused by the tissue destruction that has occurred.

HEALTH & SAFETY

Covering electrodes

Some manufacturers do not require the indifferent electrode to be covered. Check the manufacturer's instructions for recommended settings.

HEALTH & SAFETY

Effective delivery of current

It is not recommended that insulated needles are used with blend current.

ACTIVITY FUNCTIONAL SKILLS

Case study

Plan and write up the full service programme for a client with fine upper lip hair and coarse chin hair.

4 Insert the needle into the follicle.

5 Apply the current using the foot pedal, wait for the time to be completed, then switch the current off. (Some machines automatically switch the current off.) It will be necessary to adjust the current intensity and the time in order to treat different strengths of hair growth.

6 Remove the needle from the follicle and gently remove the hair from the follicle. Place the hair onto a dry piece of tissue or cotton wool.

7 Repeat steps 14 to 21 from pages 321–322.

Units of lye chart and recommended settings

Sodium hydroxide (lye) is produced in the follicle by dc. The lye helps to chemically decompose the follicle.

A unit of lye is a tiny quantity of lye solution made in the follicle. The formula for assessing how much lye is made is: one-tenth of a milliampere of galvanic current flowing for 1 second will produce one 'unit' of lye, *or* one-tenth milliamperes × seconds = units of lye. The table shows approximately how much lye is needed to destroy which size of follicle. The intensity and duration for each follicle can then be calculated.

Approximate units of lye for different follicle sizes

Follicle size/service area	*Units of lye*
Shallow insertion: vellus hairs on upper lip, eyebrows, face, arms	15
Medium insertion: side of face (cheeks), chin, eyebrows, arms, stomach, medium leg hair	45
Deep insertion: chin, back, legs, thigh, underarms, bikini, shoulders	60
Very deep insertion: man's beard, back, shoulders, thighs	80

Table of suggested probe and currents for services areas. The services must be assessed individually, these are recommendations only, not a definitive list.

Service area	*Probe/needle type*	*Probe/needle size*	*Current type*
Upper lip	Two piece insulated or gold	.002 or .003	High frequency ac/ diathermy
Chin	Two piece insulated or gold	.003 or .004	Blend or diathermy
Neck	Two piece or one piece	.003 or .004	Blend or diathermy
Eyebrow	Two piece or one piece	.003 or .004	Diathermy or blend

Service area	*Probe/needle type*	*Probe/needle size*	*Current type*
Underarm	One piece	.004 or .005	Blend
Breast	One piece	.003 or .004	Blend
Bikini line	Two piece or one piece	.004 or .005	Blend

Hair regrowth

Hair regrows after epilation, but the growth eventually becomes weaker and finer. There are several reasons for the occurrence of regrowth.

Tweezing, waxing and threading can, in theory, increase the strength of the individual hairs present. However, waxing of larger areas such as legs does seem to lessen the hair growth on some clients over the years. Depilatory creams dissolve the hairs at the surface and can make the regrowth seem brittle. The skin can also be sensitized showing either reddening or dry and thickened areas. Bleaching can dry out the hair and skin although this is usually temporary.

Hormonal imbalance If the client has a medical condition and is taking hormonal tablets or steroids, these can influence the blood supply to the follicle. The hairs will be nourished and continue to grow so medical advice should be sought to help determine an effective service plan and outcome as appropriate.

Partial destruction of the follicle If the hair was not in the anagen stage of hair growth only partial destruction will occur because the bulb was not attached to the dermal papillae. Alternatively, the beauty therapist may not have applied sufficient current to effectively destroy the dermal papillae.

Incorrect technique

- Incorrect probing – the beauty therapist has not probed to the base of the follicle therefore insufficient current has been distributed to effectively destroy the blood supply.
- Incorrect needle size – if the needle size is too small, insufficient current will disperse to effectively destroy the dermal papilla and follicle, therefore regrowth will occur.
- Previous methods of removal – if the client has previously had the hairs removed by temporary measures this can cause distortion of the follicle. This makes it harder for the beauty therapist to effectively probe the follicle, so reducing the effectiveness of the service.

Aftercare

Outcome 4: Provide aftercare advice

Provide aftercare advice

1. Giving **advice** and recommendations accurately and constructively.
2. Giving your clients suitable **advice** specific to their individual needs.

Following the epilation service, the skin will be prone to infection because of the heat and tissue destruction. To avoid infection the area should be kept clean. The following aftercare procedures must be explained to the client:

- Apply the recommended soothing antispetic lotion for 48 hours following each service. If any redness remains the client should continue using the lotion. unless obviously it is a contra-action to the aftercare lotion. The skin should be treated gently and carefully. Always wash hands before touching the area.

Cataphoresis for reducing post-service skin reaction

Cataphoresis in electrical epilation service has the meaning of using a positive polarity galvanic current to produce an acid on the skin.

When using the galvanic or blend current it is possible to apply cataphoresis after the service to sooth the skin and reduce the reddening and skin reaction. There are epilation machines available that have this facility already built into the machine.

When the galvanic current is used either on its own or as a blended current, the alkali 'lye' is produced in the follicle. Cataphoresis is the procedure applied with a positive electrode, usually a roller, using galvanic current to produce acid over the treated area. This has the effect of neutralizing any lye action left in the follicle and also to have a soothing effect by the tightening and contraction of the small blood vessels in the skin which dilate and cause reddening. This can be beneficial in a sensitive facial area and also on a larger body area such as the bikini line. If the machine being used does not have this built in then it is possible to use a galvanic facial machine on the positive polarity in the same way. It is best to refer to the manufacturer's instructions to ensure that the cataphoresis is carried out correctly. The aftercare gel or liquid solution is normally used to conduct the current.

- Report any scabbing or pustular infection to the beauty therapist. Do not pick or rub the skin this may cause scarring. Do not expose the area to UV light, either through sunbathing or use of sunbeds because this will possibly cause skin pigmentation. Protect the area with sun protection factor (SPF) 15 lotion but do not apply self-tan(ning) lotion or heavily perfumed creams to the area this may cause skin irritation.
- Do not pluck or wax the area between services because this will stimulate the hair growth making them become thicker and coarser. If necessary, trim the hairs – this does not affect hair growth.
- Facial hair can be trimmed with scissors or, if necessary, shaved between services where growth is extensive but not within 48 hours of the next service. Bleaching the hair is a useful method of disguising the remaining growth between services but can cause skin irritation.
- For body services, keep the area clean and fresh. Do not wear tight or constricting clothing which may rub or irritate the area.
- Some scabbing may occur occasionally when strong hairs, such as those in the bikini line, are being treated. Do not remove any such scabs otherwise scarring may occur. The beauty therapist should be advised if any scabbing does occur.

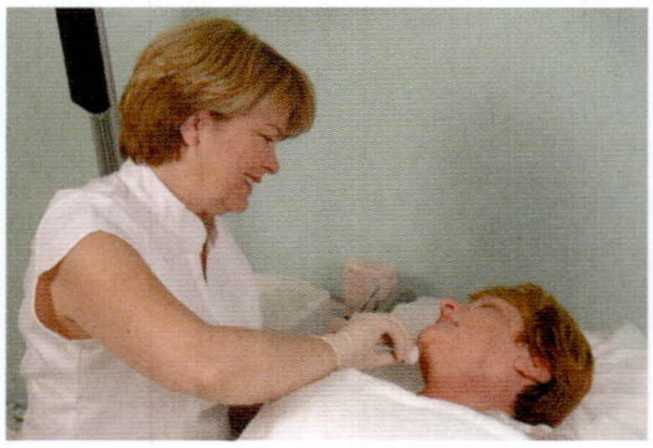

Position for facial aftercare

- Do not use heat services such as sauna, and do not swim for 48 hours after the service.
- Do not have a hot bath or shower for the following 48 hours due to skin sensitivity. Wash in lukewarm water no hotter than body temperature.

> Ensure you give ongoing support and motivation to clients during this long-term but permanent method of hair removal.
> Make sure your client is aware of, and understands, the hair management techniques they can use in between appointments.
>
> **Gill Morris**

These aftercare instructions need to be explained after every service and the client must be advised to follow them to prevent infection or scarring. Epilation irritates the skin which can easily become infected if proper procedures are not followed.

Keep the working area clean and tidy for each client. Discard waste, disinfect surfaces, sterilize equipment, and renew towels and paper tissue bedroll.

Managing hair growth between services is essential. Clients are having electrical epilation service because they don't want their hair so will not want to leave it showing. Discuss how to treat the growth with your client and explain which methods are best for the area being treated. Be watchful for the signs that your client is doing more than they should, e.g. waxing in between services may result in you having no regrowth at all to work on. Explain this can reduce the effectiveness of the service or stop it working all together. Be prepared to have clients who sometimes will still do this even though they are paying to have an epilation service.

HEALTH & SAFETY

Principles for avoiding cross-infection

- Disposal of chemical waste and sharps in accordance with local EHO recommendations.
- Personal protective equipment – gloves, masks.
- Sterilization: tweezers, dispose of caps if used.
- Pre-sterilized, single use, disposable needles – i.e. Probex, Sterex.
- Sanitizing client's skin.
- Washing hands.

Contra-actions

These are effects which might occur particularly if the area is very delicate or the beauty therapist's technique is incorrect. The table describes some common contra-actions.

Common contra-actions following epilation

Contra-action	*Cause*	*Action*
Bleeding – a spot of blood appears at the follicle opening	This may be as a result of the needle having been mis-probed, piercing the follicle wall or base of the follicle and breaking blood capillaries.	Wearing disposable gloves, apply dry cotton wool with a light pressure to stop the bleeding. Contaminated waste must be incinerated or placed in a sharps box. Take care to make sure insertions are accurate.
Palpitations	A rapid heartbeat which some people are liable to experience when stressed.	Stop the service and allow the client time to calm down and let the palpitations stop normally. If the client has not experienced them before then ask them to seek medical advice. Resume the service another day, being especially careful to keep the client calm and comfortable.
Profuse sweating	Some people may sweat profusely if they are under stress or feel pain. This is often most obvious on the upper lip, under arm and bikini line areas.	It will be difficult to continue the service if the skin is very damp as the current can dissipate on the surface of the skin. This may result in surface damage. Keep the client cool, relaxed and work on small areas at a time. The overall service plan may take longer.
Oedema	Swelling of the area due to fluid in the tissues may result along with reddening (erythema) of the skin.	Keep the current intensity as low as possible to be effective and do not treat hairs very close together. Space out the insertions in a treat one, miss one, treat one pattern.
Small white pus-filled spots	Usually a bacterial infection (staphylococcus) introduced either during the service or by the client after service.	Advise the client to use an antiseptic cream to aid healing. Review your sterilization, disinfection and sanitizing techniques to make sure they are in place. Explain the aftercare to the client again and make sure they understand the importance of looking after their skin properly to avoid infection.
Bruising – a blue lump appears under the skin where the insertion has been made	The needle has gone through the base of the follicle or the side of the follicle, causing bleeding into the dermis.	A cold compress with ice or witch hazel can be applied to reduce swelling and bruising. Make sure insertions are accurate.
Erythema (redness) – a reaction to injury being caused to the skin during the service	While some redness is inevitable, too much, together with associated swelling, indicates over-service.	Apply a soothing compress such as witch hazel. A shorter service time and spacing insertions are needed for the next service.
Brown scabs or crusts	High-intensity, high-frequency currents can cause scabbing, often seen on serviced areas such as the bikini line and abdomen. Scabbing can also be caused by incorrect placement of the electrical current in the hair follicle, e.g. too shallow, and applying the current when entering or leaving the hair follicle.	Advise the client to continue to apply a soothing antiseptic cream as the skin heals. The client must not remove the scabs or scarring may occur. Keep the current intensity levels low while still maintaining effectiveness. Ensure the insertions are deep enough.

Common contra-actions following epilation (Continued)

Contra-action	*Cause*	*Action*
Blanching – immediate whitening of the skin around the needle when a high intensity of current is applied	The skin has dried too quickly.	Apply a soothing cool compress. In future, make sure the current intensity is kept lower, or is applied for a slightly shorter time.
Weeping follicles – the follicles weep clear tissue fluid after the service	Too much galvanic current, either on its own or when using blend, will result in weeping follicles.	Keep the current intensity lower or the time shorter.
Brown spots or hyper-pigmentation – the pigment layer is disrupted and the skin becomes darker in the treated areas	This happens when the current intensity is too high using any of the methods.	Keep the current intensity lower, make sure the probe insertion is deep enough. Asian and African–Caribbean clients are particularly prone to hyper-pigmentation.
White spots or hypo-pigmentation – the pigment layer is disrupted and the mel-anocytes are damaged, resulting in small white spots around the treated follicles	This occurs when the current intensity is too high.	Keep the intensity lower and make sure the probe depth is correct.
Keloids – raised, shiny scarring	Caused by incorrect needle insertion and current application. African–Caribbean clients are susceptible to these.	With clients with a predisposition, assess skin tolerance and healing by perform-ing shorter services; identify the most suitable current intensity to promote safe skin healing.
Pitting and dermal contraction scars – small, round indentations, giving the skin a pitted look; sometimes described as 'orange peel' in texture	This is caused by scars in the dermis. Over-treatment and too high current intensities are the usual causes.	Keep current intensities and service time to the minimum necessary.
Indifferent electrode rash – reddening and irritation of the skin on the palm of the hand in which the indifferent elec-trode has been held	The positive electrode produces hydro-chloric acid.	Make sure the indifferent electrode is covered with dampened tissue or as recommended by the manufacturers.

ASSESSMENT OF KNOWLEDGE AND UNDERSTANDING

Having covered the learning objectives for **Provide electrical epilation treatments** – test what you need to know and understand answering the following short questions below. These will help to prepare you for your summative (final) assessment.

Anatomy and physiology questions required for these units are found on pages 97–99.

FUNCTIONAL SKILLS

Organizational and legal requirements

1 Summarize your responsibilities for **four** current legisla-tive requirements, e.g. Health and Safety at Work Act.

2 What are you responsibilities under your local author-ity licensing regulations for yourself and your premises and how might these vary depending upon where you have your business?

3 How can you ensure that people with illnesses and disabilities are not discriminated against when performing electrical epilation services?

4 At what age is a person classed as a minor and how does this affect how you can proceed with delivering this service?

5 Why must you check your insurance guidelines for the delivery of electrical epilation service?

6 What are the local authority and organizational requirements for contaminated waste disposal?

7 In relation to the Data Protection Act, what are the correct storage requirements for client record cards?

8 What are your responsibilities and reasons for maintaining a high standard of personal hygiene, appearance and wearing personal protection according to accepted industry and workplace requirements?

9 What are your workplace requirements for client preparation?

10 What are your workplace service times for the following electrical epilation services: upper lip, leg and eyebrows for a client who is commencing the service?

11 What are your workplace and manufacturer's requirements to maintain an asepsis working environment?

How to work safely and effectively when providing electrical epilation services?

1 How would you set up the work area for electrical epilation?

2 What are the necessary environmental conditions for electrical epilation services and why are these important refer to lighting, heating, ventilation and general client comfort?

3 What type of personal protective equipment should be worn for electrical epilation service and which legislation does this comply with?

4 What is contact dermatitis and how would you avoid developing it while carrying out electrical epilation services?

5 What is repetitive strain injury and how can you avoid developing it when delivering electrical epilation services?

6 Why is it important to disinfect your hands? Explain an effective method.

7 How would you position yourself and your client for electrical epilation services on the face and body areas?

8 What are the reasons for maintaining client modesty, privacy and comfort during the service?

9 Why is it important to check on the client's well-being at regular intervals during service?

Client consultation

1 What is the importance of effective client communication and discussion at consultation?

2 Why should you allow time for and encourage clients to ask questions at consultation?

3 At what stages of the service would you give advice and recommendations to the clients?

4 Why is it important to explain the commitment required to the service to gain the best possible results?

5 Why is it important to identify the client's skin type when planning the service?

6 How would you conduct a skin sensitivity test to identify possible allergies prior to the service?

7 What pigmentation issues may occur during the service. Why may theses occur?

8 If there are contra-indications to electrical epilation service either before or during the course which services could you recommend as an alternative?

9 How would you describe the sensation of the treatment and how it varies in different areas and for each electrical epilation method used?

10 How might skin sensitivity be affected by other skincare services which may inhibit electrical epilation?

11 Why should you read previous record cards?

Anatomy and physiology

1 Describe the basic structure and function of the skin.

2 Draw and describe the structure of the pilosebaceous unit.

3 What is the hair growth cycle and how does this influence epilation services?

4 Define three **types** of hair growth.

5 List and describe **four** types of endocrine system malfunction which have an effect on hair growth.

6 How are hormones circulated through the body?

7 Define the types of hair growth: superfluous, hirsutism and hypertrichosis.

8 Discuss the causes of hair growth: topical, congenital and systemic.

Contra-indications and contra-actions

1 State **three** contra-indications that prevent service and why?

2 What are the conditions that require medical approval before service can proceed?

3 State **three** conditions that restrict service and why?

4 What might be the potential consequences if you carried out a service on a contra-indicated client?

5 State **four** possible contra-actions which may occur during a service and how you would deal with them?

6 Why is it important to encourage clients with suspected contra-indications to seek medical advice?

Equipment and materials

1 What are the different types of equipment available for electrical epilation services?

2 Why is it important to follow manufacturer's instructions?

3 What types and sizes of needle are available for electrical epilation? When would you choose each?

Service-specific knowledge

1 Why should you communicate with and reassure the client during service?

2 How would you adapt your service application technique when treating dense and scattered hair growth?

3 Compare the benefits of each hair removal system such as galvanic, ac and blend techniques.

4 How would you select the type and size of needle to suit the hair and skin type and the area to be treated?

5 How would you consider to correctly insert the needle into the hair follicle?

6 What would be the effect of incorrect insertion technique?

7 How would you adapt your electrical epilation service technique to suit the client's skin condition, hair type and area to be treated?

8 How can you effectively remove hair from single follicles, compound follicles and distorted follicles?

9 Why can it be beneficial to apply post-service cataphoresis and what are the effects?

10 How does the moisture content of the hair follicle affect the electrical epilation service?

Aftercare

1 Why is it so important to give aftercare advice to clients relating to skin hygiene and hair management in between services?

2 What are the normal skin reactions that occur following a service?

3 What activities should be avoided 24–48 hours after a service?

4 What aftercare products should be recommended for home use which will benefit and protect the area that has been treated?

5 Which hair removal methods would you recommend for dealing with regrowth between services?

10 Body massage

SHUTTERSTOCK/MONKEY BUSINESS IMAGES

Learning Objectives

This chapter covers the unit on how to **Provide body massage treatments**.

This unit is all about how to provide the service body massage to different areas of the body. This may be carried out *manually*, where the beauty therapist's hands manipulate the client's skin, tissue and underlying muscles, or *mechanically* using a machine. Treatment application is modified to achieve the client's service objectives which may be a psychological/physiological-related outcome or both. This will be identified at consultation. To help you achieve these objectives, further equipment may be beneficial to use which are suggested and their use explained.

There are **five** learning outcomes which you must achieve competently:

1. **Maintain safe and effective methods of working when providing body massage services.**
2. **Consult, plan and prepare for services with clients.**
3. **Perform manual massage services.**
4. **Perform mechanical massage services.**
5. **Provide aftercare advice.**

(continued on the next page)

BSON

ROLE MODEL

Katie Harris

Holistic Therapist at Equilibrium Complementary Health Centre and Mobile Holistic Therapist

"I started work at The Treatment Rooms, a spa in Brighton. Work at the spa was very busy, with back-to-back clients all day. Here I did Swedish massage, aromatherapy and reflexology; the company then trained me in Ayurvedic massage, La Stone Massage, scrubs, wraps and massage-based facials. This was really nice, as I had a real variety of services that broke up the day from doing just massage. Also the scrubs, wraps and facials gave my hands a break from massage. I am now able to use all these skills in my current job in the complementary health clinic.

(continued)

When providing massage services you will be required to:

- use different **consultation techniques** to correctly identify your client's needs
- use of **equipment** suitable to the area and which will enhance the service
- use different **massage mediums** suitable for your different clients
- adapt your service to suit the client's **physical characteristics**
- take the **necessary actions** where a contra-action, contra-indication or service modification is required
- meet different **service objectives** when performing the treatment
- use different **massage techniques** modified to meet your clients massage requirements
- covered all **body massage treatment areas**
- provide relevant aftercare **advice** to meet your clients present and future service objectives.

When providing a body massage service it is important to use the skills you have learnt in the following units:

Monitoring safe work operations.

Promotional activities.

Essential anatomy and physiology knowledge required for this unit is identified on the checklist in Chapter 2, pages 12–13 and is also discussed within this chapter.

COURTESY COLLIN UK © COLLIN PARIS

Female client receiving a relaxation massage

Types of massage application

Manual massage has been practised for thousands of years and benefits the client both physiologically (the health and functioning of the body) and psychologically (mentally). The soft tissues of the body, are manipulated, producing heat and stimulating the vascular, lymphatic and nervous system. Massage can achieve different results including relaxation and stimulation followed by a feeling of well-being.

Electrical equipment as an alternative can also be applied, which achieves similar effects to manual massage. Electrical equipment may be combined with manual massage to enhance the effect achieved.

Mechanical massage, also referred to as gyratory massage, is a hand-held electrical body massage service providing a stimulating massage from a vibratory head to which different applicator heads are attached. This massage service is often used to soften fatty tissue and stimulate the lymphatic system.

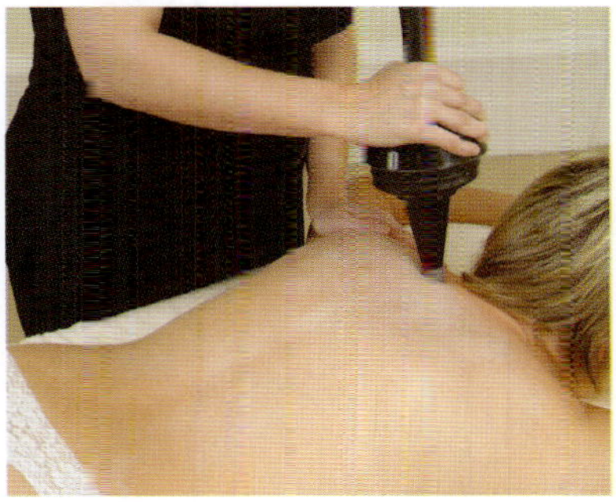

CARLTON BEAUTY + SPA LTD

Mechanical massage being applied to the client

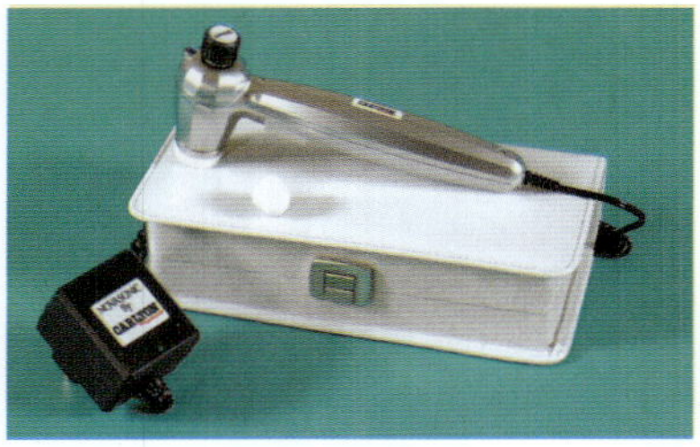

Audio sonic machine

Audio sonic is a hand-held electrical vibratory machine which gently compresses and decompresses the soft tissues using sound waves which are created as the machine head passes over the skin. This vibratory service creates a deep stimulating action without irritating the skin surface, ideal for a sensitive skin.

The knowledge requirements for mechanical and audio sonic massage are found in **Facial and body electrical services, Chapter 8.**

Effects of manual massage

Physiological effects

- increases the blood circulation, bringing fresh nutrients and oxygen to the body cells and systems
- warms the tissues and produces skin erythema
- superficial and deeper layers of the skin are stimulated, increasing cellular function and regeneration of body cells
- aids desquamation – the removal of dead skin cells
- sebaceous secretions of the skin are increased, naturally moisturising the skin
- reduces fibrous growth formation such as skin tags (verruca filliformis) and aids the dispersion of milia
- increases lymphatic flow, aiding the removal of waste products and toxins
- relaxes tense and contracted muscles, improving muscle tone
- stimulates the nerve endings, relieving muscular pain and fatigue
- softens and breaks down localized fatty deposits and loosens scar tissue

TOP TIP

Pre-blended massage medium

Pre-blended massage oils and creams can be used for massage. When inhaled and absorbed through the skin they can help relax or energize the client.

Psychological effects

Each massage is adapted to meet the client's psychological needs; these are identified at the client consultation. A stimulating massage application will invigorate, while a slow, deep massage will aid relaxation, helping to relieve tension and stress. The client will also feel energized as the body systems such as blood and lymphatic circulation are stimulated. A feeling of well-being can also increase the client's confidence and self-esteem.

> Be always willing to do as many different services as possible, especially massage. This makes you more employable, as body massage is often a big part of the job.
>
> **Katie Harris**

Effects of body massage on the systems of the body

Circulatory and lymphatic systems The circulatory system is improved with massage to the tissues in the area. This is known as hyperaemia. The blood flow in the arteries is increased by massage techniques and the vessels dilate (vasodilation), bringing about an erythema, redness of the skin. The arteries assist the transportation of oxygen and nutrients to the cells. Massage improves the gaseous exchange, helping to promote healthier cells. The venous return helps to remove waste products, toxins and carbon dioxide from the cells, creating a feeling of well-being.

Lymph capillaries have a single layer of cells, They begin as blind-ended tubes in areas that contain tissue fluid and eventually join together to form lymph vessels. Some waste products and toxins pass into lymph vessels via the lymph capillaries, which have larger pores than those in the blood capillaries. Before re-entering the bloodstream, lymph passes through lymph nodes where many toxins are removed by the actions of white blood cells.

Muscular system The increased blood circulation feeds the muscle tissue, bringing extra oxygen and nutrients and aiding the removal of waste products in the venous return. This helps muscles to function to their full potential, keeping them toned and maintaining their elasticity and extensibility. The increased production of heat created by vasodilation produces a warming effect and the skin's surface temperature is raised. Muscles that are tense and shortened can be relaxed and stretched; weakened muscles can increase in tone.

Nervous system The peripheral nerve endings can be either soothed or stimulated, depending on the massage techniques being performed. Vigorous techniques can have a stimulating effect – tissues and organs can be encouraged to work more efficiently. Slow, rhythmically applied techniques can induce relaxation and sleep. Massage can also have a soothing effect on the nerves when performing the massage techniques effleurage and vibrations, causing temporary pain relief.

The autonomic nervous system parasympathetic division is stimulated in times of relaxation such as when receiving massage which has a calming effect on the body.

The skin Massage helps the skin to perform its various functions. Stimulation of the sebaceous glands by general massage techniques produces more sebum, which helps to soften and moisturise the skin making it more resistant to infection due to its anti-bacterial property. The vasodilation action creates warmth in the skin, increasing the output of the sudoriferous sweat glands. This helps to remove the waste products and urea from the body more efficiently. Frictions used in the massage routine will aid desquamation of the dead skin cells, leaving the skin smoother and softer. Sensory nerve endings can either be soothed or irritated depending on the massage technique used, e.g. effleurage or tapotement (percussion).

The lungs Percussion technique can have an effect on lung tissue. The circulation to the bronchioles is increased, helping to feed and nourish the tissues. This in turn promotes good elasticity and gaseous exchange within the lungs.

Heat services

Pre-heating services To increase the service objectives of the massage, such as relaxation, a pre-heating service may be given. This will increase the attainment of the circulatory response to massage.

Services that may be used include infrared, paraffin wax therapy, steam or sauna service and hot towels.

HEALTH & SAFETY

Erythema

The skin will gain an erythema during massage due to increased blood flow. However, excessive erythema could indicate skin intolerance – a contra-action to treatment. Stop service and identify the cause. Note this on the client treatment record card.

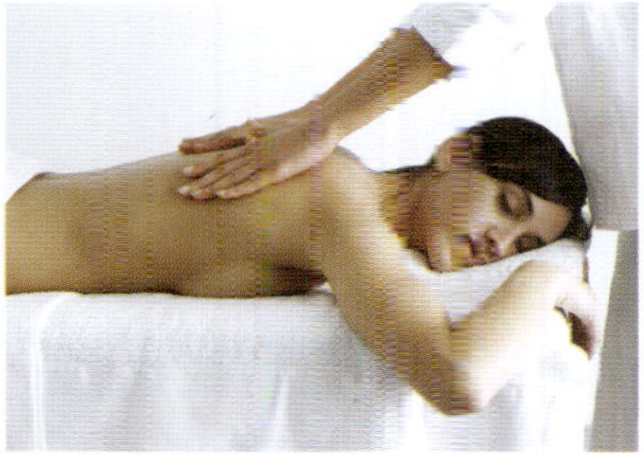

Massage benefits physiologically the whole body systems

HEALTH & SAFETY

Infrared heat lamp safe use

Ensure the infrared heat lamp has a stable surface before use and that all joints are tight, enabling accurate positioning and preventing accidental harm to clients.

HEALTH & SAFETY

Infrared bulbs safety

A protective grille or guard should be used in the event of the bulb breaking during use.

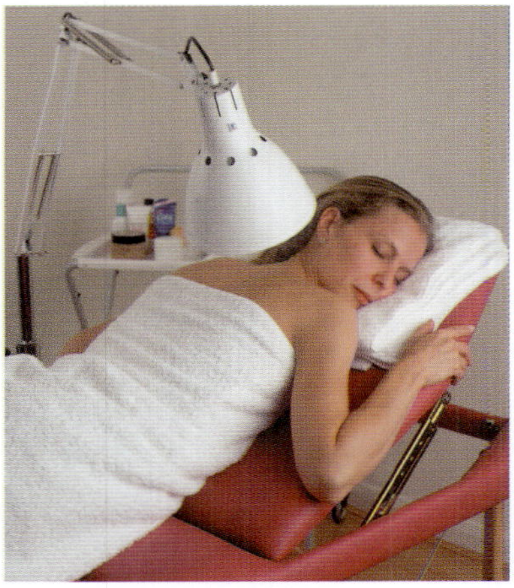

Infrared application to the body

Infrared Infrared lamps emit infrared rays through an infrared treatment bulb, which have a heating therapeutic effect on the epidermal tissue. The skin becomes warmer, sweating increases and hyperaemia occurs as blood circulation increases locally in the area as the blood vessels dilate. A soothing effect on the sensory nerve endings in the area occurs as a result of the heating action.

The underlying muscle tissue relaxes due to this heating action. Heat is applied to localized areas because of the limitations of the arc of light from the lamp. Popular areas for using this service are the face, back and chest.

Infrared is applied to skin that is clean and free from any products and jewellery. It is important that a tactile and thermal skin sensitivity test is performed before the service application to assess skin sensitivity to heat. It is also important to check for general body electrotherapy contra-indications. As a precaution it is best practice for the client to wear protective eye shields or prevent eye exposure to prevent injury to the eyes.

The infrared lamp is heated in advance of the service application and then applied at a distance of 45–90 cm dependent upon skin sensitivity and the body part being treated. The rays from the bulb must strike the skin perpendicularly (at right angles) for maximum penetration. Always refer to manufacturer's instructions for service application guidance. The service application may be 10–30 minutes dependent upon the area of the service, skin sensitivity and positioning of lamp distance from the skin.

The client must be asked to inform you if the area feels uncomfortably hot, which would be a contra-action.

As a pre-heating service, infrared is usually applied 10 minutes before massage application.

Traditional wood sauna dry heat service

HEALTH & SAFETY

Contra-action-Infrared service over exposure – lamp too close or length of application too long.

Incorrect exposure can result in the following contra-actions:

- burns
- headaches
- fainting

Steam room wet heat service

Paraffin wax A wax heated in a specialized bath which is then applied to the skin usually with a brush. The wax sets and is left in contact with the skin where the heating effect stimulates blood circulation, increases perspiration, softens the skin and eases discomfort in arthritic and rheumatic conditions.

Sauna service A dry heat service where air is heated. This has the benefits of quickly heating the body which enables the muscles to relax due to the rise in body temperature and increased blood circulation.

Steam service A wet heat service where water is heated to produce a steam environment. The effects are as those of a sauna service.

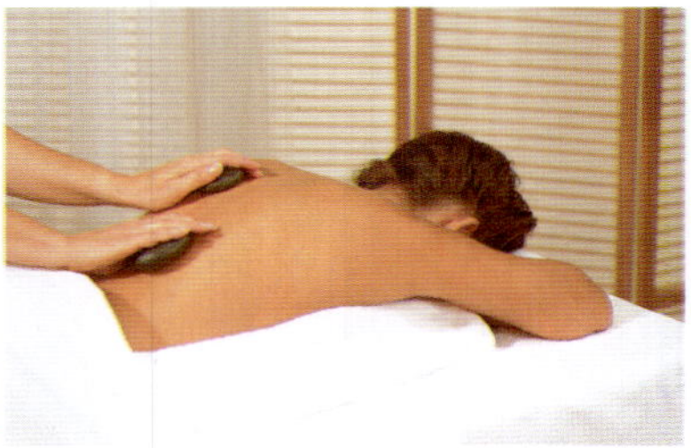

Client receiving hot stone massage

Hot stone therapy Hot stone therapy uses stones. The application of both hot and cold stones to the body has proven therapeutic effects. Placement of heated stones balance the energy centres of the body and heal while cold stones can be placed to relieve stress. One stroke with a stone is considered to achieve the equivalent of 5–10 strokes with the hand, thus the therapeutic benefits can be considered to be achieved much more quickly.

Hot stone therapy can be offered within a massage service programme or as a service on its own.

Hot towels Towels are heated, usually in a specialized hot towel cabinet. The towels become steamed and moist which when applied immediately to the skin can be used to soften and warm the skin and aid absorption of products used to massage the skin. Essential oils can be infused to relax or stimulate your client's skin and senses. Hot towels can also be used to remove excess oil following massage.

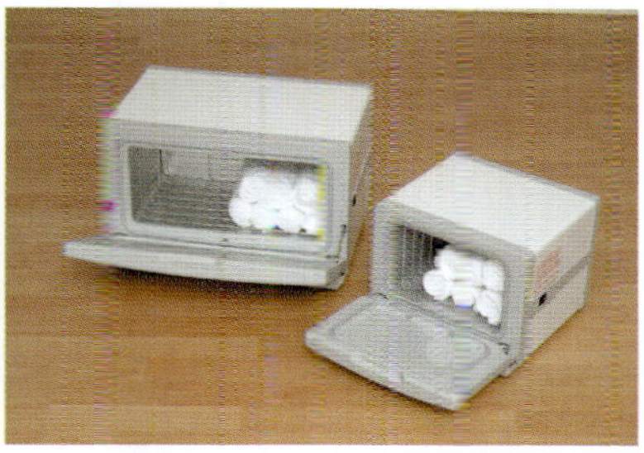

Towel warmer (large) cabinet

Massage techniques

There are several different massage techniques which are selected and applied according to the desired effect. These are described below.

Effleurage (stroking)

Effleurage movements have a sedating and relaxing effect on the skin. They are performed with the whole palm and depending on the pressure applied, can either be performed superficially or deeply. Effleurage always commences and completes a massage sequence and can also be used as a link movement.

Effects of effleurage

- increases lymphatic and blood circulation
- relieves tension
- helps reduce non-medical oedema
- aids desquamation
- induces relaxation

ALWAYS REMEMBER

Effleurage application
Deep effleurage movements are always directed towards the heart and bring about a physical change to the surface capillaries, producing an hyperaemia. Superficial effleurage is used to bring the beauty therapist's hands back to the starting position.

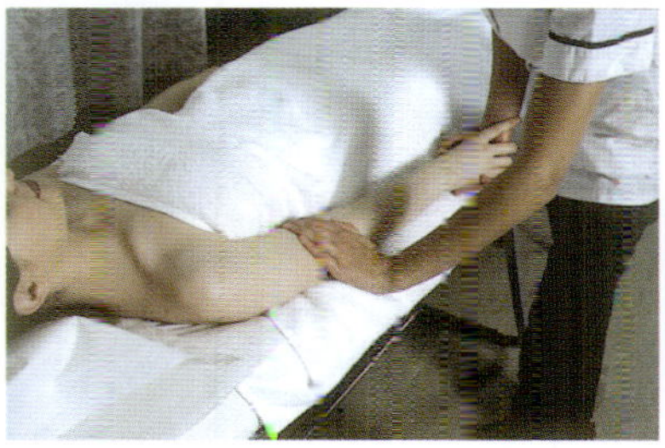

Effleurage to the arm

TOP TIP

Effleurage application technique
Keep the hands relaxed with the fingers and thumbs of the hand together maintaining required pressure and contact with the area being treated.

Petrissage (compression)

Petrissage techniques include kneading, knuckling, lifting, rolling and wringing. Using the fingers and thumbs, intermittent pressure is applied smoothly and firmly to the tissues of the skin, squeezing and lifting it from the underlying structures. This manipulation is then followed by relaxation of the tissues. Petrissage helps to tone and relieve muscular fatigue, leading to an improvement in elasticity within the muscle.

Effects of petrissage:

- increases lymphatic and blood circulation
- increases venous return
- breaks down tight nodules in the muscles
- aids removal of waste products from the tissues
- promotes relaxation in the client
- helps to soften and mobilize fatty tissue

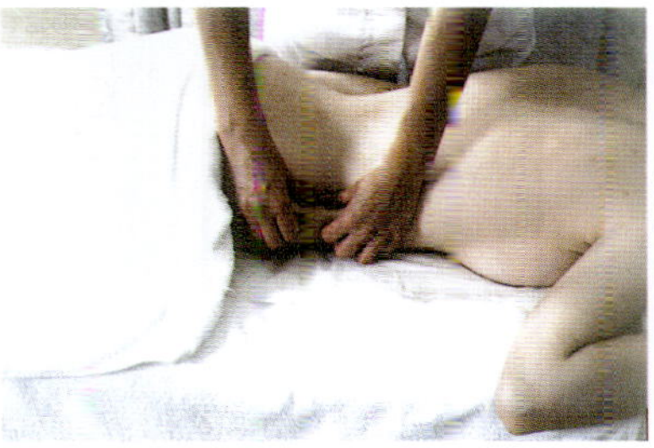

Petrissage skin-rolling technique to the lateral, side walls of the abdomen

Tapotement (percussion)

Tapotement techniques are used for general toning and should not be included in a relaxing massage. Tapotement movements include beating, clapping/cupping, hacking and pounding. The client must have suitable body mass to receive this service (the client's

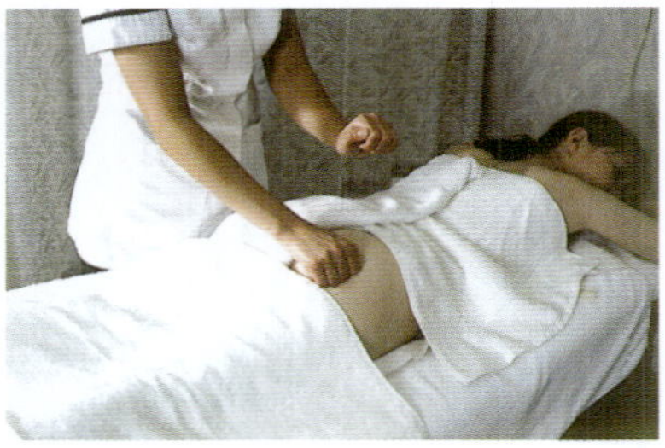

Percussion-beating technique to the gluteal area

weight needs to be within the correct range for their height) otherwise it can be very uncomfortable.

Effects of tapotement/percussion:

- increases sluggish lymphatic and blood circulation
- stimulates the sensory nerve endings
- improves muscle tone and response
- helps to loosen mucus in chest respiratory conditions
- helps to soften areas of fatty, adipose tissue

Tapotement technique is particularly beneficial for stimulating the surface and underlying tissues to improve overall appearance.

HEALTH & SAFETY

Tapotement

Tapotement technique should be avoided on thin or elderly clients because they could lead to bruising and possible damage to the bones if they have osteoporosis. Also avoid application over the abdomen due to lack of bony support.

ALWAYS REMEMBER

Distal phalanx

The distal phalanx is the smallest bone in the thumb, forming the tip of the thumb.

Vibrations

Vibrations technique is used to help relieve pain and fatigue, stimulate the nerves and produce a sedative effect. They are fine, trembling movements, performed with one or both hands. They can vary between static and running vibrations. The palmar surface of the hand, the pads of the fingertips and the distal phalanx of the thumb can all be used for vibrations.

Effects of vibrations:

- relieves tension in the neck and long muscles of the back
- increases the action of the lungs
- helps to increase peristalsis (muscular contractions of the gut that move food along) in the colon

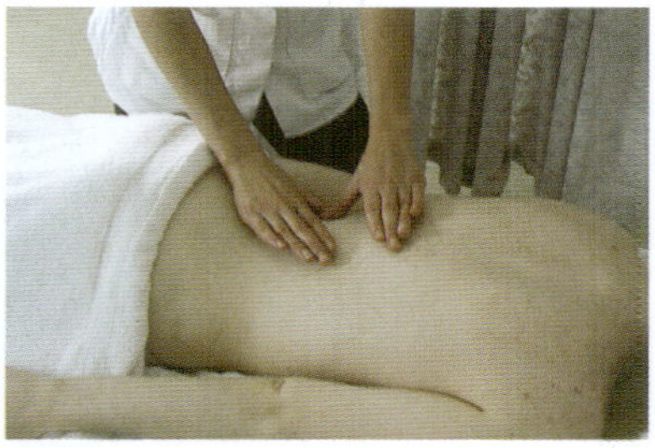

Frictions technique to the forearm

Frictions

Frictions cause the skin and superficial structures to move together over the deeper, underlying structures. They are concentrated in a particular area and applied with regulated pressure. This technique helps to break down fibrous thickening and fat deposits, and aids the removal of any non-medical oedemas.

Effects of frictions:

- aid relaxation
- break down tight nodules
- increase lymph and blood circulation

Any massage service should include a full range of techniques applied to suit the client's physiological and psychological needs. For example, if the client has tension in the neck and shoulders, the beauty therapist should adapt the techniques to focus upon and provide benefit to this area. More time should be spent concentrating on this area and correspondingly less on other parts of the body. This will be agreed with the client at the consultation.

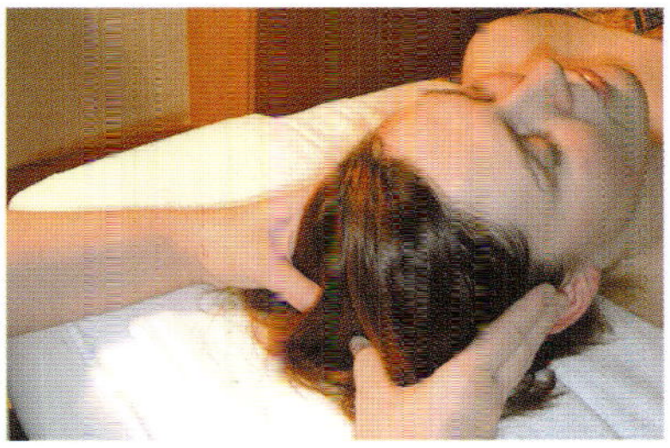

Pressure point technique to the scalp

Pressure points

Pressure points is the application of pressure on specific points of the head, face or body using fingertips and thumbs. This helps to release blocked energy channels flowing through the body, improving circulation, stimulating the nervous system, improving the body's ability to function and repair.

TOP TIP

Oedema test

To test whether an oedema is medical or non-medical, gently press the centre of the swelling. If the indentation in the skin springs back quickly it is non-medical; if it takes a few seconds to return to normal it may be a medically related oedema. Advice the client to consult their GP in this case.

Outcome 1: Maintain safe and effective methods of working when providing body massage services

Learn how to maintain safe and effective methods of working when providing body massage service by:

1. Setting up and monitoring the service area to meet organization procedures and manufacturer's instructions.
2. Making sure that environmental conditions are suitable for the client and the service.
3. Ensuring your personal hygiene, protection and appearance meet accepted industry and organizational requirements.
4. Ensuring that your nails are short, clean, well manicured and free of polish.
5. Effectively disinfecting your hands prior to and after service.
6. Ensuring your own posture and position minimizes fatigue and risk of injury while working.
7. Ensuring all tools and **equipment** are cleaned using the correct methods.
8. Positioning **equipment** and **massage mediums** for ease and safety of use.
9. Ensuring the client is in a comfortable and relaxed position suitable for the service.
10. Maintaining accepted industry hygiene and safety practices throughout the service.
11. Adopting a positive, polite and reassuring manner towards the client throughout the service.
12. Maintaining the client's modesty, privacy and comfort at all times.

TOP TIP

Cellulite

Cellulite is caused by a build-up of waste products and toxins in the cells around adipose tissue which stagnate and cause fluid retention. Cellulite can affect any age, weight or shape of client. It can appear around the lateral aspect of the thigh (tensor fasciae latae muscle), the abdomen (rectus abdominus), the back of the arm (triceps) and the buttocks (gluteals). When touched, the area feels cold and can take on a dimpled, puckered appearance.

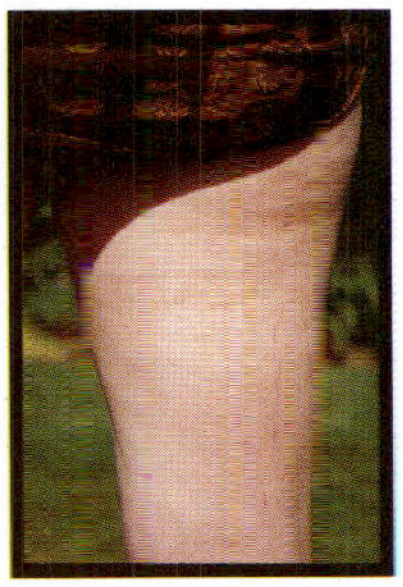

(Continued) Learn how to maintain safe and effective methods of working when providing body massage service by:

13. Disposing of waste materials safely and correctly.
14. Ensuring the service is cost-effective and is carried out within a commercially viable time.
15. Ensuring client record cards are up-to-date, accurate, complete, legible and signed by the client and practitioner.
16. Leaving the service area and **equipment** in a condition suitable for future services.

Before beginning the body massage service, check that you have the necessary equipment and materials to hand and that they meet legal, hygiene and industry requirements for body massage.

EQUIPMENT AND MATERIALS LIST

ELLISONS

Massage couch
With sit up and lie down positions and an easy to clean surface This may feature a face hole in its design

Stool
Adjustable in height, to ensure correct therapist working position

BEAUTY EXPRESS LTD

Large and small towels
Two large and approximately four small plus a large towel or bathrobe for the client. Towels may be used for both support and protection

TISSERAND AROMATHERAPY

Massage medium – oil
Choice to suit different skin types/ conditions

BEAUTY EXPRESS LTD.

Massage medium – cream
Choice to suit different skin types/ conditions

BEAUTY EXPRESS LTD.

Purified talc If preferred as a massage medium, suitable for an oily skin type or very hairy area

Trolley To hold all necessary equipment and materials

Damp cotton wool
To apply and remove skin cleansing products

Large tissues
To blot the skin dry after cleansing

Spatulas
To remove products hygienically from containers

Four plastic bowls
Two large and two small to dispense products into and hold consumables

Client record card
Confidential card recording details of each client to record personal details, products used, retail purchases made and details of the service

ELLISONS

Hot towel heater
Towels can be used to cleanse the area and remove products from the skin

CARLTON PROFESSIONAL

Mechanical massage equipment

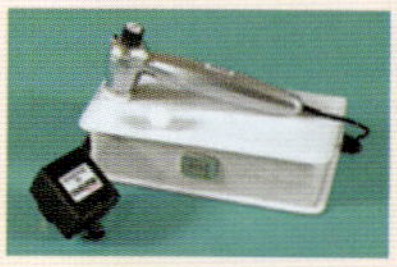
CARLTON PROFESSIONAL

Audio sonic equipment
Vibratory service where attachments are selected and applied to create a deep stimulating action

DAYLIGHT

Infrared unit equipment
Pre-heating service used prior to massage application

YOU WILL ALSO NEED:

Removable protective couch cover To maintain hygienic working practice and prevent cross-contamination

Disposable paper tissue bedroll To cover the couch and can prevent towel staining from massage oils

Skin cleanser, e.g. witch hazel or eau de cologne to remove excess massage medium following treatment

Cosmetic cleansing preparations to suit different skin types To remove facial make-up, dead skin cells and sebum

Waste container with lid Bin lined with a disposable bin liner

Aftercare advice Recommended advice for the client to refer to following the service and products to purchase/further recommended services

Sterilization and disinfection

Manual massage Before the massage service, make sure the couch and trolley have been wiped over with warm soapy water and chlorine-based preparation. Plastic spatulas if used should be cleaned and placed in an UV cabinet prior to use, to ensure they are hygienic. Preferably use disposable items to avoid contamination and cross-infection. Clean towels and bedroll should be provided for each client to prevent cross-infection.

Mechanical massage Attachments used should be washed in warm soapy water to remove talc, dead skin cells and sebum. They should then be dried and disinfected in the UV cabinet. Disposable protective attachment covers may be purchased.

Audio sonic Heads should be cleaned with a disinfectant spirit-based cleaner after use and disinfected in the UV cabinet.

ELLISONS

Disposable mechanical massage sponge heads

ELLISONS

Mechanical massage heads with disposable covers

Preparation of the work area

The service area should be clean and at a comfortable working temperature for both the client and beauty therapist, between 18 and 21°C. One large towel should be placed over the length of the couch and a small towel over the head end. Further towels should be used as appropriate to preserve the client's modesty. All products, equipment and materials should be placed on the trolley prior to the service, so that the beauty therapist does not need to break the continuity of the massage to go in search of them. The trolley should be positioned for ease of access for the beauty therapist.

Adequate ventilation should be provided to create a hygienic environment, preventing cross-infection through viral airborne spores, drowsiness through carbon dioxide-saturated air and the removal of stale smells and odours. Lighting should be soft, decor subtle and non-gender biased. Sound levels should be low for relaxation. An electric point should be available for electrical equipment.

The service area should remain in a safe and hygienic state throughout the day, ready for further use. Waste at conclusion of the service should be disposed of in a sealed polythene bag and towels laundered.

HEALTH & SAFETY

Legislation

It is important that you comply with all relevant health and safety legislation while performing body massage.

Examples include:

Workplace (Health, Safety and Welfare) Regulations (1992)

Control of Substances Hazardous to Health Regulations (COSHH) (2002)

Electricity at Work Regulations (1989).

Remember to use the knowledge and skills you have learnt in the chapter on **Monitoring safe work operations.**

ELLISONS

Mechanical massage attachment heads

TOP TIP

Accommodating disabilities

Hydraulic couches are effective as they allow clients with mobility problems easier access onto the couch.

They also benefit the beauty therapist as they are height adjustable, preventing unnecessary strain caused by stretching during manual application.

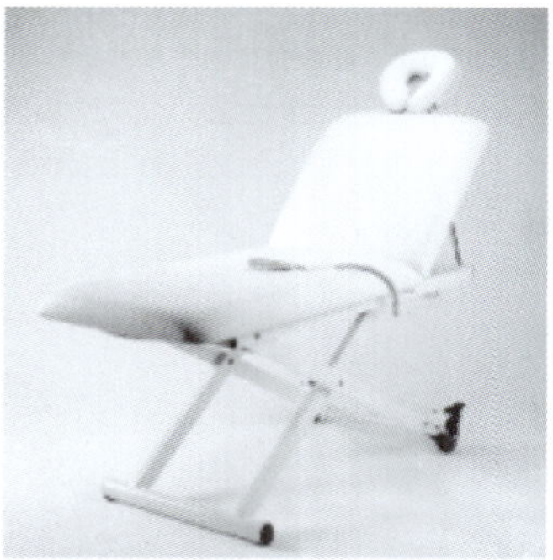
BEAUTY EXPRESS LTD

Electric couch

ALWAYS REMEMBER

Record card completion

Accurately record your client's answers to questions asked at consultation on the record card. This is a legal requirement.

> Know your products well in order to get the best possible result from their use.
>
> **Katie Harris**

> Always leave the room tidy and set up ready for the next client, even if you're not in it next. Impressions count!
>
> **Katie Harris**

HEALTH & SAFETY

Avoiding cross-infection

Strict hygiene procedures should be complied as cross-infection can easily occur if they are not followed exactly.

Products

Check that all products are clean at all times and that the 'use by' date has not expired. Ensure all containers are wiped over and lids are securely replaced after use to prevent contamination.

Plan and prepare for the massage service

Outcome 2: Consult, plan and prepare for services with clients

Learn how to use consultation techniques to effectively plan and prepare for massage service by:

1. Using **consultation techniques** in a polite, sensitive and friendly manner to determine the client's service needs.
2. Obtaining signed, written informed consent from the client prior to carrying out the service.
3. Ensuring that informed and signed parent or guardian consent is obtained for minors prior to any massage service.
4. Ensuring that a parent or guardian is present throughout the massage service for minors under the age of 16.
5. Clearly explaining to the client what the service entails in a way they can understand.
6. Using suitable **consultation techniques** to identify your client's medical history, **physical characteristics** and lifestyle pattern.
7. Asking your client appropriate questions to identify if they have any contra-indications to massage services.
8. Accurately recording your client's responses to questioning.
9. Actively encouraging clients to ask questions and clarify any points.
10. Taking the **necessary action** in response to any identified contra-indications.
11. Ensuring client advice is given without reference to a specific medical condition and without causing undue alarm and concern.
12. Clearly explaining and agreeing the projected cost, likely duration, frequency and types of service needed.

(Continued) **Learn how to use consultation techniques to effectively plan and prepare for massage service by:**

3. Agreeing in writing the client's needs, expectations and **service objectives**, ensuring they are realistic and achievable.
4. Ensuring that the client's skin is clean and prepared to suit the type of massage to be used.
5. Ensuring that clothing, hair and accessories are effectively protected or removed.
6. Selecting suitable **equipment** and **massage mediums** to meet the **service objectives**.

Client consultation

Reception

Massage services in the salon can range from a full-body massage to massage only for specific areas of the body, e.g. a back massage or a neck and shoulder massage. When the appointment is made identify the client's requirements where possible so that a suitable time can be allocated for the service required. Allow an hour for a full-body massage excluding head and face massage. If head and face massage is required allow 75 minutes. Allow 30 minutes for a back massage service. Service times for other specific areas will vary according to the of the areas being treated.

> Be prepared to think on your feet if your client has different needs or requests, always make them feel comfortable and not like its an effort.
>
> **Katie Harris**

Massage times for specific body areas

Area	*Time (minutes)*
Arms, each	5
Neck/chest	5–8
Abdomen	5–8
Legs, each	5
Buttocks	5–8
*Back	20–30
Head and face	15

*If performed as part of a full-body massage 20 minutes is usually allowed for back massage and 30 minutes if performed as an individual massage service.

Consultation techniques

The beauty therapist needs to obtain personal information from the client, which will inform service delivery, before commencing the massage service. For this reason a full consultation should always be performed, which should be reviewed at every further appointment, conducted in a quiet private area without unnecessary interruptions. This may be the area where the massage service will be received. Client modesty and privacy should be considered at all times

ALWAYS REMEMBER

Client privacy and respect at consultation

Commence the consultation with the client fully clothed in the case that you find they have a contra-indication which means the service may not go ahead. Details of how to conduct the consultation to identify physical characteristics and lifestyle factors are found on pages 346–347. The client should be made to feel welcome and at ease throughout the service. Remember the importance of communication through body language. A positive rapport should be established between the client and beauty therapist in order that the client feels relaxed and comfortable.

Personal details taken are recorded on the client record card. These include the client's medical history, GP's details, any contra-indications that prevent or restrict service and the requirements for the massage service. The contra-indications that prevent or restrict the beauty therapist from performing manual massage are listed in the table below, but if in doubt a letter of approval should always be obtained from the client's GP before massage is received.

ALWAYS REMEMBER

Contra-indications

A contra-indication is a disease or disorder that prevents a client receiving service because of a risk of cross-infection (e.g. scabies, shingles, ringworm) or because the client may experience discomfort or even harm as a result of the contra-indication.

Contra-indications to massage

These are divided into three categories as illustrated in the table: general affecting the, local and temporary. **General** contra-indications affect the whole body or part of the body; **local** contra-indications are concentrated in a particular area; the symptoms of **temporary** contra-indications prevent treatment but the service can proceed when the condition or restriction no longer exists or there is medical approval. If the beauty therapist has any concern over the client's health or well-being, medical advice should be sought prior to the service.

Those contra-indications requiring GP referral should be tactfully and clearly discussed to ensure client understanding and avoid causing necessary client worry or concern.

HEALTH & SAFETY

Abrasions

An adhesive dressing can be applied to a small abrasion to prevent secondary- infection or cross-infection when preparing the client for massage.

Contra-indications to massage

General	*Local*	*Temporary*
Heart conditions	Recent operations	Medication
High and low blood pressure	Recent scar tissue	Skin bruising
Certain medication		Skin abrasions
Diabetes	Skin diseases	Medical oedema
Cancer	Skin disorders	Skin diseases
Rheumatism		Skin disorders
Undiagnosed lumps, bumps or swelling		During chemotherapy or radiotherapy
Loss of skin sensation		Product allergies
Postural deformities		
Over-bulbous varicose veins		
Phlebitis		
Deep vein thrombosis (DVT)		
High temperature		
Epilepsy		

HEALTH & SAFETY

Product allergies

If the client has a sensitive skin or suffers from allergies, recommend they receive a skin sensitivity 'patch test' before you proceed with the massage service.

A small amount of the product to be used within the massage procedure is applied to the skin at least 24 hours beforehand. A 'positive' reaction indicates that the product is unsuitable and an alternative should be sought.

HEALTH & SAFETY

Service for minors

Any client under 16 years must not receive a massage service unless accompanied by a parent/guardian who must sign a consent form. Also, follow your salon policy on the service of **minors.**

Contra-actions

A contra-action is an unwanted reaction to body massage service which may occur during or following service. These should be discussed with the client at the consultation.

These might include:

- sickness, caused by the increased circulation of waste products transported in the lymphatic system
- fainting, caused by dilation of the blood capillaries, altering blood-pressure levels
- skin reactions, such as an allergy to the **massage medium** used
- bruising, caused by incorrect application of the technique, e.g. excessive pressure during tapotement application

If the client suffers any contra-action, whilst in the salon:

- In the instance of respiratory allergy, Ensure the client can breathe properly and that the room is well ventilated.
- Offer the client a glass of water if they feel sick.
- Apply a cold compress if a skin reaction occurs.
- Advise the client to seek immediate medical advice if the symptoms persist.

Any contra-action, with actions taken should be noted on the clients record card for future reference. Discuss and confirm with the client their service requirements. Explain clearly to the client what the massage service involves and the benefits to be gained. Treatment objectives must be suitable for the client realistic and achievable. Discuss the ways in which the service can be modified or adapted to meet their specific physiological, psychological treatment needs including the use of any massage equipment. Agree the service plan and if this will be a manual or mechanical massage

Allow time and invite the client to ask questions – the client should fully understand what the service involves including costs, duration, frequency and use of equipment if used. Expected and possible post-service reactions should be discussed.

Effective questioning on the client's expectations can ensure client satisfaction. The client will also require a postural check at the time of consultation. This is to assess if the client has any noticeable posture conditions which the beauty therapist may provide advise for within their professional responsibility, and which may require adaption of massage application including massage techniques incorporated. Postural assessment is discussed on pages 202–204.

Once the consultation is complete the beauty therapist should ensure that all the details are recorded accurately and that the client has signed their record card.

HEALTH & SAFETY

Contra-indications

Phlebitis and deep vein thrombosis

Venous problems can lead to vein inflammation and skin ulceration.

Phlebitis is when the vein becomes inflamed.

Thrombosis is where a blood clot forms in a blood vessel.

Thrombophlebitis is where a blood clot forms in an inflamed vein.

Massage is unsuitable for the above contra-indications due to possible client harm. Massage may cause a blood clot to move through the bloodstream, causing a blockage elsewhere which could prove fatal!

Medication

Massage increases circulation, therefore certain drug therapies such as chemotherapy may increase in rate, possibly altering the drug's effect.

BEST PRACTICE

Contra-indications and service modification

If the client has a contra-indication, the beauty therapist should use their discretion to determine whether or not the client is suitable for the service, offering alternatives where possible. For example, varicose veins can be a contra-indication but a back, neck and shoulder massage could be offered if appropriate..

BEST PRACTICE

Postural conditions

Examples of postural conditions the beauty therapist will be looking for are kyphosis, lordosis and scoliosis. Some of these may be linked to postural habits or poor working related posture. The massage application may be modified for the postural condition.

Record card for providing body massage services

Date	Beauty therapist name	
Client name	Date of birth (Identifying client age group.)	
Home address	Postcode	
Email address	Landline phone number	Mobile phone number
Name of doctor	Doctor's address and phone number	
Related medical history (Conditions that may restrict or prohibit service application, i.e. diabetic client if receiving infrared service as their skin sensitivity may be impaired.)		
Are you taking any medication? (This may affect the appearance of the skin or skin sensitivity.)		

CONTRA-INDICATIONS REQUIRING MEDICAL REFERRAL
(Preventing **head and body massage** service application.)

- ☐ skin disorders – active
- ☐ high or low blood pressure
- ☐ recent head and neck injury
- ☐ severe varicose veins
- ☐ recent scar tissue
- ☐ pregnancy
- ☐ heart disease
- ☐ dysfunction of the nervous system
- ☐ skin disease
- ☐ severe bruising
- ☐ severe cuts and abrasions
- ☐ medical conditions
- ☐ deep vein thrombosis
- ☐ during chemotherapy and radiotherapy

SERVICE AREAS

- ☐ head
- ☐ arms and hands
- ☐ back
- ☐ full body
- ☐ gluteals
- ☐ face
- ☐ chest and shoulders
- ☐ abdomen
- ☐ legs and feet

LIFESTYLE

- ☐ occupation
- ☐ dietary and fluid intake
- ☐ exercise habits
- ☐ hobbies, interests, means of relaxation
- ☐ family situation
- ☐ sleep patterns
- ☐ smoking habits

MASSAGE TECHNIQUES

- ☐ effleurage
- ☐ tapotement (percussion)
- ☐ vibrations
- ☐ petrissage
- ☐ frictions
- ☐ pressure points

MASSAGE MEDIUMS

- ☐ oil
- ☐ powder
- ☐ cream

CONTRA-INDICATIONS THAT RESTRICT SERVICE
(Service may require adaptation.)

- ☐ cuts and abrasions
- ☐ skin disorder
- ☐ high or low blood pressure
- ☐ recent scar tissue (avoid area)
- ☐ cuts and abrasions
- ☐ mild eczema/psoriasis
- ☐ undiagnosed lumps, bumps, swellings
- ☐ varicose veins
- ☐ asthma
- ☐ product allergies
- ☐ recent injuries to the area of the service
- ☐ certain medication
- ☐ abdomen during menstruation
- ☐ migraine
- ☐ epilepsy
- ☐ diabetes

PHYSICAL CHARACTERISTICS

- ☐ weight
- ☐ muscle tone
- ☐ health
- ☐ size
- ☐ age
- ☐ skin condition
- ☐ height
- ☐ posture

OBJECTIVES OF SERVICE

- ☐ relaxation
- ☐ sense of well-being
- ☐ uplifting
- ☐ anti-cellulite
- ☐ stimulating

EQUIPMENT AND MATERIALS

- ☐ gyratory massager
- ☐ audio sonic
- ☐ infrared

Beauty therapist signature (for reference)

Client signature (confirmation of details)

Record card for providing body massage services (continued)

SERVICE ADVICE

Head and body massage service – *this service will take 75 minutes*

Body massage without head – *60 minutes*

Partial body massage – *differs according to areas to be treated, i.e. back massage 30 minutes*

SERVICE PLAN

Record relevant details of your service and advice provided for future reference.

Ensure the client's records are up-to-date, accurate and fully completed following service. Non-compliance may invalidate insurance.

DURING

- explain choice of massage medium and its benefits
- explain the service procedure at each stage of the massage to meet the service needs
- explain how the massage products should be applied and removed at home
- note any adverse reaction, if any occur, and action taken

AFTER

- record the areas treated
- record any modification to service application that has occurred
- record what products have been used in the head and body massage service as appropriate
- provide postural advice
- provide advice to follow immediately following service, to include suitable rest period following service, general advice regarding food and drink intake, avoidance of stimulants
- recommended time intervals between services
- discuss the benefits of continuous services
- record the effectiveness of the service
- record any samples provided (review their success at the next appointment)

RETAIL OPPORTUNITIES

- provide guidance on progression of the service plan for future appointments
- advise regarding products that would be suitable for home use and on how to gain the maximum benefit from their use to care for their skin and continue the service benefits
- recommendations for further services including heat services and electrical massage services
- advise on further products or services that you have recommended that the client may or may not have received before.
- note any purchases made by the client

EVALUATION

- record comments on the client's satisfaction with the service
- record if the service objectives were achieved, e.g. relaxation; if not, explore the reasons why not
- record how you will progress with the service to maintain and advance the service results in the future

HEALTH AND SAFETY

- advise on avoidance of activities, and product application that may cause a contra-action
- advise on appropriate necessary action to be taken in the event of an unwanted reaction (e.g. aching, tiredness, heightened emotional state)

SERVICE MODIFICATION

Examples of service modification include:

- altering the pressure or choice of manipulations during massage to suit the client's skin and muscle tone
- adapting the massage to achieve an effect of relaxation or stimulation
- altering the choice of massage medium to suit the area or the service

Preparation of the beauty therapist

The beauty therapist should wear protective workwear which does not restrict movement. Full, enclosed shoes should be worn with low or medium-height heels. Very high heels can lead to serious foot and postural problems for the beauty therapist. The client's record card should be collected prior to their arrival and the beauty therapist should identify the client's massage requirements. A full consultation, including a postural check, should have been carried out before the service commences.

Beauty therapist's hands The beauty therapist should always clean their hands thoroughly prior to the service. The hands also need to be flexible in order to fit the contours of the client's body. Mobilizing the joints of the hands and fingers will loosen the hands and facilitate good manipulations. Hand exercises should be practised on a regular basis. Examples of some exercises the beauty therapist can practice are illustrated.

Step-by-step: Hand exercises

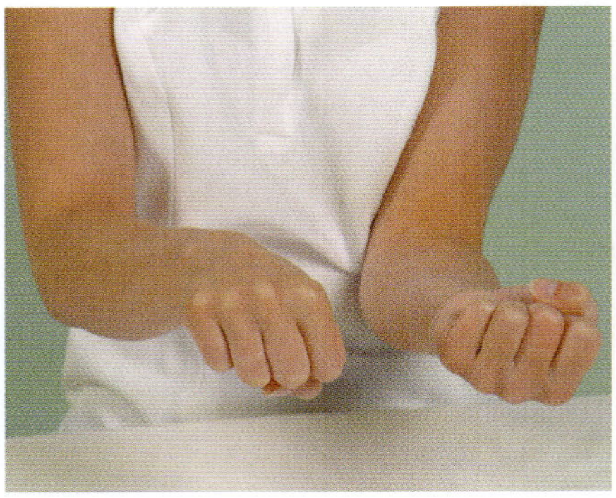

1 Rotate wrists clockwise then anti-clockwise to loosen the wrists

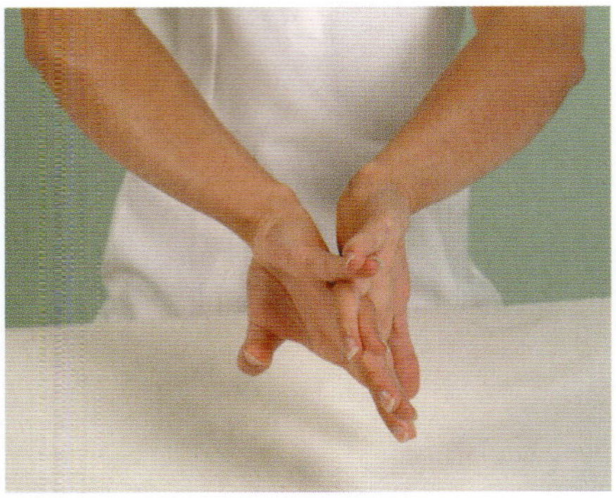

2 Clench the fingers together with backs of hands facing. Pull fingers apart but maintain contact

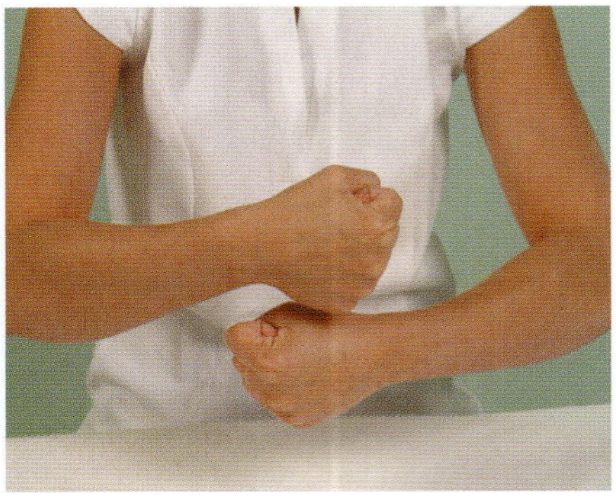

3 Rotate fists in a circular motion

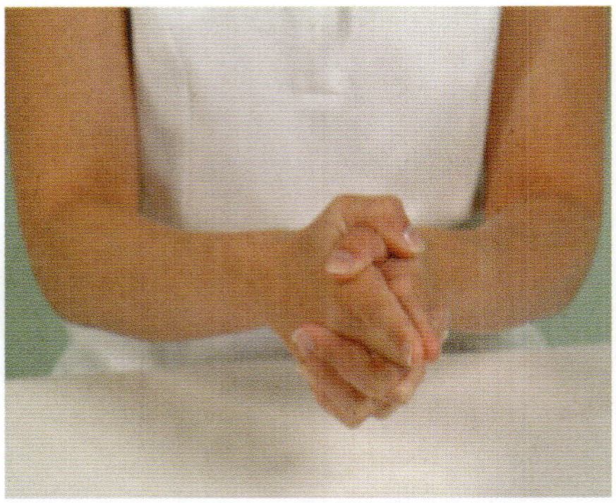

4 Finger-pad resistance – press the fingers against each other one by one

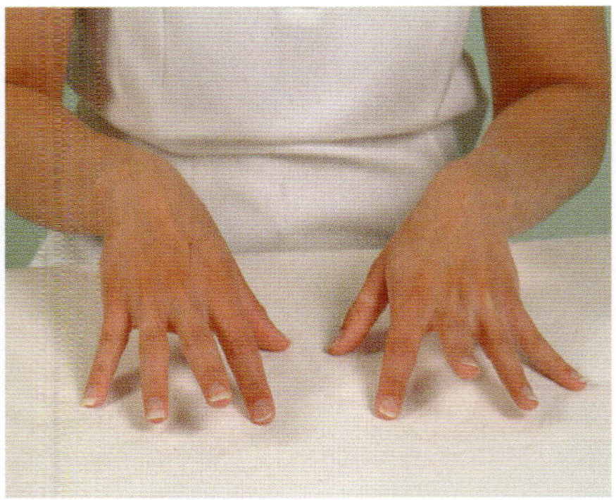

5 Place alternate fingers down on a hard surface as if playing a piano

6 Place palms together and apply slight pressure, maintaining the contact

HEALTH & SAFETY

Repetitive strain injury

When performing massage you will strengthen certain muscles used to perform the massage movements. To avoid repetitive strain injury, and damage to yourself, your muscles must not be tight especially those of the neck, shoulders, back, arms and hands. Stretching exercises should be performed slowly to avoid muscle fibre damage.

> Repetitive strain in the hands and arms is probably the most challenging part of a Massage or Beauty Therapist's job. You should be very aware of your posture too, to avoid putting strain on your back when massaging.
>
> **Katie Harris**

Preparation of the client

- Instruct the client to remove their clothing down to their undergarments. It is important that you maintain the client's modesty and privacy at all times.
- Provide a private changing area for the client. A large towel or bathrobe may be provided for the client to wear. Paper disposable slippers may also be provided to avoid potential cross-infection if bare footed.
- Ask the client to remove all jewellery and accessories (including hair accessories) and store them in a safe place – either in a bowl on the bottom of the trolley or pass to the client for safekeeping. (Follow your workplace policy.)
- Position the client for the service. Instruct the client to lie on the couch in a supine or prone position according to the area being treated. If using a hydraulic couch, adjust to suitable height. Provide steps to assist if required.
- Place towels over the client in a way which will allow minimal interruption to the service and keep them warm. (Modesty towel or bathrobe should be removed.)
- Cover any minor skin defects, cuts or abrasions with an adhesive dressing prior to the service.
- If the client has long hair it may need to be secured in a clip while you treat the neck area.
- Support pillows or rolled towels can be placed to improve client comfort. Support may be provided in supine position under the neck and under the knees avoiding strain to the client's back. In prone position support may be provided under the shoulders and ankles.
- If facial massage is to be performed cleanse the face using suitable facial products for the client's skin type using your regular cleansing routine.

Planning body, head and face massage services

A thorough consultation will have included details of the client's age, weight, size, posture, muscle tone and psychological needs. This will help to determine whether the massage is to be provided for relaxation or uplifting effect, toning or maintenance of physical health. (Maintenance of physical health refers to such things as relief of muscle tension and fatigue, improvement of blood and lymph circulation and improvement of skin condition.)

The massage routine should be planned before you start so that continuity of the massage service occurs. The sequence that is normally followed for full-body massage is:

ALWAYS REMEMBER

Supine position
The supine position is lying on the back, facing upwards.

Prone position
The prone position is lying on the front of the body, facing downwards.

BEST PRACTICE

Positioning of the towels
Place towels according to your workplace practice. For example, two towels can be used to cover the client: one to cover the lower body and one to cover the upper body. Towels provide modesty and also keep the area warm.

BEST PRACTICE

Small steps should be provided to enable clients to easily position themselves onto the couch.

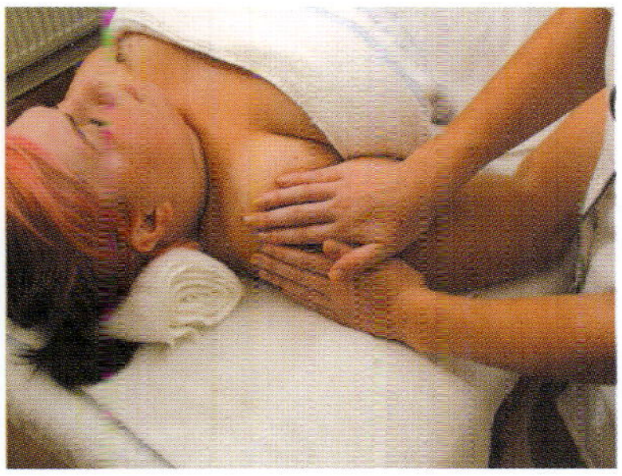

Rolled towel to support the neck

With the client lying supine:

- left arm
- right arm
- chest and shoulders
- abdomen
- right leg and foot
- left leg and foot
- face
- head

Then with the client lying prone:

- gluteals
- back and shoulders

> Bend the knees and don't forget to breathe when massaging, this really helps in your massage application and maintaining good postural health.
>
> **Katie Harris**

The massage techniques should be adapted to suit the needs of each client. The sequence of application may also differ according to your workplace or particular training recommendations specific to a beauty company.

The correct stance for massaging the body

Beauty therapists need to ensure they are correctly positioned when massaging. This will prevent strain and fatigue to the beauty therapist while working. Failure to adopt the correct stance will result in the beauty therapist being unable to work a full day and eventually serious muscle or joint strain could occur. Working positions are walk standing and stride standing (see table and illustrations).

Correct positioning allows maximum mobility and the correct pressure to be applied when applying each massage technique.

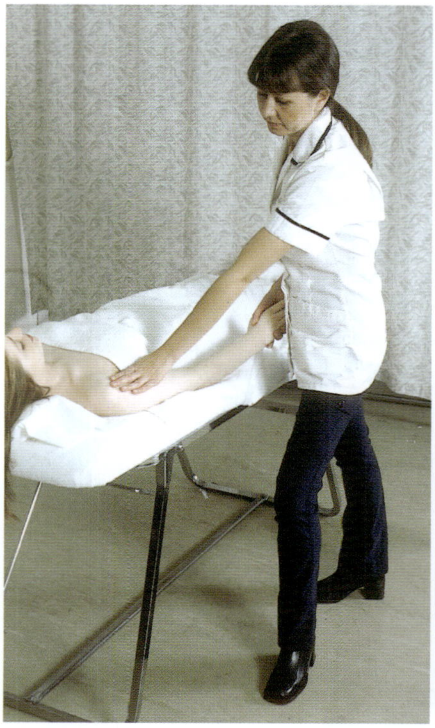

LORRAINE NORDMANN

Walk standing

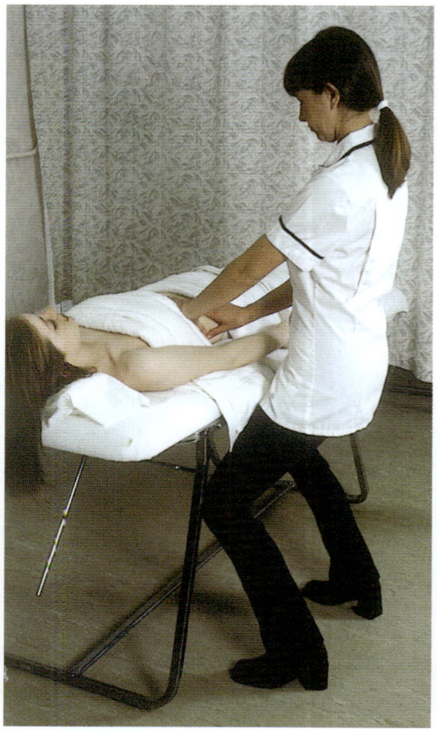

LORRAINE NORDMANN

Stride standing

Working positions for the beauty therapist

Name	*Description*
Walk standing	This stance enables the beauty therapist to work longitudinally over the body. The beauty therapist stands with one foot in front of the other and moves their body weight forwards and backwards through the ball and heel of the foot with the massage. The knees must be flexible, allowing the beauty therapist to move forwards along the body.
Stride standing	This enables the beauty therapist to work transversely across the body. The beauty therapist faces the couch with their back upright feet apart on a firm base and knees slightly bent.

Selecting the massage medium

The choice of massage medium is important in order to provide an effective service. This will be determined by the skin type of the client, but on occasion the client will state which medium they prefer. The massage medium chosen should be used sparingly and always applied to the beauty therapist's hands first and not directly onto the client's skin. The massage medium should be rubbed in the beauty therapist's hands to warm it and distribute it over the hands before application.

Type of massage medium

Name	*Use*
Massage cream  BEAUTY EXPRESS LTD.	Used for normal-to-dry skin; helps to soften and nourish the skin; is readily absorbed requiring more frequent application.
Massage oil  TISSERAND AROMATHERAPY	Good for normal-to-dry skin; helps to nourish and lubricate the skin; helps the beauty therapist to provide a deeper massage and prevents the skin from tearing while being stretched.
Purified talc powder  BEAUTY EXPRESS LTD.	Used on combination and oily skins; helps to absorb excess sebum and perspiration on the skin; allows the hands to slide over the skin and provides adequate slip. Provides a deeper massage to the tissues.

HEALTH & SAFETY

Aromatherapy oils

Undiluted aromatherapy essential oils can be highly irritant or poisonous. Aromatherapy oils, if used, should be pre-blended unless you are qualified and insured to blend essential oils.

BEST PRACTICE

Dispensing massage medium

To ensure that the cross-contamination of the massage medium is avoided, dispense the product amount required from its container into a small bowl before you commence your service.

TOP TIP

Massage cream quantity required

Remember you will require more massage cream than other mediums when performing a massage as it is readily absorbed by the skin. Consider this if decanting the massage medium.

ALWAYS REMEMBER

Femoral triangle

The femoral triangle refers to the area covering the space on the medial side of the upper thigh, and can be seen as a slight depression.

Once you have decided on the type of massage the client requires and have selected a suitable massage medium, wipe over each part of the client's body to be massaged with a skin cleansing medium i.e. eau de cologne. Dry the skin, by blotting the area immediately with a clean tissue.

Adapting the massage

There are several reasons why you might need to adapt your massage. These will become evident at consultation.

- *Relaxing massage.* Used to relieve stress and tension, avoid all stimulating techniques and concentrate on effleurage and petrissage techniques. The speed of application and pressure should be firmer and the rhythm slower. Incorporate pressure points, beginning lightly and gaining pressure with each repeated movement application. A pre-heating service would be beneficial before massage application.
- *Tight or contracted muscles.* Tapotement movements should be avoided, and slow and rhythmical movements should be used to help stretch the muscle.Effleurage and stroking movements are beneficial to link massage movements. Concentrate your massage application on key sites of tension, e.g. the trapezius muscle.
- *Slack muscles.* Elasticity of the muscles is reduced and the circulation needs to be improved. Deep petrissage and stimulating tapotement massage movements should be used to help to tone and firm the area being treated.
- *Massage for weight problems.* Include stimulating techniques such as deep petrissage and tapotement on the areas of excess fat and where cellulite is present applying increased pressure. This helps to mobilize the fat deposits. Intersperse effleurage strokes to aid lymphatic drainage and the removal of toxins between massage manipulations. A reduced calorie nutritionally balanced diet and exercise programme is recommended if the client wants to gain maximum benefits from weight loss and improvement in the appearance of skin condition.
- *Massage for males.* Muscle bulk in men is larger and stronger than in women. The muscles are firmer, the skin thicker and there is less fatty tissue. Apply full-body weight when performing the massage which should also be firmer. When massaging men, the anatomical space femoral triangle is avoided. If the client is particularly hairy, select a massage medium that provides slip and avoids 'dragging' body hair. If excessively hairy, oil is often a preferable choice of medium.
- *Skin condition.* Dead skin cells are removed during massage, blood circulation is increased and sebaceous gland activity is increased. The skin appears healthier and functions more efficiently. This is beneficial for all skin types. However, if the client has oily skin with pustules and papules present, avoid over-stimulating the skin and select a purified talc massage medium. In some cases, it will be necessary to avoid the area to prevent client discomfort and secondary infection. If the skin lacks elasticity, e.g. due to stretch marks or aged skin, avoid stretching massage manipulations such as wringing and rolling and incorporate toning massage manipulations in preference. Home application of both massage and skin care products. will help maintain the condition of the skin.
- *Older clients.* As the client ages, the skin becomes thinner: bony areas may become more prominent and possibly brittle (osteoporosis) and the skin reduces in elasticity and tone. Avoid over-stimulating the skin, unnecessarily stretching the skin and excessive pressure during massage application. Check with the client to ensure they are comfortable during the service.
- *Postural condition.* At the consultation, assessment of the client's postural condition is important. Good posture exists when all parts of the body are held in a state of balance. This avoids unnecessary stress on the joints and skeletal

muscles responsible for posture. If any muscles become stretched through poor posture, other muscles are affected: they work harder to correct this imbalance, which can lead to injury. Common figure faults are discussed in client services on pages 202–204. Where muscles have become tightened and shortened, apply deep effleurage and petrissage movements slowly to relax the muscles, remove physical tension in the muscles such as tension nodules and stretch the muscles. Where muscles have become overstretched, perform stimulating petrissage and tapotement movements briskly to help these weakened muscles improve in strength, tone and shorten.

- *Pregnancy.* Avoid massaging over the abdomen in early stages of pregnancy. Future massage should be light, avoiding stimulating massage manipulations.

TOP TIP

Massage pressure

The pressure should be varied according to the area being treated, skin reaction and after confirming client comfort with pressure applied.

ACTIVITY

Postural conditions

State how you would adapt your massage application in terms of choice of massage movement, depth of pressure and speed of application for a client who has the following postural conditions:

- lordosis
- scoliosis
- round shoulders

Identify which muscles have been shortened and which ones have been lengthened.

BEST PRACTICE

Adapting the massage to meet your client's service needs

This can be achieved by:

- depth of pressure used
- choice of massage techniques
- speed of application
- choice of massage medium

Manual massage service application

Outcome 3: Perform manual massage services

Learn how to perform manual massage service to meet your clients needs by:

1. Providing suitable support and cushioning to specific areas of the body during the service if necessary.
2. Adapting your **massage techniques**, sequence and **massage mediums** to meet the client's **physical characteristics** and **area**(s) treated.
3. Effectively varying the depth, rhythm and pressure of massage movements to meet **service objectives, area**(s) treated and client's **physical characteristics** and preferences.
4. Ensuring the application and use of **massage medium** minimizes waste.
5. Taking appropriate and prompt remedial action if contra-actions or discomfort occur during the course of service.
6. Allowing the client sufficient post-service recovery time.
7. Ensuring the finished result is to the client's satisfaction and meets the agreed **service objectives**.

Step-by-step: Arm massage

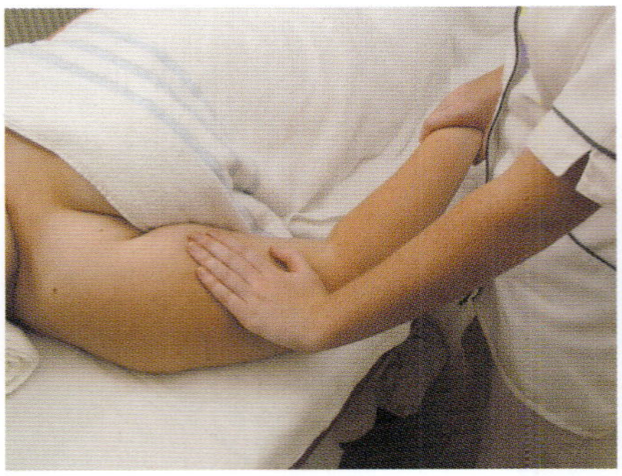

1 Support the client's arm with one hand and effleurage the whole arm from the wrist to the shoulder with the free hand. Repeat this step at least three times and up to six times until the client feels relaxed.

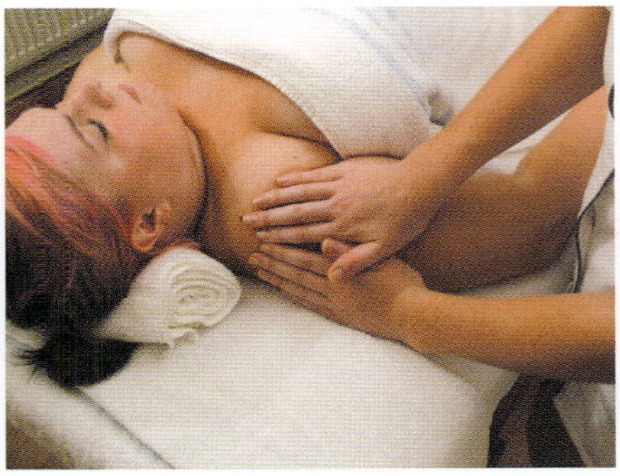

2 Still supporting the client's arm, apply deep effleurage to the deltoid muscle ensuring the palm of the hand is contoured around the muscle. Rotate the movement three times clockwise and then repeat three times anti-clockwise.

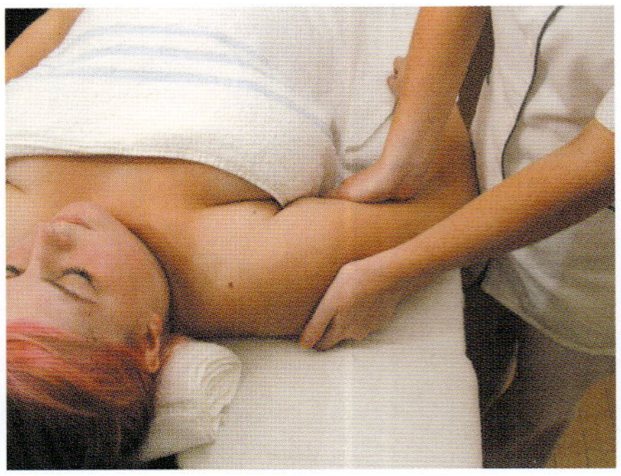

3 Supporting the arm, use alternate palmar kneading to the biceps and triceps muscles, working upwards with the movement three times and then sliding back to the elbow.

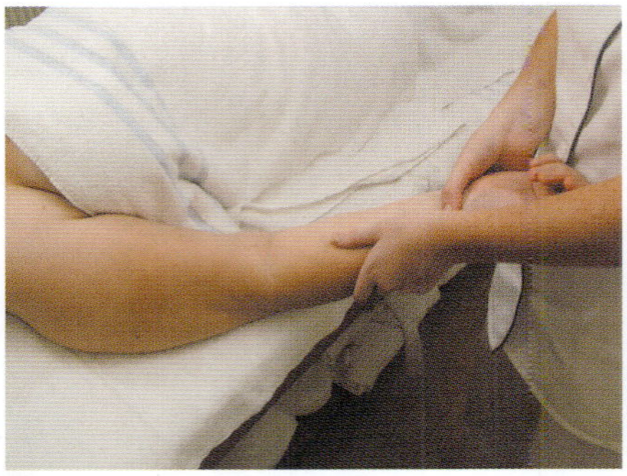

4 On completion of alternate kneading, slide your hands down from the elbow to the wrist joint. Whilst supporting the client's arm with one hand, pick up the extensors and then flexors three times, working from elbow to wrist, and slide back up to the elbow.

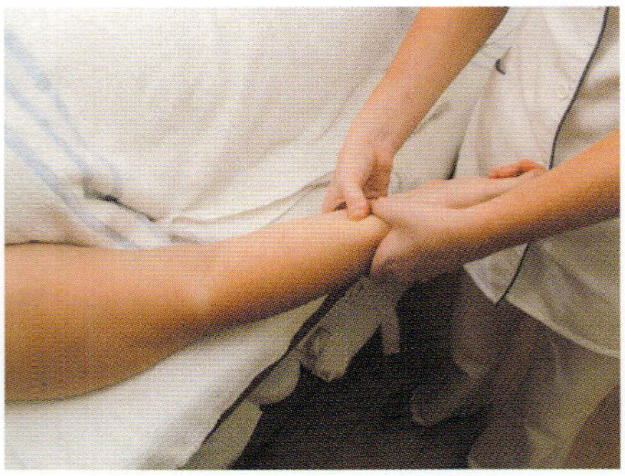

5 Support the client's arm at the wrist and thumb knead along the interosseous membrane up to the elbow. Work up in small friction movements three times and slide back down to the wrist.

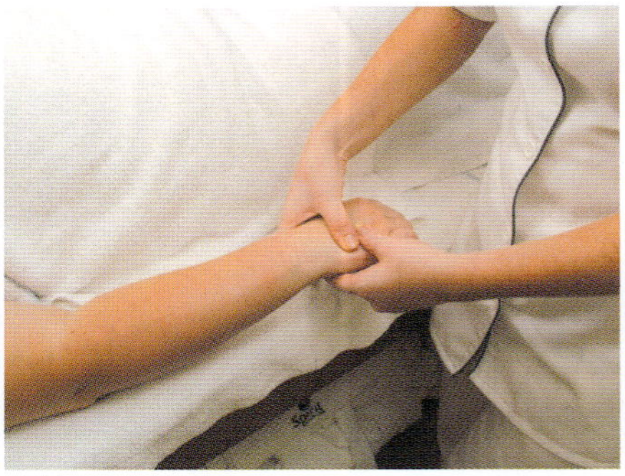

6 With the arm still supported, thumb knead the metacarpals down between each bone, adapting the pressure so as not to cause discomfort.

ALWAYS REMEMBER

Interosseous membrane

The interosseous membrane is a fibrous sheet of tissue that connects the radius and ulna bones of the arm.

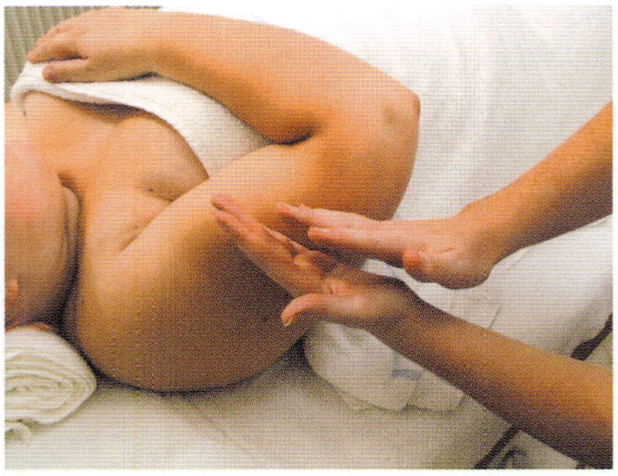

7 Supporting the client's arm, place the hand to the opposite shoulder and on the lateral aspect of the upper arm, perform hacking up and down the arm from shoulder to elbow.

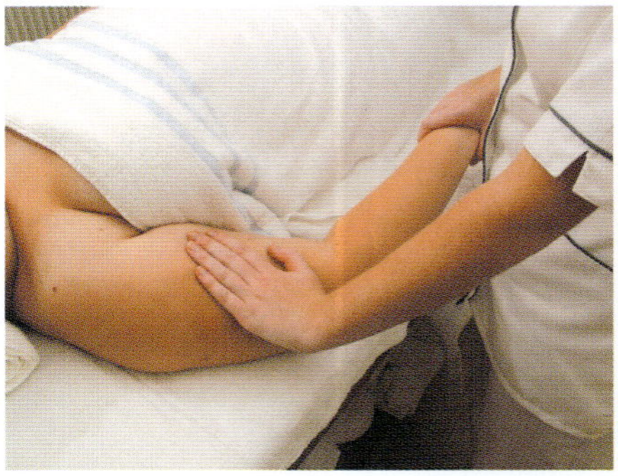

8 Complete the arm routine with effleurage as step **1**. Place the client's arm back onto the couch and repeat the movements on the other arm. Proceed to the neck and chest routine.

Step-by-step: Neck and chest massage

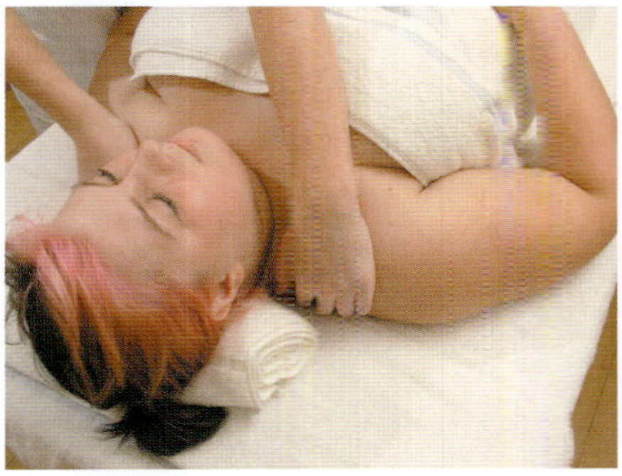

1 Facing the client, effleurage across the clavicle, around the shoulders and up behind the neck, ensuring that the pressure is adapted to suit the client. Keeping the hands in contact with the client, slide back to the sternum, cross the hands over and effleurage to the deltoids, pausing for a few seconds with a slight stretch on the movement, keeping the palms of the hands on the deltoids.

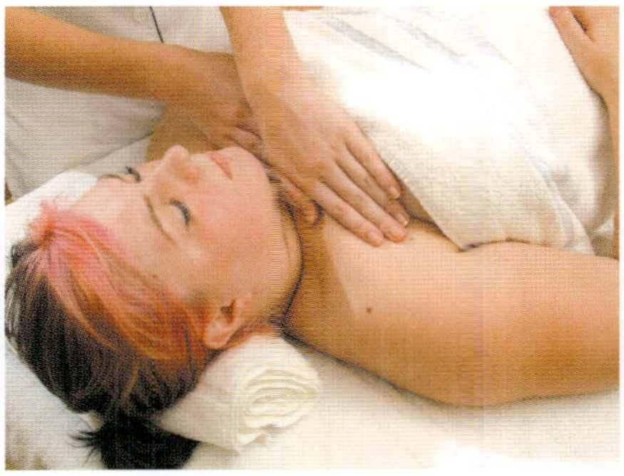

2 Apply superficial stroking across the chest with alternate hands moving from axilla to axilla towards you, ensuring that one hand begins as the other is leaving the body in order to remain contact.

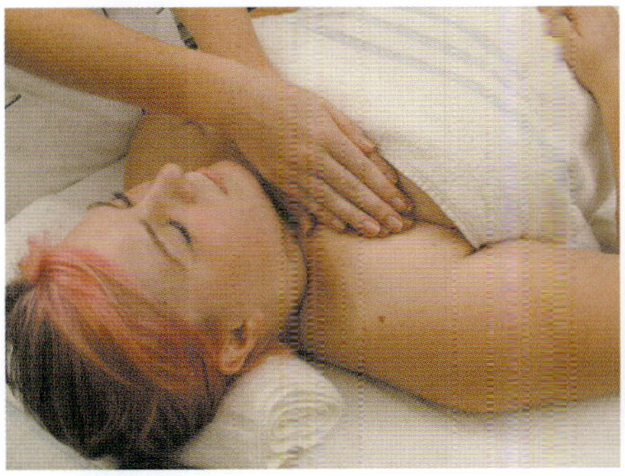

3 Follow with double-handed (reinforced) kneading over the chest, repeated three times, making sure the pressure is appropriate and comfortable for the client.

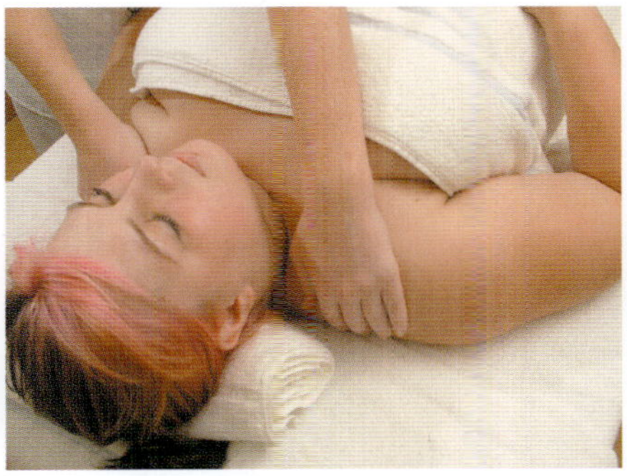

4 Knead the trapezius muscle, working inwards from the shoulders up to the occiput and sliding back around. Repeat the procedure three times or, if the client is tense, up to six times.

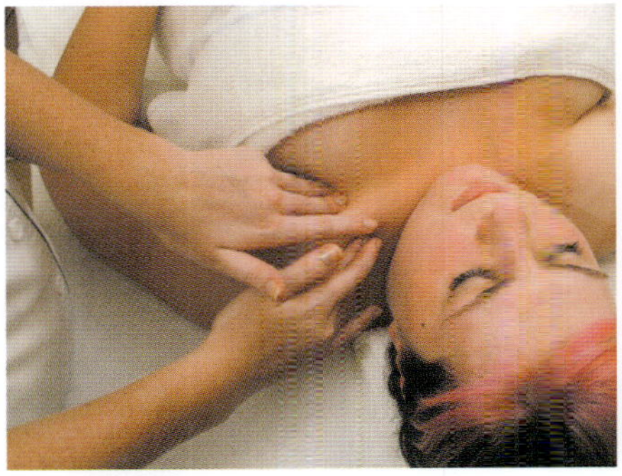

5 Working from the front of the client, knead above and below the clavicle three times with index and middle finger.

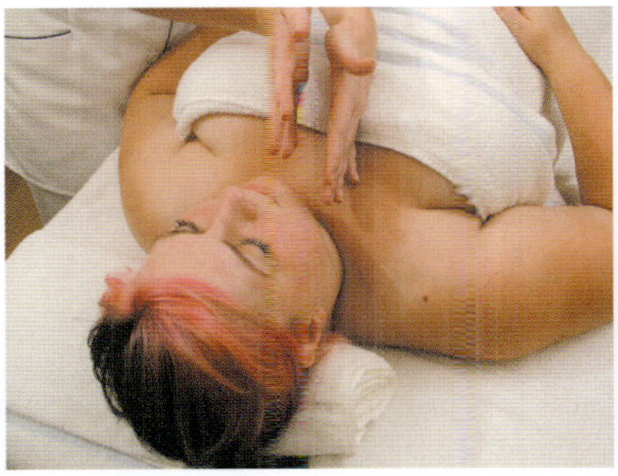

6 Perform light hacking technique across the chest. Place the hands on the sternum area and move the hands outwards towards each axilla. Continue the technique returning the hands towards the sternum. Repeat the technique until a slight erythema of the skin appears.

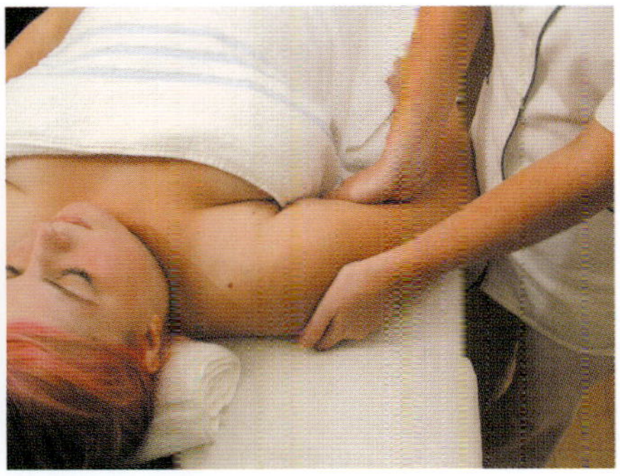

7 Repeat effleurage technique, as step **1**, three to six times to complete the neck and chest massage. Proceed to the abdominal routine.

TOP TIP

Larger-framed clients

If the client has a larger frame, support the arm on a pillow or a support so that the massage movements can be applied with ease.

TOP TIP

Tapotement

Only perform tapotement movements if the client has sufficient tissue present in the area. Techniques such as hacking will increase the blood circulation and lymphatic drainage in the area, promoting a better appearance and texture.

BEST PRACTICE

Medium providing slip

Ensure there is sufficient massage medium to provide adequate slip to perform massage techniques effectively and efficiently.

Where excess massage medium has been applied, remove it – you will not be able to apply massage techniques correctly.

COURSEMATE

For a video on body massage (including aftercare and skin tests), please visit this book's accompanying CourseMate.

Step-by-step: Abdominal massage

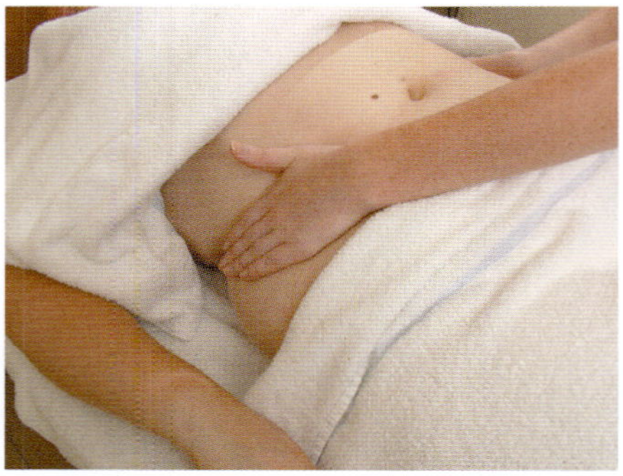

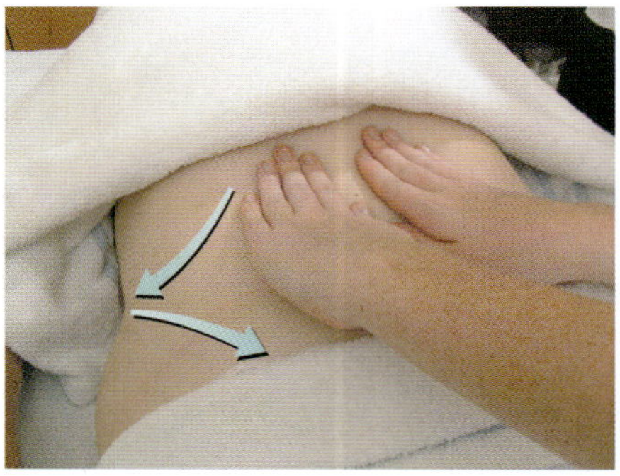

1 Ensure the client's modesty is maintained by placing a small towel over the chest area and pulling the large towel down to the hips. Place the palms of the hands at the waist and effleurage up to the sternum, back to the waist and then down towards the pubic symphysis, the joint that holds the pelvis together. This is known as diamond effleurage. Repeat this technique slowly three times.

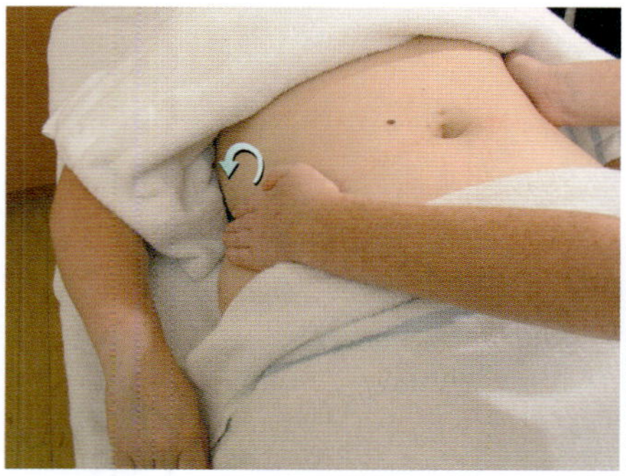

2 Place the hands on the lateral walls of the abdomen and apply alternate, kneading three times.

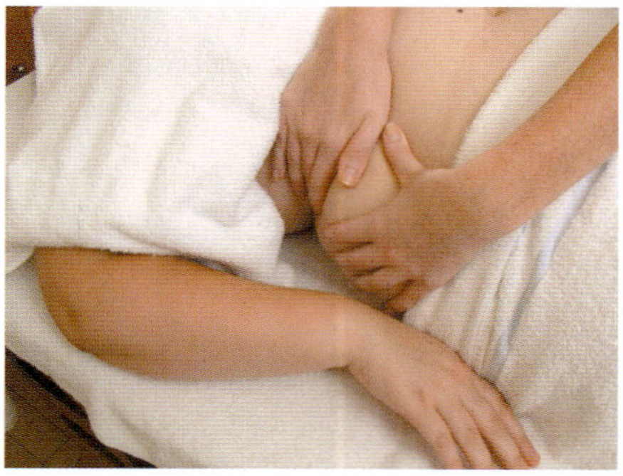

3 Follow kneading with wringing technique to the lateral walls of the abdomen. The skin and underlying muscle is lifted from the underlying structures and gently twisted alternately with each hand. Ensure the client has enough subcutaneous tissue to manipulate, otherwise it can be uncomfortable for the client.

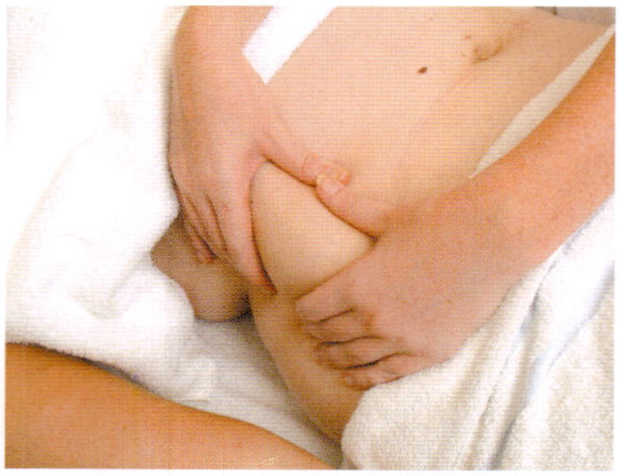

4 Progress from the wringing technique to skin rolling, applied with the palms of the hands underneath the posterior aspect of the abdomen and the thumbs placed on the anterior aspect of the abdomen. Roll the thumbs down towards the palms of the hands with visible skin movement underneath the thumbs.

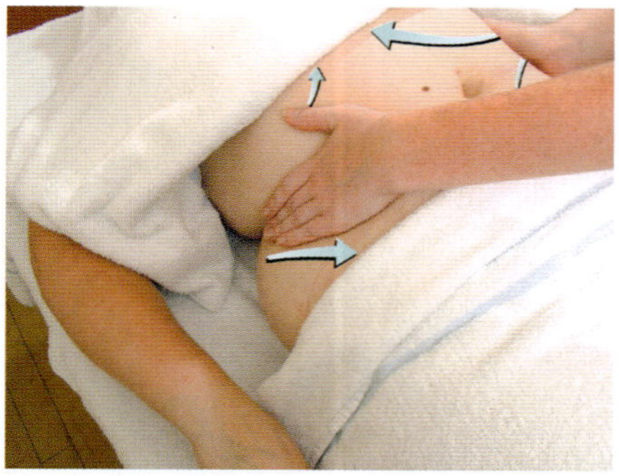

5 Complete the abdominal routine with three diamond effleurage sequences (step **1**). Reposition the towel to cover the abdomen and proceed to the leg routine.

TOP TIP

Constipation

If the client is constipated, using a double-handed (reinforced) kneading technique trace the colon to stimulate peristalsis. This will encourage the wave-like muscular contractions that move food through the digestive tract.

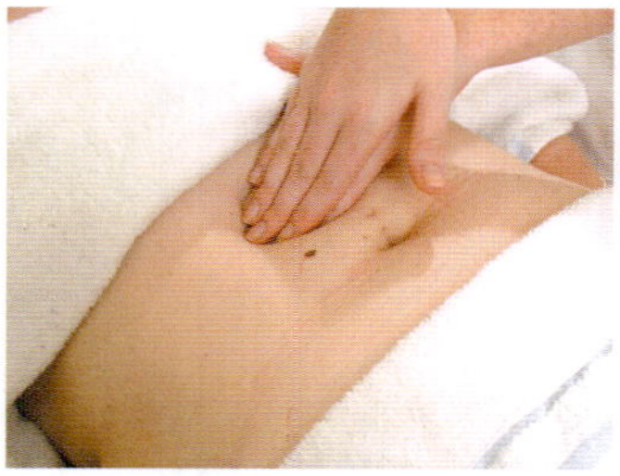

Reinforced kneading technique around the colon

Step-by-step: Leg massage

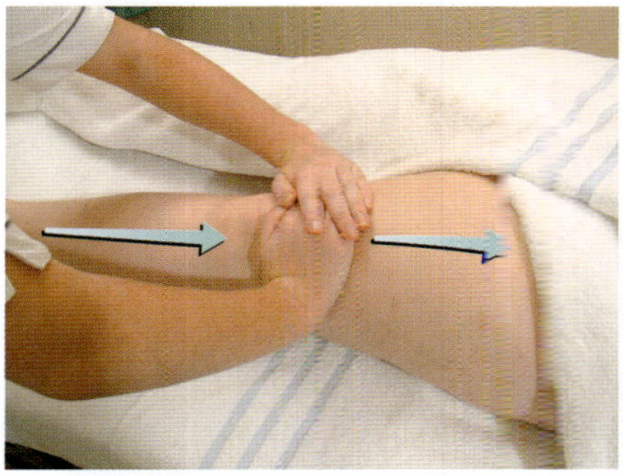

1 Uncover the leg you are going to work on and place a towel in the middle of the legs so that the other leg remains covered.

2 Effleurage the entire leg, covering the anterior, lateral and medial walls three times from the tarsals up to the femoral triangle. Pressure should be applied towards the heart with superficial effleurage to return the movement back to the tarsals.

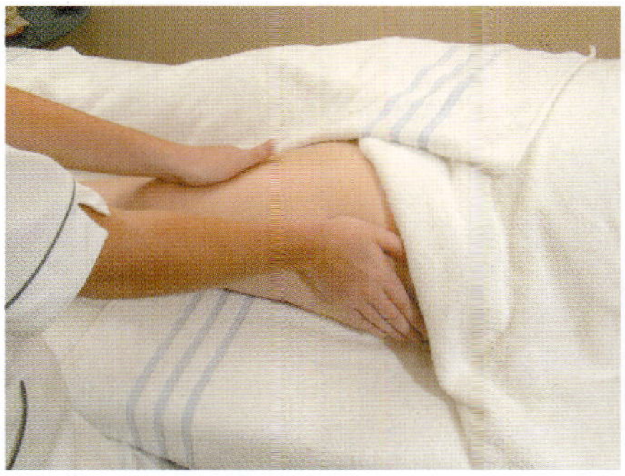

3 Alternate hand-knead three times from the hip to the patella, starting at the lateral aspect of the thigh – when both hands are parallel they will knead alternately.

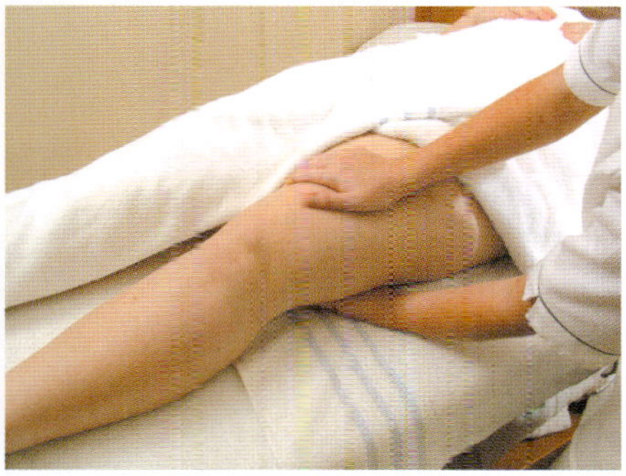

4 Slide the palms of the hands around the anterior and posterior aspect of the legs so that they are positioned on the quadriceps and hamstrings. Alternate hand-knead the muscles three times. If the movement is difficult because the client is large, place a support underneath the patella to aid movement.

If the client suffers from poor circulation or cellulite on the upper lateral or posterior aspect of the thigh, tapotement technique will be beneficial to stimulate the circulation. Standing in stride stance, use hacking (4a) and clapping (4b) beating (4c) and pounding (4d) techniques

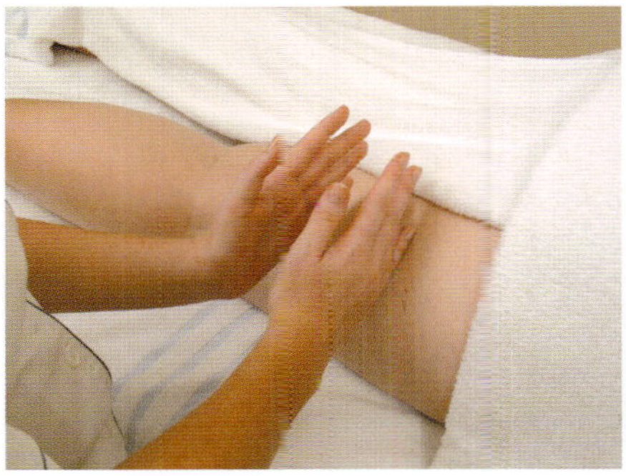

4a Hacking

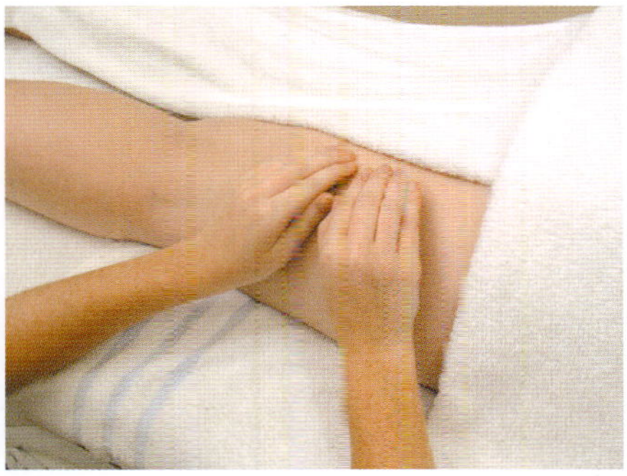

4b Clapping

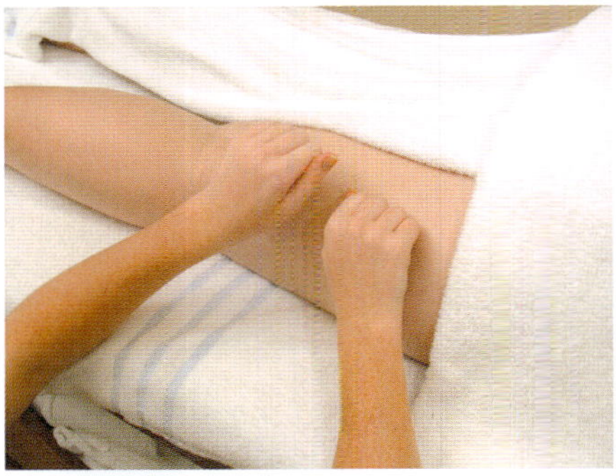

4c Beating

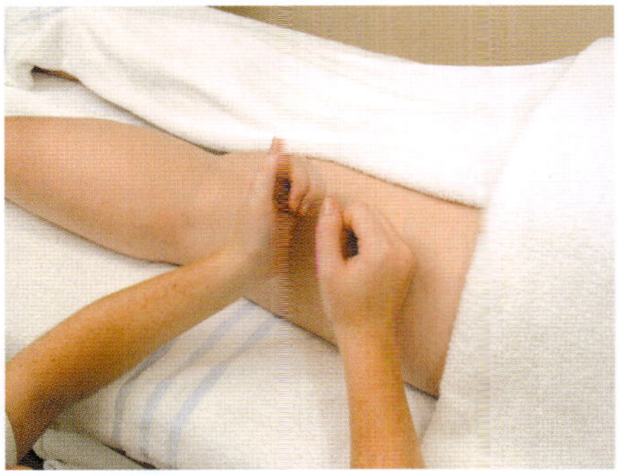

4d Pounding

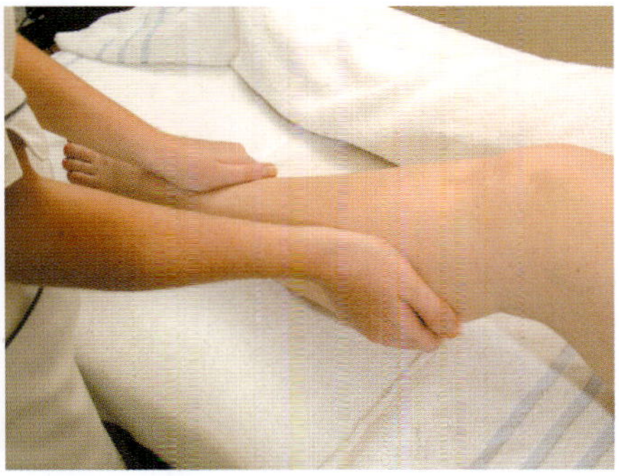

5 Effleurage the upper thigh three times and then around the patella three times in slow rhythmical movements.

6 Flex the client's knee palmar, knead up and down the gastrocnemius muscle three times.

HEALTH & SAFETY

If a contra-action occurs, discontinue the service and provide appropriate action and advice.

TOP TIP

Scissoring technique

When performing scissoring movement to the foot, enough pressure needs to be applied to prevent irritation to the client.

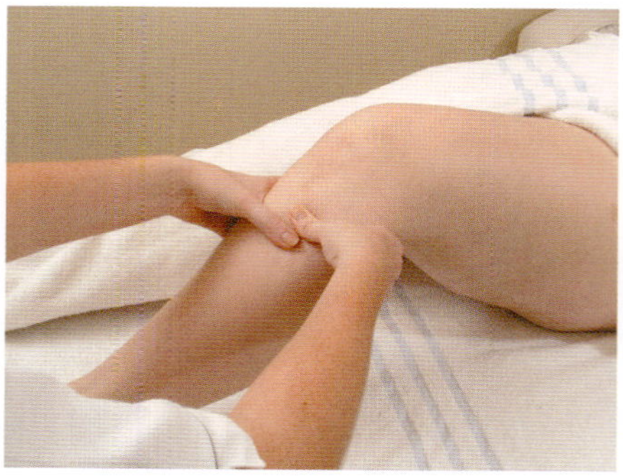

7 Slide the palm down to the ankle on the last apply friction technique thumb-kneading over the tibialis anterior on the outer shin three times, working upwards.

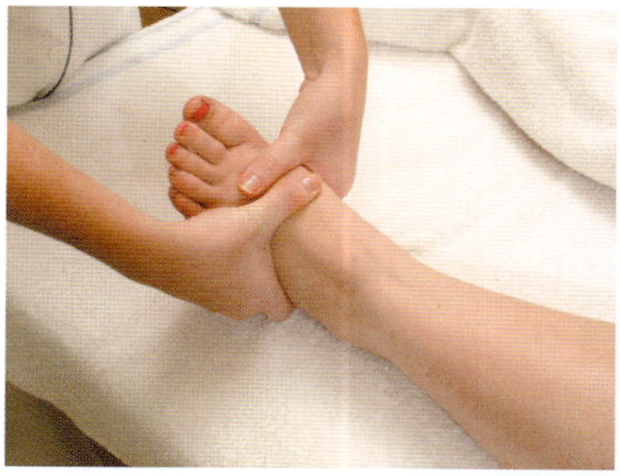

8 Thumb knead the top of the foot down between each metatarsal bone and slide back to the ankle.

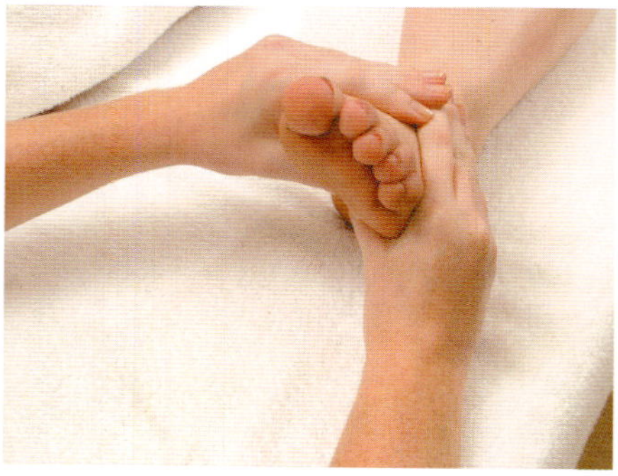

9 Apply friction technique, scissoring to the plantar region of the foot three times, scissoring down and stroking firmly back up.

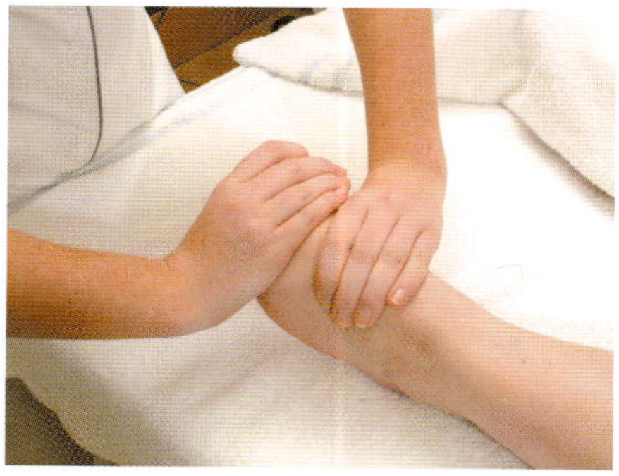

10 Place the hands either side of the phalanges (toes); and gently press together rotating three times clockwise and three times anticlockwise (phalange circling). Effleurage the foot three times. Complete the leg massage with effleurage (step 1) to cover the whole leg three times. Progress to gluteals, if included.

How to massage buttocks (gluteals)

1. Work on one side of the gluteals at a time. Cover the other side with a small towel so minimal exposure is achieved. Stand on the opposite side to the gluteals being massaged. This will enable you to work inwards with the movements performed.
2. Effleurage inwards with one hand to cover the buttocks. The free hand can be placed on the towel on the other buttock to keep it in place. Knead the gluteals three times with deep movements, then use reinforced kneading to follow.
3. To stimulate the area, use tapotement technique: hacking, clapping, beating and pounding in that order (see table on page 359), ensuring that the whole buttock is covered. This will help to improve the area.
4. Effleurage the area to complete the routine.
5. Cover the client's buttock with the towel and change positions to enable you to work on the other side. Uncover the buttock and repeat the procedure.

Tapotement movements

Name	*Description*
Hacking 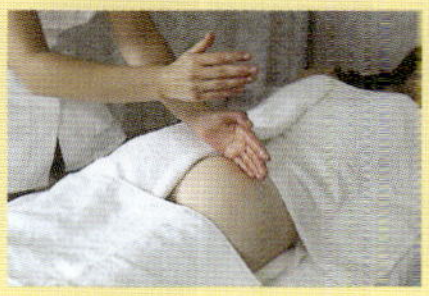	Hands are placed at right angles to the wrist with palms facing. The movement is applied with a light, fast action and the fingers are flicked against the skin.
Clapping 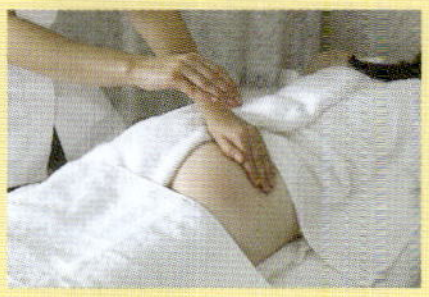	This is a stimulating technique and is used over adipose tissue. The hands are formed into cups and strike the body rhythmically; a hollow sound can be heard.
Beating 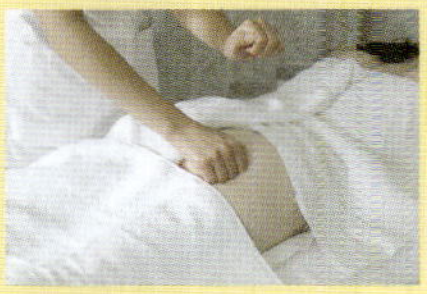	The hands are held in loose fists and moved rhythmically, either quickly or slowly, depending on the response required. The hands are moved from shoulder height and alternately placed on the buttocks and brought back to the starting position.
Pounding 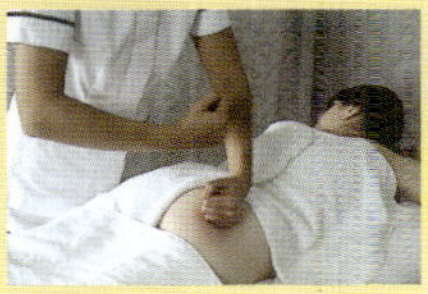	A stimulating technique used over adipose tissue and the deep gluteal muscle. The hands are loosely closed and as one hand strokes the area, it is closely followed by the other, in a rapid rhythmical manner.

TOP TIP

Couch with face hole

For client comfort, some couches have an optional face hole so that when the client receives back massage they can breathe easily without strain on the neck.

BEST PRACTICE

Tapotement technique

Ensure the hands are loose and relaxed when performing tapotement movements to avoid discomfort and skin bruising. This will also prevent repetitive strain injury (RSI) to the beauty therapist's hands and wrists.

Step-by-step: Back and neck massage

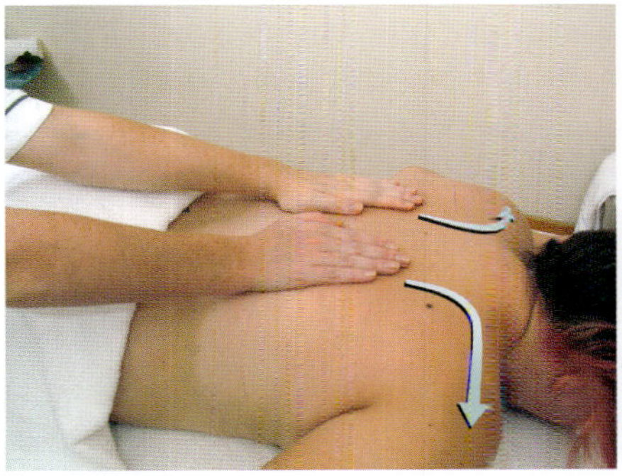

1 With the client in the prone position, effleurage up the back from the sacrum, splitting the hands at the scapula and massaging to the deltoid muscles. Slide the hands back down the same channel to the starting position. Repeat the effleurage technique, covering the trapezius muscle.

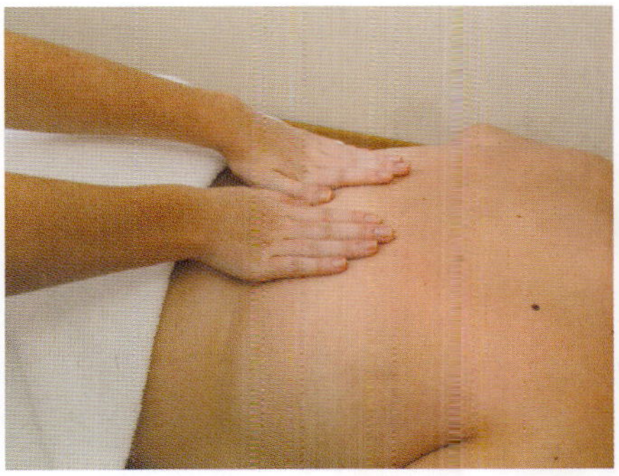

2 Single-hand knead from the scapula to the sacrum in three channels on either side of the spine.

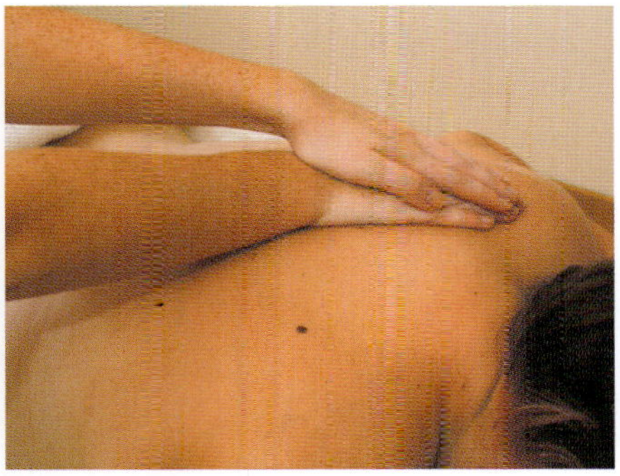

3 Continue with double-handed (reinforced) kneading three times down either side of the spine.

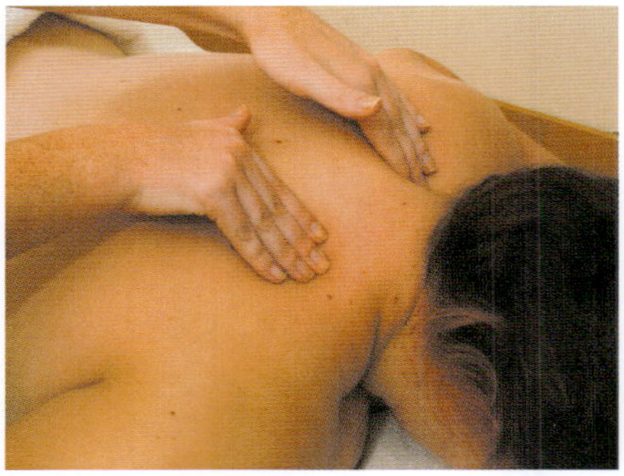

4 Knead along the trapezius muscle to the base of the neck. Depending on how tense the client is, repeat the movement three to six times.

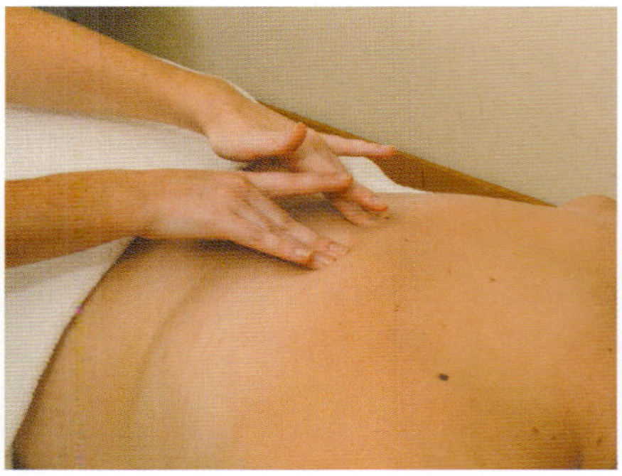

5 Knead around the sacrum and then knead up towards the scapula on either side of the spine. Repeat the movement one to three times.

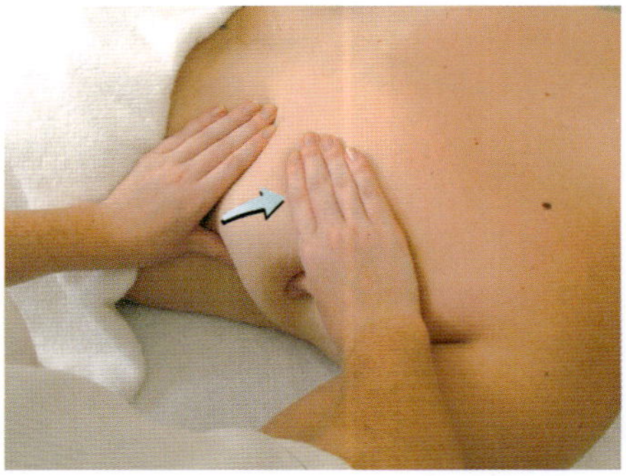

6 Wring the lateral walls, working around the back. Wringing may also be applied over the trapezius muscle at the shoulders.

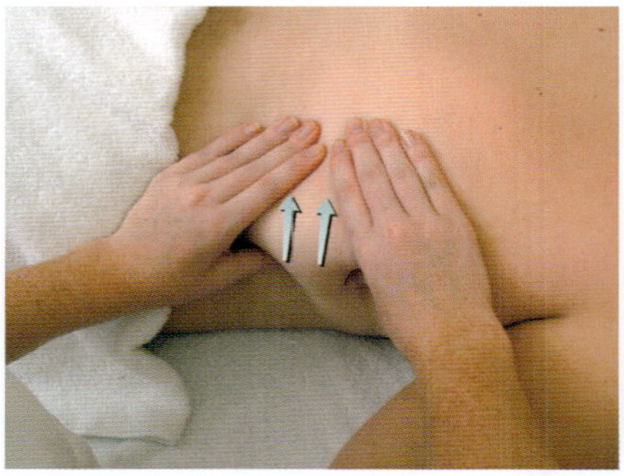

7 Skin roll the lateral walls of the back. Rolling may also be applied over the trapezius muscle at the shoulders.

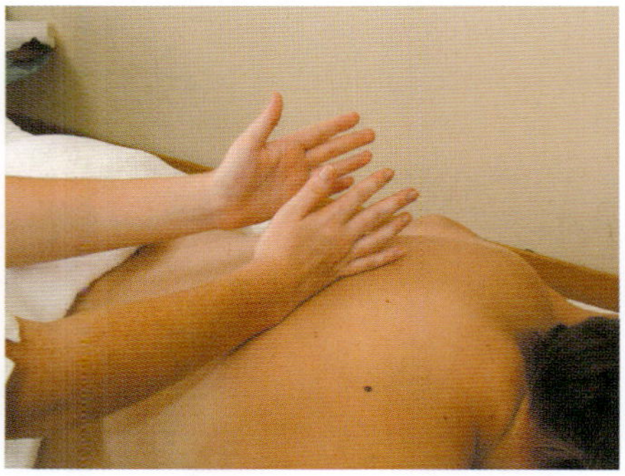

8 Follow with gentle hacking three times. Further tapotement techniques may be applied dependant upon the objectives of the treatment.

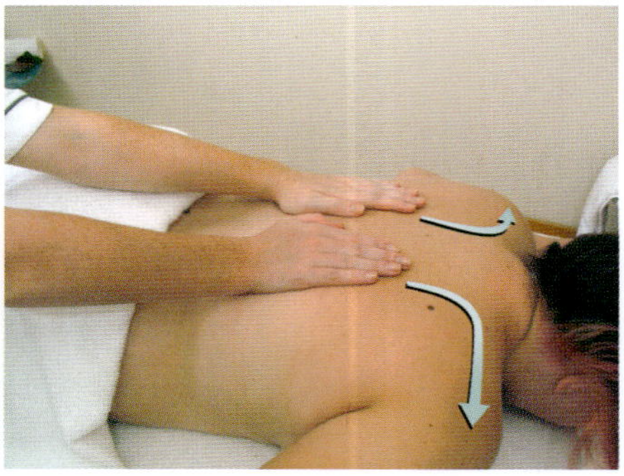

9 Complete the back routine with effleurage three to six times.

TOP TIP

Tense client

If the client feels tense, more effleurage and petrissage techniques can be performed on the back and time reduced on other areas to compensate.

TOP TIP

Hydrotherm massage cushion

A hydrotherm massage cushion filled with warm water and maintained at a constant temperature enables the beauty therapist to slide their hands between the client and cushion when the client is lying in a supine position on the bed. This is beneficial for clients who cannot lie in a prone position, e.g. pregnant clients. The warmth of the water soothes the nerves and warms the muscles, enabling the client to receive a relaxing massage.

Head massage

A head massage to the scalp may follow the body massage. Allow approximately 15 minutes to complete the service if incorporated. If preferred, an oil may be applied to the scalp, use approximately 4 ml. This will nourish the skin of the scalp and the hair. As part of the aftercare advice it is recommended that the oil is left on the hair for the remainder of the day, if practicable, to continue its conditioning effect.

Discuss if the client wishes to have oil applied to the scalp during the consultation and explain the benefits.

Step-by-step: Head massage

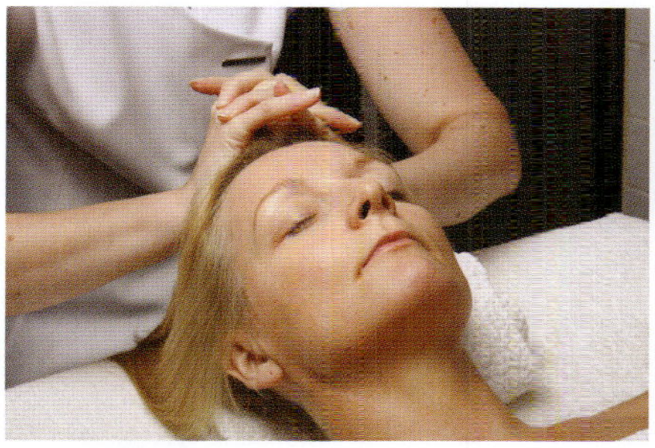

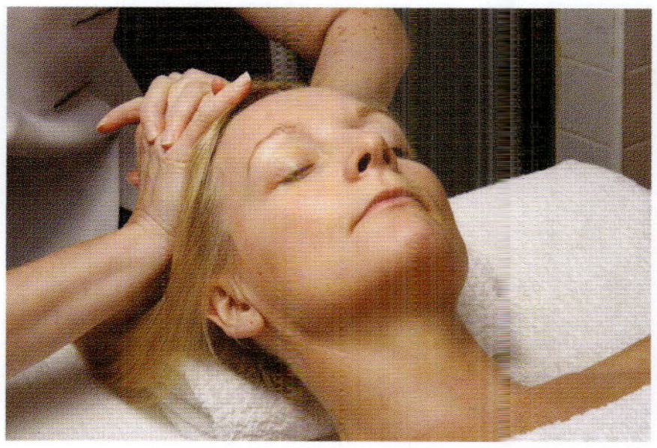

1 Interlock fingers and place joined hands on the forehead. Using the heel of the hands simultaneously perform circular, petrissage movements, moving the hands to cover the scalp.

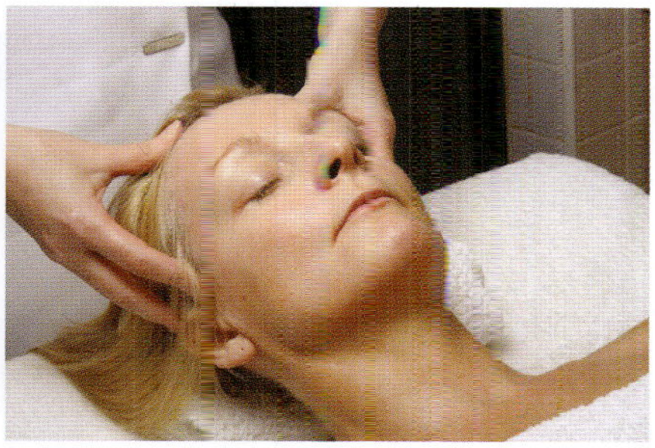

2 Place the thumbs on the scalp at the hairline and gently apply pressure point technique. This helps to relieve stress and tension as the pressure points are on the meridians of energy pathways that connect the body. This in turn stimulates the nerve pathways, frees blockages on the meridian lines of the body and helps to balance the body.

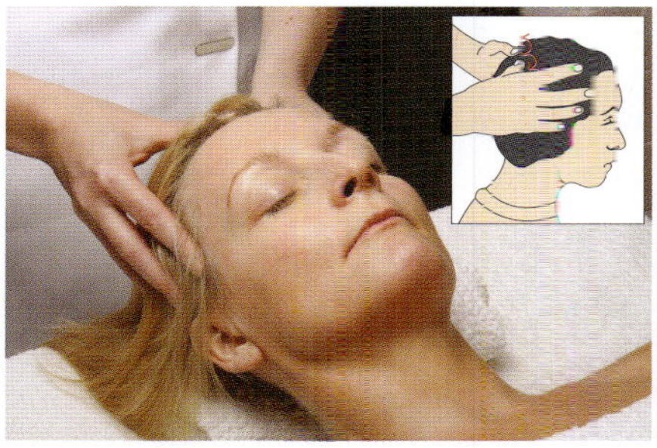

3 Place one thumb above the other. Each thumb alternately applies pressure in a 'C' shape moving from the hairline towards the crown area.

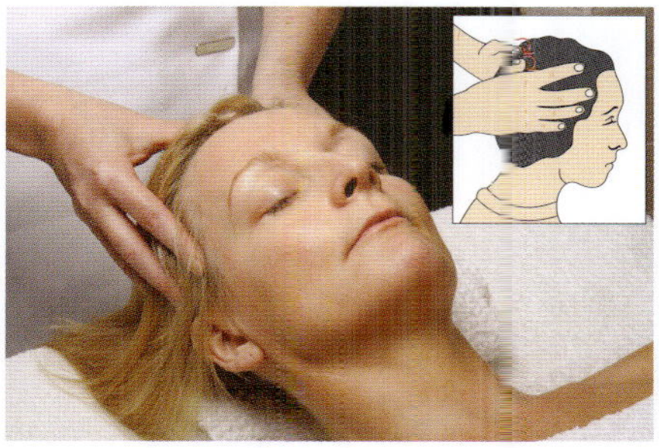

4 Position both thumbs at the crown area. Rotate both thumbs simultaneously in a clockwise direction, increasing pressure with each rotation: check pressure with client for comfort. Follow by rotating thumbs anti-clockwise, reducing pressure with each rotation.

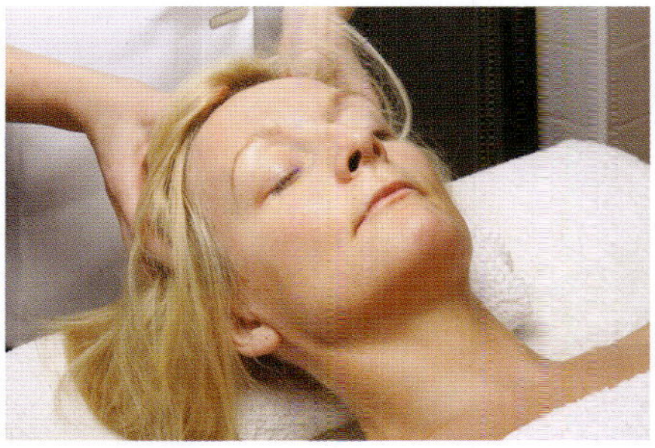

5 Apply petrissage movement over the scalp as if shampooing the scalp, using the fingertip pads to move the scalp gently.

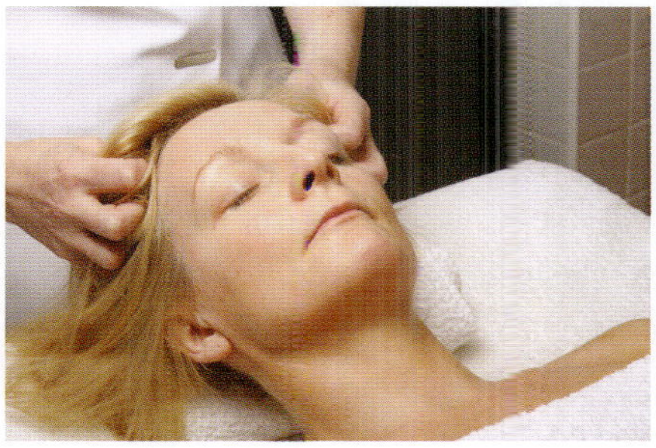

6 Place the knuckles of each hand against the scalp and apply gentle pressure, rotating the knuckles of each finger to cover the scalp.

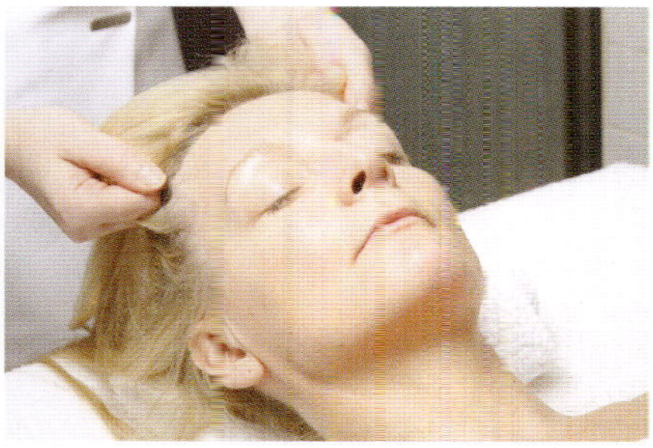

7 Grasp sections of hair between the fingers of each hand and gently pull the hair at the roots.

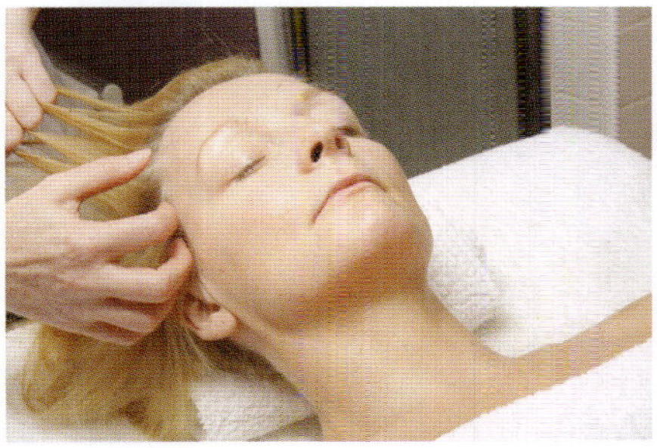

8 Alternating the fingers of each hand, use the fingers to slowly comb through the hair from the scalp to the end of the hair. Cover the scalp.

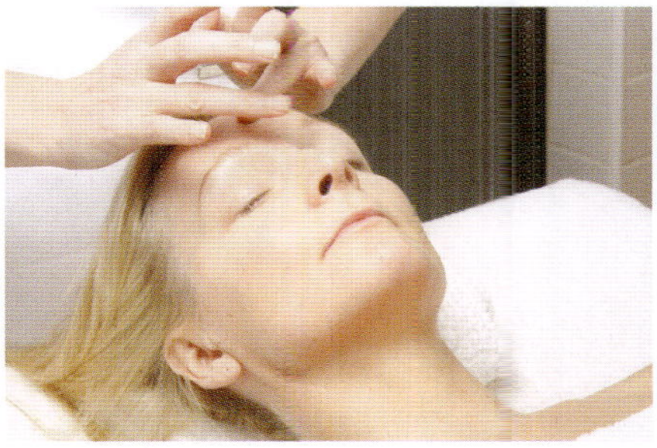

9 Using the third finger of each hand alternately stroke the forehead from above the nose towards the hairline

Face massage

Hot towels may be applied to the face to warm the tissues before facial massage. The face will have been previously cleansed.

Select a massage medium to suit the client's skin type.

Step-by-step: Face massage

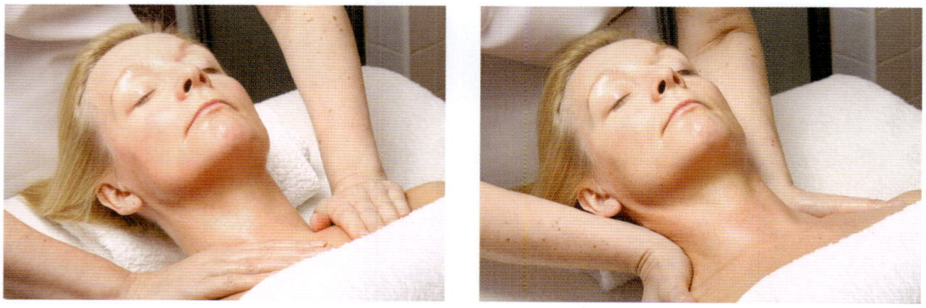

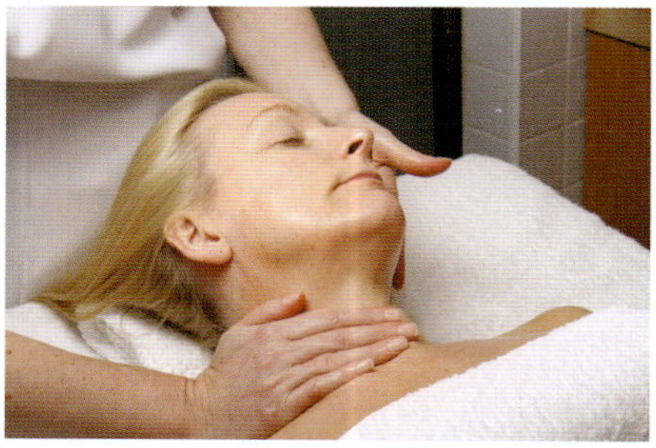

1 Effleurage to neck and shoulders

Slide the hands down the sides of the neck, across the pectoral muscles around the deltoid muscle and across the upper fibres of the trapezius muscle. Slide the hands to the back of the neck to the base of the skull.

Repeat step **1** a further five times.

2 Stroking to the side of the neck

Turn the client's head to the side and support the head with one hand. With the other hand stroke firmly, covering the trapezius, sterno-cleido mastoid and platysma muscles moving up towards the ear and return using a stroking movement downwards to the start.

Repeat step **2** a further four times to each side of the neck.

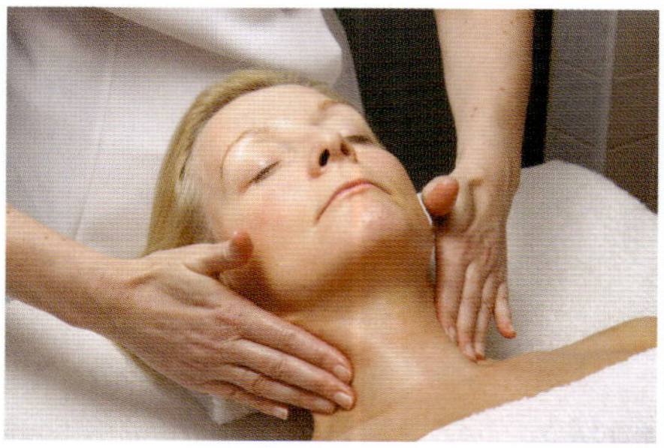

3 Circular massage to the neck

Perform small circular petrissage technique to the front and sides of the neck over the platysma and sternomastoid muscle.

Repeat the movements to cover the neck area several times.

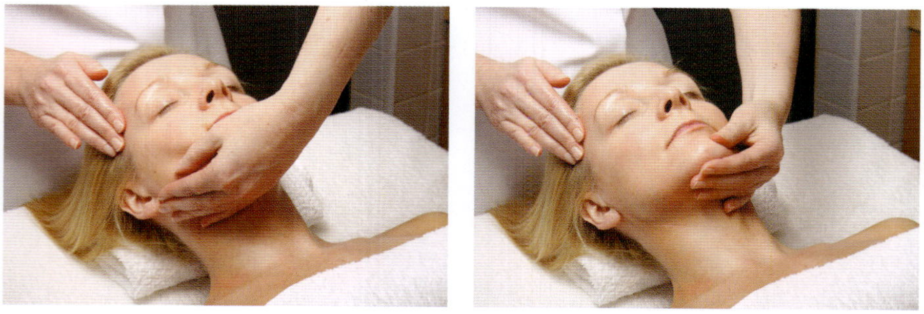

4 Effleurage across chin

Support the sides of the head with one hand, and with the other apply a smooth effleurage stroke from one angle of the mandible to the other. Swap hands and repeat on the other side.

Repeat step **4** a further three times to each side of the mandible.

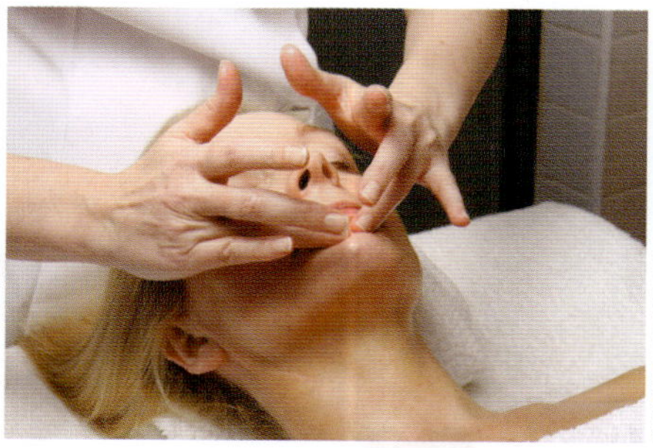

5 One finger effleurage around the lips.

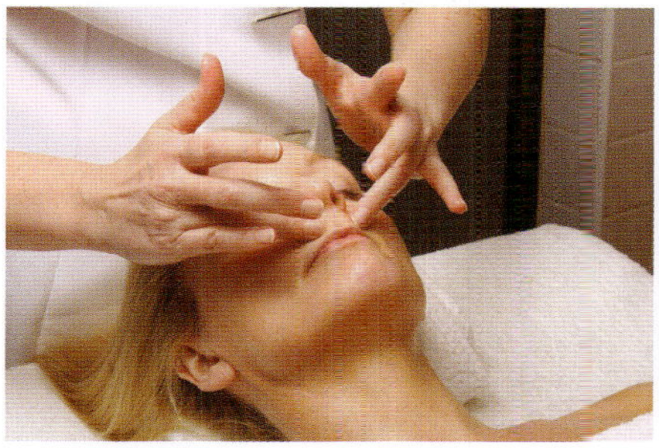

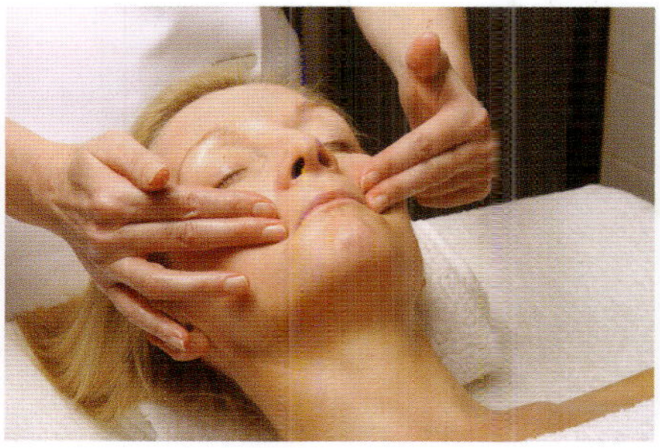

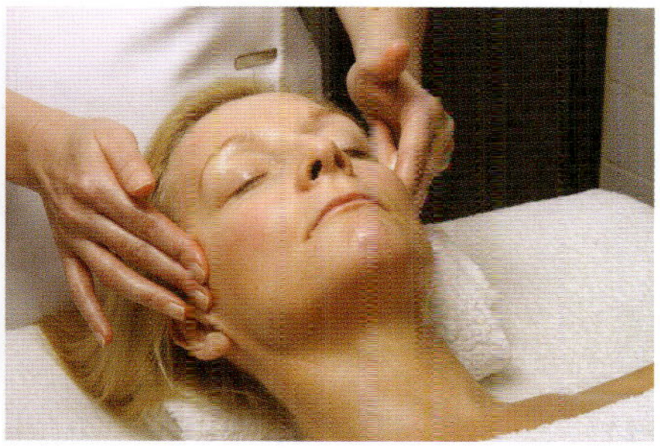

With the ring fingers of both hands placed beneath the centre of the lower lip, apply a light effleurage stroke around the mouth to the nose, reverse and return to starting position.

Repeat step **5** a further three times.

6 Drain from nose to ears

Place the first and middle fingers of each hand on either sides of the nostrils. With a light even pressure sweep across the cheeks beneath the zygomatic bones to the ear and return to starting position.

Repeat step **6** a further three times.

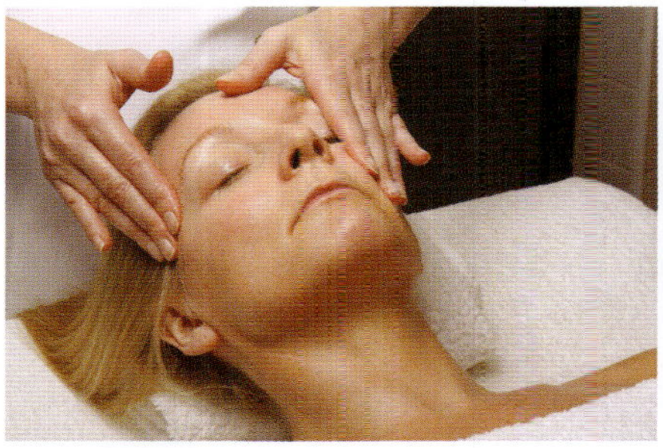

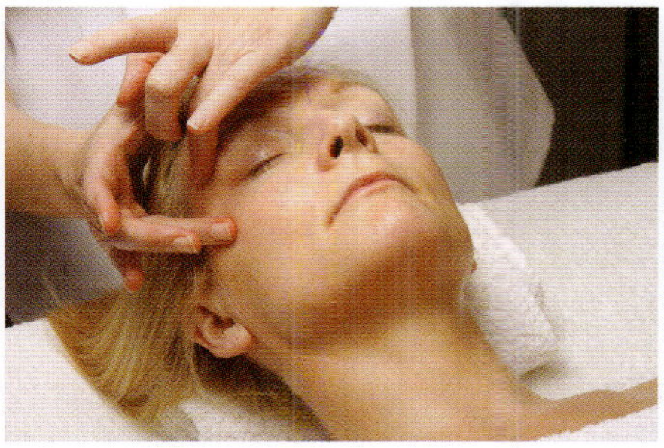

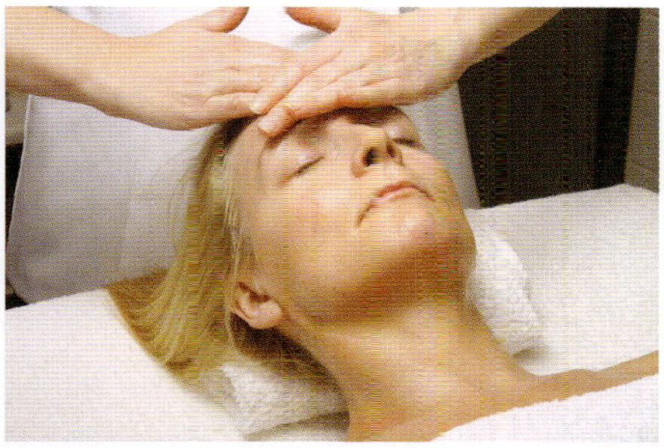

7 Circle around eyes

Place both thumbs on the forehead with one hand on the side of the head for support. With the fingers of the other hand, circle around the eyes towards the nose.

Repeat step **7** a further three times.

8 Alternate finger stroking at the outer corner of the eye

Using the ring finger, gently stroke downwards at the outer corner of each eye.

Repeat step **8** a further three times.

9 Alternate stroking to the forehead

Place one hand on the forehead and stroke from the eyebrows to the hairline using a slow controlled effleurage stroking movement. Repeat with alternate hands covering the whole forehead.

Repeat step **9** a further three times to cover the frontalis muscle.

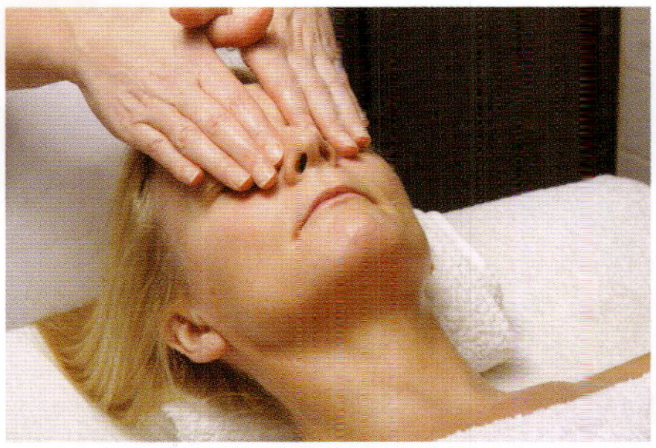

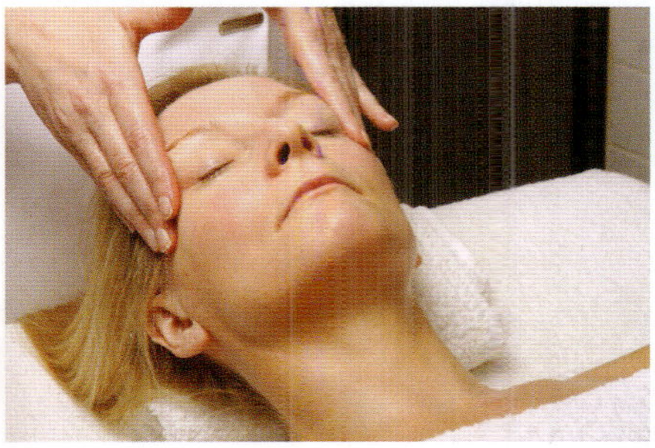

10 Finger curtains to eyes

Slide the fingertips of both hands down the bridge of the nose, relax the fingers onto the cheeks and slowly draw the hands over the eyes. Hold for a count of three. Slide finger tips out to the temples, apply a slight vibration, then move.

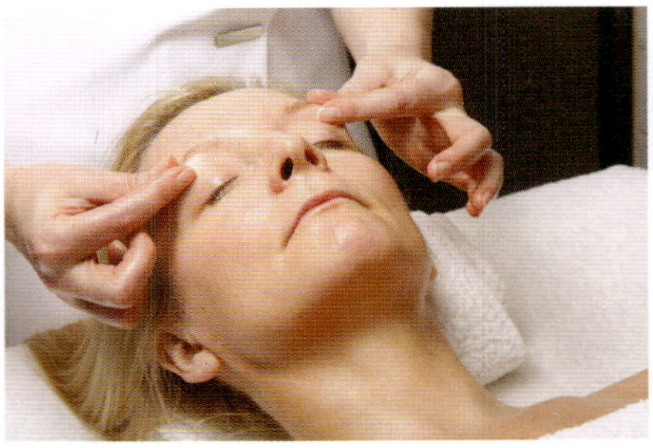

11 Pinch along the eyebrows

Gently pinch the length of both eyebrows simultaneously, using the finger and thumb of each hand.

Repeat step **11** a further three times.

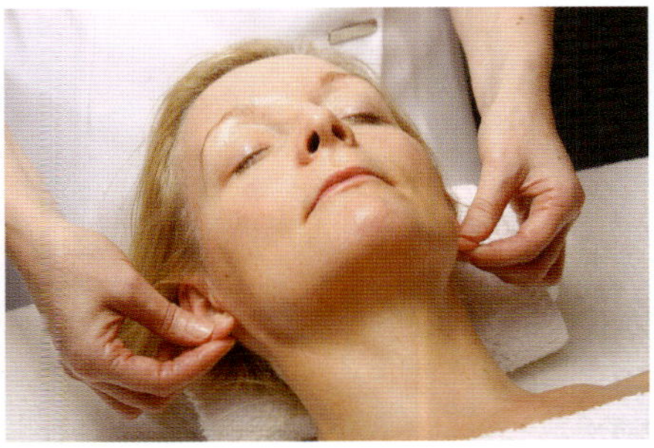

12 Pinching and rolling to the ears

Gently holding the tip of each ear apply a pinching and rolling movement using the pads of the fingers to cover the outside edge of each ear.

Repeat step **12** a further three times to cover the ear.

13 Repeat step **1**.

Concluding the face massage

To conclude the massage, apply gentle pressure at the temples, cradling the sides of the head with each hand. Slowly remove hands.

Maintain the correct atmosphere throughout, including at the end of the massage sequence. Avoid startling the client if asleep.

In a gentle manner, quietly inform the client that the service has ended. Advise them to rest and get up slowly to avoid feelings of dizziness. A glass of water may also be provided for the client.

Before the client gets up from the couch, gently remove any remaining massage medium with a small clean towel, hot towel or soft strong tissues. Eau de cologne may be applied to remove excess oil. You may provide these for the client to perform themself. Where possible the massage medium should be left upon the skin to condition and regulate for several hours. The client should be covered with a towel and allowed to rest for a few minutes to allow the blood circulation to return to normal. If they were to get up immediately they might feel light-headed as the brain is temporarily starved of blood. They might even faint. A relaxation room may be available in your workplace for the client to continue to rest and benefit from the peaceful, warm environment.

Ensure client satisfaction and that the results meet the agreed service plan. Ask the client how they feel to assess if the service needs have been met.

Ensure that the client's records are up-to-date and accurate. This enables continuation of the service to be tracked and any adverse reactions noted.

Faults during massage

Ensure the hands are warm before commencing massage to induce relaxation, and the nails are short to avoid scratching the client and to competently manipulate the skin and muscles.

If the beauty therapist does not apply the correct pressure and their massage is too light or too heavy, the client will not feel the benefits. Inconsistent massage will not relax the client and will not feel as though it is flowing.

The beauty therapist should ensure that the client is appropriately positioned to prevent discomfort and that the massage service provided is not too rough.

It is important that the client is kept warm during body massage application and that modesty and privacy are maintained at all times.

Ensure that the correct massage medium is selected and that adequate medium is applied. Too little may cause client discomfort, too much will make the skin too slippery to manipulate correctly.

Observing your clients body language and how tense their body is during massage is a good indicator of client comfort and if suitably relaxed .

Mechanical massage services

Outcome 4: Perform mechanical massage services

Learn how to use equipment to enhance and compliment the service benefits of manual massage and meet the needs of your client.

1. Clearly explaining the sensation created by the **equipment** being used.
2. Explaining the service procedure to the client in a clear and simple way at each stage in the process.
3. Providing suitable support and cushioning to specific areas of the body during the service if necessary.
4. Safely using the correct service settings, application and applicator heads on the body throughout the service to meet manufacturer's instructions.
5. Adjusting the intensity and duration of the service to suit the client's **physical characteristics** and the **service area**(s).
6. Effectively varying the sequence, depth and pressure of massage movements to meet **service objectives** and **service area**(s).
7. Checking the client's well-being throughout the mechanical massage service.
8. Taking appropriate and prompt remedial action if contra-actions or discomfort occur during the course of service.
9. Allowing the client sufficient post-service recovery time.
10. Ensuring the finished result is to the client's satisfaction and meets the agreed **service objectives.**

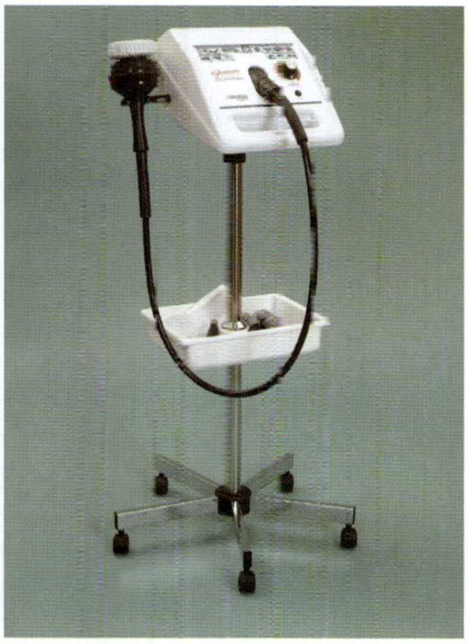

CARLTON BEAUTY + SPA LTD

Mechanical massage G5 machine

Mechanical massage using G5 Massage (CC500) equipment

CARLTON BEAUTY + SPA LTD

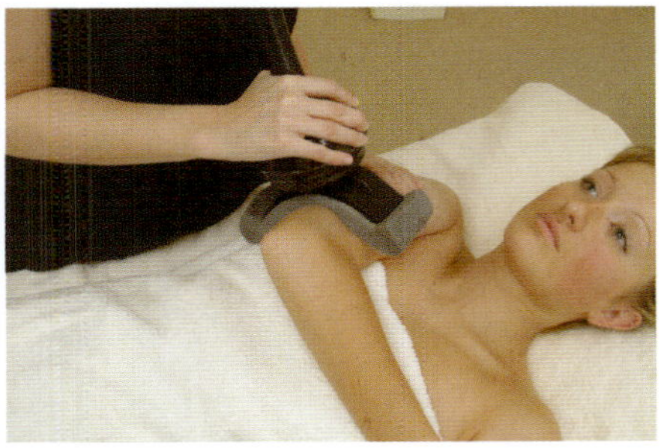

Effleurage to the arms, application to the triceps where fatty tissue can deposit.

CARLTON BEAUTY + SPA LTD

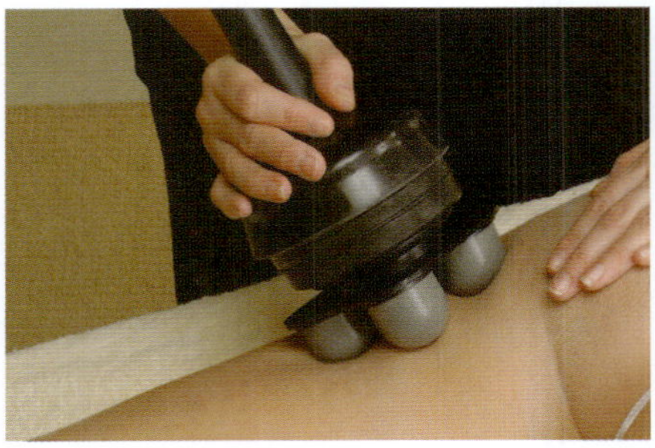

Petrissage 'egg-box' application to legs, hip and gluteal area

CARLTON BEAUTY + SPA LTD

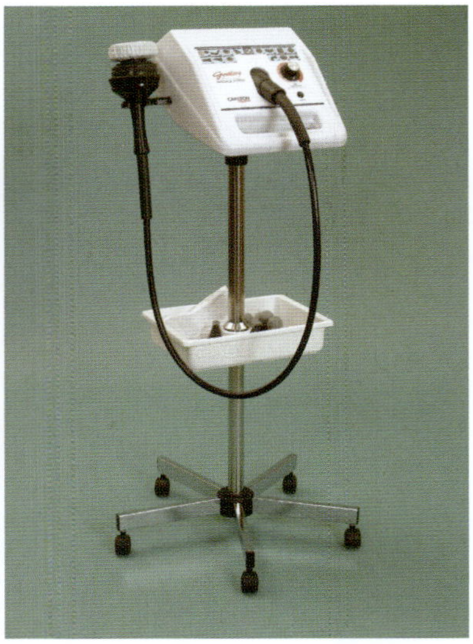

Mechanical massage (G5) equipment

CARLTON BEAUTY + SPA LTD

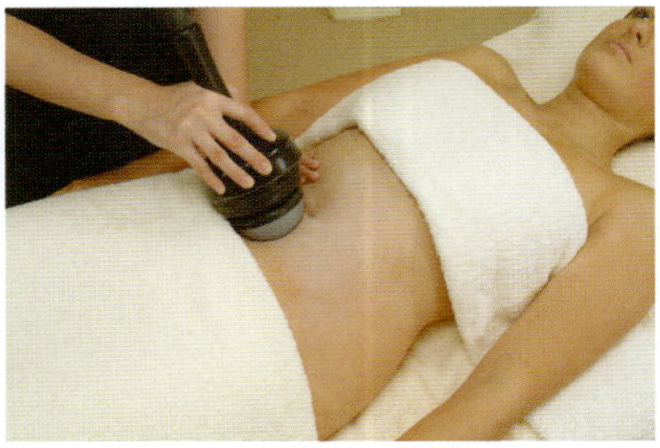

Petrissage 'football' application applied over the colon to aid peristalsis

CARLTON BEAUTY + SPA LTD

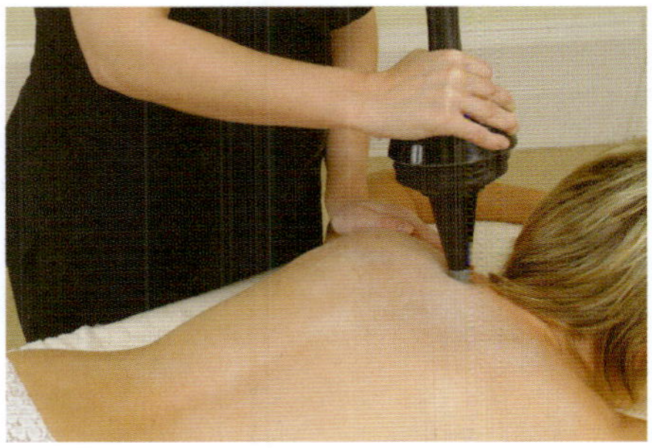

Friction 'lighthouse' application to upper fibres of the trapezius

CARLTON BEAUTY + SPA LTD

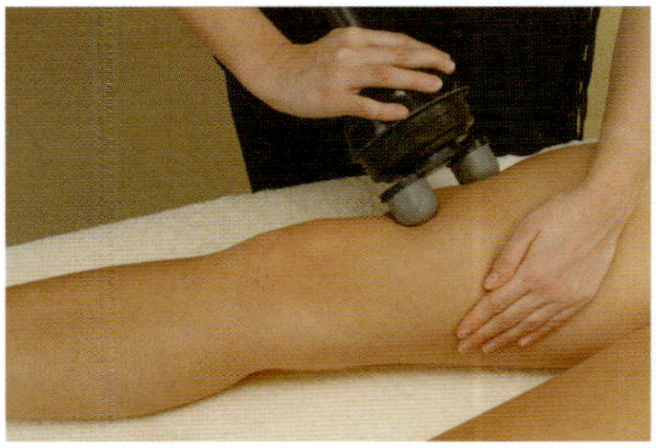

Petrissage two-ball rubber application to the thigh

Mechanical massage

Mechanical massage is an electrical body massage service which produces friction on the skin's surface, creating a heating effect as a result, the capillaries dilate and the skin becomes red, creating an erythema in the area. The benefits resemble manual massage but with less effort required by the beauty therapist. It is less personal and relaxing than manual massage.

It provides a deep massage and is therefore beneficial when a toning or slimming effect is required from the service as fatty tissue is softened and lymphatic circulation is stimulated, encouraging the removal of waste and toxins and excess fluid elimination. This is often referred to as 'spot reduction'. A dry skin is also improved by removal of dead skin cells and improvement of sebaceous gland activity.

It is unsuitable for use on the chest area and other bony areas.

The massage head is driven by a powerful electric motor so the expected sounds and service sensation should be explained to facilitate client relaxation and service understanding.

When performing a mechanical massage it is important to correctly position yourself, observing a good postural technique to prevent strain, fatigue or injury.

Client satisfaction should be checked during service application providing verbal reassurance and further service explanation as necessary. Observe client body language also. Mechanical massage equipment should be used in accordance with manufacturer's instructions. The service technique can be adapted by intensity, pressure and duration to achieve the physiological requirements.

Refer to **Facial electrical services** and **Body electrical services** in **Chapter 8** to learn the techniques for performing mechanical massage service to the face and body see page 205 onwards.

The knowledge and understanding questions in this chapter will include assessment for mechanical massage services.

Outcome 5: Provide aftercare advice

Learn how to provide aftercare advice which supports and meets the needs of your clients by:

1. Giving **advice** and recommendations accurately and constructively.
2. Giving your clients suitable **advice** specific to their individual needs.

This resting time could be used to discuss with the client suitable aftercare and homecare products to complement the massage. This might involve advice on healthy eating and exercise, including specific exercises that might be necessary to alleviate any postural problems. You should also advise the client to rest for a few hours when they get home, avoid strenuous exercise, not to eat a heavy meal and to avoid alcohol.

Explain that for 24 hours following service stimulants such as alcohol and caffeine should be avoided.

Warn the client of possible post-service reactions including:

- feeling of sickness
- emotional anxiety
- headache

The above reactions will normally subside in 24 hours.

Reconfirm possible contra-actions that may occur and advise on the appropriate action to take.

As the client's circulation continues to return to normal, the blood vessels will constrict, resulting in a need to visit the toilet frequently. Advise the client to drink plenty of fluids, preferably water, to replace the fluids lost. (Eight glass per day is recommended.)

If the massage was for relaxation, you might give advice on relaxing bath products, breathing and massage techniques that could be used at home. The massage could, of course, form part of a comprehensive service plan, including heat services such as infra-red, sauna, steam and electrical services, which will further benefit the client.

Inform the client of the cumulative benefits of regular massage services.

Services should be recommended as follows:

- Body massage 1–2 times per week
- Mechanical massage 2–3 times per week
- Audio sonic 1–2 times per week

The above recommendations will vary according to the service plan/aim.

Allow the client to dress in a private changing area and make client aware of facilities for personal grooming.

ASSESSMENT OF KNOWLEDGE AND UNDERSTANDING

FUNCTIONAL SKILLS

Having covered the learning objectives for **Provide body massage treatments**, test what you need to know and understand by answering the following short questions below. The information covers:

- organizational and legal requirements
- how to work safely and effectively when providing body massage services
- client consultation
- preparation for service
- anatomy and physiology
- contra-indications and contra-actions
- equipment and massage mediums
- service specific knowledge
- aftercare advice for clients

Additional anatomy and physiology questions required for this unit are found on pages 97–99.

Organizational and legal requirements

1 Which health and safety legislation are you responsible for implementing when performing a body massage service?

2 When using electrical equipment such as gyratory massage, what are your responsibilities under the Electricity at Work Act?

3 How can cross-infection be avoided when carrying out a body massage service?

4 What is the commercially acceptable timing for the following:
- a back massage?
- a full-body massage, including head and face massage?

5 Why is it important to allow sufficient time to complete a service?

6 Why is it important to obtain the client's signature and keep detailed records of the client's service(s)?

7 What information should be recorded on the client's record card before service application?

How to work safely and effectively when providing body massage services

1 How should the service environment be prepared to ensure client comfort and maximum benefit from the service? Consider temperature, lighting and sound.

2 Why is it important to maintain correct posture when performing body massage?

3 How would you dispose of general waste generated while completing a body massage service?

4 How can you check client well-being during manual and mechanical massage service?

5 How can you maintain client modesty and privacy during the service? Give **three** examples. Why is this important?

6 How can muscle fatigue and injury be avoided when performing regular body massage services?

Client consultation

1 What is the purpose of the consultation before body massage service?

2 Name three postural conditions that may be identified at consultation that you would consider in your massage application and modification.

3 What lifestyle factors should be discussed with a client when planning a massage service plan and deciding their service needs?

4 Why is it important to discuss potential contra-actions with a client at the consultation?

5 How can you assess the physical characteristics weight, height, muscle tone, health and skin condition?

6 How would you recognize the following skin types/ conditions:

- dry?
- oily?
- sensitive?
- aged?

Preparation for service

1 How should the client be prepared before the body massage service commences?

2 Which massage medium would be most suitable for the skin types listed in client consultation question number 6 conditions above?

3 Why can it be beneficial to perform a pre-heating service before body massage service?

4 What verbal instructions should be given on general preparation of the client for service consider clothing and accessory removal? How can client modesty and privacy be maintained at this stage?

Anatomy and physiology

1 What effect does massage have on the following:

- skin?
- bones?
- muscle?
- blood system?
- lymph system?
- nervous system?

2 What do you understand by the term *muscle tone*? How may this be affected by body massage?

3 What are the physiological and psychological benefits of massage service?

Contra-indications and contra-actions

1 Why is it important to refer clients to their GP if you identify a contra-indication?

2 When would you need to refer a client to their GP before service could be given?

3 State **three** contra-indications that *prevent* body massage service.

4 State **three** contra-indications that *restrict* body massage service.

5 What are the possible contra-actions which may occur during and post service/how would you deal with them if they occurred?

Equipment and massage mediums

1 How may massage equipment be adjusted to assist body massage application to the body parts during application?

2 What considerations should be given to supporting and positioning of the client during the service? How is this provided?

3 How is the following equipment cleaned and maintained to prevent cross-infection:

- gyratory massage heads?
- audio sonic attachment heads?
- service couch?

4 When would you select to use the following mediums:

- oil?
- cream?
- powder?

5 Name a suitable product to use with mechanical massage and audio sonic to provide slip.

Service-specific knowledge

1 What do you understand by the terms erythema and hyperaemia, and what are the causes?

2 How would body massage techniques, choice of medium, speed of application and pressure be adapted for the following clients:

- a young, athletic male client?
- a female client with poor skin tone and stretch marks?
- an overweight client on a weight reducing client?
- an elderly client requiring a relaxation massage?

3 What are the advantages of combining mechanical and manual massage?

4 How can massage be adapted to achieve relaxation; anti-cellulite, uplifting and stimulating service objectives?

5 In which direction and at what systems of the body is body massage application directed towards?

6 Why should correct posture be adopted at all times when performing a body massage?

7 How can client satisfaction be assessed during service application?

Aftercare advice for clients

1 Why is it important to gain feedback from the client and give relevant advice to them following service?

2 State three contra-actions that could occur during or following body massage.

3 Why is it important to record any contra-action either during or following service on the client record card?

4 What aftercare products may be recommended to your client?

5 How often would you recommend a client receives body manual massage and body mechanical massage?

6 What other service(s) could be recommended to a client who was following a weight reduction programme?

7 What recommendations to lifestyle habit would enable a client to continue to benefit from the service for:

- relaxation?
- sense of well-being?

11 Indian head massage

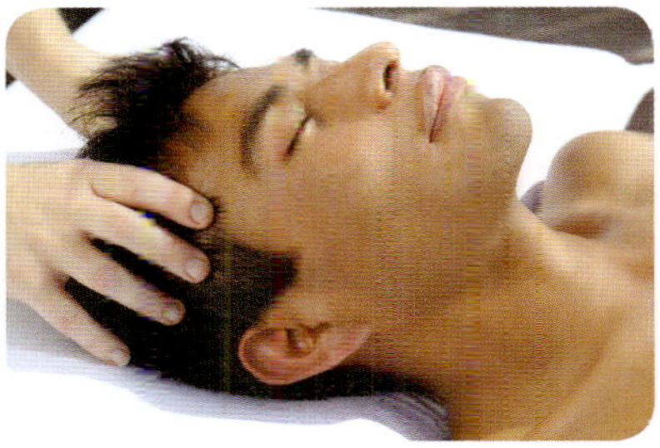

SHUTTERSTOCK/HOLBOX

Learning Objectives

This chapter covers the **Provide Indian head massage treatments** unit.

This unit is all about how to provide the service Indian head massage an ancient massage technique. The massage is applied to the face, head and upper body, achieving both a physiological and psychological effect. Application technique is modified to achieve the client's service objectives identified at consultation. Oils may be used, selected to enhance the service results applied to the skin and hair.

There are **four** learning outcomes which you must achieve competently:

1. **Maintain safe and effective methods of working when providing Indian head massage service.**
2. **Consult, plan and prepare for services with clients.**
3. **Perform Indian head massage.**
4. **Provide aftercare advice.**

For each unit your assessor will observe you on **at least three separate occasions,** each involving different clients; **one** massage must include the use of massage oil and **one** massage must exclude the use of oil.

From the **range** statements, you must show that you have:

- used all **consultation techniques**
- dealt with all the client's **physical characteristics**

(continued on the next page)

ZOE CROWLEY

ROLE MODEL

Zoe Crowley

Aqua Sana Manager, Elveden Forest Center Parcs

"I qualified as a Beauty Therapist in 1996 and then worked for Steiner Transocean onboard cruise ships. I loved life at sea and stayed for seven contracts, working my way up from Beauty Therapist, to Senior Beauty Therapist, Assistant Spa Manager until I became Spa Director and managed my own ships. Once I returned to dry land I worked for Molton Brown in a retail store before setting up a brand new day spa in the Malmaison Hotel in Birmingham. That was a great challenge and very rewarding to see the project through from start to finish, choosing the decoration, employing the team, opening orders of stock, etc.

I then relocated and joined Center Parcs and have now been here for 5 years. I manage the Aqua Sana team of around 90 which includes beauty therapists, spa attendants, hairdressers and reception staff, I also have four assistant managers who help me with the operation.

Our facilities include 21 treatment rooms including a dry floatation room and dual-treatment rooms, and over 16 experiences to try in our wonderful World of Spa including Tyrolean sauna, Turkish Hammam, Aqua Meditation room and water beds. It is a fantastic spa and no two days are ever the same.

(continued)

- dealt with at least **one** of the **necessary actions** where a contra-action, contra-indication or service modification occurs
- met all **service objectives**
- used all **massage techniques**
- covered all **service areas**
- provided all types of relevant aftercare **advice**

However, you must prove that you have the necessary knowledge and understanding to be able to perform competently across the range.

When providing Indian head massage services it is important to use the skills you have learnt in the following chapters:

Monitoring safe work operations.

Promotional activities.

Essential anatomy and physiology knowledge requirements for this unit are identified on the checklist in Chapter 2, pages 12–13. This chapter also discusses anatomy and physiology specific to this unit.

Introduction

Indian head massage is a service applied to the upper part of the body (the shoulders, upper arms, neck and head) using the hands. It helps to relieve stress and tension, and creates a feeling of well-being. This type of massage has developed over a thousand years from traditional techniques practised in India. The family tradition of massage plays a central role in daily life in India and dates back to the beginnings of Hinduism, the main religion of that country. Indian head massage is known as 'champissage' in India and is part of the system of **Ayurveda** – the science of life – an ancient form of medical treatment which is nearly 4000 years old. Ayurveda is a method of relieving pain and healing through the balance of the body.

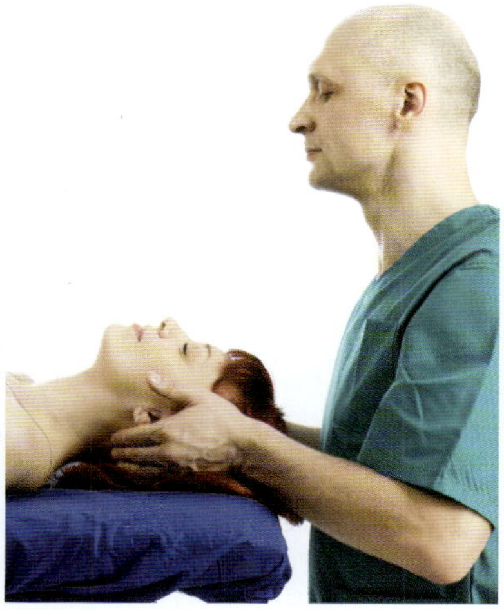

Indian head scalp massage application

The Ayurveda (science of life), a sacred Hindu text, was written around 1800 BC. In Ayurveda, life consists of body, mind and spirit and each person is different. Massage is included among its principles of achieving balance of the body. By restoring the balance and harmony of the body, mind and spirit the health and well-being of the individual improves.

Practices adopted to achieve this balance include daily meditation, exercise, the receipt of alternative therapies and medication.

Swedish body massage techniques are also adopted and incorporated into the massage combining ancient and modern massage techniques.

As the therapeutic effects of massage become more popular, Indian head massage is an ideal service to offer and has many advantages that can meet the needs of different clients. There is no need for the client to undress, it is relatively quick to perform, can be performed almost anywhere and does not require expensive equipment.

Oils may be incorporated into the massage to condition the skin of the scalp and hair. It also helps to induce relaxation.

The massage is adapted to the client's physiological and psychological needs. These are determined during the client consultation and are termed the objectives of the service.

These objectives may include:

- relaxation
- maintaining a feeling of well-being
- an uplifting effect
- to improve the condition of the scalp and hair

Physiological effects of Indian head massage

- The muscles receive an improved supply of oxygenated blood, essential for cell growth. The tone and strength of muscles are improved. Areas of muscular tension will become relaxed. This can increase energy levels.
- Increased joint mobility in the neck area occurs through massage manipulation to the area.
- The increased blood circulation in the area warms the tissues. This induces a feeling of relaxation, which is particularly beneficial when treating tense muscles.
- As the blood capillaries dilate and bring blood to the skin's surface, the skin colour improves.
- The lymphatic circulation and the venous blood circulation increase. These changes speed up the removal of waste products and toxins. The removal of excess lymph improves the appearance of a puffy oedematous skin; it also improves production of white blood cells to fight infections.
- Sensory nerve endings can be soothed or stimulated, depending on the massage manipulations selected.
- Massage stimulates the sebaceous and sudoriferous glands and increases the production of sweat and sebum. This increases the skin's natural oil and moisture balance.
- Applying oil to the head (optional) adds moisture and improves the condition of dry hair or scalp.
- Massage to the scalp may stimulate hair growth by increasing blood supply to the hair follicle, e.g. in cases of alopecia, hair loss.

TOP TIP

Popularity and benefits

Indian head massage is popular in the hairdressing and beauty sector due to it being a relatively quick service which can be received with minimal client preparation.

Airlines are increasingly offering this to their customers as an in-flight service.

Also, it is popular in many companies which enable their employees to receive the service during work hours to relieve stress and maintain well-being.

ACTIVITY

Ayurveda

Ayurveda, pronounced 'are-you-vay-da' means the 'science of life' and is based on the principle that health is maintained through achieving balance of three important energies or *dosha*, responsible for all the physiological and psychological processes in the body–mind system: referred to as *vata*, *pitta* and *kapha*.

Research what each *dosha* is responsible for in the health of the body.

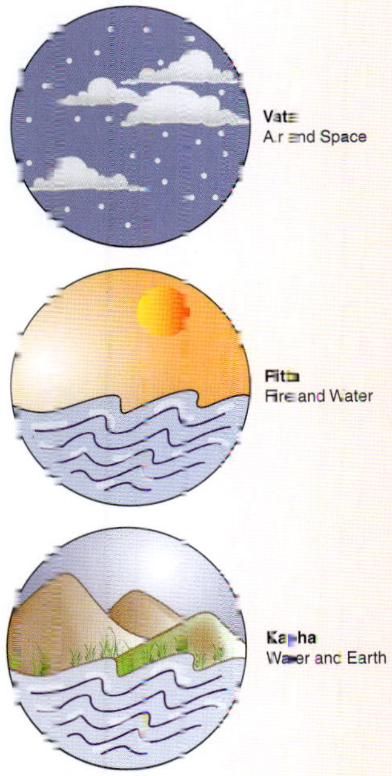

The three doshas

COURTESY OF TREATMENTS TAUGHT BY DIAMOND WAY AYURVEDA

ALWAYS REMEMBER

Emotional effect

Clients may become tearful following Indian head massage. This is because clients relax and they may then wish to talk about their problems.

If this happens, *listen* – unless qualified you should not *counsel*.

The psychological effects of massage are broad and, when performed on a regular basis, can relieve stress and tension in the client. The client may feel fresh, invigorated and healthier.

Psychological effects of Indian head massage

- helps to improve concentration – oxygen is increased to the brain
- relieves stress, tension and anxiety
- induces relaxation
- Improves sleep in the case of poor sleep patterns
- confidence-raising following the removal of tension

Anatomy and physiology

Essential anatomy and physiology knowledge requirements for this unit are identified on the checklist in Chapter 2, pages 12–13. This chapter also discusses the anatomy and physiology specific to this unit.

The Indian head massage has a beneficial effect, maintaining the health of the sinuses. These are hollow spaces in the facial and cranial bones containing air and lined with a mucous membrane, producing mucus which drains into the nose and keeps the nasal cavities moist and traps bacteria and dirt. The mucous membrane is continuous with the nasal cavities. They can also get blocked by airborne allergens, i.e. pollen, air pollution and chronic drug misuse. They connect with the inside of the nasal cavity through small openings called ostia. The main sinuses are the

- maxillary, in each cheekbone
- frontal, either side of the forehead, above the eyes
- sphenoid, between the upper part of the nose and between the eyes
- ethmoid, behind the bridge of the nose and between the eyes

The sinuses contain fibres that slow the flow of lymph fluid through them and which enables macrophages to ingest microorganisms that could lead to infection.

Following massage there is often an increase of mucous secretion from the sinuses.

HEALTH & SAFETY

Sinusitis is infection of the mucous membranes by a virus, bacteria or fungus. This causes a blockage of the involved sinus into the nose resulting in pain and swelling. With GP permission to treat, the condition sinusitis may be relieved when the infection has been treated. Massage will bring temporary relief and possible reduction in swelling.

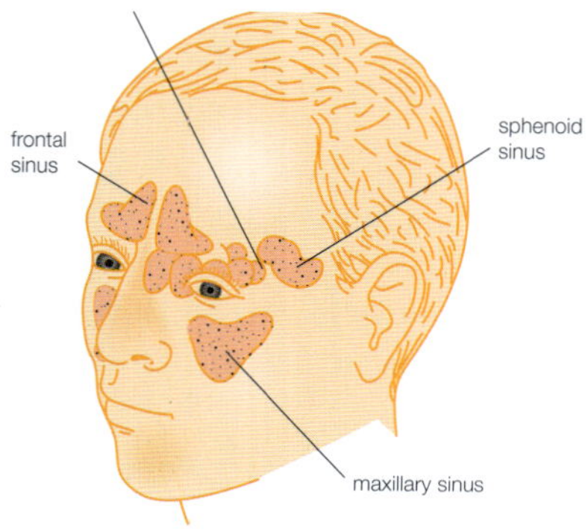

Sinuses

Massage techniques

Indian head massage is based on a series of classic westernized and Indian massage movements, used to create different effects. There are six basic types of massage techniques:

- effleurage
- petrissage
- percussion (tapotement)
- frictions
- vibrations
- pressure point (**marma**)

The beauty therapist can adapt the way each of these movements is applied, according to the needs of the client. Either the *speed* of application or the *depth of pressure* can be altered.

Effleurage Effleurage is a stroking movement, used to begin the massage, as a link manipulation, and to complete the massage sequence. This manipulation can be applied lightly or briskly, has an even pressure and is applied in a rhythmical, continuous manner to induce relaxation. The speed of application depends upon the effect to be achieved and according to the underlying structures and tissue type, but it must *never* be unduly heavy. Movements also include stroking. Effleurage has the following effects:

- desquamation (skin removal) is increased
- arterial blood circulation is increased, bringing fresh nutrients to the area, energizing the client and warming the tissues
- venous circulation is improved, aiding the removal of congestion from the veins
- lymphatic circulation is increased, improving the absorption of waste products and elimination of toxins from the tissues
- the underlying muscle fibres are relaxed
- relaxes and soothes sensory nerve endings

Uses in service: to relax tight and contracted muscles.

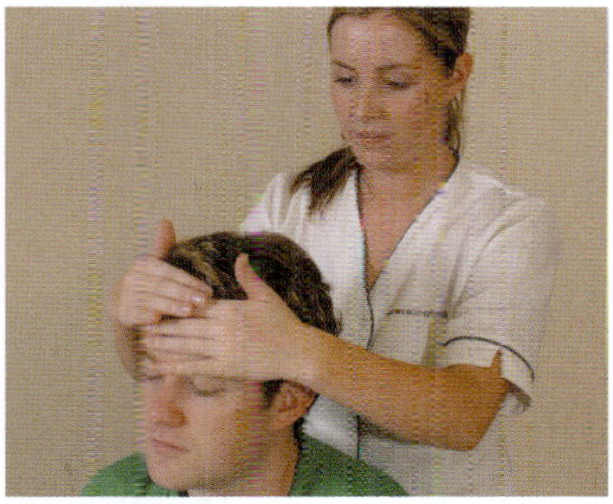

Effleurage – stroking technique to the forehead frontal bone

TOP TIP

Relief from tension and stress

Massaging the scalp neck and face can relieve symptoms of stress such as eyestrain, stiffness in the neck and headaches.

Petrissage Petrissage involves a series of movements in which the tissues are lifted away from the underlying structures and compressed, including kneading and squeezing and releasing the muscles along their length. The whole hands or just the fingers and thumbs may be used. Pressure is intermittent, and should be light yet firm. Petrissage has the following effects:

- improvement of muscle tone, through the compression and relaxation of muscle fibres
- improvement in blood and lymph circulation, as the application of pressure causes the vessels to empty and fill
- increased activity of the sebaceous glands, due to the stimulation effect on the skin tissues

Movements include picking up, kneading, pinching and rolling.

Uses in service: to stimulate a sluggish circulation; to increase sebaceous gland and sudoriferous gland activity when treating a dry skin condition.

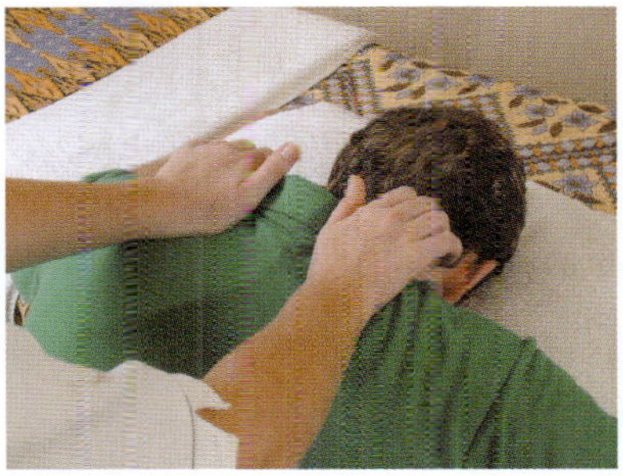

Petrissage – kneading to the trapezius muscle

Percussion **Percussion**, also known as **tapotement**, is performed in a brisk, stimulating manner. Rhythm is important as the fingers are continually breaking contact with the skin; irritation or damage can occur if this movement is performed incorrectly. Percussion has the following effects:

- stimulation of the nerves
- a fast vascular (skin reddening) reaction because of the skin's nervous response to the stimulus – this reaction, erythema, is a sign of skin stimulation

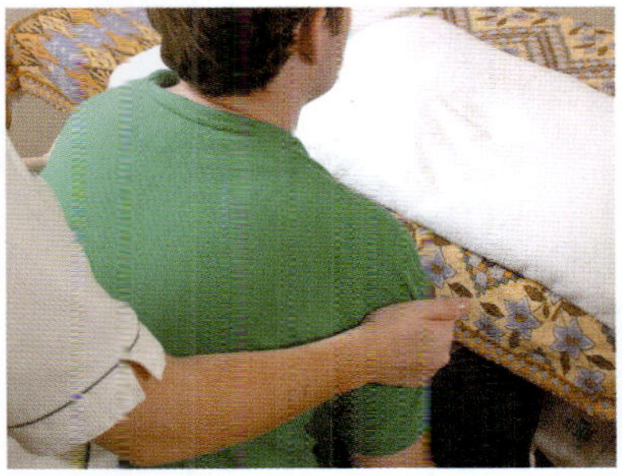

Squeezing movements to the upper arm deltoid muscle

- increased blood supply, which nourishes the tissues
- improvement in skin and muscle tone in the area

Movements include hacking and **tapping**. When performed on the scalp, only light pressure should be used. In facial massage only light tapping should be used.

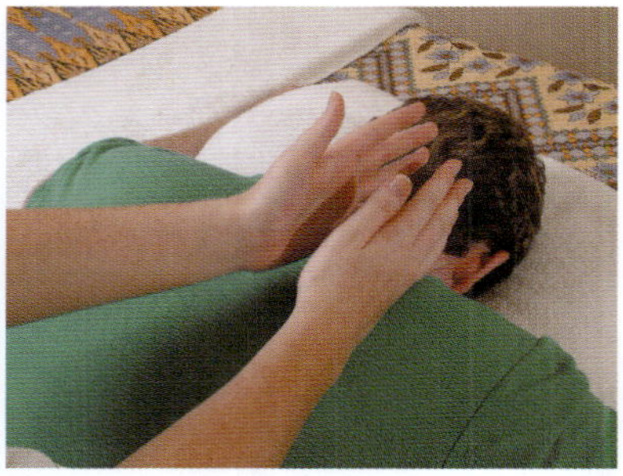

Percussion – hacking to the trapezius muscle

HEALTH & SAFETY

Skin elasticity

As the skin ages it becomes thinner and less elastic. Take care when using petrissage movements to avoid skin tissue damage.

Also, any areas of scar tissue will not be as supple as normal skin, care in handling is required.

Uses in service: to tone areas of loose skin and improve circulation in the area.

Frictions Frictions cause the skin and superficial structure to move together over the underlying structures. These movements are performed with either the fingers or the thumbs and concentrated in a particular area, applied with regulated pressure. Frictions have the following effects:

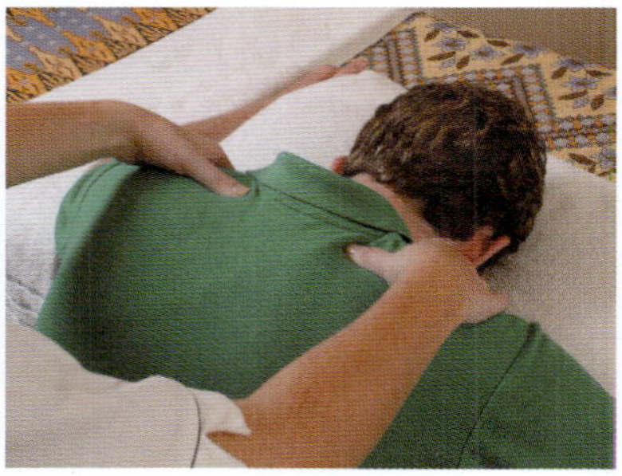

Frictions to the trapezius muscle

- desquamation (skin removal) is increased
- gentle stimulation of the skin and superficial tissues improving functioning
- improves scar tissue by breaking down the tissue adhesions
- improved lymphatic and blood circulation
- breaks down tight nodules (tension in the muscle fibres), improving mobility

Uses in service: to help break down fatty deposits, fibrous thickening and the removal of non-medical oedema (fluid retention). To stimulate and improve a dry skin condition.

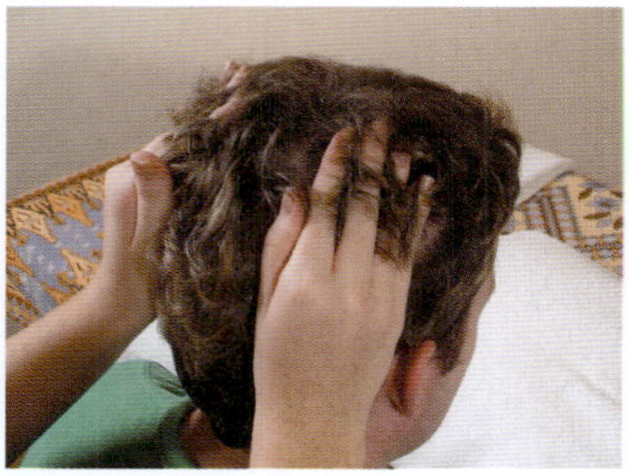

Vibrations to the scalp

Vibrations Vibrations are applied on the nerve centre. They are produced by a rapid contraction and relaxation of the beauty therapist's arm, resulting in a fine trembling movement. Vibration has the following effects:

- stimulation of the nerves, inducing a feeling of well-being
- gentle stimulation of the skin

Movements include *static* vibrations, in which the pads of the fingers are placed on the nerve and the vibratory effect created by the beauty therapist's arms and hands is applied in one position; and running vibrations, in which the vibratory effect is applied along a nerve path.

Uses in service: to stimulate a sensitive skin in order to improve the skin's functioning without irritating the surface blood capillaries.

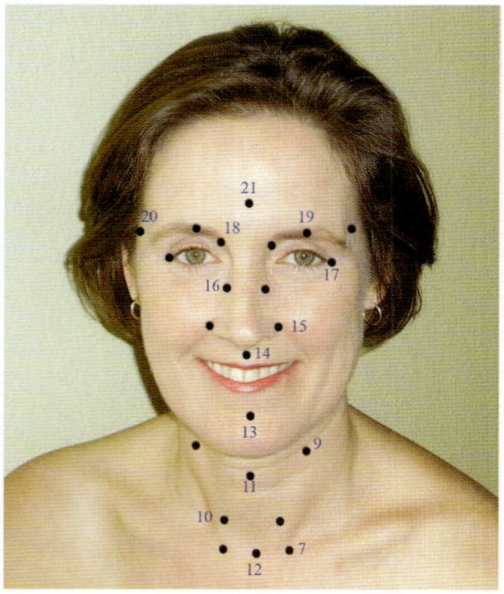

Marma pressure points on the face

Pressure point technique *Pressure point* application is also incorporated into Indian head massage. It is based on the principles and ancient Indian practices of **marma**, translated as 'vital', 'hidden' or 'secret energy point'. Pressure is applied using the thumb or index finger to nerve junctions which stimulates these vital energy points on the head, face and ears to improve circulation, relieve tiredness and induce relaxation. These points along the meridians of the body release blocked energy. Meridians are often described as channels of living magnetic energy, which flow through the body and connect the main vital organs. This energy helps keep our bodies active and the energy balance affects our well-being, including our metal, physical, spiritual and emotional conditions. An imbalance of energy manifests itself in poor health. The aim during the massage is to restore balance of energy flow in the body.

- Circulation is improved.
- Energy is created as decongestion of the body occurs.
- The nervous system is stimulated.

Marma pressure point technique balances the body. If blocked, pressure will initially feel uncomfortable for the client. Small clockwise movements gradually increase in size and pressure to the area.

Before beginning the Indian head massage service, check that you have the necessary equipment and materials to hand and that they meet the legal, hygiene and industry requirements for Indian head massage service.

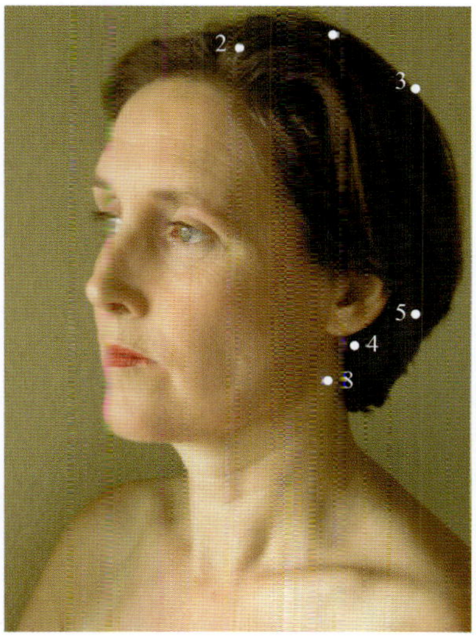

COURTESY OF TREATMENTS TAUGHT BY DIAMOND WAY AYURVEDA

Marma pressure points on the scalp and neck

Outcome 1: Maintain safe and effective methods of working when providing Indian head massage

Learn how to maintain safe and effective methods of working when providing body massage service by:

1. Setting up and monitoring the service area to meet organization procedures and manufacturer's instructions.
2. Making sure that environmental conditions are suitable for the client and the service.
3. Ensuring your personal hygiene, protection and appearance meet accepted industry and organizational requirements.
4. Ensuring that your nails are short, clean, well manicured and free of polish.
5. Effectively disinfecting your hands prior to and after service.
6. Ensuring your own posture and position minimizes fatigue and risk of injury while working.
7. Ensuring all tools and equipment are cleaned using the correct methods.
8. Positioning equipment and massage medium for ease and safety of use.
9. Ensuring the client is in a comfortable and relaxed position suitable for the service.
10. Maintaining accepted industry hygiene and safety practices throughout the service.

(*Continued*) Learn how to maintain safe and effective methods of working when providing body massage service by:

11. Adopting a positive, polite and reassuring manner towards the client throughout the service.
12. Maintaining the client's modesty, privacy and comfort at all times.
13. Disposing of waste materials safely and correctly.
14. Ensuring the service is cost-effective and is carried out within a commercially viable time.
15. Ensuring client record cards are up-to-date, accurate, complete, legible and signed by the client and practitioner.

EQUIPMENT AND MATERIALS LIST

HOF

Chair
With adjustable height, low back support, without an arm rest

BEAUTY EXPRESS LTD

Organic massage oil
e.g. almond, olive, mustard or coconut oil. The oil is warmed before application to aid absorption and induce relaxation

ELLISONS

Trolley
Or other surface on which to place everything

Combs
To allow the client to comb their hair following service

ELLISONS

Plastic bowls
Two, to dispense products into as necessary and hold consumables

BEAUTY EXPRESS LTD

Clean towels
Freshly laundered for each client
A towel may be placed over the client's shoulders if using oils

Hair clips
Used to secure long hair away from the neck area

ELLISONS

Client record card
Confidential card recording details of each client registered at the salon to record personal details, products used and details of the service.

YOU WILL ALSO NEED:

Paper tissue disposable bedroll To cover the service couch cover if used

Dry and damp cotton wool and tissues To apply skin-cleansing agents and dry the skin

Skin cleansing agent Such as witch hazel or eau de cologne

Cosmetic cleansing preparations To remove facial make-up (as necessary)

Waste container – Bin lined with a disposable bin liner

Aftercare advice – Recommended advice for the client to refer to following the service

Plan and prepare for the service

Sterilization and disinfection

Prior to the Indian head massage service, make sure that the work area is hygienic. The surface of the massage couch and the trolley surface should be wiped over with warm soapy water and disinfectant.

Plastic spatulas should be cleaned and placed in an UV cabinet prior to use to ensure they are free from bacteria.

An **aseptic** condition should be maintained, a situation trying to eliminate bacteria. The service area should remain in a safe and hygienic state throughout the day, ready for further use. Waste at the conclusion of service should be disposed of in a sealed polythene bag and towels laundered.

Clean towels should be provided for each client to prevent cross-infection.

HEALTH & SAFETY

Legislation

It is important that you comply with all relevant health and safety legislation while performing Indian head massage.

Examples include:

Workplace (Health, Safety and Welfare) Regulations (1992)

Control of Substances Hazardous to Health Regulations (COSHH) (2002)

Electricity at Work Regulations (1989).

Remember to use the knowledge and skills you have learnt in the chapter on **Monitoring safe work operations**.

> When applying for a beauty therapy position make sure you are prepared. Research the spa or salon. Consider a 'dry run' of the journey to prevent you from being late for the interview. Remember to be yourself and show your personality.
>
> **Zoe Crowley**

Preparing the work area

Prepare the work area to meet all health and safety legislation requirements.

The service area should be clean and at a warm, comfortable working temperature for both the client and the beauty therapist, between 18 and 21 °C. Adequate ventilation should be provided to create a hygienic environment, preventing cross-infection through viral airborne spores, drowsiness through carbon dioxide-saturated air and the removal of stale smells and odours. The service area should induce relaxation and client comfort. Lighting should be soft, the colour of the decor should be subtle and non-gender biased. Sound levels should be low and selected for relaxation. If performing the service over a couch there should be adequate support in the form of a bolster (a pillow) cushion to support the head and neck and ensure client comfort. Place all the equipment and materials required on the trolley prior to the service, to ensure that an efficient service is provided without unnecessary disruptions.

ALWAYS REMEMBER

Avoid getting emotionally involved

It can be tiring performing massage, as the client may become emotional and wish to talk about their problems. Listen, but do not pass judgement. When the client's service finishes it is important that you have the ability to 'switch off'.

Preparation of the beauty therapist

The beauty therapist should wear a professional work uniform which does not restrict movement. Full, enclosed shoes should be worn with low or medium-height heels. Optionally shoes may be removed when performing the massage to assist energy flow. Jewellery must be removed from the hands and wrists.

Before preparing the client for the service, wash your hands. The hands need to be flexible in order to fit the contour of the client's upper body. Shake the hands to remove any tension

HEALTH & SAFETY

Allergies

Refer to the record card to check for any known allergies to products, which could cause a contra-action, e.g., sesame oil can cause skin irritation, where possible select an alternative such as olive oil.

from the wrists and hands. Practise a deep slow breathing technique before applying massage. This will help you to relax and focus your concentration on the massage service.

Collect the client's record card from reception prior to their arrival. A full client consultation should be carried out before the service commences, including a postural check.

Beauty therapist's hands The beauty therapist should always sanitize their hands prior to the service. Nails should be short, to avoid scratching the client and to facilitate massage application. The hands also need to be flexible in order to fit the contours of the client's body. Mobilizing the joints of the hands and fingers will loosen the hands and facilitate good manipulations. Hand exercises should be practised on a regular basis.

> As a beauty therapist it is important to be able to work using your own initiative but also as part of a team. Helping out colleagues, giving advice and swapping techniques will help the operation run smoothly and create a happy working environment.
>
> **Zoe Crowley**

ALWAYS REMEMBER

Local Authority Licensing Regulations (2003)

Massage services must apply for a license to practice from their local authority's environmental health department. Your local authority will advise you on the requirements for license and how to obtain a license.

ALWAYS REMEMBER

Massage and chakras

When working on a chakra you may feel heat or cold in your hands from the energy channels opening.

Application technique

The massage movements should be adapted to suit the needs of each client. The sequence of application may also differ according to your workplace.

The service commences by *grounding* or *levelling*, a technique to balance the body's *chakras*. Chakras are non-physical energy centres, located about an inch away from the physical body, which cannot be seen. If energy levels become blocked due to stress, negative energy becomes stored in the chakra and it becomes unbalanced. This can then result in physical or mental illness. An imbalance in one energy centre can affect others. Massage helps restore the balance of the chakra, enabling energy to flow more freely. Grounding is where the beauty therapist and client begin to communicate, energy channels open and healing begins.

> It is very important to communicate with your client at all times. Make sure you confirm the service your client is expecting, ask what your client hopes to get out of the service, check throughout the service that your client is warm enough and comfortable and that the pressure is OK for her or him.
>
> Indian head massage is designed to de-stress and relive tension, so make sure you do everything within your power to ensure your client leaves your room feeling better.
>
> **Zoe Crowley**

TOP TIP

Beauty therapist's hands

Mobilizing the joints of the hands and fingers will loosen the hands and facilitate good manipulations.

Hand exercises should be practised on a regular basis.

Nails should be short, to avoid scratching the client and to facilitate massage application.

Chakras

In ancient Eastern belief the body is said to have seven major chakra centres, each with a function, which all work together in balance with each other. **Chakras** have many associations including flower representation, differing in petal number depending upon the chakra. They are also associated with different colours and elements.

1 The **base** chakra, also known as root, associated colour red, element earth. Concerned with connection to earth, health and survival.

2 The **sacral** chakra, associated colour orange, element water. Concerned with relationships, especially sexual relationships.

3 The **solar plexus** chakra, associated colour yellow, element fire. Concerned with memory, personal harmony and energy.

4 The **heart** chakra, associated colour green, element air. Concerned with physical and emotional balance and empathy with others.

5 The **throat** chakra, associated colour blue, element sound or ether. Concerned with creativity, communication and expression.

6 The **brow** chakra (also known as the *third eye*), associated colour indigo, element light. Concerned with inner vision.

7 The **crown** chakra, associated colour white, element spirit. Concerned with imagination and thought.

In Indian head massage we are concerned with restoring the balance of the higher chakras: the throat, brow and crown. The crown chakra is the master chakra and can help restore the energy and balance of the other chakras. The Indian head massage usually starts and ends by the placement of the therapist's hands over the crown chakra.

At the end of the service the beauty therapist may sometimes feel tired. Through energy channels created during massage, energy may have been taken from the beauty therapist to the client. For more information on chakras see Chapter 13, page 444.

BEST PRACTICE

Breathing technique

Advise the client that breathing should be deep and slow, not shallow and rapid.

Before service encourage to practice abdominal breathing. The client should be advised to breathe in slowly through the nose – the stomach should move out slightly – and out through the mouth.

Outcome 2: Consult, plan and prepare for services with clients

Learn how to use consultation techniques to effectively plan and prepare for massage service by:

1. Using **consultation techniques** in a polite, sensitive and friendly manner to determine the client's service needs.
2. Ensuring that informed and signed parent or guardian consent is obtained for minors prior to any massage service.
3. Ensuring that a parent or guardian is present throughout the massage service for minors under the age of 16.
4. Clearly explaining to the client what the service entails in a way they can understand.

BEST PRACTICE

Long hair

If the client has long hair it may be necessary to secure it with a clip while performing massage to the neck, shoulder and back.

HEALTH & SAFETY

'Use by' dates and safe storage

Products used should conform with the **General Product Safety Regulations**. They require that cosmetics are safe and correctly labelled.

Check that all products are clean and that the 'use by' date has not expired. Ensure all bottles are wiped over and lids are securely replaced after use to prevent spillage and the spread of bacteria.

To maintain the quality of organic oils they must be kept in cool dark conditions away from heat and light.

BEST PRACTICE

Client seating position for treatment

The client chair must not be on castors or they could move when the service is performed.

The chair must support the client and the height adjustable to avoid the beauty therapist having to adopt poor posture or strain which could lead to repetitive strain injury.

HOF

On-site massage chair

***(Continued)* Learn how to use consultation techniques to effectively plan and prepare for massage service by:**

5. Using suitable **consultation techniques** to identify your client's medical history, **physical characteristics** and lifestyle pattern.
6. Asking your client appropriate questions to identify if they have any contra-indications to massage services.
7. Accurately recording your client's responses to questioning.
8. Actively encouraging clients to ask questions and clarify any points.
9. Taking the **necessary action** in response to any identified contra-indications.
10. Ensuring client advice is given without reference to a specific medical condition and without causing undue alarm and concern.
11. Clearly explaining and agreeing the projected cost, likely duration and frequency service needed.
12. Agreeing in writing with the client's needs, expectations and **service objectives**, ensuring they are realistic and achievable.
13. Adapting client preparation procedures to suit the environment in which the massage is to be undertaken.
14. Ensuring that clothing, hair and accessories are effectively protected or removed.
15. Selecting suitable resources and massage medium, if required, to meet the **service objectives**.

Consultation

Reception

Indian head massage can be carried out as required, but is usually recommended once or twice a week, and preferably as a course for maximum effect. Regularity of service will depend upon the client's personal circumstances, including their financial position and time constraints. When a client is booking for this service, allow 45 minutes (excluding consultation and preparation time), which includes consultation, practical service and aftercare advice. The Indian head massage service itself should take 30 minutes. Warn the client that they may have a reaction after service. Symptoms can include sickness, tiredness, emotional anxiety and headaches. These contra-actions can be termed a *healing crisis*. This reaction will normally subside after 24 hours. If the client is wearing a false hair piece warn them that this will have to be removed.

Discuss with the client their service requirements. Explain clearly to the client what the Indian head massage service involves and the effects that can be gained. Service objectives must be realistic and achievable. Discuss the way the service application can be modified or adapted to meet their specific needs including the use of oil. Agree a massage service plan with the client to meet their needs, both physically and psychologically. Allow time and invite the client to ask questions – the client should fully understand what the service involves including costs, duration, frequency recommendations including post-service reactions.

The beauty therapist needs to obtain relevant details from the client before starting the Indian head massage service. The beauty therapist must ensure that their communication skills make the client feel welcome and comfortable. The client should be at ease throughout the service and a good, professional rapport should be built between client and beauty therapist. Personal details taken from the client are recorded on a record card. These should include medical history, doctor's details, and contra-indications that may be present.

ALWAYS REMEMBER

Service timing

It is important to complete service in the given time. This will ensure that:

- each client receives a competent service meeting their service requirements
- clients are not disadvantaged by receiving a hurried service
- a relaxing service environment in which clients are not made to feel anxious or stressed due to service delay is maintained

Contra-indications

Certain contra-indications preclude Indian head massage. These can be divided into three categories: general, local and temporary. **General** contra-indications affect the whole body or part of the body; **local** contra-indications are concentrated in a particular area; the symptoms of **temporary** contra-indications have only a short time span and clear up quite quickly. If the beauty therapist has any concern over the client's health or well-being, medical advice should be sought prior to the service. A doctor's note should be obtained before service is carried out.

Those requiring GP referral should be tactfully and clearly discussed to ensure client understanding.

Contra-indications

General	*Local*	*Temporary*
Heart conditions	Recent operations*	Medication
High or low blood pressure	Recent scar tissue (up to 6 months)*	Severe bruising*
Medication	Psoriasis or eczema*	Skin cuts and abrasions*
Diabetes	Skin disease	Pregnancy
Cancer	Skin disorder	Medical oedema
Rheumatism and arthritis (especially of the neck)	Recent injury*	Skin disease
Undiagnosed, lumps, bumps and swelling		Skin disorder
Loss of skin sensation		Intoxication
High temperature		Flu, cold symptoms
Migraine or severe headaches		Scalp disorders
Disorders of the nervous system		

* Only apply if located in the area.

HEALTH & SAFETY

Service to minors

Anyone under 16 years of age must not receive a massage service unless accompanied by a parent or guardian who must also sign a consent form.

Follow your salon policy on supplying a service to minors.

ALWAYS REMEMBER

Energy balance is disturbed by:

- stress
- alcohol
- nicotine
- processed foods
- medication

Discuss how lifestyle change can affect energy levels at consultation.

TOP TIP

Postural conditions

Examples of postural conditions the beauty therapist will be looking for are kyphosis, lordosis and scoliosis. The massage application will be modified for the postural condition.

"Retail sales are part of performing your services and should come naturally if you have completed your consultation. Look and listen to your guest and offer solutions in their homecare programme.

Zoe Crowley

Check for contra-indications at the consultation, and if present do not proceed with the service.

If in doubt as to the client's suitability for service the beauty therapist should first obtain a letter of approval from the client's doctor. It is important to find out about the lifestyle habits of the client. These include:

- *Occupation*. The client's occupation may be stressful or contribute to poor posture and muscle fatigue.
- *Family situation*. The client's domestic situation may affect their stress levels and limit their opportunities to take exercise or relax.
- *Dietary and fluid intake*. A nutritionally balanced diet is vital to the health of the body and the appearance of the skin. Lack of energy, skin allergies and disorders are, in part, the result of a poorly balanced diet. A healthy diet contains all the nutrients we need for health and growth. *Caffeine*, which is a stimulant, is found in tea, coffee and some fizzy drinks. Excessive amounts can interfere with digestion and block the absorption of vitamins and minerals. *Water* is important to avoid dehydration of the body and *at least* one litre of natural water should be drunk per day.
- *Alcohol*. Alcohol is a toxin (poison) and deprives the body of vitamin reserves, especially vitamins B and C. It also causes dehydration.
- *Hobbies and interests*. These leisure activities can be a form of relaxation and method to alleviate stress.
- *Exercise taken and regularity*. A lack of exercise leads to poor lymph and blood circulation and poor muscle tone, resulting in slack contours and weight gain due to inactivity. Lack of exercise also results in lethargy.
- *Smoking habits*. Smoking interferes with cell respiration and slows down the circulation. This makes it more difficult for nutrients to reach the skin cells and for waste products to be eliminated. The skin looks dull with a tendency towards open pores. Nicotine is a toxic substance.
- *Sleeping patterns*. Disturbed sleeping patterns are often a result of raised stress levels. Disturbed sleep can result in exhaustion, fatigue, irritability and poor concentration.

"Best practice for Indian head massage

- Prepare your room to help the client start to relax as soon as they enter.
- Don't think of this service as for the head only, it will benefit the whole body.
- Ensure the client is seated comfortably and positioned so you can reach the head, neck, shoulders and spine.
- Adapt the service to suit your client's individual needs.
- Ensure you offer the client the chance to relax and unwind in an appropriate area after the service has finished.

Zoe Crowley

Questioning the client on expectations and outcomes ensures that the client gains satisfaction from the service. Listen carefully to make sure you fully understand the client's service requirements. You will need to assess the client's skin type, hair and scalp condition in order to check client suitability for service, plan the service and select suitable service massage medium oils. The client will also require a postural check at the time of consultation. This is to assess whether the client has any postural conditions which the beauty therapist may advise exercise for, or whether the beauty therapist needs to adapt the massage service in any way for the comfort of the client. Postural assessment is discussed on pages 202–204.

Selecting massage oils

Suitable massage oils If using oils, organic oils are the most suitable oils when massaging the scalp. High in polyunsaturated fats, they are very soft and liquid at room temperature. They have healing benefits from their fatty acid, vitamin and nutrient content. They absorb easily through the skin, and have both an internal and external effect. Approximately 2–5 ml is required for the scalp massage, this will, of course, vary according to the length of the client's hair and condition of the scalp. The choice of oil depends on its texture, smell and specific properties. Popular oils are sesame, mustard, almond, olive and coconut.

HEALTH & SAFETY

Oil quantity

Avoid excessive use of oil which would hinder effective service application and during facial application could enter the eyes.

Massage oils

Name	*Plant*	*Use*
Sesame oil		This oil is high in minerals which nourish the skin and hair. Sesame oil has a high lecithin content (a fat-like substance) thought to relieve swelling and muscular pains. Sesame oil may irritate sensitive skin and scalps
Mustard oil		A strong-smelling oil which creates an intense heating, invigorating action. Popular for use in winter due to its warming action. The increase in body heat relieves pain, swellings and relaxes stiff muscles. The skin's pores open and a cleansing action is created. Not suitable on sensitive skin and scalps as it may cause irritation.
Almond oil		A light-textured oil, it is warm pressed and good to moisturise normal and dry skin and hair as it is high in unsaturated fatty acids (essential fats derived from food), protein and vitamins A, B, D and E.
Olive oil	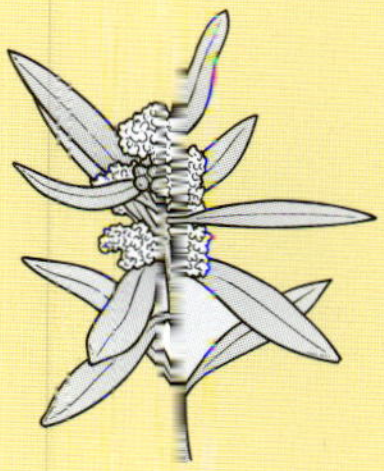	Cold pressed from olives and has an emollient, healing and nourishing effect. It has a thick consistency high in unsaturated fatty acids, suitable for excessively dry hair and skin. It also creates a heating action which helps to relieve pain, swellings and relax stiff muscles.

Name	*Plant*	*Use*
Coconut oil		A medium-to-light oil with skin and hair conditioning and emollient properties; particularly suitable for dry, brittle, chemically treated hair. Popular for use in summer as it induces a cooling action on the scalp.

ALWAYS REMEMBER

Olfactory nerve

The smell of the oil is picked up when inhaled by the olfactory nerve. The odour molecules disolve in the nasal mucus. The receptor cells cause a nerve impluse to the olfactory nerves. The smell can influence the behaviour of the person causing stimulation or relaxation.

ALWAYS REMEMBER

Frame size

Look at the client's frame size: this will guide you on how to adapt your massage.

Small frame

If the client has a small frame, avoid heavy pressure, especially over bony areas. However, pressure must be firm if that is required.

Large frame

If the client has a large frame, pressure will be firmer, especially over fatty areas.

With all clients, check their comfort with regard to the pressure you apply during the massage.

Benefits of Indian head massage

There are many general benefits of Indian head massage that address the symptoms of everyday working, including:

- headaches caused by stress and tension
- aches and pains caused by poor posture in the neck and shoulder area, e.g. long periods working on a computer
- eyestrain is relieved
- poor sleeping problems are improved

Indian head massage service should be adapted in application to meet the client's needs and physical characteristics obtained at the consultation.

Once the consultation is complete, the beauty therapist should ensure that all details are recorded accurately and that the client has signed her record card. This enables continuity of service and up-to-date tracking of the services received. An example of a typical record card is provided in this chapter.

ALWAYS REMEMBER

Accurately record your client's answers to necessary questions to be asked at consultation on the record card.

Record card for providing an Indian head massage

Date	Beauty therapist name	
Client name		Date of birth (Identifying client age group.)
Home address		Postcode
Email address	Landline phone number	Mobile phone number
Name of doctor	Doctor's address and phone number	
Related medical history (Conditions that may restrict or prohibit service application.)		
Are you taking any medication? (e.g. if taking medication to control blood pressure, Indian head massage will alter blood pressure temporarily.)		

CONTRA-INDICATIONS REQUIRING MEDICAL REFERRAL
(Preventing Indian head massage service application.)

- ☐ bacterial infection, e.g. impetigo
- ☐ viral infection, e.g. herpes simplex
- ☐ fungal infection, e.g. tinea unguium
- ☐ skin disorders, i.e. sebaceous cyst, eczema, acne vulgaris
- ☐ skin disease
- ☐ hair and scalp disorders
- ☐ high or low blood pressure
- ☐ recent head and neck injury
- ☐ severe bruising
- ☐ severe cuts and abrasions
- ☐ hair disorders
- ☐ medical conditions
- ☐ diabetes
- ☐ recent scar tissue
- ☐ dysfunction of the nervous system
- ☐ epilepsy
- ☐ during chemotherapy and radio therapy

SERVICE AREAS

- ☐ scalp ☐ head ☐ face
- ☐ chest ☐ neck ☐ shoulders
- ☐ upper back ☐ arms ☐ hands
- ☐ primary chakra areas

MASSAGE TECHNIQUE

- ☐ effleurage ☐ petrissage
- ☐ tapotement ☐ frictions
- ☐ vibrations ☐ pressure points

MASSAGE MEDIUM (IF USED)

- ☐ organic oil – type__________ ☐ cream

CONTRA-INDICATIONS THAT RESTRICT SERVICE
(Service may require adaptation.)

- ☐ cuts and abrasions ☐ bruising and swelling
- ☐ recent injuries to the service area
- ☐ medication ☐ mild eczema/psoriasis
- ☐ recent scar tissue (avoid area)
- ☐ undiagnosed lumps, bumps, swellings
- ☐ migraine ☐ allergies

LIFESTYLE

- ☐ occupation __________
- ☐ family situation __________
- ☐ dietary and fluid intake (including allergies) __________
- ☐ hobbies, interests, means of relaxation __________
- ☐ exercise habits __________
- ☐ smoking habits __________
- ☐ sleep patterns __________

PHYSICAL CHARACTERISTICS

- ☐ posture ☐ hair condition
- ☐ health ☐ scalp condition
- ☐ muscle tone ☐ age
- ☐ skin condition

OBJECTIVES OF SERVICE

- ☐ relaxation ☐ uplifting
- ☐ maintenance of health and well-being
- ☐ improvement of hair and scalp condition

EQUIPMENT AND MATERIALS

- ☐ towels ☐ comb
- ☐ spatulas ☐ protective covering
- ☐ consumables ☐ hair clip
- ☐ massage chair

Beauty therapist signature (for reference)

Client signature (confirmation of details)

Record card for providing an Indian head massage (continued)

SERVICE ADVICE

Indian head massage service – *this service will take 45 minutes.*

SERVICE PLAN

Record relevant details of your service and advice provided for future reference. Ensure the client's records are up-to-date, accurate and fully completed following service. Non-compliance may invalidate insurance.

DURING

- explain choice of massage medium and its benefits
- explain the service procedure at each stage of the massage to meet the service needs
- explain how the massage products should be applied and removed for home use
- note any adverse reaction, if any occur, and action taken

AFTER

- record the areas treated
- record any modification to service application that has occurred
- record what products have been used in the service as appropriate
- provide postural advice
- provide hair and scalp advice
- provide advice to follow immediately following service, to include suitable rest period following service, general advice regarding food and drink intake, avoidance of stimulants
- recommended time intervals between services
- discuss the benefits of continuous services
- record the effectiveness of service
- record any samples provided (review their success at the next appointment)

RETAIL OPPORTUNITIES

- provide guidance on progression of the service plan for future appointments
- advice regarding products that would be suitable for home use and how to gain maximum benefit from their use to care for the skin and continue the service benefits
- recommendations for further services including heat services and body massage services
- advice of further products or services that you have recommended that the client may or may not have received before.
- note any purchase made by the client

EVALUATION

- record comments on the client's satisfaction with the service
- record if the service objectives were achieved, e.g. relaxation, if not, explore the reasons why not
- record how you will progress the service to maintain and advance the service results in the future

HEALTH AND SAFETY

- advise on avoidance of activities that may cause a contra-action, including strenuous exercises and stimulants such as caffeine and alcohol
- advise on appropriate necessary action to be taken in the event of an unwanted reaction (an allergy to the oil used, flu-like symptoms including raised temperature, aching muscles, caused by release of toxins)

SERVICE MODIFICATION

Examples of massage service modification include:

- altering the pressure or choice of manipulations during massage to suit the client's skin and muscle tone
- adapting the massage to achieve an effect of relaxation, stimulation
- altering the choice of massage medium to treat the skin/hair condition

Contra-actions

A contra-action is an unwanted reaction to Indian head massage service which may occur during or following the service. Contra-actions to the service should be discussed at the consultation so the client would recognise symptoms if experienced.

Contra-actions occur mainly as a result of the increased circulation of waste products following the massage. Monitor the contra-action to confirm client suitability for further service.

These might include:

- sickness, caused by increased circulation of waste products transported in the lymphatic system. This is often termed a 'healing crisis'
- headache, caused by the release of toxins
- fainting caused by dilation of the blood capillaries, altering blood pressure levels
- tiredness caused by release of toxins and increased energy channels
- skin reactions, such as an allergy to the massage oil
- heightened emotional state including tearfulness
- flu-like symptoms, including raised temperature
- aching muscles, caused by the release of toxins

If the client suffers any contra-action, you must assist the client before letting them leave the salon:

- Ensure the client can breathe properly and that the room is well ventilated.
- Offer the client a glass of water if they feel sick.
- Apply a cold compress if a skin reaction occurs.
- Advise the client to seek medical advice if the symptoms persist.

Allow time and invite the client to ask any questions before service commences. Be honest and concise in your answers. Confirm the objectives of the service.

Preparation of the client

Take the client through to the service area. The client may need to remove any outdoor clothing such as a coat or jacket. Footwear should be removed and the feet placed flat on the floor. Clients generally receive Indian head massage through their outdoor clothing, but bulky clothing which may restrict service application should be removed. Shirt or blouse collars should be loosened to allow access to the neck region. If oil is to be used for the massage, upper clothing should be removed and the client provided with a towel. Any jewellery in the area of massage application should be removed – this includes earrings, necklaces, bracelets and watches. Other accessories such as glasses should also be removed. False hairpieces will also need to be removed before service. If you are using screens, ensure that these are fully closed to maintain the client's privacy. This will enable the client to feel more comfortable and relaxed – essential if they are to gain service benefit. Seat the client on a low-backed massage chair facing the service couch. If the client is in a wheelchair it may be possible to treat them while sitting in their chair, which means minimum disturbance to

HEALTH & SAFETY

If a contra-action occurs during the service discontinue and provide appropriate action and advice.

HEALTH & SAFETY

Pregnancy

It is best not to treat a client in the early stages of pregnancy, as the side-effects may include feelings of nausea. This is a common symptom in the early stages of pregnancy and could cause a client to feel worse.

> While performing Indian head massage and all services it is very important to remember the medical contra-indications and the health and safety aspects at all times.
>
> Make sure you are aware of your spa or salon's operating procedures and follow them with every service to continually provide safe services to a high standard.
>
> **Zoe Crowley**

TOP TIP

Hair products

If the client has styling/setting products on the hair, brush through as part of client preparation to ensure continuity of the service application and avoid client discomfort.

TOP TIP

Relaxation practices

Audio tapes have been manufactured for the purpose of relaxation and these make an excellent accompaniment to create a calm environment in the service room.

Aromatherapy burners can be used to create a specific atmosphere in the service room. Essential oils which create different therapeutic effects when inhaled can be burnt.

Crystals may be placed in the work area.

Selected for their therapeutic properties, crystals mined for thousands of years have their own energy and are used to help balance the body's energy channels.

the client. Ensure the client is seated comfortably; correct positioning opens up the central channel energy flow.

Before the Indian head massage is applied, the face may be cleansed to remove facial make-up using suitable facial products for their skin type using your regular cleansing routine.

After preparing the client, and before touching the skin, wash your hands again.

If your client is having a service using oils you will need to select and warm a suitable oil to use.

Place a towel over their shoulders if applying a massage oil medium.

Outcome 3: Perform Indian head massage

Learn how to perform Indian head massage service to meet your client's needs by:

1. Providing suitable support and cushioning to specific areas of the body during the service if necessary.
2. Adapting your massage techniques, sequence and use of massage medium to meet the client's **physical characteristics** and **service area(s)**.
3. Effectively varying the depth, rhythm and pressure of massage movements to meet **service objectives**, **service area(s)** and client's **physical characteristics** and preferences.
4. Ensuring that correct breathing techniques are coordinated with that of the client.
5. Ensuring the application and use of massage medium minimizes waste, when used.
6. Taking appropriate and prompt remedial action if contra-actions or discomfort occur during the course of service.
7. Allowing the client sufficient post-service recovery time.
8. Ensuring the finished result is to the client's satisfaction and meets the agreed **service objectives**.

Massage stance

When performing the Indian head massage it is important to position yourself correctly. This will prevent pain and fatigue while working. Working positions are *walk standing* and *stride standing*.

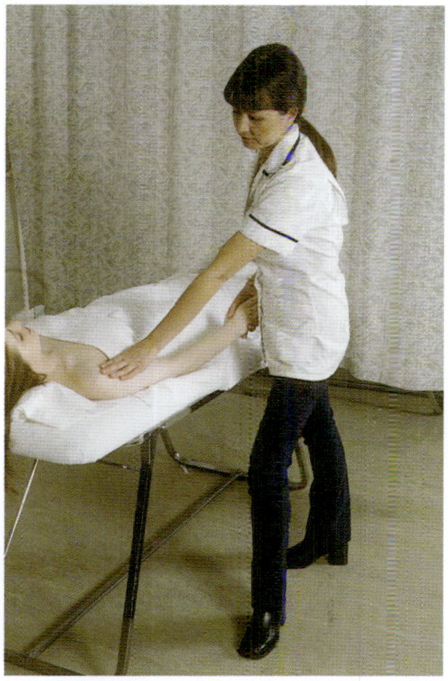

Walk standing

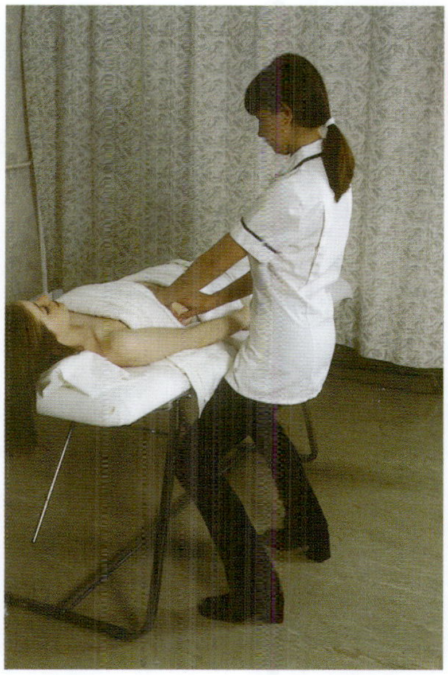

Stride standing

TOP TIP

Tension

Tension accumulates in the head, neck and shoulders. Through massage, pressure in these areas will be released.

HEALTH & SAFETY

Failure to adopt the correct stance will result in the beauty therapist not being able to work a full day and eventually serious neck or back injury could occur.

Walk standing The beauty therapist stands with one foot in front of the other. This enables the beauty therapist to work longitudinally (along the length) of the body.

Stride standing The beauty therapist works transversely (across) the body. This is the most common position when performing Indian head massage services.

COURSEMATE

For a video on Indian head massage, please visit this book's accompanying CourseMate.

Step-by-step: Grounding or levelling

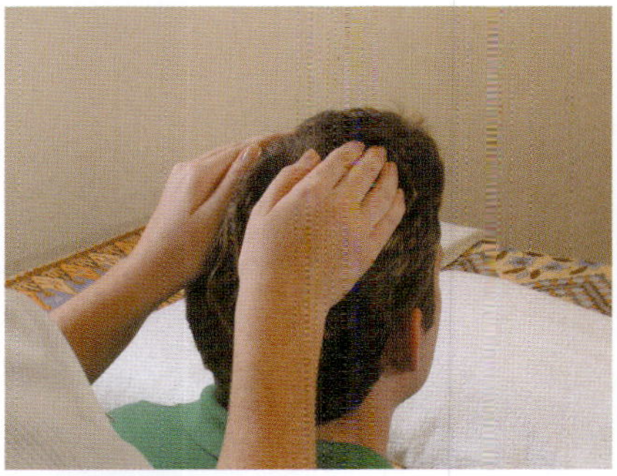

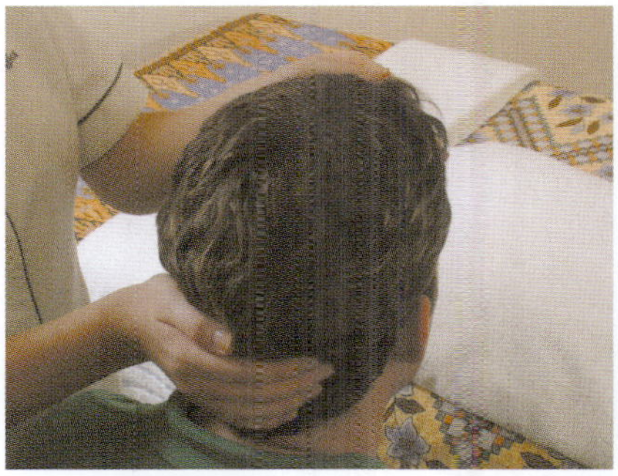

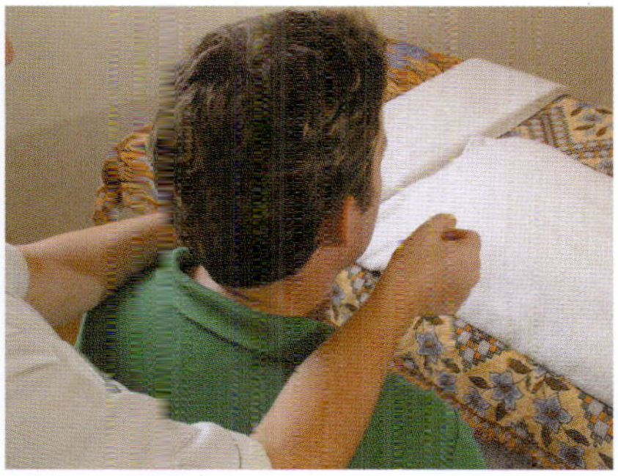

1 With both feet placed firmly on the floor, place the hands on the client's shoulders. Ask the client to close his eyes and relax. At this point outside energies pass through your body to the client.

2 Place your hands on the client's scalp on the crown area, the crown chakra.

3 Then place the hands, one on the forehead and one on the occiput, hold this position for 2 minutes.

4 Rest your forearms on the client's shoulders – ask the client to breathe in and then breathe out. This will cause the client to relax and feel calmer. As the client breathes out apply gentle pressure with your forearms onto the client's shoulders. If oil is to be used when performing the scalp massage this is applied now, selected according to the service effect required. The hair is gently parted and oil is applied to the partings.

Step-by-step: Shoulders and back

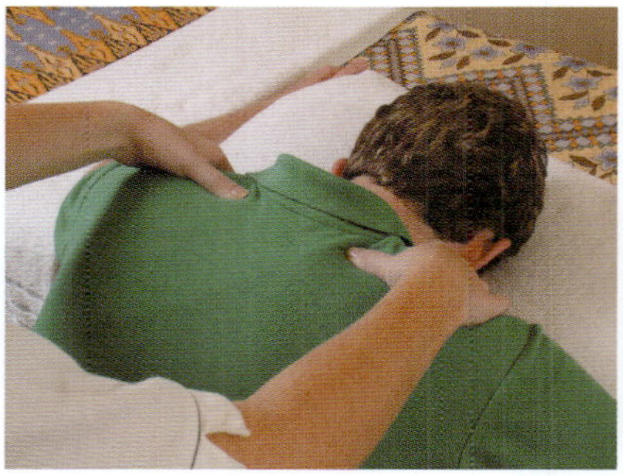

5 Ask the client to place their head forwards supported by pillows or towels.

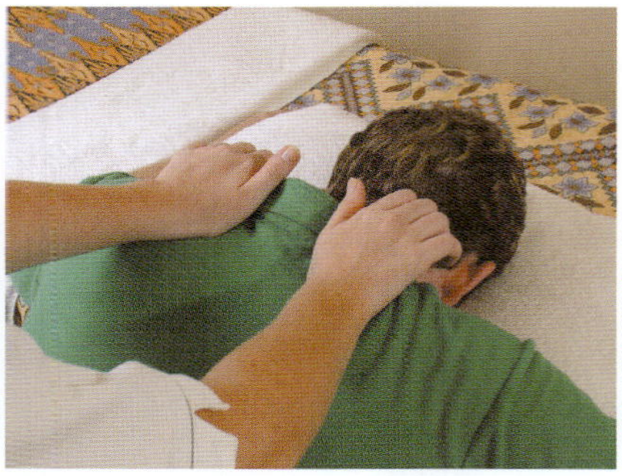

6 Frictions are applied over the tops of the shoulder area, small circular movements are applied with the thumbs to the muscle fibres of the trapezius.

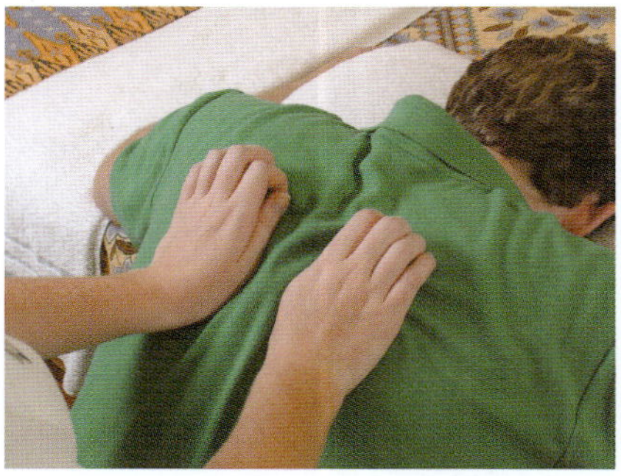

7 Kneading is applied to the shoulder and back, the heels of the hand apply pressure gently in a rotary movement along the trapezius and either side of the spine.

BEST PRACTICE

Checking body language for effectiveness

The client posture should become more relaxed during application of the service. The shoulders should drop and breathing should become deeper, allowing energy to flow more freely through the body.

Encourage the client to relax if they appear stiff.

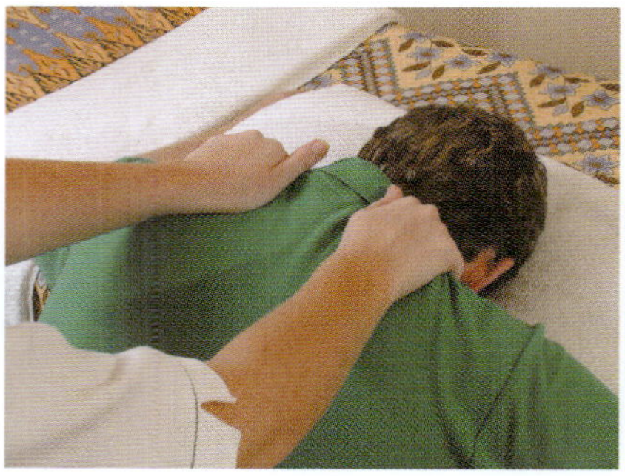

8 Picking up is applied along the trapezius; the muscle is lifted and gently squeezed using the whole hand.

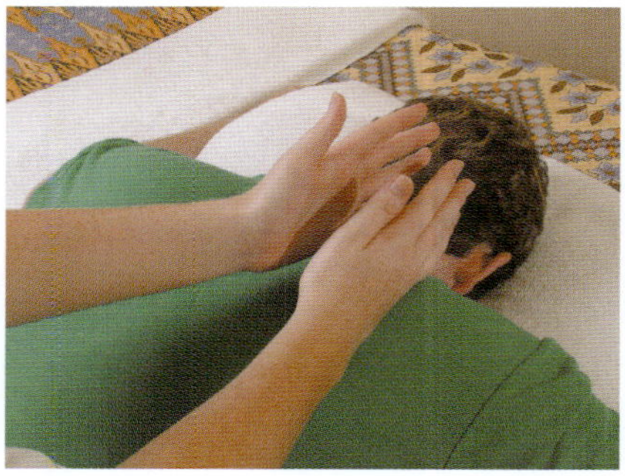

9 Hacking is applied across the top of the shoulders.

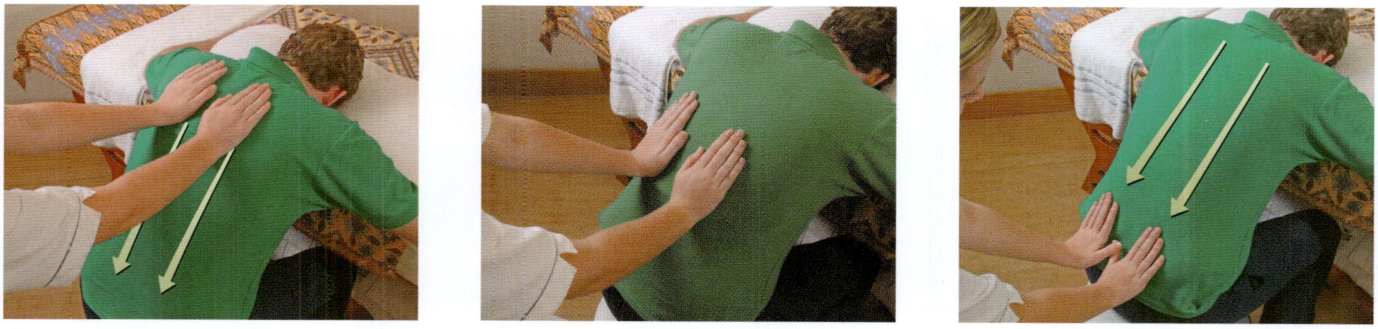

10 Lurching is applied down either side of the spine. The hands are placed flat on the shoulders and then swiftly drawn down the body, either side of the spine, flicking off the body at the base of the spine.

Step-by-step: Neck

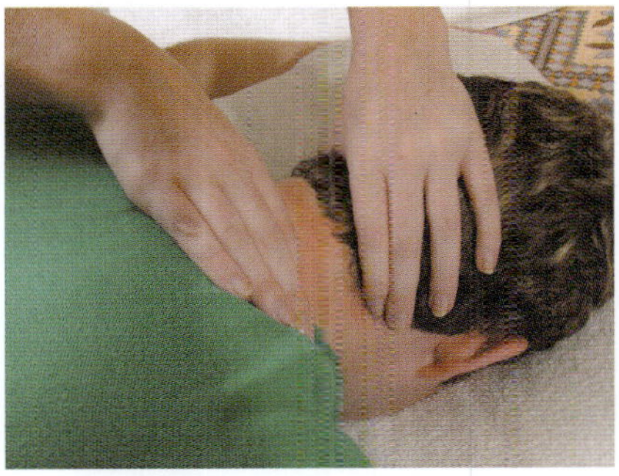
© CENGAGE LEARNING LTD

11 Pick up the muscle and skin at the back of the neck. Gently lift the tissue with each hand alternately.

12 Apply frictions under the occiput. Using both thumbs apply gentle pressure in a circular movement.

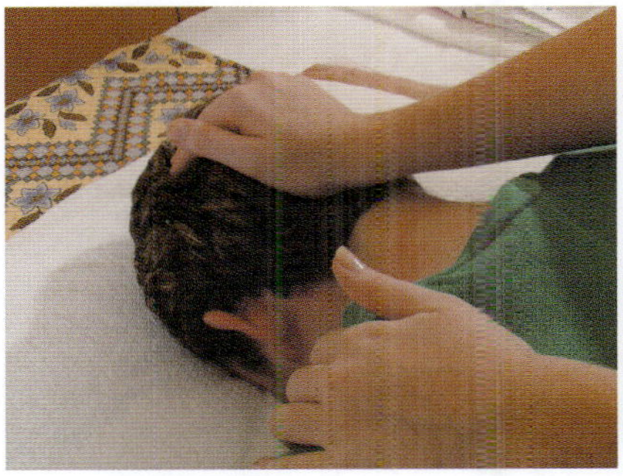
© CENGAGE LEARNING LTD

13 Apply petrissage under the occiput. Using the heel of one hand, apply a gentle circular pressure.

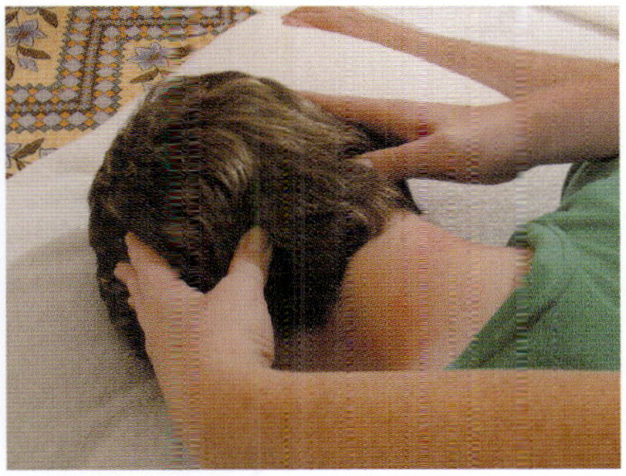
© CENGAGE LEARNING LTD

14 Apply pressure points with both thumbs in a triangular movement under the occiput.

Step-by-step: Arms

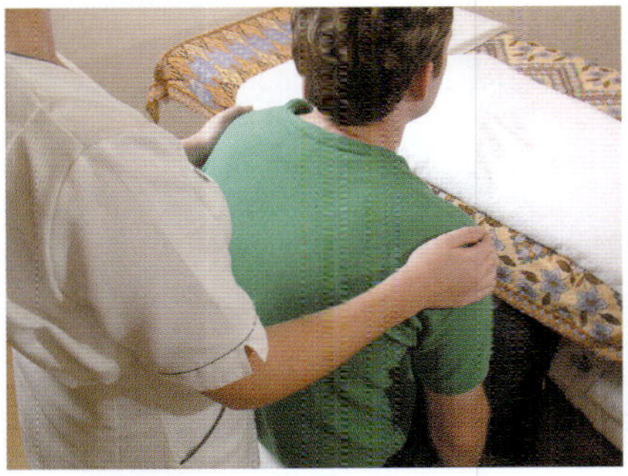
© CENGAGE LEARNING LTD

15 Ask the client to slowly lift their head.

16 Place your hands flat on the upper shoulders. Swiftly draw the hands down the length of the upper arm and flick off hands at the client's elbow.

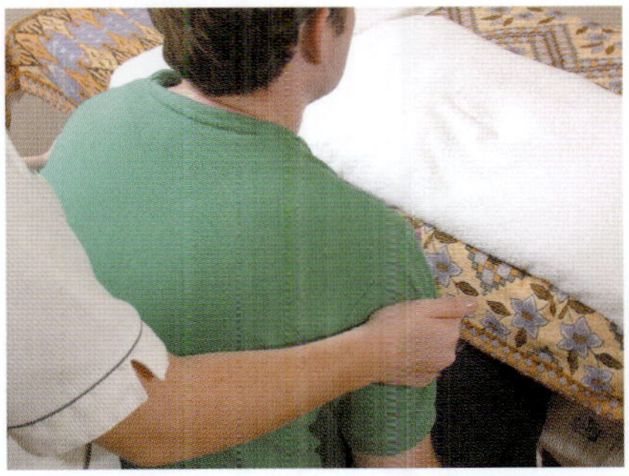
© CENGAGE LEARNING LTD

17 Squeezing. Lifting and release movement to the upper arm.

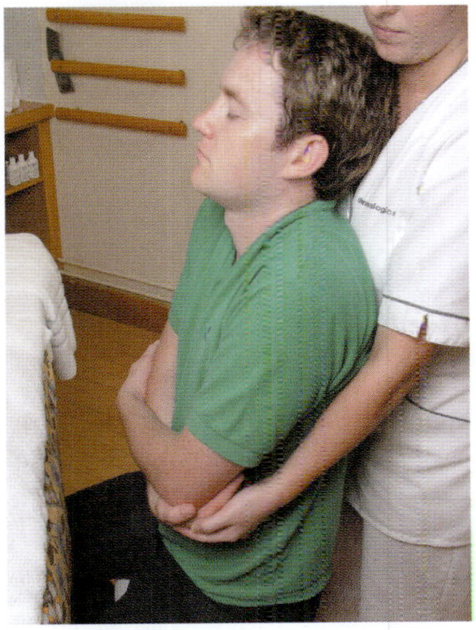

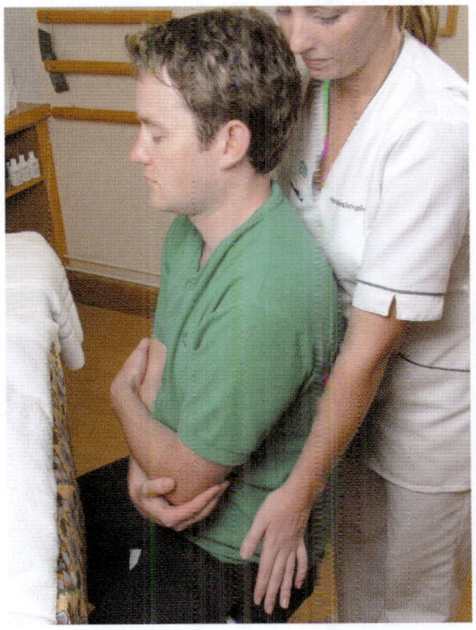
© CENGAGE LEARNING LTD

18 Place your hands firmly on the client's upper arms. Ask the client to fold their arms in front of them, ask them to breathe in deeply, gently apply a lifting pressure as they do this. Ask the client to breathe out, remove your hands from their supporting position and the client's body will gently drop.

HEALTH & SAFETY

Posture

It is important to ensure that the client and beauty therapist are correctly positioned when performing the massage. This will prevent strain and fatigue to the beauty therapist. Failure to maintain good posture may lead to serious back injury.

If the client is uncomfortable, they will be unable to relax and will not gain maximum benefit from the service. Check on client comfort during service application.

Step-by-step: Scalp

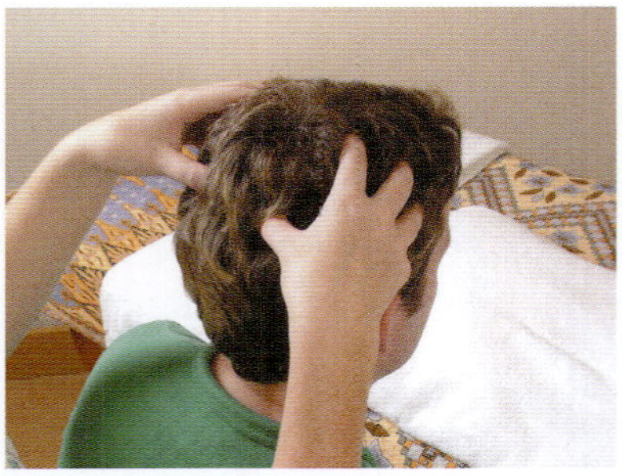

19 Apply effleurage strokes to the scalp. Place each hand alternately on the hair line and stroke hand upwards, covering the whole scalp.

20 Apply frictions to the scalp (shown) – using the pads of the fingers to apply small circular movements.

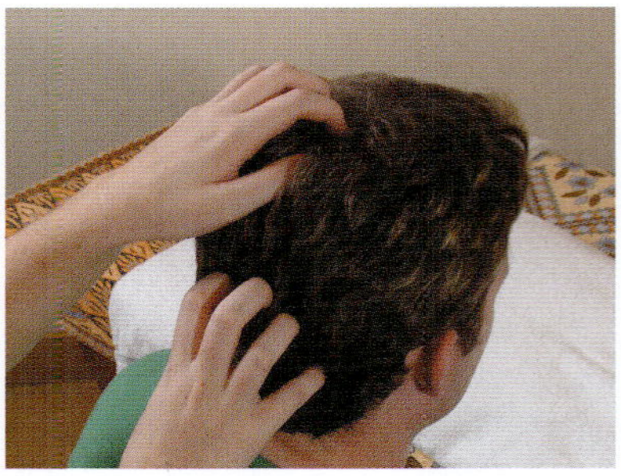

21 Apply finger stroking, place the fingertips on the hairline and draw them in a combing action through the hair.

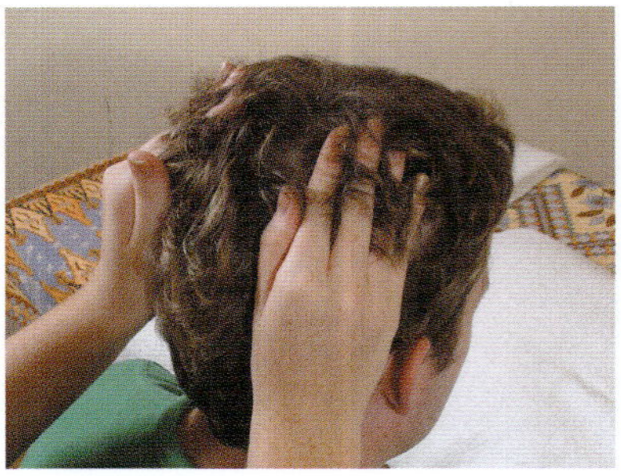

22 Apply vibrations: gently grasp the hair and pull in a vibrating manner (shown).

23 Apply hacking using both hands to cover both sides of the head.

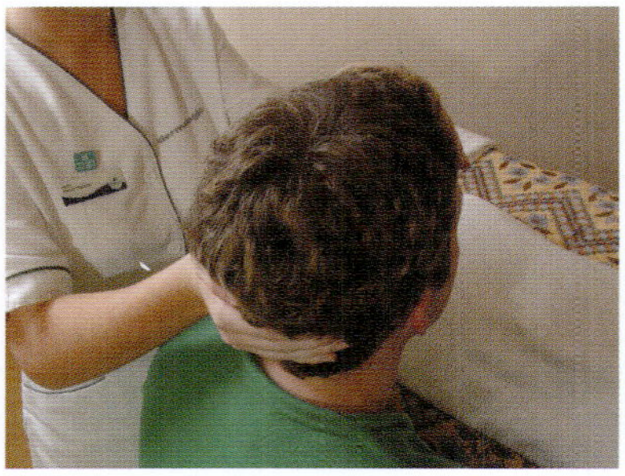

24 Using flat hands, place one hand on the forehead and the other over the occipital bone and gently lift the head. Move the hands, place one hand over the corner of the forehead the other over the corner of the back of the skull and lift. Repeat on remaining corners of the head.

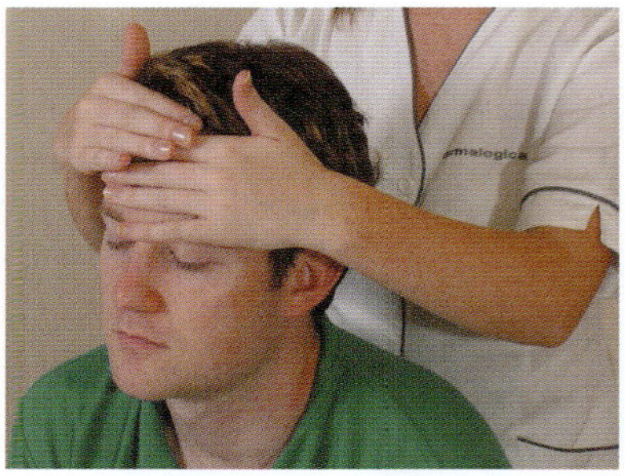

25 Stroke over the forehead using alternate hands.

26 Finally, apply effleurage to the scalp. Wash your hands following scalp massage.

TOP TIP

Scalp mobility

When working on the scalp you will be able to assess the client's state of tension: how does the scalp feel – mobile or tight? If tight, the client is tense. Manipulation of the scalp will relieve tension by improving blood circulation and soothing the nerves.

Step-by-step: Pressure points

27 Place a folded or rolled towel behind the client's head and ask the client to lean their head against your body. Apply pressure points: using the index and middle finger apply firm pressure at intervals moving upwards from the top of the nose to the forehead. Move outwards about 12 mm and work downwards to the eyebrows.

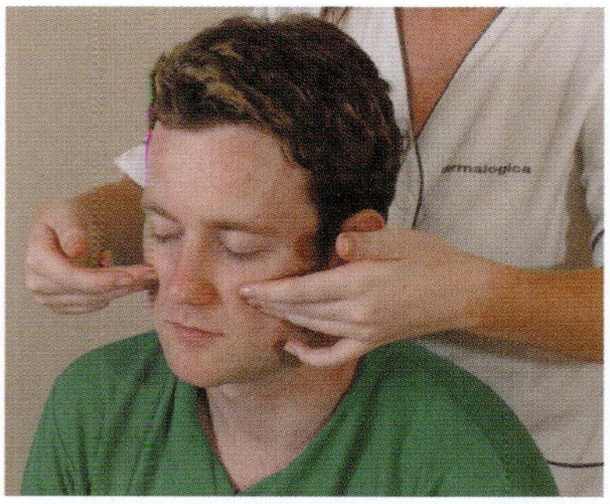

28 Apply pressure points along the zygomatic (cheek) bone. Work from either side of the nose out to the anterior auricular lymph nodes.

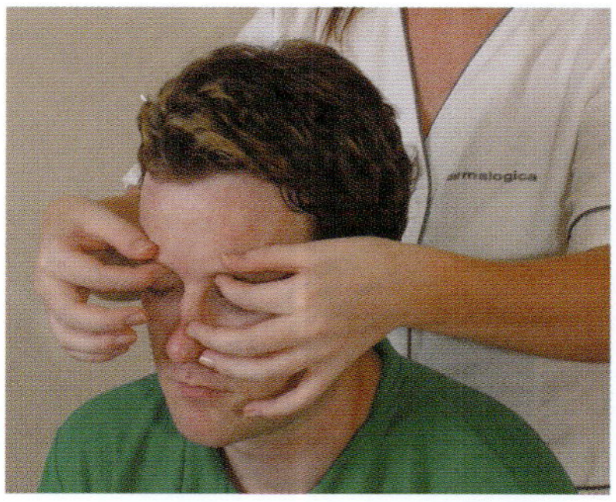

29 Gently pinch the length of both eyebrows simultaneously, using the finger and thumb of each hand. Move to the lower eye socket and apply pressure with the index finger from the outer eye in towards the nose and repeat.

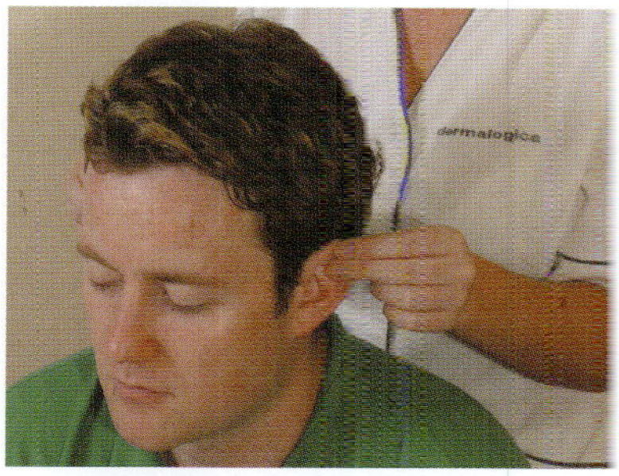

30 Gently hold the tip of each ear using the finger pads and simultaneously apply a pinching and rolling movement to cover the outside of each ear.

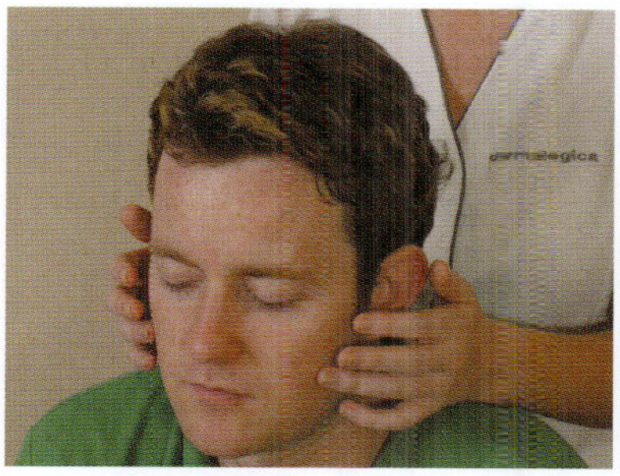

31 Using the pads of the fingers apply a light tapping movement to cover the face from jaw to forehead.

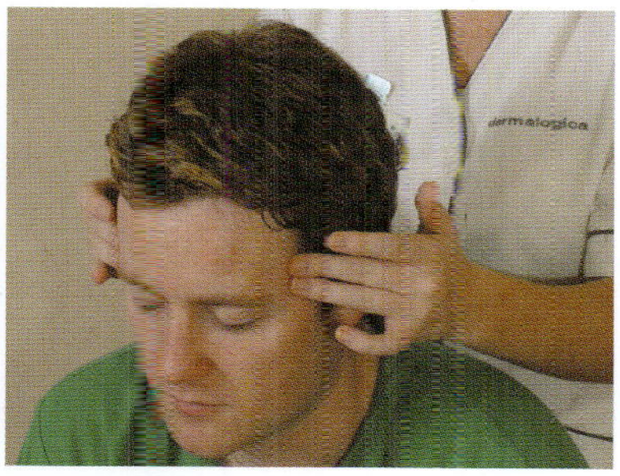

32 Apply circular pressure to the temples simultaneously using the fingertips.

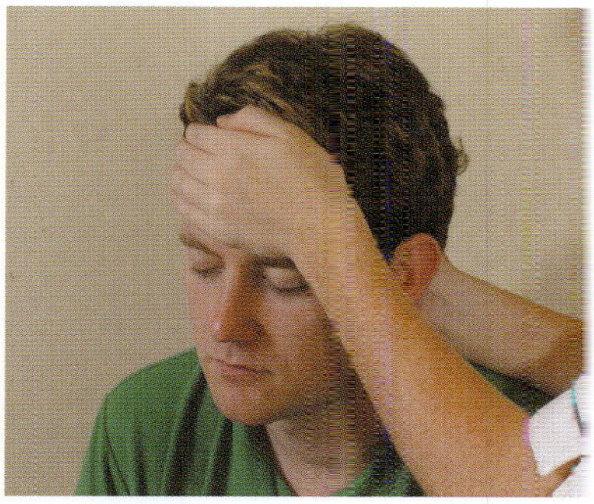

33 Finally, place the hands, one on the forehead and one on the occiput, and hold this position briefly. This will indicate to the client that the massage has finished.

34 Wash your hands. Remove excess oil if used using damp warm towelling mitts or sponges and warm water.

TOP TIP

Application of pressure point to the zygomatic (cheek)-bone will relieve blocked sinuses.

Adapting the massage

Relaxing massage: avoid stimulating movements and incorporate more effleurage, light petrissage movements. Pressure should be firm and rhythm slower. Concentrate massage application on areas of tension. Remember these areas may feel uncomfortable initially until the muscle warms and relaxation is induced.

Tight or contracted muscles: avoid excessive use of percussion movements. Slow, rhythmical movements should be used to stretch the muscles. Again, concentrate massage application on these areas and recommend the client has a regular massage service to gain cumulative benefits.

Slack muscles: stimulating percussion massage movements should be used to help to tone and firm the area being treated.

Massage for excess weight: incorporate stimulating movements such as hacking over fatty areas, to help mobilize adipose (fatty) tissue.

Massage for males: muscle bulk tends to be larger and firmer. The skin is thicker and generally there is less fatty tissue. The massage usually needs to be firmer.

ALWAYS REMEMBER

Not all clients like their ears touched, although it is very relaxing – do not include if this is the case and make a note on the client's record card.

ALWAYS REMEMBER

Faults during massage

- Incorrect pressure applied. If it is too light or too heavy the client will not feel the benefits.
- Avoid placing excessive pressure on top of the client's head: this can cause discomfort to the head and neck.
- Inconsistent massage movements will not relax the client and the massage will not flow.
- Ensure the client is appropriately positioned. This prevents discomfort to yourself and the client.

Outcome 4: Provide aftercare advice

Learn how to provide aftercare advice which supports and meets the needs of your clients by:

1. Giving **advice** and recommendations accurately and constructively.
2. Giving your clients suitable **advice** specific to their individual needs.

BEST PRACTICE

Drink and rest

Offer the client a glass of water following the service to rehydrate and allow a suitable rest period to avoid feelings of dizziness caused by changes to blood pressure.

ACTIVITY

Massage techniques for client application

As part of the client's homecare programme, simple massage techniques could be taught.

Think of three simple self-massage techniques that the client could use at home.

These may also be applied to relax the face during the day if working in an office, looking at the computer screen for long periods.

Before the client gets up, encourage them to rest for a few minutes to allow the blood circulation to return to normal. A deep relaxation massage can leave the client feeling light-headed. Sudden movement may result in a light-headed feeling as the brain is temporarily starved of blood; they may even faint. You may have a relaxation room where the client could go following service. You can also assist the client as they stand.

A warm towel can be placed over the clients shoulders immediately following service application to further induce relaxation.

Excess oil can be removed from the skin with hot towels.

As the client's circulation returns to normal, the blood vessels will constrict.

As the body rids itself of toxins and excess fluids there will be an increased need to urinate.

While resting, use the time to discuss with the client suitable aftercare and home care to complement the massage. The client will probably feel extremely relaxed at this point.

If the massage was for relaxation, you might give advice on relaxing bath products and massage techniques that could be used at home. Recommend the client increases their water intake to help detoxification and encourage good eating habits.

Remind the client about the benefits of deep breathing. Encourage them to practise breathing exercises at home, and at any time of anxiety.

Provide hair and scalp care advice, including the avoidance of excessive chemical hair services, the importance of hair protection when exposed to UV, and the application of specialized hair/scalp service products. If the service was for alopecia to stimulate new hair growth, clients should massage their scalp at home between services.

For the following 24 hours avoid:

- stimulants such as caffeine or alcohol
- heavy or highly spiced meals
- strenuous exercise

For several hours:

- avoid shampooing the hair, especially if oils have been used to maximize service effects

Warn the client of post-service reactions including:

- sickness
- emotional anxiety
- headaches
- aching muscles
- increase in production of mucus from the nasal passages

These reactions will normally subside within 24 hours.

Ask the client how they feel to establish if the service has achieved the outcome agreed at consultation. Explain the benefits of regular service to achieve maximum benefit.

You should complete the client's record card fully so that continuation of the service can be tracked and any adverse reactions noted for future reference.

ASSESSMENT OF KNOWLEDGE AND UNDERSTANDING

FUNCTIONAL SKILLS

Having covered the learning objectives for provide Indian head massage treatments–test what you need to know and understand by answering the following short questions below.

The information covers:

- organizational and legal requirements
- how to work safely and effectively when providing Indian head massage
- client consultation
- preparation for service
- anatomy and physiology
- contra-indications and contra-actions
- Indian head massage mediums
- service specific knowledge
- aftercare advice for clients

Anatomy and physiology questions required for this unit are found on pages 97–99.

Organizational and legal requirements

1. What responsibility does the beauty therapist have to comply with Control of Substances Hazardous to Health (COSHH) regulations?
2. Why is positioning of the client an important consideration when performing Indian head massage service?
3. Where should information relating to the client's consultation, service plan and Indian head massage service be stored following service?
4. Why is it important to complete the service in a commercially viable time?

How to work safely and effectively when providing Indian head massage

1. How should the service environment be prepared to ensure client comfort and maximum benefit from the service? Consider temperature, lighting, ventilation, colour, smells and sound.
2. How can you ensure the client's modesty, privacy and comfort during the service. Give an example for each.
3. How can you avoid developing repetitive strain injury when delivering an Indian head massage service. Give **three** examples of how this can be avoided when preparing for and delivering the service.
4. Give **five** examples how an aseptic environment be created when providing an Indian head massage service.

Client consultation

1. How should the client be greeted for service? Why is this important?
2. To perform an effective consultation you need the client to feel confident about providing you with positive, honest answers to your questions.
   You should have good:
   a communication skills
   b questioning techniques
   c listening skills
   d answering techniques

   Give examples of what you understand by good skills and techniques for each of the above.
3. What details are required on your client's record card?
4. Why is it important to discuss the client's lifestyle?
5. Give **four** physiological/psychological benefits that the client can expect from the service.

Preparation for the service

1. When preparing the service plan, how is the massage oil selected for the client?
2. What is the importance of self-preparation when delivering Indian head massage?
3. How should the client be positioned to gain maximum benefit from the Indian head massage service?
4. How should the client be prepared to receive Indian head massage?

Anatomy and physiology

1. How is the lymphatic system affected during an Indian head massage service? Name **three** lymph nodes that can be found in the area where Indian head massage is applied.

2 State **three** benefits to the skin that occur as a result of an Indian head massage service.

3 Name **two** muscles of the:
- face
- neck
- back
- arm

4 Name the bones that form the cranium (there are eight).

5 Briefly describe the function of the central nervous system and autonomic nervous system.

6 What is good posture? Name **three** postural faults and how they can be recognized.

Contra-indications and contra-actions

1 Name **three** contra-indications identified at the consultation which would prevent a service being carried out.

2 Name **three** contra-indications that may restrict service application.

3 When would you need to refer a client to their general practitioner before service could be given?

4 If a client became ill during the service what action should be taken?

Indian head massage mediums

1 How should Indian head massage mediums be stored and why?

2 What checks should be made at consultation to ensure the oil selected is safe to use?

3 Oils may be used as a massage medium for Indian head massage. Name **four** oils that you could use for Indian head massage, giving a brief description of each.

Service-specific knowledge

1 Name the main massage techniques performed with Indian head massage and their effect.

2 Name the **three** primary chakra areas treated when performing Indian head massage.

3 How can the massage service be adapted to achieve different effects?

4 How should the client be advised to breathe to induce relaxation?

5 What should be checked with the client during the service application?

6 Why is it important to observe body language during the service?

7 What should be offered to the client at conclusion of the service?

8 What is the suitable rest period following Indian head massage? Why is this necessary?

Aftercare advice for clients

1 Why is it important to gain feedback from the client and give relevant advice to them following the service?

2 What is a healing crisis? What reactions should you advise the client they may experience from a healing crisis?

3 Why is it important to record any contra-action either during or following the service on the client record card?

4 After the Indian head massage the client should be given advice to follow to ensure that they gain maximum benefit from the service. Discuss the advice to be given.

5 What recommendations to lifestyle habits would enable them to continue the benefits from the service?

6 How often would you recommend a client receive Indian head massage service?

12 Massage using pre-blended aromatherapy oils

ISTOCK/© GEORGINA PALMER

Learning Objectives

This chapter covers the **Carry out massage using pre-blended aromatherapy oils** unit.

This unit is all about how to provide the massage service using pre-blended aromatherapy oils. The massage is applied to the face, head and body providing both a physiological and psychological effect. Application is modified to achieve the client's service objectives identified at consultation. Pre-blended aromatherapy oils are used to enhance the service results.

There are **four** learning outcomes which you must achieve competently:

1 **Maintain safe and effective methods of working when providing massage when using pre-blended oils.**

2 **Consult, plan and prepare for services with aromatherapy clients.**

3 **Massage the body using pre-blended aromatherapy oils.**

4 **Provide aftercare advice.**

For each unit your assessor will observe you on **at least four separate occasions each involving different clients**, which must include **two full-body massage** services incorporating the **face**.

From the **range** statements, you must show that you have:

- used all **consultation techniques**
- dealt with all the client's **physical characteristics**

(continued on the next page)

KATIE WHITEHOUSE

ROLE MODEL

Katie Whitehouse

Director of Vital Touch Ltd and Complementary Therapist: Sports and Holistic Massage, Aromatherapy, Pregnancy Massage & Reflexology

"I am a Founder Director of Vital Touch Ltd. We are based in Devon where we make gorgeous organic skincare and aromatherapy products which are sold to beauty therapists, spas and retail outlets nationwide and abroad. Our passion is positive touch and our mission is to promote the benefits of this through the use of our natural products and massage guides.

I have been a practising Massage Therapist, Aromatherapist and Reflexologist for 20 years. I have taught massage, sports massage, anatomy and physiology in many colleges in the UK and currently run courses specializing in training beauty therapists to be confident in massaging pregnant clients.

I am also involved in trainings for midwives, doulas and antenatal teachers – enabling fathers-to-be to connect with their partner and unborn baby through simple touch and massage.

Currently Vice Chair of the APNT (Association of Physical and Natural Therapists) I am also an assessor for the Association. I have also been involved with the Aromatherapy Consortium – I was Secretary for the Research and Scientific Subcommittee.

(continued)

- dealt with **at least one** of the **necessary actions** where a contra-action, contra-indication or service modification occurs
- met all **service objectives**
- used all **massage techniques**
- covered all **service areas**
- provided all types of relevant aftercare advice

However you must prove that you have the necessary knowledge, understanding and skills to be able to perform competently across the range.

When providing massage using pre-blended aromatherapy oils it is important to use the skills you have learnt in the following units:

Monitoring safe work operations.

Promotional activities.

Aromatherapy derived services and products are is an important attribute of spa services

Essential anatomy and physiology knowledge requirements for massage using pre-blended oils are identified on the checklist in Chapter 2, pages 12 and 13. This chapter also discusses anatomy and physiology specific to this unit.

Introduction

The principle of this unit uses the psychological and physiological benefits of the clinical service aromatherapy. To assist your understanding on the benefits of essential oils and their application, additional background information is provided to that required for your competence in this unit. Remember to only carry out services within your level of occupational expertise and competence.

Aromatherapy could be defined as the use of aromas (or smells) for their ability to bring about feelings of well-being. Aromatherapy massage has been used for thousands of years by people from many different cultures across the world. In Babylon, essential oils were used to perfume building materials for temples. Egyptians used oils for cleansing and embalming. Essential oils and the use of aromatic substances are mentioned in many historical texts and scriptures which allows their historical uses to be dated from as early as 2000 BC.

In today's fast-paced society, stress is a major contributing factor in many diseases and disorders such as heart disease, high blood pressure and tension, and many people are looking to alternative methods to help them to achieve a better quality of life. The beauty therapist plays a major role here – using massage with pre-blended aromatherapy oils to help reduce the symptoms of modern-day living.

ALWAYS REMEMBER

Massage using pre-blended aromatherapy oils is one of the many complementary and holistic therapies available to study and practice in professionally.

Essential oils and carrier oils

TOP TIP

You can progress your skills in this area by studying aromatherapy where you will develop the competence to select and blend oils from concentrated plant essences yourself to meet the client's service requirements both psychologically and physiologically. You could practice as a clinical aromatherapist when qualified.

Essential oils

Essential oils are the aromatic substances in the **pre-blended oils** used in aromatherapy massage. They have an infinite range of aromas and also come in a variety of colours including yellow, green, brown, blue and red. Being extracted from the many parts of plants, including flowers, seeds, roots, fruits and bark, these organic compounds have many uses.

Essential oils are made up largely of three elements: **carbon**, **hydrogen** and **oxygen**. The molecular structure of essential oils is relatively small, and this explains why they are able to penetrate the skin and enter the bloodstream. Their fat solubility also helps them to penetrate more easily. Although the individual components of an oil are relatively simple in structure, an oil can be made up of hundreds of components, some of them being present in very small amounts. It may be these trace components of a natural oil which have the therapeutic effect; these may not be present in a synthetic oil, which is why chemically reproduced or synthetic oils may have the same smell as the natural oil but not the same therapeutic properties. It is also said that naturally occurring oils have a 'life force' that cannot chemically be reproduced.

Essential oils have only a simple molecular structure, yet the active constituents which make up each oil are complex. The complexity of these active constituents gives the oils their own distinctive aromas and therapeutic qualities. The active constituents work **synergistically**, that is, they are more powerful when combined than if each were used separately.

Essential oils are not only used in massage, in fact of all the essential oils produced commercially, only a tiny percentage is actually used in holistic/complementary therapy. The majority of the oils are used in food flavourings, with the remainder being used in perfumes and the pharmaceutical industry.

It is important to know the Latin names of the plants used in aromatherapy to ensure that services are both safe and effective. There are many plants with similar names but very different effects. Knowing the different names can also help you to identify an oil's quality. The best rose oil usually comes from Bulgaria and is commonly known as Rose Bulgar (*Rosa damascena*) made from the damask rose.

Some essential oils may sound similar but come from very different plant families and will have very different therapeutic effects. For example, lemon oil (*Citrus limon*) and lemongrass (*Cymbopogon citrates*) are quite different! Like wine, the quality of harvest will depend on the weather and other factors, so essential oil qualities and prices will vary from year to year.

TISSERAND AROMATHERAPY

Essential oils are sourced from highly aromatic oils found in natural plants, for example lavender

Properties of essential oils

All essential oils have the same basic properties that identify them as an essential oil. These are that they:

- do not mix with water
- mix with alcohol
- mix with mineral oil
- mix with vegetable oil
- are volatile and evaporate
- have an aroma
- are not greasy

All essential oils as stated are volatile, but their evaporation rates vary. These evaporation rates can be used to group certain types of essential oils together. Oils with rapid evaporation rates are known as **top notes**. Oils with moderate evaporation rates are known as **middle notes** and those with very slow rates of evaporation are known as **base notes**.

Top notes Top notes have the highest evaporation rates of all essential oils. They are absorbed into the skin very quickly and last for about 24 hours in the body. They commonly have a very sharp aroma and a stimulating effect. Examples of top notes are citrus oils like orange, lemon and grapefruit, and herb oils such as peppermint and clary sage.

Middle notes Middle notes evaporate moderately quickly, and last for about 24 hours in the body. Once applied, they are absorbed into the skin moderately quickly. Middle notes are generally produced from herbs, having a recognizable herby aroma. Their effect is generally therapeutic. Examples of middle notes are lavender, camomile and geranium.

Base notes Base notes have the slowest evaporation rate of all essential oils. They are absorbed slowly into the skin, taking up to 100 minutes to be fully absorbed and last up to 5–7 days in the body. Base notes tend to be produced from gums and resins, and have a rich, heavy aroma with relaxing, sedating effects. Examples of base notes are sandalwood, rose and jasmine.

Best possible ingredients Be sure about the ingredients of products you use. Purity, organic, natural and blended with expertise are all points I look out for. Skin absorbs up to 60 per cent of what we put on it – and so we need to take responsibility not to be putting loads of chemicals on our clients' skin.

Katie Whitehouse

Classification of essential oils

Top note	*Middle note*	*Base note*
Clary sage	Roman Camomile	Neroli
Eucalyptus	Geranium	Rose Bulgar
Grapefruit	Lavender	Ylang-ylang
Lemon	Marjoram	
Lemongrass	Rosemary	
Tea tree		

Storage of pre-blended aromatherapy oils

Essential oils can be spoiled if incorrectly stored, and this can lead to increased evaporation which causes loss of their therapeutic properties, fragrance and colour. The ideal storage conditions for essential oils is cool and dark, away from sunlight. The storage container should be airtight and usually made of dark-coloured glass. Bottles should be well labelled to avoid misuse and dated to ensure its quality, as some essential oils have a shorter shelf life than others.

ACTIVITY

Evaporation of essential oil
Put a few drops of a base essential oil on a piece of blotting paper and place in a cupboard. Go back each day to see if the oil still has an aroma. How many days did the base oil keep its aroma?

Purchasing pre-blended aromatherapy oils

Pre-blended aromatherapy oils should always be purchased from a reputable supplier who has a quick turnaround of stock; this way you can be relatively confident that the oil has not been left on a shelf for many months before purchasing. Avoid buying large amounts of products if you cannot guarantee their use or sale to avoid waste.

Extraction of essential oils

There are a number of different ways to extract essential oils from plants. The yield of essential oil per tonne of plant material reflects the price of the oil. For example, it takes 5 tonnes of rose-flower petals to produce 1 kilogram of rose oil; it is therefore very expensive to produce. Many kilograms of lemon oil may be obtained from 1 tonne of lemon rind, making lemon oil relatively inexpensive.

Essential oils can be extracted from different parts of the plant, such as flowers, leaves and stems:

- Lavender, ylang-ylang, rose, camomile and jasmine essential oils are all extracted from the flowers of the plants.
- Sandalwood and cedarwood essential oils are extracted from the woody parts of the plants.
- Frankincense essential oil is extracted from a gum which is present in the plant.
- Rosemary, clary sage and thyme essential oils are all extracted from the leaves of the plants.
- Lemon, bergamot, orange and grapefruit essential oils are extracted from the rind of the fruits.

Methods of extracting essential oils include distillation, enfleurage, comminution, maceration, solvent extraction and expression.

Distillation Steam distillation is the most common method of extraction of essential oils from plants. The process involves heating the plant material with steam. The steam evaporates out the essential oil and a condenser turns the vapour to a liquid made up of essential oil and water. The essential oil floats on the surface of the water and is then siphoned off. The water that is left is known as **flower water**. Oils produced by distillation include rose, lavender and ylang-ylang.

Water distillation involves heating the plant material in water to boiling point then condensing the steam. Essential oils are extracted in this way from hard seeds, fruits and woods which have been thoroughly chopped.

Enfleurage Enfleurage is a method that is now largely outdated. It involves the use of cold fat and is used for flowers which continue to produce essential oils after they have been picked. Fatty substances can easily absorb essential oils and the fat which is used in this process is pure and odourless. A thin layer of the fat is spread on a glass frame and the fresh flowers are put in layers on top of this. The essential oils are absorbed into the fat. Periodically, the dead flowers are taken off and new flowers are re-spread on the fat. At this stage the fat and essential oil mixture is known as a **pomade**. When the fat has become saturated with essential oils (i.e. has absorbed the maximum amount) it is washed in alcohol and the essential oils pass into the alcohol. The pomade and alcohol mixture is known as an **absolute**. The alcohol is then evaporated, leaving pure essential oil. Enfleurage is used to extract essential oils from delicate flowers that cannot be heated, e.g. jasmine.

Comminution During this method, the whole fruit is liquidized for 'whole fruit' drinks and left to stand. The oil rises to the top and is skimmed off.

Maceration Maceration is a method whereby essential oils are extracted from plants by dipping them into hot fat. The process is repeated with fresh flowers until the fat is saturated. It is then washed in alcohol, which evaporates, leaving pure essential oil. The

HEALTH & SAFETY

Plastic bottles

As polythene is basically a solid oil, essential oils can escape from polythene bottles!

type of plants used in this method are those which do not produce essential oils after they have been harvested. This method is rarely used today to produce pure essential oil but is used to produce infused oils.

Solvent extraction During solvent extraction, plants are covered with a solvent such as ether, benzene, petroleum or acetone and then heated gradually until the solvent extracts the essential oils from the plant. After filtration, the dark paste or 'concrete' is mixed with alcohol and cooled. The essential oil dissolves in the alcohol which then evaporates, leaving the essential oils. Gums and resins, which are dissolved in acetone, produce resinoids. Flowers, which are dissolved in ether, benzene or petroleum, produce an absolute.

Expression Expression is the most common method of extraction used to obtain citrus oils such as lemon and orange essential oil. Machines are used to crush, grate or express the essential oil from the rind of the fruit.

ACTIVITY

Dig your fingernail into the peel of a ripe orange. You will be able to smell the essential oil being released.

Methods of entry of essential oils into the body

Essential oils enter the body via four basic routes: the skin, the lungs, the olfactory system and the digestive system.

Skin Essential oils penetrate the skin when they are applied via massage. The warmth and pressure of the hands during massage speeds up the penetration of the essential oils, which may take up to 100 minutes. The most likely places of entry are sebaceous glands, sudoriferous glands and hair follicles. The lipophilic (fat-loving) nature of essential oils allows penetration between the cells via the lipid or glue that holds cells together, and even through the lipid component of cell membranes.

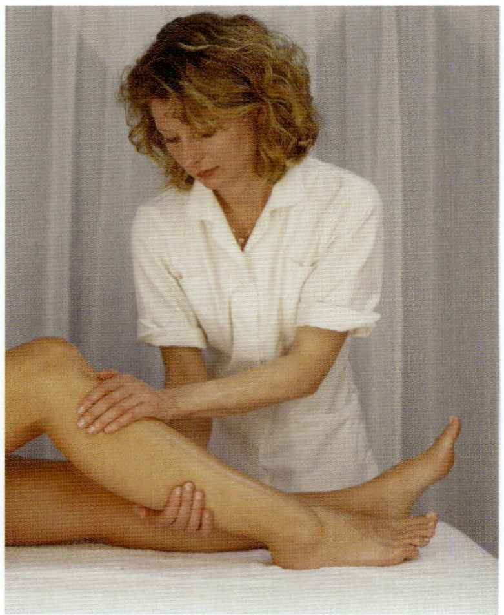

TISSERAND AROMATHERAPY

Essential oils penetrate the skin via massage

Some areas of the skin are more permeable than others – the palms of the hands, soles of the feet, forehead, forearms and scalp are more permeable than the abdomen, legs and trunk. Essential oils penetrate to the dermis where they then pass through the capillary walls into the bloodstream. The blood then transports the essential oils all around the body, which may take only about 28 seconds! Other substances with a small molecular structure that can be absorbed through the skin to the dermis include hormones, vitamins and certain types of drugs. Carrier oils, like acids, alkalis and alcohols, can only penetrate to the epidermis as their molecular structure is too large to allow them to penetrate further.

Lungs Essential oils, being volatile substances, penetrate the lungs when they are inhaled. They pass through the lining of the lung tissue, through the capillary walls and into the bloodstream where they are then transported around the body.

Olfactory system The olfactory system is located high up inside the nose and is responsible for the sense of smell. When we smell something, the nerve endings in the olfactory system are stimulated and relay messages to the brain, which then causes the body to respond. For example, the smell of freshly baked bread may cause a person to salivate. The smell of a particular substance may also trigger certain memories or emotions associated with a particular smell:

- The primary olfactory cortex and higher olfactory areas in the brain are responsible for recognizing what we have smelled and associating it with other information. For example, lavender oil may remind you of a favourite aunt who wears a lavender fragrance.
- The limbic system activates instinctual behaviour and emotion. For example, smelling grapefruit oil may cause you to salivate and desire food.

"If your client is pregnant you must be extra careful what you use on their skin, as what gets absorbed by the mother's skin can also be transferred to her unborn baby. Make sure you use brands you can trust (Natalia by Vital Touch for example!).

Katie Whitehouse

The volatile essential oils penetrate the olfactory system when they are inhaled through the nose. The olfactory surface (the ends of the olfactory nerves) is coated with a very thin layer of mucus. The essential oils pass through the mucous membranes and fatty tissues, where they bond temporarily to register their odour and stimulate the olfactory nerves. If the mucous membranes are blocked, for example during the common cold, substances have difficulty passing through and we therefore find it difficult to identify different smells. An illustration of the olfactory system and associated nerves can be found on page 73.

Digestive system Essential oils pass into the digestive system when they are taken orally. Clients should be warned against using this method as essential oils have a high risk of toxicity and irritation of the delicate membranes lining the digestive system.

TISSERAND AROMATHERAPY

An essential oil vaporizer helps the essential oils enter the lungs and olfactory system

Elimination of essential oils

Although essential oils may stay in the body for some time, especially in the deeper organs, eventually they are eliminated from the body in several ways. The skin helps with elimination through perspiration. Essential oils (garlic, for example) are eliminated in the breath during exhalation and traces of essential oils may also be found in the urine.

ACTIVITY

Smell an open bottle of lemon oil. Immediately you will begin to salivate more. This is the olfactory system in action!

Physiological effects of essential oils

Essential oils can affect the body physiologically in a number of ways:

- The cardiovascular system can be stimulated by rosemary, eucalyptus and black pepper, resulting in increased local circulation.
- Camphor can raise the body temperature, while camomile can help to lower it.
- Blood pressure can be decreased by lavender and heart rate can be stimulated by camphor.
- Most oils have an antibacterial effect.
- Phagocytosis is stimulated by camomile, lemon and thyme.
- Fennel, peppermint, rose and clary sage have an antispasmodic effect on the respiratory system, which helps to lessen muscle spasms.
- An expectorant effect can be produced by eucalyptus, lemon and benzoin.
- Lavender, rosemary, sandalwood and rose have an antispasmodic effect on the digestive system, while marjoram and rosemary have a laxative effect.
- The pH of gastric juices can be raised with clove oil.
- Lemon, fennel, cinnamon and cardamom have a stimulating effect on the nervous system, while melissa, lavender, sandalwood and ylang-ylang have a sedative effect.
- Peppermint has an analgesic effect.
- Juniper, sandalwood, fennel and rosemary all have diuretic properties.

HEALTH & SAFETY

Toxicity
Due to the toxic nature of some essential oils, all essential oils should be stored out of the reach of children.

TISSERAND AROMATHERAPY

Peppermint has an analgesic effect

- Jasmine, ylang-ylang and rose are said to have an aphrodisiac effect.
- Aniseed, garlic and fennel oil stimulate oestrogen production.

Psychological benefits

The psychological effect is achieved through the stimulation of the nerve endings in the olfactory system which relay messages to the limbic part of the brain, the area associated with memory, emotions and instincts which causes a response.

It is important, therefore, when selecting your pre-blended oil following consultation that it is suitable for the client's service requirements, i.e. stimulation, relaxation, etc.

Essential oils

Name of oil and plant(s) of origin		*Details*
Camomile *Chamaemelum nobile* *Matricaria recutita* *Ormenis mixta*	 TISSERAND AROMATHERAPY	Camomile has three sources: Roman Camomile (*Chamaemelum nobile*) – yellow/brown; German camomile (*Matricaria recutita*) – deep blue; Moroccan camomile (*Ormenis mixta*) – yellow. German camomile essential oil is distilled from the flowers and seeds of the camomile plant – a small daisy-like flower with feathery green leaves. Roman Camomile is distilled from the flowers only. Grown commercially in Europe, North Africa and Asia, this middle note essential oil is best known for its calming and anti-inflammatory properties. The oil has a sweet smell and is ideal to use in massage blends for clients suffering from tension and stress. Due to its high azulene content, German camomile turns blue in colour during distillation. Azulene is a fatty substance responsible for the soothing, anti-inflammatory effect of camomile.
Basil *Ocimum basilicum*	 SHUTTERSTOCK/LUBASHI	A native of India and a popular European herb. It can grow up to 3 feet and has small white flowers. The oil is distilled from the leaves of the plant. It has an invigorating effect and is good to stimulate blood circulation and also as an uplifting oil for tiredness and mental fatigue.
Black pepper *Piper nigrum*	Bottle or plant  TISSERAND AROMATHERAPY	The black pepper plant, which is grown in India and South East Asia is a vine which grows in the wild to a height of 20 m or 30 feet but for the purpose of essential oil productions its growth is restricted. The fruit which is used to produce the essential oil, appears as small red berries, which when dried become peppercorns. Its analgesic (pain relieving) and rubefacient properties make it ideal for massage when soothing muscular tension aches and pains. Black pepper is a middle note and is extracted by distillation.

ALWAYS REMEMBER

Black pepper

Due to the stimulating nature of black pepper essential oil, use with caution on clients with sensitive skin.

Name of oil and plant(s) of origin		*Details*
Juniper *Juniperus communis*	TISSERAND AROMATHERAPY 	Juniper is a small evergreen tree or shrub with short, spiny leaves closely arranged in whorls of three. It is usually 3 or 4 foot tall and has small deep-purple berries. The fruits or berries of this plant are distilled to produce the middle note essential oil. Grown in the Far East, Europe and the USA, juniper has good antiseptic and diuretic properties. It is often used in the service of acnefied skin conditions for its antiseptic effect and cellulite because of its diuretic effect.
Patchouli *Pogostemon patchouli*	TISSERAND AROMATHERAPY 	A native of India, the essential oil is obtained from the leaf of the plant. It has skin healing properties, is uplifting and is also used in the service of cellulite because of its diuretic effect.
Orange, sweet *Citrus sinensis* Orange, bitter *Citrus aurantium*	TISSERAND AROMATHERAPY 	Originating from China, the sweet and bitter oils are similar and are extracted by cold pressing of fresh orange peel. It has an uplifting, stimulating and an anti-depressant action.
Clary sage *Salvia sclarea*	TISSERAND AROMATHERAPY 	Clary sage is a top note and comes from a plant with broad, wrinkled, green/purple-blue flowers similar to common sage. This herb is grown commercially in France and Russia and the essential oil is obtained by distillation from the flowers. Its sedative properties make clary sage the ideal choice for clients who have difficulty relaxing. Clary sage may induce feelings of euphoria and should be used with care.

ALWAYS REMEMBER

Clary sage and alcohol

Clients should not drink alcohol before or after a service with clary sage as its enhancing effect on alcohol may produce unpleasant side-effects.

Name of oil and plant(s) of origin		*Details*
Eucalyptus *Eucalyptus globulus*	 TISSERAND AROMATHERAPY	Eucalyptus is a tall tree with whitish, papery bark and long, pointed leaves. A native plant of Australia and Tasmania, the leaves of the eucalyptus are distilled to obtain the essential oil. It is a good antiseptic and expectorant and is effective for colds, catarrh, flu and sinus problems. Eucalyptus is a top note and is good to use in blends for clients with oily skin.
Geranium *Pelargonium odoratissimum* *Pelargonium robertianum*	 TISSERAND AROMATHERAPY	The geranium plant comes in a variety of shapes and sizes, but in its most recognizable form it is about 2 feet high with pink and red flowers. The leaves of this plant are distilled to produce the sweet, floral, middle note essential oil. Geranium has sedative and antiseptic qualities and is often used in skincare preparations. It also has an uplifting, anti-depressant effect and is ideal for use with clients suffering from stress or those who want an uplifting massage. Geranium is grown commercially in Africa, southern France and Spain.
Grapefruit *Citrus paradise*	 TISSERAND AROMATHERAPY	Grapefruit oil has a very fresh, sweet smell and has an uplifting effect when used. It is obtained by expression from the peel of the grapefruit and is grown commercially in North America and Israel. It is an effective oil to use on clients who require their service to be invigorating, uplifting, refreshing and reviving. It is an appropriate choice for clients whose consultation identifies stress, tiredness and muscular aches. Safety Note – Grapefruit is phototoxic and should not be used on clients prior to exposure to the sun (ultraviolet light).
Lavender *Lavandula officinalis*	 TISSERAND AROMATHERAPY	Lavender is the most widely used and versatile of all essential oils. Distilled from the lavender plant, a bush with green-blue leaves and lavender/blue flowers, this essential oil has a multitude of uses and effects. It is an excellent antiseptic and in emergencies can be used undiluted on the skin for bites and stings, etc. Lavender is an oil that will enhance the effect of other oils that are blended with it. It has a balancing and harmonizing effect on the body and is therefore useful for all kinds of conditions. The oil is distilled from the flowers, which are grown in southern Europe and many other parts of the world.

Name of oil and plant(s) of origin		*Details*
Lemon *Citrus limon*	 TISSERAND AROMATHERAPY	Lemons grow on a small tree that has dark-green, shiny leaves and produces white flowers before the fruit. Lemon is a stimulating top note, expressed from the skin of the fruit. Grown in northern India, Europe, California and Australia, this inexpensive essential oil has a sharp, tangy, distinctive aroma. Lemon has strong antiseptic and antibacterial properties, and has an invigorating effect. It is ideal in blends designed to uplift clients or for those with oily or acnefied skin types.
Lemongrass *Cymbopogon citratus*	 TISSERAND AROMATHERAPY	This top note has a sharp, lemon-scented aroma and is extracted from the grass itself. Grown in Brazil, Sri Lanka, the USA and China, it has a deep yellow colour. The plant is a common ingredient in Oriental cooking. Lemongrass has sedative, antiseptic, anti-fungal and insect-repelling properties. It is often used as a general tonic to stimulate the circulation in cellulite conditions.
Marjoram *Origanum majorana*	 TISSERAND AROMATHERAPY	Marjoram oil is extracted from the leaves of the plant. It is pale yellow in colour and is grown commercially in Europe and Egypt. Its calming, relaxing and sedative properties make it useful in blends for rheumatism and arthritis.
Neroli *Citrus aurantium*	 TISSERAND AROMATHERAPY	Neroli oil is obtained from the flowers of the bitter orange tree and is an ingredient of eau de cologne. It is useful in blends for insomnia, stress, muscular tension and nervousness, and is soothing for dry, sensitive skin. The rejuvenating properties of neroli make it a popular choice for blends used on stretch marks and scars.

Name of oil and plant(s) of origin		*Details*
Rose Bulgar *Rosa damascena* *Rosa centifolia*	 TISSERAND AROMATHERAPY	The rose is a well-known, beautiful, scented flower with numerous white to red petals on a thorny stem. The plant is grown all over the world, but most commercially grown roses come from Bulgaria, France and North Africa. The flowers are used in the steam distillation process to produce rose essential oil. A base note, rose's many properties include antidepressant, antiseptic, aphrodisiac, astringent and sedative. It is useful in massage blends needed to relax clients and for those with dry or mature skin types.
Rosemary *Rosmarinus officinalis*	 TISSERAND AROMATHERAPY	Rosemary is a top note essential oil with a camphorous aroma that is distilled from the plant and its roots. A shrub with needle-like leaves and pale blue flowers, Rosemary is grown in southern Europe, northern Africa and the Mediterranean. Its rubefacient and stimulating properties make it a good oil for use in massage prior to exercise. Its astringent properties also make it useful for clients with oily skin.
Sandalwood *Santalum album*	 TISSERAND AROMATHERAPY	Sandalwood essential oil is obtained by distillation from the wood of the small, evergreen sandalwood tree that is grown commercially in India and Australia. Sandalwood is particularly useful when treating male clients as it has a masculine fragrance. It is a base note with relaxing and antiseptic properties and is also said to be a strong aphrodisiac. Sandalwood is beneficial to dry and dehydrated skins.
Tea tree *Melaleuca alternifolia*	 TISSERAND AROMATHERAPY	The tea tree plant is a native of Australia and is a small tree with frond-like leaves. It has very good anti-fungal, anti-viral, antibacterial and antiseptic properties due to its high terpene content, making it invaluable for many kinds of problems. Like lavender, tea tree may be used directly on the skin with safety in emergencies. This essential oil is distilled from the leaves of the plant and is a top note.

Name of oil and plant(s) of origin		*Details*
Ylang-ylang *Cananga odorata*	 TISSERAND AROMATHERAPY	The ylang-ylang is a tree that grows to about 50 feet tall and produces yellow flowers, from which the essential oil is distilled. A base note oil is produced that has a very rich, sweet, floral fragrance. Native to Indonesia and the Philippines, ylang-ylang has sedative calming properties which make it an ideal choice for insomnia. It is also reputed to be an excellent aphrodisiac.

Essential oil safety

The use of essential oils on the skin may present a potential hazard to both the client and the beauty therapist if not used correctly. These risks include toxicity, irritation and sensitization.

- *Toxicity* is often termed 'poisoning'. If an oil is toxic, it means that at a certain level it becomes fatal whether taken orally or applied to the skin. Toxicity is dose-dependent and varies according to the size of the person concerned. Babies and children should be exposed to a much lower percentage of essential oils per carrier oil, e.g. 10 times lower, and services should be less frequent. Some oils are known to be phototoxic, which means that they make skin more sensitive to sunlight.
- *Irritation* from essential oils is localized and may affect the skin or mucous membranes. Irritation is also dose-dependent.
- *Sensitization* is an allergy to an essential oil. Only a small amount of oil is needed to trigger a response, therefore it is not dose-dependent.

It is important to keep very detailed records of essential oil blends used on every client so that if any problems are reported such as irritation or sensitivity, the beauty therapist can identify the oil or quantity involved and change it accordingly for the next service.

Carrier oils

As essential oils are not actually oily in texture, an oily medium is needed in which to mix the essential oils before they can be massaged into the skin. The skin will absorb fat-soluble substances more readily than water-soluble substances, therefore essential oils will penetrate more efficiently if applied to the skin via a carrier oil. This efficiency will be enhanced by the use of an oil with a low viscosity.

The most effective medium for this purpose is a vegetable carrier oil. Mineral oils such as baby oil are not suitable for use in aromatherapy as their molecular structure is too large

HEALTH & SAFETY

Flammability

Essential oils are flammable. Never leave used towels, bed linen or tissues near a heat source as they pose a fire hazard.

HEALTH & SAFETY

Unsafe oils

The following essential oils should never be used in aromatherapy and should not appear in pre-blended oils:

Bitter almond
Boldo leaf
Calamus
Horseradish
Jaborandi leaf
Mugwort
Mustard
Pennyroyal
Rue
Sassafras
Savin
Southernwood
Tansy
Thuja
Wintergreen
Wormseed
Wormwood
Yellow camphor

to allow penetration of the epidermis and they would therefore not assist the penetration of essential oils.

Almost any vegetable oil can be used as a carrier oil, but an oil that has been cold pressed and not processed is most suitable as it contains valuable nutrients for the body and will not adversely affect the therapeutic properties of the essential oils diluted in it.

The properties of carrier oils are that they:

- have a medium viscosity
- have little or no aroma
- are not soluble in water or alcohol
- have low volatility

Carrier oils that are high in polyunsaturates absorb more readily into the skin than those high in monounsaturates or saturates.

HEALTH & SAFETY

Wheat germ

Wheat germ carrier oil should not be used on clients with wheat allergies.

VITAL TOUCH

Carrier oils

VITAL TOUCH

Organic pure base oil

ALWAYS REMEMBER

Approximately 20 drops of essential oil equals 1 millilitre.

Extraction of carrier oils

Cold pressing Cold pressing is a method of extraction that is most desirable for carrier oils used in aromatherapy massage. The plant material is crushed using great pressure, literally squeezing the oil from the plant. No chemicals or solvents are used, resulting in a pure, unrefined oil.

Solvent extraction Solvents such as petroleum are heated and washed through the plant material to dissolve any oil that is present. The solvents are then evaporated, leaving a refined oil that is unsuitable for aromatherapy massage.

Your pre-blended aromatherapy massage oil will already be in a carrier oil.

The choice of carrier oil will affect the texture, smell and specific properties. For dry skin use an oil with a thicker consistency, and for an oily skin, or fine skin such as that on the face, use a finer or lighter oil with a lower viscosity.

Creams can also be used as a carrier. Although not as good as vegetable oil for body massage, cream bases are ideal for use on smaller areas – hands or feet for example. Any unperfumed and unmedicated cream can be used for this purpose and there are many bland creams designed for use by aromatherapists. These are known as base creams. Less essential oil is needed when blending with base creams due to their denser consistency. Approximately one drop of essential oil is used per 5 grams of cream.

ALWAYS REMEMBER

FUNCTIONAL SKILLS

Blended oils

Essential oils are measured in drops. The percentage used in most blends is 2.5 per cent essential oil and 97.5 per cent carrier oil and less if using a base cream.

To achieve a lower percentage of oil in a blend, the original blend is divided in half to a dilution of 1.25 per cent.

Carrier oils

Name of oil and plant of origin	*Details*
Aloe vera *Aloe barbadenesis*	Aloe vera is a low-viscosity carrier and is therefore often blended with thicker oils to improve its texture for massage services. Its soothing, anti-inflammatory properties make it ideal for use on sensitive skins.
Apricot kernel oil *Prunus armenica*	Apricot kernel oil is a pale yellow colour and is an ideal facial massage oil due to its nourishing and protective properties.
Avocado oil *Persea americana*	In its refined state, avocado oil is a pale yellow colour, but cold-pressed avocado oil is green. It is a very rich oil which penetrates to the deep epidermis, making it ideal for very dry skin. Its high vitamin E content also makes it a good antioxidant. Due to its cost and thick consistency, avocado oil is usually blended with other lighter carrier oils before use.
Evening primrose oil *Oenothera biennis*	Evening primrose oil is a pale yellow oil which is ideal for use on dry, irritated skin conditions such as eczema and chapped hands. Due to its cost, evening primrose oil is usually blended with a cheaper carrier oil.
Grapeseed oil *Vitis vinifera*	Grapeseed oil is a very inexpensive, light oil commonly used in aromatherapy. It has a very pale yellow-green colour and can be used on all types of skin.
Hazelnut oil *Corylus avellana*	Hazelnut oil is obtained from the kernel. It is a yellow, fine-textured oil that is particularly suitable for dry sensitive skin.
Jojoba *Simmondsia chinesis*	Jojoba is cold pressed and is semi-solid at room temperature. It therefore needs to be warmed in the hands prior to use. Jojoba is very expensive but very stable and is therefore often blended with cheaper oils.
Macadamia nut oil *Macadamia ternifolia*	Macadamia nut oil has a slight odour and is pale yellow in colour. It is easily absorbed and is particularly suitable for mature dry skin.
Olive oil *Olea europea*	Olive oil is cold pressed and green in colour with soothing properties. As its consistency is quite thick, it is often blended with a lighter oil prior to massage.
Rose-hip oil *Rosa canina*	Rose-hip oil is produced by solvent extraction and is a warm golden colour.
Safflower oil *Carthamus tinctorius*	Safflower oil is pale yellow in colour. It is not very stable so needs the addition of an anti-oxidant such as avocado or wheat germ to prevent it spoiling quickly.
Sunflower oil *Helianthus annus*	Sunflower oil has a light texture and pale yellow colour. It contains vitamins A, B, C, D and E.
Sweet almond oil *Prunus amygdalus*	Sweet almond oil is a light-textured, pale yellow oil that is good for facial massage as it soothes and protects the skin. It is warm pressed and is particularly good for dry, sensitive skin.
Wheat germ oil *Triticum vulgare*	Wheat germ oil is a warm orange colour and is rich in vitamins E and C. It is a cold-pressed oil that is a very good antioxidant due to its high vitamin E content. It is often added to other blends in small quantities to prolong their shelf life. Wheat germ oil is very thick and has a strong wheat germ smell, so it should be blended with a lighter oil prior to massage.

The benefit of using a pre-blended aromatherapy oil as opposed to blending your own is as follows:

- a brand name is instantly recognizable
- large companies advertise in magazines and on the Internet which is free advertising for your product
- wide range of products available, including retail products from which to choose from

ALWAYS REMEMBER

Massage adaptation

In addition to those techniques discussed on page page 352, body massage chapter you may consider the following massage adaptations:

Relaxation

- advise client abdominal breathing
- spend more time on ares of tension such as the scalp, neck and shoulder area

Uplifting

- incorporate more tsubo pressure points within the massage routine

Well-being

- increase application time over the feet and abdominal area and encourage client abdominal breathing

- glossy promotional material available
- no messy, health and safety concerns filling bottles

Sometimes there are disadvantages such as:

- high cost minimum orders (dependent upon company)
- the beauty therapist is not involved in the essential oil blend
- the service is less personal to meet the clinical needs of the client. If this is required she should be referred to a reputable clinical aromatherapist.

VITAL TOUCH

Retail products and promotional material are simple when using pre-blended aromatherapy oils

Types of massage used in aromatherapy

The reasons for using massage with aromatherapy pre-blended oil are threefold. The pressure from the hands helps to spread and push the oils into the skin, heat helps the oils to be absorbed more easily and the effects of the manual manipulations help the client to relax.

There are three basic types of massage used in an aromatherapy massage service:

- Swedish
- neuromuscular
- shiatsu (pressure point)

When performing massage using pre-blended aromatherapy oils you will incorporate these massage techniques and adapt them to meet the service objectives.

Swedish massage

Swedish massage uses effleurage, petrissage, tapotement and vibrations to increase the blood supply generally to muscles and skin and to improve the efficiency of the lymphatic system by increasing drainage to the lymph nodes. It can be either a relaxing or stimulating massage depending on the movements used, with emphasis placed on the smooth continuity of strokes.

Neuromuscular massage

Neuromuscular massage uses strokes that are designed to affect the nerves rather than blood and lymphatic flow. The pressure is much firmer than Swedish strokes and the direction is related to the direction of the sensory nerve roots rather than the direction of blood and lymphatic flow. As the pressure is very firm it may cause mild discomfort. The overall effect of these strokes is to stimulate the nerves.

Shiatsu massage

Shiatsu is an Oriental massage technique with strokes which relate to energy paths within the body rather than nerves, blood flow or lymphatic flow. Adapted forms of shiatsu are often incorporated in aromatherapy massage and the strokes are designed to either increase or decrease energy levels within the body. The massage is performed with long flowing strokes along meridians (energy channels) or with pressures on the tsubo points. Tsubo points connect directly from the body's surface to meridians within the body. Meridians help to keep the body systems in balance. The pressures are quite firm and may sometimes be quite uncomfortable for the client.

During massage, tsubo points should be pressed with the fingertips or thumb using the beauty therapist's body to apply pressure. Apply a light-to-moderate pressure for 3–5 seconds, and 5–7 seconds on the back when the client is breathing out. The client should be instructed to breath in between pressures. Pressure applied to these points helps to unblock the energy flow along the meridian, promoting greater well-being of the client, helping the body to heal itself. Pressures are usually applied once over an area.

Outcome 1: Maintain safe and effective methods of working when carrying out massage using pre-blended aromatherapy oils

Learn how to maintain safe and effective methods of working when performing massage using pre-blended oils service by:

1. Setting up and monitoring the service area to meet organization procedures and manufacturer's instructions.
2. Making sure that environmental conditions are suitable for the client and the service.
3. Ensuring your personal hygiene, protection and appearance meets accepted industry and organizational requirements.
4. Effectively disinfecting your hands prior to and after service.
5. Ensuring your own posture and position minimizes fatigue and risk of injury while working.
6. Ensuring all equipment is cleaned using the correct methods.
7. Positioning equipment and pre-blended oils for ease and safety of use.
8. Ensuring the client is in a comfortable and relaxed position suitable for the service.
9. Maintaining accepted industry hygiene and safety practices throughout the service.

BEST PRACTICE

Relaxing services

If a client desires a relaxing service, minimize or completely omit tapotement movements.

TOP TIP

Shiatsu massage

Pressure point massage may be performed with the client fully clothed.

ALWAYS REMEMBER

Pain during pressure point application

If the client experiences sharp or sudden pain, stop applying pressure immediately.

ALWAYS REMEMBER

Safety in application of pressure point technique

Keep your nails short in order to effectively perform the pressure point technique without causing client discomfort.

ACTIVITY

Care Standards Act (2000)

You must comply with all your responsibilities under current health and safety legislation including the Care Standards Act. The **Care Standards Act (2000)** is the regulatory framework for social care to ensure high standards of care and protection of vulnerable people. This includes care for those in hospitals, children homes, residential homes and nursing homes for example. Research how you conform with the requirements of this piece of legislation.

(Continued) Learn how to maintain safe and effective methods of working when performing massage using pre-blended oils service by:

10. Adopting a positive, polite and reassuring manner towards the client throughout the service.
11. Maintaining the client's modesty, privacy and comfort at all times.
12. Disposing of waste materials safely and correctly.
13. Ensuring the service is cost-effective and is carried out within a commercially viable time.
14. Ensuring client record cards are up-to-date, accurate, complete, legible and signed by the client and practitioner.
15. Leaving the service area and equipment in a condition suitable for future services.

Ensure the work area is peaceful

Preparation of the work area

The work area should be clean and at a comfortable working temperature for both client and beauty therapist, between 18 and 21°C.

The use of subdued lighting and gentle relaxing music may help to enhance the mood of the service cubicle and encourage relaxation. Listed below is everything that your working area should contain to carry out a full body massage using pre-blended aromatherapy oils.

The work room should be warm, quiet, private, well ventilated and with soft lighting, and must be kept clean and tidy at all times. The working area should be adequately screened to allow the client privacy.

One large towel should be placed over the length of the couch and a small towel over the head end The remaining towels should be used as appropriate to preserve the client's modesty and for support. All products and materials should be placed on the trolley prior to the service, so that the beauty therapist does not need to break the continuity of the massage to go in search for them. The trolley should be positioned for ease of access for the beauty therapist.

Adequate ventilation should be provided to create a hygienic environment, preventing cross-infection through viral airborne spores, drowsiness through carbon dioxide saturated air and the removal of stale smells and odours.

Before beginning the body massage service, check that you have the necessary equipment and materials to hand and that they meet legal, hygiene and industry requirements for massage using pre-blended oils.

TOP TIP

Accommodating disabilities

Hydraulic couches are effective as they enable clients with mobility problems easier access onto the couch.

They also benefit the beauty therapist as they are height adjustable.

EQUIPMENT AND MATERIALS LIST

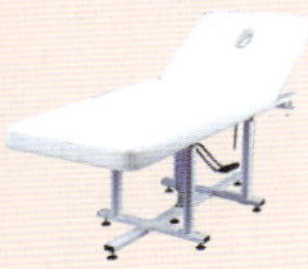

Service couch
Service couch, with sit-up and lie-down positions and an easy to clean surface

Support pillows
One to support the head and the other to support the limbs. Each pillow should be covered with a clean, removable pillow case

BEAUTY EXPRESS LTD

Towels
Two small towels to protect the bedding and two large towels to cover the client during the service. Additional towels may be used during the service for client comfort and support

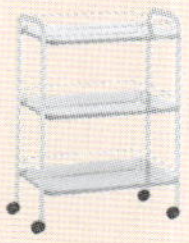

ELLISONS

Trolley
To hold all the necessary materials and equipment

ELLISONS

Small bowls
To dispense products into and hold consumables

BEAUTY EXPRESS LTD

Tissues
To wipe excess oil from the client's skin or the beauty therapist's hands, or to blot and absorb excess product following skin cleansing

ELLISONS

Record card
Confidential card recording details of each client registered at the salon to record personal details, products used and details of the service

ELLISONS

Gown
To protect the client's modesty if required

HOF

Range of pre-blended essential oils
To meet a variety of service objectives

Cleansing lotion
To remove make-up, skin oils, dead skin and debris prior to facial massage

Toner, witch hazel or eau de cologne
To freshen the skin after cleansing, to cleanse the area being massaged and remove excess medium

YOU WILL ALSO NEED:

Spatulas To remove products hygienically from containers

Damp cotton wool To remove make-up and cleansing lotion

Cleansing wipes Moist tissues to cleanse and deodorize the feet before the service

Headband To keep the client's hair away from the face during cleansing if required

Waste container with lid Bin lined with a disposable bin liner

Aftercare advice Recommended advice for the client following the service

Sterilization and disinfection

The following table gives details of sterilization and disinfection procedures to be carried out prior to and following the massage service.

Equipment item	*Procedure*
Service couch	Prior to the service, the surfaces should be wiped with warm soapy water and disinfectant. During the service, the couch may be covered with disposable tissue, towels or a loose cover. This must be replaced after each service.
Couch cover	Machine wash at 60°C in soapy water.
Towels	Replace after each service. Machine wash at 60°C in soapy water.
Trolley	The surfaces should be wiped with warm soapy water and disinfectant at the beginning of each session, then covered with disposable tissue.
Bowls	Wash in hot, soapy water.
Gowns	Clean gowns to be provided for each client. Machine wash at 60°C in soapy water.
Headband	Machine wash at 60°C in soapy water.
Bin	Line with a disposable liner and wipe regularly with disinfectant. Empty immediately following the service.

HEALTH & SAFETY

Products

Check that all products are clean and that the 'use by' date has not expired. Ensure all containers are wiped over and lids are securely replaced after use to prevent any bacteria multiplying, leading to contamination.

Presentation of the beauty therapist

In order to promote professionalism, and to promote a healthy and safe working environment, the beauty therapist must:

- maintain a high standard of personal hygiene
- have fresh breath, free from cigarette or food odours
- wear a clean, pressed overall
- wear clean, low-heeled shoes
- not wear rings or any jewellery on the arms, including watches (plain wedding bands, however, are acceptable)
- ensure that any earrings or necklaces are discreet
- ensure that any make-up is discreet and provides a professional appearance
- style long hair neatly away from the face and shoulders
- ensure that nails are short, smooth, clean and free from nail polish
- ensure that any cuts are covered with a clean plaster
- ensure that hands are washed immediately before and after physical client contact

The beauty therapist should adopt a calm and professional manner at all times.

The hands also need to be flexible in order to fit the contours of the client's body. Mobilizing the joints of the hands and fingers will loosen the hands and facilitate good massage techniques. Examples of some the beauty therapist can practice are illustrated on page 346.

Outcome 2: Consult, plan and prepare for services with clients

Learn how to use consultation techniques to effectively plan and prepare for massage using pre-blended oils by:

1. Using **consultation techniques** in a polite, sensitive and friendly manner to determine the client's service needs.
2. Obtaining signed, written informed consent from the client prior to carrying out the service.
3. Ensuring that informed and signed parent or guardian consent is obtained for minors prior to any service.
4. Ensuring that a parent or guardian is present throughout the massage service for minors under the age of 16.
5. Clearly explaining to the client what the service entails in a way they can understand.
6. Using suitable **consultation techniques** to identify your client's medical history, **physical characteristics** and lifestyle pattern.
7. Asking your client appropriate questions to identify if they have any contra-indications to massage services.

(Continued) Learn how to use consultation techniques to effectively plan and prepare for massage using pre-blended oils by:

8. Accurately recording your client's responses to questioning.
9. Encouraging your client to ask questions to clarify any points.
10. Effectively carrying out a sensitivity test to establish response and suitability for service.
11. Taking the **necessary action** in response to any identified contra-indications.
12. Ensuring any referral is given without reference to a specific medical condition and without causing undue alarm and concern.
13. Actively encouraging your client to ask questions and clarify any points.
14. Clearly explaining and agreeing the projected cost, likely duration, frequency and types of service needed.
15. Agreeing in writing the client's needs, expectations and **service objectives**, ensuring they are realistic and achievable.
16. Ensuring that the client's **service area(s)** are clean and suitably prepared.
17. Ensuring that clothing, hair and accessories are effectively protected or removed.
18. Selecting suitable pre-blended aromatherapy oils which meet the **service objectives** which are fit for purpose.

When the client arrives they should be treated with courtesy and respect. Always address the client by their name and inform them of yours. This step is important, not only to elicit information but also to help the client to relax in the knowledge that they are being treated by a professional.

First, ask for basic details such as name, address, date of birth, etc., and record them on the client's record card. Second, ask the client about their general lifestyle, hobbies, work, eating patterns, smoking, etc. This will help you to take a more holistic approach to the service. By knowing and understanding the client's lifestyle you can perhaps discover not only the correct help for their problems but also gain an understanding of how the problems may have arisen in the first place. For example, if a client suffers with headaches and eyestrain, a contributory factor to these conditions could be that

TOP TIP

Mind and body

When performing a massage using pre-blended aromatherapy essential oils, adequate time must be given to the consultation to ascertain the state of mind and body of the client. Is the need physical, psychological or both?

ACTIVITY

Think of three open questions you could ask a client at consultation to find out information about their lifestyle and service needs and suitability for the service.

they watch a lot of television, spend long periods of time on the computer or that they read a lot but do not wear glasses, and may need to seek the advice of an optician. Ask what their needs are for attending the service. Do they want to be relaxed or uplifted? Remember to use an open questioning technique to encourage the client to give you as much information as possible.

The verbal consultation will also reveal whether any medication is being taken and whether the client is suffering from conditions that cannot be seen with the eye, e.g. period pain or premenstrual tension. Other conditions which are visually obvious, such as varicose veins, can be identified during the visual part of the consultation.

Check that the client does not have a dislike of, or allergy to any particular essential oil which may be contained in your blend.

Skin sensitivity (patch) test A patch test should be carried out 24 hours prior to the service. This will help to determine the client's suitability for the service. Carry out the sensitivity test in the crook of the elbow or behind the client's ear. Ensure that the skin is clean and then apply a pre-blended essential oil to the area. Ask the client to inform the salon immediately if any contra-actions are identified, e.g. redness, itching or swelling. Also remember the effect aroma has on memory and emotion. The client may dislike a particular aroma, check first. If any contra-actions occur service must not be carried out.

Contra-indications Certain contra-indications preclude massage using pre-blended aromatherapy massage oils. These are:

Contra-indications to massage

General	*Local*	*Temporary*
Heart conditions	Recent operations	Medication
High and low blood pressure	Recent scar tissue	Bruising
Certain medication	Psoriasis or eczema	Skin abrasions
Diabetes	Skin diseases	Medical oedema
Cancer	Skin disorders	Skin diseases
Rheumatism		Skin disorders
Undiagnosed lumps, bumps or swelling		During chemotherapy or radiotherapy
Loss of skin sensation		Product allergies
Postural deformities		Fever
Over bulbous varicose veins		Soon after or before alcohol consumption
Phlebitis		Immediately after a heat service such as sauna or steam bath
Deep vein thrombosis		
High temperature		
Epilepsy		
Pregnancy (to a large extent)		

Those contra-indications requiring GP referral should be tactfully and clearly discussed to ensure client understanding.

> Employers like to see that you keep up-to-date with training. Look out for continuous professional development activities undertaken to develop technical skill and expertise to ensure current professional experience in the beauty therapy industry.
>
> **Katie Whitehouse**

HEALTH & SAFETY

Product allergies

If the client has a sensitive skin or suffers from allergies, recommend they receive a skin sensitivity 'patch test' before you proceed with a massage service.

A small amount of the product to be used within the massage procedure is applied to the skin at least 24 hours beforehand.

ACTIVITY

Client suitability

A client presents for a service with a medical condition that you are unsure is suitable for the service. State two actions you should take.

Contra-actions

After a massage using pre-blended aromatherapy oils, some clients may feel excessively sleepy or relaxed, depending upon the essential oils used. Clients reacting in this way must be recommended not to drive or operate dangerous machinery until they feel more alert. Some clients may also experience a feeling of light-headedness or headaches, this is due to the release of toxins and may also depend on which oils were used and the degree of sensitivity of the client. Advise increased consumption of water and avoidance of tea/coffee and alcohol for at least the next 24 hours. Clients with very sensitive skin may experience skin irritation if stimulating essential oils are used unwanted skin reactions include red,swollen areas of skin, even blister may occur. All product should be removed immediately from the skin clients should report any adverse effects to the beauty therapist immediately so that notes can be made on their record cards and future services adjusted accordingly. If symptoms do not improve in 2–3 days the client should contact their GP.

ACTIVITY

Postural faults

How would you recognize the following postural faults:

- kyphosis?
- lordosis?
- scoliosis?

How would you modify your massage techniques for each condition?

Visual assessment

Following the verbal consultation complete a visual assessment of the client's posture and skin condition.

Advise the client which articles of clothing and accessories they need to remove and provide a gown for modesty according to client preference. Allow the client to undress in a private changing area.

With the client seated on the treatment couch, ask the client to sit up straight. Look at their spinal column to see if it is straight. If not, is it due to poor posture, trauma or a genetic condition? (Postural assessment is discussed on pages 202–204.) Check their skin visually and physically for colour and texture. Encourage the client to ask questions as these may lead to further discussions about their needs. If the scalp is to be massaged check that the oil may be used on the hair. Record all relevant details accurately on the client's record card and obtain the client's signature to confirm the details. This enables continuity of the service and up-to-date tracking of the services received. An example of a typical record card is illustrated on the next page.

ALWAYS REMEMBER

Ensuring your treatment meets your clients needs

If the client has had a service previously or this is a course of treatment, always discuss the effects of the previous service to check the suitability of the massage techniques used and choice of pre-blended aromatherapy oils. Always be prepared to modify your service plan to meet your client's needs.

Record card for massage using pre-blended oils

Date	Beauty therapist name	
Client name	Date of birth (Identifying client age group.)	
Home address	Postcode	
Email address	Landline phone number	Mobile phone number
Name of doctor	Doctor's address and phone number	
Related medical history (Conditions that may restrict or prohibit the service application.)		
Are you taking any medication? (This may affect the appearance of the skin or skin sensitivity.)		

CONTRA-INDICATIONS REQUIRING MEDICAL REFERRAL
(Preventing aromatherapy massage service application.)

- ☐ bacterial infection e.g. impetigo
- ☐ viral infection, e.g. herpes simplex
- ☐ fungal infection, e.g. tinea corporis
- ☐ systemic medical conditions
- ☐ severe skin conditions
- ☐ during chemotherapy and radiotherapy
- ☐ patients
- ☐ deep vein thrombosis
- ☐ pregnancy
- ☐ high/low blood pressure
- ☐ recent head and neck injury

CLIENT

- ☐ male
- ☐ female

PHYSICAL CHARACTERISTICS

- ☐ weight ___
- ☐ height ___
- ☐ health ___
- ☐ skin condition ___
- ☐ size ___
- ☐ muscle tone ___
- ☐ age ___
- ☐ posture ___

SERVICE AREAS

- ☐ neck, face and scalp
- ☐ arms and hands
- ☐ back and gluteals
- ☐ full body
- ☐ chest and shoulders
- ☐ abdomen
- ☐ legs and feet

MASSAGE TECHNIQUE

- ☐ effleurage
- ☐ tapotement
- ☐ vibrations
- ☐ petrissage
- ☐ frictions
- ☐ pressure points

CONTRA-INDICATIONS THAT RESTRICT SERVICE
(Service may require adaptation.)

- ☐ cuts and abrasions
- ☐ bruising and swelling of known origin
- ☐ recent scar tissue
- ☐ pregnancy
- ☐ during lactation
- ☐ epilepsy
- ☐ post epilation/hair removal in the area
- ☐ allergies
- ☐ varicose veins
- ☐ diabetes

LIFESTYLE

- ☐ occupation ___
- ☐ family situation ___
- ☐ dietary and fluid intake ___
- ☐ oils to avoid (including allergies) ___
- ☐ hobbies, interests, means of relaxation ___
- ☐ exercise habits ___
- ☐ smoking habits ___
- ☐ sleep patterns ___

OBJECTIVES OF SERVICE

- ☐ relaxation
- ☐ sense of well-being
- ☐ uplifting
- ☐ anti-cellulite
- ☐ stimulating

Beauty therapist signature (for reference)

Client signature (confirmation of details)

Record card for massage using pre-blended oils (continued)

SERVICE ADVICE

Massage using pre-blended aromatherapy oils – *this service will take 1–$1\frac{1}{2}$ hours*

Back massage – *approximately 30 minutes*

SERVICE PLAN

Record relevant details of your service and advice provided for future reference.

Ensure the client's records are up-to-date, accurate and fully completed following the service. Non-compliance may invalidate insurance.

DURING

- explain choice of massage medium and its benefits
- explain the service procedure at each stage of the massage to meet the service needs
- explain how the massage products should be applied and removed for home use
- note any adverse reaction, if any occur, and action taken

AFTER

- record the areas treated
- record any modification to the service application that has occurred
- record what products have been used in the service as appropriate
- avoid bathing for 6 hours after the service to allow oils to penetrate the skin thoroughly
- drink plenty of water or herbal teas to keep the body cleansed and hydrated
- appropriate relaxation techniques
- how to use pre-blended oils at home
- recommended time intervals between services
- discuss the benefits of continuous services
- record the effectiveness of the service
- record any samples provided (review their success at the next appointment)

RETAIL OPPORTUNITIES

- provide guidance on progression of the service plan for future appointments
- advice regarding products that would be suitable for home use and how to gain maximum benefit from their use to care for the skin and continue the service benefits (pre-blended oils, aromatherapy bath products)
- recommendations for further services including heat services and body massage services
- advice of further products or services that you have recommended that the client may or may not have received before
- note any purchase made by the client

EVALUATION

- enter all service details on a record card including products and methods used, any service adaptations and client's approval of result
- record how you will progress the service to maintain and advance the service results in the future

HEALTH AND SAFETY

- in the event of a contra-action contact the salon immediately
- avoid alcohol before and after the service as it may produce unpleasant side-effects
- advise on appropriate necessary action to be taken in the event of an unwanted reaction (an allergy to the oil used, flu-like symptoms including raised temperature, aching muscles, caused by release of toxins)

SERVICE MODIFICATION

Examples of service modification include:

- altering the pressure or choice of manipulations during massage to suit the client's skin and muscle tone
- adapting the massage to achieve a specific effect (e.g. relaxation, stimulation)

ACTIVITY

Broken wrist

A client presents for a full-body massage service but has a broken wrist in plaster. What action do you take?

HEALTH & SAFETY

Cuts and abrasions

Why is it important to ensure that any cuts and abrasions that the client may have are covered during the service?

Preparation of the client

Following the visual inspection at consultation the client is prepared for the service to proceed. It is a good idea if the client is advised to empty their bladder before the service commences as the oil may have a diuretic effect.

Ask the client to remove all jewellery (including hair accessories) and store them in a safe place (follow your workplace policy).

Position the client for service. Instruct the client to lie on the couch in a supine or prone position according to the area to be treated. If using a hydraulic couch adjust to a suitable height.

Place towels over the client in a way which will allow minimal interruption and keep them warm. (At this stage the modesty towel or bathrobe should be removed.)

Cover any minor skin defects, cuts or abrasions with an adhesive dressing prior to the service.

If the client has long hair it may need to be secured in a clip while you treat the neck area.

Support pillows or rolled towels can be placed to improve client comfort. Support may be provided in supine position under the neck and under the knees avoiding strain to the client's back. In prone position, support may be provided under the shoulders and ankles. If facial massage is to be performed, cleanse the face using suitable facial products for their skin type using your regular cleansing routine. The feet should be cleaned using alcohol-impregnated foot wipes.

Help the client onto the couch and allow them to get comfortable in a prone (face down) position. Cover them with towels and ensure that they are warm and comfortable.

Selecting pre-blended aromatherapy oils

For this unit you are required to select a suitable pre-blended aromatherapy oil to meet the client's needs. The table shown below will help you easily to select pre-blended oils that are required for particular outcomes.

Initially you may select the oil guided by the generic effect, i.e. 'uplifting' provided on the product label literature.

Compatibility of essential oils to treatment objectives

Relaxing	*Uplifting*	*Sense of well-being*	*Anti-cellulite*	*Stimulating*
Roman Camomile	Eucalyptus	Roman Camomile	Juniper	Basil
Clary sage	Grapefruit	Clary sage	Patchouli	Geranium
Geranium	Lemon	Geranium	Rosemary	Orange
Lavender	Lemongrass	Lavender	Grapefruit	Black pepper
Marjoram	Rosemary	Neroli		Rosemary
Neroli	Tea tree	Rose Bulgar		
Rose Bulgar		Ylang-ylang		
Ylang-ylang				

Carry out massage using pre-blended aromatherapy oils

Service procedures

- Following the consultation, choose the appropriate pre-blended oils, then inform the client which oils you are using and why. Confirm the clients agreement with the choice and confirm their understanding with the choice.
- Measure out the chosen blend according to the body area being treated.
- Wash your hands.
- Apply massage techniques using the procedure outlined on the following pages, ensuring client comfort and discretion at all times.
- Provide water for the client to rehydrate.
- At the end of the service, offer the client aftercare advice.
- Allow sufficient post-service recovery time to avoid a contra-action.
- Ask the client if they have any queries that you may be able to answer.
- Offer to assist the client in getting off the couch.
- Tell the client where you are going, then leave them to dress in privacy.

Outcome 3: Massage the body using pre-blended aromatherapy oils

Learn how to perform massage using pre-blended aromatherapy oils by:

1. Providing suitable support and cushioning to specific areas of the body during the service if necessary.
2. Adapting your **massage techniques**, sequence and use of pre-blended oil to meet the client's **physical characteristics** and **service area(s)**.
3. Effectively varying the depth, rhythm and pressure of massage movements to meet **service objectives**, **service area(s)** and client's **physical characteristics** and preferences.
4. Ensuring the application and use of pre-blended oil minimizes waste.
5. Taking appropriate and prompt remedial action if contra-actions or discomfort occur during the course of the service.
6. Allowing the client sufficient post-service recovery time.
7. Ensuring the finished result is to the client's satisfaction and meets the agreed **service objectives**.

TOP TIP

Seated service

A client may receive the service for the head and neck while sitting in a chair, leaning over a couch or leaning against the beauty therapist.

This is a popular de-stressing massage and is suitable for clients who are unable to get on to the beauty couch.

ALWAYS REMEMBER

Beauty therapist's posture

It is important that the beauty therapist maintains the correct posture throughout the service. This will ensure the health and well-being of the beauty therapist and the effectiveness of the service. Refer to pages 350–351, body massage chapter for guidance on the correct postural stance.

HEALTH & SAFETY

Contra-actions

Remember that irritation or sensitivity to pre-blended aromatheray oils may be dose-dependent, so contra-actions may not show up in patch skin 'sensitivity' test but could appear in or following the service.

TOP TIP

Consultation during service

In aromatherapy massage the consultation continues during the service as the client usually provides more information about themselves that may influence your future massage requirements for them.

Order of massage using pre-blended aromatherapy oils

Start the full-body massage with the back. As this is the largest area, the oils will begin to penetrate the skin and enter the bloodstream quickly, therefore allowing a more immediate effect of the service. Then proceed in this order:

Order for massage

back
↓
gluteals
↓
back of legs
↓
face, neck and scalp
↓
chest and shoulders
↓
arms and hands
↓
abdomen
↓
front of legs
↓
feet

> Any employer will value a beauty therapist who uses their initiative appropriately – someone who is always looking out for ways of improving efficiency. If you're unsure about an idea you've had, though, talk it through with your employer before going ahead!
>
> **Katie Whitehouse**

Before commencing the service on each body part, carry out a friction rub. Using the flat palms of both hands, quickly rub back and forth a number of times. This will help to warm the skin and brush off dry, superficial skin cells, aiding the absorption of the oils.

Contra-indicated essential oils

Some essential oils are contra-indicated to particular conditions as shown in the table. However, this is not an exhaustive list. The beauty therapist should always check for contra-indicated essential oils associated with any conditions that the client may have.

Condition	*Contra-indicated oils*
Pregnancy	Aniseed, basil, camphor, carrot seed, cinnamon, clove, cedarwood, clary sage, cypress, fennel, hyssop, juniper berry, jasmine, lemongrass, marjoram, origanum, nutmeg, parsley, peppermint, rose, rosemary, sage, savoury, thyme
High blood pressure	Hyssop, rosemary, sage, thyme
Epilepsy	Hyssop, fennel, sage
Prior to exposure to sunlight	Angelica, bergamot, lemon, lime, orange

Step-by-step: Massage routine for the back

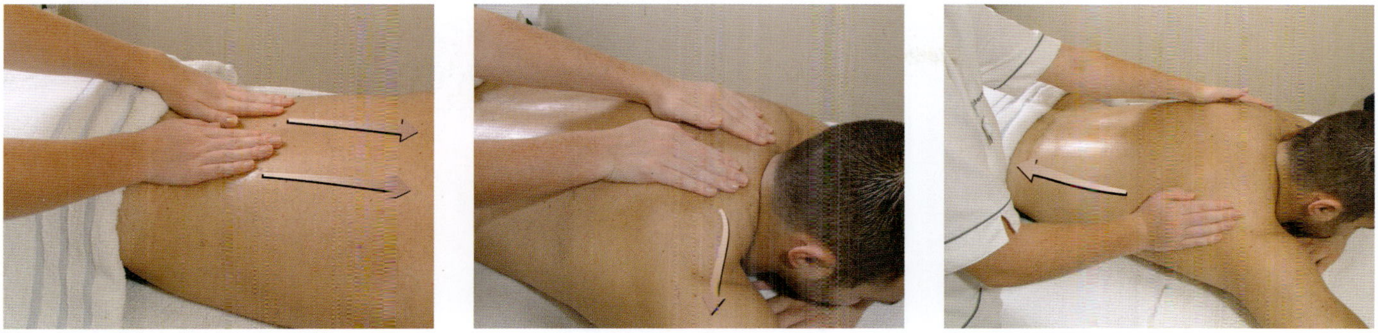

1 Effleurage From the base of the back, effleurage up the erector spinae area, across the shoulders and back down to the base of the spine. Repeat this step a further two times.

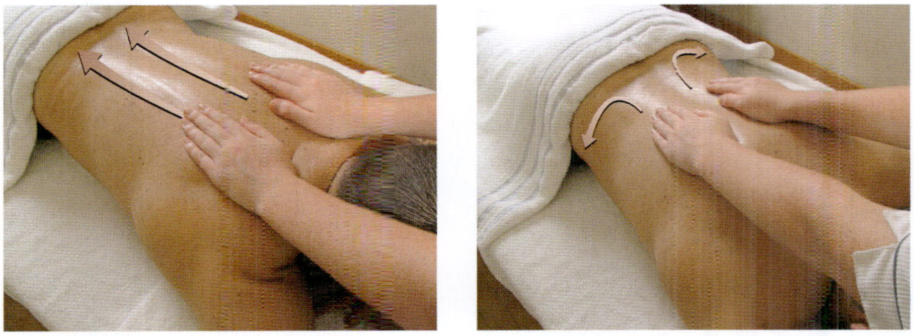

2 Reverse effleurage Standing at the client's head, effleurage from the back of the neck down over the erector spinae area, across the base of the back, and back up to the back of the neck. Repeat this step a further two times.

ALWAYS REMEMBER

Spinal column safety

Never massage directly over the spinal column.

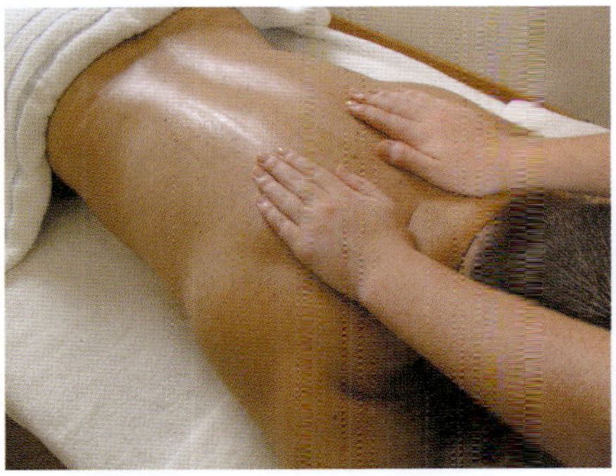

3 Double-handed kneading Starting at one shoulder, place the hands side by side and knead together, compressing the tissue between the hands. Work down to the base of the back, then move the hands slightly towards the trapezius area, and finally work down again to the base of the back. Continue until the whole of the back has been treated. Repeat this step a further two times.

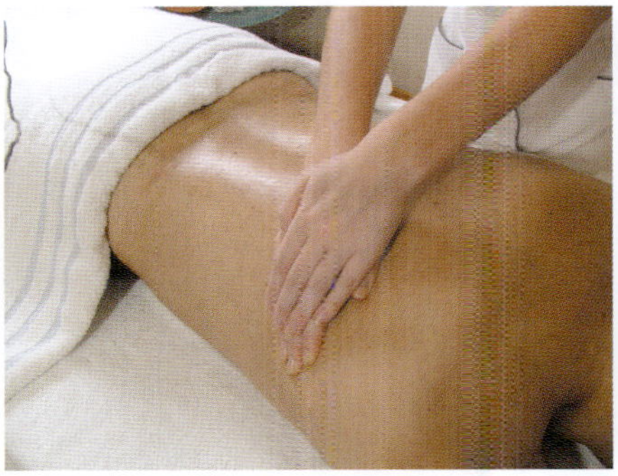

4 Reinforced kneading Starting at one shoulder, place one hand on top of the other and knead the tissues. Work down to the base of the back, then move the hands slightly towards the trapezius area, and finally work down again to the base of the back. Continue until the whole of the back has been treated. Repeat this step a further two times.

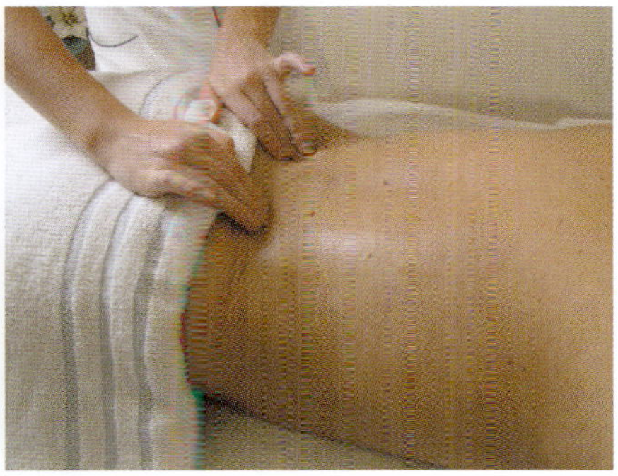

5 Kneading to the intercostal nerves Starting at the base of the spine, on either side of the spinal column, work outwards with both hands simultaneously. Using the first and middle fingers of each hand, knead in small circles, gradually working to the sides of the body. Slide the fingers back to the original position, then move up slightly and repeat the movement. When the fingers reach the ribs, the kneading should be done between the ribs on the intercostal nerves and the fingers should slide back on the rib. This movement is continued up to the occiput.

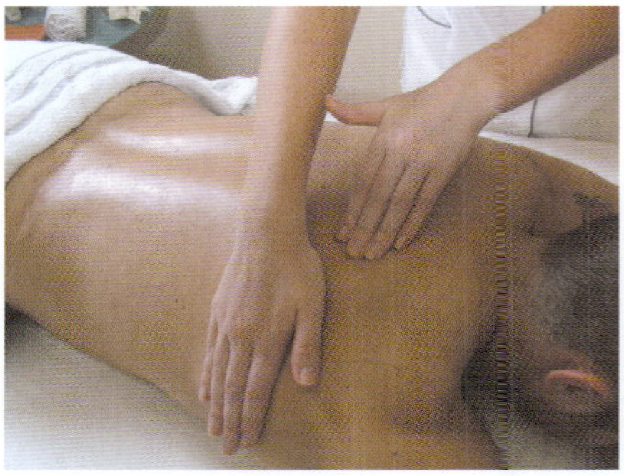

6 Single-handed stroking to intercostal nerves Starting at the top of the spine, use the whole of the hands to alternately stroke away from the spine in the direction of the intercostal nerves. Stroke down one side of the spine, then repeat on the other side. Work with moderate-to-slow speed.

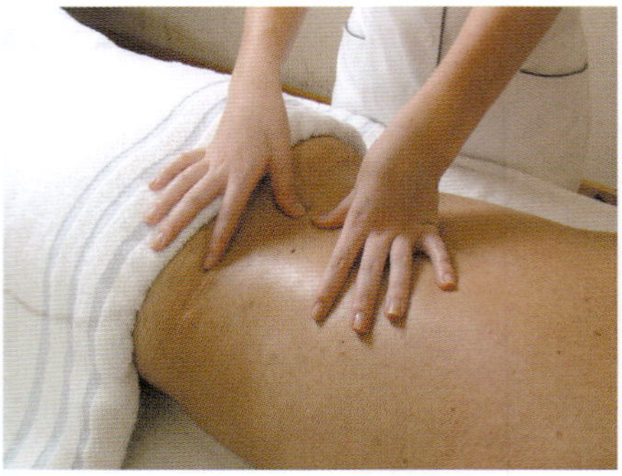

7 Thumb kneading to erector spinae Starting at the base of the spine, place the thumbs one in front of the other on the erector spinae muscle. Slowly slide the thumbs back and forth while also moving slowly up the muscle. Continue to the top of the back then repeat on the other side of the muscle.

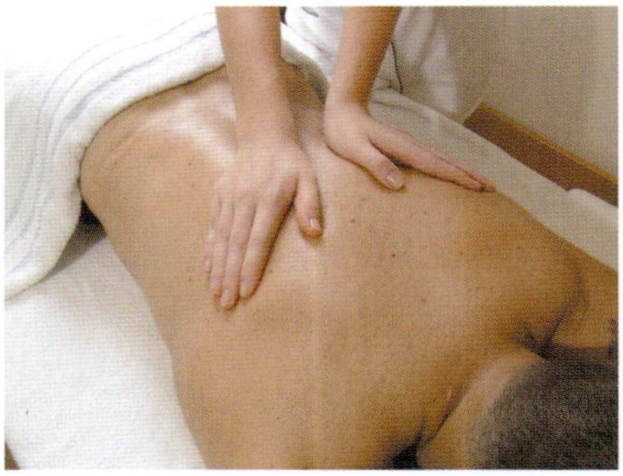

8 Double-handed stroking to intercostal nerves Place both hands either side of the spine, then gently stroke both hands outwards simultaneously in the direction of the intercostal nerves. Repeat the movement while working down towards the base of the spine.

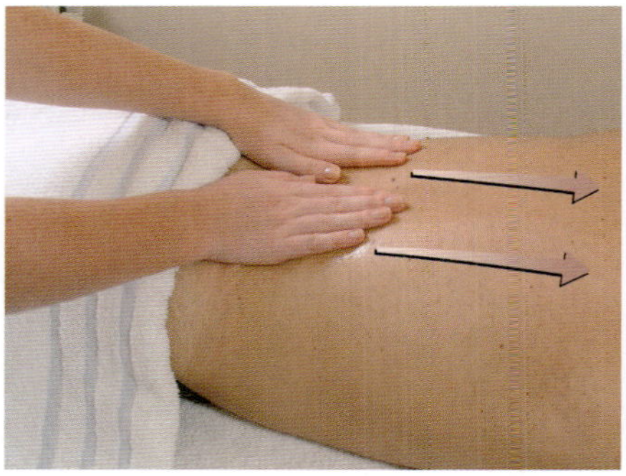

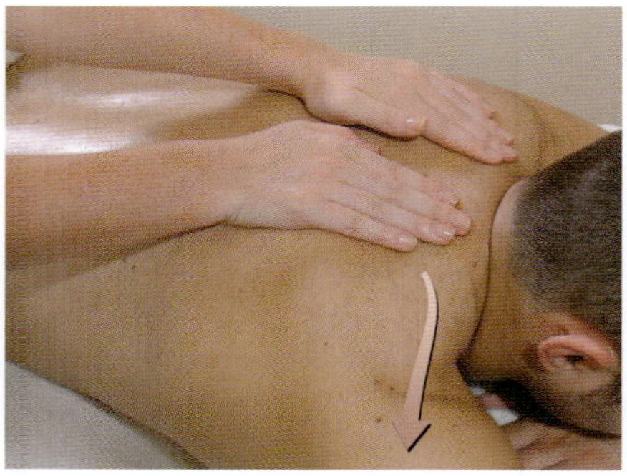

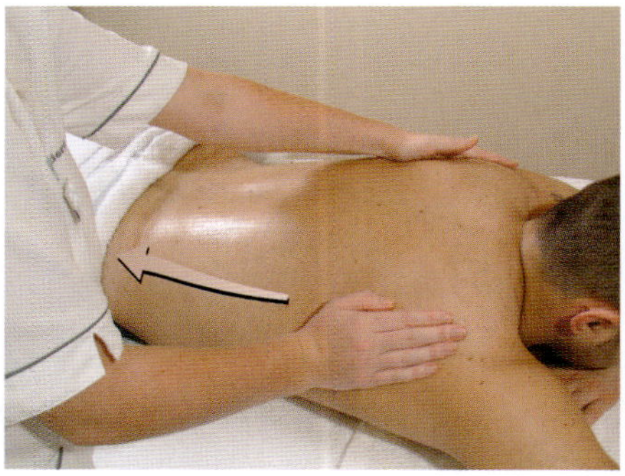

9 Repeat step 1 a further three times

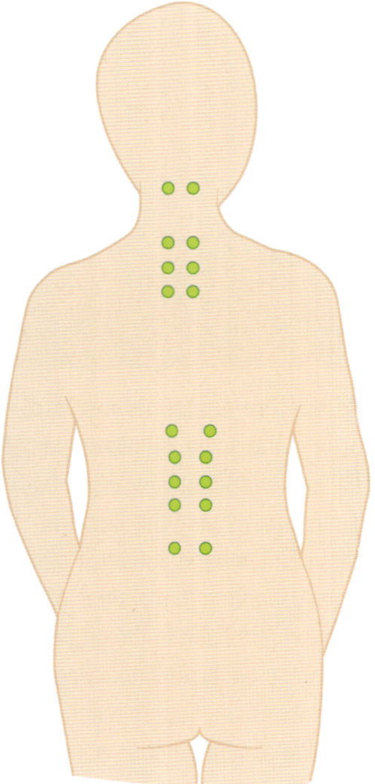

10 Apply pressure to the tsubo points shown in the diagram.

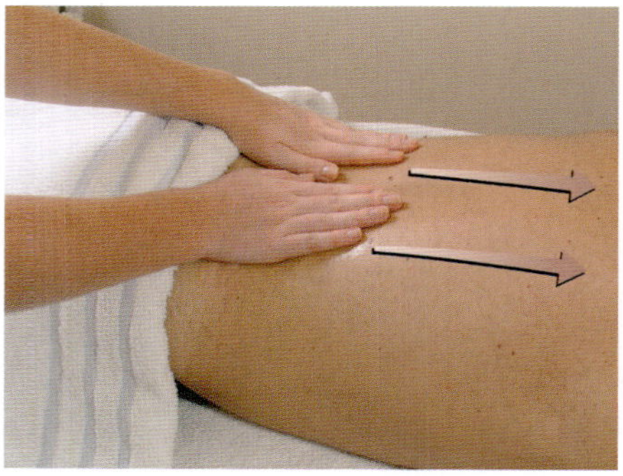

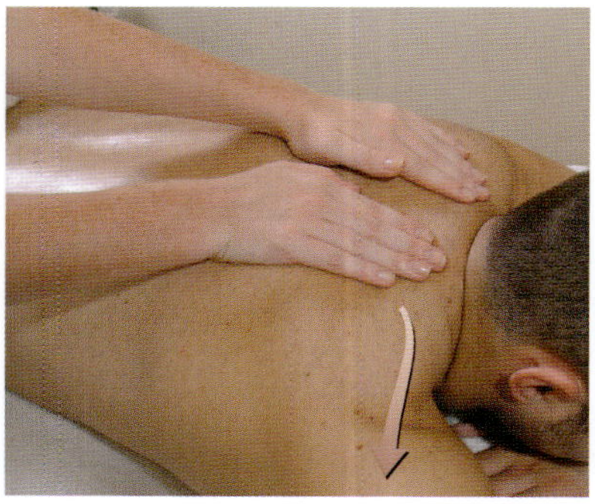

11 Repeat step 1 a further three times.

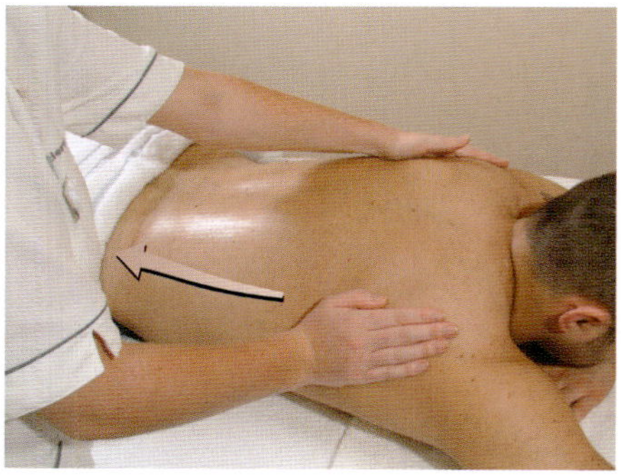

COURSEMATE

For a video on massage using pre-blended oils (including back, neck and back of leg), please visit this book's accompanying CourseMate.

How to massage the gluteals

1. Effleurage to whole of one side of gluteals. Use the whole of the hand and work from the lateral aspect to the midline. Repeat this step a further two times.
2. Kneading to whole of one side of gluteals. Knead in a circular motion from the lateral aspect to the midline. Repeat this step a further two times.
3. Apply pressure to the tsubo points as shown in the diagram opposite.
4. Repeat step 1 a further three times.

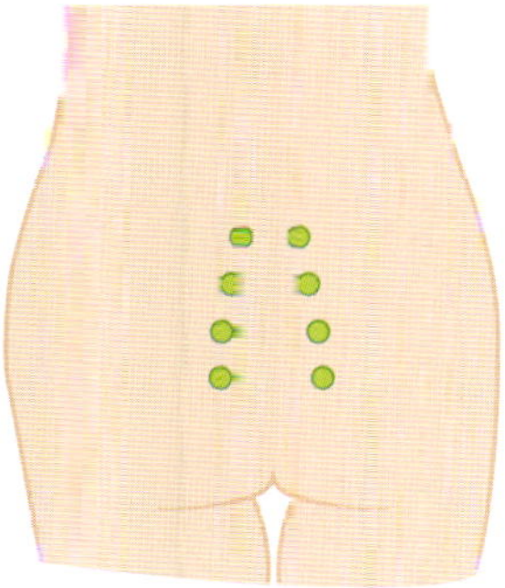

Tsubo points for gluteal massage

Step-by-step: Massage routine for the back of the legs

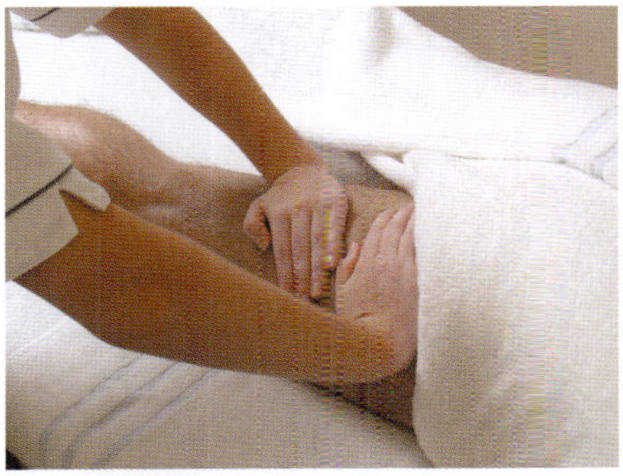

1 **Effleurage to whole leg** Starting at the tips of the toes, use the whole of the hands to apply effleurage over the whole posterior aspect of the leg, finishing at the gluteal area. Repeat this step a further two times.

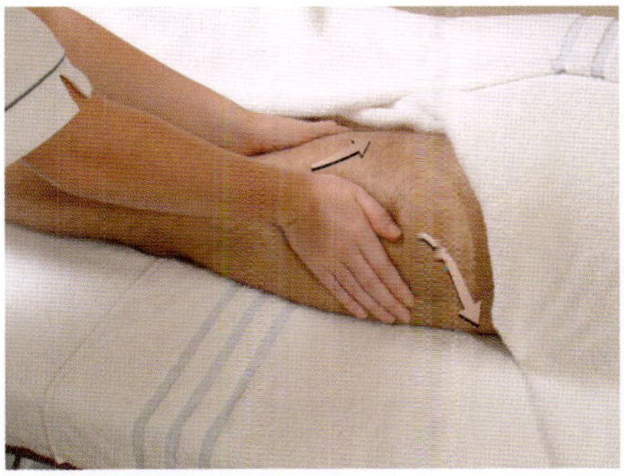

2 **Alternate kneading to whole leg** Start at the top of the thigh with the hands on either side. Knead the tissues in an alternate movement, applying pressure on the upward movement. Work down to the foot and include the plantar aspect of the foot. Repeat this step a further two times.

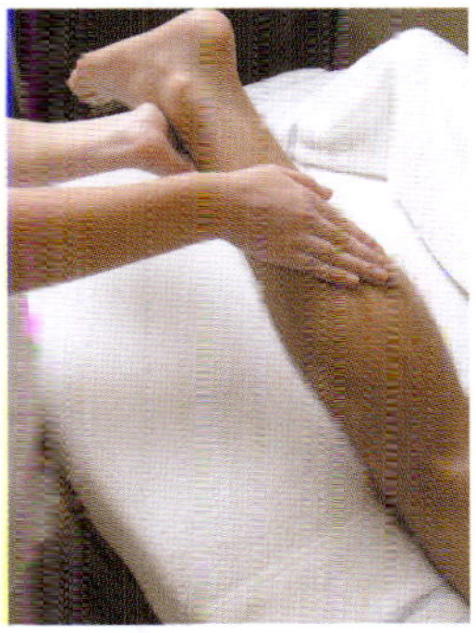

3 **Effleurage to lower leg (with knee bent)** With one hand, raise the lower leg and support it at the ankle. With the other hand, apply effleurage strokes from the ankle to the knee. Repeat this step a further five times.

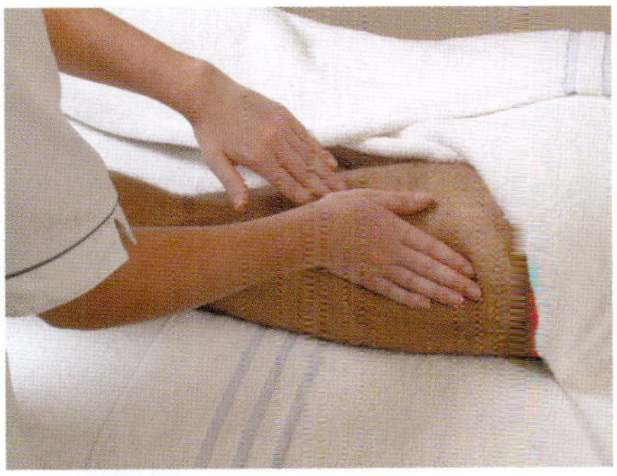

4 **Four-finger stroking to hamstring area** Place both hands on the upper thigh just below the gluteals. Stroke both hands away from the midline in a diagonal movement. Bring the hands back to the midline just below their previous position and repeat the movement. Carry the movement on to the knee.

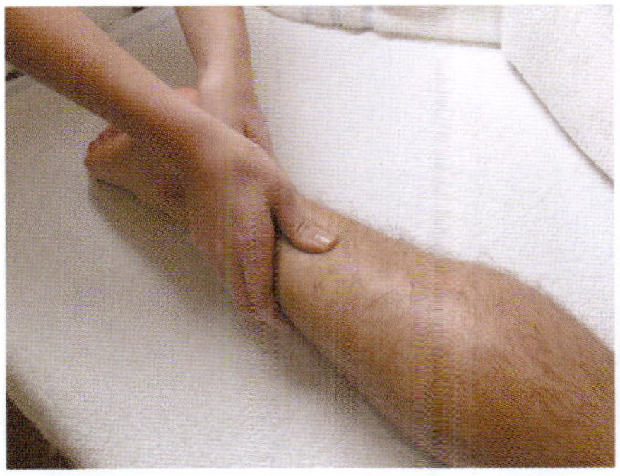

5 **Thumb stroking of sciatic nerve** Place the thumb over the base of the Achilles tendon and gently slide the thumb up the centre of the calf towards the knee. Use a firm, even pressure and stop just below the knee. Repeat this step a further two times.

TOP TIP

Supporting the leg

Two large, folded towels may be used to support the raised leg in step 3, instead of the beauty therapist holding the foot.

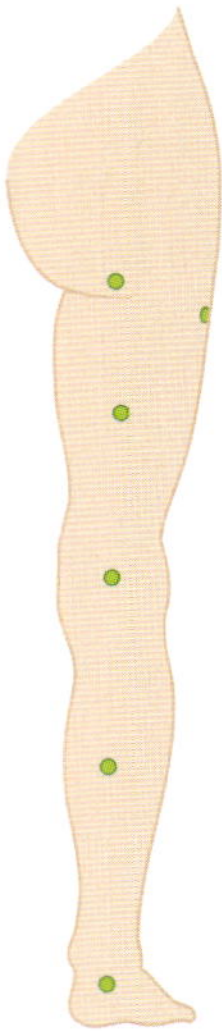

6 Apply pressure to the tsubo points as shown in the diagram.

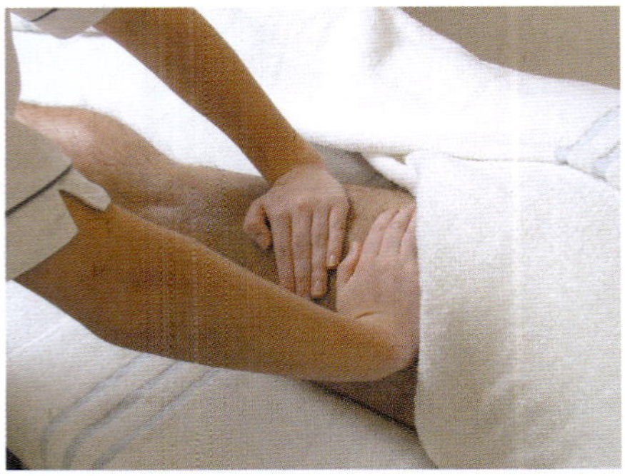

7 **Effleurage to whole leg** Repeat step 1 a further three times.

Step-by-step: Massage routine for the face, neck and scalp

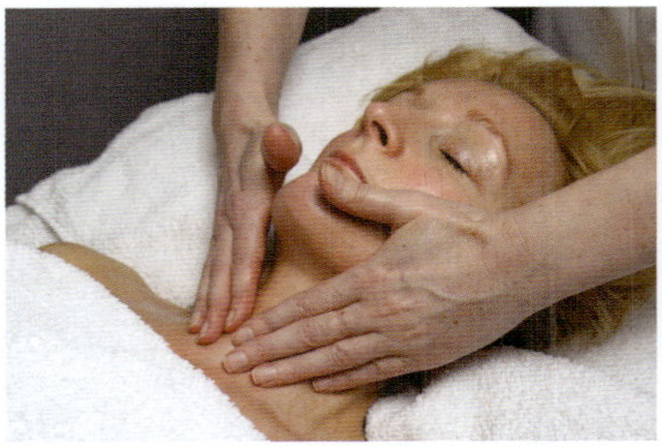

1 **Effleurage to front of neck (shown), face, scalp and back of neck** Repeat step 1 a further two times.

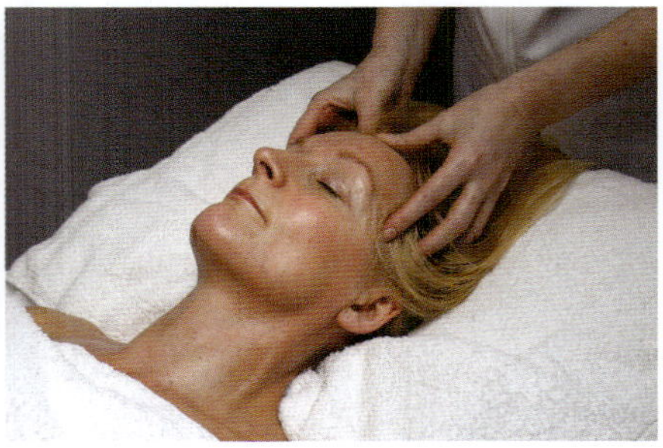

2 **Finger kneading to scalp** Starting at the temple, use the finger-tips to slowly but firmly knead the scalp all over. This movement is similar to that of shampooing the hair, but with a slower action.

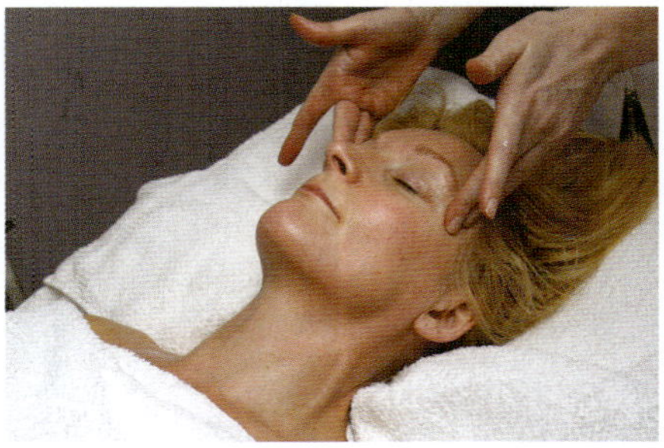

3 **Effleurage to neck and cheeks** Place both hands on the sternum and effleurage up the neck to the chin, out across the jaw line, up over the cheeks to the temples. Apply a slight vibration to the temples with the fingertips before lifting the hands. Repeat step 3 a further two times.

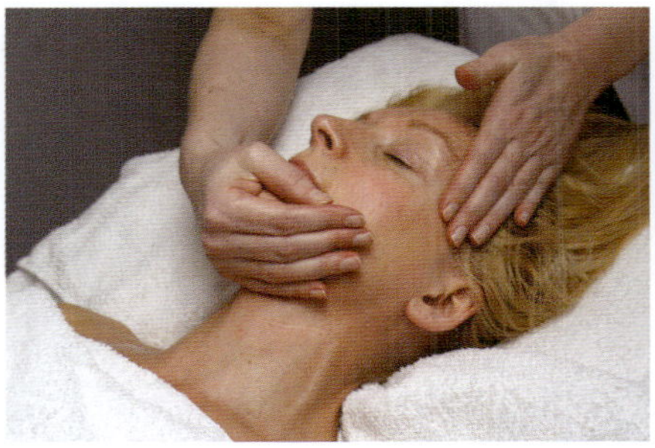

4 **Effleurage across chin (shown)** Support the side of the head with one hand, and with the other hand apply a smooth effleurage stroke from one angle of the jaw to the other. Swap hands and repeat on the other side. Repeat step 4 a further three times.

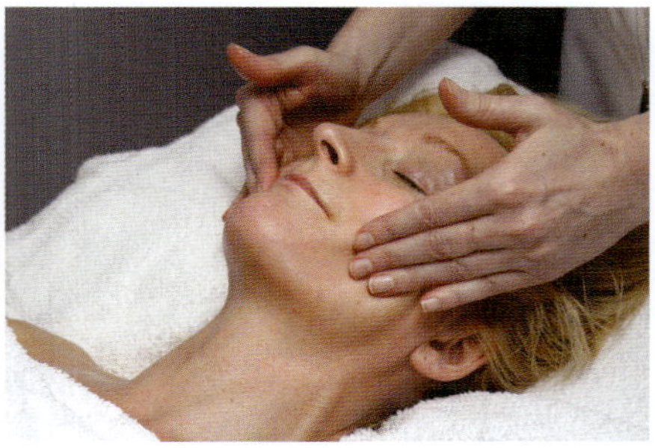

5 **Finger kneading to jaw line** Starting on the chin apply effleurage over the jaw line to the ears with both hands simultaneously. With the fingertips apply circular kneading movements back across the jaw line to the chin. Repeat step 5 a further three times.

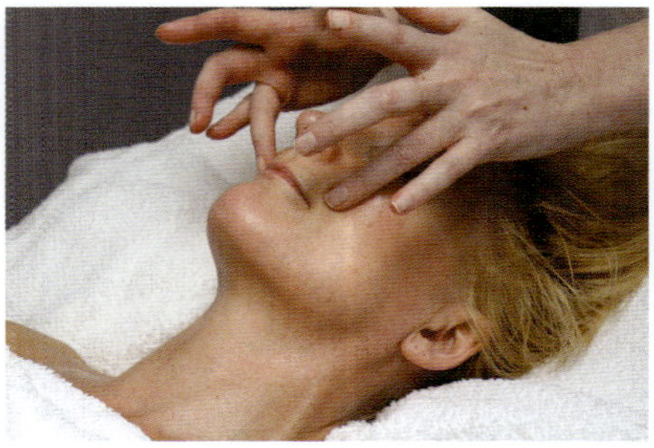

6 **One finger effleurage around lips** With the ring fingers of both hands placed beneath the centre of the lower lip, apply a light effleurage stroke around the mouth to the nose. Take the fingers off the skin and repeat the movement three times.

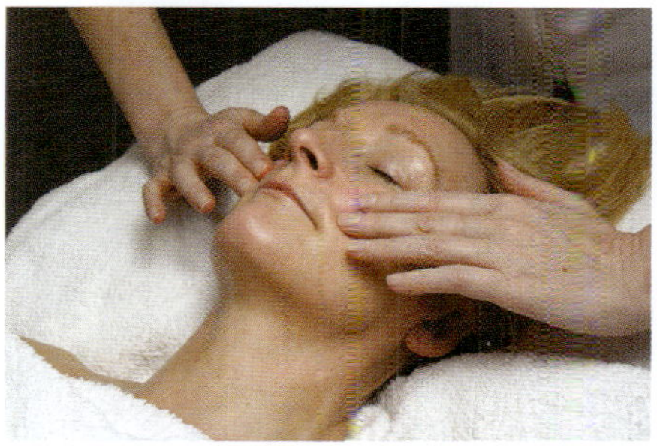

© CENGAGE LEARNING LTD

7 Drain from nose to ears Place the first and middle finger of each hand on either side of the nostrils. With a light even pressure sweep across the cheeks beneath the cheekbones to the ear. Repeat step 7 a further two times.

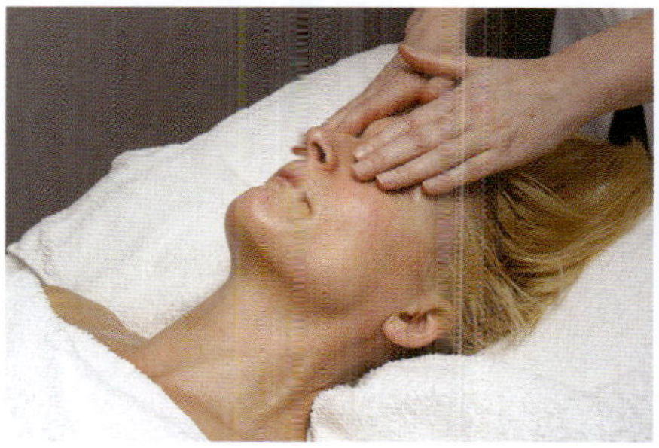

© CENGAGE LEARNING LTD

8 Circle around eyes Place both thumbs on the forehead with one hand on the side of the head for support. With the fingers of the other hand, circle around the eyes towards the nose. Repeat three times. Keeping the thumbs in contact with the skin, support the other side of the head with the other hand and draw circles around the eye. Repeat three times. Repeat step 8 a further two times.

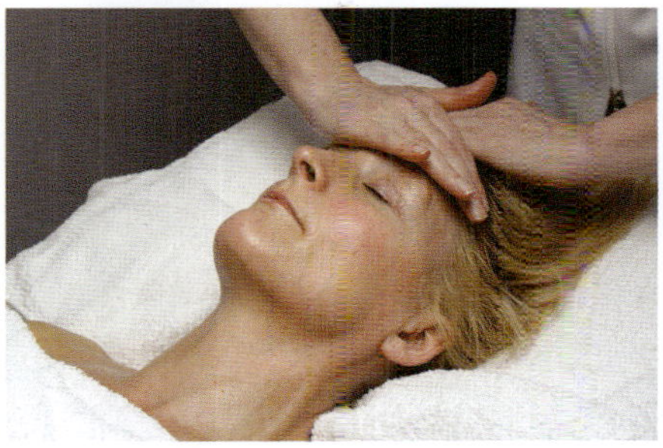

© CENGAGE LEARNING LTD

9 Alternate stroking to forehead Place one hand on the forehead and stroke from the eyebrows to the hairline. Repeat with alternate hands covering the whole forehead. Use a slow controlled effleurage movement.

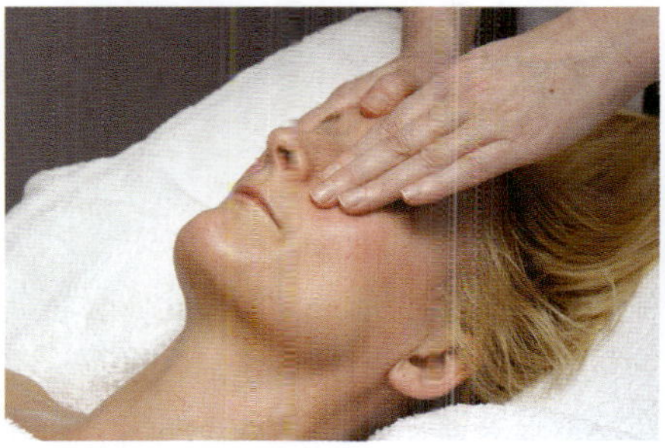

© CENGAGE LEARNING LTD

10 Finger curtains to eyes Slide the fingertips of both hands down the bridge of the nose, relax the fingers onto the cheeks and slowly draw the hands over the eyes. Hold for a count of three. Slide finger tips out to the temples, apply a slight vibration then remove.

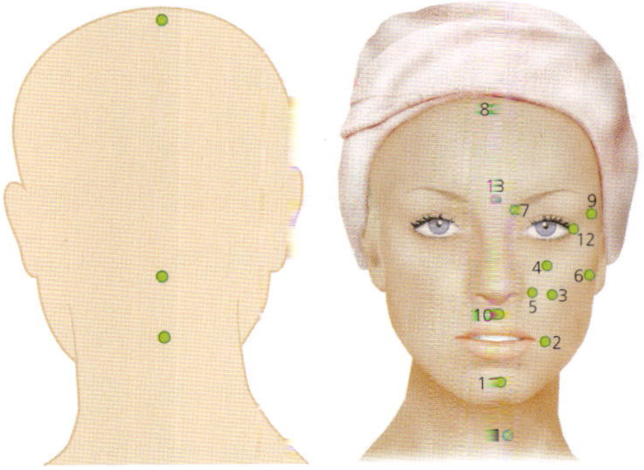

11 Apply pressure to the tsubo points as shown in the diagrams.

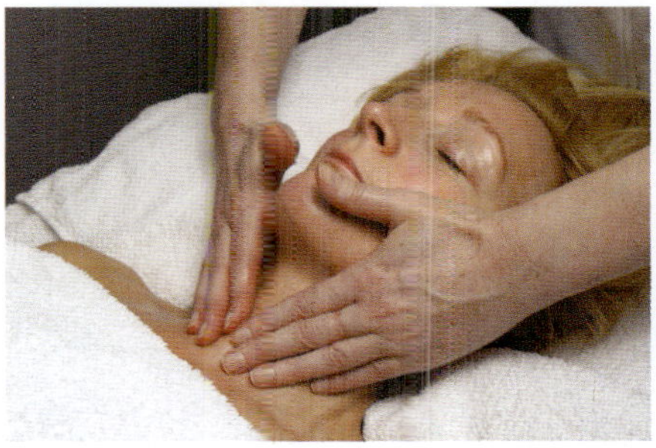

© CENGAGE LEARNING LTD

12 Repeat step 11 a further three times.

HEALTH & SAFETY

Oils and eyes

Keep essential oils away from the eyes to avoid irritation.

> The best clinics I have worked in have operated as a team, with staff meeting regularly to discuss work issues as well as informing each other about their own specialisms, such as reflexology and why that could be beneficial. The more you know about your team-mates and the more they know about you, the more you'll be able to refer clients to each other.
>
> **Katie Whitehouse**

Step-by-step: Massage routine for the chest and shoulders

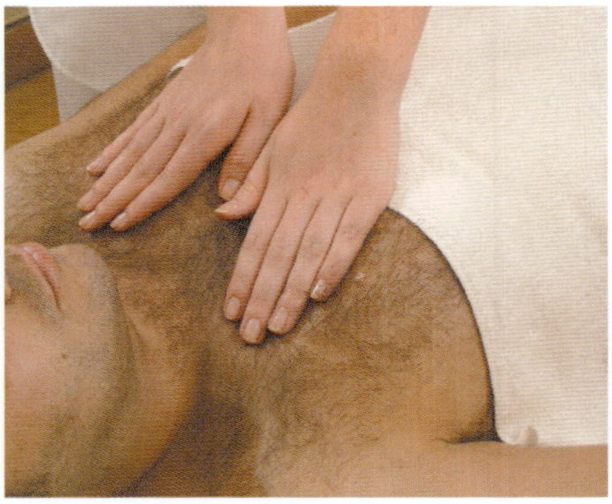

1 **Effleurage to chest and shoulders** Place both hands on the sternum and effleurage out across the chest, behind the shoulders and up the back of the neck. Repeat step 1 a further two times.

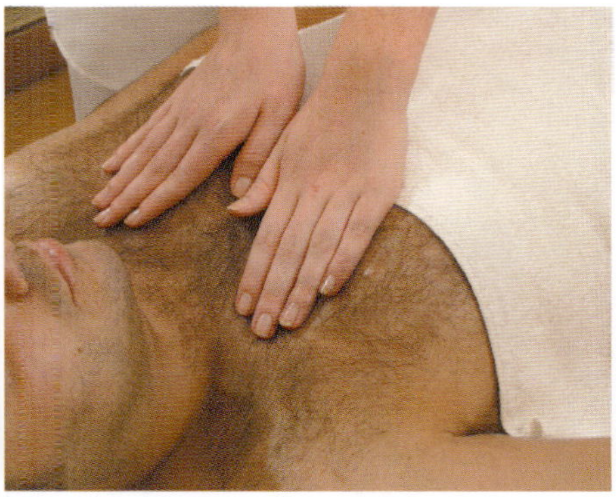

2 **Kneading to chest and shoulders** Place both hands on the sternum in a relaxed fist with fingers underneath the hand. Using circular movements knead out across the chest, behind the shoulders, over the upper trapezius area and back of the neck. Repeat step 2 a further two times.

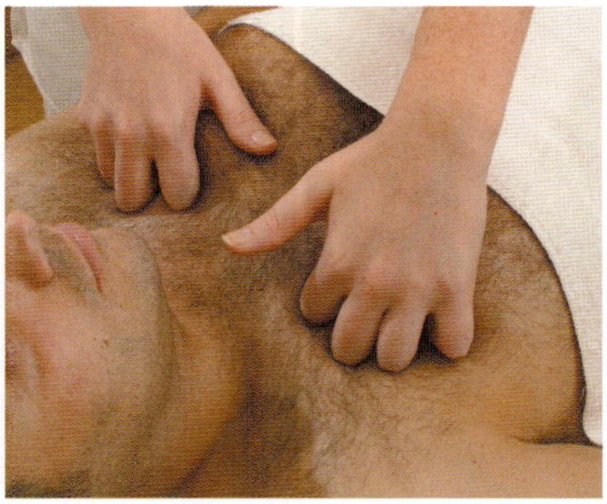

3 **Effleurage to chest and shoulders** Place both hands on the sternum and effleurage out across the chest, behind the shoulders and up the back of the neck. Repeat step 3 a further two times.

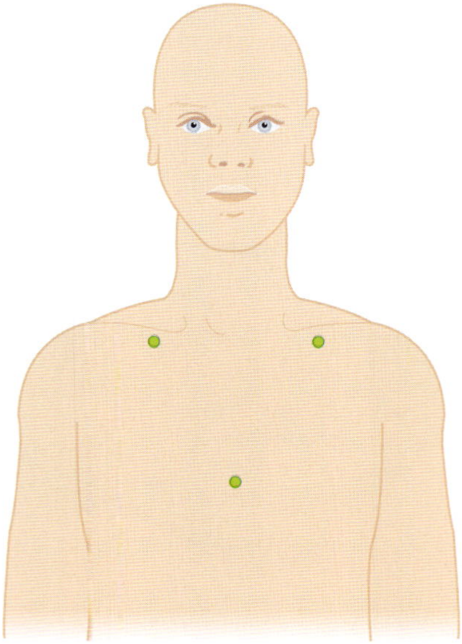

4 Apply pressure to the tsubo points as shown in the diagram.

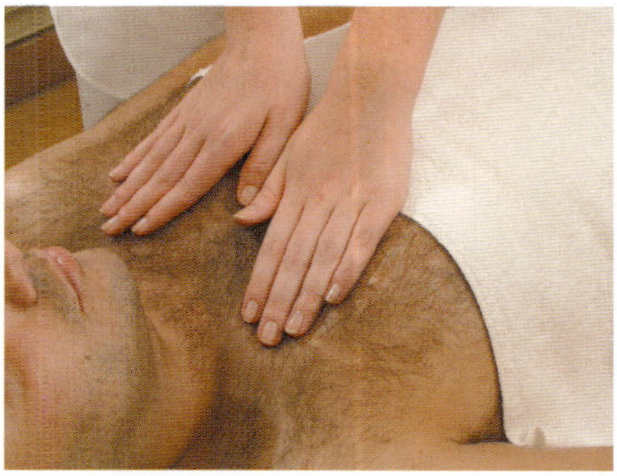

5 Repeat step 1 a further three times.

Step-by-step: Massage routine for the abdomen

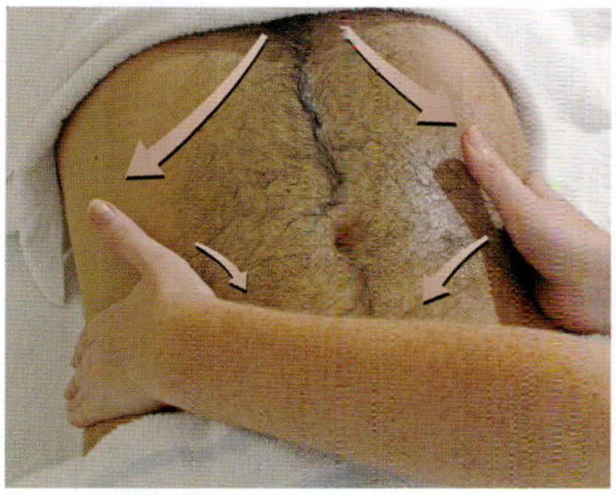

1 **Effleurage** Place both hands on the abdomen just below the sternum. Stroke outwards to the waist, then inwards down towards the pubic bone. Repeat the stroke in reverse. Repeat this step a further two times.

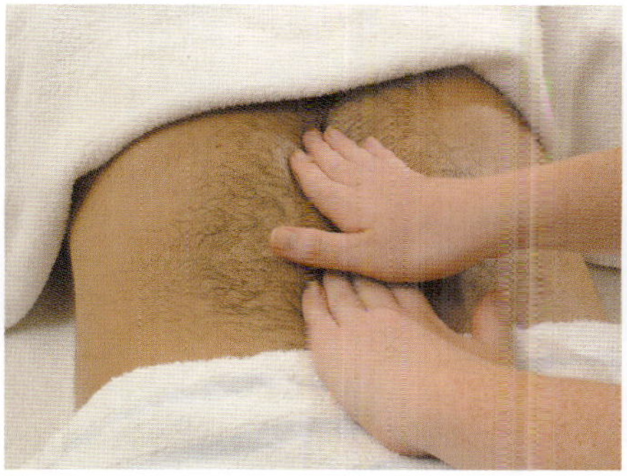

2 **Single-handed stroking to rectus abdominus** Place one hand just below the sternum and apply a smooth effleurage stroke down the rectus abdominus muscle. Repeat the movement using alternate hands. Repeat this step a further five times.

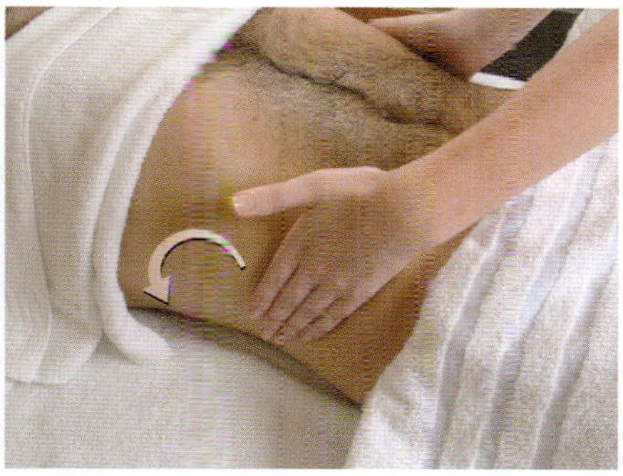

3 **Kneading the abdominal walls** Place the hands either side of the waist just below the ribcage. Using upwards, circular movements, knead down towards the hip. Effleurage back to the ribcage. Repeat this step a further two times.

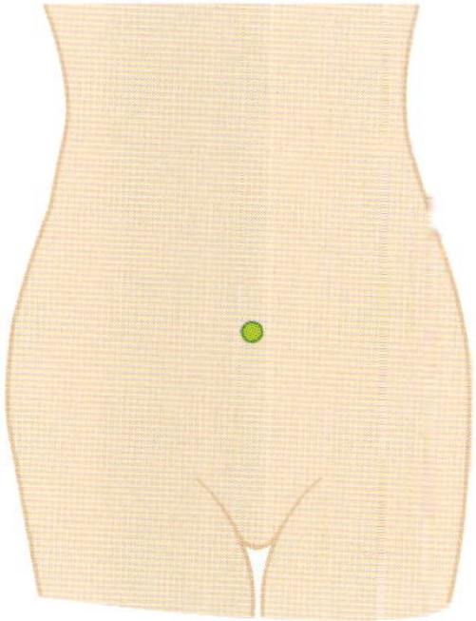

4 Apply pressure to the tsubo point as shown in the diagram.

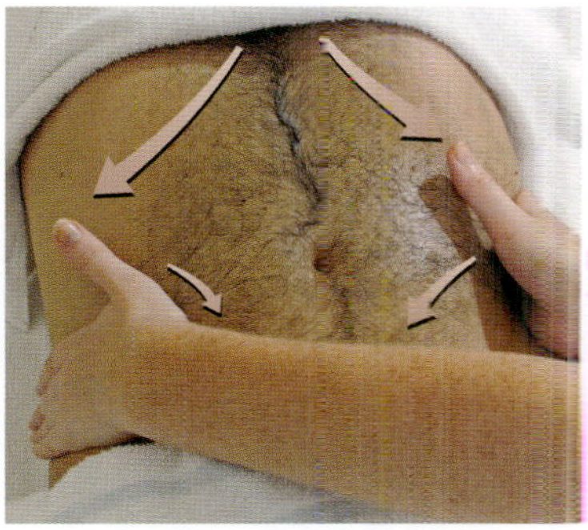

5 Repeat step 1 a further three times.

Step-by-step: Massage routine for the front of the legs

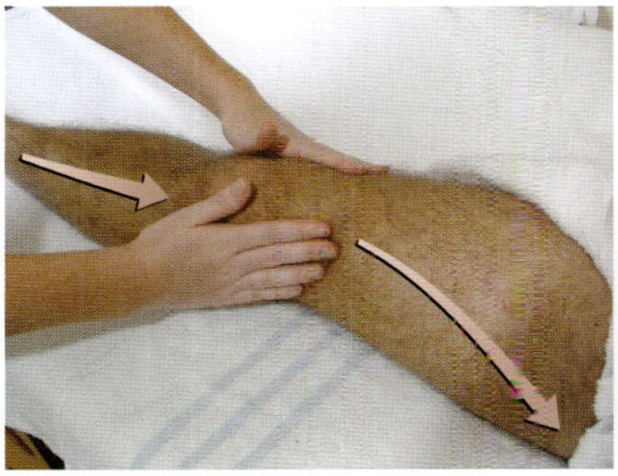

1 **Effleurage to whole leg** Starting at the tips of the toes, use the whole of the hands to apply effleurage over the whole anterior aspect of the leg, finishing at the inguinal gland area. Repeat this step a further two times.

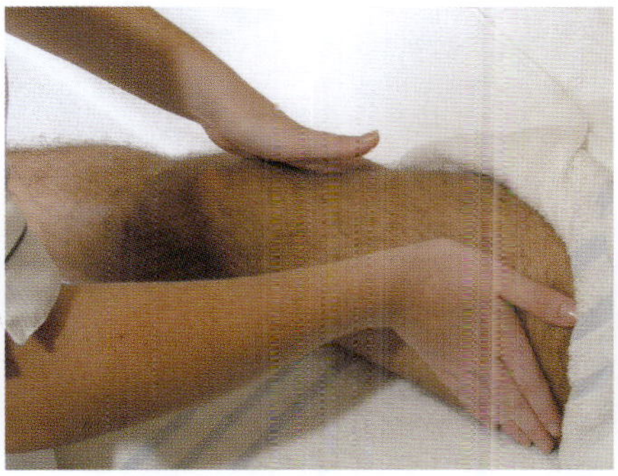

2 **Alternate kneading to whole leg** Start at the top of the thigh with the hands on either side. Knead the tissues in an alternate movement, applying pressure on the upward movement. Work down to the foot and include the plantar aspect of the foot. Repeat this step a further two times.

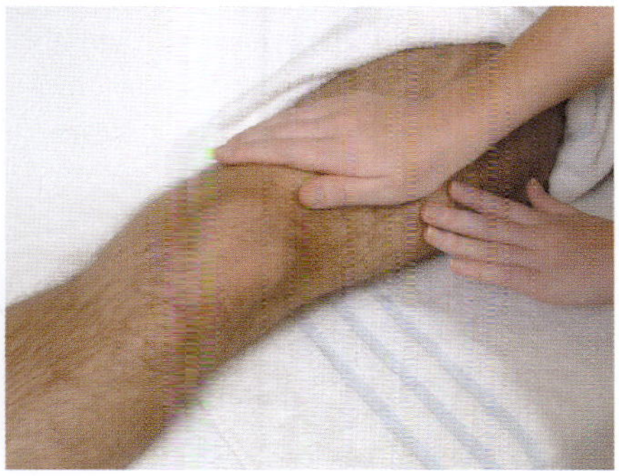

3 **Reverse diagonal stroking across thigh** Standing with your back towards the client's upper body stroke from the medial aspect of the knee, across the thigh to the hip, with alternate hands. Use a light pressure and moderate speed. Repeat this step a further three times.

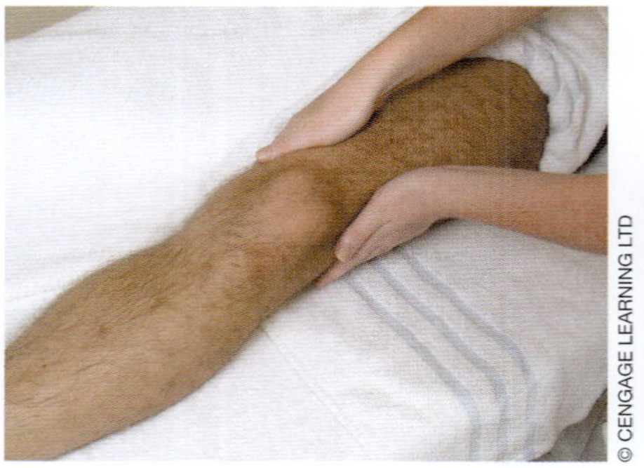

4 Reverse double kneading to thigh Stand with your back towards the client's upper body with the hands on either side of the thigh just above the knee. Knead the tissues in an alternate movement, applying pressure on the upward movement, working towards the hip. Repeat this step a further two times.

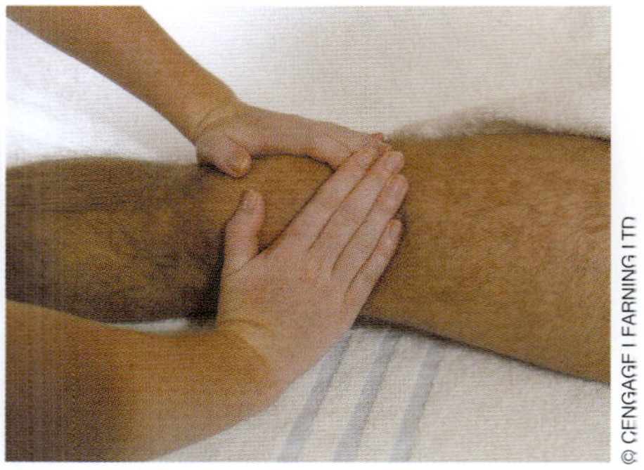

5 Effleurage around knee After crossing your wrists, place the hands on either side of the knee and effleurage around the knee until the thumbs meet again at the front. Using the thumbs, stroke towards the back of the knee. Repeat this step a further two times.

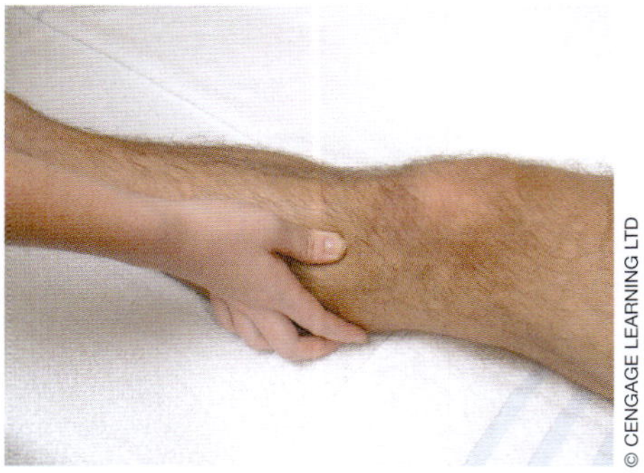

6 Thumb kneading to tibialis anterior Starting just below the knee, use the thumb to apply small, circular kneading movements to tibialis anterior. The fingers may be used to steady the thumb in this movement but do not use them to apply pressure. Work down towards the ankle. Repeat this step a further two times.

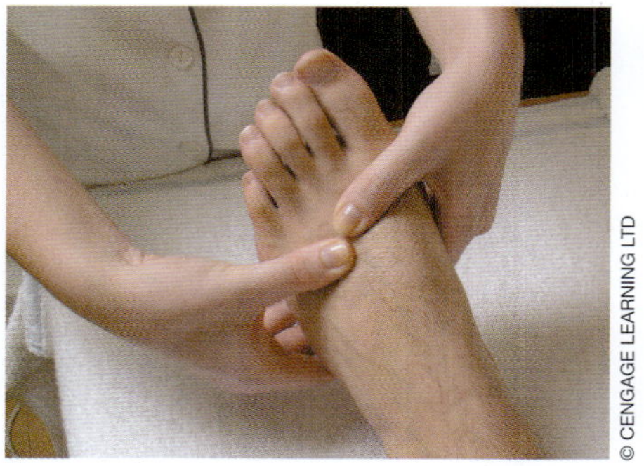

7 Cross-thumb kneading to dorsal aspect of foot Hold the foot with both hands, fingers supporting the plantar surface and thumbs on the dorsal surface. Keeping the fingers still, push the thumbs back and forth across the foot with moderate speed, covering the whole surface from toes to ankles.

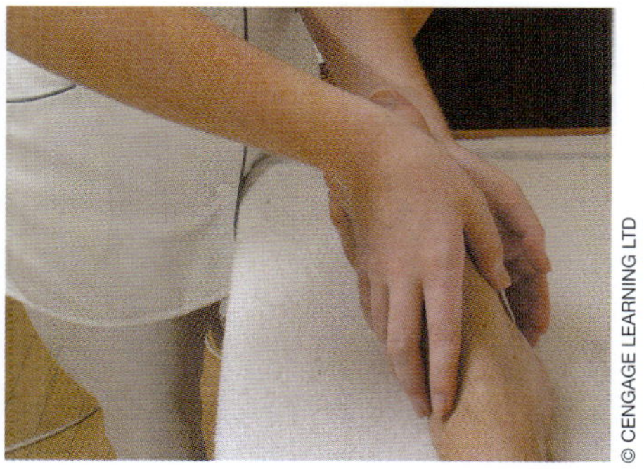

8 Palm kneading to sole of foot Supporting the dorsal aspect of the foot with one hand, use the base of the other hand to apply deep circular kneading to the plantar surface of the foot. Movement should be slow with moderate-to-deep pressure to avoid tickling the client.

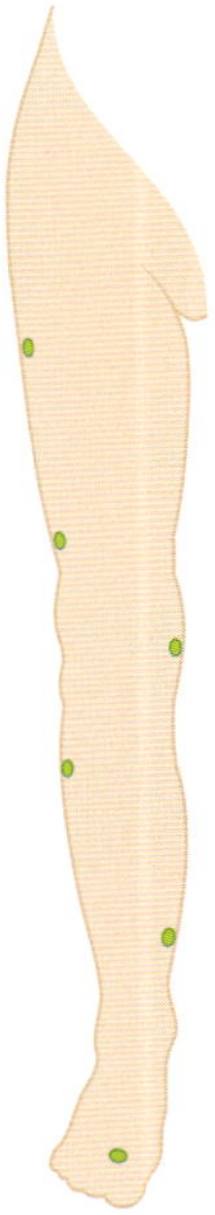

9 Apply pressure to the tsubo points shown in the diagram.

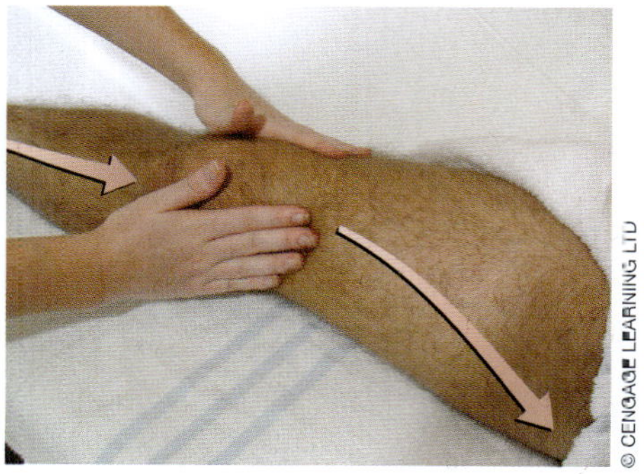

10 Repeat step **1** a further three times.

Step-by-step: Massage routine for the arms

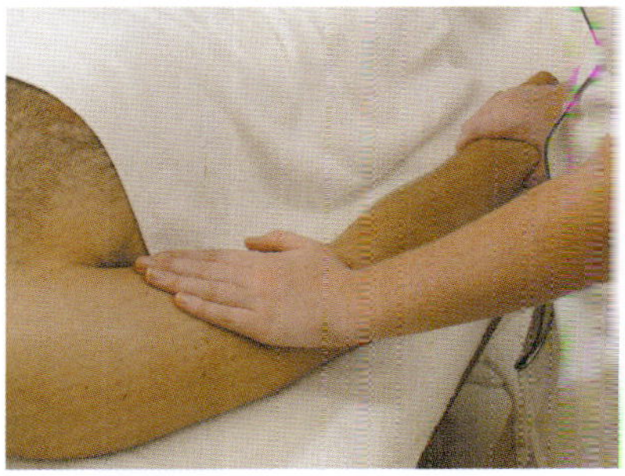

1 **Effleurage to whole arm** Starting at the fingertips, use both hands to apply alternate effleurage strokes up to the shoulder. Repeat this step a further two times.

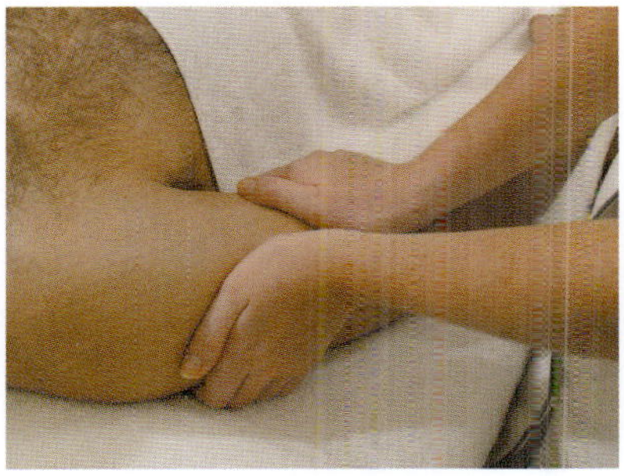

2 **Alternate kneading to whole arm** With the hands on either side of the arm, just below the shoulder, apply alternate kneading movements with pressure on the upwards movement. Work down over the forearm to the hand. Repeat this step a further two times.

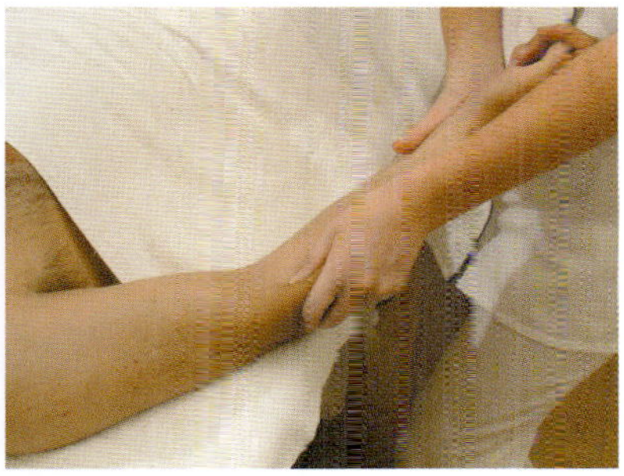

3 **Picking up over forearm** Using both hands, alternately pick up the tissues of the forearm. Repeat this step a further two times.

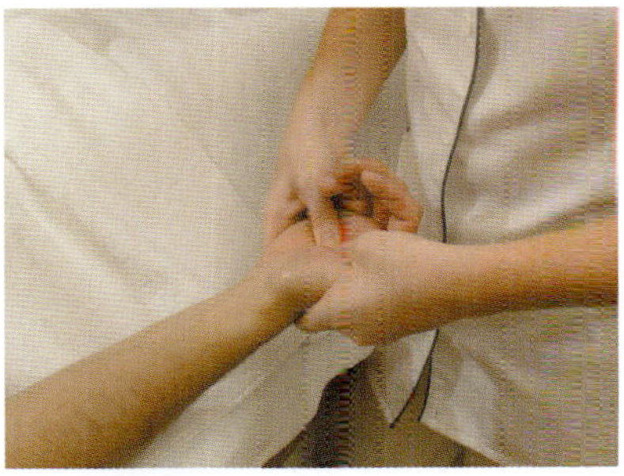

4 Thumb kneading to palms. Repeat this step a further two times.

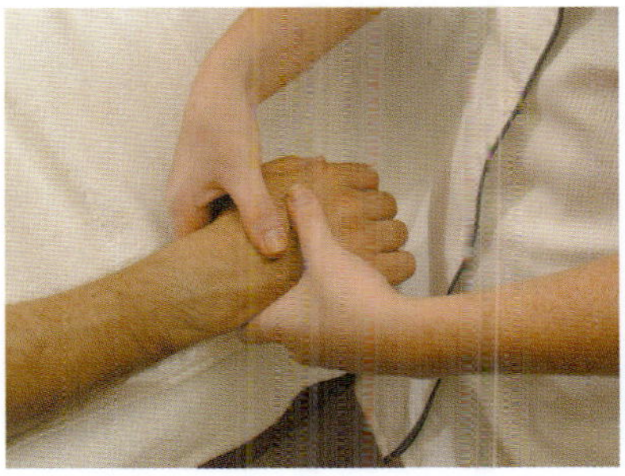

5 Cross-thumb kneading to backs of hands. Repeat this step a further two times.

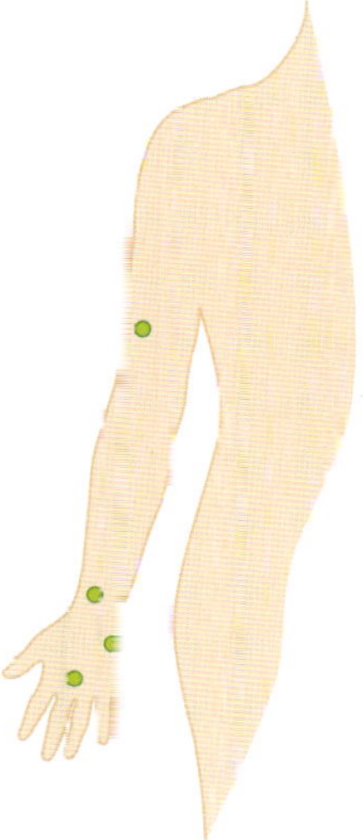

6 Apply pressure to the tsubo points shown in the diagram.

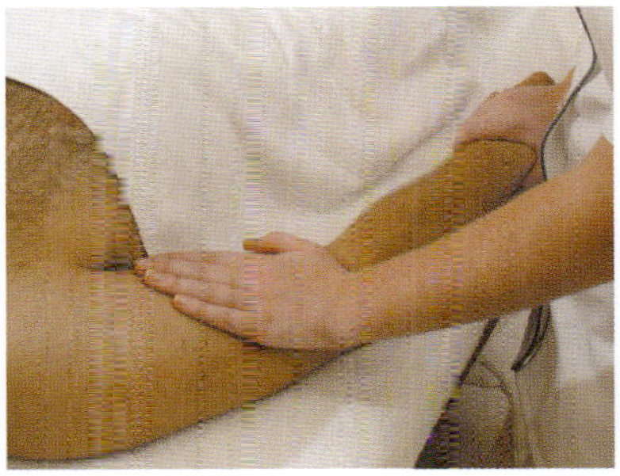

7 Repeat step 1 a further three times.

Before client gets up from the couch, gently remove any remaining massage medium with a small clean towel, hot towel or strong tissues

Where possible the pre-blended aromatherapy oils should be left on the skin to condition and continue their physiological/psychological effect for several hours. The client should be covered with a towel and allowed to rest for a few minutes to allow the blood circulation to return to normal. If they get up immediately they might feel light-headed as the brain is temporarily starved of blood. They might even faint.

Following the massage ensure that the massage meets the agreed service plan and the effect meets the client's satisfaction.

Provide accurate aftercare advice to enhance the service.

Update the client's records by recording the pre-blended oils used and leave the work area in an appropriate condition.

Provide the client with a glass of water to replace any fluids lost and to re-hydrate.

TOP TIP

Client comfort

For extra client comfort, and to stabilize the arms, place a pillow beneath the arm during massage.

Outcome 4: Provide aftercare advice

Learn how to provide aftercare advice which supports and meets the needs of your clients

1. Giving **advice** and recommendations accurately and constructively
2. Giving your clients suitable **advice** specific to their individual needs.

Aftercare advice

After the massage service it is important to give the client aftercare advice. This will ensure that they get the maximum benefit from their service and will also promote retail sales. Aftercare advice should include the following:

- healthy eating and exercise advice
- a recommendation against bathing for at least 6 hours to allow the oils to penetrate the skin completely
- avoid ultraviolet light exposure (artificial or natural) for 24 hours as some oils may cause photo-sensitization
- a recommendation to drink plenty of fluids, e.g. water and herbal tea, to promote a cleansing effect on the body and to replace any fluids lost
- explain that for 24 hours following the service to avoid stimulants such as alcohol and caffeine
- suitable relaxation techniques, relaxing bath products, breathing and massage techniques
- methods of using essential oils at home
- modification to obvious lifestyle patterns where immediate improvements are required to support the service aim

Warn the client of possible post-service reactions including:

- feeling of sickness
- emotional anxiety
- headaches
- Increased urination - as the excretory system is stimulated during lymphatic drainage massage, toxins are removed further increased if anti-diuretic oils are used.

The above reactions will normally subside in 24 hours.

Re-confirm possible contra-actions that may occur and advise on the appropriate action to take.

The massage may form part of a comprehensive service plan. Inform the client of the cumulative effects of regular massage services. Massage using pre-blended aromatherapy oils may be recommended weekly.

Retail products

Provide suitable retail products that the client can use at home to continue the service effect. These include:

- pre-blended essential oils in a roller ball applicator to apply to the temples
- pre-blended essential oil bath products

TOP TIP

After a scalp massage service

Advise the client to add shampoo to their hair before they add water, as this will make the oil easier to wash out.

- pre-blended essential oil facial and body care products
- essential oil fragranced candles

Essential oil burners are now widely available in a variety of shapes and colours. They usually contain a small dish in which to place the essential oils, with a space beneath for a small candle. When lit, the candle heats the oil, speeding up the evaporation rate and filling the room with fragrance.

> Find out as much as you can about the products you're using and focus on your favourites. If you believe in a product – your enthusiasm will shine through and selling becomes a natural process.
>
> **Katie Whitehouse**

TOP TIP

Practice deep breathing performed slowly to combat stress and induce relaxation. This can be practised in stressful situations.

© DALLAS EVENTS INC., 2008; USED UNDER LICENSE FROM SHUTTERSTOCK.COM

Deep breathing

© YURI ARCURS / MAXIM, 2009; USED UNDER LICENSE FROM SHUTTERSTOCK.COM

Bathing with essential oil based products – an ideal retailing opportunity

VITAL TOUCH

A candle essential oil burner

ASSESSMENT OF KNOWLEDGE AND UNDERSTANDING

FUNCTIONAL SKILLS

Having covered the learning objectives for **Carry out massage using pre-blended aromatherapy oils** – test what you need to know and understand by answering the following short questions below.

The information covers:

- organizational and legal requirements
- how to work safely and effectively when carrying out massage using pre-blended aromatherapy oils
- client consultation
- preparation for service
- anatomy and physiology
- contra-indications and contra-actions
- pre-blended aromatherapy oils
- service-specific knowledge
- aftercare advice for clients

Anatomy and physiology questions required for this unit are found on pages 98–99.

Organizational and legal requirements

1. What are the health and safety implications of using pre-blended aromatherapy oils on a client?
2. Why is it important to ensure that records are kept up-to-date and accurate?
3. How should waste from an aromatherapy massage service be disposed of?

4 What is a cost-effective and commercial timing for a full-body aromatherapy massage service including the face and head?

5 Describe the correct way to store pre-blended aromatherapy oils.

6 What is your salon's organizational requirements for client preparation?

7 What are your compliance responsibilities with regard to the Disability Discrimination Act when considering the suitability for service of clients with illnesses and disabilities?

How to work safely and effectively when carrying out massage using pre-blended aromatherapy oils

1 Why is it important to use a service couch that is adjustable?

2 How should the service area be kept in an asepsic condition?

3 Describe the appropriate environmental conditions for massage using pre-blended aromatherapy oils.

4 How can you ensure that the client's modesty, privacy and comfort is maintained throughout the service?

5 What are examples of good posture when performing body massage and why should this be adopted at all times?

Client consultation

1 State four consultation techniques used to assess the client's service requirements and suitable choice of oils.

2 How can a sensitive and supportive manner be demonstrated to the client?

3 Why is it important to determine the client's lifestyle pattern prior to the service?

4 Why is it important to agree the objectives of the service prior to service planning?

5 When is a skin sensitivity patch test carried out?

6 Why is it important to agree the content of the consultation record with the client before asking for their signature?

7 Why should a parent or guardian be present when treating minors?

8 Describe a possible allergic response from a client with an allergy to almond oil contained in an essential oil blend.

Preparation for service

1 What should be considered when choosing your aromatherapy oil blend for your client?

2 How would you cleanse different body areas for service including the face and the feet?

3 Why is it important to have all equipment and materials to hand during the service?

4 Give **two** reasons for discussing the different stages of the service with the client.

Anatomy and physiology

1 How do essential oils enter the body?

2 Describe how the olfactory system is affected by the inhalation of the aromatherapy oils.

3 Describe **five** physiological effects of essential oils on the body.

4 Describe **three** psychological effects of essential oils on the body.

5 What is a postural fault? How may a postural fault be benefited by massage using pre-blended aromatherapy oils within a service plan?

Contra-indications and contra-actions

1 State **three** conditions that would contraindicate a massage service using pre-blended aromatherapy oils.

2 State **three** conditions that may restrict the service.

3 List **three** possible contra-actions which may occur during and post-service when providing massage using pre-blended aromatherapy oils? How would you deal with each if they occurred?

Pre-blended aromatherapy oils

1 List three carrier oils that are obtained from nuts.

2 List three essential oils that are obtained from flowers.

3 Why is it important to know the properties of carrier oils?

4 Which pre-blended aromatherapy oils would you choose for a client requiring an uplifting service outcome?

5 How should pre-blended aromatherapy oils be stored to maintain their quality and to comply with health and safety requirements?

6 How can you ensure the safe and effective use of essential oils upon the client?

Service-specific knowledge

1 What is the cause of the skin condition 'erythema'?

2 Why are the following massage techniques incorporated into the massage effleurage, petrissage, tapotement and pressure point technique?

3 What is the difference in massage technique when treating a male and female client?

4 The use of pre-blended aromatherapy oils has a limited effect, who can you refer the client to for further clinical service using aromatherapy oils?

5 Explain how massage can be adapted in its application?

6 Case studies:

If the clients below presented themselves for service:

- client on a weight reduction programme who does not take regular exercise, does not drink the recommended daily intake of water and has cellulite on their thighs
- client who is driving a lot with work, smokes, eating a lot of fast food and is suffering from insomnia
- a young mother who is feeling generally lethargic and has received the service as a gift

a What action would you take?

b What questions would you ask when preparing their service plan?

c Which oils would you choose?

d Approximately how much oil would you use (this will reflect the service application selected)?

e How would you adapt the service?

f What aftercare advice would you give?

Aftercare advice for clients

1 Why is it important to find out about client lifestyle at the consultation to inform your aftercare care advice?

2 What are the post-service restrictions for a client to follow following the service?

3 What products can you recommend a client to use at home to extend the benefits of the service?

4 What aftercare advice recommendations would you advise to a client to enhance their health benefits for:

- healthy eating
- active exercise

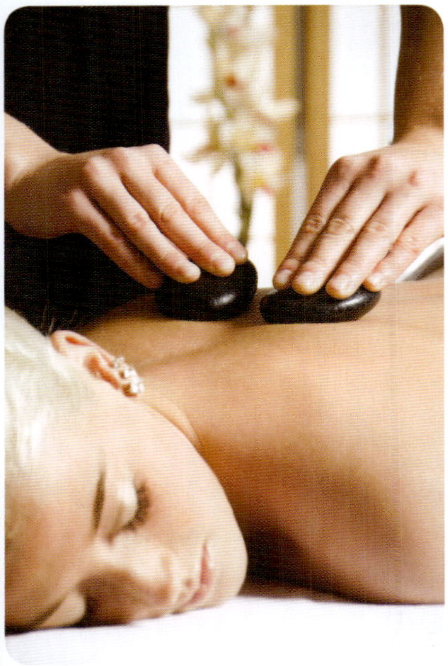

ISTOCK/© YANIK CHAUVIN

13 Stone therapy

Learning Objectives

This chapter covers the **Provide stone therapy treatments** unit.

This unit is all about how to provide hot and cold stone therapy services to the head, face and body whilst incorporating massage. The selection of different types of stones, chakras, and the placing and using of stones are all important considerations for the service. Application is modified to achieve the client's service objectives, both psychological and physiological, that are identified at the initial consultation.

There are **four** learning outcomes which you must achieve competently:

1 **Maintain safe and effective methods of working when providing stone therapy services.**

2 **Consult, plan and prepare for services with clients.**

3 **Perform stone therapy services.**

4 **Provide aftercare advice.**

For each unit your assessor will observe you on **at least four separate occasions involving different clients**. **Two** will include full-body stone therapy services including the face.

From the **range** statement, you must show that you have:

- used all types of **equipment**
- used all **consultation techniques**

(continued on the next page)

SAM DAVIES

ROLE MODEL

Sam Davies

Beauty therapist at Ki Day Spa, Altrincham, Cheshire

"I trained at Trafford College and have worked at Ki Day Spa for almost 3 years. My job role is to deliver all the services we offer to an exceptional standard; including the overall 'service', the delivery of the treatment and the aftercare advice and recommendations. I love my job, I meet lots of different clients and each day is different. Although the job can be physically and emotionally tiring, it feels fantastic to know that your client is more relaxed and de-stressed, and has thoroughly enjoyed the service.

I find it rewarding when I achieve the results that exceed the client's expectations. It can be very challenging, as every client is unique. You have to constantly adapt the treatment and your approach, to meet the many different requests and needs of your clients. There is also a lot of product knowledge, it can be challenging to remember the detail of all the ingredients and the features and benefits of each product.

(continued)

- dealt with all the client's **physical characteristics**
- dealt with at least one of the **necessary actions** where a contra-action, contra-indication or service modification occurs
- met all **service objectives**
- used three out of the four **types of stones**
- used all the **stone therapy techniques**
- covered all **service areas**
- given all types of relevant aftercare **advice**

However, you must prove that you have the necessary knowledge and understanding to be able to perform competently across the range.

When providing stone therapy services it is important to use the skills you have learnt in the following units:

Monitoring safe work operations.

Promotional activities.

ACTIVITY

FUNCTIONAL SKILLS

If you are giving stone therapy treatments, research some websites to see how you can advance your studies, e.g. www.lastoneuk.co.uk

Essential anatomy and physiology knowledge requirements for this stone therapy massage is identified on the checklist in Chapter 2, pages 12–13. This chapter also discusses anatomy and physiology specific to this unit.

Stone therapy

Stone therapy has become increasingly popular over the last few years. It is now accepted as one of the main services on offer in many salons and spas. Many clients prefer a stone therapy service to a more traditional manual massage, because of the combined effect of heat and massage, and the deep massage technique that can be achieved. Although the development of stone therapy into a professional service is relatively recent, the foundations of the service date back many millions of years. The combination of stones, heat and massage is very powerful and has been used by many cultures for centuries. Stones were used for healing, worship and guidance as long ago as 1500 BC in countries such as China and Egypt, and the Incas and Native Americans used them in ceremonies and treatments. Traditionally basalt stones are used, sourced from riverbeds and seashores. These stones are said to be closely connected to the earth and have a life and energy of their own. This energy needs to be nurtured and protected to maintain the healing ability of the stone therapy service.

The original stone therapy service was introduced by Mary Nelson of Arizona, USA in 1993. As a massage beauty therapist, she needed a method of working deeply on the body for long periods of time without causing damage to her own wrists and joints. Mary developed the La Stone Therapy service, which uses heated and chilled stones to deliver a very relaxing, therapeutic, deep-tissue service. There are now many companies offering their own form of stone therapy, some using both hot and cold stones, others just the hot ones. Techniques can differ, and it is important to follow the guidelines laid down by the company.

ALWAYS REMEMBER

Holistic

The word 'holistic' comes from the Greek word 'holos' meaning the whole: that is why holistic therapies treat the 'whole person': mind, body and spirit.

ISTOCK/© MARCUS LINDSTRÖM

TOP TIP

Stone therapy can be incorporated into many other services such as facials and pedicures.

Effects of stone therapy

Physiological effects

Different effects can be achieved depending on the temperature of the stones used.

Heat services raise the body temperature, the main effects on the body of using hot stones are:

- blood circulation is increased, the temperature of the body is raised
- the increased body temperature causes an increase in the heart rate and the pulse rate quickens
- superficial capillaries dilate in an attempt to cool the body. This vasodilation means an increase in the blood flow to the area, nourishing every cell
- a hyperaemia is produced, the skin reddens and warms. The overall skin colour can be improved
- blood pressure is lowered as a result of the vasodilation
- lymphatic circulation is increased, speeding up the removal of waste products and toxins
- sensory nerve endings are soothed, there is a feeling of relaxation
- tense, tight muscles are relaxed. After exercise it can prevent a build-up of lactic acid which can cause stiffness

© CENGAGE LEARNING LTD

Tense muscles can be relaxed with hot stones

Stone therapy can often be performed with cold stones (or neutral temperature) usually made from marble or white quartzite. Cold/chill treatments lower the body temperature. The main effects on the body of using cold stones are:

- blood circulation is decreased, the temperature of the body is lowered
- superficial capillaries constrict in an attempt to conserve body heat – vasoconstriction. Blood circulation is decreased to the area
- the skin goes pale, as the capillaries constrict
- there is an analgesic effect on superficial nerve endings – blocks out pain impulses, numbs the area
- there is a tightening effect on the skin, can help skin tone when reducing weight

ISTOCK/© WEBPHOTOGRAPHEER

Stone therapy can achieve a sense of well-being

For a more detailed explanation of the effects of massage and heat on the systems of the body, refer to **Chapter 10, Body Massage**. You will also need to have a thorough knowledge of all the systems of the body, this is covered in detail in **Chapter 2, Anatomy and Physiology**.

ALWAYS REMEMBER

Geothermotherapy

Geothermotherapy is the name given to the alternate use of hot and cold temperatures on the body. It can also be referred to as Kneipp therapy.

Psychological effects

Each service performed is adapted to meet the client's psychological needs; these are identified at the client consultation. A hot stone therapy service will relax and help relieve tension and stress, with a nurturing feeling. If cold stones are used or the temperature of the stone is alternated, this will provide more of a stimulating, refreshing and invigorating effect. Generally the stone therapy service will leave the client feeling energized as the body systems such as blood and lymphatic circulation are stimulated. A feeling of well-being can increase the client's confidence and self-esteem.

Many stone therapy services work on the chakras and the person's 'aura'. This results in a more spiritual service, with the client often feeling more grounded, cleansed and with renewed energy, both physically and mentally.

Uses of stone therapy

Stone therapy is a blend of heat, massage and stone placement. It is said that one stroke of the stone is equivalent to 5–10 manual massage strokes. Generally stone therapy is used for:

- deep tissue massage
- relaxation
- ideal for pain relief, e.g. back pain
- stress related conditions
- sleep related problems
- balancing energy levels

Specific uses of hot stone therapy:

- heat penetrates muscles, causing immediate relaxation
- muscular aches and pains are relieved
- warming, relaxing, sedative effect, stress and anxiety can be reduced
- warms body on a cool day
- removes need to give a pre-heat service before a massage
- stimulate sluggish blood and lymphatic circulation, helping circulatory problems
- feeling of well-being

Specific uses of cold stone therapy:

- blood vessels constrict, calming an inflamed area
- cools body on a hot day, or after overexertion
- refreshing and stimulating, a revitalizing tonic effect
- soothes irritated skin
- relieves congestion, such as sinus congestion
- after a sports massage service, can help reduce swelling and puffiness
- feeling of well-being

Often cold stones are used to provide balance during a hot stone therapy service. This is done to avoid overheating the body and involves the placement of cool/cold stones over certain chakras. Another method is to use hot and cold stones alternately, by massaging the body first with hot stones and then cold. This technique does not suit all clients, as a person who has circulatory problems or feels the cold quickly is best recommended to have only the hot stone therapy.

BEST PRACTICE

Cool stones can be used for a refreshing and stimulating effect.

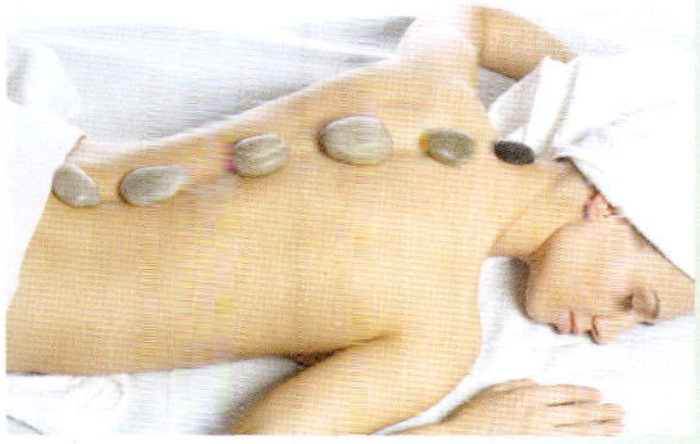

ISTOCK/© SERGUEI KOVALEV

ALWAYS REMEMBER

Sports massage
Sports massage is a massage technique applied to improve performance or aid recovery following sporting activity.

ACTIVITY

Research: repetitive stain injury (RSI)

Why do beauty therapists need to be very aware of this condition?

Find out what you can do to avoid getting this condition when performing stone therapy services.

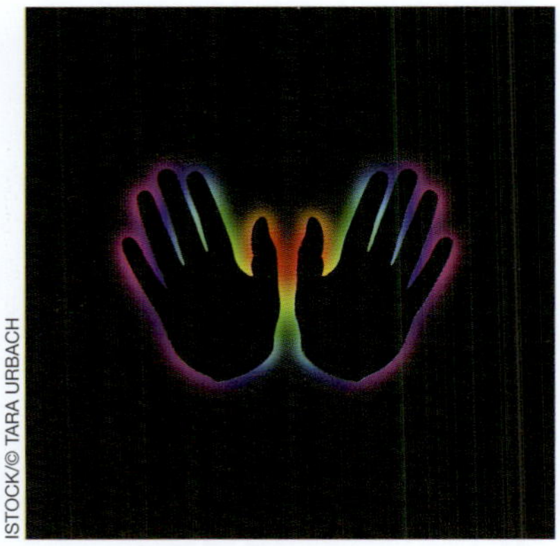

An aura or energy field is often described as a 'luminous radiation'

'Aura' or energy field

Ancient Far Eastern cultures believed that the body was surrounded with an energy field or 'aura'. This has been described as a 'luminous radiation', which surrounds structures such as the body, plants, etc. and provides a protective field. Those that work in the 'healing' field often see the colour of this light, and it helps them assess what is needed to help balance the body. The auric field is said to be a series of layers, each corresponding to a different aspect of the person and to a different chakra. The aura can be seen in colours, which differ from person to person depending on how they are feeling physically and their emotional levels.

Chakras

A **chakra** is often referred to as an energy centre, and is a focus for the stone therapy service. There are seven major chakras in the body, running in a vertical straight line along the centre of the body, from the base of the spine to the top of the head. In order to function at their peak, chakras need to be 'open' so that energy is free to flow in and out of the body's 'aura'.

For more information on chakras see **Chapter 11, Indian Head Massage**, page 381.

1. The **base** chakra, also known as root, associated colour red, element earth. Concerned with connection to earth, health and survival.
2. The **sacral** chakra, associated colour orange, element water. Concerned with relationships, especially sexual relationships.
3. The **solar plexus** chakra, associated colour yellow, element fire. Concerned with personal harmony and energy.
4. The **heart** chakra, associated colour green, element air. Concerned with empathy with others.
5. The **throat** chakra, associated colour blue, element sound or ether. Concerned with communication and expression.
6. The **brow** chakra (also known as the *third* eye), associated colour indigo, element light. Concerned with inner vision.
7. The **crown** chakra, associated colour white, element spirit. Concerned with imagination and thought.

Seven principle chakras

Chakra	*Colour*	*Layer of aura/ aspect of the person*
Crown	Violet or white	Spirituality
Third eye	Indigo	Intuition
Throat	Blue	Communication
Heart	Green	Humanity, forgiveness
Solar plexus	Yellow	Emotion
Sacral	Orange	Creation
Root	Red	Physical and material health

Five elements

In Chinese medicine, balance is provided by the inclusion of the five elements. These elements are earth fire, metal, wood and water. It is thought that stone therapy provides balance as it encompasses all five elements and how these are related within the service:

- earth – the stones are from the earth
- fire – the electricity of the heater
- metal – heater
- wood – wooden spoon can be used, also the sage, and the towels (cotton comes from plants which is a wood element)
- water – water is used to heat the stones, and in the ice used to cool the marble

ISTOCK/© CHRISTIAN NASCA

The five elements work in balance in the environment

ALWAYS REMEMBER

In a chakra layout, the appropriate semi-precious stones are placed on the chakras to help balance mind, body and spirit

ISTOCK/© MARTIN NOVAK

Types of stones

Basalt

Basalt is one of the most common stones in the world. It is a type of volcanic rock, rich in the minerals iron and magnesium, formed from molten lava as it cools. Basalt is very plentiful in regions that have undergone a lot of volcanic activity. Over time the rock's composition changes, resulting in a dense stone with a variety of colour ranging from grey through to black, some with purple or green tones. Over millions of years the rock has been washed along the seashore or river beds, ending up as smooth pebbles. Basalt stone heats up easily and retain their heat over a long period of time.

Marine

Sourced from the water, Formed from sedimentary rock, which results in a very dense but smooth, silky texture, which retains the cold well and are useful when required to cool an area. Very popular for stone therapy service.

WAVEBREAKMEDIA LTD/WAVEBREAK MEDIA/THINKSTOCK

Basalt stones contain iron and magnesium which helps retain the heat

Marble

Formed from limestone, which over time, changes into an extremely hard marble. Marble pebbles are not usually found naturally, as this stone would break up if it was washed over seashores and riverbeds. The marble stones for stone therapy services are designed carefully to ensure the shape and size are perfect for the service. The marble is naturally cool and these stones are used for the cold stone therapy, or combined with hot stone as appropriate.

Semi-precious stones

Crystals and **semi-precious stones** may be used within the service. Stones such as rose quartz can be incorporated into the stone therapy service. Each semi-precious stone is said to have unique characteristics, effects and uses. For example, rose quartz stone corresponds to the heart chakra. A heart-shaped rose quartz stone may be placed on the body over the heart chakra to balance the upper four chakras helping to ease emotional imbalance, replace negativity and enhance self-confidence.

Often a semi-precious stone is placed on the chakras during stone therapy. A stone is chosen to match the colour of the chakra, so that it can help 'open' the chakra, e.g. a blue stone such as lapis lazuli on the throat chakra, or an amethyst on the third eye.

ISTOCK/© NICHOLAS SUTCLIFFE

Rose quartz is a semi-precious stone that is thought to correspond to the heart chakra

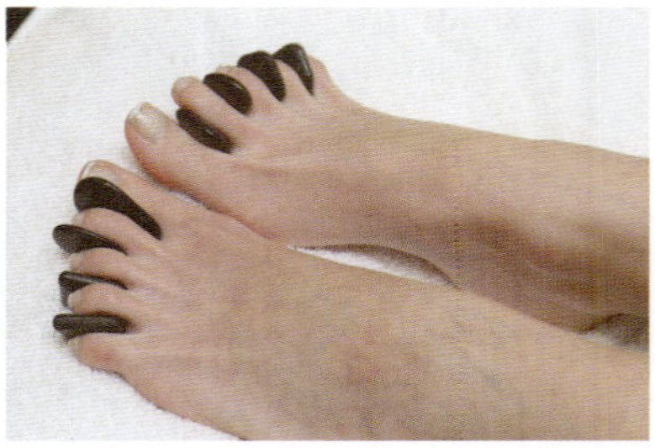

© CENGAGE LEARNING LTD

Toe stones are used between the fingers and toes

Sizes/types of stone	Uses	Appropriate for which area of the body?
Contour stone	A placement stone that is curved	Back of neck, sole of foot
Extra large	A placement stone for use on larger areas	Sacrum, solar plexus
Large stone	A placement stone, or for massaging larger areas	Back, thighs
Medium stone	A massage stone for medium-sized areas	Arms, lower legs, abdomen
Small stone	Stones for massaging smaller areas of the body	Face, foot, hands
Toe/finger stones	Small placement stones for between the toes and fingers	Fingers and toes
Trigger stones	Oval shaped placement stone, or can be used on trigger points to release tension	Around the scapula, shoulders
Facial stones	Small stones for facial massage	Face and neck
Chakra stones	Seven semi-precious stones, that are placed on the chakras to help remove blocked energy	Chakras

ISTOCK/© TINA SPRUCE

Stones can recharge when placed in a circle (mandala)

Re-energizing or recharging the stones

To get the best from the stones, it is essential to look after them carefully, if not they may not heat up effectively or lose heat very quickly. Wash them after every service, and use fresh water, never use stagnant or dirty water. If oil has made them sticky, wash with hot soapy water and wipe with disinfectant. It is thought that the stones can be 'energized' by some of the following:

- Use labradorite crystal to recharge/energize basalt stones.
- Use moonstone to recharge/energize marble stones.
- Place in a circle (mandala) in the treatment room, or better still on the earth (their natural home).
- Sprinkle with natural salt, or 'smudge'/burn a bundle of wild/white sage over them.
- Leave them out in a full moon, every month, or out in the sun.

ELLISONS

The labradorite stone can help recharge the stones

Service techniques

When massaging, the stones are used as an extension of the hand, and traditional massage techniques are used such as effleurage. Ensure there is sufficient oil on the body to allow the stone to easily glide over the skin. The stones can be used in a variety of ways to suit the client's physical characteristics and the aims of the service:

- Effleurage – the basic stroke – long, flowing, smooth, continuous. Flat side of the stone is used.

- *Petrissage.* Kneading, compression-type strokes, usually the flat side of the stone is used.
- *Friction.* Localised deep circular movements, the tip of an oval stone can be used. The side of the stone is used to work deeper into the body tissues. The stone is gripped between the fingers and thumb, and a deeper pressure is used to help relax areas of tension, e.g. around the scapula.
- *Tapping.* The stone is tapped directly on a tight muscle as a type of vibration to help release and relieve tension.
- ***Tucking.*** The placing of stones around the body for warmth and the feeling of being 'nurtured'. Stones can be 'tucked' under the sides of the body, in palms of hand, etc.
- *Placement.* The placing of stones on specific parts of the body such as chakras.
- ***Trigger point.*** Deep localized movement, the edge or end of a stone can be used. A trigger point usually refers to a small contraction knot and can be a common source of pain.

'Cocooning' is often used to describe a hot stone therapy technique that can be used to treat a specific area, such as an inflamed ankle

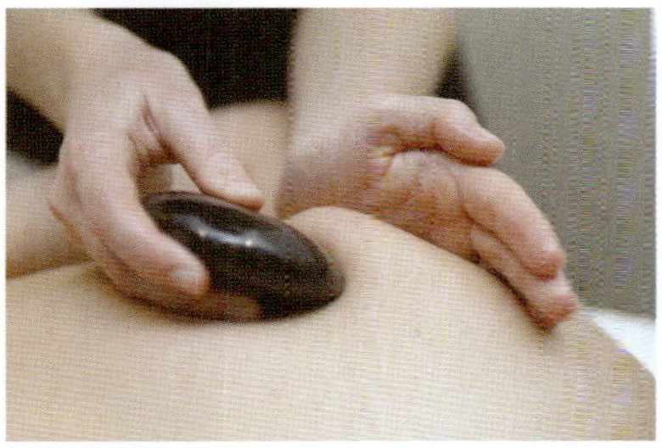

Tension around the scapula can be improved with stone therapy

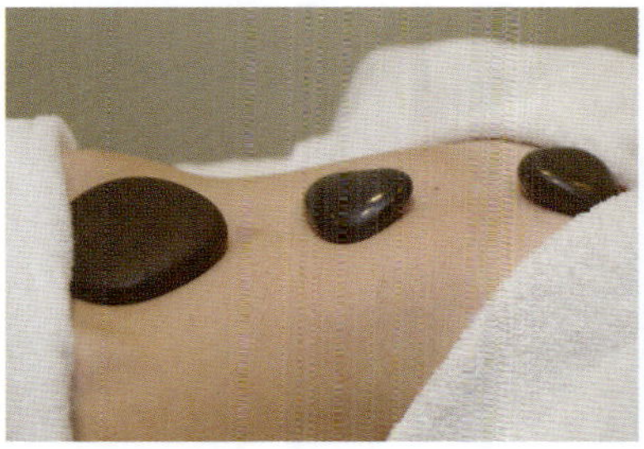

Stones are placed on specific areas of the body such as the solar plexus area (network or group of nerves situated in the abdomen, below the diaphragm)

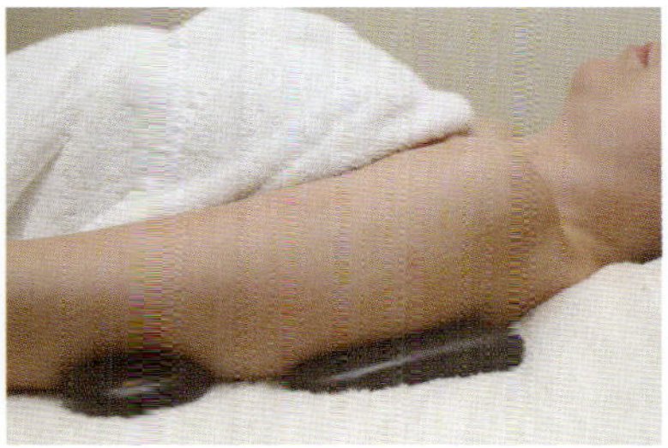

Warm stones can be 'tucked' around the body

Chapter 10, Body massage has all the details on body massage, including the individual massage movements, their effects and uses.

HEALTH & SAFETY

Posture

Correct posture is so important, it means the beauty therapist gets less tired and gives a better service. It also helps prevent the beauty therapist getting a backache.

ALWAYS REMEMBER

LA stone therapy

La stone therapy is the original hot and cold stone massage created by Mary Nelson from Arizona, USA. There are now many different 'followers' and 'expressions of stone therapy' and it has become a mainstream service in many salons and spas around the world.

Massage medium

A good quality oil is needed to ensure the stones glide smoothly over the body. Great care has to be taken to apply only the correct amount of oil: too little and the stone will drag and cause irritation, too much and it will be difficult to massage the area and the stone will keep slipping off the body. The purpose of the service has to be taken into account, as well as the client's skin type. Some beauty therapists favour a traditional carrier oil such as grapeseed, jojoba, coconut, avocado or sunflower seed oil. Others prefer to use a ready-blended oil containing essential oils to enhance the overall effect of the massage. For example, a blend containing lavender would provide a calming relaxing service, and one containing geranium and rose would help provide more of an emotionally balancing outcome. Many manufacturers now provide special ready-blended 'hot stone massage oil'.

TOP TIP

Massage medium

Be careful to apply sufficient oil, or the stone will drag and cause irritation, even bruising.

THERMAL STONE

Many companies now offer specially blended 'stone oils'

> Always promote the 'benefits' of stone therapy service: how it can address the client's problems and concerns, the main ingredients in the oil and how much value for money it represents.
>
> **Sam Davies**

HEALTH & SAFETY

Care handling stones

Be very careful when transferring stones from the heating unit, don't pass directly over the body, especially over the face. The stones can become slippery with oil and you don't want to drop one on the client.

> You can put your oil bottle in the heater for a few minutes (if appropriate) – this will warm the oil and feel lovely and soothing when you apply it to the body.
>
> **Sam Davies**

Outcome 1: Maintain safe and effective methods of working when providing stone therapy services

Learn how to maintain safe and effective methods of working when providing stone therapy service by:

1. Setting up and monitoring the service area to meet organization procedures and manufacturer's instructions.
2. Making sure that environmental conditions are suitable for the client and the service.
3. Ensuring your personal hygiene, protection and appearance meets accepted industry and organizational requirements.
4. Ensuring that your nails are short, clean and well manicured and free of polish.
5. Effectively disinfecting your hands prior to and after service.
6. Ensuring your own posture and position minimizes fatigue and risk of injury while working.
7. Removing and handling stones in a way which avoids injury to yourself and the client.
8. Ensuring all tools and **equipment** are cleaned using the correct methods.
9. Effectively disinfecting stones after each service.
10. Leaving stones to dry overnight and stored in a way which effectively energizes them.
11. Positioning **equipment** and service products for ease and safety of use.

HEALTH & SAFETY

Heating stones

Stones must only be heated in a professional heater, following manufacturer's instructions. Otherwise the salon or beauty therapist may not be fully insured.

THERMAL STONES

(Continued) Learn how to maintain safe and effective methods of working when providing stone therapy service by:

12. Ensuring the stones are heated and cooled following heater manufacturer's instructions prior to use.
13. Ensuring the client is in a comfortable and relaxed position suitable for the service.
14. Using suitable materials to protect the client's skin against extremes of temperature during stone placement
15. Maintaining accepted industry hygiene and safety practices throughout the service.
16. Adopting a positive, polite and reassuring manner towards the client throughout the service.
17. Maintaining the client's modesty, privacy and comfort at all times.
18. Using service products effectively to minimize waste.
19. Disposing of waste materials safely and correctly.
20. Ensuring the service is cost-effective and is carried out within a commercially viable time.
21. Ensuring client record cards are up-to-date, accurate, complete, legible and signed by the client and practitioner.
22. Leaving the service area and **equipment** in a condition suitable for future services.

ELLISONS

Many salons purchase a full stone service kit, including heater, stones, net, spoon, etc.

Equipment and materials list

Before beginning the stone therapy service, check that you have the necessary equipment and materials to hand and that they meet legal, hygiene and industry requirement for stone therapy.

Hot stone heaters

Hot stone heaters are designed for professional use and should always be used in the salon or spa. Never use a domestic heater that is designed to heat food, as they are not safe or efficient for hot stone therapy. They may overheat the stones, cause burning and may not be covered by the salon's insurance policy. Professional heaters are made of purpose build materials that will contain the heat, with a safe 'bath' for the water that heats the stones. The heaters are thermostatically controlled and keep the stones at a constant temperature ready for use. Professional heaters are available in a variety of sizes; the larger ones can hold 50 or more stones, but there are smaller version available and models specifically for facial stones.

BEST PRACTICE

There are many professional stone therapy heaters on the market, take time to choose the one most suitable for the salon.

HOF

Professional stone therapy heater

It is important to lay the stones evenly in the heater, so they warm up evenly. Each heater may differ slightly, but the usual working temperature is 50–55°C. It may take approximately half an hour for the heater to get to the working temperature. Some models will allow hot water to be poured into the heater to speed the process up.

EQUIPMENT AND MATERIALS LIST

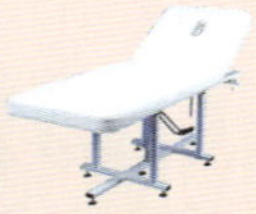
ELLISONS

Massage couch
With sit up and lie down positions, with a face hole. Easy to clean

THERMAL STONES

Thermostatically controlled professional heater

THERMAL STONES

Range of stones
Hot and cold

BEAUTY EXPRESS LTD

Towels
Clean large and small

ELLISONS

Trolley
Two shelves, easily moved

THERMAL STONES

Scoop/net/spoon
To help handle the hot stones

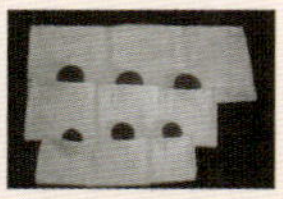
THERMAL STONES

Pouches or linen
To hold stones to help keep the temperature appropriate.

THERMAL STONES

Massage oil
Can be a special 'stone therapy oil'

ISTOCK/© MACIEJ WINER

Ice
For cooling marine and marble stones

YOU WILL ALSO NEED:

Removable protective couch cover To maintain hygienic working practices and prevent cross-contamination

Trolley To hold all the necessary equipment and materials

Pillows, props or rolled towels For support, e.g. under the knees

Disposable paper tissue bedroll To cover the service couch

Aroma-burner To give the treatment room a relaxing aroma

Cosmetic cleansing preparations To remove facial make-up

Waste container with lid Bin lined with a disposable bin liner

Spatulas To remove any products hygienically from containers

Bowls To hold cotton wool, etc.

Cotton wool, tissues To cleanse the face and other areas of the body

Foot-wipes To cleanse the feet

Record cards To record all the client's details.

Aftercare advice Recommended advice for the client to refer to following service

ISTOCK/© PIXHOOK

Stones need to be disinfected before every client

Team work is essential when delivering stone therapy services: you need to support and help other members of the team. After you have completed your service, leave the equipment immaculate, so it is ready to be used again and doesn't hold your colleagues up, or delay a client's service. If you have some spare time, offer to help other team members who are busy and would appreciate help preparing rooms and/or equipment.

Sam Davies

Sterilization and disinfection

The following table gives details of sterilization and disinfection procedures to be carried out prior to and following the hot stone service.

Equipment item	*Procedure*
Service couch and trolley	Prior to the service these should be wiped with warm soapy water and disinfectant.
Bed linen/towels	Should be washed at hot temperatures to remove oil and grease.
Floors	Should be disinfected daily.
Towels	Use clean fresh towels and gown for each client.
Stones	Need to be disinfected between every client. They are washed and then wiped with disinfectant.
Sterilizing equipment	A sterilizing tablet or disinfectant solution is used in the water in the heater, follow manufacturer's instructions.
Hand gel	Hands need to by hygienic so not to cause cross-infection, a disinfectant hand gel can be used.

> Creams and gels can leave a film in the water heater and can stain the stones – use only the recommended oil during the stone therapy service.
>
> **Sam Davies**

Preparation of the work area

1. The service room should be clean and at a comfortable working temperature for both the client and beauty therapist.
2. The service room should be set up to enhance the stone therapy service. Ensure the temperature and lighting are appropriate. Soft music and an aroma-burner will help create the perfect ambience for relaxation.
3. Cover the couch with a large clean towel, with a small one at the head end.
4. All products and materials should be laid out neatly on the trolley, which should be positioned for ease of access.
5. Place a towel under the heater, so that it catches any drips when stones are lifted out.
6. Place a towel next to the heater, so the stones can be set on it. This will remove excess water before the stones are taken over to the body, avoiding water drips/spills on the floor.
7. Some manufacturers encourage the use of a small white towel placed in the base of the heater. Stones are placed on it, so that it is easier to see the stones in a dimly lit room.
8. The heater must be placed on a stable surface and be easily accessed. Cover the stones with water and set the thermostat to 50–55°C, allow about 30–45 minutes for the water to warm. The temperature of the water will be maintained during the service.
9. Cold stones can be used as they are (neutral temperature) or chilled. Prepare the stones by placing them in a bowl with ice cubes.

BEST PRACTICE

Create the best ambience possible for your stone therapy service.

JOAN SCOTT

HEALTH & SAFETY

Stone hygiene

Some companies provide a sterilizing tablet for the stone heater, to ensure the service is hygienic for each client.

BEST PRACTICE

Cold stones can be chilled by placing them in a bowl with ice cubes

ISTOCK/© DARREN BAKER

ALWAYS REMEMBER

The beauty therapist should look professional at all times.

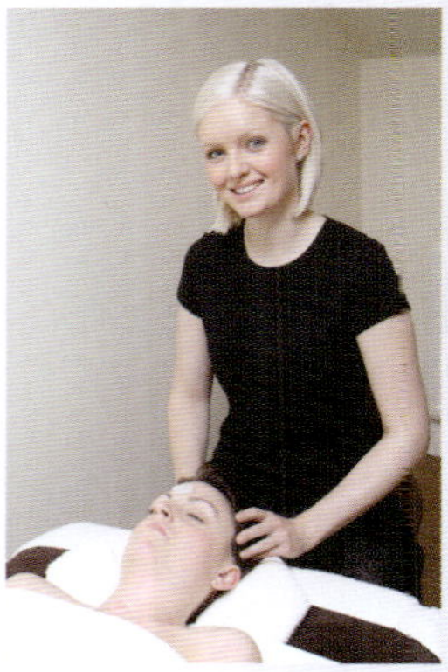

SAM DAVIS

Preparation of the beauty therapist

The beauty therapist should look professional at all times. Importance should be given to workwear, wearing of low-heeled shoes, personal hygiene and presentation. Hands should be washed thoroughly before each service, with well manicured, short nails free from nail polish. The client's record card should be collected prior to their arrival and the beauty therapist should identify the client's service requirements. A full consultation, including a postural check, should be carried out before the service commences.

HEALTH & SAFETY

Dermatitis can develop to such an extent that beauty therapists have to change career. It is essential that you look after your hands, always dry hands thoroughly after being in water, so they don't get irritated and chapped. Protect hands with hand cream, look after them carefully, don't abuse them. For more advice visit the Habia website (www.habia.org) and check out the 'bad hand day' campaign.

HABIA

ALWAYS REMEMBER

It is said that each stroke of stone therapy is equivalent to 5–10 strokes of manual massage. This makes the service suitable for those beauty therapists who are worried about straining their wrists.

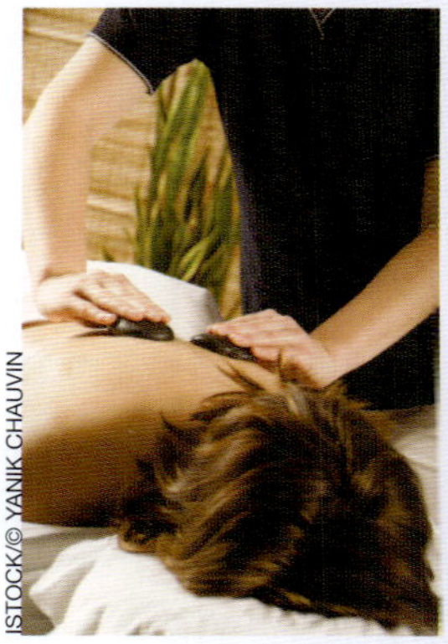

ISTOCK/© YANIK CHAUVIN

Outcome 2: Consult, plan and prepare for service with clients

Learn how to use consultation techniques to effectively plan and prepare for stone therapy service by:

1. Using **consultation techniques** in a polite, sensitive and friendly manner to determine the client's service needs.
2. Obtaining signed, written informed consent from the client prior to carrying out the service.
3. Ensuring that informed and signed parent or guardian consent is obtained for minors prior to any stone therapy service.
4. Ensuring that a parent or guardian is present throughout the stone therapy service for minors under the age of 16.
5. Clearly explaining to the client what the service entails in a way they can understand.
6. Using suitable **consultation techniques** to identify your clients medical history, **physical characteristics** and lifestyle pattern.
7. Asking your client appropriate questions to identify if they have a contra-indication to stone therapy services.
8. Accurately recording your client's responses to questioning.

(Continued) **Learn how to use consultation techniques to effectively plan and prepare for stone therapy service by:**

9. Actively encouraging clients to ask questions to clarify any points.
10. Correctly carrying out a patch test to accurately determine the client's skin response to hot and cold temperatures.
11. Taking the **necessary action** in response to any identified contra-indications.
12. Ensuring client advice is given without reference to a specific medical condition and without causing undue alarm and concern.
13. Clearly explaining and agreeing the projected cost, likely duration, frequency and types of service needed.
14. Agreeing in writing to the client's needs, expectations and **service objectives**, ensuring they are realistic and achievable.
15. Ensuring that the client's skin is clean and prepared to suit the areas to be treated.
16. Ensuring that clothing, hair and accessories are effectively protected or removed.
17. Selecting **types of stone** suitable to meet the **service objectives**.

Client consultation

Reception

A stone therapy service is usually a full-body service, including the head and face. Some salons and spas may offer an individual back service, and also incorporate stone therapy in other services such as facials. The receptionist should identify the client's requirements at the time of booking so that a suitable time can be allocated for the service required. 75 minutes is usually allocated for a full-body service, with approximately half an hour for a back service.

JOAN SCOTT

A full consultation is essential before stone therapy service

Consultation techniques

Before commencing the stone therapy service, the beauty therapist needs to obtain relevant details from the client. For this reason a full consultation should be performed. The consultation should be conducted in a quiet private area. Client modesty and privacy should be considered at all times. Details of how to conduct the consultation to identify physical characteristics and lifestyle factors are found on pages 194–197.

The beauty therapist must be professional in manner and make the client feel welcome. The client should feel at ease throughout the service and a good rapport should be built up between client and beauty therapist. Personal details should be taken and recorded on a record card. These should include medical history, doctor's details, any contra-indications that may be present and the service required. If in any doubt about a medical condition, a letter of approval should first be obtained from the client's GP.

Questioning the client on expectations and outcomes can ensure the client gains satisfaction from the service. The client will also require a postural check at the time of the consultation. This is to assess whether the client has any postural conditions which the beauty therapist may advise exercise for, or whether the beauty therapist needs to adapt the stone therapy service in any way for the comfort of the client. For more details on postural assessment go to pages 202–204.

If the client hasn't had stone therapy before then a thermal skin sensitivity test needs to be carried out. Two test tubes are used, one filled with warm water and one with cold water. The client closes their eyes, and then asked to differentiate between the temperatures on different areas of the body. If successful, the service can go ahead, but if the client can't feel the difference then it is best not to proceed, as there is a risk of burning.

ACTIVITY

Healthy lifestyle

Stress and anxiety in a client's life comes from all kinds of sources. Devise a leaflet that gives advice on a healthy lifestyle. This could include the following topics:

Lack of fresh air	Lack of sleep	Chemicals and pollution
Stress	Lack of exercise	Fluid intake
Computers and mobile phones	Processed food	Managing time

Contra-indications

Conditions that prevent service:

- Deep vein thrombosis
- Heart disease and cardiovascular conditions
- Pregnancy for the first trimester
- During chemotherapy and radiotherapy
- Under the influence of recreational drugs or alcohol
- Epilepsy (GP permission needed)
- Any infection, disease or fever
- Clinical obesity
- Diarrhoea and vomiting
- Diabetes (GP permission needed)
- Loss of skin sensitivity

Any condition where massage and heat is contra-indicated, then hot stone therapy will also be contra-indicated (for details go to Chapter 10, pages 339–340).

Localized contra-indications:

- Localized swelling
- Inflammation
- Varicose veins
- Skin disease
- Undiagnosed lumps and bumps
- abrasions
- sunburn
- hormonal implants
- haematoma
- hernia

HEALTH & SAFETY

If the client hasn't had stone therapy before then a thermal skin sensitivity test needs to be carried out, to avoid burning the skin.

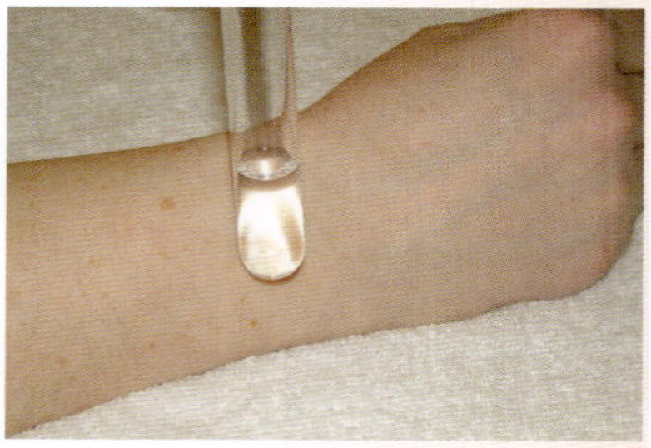

LORRAINE NORDMANN

Thermal skin sensitivity test

> You're usually so busy when doing stone therapy services, that its essential you use your initiative: prioritize what is important, plan your day carefully, organize all the relevant equipment and products and stay calm and focused so you can deliver an outstanding service.
>
> **Sam Davies**

HEALTH & SAFETY

Pregnancy is a contra-indication to stone therapy, unless the GPs permission is given.

ISTOCK/© DIGITALSKILLET

Cuts, bruises	gastric ulcers
Recent fractures (minimum 3 months)	after a heavy meal
Scar tissue – major operation (2 years)	pregnancy (abdomen)
Scar tissue – minor operation (6 months)	cervical spondylitis
Conditions affecting the neck	abdomen (first few days of menstruation)
Areas of sensitive skin, e.g. cheeks	

HEALTH & SAFETY

Sunburn is a local temporary contra-indication to stone therapy.

Contra-actions

A contra-action is an unwanted reaction to the stone therapy service, which may occur during or following service. These might include:

- skin irritation, caused by the temperature of the hot stones
- burn or scald, caused by excessively hot stones
- sickness, caused by the increased circulation of waste products transported in the lymphatic system
- fainting, caused by dilation of the blood capillaries, altering blood-pressure levels
- skin reactions, such as an allergy to the massage oil used
- bruising, caused by incorrect technique with the stones, e.g. excessive pressure, too large stones used for the area

If a client suffers any contra-actions, you must assist the client before letting them leave the salon:

- The client can take a shower to lower their body and skin temperature, a soothing cream can be applied to reduce any reaction or irritation.
- Run cold water over the area, apply a sterile dressing that will not adhere to the skin and cause further damage, this prevents any infection from entering the skin. If the burn is severe or does not heal, the client must seek medical advice.
- Ensure the client can breathe properly and that the room is well ventilated.
- Offer the client a glass of water if they feel nauseous or sick.
- Apply a cold compress if a skin reaction occurs.
- Advise the client to seek medical advice if the symptoms persist.

BEST PRACTICE

Always offer the client a glass of water after service, to help balance and rehydrate the body and avoid headaches.

JOAN SCOTT

Service plan

Discuss with client their service requirements. Explain clearly to the client what the stone therapy service involves and the effects that can be gained. Service objectives must be realistic and achievable. Discuss the way the service application can be modified or adapted to meet their specific service needs including the use of hot and cold stones, and semi-precious stones. Agree a service plan, that will meet the client's needs, both physically and psychologically. Allow time and invite the client to ask questions – the client should fully understand what the service involves, including costs, duration, frequency and type of service required including post-service reactions.

Record card for stone therapy

Date	Beauty therapist name	
Client name	Date of birth (Identifying client age group.)	
Home address	Postcode	
Email address	Landline phone number	Mobile phone number
Name of doctor	Doctor's address and phone number	
Related medical history (Conditions that may restrict or prohibit service application.)		
Are you taking any medication? (This may affect the condition of the skin or skin sensitivity.)		

CONTRA-INDICATIONS REQUIRING MEDICAL REFERRAL
(Preventing stone therapy service application.)

- ☐ deep vein thrombosis
- ☐ hear disease/cardio-vascular conditions
- ☐ during chemotherapy & radiotherapy
- ☐ epilepsy
- ☐ diabetes
- ☐ loss of skin sensation
- ☐ clinical obesity
- ☐ any infection, disease or fever
- ☐ pregnancy for the first trimester

PHYSICAL CHARACTERISTICS

- ☐ weight
- ☐ height
- ☐ posture
- ☐ muscle tone
- ☐ age
- ☐ health
- ☐ skin condition

STONE THERAPY TECHNIQUES

- ☐ rotation of stones
- ☐ alternation of hot and cold stones
- ☐ use of hot stones only
- ☐ use of cold stones only
- ☐ combination of stone types and sizes
- ☐ temperature management

SERVICE AREAS

- ☐ face
- ☐ head
- ☐ neck, chest and shoulders
- ☐ arms and hands
- ☐ abdomen
- ☐ back
- ☐ legs and feet

TREATMENT TECHNIQUES

- ☐ effleurage
- ☐ petrissage
- ☐ friction
- ☐ tapping
- ☐ tucking
- ☐ placement
- ☐ trigger point

CONTRA-INDICATIONS THAT RESTRICT SERVICE
(Service may require adaptation.)

- ☐ localised swelling/inflammation
- ☐ varicose veins
- ☐ sunburn/abrasions
- ☐ cuts/bruises
- ☐ recent fracture
- ☐ scar tissue
- ☐ areas of sensitive skin e.g. cheeks
- ☐ hernia
- ☐ after a heavy meal
- ☐ pregnancy (abdomen)
- ☐ abdomen (first few days of menstruation)

TYPES OF STONES

- ☐ basalt
- ☐ marine
- ☐ marble
- ☐ semi-precious stones

OBJECTIVES OF SERVICE

- ☐ relaxation
- ☐ sense of well-being
- ☐ balancing
- ☐ uplifting
- ☐ relief from muscular tension
- ☐ local decongestion
- ☐ stimulating

Beauty therapist signature (for reference)

Client signature (confirmation of details)

Record card for stone therapy (continued)

SERVICE ADVICE

Full-body stone therapy service – *this service will take 1 hour 15 minutes*

Back stone therapy service – *30 minutes*

SERVICE PLAN

Record relevant details of the service and advice provided for future reference.

Ensure the client's records are up-to-date, accurate and fully completed following service. Non-compliance may invalidate insurance.

DURING

- explain choice of stones, and temperature
- explain placement of stones, why and on which chakra
- explain choice of massage oil and its benefits
- explain how massage oil should be applied and removed at home
- note any adverse reaction, if any occur, and action taken

AFTER

- record the areas treated
- record any modifications to service application that has occurred
- record which products have been used in the body, face and head service as appropriate
- provide postural advice
- provide advice for client to follow immediately following service, to include suitable rest period following service, general advice regarding food and drink intake, avoidance of stimulants
- recommended time intervals between services
- discuss the benefits of continuous services
- record the effectiveness of service
- record any samples provided (review their success at next appointment)

RETAIL OPPORTUNITIES

- provide guidance on progression of the service plan for future appointments
- advise regarding products that would be suitable for home use and on how to gain the maximum benefit from their use to care for their skin and continue the service benefits
- Recommendations for further services including those that enhance the stone therapy
- advise on further products or services that you have recommended that the client may or may not have received before
- note any purchases made by the client

EVALUATION

- record comments on the client's satisfaction with the service
- record if the service objectives were achieved, e.g. relaxation, if not, explore the reasons why not
- record how you will progress the service to maintain and advance the service results in the near future

HEALTH AND SAFETY

- advise on avoidance of activities and product application that may cause a contra-action
- advise on appropriate necessary action to be taken in the event of an unwanted reaction (e.g. dizziness, burning).

SERVICE MODIFICATION

Examples of stone therapy service modification include:

- adapting the temperature of the stones to suit the objective of the service, for example cold stones to decongest
- altering the pressure or choice of manipulations during the service to suit the client's skin and muscle tone
- using different-sized stones to suit the body and physical characteristics
- adapting the service for male and female clients
- adapting the techniques to achieve an effect of relaxation or stimulation

Preparation of the client

- Instruct the client to remove their clothing down to their undergarments. It is important that you maintain the client's modesty and privacy at all times.
- Provide a private changing area for the client. A shower can be advised to ensure the skin is clean before the service begins. A large towel or bathrobe may be provided and paper disposable slippers to avoid cross-infection.
- Ask the client to remove all jewellery and accessories (including hair accessories) and store in the client's own bag or in a safe place (follow your workplace policy).
- Position the client for the service. Instruct the client to lie on the couch in a supine or prone position, depending on the area to be treated. If using a hydraulic couch, adjust to a suitable height.
- Place towels over the client in a way which will allow minimal interruption to the service and keep them warm. Modesty towel or bathrobe should be removed.
- If the client has long hair it may need to be secured in a clip while the back and neck areas are treated.
- Support pillows or rolled towels can be placed to improve client comfort. Support may be provided in supine position under the neck, and under the knees to avoid strain to the client's back. In the prone position, support may be provided under the shoulders and ankles.
- Cleanse the face using suitable facial products for the skin type, using the regular cleaning routine.

BEST PRACTICE

Use pillows, props and rolled towels to support the body and avoid strain.

ISTOCK/© BTRENKEL

BEST PRACTICE

Providing modesty and efficiency

Use large towels and position one over the top of the client's body and one over the lower part. This makes it much easier to provide a smooth flowing service without unnecessary interruptions and delays.

TOP TIP

A hot stone in a towel provides good support for the neck.

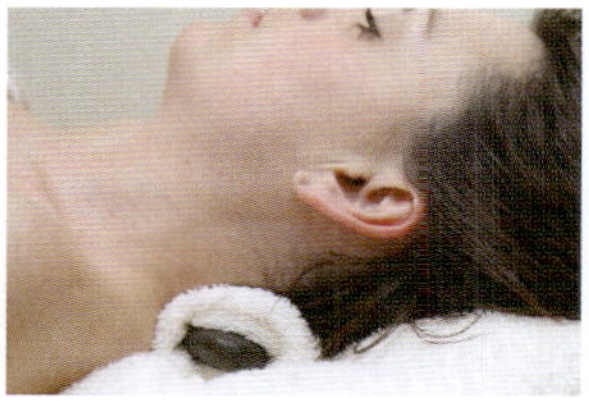
© CENGAGE LEARNING LTD

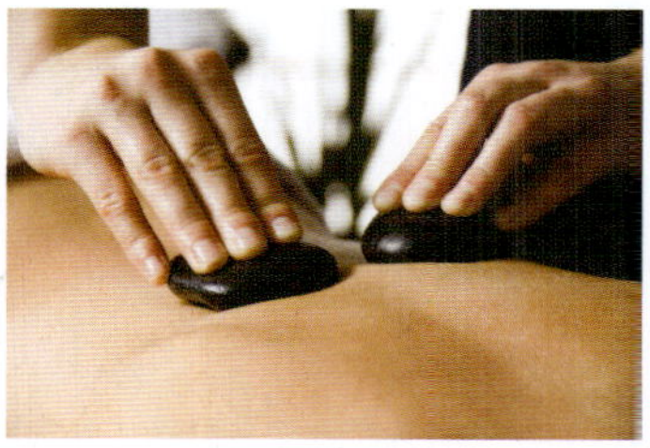
ISTOCK/© YANIK CHAUVIN

Special oils are available called 'stone oils' that work well with the stones, they can be rubbed over the stone and on the body to provide 'slip'

Stone therapy service

A thorough consultation will have included details of the client's age, weight, posture, muscle tone and psychological needs. This will help to determine whether the service is to be provided for:

Relaxation	Balancing	Uplifting
Sense of well-being	Local decongestion	Relief from muscular tension

The stone therapy service should be planned before it is started, so that it is carried out smoothly with a continuity of service. The sequence is usually:

With the client lying prone and stones placed on the back:

- back of right leg
- back of left leg
- back

With the client lying supine and stones placed on the abdomen:

- front of left leg
- front of right leg

- abdomen
- left arm
- right arm
- upper chest and neck
- face and head

Adapting the service

As with any form of massage, the beauty therapist needs to adapt the stone therapy to suit the physical characteristics of the client and the planned outcomes/objectives of the service. During the consultation it will become evident if adaptations need to be made, for reasons such as:

Tight or contracted muscles – use hot stones and concentrate on the kneading movements, frictions, tapping and trigger point techniques.

Male clients – larger stones are usually needed, more pressure can be applied, take care in areas of excess hair such as on the legs.

Female clients – smaller stones may be more appropriate, lighter pressure, avoid bony areas and the breast area.

Relaxing outcome – use mainly hot stones, with techniques such as placement, lots of effleurage, and kneading. Use with a ready-blended oil specifically for relaxation.

Energizing outcome – use alternate hot and cold stones to stimulate blood circulation and refresh the client. Brisker strokes may be used, with a ready-blended energizing oil.

Older clients – be very careful, apply lighter pressure and avoid bony areas. There may be extra sensitivity to heat, so ensure stones are not too hot and avoid any overstretched skin.

Postural conditions – depending on the condition, use techniques for relaxation on tight contracted areas (e.g. pectorals) and the more cooler energizing techniques for overstretched muscles.

For more details on adapting massage techniques go to **Chapter 10, Body massage**.

Stone therapy service application

Outcome 3: Perform stone therapy services

Learn how to perform stone therapy service to meet your clients needs by:

1. Clearly explaining the sensation created by the stones.
2. Explaining the service procedure to the client in a clear and simple way at each stage in the process.
3. Providing suitable support and cushioning to specific areas of the body during the service if necessary.
4. Using suitable material to protect the client's skin against extremes of temperature during front and back placement.
5. Correctly placing suitable **types** of **stones** on the chakra points, when required, to meet the agreed **service objectives**.

HEALTH & SAFETY

Stone hygiene

Always ensure the stones are smooth with no chips or cracks, as this can cut the client and could harbour bacteria.

JOHN SCOTT

BEST PRACTICE

You will need to adapt your service for male clients, and may need to use larger stones, with more pressure and take care in areas of excess hair such as on the legs.

ISTOCK/© BEN BLANKENBURG

HEALTH & SAFETY

Select stones that are the correct size for the your hands and for the body area to be treated. Too small and you will need more repetition to give an effective service. Too large and they will be impossible to massage with and could cause discomfort and bruising.

ISTOCK/© CLIFF PARNELL

ALWAYS REMEMBER

It is thought that if the stones lose heat quickly in a particular area, it is because that area needs the heat to help heal.

HEALTH & SAFETY

Never put warm or hot stones directly on the eye area.

ISTOCK/© JUSTIN HORROCKS

TOP TIP

Be very careful when getting stones from the heater, don't bang and splash about as this may damage the stones but can also alarm the client and isn't very relaxing.

BEST PRACTICE

There are many companies offering stone therapy equipment and training. Always follow the manufacturer's instructions, to ensure the service is effective and you are fully covered for insurance purposes.

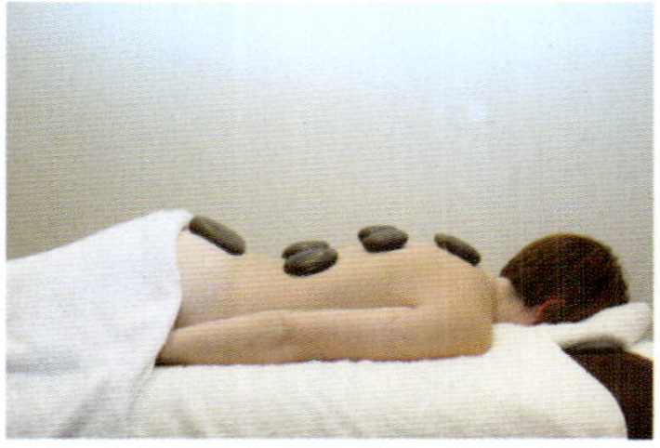

© CENGAGE LEARNING LTD

Start by placing stones on the back

> Stones that have been placed on the body will retain their heat if they are covered with a towel once positioned.
>
> **Sam Davies**

***(Continued)* Learn how to perform stone therapy service to meet your clients needs by:**

6. Correctly placing suitable **types** of **stone** under the body, when required ensuring client comfort.
7. Ensuring the skin is sufficiently lubricated to allow the smooth, continuous movement of the stones over the skin to avoid the risk of overheating.
8. Effectively introducing and using **stone therapy techniques** in a way which avoids alarm to the client, is suitable for their **physical characteristics**, the **service area**(s) and **service objectives**.
9. Adapting your **service techniques** and sequence to meet the client's **physical characteristics** and **treated area**(s).
10. Effectively varying the depth, rhythm and pressure of the **service techniques** to meet the **service objectives**, **treated area**(s) and client's **physical characteristics** and **preferences**.
11. Checking the client's well-being throughout the stone therapy service.
12. Handling stones to avoid excessive noise and disturbance to the client throughout the service.
13. Assisting to reposition the client in a controlled manner to minimize disturbance of the treatment process.
14. Taking appropriate and prompt remedial action if contra-actions or discomfort occur during the course of the service.
15. Allowing the client sufficient post-service recovery time.
16. Ensuring the finished result is to the client's satisfaction and meets the agreed **service objectives**.

Service application

Start the service with the client lying face down (prone). Select the appropriate pre-blended massage oil, a few drops can be applied along the spine and on the sole of each foot. Take the client through slow, deep breathing exercises so they start to fully relax.

Placement of stones on the back

1. Take a hand towel and place it on the client's back. As the client exhales, place the 'sacrum' stone securely on the lower back area, over the coccyx.
2. Fold the towel back, and place 3–4 large stones along the client's spine. Be careful to choose appropriately sized stones, to suit the client's physical characteristics.
3. Fold the towel back to cover the stones, cover the back area with a large towel, sheet or blanket to keep the client warm.

Back of the legs

1. Place a dry towel close to the leg area.
2. Place a few drops of oil in the hands and perform three to four standard effleurage strokes.
3. Select two stones, place them on the dry towel, then roll them in the hands to check the temperature and disperse some of the heat.
4. Perform two more effleurage strokes with warmed hands.
5. With a stone in each hand, start to massage the leg. Use long strong strokes to spread the heat.
6. Start at the top of the leg, following a simple leg massage routine. Use effleurage, kneading and stroking movements in a slow rhythm.
7. When the stones start to cool, place them on the leg. Select two more stones from the heater and roll them in the hands to check the temperature and disperse the heat.
8. Place the two original stones back in the heater. Perform a simple lower leg massage with the two stones, using similar strokes to those used on the upper leg.
9. Once the stones start to cool, replace them back in the heater and complete the leg massage with three-to-four strokes of manual effleurage.
10. Select a small stone and massage the sole of the foot.
11. Cover the leg with a large towel or blanket to keep it warm.
12. Repeat on the other leg and foot.

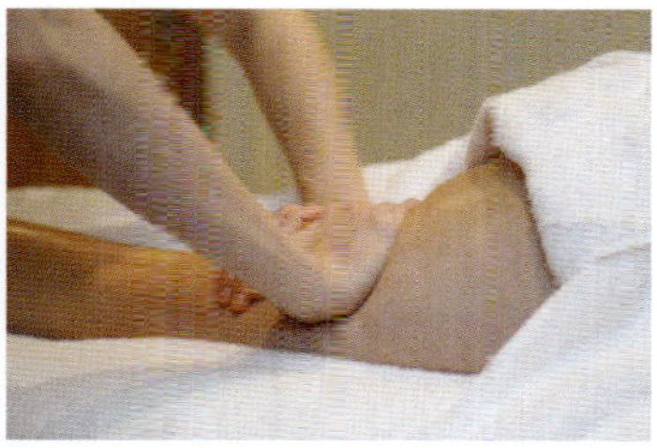

Effleurage to the back of the leg

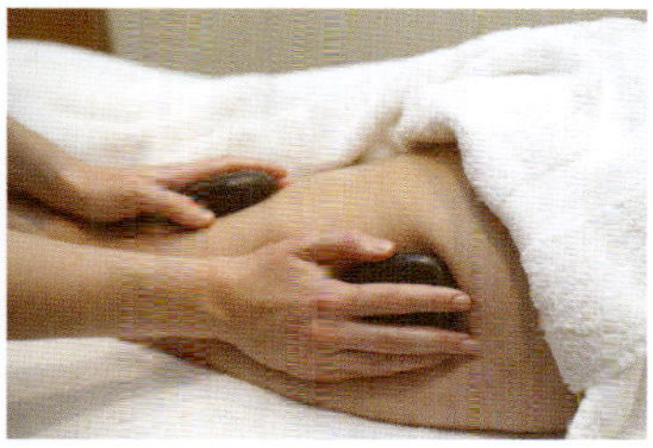

Kneading to the back of the leg

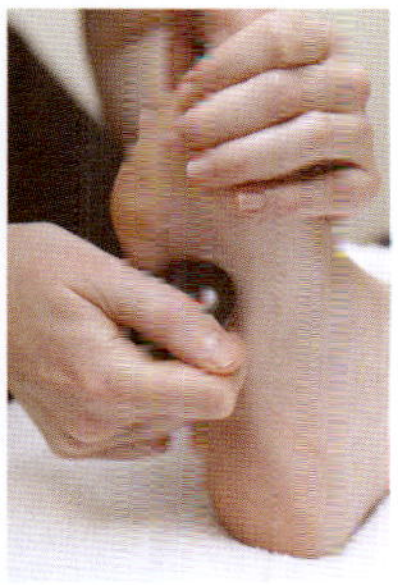
Massaging the sole of the foot

Back

1. Ensure the client is breathing slowly.
2. Remove the stones from the back and return to the heater.
3. Place a dry towel close to the back area.
4. Place a few drops of oil in the hands and perform three-to-four standard effleurage strokes.
5. Select two stones, place them on the dry towel, and again roll them to check the temperature and disperse some of the heat.
6. Perform two more effleurage strokes with warmed hands.
7. With a stone in each hand, start to massage the back using long strong strokes to spread the heat.
8. Follow a simple back massage routine, using effleurage, kneading and stroking movements in a slow rhythm. Use the edges of the stones to give a deeper effect on any areas of tension, around the scapula, etc.
9. As on the leg, when the stones start to cool, leave them on the back and choose two new stones from the heater, roll in hands, then continue the massage.

BEST PRACTICE

Always provide adequate support, placed under the ankles, chest, knees and neck as required.

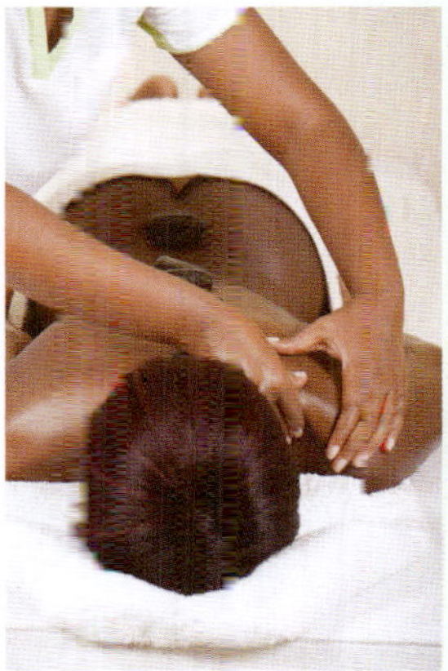

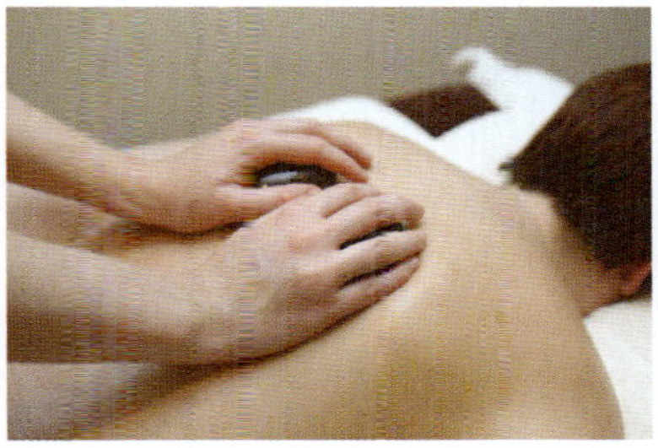

Use the stones to 'effleurage' the back

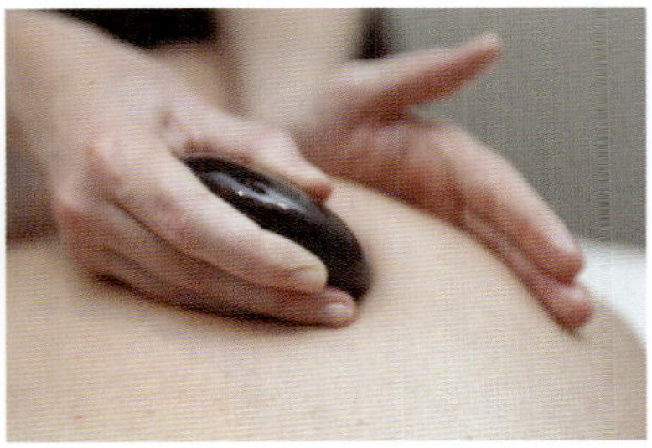

© CENGAGE LEARNING LTD

Concentrate on areas of tension

ISTOCK/© DARREN BAKER

Tight muscles really benefit from the hot stones

BEST PRACTICE

After massaging with the hot stone, when it has started to cool down, place it under the clients hand.

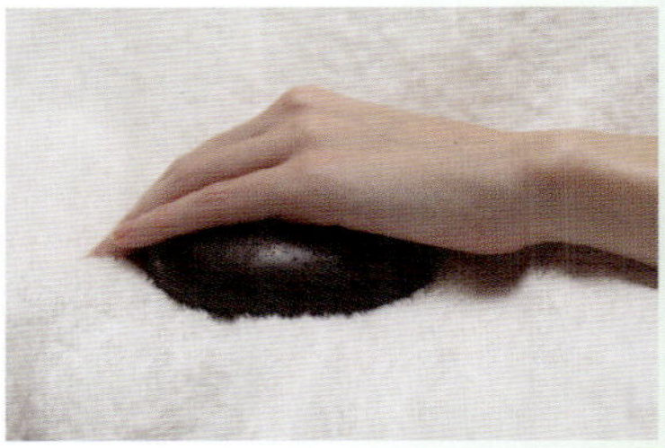

© CENGAGE LEARNING LTD

TOP TIP

You can cool down stones by rolling them in your hands before applying them to the body.

© CENGAGE LEARNING LTD

10 Once these stones start to cool, replace them back in the heater and complete the back massage with three-to-four strokes of manual effleurage.

11 Cover the back with a large towel or blanket to keep the client warm

Placement of stones on the abdomen

1 Turn the client over so they are lying on their back, face up (supine).

2 Eight medium-sized flat stones can be placed on the bed, in pairs, 2 inches apart so that the client when they lie back will feel the warmth of the stones either side of their spine. Adjust the location of the stones to ensure it feels very comfortable for the client.

3 Massage a few drops of the chosen oil onto the abdomen area.

4 Encourage the client to breathe slowly and deeply.

5 Take a hand towel and place it on the abdomen. As the client exhales, place the 'sacrum' stone securely on the abdomen covering the base chakra.

6 Choose two stones and place on the chest, covering the solar plexus and heart chakra.

7 Place a cold stone over the third eye chakra, to help balance the body.

8 Place the hot 'neck' stone in a towel under the neck, for support.

9 Place a hot stone under each hand, palm resting downwards.

10 Cover the abdomen and chest with a large towel, sheet or blanket to keep the client warm.

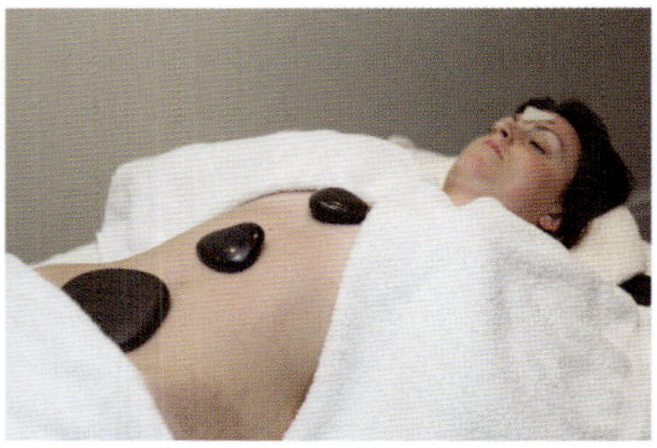

© CENGAGE LEARNING LTD

Stones are placed over the base, solar plexus and heart chakras

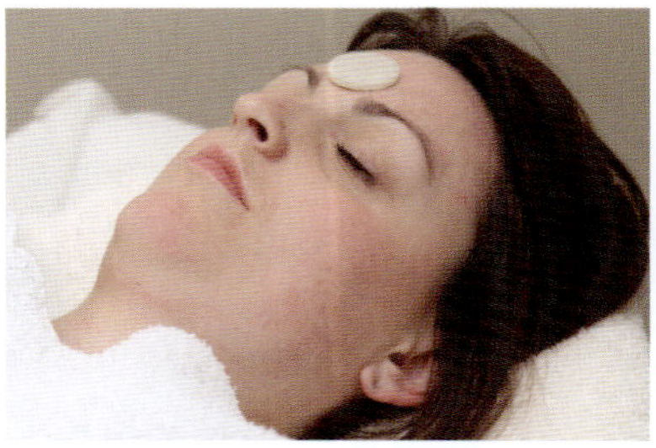

© CENGAGE LEARNING LTD

A cold stone is placed on the third eye chakra, to help balance the body

Front of the legs

1 Place a dry towel close to the leg area.

2 Place a few drops of oil in the hands and perform three-to-four standard effleurage strokes.

3 Select two stones, place them on the dry towel, then roll them in the hands to check the temperature and disperse some of the heat.

4 Perform two more effleurage strokes with warmed hands.

5 With a stone in each hand, start to massage the leg. Use long strong strokes to spread the heat.

6 Start at the top of the leg, following a simple leg massage routine. Use effleurage, kneading and stroking movements in a slow rhythm.

7 When the stones start to cool, place them on the leg. Select two more stones from the heater and roll them in the hands to check the temperature and disperse the heat.

8 Place the two original stones back in the heater. Perform a simple lower leg massage with the two stones, using similar strokes to those used on the upper leg.

9 Once the stones start to cool, replace them back in the heater and complete the leg massage with three-to-four strokes of manual effleurage.

10 Select four small stones and place between the toes

11 Cover the leg with a large towel or blanket to keep it warm.

12 Repeat on the other leg and foot.

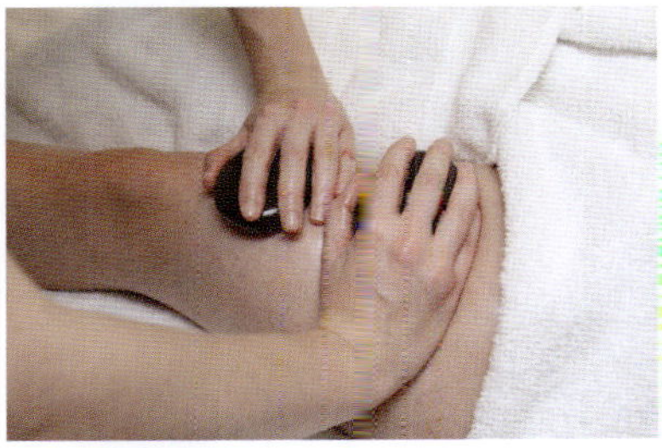

Use the stones to perform kneading movements on the front of the thigh

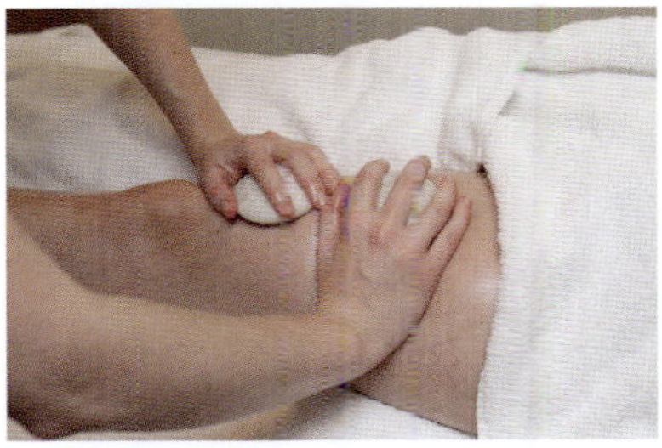

Cold, chilled stones can be used to provide a more invigorating effect. They are used alternately with hot stones.

Four small toe stones are placed between the toes on each foot.

Abdomen

1 Slowly remove the three placement stones.

2 Place a few drops of oil in the hands and perform three to four standard effleurage strokes.

3 Select two stones, roll them to check the temperature and position on the dry towel.

4 Perform two more effleurage strokes with warmed hands.

5 With a stone in each hand, massage the abdomen with effleurage strokes.

6 Follow the digestive tract with alternating hands in long slow gliding movements.

7 Once the stones start to cool, replace them back in the heater and complete the abdomen massage with three to four strokes of manual effleurage.

8 Replace the placement stones over the chakras.

TOP TIP

Stones can be cooled down by leaving them on a towel alongside the body until they are ready to be used.

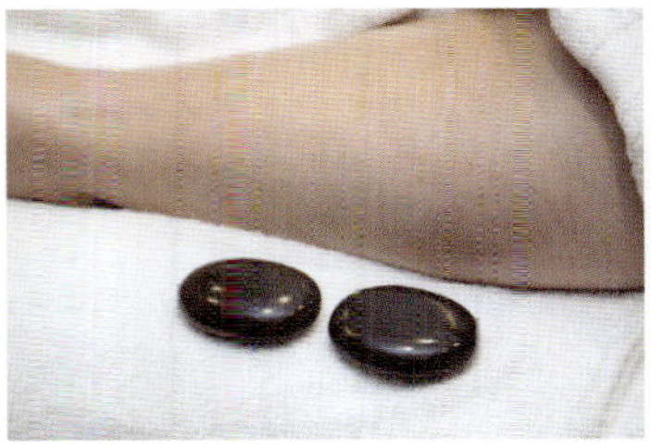

Arm

1 As with the legs, perform three to four strokes of manual effleurage on the arms.

2 Select one stone to suit the size of the arm, roll it in the hands to check the temperature.

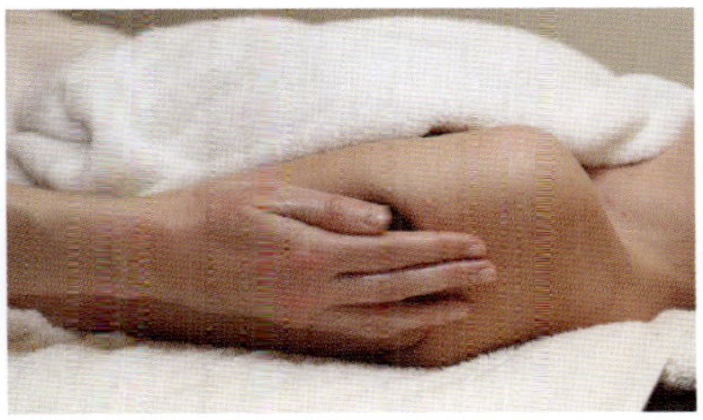

The stone is used to knead the upper arm

BEST PRACTICE

Monitoring service satisfaction
Throughout the service, ask the client if the temperature of the stones is comfortable.

BEST PRACTICE

Stones can be placed in special pockets/pouches, or simply wrapped in linen to ensure the temperature isn't too hot.

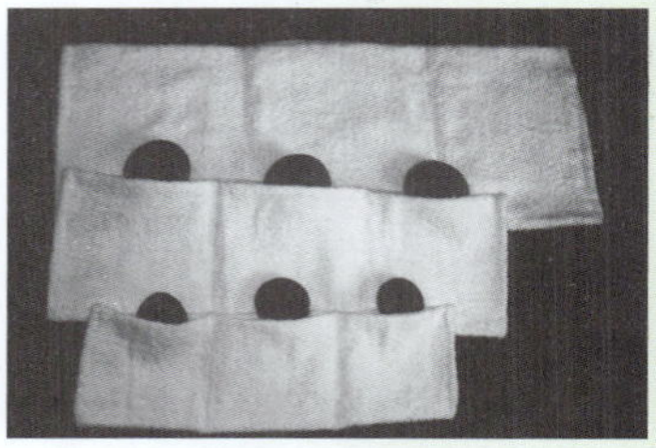

THERMAL STONES

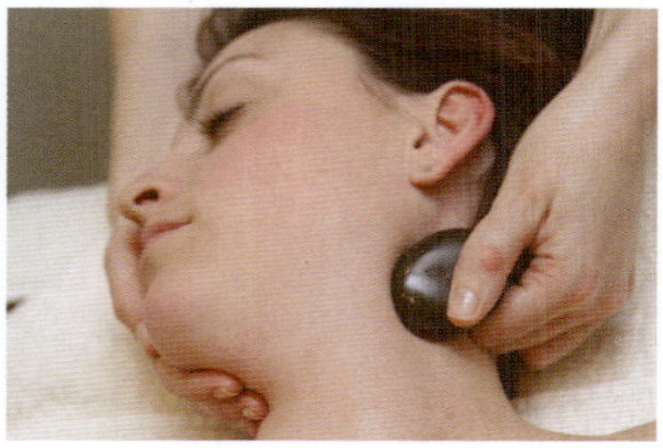

© CENGAGE LEARNING LTD

Use deep circular movements to the sterno-cleido-mastoid neck muscle

3 Perform two more effleurage strokes with warmed hands.
4 Perform effleurage and kneading movements with the stone, replace when the stone cools (as on the leg).
5 Finish with a short hand massage.
6 Leave the warm stone in the client's palm.
7 Cover the arm with a large towel or blanket to keep it warm.
8 Repeat on the other arm.

Upper chest and neck

1 Remove the neck and third eye stones.
2 Massage the area manually with the oil.
3 Select two small stones, disperse the heat as before.
4 With the stones, perform gentle effleurage and stroking movements along the chest area.
5 Select two facial stones and glide up and down each side of the neck.
6 Turn the client's head into the hand, and use deep circular movements to the sterno-cleido-mastoid muscle. Repeat on both sides of the neck.
7 Finish with manual effleurage strokes across the chest area.

Face

1 Select a gentle facial oil, don't apply too much.
2 Select two facial stones, disperse the heat as before.
3 With the warm stones perform gliding movements along the jaw line to the temple, under the cheekbone to the temple, and across the forehead and back to the temple.
4 Use the stones in gentle stroking movement across the face.
5 Replace the cold stone over the third eye chakra.
6 Perform a gentle but deep, soothing scalp massage.
7 Remove all stones from the body, the third eye stone should be the last to be removed.

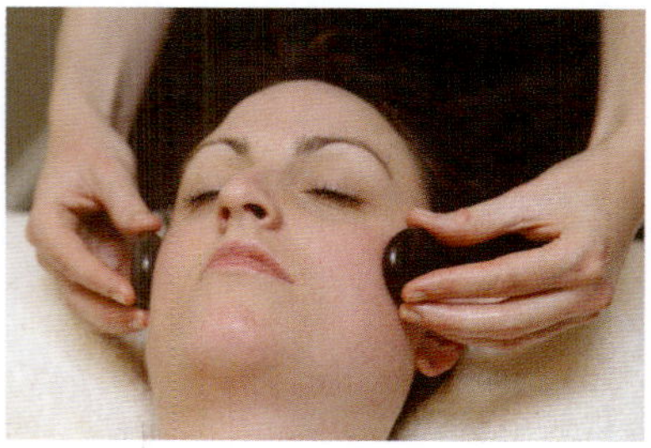

© CENGAGE LEARNING LTD

Perform gliding movements under the cheekbone towards the temple

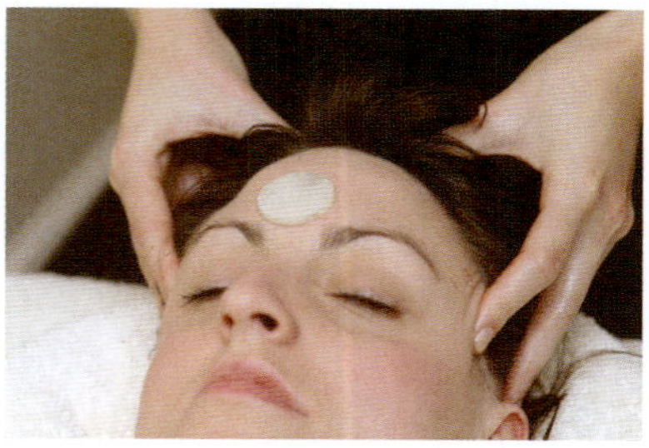

© CENGAGE LEARNING LTD

Perform a gentle but deep, soothing scalp massage

Step-by-Step: Full body stone therapy service

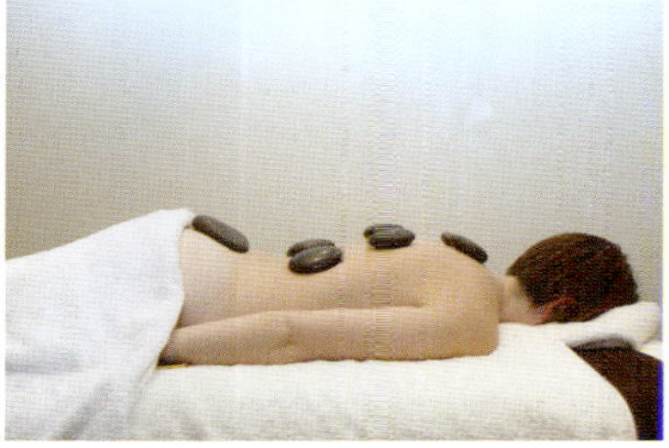

1 Place the 'sacrum' stone securely on the lower back area, then place three to four large stones along the spine.

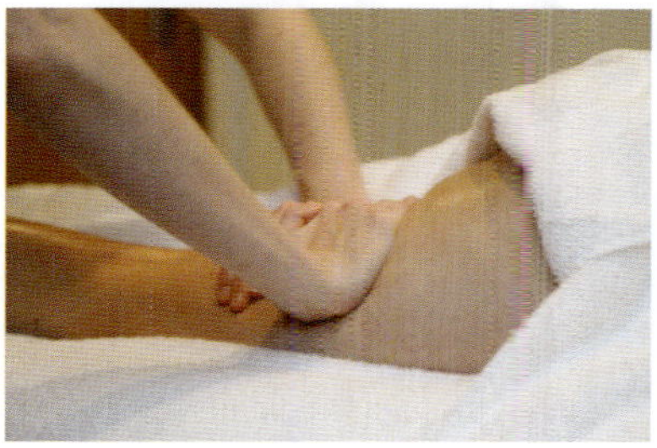

2 Select two appropriately sized stones, roll them in the hands to check the temperature, and then perform three to four effleurage strokes with warmed hands.

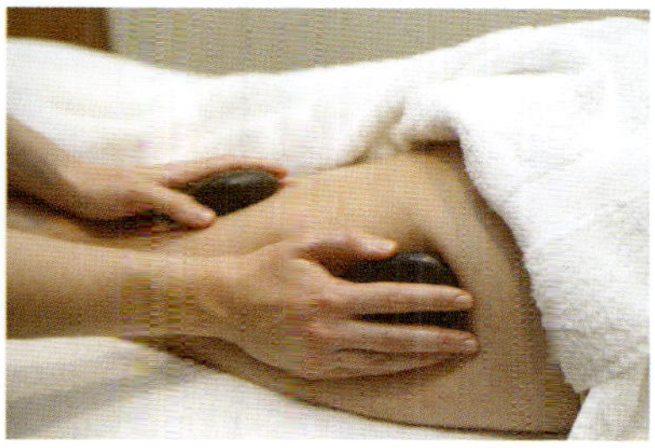

3 Massage the back of the leg with the warm stones using strong strokes to disperse the heat. Use effleurage, kneading and stroking movements.

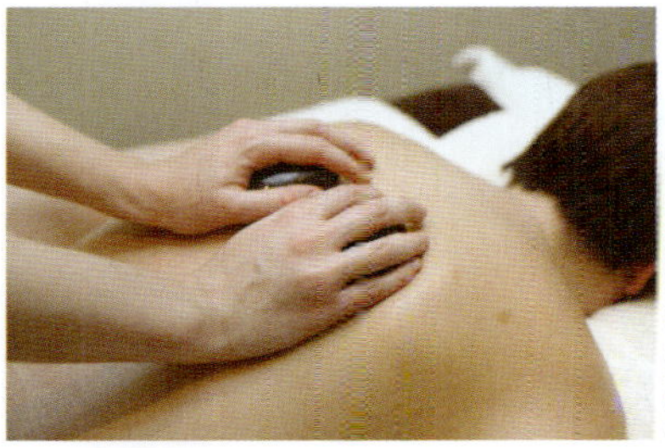

4 With the warm stone, begin massaging the back with long, strong strokes. Start with effleurage movements over the entire back.

5 Continue with kneading, stroking and deeper movements. Use the edge of the stone in any areas of tension and around the scapula.

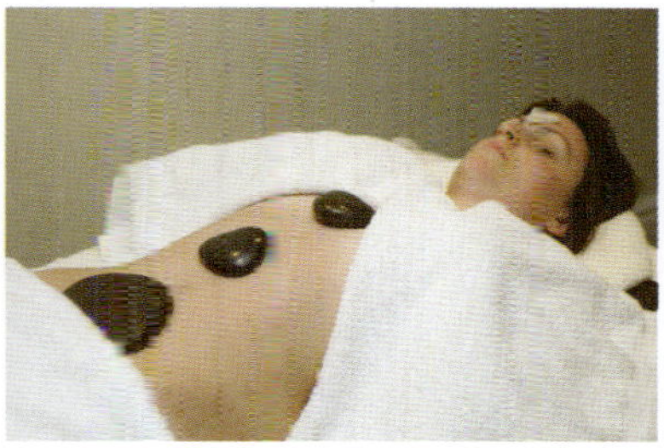

6 Place the hot 'sacrum' stone on the base chakra, and two hot stones over the solar plexus and heart chakra. A cold stone is placed on the third eye to have a balancing effect on the body.

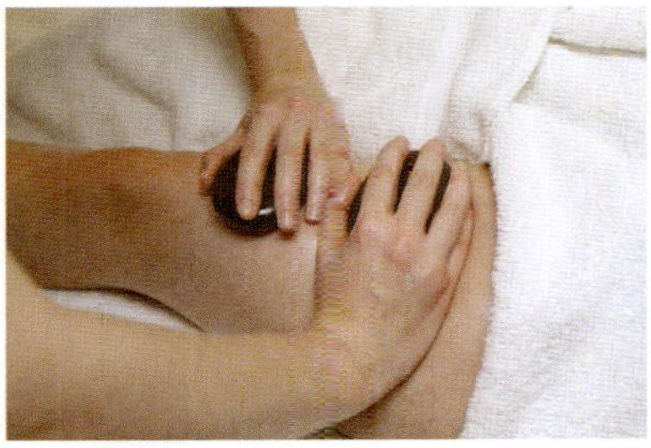

7 Massage the front of the leg with the warm stones using strong strokes to disperse the heat. Use effleurage, kneading and stroking movements. At the end, place four small stones in between the toes

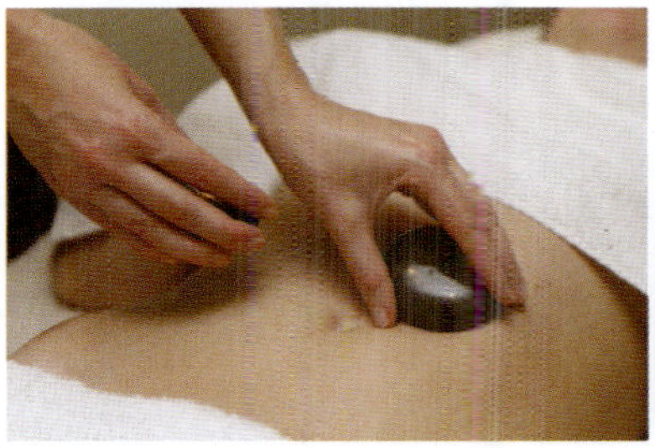

8 On the abdomen use gentle effleurage movements. Use alternating hands, following the digestive tract, in slow gliding movements.

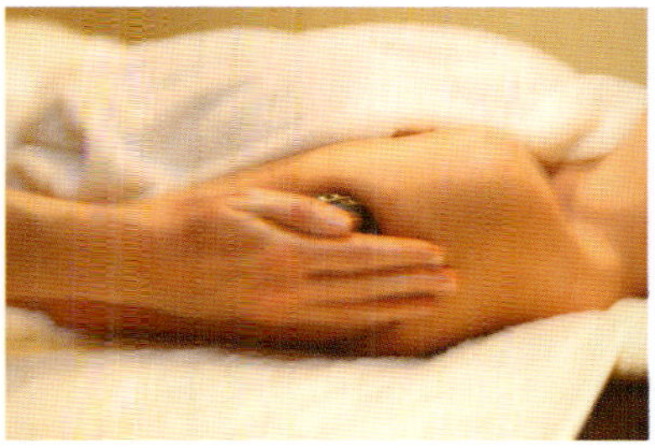

9 Choose one medium-size stone, perform effleurage and kneading movements, ending with a short manual hand massage.

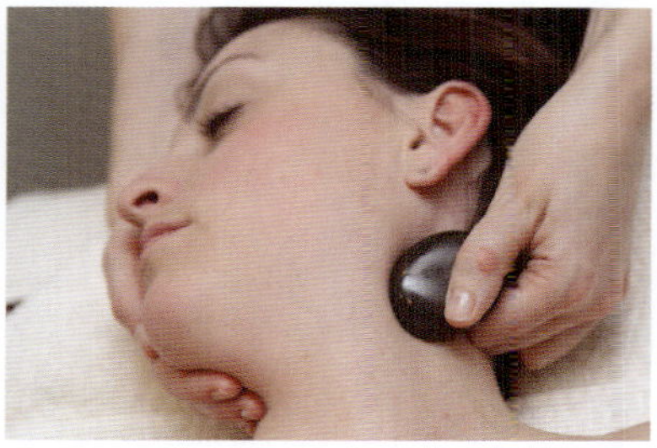

© CENGAGE LEARNING LTD

10 Use gentle effleurage and stroking movements along the chest area. Use two face stones to glide up the neck, turn the head into the hand and use deep circular movements down the sterno-cleido-mastoid muscle.

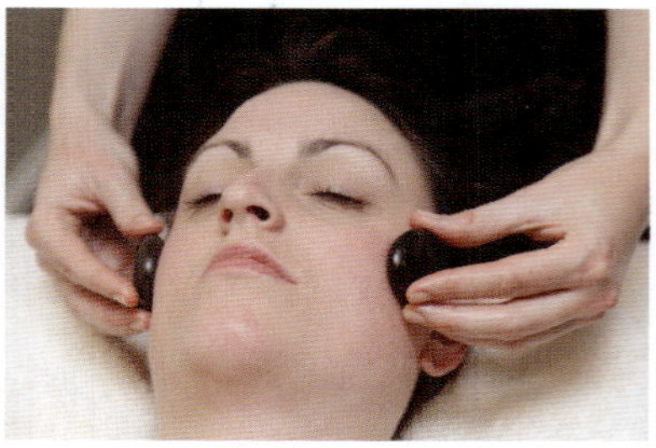

© CENGAGE LEARNING LTD

11 Using two facial stones perform gliding movements from the jaw to temple, under the cheekbones to the temple, and across the forehead to the temple .Gently stroke across the face.

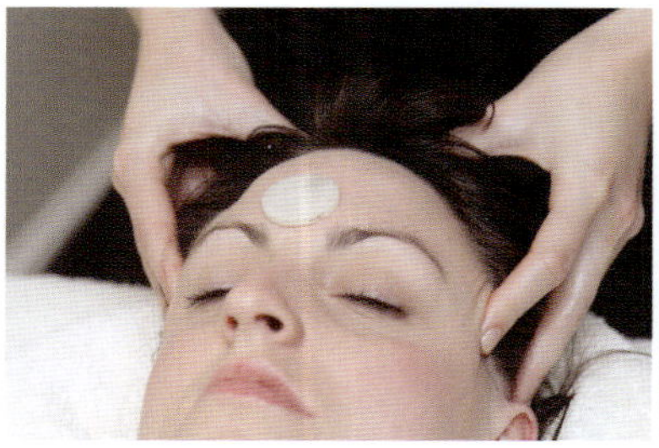

© CENGAGE LEARNING LTD

12 Replace the cold stone on the third eye chakra and perform a gentle but deep, soothing scalp massage. Calmly and quietly, remove 'tucked', stones placed on the client and from the treatment couch at the end of the service. This will indicate to the client the service has finished.

COURSEMATE

For a video on stone therapy, please visit this book's accompanying CourseMate.

ALWAYS REMEMBER

Some techniques can involve no oil and the clothes are kept on. Stones are placed on various parts of the body. The techniques such as holding, tucking, vibrations and rocking can be done through clothes.

TOP TIP

Stone can be used to relieve the tension in the shoulder area.

ISTOCK/© STILLS

Outcome 4: Provide aftercare advice

Learn how to provide aftercare advice which supports and meets the needs of your clients by:

1. Giving **advice** and recommendations accurately and constructively.
2. Giving your client's suitable **advice** specific to their individual needs.

ALWAYS REMEMBER

Complimentary exercise
Stretching between massage sessions can be beneficial for the client and help keep the muscles relaxed, e.g. yoga.

ISTOCK/© DIEGO CERVO

Aftercare and advice

The client should be encouraged to relax immediately after the stone therapy service so that the body can normalize. Offer the client a glass of water while resting. Explain any reaction they may experience and their home-care advice:

- Drink plenty of water to re-hydrate the body and avoid dehydration.
- Avoid activities such as exercise in the immediate hours after the service.
- Avoid services such as waxing, epilation, ultraviolet, as the skin will be sensitized from the stone therapy service.
- Recommend the use of body and facial products at home to nourish the skin, and enhance the effectiveness of the service, e.g. body scrubs, body butters, body oils, shower/bath products, loofah, body brush.

- Give general advice on living a healthy well-balanced life, including the benefits of healthy eating, drinking plenty of water, regular exercise and relaxation activities.
- Stretching between massage sessions can be beneficial and help keep the muscles relaxed, e.g. yoga.
- Stone therapy service can be carried out every 2–3 weeks depending on the individual client's needs. A more concentrated programme may be needed if the service is for a specific problem such as tense and tight muscles. In this case, stone therapy for approximately 20–30 minutes may be combined with manual massage.

BEST PRACTICE

Recommend complimentary retail

Recommend the use of appropriate body and facial products at home to nourish the skin, and enhance the effectiveness of the service.

ALWAYS REMEMBER

Many services work well with stone therapy and can be combined to provide a tailor-made/bespoke package for the client. Services such as:

- aromatherapy/pre-blended oil massage
- Indian head massage
- facials
- body exfoliation
- milk bath service
- manicures
- pedicures

ELLISONS

Body exfoliation can link well with stone therapy

ASSESSMENT OF KNOWLEDGE AND UNDERSTANDING

FUNCTIONAL SKILLS

Having covered the learning objectives for **provide stone therapy treatments** - test what you need to know and understand by answering the following short answer questions below.

The information covers:

- organizational and legal requirements
- how to work safely and effectively when providing stone therapy services
- client consultation
- preparation for service
- anatomy and physiology
- contra-indications and contra-actions
- stone therapy equipment
- service-specific knowledge
- aftercare advice for clients

Organizational and legal requirements

1 When performing a stone therapy service, what are your responsibilities under the Health and Safety at Work Act?

2 Why is it important to check out the salon's insurance guidelines when offering stone therapy services?

3 Why is it important to have a parent/guardian present when treating minors?

4 What is the importance of storing client records in relation to the Data Protection Act?

5 What are the reasons for keeping records of services and gaining client signatures? Why is it so important?

6 Why should your nails be short, clean, well-manicured and free of polish for stone therapy services?

7 What is the correct timing for the following stone therapy services: full body, including the face, the back and legs and feet and the back only? Why is it important to complete the service in a commercially viable time?

How to work safely and effectively when providing stone therapy services

1 How should the service environment be prepared to ensure comfort and maximum benefit from the service? Consider lighting, heating, ventilation.

2 Why is it important to disinfect stones after each service? And how would you do this?

3 What is repetitive strain injury (RSI)? What advantages does stone therapy have as a means of avoiding it compared to manual massage?

4 Why is it important to use the correct sized stones for the size of your own hands and the client's physical characteristics?

5 Why is it important to maintain correct posture when performing a stone therapy service?

6 How can you check the client's well-being during stone therapy service?

Client consultation

1 Why would you encourage clients to ask questions during the consultation?

2 Why is it important to record the client's responses to questioning? What is the legal significance of these records of questions asked and responses?

3 Describe how you would visually assess the client's physical characteristics.

4 Why would you carry out a thermal test before a stone therapy service?

5 How would you adapt and change the stone therapy service to different posture and skeletal conditions?

6 Why is it important that you don't name specific contra-indications when encouraging clients to seek medical advice?

7 What advice would you give the client about their lifestyle pattern, to help the effectiveness of the service.

Preparation for service

1 Why is it important to give clients clear instructions on the removal of relevant clothing and general preparation for the service?

2 Why is it important to reassure clients during the preparation process?

3 How do you select the correct oil that is suitable for each stone therapy service?

4 How would you cleanse different areas of the body in preparation for stone therapy service, including face and feet.

Anatomy and physiology

1 Describe the physical effects of hot and cold stone therapy service.

2 List **five** functions of the skin.

3 What are the **three** main bones of the leg?

4 Describe lordosis, kyphosis, scoliosis.

5 Describe the main muscle groups of the leg, and their position and action.

6 Name **four** lymph glands/nodes of the body.

7 Describe the psychological effects of hot and cold stone therapy service.

Contra-indications and contra-actions

1 Describe **six** contra-indications that would prevent a stone therapy service from going ahead.

2 Describe **four** contra-indications that may restrict a stone therapy service.

3 What are the possible contra-actions which may occur during and post-service? How would you deal with them?

Stone therapy equipment

1 Why should you never use non-professional stone heating equipment? What are the insurance implications?

2 Describe the different types of stones used during stone therapy service, their properties and uses.

3 What is the correct way to dry and store different types of stones to effectively energize them?

4 What is the recommended operating temperatures for hot and cold stones?

5 How would you protect the client's skin against extremes of temperature during stone therapy service?

6 Describe the different types of oil suitable for stone therapy and their purpose.

Service-specific knowledge

1 What are the '**five elements**' of stone therapy?

2 What are the **seven major** chakras? describe their characteristics.

3 Why would you place stones on the major chakras, what is the purpose and benefits?

4 Why is the temperature and time management of the stones so important during the service?

5 Which areas of the body and body characteristics need particular care when performing a stone therapy service?

6 What advantages could you discuss with the client when promoting stone therapy services?

7 Describe how stone therapy could be used to enhance other services?

8 What are the recommended timings for stone therapy service? How would you adapt the timing to suit the client's individual needs?

Aftercare advice for clients

1 What advice would you give your client regarding their lifestyle to improve the effectiveness of the stone therapy service?

2 Which activities should be avoided after the stone therapy service?

3 Which products would you recommend for home use that will benefit the client? Any that you would advise they avoid and why?

4 Which other services would you recommend the client had to enhance the effect of the service?

SHUTTERSTOCK/RIDO

14 UV tanning

Learning Objectives

This chapter covers the unit on **Provide UV tanning services**.

This unit is all about how to provide and monitor the service UV tanning using UV equipment. Choice of UV equipment and application is modified to suit the client's skin type and achieve the service objectives identified at consultation. Relevant health and safety legislation, hygiene and industry codes of practice must be effectively implemented throughout the service.

There are **four** learning outcomes which you must achieve competently:

1 **Maintain safe and effective methods of working when providing UV tanning services.**

2 **Consult, plan and prepare for services with clients.**

3 **Monitor UV tanning services.**

4 **Provide aftercare advice.**

For each unit your assessor will observe you on **at least three separate occasions each involving different clients.**

From the **range** statements, you must show that you have:

- used all **consultation techniques**
- dealt with **at least one** of the **necessary actions** where a contra-action, contra-indication or service modification occurs
- provided all types of relevant aftercare **advice**

(continued on the next page)

ALEX WIDDOWS SUN CHIC TANNING, WWW.SUNCHIC.COM

ROLE MODEL

Alex Widdows

Managing Director of Sun Chic Luxury Tanning Salon

“As Managing Director I am primarily focused on marketing and promotions, improving customer service and staff recruitment and training.

I came into the tanning industry only relatively recently, about 2.5 years ago, but have always worked in customer-facing roles. Initially I worked in restaurant management and then as Project Manager for a large engineering firm. In each position I have held I have always worked with a diverse spectrum of people.

In 2007, I purchased an existing tanning salon in Hove, originally called 'Tanarama'. The salon was completely refitted and re-named 'Sun Chic'. Not only did we go out of our way to open the friendliest and most luxurious salon we could, we also wanted it to provide the latest tanning technology as well.

In July 2007, scientific guidelines were published on the safest levels of UV to be used in tanning; known as the 'Zero·3' guidelines; the name relates to a suggested maximum UV level of 0.3 Wm^2. These guidelines have subsequently become law in a number of European countries and it is only a matter of time before Zero·3 becomes compulsory in the UK. We

(continued on the next page)

(continued)

However, you must prove that you have the necessary knowledge, understanding and skills to be able to perform competently across the range.

When providing UV tanning services it is important to use the skills you have learnt in the following units:

Monitoring safe work operations.

Promotional activities.

(continued)

already offer Zero·3 tanning in our salon and as lamp technology continues to improve we will ensure that we are fully aware of the latest developments so we can offer the safest tanning with the best results.

Working in the tanning industry I have met some fantastic people and opening and developing the business has been a very rewarding experience. It was an uphill struggle initially, but with a lot of persistence and hard work it is now one of the most successful tanning salons in the area. The salon environment is an enjoyable place to work, we know most of our customers by name and there is always a very friendly sociable atmosphere.

Essential anatomy and physiology knowledge requirements for UV tanning services is identified on the checklist in Chapter 2, pages 12–13. This chapter also discusses anatomy and physiology specific to this unit.

“When setting up a salon, or any other business, always get a solicitor to review any documents before signing; this includes building contracts, equipment leases, warranties, maintenance contracts, etc. It is money very well spent in the long term.

Alex Widdows

Introduction

Tanning is where the skin darkens in response to ultraviolet light (UVL) in order to protect itself from further sun exposure. UV light may be outdoor (natural sunlight) or indoor (artificially created by UV tanning equipment).

UV tanning equipment emits UV rays the same type of radiation as that found in natural sunlight. Equipment includes lie-down sunbeds, canopy sunbeds, vertical stand-in sun beds, sun showers and sun lamps.

Sensible UV exposure minimizes the associated risks and enables the associated benefits of tanning. This should be the aim of the sunbed operator where UV tanning is provided including beauty salons, leisure centre gyms, sports and fitness clubs and hotels.

Beneficial effects of UV exposure:

- the treatment of seasonal affective disorder (SAD) – an emotional disorder that occurs between winter and spring and is related to a lack of sunshine
- a feeling of well-being and relaxation
- production and release of vitamin D into the bloodstream – essential for healthy skin and bones as it increases calcium absorption and is important for blood clotting
- increased blood circulation, which increases skin healing
- the treatment of certain skin disorders, including:
  - acne vulgaris, through its healing and disinfecting effect
  - psoriasis, can respond well to medical treatment using a lamp providing narrow band or broad band UVB or UVA.
  - neuro-dermatitis, an inflammatory skin condition

HEALTH & SAFETY

Medical benefit of UVL

The skin disorder psoriasis appears to improve in the summer months in the presence of sunlight. UV as a service for the condition should only be provided by the medical profession. Medical treatment is the only exemption for those under 18 years of age to receive UV, administered by the medical profession.

Medical treating with UV is known as phototherapy. The treatment of children under 18 years of age with tanning equipment is the only exemption

BEST PRACTICE

UV tanning service regulation

To ensure regulation of UV tanning services the Sunbed Association offers membership and professional guidance to tanning salon operators, manufacturers and distributors of indoor tanning equipment. The Sunbed Association logo shows your client your commitment to being aware of your responsibilities and compliance with the sunbed code of practice. www.sunbedassociation.org.uk

ALWAYS REMEMBER

Minimizing UV exposure risk

The associated risks may be both short term and long term. Safe working practices should reduce the risk of both. Refer to HSE publication – ***Reducing Health Risks From the Use of Ultraviolet (UV) Tanning Equipment***. Specific advice for customers, based on current medical opinion, is provided on the poster ***UV tanning equipment***.

When carrying out a risk assessment you should consider the **Sunbeds (Regulation) Act (2010).** The main purpose of this Act is to prevent the use of sunbeds on commercial business premises by children and young people under the age of 18. They must also not be present in a restricted zone, this is where the sunbed is located. The Act additionally requires operators to provide sunbed users with information on the health effects of sunbeds.

Guidance on the implementation is available, provided by the Department of Health. Local Authority officers enforce these regulations.

Associated risks of UV overexposure

- UV burning and skin dryness
- thickening of the skin, as the basal cells reproduce more quickly
- photo-ageing – sun damage, causing premature ageing with the signs of loose skin and wrinkling, mainly caused by damage to the collagen fibres in the skin
- skin cancer – commonly basal cell cancer, squamous cell cancer and, the most harmful, melanoma cancer
- irritation and damage to the eyes – acute UV exposure can lead to photokeratitis, inflammation of the cornea and iris; photoconjunctivitis, inflammation of the conjunctiva; and cataracts

HEALTH & SAFETY

Moles

If the client has moles (cellular naevi), ask them to keep a close check for any changes, including irregular borders, darkening, colour change, bleeding and crusting. These may be an indication of a melanoma, a rare and serious type of cancer that begins in the skin and can spread to other organs in the body. The chart below shows how a skin melanoma can be differentiated from a normal mole.

Normal mole	Melanoma	Sign	Characteristic
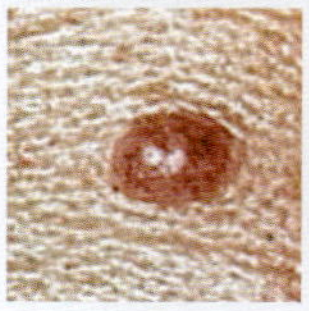	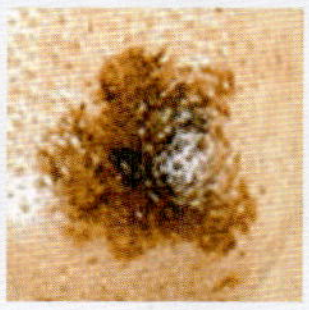	Asymmetry	When half of the mole does not match the other half
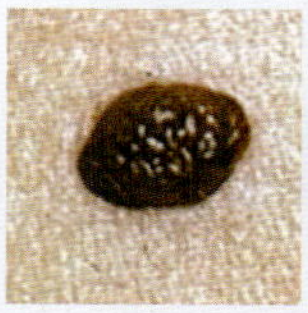	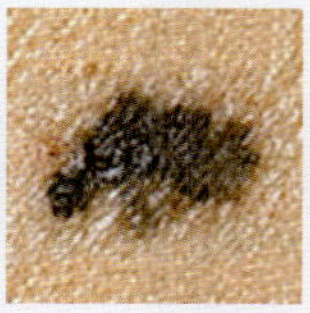	Border	When the border (edges) of the mole are ragged or irregular
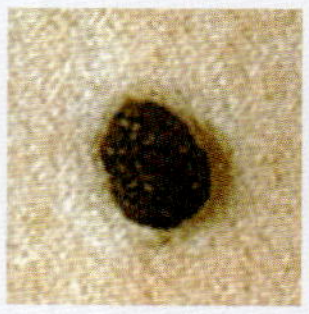	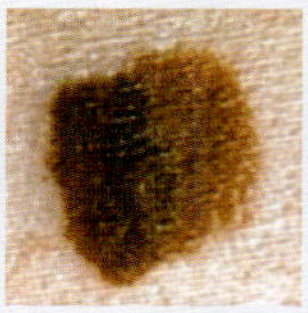	Colour	When the colour of the mole varies throughout
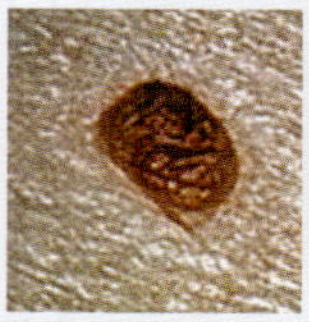	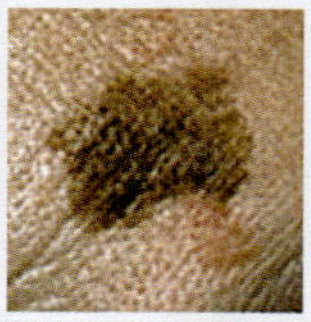	Diameter	If the mole's diameter is larger than a pencil's eraser

PHOTOGRAPHS USED BY PERMISSION: NATIONAL CANCER INSTITUTE

How to differentiate a skin melanoma from a normal mole

Always refer the client to their GP in this instance, and *never* name a specific contra-indication. Habia Skills Academy launched a Skin Cancer Awareness Campaign in 2013 to encourage professionals employed in the sector, to identify the possible early symptoms of skin cancer, through their role in working closely with clients.

Anatomy and physiology

A tan is the skin's method of protecting the body from exposure to the sun. The **melanocytes**, cells in the epidermis which create skin pigmentation, are stimulated to produce melanin. Melanosomes found in the melanocyte cell are organelles which synthesize and store the pigment melanin. The melanocytes increase melanin production as a protective measure to absorb harmful rays of UV light. Pigmentation changes can occur in the skin due to the changes in activity and numbers of melanocytes. This can result in increased ephelides (freckles), solar lentigines or chloasma (liver spots) and irregular pigmentation. Pigmentation changes are not uncommon in Asian skin and often result in large hyper-pigmentation marks. The skin also thickens as the cells in the epidermis multiply to absorb UV and reduce its penetration.

The quantity and distribution of melanocytes differs according to race. In a white Caucasian skin the melanin tends to be destroyed when it reaches the stratum granulosum layer of the epidermis. With stimulation from UV exposure, however, melanin will also be present in the upper epidermis. In a black-skinned person, melanin is present in larger quantities throughout all the layers, a level of protection that has evolved to deal with bright UV light. The increased protection allows less UV to penetrate the dermis below. The less melanin there is in the skin the less natural protection the skin has from the harmful UV rays.

On exposure to UV the melanin that is already available will produce a tanned effect, which will quickly disappear. It can take up to 3–7 days before new melanin is released following UV exposure, so the tanned appearance gradually develops. The development of a gradual tan without burning should be aimed for.

Overexposure to the sun results in an erythema of the skin as the blood capillaries dilate. The skin will also feel sore as the nerve endings become stimulated. The skin may then form a blister and then form a crust as the skin begins to heal. This can lead to skin hyper-pigmentation and hypo-pigmentation. In hypo-pigmentation the skin loses colour caused by decreased melanin production and therefore has less protection.

The electromagnetic spectrum The sun's spectrum comprises of different electromagnetic rays which travel in waves. The full range of radiations in the electromagnetic spectrum is:

- radio waves – radio, TV and radar
- infrared rays – heat rays
- light
- UV rays
- x-rays
- gamma rays – from radioactive substances
- cosmic rays – in outer space

The electromagnetic spectrum is an arrangement of these waves in order of wavelength. Wavelength is measured in nanometres (nm) – 1 nanometre is 1 billionth of a metre.

Natural UV UV is part of this spectrum, which ranges from short rays including UV light (tanning) to visible white light (daylight) to infrared rays (warmth) which are invisible.

HEALTH & SAFETY

0.3 UV Tanning Regulations

In 2003 a European Standard on UV radiation levels was introduced, followed in 2009 with new regulations limiting the amount of UV radiation permitted in UV tanning equipment in the UK to a maximum of 0.3 watts of energy per square metre (0.3W/m²).

All equipment should be 0.3 compliant.

The UV emissions being no higher than the midday Mediterranean sun.

HEALTH & SAFETY

UV risk short term:

- Burnt skin
- Skin which is dry with signs of irritation such as a rash
- Eye irritation or conjunctivitis
- Mechanical failure of equipment causing injury

Long-term UV risk:

- Skin cancer
- Cataracts of the eyes
- Photo-ageing: premature ageing of the skin

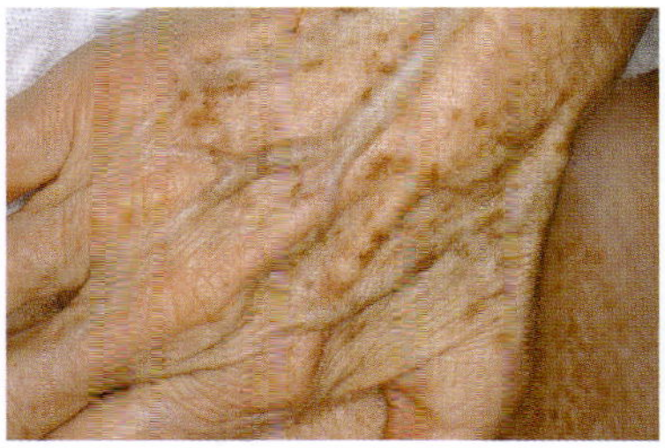

Chloasma is concentrated melanin caused by sun damage

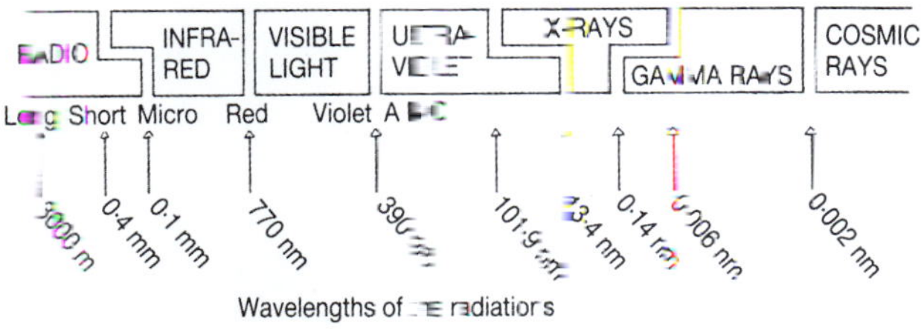

The electromagnetic spectrum

UV wavelengths can be divided into three types according to their wavelengths: UVA, UVB and UVC.

- **UVA** rays are the longest (within the range 315–400 nm), providing 95 per cent of natural UV light.
- **UVB** rays are shorter rays (within the range 280–315 nm), providing 4–5 per cent of natural UV light. These are much stronger than UVA rays and the most active.
- **UVC** rays are the shortest (within the range 100–280 nm) and fail to reach the Earth as they are almost completely absorbed by the atmosphere.

ALWAYS REMEMBER

UV wavelength

Two types of UV wavelength reach the earth: UVA and UVB rays.

HEALTH & SAFETY

UVL exposure for medical and therapeutic use

UVB rays are mainly used for medical purposes and do not penetrate deep into the skin.

Artificial UV Artificial UV is produced by high or low-pressure tubes and lamps. The term pressure relates to the wattage of the lamps. Most suntanning units emit both UVA and UVB rays. Tanning beds produce between 3–8 times the UVA the natural sun produces at noon in the summer.

Physiological effects The shorter the wavelength, the higher the energy and possible damage. UVA rays have a longer wavelength. These stimulate melanin production, creating a rapid but short-lived tan. They also penetrate deeply into the dermis, damaging the elastin and collagen fibres which give the skin its strength and elasticity. UVA exposure leads to premature skin ageing, seen as pigmentation disorders and wrinkling.

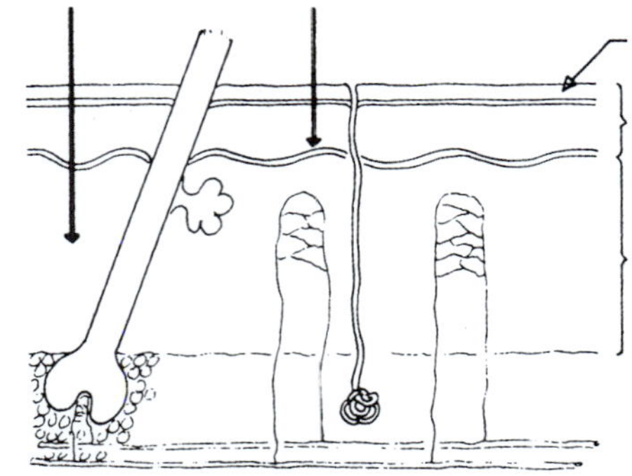

Penetration of UV rays into the skin

UVB rays have a shorter wavelength than UVA and penetrate only as far as the lower layers of the epidermis. They cause skin erythema, skin burning (sunburn) and stimulate the pigment cells, melanocytes, to increase melanin production, creating a longer-lasting tan than UVA. UVB also stimulates vitamin D production. When UV hits the skin, a chemical in the skin changes it to vitamin D. This then aids the absorption of calcium.

When exposure to UV ceases, the tan eventually fades. This is because the pigmented cells are gradually lost and replaced through the process of desquamation.

Fitzpatrick classification scale It is important to have an understanding of the Fitzpatrick skin classification scale as this is used to categorize skin types in order to measure the skin's ability to tolerate UV exposure.

The **Fitzpatrick classification** can be measured more accurately by asking a client a series of questions, and allocating an associated point score to client responses. When totalled, the cumulative score will provide their Fitzpatrick skin type. This will guide you on how to assess what UV exposure would be appropriate.

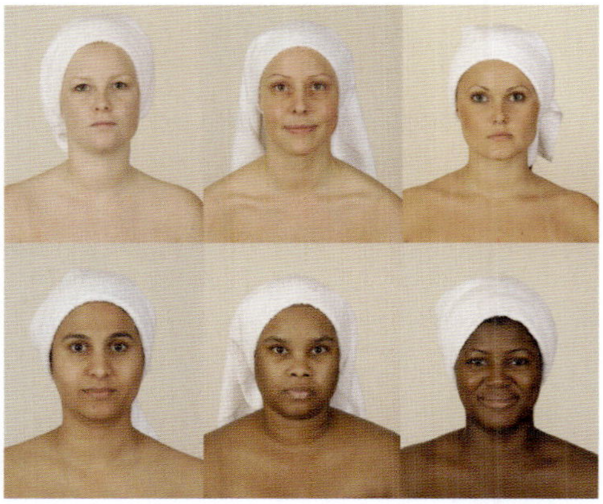

Fitzpatrick skin typing helps predict the skin's response to the services

SKIN TYPE	SKIN COLOUR	HAIR AND EYE COLOUR	REACTION TO SUN	COMMON ETHNIC CONSIDERATIONS
Type I	White	Blond hair and green eyes	Always burns, freckles	English, Scottish
Type II	White	Blond hair and green/blue eyes	Always burns, freckles, difficult to tan	Northern European
Type III	White	Blond/brown hair and blue/brown eyes	Tans after several burns, may freckle	German
Type IV	Brown	Brown hair and brown eyes	Tans more than average, rarely burns, rarely freckles	Mediterranean, southern European, Hispanic
Type V	Dark brown	Brown/black hair and brown eyes	Tans with ease, rarely burns, no freckles	Asian, Indian, some Africans
Type VI	Black	Black hair and brown/black eyes	Tans, never burns, deeply pigmented never freckles	Africans

Fitzpatrick skin type scale

Fitzpatrick identification form genetic disposition part I

POINTS						
Question	**0**	**1**	**2**	**3**	**4**	**Score**
What colour are your eyes?	Light blue, grey, green	Blue, grey, or green	Blue	Dark brown	Brownish black	
What is the natural colour of your hair?	Sandy red	Blond	Chestnut/Dark blond	Dark brown	black	
What colour is your skin (unexposed areas)?	Reddish	Very pale	Pale with beige tint	Light brown	Dark brown	
Do you have freckles on unexposed areas?	Many	Several	Few	Incidental	None	
					Genetic Disposition Total	

Reaction to sun exposure part II

POINTS						
Question	**0**	**1**	**2**	**3**	**4**	**Score**
What happens when you stay too long in the sun?	Painful redness, blistering, peeling	Blistering followed by peeling	Burns sometimes followed by peeling	Rare burns	Never had burns	
To what degree do you turn brown?	Hardly or not at all	Light colour tan	Reasonable tan	Tan very easy	Turn dark brown quickly	
Do you turn brown with several hours of sun exposure?	Never	Seldom	Sometimes	Often	Always	
How does your face react to the sun?	Very sensitive	Sensitive	Normal	Very resistant	Never had a problem	
					Reaction to Sun Exposure Total	

Tanning habits part III

POINTS						
Questions	**1**	**2**	**3**	**4**	**5**	**Score**
When did you last expose your body to sun (or artificial sunlamp/tanning cream)?	More than 3 months ago	2–3 months ago	12 months ago	Less than 1 month ago	Less than 2 weeks ago	
Did you expose the area to be treated to the sun?	Never	Hardly ever	Sometimes	Often	Always	
					Tanning Habits Total	

Skin-type scores

SKIN TYPE SCORES	
Total for Genetic Disposition	
Total for Reaction to Sun Exposure	
Total for Tanning Habits	
Total Skin Type Score	

Fitzpatrick skin type scale

Fitzpatrick skin type

SKIN TYPE SCORE	FITZPATRICK SKIN TYPE
0–7	I
8–16	II
17–25	III
25–30	IV
Over 30	V–VI

A Wood's lamp, a high-pressure mercury vapour lamp covered with a dark filter which contains nickel oxide, can be used to assess skin further including the diagnosis of skin type, skin condition, pigmentation and blood flow. It works by measuring the fluorescence given off by different matters when they are irradiated with UV of a particular wavelength about 365 nm. UV damage to the skin can be assessed using this lamp which can be provided with a powerful magnifying lens.

BEST PRACTICE

UV overexposure

UV overexposure is harmful to **all** skin types. However, immediate damage seen as erythema is more visible on skin type I than skin type VI. Always start at the minimum recommended service exposure time to assess skin tolerance and avoid erythema.

Calculating session times

When calculating the duration of exposure to a tanning service and the frequency of sessions, the client's skin type must always be taken into account as numbered:

1. light sensitive – burns easily, never tans
2. light – burns easily but tans slightly
3. medium colouring – burns moderately, tans slowly
4. medium colouring – rarely burns, tans easily
5. darkly pigmented – rarely burns and tans immediately
6. dark, deeply pigmented – never burns and tans immediately

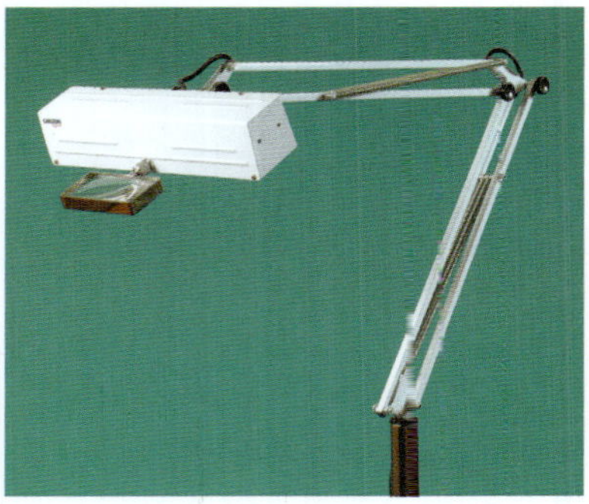
CARLTON BEAUTY + SPA LTD

A Wood's lamp is used to measure the skin's fluorescence

HEALTH & SAFETY

Skin type non-exposure recommendations

Because clients with Fitzpatrick skin types I and II have risk factors of poor protection because the skin has a poor tanning response and burns easily, these clients should avoid UV tanning as a service. Offer an alternative service such as self-tanning.

Extra care should be taken by clients whose skin has lots of freckles and moles.

ALWAYS REMEMBER

Using the Wood's lamp to measure skin fluorescence

A dry skin will project a weak fluorescence when exposed to the Wood's lamp and a greasy skin a bright fluorescence.

Hypo-pigmentation will show as a bright fluorescence.

Electrical science

Starters send the high voltage required to get the tubes operating and a ballast device maintains and limits the electric current in a circuit. The ballast in the sunbed varies in size and weight, and it is important that the tube wattage is correct for the ballast of the sunbed.

Suntanning units may use tubes filled with mercury vapour at low pressure, which is transformed to UV when the equipment is switched on, or quartz tubes, which are filled at a higher pressure. High-powered compact lamps known as burners are featured in some tanning equipment; this intensifies the UV. They emit high levels of UVB and some UVC, which requires filtering.

Modern tanning units contain filter screens which control the intensity of the UV emitted. The short wavelengths which create skin burning are screened, but may still be sufficient to cause burning dependent upon application.

Filters must always be in good repair or skin burning could occur.

Modifications to the tubes can determine whether more UVA or UVB is emitted, through the different fluorescent linings.

BEST PRACTICE

Skin tanning response

Ask the client what their skin's normal reaction to UV light is and when their last exposure to UV light was.

Viable radiation is also produced, seen as blue or pink when the UV tanning equipment is in operation.

Reflectors are fitted so that the UV is directed onto the skin's surface.

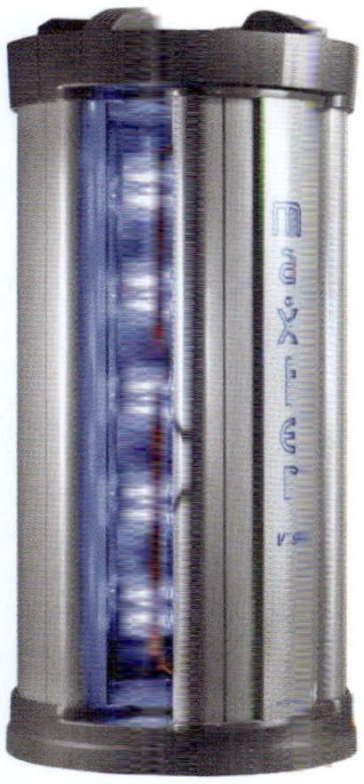
ALEX WIDDOWS, SUNCHIC TANNING. WWW.SUNCHIC.COM

A vertical tanning unit

Choice of tanning equipment

There is a variety of tanning equipment available. They all have different types of tubes which provide different levels of UV output, dependent upon the amount and their strength (pressure). The BS EN safety standard BS EN 60335-2-27: European Standard controls the safety of sunbed equipment, which sets a safety limit of 0.3 W/m² UV radiance for skin exposure to ultraviolet radiation. They are usually either **vertical**, where the client stands, **horizontal**, where the client lies down or UV chairs designed for upper body tanning. These units provide either total or partial tanning. They incorporate high-performance tanning tubes, closely packed together and protected with a safety layer of acrylic which provides a barrier between client and UV lighting. Fans are also fitted to prevent the equipment overheating. Additional equipment features include facial tanning tubes, shoulder tanning features, cooling body/facial fans to prevent overheating, stereo speakers, or the facility for the client to play their own audio device for entertainment and the facility to produce aromas. Many are coin token operated.

High-pressure tanning units These units achieve a tan very quickly as they emit a lot of UV rays. Application time is very short, commencing at 4–5 minutes with a maximum of 9–15 minutes dependent upon the unit. High-pressure units have an increased level of UVB to speed the tanning process and as such, overexposure will result in burning of the skin.

TOP TIP

Vertical tanning

Vertical tanning is not recommended for clients who suffer from claustrophobia due to the small, confined area of the tanning unit. Check this at consultation.

BEST PRACTICE

Data Protection Act (1998)

It is necessary to ask the client questions before the service plan can be finalized: the details are recorded on the client record card.

Remember *this information is confidential* and should be stored in a secure area following the service.

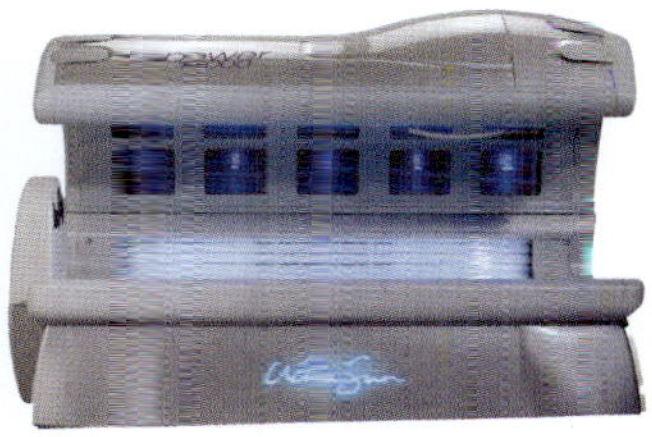
HELIONOVA

High-pressure, horizontal tanning unit

Outcome 1: Maintain safe and effective methods of working when providing UV tanning services

Learn how to maintain safe effective methods of working when providing UV tanning services by:

1. Setting up the service area to meet organization procedures and manufacturer's instructions and the current sunbed Code of Practice.
2. Wearing suitable personal protective equipment, when necessary.
3. Ensuring the client is provided with the personal protective equipment recommended by the current sunbed Code of Practice.

BEST PRACTICE

Maintenance checks

- Daily when turning on UV equipment check all lamps/ tubes are lit
- Check for unusual smells and noises which may indicate an electrical fault
- Check all vents are clear
- Clean acrylic shields,reflectors and lamps as recommended by manufacturer

(Continued) Learn how to maintain safe effective methods of working when providing UV tanning services by:

4. Making sure that the environmental conditions are suitable for the client and the service.
5. Ensuring your personal hygiene, protection and appearance meets accepted industry and organizational requirements.
6. Providing suitable skin preparation products for client use prior to UV tanning sessions.
7. Positioning equipment cleaning products for safety and ease of use by the client.
8. Ensuring equipment is cleaned and maintained using the correct methods and at time intervals required by the local authority.
9. Maintaining the client's modesty, privacy and comfort at all times.
10. Disposing of waste materials safely and correctly.
11. Ensuring the service is completed within a commercially viable time.
12. Ensuring client record cards are up-to-date, accurate, complete, legible and signed by the client and practitioner.
13. Ensuring the service area and equipment is left clean and in a condition suitable for future services.

> "The backbone of our industry is repeat custom and without exceptional customer service and a first-class relationship with our tanners, we would not be in business.
>
> **Alex Widdows**

ALWAYS REMEMBER

The Management of Health and Safety at Work Regulations (MHSWR) (1999) requires a risk assessment for every workplace to be carried out.

The main risk associated with the provision and use of UV tanning equipment is the the UVL radiation emitted.

The necessary procedures must be put in place to prevent or control UV radiation exposure levels for people working near or using the UV tanning equipment.

UV equipment must be separated with adequate screening if there is more than one piece of equipment in a room to comply with legislation and prevent overexposure to UV radiation and for privacy.

Equipment should be installed and serviced regularly testing for efficiency and safety in line with European standards, by a qualified electrician in compliance with the Electricity at Work Regulations (1989). A service record must be maintained and available for checking by local authority enforcement officers.

Under the Health and Safety at Work Act (1974) and the Management of Health and Safety at Work Regulations (1999) there is a legal requirement for the employer or other appointed competent person to carry out a risk assessment for the use and operation of the UV tanning service. If the business has five or more employees, the findings must be recorded. Measures must be taken to control as is 'reasonably practicable' the risks. All staff must be made aware of the findings of the risk assessment and be competently trained all aspects of its use. It is recommended this risk assessment is carried out annually. Health and safety training should be provided on-going to ensure implementation of current associated legislation.

Before providing the UV tanning service, check that you have the necessary equipment and materials to hand and that they meet legal, hygiene and industry requirements for UV tanning.

EQUIPMENT AND MATERIALS LIST

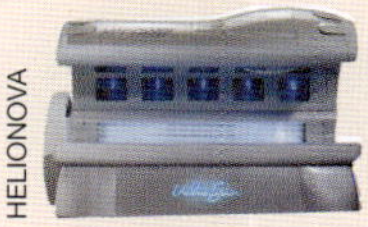

HELIONOVA

Sunbed equipment
Sited in a fully screened area to avoid irradiation of other clients or beauty therapists

ELLISONS

Client record card

UV-POWER UK

Protective eye goggles or shields
To prevent eye disorders. Goggles should offer side protection and be in sizes to suit a variety of clients' needs

IPGGUTENBERGUKLTD/ ISTOCK/THINKSTOCK

Shower
To cleanse the skin before tanning

Unperfumed soap
To cleanse the skin

BEAUTY EXPRESS LTD

Towels
To dry the skin and protect the hair

UV-POWER UK

Tanning cosmetic preparations
To aid tanning and to care for the skin

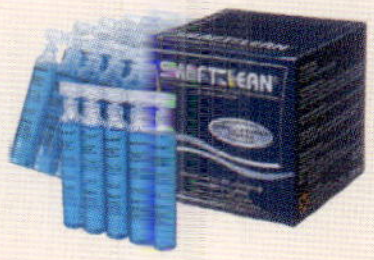

UV-POWER UK

Sunbed cleaning agent
To clean the UV tanning system

YOU WILL ALSO NEED:

Tanning guidelines Displayed in the service area

Cosmetic cleansers To remove make-up if worn

Cotton wool and tissues To remove cleansing preparations

Hydrating body lotions To replace moisture lost from the skin following service

Covered, lined waste bin In the area to dispose of consumable items

Water For client consumption to replace lost body fluids and cool following the service

Tanning guidance leaflet To advise the client of sensible UV exposure, effects and care of the skin

Sterilization and disinfection

- The surface of horizontal tanning units must be cleaned after each client with an appropriate cleaning agent recommended by the equipment supplier to remove tanning products if used and skin debris. Vertical tanning units do not come into contact with the client's skin and do not require cleaning after each client.
- Flooring in the area must be cleaned to avoid contamination and cross-infection. Disposable floor covering may be made available where possible.
- Goggles should be disinfected for each client to prevent cross-infection. Preferably, disposable eye protection should be used.
- The shower must be cleaned after each client to avoid cross-infection and to prevent slippage from wet floors.
- The tanning system should be wiped down daily with an appropriate cleaning agent. Cleaning maintenance should take place as recommended by the equipment manufacturer.
- Waste bins in the area should be emptied after each client. These should be lined using a disposable bag and covered.

ELLISONS

Disposable protective eye shields are preferable as they do not require disinfection

TOP TIP

Disposable film covers

A film that covers the surface of the sunbed and is provided for each client, maintains hygiene and may be used in conjunction with certain tanning equipment.

ALWAYS REMEMBER

The incorrect choice of cleaning agent can damage the acrylic shield of the sunbed.

UV-POWER UK

Sunbed cleaners

> Cleanliness is next to godliness! The reality is that a tanning salon is a place where people come and get undressed and no one wants to do that in a dirty cubicle.
>
> **Alex Widdows**

HEALTH & SAFETY

Guidance on ventilation for equipment installation is available in the Chartered Institute of Building Services Engineers (CIBSE) Guide B–2004, covering heating, ventilation, air conditioning and refrigeration.

Check ventilation requirements with your manufacturer's supplier also.

Preparation of the work area

- Where there are 2 UV units in the same area, they should be screened to prevent increased exposure.
- Ensure there is adequate ventilation in the tanning area. This is important for client comfort, to maintain a reasonable temperature, to prevent the build-up of ozone and to ensure that the equipment can operate efficiently.
- Cubicle doors should be able to be opened from the outside in the event of an emergency – check this.
- Check all general electrical safety precautions. Any defective equipment must be removed from use and reported on.
- Ensure the tanning unit is cleaned with a recommended proprietary equipment cleaner between each client. Certain cleaning agents may cause skin sensations or photo-chemically react with the skin when exposed to UV light and must not be used.
- Ensure that the distance between the overhead surface of the tanning unit and the client is fixed and stable.
- Ensure other components of the machine are clean and dust-free, i.e. filters and fans, clean regularly.
- Refill consumable items as necessary in the shower, changing and tanning area.
- Provide a clean towel for use after showering.
- Guidance notice should be provided in the area on exposure, how to safely use the equipment and post service advice.

HEALTH & SAFETY

Equipment maintenance

- Have a regular system for examining electrical equipment.
- Check daily that the tubes are working, that they are lit up and that filters are not cracked. This task should be performed using protective eyewear. Spare stock should be available for replacement. These will be mainly tubes and starters. Any maintenance should be in your competence level and area of responsibility.
- Regularly check that the equipment is operating efficiently. Know what action you would take if a piece of equipment failed mechanically.
- A record should be kept to calculate equipment usage as the tubes/burners will become less efficient, emitting less UV and require replacement after a specific time. Some equipment is able to store this information, which can be accessed as necessary. This is generally between 400 and 800 hours. Only replace tubes with those recommended by the equipment manufacturer.
- The BS EN 60335-2-27 standard on manufacturing UV tanning equipment controls how sunbeds are built. All sunbeds should meet **Standards** for maximum irradiance. It is important when purchasing any equipment it conforms to this standard and should be labelled as such.
- Technical equipment must be serviced annually by a professional, and tested for efficiency and safety in line with European standards. Starters need to be replaced on average after 1000 hours of service.

Outcome 2: Consult, plan and prepare for services with clients

Learn how to use consultation techniques to effectively plan and prepare for UV tanning services by:

1. Using **consultation techniques** in a polite and friendly manner to determine the client's service needs.
2. Obtaining signed, written informed consent from the client prior to carrying out the service.
3. Ensuring that informed and signed parent or guardian consent is obtained for minors prior to any service, where relevant.
4. Refusing service to minors under 18 years of age.
5. Clearly explaining to the client what the service entails, its potential benefits and any restrictions to use in a way they can understand.
6. Asking your client appropriate questions to identify if they have any contra-indications to UV tanning services.
7. Accurately recording your client's responses to questioning.
8. Encouraging clients to ask questions to clarify any points.
9. Accurately establishing, agreeing and recording the client's skin type and colouring following current sunbed Code of Practice classifications.
10. Taking the **necessary action** in response to any identified contra-indications.
11. Ensuring client advice is given without reference to a specific medical condition and without causing undue alarm and concern.
12. Recommending alternative tanning services which are suitable for the client's skin type and needs if contra-indicated for UV tanning service.
13. Clearly explaining and agreeing the projected cost, duration and frequency of the sessions needed.
14. Agreeing in writing to the client's needs, expectations and session outcomes, ensuring they are realistic and achievable.
15. Giving your client clear and accurate advice on how to clean and prepare their skin prior to UV tanning services.
16. Clearly explaining how to use the equipment correctly and confirming their understanding of this and the current sunbed Code of Practice for safe tanning.

HEALTH & SAFETY

Disconnect equipment from the mains when cleaning and only use cleaning products in the quantities directed by the manufacturer.

ACTIVITY

What action would you take if a client was unable to get off a horizontal sunbed because it had mechanically malfunctioned?

> Use each piece of tanning equipment yourself, or at least go through the motions. Do this on a regular basis, to see your salon from your customer's point of view. Only when you get into the role of the customer can you see where the service you offer can be improved.
>
> **Alex Widdows**

HEALTH & SAFETY

Service area

During UV application, nobody should enter the service area as this would expose them to the UV rays.

Drinks must be prohibited in the service area to avoid slips and contact with live electrical equipment.

> Ensure your employees and your tanners are always fully informed. Educating your customers will build their confidence and consequently their loyalty.
>
> **Alex Widdows**

ACTIVITY

UV tanning risk assessment

Identify the risks that could occur when providing the work activity UV tanning. State who could be at risk and how and what procedures must be taken or put in place to control them. HSE ***Five steps to risk assessment*** provides advice on completing a risk assessment.

ALWAYS REMEMBER

Consultation

Following consultation and their Fitzpatrick classification, inform the client of your recommendations, including:

- duration of their tanning session
- interval between each session
- total number of sessions

Clients should be provided with information on the health effects of artificial UV exposure.

Information provided at consultation must be adequate to enable the client to make an informed decision about their reasons for service, suitability and safety.

HEALTH & SAFETY

UV tanning equipment safety

Sunbeds should be supplied by a reliable source and comply with relevant British and European Standards indicated by a BS EN number and CE mark. This standard identifies that the irradiance limit of 0.3 W/m^2 is not exceeded. Equipment should be professionally installed and maintained. Equipment must meet also if new or second hand, the UK Electrical Equipment (Safety) regulations 1994.

A record of sunbed usage and maintenance should be kept.

When tubes are replaced, service sessions should be reduced usually for the first 50 hours, as the UV output will be 50 per cent stronger than the old lamps.

Reception

If an enquiry is made through reception, the client should be questioned to check for suitability and for possible contra-indications.

A consultation should always occur before a tanning service.

Consultation

Collect the client record card and carry out a consultation to assess the client's tanning requirements.

Remember to assess:

- skin type
- natural hair colour
- eye colour
- if the client has freckles
- how the skin tans
- sensitivity to UV exposure
- check if they have recently been exposed to natural or artificial UV

Contra-indications

Certain contra-indications preclude the UV tanning service. If there is any concern over the client's suitability, medical advice should be sought before the service proceeds.

During the client assessment, if you find any of the following, UV service must not be recommended or carried out:

- client is under 18 years of age – childhood exposure to UV radiation can be a high contributory factor to developing skin cancer in later life
- vitiligo, hypersensitive skin or vascular skin disorders
- history of cancerous conditions
- recent x-ray treatment (within the last 3 months)
- infectious skin diseases – fungal, viral or bacterial
- medical conditions, such as liver, heart, lung and kidney disease
- medication which causes the skin to be UV sensitive – known as **photosensitizers**: these include antibiotics, medication for blood pressure, diabetes and tranquillizers; the reaction can result in an itchy rash, sometimes followed by pigmentation
- pregnancy – uneven pigmentation may occur
- in conjunction with services which have affected skin structure/function temporarily, i.e. skin injectables, micro-dermabrasion, laser and chemical peels
- immediately after other heat or sensitizing services such as waxing hair removal, sauna or electrolysis
- immediately following use of essential oils on the skin which may be phototoxic, which means they make the skin more sensitive to sunlight
- light skin unable to tan, sensitive skin and those skins with a tendency to burn in natural sunlight

- excessive moles – more than 50
- excessive freckles indicating a high risk of burning in natural UV, therefore unsuitable for artificial UV exposure
- alcohol consumption before service
- contact lenses, unless removed – to avoid eye damage caused by ray concentration

Those requiring GP referral should be tactfully and clearly discussed to ensure client understanding. GP approval must be sought if the client has a medical condition or is taking medication which contra-indicates service as listed above.

Inform the client of the possible contra-actions that could occur following UV exposure and the aftercare recommendations.

TOP TIP

Light-skinned clients

For those skinned clients for whom UV service would be unsuitable, a self-tanning service could be offered as an alternative.

Perform a patch test if you feel the client has indications of sensitivity.

Contra-actions

- *Erythema* (reddening of the skin.) In severe cases this leads to blistering and peeling of the skin and free radical formation caused by UV overexposure. Tanning should not be received until all skin reddening has gone. Medical advice should be sought with excessive UV overdose.
- There are four degrees of erythema following UV exposure:
  - **First degree** the skin develops a slight redness with no skin irritation, which will disappear after 24 hours.
  - **Second degree** the skin has increased redness due to increased blood circulation in the area to repair the damage. There will be some irritation, this will take 2–3 days to disappear followed by skin peeling.
  - **Third degree** the skin will have excessive redness, will feel hot to the touch, with some swelling, blistering and the nerve endings will be stimulated making the skin feel prickly. This will take up to a week to disappear.
  - **Fourth degree** this is the severe case leading to excessive skin redness, skin blistering and peeling

    Permanent photo-damage in varying degrees may follow stages 2–4 when the skin has repaired including pigmentation, scarring or possibly even skin cancer.
- *Tinea versicolor.* A **fungus** condition appearing as white spots where the melanocytes, ability to produce melanin is affected giving the skin areas without pigment.
- *Prickly heat.* A skin rash caused by overexposure to UV. Antihistamine tablets and a cooling, soothing lotion are usually prescribed, together with a period of absence from UV tanning. At the next session, tanning time should be reduced.
- *Eye disorders.* Such as swelling and inflammation, resulting from failure to wear protective eyewear. Both UVA and UVB light can pass through the eyelids if protective eyewear is not worn and can affect the cornea and the lens of the eye. There is a possibility with excessive exposure that the following eye disorders may occur:
  - **Photokeratitis** – inflammation of the cornea caused by UVB rays: cloudy vision can occur and they eyes become light sensitive and feel itchy.
  - **Photoconjunctivitis** – inflammation of the conjunctiva.

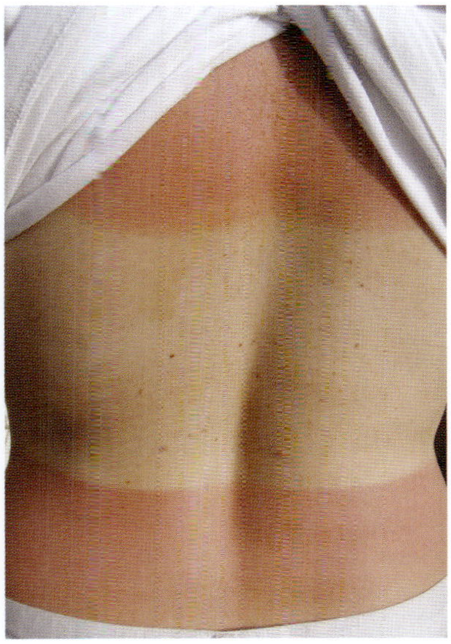

ISTOCK/© CHRISTINE GONSALVES

Skin erythema following excessive UV exposure (see http://dermnetnz.org/reactions/sunburn.html)

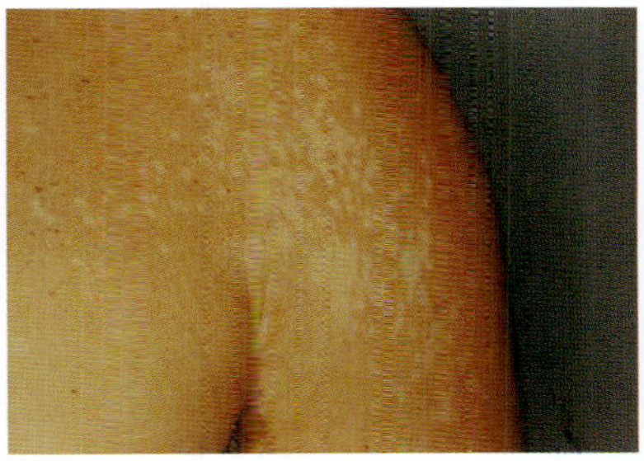

RUBE J. PARDO, M.D., PH.D.

Tinea versicolor

ALWAYS REMEMBER

Cosmetic tanning lotion

To reduce the drying effect of UV exposure and anti-oxidants, a cosmetic tanning lotion is recommended. The surface epidermis layer is moisturised with ingredients such as aloe vera which aids absorption of the tanning rays. Tanning accelerator ingredients such as the amino acid tyrosine which stimulates the skin to produce more melanin, optimizing the tanning result.

Their formulation is different to those prepared for natural UVL exposure.

HEALTH & SAFETY

Health and Safety Executive

Copies of the HSE poster *UV tanning equipment* should be displayed and available for clients to read and made available to all suntan service clients.

Copies of the HSE publication *Reducing Health Risks From the Use of Ultraviolet (UV) Tanning Equipment* provides guidance for people responsible for operating UV tanning equipment.

It is important that you check that you are complying with local and national legal requirements. Some local authorities require licensing of UV salons to regulate them. Check with your local authority's Environmental Health Department.

The Sunbed Association (TSA)

This industry body sets the standards for safe tanning and provides supporting guidelines and training for its members to promote a Code of Good Practice. (See www.sunbedassociation.org.uk/.)

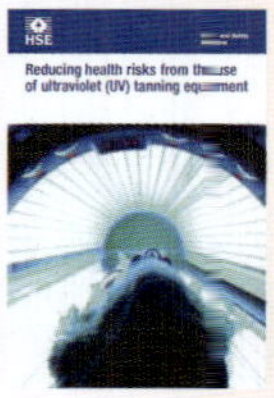

HSE

HSE publication providing guidance for beauty therapists of UV tanning equipment

- ○ **Cataracts** caused by the UV rays penetrating the cornea and lens of the eye, causing the lens to thicken, becoming opaque and resulting in blurred vision.
- ○ **Carcinomas** (cancer) of the delicate eye tissue caused by excessive UV exposure.
- *Feeling faint.* Due to sudden movement following heat service.
- *Nausea.* Caused by increased body temperature and excessive exposure.
- If any abnormal skin reaction occurs either during or following service, the client must be advised to consult a GP before further tanning exposure.
- Uneven pigmentation due to skin damage or overexposure, commonly on darker skin types.

Explain the service procedure to the client and the expected outcome.

When using sunbeds, recommended UV session times should be given according to the manufacturer's recommendations, taking into consideration the sessions already received and skin type and, if carried out, the results of the skin patch test.

Skin exposure schedule

To assess skin tolerance to UV and calculate the correct tanning dosage, exposure should be gradually built up to avoid short-term and long-term effects of UV exposure. Exposure time will depend upon the skin type of the client and output of lamps in tanning equipment. Tan should be gradually achieved without the risk of erythema. The manufacturer will provide an exposure schedule and recommended exposure time for differing skin types. It is the responsibility of the tanning operator to classify the skin and photo sensitivity based upon findings at the consultation and guided by manufacturer's instructions.

Exposure should be gradually built up to avoid short term and long term effects of UV exposure. Exposure time will depend upon the skin type of the client and output of lamps in tanning equipment. Tan should be gradually achieved without the risk of erythema. The manufacturer will provide an exposure schedule and recommended exposure time for differing skin types. It is the responsibility of the tanning operator to classify the skin and photo sensitivity based upon findings at the consultation and guided by manufacturer's instructions.

HEALTH & SAFETY

Light skins

Light-skinned clients are more at risk than those with darker skins on exposure to UV light.

Skin type based on the Fitzpatrick system is arranged from lightest to darkest colouring. It is determined by exposure following response to initial UVL exposure (see pages 474–476). It can take 6-10 sessions to safely achieve a base tan.

Tanning colour takes from 48 up to 72 hours after exposure to be seen as a result of increased melanin production. Clients must be informed of this, to avoid the risk of over-exposure if further tanning is received within this time period.

Often, the tanning services are booked as part of a course and a discounted price may be offered. Vouchers are usually provided for each session as proof of payment. Where the tanning unit is operated by coins or tokens it will be necessary to have a store of these, which are issued at reception.

At each repeat service, check the client's skin reaction to the previous tanning exposure and discuss service progression as necessary.

Agree on an appropriate service plan and complete the record card. Ask the client to sign the record card confirming understanding of the tanning service.

Record card for UV tanning services

UV SERVICE TREATMENT CARD

	Name
	Tel (Work) (Home)
Address	Mobile Email
Postcode	D.O.B.
Doctor	(Client must be over 18 years of age.)

ARE YOU UNDER MEDICAL SUPERVISION?				Prescribed or taking any form of drug			
Diabetic		Diuretic		Pregnant		Tranquilliser		Antibiotic		Steroid	

Are You Hypersensitive to Sunlight	Do You Have a Sensitive Skin?

DO YOU OR HAVE YOU HAD ANY OF THE FOLLOWING				Allergies/Asthma		Blood Disorder	
Epilepsy		Heart Disorder		Cold Sores		Renal Disorders	
Skin Ulcers		Hypertension		Fainting		Skin Cancer	
Verrucas		Prickly Heat		Headaches		Migraine	
Athlete's Foot		Vitiligo		Skin Disorders		Eczema	

Ill Effects from Normal Sunbathing	Abnormal Blood Pressure

PREVIOUS SERVICES

Heat services		Laser service		IPL service		Micro-dermabrasion		Recent chemical peels	

If your client answers in the affirmative to any of the above questions **you should advise them** to consult their doctor **prior to treatment.**

I confirm that to the best of my knowledge I have answered the questions correctly.
I understand that if the answer is yes to any question I should consult my doctor before using suntanning equipment.
I have read and understood the above and am satisfied that I am suitable for UVA suntanning service.

Client signature .... Date .... Update .... Update ....

Always re-check contra-indictions before treatment.

E.A. Ellison & Co. Ltd. Birmingham, Coventry, Leicester

Record card for UV tanning services (continued)

UV SERVICE TREATMENT CARD	Name:

SKIN TYPE	Type I		Type II		Type III		Type IV		Type V		Type VI	

SUNBED	High Pressure		Low Pressure UVA		Low Pressure R-UVA	

Date		No. of Sessions Booked		Length of Session		Amount Paid £	
Date		No. of Sessions Booked		Length of Session		Amount Paid £	
Date		No. of Sessions Booked		Length of Session		Amount Paid £	
Date		No. of Sessions Booked		Length of Session		Amount Paid £	

No.	Date	Time	Length	Paid	No.	Date	Time	Length	Paid	No.	Date	Time	Length	Paid
1					13					25				
2					14					26				
3					15					27				
4					16					28				
5					17					29				
6					18					30				
7					19					31				
8					20					32				
9					21					33				
10					22					34				
11					23					35				
12					24					36				

Special advice to the Client on Home Skincare and Hygiene.

Products purchased for Home Care. Date Purchased.

ET1 AB64

HEALTH & SAFETY

Repeated services

The UV service should never be received twice in one day. If the client has already been exposed to natural UV, artificial UV should not be received.

HEALTH & SAFETY

Jewellery

All jewellery should be removed as this could cause skin burning and uneven tanning.

Preparation of the client

Draw the client's attention to the safe tanning notice displayed in the service area. This information is sometimes also included on the record card. This will ensure that the client understands the health risks associated with the tanning service.

Show the client all the service facilities, e.g. shower, how they operate, use and availability of associated skincare products.

Tanning gels, creams and lotions for use with UV tanning equipment do not contain a sun protective factor (SPF) as this would have a negative effect on the service. They often contain tyrosine, an amino acid occurring naturally in the skin which activates melanin production, increasing the production of the required tan. Concentration may vary according to the client's skin type and history of UV exposure. Its inclusion is thought to speed the tanning process. Other ingredients have anti-ageing properties such as vitamin E and moisturisers. Formulations are available for both the face and the body. Samples of retail products may be provided for your client for their first use to assess suitability or you may cost the product into your service.

The client should remove any jewellery, contact lenses and make-up. A shower should be taken using unperfumed soap to remove skin creams, deodorants, perfumes and lotions which could cause a photochemical reaction causing skin sensitization. A secure area may be provided for clients' belongings following your salon policy.

It is recommended that briefs be worn while tanning. Similar clothing should be worn for subsequent services to avoid exposure of new skin, which may result in burning. Advise the client to protect their hair if it has been chemically treated, to avoid colour change or drying.

Explain how the tanning equipment operates and the most suitable tanning position. Explain that a trained beauty therapist will be within calling distance at all times. Demonstrate the safety features including the emergency button. If this facility is not provided an alternative should be provided instead, e.g. an intercom in the room. Provide clean, disinfected goggles or disposable eyewear to protect the eyes.

Ensure the client is confident with the use of equipment. Provide the client with the coin token to operate the machine if required. Wash your hands as appropriate during client preparation, demonstrating to your client that you work hygienically.

A specialized tanning preparation may be recommended. This protects the skin, promotes tanning and keeps the skin hydrated as it contains moisturisers.

Exfoliation is not recommended directly before tanning as it may sensitize the skin. However, it is recommended before use, say 8–24 hours before, as excess dead skin cells reflect UV rays and reduce the tanning response. It is also beneficial following tanning to remove dead skin cells and brighten the skin.

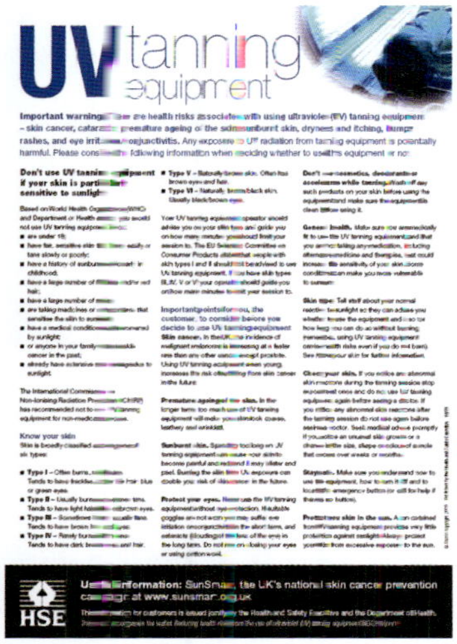

HSE

Safe tanning notice poster (see HSE UV tanning equipment poster at www.hse.gov.uk/PUBNS/misc869.pdf)

HEALTH & SAFETY

Eye protection

Traditional goggles must be disinfected before every use to prevent cross-infection and placed in the UV cabinet. A reputable professional disinfectant solution should be used and the goggles should be thoroughly rinsed and dried before use to avoid skin/eye sensitization.

Disposable eye protection can be retailed to your client. This protects the eyes from UVA and UVB rays while allowing the client to see through them. They are disposed of after use.

Sensitive areas

Body parts respond differently to UV exposure. Areas not regularly exposed may burn and become sensitive more quickly. These areas include the neck, chest, shoulders and back.

Pressure points on the body may not tan as efficiently. This is because the reduced blood supply to the area prevents the melanin being oxidized.

ALEX WIDDOWS SUNCHIC TANNING. WWW.SUNCHIC.COM

Client cubicle, enabling the client to prepare for a UV tanning service and provide a secure area for personal belongings

> Have a comprehensive salon training manual. This will ensure that all employees give a consistent message to your customers. Make sure that the manual is regularly updated and a regular part of an ongoing staff training programme.
>
> **Alex Widdows**

UV-POWER UK

Specialized tanning preparations

Outcome 3: Monitor UV tanning services

Learn how to apply UV tanning service to meet the needs of your client by:

1. Carrying out and recording UV tanning equipment safety and function tests at the specified intervals.
2. Ensuring that portable appliance testing and tube replacement is carried out at the manufacturer's specified intervals and recorded on the maintenance log.
3. Promptly reporting any equipment problems to the relevant person(s).

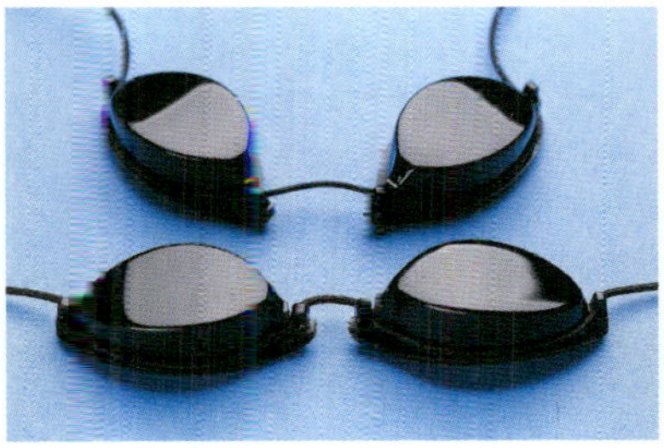

SMART BUY

Actinotherapy goggles

ISTOCK/© OKAN METIN

UV tanning

HEALTH & SAFETY

Beauty therapist protection

This risk is identified under the Management of Health and Safety at Work Regulations (1999).

Gloves must be worn when cleaning equipment, to prevent the possibility of contact dermatitis and protective eye shields must be worn by the beauty therapist if exposure to UV is likely when carrying out their job role. In compliance with the Personal Protective Equipment at Work Regulations (1992).

HEALTH & SAFETY

Sessions per year

It is recommended by the Health and Safety Executive that clients should have no more than 20 tanning sessions per year. Many tanning beauty therapist have a policy to notify their users of this, formally notifying them when the level is exceeded.

> "Create a desirable environment. It is not just your products that set you apart from your competition, it is the complete package. Choosing your decor and how you greet your customers, is just as important as choosing your tanning equipment.
>
> **Alex Widdows**

(Continued) **Learn how to apply UV tanning service to meet the needs of your client by:**

4. Ensuring that the timing of the session is suitable for the client's skin type and colouring.
5. Ensuring that repeat sessions are carried out following current sunbed Code of Practice guidelines for the client's skin type.
6. Ensuring that the clients do not exceed the total number of annual sessions recommended by the current sunbed Code of Practice or any local authority restriction.
7. Adjusting session times following manufacturer's instructions as a result of tube replacement.
8. Discontinuing service where contra-actions occur and taking the appropriate remedial action.
9. Checking the well-being and satisfaction of the client at the end of each session.

How to provide UV tanning service

Always start at the minimum recommended service exposure time to assess skin tolerance and avoid erythema. Service time exposure should be increased as recommended by the equipment manufacturer. Ideally, no more than three sessions should be received per week. A time interval of at least 48 hours should be taken between tanning services to allow for repair if UV damage in skin cells.

Once the tan has been achieved, a service may be received once per month. Client posters and leaflets should be made available to provide advice on sensible tanning and the risks of misuse.

All equipment must be operated and maintained according to manufacturer's instructions.

All staff operating UV tanning equipment must be trained and competent in its use.

1. Switch the tanning unit on.
2. Set exposure time according to the client's skin type and stage of UV service exposure. At the end of the timed session, the machine will automatically switch off. Timer mechanisms should be designed to stop the UV equipment if a fault occurred with the timer mechanism.
3. Allow the client to rest for a short period after the tanning service. The client may wish to shower following the service to remove perspiration.
4. After sun lotion may be used following the session.
5. Record the date and duration of the service on the client's record card. An accurate record keeping system is required. The recommended service time and number should not be exceeded. The Health and Safety Executive recommend a maximum of 20 sessions per year.

HEALTH & SAFETY

Tanning tips

When using horizontal lie down tanning beds, pressure points can sometimes occur where there is poor oxygenation of the tissues, resulting in paler areas. Advise the client to change their position regularly, e.g. sometimes lying on their front instead of their back.

To minimize white patches in unexposed areas, the client may be advised to place their hands behind their head to prevent white patches under their arms.

Outcome 4: Provide aftercare advice

Learn how to provide aftercare advice which supports and meets the needs of your clients by:

1. Giving **advice** and recommendations accurately and constructively.
2. Giving your clients suitable **advice** specific to their individual needs.

Aftercare

- The client must not rise quickly from a horizontal position or fainting may occur.
- Advise the client to shower after service – this removes perspiration, which could cause a skin rash.
- Skincare preparations should be available and recommended to moisturise the skin and prevent skin dehydration.
- Drinks must be available for the client, to rehydrate to replace body moisture lost through sweat.
- Avoidance of heat services and further UV services must be recommended within the next 24 hours.
- Details of the service should be entered on the record card, to include date of session, period of session, any adverse reaction.
- Artificial tanning does not protect against burning in natural UV – a sunscreen should always be worn.
- Provide the client with a tanning guidance leaflet.
- Lumps, skin irritation or unusual moles should be reported

Artificial tanning is popular before 'sun' holidays and advice should be given on continued safe tanning. This provides an opportunity to increase retail sales of suncare cosmetics which protect against UVA and often also UVB damage. The correct SPF should be selected according to how long the client can safely stay in the sun without burning.

Self-tanning cosmetic preparations or self-tanning service can be offered as a complimentary product/service.

ELLISONS

Tanning guidance leaflet

SMART BUY

Retail products for clients going on holiday

ASSESSMENT OF KNOWLEDGE AND UNDERSTANDING

FUNCTIONAL SKILLS

Having covered the learning objectives for **Provide UV tanning services** – test what you need to know and understand by answering the following short questions below.

The information covers:

- organizational and legal requirements
- how to work safely and effectively when providing UV tanning services
- client consultation
- contra-indications and contra-actions
- equipment and products
- anatomy and physiology
- tanning services
- aftercare advice for clients

Organizational and legal requirements

1 How can a hygienic environment be maintained when providing UV tanning services? Give **five** examples of necessary cleaning regimes

2 Why is it necessary to keep records of all UV tanning services? What information needs to be recorded?

3 What health and safety legislation should be considered when performing UV tanning services?

4 Why is ventilation important in the delivery of UV tanning service?

5 Why is it necessary to complete a risk assessment for UV tanning service?

6 What would need to be checked with the local authority before providing UV tanning services?

How to work safely and effectively when providing UV tanning services

1 What types of personal protective equipment must be worn by the beauty therapist when maintaining and operating UV equipment and why?

2 Why should UV tanning not be received by clients less than 18 years of age?

3 What guidance should be provided to the client with regard to positioning when receiving UV tanning service?

4 What environmental conditions should be checked when providing UV tanning services?

5 When should a client's well-being be checked when providing UV tanning service? Why is it necessary to do this?

Client consultation

1 When planning the client's UV tanning service, state the questions it will be necessary for you to ask the client. How will the client's responses enable you to plan the UV tanning service?

2 What information and advice would be given to a client who made a telephone booking in preparation for the UV tanning service?

3 Why is it important to confirm the client's understanding of the UV tanning service following the consultation?

4 Why is it important that all responses to questions asked are recorded on the record card?

5 Why is it necessary to assess the client's skin type at the consultation?

Contra-indications and contra-actions

1 Name **three** contra-indications observed at consultation which would prevent self UV tanning service

2 What other beauty therapy services offered would restrict UV exposure?

3 State three contra-actions that occur following a UV tanning session and why these may occur

4 Why is it important not to name specific contra-indications when encouraging clients to seek medical advice before service?

Equipment and materials

1 What are the differing types of UV equipment available?

2 What skin products can be used in conjunction with UV tanning service? What is their benefit?

3 How is the work area prepared for service to prevent cross-infection when carrying out UV tanning service?

4 What is the purpose of the sunbed Code of Practice? Give **three** examples of guidance provided in terms of equipment maintenance.

Anatomy and physiology

1 What vitamin is formed on exposure to UV in the skin? What is its function?

2 How do UVA rays differ from UVB rays with their effect upon the skin and its structures?

3 What are the associated risks to the skin of UV over-exposure?

4 What is the Fitzpatrick skin type classification system and how is it used in relation to planning UV skin exposure?

5 How does a person's melanin production affect their tanning capability?

6 What are the beneficial effects to the skin of UV exposure?

Tanning services

1 How should the skin be prepared for UV tanning service?

2 Why should a skin sensitivity patch test be performed before a UV tanning service? How is this performed?

3 What personal protective equipment should a client be provided with before UV exposure and why must these be worn?

4 Why should the skin be thoroughly clean before a UV tanning session?

5 Why must shower facilities be provided in conjunction with UV tanning service?

6 What is the electromagnet spectrum?

7 At what stage does a skin erythema it become a contra-action? What are the **four** degrees of erythema?

Aftercare advice for clients

1 How often would you recommend the client receives a UV tanning service? What is the recommended interval between appointments and why is this necessary?

2 State the skincare instructions a client should follow after UV exposure.

3 What retail products could you recommend to a client in conjunction with a UV tanning service?

4 State **three** post-service restrictions following UV tanning application.

5 If a client experiences excessive erythema following UV tanning service, what action should the client be advised to take?

15 Self-tanning

SHUTTERSTOCK/EVGENY KORSHENKOV

Learning Objectives

This chapter covers the **Provide self-tanning services** unit.

This unit is all about how to provide the service self-tanning using self-tan equipment and products. Application is modified to achieve the client's service objectives identified at consultation. Relevant health safety and hygiene practice must be effectively implemented throughout the service.

The communication of pre- and post-self-tanning information and advice is essential to ensure the effectiveness of the service.

There are **four** learning outcomes which you must achieve competently:

1. **Maintain safe and effective methods of working when providing self-tanning services.**
2. **Consult, plan and prepare for services with clients.**
3. **Apply self-tan products.**
4. **Provide aftercare advice.**

For each unit your assessor will observe you on **at least three separate occasions each involving different clients**, which must include **one** spray-tan using a spray-gun and compressor and **one** manually applied self-tan using the hands to apply the product to the skin.

From the **range** statements, you must show that you have:

- used all **consultation techniques**
- used all **types of equipment**

(continued on the next page)

TAMMY BAKER, ST TROPEZ

ROLE MODEL

Tammy Baker

Education and Events Manager for St Tropez

" I have been involved in the beauty, hair and wellness industry for over 17 years. During this time I also competed in fitness competitions, which built the base for my career within the television industry and my being selected to participate as 'Fox' in the hit TV series 'Gladiators'. I continued studies in personal training, sports nutrition/psychology and personally trained pop star Robbie Williams, attending to his training, massage and nutritional needs. I co-published and edited a health and wellness-based publication which gave me a platform to educate the masses in related topics for total self-improvement and wellness for men and women.

My role as Education and Events Manager includes the continuous improvement of teaching material, techniques and development of the Education team. I organize, attend and present business seminars, exhibitions and events related to promotion and education in tanning. I regularly train and update internal staff and deliver training to international accounts and press/TV and support the marketing department in implementing brand communication and education of new products.

I have developed my knowledge through several industry-related career choices and I have enjoyed the diversity of my career to date which includes make-up, fitness and nutrition, sales/retail and salon management through to teaching/training and development.

(continued)

- used at least **four out of the six products** which include tanning creams and gels, spray-tan liquid, barrier cream, exfoliators and moisturisers*
- dealt with **at least one** of the **necessary actions** where a contra-action, contra-indication or service modification occurs
- provided all types of relevant aftercare **advice**

*However, you must prove that you have the necessary knowledge, understanding and skills to be able to perform competently across the range.

When providing self-tanning services it is important to use the skills you have learnt in the following chapters:

Monitoring safe work operations.

Promotional activities.

ALWAYS REMEMBER

Faux tan is an alternative word for fake tan.

Essential anatomy and physiology knowledge requirements for self-tanning are identified on the checklist in Chapter 2, pages 12–13. This chapter also discusses anatomy and physiology specific to self-tanning services.

The application of self-tanning products creates a healthy, tanned appearance to the skin without any of the harmful effects of UV. The effect is temporary as dead skin cells are shed, so too is the colour. This process of losing the tan usually takes 5–6 days. The life of the tan can be extended through client maintenance following the service.

There are many different self-tan applications to choose from for professional or retail use, including self-tan tissues, mousses, **spray-gun**, airbrush, automated spray booth, cream and gel.

Formulations differ as they are often designed for different parts of the face or body, and for various skin tones – fair or dark – to achieve a realistic result. Maximum tanning effect takes between 8 to 24 hours depending upon the tanning product and the client's natural skin type/colour.

Self-tanning is ideal for clients who want an immediate colour, have fair skin with a tendency to burn in UV light or who are concerned with the associated risks of UV exposure.

MYSTIC TAN

Self-tan automated spray booth

"When providing self-tanning services the beauty therapist needs to ensure that their own tan (if worn) is perfect. Your appearance is a sales tool!

Tammy Baker

Anatomy and physiology

The main active ingredient in **self-tan products** is **dihydroxyacetone** (DHA), a colourless sugar which reacts with the amino acids – proteins of the stratum corneum, the skin's epidermal skin cells and oxygen – creating the pigmented tanned look. DHA reacts differently to the skin's amino acids, producing different tanning colourations. DHA concentrations range from 1–15 per cent affecting the depth of colouration. The higher the percentage content of DHA the darker the tan result. A fast-acting solution will be 10–12 per cent DHA.

HEALTH & SAFETY

DHA

DHA is only recommended for external use to the body, so care must be taken to avoid inhaling the product, ingesting the product or contact with the eyes.

HEALTH & SAFETY

Manufacturer's guidance

The product manufacturer will guide you if SPF is required – inform the client of this requirement as necessary.

ALWAYS REMEMBER

Development time

Dihydroxyacetone begins to tan the skin after 1 hour following application and continues darkening during the following 24–72 hours, depending on formulation. Explain this to the client.

TOP TIP

Skin colour

The lighter the clients skin, choose a self-tanning product with a lower percentage DHA.

Some contain UV protection and have a SPF, however, the skin still requires protection.

It is essential that exfoliation is carried out before the service is performed to remove dry, flaky skin cells which would create a patchy uneven colouration.

Outcome 1: Maintain safe and effective methods of working when providing self-tanning services

Learn how to maintain safe effective methods of working when providing self-tanning services by:

1. Setting up and monitoring the service area to meet organization procedures and manufacturer's instructions.
2. Wearing suitable personal protective equipment.
3. Ensuring the client is provided with suitable personal protective equipment.
4. Making sure that environmental conditions are suitable for the client and the service.
5. Ensuring your personal hygiene, protection and appearance meets accepted industry and organizational requirements.
6. Effectively disinfecting your hands prior to service.
7. Ensuring all tools and **equipment** are cleaned using the correct methods.
8. Positioning **equipment** and **products** for safety and ease of use.
9. Maintaining accepted industry hygiene and safety practices throughout the service.
10. Maintaining the client's modesty, privacy and comfort at all times.
11. Checking the client's well-being at regular intervals throughout the service.
12. Disposing of waste materials safely and correctly.
13. Ensuring the service is cost-effective and is carried out within a commercially viable time.
14. Ensuring client record cards are up-to-date, accurate, complete, legible and signed by the client and practitioner.
15. Leaving the service area and **equipment** clean and in a condition suitable for future services.

Before beginning the self-tanning service, check that you have the necessary equipment and materials to hand and that they meet legal, hygiene and industry requirements for self-tanning.

EQUIPMENT AND MATERIALS LIST

ELLISONS

Record card
Confidential card recording details of each client registered at the salon to record personal details/products used and details of the service

SHUTTERSTOCK/SANDRA VAN DER STEEN

Disposable gloves
Thin enough to enable even application and protect the beauty therapist's hands from staining and skin irritation

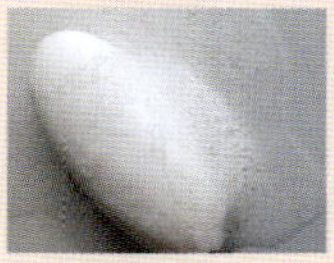
JOHN PAUL ENDRESS

Unperfumed soap
To cleanse the skin

ELLISONS

Self-tan products

ELLISONS

Bin
With a lid, lined with a disposable liner

HORST GOSSMANN/ISTOCK/THINKSTOCK

Mirror
To allow the client to prepare skin before service and to view afterwards

IPGGUTENBERGUKLTD/ISTOCK/THINKSTOCK

Shower
To cleanse the skin, if applicable to the self-tan system

MILADY

Beauty therapist face mask
With carbon filter to filter out any excess airborne particles

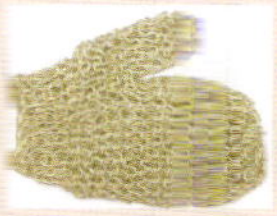
IGOR DUTINA/ISTOCK/THINKSTOCK

Exfoliating mitt
Used to remove dead skin before self-tanning application

YOU WILL ALSO NEED:

Cosmetic cleansers To remove make-up if worn

Cleansing wipe Used following tanning application to remove product from the fingers, toe nails and palms of the hand

Buffing mitt To remove excess tanning product during manually-applied self-tan

Self-tanning guidance instructions If using the spray booth system

Barrier cream/oil For the palms of the hands, soles of the feet and any area of dry skin, e.g. ankle area

Self-tan equipment As appropriate, e.g. spray-gun and compressor

Disposable briefs (If required)

Protective nose filters or mask For client to use to avoid inhalation of airborne particles during spray-tanning techniques

Protective hair covering To prevent hair staining

Protective eyewear To avoid eye irritation during spray-tanning application techniques

Cotton wool and buds To remove self-tan from parts not required and to remove cleansing preparations

Tissues To protect against staining and for removing cleansing preparations and self-tan product

Protective disposable coverings, e.g. a paper bedroll for trolley surfaces and flooring and for cleaning the area

Cleaning agents To clean equipment and work area

Aftercare advice Recommended advice for the client to refer to following the service

HEALTH & SAFETY

Products and equipment
Check that all products are kept clean and airtight. Check the use by date has not expired. Equipment should be safely stored i.e. spray hose when not in use to avoid tripping.

ST. TROPEZ, THE SKIN FINISHING EXPERTS

St Tropez tan range

ST TROPEZ, THE SKIN FINISHING EXPERTS

St Tropez Elegance spray booth

HEALTH & SAFETY

COSHH assessment

The safety of the selected tanning product should be assessed by obtaining a Material Safety Data Sheet (MSDS) to learn the safe use and handling of the product. Obtain this from the product supplier.

HEALTH & SAFETY

Occupational exposure limit (OEL)

Each self-tanning product contains different ingredients. Check with your supplier the ventilation/ extraction requirements for the tanning system.

TOP TIP

Choice of self-tanning preparations

There is an extensive range of self-tanning products available for both manual application and spray-tanning techniques, taking into consideration both skin colour and skin type.

Skin colours range from light to medium and medium to dark. Ingredients which enhance the cosmetic effect such as metallic, sparkly finishes should be avoided on coarse, uneven skin textures and mature skin types. This will accentuate the characteristics and appearance of the skin condition.

Sterilization and disinfection

The shower, if used, must be cleaned after each client to avoid the risk of cross-contamination. The floor where the client stands during treatment application must be cleaned with an effective disinfectant cleaning agent and protected as appropriate using a disposable non-slip covering. The self-tan liquid used in spray systems is a hazard if not adequately removed through ventilation systems and could cause slippage if not removed with effective cleaning procedures.

An automatic wash cycle cleans the automated spray-tanning booth automatically cleans after each use. Waste is collected in floor filters which will require regular cleaning as recommended by the manufacturers.

Spray-tan extraction booths require cleaning after each use and have filters which may be disposable or can be cleaned. Follow your manufacturer's instructions.

Airbrush spray-tanning has less opportunity for cross-infection in application as there is no direct contact apart from with the floor, and sole protectors should be worn. The spray tan unit requires regular dismantling and cleaning in accordance with manufacturer's instructions.

Waste bins in the area should be covered, lined and emptied after each client.

Waste generated from automated spray-tan systems is classed as trade effluent requiring a trade effluent license. Check your responsibilities with the local water authority.

As water is held in small holding tanks in automated spray booths it is necessary to carry out a risk assessment of the safety levels of bacteria and possible legionnella bacteria which can lead to legionnaires' disease by inhaling small droplets of water suspended in the air, which contain the bacteria.

Preparation of the work area

Floors in the work area should be non-slip and easy to clean.

Ensure that tanning equipment is serviced regularly as per the manufacturer's instructions.

Some compressors are noisy, consider this is where the service is carried out.

For the spray-tan automated application technique a cold water supply and waste pipe for drainage is required. It is essential that spray-tan booths are sealed adequately to prevent chemical leakage into the atmosphere. Ventilation must also be adequate for all systems, airborne particles will affect breathing of employees and clients. Filters and extraction systems should be checked for efficiency.

Ensure there is sufficient tanning product to operate the spray-tanning systems.

For automated booth spray systems check pressure gauges and fluid tank levels.

There must be sufficient room in the working area to adequately perform the service.

Ensure there is adequate lighting to ensure an even application and avoid shadows which will affect the result. A daylight lamp is effective for optimum light.

The room needs to be warm enough for the client, too hot and the client could perspire causing streaking.

After each use clean any equipment that comes into contact with skin, i.e. protective eyewear, using cleaning materials specified by the manufacturer.

Trolley surfaces should be protected against accidental spillage of self-tan product from manual and spray-tan techniques.

Disposable floor coverings or sole protectors should be provided if providing spray-tanning technique. Avoiding contact with product residue on the floor.

Service couches required for the application of manual self-tan applications must be adequately protected with disposable coverings to prevent staining and cross-infection.

HEALTH & SAFETY

Compressors

The automated spray booth and spray-gun tanning systems use a compressor to apply the tanning product.

The use and system must comply with the Pressure Safety Regulations (2000).

A pressure system is a piece of equipment containing a fluid under pressure.

Portable appliance testing (PAT) will also be required, annually.

Preparation of the beauty therapist

For manual and spray tan application the beauty therapist's hands should be protected with disposable gloves, this will also prevent skin/nail staining. The hands should be disinfected before the protective gloves are applied. Regular exposure of the skin to self-tanning preparations without protection may lead to allergic reaction and skin disease contact dermatitis.

It is recommended that the beauty therapist wears additional personal protective equipment such as a protective apron to protect workwear from staining, especially during manual application technique.

A face mask can be worn to filter excess airborne particles that are transient in the tanning mist created. A charcoal filter may be fitted in the face mask to remove the perfume component of the self-tanning product.

Safety goggles must also be worn to protect the beauty therapist's eyes.

Long hair should be tied back

TOP TIP

Self-tan product ingredients

Some self-tan products contain alpha hydroxy acids (AHA) which continue to gently remove dead skin cells, aiming to produce a more even colour as the product achieves the skin's colour change.

Some products contain ingredients to achieve a sparkly finished effect.

Outcome 2: Consult, plan and prepare for services with clients

Learn how to use consultation techniques to effectively plan and prepare for self-tanning services

1. Using **consultation techniques** in a polite and friendly manner to determine the client's service needs.
2. Ensuring that informed and signed parent or guardian consent is obtained for minors prior to any service.
3. Ensuring that a parent or guardian is present throughout the service for minors under the age of 16.
4. Clearly explaining to the client what the service entails, its potential benefits and any restrictions to use in a way they can understand.
5. Accurately carrying out a skin sensitivity test to determine skin sensitivity and colour preference, when necessary.

HEALTH & SAFETY

Contact dermatitis

Contact dermatitis is caused by intolerance of the skin to a particular substance or a group of substances. On exposure to the substance the skin quickly becomes irritated and an allergic reaction occurs. This may occur when a beauty therapist's skin is exposed to self-tanning chemicals on a regular basis.

TOP TIP

Link selling

It is a good idea for clients to receive a professional exfoliation service before their service. This must be compatible with the self-tanning product or the final tan colour may be affected and the desired colour not achieved.

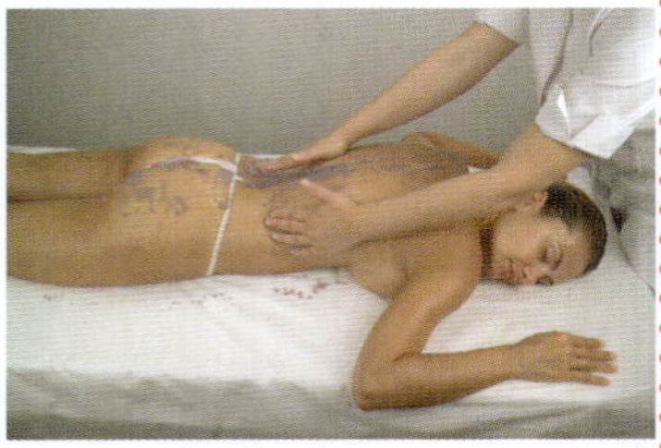

DEPILEX

Depilex manufacturer exfoliating service

***(Continued)* Learn how to use consultation techniques to effectively plan and prepare for self-tanning services**

6. Asking your client appropriate questions to identify if they have any contra-indications to self-tanning services.
7. Accurately recording your client's responses to questioning.
8. Taking the **necessary action** in response to any identified contra-indications.
9. Recommending alternative tanning services which are suitable for the client's skin type and needs, when necessary.
10. Clearly identifying and agreeing the projected cost, duration and frequency of service needed.
11. Agreeing in writing the client's needs, expectations and service outcomes, ensuring they are realistic and achievable.
12. Ensuring that the client's skin is clean and prepared to suit the **type** of **product** to be used.
13. Selecting suitable **equipment** and **products** for the service.

Consultation

Carry out a client consultation to assess the client's service requirements and expectations and suitability in choice of products.

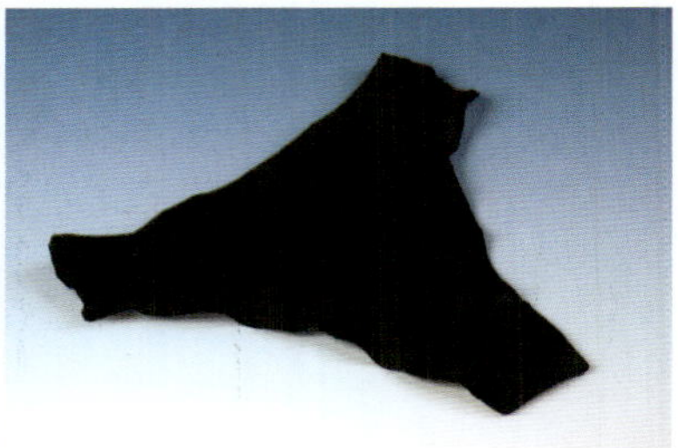

BEAUTY EXPRESS LTD

Disposable underwear

Reception

Preparation procedures should be given in advance of the service where possible so that the client's skin is compatible with effective tanning. A skin preparation information sheet or verbal instruction is a good idea to give your client when booking the appointment which can detail all aspects of the service including aftercare requirements.

If the client has hypersensitive skin or known allergies, a skin sensitivity patch test should be performed to assess skin suitability, recording the results on the record card.

Depending on the system used, time should be allowed when booking the service for client preparation, self-tan application and drying off.

During service application advise the client what may be worn. Disposable underwear may be provided, which will be costed into the service. Some clients, may wear old swimwear or will be happy not to wear underwear (follow your workplace policy). Loose, dark-coloured clothing should be worn to avoid removal of product and staining following the service. Recommend footwear such as flip flops to avoid spoiling tan application to the feet.

Waxing, shaving, electrical epilation or injectable services such as Botox® injections should be carried out 24 hours prior to service to avoid skin irritation.

Body lotions, especially those containing therapeutic/perfumed ingredients, should not be applied to the skin on the day of self-tan application as this may affect the result obtained.

ALWAYS REMEMBER

Beauty therapy services where therapeutic products are applied to the skin or remove the surface skin cells should not be performed before or after the service, such as galvanic therapy, micro-dermabrasion or massage using pre-blended aromatherapy oils.

If you require the client to shower and exfoliate before the service, explain this when they book. Attention should be given to the ankles, elbows and knees to remove dead skin. On arrival, complete the client's personal details on the client record card. Question the client to check for suitability and for possible contra-indications.

HEALTH & SAFETY

Skin sensitivity patch test

In order to assess skin tolerance to the self-tan product, a skin test may be performed on a small area of skin. This is usually done in the crook of the elbow or behind the ear.

Some products contain nut extracts such as Juglans Regia, 'walnut oil', which creates a dark toned effect. This may be unsuitable for use on a client with nut allergies.

Storage

Ensure all products are clearly labelled and stored at room temperature away from heat and sunlight, ideally in a cupboard.

Temperatures in excess of 40°C should be avoided as this will affect the quality and effectiveness of the product.

TOP TIP

Avoid clothes staining

Recommend the client avoids wearing silk or leather clothing as the pigment can cause staining.

If the client has stretch marks or recently healed skin, the colour result will differ. Inform the client of this.

If the client is a minor or under the age of 16 years of age, it is necessary to obtain parent/guardian permission for service. The parent/guardian will also have to be present when the service is received.

Explain what is involved in the different self-tanning services: timing, how long the effect will last and costs – a choice will then be able to be agreed on the most suitable technique.

Agree with the client the colour required and what can be achieved with the chosen tanning system. Consider the client's natural skin colouring. Ideally the colour should be 2–3 shades darker. A lighter skinned client will not achieve the possible dark tanning of a darker skinned client. The tan may initially appear too dark for a light skinned client as they do not usually tan, explain this, but cautiously apply a lighter application of tan if spray-tanning using a spray-gun on a client's first service.

Explain how the client will be prepared for the service and how long the service will take.

If the client is receiving an automated spray-tan booths application they will need to be instructed to adopt typically four different poses between each spray application exposure. For some clients with mobility issues these may be difficult to adopt and they should be advised accordingly. For clients who suffer from claustrophobia this method of self-tanning service may be an unsuitable choice.

Discuss the expected skin colour, expected skin reactions following service and aftercare requirements. If the client has a tattoo it will appear faded when the tan is initially applied.

Once the consultation is complete, the beauty therapist should ensure that all details are recorded accurately and that the client has signed their record card. This enables reference for future services and up-to-date tracking of services received. A sample record card is shown on the following page.

Invite the client to ask questions, the client should fully understand what the service involves.

Check for contra-indications at the consultation and if present do not proceed with the service.

" To ensure that your client's tan fades evenly it is crucial to recommend aftercare advice. Simple tips include polishing every 2–3 days to remove dead skin cells to help the tan fade evenly and to moisturise the skin every day to maintain hydration to help the tan last longer.

Tammy Baker

" Customers generally fall into two categories: those who think and behave similarly to you, and those who don't. The most successful service providers have learned how to work with both groups. When you are able to speak another person's language, it becomes easier to understand – and be understood by – them. Being able to adapt to various personalities will create and build strong relationships.

Tammy Baker

ST.TROPEZ

TANNING TREATMENT CONSULTATION

	YES	NO
Have you used self-tanning products before?	☐	☐
How were the results? POOR ☐	AVE ☐	GOOD ☐
Have you had a St.Tropez tan before?	☐	☐
If yes, were you pleased with the results?	☐	☐
Do you require an all over tan?	☐	☐
Is the tan for a special occasion?	☐	☐
Are you going on holiday?	☐	☐
Is your skin free from SPF and salt water?	☐	☐
Have you removed all deodorant/perfume/make-up?	☐	☐
Have you shaved or waxed less than 24 hours ago?	☐	☐
Do you have bleached hair or eyebrows?	☐	☐
Are you on any medication?	☐	☐
Have you recently had a course of antibiotics or chemotherapy?	☐	☐
Have you any known allergies?	☐	☐
Have you any open cuts, wounds, rashes or grazes?	☐	☐
Do you suffer from any skin disorders?	☐	☐
Do you have any pigmentation patches or pigmentary disorders?	☐	☐
Would you describe your skin as hyper-sensitive?	☐	☐
Do you suffer from any respiratory problems?	☐	☐
Are you pregnant or breastfeeding?	☐	☐
Have you recently had any body piercings or tattoos?	☐	☐
Have you received a pre-treatment advice slip?	☐	☐
Have you any queries from this advice or any other questions?	☐	☐

How will you maintain your tan?

What concerns do you have with home tanning?

PATCH TEST
We recommend that you have a patch test prior to every treatment.

	YES	NO
Have you taken the patch test?	☐	☐
If no, are you happy to receive a tan without a patch test?	☐	☐

DETAILS

Name:

Address:

Date of Birth:

Telephone:

E-mail:

INDEMNITY

I have read and understood the recommendations. To the best of my knowledge, there is no reason why I should not tan.

Signed:

St.Tropez and its agents would like to be able to advise you of products, services and special promotions in the future. If you do not wish to receive further communications, please tick the box ☐

ST.TROPEZ

ST TROPEZ, THE SKIN FINISHING EXPERTS

DATE	TREATMENT/COMMENTS	INITIALS

Record card for self-tanning

Contra-indications

Certain contra-indications preclude a self-tanning service. If there is any concern over the client's suitability, medical advice should be sought before the service proceeds.

During the client assessment, if you find any of the following, self-tan service must not be recommended or carried out.

- Pregnancy – due to the hormonal changes in the body, the colour result may change. There is also an insurance implication as no body services should be carried out in the first 3 months of pregnancy.
- Hypersensitive, allergenic skins – an allergic reaction can occur caused by the ingredients in the self-tan product.
- Infectious skin conditions – fungal, viral or bacterial.
- Cuts and abrasions in the area – skin irritation and secondary infection could occur.
- Recent tattoo as scar tissue will not tan evenly and there may be a risk of bacterial infection.
- Immediately after other heat or sensitizing services such as waxing hair removal, electrolysis or sauna. Again, skin irritation and secondary infection can occur if the skin has been damaged.
- Contact lenses, unless removed – to avoid eye irritation.
- Respiratory conditions – these may be aggravated by the chemical fumes with spray-tan technique.
- Skin conditions where the skin is thickened and broken such as psoriasis, eczema and dermatitis. Excessive skin plaques will also result in uneven tanning.
- Positive (allergic) reaction to a skin sensitivity patch test.
- Skin erythema – the skin is already sensitized.

Those requiring GP referral should be tactfully and clearly discussed to ensure client understanding.

Inform the client at consultation of any relevant contra-actions that may occur and the action to take.

Contra-actions

- **Erythema** (reddening of the skin) **irritation, burning** sensation and **swelling** caused by an allergic reaction to the self-tanning product used. The allergic reaction is rarely to DHA but other ingredients such as perfume and preservatives. If this occurs, advise that the client showers to remove the product and make a record of the skin response on the client's **record card**. If the redness does not reduce, the client may require to seek medical attention.

  A skin sensitivity patch test may take place in the future using a different skin self-tanning product to assess skin tolerance.

- **Respiratory problems** due to inhalation of airborne self-tanning particles or inadequate ventilation leading to shortening of breath and tightening of the chest. If this occurs the service should stop and the service may be unsuitable.

  Respiratory problems should be checked for at consultation and appropriate action taken. A mask or nose filters may be provided for client use and used as a precautionary measure.

TOP TIP

Vitiligo

Self-tan application can help disguise the appearance of the skin condition vitiligo (lack of skin pigment), especially when the self-tan is applied specifically to one area, e.g. using spray-tan airbrush technique. Choose a colour close to the client's natural skin tone.

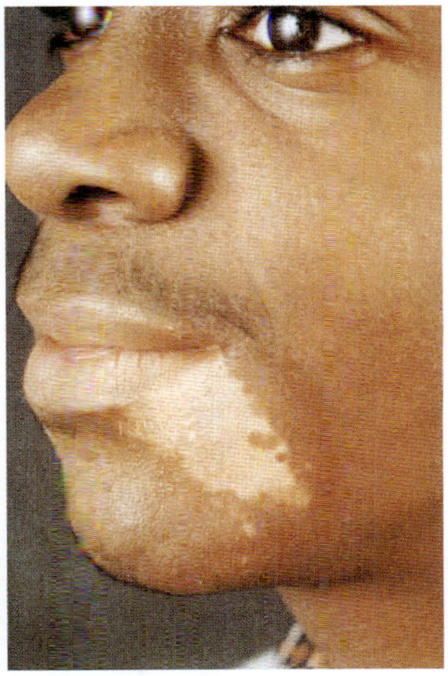

DERMA COLOUR

Vitiligo

HEALTH & SAFETY

Respiratory contra-indications

Severe asthma is unsuitable for exposure to spray-tanning. An alternative would be manual application technique.

TOP TIP

Hair protection

Ensure clients with lighter or white hair adequately protect their hair with a cap when receiving spray-tanning or the hair may become discoloured where not protected.

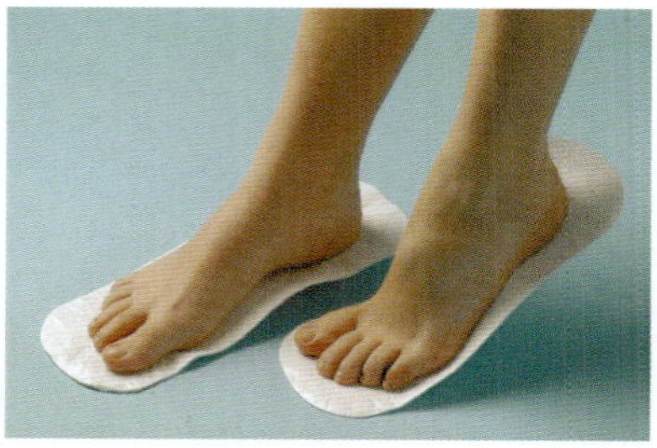

SMART BUY

Disposable sole protectors provide hygiene and prevent skin staining

TOP TIP

Exfoliation

Dry exfoliation can be performed using an exfoliating mitt before the service.

ST TROPEZ, THE SKIN FINISHING EXPERTS

Buffing/exfoliating dual purpose mitt

TOP TIP

Avoid stained nails

If the client has long nails, barrier cream may be applied under the free edge to avoid staining.

- **Watery eyes** caused by an irritant effect to the self-tanning product. Protective eyewear is available for use as a precautionary measure.
- **Fainting** may occur if standing during spray-gun tan applications. Check client comfort during application. Have water available to ensure client hydration. Ensure the work area is free from obstacles that could harm the client if they fainted. Have an awareness of what action to take if a client fainted.
- **Nausea** ingestion of the self-tanning product can occur when using spray systems which may cause nausea. Discuss the procedure at consultation to avoid unnecessary ingestion.

Have tanning instructions clearly displayed for use with automated spray-tanning systems.

Preparation of the client

Choose the correct shade for the skin colour – light, medium or dark. Some manufacturers provide shade charts to enable the client to identify the colour. If an automated spray-tan booth is used this cannot be accommodated for. The service cannot be personalized. The client must be confident of the poses to adopt during spray-tan application and the service sensations.

Best results are achieved on clean skin which has been cleansed and exfoliated to remove skin lotions, sebum and dead skin cells, all of which will act as a barrier. This type of cleansing enables an even application, although not all tanning systems require this.

Poor skin preparation can result in streaking, darker uneven patches or a lack of colour development.

For automated booth spray systems check pressure gauges and fluid tank levels.

Exfoliation may be performed in the salon or by the client at home, depending on the self-tan product. Areas requiring exfoliation attention are the elbows, knees and ankles, where dead skin cells build up.

A lip balm may be applied before spray-tanning technique to avoid skin staining. Glasses and jewellery should be removed from the treatment area to ensure an even application, and make-up should be removed.

It is recommended to provide paper underwear to prevent staining the client's underwear. It is the client's choice if worn.

In the self-tan spray techniques a barrier cream is applied to the palms of the hands, soles of the feet, ankles and nails of the client to prevent staining. Disposable sole protectors may be used. Ask the client to step firmly onto the adhesive surface.

A protective cap is worn to cover the hair. This is lifted at the hairline to expose the ears. Ensure this is not too low on the forehead or a demarcation line will occur. The eyebrow hair may also be protected with a barrier cream.

Remind the client of the procedure and sensations. Invite any questions from the client to confirm understanding. It is a good idea if you ask them to signal to you if you need to stop for any reason during spray-tan manual application.

If using an automated tanning booth, ensure the client is confident on the procedure to ensure their safety and efficiency of the tanning application. Have instructions clearly placed for the client to refer to.

Outcome 3: Apply self-tan products

Learn how to apply a self-tanning service to meet the needs of your client by:

1. Ensuring that exfoliation is carried out prior to the service according the manufacturer's instructions.
2. Ensuring that exfoliation leaves the skin smooth and free from dry, flaky skin.
3. Effectively applying moisturisers and barrier creams following manufacturer's instructions to prevent over-development of tanning products.
4. Correctly testing the pressure and operation of the spray-gun prior to use.
5. Using **equipment** and **products** to meet client requirements and following manufacturer's instructions.
6. Using spray-tanning techniques in a controlled way and at a correct distance from the body to achieve the desired effect.
7. Applying **products** evenly in the correct sequence to achieve the desired effect.
8. Using techniques that minimize the risk of **products** being spread outside the services area and surrounding environment.
9. Effectively correcting any problems occurring during the application process.
10. Ensuring that the finished result is to the client's satisfaction.

HEALTH & SAFETY

When performing a self-tanning service consider your responsibilities under the following legislation at all times:

- **Health and Safety at Work Act (1974)**
- **Control of Substances Hazardous to Health Regulations (2002)**
- Pressure Systems Safety Regulations (2000)
- **Workplace (Health Safety and Welfare) Regulations (1992)**
- **Management of Health and Safety at Work Regulations (1999)**.

ST TROPEZ, THE SKIN FINISHING EXPERTS

Self-tanning products – pre-service clarifier, tanning fluid, pure pigment, hydrating mist

How to apply self-tanning products

The following tanning systems application techniques are discussed: automated spray booth, spray-tan using an airbrush or gun and manual hand-applied technique. Always follow the manufacturer's instructions to ensure the optimum effect is achieved.

When applying self-tan to the face, the eyes should be closed or protected as per the manufacturer's instructions and system used. Hair should be protected and covered. Nose filters should be provided to prevent inhalation of tanning particles if using spray systems.

BEST PRACTICE

Spray booths

Spray booths provide privacy during application of the spray-tan. The booth features fans to clean the air following application and a protective floor cover.

> It is important to be self-motivated, but you must be able to work equally well as part of a team. Nominating a 'St Tropez specialist' within your team will ensure that one person is solely responsible for updating the team on new product releases and tanning techniques to ensure you are all offering the ultimate service.
>
> **Tammy Baker**

SUNQUEST TANNING SYSTEMS LTD

Spray-tanning booth

How to apply self-tan using spray-tan automated booth application technique

1. The client and their skin are prepared for spray application.
2. A large air compressor sprays liquid product in a mist evenly all over the client's skin from a set of spray nozzles in a large self-contained booth constructed from fibreglass, acrylic or aluminium. The design of the booth produces a downward flow of air and contains filters to remove chemical particles from the air. Some systems also have inbuilt heaters so that the environment is temperature regulated to prevent the skin drying too quickly.
3. The client stands in the cubicle in front of the nozzles where, after operating a start button, the front and then the back of the body are sprayed with self-tan from the set of spray nozzles, which move sideways creating an even application of self-tan product. Different positions are adopted by the client, usually four simple standing positions to ensure even application. The client then strokes the product over the skin until it has dried. Excess product should be removed using a paper towel from the skin, including the palms of the hands and soles of the feet. This system offers additional privacy for the client.

   Application and drying time: *5–10 minutes depending on the system*.
4. If required, a second application may be given when the skin has dried. An immediate colour is achieved and then the tan continues to develop.
5. Ensure the client is satisfied with the finished result and understands how the finished result will appear.

A disadvantage of the automated systems is that you cannot control where the product is applied by taking into consideration the size, shape and skin condition of the client which can be achieved with a personal manual application.

Automated spray-tanning has the following benefits:

- it is the quickest self-tanning service
- there is little time required as a resource for the beauty therapist
- it offers the client total privacy

How to apply self-tan using spray-gun application technique This technique uses a compressor unit, which generates pulses of air pressure producing a stream of compressed air, to direct a fine mist of self-tan product from a small container of tanning solution onto the skin through a flexible hose and a spray-gun nozzle.

Normally two full-body applications will be given during the service which takes between 15-20 minutes to carry out. However, only one application to the hands and feet occurs to achieve a realistic result.

- The client and their skin are prepared for application. Explain to the client the service sensation of a cool mist of moisture.
- The client stands in a booth or working area protected from spray, while the beauty therapist applies self-tan with an air gun. It is important that the client does not touch the skin during application to avoid uneven coverage.
- The client should stand upright with legs a part facing the beauty therapist with arms relaxed at their side. It is important to explain throughout the application how you want them to stand and move different parts of their body.
- Start spraying the body starting at the face and working your way down.

TOP TIP

Avoiding stained hands

When removing the protective hair covering advise the client uses a paper towel to avoid contact with the skin of the hand which could lead to skin staining.

HEALTH & SAFETY

Spillages

If product is spilt during application, soak up excess liquid with tissue while wearing hand protection and dispose of in accordance with Waste Regulations.

- When spraying the face the client should be advised to hold their breath and close their eyes.
- Overlap each stroke as you work down the body, keeping the spray-gun level.
- Ensure that you spray underneath the breasts, this will be achieved by asking the client to raise their arms to the sides of the body.
- Hold and rotate the arms spraying down towards the hand (without spraying the hands) spraying the inside and side of each arm.
- Spray down each leg (without spraying the feet) and release the trigger on the gun as you reach the ankles. A lighter application is required over the knees where the area is drier.
- Ask the client to turn around and face the back of the booth.
- The client should tilt their head forward while you spray the neck. Work your way down the body spraying over the shoulders and back.
- Ask the client to point their hands towards the back of the booth with palms facing down and arms held slightly away from their trunk while you spray the back of the arms.
- Continue spraying down the body, the client may bend forward slightly when spraying over the buttocks in order to tan the crease underneath the buttocks or a lighter line will result in this area. Spray the outside to inside of one leg and the inside to outside of the other. Stop at the ankle.
- Spray the sides of the body asking the client to turn to one side so that they are facing side on to you. This will require the client to position themselves with one leg in front of the other and one arm raised above their head and elbow pointed back. Spray the sides of the breast and trunk.
- Spray down the inside of the back leg and then the outside. Repeat this application to the other side of the body which will require the client to alter the position and raise the other arm.
- Repeat the spray application again.
- Finally, increase the distance from the client and lightly spray each foot and hands. The hands will require the client to move their hands into different positions in order to cover the backs and sides of their hands effectively.
- Apply the tan in a specific sequence to ensure even coverage. Adjust pressure according to the effect required. Follow your manufacturer's application, including vertical, horizontal and circular spray patterns. Always try to use the lowest pressure as less fumes will be created and a good coverage achieved.
- Any area which appears wet should be gently patted dry.
- A cleansing wipe can be used following application to remove product from the fingers, toe nails and palms of the hand.
- Ensure the client is satisfied with the finished result and understands how the finished result will appear. Advise the client to allow the product to dry for approximately 5–10 minutes before dressing.
- Body moisturiser may be applied to areas that typically can crease and stain such as the wrists, knees and ankles.
- Following application the client stands in the booth to allow the warm air to dry the skin.

SUNQUEST TANNING SYSTEMS LTD

Airbrush spray booth

TOP TIP

Spray tan booth

Spray booths provide privacy during application of the spray tan. The booth features fans to clean the air following application and a protective floor cover.

ACTIVITY

FUNCTIONAL SKILLS

PSI is often referred to as a feature in the sale of spray-guns. This means pounds per square inch and refers to the pressure of the air generated by the compressor. This requires adjustment of the pressure to create the result required.

Research different spray-gun tan systems and identify their PSI and other technology features.

Remember, technology advances all the time and it is important to be using the equipment that will give your clients the best result wherever possible.

HEALTH & SAFETY

Safe posture

It is important to follow recommended posture positions as advised by the HSE in an exploratory study, 2009, to avoid risk of repetitive strain injury. Your manufacturer's guidance instructions will also advise you of these.

- The sole protectors are removed and any sticky residue may be removed with a cleansing tissue.
- Clean the work area and dispose of waste.

Application and drying time: *20–30 minutes*.

Spray-gun tanning application technique

- To ensure even application a small rotating platform, which the client stands on, can be used to facilitate application.
- To create a more natural, lighter result reduce pressure and increase the distance.
- Start moving the air gun before you start spraying to avoid darker areas of application.
- Ensure no body parts are missed, e.g. under the chin!
- Wipe over light brow hair with a tissue to avoid staining, following face application.
- If application is excessive, blot the area to avoid too dark a colour developing.
- Keep the airbrush at 90 degrees and move at all times to ensure even application. A repetitive finger, hand and arm movement is required. Safe working must be considered to prevent repetitive strain injury.
- Spray the legs first at they take the longest to dry.
- Do not over-wet the skin. This can also result in a scaly appearance to the skin.
- If the client has any folds of skin, e.g. on the back, it will be necessary for them to stretch while these body parts are sprayed.
- When spraying the face, ask the client to inhale through the nose and as they exhale through the mouth spray the face from the chin to forehead to avoid inhalation of the spray. The client's eyes are closed at all times.
- Blemished areas, and areas of dry skin absorb more colour and lighter application is required over such areas.

Step-by-step: Airbrush tanning application techniques

Fill the spray tan product to the correct level in the container. A small pen-like spray-gun applicator atomises the spray-tan liquid into tiny particles. Again, operated by a compressor. This is useful for performing corrective work, e.g. concealment of vitiligo.

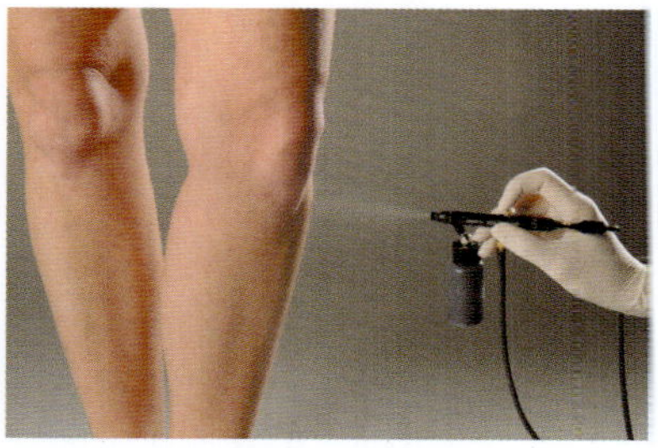

ELLISONS

1 Test the gun is working before the service commences. Switch on the compressor and adjust the pressure to create the desired result. Leg application – apply tan to the client's legs as these take the longest to dry. Work down the leg at a distance of 13–21 cm to ensure full, even coverage.

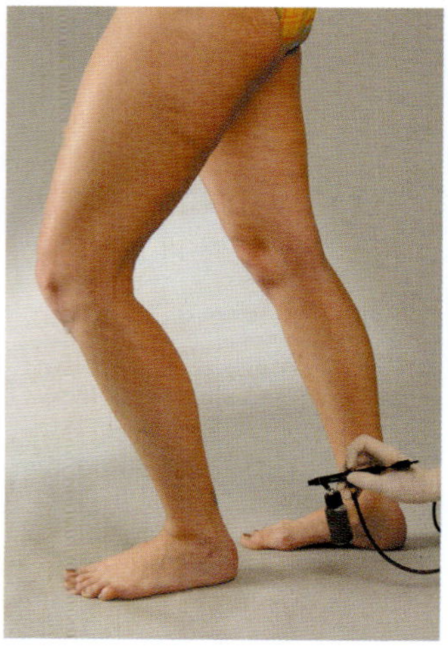

ELLISONS

2 Ankle application – this area can be dry, creating a darker effect, so a lighter application is required. Lightly spray the tops of the feet. Increase distance and reduce pressure. Advise the client to lean forward to stretch the skin in this area. Continue to apply tan to the upper body front and back by applying tan in a downwards direction until the area is evenly covered. Ask the client to move their body as required to facilitate application.

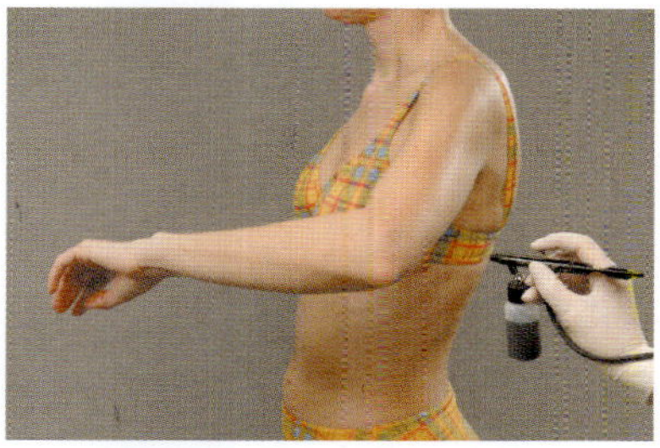

ELLISONS

3 Arm application – apply tan to the client with their arm raised, working from the wrist down the arm and then apply to the rest of the arm, asking the client to move their arms as required to ensure full, even coverage.

BEST PRACTICE

Self tan product application

Check your application of the product as you are working. The skin should look initially as if it has a fine mist on its surface which dries quickly. If it is too wet it will run resulting in streaking.

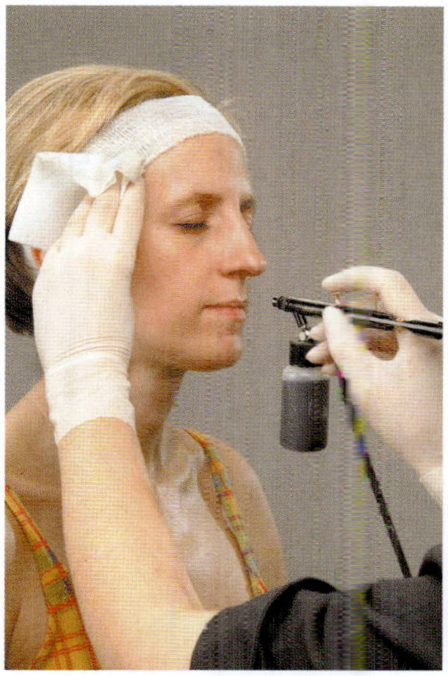

ELLISONS

4 Facial application – protect the hair (including brow hair) to prevent staining. Ask the client to close their eyes and take a deep breath while you apply tan to the face. Include the ears, around the ears and the neck area.

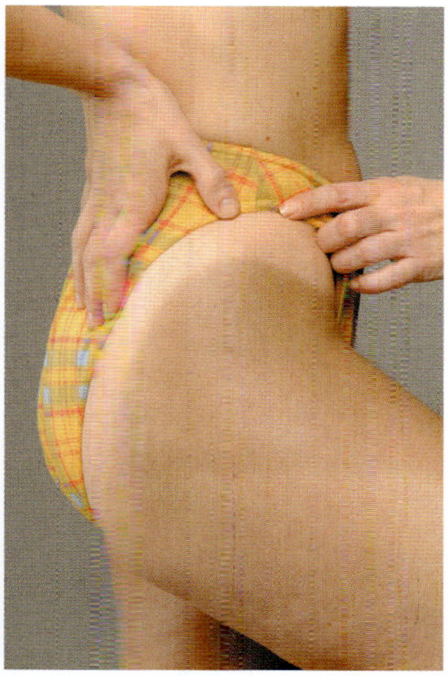

ELLISONS

5 Finished result – ensure the client is satisfied with the finished result and that the application is even. Reapply to any lighter areas.

Rinse the air gun immediately with warm, clean water to prevent clogging with dried product. Self tanning product is water-based.

ALWAYS REMEMBER

Care of the spray-gun

Temporarily, between use, store the air gun in water to prevent clogging.

When not in use, store the air gun in an air gun holder.

If clogged, the air gun will not apply the product evenly and will spit the product.

> The most common cause of a patchy tan is dry skin, so it is crucial to polish the entire body and moisturise problem areas such as hands, elbows, knees and feet prior to self-tan applications.
>
> **Tammy Baker**

TOP TIP

Uneven application

If you make a mistake during application, pat the area dry, do not rub the skin as this will lead to uneven patchy colouration.

You can always apply a further application to produce an even result.

TOP TIP

Protecting the hands

The palms of the hands have more pores than other body areas and will soon tan. To prevent staining wear thin gloves during application. This is true for your clients also, so care must be taken to avoid tan getting onto the hands being transferred following service application.

How to apply self-tan using manual hand-applied application technique

This is a luxurious service which is recommended if the client would like to benefit from a relaxing massage to the skin's surface

1 The client should be dressed in disposable underwear, hair secured from the face and covered on the couch with towels for modesty and to keep warm. The client and their skin are prepared for self-tan application. This usually requires showering and the application of an exfoliant.

2 Moisturiser may be applied to the elbows, knees, ankles and feet. Adding moisturiser lightens the result but should only be used if recommended by the manufacturer as it can also create a barrier if too much is used.

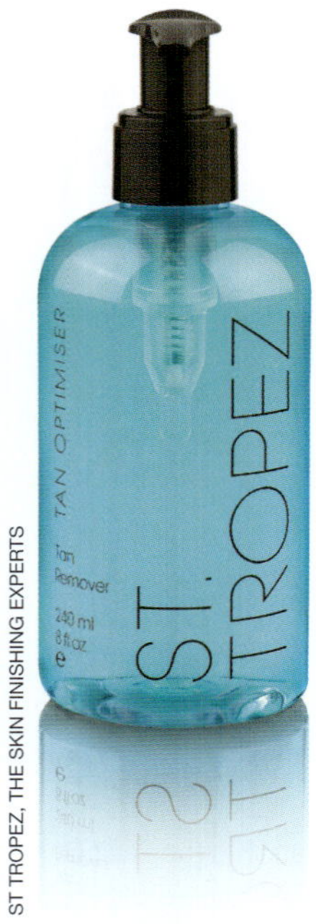

Tan corrector

ALWAYS REMEMBER

Medical suitability
Some forms of medication can affect how the skin responds to self-tanning product.

TOP TIP

Lightening the result
Moisturiser may be used to lighten the result for the areas: face, hairline, inner arm, underarm, hands, ankles, knees and feet to avoid the result in these areas becoming too dark.

TOP TIP

Removing unwanted product
Any product applied to unwanted areas should be removed with cotton wool or tissue during the application.

3 The self-tan product is applied over the body following the manufacturer's guidelines for application using the hands, which are usually protected with gloves to prevent staining.

4 Service must be methodical to ensure no body parts are missed and that an even coverage is obtained.

5 Product should be removed immediately during application, using a clean tissue, from the palms of the hands, toes and fingernails to prevent staining.

6 Time should be allowed for the product to dry, *approximately 10 minutes*.

7 The skin is then buffed to remove excess product, avoid rubbing the skin which could result in uneven colouration. Pay particular attention to areas where the skin is drier, e.g. ankles and wrists.

8 Ensure the client is satisfied and understands how the finished result will appear. Application and drying time: *approximately 1 hour 20 minutes* including pre-exfoliation and post skin buffing.

Poor tanning results These are commonly caused by the beauty therapist and their choice and application of products, or the client not following the necessary skin preparation/aftercare instructions.

- *Tan too light in colour.* Incorrect colour shade selected. Insufficient application of product to area if using spray-gun tanning, the pressure may have been too low or distance too far away. The addition of too much moisturiser to the tanning product during manual hand application technique.
- *Tan too dark.* Incorrect colour shade selected. Incorrect formulation, percentage of DHA too high for skin colouring. If using spray-gun tanning the pressure used was too high or application distance too near the client.
- *Uneven application.* The client may have products on the skin which have not been effectively removed before tanning, e.g. perfume around the neck-line. Insufficient exfoliation and moisturising of the skin before service. Confirm that the client has followed aftercare instructions if occurs following application.
- *Incorrect application technique.* This must be methodical to avoid missing areas of skin. Excessively dry skin conditions can result in a patchy uneven result. Not allowing the skin to dry properly before dressing can result in removal of some of the product. There may be a problem with the quality of the product, if it happens again contact the supplier for guidance.
- *Tan corrector products***.** These are available which can be used with leading tanning manufacturer products usually within 5 hours of application to correct streaking. Alternatively, an exfoliant may be used. Self-tan can be reapplied to the area to even the result, the application may be modified to create the necessary result, i.e. darker or lighter.
- *Orange or ashy cast to the skin.* Caused by over-application or incorrect choice of formulation for the client's skin colour. There may be alkaline products on the skin which will create an orange colour to the skin.

> Self-tan and gradual tan can stain blonde or bleached hair. Put a little extra moisturiser on the eyebrows and the hairline prior to application.
>
> **Tammy Baker**

> Excellent customer service and product knowledge will result in an increase in sales revenue, repeat business and customer retention. With the ultimate consultation the customer/client will receive the correct advice to follow up any professional service with the best product choices and achieve the best results.
>
> **Tammy Baker**

Outcome 4: Provide aftercare advice

Learn how to provide aftercare advice which supports and meets the needs of your clients by:

1. Giving **advice** and recommendations accurately and constructively.
2. Giving your clients suitable **advice** specific to their individual needs.

SPRAY TAN ADVICE

A St.Tropez Spray Tan Treatment gives you a fast, flawless tan in a controlled environment. Now with Aromaguard™ fragrance technology which eliminates the tell-tale self tan aroma by a minimum of 70%. The tan is applied and tailored by an expert and takes no more than 15 minutes. You need to allow some time to prepare and dress.

To ensure your tan is flawless and even, please follow this simple guide:

Before Treatment Advice

- It is preferable not to apply any type of perfume, deodorant or aromatherapy oils on the day of your treatment as these reduce the results.
- Waxing or shaving should be completed at least 24 hours prior to the treatment to reduce sensitivity.
- The evening before or morning of your treatment, exfoliate your entire body using St.Tropez Body Polish. Pay special attention to dry areas of your body such as hands, elbows, knees and feet.
- Wear dark, loose fitting clothing with a dark coloured bra or preferably no bra at all. Please be aware the guide colour can stain light hair, man-made fibres and wool.
- We recommend you have a patch test prior to every St.Tropez Spray Tan Treatment.

The Treatment

The application takes up to 15 minutes to cover the whole body. The Bronzing Mist will dry on your skin in just a few minutes so you can dress straight after the treatment. Avoid touching or rubbing the applied tan once the treatment is completed.

- For the short period that your face is sprayed, close your eyes and do not inhale. If you suffer from respiratory problems, please contact your doctor before having a treatment.

After Treatment Advice

Your tan will begin to develop immediately after your treatment.

- Do not shower or bathe for a minimum of 4 hours after your treatment
- Do not participate in any activity which may cause perspiration for at least 12 hours after the treatment.
- It is fine to leave the guide colour on overnight and wash in the morning. Some guide colour may transfer to bed linen. This will wash out of cotton but not so easily from man-made fibres or wool.

Tan Maintenance Tips

With the correct aftercare your tan will last longer

- Apply St.Tropez Body Moisturiser or NEW St.Tropez Body Butter daily in between self tan applications to maintain your tan for longer and to ensure even fading.
- Exfoliate your skin with St.Tropez Body Polish every 2 days to ensure your tan fades evenly.
- Do not rub but pat your skin dry after showering or bathing.
- Avoid swimming pools as chlorine can bleach the tan.

WARNING St.Tropez products do not contain a sunscreen and do not protect against sunburn. Repeated exposure of unprotected skin while tanning may increase the risk of skin ageing, skin cancer and other harmful effects to the skin, even if you do not burn.

ST TROPEZ, THE SKIN FINISHING EXPERTS

Aftercare leaflet

Aftercare advice

- Details of the service should be entered on the record card, to include date, colour, result, any adverse skin reaction. To ensure effective tan development, avoid streaking and to maintain the result:
  - Avoid anything that will make you sweat immediately following service as this will dilute the product, disturb application affecting the finished effect. Therefore no strenuous exercise for approximately 6–8 hours.
  - Cosmetic products which remove the surface cells such as facial peeling masks should be avoided.

- Avoid tight clothing or friction with any body part immediately following application to avoid product removal.
- Do not bath/shower for at least 8 hours following service application. Care should be taken when washing the hands to avcid product removal following service.
- Avoid chlorinated pools, excessive bathing and heat services such as sauna as they encourage fading. Avoid long baths and showers as they will encourage exfoliation.
- On showering, excess lotion referred to as the guide colour will be removed making the water appear brown. The skin should be gently patted dry with a soft towel.

- Encourage the retail of self-tanning preparations. Tinted products are useful as this assists in even application. They often contain ingredients, such as vitamins and plant extracts, to keep the skin moisturised.
- Other relevant products are exfoliators, which can be used between services as advised by the beauty therapist and to prepare the skin for future self-tan applications. These must be used cautiously as they will recuce the life of the tan if used incorrectly or too often.
- Moisturiser should be applied daily to prevent the skin becoming dry and to keep the skin hydrated. Avoid the use of AHA products, which will encourage skin removal and loss of skin colour.
- Encourage the client to use a tan enhancer to maintain and enhance the result.
- If a contra-action occurs, contact the salon for professional advice.
- Encourage a repeat appointment booking, usually every 2 weeks as the tan fades. A client, however, requiring a deeper tan could return in 48 hours for a second application if suitable.
- Sun protection is necessary on exposure to UV.

> Always describe the features, advantages and benefits of a product and allow your client to feel, smell and experience the products you are recommending.
>
> **Tammy Baker**

> The tan will not deepen the longer it is left on. Once it has been left on for the required amount of time, generally 4–12 hours, it will have developed into a natural looking golden tan. For a deeper tan you should reapply on 2 successive days which is known as a 'Double Dip' and will result in a really deep, rich bronze tan.
>
> **Tammy Baker**

TOP TIP

Retail opportunities

Many self-tanning product suppliers have extensive retail ranges to care for and enhance the tanned skin.

TOP TIP

Oily skin

The result will be better on a client with an oily skin, however, all skin will require moisturising to avoid dry, uneven, flaky patches, resulting in uneven desquamation.

TOP TIP

Tan enhancer

The use of tan enhancer will extend the life of the tan as it will keep the skin moisturised and has a small amount of self-tan in its formulation.

ASSESSMENT OF KNOWLEDGE AND UNDERSTANDING

FUNCTIONAL SKILLS

Having covered the learning objectives for **Provide self-tanning services** – test what you need to know and understand answering the following short questions below:

The information covers:

- organizational and legal requirements
- how to work safely and effectively when providing self-tanning services
- client consultation
- contra-indications and contra-actions
- equipment and products
- tanning services
- aftercare advice for clients

Organizational and legal requirements

1 How can a hygienic environment be maintained when providing self-tanning services? Give **five** examples of necessary cleaning regimes.

2 Why is it necessary to keep records of all self-tanning services? What information would need to be recorded?

3 What health and safety legislation should be considered when performing self-tanning services?

4 What is the differences in service timing for each of the self-tanning services?

5 Why is ventilation important in the delivery of spray self-tanning service?

How to work safely and effectively when providing self-tanning services

1 How should waste generated from the different self-tanning services be disposed of following service to comply with the Waste Disposal Regulations?

2 What types of personal protective equipment must be worn by the beauty therapist when performing the different self-tanning services and why?

3 Self-tanning manual application techniques requires you to adopt different awkward positions. How may continued poor posture affect you?

4 How can the client's modesty and privacy be maintained during the different self-tanning techniques?

5 What should personal protective equipment be made available for the client's use and safety when performing self-tanning services?

6 Why is good lighting important when providing manual hand-applied self-tan technique?

Client consultation

1 When planning the client's self-tanning service state **three** questions it will be necessary for you to ask the client and explain why.

2 What information and advice would be given to a client who made a telephone booking in preparation for the service?

3 What advice would you give to the client in preparing them for the service at the consultation on the day of the service?

4 Why is it important that all responses to questions on the record card are recorded?

Contra-indications and contra-actions

1 Name **three** contra-indications observed at consultation which would prevent self-tanning service.

2 State **three** contra-actions that occur following self-tanning application.

3 Why is it importance not to name specific contra-indications when encouraging clients to seek medical advice before service?

Equipment and products

1 What are the advantages and disadvantages of the following systems?
   - manual hand-applied self-tan
   - airbrush/gun spray application technique
   - spray booth application technique

2 How is the choice of self-tan product and colour selected?

3 What problems can occur if the airbrush applicator is not cleaned after every self-tan application?

4 What is the meaning of the term PS and which self-tanning system does this relate to?

Tanning services

1. How should the skin be prepared for self-tanning service?
2. How does self-tanning product react with the skin to create the artificial tanned appearance?
3. What is the ingredient in self-tanning product that provides the tanned appearance of the skin?
4. Why should a skin sensitivity test be performed before each self-tanning service? How is this performed?
5. How would you adapt service application for the following skin disorders hyper-pigmentation and hypo-pigmentation?
6. What is the purpose of a tanning corrector?
7. Describe **three** results that could occur if the client did not follow the pre and post-service instructions?

Aftercare advice for clients

1. How often would you recommend the client receives a self-tanning service if they wish to maintain the skin's tanned appearance?
2. State the skincare instruction a client should follow to ensure that an optimum result is achieved from the self-tan.
3. What retail products could you recommend to a client following a self-tanning service?
4. What are the post-service restrictions following self-tan application?
5. If a client experienced an allergic reaction to the self-tanning service what action would the client have been advised to take at consultation?

16 Male and female intimate waxing

SHUTTERSTOCK/VALUA VITALY

Learning Objectives

This chapter covers **Provide female intimate waxing services** and **Provide male intimate waxing services**.

These units are all about how to remove and shape body hair from intimate areas using temporary methods including hot wax, warm wax and sugar paste waxing techniques.

Aftercare instruction is an important part of this service to promote skin healing.

There are **four** learning outcomes which you must achieve competently:

Provide female intimate waxing services

1. **Maintain safe and effective methods of working when providing female intimate waxing services.**
2. **Consult, plan and prepare for waxing services with clients.**
3. **Remove unwanted hair.**
4. **Provide aftercare advice.**

Provide male intimate waxing services

1. **Maintain safe and effective methods of working when providing male intimate waxing services.**
2. **Consult, plan and prepare for waxing services with clients.**

(continued on the next page)

©ANDY ROUILLARD AND JPB-IMAGERY.COM

ROLE MODEL

Andy Rouillard

Owner of Axiom Bodyworks male grooming salon and freelance trainer for Perron Rigot waxes

"While working as a massage beauty therapist several years ago, an increasing number of my male clients started asking for various skin care services, particularly waxing. At the time there were very few places in the UK offering grooming services for men. Sharing their frustration, I took up the mantle and trained in waxing before going on to complete my full beauty therapy NVQ.

I joined forces with a local barbershop to open a one-stop male grooming centre in Hampshire.

Hair removal is still our most popular service. Some clients regularly travel over an hour just to get their monthly defuzzing. The male Brazilian (or 'Boyzilian') is our signature service.

I am also a trainer for a leading international wax brand and am passionate about helping fellow beauty therapists become better waxers. My work takes me all over the UK and further afield, speaking at industry events, writing for magazines and demonstrating the art of waxing across Europe. It is tremendously rewarding to work in an industry that is all about helping customers to look and feel their best.

(continued)

3 **Remove unwanted hair.**

4 **Provide aftercare advice.**

For each unit your assessor will observe you on **at least four separate occasions** involving a different waxing service on different clients which will be recorded.

The range to be completed is the same for each service apart from waxing services to be covered which are both shown*.

From the **range** statement, you must show that you have:

- used all **consultation techniques**
- carried out all **four waxing services** listed including: Hollywood, Brazilian, Shaping and Playboy female intimate waxing
- carried out **four** of the **five** following **waxing services:** lower back, buttocks, anal area, scrotum and penis male intimate waxing
- dealt with at least **one** of the **necessary actions** where a contra-action, contra-indication or service modification occurs
- carried out all types of **preparation of the client**
- used **two** of the **three** types of wax products: hot wax, wax warm and sugar paste
- used **one** of the **two** types of **pre-wax application products:** oil and powder
- used all intimate waxing **work techniques**
- provided all types of relevant aftercare **advice**

However, you must prove that you have the necessary knowledge and understanding to be able to perform competently across the range.

When providing intimate waxing services it is important to use the skills you have learnt in the following units:

Monitoring safe work operations.

Promotional activities.

ROLE MODEL

Annette Close

Sales & Marketing Manager, Australian Bodycare UK Ltd

"My background began traditionally – I trained in all aspects of beauty therapy and hairdressing in the mid-70s, worked in salons for a couple of years then moved abroad and worked in spa therapy. When I returned to the UK, I opened my own salon, went back to college to do my teaching certificates, and worked as an examiner for the IHBC.

After the birth of my fourth baby, I sold the salon and taught beauty therapy full-time in various colleges throughout Kent, ending up working for adult education and implementing fully accredited beauty therapy and alternative therapy courses to adult learners in Kent.

From here I decided to change direction and applied to an international company as a UK development manager where I stayed for 8 years and became the UK marketing manager.

I was then approached by Australian Bodycare and, after 3 years, have established a solid foundation for our brand throughout the UK and Ireland. I am actively involved in new product development and research along with all the marketing aspects, PR, creation of new POS [point-of-sale] and information brochures and development of a professional website. The job is challenging and rewarding and allows me to be creative and exercise management skills all in one role.

Essential anatomy and physiology knowledge requirements for male and female intimate waxing are identified on the checklist in **Chapter 2, Anatomy and Physiology,** pages 12–13. This chapter also discusses anatomy and physiology knowledge requirements specific to intimate waxing.

Introduction

Hair removal is a popular service in the salon, where both temporary and permanent methods of hair removal are often available and used.

Intimate waxing involves applying depilatory wax products to the pubic area of the body, which embeds the hairs to be removed in the wax. When the wax is removed from the area, the hairs are removed at their roots. They grow again in approximately 3–4 weeks when it is recommended that the service is repeated. Both female and female waxing is achieved in much the same way with the omission of handling the male genitals.

Intimate waxing includes different hair removal services.

Intimate waxing technique	*Description*	*Image*
Hollywood	All hair is removed from both the pubic area and the anal area	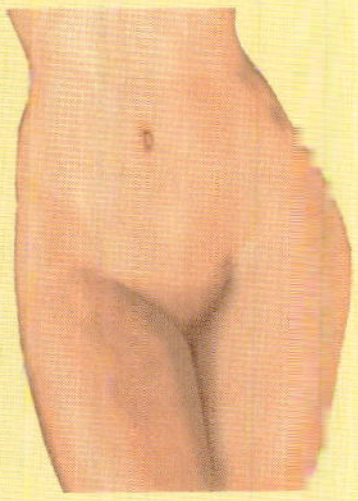
Brazilian	Hair is removed from the pubic area, sometimes a strip of hair approximately 2.5 cm wide remains up and over the pubic mound in the shape of a square, rectangle, oval or triangle, based on personal preference	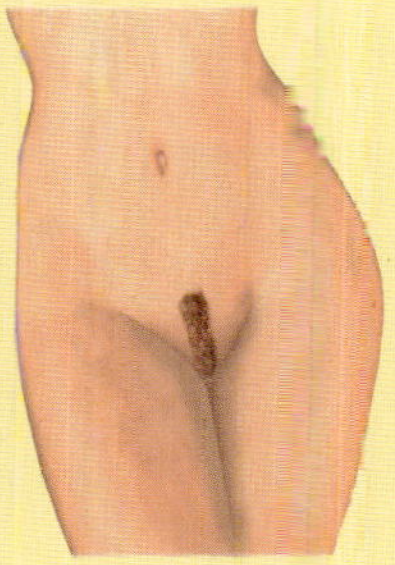
Shaping	Hair is shaped over the pubic mound using a template, e.g. heart shape	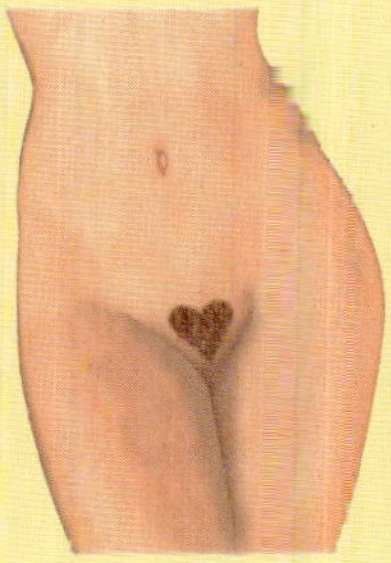

> "When it comes to intimate waxing, if you feel uncomfortable about doing it ***then don't***! Your disposition will be transferred to your client and he/she will feel awkward and possibly embarrassed. If you do carry out this service be professional, thorough and totally in control at all times. If you blush easily this is not for you.
>
> **Annette Close**

TOP TIP

Male waxing

Hair removal from male intimate areas includes skin surrounding the penis, scrotum, chest and anal areas. This is often referred to as 'back, sac and crack' or 'BSC'.

> Although 'looks' aren't everything, appearance most certainly is. Being a beauty therapist means you are not only selling yourself as a service provider but also the products you work with, making sure you are well groomed, have a clean uniform, and are well manicured will all instil confidence in your colleagues and clients
>
> **Annette Close**

HEALTH & SAFETY

Waxing service legal requirements

Habia have provided a Code of Practice for Waxing. This should be referred to, ensuring that you are complying with your responsibilities under relevant health and safety.

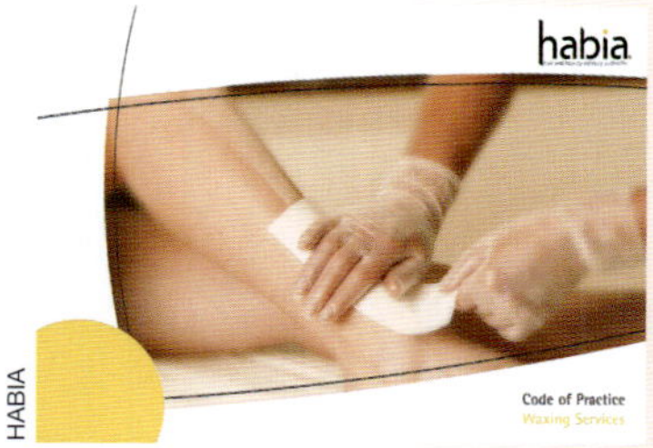

Habia code of practice for waxing

Intimate waxing technique	*Description*	*Image*
Playboy	Hair is removed from the pubic mound, buttock and anal area leaving a pencil-wide strip of hair over the pubic mound	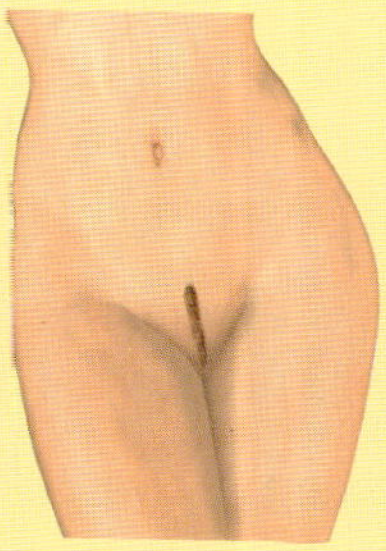
Male	Hair is removed from the following areas: lower back, buttocks, penis, scrotum and anal areas	

Anatomy and physiology

When performing intimate waxing you are required to be aware of the structure and function of the skin including different skin characteristics. The structure of the hair, the types of hair growth and the basic principles of the hair growth cycle. The correct medical terminology for the external genitalia and its structure and more information about the anatomy and physiology of male and female genitalia are discussed in Chapter 2, pages 93–94.

Outcome 1: Maintain safe and effective methods of working when providing male/female intimate waxing services

Learn how to maintain safe and effective methods of working when providing male/female intimate waxing services by:

1. Preparing the work environment to meet legal, hygiene and industry Code of Practice for Waxing requirements.
2. Ensuring your personal appearance meets accepted industry Code of Practice for Waxing and organizational requirements.
3. Wearing suitable personal protective equipment for the work that conforms to the industry Code of Practice for Waxing.
4. Preparing the client and providing suitable personal protective equipment to conform to the industry Code of Practice for Waxing.
5. Making sure that environmental conditions are suitable for the client and the service.
6. Ensuring all tools and equipment are cleaned using the correct methods.

(Continued)
Learn how to maintain safe and effective methods of working when providing male/female intimate waxing services by:

7. Effectively disinfecting your hands prior to waxing services.
8. Maintaining accepted industry hygiene and safety practices throughout the service.
9. Selecting and correctly positioning suitable equipment, materials, applicators and **products** for the **waxing service**
10. Ensuring your own posture and position minimizes fatigue and the risk of injury while working.
11. Maintaining the client's modesty and privacy at all times.
12. Minimizing wastage of product during application
13. Disposing of hazardous waste correctly to meet local authority requirements.
14. Ensuring that the service is cost-effective and is carried out within a commercially viable time.
15. Ensuring the client's records are up-to-date, accurate, easy to read and signed by the client and practitioner.
16. Leaving the work area and equipment in a condition suitable for further **waxing services**.

HEALTH & SAFETY

Electricity at Work Regulations (1989)
Ensure that electrical appliances such as your wax heater and autoclave are maintained in accordance with the Electricity at Work Regulations (1989). Records of maintenance should be available for inspection.

> Consider adding service codes to your waxing price list, which allows customers to book an appointment without the embarrassment of others overhearing what they are having done.
>
> **Andy Rouillard**

Before beginning the intimate waxing service, check that you have the necessary equipment and materials to hand and that they meet legal, hygiene and industry requirements for waxing services.

EQUIPMENT AND MATERIALS LIST

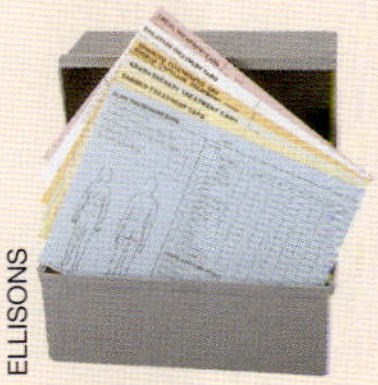

ELLISONS

Client record card
Confidential card recording details of each client registered at the salon to record the client's personal details, products used and details of the service

ELLISONS

Wax-removal strips
(Bonded-fibre) – thick enough that the wax does not soak through, but flexible enough for ease of work. These strips should be cut to size and placed ready in a covered container

MILLENNIUM NAILS

Self-adhesive bikini-line gem skin adornments
(if used)

ELLISONS

Wax heater
With a thermostatic control

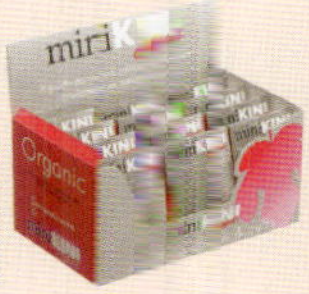

MINIKINI

Specialist pubic hair colourant
Special hair colourants may be applied to pubic hair in natural and artificial colours, e.g. black, brown, pink and bright orange

CLEAN+EASY

Waxing products
Hot wax (hard wax), warm wax or sugar paste (soft wax)

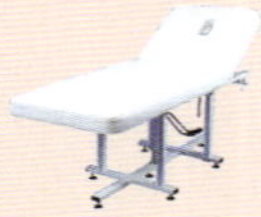
BEAUTY EXPRESS LTD

Couch
With sit-up and lie-down positions and an easy to clean surface

CLEAN+EASY

Professional alcohol-based pre-wax skin cleanser
(Also known as pre-wax lotion) and antiseptic wipes

BEAUTY EXPRESS LTD

Tweezers
(Sterilized) – to remove stray hairs following wax depilation

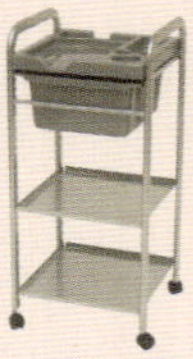
BEAUTY EXPRESS LTD

Trolley
To hold all necessary equipment and materials

GIGI

Disposable paper briefs
Templates are available to create a variety of shapes on hair removal

SHUTTERSTOCK/ SANDRA VAN DER STEEN

Single use synthetic/powder-free disposable gloves
To ensure a high standard of hygiene and reduce the possibility of contamination. These can be worn by the client as well as the beauty therapist if assisting holding the skin taut during hair removal and if applying after-wax lotion

ELLISONS

Disposable wooden spatulas
A selection of differing sizes, for use on different areas

BEAUTY EXPRESS LTD

Towels
(Medium sized) – for draping over the client and providing modesty

ELLISONS

Waste container
Metal bin with a lid – lined with a disposable heavy duty yellow medical bin liner

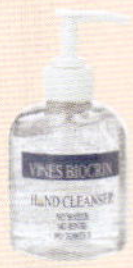
BEAUTY EXPRESS LTD

Hand disinfectant gel
To clean hands before each waxing service

GIGI

Pre-depilation dusting powder
Absorbs the oil and moisture present on the skin's surface, facilitating warm wax removal techniques

GIGI

Pre-epilation oil
Conditions the skin before hot wax application, facilitating hair removal

YOU WILL ALSO NEED:

Skin thermal sensitivity test applicators

Protective plastic couch cover

Protective disposable paper tissue roll

Cotton wool pads For cleaning equipment and the client's skin

Large tissues To blot the skin dry

Cleansing wipes For the client to cleanse the body part to be treated

Wax solvent commercial cleaner Designed for cleaning equipment to remove wax residue

Autoclave To sterilize metal implements (e.g. tweezers and scissors) prior to use

Small scissors (sterilized) or small clippers For trimming long hair

Disinfecting solution In which to immerse all sterile metal tools following sterilization in the autoclave this must be changed regularly as stated in manufacturer's instructions

After-wax lotion With soothing, healing and antiseptic qualities

Disposable apron To protect workwear from spillages and for hygiene

List of contra-indications To discuss with the client prior to service

Aftercare leaflets Recommended advice for the client to refer to following the service

Prepare for intimate waxing services

Sterilization and disinfection

Modesty towels used in the service should be washed at a sufficient temperature setting to avoid contamination and comply with hygiene legislation.

Hands must be washed before and after client service with an antibacterial soap. A hand disinfectant may also then be applied.

Any cuts or abrasions on the hands should be protected with a sterile adhesive dressing.

Hands should then be protected with disposable gloves.

A protective disposable apron should be worn to minimize cross-contamination and protect workwear from spillage.

All metal tools should be sterilized in the autoclave before use and following service, as they are at high risk for infection transfer.

Poor working practice can lead to cross-contamination, the risk of which must be minimized at all times

- Never re-dip the spatula into the wax.
- When using wax pot/spatula technique never sieve hot wax and re-heat!

Disposable waste from intimate waxing will have body fluids on it referred to as clinical waste and potentially a health risk through cross-contamination. It must be disposed of according to the local Environmental Health Regulations. The **Code of Practice for Waxing** recommends the disposal of such waste into a separate closed bin liner with a medical yellow bin liner.

All work surfaces including the couch should be disinfected /protected with fresh coverings following each service.

Arrangements for collection should be made with the council to be disposed of appropriately in accordance with the **Controlled Waste Regulations (1992)**.

Arrangement must be in place to provide every client with comprehensive aftercare advice - which is preferably in written format such as an aftercare leaflet.

HEALTH & SAFETY

Disposal of waste

Waste matter following intimate waxing is contaminated waste. Infections such as viruses can be carried in such waste, for example Hepatitis B and C and HIV. This waste includes hygiene wipes used to cleanse the treatment area before service and disposable panties.

All staff must be trained in the risk of handling such waste and procedures to be followed.

Preparation of the work area

Prepare for intimate waxing service by:

- making sure the couch is clean, having been previously washed with hot soapy water and wiped thoroughly with a disinfectant which is bacterial, fungicidal and virucidal

HEALTH & SAFETY

All metal tools should be sterilized in the autoclave.

HEALTH & SAFETY

Accommodating disabilities

Hydraulic couches are effective as they enable clients with mobility problems easier access onto the couch.

CLEAN+EASY

Wax product formulated for intimate waxing service

BEST PRACTICE

Choice of wax for intimate waxing

The hair to be treated is coarse and terminal in type and the area is sensitive and delicate. You need a wax that will remove hairs efficiently with minimum discomfort. Waxes are available on the market specifically formulated for intimate waxing.

MOOM

Moom 4 Men, depilatory wax designed for male hair removal

- protecting the service couch with a clean, disinfected plastic couch cover
- covering the surface of the plastic couch cover with disposable paper roll
- checking the trolley to ensure that you have all you need before carrying out the service and that it is suitably positioned to prevent unnecessary stretching or walking which will affect the commercial timing and could cause repetitive strain injury
- heating the wax to its optimum temperature for service as guided by the manufacturer's instructions
- checking all electrical safety precautions
- ensuring all metal tools have been sterilized before use
- the service area should be well lit and warm. If the client is cold the hair follicles will constrict, making hair removal more difficult. Ensure ventilation is adequate to remove odours and stale air providing sufficient air movement to keep the air fresh.

Outcome 2: Consult, prepare and plan for waxing service with clients

TOP TIP

After-wax skin care formulation

Choose an after-wax product that conditions and moisturises the skin and removes any residual wax from the body part treated.

Learn how to use consultation techniques to effectively plan and prepare for intimate waxing services by:

1. Using suitable **consultation techniques** in a polite and professional manner to determine the client's service.
2. Ensuring that informed and signed parent or guardian consent is obtained for minors prior to any intimate waxing service.
3. Ensuring that a parent or guardian is present throughout the intimate waxing service for minors.
4. Obtaining signed written informed consent from the client prior to carrying out the service.
5. Asking your client appropriate questions to identify if they have any contra-indications to **waxing service**.
6. Encouraging clients to ask questions to clarify any points.
7. Accurately recording your client's responses to questions.
8. Conducting a patch test correctly on a suitable area of the skin in the groin following the industry Code of Practice for Waxing.
9. Informing the client in a tactful way if there is an adverse reaction to the test patch and the service cannot be carried out.
10. Taking the **necessary action** in response to any identified contra-indications and the client's suitability for **waxing service**.
11. Clearly explaining the possible contra-actions to the client prior to agreeing to the **waxing service**.

"Waxing is a staple service in the salon and one which creates approximately 40 per cent of a salon's turnover, so becoming an expert is essential."

Annette Close

(Continued)
Learn how to use consultation techniques to effectively plan and prepare for intimate waxing services by:

- 12 Ensuring client advice is given without reference to a specific medical condition and without causing undue alarm and concern.
- 13 Agreeing the **waxing services** and outcomes that are acceptable to the client and meets their needs.
- 14 Making sure the **preparation of the client** meets the agreed service plan and the industry Code of Practice for Waxing.

Reception

When the client is booking their service they should be asked whether they have had a wax service before in the salon. It is important to discuss the type of intimate waxing service that is required so that sufficient time is allowed, any necessary skin test is received in advance of the service and the work area can be prepared with appropriate resources. If they have not received the service before, a small area of waxing should be carried out as a skin sensitivity patch test, to ensure that they are not sensitive to the technique or allergic to any of the products to be used, such as pre-wax skin cleanser or after-wax lotion. If this patch test causes an unwanted reaction, a contra-action within 48 hours, then the service must not be undertaken. A patch test should also be performed at **consultation**. A thermal skin sensitivity test should also be used at consultation where two test tubes or similar containers are filled with water, one containing cold water the other warm. Each test tube is held alternately next to the client's skin and they should be able to identify which is cold and which is warm. Failure to do so may mean that the client has defective sensation and may be at risk by being unable to identify if the wax is too hot.

It is advisable before any colour application; a skin sensitivity patch test is carried out. Incompatibilities and/or allergies can occur at any time and for any reason, therefore it is best to be cautious. The manufacturer's instructions will guide you through the recommended test process.

Advise the client not to apply any lotions or oils to the area on the day of their service – these could prevent the adhesion of the wax to the hairs to be removed.

Advise the client to have showered or bathed where possible before arrival for service.

Ask the client to allow at least 1 week, and preferably 2, between any home shaving or other depilatory methods and a salon waxing service.

This will allow the hairs to be a sufficient length for the hairs to be removed effectively and efficiently.

Allow a 3–4 week interval between successive intimate waxing appointments.

Some colours applied to pubic hair last the duration so if required again would be rebooked every 3–4 weeks.

Service time Allow approximately 45 minutes for a female intimate waxing service and up to 60 minutes for a male intimate waxing service. Where all hair is to be removed in the area, 'Hollywood', for both males/females allow 60 minutes.

It is important to complete service in the time allowed in order to be efficient in service application and to ensure that the appointment schedule runs smoothly and clients are not kept waiting.

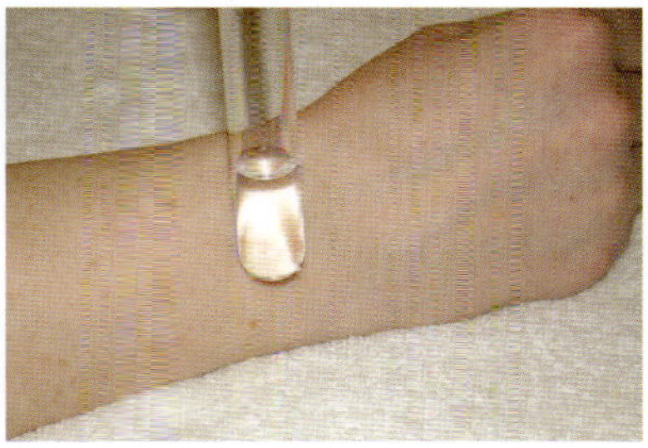

LORRAINE NORDMANN

Thermal skin sensitivity test

> "When pricing your male waxing services, consider a flexible tariff that allows you to pitch your price according to how hairy the client is and how long the service takes you. For example, back and shoulder wax: £20–£30."
>
> **Andy Rouillard**

ALWAYS REMEMBER

Accurately record your client's answers to necessary questions to be asked at consultation on the record card

Record card for providing female and male intimate waxing services

Date	Beauty therapist name	
Client name	Date of birth (Identifying client age group.)	
Home address	Postcode	
Email address	Landline phone number	Mobile phone number
Name of doctor	Doctor's address and phone number	
Related medical history (Conditions that may restrict or prohibit service application.)		
Are you taking any medication? (This may affect the sensitivity, skin healing and skin reaction following service, e.g., Roaccutane used to thin the blood.)		

CONTRA-INDICATIONS REQUIRING MEDICAL REFERRAL
(Preventing **intimate hair removal** service.)

- ☐ bacterial infection (e.g. impetigo, folliculitis)
- ☐ viral infection (e.g. warts/HIV)
- ☐ fungal infection
- ☐ severe skin conditions
- ☐ diabetes
- ☐ severe varicose veins
- ☐ defective circulation
- ☐ blood disorders (e.g. hepatitis B)
- ☐ infestation (e.g. pubic lice)
- ☐ haemorrhoids

TEST CONDUCTED

- ☐ self (temperature test)
- ☐ client skin sensitivity thermal test
- ☐ client skin sensitivity product patch test

WAX PRODUCTS

- ☐ hot wax
- ☐ warm wax – spatula method
- ☐ warm wax – disposable cartridge system
- ☐ strip sugar
- ☐ sugar paste

WORK TECHNIQUES

- ☐ keep the skin taut during application and removal
- ☐ speed of product removal
- ☐ direction and angle of removal
- ☐ ongoing wax product temperature checks

CONTRA-INDICATIONS THAT RESTRICT SERVICE
(Service may require adaptation.)

- ☐ cuts and abrasions
- ☐ bruising and swelling
- ☐ self tan
- ☐ skin disorders
- ☐ heat rash
- ☐ sunburn
- ☐ warts or hairy moles
- ☐ mild eczema/psoriasis
- ☐ skin tag
- ☐ scar tissue
- ☐ thin, fragile skin

WAXING SERVICES

- ☐ Hollywood
- ☐ Brazilian
- ☐ playboy
- ☐ shaping
- ☐ male
- ☐ other ______________________

AFTERCARE ADVICE

- ☐ avoidance of activities which may cause contra-actions
- ☐ future service needs
- ☐ home care
- ☐ personal hygiene

Beauty therapist signature (for reference)
Client signature (confirmation of details)

Record card for providing female and male intimate waxing services (continued)

SERVICE ADVICE
Female intimate waxing service – *allow 45 minutes*
Male intimate waxing service – *allow 60 minutes*
*Waxing timings may differ according to the system used. Always allow slightly longer when using hot wax.

SERVICE PLAN
Record relevant details of your service and advice provided for future reference. Ensure the client's records are up-to-date, accurate and fully completed following service. Non-compliance may invalidate insurance

DURING
- monitor client's reaction to service to confirm suitability
- note any adverse reaction, if any occur and take appropriate action

AFTER
- record results of service
- record any modification to service application that has occurred
- record what products have been used in the wax removal service:
  - aftercare products following service to soothe and care for the skin to reduce redness, irritation and prevent secondary infection
  - skincare products following wax removal service
- provide maintenance advice
- discuss the recommended time intervals between services
- record the effectiveness of service
- record of any samples provided (review their success at the next appointment)

RETAIL OPPORTUNITIES
- advise on products that would be suitable for the client to use at home to care for and maintain the service area and prevent ingrowing hairs (these include body exfoliation and moisturising skincare products)
- recommend further hair removal services
- advise on further products or services that you have recommended that the client may or may not have received before
- note any purchase made by the client

EVALUATION
- record comments on the client's satisfaction with the service
- if poor results are achieved, record the reasons why
- if applicable, note how you may alter the service plan to achieve the required service results in the future

HEALTH AND SAFETY
- advise on how to care for the area following service to avoid an unwanted reaction
- advise on avoidance of any activities, actions or services that may cause irritation and poor skin healing:
  - avoid exposure to UV services to avoid irritation and skin pigmentation
  - avoid perfumed or chemical-based products such as body lotions and self-tan preparations to avoid skin irritation
  - avoid wearing tight-fitting clothing immediately following service
  - stress the importance of maintaining a high standard of personal hygiene in the area
  - avoid touching the treated area to prevent skin infection
- advise on appropriate necessary action to be taken in the event of an unwanted skin reaction

SERVICE MODIFICATION
Examples of waxing service modification include:
- hair removal around contra-indications that restrict service, such as hairy moles and skin tags
- altering the choice of wax to suit skin sensitivity and hair type

HEALTH & SAFETY

Hygiene awareness

As clients may not always be aware if they have contracted a sexually transmitted infection it is essential to implement a high level of hygiene practice with due regard to health and safety at all times to prevent cross-infection and contamination.

"Discuss the importance of home care during the consultation, not at the till; this way you have your client's undivided attention and your advice becomes a natural extension of the service itself. Back it up with written aftercare instructions that you give to the customer at the end of every appointment.

Andy Rouillard

Contra-indications

If the client has any of the following, intimate waxing must not be carried out:

- skin allergy to products and ingredients, e.g. rosin (a resin found in wax), colourant used to colour pubic hair
- skin disorders, such as bruising or recent haemorrhage
- swellings (oedema)
- sunburn
- heat rash
- diabetes
- defective circulation
- folliculitis (infection of the hair follicle)
- recent scar tissue
- loss of skin sensation
- thin and fragile skin – this skin lacks strength and elasticity and tears easily when subject to tissue trauma
- excessive surface veins – these could be made worse.
- keloid scarring – this service could make the condition worse, blood disorders such as hepatitis B and AIDS caused HIV – there may be a risk of cross-infection as the viruses are transmitted by body fluids.
- urinary infections or disease
- external haemorrhoids
- sexually transmitted infections (STI) – although clients may not always be aware if they have contracted a STI
- infestation – such as pubic lice
- medication used to thin the blood, such as Roaccutane
- clients under 16 years of age – it is recommended that intimate waxing is not carried out on clients under 16 years of age, even with parental consent

Certain contra-indications restrict service application. This may mean that the service has to be adapted for the client. For example, in the case of a small localized bruise, the area could be avoided. Contra-indications that restrict service include:

- minor bruise
- skin tag
- hairy mole
- body piercing jewellery

The beauty therapist must not carry out a wax service immediately after a heat service, such as sauna, steam or UV services, as the heat-sensitized tissues may be irritated by the wax service.

If you are unsure if service may commence, tactfully refer the client to their GP for permission to treat. If the service cannot be carried out for any reason, always explain why without naming a contra-indication, as you are not qualified to do so. Clients will respect your professional advice.

Contra-actions

A contra-action is an unwanted reaction which may occur during or following the service. Contra-actions should be discussed with the client at consultation.

All the contra-actions listed below may be caused by incorrect wax removal technique:

- excessive erythema, skin irritation
- excessive swelling
- ingrowing hairs
- skin removal
- burn
- bruising
- blood spots
- abrasions
- broken hair
- allergic/histamine reaction

In the case of an allergic reaction, if it occurs during waxing application, stop the service and remove any remaining product. Apply a cool compress and soothing agent to the area to reduce redness and irritation. Identify the possible cause of the allergic reaction. If symptoms persist, ask the client to seek medical advice.

Always record any contra-actions on the client's record card, with actions taken/recommendations provided and the outcome. In the case of an allergy, the offending product can then be avoided in the future. Try alternative waxing products to assess skin tolerance. In some cases the skin may be too sensitive and intolerant to waxing service.

In cases of extreme skin reaction to service it will be advisable that the client does not receive the service again due to unsuitability.

If burning of the area occured, it would be necessary to record the details in the workplace accident book.

Many contra-actions will be avoided if the correct aftercare is applied and instructions followed by the client.

HEALTH & SAFETY

Contra-actions during hair removal

Avoid over-working an area by repeated wax application and removal. This would be recognized by *excessive skin cell removal* (the skin appears shiny), *excessive erythema, swelling* or *bruising*.

A *burn* should be treated as skin removal. If blisters form they should not be broken – they help prevent the entry of infection into the wound. Medical attention should be sought. If the hairs are too short or the area has not been prepared suitably according to the hair removal technique to be used, this could result in a contra-action and ineffective hair removal.

With experience you will be able to recognize and assess skin tolerance.

Ingrowing hairs may be caused by over-reaction to skin damage. Extra cornified cells are made, which may block the surface of the follicle causing the newly growing hair to turn around and grow inwards.

"Be a 'bossy' beauty therapist. Don't be afraid to move your client into a position that makes your job easier and more comfortable, and get your client to help with stretching the skin if necessary. If it is easier for you, it is going to be easier and more comfortable for your client."

Andy Rouillard

HEALTH & SAFETY

Disposable glove safety

Avoid latex, the traditional material used in glove formulation. Other choices to consider in the case of allergy are nitrile or PVC.

SHUTTERSTOCK/SANDRA VAN DER STEEN

Disposable gloves supplied by manufacturer with wax removal system

HEALTH & SAFETY

Skin allergens

Ingredients such as pine resins and rosin are often excluded in specialist intimate wax formulations to avoid skin sensitivity as they are known allergens.

ALWAYS REMEMBER

Expected service sensation and effect

Explain to the client that the treated skin will appear red and slightly swollen. Small bumps may appear around the hair follicles where the hairs have been removed but this will subside following service. If it does not, the client must continue to apply a soothing after wax preparation that is recommended for purchase following service, which ensures effective skin healing. The client must contact the salon if there is continued redness and irritation.

A small amount of blood may appear due to trauma of the coarse hair being removed from the hair follicle.

Due to the effect of hair removal and increased blood circulation in the area a pinprick effect occurs around the hair follicles.

The beauty therapist should prepare for the intimate waxing service by:

- complying with the industry Code of Practice for Waxing
- collecting the client's record card
- obtaining the client's personal details
- carrying out a client consultation, explaining the service procedure – including expected skin sensations, outcomes and post-service advice

This information includes:

- advice on products that would be suitable for a client to apply at home to soothe and care for their skin to reduce redness and irritation and prevent secondary infection
- contra-action advice and action to be taken in the event of an unwanted skin reaction
- recommendations for further temporary hair removal services
- the recommended time intervals between hair removal services

HEALTH & SAFETY

Insurance

The business must have Public (Third Party) Liability Insurance, including treatment liability and salon owners must have Employers Liability Insurance protecting the employee and client. It is important to check current insurance guidelines for delivery of intimate waxing services for compliance.

Ensure that the client fully understands the importance of carrying out the aftercare advice following service and ask them to sign to confirm this. If they are not willing to sign, do not perform the service.

- Discuss the hair growth cycle with the client. This will help the client to understand that the hairs growing through following hair removal were at different stages of the hair growth cycle and were below the skin's surface at the time of the service. It is also beneficial to support the need for regular intervals between waxing appointments as hairs will be at a similar hair growth pattern.
- Assess the client; question the client and discuss the effect to be achieved.
- Agree on an appropriate intimate waxing procedure.
- Invite the client to ask questions. It is important that they understand fully what the service agreed includes.
- Confirm the client's consent and understanding of the service information by obtaining the client's signature, and signing and dating the record card.

Conduct a patch test on a suitable area of skin in the groin area following the industry Code of Practice for Waxing. If there is a contra-action to the patch test, the client should be tactfully informed of this. Unwanted reactions include erythema, swelling, itching and blisters.

> You can never know too much. I'm still learning after all these years and I love having the opportunity to retrain, learn a new skill or just speak with other industry people. If you have sound knowledge, based on training, experience and personal development, your career will flourish and you will be seen and regarded as an 'expert' in your field.
>
> **Annette Close**

Outcome 3: Remove unwanted hair

Learn how to remove unwanted hair using intimate waxing techniques to meet your client's needs by:

1. Using the correct **pre-wax application** products prior to waxing following manufacturer's instructions.
2. Ensuring the wax is the correct temperature for the client and the area to be treated immediately prior to the intended **waxing service**.
3. Establishing the hair growth pattern prior to the application of the product.
4. Using methods of application correctly and following manufacturer's instructions.
5. Applying and removing the product in the service area according to the requirements of the hair removal method and hair growth pattern.

BEST PRACTICE

Pain threshold

A woman's pain threshold is at its lowest immediately before and during her period. The hormones that stimulate the regrowth of hair are always at their most active during this period. For these two reasons avoid intimate waxing at this time if possible.

TOP TIP

Describe the sensation

Here are some explanatory phrases to explain the service sensation at consultation. 'It's a bit like ripping a plaster off, and taking the hairs with it.' 'It isn't so bad, or so many people wouldn't have it done time and time again!'

ALWAYS REMEMBER

Client records

In accordance with the **Data Protection Act (1998)** confidential information on clients should only be made available to persons to whom consent has been given. All client records should be stored securely and be available to refer to at any time as required.

(Continued) **Learn how to remove unwanted hair using intimate waxing techniques to meet your client's needs by:**

6. Conducting yourself in a professional manner throughout the **waxing service** in line with the industry Code of Practice for Waxing.
7. Correctly removing hazardous waste from your work area throughout the **waxing service**.
8. Providing clear instructions to the client on how and when to support their skin during the **waxing service**.
9. Ensuring your **work techniques** minimize discomfort to the client.
10. Checking the client's well-being throughout the **waxing service** and giving the necessary reassurance.
11. Discontinuing the **waxing service** and providing advice and recommendations for any other relevant service where contra-actions occur.
12. Ensuring the client's service area is left free of product and hair and is treated with a suitable soothing product.
13. Ensuring that the finished result is to the client's satisfaction and meets the agreed service plan.

Preparation of the client

- After an initial consultation, the correct technique for the client's hair removal requirements is identified and agreed with the client. Perform a thermal sensitivity test to ensure that the client will be able to inform you if the wax is too hot.
- Ask the client to inform you if any part of the service becomes too painful to tolerate during service.
- Wash your hands with an antibacterial hand cleanser before handling the client. An antibacterial hand gel may also be applied.
- Wear disposable gloves, taking care on application not to contaminate the inside of the second glove with the first in putting them on.
- Instruct the client to remove clothing and jewellery (where possible) from the area being treated. Where body piercings cannot be removed, the beauty therapist must work carefully around these areas.
- Provide the client with disposable hygiene wipes to cleanse their own intimate areas. Advise the client where these should be disposed of after use. The client should also be advised where they may wash their hands after intimate cleansing.
- Provide the client with disposable paper briefs to wear. These may be a minimal thong with a template attached for ease of shaping procedure (if used).
- Position the client comfortably on the couch and cover with a clean modesty towel. Alternatively, paper roll may be used for this purpose. Modesty and client privacy should be considered at all times during service delivery.
- Question the client further where necessary to check information in relation to the suitability if contra-indications are apparent on further inspection of the area.

HEALTH & SAFETY

Wax and related products usage

All products used in the waxing service should be used in accordance with The Cosmetic Products (Safety) Regulations (2008).

BEST PRACTICE

Professional manner and conduct

Due to the intimate nature of the service being provided it is important to perform your service in a professional efficient manner.

There should also be a procedure for dealing with any inappropriate conduct from a client should it occur. Unsuitable clients can be refused service.

- Cleanse the skin using an appropriate pre-wax skin-cleansing preparation then blot the skin dry.
- If the hair is long in the area, it is advisable to trim the hair using sterilized scissors. Trimming long hair minimizes client discomfort and enables you to observe hair growth directions and possible contra-indications such as skin tags. Discarded hair should be collected on a clean tissue, which is disposed of in the waste bin. The paper tissue should then be replaced before service continues.
- Pre-depilation powder may be applied if recommended with the waxing technique, typically warm wax, soft wax formulations, to absorb body moisture and oil, facilitating wax removal. Alternatively, pre-epilation oil may be applied to condition the skin, again facilitating hair removal for hard wax techniques, i.e. hot wax.

BEST PRACTICE

Communication

During service aim to keep conversation professional and specific to the service in terms of guiding the client in positioning him/themself and supporting the area and confirming the client's tolerance to the service. This will enable you to perform an efficient service

Further intimate waxing styles

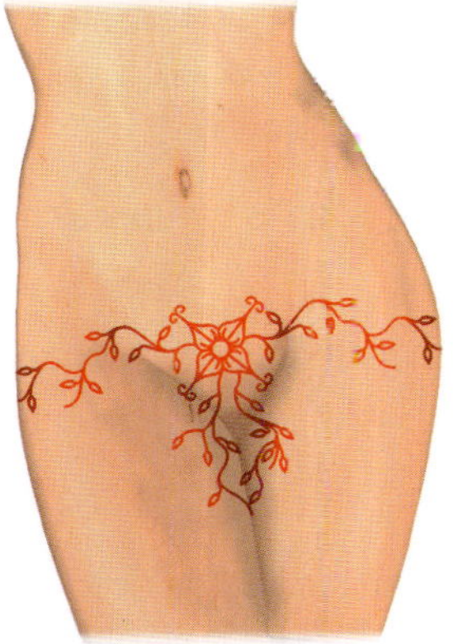

Bollywood: The removal of all hair in the pubic, buttock and anal area is followed by henna decoration of the pubic mound.

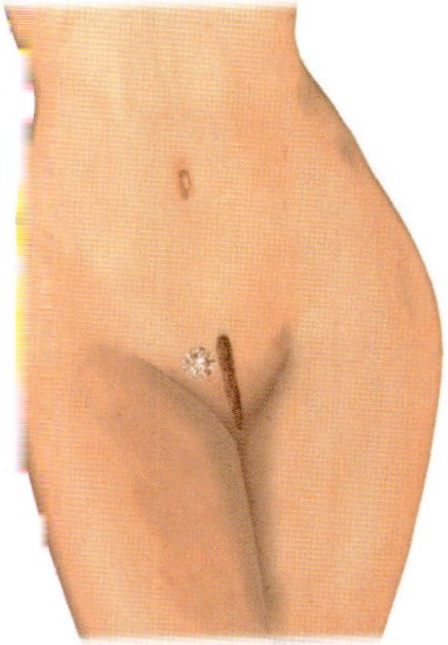

Las Vegas: A Brazilian or Playboy hair removal technique with diamante decoration application.

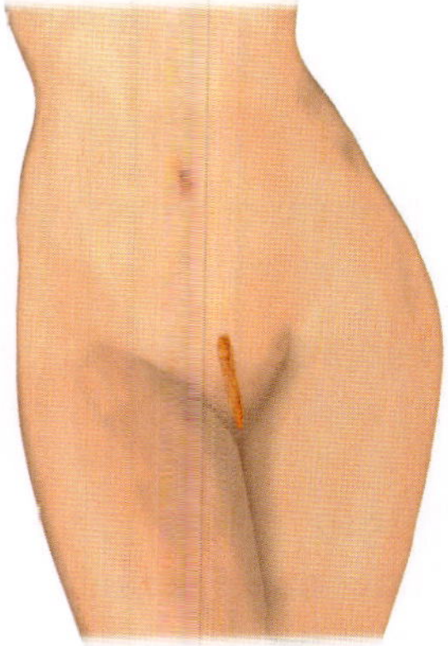

Californian: A Brazilian with the remaining hair coloured.

SIMONE ANDRESS/ISTOCK/THINKSTOCK

Diamantes can be secured to the body part following intimate waxing

Removing unwanted hair

Inform the client of the sensation and expected appearance of the skin following service. Engage your client in conversation during the service, this will help them to relax and provide reassurance and confidence in the service.

Ensure the wax is at the correct working temperature according to manufacturer's instructions. Test temperature on your self and then client, the wax must not be too hot.

Prepare the hair for wax application according to the waxing techniques to be used. These are discussed below.

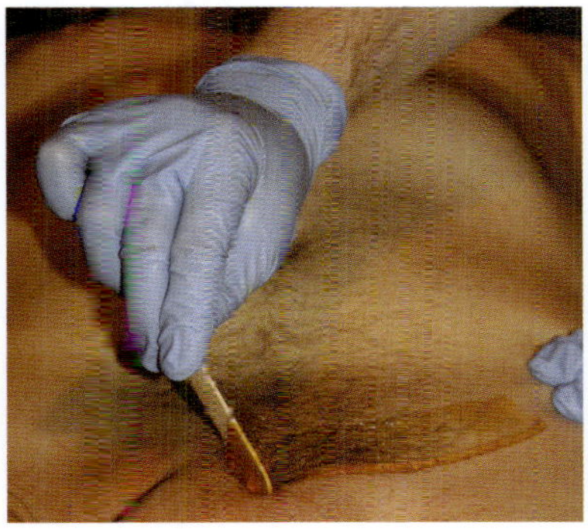

© ANDY ROUILLARD AND JPB-IMAGERY.COM

Hot wax application

Waxing systems

Hot wax

Hot wax technique Hot wax is heated to approximately 50°C until it reaches a thick consistency. It is then applied firmly using a spatula with or against the direction of hair growth, dependent upon the manufacturer's instructions.

When the wax cools, becoming matt in appearance, remove it against hair growth while the wax is still soft and pliable.

Formulation Hot waxes tend to be a blend of waxes and resins so that they stay reasonably flexible when cool.

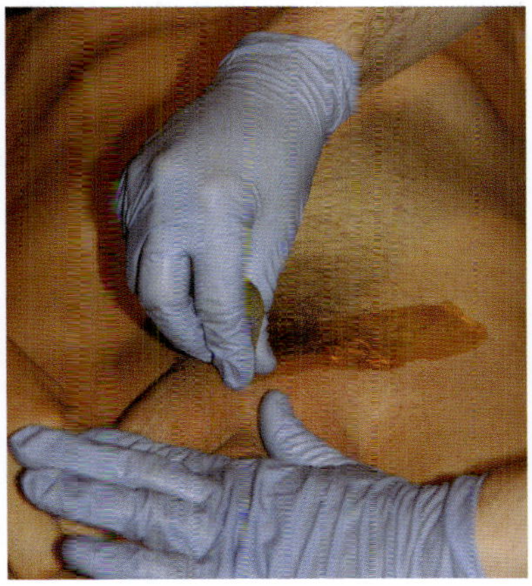

© ANDY ROUILLARD AND JPB-IMAGERY.COM

Hot wax removal

TOP TIP

Disposable applicator technique, warm wax, sugar techniques:

- apply product with the direction of hair growth
- remove product against the direction of hair growth

TOP TIP

Hot wax technique:

- apply with/against the direction of hair growth (follow manufacturers instructions)
- remove against the direction of hair growth
- the layer must have even borders and be thick enough to effectively grip the hairs in the area as it contracts. This thickness will also reduce discomfort on removal. Too thin and the hair will not be effectively removed and a layer of wax may remain on the skin which is difficult to remove.

Beeswax is a desirable ingredient often comprising 25–60 per cent of the finished product. The beeswax sets and grips the hair; the addition of resin keeps the wax pliable on removal.

Hair preparation Pre-depilation talc or pre-depilation oil may be applied to the body part to facilitate wax removal. Choice will be dependent upon the hot wax system used.

Warm wax

Spatula technique Warm wax is heated to a runny consistency of 43°C. A disposable spatula is used to apply the wax in the direction of hair growth. A bonded fibre strip is used to remove the wax, against the hair growth.

Disposable applicator head technique *Roller head* and *flat applicator head* techniques are hygienic warm wax systems using disposable applicator heads. A disposable applicator head screws onto the wax applicator tube/cartridge in place of the cap for each client. This reduces the risk of contamination through cross-infection. The tubes/cartridges of wax vary in size, as does the applicator head to treat the different body areas. Each tube/cartridge of wax is heated to working temperature. A thin film of wax is applied in the direction of hair growth. A strip is used to remove the wax against hair growth.

Formulation Warm waxes are frequently made from mixtures of glucose syrup, resins and zinc oxide.

Hair preparation Pre-depilation talc is applied to absorb body moisture and oil, facilitating wax removal.

Sugar paste

Sugar paste technique Sugar paste is applied to the hair with the hands in the direction of hair growth. The hairs embed in the wax, which is then removed swiftly against hair growth.

Formulation Sugar wax has pure sugar as the main ingredient, plus other natural ingredients such as lemon.

Hair preparation Pre-depilation powder is applied to absorb body moisture and oil, facilitating wax removal.

Step-by-step: Female intimate brazilian waxing service (hot wax)

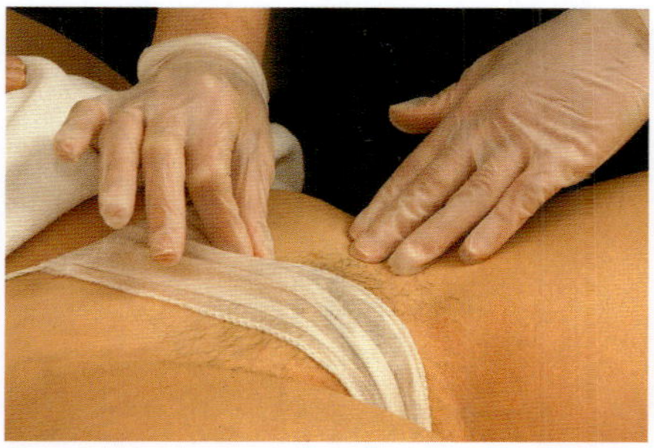

1 Evaluate the hair length. If the hair is so long that it curls, it should be trimmed to 12.7 mm using scissors or a clipper.

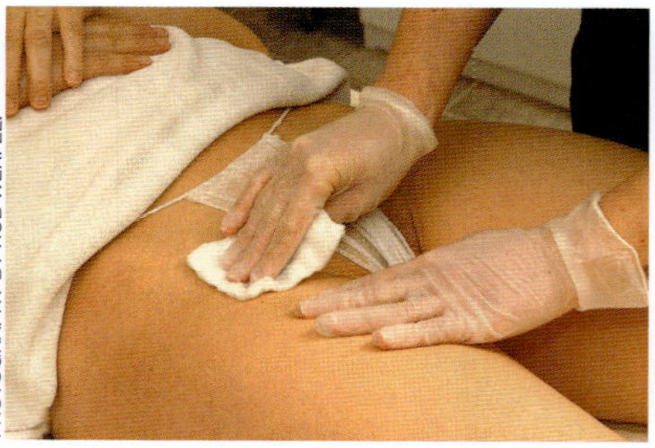

2 Cleanse the upper leg and the bikini area with an antiseptic cleaner, and pat dry.

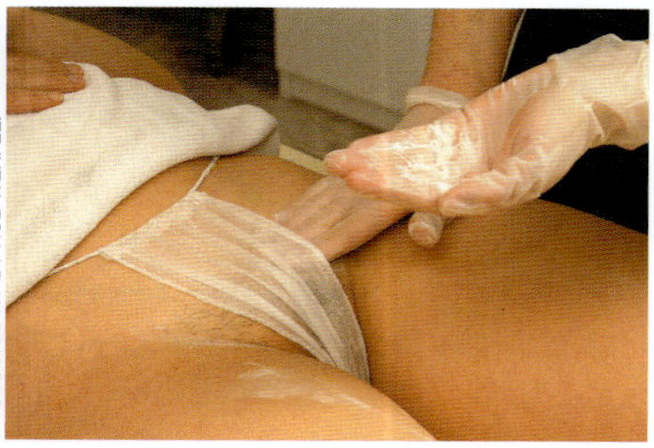

3 Dust the area with powder. Offer the client gloves. This will ensure non-contamination of the area if the client is assisting holding the skin taut during hair removal.

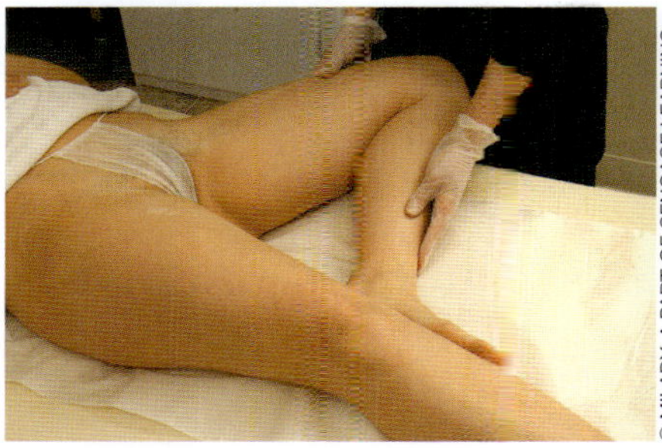

4 Have the client leave one leg straight and bring the sole of the other foot to the level of the knee. Test the wax on a small area to ensure that the temperature is suitable for application. This should be checked throughout the service.

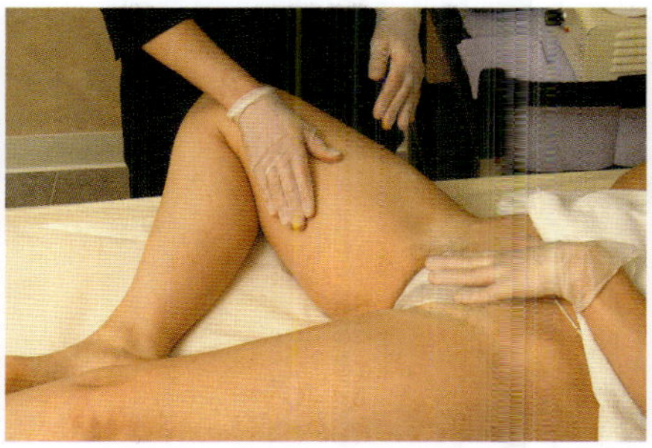

5 Starting first on the right side of the client's bikini area, have the client place the left hand firmly on the skin, stretching with fingers straight downwards. Check client well-being and reassure throughout.

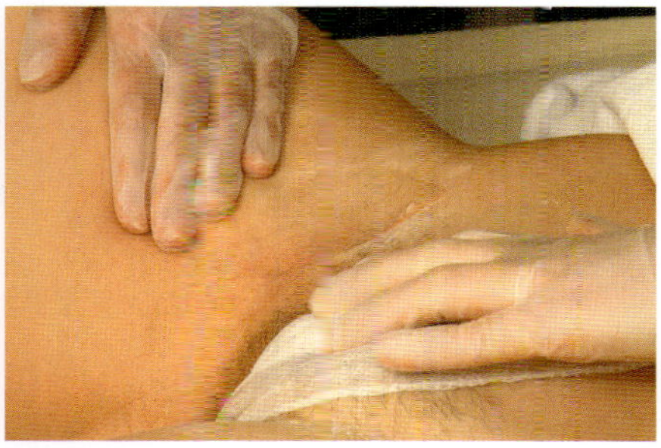

6 Have the client place her free hand on the outer edge of the thigh to help pull the skin taut. This avoids potential legal implications of unnecessary contact with sexual areas.

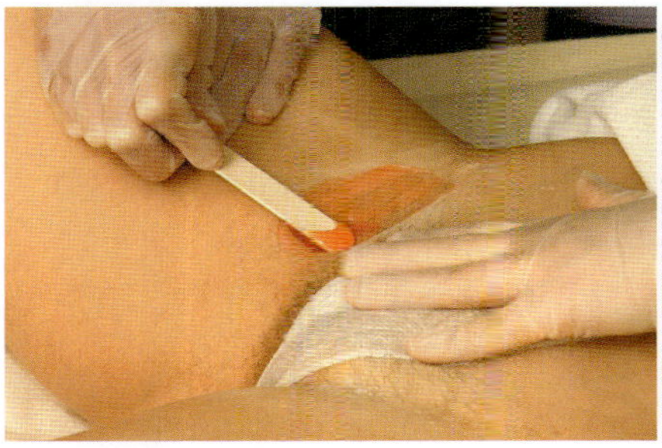

7 Working on the bent leg, apply the wax with the edge of a spatula in the direction of hair growth. The first application should be to the section farthest away from the bikini line and only up to the femoral ridge (an anatomical area as shown), following the downward direction of hair growth. Dispose of each spatula applicator after you have used it

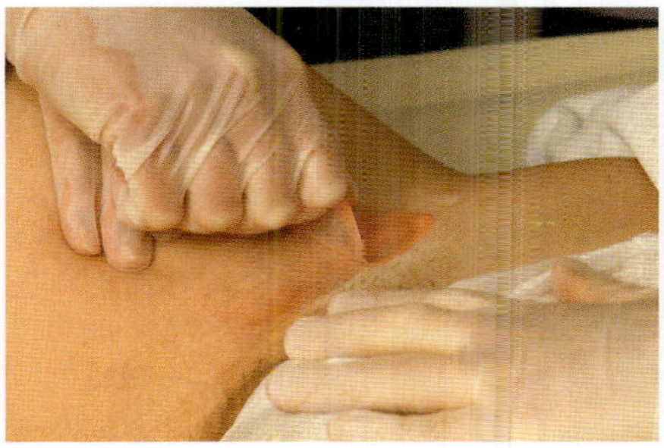

8 As soon as the wax has set, flick the free edge to loosen it. Grasp the free edge with one hand and stretch the skin taut with your free hand. Remove the wax backwards in a swift, continuous manner, as close to the skin as possible.

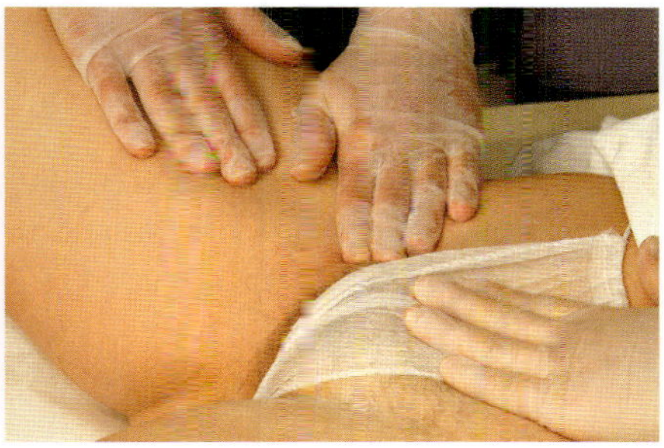

9 Apply immediate, firm pressure to alleviate the discomfort. Repeat the process, working towards the bikini line

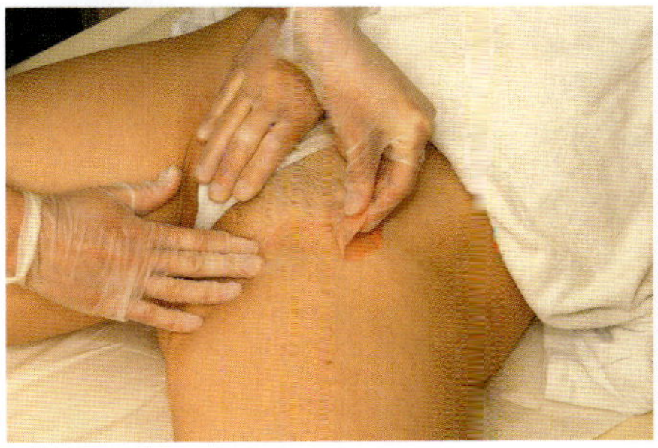

10 Repeat on the left side of the client's bikini line. Move to the hair that grows down from the femoral ridge.

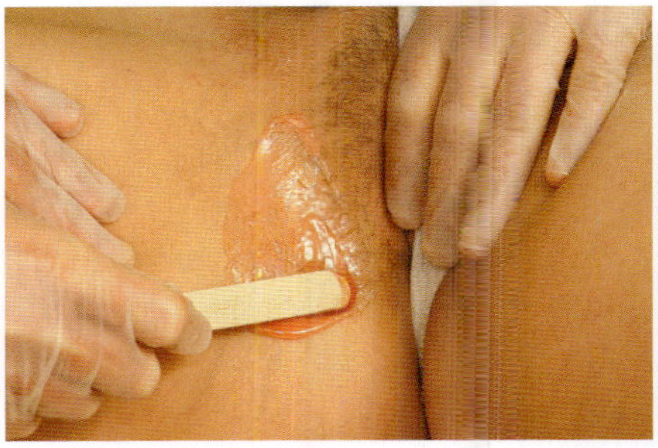

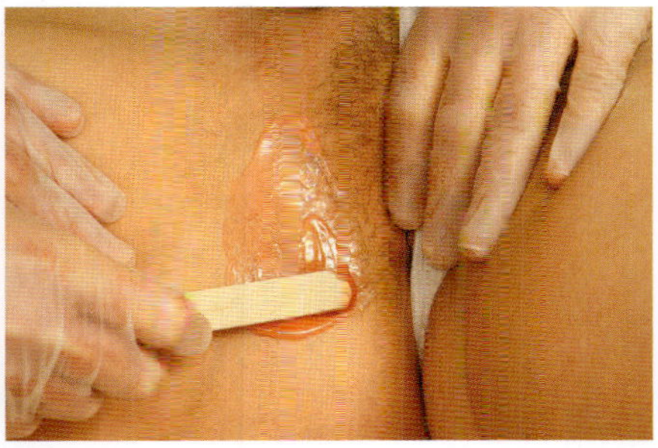

11 Apply wax two-thirds of the way down in the downward direction of hair growth, leaving enough space at the bottom to place your client's hand to hold the skin taut. Allow the wax to set. Take hold at the free edge, using the other hand to hold skin taut. Remove hair and follow by quickly placing your hand firmly on the area for relief.

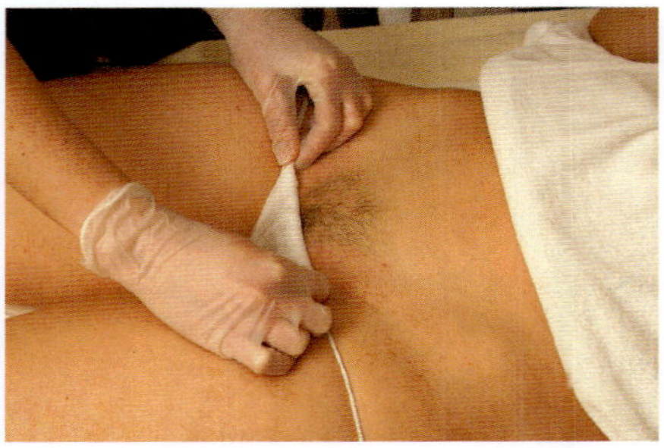

12 Move to the pubis and remove hair. Apply wax in direction of growth in 25.4 by 76.2 mm segments.

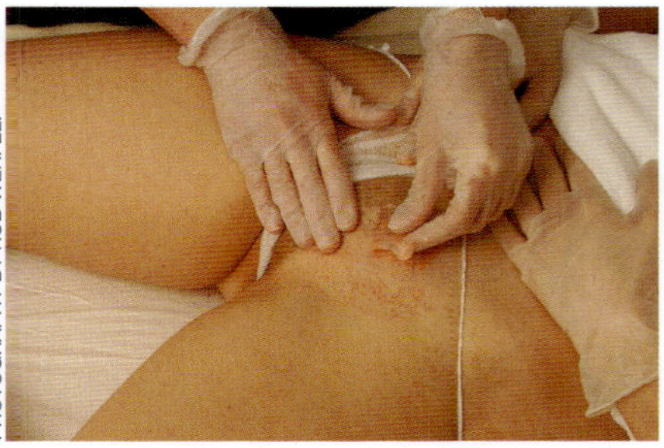

13 Allow wax to set and remove it, followed by pressure. Repeat this process across the pubis until you have removed all hair.

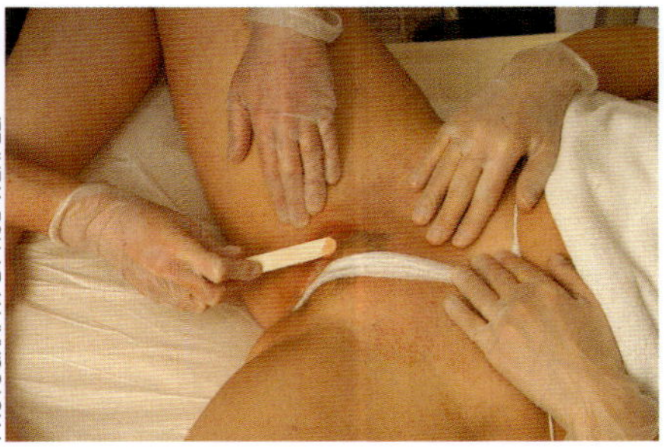

14 For removing the hair on the labia, apply the wax in the direction of growth in a 1- by 76.2 mm section. Allow the wax to set and remove it in an upward, not outward pattern.

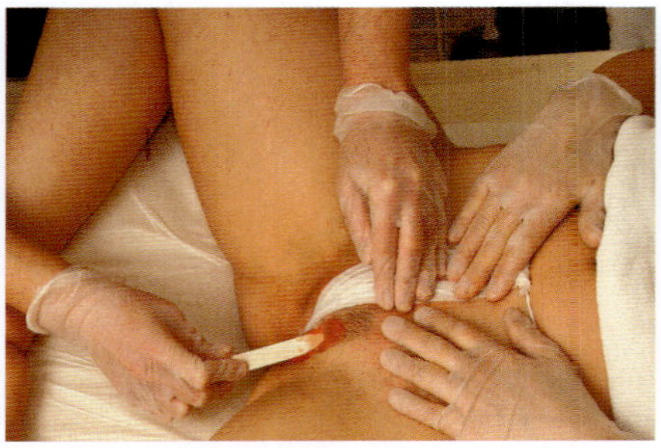

15 Repeat until you have removed all hair on both sides of the labia, working in small sections to minimize client discomfort.

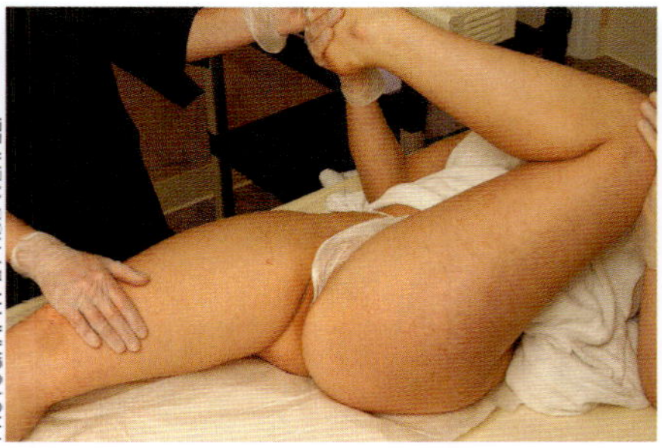

16 Have the client lift one leg toward her chest, grasping the ankle with the opposite hand and drawing the leg across the body. This should expose the last remaining third of the hair that was too near the labia to apply the wax. This position also ensures that the skin is very taut.

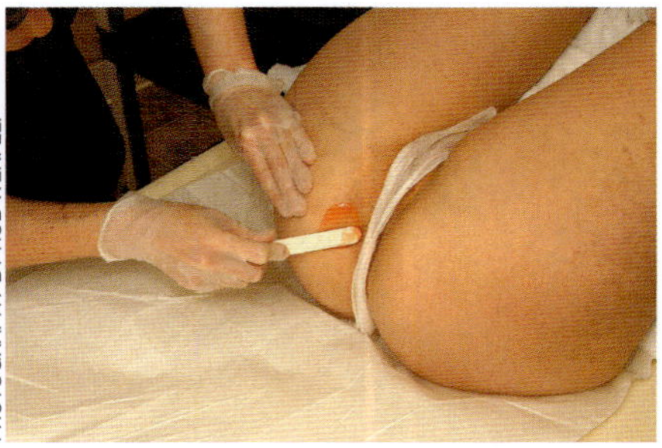

17 Apply the wax downward as before, with the pull upward.

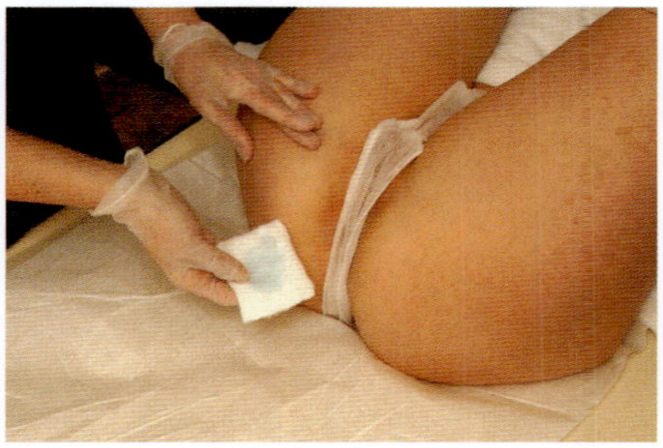

18 Use soothing antiseptic after wax lotion on the entire area that has been waxed.

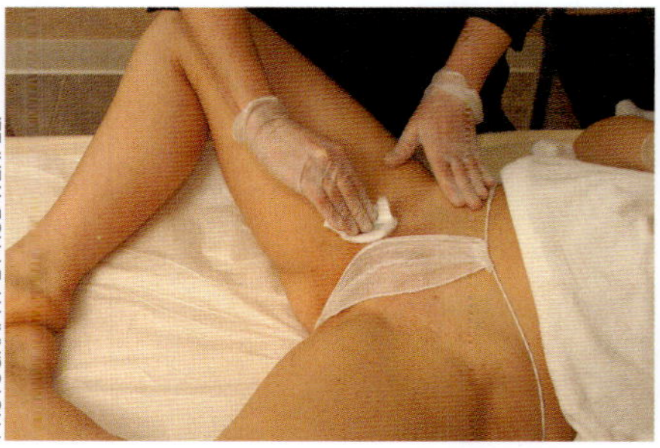

19 Remove any traces of excess wax from the area that has been waxed.

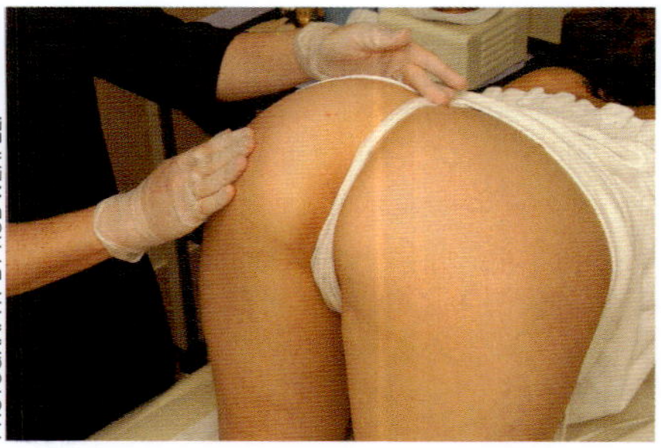

20 Have the client turn over into a kneeling position with one forearm resting on the couch in front of her. Disinfect the area and apply powder.

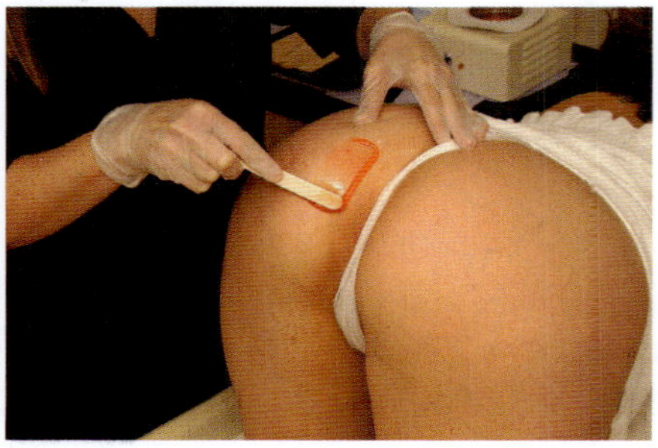

21 Start at the rear of the buttocks, apply the wax in 25.4-by 76.2 mm strips in the direction of hair growth towards the anus, enlisting the client's assistance to make the area available to wax. Allow the wax to set and then remove against growth. Apply pressure. Repeat until all hair is removed.

ALWAYS REMEMBER

When removing wax use the non-working hand to stretch the skin to minimize discomfort, or ask the client to support the area as required. It is best practise if the client wears gloves to maintain hygienic working practice if assisting.

Check client well-being and reassure throughout.

Success of removal required effective stretching and manipulation of the skin in the area during application and removal and speed of application and removal technique.

Stray and very short hairs may be removed using a pair of sterilized tweezers.

An after-wax lotion should be applied following the service using clean cotton wool. This breaks down any wax residue, helps to guard against infection and irritation and reduces discomfort in the area. For more intimate areas that have been treated you may request the client applies the after-wax product to these parts themself ensuring that their hands are clean before application. They should also be advised where to dispose of the waste.

Ensure that the finished result is to the client's satisfaction and that the results meet the agreed service plan.

TOP TIP

Soothing product application

Before application of a soothing product, the area treated should be checked thoroughly to make sure that it is product and hair free.

TOP TIP

Hair growth pattern

If there are different hair growth patterns in the area, apply smaller sections of wax to these areas to ensure effective application and removal technique. This will also avoid contra-actions including skin damage caused by bruising or hair breakage leading to early re-appearance of hair growth and ingrowing hairs.

ALWAYS REMEMBER

During hair removal

- ensure wax is comfortable for the client, ask the client
- observe client body language; this will indicate their 'pain threshold and tolerance to the service being provided.
- assess the client's skin reaction to the service
- reassure the client
- keep communication professional at all times to avoid misinterpretation

Step-by-step: Male intimate full Brazilian waxing (hot wax)

Clear instructions must be provided throughout the service to guide the client on how and when to hold and stretch skin to minimize discomfort. Follow Steps 1–3 as for female intimate waxing on page 530.

Apply and remove wax according to the waxing technique used and hair growth pattern.

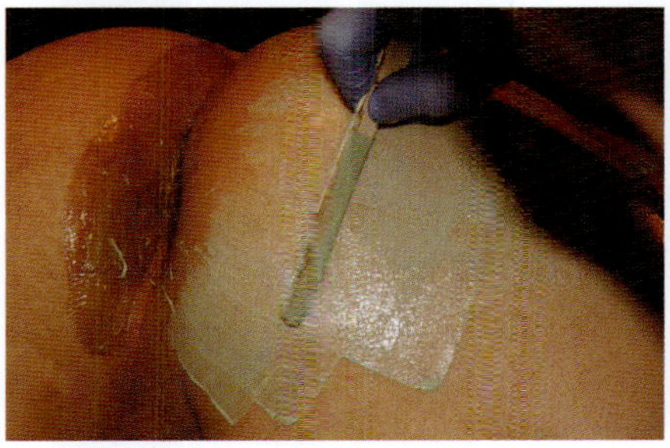

ANDY ROUILLARD AND JPB-IMAGERY.COM

1 Position the client on his knees, leaning forward supporting himself on one hand while the other hand supports the genitals. Test the wax on a small area to assess temperature is suitable for application. Apply and remove wax from the buttocks and anal area if required. Warm wax may be used shown to remove hair from the buttock area, while hot wax is preferred for coarser hair nearer the anal area.

2 With the client in the same position, apply and remove wax to the back of the scrotum while the client holds the genitals forwards.

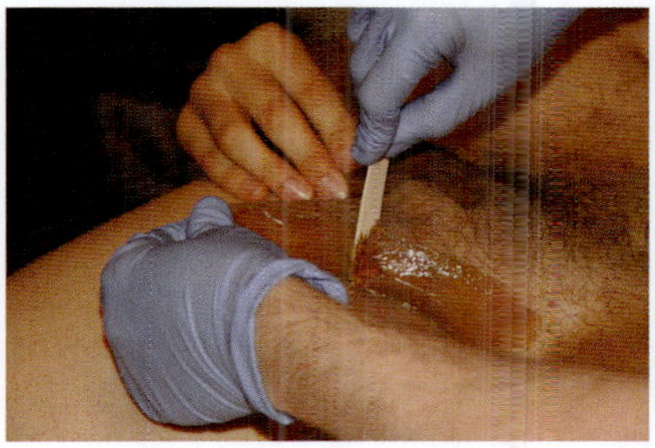

ANDY ROUILLARD AND JPB-IMAGERY.COM

3 Position the client lying on his back with his legs abducted (opened) at the knees. Apply and remove wax to the front and sides of the scrotum. the client should be asked to hold ther genitals away from the area.

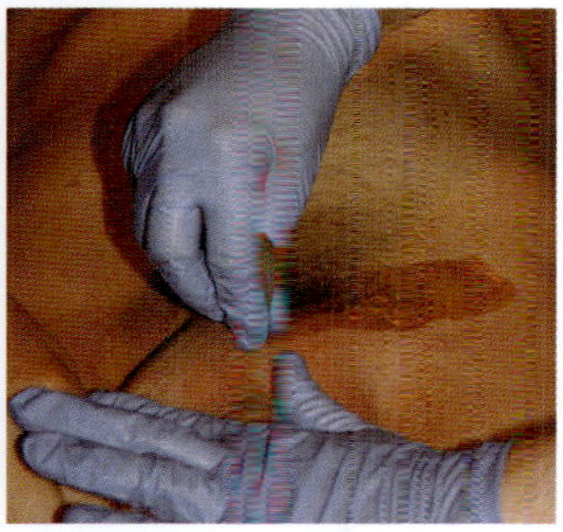

©ANDY ROUILLARD AND JPB-IMAGERY.COM

4 With the client holding his genitalia, apply and remove remaining hair from the area. stray and very short hairs may be removed using a pair of sterilized tweezers.

5 An after wax lotion should be applied following service using clean cotton wool. For more intimate areas request the client applies the after wax product to these parts themselves. Gloves should be worn by the client to prevent secondary infection by contamination. Ensure that the finished result is to the client's satisfaction and meets the agreed service plan.

HEALTH & SAFETY

Spot bleeding

If spot bleeding occurs during service, remove blood immediately with an antiseptic wipe avoiding cross-contamination. The contaminated waste should be disposed of correctly. Aftercare products and instructions should be provided to prevent secondary infection.

Outcome 4: Provide aftercare advice

Learn how to provide aftercare advice which supports and meets the needs of your client by:

1. Giving **advice** and recommendations accurately and constructively.
2. Giving your clients suitable **advice** specific to their individual needs.

TOP TIP

Ingrowing hair prevention

Products have been formulated to apply to the skin following wax depilation to slow hair re-growth. The product when entering the empty hair follicle aims to weaken the cells of matrix, slowing cell division in this area which is responsible for creating the new hair. These are available for your client to purchase as a retail product.

GIGI

Aftercare advice

Inform the client following the service that they may experience signs of skin irritation such as redness, dryness and itching. This will vary according to the service application technique applied and the skin type treated. Soothing, antiseptic after-wax skincare preparations should be recommended and the client must avoid scratching the skin.

If a contra-action occurs, recommend that the client contact the salon immediately to receive appropriate professional advice. Reinforce the contra-action advice provided at the consultation.

The client should:

- avoid UV exposure for up to 7 days following service, as the skin is more susceptible to sun damage
- wear a UV sunblock on exposure of the service area to sunlight at all times
- use recommended retail products to care for the skin at home, to soothe and promote skin healing and prevent ingrowing hairs
- avoid perfume and chemical-based preparations such as deodorants and self-tan for 24 hours to avoid skin irritation and sensitization
- friction with the area should be avoided following service; this includes restrictive tight-fitting clothing
- all skincare preparations should be applied with clean hands and clean cotton wool
- avoid touching the area with unclean hands
- personal hygiene, including toilet hygiene, is important to prevent secondary infection of the service area – recommend the area is bathed regularly with clean, lukewarm unperfumed water
- heat services, avoid hot baths/showers, swimming and exercise should be avoided for 24 hours following service
- following verbal instructions, provide the client with an aftercare leaflet that states all necessary after instruction following intimate waxing procedure
- all clients should be recommended to exfoliate once to twice per week to avoid ingrowing hairs or recommend the use of a specialised retail product for this purpose as shown
- ensure that the client records are up-to-date, accurate and complete

"Waxing is an area where the sale of home-care items is often overlooked, and yet it provides a number of unique retail opportunities and benefits. Many clients will not know what or where to buy suitable products outside of the salon, so don't leave them guessing. Offer customers the convenience of a one-stop shopping service by stocking up on post-wax essentials such as soothing gels or creams, antibacterial skinwash, exfoliating mitts, body scrubs and lotions.

Andy Rouillard

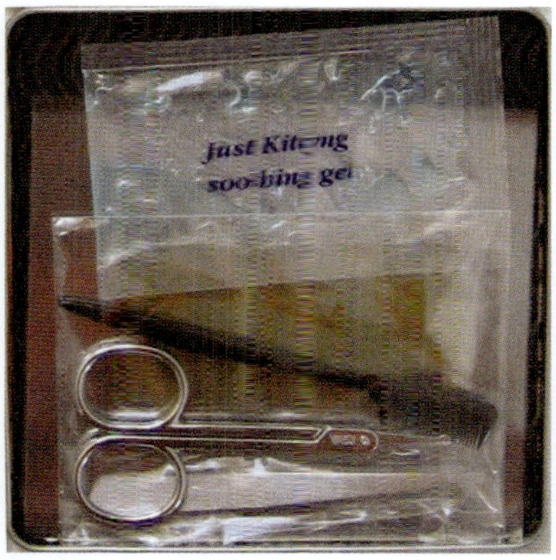

JUST KITTYNG WWW.JUSTKITTYNG.COM

Retail bikini art kits for self-maintenance

Appointment .... Date

....

....

....

....

....

....

....

AUSTRALIAN BODYCARE

Product suppliers supporting waxing aftercare literature

Waxing aftercare information

It is essential to take special care of your skin after your wax treatment.

Please read the guidelines below and remember to contact your therapist if you experience any persistent redness or irritation.

Legs, Arms, Bikini Area, Backs, Chests:
We recommend Australian Bodycare Antiseptic Hand & Body Lotion. Use daily to keep skin smooth and healthy and prevent ingrown hairs.

Facial:
Use Australian Bodycare Active Face Cream to calm and protect the delicate skin on the face.

Underarm:
Use Australian Bodycare alcohol & aluminium free Deodorant. Non stinging and gentle for everyday use.

For the next 24 - 48 hours please avoid the following:

Sunbathing - natural & artificial, friction from tight clothing, swimming, hot baths or showers, highly perfumed soaps and body lotions and scratching the waxed area.

To ensure your skin is kept in optimum health use Australian Bodycare Skin Wash.

Have you booked your next appointment ....

AUSTRALIAN BODYCARE

TOP TIP

Retail sales

Preparations that can be applied to the skin to ensure the skin heals without infection should be recommended. Some products aim to reduce the possibility of ingrowing hairs and slow future hair growth containing ingredients such as Alpha Hydroxy Acids (AHA).

GIGI

Soothing cream

Their benefit should be reinforced to the client at the consultation stage and when providing the aftercare advice.

ASSESSMENT OF KNOWLEDGE AND UNDERSTANDING

FUNCTIONAL SKILLS

Having covered the learning objectives for **Provide female intimate waxing services** and **Provide male intimate waxing services** – test what you need to know and understand by answering the following short questions below.

The information covers:

- organizational and legal requirements
- how to work safely and effectively when providing waxing services
- consult, plan and prepare for services with clients
- anatomy and physiology
- contra-indications and contra-actions
- equipment and materials
- service-specific knowledge
- aftercare advice for clients

Organizational and legal requirements

1 What is the purpose of the Code of Practice for Waxing? Why is it important to follow its provisions?

2 State the main health and safety legislation that should be followed in relation to intimate waxing service.

3 What is clinical waste and how should it be disposed of?

4 Name **five** actions to take that will minimize cross-infection when performing intimate waxing services.

5 Why is it important to keep accurate records of all services provided?

6 How long would you allow commercially to complete a male and female intimate waxing service?

How to work safely and effectively when providing waxing services

1 In compliance with your responsibilities under health and safety legislation, what personal protective equipment should be worn? Which piece of health and safety legislation does this come under?

2 How can you minimize the risk of acquiring the skin condition *contact dermatitis* when performing intimate waxing services?

3 Give **three** examples of when both sterilization and disinfection methods are used to comply with hygiene regulations when performing an intimate waxing service.

4 What are the necessary environmental conditions required for intimate waxing? Consider lighting, heating and ventilation in your answer.

5 How can cross-infection be prevented when carrying out intimate waxing service. Provide **three** examples.

6 Poor posture could lead to muscle fatigue, poor removal techniques and repetitive strain injury. Explain how you can avoid personal injury by positioning equipment, materials and the client for the service.

Consult, plan and prepare for services with clients

1 How can a professional rapport be maintained with your client throughout an intimate waxing service?

2 Why would you refer to the menstrual cycle when performing a waxing service on a female client?

3 What is a skin sensitivity patch test and a skin sensitivity thermal test? When and why would you perform each?

4 How should the area to be treated for wax depilation be prepared to ensure effective hair removal? What other products can be applied to facilitate hair removal?

5 Why is it necessary to explain contra-actions that may occur with the client at the consultation?

6 It is necessary to consider the direction of hair growth for the waxing hair removal technique chosen. Why is this?

Contra-indications and contra-actions

1 What would be **three** undesirable post-service skin reactions? How would these be avoided?

2 What contra-indications restrict service, meaning that the service may proceed, but the area contra-indicated must be avoided?

3 What contra-indications identified at consultation would require medical referral?

4 When observing the area for hair removal you identify what you think to be a contra-indication requiring referral. What action would you take?

5 Why is diabetes normally regarded initially as a contra-indication to waxing service?

Equipment and materials

1 Certain ingredients may cause an allergic reaction; therefore it is important that you know what the product contains. What are the main ingredients in:
- sugar paste?
- hot wax?

2 What is the purpose of pre-wax lotion when used in a waxing service?

3 What should be applied to the skin following wax depilation? What action does this product have on the treated area?

4 When and why might you apply powder to the skin in a waxing service?

Service-specific knowledge

1 Explain **three** other temporary methods of hair removal and **three** permanent methods of hair removal. If a client had received these services previously how would this affect the service plan for waxing?

2 How should the skin be supported during the intimate waxing service by the beauty therapist and the client avoiding inappropriate contact?

3 What is the expected skin reaction to intimate waxing service that should be explained to the client at the consultation.

4 What additional precautions should be taken to ensure that the wax is used at a comfortable temperature for the client?

5 What action would you take if the client's actions were inappropriate to the context of the service?

6 Describe how you would explain the following intimate waxing services to a female client:
- Hollywood
- Brazilian
- shaping

Male client:
- lower back, buttocks, scrotum and penis.

Aftercare advice for clients

1 What is the recommended interval between intimate waxing services?

2 What home-care products could you recommend for your client to use at home?

3 What personal hygiene instructions be followed by the client following intimate waxing service?

4 What advice can you give to your client to prevent ingrowing hairs occurring following service?

5 What aftercare instructions should be given to your client following intimate waxing service?

ISTOCK© INGA IVANOVA

17 Single eyelash extensions

Learning Objectives

This chapter covers the **Provide single eyelash extension services** unit.

This unit is all about how to provide the service single eyelash extensions to enhance the appearance of the natural eyelashes artificially increasing length, thickness and curvature while maintaining a natural or glamorous look dependent upon the requirements of the client. Relevant health and safety and hygiene practice must be effectively implemented throughout the service.

There are **five** learning outcomes which you must achieve competently:

1 **Maintain safe and effective methods of working when providing single eyelash extension services.**

2 **Consult, plan and prepare for the service with clients.**

3 **Attach single eyelash systems.**

4 **Maintain and remove single lash systems.**

5 **Provide aftercare advice.**

For each unit your assessor will observe you on at least **three separate occasions** each involving different clients, which must include **a full set of single lash extensions** and **a partial set of single lash extensions**.

From the **range** statements, you must show that you have:

- used all **consultation techniques**
- dealt with at least **one** of the **necessary actions** where a contra-action, contra-indication or service modification occurs
- provided all types of relevant aftercare **advice**

(continued on the next page)

SHAVATNA SINGH

ROLE MODEL

Shavata Singh

Brand Director, Shavata UK (encompassing Shavata Brow Studio and Lash Lounge by Shavata)

"I have been in the beauty industry for over 20 years. A passion for eyebrows and eyelashes is one of the reasons I founded my first Brow Studio at the Urban Retreat, Harrods, followed by Lash Lounge by Shavata (available at Debenhams, Harvey Nichols and House of Fraser). These studios are my perfect solution for men and women who need a quick, efficient, effective service that takes just minutes and can transform your look. Shavata Brow Studios and Lash Lounges are now available in selected locations across the UK to help meet the demands of our clients.

I have also developed my own range of fabulous products, which can help you to create the perfect brow or lash in between your studio appointments.

(continued)

However, you must prove that you have the necessary knowledge, understanding and skills to be able to perform competently across the range.

When providing single eyelash extension services it is important to use the skills you have learnt in the following chapters:

Monitoring safe work operations

Promotional activities

Essential anatomy and physiology knowledge requirements for single eyelash extensions are identified on the checklist Chapter 2 pages 12 and 13. In addition it is necessary to have an understanding of the basic structure and function of the eye. This is discussed in **Chapter 2, Anatomy and physiology,** pages 36–38.

Introduction

Single lash extensions

Formed from synthetic fibre polyester material to resemble natural lash hair, single eyelash extensions are bonded to the natural lashes using a strong adhesive (usually cyanoacrylate), which sets rapidly and can be harmful if in contact with the skin. As the client loses their natural lash, after approximately 60 days, they will also lose the artificial lash. From 30–70 **single lashes** are applied to the eyelashes, which can take up to 2 hours. This requires the client to have their eyes closed continuously during this period. Single lash extensions can be worn from 3 to 8 weeks, depending upon the cyclic nature of the natural hairs; the natural functioning of the eyes – single lashes applied to clients who have oily eyes will not be as durable as the oil weakens the adhesive; and the lifestyle and aftercare procedures followed by the client following application. To keep them looking their best it is necessary to have a maintenance service every 3 weeks, where lost lashes are replaced.

ALWAYS REMEMBER

Lash thickness

The upper lashes are thicker and more numerous than those of the lower lashes. The quantity and type of lash hair will be different for each client and will influence your choice of artificial lash and application.

Anatomy and physiology

For more information about the anatomy and physiology of the eye, see Chapter 2, pages 36–38.

Eyelashes are short, coarse, terminal hairs situated on the outer portion of the eyelid in rows of three to five. The eyelash hair protects the eyes from bright light, dust and debris. There are up to 150 lashes on the upper lid and 80 on the lower eyelid. They are between 7–9 mm in length.

TOP TIP

Maintenance service

This will be influenced by client lifestyle. If the client takes part in active exercise, swims or receives heat services the lashes may not be as durable.

Vision can be affected following single lash extensions

Thickening of the cornea can occur as a result of swelling behind the cornea. This is if the eyes are closed for long periods. Once the eyes re-open the cornea reduces its thickness as swelling reduces, restoring normal vision.

Over-stimulation of the meibomian gland, the sebaceous glands found on the eyelash line. This could occur due to incorrect choice of lash length, thickness and wearing of the single lash extensions for long periods.

Outcome 1: Maintain safe and effective methods of working when providing single eyelash extension services

Learn how to maintain safe and effective methods of working when providing single eyelash extension services by:

1. Setting up the work area to meet legal, hygiene and service requirements.
2. Making sure that environmental conditions are suitable for the client and the service.
3. Ensuring your personal hygiene, protection and appearance meets accepted industry and organizational requirements.
4. Ensuring all tools and equipments are cleaned using the correct methods.
5. Effectively disinfecting your hands prior to extending eyelashes.
6. Maintaining accepted industry hygiene and safety practices throughout the service.
7. Positioning equipment and materials for ease and safety of use.
8. Ensuring your own posture and position minimizes fatigue and the risk of injury while working.
9. Maintaining the client's modesty and privacy at all times.
10. Disposing of waste materials safely and correctly.
11. Ensuring that the service is cost-effective and is carried out within a commercially viable time.
12. Leaving the work area in a condition suitable for further services.
13. Ensuring the client's records are up-to-date, accurate, easy to read and signed by the client and practitioner.

Before beginning the single lash system application, check that you have the necessary equipment and materials to hand to meet legal, hygiene and industry requirements for eye services.

EQUIPMENT AND MATERIALS LIST

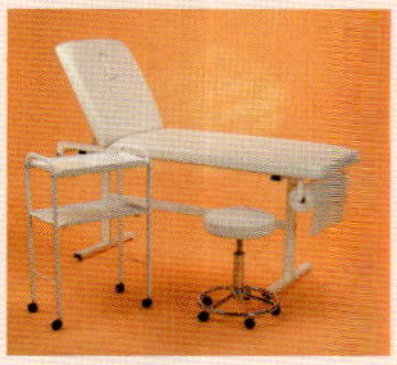
BEAUTY EXPRESS

Couch or beauty chair
With sit-up and lie-down positions and an easy to clean surface

Trolley on which to display everything

ELLISONS

Headband bonnet (disposable)
Clean, to keep hair away from the service area and the beauty therapist from direct contact

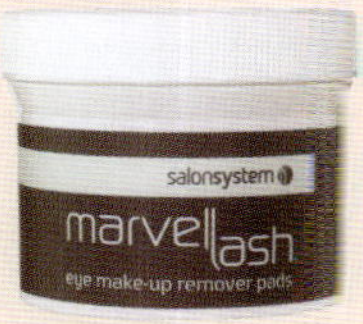

BEAUTY EXPRESS

Eye make-up remover (non-oily formulation)
To remove cosmetics from the eye area and general skin debris and natural oils from the area

BEAUTY EXPRESS

Facial tissues (white)
For blotting the eyelashes dry and collecting any moisture from the eye area during application

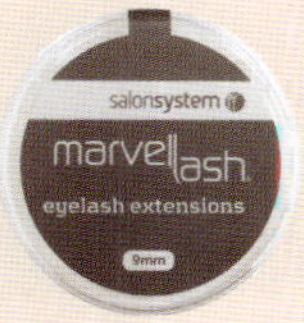

BEAUTY EXPRESS

Single synthetic lash extensions
In a variety of lengths, thicknesses, curvatures and colours (as available from you manufacturer)

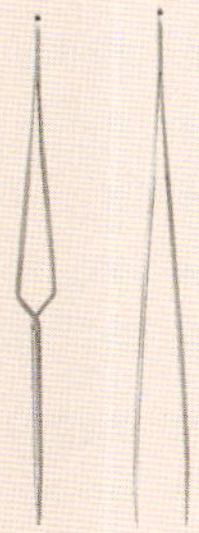
BEAUTY EXPRESS

Sterilized tweezers
Of long pointed design to enable single lash hairs to be isolated during application and precision application. Two pairs are required for each service. Several pairs are required to allow for sterilization after use

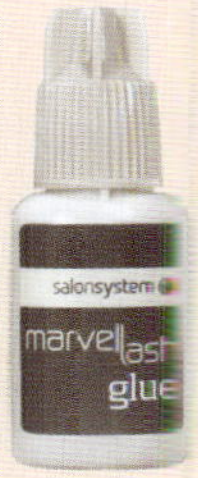

BEAUTY EXPRESS

Single lash system adhesive
To attach the artificial lash to the natural lash. Some glues are odourless which are more suitable for clients with sensitive eyes

BEAUTY EXPRESS

Single lash system solvent
Used to remove lashes during application if incorrectly applied following in the event of a contra-action or when performing a maintenance service

BEAUTY EXPRESS

Small micro-applicators
For the application of adhesive solvent to smooth and even the application of adhesive coating during application

Eyelash blower
To apply air over the area speeding the lash adhesive drying time.

YOU WILL ALSO NEED:

Towels (2 medium sized) Freshly laundered for each client

Disposable tissue roll To cover the couch before each service

Hand mirror To show the client the finished result

Scissors (sterile) To cut the micropore tape to size

Client record card To record the client's personal details, products used and details of the service

Single lash system sealer To seal the lashes following application

Eye shields Single use, disposable, usually gel pads to cover and prevent the upper and lower lashes from sticking together and also providing a conditioning service for the lower eye tissue if impregnated with therapeutic products

Clear surgical tape Cut to size, used to secure the lower lashes in place following eye shield application and to attach single lashes prior to application, to facilitate application

Eyelash combs Used to brush though the artificial and natural lashes. These are disposable, preventing cross-infection

Support cushion To place under the client's knees when positioned for treatment to avoid discomfort.

"With lashes take your time, the more precise the application the better the result.

Shavata Singh

TOP TIP

Adhesive holders

Small plastic containers to hold the adhesive, worn as a ring on the non-working hand, are used by some beauty therapists, facilitating application.

HEALTH & SAFETY

Repetitive strain injury

Support of the back and correct working height should be adequate to avoid straining, which may lead to permanent injury. Breaks should be taken to relax and lengthen muscles used excessively during this service procedure, e.g. the neck.

Preparation of the work area

Before the client is shown through to the work area, check it to ensure that the required equipment and materials are available and the area is clean and tidy. The plastic covered couch should be clean, having been thoroughly washed with hot, soapy water and wiped thoroughly with a professional disinfectant cleaner. The couch or chair should be protected with a long strip of disposable tissue paper bedroll, placed to cover a freshly laundered sheet or bath towel. A small towel should be place neatly at the head of the couch, ready to be draped across the client's chest for protection during service. (The paper tissue will need changing and the towels will need to be laundered for each client.)

A support may be available to place under the clients knees. This helps to to avoid discomfort and strain on pressure points when positioned in one place for for a long period of time.

The couch or beauty chair should be in a slightly elevated position, to give the optimum position for the beauty therapist when applying the single lashes.

Check the lighting, temperature and ventilation is adequate for the service. If the temperature is too warm the adhesive will set very quickly which may cause problems when fixing the lashes in place.

Sterilization and disinfection

Hygiene must be maintained in a number of ways:

- When preparing the single lashes remove from the container and apply to surgical tape when required to reduce contamination.
- Always have spare tweezers to ensure if you were to drop a pair you will always have access to a clean, sterile pair. All metal tools, e.g. tweezers and scissors, should be cleaned with disinfectant and then sterilized in the autoclave after use.
- Always dispense products into clean containers, e.g. adhesive.
- Discard dispensed products following the service that have been exposed to the atmosphere.
- Maintain high standards of personal hygiene.
- Disinfect work surface after every client and replace consumables.
- Protective client coverings such as towels and head bands should be freshly laundered for every client.
- Dispose of waste into a covered, lined bin at all times.

Preparation of the beauty therapist

In order to promote professionalism and to promote a healthy and safe working environment, the beauty therapist must:

- maintain a high standard of personal hygiene
- have fresh breath, free from cigarette or food odours as you will be working in close proximity to the client
- wear a clean pressed overall daily
- wear clean, low-heeled shoes
- not wear rings or any jewellery on the arms (including watches); plain wedding bands, however, are acceptable
- ensure other jewellery, e.g. necklaces and earrings, should be discreet
- make sure that make-up if worn is expertly applied
- neatly style long hair away from the face and shoulders
- keep nails should be short and free from polish
- wear the recommended face mask be worn to avoid inhalation of chemicals, i.e. solvents, and to reduce the risk of cross-contamination through airborne viruses, etc. when working in close proximity to the client
- wash the hands regularly and apply a hand disinfectant

HEALTH & SAFETY

Disposable equipment

Wherever possible use disposable containers/applicators/protective accessories such as head bonnets/face masks to prevent cross-infection and maintain high standards of hygiene.

TOP TIP

Shelf life of products

Always note when products have been opened to ensure their quality. Some will only be effective for a specific period. Eyelash adhesive usually has a shelf life of 6 months, which is halved when opened.

Outcome 2: Consult, plan and prepare for the service with clients

Learn how to use consultation techniques to effectively plan and prepare for single eyelash extension service by:

1. Using **consultation techniques** in a polite and friendly manner to determine the client's service.
2. Obtaining signed, written informed consent from the client prior to carrying out the service.
3. Ensuring that informed and signed parental or guardian consent is obtained for minors prior to any service.
4. Ensuring that a parent or guardian is present throughout the service for minors under the age of 16.
5. Asking your client appropriate questions to identify if they have any known contra-indications to the service.
6. Accurately recording your client's responses to questioning.
7. Encouraging clients to ask questions to clarify any points.

(Continued)
Learn how to use consultation techniques to effectively plan and prepare for single eyelash extension service by:

8 Helping the client into a safe, comfortable and relaxed position for the service.

9 Carefully examining the eye area to identify any **factors** that may affect the service.

10 Correctly performing a skin sensitivity test on the client according to manufacturer's instructions and organizational requirements and recording the results.

11 Taking the **necessary action** in response to any identified contra-indications.

12 Informing the client in a tactful way if there is an adverse reaction to the skin sensitivity test and they cannot be treated.

13 Ensuring client advice is given without reference to a specific medical condition and without causing undue alarm and concern.

14 Basing your recommendations on an accurate evaluation of your client's eyelashes and the potential to achieve the required look.

15 Agreeing the service and realistic outcomes that are acceptable to your client and which meet their needs.

16 Selecting and using single lash systems which are:

- of a suitable colour
- of a suitable curvature
- custom blended
- of a suitable length
- of a suitable thickness

17 Preparing the single lash extensions to avoid wastage, tangling and to meet the manufacturer's instructions.

18 Ensuring your client's clothing is effectively protected and all hair away from the face prior to service.

19 Ensuring any lashes not to be treated are effectively secured and protected.

20 Leaving the client's eye area free of all make-up and oil prior to service.

Provide single eyelash extensions

Reception

When making an appointment for single lash service, find out why the client wants artificial lashes and determine which type would be most appropriate. It may be that strip or individual flare lashes may be most appropriate.

Although single lashes may be worn for up to 8 weeks they look effective for up to 2 to 3 weeks when through the natural cyclic shedding of the client natural lash hair, gaps may become evident which will require replacement. The lash extensions may also lift as the adhesive weakens, sometimes twisting from their original placement. This will require a maintenance service and the client should be informed of this. The client must be reminded of this service as part of the consultation and aftercare advice.

When a client makes an appointment for single lash service, they should be asked:

- Have they had the service or other artificial lash service before? If they have not, they should visit the salon beforehand for a skin sensitivity test to assess any skin intolerance to the products used, e.g. adhesive. Results should be recorded on the client record card.
- Are they having the lashes applied for any particular reason, such as a holiday or special occasion?

In deciding which type of artificial lashes would be most appropriate, take into consideration the effect required, how long the lashes are to be worn for. In addition, consider their occupation to see it is compatible to maintaining the lashes, their commitment to the time required for an initial lash application, aftercare requirements and their agreement to the cost of the service.

Also question the client about other chemical service they may have received e.g. eyelash tinting and eyelash perming, ask when this was, its success and if there were any comments with regard to the service that should be noted, e.g. eye irritation.

ISTOCK/© VALUA VITALY

Has the client had lash services or artificial eye lashes before?

> Think on your feet, for example, if a client is running late and there is a way to fit them in, then do it!
>
> **Shavata Singh**

TOP TIP

Contact lense wearers

Contact lenses are required to be removed before service application. Advice your client of this, and suggest they may prefer to wear glasses for the appointment. This will avoid disturbing the eye immediately following the service.

Planning the service

A variety of lashes are available, these can be applied for corrective purposes as well as to lengthen the natural lash. Lash length may be short, medium or long; their texture may be fine, medium or thick. A Y-shaped lash is also available, which gives the appearance of having applied two lashes reducing application time to achieve a result and is ideal when immediate volume is required.

They are also available in a variety of colours, the most popular colours commercially being black and brown. For special occasions and fashion looks lashes are available in fantasy colours including metallic.

Factors when choosing single eyelash extensions

Before applying single eyelash extensions the beauty therapist should consider the following points and advise the client accordingly.

The client's age Artificial lashes can create a very bold dramatic effect, which can give an older client a harsh, unnatural look. Skin colour and the natural hair colour and the thickness, quantity of lashes change with age often becoming finer and sparser the lash chosen must enhance the client's appearance.

BEST PRACTICE

Information leaflet

It is a good idea to have an information leaflet available to provide to the client which confirms aftercare instructions. This can be provided to the client if they are unsure whether to have the service or not and would like time to consider. They are also useful to provide at any salon promotions with other reference materials.

> Always take into account the client's age and look: huge false lashes on a client that would suit a more natural look needs to be addressed. Always remain honest.
>
> **Shavata Singh**

TOP TIP

Lash length

Single lash system may be applied in a variety of lengths to create a natural look simulating the natural cyclic appearance of hair growth.

Longest lashes are usually applied in the centre of the natural lash line. Shorter lashes should be placed on the inner corner of the lash line to avoid eye irritation.

TOP TIP

Lashes behind glasses

If the client wears glasses ensure that if the lens provides magnification to the eye, the lash length and thickness is taken into account to create a flattering effect.

ALWAYS REMEMBER

Always discuss with the client their previous services. A client's lashes may appear dark and curly but they may have received the chemical lash services eyelash tinting and eyelash perming.

ACTIVITY

What lash length and thickness would you select for the following?

- short, stubby lashes?
- sparse lashes?
- long, thick lashes?
- fine lashes?
- curly lashes?

The client's natural lashes Look at the client's natural lashes: are they short, long, sparse or thick, curly or straight – also their natural curvature? Choice of curvature of the single eye lash extension ranges from natural to dramatic. The single lash should be chosen to complement the natural lash or the result may be unsuitable in terms of appearance and durability. For a natural look, select slightly longer lashes and they eye application will make the eyelashes look fuller.

For a dramatic look increase the length by half again and select a thickness of 0.2–0.25.

Choose a lash that is 1/2 to 1/3 longer than the client's natural eyelashes. If the single lashes are too long this will affect the durability of the attachment and may cause stress to the natural lash causing it to weaken.

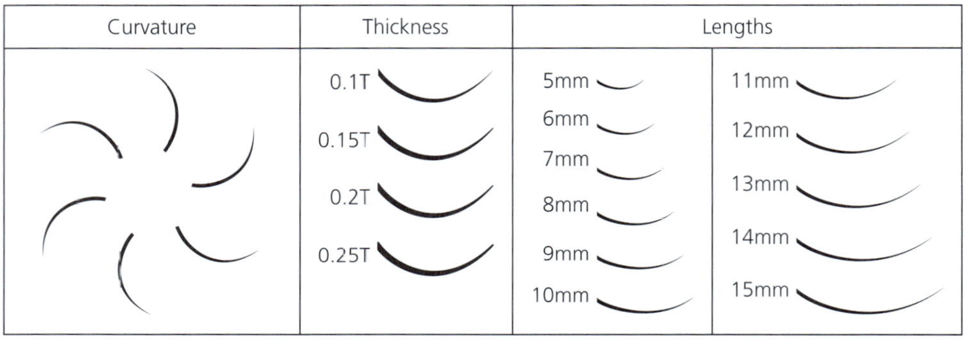

Sample single lash lengths, thicknesses and curvatures

Eyelash and skin colour Select lashes that complement the hair and skin tone. Remember a client may have their lashes tinted so the lash natural colour should be considered.

Natural eye shape

Using single lash systems for corrective purposes Below are some examples of corrective techniques for various eye shapes.

Eye shape	*Corrective steps*
Small eyes	Use medium-length lashes at the outside of the eye, longer in the middle and shorter on the insides.
Close-set eyes	Apply differing lengths of medium and longer lashes at the outside corners of the eyes and shorter on the insides.
Wide set	Use medium lashes from the inner portion of the eye with longer in the centre and a mixture of shorter and medium at the outsides.

Record card for provide single eyelash extension services

Date	Beauty therapist name	
Client name	Date of birth (Identifying client age group.)	
Home address	Postcode	
Email address	Landline phone number	Mobile phone number
Name of doctor	Doctor's address and phone number	

Related medical history (Conditions that may restrict or prohibit service application.)

Are you taking any medication? (This may affect the appearance of the skin or skin sensitivity.)

CONTRA-INDICATIONS REQUIRING MEDICAL REFERRAL
(Preventing eye service application)

- ☐ severe skin disorders (e.g. severe eczema in the area)
- ☐ infectious skin diseases
- ☐ eye infections (e.g. conjunctivitis)
- ☐ eye disease
- ☐ inflammation of the skin
- ☐ chemotherapy
- ☐ trichlotillomania
- ☐ recent eye surgery
- ☐ blepharitis

FACTORS AFFECTING THE SERVICE

☐ occupation/lifestyle (to check suitability)

____

____

☐ natural eye shape (e.g. small, large, close-set)

____

☐ Effect required i.e. natural/dramatic

____

COLOUR OF NATURAL LASHES

☐ fair ☐ brown ☐ black ☐ red ☐ grey/white

THICKNESS OF NATURAL LASHES

☐ fine ☐ medium ☐ thick

LENGTH OF NATURAL LASHES

☐ short ☐ medium ☐ long

DENSITY AND GROWTH OF NATURAL LASHES

☐ sparse ☐ dense ☐ curly

☐ direction (e.g. downwards, crossed) ______________

CONTRA-INDICATIONS THAT RESTRICT SERVICE
(Service may require adaptation.)

- ☐ cuts and abrasions
- ☐ bruising
- ☐ eye disorders
- ☐ skin allergies
- ☐ skin disorders (e.g. non-active psoriasis)
- ☐ dry eye syndrome
- ☐ glaucoma
- ☐ contact lenses
- ☐ thyroid disturbance

TYPE OF SERVICE

- ☐ full service
- ☐ maintenance service

CHOICE OF SINGLE LASH

- ☐ curvature selected ______________
- ☐ lash length ______________
- ☐ lash thickness ______________
- ☐ lash colour/finish ______________
- ☐ application details (i.e. number applied upper lash line, lower lash line) ______________

SKIN SENSITIVITY TEST

(recommended for clients with prior history of sensitivity)
Date ______________

CHEMICAL EYELASH SERVICE

☐ eyelash tint Date ________ ☐ eyelash perm Date ________

Beauty therapist signature (for reference)

Client signature (confirmation of details)

Record card for provide single eyelash extension services (continued)

SERVICE ADVICE
A full set of single lash extensions allow 120 minutes
Partial application allow between 30–60 minutes

SERVICE PLAN
Record relevant details of your service and advice provided for future reference.
Ensure the client's records are up-to-date, accurate and fully completed following service. Non-compliance may invalidate insurance. The client should sign the record card after each service to show it has been agreed.

DURING
Find out:

- what products the client is currently using to cleanse and care for the skin of the eye area
- satisfaction with these products

Explain:

- how the different eye products should be applied and removed

Note:

- any adverse reaction, if any occur

AFTER
Record:

- results of service
- any modification to service application that has occurred
- what products have been used in the eyelash service
- the effectiveness of service
- details of the choice of single lash and application
- any samples provided (review their success at the next appointment)

Advise on:

- product application and removal in order to gain maximum benefit from product use, e.g. mascara formulated to be worn with the single eyelash extensions
- use of aftercare products following eye service
- maintenance procedures
- recommended time intervals between services

RETAIL OPPORTUNITIES
Advise on:

- progression of the service plan for future appointments
- products that would be suitable for the client to use at home to care for/enhance the eye area
- recommendations for further services
- further products or services that the client may or may not have received before, e.g. eyelash tinting

Note:

- any purchase made by the client

EVALUATION
Record:

- comments on the client's satisfaction with the service
- if poor results are achieved, or the client is dissatisfied the reasons why
- how you may alter the service plan to achieve the required service results in the future, if applicable

HEALTH AND SAFETY
Advise on:

- how to care for the area following service to avoid an unwanted reaction
- avoidance of any activities or product application that may cause a contra-action
- appropriate necessary action to be taken in the event of an unwanted skin or eye irritation or other contra-action

Contra-indications

Certain contra-indications preclude or restrict single lash extension service. If there is any concern over the client's suitability, medical advice should be sought before the service proceeds. If following completion of the record card or inspection of the eye area you have found any of the following, do not apply single eye lash extensions:

- skin disease
- skin disorder in the eye area
- recent eye surgery
- skin trauma in the area, e.g. burns
- inflammation or swelling around the eye area
- hypersensitive skin
- conditions such as stroke or bells palsy where it makes it difficult to close the eye
- any eye disorder such as styes or hordeola, conjunctivitis; blepharitis; watery eye or cysts and dry eye syndrome
- alopecia, this is where hair is lost and may be partial or total. It is not known if this service could aggravate hair loss further. In some cases where hair loss is total in the area, there will be no natural hair to attach the eyelash extension to
- trichotillomania, this is a body focused repetitive disorder where the client pulls out their hair voluntarily commonly the eyelash hair
- a positive (allergic) reaction to the skin sensitivity adhesive patch test
- chemotherapy, while undertaking this medical radiation service commonly used to treat cancer the sides-effects can be hair loss, as all cells of the body are affected by the service, not just the cancer cells
- contact lenses (unless removed)
- previous eye service chemical services that may have weakened the natural lashes, e.g. eyelash perming
- if the client suffers from allergies such as hay fever there may be occasions when it is impractical for the lashes to be applied as they will be lost more quickly as the eyes become irritated and water

HEALTH & SAFETY

Eye disorders

It is best practice to wait at least a month following any eye disorder such as conjunctivitis to ensure the condition has fully cleared the area for service is healthy and there is no risk of cross-infection.

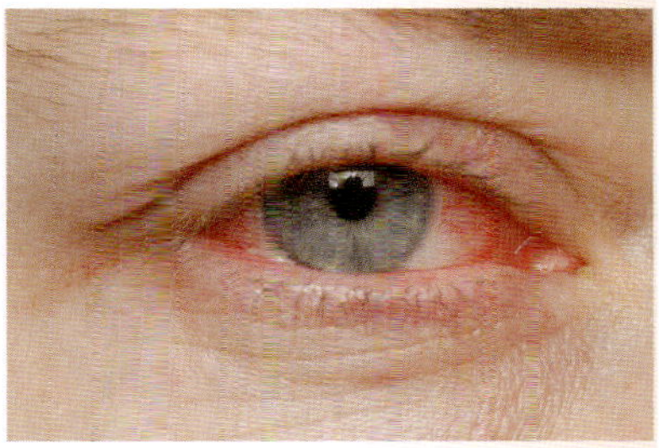

ISTOCK/© TIMMCCLEAN

Conjunctivis (pink eye) – ensure the condition has fully cleared before service

> Always ensure that you conduct a patch test with the glue if a client has not used lashes before, particularly if they are going to a special event or a wedding.
>
> **Shavata Singh**

HEALTH & SAFETY

The following disorders restrict service

Dry eye syndrome In this condition there is decreased tear production or excessive tear evaporation which may be caused by age, medical conditions and certain medications such as antihistamines. Its presence may be temporary or permanent. Refer your client to their GP before service proceeds.

Glaucoma an eye disorder in which the optic nerve is damaged at the point where it leaves the eye. This can be caused by raised eye pressure or damage occurs because there is a weakness in the optic nerve. This can lead to loss of sight. Refer your client to their GP before service proceeds.

HEALTH & SAFETY

Herpes simplex

If a client suffers from the virus herpes simplex, this in some instances can occur in the eye area affecting the top layer of the cornea. If severe, this can affect the deeper layers of the cornea leading to scarring, resulting in permanent damage to vision. Be aware if your client suffers from this viral condition.

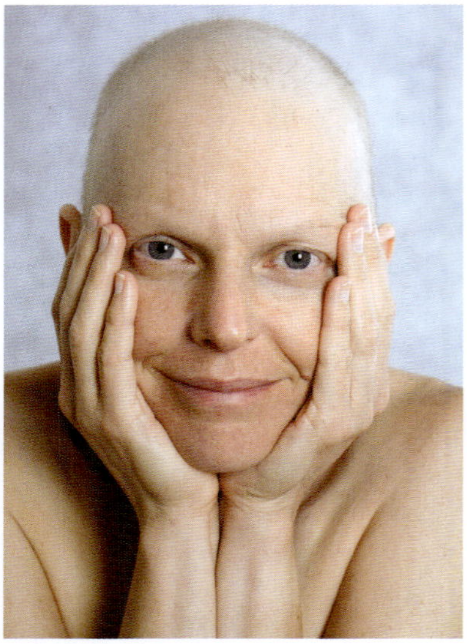

ISTOCK/© MICHAEL COURTNEY

Post chemotherapy, a client may request a service – seek medical confirmation if hair growth is new

HEALTH & SAFETY

Post-chemotherapy treatment

A client may request service following chemotherapy. It usually takes 3–6 months following treatment for hairs to grow back. Hair re-growth may be different from previously, changing texture and becoming curly when previously straight. Seek medical confirmation to treat if the hair growth is new.

An unduly nervous client with a tendency to blink could prove hard to treat in this way. Use your discretion in deciding the suitability for the service.

Those contra-indications requiring GP referral should be tactfully and clearly discussed to ensure client understanding.

Explain to the client what actions to take if a contra-action was to occur.

Contra-actions

If during application of single lashes the eyes start to water, blot the tears with the corner of a clean tissue. The tears can affect the adherence of the adhesive. Any possible irritation of the eyes should therefore be avoided, during the preparation of the eye area and application itself.

If the adhesive has accidentally seeped and glued to the protective eye shield, apply adhesive solvent with an applicator, and gently roll it over the area to dissolve the adhesive. To prevent this you should regularly check during application that the adhesive has not stuck to the shield. This is achieved by lifting the upper eyelid slightly.

If solvent accidentally goes into the client's eye, remove excess product, rinse the eye thoroughly and immediately, using clean water if necessary. Repeat this until discomfort is no longer experienced.

Allergic reaction to the products used – the client will need to have the products removed immediately and a record made of the reaction and action taken. It will be necessary to perform skin sensitivity tests with the products used to identify the allergen.

Skin sensitivity patch test

The adhesive used for single lash extension service should not come into contact with the skin which means a skin sensitivity test should not be necessary. However, accidental contact may be made with the skin and some clients may be sensitive to the lash adhesive, producing an allergic reaction immediately on contact with it; others may become allergic later. For this reason, therefore, it is recommended to carry out a skin sensitivity test before each single lash extension service.

This test should be given on either the skin on the inside of the elbow or behind the ear.

Two responses to the skin sensitivity test are possible – positive and negative:

- A positive skin sensitivity test result is recognized by irritation, swelling or inflammation of the skin.

- A negative skin sensitivity test result produces no skin reaction – in this case you may proceed with the service.

Before you proceed with the service question your client to confirm their understanding of all aspects of the service procedure.

The record card should be signed and dated by the client and beauty therapist following the consultation to confirm the suitability and consent of the agreed service.

It is important that accurate records are kept and stored in compliance with the Data Protection Act (1998) and for future reference.

Remember clients classed as minors cannot be treated without signed parental/guardian consent and they must be present throughout the service if received.

Preparation of the client

Show the client to the prepared work area after the record card has been completed. Consult the record card and check for any contra-indications to service. All accessories must be removed from the eye area including contact lenses. Explain the preparation process for the service explaining how the area will be prepared, the sensations to be experienced and how long the eyes will be closed for. It is important that they understand they cannot open their eyes while the service is being carried out.

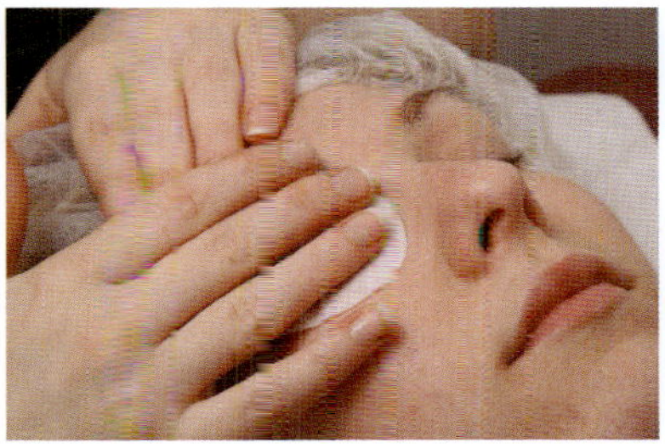

PHOTOS COURTESY OF E'LAN LASHES EYELASH EXTENSIONS

Cleanse the eye using the manufacturer's recommended eye make-up remover

1. Position the client comfortably, and ensure they are relaxed this is important as the service can take any time between 2 hours if applying a full set of single lashes or 30–60 minutes if providing a maintenance service. The back of the couch should be slightly elevated without causing unnecessary strain to you while working. Support the client's head or neck with a cushion or pillow. A support cushion may be also placed under the knees to take the strain of the back while lying for a long period.
2. Protect the client's hair with a hair head band, preferably disposable. This ideally must cover the whole head, e.g. a head bonnet to avoid beauty therapist contact with the client's scalp hair while working.
3. Protect the client's upper clothing with paper tissue, cape or small towel according to your workplace policy.

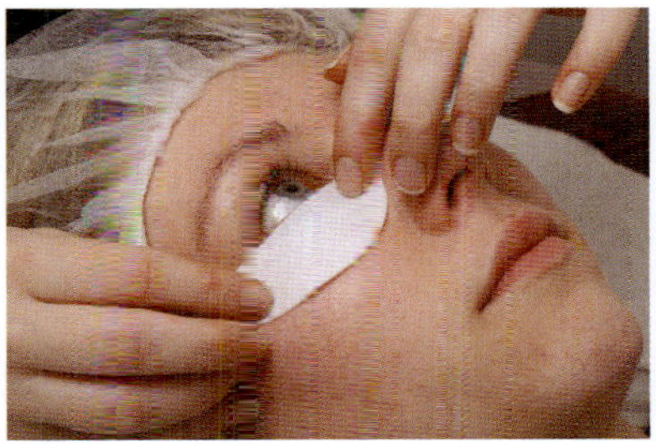

PHOTOS COURTESY OF E'LAN LASHES EYELASH EXTENSIONS

Apply protective eye shield to cover the lower lashes

4. Wash your hands and apply a hand disinfectant after preparing the client. Protective gloves may be worn, especially if the beauty therapist has intolerance to any of the products use in the service.
5. Cleanse the eye area using the specialized eye make-up remover provided by your manufacturer. This will remove natural oils from the lashes which will affect adherence
6. Comb through the lashes to separate them, allowing them to dry. Check client comfort.
7. Remove the adhesive backing on the reverse of the eye shield. Ask the client to look upwards towards you, holding the skin around the lower eye taut, usually with the ring finger, apply a protective eye shield to cover the lower lashes of each eye. Ensure that this fits snugly around the eye contour and covers the lower lashes.

   Comb through the lashes again as necessary, this straightens the lashes, avoids tangling and loosens any lashes that may be ready to naturally shed.

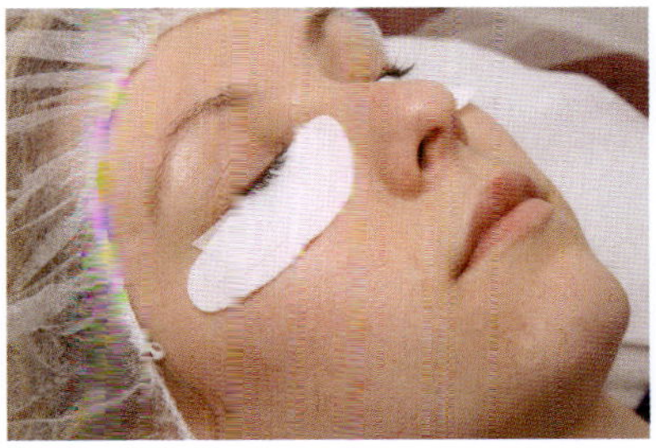

PHOTOS COURTESY OF E'LAN LASHES EYELASH EXTENSIONS

Apply surgical tape to cover any exposed lashes

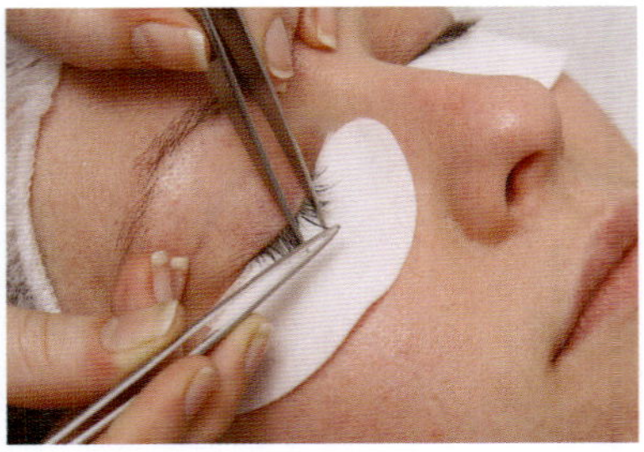
PHOTOS COURTESY OF E'LAN LASHES EYELASH EXTENSIONS

Single eyelash extension application

8 Ask the client to close her eyes. They must now remain closed.

9 Finally, check that the client is comfortable before single lash application.

ALWAYS REMEMBER

Avoid eye cosmetics before service application

It is best if the client arrives for the service wearing no cosmetic products on the eye area. This is because it will take time to remove and the cleansing process may affect the adherence of the lash system and sensitize the eye, causing it to water or create oils, again which will impede adherence.

HEALTH & SAFETY

Allergy

The adhesive used on the eye shield and surgical dressing to cover the lower lashes may cause irritation/allergy if the client/beauty therapist has an allergy to adhesive. Allergy to plasters must be checked for at consultation. The beauty therapist, if allergic, may have to wear gloves.

TOP TIP

Protective shields

The protective shield is usually impregnated with soothing, nourishing ingredients and acts as a service itself for use around the eye.

TOP TIP

Eyelash blower

If using air to assist drying, blow air from the top of the lash downwards towards the nose. For some clients this may cause the clients eye to water if the cornea becomes dry, so use with caution.

Outcome 3: Attach single lash systems

Learn how to attach single lash systems to meet the needs of your clients by:

1. Effectively isolating single lashes to meet the requirements of the system to be used.
2. Placing and securing the single lash systems in a way that will allow them to lie in the direction required.
3. Effectively securing lash extensions into your client's lashes with an even application of adhesive.
4. Leaving a gap between the eyelash extension and the eyelid to meet manufacturer's instructions.
5. Adding and attaching single lash systems in a way that takes into account the **factors** influencing the service.
6. Effectively releasing lashes and eye pads at regular intervals throughout the service to avoid unwanted adhesion.
7. Effectively removing any excess adhesive and debris throughout the attachment process, minimizing any discomfort to the client.
8. Checking the comfort of your client at regular intervals throughout the service.
9. Giving suitable reassurance to the client, if necessary.
10. Identifying and resolving any problems occurring during the service.
11. Effectively sealing the eyelashes following manufacturer's instructions.
12. Ensuring, on completion, that the single lash systems give a balanced and well-proportioned finish suitable for the intended look and your client's natural eyelashes.

On completion the single lashes should give a balanced, well-proportioned look complementing the client's eye shape and the agreed desired effect.

1 Select the length of lashes, thickness, colour and curvature to suit your client and agreed in the service plan.

2 Place the selected hairs on surgical tape where they are easily visible and accessible.

3 Dispense the adhesive in measured amount into a container.

4 The surgical tape holding the lashes may be applied to the back of the hand.

5 Working from behind the client commence application placing the first lash in the centre, this is usually a longer length of lash. Isolate the natural eyelash by holding the tweezers at a 45° angle in your non-working hand.

Select a hair by its tip, the tapered end and using the pointed tweezers in your working hand, apply adhesive to two-thirds of its length from its base so it appears in small droplets, keeping the adhesive away from the tip.

6 Coat the surface of the isolated natural lash by running the single lash extension in an upward direction, against its length, avoiding contact with the skin.

Secure the lash into position ensuring there are no gaps with the natural hair, approximately 0.5 mm to 1.0 mm from where the base of the lash leaves the skin. Smooth the surface of the small droplets of adhesive so that as it dries a natural appearance is achieved using a cocktail stick or micro-applicator.

7 To create a balanced look and to allow the adhesive to dry, isolate and position the next single lash on the outer portion of the eyelid.

8 Lashes should be positioned at spaced intervals along the lash line in order to achieve a balanced look and to avoid adjacent lashes sticking together during application.

TOP TIP

Bonding the single lash securely

If the adhesive has not coated securely the natural lash and artificial lash along its length it will soon be lost as lifting and separation of the lashes occurs.

Too much adhesive can cause lashes to stick together causing a 'clumping' unnatural effect. This may also affect the natural hair growth.

If single lash placement is incorrect when checking, e.g. lifting or crossing other lashes, remove and replace.

ALWAYS REMEMBER

Never apply more than one single lash to a natural lash, this will be too heavy for the natural lashes and may affect their growth and cause lash loss.

BEST PRACTICE

Apply sufficient lashes so that when the natural lash is naturally lost through the hair growth cycle which will mean the loss of the artificial lash also there will be sufficient remaining artificial hairs for the effect to be maintained until the maintenance service 2–3 weeks after application.

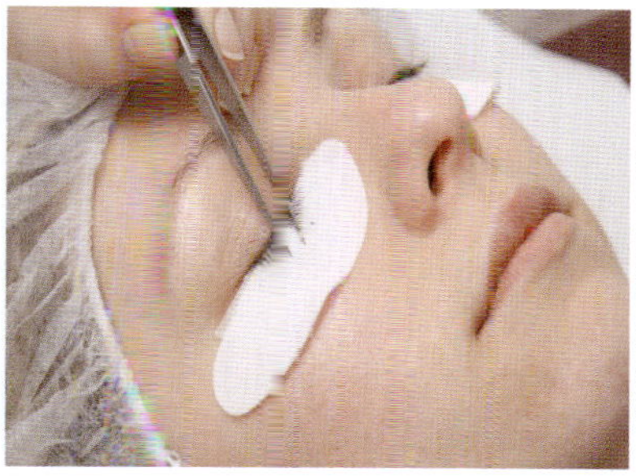
PHOTOS COURTESY OF E'LAN LASHES EYELASH EXTENSIONS

Isolate the natural lash hair

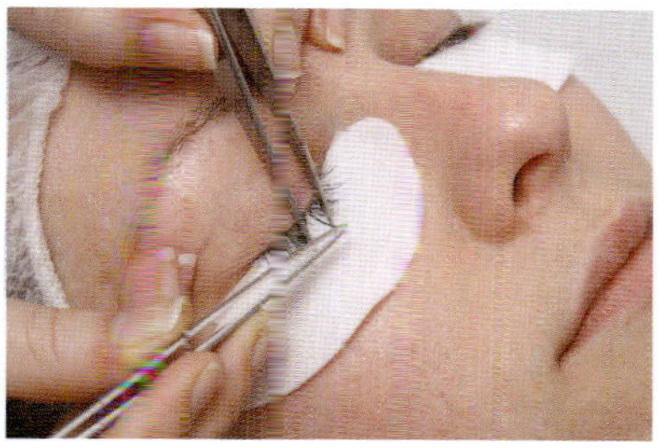
PHOTOS COURTESY OF E'LAN LASHES EYELASH EXTENSIONS

Secure the single lash extension into position

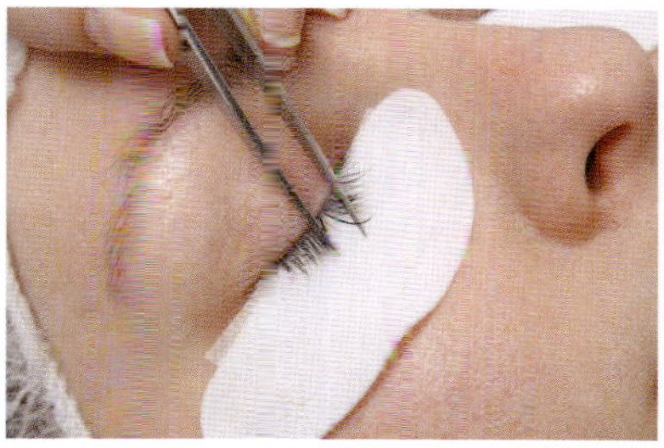
PHOTOS COURTESY OF E'LAN LASHES EYELASH EXTENSIONS

Allow the adhesive to dry

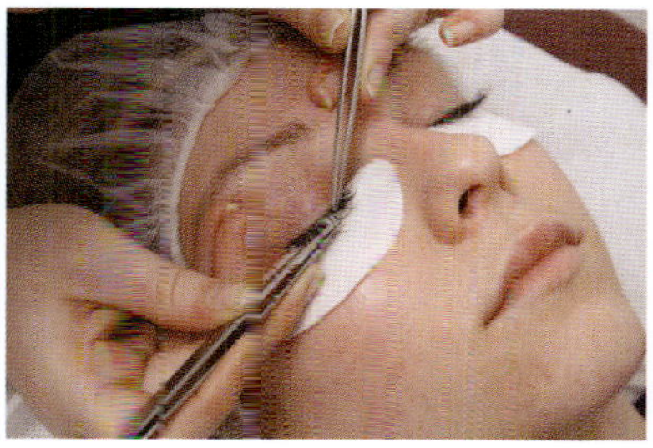
PHOTOS COURTESY OF E'LAN LASHES EYELASH EXTENSIONS

Position lashes at spaced intervals

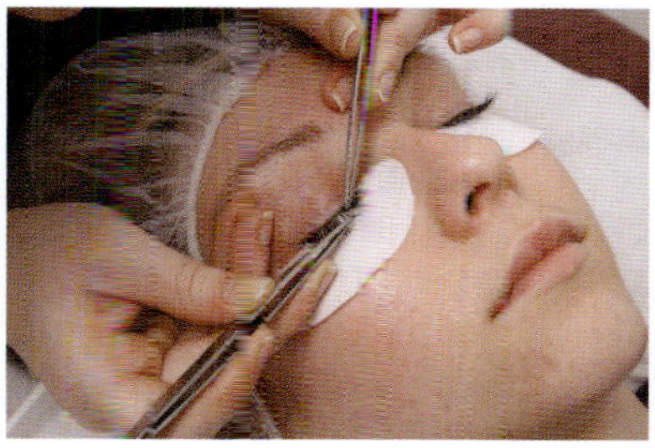
PHOTOS COURTESY OF E'LAN LASHES EYELASH EXTENSIONS

Avoid adjacent lashes sticking together

COURSEMATE

For a video on the single lash extension service, please visit this book's accompanying CourseMate.

TOP TIP

Excess adhesive

If there is excess adhesive anywhere following placement, remove immediately while soft, using the professional tool or small applicator provided by manufacturers for this purpose. Also, if the lashes become stuck together, clean and release them immediately.

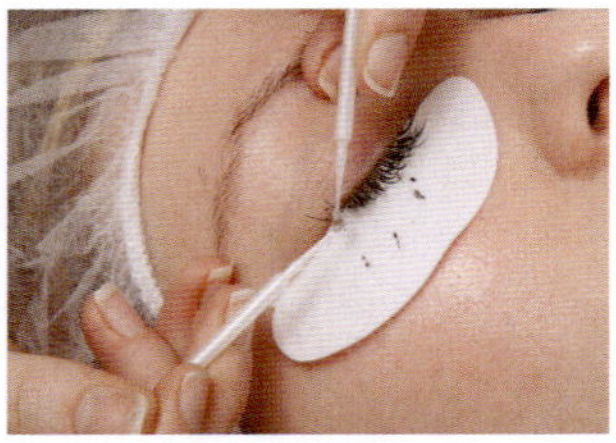

PHOTOS COURTESY OF E'LAN LASHES EYELASH EXTENSIONS

Remove excess adhesive

Once the glue has dried, this task will become more complicated and irritating for the client. A clean small applicator will be required to gently separate them using a small amount of adhesive. Clean tweezer points can also be used to separate the lashes.

ALWAYS REMEMBER

Check under lashes

During application gently lift the lashes, lifting the lash line to check underneath that they have not become stuck to the lower lashes/ eye shield below.

Repeat this check several times during application.

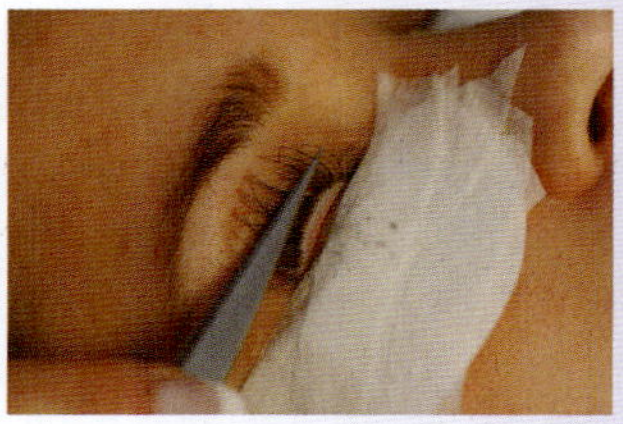

PHOTOS COURTESY OF E'LAN LASHES EYELASH EXTENSIONS

Lift lashes to check underneath

9 On completion of application the lashes may be combed through.

A protective sealer is applied to coat the adhesive and lash by improving the longevity.

10 Remove the adhesive tape and then the protective eye shield from the outside of the eye inwards. This should be easily removed. If excess adhesive has been used or the lower lashes have not been properly covered there can be resistance on removal which is poor practice. The lashes should feel weightless and totally natural.

11 Provide the client with a mirror and show the client the finished result.

12 Discuss aftercare advice and book a maintenance service.

13 Tidy the work area and dispose of any waste.

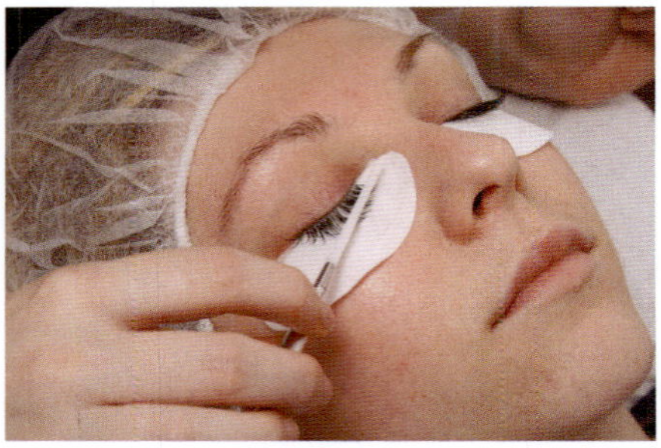

PHOTOS COURTESY OF E'LAN LASHES EYELASH EXTENSIONS

Combing through the lashes

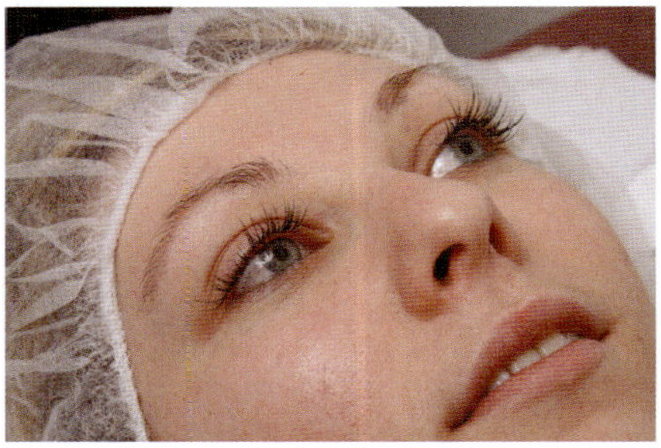

PHOTOS COURTESY OF E'LAN LASHES EYELASH EXTENSIONS

Finished result

> Never agree to conduct a service that you do not feel is correct for the client, for example if the client wants to create something that you simply know will not suit her then be honest, she will appreciate it in the long run.
>
> **Shavata Singh**

BEST PRACTICE

Application techniques

Outside working inwards

Lash application can commence from the outside working inwards with spaced intervals between each single lash application along the lash line until completed. Each single lash application should be alternated between each eye.

Completing application to one eye, before moving to the other

Commencing lash application in the middle of the lash line, move to the outermost lash then halfway between these two lashes, then halfway again until application to the whole lash line on one eye is completed, before moving to the other.

Outcome 4: Maintain and remove single lash systems

Learn how to maintain and remove single lash systems by:

1. Maintaining and removing single lash systems following manufacturer's instructions.
2. Using the correct tools effectively and minimizing damage to the client's natural eyelashes and injury to the eye area.

(Continued) Learn how to maintain and remove single lash systems by:

3 Using the correct products to remove single lash systems avoiding damage to the client's natural eyelashes and injury to the eye area.

4 Leaving the client's natural eyelashes free of product build-up and debris.

5 Leaving the client's natural eyelashes clean, even and tangle free.

Maintenance of single eyelash extensions

1. Position the client lying on the couch.
2. Refer to the client's records and check the lashes.
3. Wash your hands.
4. Prepare the lashes as discussed previously for application.
5. It may be necessary to remove some single lashes that require replacement, this is discussed below in removal.
6. Apply replacement lash extensions, required following the chosen application procedure. This will take between 30–45 minutes depending upon the quantity of lash replacement required.
7. Show the client the finished result and review aftercare procedures.
8. Re-book the next maintenance service.
9. Tidy the work area and dispose of any waste.

DELMAR CENGAGE LEARNING

Application of adhesive solvent

Removal of single eyelash extensions

1. Position the client lying on the couch.
2. Refer to the client's records and check the lashes.
3. Wash your hands.
4. Remove make-up from the eye area, cleansing the skin with a suitable eye make-up remover.
5. Protect the lower lashes and eye by placing a protective eye shield over them. The eye shields should fit snugly to the contour of the lower eye.
6. Dispense the solvent in the required amount into a container.
7. Apply solvent to an applicator and by treating one eye at a time, gently stroke down the lash extensions with the adhesive solvent until the adhesive dissolves, and the false lash begins to loosen. Use a dry applicator in the other hand to loosen the single eyelash extension.
8. When you are satisfied that the eyelash adhesive has been dissolved, gently attempt to remove the lash extensions. Support the upper eyelid with the fingers of one hand, using the other hand to remove the false lash with a sterile pair of tweezers. If the adhesive has been adequately dissolved, the eyelash will lift

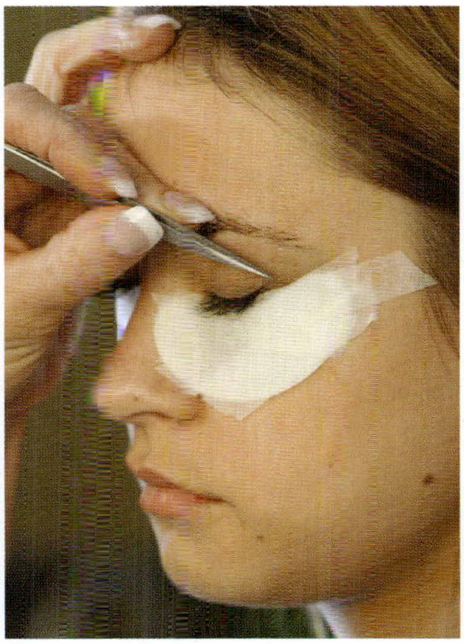

PHOTOS COURTESY OF E'LAN LASHES EYELASH EXTENSIONS

Removal of single eye lash extension using tweezers

away easily from the natural eyelash. If there is any resistance, repeat the solvent application until the eyelash comes away readily.

9 As the lash extensions are removed, collect them on a clean white facial tissue or a clean cotton wool pad.

10 Having removed all the lash extensions lashes from one eye, soothe the area by applying damp cotton wool pads soaked in cool water. (This will remove any remaining solvent.) A damp cotton wool pad may be placed over the eye, while you remove the lash extensions from the other eye.

11 Tidy the work area and dispose of any waste.

HEALTH & SAFETY

Client comfort

Never attempt to remove the artificial lashes until they have begun to loosen – if you do, the client's natural eyelashes will also be removed, causing them discomfort.

Avoid excessive use of solvent which could run and enter the client's eye or cause skin irritation.

> Keep yourself updated with the latest celebrity trends, particularly when it comes to lashes. For example, if someone comes into the studio and says that they have seen a certain look on a celebrity, you should always be one step ahead.
>
> **Shavata Singh**

Outcome 5: Provide aftercare advice

Learn how to provide aftercare advice which supports and meets the needs of your clients by:

1. Giving **advice** and recommendations accurately and constructively.
2. Giving your clients suitable **advice** specific to their individual needs.

Aftercare advice

- Avoid rubbing the eyes, or the artificial lashes may become loosened.
- Do not use oil-based eye make-up remover as its cosmetic constituents will dissolve the adhesive.
- Use only dry or water-based make-up (as these may readily be removed with a non-oily eye make-up remover).
- Avoid extremes of heat, e.g. sauna service.
- Do not use regular mascara. If necessary to use mascara, this should be especially formulated to wear with single lash extensions.
- Do not use mechanical eyelash curlers, which may loosen the artificial lash and could damage the natural lash, causing loss.
- Do not touch the eyes for 1½ hours after application, while the adhesive dries thoroughly. If showering avoid contact with the face. Use a cloth with water to cleanse the face as necessary.
- Avoid swimming for 24 hours or other exercise activities that may cause sweating.
- Do not attempt to remove the lashes – pulling at the artificial lash will also pull out the natural lashes.

PHOTOS COURTESY OF E'LAN LASHES EYELASH EXTENSIONS

Mascara formulated for use with single eyelash extensions

- After bathing or swimming, gently pat the eyes dry with a clean towel. As the lashes are synthetic they will not dry like natural lash hair.
- An eyelash comb may be used to comb through the lashes to separate them after exposure to moisture, i.e. after showering.
- Any contra-action should be reported immediately to the salon.

Clients with single lash extensions should have their lashes maintained by regular visits to the salon. Lost single lashes can be replaced as necessary; this is often described as an infill service. Schedule every 2–3 weeks, this will enable you to maintain the appearance of the lashes and allow you to assess the health of the natural lashes.

Also recommend the purchase of the mascara formulated for use with the lashes. A sealant is also provided by some manufacturers for use following lash extensions to protect from moisture helping maintain their appearance.

If the client wishes to have their single lashes removed, this must be done professionally. Recommend other eye services to enhance the eye area.

ASSESSMENT OF KNOWLEDGE AND UNDERSTANDING

FUNCTIONAL SKILLS

Having covered the learning objectives for **provide single eyelash extension services** – test what you need to know and understand by answering the following short questions below.

The information covers:

- organizational and legal requirements
- how to work safely and effectively when providing single lash system services
- client consultation, service planning and preparation
- contra-indications and contra-actions
- equipment and products
- anatomy and physiology
- equipment, materials and products
- attaching, maintaining and removing single lash systems
- aftercare advice for clients

Organizational and legal requirements

1. Why is it necessary to keep records of each eyelash extension service?
2. What information needs to be recorded in relation to each service?
3. How long should be allowed for an initial single lash extension service to the upper lashes and for a maintenance service?
4. What exercises can you perform to prevent repetitive strain injury and fatigue from performing regular single eyelash extension services?
5. What systems of sterilization and disinfection should be used to maintain the equipment in a clean and hygienic condition?

How to work safely and effectively when providing single eyelash extension services?

1. What types of personal protective equipment must be worn by the beauty therapist when providing the service?
2. How should the client be positioned to ensure their comfort during service application and to prevent beauty therapist poor working posture?
3. What safety considerations should occur when using single eyelash extension systems?
4. Why is it important to check if other chemical eye services have been received before application?
5. When should lash application be checked when providing the service? Why is it necessary to do this?

6 What is checked for when carrying out an examination of the client's natural eyelashes before service application?

Client consultation, service planning and preparation

1 How is a skin sensitivity test conducted? Why is this necessary?

2 What should be checked for at the consultation in order to select the most suitable lashes and confirm the suitability of the eye area for the service?

3 Why is it important to confirm the client's understanding of the service following the consultation?

4 Why is it important that all responses to questions asked are recorded on the record card?

5 How should the area be cleansed before the service?

Contra-indications and contra-actions

1 Name **three** contra-indications observed at consultation which would prevent single eyelash extension service.

2 What contra-indication would restrict service application and why?

3 State **three** contra-actions that could occur following the service and why these may occur.

4 Why is it importance not to name specific contra-indications when encouraging clients to seek medical advice before service?

Equipment, materials and products

1 How would you select lashes appropriate for the client's natural lashes while meeting the client's service expectations?

2 How would you prepare the single lashes for application to avoid wastage and tangling?

3 How should the client's natural lashes be prepared for single eyelash extension application to ensure their durability?

4 What limitations must you be aware of that will affect client suitability for the service?

Attaching, maintaining and removing single lash systems

1 What is the generally accepted application procedure for single eyelash extension application when applying a full set of lashes?

2 When would it be beneficial to apply a 'Y' lash?

3 Which lashes would you select and how would you apply them to suit a client with small eyes?

4 When would you recommend a client received maintenance service? What maintenance procedures are performed at this service to restore the appearance of the lashes?

5 When applying single lash extensions how can you avoid a build-up of excessive adhesive during application?

6 Why is it necessary for the client to return to the beauty therapist to have their artificial eyelashes removed?

Aftercare advice for clients

1 How often would you recommend the client receives a single lash extension service? What is the recommended interval between appointments?

2 State the products and tools that a client may use at home to cleanse and maintain the area? What skincare products should be avoided?

3 What retail products could you recommend to a client in conjunction with a single eyelash extension service?

4 State **three** post-service restrictions following the service?

5 If a client experienced a contra-action following the service what action should the client have been advised to take?

Glossary

Acid mantle the combination of sweat and sebum on the skin's surface, which creates an acid film. The acid mantle is protective and discourages the growth of bacteria and fungi.

Adipose tissue body tissue layer that stores fat.

Aftercare advice given to the client following service to continue the benefits of the service.

Allergen a substance that the skin is sensitive to and which causes an allergic reaction.

Alternating current (ac) an interrupted electrical current which reverses the direction of flow of electrons.

Anagen the active growth stage of the hair growth cycle.

Anion a negative ion, an atom that has gained more electrons than protons.

Anode a positive electrode or pole of a constant electrical current.

Aromatherapy the use of essential oils combined with massage to bring about a feeling of well-being.

Assessment techniques used to assess the needs of the client to ascertain the service objectives, including questioning and natural observation.

Aseptic The opposite of sepsis, a situation trying to eliminate bacteria. All service procedures must be aseptic, i.e. wearing personal protective equipment, hand washing, disposal of waste, etc. (from British Standards glossary of terms relating to Disinfectants).

Audio sonic a hand-held electrical massage service applied to the face or body. The equipment produces sound waves, which vibrate through the skin's cells and tissues. The service is used for its physiological benefits on the skin and muscle tissues.

Ayurveda (art of life) a sacred Hindu text written around 1800BC. In Ayurveda life consists of body, mind and spirit – each person is different. By restoring balance and harmony of the body, mind and spirit, the health of the individual improves.

Base note a measure of the evaporation rate of essential oils – base notes have the slowest evaporation rate of all essential oils and are absorbed slowly into the skin.

Benefit the gain to me made from using a product or service.

Blend epilation the combined use of both high frequency and direct current to destroy the hair; both currents retain their individual effects in the hair.

Blood nutritive liquid circulating through the blood vessels; it transports essential nutrients to the cells, removes waste products and transports other important substances such as oxygen and hormones.

Blood vessels there are three main types of blood vessel: arteries, veins and capillaries which differ in their structure and role in blood transportation.

Body language communication using the body rather than speech.

Bone a specialized form of connective tissue, a structural tissue that supports, surrounds and connects different parts of the body. They have an important function of support; protection; movement; blood cell production and mineral storage.

It is made up of water; non-living (inorganic) material including calcium and phosphorus and living (organic) material such as the cells which form bones called osteoblasts.

Care Standards Act (2000) You must comply with all your responsibilities under current health and safety legislation including the Care Standards Act. The Care Standards Act (2000) is the regulatory framework for social care to ensure high standards of care and protection of vulnerable people.

Cataphoresis this is usually applied after an epilation service by galvanic electrolysis to soothe and reduce redness on the skin.

Catagen a brief, transitional stage in the cycle of hair growth – anagen, catagen and telogen – in which the hair moves up the hair follicle.

Cathode a negative electrode or pole of constant electrical current.

Cation a positive ion; an atom that has lost an electron and has more protons than electrons.

Cell the smallest and simplest unit capable of life.

Cellulite terminology used to describe fatty tissue that causes the overlying skin to appear dimpled.

Central nervous system (CNS) composed of the brain and the spinal cord co-coordinating the activities of the whole body.

Chakras non-physical energy centres, located about an inch away from the physical body, which cannot be seen. In ancient Eastern belief the body is said to have seven major chakra centres each with a function, all of which work together in balance with each other.

Circulatory system transports material around the body. It supplies cells with oxygen and nutrients and then carries away waste products.

Codes of practice are also available from the hairdressing and beauty industry authority (Habia) sharing best and mandatory working practice approved by both industry experts and health and safety advisors. A Sunbed Code of Practice is also provided by The Sunbed Association (TSA).

Collagen a protein fibre providing strength to the skin. They are produced by specialized cells called fibroblasts, and are held in a gel called the ground substance.

Compressor a piece of equipment used to compress air, the air pressure is then regulated by the attachment of a regulator. Used in the application of make-up and nail art, airbrushing and self-tan application techniques.

Conductor a substance that conducts electricity and heat. Good conductors include metals and solutions which have conducting properties such as acids and alkalis.

Connective tissue sheath surrounds both the hair follicle and sebaceous gland, providing both a sensory supply and a blood supply. The connective tissue sheath includes and is a continuation of the papilla.

Consultation assessment of the client's needs using different techniques, including questioning and natural observation.

Consumer Protection (Distance Selling) Regulations (2000) these Regulations are derived from a European Directive and cover the supply of goods/services made between suppliers acting in a commercial capacity and consumers. They are concerned with purchases made by telephone, fax, Internet, digital television and mail order.

Continuing professional development activities undertaken to develop technical skill and expertise and to ensure current, professional experience in the beauty therapy industry is maintained.

Contra-action an unwanted reaction occurring during or after service application.

Contra-indication a problematic symptom which indicates that service may not proceed.

Control of Noise at Work Regulations (2005) as an employer a safe working environment should be provided, therefore noise levels should be kept within safe levels. There is a duty to assess any risks in the workplace in this.

Control of Substances Hazardous to Health (COSHH) (2002) these Regulations require employers to identify all hazardous substances used in the workplace and state how they should be stored and handled.

Controlled Waste Regulations (1992) categorizes waste types. The Local Authority provides advice on how to dispose of waste types in compliance with the law.

Cosmetic Products (Safety) Regulations (2004) part of consumer legislation that requires that cosmetics and toiletries are safe in their formulation and are safe for use for their intended purpose as a cosmetic and comply with labelling requirements.

Cross-infection the transfer of contagious microorganisms.

Data Protection Act (1998) legislation designed to protect client privacy and confidentiality.

Demonstration an activity that allows you to show the client a product or service to enhance their awareness and understanding of it.

Dermal papilla an organ that provides the hair follicle with blood, necessary for hair growth.

Dermis the inner portion of the skin, situated underneath the epidermis composed of dense connective tissue containing other structures such as the lymphatic system, blood vessels and nerves. It is much thicker than the epidermis.

Desincrustation ionization of a solution forming alkalis during galvanic therapy which softens dead skin and the fatty acids of sebum. Used to achieve a cleansing action.

Diathermy uses a high frequency alternating oscillating current, oscillating at millions of cycles per second. The current is introduced into the skin via a needle which produces heat as the water molecules in the cells are agitated by the high frequency energy.

Digestive system breaks down food into nutrients that can be absorbed by the body into the bloodstream.

Dihydroxyacetone (DHA) the active ingredient in self-tan products. A colourless sugar which reacts with amino acids in the skin creating the pigmented look.

Direct current (dc) an electrical current using the effects of polarity. The electrons flow constantly, uninterrupted, in one direction.

Disability Discrimination Act (DDA) (1995) this Act makes it unlawful to discriminate on the grounds of disability.

Disinfectant a chemical agent that destroys most micro-organisms.

Ectomorph a body figure type, usually with long limbs and a slender body.

Effleurage a massage movement which has a sedating and relaxing effect; applied with the whole palm it can be made superficially or deeply.

Elastin a protein fibre giving the skin elasticity. They are produced by specialized cells called fibroblasts, and are held in a gel called the ground substance.

Electric current the flow of electrons along an electric circuit between the electrical supply and the appliance.

Electricity at Work Regulations (1989) these Regulations state that every piece of equipment in the workplace should be tested every 12 months by a qualified electrician. It covers the installation, maintenance and use of electrical equipment. It is the responsibility of the employer to keep records of the equipment tested and the date it was checked in order to keep it in a safe condition.

Electrolysis the chemical reactions that occur when ions arrive at their respective electrodes. Acids are formed at the anode and alkalis at the cathode.

Electrolyte solution of electrically charged particles capable of conducting electricity.

Electrotherapy the use of mechanical or electrical equipment to improve the condition and appearance of the face and/or body.

Electro-muscle stimulation (EMS) an electrical service applied to both the face and body to specifically exercise muscles by electrical current by creating a tightening, toning effect.

Employers Liability (Compulsory Insurance) Act (1969) this provides financial compensation to an employee should they be injured as a result of an accident in the workplace.

Endocrine system coordinates and regulates processes in the body by means of chemicals (hormones), released by endocrine glands into the bloodstream. Hormones control activities such as growth or the development of the secondary sexual characteristics.

Endomorph a body figure type, usually with short limbs and a plump, rounded body, often pear-shaped.

Epidermis the outer layer of the skin located directly above the skin dermis. Composed of five layers, with the surface layer forming the outer skin with a protective function.

Epilation total follicle destruction.

Erythema reddening of the skin

Essential oils the aromatic substances used in aromatherapy. They have an infinite range of aromas, being extracted from flowers, seeds, roots, fruits and bark.

Evaluation method used to gain feedback which can be used to measure the success/effectiveness of an activity.

Exfoliant a cosmetic service preparation of chemical or vegetable origin to accelerate the process of natural skin loss – called desquamation. It is normally applied to the face after facial cleansing and steaming. Exfoliants may also be applied to the skin of the hands and feet, which tend to be coarser in texture.

Exfoliation a salon service used to remove excess dead skin cells from the surface of the skin, which has a skin cleansing action. This process can be achieved using a specialized cosmetic, or mechanically, using facial equipment applied over the skin surface.

Facial a service to improve the appearance, condition and functioning of the skin and underlying structures.

Faradic service also known as electro-muscle stimulation. This is an electrical service applied to both the face and body. An electrical current is used to exercise muscles by stimulation, which creates a tightening and toning effect.

Faux tan alternative word for fake tan.

Features the uniqueness or individuality of a product or service.

Fibres these are found in the dermis and give the skin its strength and elasticity. Yellow elastin gives the skin its elasticity, white collagen gives skin its strength.

Fitzpatrick Classification system devised in 1975 at Harvard University, this is a skin classification on a scale of 1 to 6 based on photosensitivity reaction to UV irradiation.

Frictions a massage manipulation which causes the skin and superficial structures to move together over the deeper, underlying structures. The movements help to break down fibrous thickening and fat deposits, and aid the removal of any non-medical oedemas (areas of fluid retention).

Fungus microscopic plants, which are parasites. Fungal diseases of the skin feed on the waste products of the skin. They are found on the skin's surface or they can attack deeper tissues.

Galvanic current a constant direct current which creates chemical effects.

Galvanic epilation hair removal using direct current. The needle from the electrical epilation machine is inserted into the follicle and direct current flows out over the length of the needle. Sodium hydroxide (lye) is formed in the moisture of the hair follicle. This chemically decomposes the follicle tissue and remains in the follicle to continue to destroy the cells.

Galvanic therapy therapeutic substances are introduced into the skin using a direct current to achieve specific effects upon the skin's surface and underlying tissues.

Gyratory massage an electrical body massage service which produces frictions on the skin's surface, creating a heating, stimulating effect.

Hair follicle a structure in the skin formed from epidermal tissue. Cells move up the hair follicle from the bottom (the hair bulb), changing in structure, to form the hair.

Health and Safety at Work Act (1974) legislation which lays down the minimum standards of health, safety and welfare requirements in each area of the workplace.

Health and Safety (Display Screen Equipment) Regulations (1992) these regulations cover the use of visual display units (VDUs) and computer screens. They specify acceptable levels of radiation emissions from the screen and identify correct posture, seating position, permitted working heights and rest periods.

Health and Safety (First Aid) Regulations (1981) legislation which states that workplaces must have first aid provision.

Health and Safety (Information for Employees) Regulations (1989) these regulations require the employer to make health and safety information via notices, posters and leaflets published by the Health and Safety Executive (HSE) available to all employees.

High-frequency current an electrical current which moves backwards and forwards at very high speed; referred to as an alternating or oscillating current.

High-frequency service service which may be applied directly or indirectly to service, which may be applied directly or indirectly to stimulate, sanitize and heal the skin.

Heart a muscular pump which keeps the blood circulating in the body.

Hirsutism hair growth pattern considered to be abnormal for the person's sex, i.e. female hair growth following a male hair growth pattern. The hair growth is usually terminal when it should be a vellus type.

Histamine a chemical released when the skin comes into contact with a substance to which it is allergic, this causes a reaction referred to as a histamine reaction. Cells called mast cells burst, releasing histamine into the tissues. This causes the blood capillaries to dilate, which increases blood flow to limit skin damage and begin repair.

Hormones chemical messengers transported in the blood. They control the activity of many organs in the body, including the cells and glands in the skin.

Hygiene the recommended standard of cleanliness necessary in the salon to prevent cross-infection and secondary infection as laid down by law, industry codes of practice or written procedures specified by the organization.

Hyper-pigmentation increased pigment production.

Hypertrichosis excessive hair growth for a person's sex, age and race. It is usually due to abnormal conditions in the body caused by disease or injury.

Hypo-pigmentation loss of pigmentation.

Indian head massage a massage service traditionally practised in India, applied to the upper body using the hands. The massage helps to relieve stress and tension and create a feeling of well-being. Oils may be applied to the scalp and hair to improve its condition.

Infrared pre-heating service usually used before massage application.

Inner epithelial root sheath grows from the bottom of the hair follicle at the papilla, both the hair and inner root sheath grow upward together until level with the sebaceous gland when it ceases to grow.

Insulators poor conductors of electricity often used to prevent the flow of electrons. Poor conductors include rubber, plastic and wood.

Intimate waxing application and removal of depilatory wax from the pubic area of the body.

Iontophoresis the introduction of water-soluble preparations into the skin during galvanic therapy to assist rehydration and cellular metabolism in the area.

Job description written details of a person's specific job role, duties and responsibilities.

Keratin a protein produced by cells in the epidermis called keratinocytes. Keratin makes the skin tough and reduces the passage of substances into our bodies. Each hair and the nails contain keratin.

Lanugo hair hair found on the unborn foetus; usually shed at the eighth month of pregnancy.

Legislation laws affecting the operation of the business: services and how they are promoted and delivered, employees, and systems and procedures in the work environment.

Limbic system is involved in emotions and memory. It consists of a group of structures that encircle the brain stem.

Local Government Miscellaneous Provisions Act (1982) legislation that requires that salons offering any form of skin piercing be registered with the local health authority. This registration includes both the beauty therapists who will be carrying out the service and the salon premises where the service will be carried out.

Lymph a clear straw-coloured liquid circulating in the lymph vessels and lymphatic system of the body, filtered out of the blood plasma.

Lymphatic drainage equipment equipment used to specifically improve lymphatic circulation, removing non-medical excess tissue fluid both locally and generally.

Lymphatic system closely connected to the blood system. Its primary function is defensive: to remove bacteria and foreign materials in order to prevent infection. The lymphatic system consists of the fluid lymph, the lymph vessels and the lymph nodes (or glands).

Management of Health and Safety at Work Regulations (1999) this legislation requires the employer to make formal arrangements for maintaining a safe, secure working environment under the Health and Safety at Work Act. This includes staff training for competently monitoring risk in the workplace, known as a risk assessment.

Manual Handling Operations Regulations (1992) legislation which requires the employer to carry out a risk assessment of all activities undertaken which involve manual handling (lifting and moving objects) the aim being to prevent injury due to poor working practice.

Marma (pressure point) incorporated into Indian head massage, this is a technique of pressure point application, based upon the principles and practice of Marma. Pressure is applied to the nerve junctures which stimulates vital energy points on the head, face and ears to improve circulation, relieve tiredness and induce relaxation. Marma pressure points also balance the body.

Mask a skin cleansing service preparation applied to the skin which may contain different ingredients to have a deep cleansing, toning, nourishing or refreshing effect. It may be applied to the hands, feet and face.

Massage manipulation of the soft tissues of the body, producing heat and stimulating the muscular, circulatory and nervous systems.

Massage medium a product used to suit the skin types, i.e. oil, cream or talc to facilitate massage manipulation of the soft tissues and dependent upon formulation to benefit the skin condition.

Massage techniques movements which are selected and applied according to the desired effect to be created, which may be stimulating, relaxing or toning. Massage manipulations include effleurage, petrissage, percussion (also known as tapotement) vibrations and frictions.

Melanin a pigment in the skin that contributes to skin colour.

Melanocytes the cells that produce the skin pigment melanin, which contributes to skin colour.

Mesomorph a body figure type, usually a muscular build with well-developed shoulders and slim hips: an inverted triangle shape.

Micro-current based on a modified direct current and as such creates similar effects to galvanic current. It is a direct current interrupted at low frequencies of one to a few hundred times per second.

Micro-current therapy an electrical service used on the face and body, which achieves an immediate skin toning and firming effect.

Micro-dermabrasion a mechanical exfoliating service for use on the body or face. Microcrystals are applied under pressure over the skin's surface: they gently break down the skin's cells to achieve a skin rejuvenating effect.

Middle note a measure of the evaporation rate of certain essential oils. Middle notes have a moderate evaporation rate and are absorbed into the skin fairly quickly.

Minors, in Scotland a minor is classed under the age of 16. In England, Wales and Northern Ireland a minor is someone under the age of 18. All minors require parental consent.

Moisturiser a skincare preparation whose formulation of oil and water helps maintain the skin's natural moisture by locking in moisture, offering protection and hydration.

Motor point a location on the muscles where the motor nerve can be most easily stimulated.

Motor nerves nerves situated in a muscle tissue and act on information from the brain, causing a particular response, typically muscle movement.

Muscle contractile tissue responsible for movement of the body made up of a bundle of elastic fibres bound together in a sheath, the fascia. Muscular tissue contracts (shortens) and creates movement.

Muscle tone the normal degree of tension in healthy muscle.

Nerve a collection of single neurones surrounded by a protective sheath through which impulses are transmitted between the brain or spinal cord and another part of the body.

Nervous system coordinates the activities of the body by responding to stimuli received by the sense organs.

Neurones nerve cell which makes up nervous tissue.

Objectives the aim or purpose of an activity that can be measured to see if it has been met or not.

Oedema the retention of fluid in the tissues, which causes swelling.

Olfactory system located high inside the nose and responsible for the sense of smell. When we breathe in aromas, nerve endings in the olfactory system are stimulated and relay messages to the brain which then cause the body to respond.

Outer epithelial root sheath forms the hair follicle wall. This does not grow up with the hair but is stationery, a continuation of the growing layer of the epidermis.

Papillae projections near the surface of the dermis, which contain nerve endings and blood capillaries. They supply the upper epidermis with nutrition

Personal Protective Equipment (PPE) Regulations (2002) this legislation requires employers to identify, through a risk assessment, those activities which require special protective equipment to be worn or used. Instruction should be provided on how the personal protective equipment should be used/worn to be effective.

Petrissage massage manipulations which apply intermittent pressure to the tissues of the skin, lifting them from the underlying structures. Often known as compression movements.

pH the degree of acidity or alkalinity measured on the pH scale.

Physical characteristics the individual features of each client to be considered when planning a service, i.e. height, weight, posture, muscle tone, age, health and skin condition.

Pilosebaceous unit hair follicles together with the sebaceous gland forms the skin structure, the pilosebaceous unit

Photosensitizers something that causes the skin to become UV sensitive such as certain medication.

Placement (stone therapy technique) placing a stone in a specific position on or underneath the body.

Posture the position of the body which varies from person to person. Good posture is when the body is in alignment.

Pre-blended oils aromatherapy oils used in massage to meet the clients physical characteristics and emotional preferences, i.e. relaxation, uplifting and sense of well-being.

Pressure points the application of pressure on specific points of the head, face or body during massage service using the fingertips or thumbs. This helps to release blocked energy channels flowing through the body, improving the body's circulation, function and repair

Promotion an activity carried out to benefit the business to meet specified objectives.

Provision and Use of Work Equipment Regulations (PUWER) (1998) this Regulation lays down important health and safety controls on the provision and use of equipment to prevent risk. They state the duties required by employers and for users.

Public Liability Insurance protects employers and employees against the consequences of death or injury to a third party while on the premises.

Race Relations Act (1976) this Act makes it unlawful to discriminate on the grounds of colour, race, nationality, ethnic or national origin.

REACH 2007 is a European Union Regulation concerning the Registration, Evaluation, Authorization and Restriction of Chemicals. It operates alongside COSHH and is designed to improve the information provided by chemical manufacturers through the provision of adequate safety data sheets.

Record cards confidential cards recording personal details of each client registered at the salon.

Regulatory Reform (Fire Safety Order (2005) this legislation requires that the employer or designated 'responsible person'

must carry out a risk assessment for the premises in relation to fire evacuation practice and procedures.

Repetitive strain injury (RSI) injury incurred through repetition of movement of a particular part of the body.

Reporting of Injuries, Diseases and Dangerous Occurrences Regulations (RIDDOR) (1995) RIDDOR requires the salon/business to notify the HSE incident contact centre (ICC) in any case of personal injury, disease or dangerous occurrence in the workplace.

Reproductive system that creates new humans. These systems include the male and female sex glands. The male testes which produces sperm required for sexual reproduction and the female ovaries which produces the egg required for sexual reproduction.

Resources the equipment, products and time required to complete a service.

Respiratory system brings air into close contact with the blood in the lungs and enables oxygen to enter the bloodstream and be transported to all cells in the body where it can be used to provide energy by cell respiration.

Sanitization the destruction of some, but not all living microorganisms when cleansing the skin.

Sauna a timber construction where the air inside is heated to produce therapeutic effects.

Sebaceous gland a minute sac-like organ usually associated with the hair follicle. The cells of the gland decompose and produce the skin's natural oil sebum. Found all over the body except the soles of the feet and the palms of the hands. It is usually associated with the hair follicle forms the pilosebaceous unit.

Sebum the skin's natural oil which keeps the skin supple.

Secondary infection bacterial penetration into the skin causing infection.

Self-tan products cosmetic products containing an ingredient which gives a healthy, tanned appearance to the skin. Different methods can be used to apply self-tan products including spray, manual and airbrush application.

Semi-precious stones these can be incorporated within stone therapy placement to enhance the benefits of the service, e.g. for clearing, balancing, etc.

Sensory nerves nerves which receive information and relay it to the brain. they are found near to the skin surface and respond to touch, pressure temperature and pain.

Service plan after the consultation suitable service objectives are established to treat the client's condition and needs.

Single lashes these are a single artificial lash, which are attached to a single natural eyelash by use of adhesive.

Skeletal system supports the softer tissues of the body and maintains the shape of the body.

Skin allergy if the skin is sensitive to a particular substance an allergic skin reaction will occur. This is recognized by irritation, swelling and inflammation.

Skin analysis assessment of the client's skin type and condition.

Skin appendages structures within the skin including sweat glands (that excrete sweat), hair follicles (that produce hair), sebaceous glands (produce the skin's natural oil sebum) and nails (a horny substance that protects the ends of the fingers).

Skin sensitivity test this is performed to determine if the client is allergic to a product (e.g. eyelash extension adhesive) being applied or to assess skin response, i.e. before application of electrotherapy services to ensure that the client can differentiate skin sensations.

Skin tone the strength and elasticity of the skin.

Skin type the different physiological functioning of each person's skin provides their skin type. Skin types include dry (lacking in oil), oily (excessive oil) and combination (a mixture of two skin types, e.g. dry and oily).

SMART an acronym used for setting objectives. Specific, Measurable, Achievable, Realistic Time-bound.

Spa pool a pool of warm water with jets of air passing through to create bubbles which massage the skin.

Spray-gun equipment used to apply liquid self-tanning preparation to the skin.

Sterilization the total destruction of all microorganisms.

Stock-keeping maintenance of stock levels to anticipate needs. Stock records note how much stock has been used and when a new order is needed. This may be achieved using manual or computerized systems.

Stress a condition which develops when a person becomes pressurized. This may result in undesirable side-effects such as insomnia, muscular tension and skin disorders.

Stretch marks (striations) scarring of the skin as a result of the skin breaking beneath the surface in the dermal layer.

Subcutaneous tissue a layer of fatty tissue situated below the epidermis and dermis.

Superfluous hair hair considered to be in excess of that of normal downy hair for the person's age and sex, but is considered unwanted.

Sweat glands or **sudoriferous glands** are small tubes in the skin of the dermis and epidermis which excrete sweat. Their function is to regulate body temperature through the evaporation of sweat from the skin's surface. There are two types of gland: eccrine gland and apocrine gland.

Tapotement also known as percussion. A massage manipulation which is used for its general toning and stimulating effect.

Tapping (stone therapy technique). Holding a stone on the body while rhythmically tapping with another to create a vibrational effect.

Target a goal or objective to achieve, usually set within a timescale.

Telogen the resting stage of the hair growth cycle where the hair is finally shed.

Terminal hair deep-rooted, thick, coarse, pigmented hair found on the scalp, underarms, pubic region, eyelash and brow areas.

Tissues groups of cells, sharing function, shape and size that specialize in carrying out particular functions. These include: epithelial, connective, muscular and nervous.

Top note a measure of the highest evaporation rate of an essential oil. These commonly have a sharp aroma and a stimulating effect.

Trigger point (stone therapy technique) deep, continuous pressure with a stone on an isolated area to achieve relief of muscular tension.

Tucking (stone therapy technique) a warm stone is positioned underneath an area of the body after it has been used for service (e.g. knees, legs, shoulder, etc.).

Ultraviolet light (UV) invisible rays of the light spectrum with a wavelength shorter than visible light rays.

Urinary system (excretory system) filters waste products from the blood, maintaining its normal composition.

UV tanning the skin is exposed to artificially produced UV and the skin darkens creating a tan. Artificial UV is produced by high or low-pressure tubes and lamps. The term pressure relates to the wattage (power or energy) of the lamps.

Vacuum suction service a mechanical service which can be applied to the face or body. External suction is applied to the surface tissues causing lift and stimulation of the underlying tissues. Locally, blood and lymphatic circulation is improved which aids removal of tissue fluid accumulation. It also improves skin texture and appearance.

Vellus hair hair which is fine, downy and soft; found on the face and body.

Vibrations massage manipulation used to relieve pain and fatigue, stimulate the nerves and produce a sedative effect. The movements are firm and trembling, performed with one or both hands.

Virilization a condition where the female body becomes more masculine resulting in heavy, facial and body hair growth in a masculine pattern.

Virus the smallest living bodies, too small to be seen under an ordinary microscope. They are considered to be parasites, as they require living tissue to survive. Viruses invade healthy body cells and multiply within the cell. Eventually the cell walls break down and the virus particles are freed to attack further cells.

Workplace (Health, Safety and Welfare) Regulations (1992) these Regulations ensure the workplace is a safe, healthy and secure working environment meeting the needs of all employees.

Index